ECONOMIC FREEDOM

Lessons of Hong Kong

ECONOMIC FREEDOM

Lessons of Hong Kong

Kui-Wai Li

City University of Hong Kong, China

World Scientific

NEW JERSEY • LONDON • SINGAPORE • BEIJING • SHANGHAI • HONG KONG • TAIPEI • CHENNAI

Published by

World Scientific Publishing Co. Pte. Ltd.
5 Toh Tuck Link, Singapore 596224
USA office: 27 Warren Street, Suite 401-402, Hackensack, NJ 07601
UK office: 57 Shelton Street, Covent Garden, London WC2H 9HE

British Library Cataloguing-in-Publication Data
A catalogue record for this book is available from the British Library.

ECONOMIC FREEDOM
Lessons of Hong Kong

ISBN 978-981-4368-84-1
ISBN 978-981-4368-85-8 (pbk)

In-house Editor: Alisha Nguyen

Typeset by Stallion Press
Email: enquiries@stallionpress.com

Printed by FuIsland Offset Printing (S) Pte Ltd Singapore

The author will donate the royalties received from the sale of this book to the Evengel Children's Home in Hong Kong SAR.

We should continue to respect each other's choice of development path and efforts to promote economic and social development and improve people's lives.

President Hu Jintao, People's Republic of China
April 15, 2011

Thinking is the most economical form of entertainment.

Preface

Why a second book on the Hong Kong economy within a few years? Since my 2006 book on *The Hong Kong Economy: Recovery and Restructuring*, I have strong urge to relate the post-1997 Hong Kong economy to the more fundamental value — economic freedom. Although quite a considerable amount of materials covered in this new book have expanded, revised and extended the coverage of the 2006 book, the theme of economic freedom is probably the clearest message one can elaborate on Hong Kong's economic achievement. Instead of referring to the different political status, the term Hong Kong is used throughout to represent the territory.

Around the late 1970s and early 1980s, the economics syllabus for the Hong Kong matriculation examination has been changed. Previously, the syllabus was very standard and covered principles of both microeconomics and macroeconomics. Another key element in the matriculation syllabus included a considerable amount of teaching on the macroeconomy of Hong Kong. The new syllabus was transformed by a well-known professor to incorporate mainly a microeconomic approach to economic studies, such as the theory of transaction cost. The section on Hong Kong's macroeconomy had since been reduced drastically. To do justice to our students, I think that those matriculated economics students graduated without a good knowledge on the local macroeconomy is a serious mistake. It did not only create a knowledge gap, it might lead to social loss if their lack of knowledge has resulted in undesirable consequences. Since not all matriculated graduates entered university for their higher degree studies, and even for those who had entered to do undergraduate studies, the Hong Kong economy may not be included in the teaching curriculum. Such a lack of knowledge on the economy of Hong Kong came to my notice when I taught the undergraduate classes. The lack of knowledge and the inability to dissect the Hong Kong economy was alarming.

As an economist majoring in development studies, I have great desire and interest to know and understand the detailed texture of the Hong Kong economy. The lack of teaching and research on the Hong Kong macroeconomy provided me with the stimulant, and a sense of duty to educate students with an appropriate knowledge on the contemporary Hong Kong economy. I hope future economics graduates, at the least, will have an adequate knowledge on the Hong Kong economy, and at the most, will help to steer the Hong Kong economy to new heights.

There is a second reason. Since the 1970s, Hong Kong has been regarded as a matured or advanced economy in Asia, along with Japan, Singapore, South Korea and Chinese Taipei (Taiwan). In many ways, the capitalist market economy has been an important factor. The successful Asian economies have succeeded the "first generation" of the western capitalist market economies. As the "second generation" of successful market economies, a number of emerging world economies has been examining the successful Asian economies. Hence, a book on the Hong Kong economy has its non-local impact. It summarizes the lessons, the context and the experience of a successful post-World War II free market economy. The condensed materials are useful inputs to others. The economic freedom of Hong Kong becomes the natural choice of study I would dwell on. The lessons of Hong Kong can be used for comparative studies with development in other emerging economies. More importantly, I wish this book can serve as a record for the future development of Hong Kong itself. With sovereignty reversion in 1997 and the framework of "one country, two systems", the challenge to Hong Kong itself is whether the post-1997 development will bring a better and economically stronger Hong Kong.

This book contains 16 chapters, and the ingredients of the chapters can conveniently be grouped under four headings of conceptual, contextual, component and conditional. Economic freedom is both conceptual and theoretical. While the theory of economic freedom relates to the quantifiable factors, it is more important to elaborate on the conceptual aspects that go beyond the quantifiable factors and relate also to other human behaviors. Once the conceptual element is understood, it will be necessary to discuss the context of economic freedom, and how they are related to each other that serves as pillars to economic freedom. Contextual can cover a large number of issues, and the book has covered only the more relevant issues. More contextual discussions can be conducted. The component part concerns the key policies practiced in Hong Kong's economic freedom. These key policy discussions aim to reflect the instruments through which the ingredients of economic freedom are conducted, preserved and promoted. Economic policies do not operate in a vacuum, but need to be complemented by relevant suitable conditions. Conditional factors include non-economic aspects of freedom. The discussion of economic freedom presented in the sequence of "conceptual-contextual-component-conditional" aims to provide step-by-step understanding of the virtue of economic freedom that Hong Kong has been enjoying. Readers are welcome to provide me with feedback on the discussions, and comments from critics will definitely be noted, as that shall be the "food for thought" for my future studies.

The first two chapters are mainly conceptual, aiming to lay the intellectual understanding and foundation of economic freedom and how it is related to Hong Kong. Chapter 1 discusses the theoretical and intellectual base of economic freedom, elaborating on the key elements and requirements. Chapter 2 examines the Hong Kong case in recent historical events. The next five chapters are contextual, with the intention to outline the texture of the free Hong Kong economy. Chapter 3 studies the income performance of Hong Kong, and Hong Kong is compared to other Asian economies. Chapter 4 extends the discussion beyond that covered in my 2006 book by elaborating on a major economic element of productivity and cost. Chapter 5 expands the productivity discussion to cover the performance and experience of small- and medium-sized enterprise, which is a core component in the economic success of Hong Kong. Another contextual chapter, Chapter 6, concentrates on Hong Kong as a knowledge-based economy. Along with the knowledge-based economy is the last contextual chapter, Chapter 7, on economic efficiency. Each of these contextual chapters is a stand-alone chapter, providing a different dimension on the texture on the economic freedom of Hong Kong.

There are five chapters on the components of economic freedom in Hong Kong. Component chapters concern mainly policy discussions. Chapter 8 begins by looking at the issue of competition and considers how the experience of other economies in dealing with competition can be made relevant to the Hong Kong economy. The next two chapters, Chapter 9 and Chapter 10, deal with the financial and currency activities in Hong Kong, respectively. What are the key to survival and expansion amidst strong competition and challenge? Chapter 11 turns to examine the fiscal policy and the role of government in the freest economy. The cost and benefits of government involvement are elaborated in details, using examples from annual budgets. The last component chapter relates to policy on land and the real estate market. Ownership freedom is important, but a resource utilization policy requires a balancing skill.

There are three chapters that elaborate on the conditions of economic freedom in Hong Kong. Chapter 13 looks at the issue of inequality and poverty, and suggests that opportunity is the answer to economic freedom. Economic integration with Mainland China has become part of the Hong Kong economy. Politics aside, the challenge is the mixture of the "two systems" that can alleviate conflicts on the one hand and promote mutual advantages on the other hand. Chapter 15 rounds up the discussion by raising the important condition of civic freedom in its totality. The last chapter, Chapter 16, serves as a summarizing chapter that reminds the reader the importance of a continued freedom path.

The writing of the books uses simple language, and the use of jargons is minimized. The technical analysis has also been kept to its bare minimum. Non-technical readers could skip the technical sections without a loss of understanding. Since the chapter has been written over a period of five years or so, some sections of the data used and the analysis presented may not be that up-to-date. There are some sections that are more current or up-to-date than other sections, but the various sections and chapters are interconnected to each other. The ultimate intention is to present consistent arguments and views. While it would be a sense of comfort if readers are supportive to the discussions in the text, critics are welcome to provide different views. It is hope that at least one agrees that the discussion and materials covered are correct, though views and analyses can differ.

The formative stage of this book began as soon as my 2006 book was published. The incentive to complete this book was raised further when the Hong Kong SAR Government had designated the City University of Hong Kong APEC Study Center, to which I was in charge, as the Hong Kong APEC Study Center in the two years of 2007–2009, as modest funding was given to support research studies related to Hong Kong. While the various "knitting" research and writing activities have been slowly conducted, the bulk of the chapters were written during my sabbatical year in 2010–2011. My first destination was the University of Geneva where I visited for 3 months from September to December 2010, and was provided with excellent facilities and support. The quiet living environment in Geneva gave me a fruitful time in catching up with the writing of chapters. Among a number of colleagues and staffs I met in the University of Geneva, international institutions and Hong Kong officials in Geneva, there are a number of professors, scholars and assistants whom I would especially like to express my gratitude, including Yves Flückiger, Henri Loubergé,

Marcelo Olarreaga, Jayalakshmi Krishnakumar, Frédéric Robert-Nicoud, Elvezio Ronchetti, Ulrich Kohli, Pierre Willa, Nicolas Zufferey, Lucio Baccaro, Roberta Piermartini, Giséle Schmid, Nicolay Markov and Donald Ng.

The second destination where I spent another three months of my sabbatical from January to March 2011 was the Asian Institute, Munk School of Global Affairs, University of Toronto. The office provided to me in the Richard Charles Lee Canada-Hong Kong Library was an excellent venue for my writing. A number of scholars, professionals and Hong Kong officials in Toronto I met during my stay in Toronto have been extremely helpful in sharping the later part of my writings. I would like to express my thanks particularly to Don Brean, Janice G. Stein, Louis Pauly, Joseph Wong, Senator Vivienne Poy, Wendy Dobson, Jack Hang-tat Leong, M. H. Franco Wong, Tong Lam, Loren Brandt, Xiaodong Zhu, Eric Fong, Marisa Ciappara, Fred McMahon, Maureen Siu, Stephen Siu and Eileen Lam.

Funding support from the Department of Trade and Industry, Hong Kong SAR Government, for the Hong Kong APEC Study Center is gratefully acknowledged. Thanks should go to those scholars supporting me with their blurbs and colleagues from the publisher whom has been seeing to the completion of the publication. I would express my gratitude to a number of scholars and professionals whom have assisted my work on economic freedom. In alphabetical orders, they are: Sven Arndt, Eamonn Butler, Beth Cave, Wallace Chan, Edwin J. Feulner, Shinichi Fukuda, James D. Gwartney, Bharat Raj Hazari, Tae-Shin Kwon, Kazuyuki Ishida, Frank Lavin, Ngok Ma, Tatsuyoshi Miyakoshi, Mark Mullins, Tom G. Palmer, Ken Sheffer, Olaf Unteroberdoerster, Ian Vasquez and Andrew Work.

The City University of Hong Kong has been supportive in both resource and time. I am grateful to all my line managers in the College of Business and the Department of Economics and Finance. Computing support has been provided by Adams Chan, Eric K. F. Ng and Simon K. M. Li in the Information Technology Services Unit. Surely, much of the background research work has been supported by a number of Research Fellow, Senior Research Assistants, Research Assistants and student helpers over the years, including in alphabetical orders, Helen K. K. Chan, Patrick W. Y. Cheung, Eddie M. L. Kwok, Helen H. K. Lam, Yiming Li, Anthony H. F. Mak, Liang Wang, Anson L. K. Wong, Douglas T. K. Wong, Joseph Y. Y. Wong, Woody K. Y. Wong, Siyang Ye, Travis C. M. Yip, Pang Yu, Ang Zhang and Xianbo Zhou.

Although experience in family life is often faced with bumps, but family support is crucial in tasks that engage a few years' of a person's time. Support from my own family has been total, and moral support from close friends has been appreciated. Nonetheless, I shall be responsible for any mistakes found in this book.

Kui-Wai Li
City University of Hong Kong
September 2011

Contents

About the Author

Dr. Kui-Wai Li lectures on the Asia-Pacific economies, including the China economy and specializes in the areas of financial and economic development, industry and trade, political economy and globalization. He has published a number of referee articles and has contributed chapters to edited books. Other previous books he authored and edited include *The Hong Kong Economy: From Recovery to Restructure* (2006), *Capitalist Development and Economism in East Asia: The Rise of Hong Kong, Singapore, Taiwan and South Korea* (2002), *Financial Repression and Economic Reform in China* (1994), and *Financing China Trade and Investment* (1997). Dr. Li has worked as a consultant to international institutions, foreign governments and business, and has regularly been interviewed by local and foreign press, radio and television on Hong Kong, Mainland China and foreign issues. Formerly, Dr. Li visited a number of universities, including Vilnius University, University of Toronto, University of Geneva and Yale University.

1 Economic Freedom: Theory, Measurement and Concepts

1.1 Introduction

The capitalistic mode of production has successfully been adopted in all industrialized and advanced countries in North America and Western Europe. One can argue that these Western capitalist economies have become the "first generation" of capitalist economies that serve as models and references for other world economies. The key element in capitalism embraces economic freedom that allows voluntary participation of individuals in a free market and the establishment of various civic institutions that provide the rule of law and the protection of property rights.

After the Second World War and since the 1950s, there have been a number of world economies that have succeeded after taking up market capitalism. In East Asia, the "dragon" economies of Japan, Hong Kong, South Korea, Singapore and Chinese Taipei (Taiwan) have attracted world attention because of their rapid economic transformation in the second half of the 20th century. Although the extent of market capitalism may have differed from countries in Europe and North America, the economic success of these "dragon" economies have in turn served as "second generation" models and references of market capitalist economies for other emerging and transitional economies. Beginning from the 1980s in Asia, the "next tier" of Southeast Asian nations that comprise of Malaysia, Thailand, Indonesia and the Philippines have followed the path of the developed Asian economies. Similarly, Mainland China's economic reform in 1978 has adopted pragmatic market economic principles and had attracted huge and continuous injection of capital from overseas Chinese. By the turn of the 21st century, the rapid growth of the Mainland China economy has led other emerging economies, such as India, Latin American and Eastern European countries, to examine the strength and virtues of market capitalism and have paid even closer and detailed attention to the post-World War II development of the Asia "dragon" economies as targets and references where development lessons can be learnt.

The post-World War II economic success of the Asia "dragon" economies and the increasing role they have in influencing other emerging world economies has led to the debate on the "Asia paradigm" of development. While capitalism has been the basic mode of production, the concerns include the various economic and non-economic ingredients, fabrics and textures that facilitated growth in these Asian economies. Among a large volume of studies that documented the successful growth in East Asia, Li (2002) has coined "economism" as the paradigm that explained how the success of Asian economies differed from the traditional "first generation" capitalist countries in North America and Western Europe.

The Hong Kong economy has been selected as the "freest" economy in the world for a number of consecutive years, and the Hong Kong economy has attracted large attention because its political sovereignty has reverted from Great Britain to the People's Republic of China on July 1, 1997, ending the status of a British colony for 155 years. The concern is whether the established economic strength of Hong Kong will be challenged by the wave of economic convergence and integration with the Mainland China economy after 1997. The changing bilateral and mutual relationship with the Mainland China economy will be of great interest for the further development of the "freest" world economy. The mutual influence will form the dynamics of the bilateral relationship. Given its openness and the colonial connections, Hong Kong also has its other "leg" in the world economy. Although Hong Kong has constantly been influenced by the world market, changes in the Hong Kong market in turn have provided necessary information to international investors.

The Hong Kong economy in first decade of the 21st century has suffered from a number of regional and international crises. The Asian financial crisis in 1997 that brought different degrees of economic hardship to a number of Asian economies has subsided by the time the new century arrives, though some of the Asian economies were still struggling with economic recovery and were drafting a new path in their economic development. Health hazards occurred with the spread of the avian flu pandemic at regular intervals in a number of Asian economies since 1997, together with the outbreak of the severe acute respiratory syndrome (SARS) in 2003 in Hong Kong and Mainland China that have spread to the other parts of the world. In early 2009, the human swine flu that first discovered in Mexico has also quickly spread to the US and other parts of the world. In the US, the September 11, 2001, terrorist attacks on the World Trade Center in New York and the Pentagon in Washington DC have lifted the curtain for a prolonged war on terrorism that drained away much economic resources. One other unintended economic consequence includes the dramatic rise in the petroleum price that has in different manner hurt the world economy.

The showdown in the series of crises in the first decade of the 21st century came in September 2008 after a sequence of financial events and difficulties in the US that led to similar financial meltdown in different world regions. The 2008 financial crisis in the US has raised a number of interesting debates. One debate concerns whether the magnitude of the 2008 financial crisis is comparable to the "Great Depression" of the 1930s. The world economy in the 21st century, however, surely differs from the economic world of the 1930s, as the developed European and Asian countries have played a part in the world economy, suggesting that the cushion for economic hardship is now larger.

Another debate that arises from the 2008 financial crisis is whether there is an excessive application of economic freedom, especially in the financial world. One question is whether financial institutions have been given too much freedom to the extent of ignoring their moral, business conduct or ethic responsibilities. There have been two views in this debate. One view simply concerns that people have taken economic freedom to their own hands and unethically exploited it. Thus, anti-freedom advocates would call for a greater control, and introduce more economic restrictions and planning, typically to be exercised by the government or the state. Those who hold this view effectively suggest a rewinding of freedom, at least in the financial world, asking the government or the state to intervene and take over the economic decisions of individuals, businesses and institutions.

The pro-freedom advocates treasure the virtues of individual freedom, but point to the importance of needed regulations in the financial world. The needed and transparent financial regulations are meant to protect, nurture and strengthen economic freedom and provide a "level playing field" platform through which market participants can rely, participate, transact and engage effectively. Economic freedom does not operate in a vacuum; and individuals and businesses in a free economy need to be protected from illegal or faulty transactions and abuse. A more open, standardized and transparent set of financial and banking regulations should be seen as a complement to the operation of financial transactions and the functioning of economic freedom.

Economic freedom is not a "free good". The exercise of economic freedom comes with the presence of a high level of civilized behaviors and manners governed by the presence of specialized and professional institutions and the presence of regulations that specify how activities are conducted equitably, transparently and openly. A somewhat simplified structure that gives the relationship between the state representing the government or the ruler and the citizens representing the public is shown in Figure 1.1. The state or the government exercises and implements appropriate policies in a timely manner, while the citizens express and voice their opinions and needs through different channels.

In Figure 1.1, institutions on the one hand and regulations on the other hand act like two arms in a free economy. Institutions represent numerous civic establishments that specify various standard practices and an extent and coverage of activities and transactions, while regulations specify how standard practices are maintained and how activities and transactions are conducted in a manner that applies to all citizens indiscriminately. In short, the exercise of freedom itself needs to be protected from coercion and abuse, and the form of protection is embedded in the presence of relevant institutions guided by comprehensive regulations.

The 2008 financial crisis has actually highlighted the relevance and importance of economic freedom. In the first instance, freedom in financial, investment, information and monetary transactions are crucial elements in civic societies. For example,

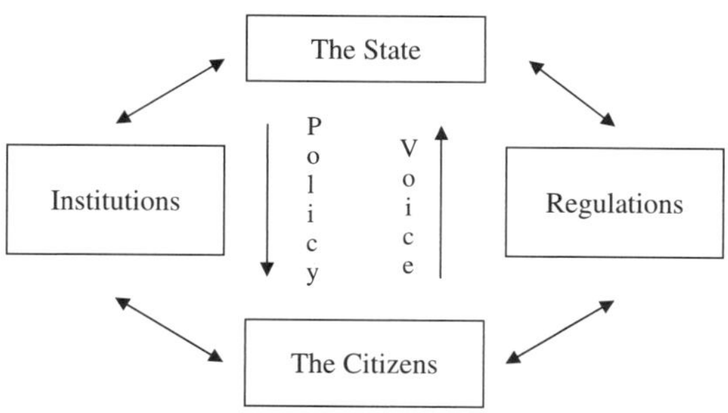

FIGURE 1.1 A simplified structure in a free economy

the knowledge about the financial products, the method used to calculate investment returns, the agent that handles the invested amount, the risk level of individual business entities and financial products, and the use and flow of private information between bankers and investment agents are equally important in order to ensure that all parties in financial transactions are fully aware of the size of monetary involvement and the responsibility of each and every individual and agent. As the financial sector involves changes and innovations constantly, it would be appropriate to establish new and timely regulations that counterbalance possible mishaps, abuse and poor governance by individuals and business entities in the financial world.

The next two sections summarize the key arguments of economic freedom, pointing out its virtues, and elaborate conceptually on its intuition and strength to show how an individual and the society can benefit and progress with it. Section 1.4 examines the way economic freedom is measured. Section 1.5 illustrates some of the key empirical studies that relate economic freedom to its causes and consequences, providing comparisons across different world economies. Most empirical studies come to the conclusion that economic freedom is surely a virtue and not a vice to humanity.

Hong Kong has been the freest economy for a number of consecutive years. Section 1.6 considers the elements that Hong Kong has performed in the *Index of Economic Freedom*. The various elements are then grouped into three headings so that other economies aim to pursue and improve their economic freedom can draft their own paths by examining the content and performance of the three economic freedom pillars.

Before concluding the chapter, the discussion in Section 1.7 looks deeper into the foundation of economic freedom. The result of economic freedom rests with the different economic outcomes experienced by individuals and enterprises. But the difference in outcome should not be contradictory or conflicting because all outcomes depend on efforts and resource endowments. Economic relativity is the ultimate accepted outcome in a free society where individuals can conduct their activities according to their resource endowments. There is no doubt inequality emerges, but inequality can be viewed dynamically because the difference can change overtime, can get larger or shrink according to individuals' effort and adjustment in endowment and business cycles.

The chapter concludes that being the freest economy in the world, Hong Kong economy is worth to be studied and documented, so that lessons can be drawn and learned by other economies. One is not projecting a perfect economy, and there are always economic faults and drawbacks. By openly studying the various components of the freest economy, one can have an insight on how a free economy operates and how different components function, complement and interact with each other. The lesson is to know how activities are being conducted successfully, and at the same time observe the continued or dynamic performance of the Hong Kong economy. Lacking natural resources of its own, Hong Kong seems to face different economic challenges at different times. Economic vibrancy seems to be a good and successful alternative to the shortage in natural resources.

1.2 Economic Freedom Advocates: Smith, Hayek and Friedman

Scholars in economic thoughts have provided a detailed sequence and classification on the contribution by different economic philosophers. The early economic philosophers of mercantilists in the 18th century gave way to the development of the classical economists in the 19th century. Economic liberalism in the form of *laissez-faire* emphasized on the pursuit of individual economic interests, and coupled with the necessary institutional setup, formed the basis of classical economic theories and arguments.

The two diverging political economy views that emerged after the classical economists are the Marxian school and the neo-classical school. Contrary to the classical school were the Marxists, whom preached for collectivism, communism and concentration of economic power in the hands of the state. Under communism, resource allocation and output would come under the monopoly of the state. According to the Marxists, imperialism and the dependency theory argue that underdevelopment in developing countries was the result of economic exploitation. The marginalist school extends the classical school by incorporating a discussion on economic efficiency, and has formed the main stream of the neo-classical school in the early 20th century. Since the end of the Second World War in 1945, the neo-classical school has gradually extended to numerous other theoretical areas, including growth and equity, macroeconomic measurement and policy, and the role of government (Wonnacoltt and Wonnacott, 1990).

The most well-known classical economist has been Adam Smith whose pioneering book, *An Inquiry Into the Nature and Causes of the Wealth of Nations* (1776) (*WON* hereafter), has defined numerous contemporary economic relationships among individuals and nations. Indeed, the "first lesson" an economic student learns in any economic textbooks is derived largely from the *WON* (Weinstein, 2001). The *WON* actually contained five books. The first book begins with the productive power of labor. The division and specialization of labor have become the basis of contemporary economic ideas. The second book that deals with the function of money and role of price in the market economy is covered in every basic economic textbook. The unequal outcome of nations' wealth due to the different ability in wealth accumulation is discussed in Book III. The political economy and external economic relationships among nations in the form of trade and economic choice of domestic production are discussed in Book IV. The sovereign state discussed in Book V concerns the fiscal role of the state, and the needed fiscal expenditure on public works and sources of revenue have lasting implications on the public finance of contemporary world economies.

Although Adam Smith is regarded as the "father of modern economics", Krueger (2003, Introduction) agrees that "many of the ideas in *WON* can be traced to earlier thinkers" and that Adam Smith had literally borrowed from his French contemporaries. It has also become popular to find ancient Chinese philosophers who, though unknown to Adam Smith at the time, advanced related ideas two thousand years earlier. Indeed, Krueger's (2003) observation has been elaborated by Zhang (2000) who has drawn a comparison between the philosophical work of Adam Smith

(1723–1790) and Confucius (551–479 BC) by examining their economic doctrines, moral sentiments and approaches to the free will of an ideal individual. Zhang (2000:29) pointed out that despite the low economic development in China at the time of Adam Smith, Confucius had influenced the "mental and spiritual states" of European philosophers. Zhang (1999:88) elaborated that Confucius "tried to construct a social environment where each individual pursues his own benefits without hurting other people". While Confucius discussed free will, Adam Smith upheld freedom and "the invisible hand" in exchange and in social order (Zhang, 1999, 2000; Butler, 2007). Before the *WON*, Adam Smith (1759) had written an earlier work on *The Theory of Moral Sentiments* that explained "human morality through the sentiment of sympathy" (Krueger, 2003, Introduction).

A key figure in the advocate of economic freedom in the last century is Friedrich A. Hayek, whose famous book *The Road to Serfdom* was published in 1944. Friedrich Hayek's economic philosophy has been documented in numerous works, notably in the nineteen volumes of *The Collected Works of F. A. Hayek*, under the general editorship of Stephen Kresge. Especially in examining the unwanted consequences of the Second World War, Friedrich Hayek (1944) considers freedom as a core value in humanity and that economic intervention by government and economic planning would take away individual freedom in economic decision making, and the growing power of the government would "enslave" the citizens. Put in modern terms, Friedrich Hayek (1944) argues that political and economic power concentrated in the hands of government officials whom planned and distributed all forms of economic resources would leave little choice and room for individuals to make their own economic progress. Friedrich Hayek (1991:385–386) concerns particularly the danger of unlimited government even in a democratic regime because "a government with unlimited power will be forced, [in order] to secure the continued support of the majority, to use its unlimited powers in the service of special interests".

In Volume 10 on *Socialism and War*, Caldwell (1997:40) notes that individuals make their own choices in a free market system, but a "code of values" will have to be imposed by the planners in a planned economy, and that "since planners are political appointees who wish to retain power, they will seek ways to justify the choices that they have made". As such, the planners tend to favor those support their plans and "authoritarian government tends inevitably to expand beyond the economic and into the political domain". Caldwell (1997:218) goes further to elaborate that central planning necessarily produces a totalitarian system because "whoever control the means must decide which ends they are to serve" and this means a control over all economic activities. Friedrich Hayek concludes that individual liberty will ultimately be sacrificed.

Friedrich Hayek was also a major critique of John M. Keynes, whom had also written extensively and advocated the strong role of the government in the economic development after World War II in Great Britain. Keynes' much quoted work is *The General Theory of Employment, Interest and Money* (1936). Caldwell (1997:33) notes that Friedrich Hayek opposes John Keynes's argument of keeping interest rate low in the economic depression of the 1930s fearing that the disruption of the production structure would exacerbate the business cycle in the long-run.

Such argument can have profound economic implications, even in financial crisis that have taken place in various parts of the world in the 1990s and the first decade of the 21st century, including the 2008 financial crisis in the US. A prolonged period of near-zero interest rate reduces the opportunity cost of money and financial resources, thereby encourages low productivity investment and speculation that would not have been possible had interest rate been set at a reasonably high level. With a near-zero interest rate, low productivity investment projects can have an easy access to financial resources. Once financial resources are given to low productivity investment projects, the same recourses may not be available to high productivity investment projects.

The most influential advocate of freedom in the latter half of the 20th century is Milton Friedman, who has in numerous occasions and writings used Hong Kong as the most successful case of economic freedom in modern time. In introducing Milton Friedman, Baird (Friedman, 1991) says Milton Friedman is "one of the most versatile members of the profession" and "in addition to methodology and macroeconomics, he has made significant contributions in the areas of economic history, statistics, international balance, risk and insurance and microeconomic theory". The two most highly-read books by Milton Friedman are *Capitalism and Freedom* (1962) and *Free to Choose* (1979, with Rose Friedman). Accordingly to Milton Friedman (1962:15–16), "the fundamental threat to freedom is power to coerce, be it in the hands of a monarch, a dictator, an oligarchy, or a monetary authority", and "the preservation of freedom requires the elimination of such concentration of power to the fullest possible extent". In a free society, individuals are free to "advocate and propagandize openly for a radical change in the structure of the society — so long as the advocacy is restricted to persuasion and does not include force or other forms of coercion".

In *Free to Choose*, Milton Friedman (1979:65–66) summarizes economic freedom in the following. "An essential part of economic freedom is freedom to choose how to use our income", and "how much of our income is spent on our behalf by government". "Another essential part of economic freedom is freedom to use the resources we possess in accordance with our own values". "Freedom to own property is another essential part of economic freedom".

Freedom is closely associated with limited government. Milton Friedman (1962:2–3) pointed out two basic principles of a limited government. The first general principle is that the major function of government "must be to protect our freedom both from the enemies outside our gates and from our fellow-citizens: to protect law and order, to enforce private contracts, to foster competitive markets". It is only "by relying primarily on voluntary co-operation and private enterprise, in both economic and other activities, we can insure that the private sector is a check on the powers of the governmental sector and an effective protection of freedom of speech, of religion, and of thought". The second general principle is that "government power must be dispersed".

Milton Friedman (1993:9) is extremely worried about excessive government power. In drawing the difference between a private enterprise and a public enterprise, Milton Friedman gives a general rule: "if a private enterprise failed, it closes down — unless it can get a government subsidy to keeps it going; if a government enterprise fails, it is expanded". Milton Friedman (1981:11–15) further explains that "it is easier to keep the government from getting involved in something than it is to get the government out once it gets involved, because vested interests are created that are extremely difficult to dislodge, not least the vested interests of the civil service". "The government is simply a mechanism which has the power to take from some to give to others. It is a way in which some people can spend other people's money for the benefit of a third party — and not so incidentally, themselves". Milton Friedman elaborates that "the fundamental principle under capitalism is that transactions shall be voluntary and no force shall be used". On the role of the government, Friedman comments that "government is essential both as a forum for determining the 'rule of the game' and as an umpire to interpret and enforce the rules decided on".

In commenting on the relationship between economic freedom, human freedom and political freedom, Friedman (1991:5–6) uses the example of Hong Kong and regarded the development of Hong Kong as a showcase in his book on *Capitalism and Freedom* (1962).

"Hong Kong has been one of the freest, if not the freest, of countries in the world in every aspect but one. Hong Kong has had an extraordinary degree of economic freedom: no tariffs and no import or export quotas... Taxes have been very low. There are few regulations on business, no price controls, no wage controls... Hong Kong has a great deal of human freedom, and has never seen any evidence of suppression of freedom of speech, freedom of the press, or any other human freedom that we regard as important... However, in one aspect Hong Kong has no freedom whatsoever. It has no political freedom".

Peacock (1997:27) points out that the study of economic freedom falls largely within the field of "political economy" that links between ethics and economics, and argues that ethics is concerned with the identification of human actions as "right" and "wrong". Economic freedom has been interpreted differently. For example, Sen (1987, 1994) distinguishes between "freedom to act" and "freedom to achieve", and argued that despite the presence of market mechanism, there is the problem in "freedom of choice" in that choice could be restricted by poverty and misfortune, and choice can lead to conflict of interest. Peacock (1997:33) doubts about Sen's (1987, 1994) interpretation of freedom, and pointed out that although resource endowment may differ among individuals, their performance can best be rewarded in a fully fetched, ethically sound market economy, and not a politically restricted, manipulated or controlled market. One should not look at exceptional or individual cases at the expense of the very fundamental principle.

1.3 Economic Freedom in Its Entirety

It is worth understanding the conceptual essence of economic freedom and how it is linked to both economic and non-economic aspects in advancing societal progress. The very fundamental of economic freedom rests in a *laissez-faire* doctrine that emphasizes private economic initiatives with production free from state or government intervention. The essence of the *laissez-faire* doctrine is liberalism. The advocates of liberalism believe that a free market capitalist system produces greater prosperity, freedom and personal achievement than other economic systems.

The society composes of individuals, who probably know the marketability of their own endowment best, given the information available in the market. Personal endowments include formal education, talent, job or industry preferences, skills, market and trade information, work experience, exposure to different business, personal visions, creativity and innovation, family relationships, heritage and so on. With freedom to interact and in order to maximize one's return and gains, an individual will naturally search for the best possible economic outcome in the market. In a modern market economy, an entrepreneur can form a business or trade using his/her own financial resources or typically getting a loan from banks, specializing in his/her own area of expertise and interest. For an individual who does not have sufficient financial capital or ability to borrow, he/she will have to offer his/her service to work in a business or institution. Either way, the individual will be rewarded either through capital gains from business or a salary payment from employment.

In modern economies, individual entrepreneurial businesses begin typically with the establishment of small- and medium-sized enterprises (SMEs) which often form the backbone of businesses in a society. SMEs usually begin with the expertise of the individuals willing to take risk, and when successful, the individual entrepreneurs can expand their business, including the ability to list in the stock market, going overseas to take advantage of the foreign market, merging or acquiring another enterprise to secure resource supply or diversifying into another business. For individuals who are employed in business, trades and other establishments, and once they have earned sufficient experience, expertise and connections, they may decide to set up their own business. Once individuals have cumulated sufficient experience, they are often provided with a higher return in the form of salary or commissions.

The first important advantage of economic freedom is that all individuals, through their own business establishment or engagement in employment, take care of their own economic welfare. In other words, their goal is to achieve economic security. With economic security, the individuals can start to accumulate, save and build up their wealth for their current and future expenses in acquiring private property, making medical expenses, education for their children and retirement plans. Thus, the achievement of economic security in turn helps the individuals to attend to their own social security, and the individuals can stand on their own feet economically and not to rely on the state or the government for economic assistance and subsidies. Indeed, the individual can even contribute to the society by paying profit tax or income tax to the government. The attainment of economic security, and subsequently social security, is the first important outcome of economic freedom.

With economic freedom, individuals are free to improve their personal market endowments and engage in different industries, trades and businesses. Given their own economic motivation, innovation and creativity, coupled with development in technology, individuals are free to explore new ideas and venture into new production areas, and subsequently new jobs are created as businesses and production prosper and have become more diversified. Armed with the legal protection of intellectual property rights, individuals are encouraged and free to innovate and be creative, and that eventually can results in the development of new industries, businesses, employment and trade. Diversification in business and employment can broaden the society's economic base, help to sustain economic growth and development, and provide new job opportunities for job-seekers. These activities further provide new opportunities for other job-seekers to achieve their economic security.

In an economically free society, individual creativity, innovative ability and entrepreneurial drive are important assets to economic diversity and progress. Although innovation in technology often requires huge capital expenses and research and development activities that can only be provided by modern corporations, often the applied usage and the commercialization of existing technology are conducted through individuals' creativity, vision, design and packaging and risk-taking in product and market development.

The provision and enlargement of economic opportunities is the second virtue of economic freedom. Indeed, it is often the scarcity of opportunity, rather than the scarcity of resources, that has been the larger constraint in economic development. Economic freedom allows individuals to establish and conduct their own economic activities, excel in their business or trade, acquire necessary input and resources through the market mechanism and utilize the market to promote their output. The common result from all these transactions is the creation of more employment opportunities for other job-seeking or job-dependent individuals and eventually a more diversified economic base can be generated. At the same time, economic diversification allows individuals to use their endowment, expertise and vision to venture into uncharted areas of development that can actually provide new economic alternatives. A more diversified economic base and the greater job opportunities can ensure a more sustainable economy and can better be prepared should sudden economic shocks or social hardship arises.

Many individuals have their own innate talents, while others can enrich their individual endowment through formal education and training. In all societies, there are always some individuals who achieve less or fall out from the formal education system, resulting in a lower level of personal endowment. The formal education system, privately or publicly provided, trains individuals to have different endowment, which in turn produce differences in the rewards. Thus, the fact that individuals are trained differently, jobs are paid differently and businesses are rewarded differently, will definitely lead to income inequality. Welfare advocates often focus on the undesirable aspects of income inequality, without admitting that individuals with different market endowments can coexist cooperatively, productively and peacefully in a society. Individuals with sufficient market endowments can economically survive and ensure economic security, though the return to their endowment differ. The more relevant concern is to look for the way out and at the same time to minimize the number of those individuals who lack sufficient market endowment and are not able to survive economically.

There are numerous possibilities that individuals have problems of securing sufficient market endowment. Examples include the downturn of a business cycle that generates economic recession, resulting in poor business outlook and ultimately a loss in the number of available jobs. The emergence of economic or industrial restructuring can result in the displacement of some outdated jobs, especially when economic or industrial restructuring has not been supplemented by the retraining of workers for other employment. It is possible that a person is deprived of formal education at a young age, either because of family condition, health, environmental or geographical reasons. Individuals making poor academic progress when they were at their young ages, and consequently did not attain sufficient formal education, qualification and skill when they grow up will have a lower chance in securing sufficient marketable endowment. A similar situation is the lack of job experience in the case of school leavers. New immigrants that do not have necessary qualifications and experience will have problem in securing employment in the market. In addition, individuals who experience different types of life hardship due to natural disaster, accidents and loss of family members can end up with inability to support themselves economically and are faced with an economic survival problem.

In other words, there is always a group of endowment-low individuals in all societies, and they are generally labeled as the poor, typically measured in the form of low income, low skill, low job opportunity and low marketability for employment. Advocates for social welfares tend to emphasize a lot on the limited amount of government assistance. For the government, the more relevant concern is not the economic achievement the endowment-high individuals have made, but how to deal with the endowment-low individuals who need help in economic and social security.

In dealing with poverty, the more relevant strategy is to make a distinction between the stock (the quantity at any time) and the flow (the new entrants and the number departing). Although the stock shows the size of poverty the government needs to concern, it is more relevant and effective to pursue economic policies that deal with the flow of the poverty. The overall pool of poverty can be reduced only when the appropriate economic policies ensure on the one hand a decline in the number of new entrants and on the other hand an increase in the number of departures. The issue of poverty should thus be seen as a "fluid" issue, meaning that dynamically there are always new entrants to the poverty pool, and there are individuals who have equipped themselves with sufficient endowment to depart from the poverty pool.

There are economic instruments that prevent individuals from entering and permit individuals to exit the poverty pool. Formal educational qualifications and technical and vocational training are always the effective mean to enrich an individual's endowment. Policies that aim to maintain macroeconomic stability and the prevention of economic shocks and economic recessions are other effective ways to avoid individuals falling into the poverty pool. Good social and personal ethics produce social equity that maximizes the chances of personal drive in the market.

On the contrary, the solution to encourage individuals to depart from the poverty pool will be the creation of market incentives so that new investment activities can create more jobs, and economic policies that lead to economic recovery after a period of shocks and hardships. If policies are properly instituted, the number of entrants into the poverty pool will be minimized while the number of departures is maximized. Given that the poverty pool is minimized, it would be appropriate to provide adequate assistance to ensure people in the poverty pool can reach the economic survival level. In short, endowment-strong individuals are free to maximize their economic achievements through market transactions, while the endowment-weak individuals that are not secured economically and socially will have to be provided with temporary assistance in the form of welfare subsidy until the new availability of jobs that can absorb them back into the market. Economic freedom thus minimizes those who are in need of assistance, and maximizes the economic opportunities available for individuals with marketable endowment.

On the question of educating the young, Milton Friedman (1982) makes a distinction between the "neighborhood effect" and the "paternalistic concern" in the provision of education. The "neighborhood effect" relates to the finance and provision of a minimum level of schooling by the government, while the "paternalistic concern" is the responsibility of the society to see to the fact that children have to be educated. While it is most desirable for a society to have a build-in policy that provides adequate formal qualifications to individuals, the individuals themselves, especially when they are at the young and learning years, should utilize the maximum educational and training opportunities and channels to learn and equip themselves with modern skill and knowledge. In-job training and adult education are additional available means, especially for those facing rapid structural changes in industries.

In a *laissez-faire* economy, economic freedom is pursued to its maximum extent, individual liberty is cherished, but market anarchism to the extent that all human issues are solved or conducted through the market is discouraged. There is a role for the government. One basic role of the government is to exercise a minimum level of income redistribution so as to provide the needed economic survival assistance to those in the poverty pool through the use of temporary cash subsidy in the form of redeemable vouchers, since subsidy recipients can also have the freedom to choose their service (Friedman, 1982). The other issues concern the provision of physical infrastructure and public goods. Basic physical infrastructure facilities, typically the construction of roads, highways, sewage system, street lighting, land formation for construction, police and national security, urban planning and ports and airport construction, museum and cultural centers, preservation of environment and heritage buildings, parks and stadiums, and recreational amenities are regarded as social capital that are best supplied by the government using the fund collected from tax revenues. The construction of physical infrastructures often requires large financial capital, and their provision is meant to create or facilitate other economic activities for the public at large.

The more controversial role is the provision of public goods, typically including such basic necessities as educational institutions, medical facilities, communications networks (radio and television), housing and transport system. Due to the high cost in the provision of public goods, the typical debate is that if they are supplied by the private sector, the price consumers paid may be too high. But if they are supplied by the government, there could be inefficiency, resulting in losses and misuse or abuse of resources. A good balance will be, where possible, the provision of public goods by both the government and private organizations. Educational institutions and medical services are good example. While economically capable parents are free to send their children to private educational institutions, government provision of education provides not only choice, but a check and balance in the quality of the education service. In the case of housing, the government should provide adequate public housing for the needy, while capable individuals are encouraged to acquire their housing needs in the private sector. Joint ventures are possible for the provision of an efficient public transport system. In many ways, there is also a need for competition in the provision of public goods. While individuals are allowed a choice, the government provision ensures that every individual has access to public goods, utilities and services.

The conceptual debate on the role of the government has always been "how much", and "to what extent" the government should involve in the economy. The government itself should behave more like a monitor than a producer, checking the orderly conduct of private sector economic activities, ensuring macroeconomic stability rather than engaging in physical production of goods and services. To strike a balance in the extent of economic involvement requires the deliberation of a doctrine that specifies certain practices, policies and strategies that maximize individual economic freedom, and at the same time there is enough room for the government to maneuver to ensure economic efficiency and social equity.

1.4 The Measurement of Economic Freedom

There are a number of sound and long established national and world institutions that advocate for individual liberty and freedom, which is considered as a value fundamental to humanity. The provision of economic freedom is thought to promote, on the one hand, individual prosperity and advancement, and on the other hand, liberate individuals from relying on government for support. It follows that with economic freedom, individuals are free within the legal boundary to conduct their economic activities, which eventually provide them with economic security. With the achievement of economic security by individuals, the role of the government will cater mainly for the provision of pure public goods and care for the truly needy in the society. Thus, economic independence of individuals can lessen the welfare burden of the government.

The two reputable world organizations that regularly provide a measure of economic freedom and rank the performance of economic freedom among world economies are the Heritage Foundation in Washington DC, United States, and the Fraser Institute in Vancouver, Canada (Hanke and Walters, 1997). For a number of years, each of these institutions produces a world-wide economic freedom index based on a number of characteristics, to measure national performance of economic freedom, and rank annually the extent of overall economic freedom across different world economies. The economic freedom index aims to rank and promote economic freedom around the world, as it can provide individuals, businesses, policy makers and government with useful information that can have implications on individual economic behavior, and directions and outcomes of government policies.

The Heritage Foundation, which publishes the annual *Index of Economic Freedom* with the support from the *Wall Street Journal*, defines economic freedom that "provides an absolute right of property ownership, fully realized freedom of movement for labor, capital, and goods, and an absolute absence of coercion or constraint of economic liberty beyond the extent necessary for citizens to protect and maintain liberty itself". A total of ten categories of economic freedom are used to construct the index (Beach and Kane, 2008). They are:

1. **Business freedom:** the ability to create, operate and close an enterprise quickly and easily, as burdensome and redundant regulatory rules is harmful barriers to business freedom.
2. **Trade freedom:** a composite measure of the absence of tariff and non-tariff barriers that affect exports and imports of goods and services.

3. **Fiscal freedom:** the burden of government from the revenue side. It includes both the tax burden in terms of the top tax rate on individual and corporate income and the overall amount of tax revenue as a portion of Gross Domestic Product (GDP).
4. **Government size:** all government expenditures, including consumption and transfers. The state should commit a minimum amount of expenditure only on true public goods.
5. **Monetary freedom:** price stability with an assessment of price controls. Both price controls and inflation distort market activity, and price stability without microeconomic intervention is the ideal state for the free market.
6. **Investment freedom:** the free flow of capital, especially foreign capital.
7. **Financial freedom:** a measure on banking security as well as independence from government control. State ownership of banks and other financial institutions gives rise to political favoritism and produces an inefficient burden to the free capital market.
8. **Property right:** an assessment of the ability of individuals to accumulate private property, secured by clear laws that are fully enforced by the state.
9. **Freedom from corruption:** based on quantitative data that assesses the perception of corruption in the business environment, including levels of government, legal, judicial and administrative corruption.
10. **Labor freedom:** a composite measure of the ability of workers and businesses to interact without restriction by the state.

The statistical data used in calculating the index come mainly from international organizations, such as the World Bank, International Monetary Fund and the Economist Intelligence Unit. Each of these ten economic freedom categories is supported by a clearly defined methodology, and all ten categories are equally weighted in order to avoid bias in the overall score. The ten freedom categories are graded using a scale from 0 to 100, where 100 represents the maximum degree of freedom. The higher the score out of 100, the better the economic environment or set of policies conducive to economic freedom. The methodology has constantly been upgraded as new data and measurement become available (Beach and Kane, 2008).

The Fraser Institute defines economic freedom as that "individuals have freedom when the property they acquire without the use of force, fraud, or theft is protected from physical invasions by others and they are free to use, exchange, or give their property as long as their actions do not violate the identical rights of others" (Gwartney *et al.*, 1996). The *Economic Freedom of the World*, which is a project "godfathered" by Milton Friedman, is co-published by a total of seventy two members of the Economic Freedom Network (Gwartney *et al.*, 2007). The Fraser Institute outlines the four key ingredients of economic freedom to include: 1) personal choice; 2) voluntary exchange coordinated by markets; 3) freedom to enter and compete in markets; and 4) protection of persons and their property from aggression by others (Gwartney and Lawson, 2003). The Fraser Institute's *Economic Freedom of the World* is based on 42 distinct factors grouped under five categories (Gwartney *et al.*, 2007). They are:

1. **Size of government:** general government consumption spending as a percentage of total consumption; transfer and subsidies as a percentage of GDP; government enterprises and investment; and top marginal income tax rate and income and payroll tax rates.
2. **Legal structure and security of property rights:** judicial independence; impartial courts; protection of property rights; military interference in rule of law and the political process; integrity of the legal system; legal enforcement of contracts; and regulatory restrictions on the sale of real property.
3. **Access to sound money:** money growth; standard deviation of inflation; inflation of most recent years; and freedom to own foreign currency bank accounts.
4. **Freedom to trade internationally:** taxes on international trade that include revenue from taxes on international trade as a percentage of exports and imports, mean tariff rate and standard deviation of tariff rates; regulatory trade barriers that include non-tariff trade barriers and compliance cost of importing and exporting; size of trade sector; black-market exchange rates; international capital market controls that include foreign ownership or investment restrictions and capital control.
5. **Regulation of credit, labor and business:** credit market regulations that include the ownership of banks, foreign bank competition, private sector credit and interest rate controls; labor market regulations that include minimum wage, hiring and firing regulations, centralized collective bargaining, mandated cost of hiring, mandated cost of worker dismissal and conscription; business regulations that include price controls, administrative requirements, bureaucracy costs, starting a business, extra payment and bribes, licensing restrictions and cost of tax compliance.

The criteria and characteristics used by the two institutions to measure economic freedom and rank the various world economies are quite similar; basically their core features are the extent of individuals' economic liberty, small size of government, property right protection, sound fiscal and monetary policies, and economic openness to foreign capital and trade.

1.5 Evidence From Empirical Studies

Empirical studies on economic freedom using data from Gwartney *et al.* (1996) and different annual *Economic Freedom of the World* reports published by the Fraser Institute have concentrated on two major areas: one area concerns the relationship between economic freedom and economic growth, while the other area relates economic freedom to political freedom, liberalization and democracy. There are others that relate the study of economic freedom to corruption, experiences in Asia, Latin America and Eastern European countries, equity returns, religion, the extent of government intervention, equality, and the role of world institutions and so on. The benefits of economic freedom are summarized in Berggren (2003), while Grubel (1998) outlines some empirical findings on economic freedom and human welfare.

In the various studies on economic freedom and growth (e.g., Haan and Siermann, 1998), the study by Gwartney *et al.* (1999) shows a number of empirical findings. Firstly, economic freedom exerts a strong and robust impact on economic growth, and along with differences in the level of investment in physical capital, differences in the level of economic freedom can explain about 40% of variation in cross-country growth rates during the two decades in 1975–1995. Secondly, increases in economic freedom can result in more rapid growth, but the higher growth does not enhance future economic freedom. In the process of economic freedom, institutions that are conducive to growth must be encouraged to expand their activities, but achievements in economic liberalization do not make it more likely that a country will enhance its economic freedom. Thirdly, political freedom is less potent than economic freedom as a determinant of economic growth. Such policies that enhance economic freedom and a greater reliance on market, freedom of exchange, openness of the economy and monetary stability is more important as a source of economic growth than the nature of political regime. Similar conclusions are provided by Haan and Sturm (2000) who show that more economic freedom fosters economic growth, but the level of economic freedom is not related to growth, implying that the change in economic freedom increases growth, while the level of economic freedom does not lead to higher growth.

Cole (2003) explores the effect of adding the economic freedom element into two growth models: the neoclassical augmented Solow growth model included such explanatory variables as initial income, investment share in GDP, population growth and a measure of human capital, and a simplified version of the model in Gallup *et al.* (1999) that explains per capita income growth in terms of the income convergence effects and other geographical variables. The empirical results showed that economic freedom and change in economic freedom are significant and positive to growth, and any given level of investment will have a higher growth impact in countries with a greater degree of economic freedom. The estimated impact of economic freedom on economic growth is stronger in the Gallup *et al.* (1999) model than in the neoclassical growth model. The paper concluded that economic freedom is a significant factor in economic growth, regardless of the basic theoretical framework, and that bad policies have a negative impact on growth, while improvements in the policy mix can enhance growth.

Ayal and Karras (1998) also use the neoclassical Solow growth model to study economic freedom. Using a sample of 58 countries for the period 1975–1990, the empirical evidence shows that aggregate economic freedom enhances growth through an increase in total factor productivity and capital accumulation. The various economic freedom factors that are shown to be statistically significantly correlated with total factor productivity and capital accumulation are a low money growth rate, a small economic role of government enterprises, and an absence of a black market exchange rate, a large trade sector and freedom in capital transaction.

Among all the components of economic freedom in the *Economic Freedom of the World* report, Carlsson and Lundström (2002) separate those components that are important to growth for a total of 74 countries for the period 1975–1995. Empirical result showed that while an increase in economic freedom enhances growth, the four economic freedom variables that are positively related to growth are economic structure and use of markets, freedom to use alternative currencies, legal structure and security of private ownership, and freedom of exchange in capital markets.

On the question of equity and equality, Scully (2002) examines the relationship between economic freedom, equity and growth and finds that economic freedom increases both the rate of economic growth and the equitable distribution of income, and there is a positive but relatively weak relationship between growth and income inequality, implying that the amount of increase in income inequality is rather small for substantial differences in growth rates across the sample of countries.

There is quite a considerable amount of empirical literature discussing about the relationship between economic freedom and political freedom or democracy (Farr *et al.*, 1998). The Freedom House in Washington DC, United States, which produces the annual report on *Freedom of the World*, examines the importance of political freedom. Vega-Gordillo and Alvarez-Arce (2002) use data for 45 countries for the 1975–1995 decades to show that both political freedom and economic freedom have a statistical significant effect in enhancing growth, and that the impact of economic freedom on growth nearly doubles the effect of political freedom. In addition, a high growth rate can foster political freedom, but a higher growth rate may undermine economic freedom, if redistributive policies are adopted after achieving economic prosperity, since by definition economic redistribution goes contrary to economic freedom. In the estimated dynamic relationship, the empirical result showed strongly that while economic freedom can foster economic growth, market liberalization seems to be an appropriate institutional factor for countries to achieve growth. The impact of political freedom on economic growth is less clear cut, but intensified democracy may result in faster growth and greater economic freedom.

Similarly, Lundström (2005) studies the long-run effect of democracy on different categories of economic freedom in developing countries, and the finding showed strongly that a higher level of democracy leads to increased reliance on the market as the allocation mechanism. This finding is supported by Haan and Sturm (2003) who conclude that the level of political freedom is positively related to increases in economic freedom. Stroup (2007) examines the effect of democratic freedom and economic freedom on the well-being of the society. The well-being of a society is indicated by six measures: years of life expectancy at birth for the total population; child mortality rate per 1,000 children at five years old or younger; the adult literacy rate as a percentage of the whole population; the percent of total population attaining at least a fifth grade education; the percentage of total population with access to improved water sources; and the percentage of two-years-old children having received adequate vaccination. The empirical results showed that economic freedom has a relatively large and beneficial influence on all six well-being measures, while the presence of democracy has a relatively smaller influence on five of the six measures. Hence, expanding the economic freedom of individuals would increase well-being to a greater extent than an equivalent expansion of democratic freedom.

Along the similar lines, Ali and Crain (2002) distinguish between the growth effects of political freedom versus economic freedom, and considered both the direct effect of the political freedom and economic freedom measures on growth, and the indirect effect on investment for a large sample of countries. Their finding show that the effect of economic freedom on growth is independent of the level of political freedom and civil liberty, as the turnover of political leaders is less important than the turnover of economic policies. In addition, the measures of freedom do not show any systematic relationship to economic growth, either directly or indirectly through investment. The conclusion is that more economic freedom lowers relative price distortions and raises the overall quality of institutions.

In the debate between "democracy first, growth later" and "growth first, democracy later", Nelson and Singh (1998) consider a threefold relationship. First, the growth and democracy relationship are examined under a set of conditioning factors that have been identified in the literature as important determinants to growth. The second relationship concerns whether political democracy contributes to economic growth after accounting for economic freedom. The third relationship concerns the causality direction between democracy and economic performance. The empirical results show that when factors that influence growth are being controlled, there is strong evidence that developing countries that have achieved a higher level of political and civil liberties experience significantly higher growth rates than those with autocratic government regimes. A lack of democracy and political freedom can seriously hurt nations' economic performance. The causality tests show that economic growth necessarily leads to more democracy.

In a cross section of 25 transition countries in Eastern Europe, Fidrmuc (2003) looks at the relationship between liberalization and growth, democracy and growth, and democracy and liberalization. The empirical results show convincingly that progress in economic liberalization is an important determinant of growth, and the implementation of democratic policies do not hurt the growth performance. Indeed, it is because of economic liberalization that democratization improves growth performance in the later part of the transition period. In addition, Easton and Walker (1997) define market socialism to include the two aspects of ownership and the ability for market to clear and examine whether practiced market socialism constituted economic growth. Various categories of economic freedom from Gwartney *et al.* (1996) are used to investigate if growth is systematically related to the two aspects of market socialism. The hypothesis of an independent relationship between public ownership and market intervention is rejected, implying that market socialism is economically inefficient and a freer economic structure would achieve further economic development.

There are other studies on economic freedom that are tangentially related to either growth or political freedom. Heckelman and Stroup (2000) question the way the economic freedom index is constructed, and that missing data can prevent consistent data aggregation because some categories actually provided a measure on economic outcome rather than policies *per se*. As a consequence, there is bound to be subjectivity and arbitration in its measurement and aggregation methods. Alternatively, rather than relying upon a subjective index, Heckelman and Stroup (2000) disaggregate the specific components of economic freedom and come up with a weighted growth-promoting economic freedom index. Their findings show that although some countries are rated below the mid-point of the economic freedom index, these countries do have relatively high degree of freedom for those components of the freedom index that contribute strongly to economic growth. Such a re-weighted index can have a higher predictive power on a country's economic growth than the economic freedom index in Gwartney *et al.* (1996).

In studying the relationship between crisis and economic liberalization, Pitlik and Wirth (2003) examine the relationship between economic crisis and economic liberalization using data in Gwartney *et al.* (1996) and find that economic liberalization is smaller after periods in which there is an absence of crisis or there is only a medium-sized crisis than after a period of deep crisis. At the business level, Bjornskov and Foss (2008) find that the level of entrepreneurial activities is significantly related to the two economic freedom categories of government size and sound monetary policy.

In relation to the question of corruption, Graeff and Mehlkop (2003) look at the impact of different components of economic freedom on corruption, and conclude that a crucial determinant of corruption might be the incentive to engage in illegal activities or the ease in conducting illegal businesses. For poor countries, the ease of winding up economic affairs can severely affect the likelihood of corruption. For rich countries, corruption is more affected by the legal structure and the extent the state supports the rule of law. Similarly, Akhter (2004) poses the hypothesis on the relationship between economic globalization, economic freedom, corruption and human development, and finds that the effect of economic globalization on economic freedom is positive and significant, but the effect of economic globalization on corruption is negative and significant. Similarly, the effect of economic freedom (corruption) on human development is positive and significant (negative and significant).

Although both Hong Kong and Singapore have been ranked highest in economic freedom, Paldam (2003) studies the economic freedom of different Asian economies. Among the five East Asian economies (Hong Kong, Singapore, Japan, Taiwan and South Korea), the evidence shows that there is a general upward trend in economic freedom during the period 1970–1999. Both Hong Kong and Singapore have consistently gained much higher level of economic freedom than the other three Japanese-style economies. Economic freedom is therefore not the only factor that accounts for economic success in the rise of the Asian "dragon" economies.

The study on the economic freedom of Latin American countries can be found in Sanchez-Robles and Calvo (2002), who look at the relationship between economic freedom, foreign direct investment and growth using panel data from 18 Latin American countries over the period 1970–1999. Their findings show that economic freedom is a relevant variable in affecting foreign direct investment decisions, which in turn attracted more potential investors. A minimum threshold of development has to exist before foreign direct investment can impact growth. Typically, those countries with a low level of human capital, distorted market and lack of social stability will benefit less from the advantages entailed by the inflow of foreign direct investment.

Bergh (2006) studied the Scandinavian and European countries and showed that high taxes have a negative impact on the division of labor, and economic openness and that free trade created more opportunities for the division of labor to rise. The conclusion is that with openness comes not only access to new products through free trade, but also access to knowledge and technologies that play a fundamental role in economic growth. In the relationship between economic freedom and return to equity investment, Stocker (2005) uses data for the period 1970–2002 to show that a significant direct relationship existed between the percentage increase in economic freedom and observed equity rate of return. Secondly, there was an inverse relationship between the beginning level of economic freedom and observed equity returns; namely less free countries have higher equity returns. Thirdly, there was an inverse relationship between the beginning level of freedom and the percentage increase in freedom; namely, less economically free countries are more likely to experience a greater increase in economic freedom than countries that already experience higher levels of economic freedom.

Davidson (2001) relates the 1997 Asian financial crisis in terms of the "grabbing hand" theory of the state, that government have incentives to involve themselves in economic activity either directly as government or indirectly by participating in business networks. High grabbing hand states have a set of policies, including non-market exchange rate regimes. Using the exchange rate regimes and the presence of civic and property rights as proxies, Davidson (2001) shows that those economies with non-market related foreign exchange rate regimes performed worse than those with market oriented exchange rate regimes. Similarly, those economies with higher levels of political and civil freedoms performed better than those with lower levels of political and civil freedoms. The results are consistent with the hypothesis that "grabbing hand" states performed poorly during the Asian financial crisis.

The study of economic freedom has been related to religion as well. Alon and Chase (2005) agree that freedom is multidimensional and contains economic, political and social aspects. The paper examines how much cross-country variation in per capita income can be explained by religious and other aspects of freedoms. The Fraser Institute's measure of economic freedom is used for 123 countries, and each country is assigned a value from 1 to 7 based on their level of religious freedom, which focuses on the denial of the right to practice one's religion. Empirical results show that economic freedom has the highest correlation with per capita GDP, followed by civil liberties, religious freedom and political freedom. Religious freedom is highly correlated with civil liberties, followed by political freedom. Civil liberties can explain about 67% of the variation in religious freedom. The conclusions are that the more economically free countries also produce richer individuals on average. Secondly, economic freedom remains one of the most influential variables affecting economic prosperity. Third, religious freedom has a positive impact on a country's prosperity. Religious tolerance goes hand-in-hand with other types of freedom, including economic freedom. It is thus in a nation's long-run economic interest to expand not only economic freedom, but also religious freedom.

Whether the operation of such world organization as the International Monetary Fund (IMF) and the World Bank has promoted economic freedom, Boockmann and Dreher (2003) use a panel of 85 countries for the period 1970–1997 to show that World Bank projects produced a positive impact on overall economic freedom, but the amount of World Bank credits yielded a negative effect on economic freedom. In the case of the IMF, their study do not show a clear relationship between the credits and programs of the IMF and economic freedom.

Economic freedom can also be related to the presence of conflicts. Using OECD countries controlled by the level of development, Tures (2003) investigates the relationship between economic freedom and internal conflict, including internal war. The results show a negative relationship between economic freedom and the number of conflicts. "Free" countries are least likely to generate conflicts, "partly free" and "not free" countries are 2.34 times and 3.3 times, respectively, more likely to have a conflict than a "free" country. In conclusion, economic freedom promotes peace, stability and prosperity.

1.6 The Freest Economy: System, Policy and Ethics

For a number of consecutive years, Hong Kong has been ranked the freest economy in the world. Table 1.1 shows the overall score and the scores of individual factors across the years for both the *Index of Economic Freedom* and the *Economic Freedom of the World*. Although Hong Kong's total score for the two indices has improved slightly over the years, there are annual fluctuations in both measures. For example, during the economic recession after the Asian financial crisis in 1997, economic hardship and the increased government intervention, typically in the use of reserve in defending the Hong Kong currency led to a fall in both fiscal freedom and monetary freedom in the *Index of Economic Freedom*, the overall score reached the lowest of 88 points in 1998.

In the case of the *Index of Economic Freedom*, Hong Kong's score has been very stable in trade freedom, investment freedom, financial freedom and property right protection. The score for trade freedom has even increased since 2007, but the score for business freedom has dropped considerably since 2006. The score for fiscal freedom has experienced minor changes over the years, but its score has remained higher than 91 at all times. Labor freedom has been introduced in the index since 2005, and Hong Kong's score has also been high and steady. The more volatile scores are size of government, monetary freedom and freedom from corruption. The score for the government size has fallen since 2000, showing a lowest score of 87.9 in 2006 before it bounced back. Despite the free movement of capital, the score for monetary freedom in Hong Kong has remained below 90 in most years, but overall the trend has risen. The score for freedom from corruption has definitely fallen considerably since 1997 to below 80, though it has been edging upwards since.

In the case of the *Economic Freedom of the World*, the scores for the size of government and the freedom to international trade have been high and steady. The score for the access to sound money has remained high since 1985. The score for the regulation of credit, labor and business has been steady, and has improved since 1995. The more unsteady score is the legal structure and security of property rights, as it has suffered a lowest score of 5.9 in 1990, though it has risen considerably since.

Although classified under different categories (eleven in the *Index of Economic Freedom* and six in the *Economic Freedom of the World*), the factors used in the calculation of the two indices by both the Heritage Foundation and the Fraser Institute are similar. It would be interesting to compare the performance of economic freedom between Hong Kong and the neighboring economies in Asia. Figure 1.2 shows the total score of five other Asian economies. Singapore, Taiwan, South Korea, China and India. Together with Hong Kong, the six Asian economies show a three-tier performance in economic freedom. Singapore ranks second in the *Index of Economic Freedom*, and the various scores are close to Hong Kong's performance. The second tier of economically free economies in Asia are Japan, Taiwan and South Korea, who ranked 17th, 25th and 41st in the 2008 *Index of Economic Freedom*, respectively. The third tier economic freedom Asian economies are India and China, which are ranked

TABLE 1.1 Hong Kong's performance in economic freedom

Index of Economic Freedom

Year	Rank	Total	Business	Trade	Fiscal	Gov Siz	Money	Invest.	Financial	Prop. Rights	Corruption	Labor
1995	1	88.6	100.0	90.0	93.0	93.5	80.8	90.0	70.0	90.0	90.0	
1996	1	90.5	100.0	90.0	91.4	92.0	81.1	90.0	90.0	90.0	90.0	
1997	1	88.6	100.0	90.0	91.8	93.0	81.1	90.0	90.0	90.0	71.0	
1998	1	88.0	100.0	90.0	91.9	92.4	78.0	90.0	90.0	90.0	70.0	
1999	1	88.5	100.0	90.0	91.8	92.9	79.2	90.0	90.0	90.0	73.0	
2000	1	89.5	100.0	90.0	93.0	92.3	82.5	90.0	90.0	90.0	78.0	
2001	1	89.9	100.0	90.0	93.7	91.0	87.4	90.0	90.0	90.0	77.0	
2002	1	89.4	100.0	90.0	93.8	90.3	83.7	90.0	90.0	90.0	77.0	
2003	1	89.8	100.0	90.0	93.6	90.2	85.5	90.0	90.0	90.0	79.0	
2004	1	90.0	100.0	90.0	93.6	89.5	84.6	90.0	90.0	90.0	82.0	
2005	1	90.2	100.0	90.0	93.6	89.7	85.1	90.0	90.0	90.0	80.0	93.3
2006	1	89.3	90.0	90.0	93.3	87.9	88.3	90.0	90.0	90.0	80.0	93.3
2007	1	90.6	88.4	95.0	92.9	91.9	91.6	90.0	90.0	90.0	83.0	93.1
2008	1	90.3	88.2	95.0	92.8	93.1	87.2	90.0	90.0	90.0	83.0	93.3

Economic Freedom of the World

Year	Rank	Total	Size of government	Legal structure and security of property rights	Access to sound money	Freedom to trade internationally	Regulation of credit, labor and business
1970	1	8.69	9.6	7.7	8.8	8.6	7.2
1975	1	8.58	9.7	6.6	9.2	9.4	7.2
1980	1	8.70	9.7	8.1	8.5	9.6	7.2
1985	1	8.33	9.4	6.3	9.3	9.6	7.2
1990	1	8.12	9.3	5.9	9.0	9.6	7.2
1995	1	9.03	9.5	8.2	9.4	9.7	8.7
2000	1	8.80	9.4	7.2	9.1	9.8	8.6
2001	1	8.70	9.1	7.0	9.4	9.8	8.3
2002	1	8.70	9.0	7.3	9.3	9.6	8.3
2003	1	8.70	9.0	7.4	9.2	9.6	8.4
2004	1	8.70	9.1	7.5	9.2	9.5	8.3
2005	1	8.92	9.1	8.0	9.5	9.4	8.6
2006	1	8.92	9.3	8.2	9.4	9.5	8.3
2007	1	8.97	9.3	8.2	9.5	9.6	8.3

Sources: The Heritage Foundation, Washington DC, and The Fraser Institute, Vancouver.

115th and 126th in the 2008 *Index of Economic Freedom*, respectively. The performance of China, whose score was higher than India before 2004, has been caught up by India. For the entire 1995–2008 period, India has been making a gradual progress in the score.

There is similarity in the score performance of the major Asian economies in the *Economic Freedom of the World*, shown in the lower portion of Figure 1.2. The performance of both Hong Kong and Singapore are ahead of other Asian economies,

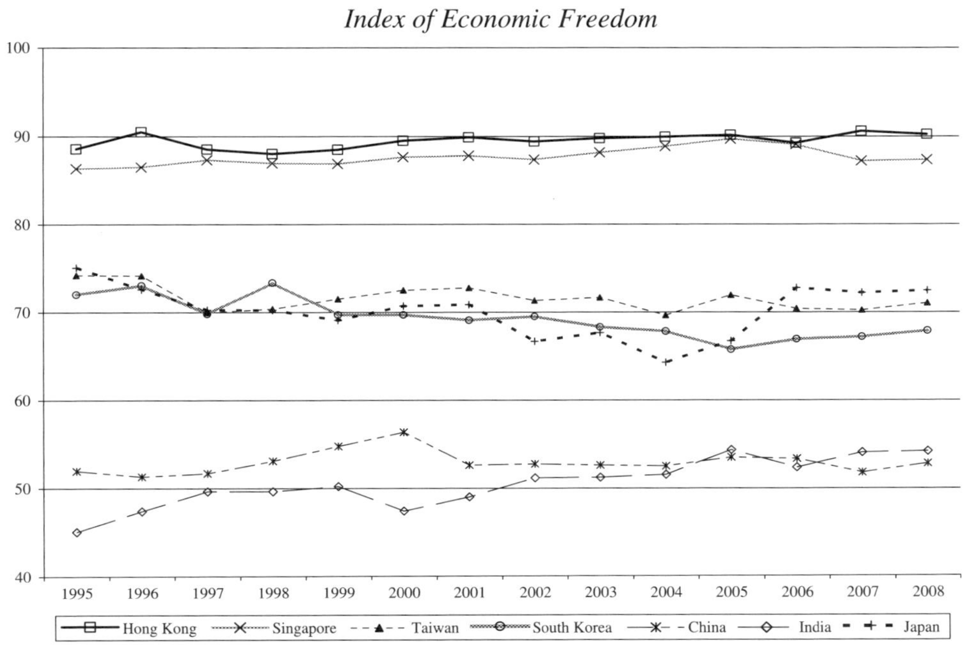

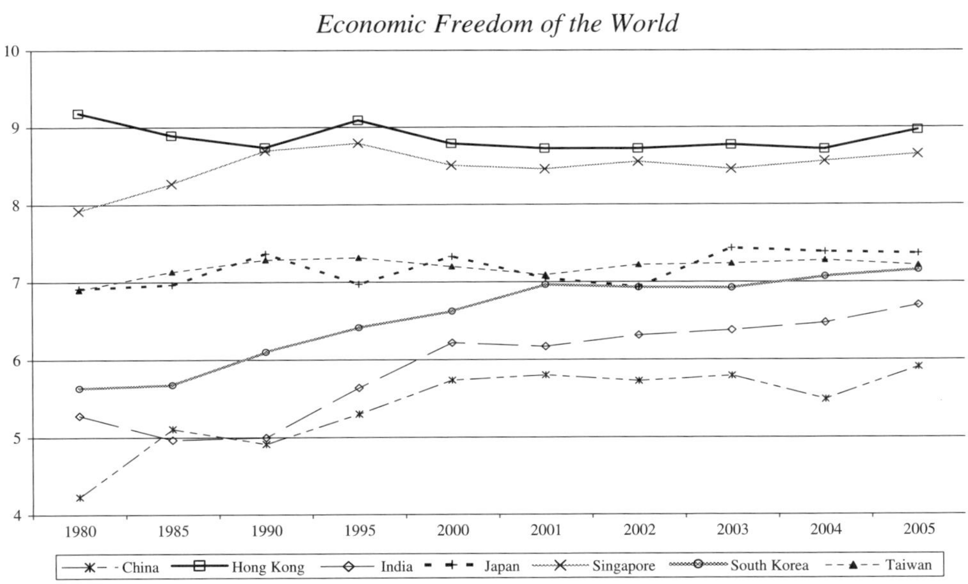

FIGURE 1.2 Performances of Hong Kong and key Asian economies

but it is notable that the scores of South Korea, India and China are rising gradually, while Japan and Taiwan have remained steady. Figure 1.3 examines the performance of the ten aspects of economic freedom used in the *Index of Economic Freedom* across the five Asian economies. In the case of business freedom, Hong Kong has performed worse than Singapore since 2006. On the contrary, South Korea has improved since 2005, while Taiwan has worsened since 2002, and China has the lowest score and has shown a weaker performance since 2006. In trade freedom, China has notably shown a great improvement all through the period. In fiscal freedom, other than Singapore whom has shown some improvement in 2003, the trend for all other four economies has been very steady. In the size of government, Taiwan has definitely made an improvement while South Korea has deteriorated over the years.

In monetary freedom, all five Asian economies have experienced an unsteady trend over the years, suggesting that the maintenance of monetary stability would be the more difficult task among all aspects of economic freedom. China is the only economy that has made considerable improvement over the years, though its improvement since 2006 has edged downwards. There is definitely wide dispersion among the different Asian economies in the two cases of investment freedom and financial freedom, though the trends for most economies are steady. Over the years, both South Korea and Taiwan have made some improvement in investment freedom. For China, there was a decline in 2001 in both investment and financial freedom. The performance of Taiwan has been unsteady in financial freedom.

In the case of property rights, the trends are steady, but the scores of Taiwan and South Korea have dropped in 2002 and 2003, respectively. China's performance in property right is much weaker than the other four economies. Freedom from corruption is probably the only aspect of freedom that shows a different level of performance among the five Asian economies, with Singapore showing the best performance, followed by Hong Kong, Taiwan, South Korea and China. Lastly, although labor freedom has been introduced in 2005, the performance of China is better than both Taiwan and South Korea.

By using Hong Kong as the example of a free economy, one can make several observations from the *Index of Economic Freedom* in Table 1.1. One can group the ten factors conveniently into three "pillars" in economic freedom. The first pillar consists of various "systemic factors" of trade freedom, investment freedom, financial freedom and adherence to property rights. These four basic factors in Hong Kong have remained unchanged all through the entire period. A system that works favorably to economic freedom gives a strong structural foundation. As an open market capitalist economy, Hong Kong economy traditionally has adopted the *laissez faire* principle dominated by the private sector with minimal government intervention. As an open and free trading post, Hong Kong has never initiated any trade restrictions on all trading partners. All legal goods and business-related services are free to move across borders.[1]

[1] Since 2005, Hong Kong has concluded a series of Closer Economic Partnership Agreements (CEPA) with Mainland China, see discussions in later chapters.

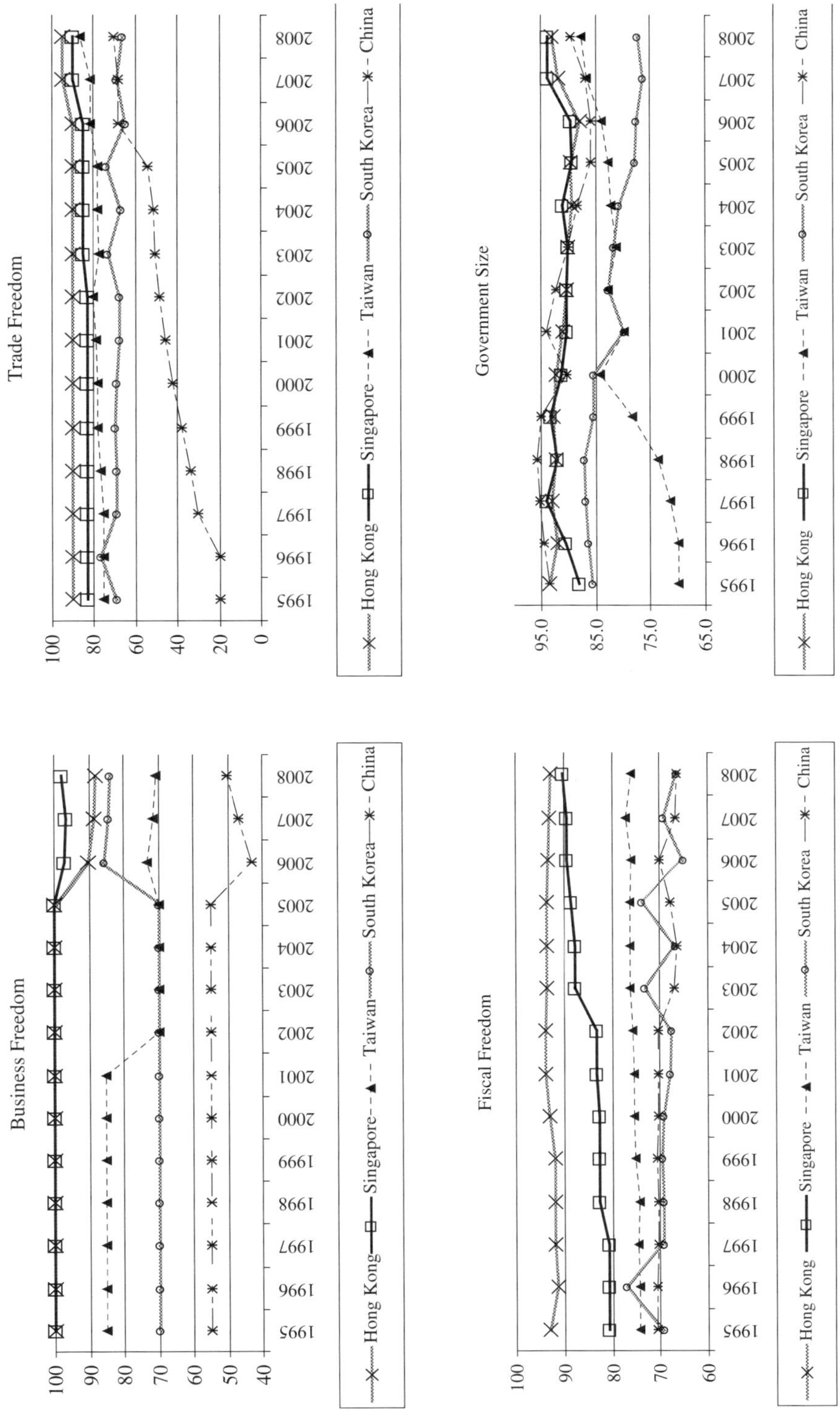

FIGURE 1.3 The ten aspects of economic freedom compared

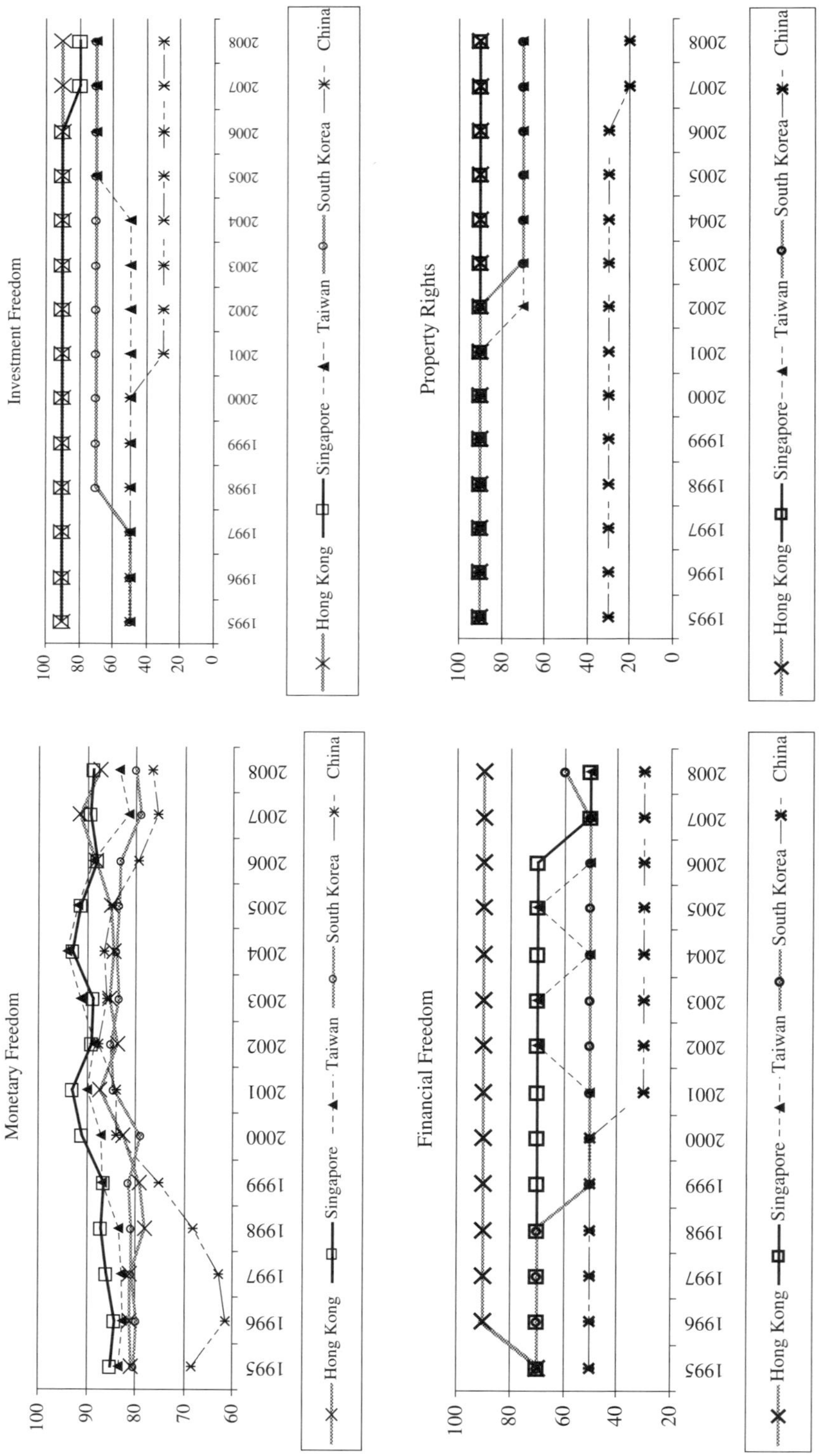

FIGURE 1.3 (*Continued*)

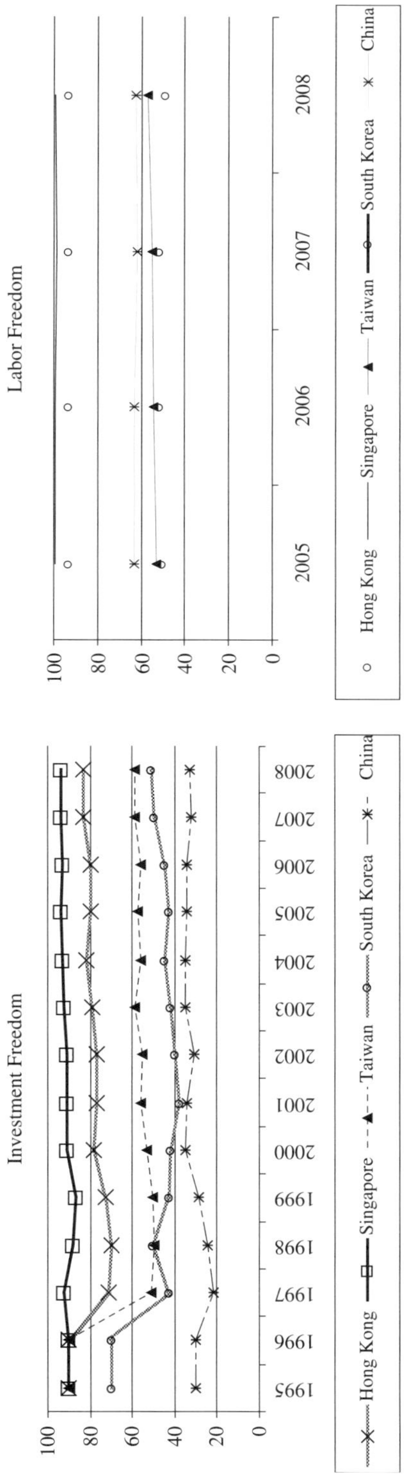

FIGURE 1.3 (*Continued*)

Free trade cannot prosper without financial freedom and investment freedom. With exports and imports, businesses require financial arrangements that involve capital flows across borders. An efficient and reliable banking system becomes a pre-requisite, when traders need to make payments in foreign currencies. As financial activities become widespread, there are new requirements for the establishment of capital markets that soon led to the development of non-bank financial institutions, typically the stock market, insurances and other formal institutions. Open trade attracts foreign investment, and investment freedom then becomes a close partner to economic freedom. Obviously, investment freedom requires sound financial institutions.

The strong and persistent performance in trade freedom, financial freedom and investment freedom indeed forms the core value and practice in economic freedom. A strong foundation of economic freedom is important; as in the case of Hong Kong, it has become rooted and benefited the entire economy indiscriminately.

The second "pillar" includes fiscal freedom, monetary freedom and the size of government. These three aspects of economic freedom relate primarily to the economic policy and the philosophy of the government. Typically, extensive intervention by the government will create distortions in fiscal and monetary performance, leading probably to fiscal deficits and unsound monetary management. Fluctuations in the business cycle would lead to changes in these three aspects of economic freedom, as interventionist policies may need to be introduced in order to rescue the economy. Among these three aspects of economic freedom in Hong Kong as shown in Table 1.1, the gap of fluctuation in the scores in the entire sample period for fiscal freedom, size of government and monetary freedom are 2.4, 4.0 and 13.6, respectively. Monetary freedom experienced its lowest score of 78.0 in 1998, when the government intervened in the stock market at the peak of the Asian financial crisis, and the highest score of 91.6 in 2007. Despite the unprecedented recession and the experience of the huge fiscal deficit that followed the Asian financial crisis in 1997, fiscal freedom is most stable due certainly to the "non-intervention" policy that effectively controls the total level of public expenditure below 20% of GDP. Hence, in addition to the "built-in" system, economic freedom has to be up-held by effective and determined policies.

The third "pillar" concerns the remaining three aspects of business freedom, freedom from corruption and labor freedom. The common characteristic among these three aspects is the ethical requirement of the engaging parties. Issues on equity, reliability, transparency, moral hazards, indiscrimination, commitment and other professional ethics are seen to have effectively been carried out. These aspects of freedom relate primarily to ethical behavior, social manner and practice, and level of education attainment, supported by a strong legal framework. Although law against corruption, for example, can be made to guard against corruption, the more basic question is whether such laws are being instituted and implemented successfully by the state or the government authority, which can have wide political implications on the various interest groups in the society.

In the case of business freedom, Hong Kong's perfect score of 100 has declined rather rapidly since 2006 to only 88.2 in 2008. The score for freedom from corruption has declined from 90.0 in 1995 to its lowest of 70.0 in 1998, though it has edged upwards to 83.0 in 2008. In other words, both the business freedom and freedom from corruption in Hong Kong have weakened. Lastly, labor freedom related to the employer-employee relationship has been maintained high since it was first introduced in 2005. However, with the demand for a minimum wage in Hong Kong in 2010, the score for labor freedom could fall in future, depending on how extensive the minimum wage law would be.

One can summarize that the achievement in economic freedom depends on three major categories of factors: a well-established economic system that provides a strong structural foundation; appropriate policy orientation that minimizes the distortion in economic resources; and sound ethical behavior that produces a high standard in social and non-economic attitudes across different sectors of the economy. These three "pillars" are complementary to each other, the successful performance of one hinges on the successful performance of the others. Secondly, it is important for these three "pillars" to be instituted as early as possible, as their good performance cannot be expected overnight and time is needed for experience to accumulate.

1.7 The Essence of Economic Freedom: Relativity

What is the essence of economic freedom? The economic freedom paradigm actually provides a framework of "relativity" in human behavior through different economic aspects and activities. Conceptually, because of difference in individual endowment, economic outcomes are different to different individuals. Equally, individuals are free to enrich their endowment through various channels and means. As such, economic outcome in a free society becomes "relative", with some gaining more returns than others. When compared inter-personally, inequality exists between individuals, but when individuals are compared intra-personally, economic improvement can allow the individual to gain more over time. While however more one individual earns, there is always another individual who will earn more when inter-personal comparison is made. Inequality always exists when a cross section comparison is made among individuals. The different and "relative" economic outcome permits economic coexistence among individuals in different businesses, trade, sector and employment. Difference in economic rewards leads subsequently to differences in consumption patterns of individuals, which in turn permits different consumer-related goods and services to be produced and supplied. Diversity in the supply of goods and services results in new employment provisions.

The "economic relativity" outcomes among individuals can further be examined conceptually. Human behavior produces either a "relative" outcome or an "absolute" outcome. A "relative" outcome in human behavior produces a "win-win" situation in which parties receive different gains. Typically, all economic activities yields "relative", "more or less" outcomes that depend on how individuals manage their time, resources and endowment, and the opportunities open to them. Investment produces different returns, education and qualifications produce different skills and knowledge which in turn yield different rewards and salaries, difference in age can also produce different rewards and returns. Similarly, individuals in different economic roles complement each other. Workers need employers and vice versa. In a market economy where employers take up the risk of their business more than employees, investment returns to the employers will differ from the fixed salary received by the employees. One thing common to human behavior with relative outcomes is the peaceful coexistence among individuals, with each attending their own individual affairs.

On the contrary, an "absolute" outcome in human behavior provides a zero-sum game, in which one party gains and the other party loses. Typical examples include political elections, wars and civil conflicts that produce opposing outcome with one party winning and another party losing. In a civilized society, human behavior that produces absolute outcomes is either personalized or organized using different economic and market tools. Sport games with absolute outcomes are organized and managed by using economic and marketing skills. Sport associations are agents that promote the games and compete with the intention to win. Preferences on sport teams become a personal choice. Other example includes religious faith, which in a civic society, is very much a personalized affair. The choice of political party in a democratic election, and even the choice of getting married produce an absolute outcome. In conclusion, economic freedom allows peaceful coexistence among individuals in that human activities produce either a "win-win" relative outcome, or personalized into individual preferences and choices.

In its entirety, economic freedom allows individuals to maximize their production potentials and rewards, achieve economic security that eventually takes care of their social security needs, create opportunities and maintain a sustainable macroeconomy for jobs and employment. Differences in rewards provide relative outcomes that permit individuals and economic sectors to coexist peacefully. Relative economic outcomes generate stability and economic progress can then be made. Activities that produce absolute outcomes become personalized, and individuals are given the choice and can freely exercise their preferences.

Given that resources, endowments and opportunities are unequal among individuals and among world economies, economic freedom that yields a "more or less" outcome becomes the acceptable, sustainable and maintainable mechanism through which individuals and societies interact with each other in a stable and peaceful manner. It is a mistaken view that critiques of capitalism and economic freedom have magnified the drawbacks and dangers in activities that produce absolute outcomes, probably with opposing extremes, such as the employer and employee relationship, landlord and tenant relationship, political elections and war or territorial conflicts. The more relevant concern is whether there are sufficient instituted and civic rules and regulations that protect the interest of all parties equitably.

While individuals interact to achieve and maximize relative economic outcomes that differ due to differences in resources, endowments and opportunities, human activities that produce absolute outcomes in a civilized society are either regulated, managed or transformed into personalized preferences. Economic freedom provides the mechanism through which relative outcomes in economic activities are materialized. The maximization of relative economic outcomes in turn minimizes absolute outcomes that are divisive and lead to unwanted conflicts. Stability, peace and expansion of opportunities are the virtues of economic freedom.

1.8 Conclusion

This chapter highlights the importance and relevance of economic freedom. By pointing out that capitalist market economy has been the successful mode of production, a key ingredient in capitalism is economic freedom that permits individuals to interact voluntarily. There is the possibility of unequal outcomes, but more importantly is the fully functioning of a free market. Expansion of economic opportunities is seen as another constrain in economics. Individuals and economies can be limited for resources and endowments, but opportunities can help to raise the returns and rewards. Comparisons have to be made across time and not just a snap shot.

The chapter also summarizes the key ideas from the "forefathers" of economic freedom; but the conceptual and contextual understanding in contemporary terms is important in showing the essence and relevance of economic freedom. In contemporary economies, economic security provides the individual the opportunity to conduct his/her own personal business, allows the economy to maximize its efficiency and productivity, produces tax revenue for the government, and most importantly, looks after the individual's social needs. Once secured economically, individuals will also ensure social security automatically. Numerous empirical studies have repeatedly pointed to the conclusion that economic freedom can benefit growth and development. The various freedom indicators can be funneled into three key freedom aspects of "system, policy and ethics".

The evidence of Hong Kong being the freest economy and its performance with the neighboring and other Asian economies are considered. Although Hong Kong stays the freest, there are indicators that show the need for Hong Kong to improve. One should not be complacent, and the resilient attitude of the people in Hong Kong will lead the Hong Kong economy to its next stage of development. Indeed, while a number of Asian and world economies have studied the past success of Hong Kong, the more challenging task is how Hong Kong can maintain its freest status in the new century. In turn, Hong Kong is being studied and observed. The success of economic freedom in Hong Kong has been noted, but its ingredient, texture and fabrics can form lessons for other emerging economies that want to achieve growth and development through the pursuit of economic freedom. In other words, learning from Hong Kong's experience enables other economies to institute appropriate policies and strategies that are conducive to economic freedom.

This chapter extends the conceptual discussion of economic freedom by examining the difference between "relative" and "absolute" outcomes in economic activities. Economic freedom is a paradigm of "relativity" where outcomes in the form of rewards and returns differ according to differences in resources and endowments. Equally important is the "scarcity of opportunity". Economic freedom allows the maximization of economic opportunities that generate economic security. In a contemporary civic society, unequal returns are acceptable provided there are ample economic opportunities for everyone. And individuals who maximize returns from their resources and endowments lead to relative economic outcomes. Activities that produce absolute outcomes are in turn personalized into individual preferences and choices. Economic freedom is thus a mechanism of sustainable and long lasting peace and stability in an economy.

The economy of Hong Kong, so as its performance in economic freedom, enters a new chapter with sovereignty reversion in July 1997 when Hong Kong is the Special Administrative Region (SAR) of Mainland China. Under the "one country two systems" home rule, the Hong Kong SAR has its own constitution, known as the Basic Law, which states the administrative and economic principles. Thus, while Hong Kong's success in economic freedom can be considered as a "showcase" to other economies, economic freedom in Hong Kong is dynamic and will be observed to see how it can be maintained and deepened or diminished and shallowed.

2 The Hong Kong Brand of Economic Freedom

2.1 Introduction

China has been a great nation with long heritage and culture. Paper, gunpowder and compass are some of the great inventions of China. The history of the world has been rewritten upon Menzies' (2002) book on *1421 The Year China Discovered the World*, where it documents that the sail from China's largest fleet on March 8, 1421, under the command of Admiral Zheng He, circumnavigated the globe in a period of two years. This discovery leads to a rewrite of world history as Admiral Zheng He's fleet had discovered the world "a century before Magellan, seventy years before Columbus reached America, and three hundred and fifty years before Cook arrived in Australia". Menzies' (2002) book also documents detailed economic activities in the 15th century between China and other Asia, near-Asia and Middle East countries of today.

The quality of life in China during Zheng He's time was much higher than life in Europe. Menzies (2002:63) made the following comparison. "The formal inauguration of the Forbidden City was followed by a sumptuous banquet. Its scale and opulence emphasized China's position at the summit of the civilized world. In comparison, Europe was backward, crude and barbaric. Henry V's marriage to Catherine of Valois took place in London just three weeks after the inauguration of the Forbidden City. Twenty-six thousand guests were entertained in Beijing, where they ate a ten-course banquet served on dishes of the finest porcelain; a mere six hundred guests attended Henry's nuptials and they were served stockfish (salted cod) on rounds of stale bread that acted as plates". Similar comparisons on the dressing materials, jewelry worn and the size of army between Emperor Zhu Di in China and Henry V in England were made.

Given the well-developed fleets and the experience of sailing to uncharted waters in much of Asia, Middle East and Africa, Menzies (2002) towards the end of his book questioned that had China in the 15th century opened up and globalized the world, China could have developed new economic epochs, progressed in science and technology and brought advancement to world civilization. As China's history unfolded, unfortunately, it turned out that Zheng He's 1421 sail was the last as the then ruler in China, instead of outward looking and turning to the world for new exploration and development, adopted a self-imposed isolation policy and the returned ships were left to rot, while the well-documented seafaring knowledge and records of seafaring journeys were destroyed (Menzies, 2002). For centuries after Zheng He, China has remained inward-looking. Emperors of different dynasties, served by concubines and surrounded by eunuchs, made little progress in governance, scientific advancement and economic development; China remained largely a primitive, feudalistic, superstitious, rural-based and agriculture-oriented economy.

The modern political and economic history of Hong Kong began in the early 19th century at the peak of the European colonial epoch when different European countries colonized different parts of Asia and the world. Great Britain saw the need to establish a trading post in the Far East as trade flourished between Asia, especially China, Great Britain and other European countries. For decades, China had imported large amount of opium from other Asian countries, but the consumption of opium had poisoned the daily life of a great number of citizens all over China. The government in the Qing Dynasty was too weak to eliminate opium import and root out opium consumption. In the meantime, the British navy had studied and surveyed the Pearl River Delta region. The deep water in the Hong Kong harbor was an attraction, as the lip-shaped harbor could ensure a strategic defensible position. At the eastern end of the Hong Kong Island, for example, Lei Yu Mun could make naval defense possible through the narrow water stripe that ships entered or exited the harbor.

The chance for Great Britain to locate a trading post in southern China came in the Opium War that began in June, 1840, and the British army soon occupied the Hong Kong Island in January and declared Hong Kong Island as a "freeport" in June, 1841. When China lost the Opium War to Great Britain, China's price in the "peace settlement" was to cede the island of Hong Kong to Great Britain in perpetuity in an unequal Treaty of Nanking on August 28, 1842. The Hong Kong Island became a British colony and immediately began to serve as a British trading post in the Far East. Economic and trade openness were the early features instituted in Hong Kong and the Treaty of Bolgue concluded on October 8, 1843, effectively opened Hong Kong to trade as full permission was given to all China natives coming to the island of Hong Kong for the purchase of goods.

The Kowloon peninsula adjacent to the Hong Kong Island was subsequently leased to the British government in perpetuity in another unequal Treaty of Peking on March 24, 1860. As virtually all basic daily necessities have to come mainly from the adjacent province of Guangdong in China, it would not be realistic for the residents in the Hong Kong Island and the Kowloon peninsula to survive independently, the British government attempted to acquire more land from China and in June 6, 1898, leased the New Territories for a period of 99 years. Thus, the political territory of Hong Kong composes of the Hong Kong Island, the Kowloon peninsula and the New Territories (Endacott, 1964).

During the Second World War, the Japanese occupied Hong Kong and took over the government from Britain on December 25, 1941, but after the defeat of Japan in 1945, Great Britain reclaimed Hong Kong from Japan on August 30, 1945. However, in a peaceful communication with Great Britain in August 1954, Premier Zhou En-Lai of China made clear that Hong Kong is part of the People's Republic of China, but the problem will be dealt with in "an appropriate time". In the early 1970s when President Richard Nixon of the US wanted to draw China away from the influence of the Soviet Union, the People's Republic of China was admitted as a member to the United Nations to replace Taiwan. In an early "anti-colonialization" statement made in the United Nations, China's ambassador to the United Nations declared on March 8, 1972, that the territories of Hong Kong and Macau are not separable from the motherland of China (Liu, 2009).

The economy of China in the early part of the 1970s was regaining its order from the devastating effect of the decade-long Cultural Revolution of the 1960s. Both Premier Zhou En-Lai and Chairman Mao Zedong died in 1976, and after the short disruption by the "Gang of Four", the ultra-leftist group led by the wife of Chairman Mao Zedong, Deng Xiao-Ping eventually secured leadership in Beijing, visited both Japan and the US and soon declared a program of economic reform in 1978 with the motto that "it does not matter if the cat is white or black, so long as it catches mice". A process of economic reform was initiated at the Communist Party's third plenary session in late 1978 within the framework of "readjustment, restructuring, consolidation and improvement". Readjustment refers to the removal of imbalances between heavy and light industries, agriculture and industry, production and construction, and investment and consumption. Restructuring refers to the reform of the economy from a centralized, bureaucratic planning system to a decentralized and market-oriented system. Scholars conclude that the four features of the 1978 economic reform in China are marketization, liberalization, pragmatization and privatization (Perkins, 1988; Bettelheim, 1988).

Hong Kong's sovereignty reversion was brought up in 1979 in a visit to Beijing by the then Governor of Hong Kong, Sir Crawford Murray MacLehose. Due obviously to uncertainty generated from the concern by the business sector and investors in Hong Kong in the light of the expiry of the 99 years lease of the New Territories, the British Government led by the Prime Minister, Margaret Thatcher, engaged in a series of Sino-British negotiation over the future of Hong Kong between 1982 and 1984. The British Government insisted on the perpetuity of the Treaty of Nanking initially, but Beijing insisted to resume the sovereignty of the entire territory of Hong Kong in 1997 regardless. The British proposal on the separation between sovereignty and governance, thinking that the sovereignty of Hong Kong would be returned to China but the British Government would remain to rule Hong Kong, was also rejected by Beijing.

The Sino-British negotiation resulted in the conclusion of a Sino-British Joint Declaration on December 19, 1984, that restored stability and business confidence in the Hong Kong economy. The Basic Law that formed the constitution for the post-1997 Hong Kong was enacted in 1990. Chapter 5 of the Basic Law primarily defines the various economic activities in Hong Kong, as it has fundamentally written down the principle and practice of the Hong Kong economic system at the time. To maintain Hong Kong's stability and its international status, the People's Republic of China specified the principle of "one country, two systems" and "self-rule" that Hong Kong can maintain its capitalist economic system for 50 years (until 2047) and will be governed by the people of Hong Kong. The notion of 50 years was suggested by the late Deng Xiao-Ping. On July 1, 1997, the political sovereignty of Hong Kong returns to and becomes a Special Administration Region (SAR) of the People's Republic of China, thereby bringing an end to Hong Kong's status as a British colony for the period of 155 years. Mr. Tung Chee-Hua was elected as the first Chief Executive to head the SAR government.

Since the establishment of the Hong Kong SAR in July 1997, further details regarding the Sino–British negotiation has been unfolded. For example, in an interview that marked the ten years anniversary of the 1997 hand-over with former British Prime Minister Baroness Thatcher who visited Beijing in 1984 to sign the Sino–British Joint Declaration, Lady Thatcher "regretted failing to persuade Beijing to let Britain lease Hong Kong for a longer period", and that she "had doubts about the 'one country, two systems' formula".[1]

Recent declassified reports from Britain's National Archives have disclosed a number of details. Although in response to the Cultural Revolution in China and in the peak of the 1967 riot in Hong Kong, the British Government thought of withdrawing from Hong Kong, the British Government saw in 1969 the need to hand-over Hong Kong to China by initially taking up an informal approach. Former Chinese Premier Zhou En-Lai assured Britain in 1972 that Beijing was in "no hurry" to take back Hong Kong and negotiation on the city's future would open in due course as China was satisfied with the state of the Anglo–Chinese relation in the 1970s.[2]

The idea of turning Hong Kong into a "special administrative district" was first thought of by the former Governor Murray MacLehose at the time of his appointment in 1971. Governor Maclehose foresaw the need to negotiate with China sometime in the 1980s for the return of Hong Kong's sovereignty to Beijing. To gain more bargaining power for Hong Kong in the handover negotiation, Governor MacLehose argued for the need to upgrade the Hong Kong economy as that could strategically place Hong Kong as a more advanced economy. Governor MacLehose believed that an advanced Hong Kong economy might convince the Chinese leaders the "merit in some continuing arrangements for Hong Kong whereby a special [administrative] regime to be established could nominally remove the colonial stigma", but maintains Hong Kong's economic status. At the same time, the "special administrative district" formula could serve three related purposes. It can "preserve for China some of the economic and political benefits of the present status [of Hong Kong], save China from having to absorb a population with different standard of living and attitude of mind, and preserve for foreigners a tolerable trading base while concentrating them in a single area where they did not affect life in the rest of China".[3]

Since 1969, Britain has been planning to handover the control of the colony back to China, and the visit by Governor MacLehose in 1979 to Beijing "merely followed a script written from the report by the British Cabinet Office drafted 10 years before the visit". The 1969 report recognized the need to cooperate with China as "there was no real prospect of any solution to the Hong Kong question which does not provide for the resumption of Chinese sovereignty over Hong Kong". The British Government had forecasted that public confidence in Hong Kong's future would slip and fear a possible wave of emigration in the 1980s if the 1997 question remained unsolved. Among the four possible scenarios that were spelled out in the 1969 report, the best was "an informal approach with a view to reaching a tacit understanding", and with the aim "at reaching an eventual withdrawal when the time is

[1] *South China Morning Post*, June 11, 2007.
[2] *South China Morning Post*, June 25, 2007.
[3] *South China Morning Post*, June 25, 2007.

ripe". To have an effective orderly transfer, the report said that the British Government "will endeavor to avoid doing anything in Hong Kong to make the transfer more difficult, for example by constitutional changes towards representative and more responsible government". Such a recommendation was seen to be "in line with Britain's post-war policy of rejecting any idea of full democracy for Hong Kong so as not to spark resentment and suspicion from Beijing".[4]

As the foreign policy advisor to the British Prime Minister Margaret Thatcher for the period 1984–1992 and prior to his long service as a sinologist in the British Foreign Office and as the British Ambassador to Beijing (1978–1984), Sir Percy Cradock (1924–2010) has been hailed as the architect of the 1984 Sino-British Joint Declaration. Much of the content of the 1984 Joint Declaration has been written into the Basic Law that has basically preserved the economic, political and social life of people in Hong Kong. Sir Percy Cradock had been instrumental in persuading "a reluctant British Prime Minister, Margaret Thatcher, into accepting the inevitably of an agreement that would return Hong Kong to China". This included persuading the Lady Prime Minister not to take "the explosive course of simply declaring independence for Hong Kong" after the June 1989 Tiananmen Square crackdown in Beijing. It was held that Sir Percy Cradock "spearheaded the negotiation strategy that persuaded China to make much more detailed commitment on Hong Kong's future than Beijing had initially intended".[5]

Critics argued that Sir Percy Cradock did not "secure more specific promises from China on the pace of democratization", and often took "too rosy a view of Beijing's intention and was always too ready to reach an agreement at any price". However, Sir Percy Cradock's influence faded upon the replacement of Margaret Thatcher by John Major as the British Prime Minister, who preferred to choose a politician rather than a sinologist to be the next Governor of Hong Kong. Chris Patten, who replaced Sir David Wilson as the last Governor of Hong Kong before the handover in 1997, took a very different attitude towards Hong Kong on responding to public pressure for more democracy.[6] It would remain as historic debates as to whether the Sino-British negotiation over Hong Kong would have a different outcome if professional politicians rather than sinologists had played the key figures.

The Tiananmen Square crackdown incidence in Beijing had sparked much political fear in Hong Kong about its future and the reliability of the post-1997 Chinese government in ruling Hong Kong. It was reported that a postponement on the return of sovereignty had been discussed in Beijing as some of the Hong Kong drafters of the Basic Law petitioned to Beijing for a delay in the resumption of Chinese sovereignty and the renewal of a British lease on Hong Kong was suggested. But both the then Premier Deng Xiao-Ping and the General Secretary of the Communist Party Jiang Zemin stood firm and assured all Basic Law drafters that Hong Kong would remain unchanged for 50 years.[7] In response to the political

[4] *South China Morning Post*, November 20, 2006.
[5] *South China Morning Post*, February 12, 2010.
[6] *South China Morning Post*, February 12, 2010.
[7] *South China Morning Post*, June 27, 2007.

uncertainty resulting from the Tiananmen Square crackdown, it was reviewed that top business tycoons from Hong Kong had proposed to Chinese officials a payment of HK$10 billion (US$1.41 billion) to Beijing in exchange for self-rule in Hong Kong for ten years after 1997, though the suggestion was regarded as "treasonous" by officials in the State Council's Hong Kong and Macau Offices in Beijing.[8]

2.2 Upholding Laissez-Faireism

From its very beginning as a British colony, Hong Kong was destined to open trade and exchange across borders and economic freedom in the form of *laissez-faire* principle was instituted. Commercial activities were conducted with minimal intervention from the colonial government. Over the years, the growing British presence of commercial interests in Hong Kong attracted other foreign business ventures. More importantly, many foreign investments not only stationed in Hong Kong, they soon settled and the favorable economic conditions convinced them to root their businesses in Hong Kong, using Hong Kong as their business base. For example, shipping and re-export trade were the very early industries after Hong Kong was colonized, but other industries began to grow, including cement, soap, salt production and textile in the early 1900s.

The *laissez-faire* economic policy provides a great degree of, if not complete, economic freedom in conducting commercial activities. In turn, the government's fiscal policy aims to minimize the level of salary and profit taxes, and a simple tax system allows investors and businesses a high degree of certainty in their business calculations. An efficient, minimal and "taking a back seat" government encourages the private sector to perform its economic activities to its fullest possible potential. The main objective of monetary policy is the maintenance of macroeconomic and currency stability so as to ensure free and open transactions in financial capital. The private sector has all along played a pivotal role in the economic development of Hong Kong.

In the early colonial days, social welfare provision was non-existed. However, the colonial government did allow religious and civic groups, either foreign or home grown, to establish institutions that acted as supplements to education, medical centers and welfare provisions. Examples include the Tung Wah Group of Hospitals, established in 1856, which provided free medical services to the poor. The Po Leung Kuk, established in 1878, provided basic social and welfare assistance to the sick, destitute and immigrants. The Maryknoll Covent School was established in 1921 by the Maryknoll sisters on a mission to Hong Kong to set up schools for local children. Numerous associations based on different Chinese dialects and geographical origins have been established over the years, thereby providing closer relationships with families and relatives from their own place of origin.

In addition to being a free and open trading port that facilitated economic, trade and commercial activities in and among Asia, Europe and America, Hong Kong soon played a new role as an immigration center. Hong Kong went through various

---

[8] *South China Morning Post*, July 4, 2007.

periods of instability, crises and threats in a number of historical timelines in the last century. Firstly, despite the outbreak of the Chinese Revolution led by Sun Yat-Sen in 1911 that ended the Qing Dynasty, there was an absence of stability in China in much of the first half of the 20th century. Although Sun established the Nationalist government and declared the three principles of "People's Livelihood, Nationalism and Democracy" (Wade, 1990), Sun made little progress in economic development and did not introduce effective control and governance. China was soon in the hands of regional or territorial warlords. Despite Sun's background as a medical doctor and he had travelled around the world, Sun had ideologically leaned more towards communism practiced in the Soviet Union than capitalism in the Western world. The Nationalist government soon faced an indecisive ideological battle between communism and capitalism, and China became a war-torn country as ideology division between the Nationalist government and the Communist Party occurred along with Japanese invasion before 1949.

The First World War in 1914–1918 and the Japanese occupation in the Second World War in 1939–1945 imposed prolong hardship to the people in Hong Kong. Communist ideology was established in China after 1949, as economic planning, nationalization of industries and the establishment of the commune system occupied much of the 1950s, and the Great Leap Forward in the mid-1950 when Mao Zedong declared that "China would caught up with Britain in a matter of eight years and the United States in a matter of ten years" ended up in famine in 1958 as farm produce dropped due to poor harvest. The power struggle between leaders in the top echelon of the Community Party led Mao Zedong to declare the Cultural Revolution in early 1960s that sent all professionals and literates to do hard labor work in remote countryside, and family units were dismantled as all individuals belonged to a commune. Extreme hardship was created and economic development and human progress was sacrificed (Chen and Galenson, 1969).

Hong Kong has naturally become an attractive shelter for large number of Chinese natives fleeing from Mainland China to Hong Kong during the different hardship periods. Indeed, political stability and the availability of ample economic opportunities in Hong Kong had pulled resources from Mainland China to Hong Kong. Thus, over the years, Hong Kong has been a popular destination for Chinese refugees. It was only after the 1960s that the Hong Kong government stopped granting free entry to refugees from Mainland China. For a long time before the 1960s, social security and welfare provision in Hong Kong was minimal, if at all existed. Chinese migrants to Hong Kong in those days, however, were not after the provision of social security from the British Hong Kong colonial government, but rather considered Hong Kong as a stable place in which they could secure, pursue and extend their private individual economic drives. Economic returns and benefits were obtained through hard work, self-reliance, ingenuity with business-driven mentality and entrepreneurship. Rather than to wait for assistance or to free-ride the system in Hong Kong, immigrants created and searched for viable economic opportunities. With few natural advantages (for example, the lack of natural resources and fertile arable land), new migrants in previous decades responded quickly with creativity and determination to challenges and overcome economic hardship. Migrants, who fled to Hong Kong either joined the labor force to work for industries and commerce, established their entrepreneurial business or came with financial capital that aided the industrialization process in the Hong Kong economy after the Second World War.

In general, migrants usually are more determined, self-reliant and enterprising than the average person in the population from which they come. Other than being in their youthful age, one peculiar attributes of immigrants is the selective bias of migratory individuals. As such, Hong Kong was the recipients of not only a large low wage labor force but people with marked potential for upgrading and, most especially, people that are positively inclined to respond to market signals. It is the advantage from such an asset that Hong Kong displayed the fullest pragmatic resiliency in response to the many challenges it has faced over the years. Looking back, this tradition was just as valuable as any physical inputs in fashioning the high-performance economic system in Hong Kong. Over the years, it has become clear that the ability to generate a creative response is an ever present or evergreen resource for Hong Kong.

The economy of Hong Kong in the pre-World War II decades was largely considered as a fishing port and a re-export center. The provision of a free port and the *laissez-faire* policy are the conventional reasons for Hong Kong's economic success (Chou, 1966; Cheng, 1982; Hsia, 1984). Hong Kong began to industrialize in the 1950s either from the financial capital brought to Hong Kong by immigrants fleeing from Mainland China or from post-war investment provided by Britain and other foreign countries. The inflow of capital occurred along with the rising number of refugees that formed the low cost labor force in Hong Kong (Szczepanik, 1958; Chow and Papanek, 1981; Riedel, 1974, 1988; Li, 2002). Beginning from the 1960s, the colonial government designated such areas as Tsuen Wan and Kwun Tong as industrial districts dominated by small- and medium-sized enterprises. The early phrase of industrialization centered on such labor-intensive manufactures as textiles, wigs, transistor radios and toys. By the 1970s, and despite the growing protectionist policies imposed on Hong Kong's textile exports in the form of the Multi-Fiber Agreements, Hong Kong has achieved a high degree of industrialization, with diversification in manufactures and in overseas markets (Chen, 1979; Chen and Li, 1994, 1997; Li, 1991).

The continuous inflow of foreign capital produced periodic dynamism in Hong Kong's changing advantages. With the experience of a re-export center and an industrialized economy, Hong Kong has rapidly become a banking and financial center in the Asia region. The buoyant international banking activities that involved trading of currencies and transactions in export and import soon spilled over to such financial activities as money market development, insurance and stock trading. In short, Hong Kong began with an international banking center that gradually spread to related financial transactions and activities before becoming a full-fetch financial center (Jao, 1974, 1988, 1997; Goodstadt, 2006a, 2007; Schenk, 2002).

The economic growth of Hong Kong has largely been based on a supply-driven strategy through recurrent economic virtuous cycles of "investment → industrial production and output → export of goods and services". Over the years, economic openness has provided an instrument for attracting inward capital in the form of foreign investment and external demand in the form of manufactured goods and services exports. It was Hong Kong's industrious labor force, ingenuity and drives to attain personal economic security, coupled with a pragmatic administration and the timely provision of appropriate infrastructure that enabled Hong Kong to supply goods and services to the rest of the world. The rise in income and demand, both locally and internationally, was the result of the successful outcome of the supply-driven economic strategy. Most important of all, the supply-driven strategy created numerous economic opportunities for jobs, employment and ultimately attracted investment.

As a British colony, there had over the years been occasional political calls of anti-colonialism in Hong Kong, such as the riots in 1967 at the peak of the Cultural Revolution in Mainland China, but little had dented the Hong Kong economy. Administrative absolutism practiced by the British colonial government produced a high degree of administrative efficiency. The colonial Governor took advice from the Executive Council before finalizing policies, while the Legislative Council took care of the law-making process. Within the administration, the Attorney General took charge of the legal department, while the Chief Justice controlled the judiciary. The Financial Secretary was responsible for drafting the annual budget and managed both economic and monetary affairs. The Chief Secretary headed a number of civil service departments. Government departments were set up to take care of various social fabrics, formulate rules, practices and systems. The division of power among the administration, the legislature and the law is seen as an asset in Hong Kong, as it permits an independent legal system free from political and administrative interference. Periodic political election and the call for a strong welfare system have not been pursued as pragmatic options (Rabushka, 1987; Lo, 1992).

With the adoption of a legal system that matches with that practiced in Great Britain, the rule of law in Hong Kong, together with growing standards exercised by numerous civic establishments, provided security to property and ensured equality in front of the law. A rule-based legal system minimized personality influences, though legal matters often become costly for low income households and under-privileged individuals. Over the decades, specialized civic institutions emerged, grew and matured. Well-established civic institutions tended to receive a high degree of public trust (Lau, 1993, 1994). Along the pursuit of profits and commercial gains by individuals and businesses, ethical issues within both the government administration and business activities have been upheld, for example, by the Independent Commission Against Corruption (ICAC) which was set up in 1974 to investigate, educate and prevent people and activities in Hong Kong from the various dangers and negative impacts of corruption. Despite the absence of regular political elections, a large number of reliable civic and professional institutions acted as the "check and balance" on the administration of the Hong Kong colonial government. Consequently, fairness, confidence and a "level playing field" across the various strata of the society could then be ensured.

In his two articles, Goodstadt (2004, 2006a) reviews and documents a number of detailed incidents about the way the colonial government handled welfare demands and determined to keep *laissez-faireism* in Hong Kong in the years between and after the two World Wars. In numerous occasions, and despite the pressure from London as a result of changes in British governments with different political ideological background and from the soaring public pressure, the various colonial governors and financial secretaries maintained a free economy with minimal intervention and welfare expenses were granted only when needed. For example, in response to the constant influx of immigrants and the increased pauperization in Hong Kong, Sir Geoffrey Northcote, the Governor in 1937, began a comprehensive social program that provided a range of improvements in health, education, nutrition, employment, housing and welfare. There was, however, an absence of drastic tax reform in favor of redistribution. Intervention through social policies was seen to undermine economic *laissez-faireism*. In the late 1930s when Sir Sydney Caine was the Financial Secretary, the tax reform was dressed in the themes of social justice and an incentive for new factory development to avoid disruption in Hong Kong's commercial well-being (Goodstadt, 2004:63–64).

After the end of the Second World War, the provision of welfare in Hong Kong was seen by the colonial government as an issue of infrastructure, housing provision and urban development. For example, a preliminary town planning report as early as in 1948 had called for a cross-harbor tunnel, a modern transport infrastructure and the creation of tourist facilities, but Governor Sir Alexander Graham (1947–1957) eventually devoted the needed resources to public housing schemes. There was reluctance in reforming the tax system, despite the pressure from London, as Governor Sir Alexander Graham considered the paramount importance of local businesses and professional classes.

The determination of the colonial government in pursuing the *laissez faire* economic policy can be shown by historic events in the 1960s, when the British government was ruled by the Labor Party and pro-welfare policies were introduced in Britain. Goodstadt (2004:71–72) reported that "a Labor government had come to power in 1945 which believed that colonial administrations should drop their traditional *laissez-faire* attitudes and accept responsibility for both economic and social development... It directed that all colonies should draw up development plans mapping out how they would promote the prosperity and well-being of their population.... Their starting point was to be the growth of business and industry because without flourishing economies, social services could not be financed". However, the Colonial Office in London "soon found that promoting development was largely irrelevant to a community already equipped with a modern trading sector and rapidly building up its industrial capacity". "Hong Kong had few peasants who needed land reform, irrigation schemes or farm cooperatives". Direct government development plans were unpopular. Similarly, in 1952 when a Conservative Secretary of State for the Colonies in London circulated a blueprint on how the colonial government could promote the growth of local industries, the Governor, Sir Alexander Grantham showed no interest to "embrace state intervention even though rapid growth of local manufacturing had become essential for survival as the traditional China trade was brought to a halt by the United Nations and the US embargoes after China entered the Korean War".

Sir John James Cowperthwaite was appointed the Financial Secretary for the decade of 1961–1971. Sir John Cowperthwaite, being a Scottish, was a disciple of Adam Smith (who is also a Scot) and an economic freedom faithful.[9] Fearing that the

[9] Information on Sir John James Cowperthwaite can be found from the webpage of the Hong Kong Lion Rock Institute (2007) at http://en-cowperthwaite.blogspot.com/.

British Labor Government would pressure the Hong Kong colonial government to adopt strong welfare that would be destructive to the *laissez-faire* policy, the Governor Sir Robert Black (1958–1964) "restricted the compilation of social statistics in the 1950s", and Sir John Cowperthwaite "did most to prevent the collection of economic data" (Goodstadt, 2006a). Although the reluctance to collect economic and social statistics was a sign of pragmatism as it was intended to minimize the need for policy interventions, the true reason was that "officials resisted the collection of data whenever they believed that the figures would empower their local critics or create additional excuses for British ministers and officials in London to interfere with Hong Kong affairs" (Goodstadt, 2006a:3).

The *laissez faire* policy was interpreted in all possible economic means by Sir John Cowperthwaite. After the end of Second World War when poverty was widespread in Hong Kong and the supply of rice was unsteady, it was reported that although some government officials preferred "to enter the rice trade directly to dampen inflation and stabilize the cost of living as Britain and other colonial territories had done"(Goodstadt, 2004: 69). Sir John Cowperthwaite rejected the idea and instead, adhered to a supply-driven strategy and argued that "it would be better to spend resources not on consumer subsidies but on incentives for rapid industrialization". The principle was simply that job creation is more useful than subsidies to consumers. Resources deployed by the government should aim for long-term job security and creation, rather than concentrating on short-term consumer subsidies. Teaching the person how to fish is always better than giving the person a fish. This documented example is important as it showed not only a lesson on the determination of *laissez-faire* policy, but on the usefulness and relevance of a supply-driven strategy for the Hong Kong economy. *Laissez-faireism*, coupled with economic pragmatism, have worked for Hong Kong, though there have been public calls for more control by the government when various aspects of economic lives in Hong Kong were in hardship. One has to distinguish that short-term demand-driven policies are necessary in a crisis situation, but in normal economic times, supply-driven economic policies are the answer to expand Hong Kong's long-term economic capacities.

2.3 The Paradigm of Economism

The economic development of East Asia that composes of Japan, Hong Kong, Singapore, South Korea and Taiwan since the end of the Second World War has over the decades been well documented by numerous scholars. Numerous studies have provided popular economic, political and social explanations on the success of economic development in East Asia. Explanations include industrialization, open market capitalist principles, market-friendliness and export-led economic policies and freedom, high saving and investment rates, attractive to foreign direct investment, disciplined labor force and improvement in human capital, "chop-sticks" culture, strong entrepreneurial spirit and adoption of Confucius principles, geographical proximities and geo-political location advantages, improvement in such domestic factors as corruption and rule of law, siege mentality due to possibilities of civic war, open conflict and unrest, and so on.

In studying the economic achievement of the four East Asia economies of Hong Kong, Singapore, Taiwan and South Korea, Li (2002) elaborates on the paradigm of "economism" that welds together a number of economic and non-economic dimensions that provide a comprehensive, integrated and in-depth analysis on the economic success of East Asia. In addition to the pursuit of capitalist market economic principles, East Asia economies pursue a pro-growth development, meaning that economic growth tends to be a top priority target, other things being secondary. The private sector forms the engine of growth, while the government provides relevant support, facilitation and infrastructures. The ultimate advantage of a pro-growth regime is the provision of economic security. With economic security, individuals can look after their economic as well as social interests. With economic security, individuals' employment is secured, and their earnings can provide a source of revenue to the government, In turn, the government can have a larger tax pool from individuals and businesses, thereby ensuring a steady inflow of tax revenue. With economic security, the provision of jobs and employment is maximized, and the number of individuals needing government social welfare assistance is simultaneously minimized. The government will then have more fiscal resources in promoting business-friendly, supply-side economic policies to widen the economic base, thereby creating a virtuous cycle of "creation of jobs and employment → income and output → rise in tax revenue → fall in poverty and welfare needs → more fiscal resources to develop new activities".

Income inequality has been a concern in other countries. In East Asia, income inequality is largely tolerated. On the contrary, the focus has been on job creation, equality in employment opportunities and reduction of poverty through supply-side economic policies. Income inequality surely can be improved in periods of prolonged economic growth as the overall level of income rises, but can be worsened in times of economic recession as the overall level of income falls. Poverty reduction tends to receive a higher priority, and poverty is seen more as a flow than a stock. The flow of poverty shows dynamically the number of poor entering and exiting the poverty pool. The stock of poverty merely takes a static point of view and considers the number of poor at a particular point in time. It is relevant to use the flow concept to solve poverty, as policies that minimize/maximize the number of entries/exits of poor should best be exercised.

In the economism paradigm, the role of the government, as Li (2002) summarizes, is indicated metaphorically by "fertilizers, pillars and carpets". To businesses and progressive individuals, the government provides a business-friendly environment by imposing a low tax regime and suitable institutional support as "fertilizers" so that business and investment can prosper without any disincentive barriers. Economic rewards, though differ among businesses and individuals, are based more on capital and personal endowments than through government redistribution policy. "Fertilizers" are regarded as indirect supports and advantages made available on an economy-wide basis. The implication of a fertilizer's role is that both businesses and individuals can benefit from the advantages should they choose to conduct their activities.

East Asian economies have successfully adopted an export-led growth strategy. This necessarily means that both the level and composition of exports have expanded and diversified over time. The trade theory of comparative advantage argues that economies should export the product that has the lowest marginal cost of production. In East Asia, the theory of comparative advantages has also been applied dynamically, meaning that new comparative advantages are created or nurtured so that newly developed goods and services can be exported and become new comparative advantages. There is thus a continuous flow of comparative advantages in exports.

The role of government can create an environment for the promotion and growth of industries and services, thereby establishing "pillars" for the economy. In construction, pillars serve to uphold the structure of the building. The metaphor is that key industries serve as pillars in upholding the structure of the economy. With changing comparative advantages, economic pillars also changes with time, with pillars of today being replaced by new pillars tomorrow. In other words, while an economy is enjoying a particular comparative advantage today, the economy should also look for and nurture future new comparative advantages so that export and trade can be prolonged and sustained. Economic growth may fall substantially if there is no replacement in new advantages. The experience of East Asia in exploring new economic pillar industries and services varies. In some cases, the government engages only in indirect support through education. In other cases, the government engages resources in research and development, or provides favorable terms on loans and capital.

While economic rewards are based on individual endowments, there is always a group of individuals that have economic survival difficulties. The economic "carpet" symbolizes a minimum level of survival, below which individuals may need help from the society probably through welfare assistance, above which individuals will not be constrained in their earnings of economic gains. "Redistribution" is needed to the extent of securing economic survival for those "below-carpets" individuals, but disincentives through high taxation will not be imposed on the economic successful individuals, and individuals are encouraged to get "above-carpet" as much as possible.

In the paradigm of economism, Li (2002) observes that economic openness is considered as a necessary condition in the growth experience of East Asia. With their export-led growth strategy, East Asian economies naturally pursue economic openness through trade and foreign connections. While export allows changes in comparative advantages, East Asia economies effectively ride on the changing demand of the external world. As foreign direct investment are attracted to East Asian economies due to low labor cost, the resulting industrial output is largely exported back to the home countries in Europe and North America. Thus, the inflow of foreign direct investment also to a large extent ensured exports.

However, an export-led strategy could not have been successful if there were a lack of corresponding improvements in domestic conditions. The eradication of corruption, respect of intellectual copy rights, improvement in human capital, advancement in ethics and moral standards are examples of domestic conditions that are seen as both a necessary and sufficient condition for economic growth and development in East Asia. Indeed, one simple observation is that although there are quite a large number of economies that have experienced inflow of foreign direct investment, the post-Second World War growth in East Asia has been unprecedented, suggesting that their economic openness and export-led strategy has been complemented successfully by improvements in domestic conditions.

Based on the capitalist development experience of economies in East Asia, Li (2002) argues that the economism paradigm does provide a set of pre-conditions or roadmap for economies to progress successfully. Indeed, the economic success of East Asia in the second half of the 20th century has served as the a new wave of capitalist market economies that radiate outwards and provide lessons to other contemporary developing and emerging countries in Asia and elsewhere that are intended to develop along the lines of a market-friendly, pragmatic and free economy.

2.4 The Macroeconomy

Hong Kong's Gross Domestic Product (GDP), by definition from the Census and Statistics Department, measures the total value of production of all resident producing units in a specified period of time. The changes of GDP at current market price reflect the combined result of changes in the price level and real production of goods and services from one period to another. The real GDP is expressed in constant market price terms, thereby removing the effect of annual change in market price. The market price of a certain year, say 2005, is considered as the base. The nominal GDP estimates of different years are expressed in the market price of the base year. The per capita GDP shows the ratio between total GDP and the population of the territory in the same year.

Table 2.1 reports at a five-year interval Hong Kong's GDP and per capita GDP since 1961, both are expressed in nominal term (at current market price) and in real term (at constant 2005 price). The trends of both GDP and per capita GDP are shown in Figure 2.1 In 1961, Hong Kong's GDP at current market price amounted to HK$7,453 million (or HK$79,354 million in constant 2005 price). By 2008, Hong Kong's nominal (real) GDP has risen to HK$1,675,171 million (HK$1,650,119 million equivalent to about US$211,553.72 million). The Hong Kong economy has experienced a two-digit GDP growth rates in a number of years in the 1960s and 1970s. There are a total of 12 years that showed a two-digit GDP growth rate between 1962 and 1987. Since 1987, Hong Kong's GDP growth rates have remained below 10%. In 1961, the per capita GDP was HK$2,353 at current market price (or HK$25,048 in constant 2005 price). Hong Kong's nominal (real) per capita GDP in 2008 has risen to HK$240,075 (HK$236,485 equivalent to about US$30,318.6).

There has been debate as to whether GDP measures can show an accurate picture on the strength of an economy. Equally, the method used in GDP measurement, and the components that are included in the measurement of GDP has been debated. For example, Kohli (2007) argues that as Hong Kong's economic openness has remained high all along, the improvements in the term of trade, measured by the price of exports relative to the price of imports, has increased by nearly 50% between 1961 and 2003. Kohli (2007) shows that when such an improvement in the term of trade has taken into account, Hong Kong's real GDP should have increased by 0.4% per annum in the sample period.

TABLE 2.1 Hong Kong's GDP and per capita GDP: 1961–2008

	GDP (HK$ Million)		Per Capita GDP (HK$)	
	Current Price	Constant 2007 Price	Current Price	Constant 2007 Price
1961	7,453	81,439	2,353	25,706
1966	14,276	136,049	3,933	37,480
1971	26,647	186,285	6,587	46,050
1976	63,141	276,022	13,975	61,094
1981	172,965	450,617	33,369	86,935
1986	319,232	604,129	57,784	109,353
1991	690,324	834,024	120,015	144,997
1996	1,229,481	1,060,217	191,047	146,745
2001	1,299,218	1,164,570	193,500	173,446
2006	1,457,357	1,518,542	215,158	221,455
2007	1,615,455	1,615,455	233,248	233,248
2008	1,675,171	1,650,119	240,075	236,485
2009*	1,633,535	1,606,155	233,239	229,329

Note: * = figures are subject to revision.
Source: Census and Statistics Department, Hong Kong.

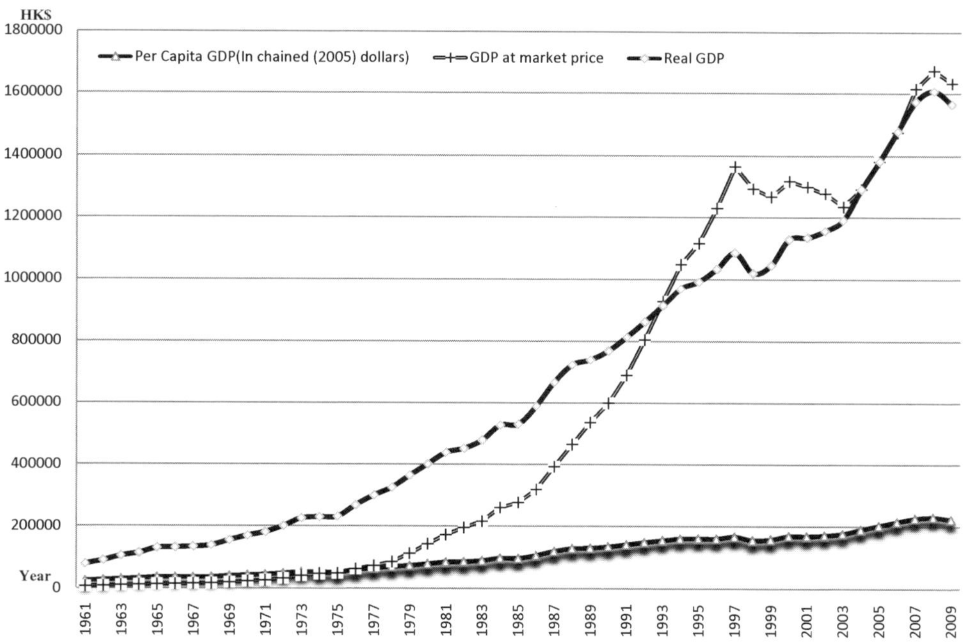

FIGURE 2.1 Trend of GDP in Hong Kong: 1961–2009

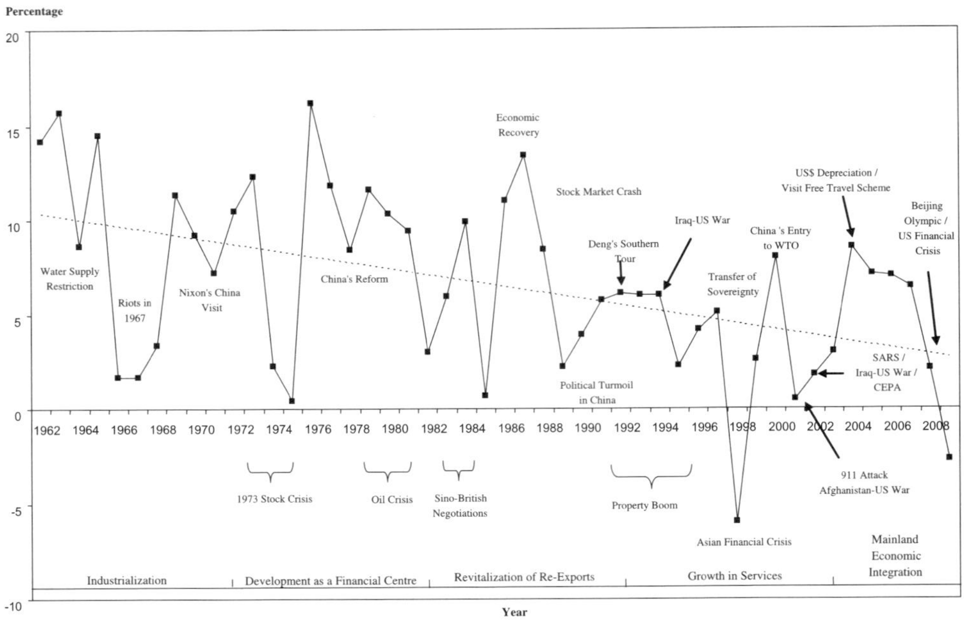

FIGURE 2.2 Hong Kong's GDP growth rates: 1962–2009

Figure 2.2 shows the trend of GDP growth rates (in constant 2005 price), and the key events during the various time periods. Clearly, the Hong Kong economy has experienced various business cycles since the early 1960s. Other than the water supply shortage in 1964, the riot in 1967 has resulted in a low GDP growth rate of 1.7% in both 1966 and 1967. The 1973 oil crisis has produced another economic downturn, resulting in a lower growth rate of 0.4% in 1975. Once again, the Hong Kong economy bounced back quickly with a 16.2% GDP growth rate in 1976, giving a record high growth rate. The second oil crisis in 1980 did not have large negative impact, but the political uncertainty generated during the Sino-British negotiation in 1982–1984 over the post-1997 political future of Hong Kong has brought another downturn, producing only 0.7% growth rate of GDP in 1985.

Since China's economic reform in 1978 and the Sino–British negotiation over Hong Kong's sovereignty reversion in 1982–1984, both economic and political events in Mainland China have become sensitive to the Hong Kong economy. For example, the political turmoil in Mainland China in 1989, commonly known as the Tiananmen Square crackdown, has resulted in a GDP growth rate of 2.2%, though its impact has quickly been defused and the GDP growth in Hong Kong has been revised steadily in the early half of the 1990s.

The economic revival, however, was soon followed by increased speculation in property and stocks that eventually contributed to the economic bubble. The economy began to show signs of weakness in 1995 when the GDP growth rate dropped to 2.3%. Between 1995 and the Asian financial crisis in late 1997, speculation continued, and GDP growth rate reached 5.1% in 1997. The GDP growth rate in much of the 1990s has been steady, suggesting that property and stock speculative activities did not result in large GDP growth. In other words, speculative activities are mainly "nominal" in nature where monetary transactions are not conducted along with increase in physical output, such as manufacturing and domestic exports, which is regarded as the "real" economy. Indeed, the 1997 issue was instrumental to a number of local and non-local people to speculate on the stock market in order to ripe windfall gains.

The biggest historic blow to the Hong Kong economy has been the outbreak of the Asian financial crisis that began in the second half of 1997, but its severe and fierce impact did not hit Hong Kong until the first quarter of 1998. The Hong Kong economy recorded the largest negative growth rate of –6.0% in 1998 and despite the quick bounce of 8.0% GDP growth in 2000, the GDP growth rate in 2001 was only 0.5%. The economic downturn has been prolonged, due probably to structural rigidities and the severe acute respiratory syndrome (SARS) in 2003, and it was not until 2004 when the trade agreement known as the Closer Economic Partnership Agreement (CEPA) with Mainland China was concluded, and visa-free travel to Hong Kong began with a number of major cities and provinces in Mainland China. As Figure 2.2 shows, economic growth regained with an increase of 8.5% in 2004. The 2008 financial crisis in the US led to another economic downturn in Hong Kong, leading to a GDP growth rate of 2.1% and –2.7% in 2008 and 2009, respectively.

Figure 2.2 reveals quite a number of important issues in the Hong Kong economy. Firstly, the dotted line shows a declining trend in Hong Kong's GDP growth. One simple explanation is that due to the increasingly larger GDP denominator over the years, GDP growth rates will be lower. In other words, the behavior of Hong Kong's matured economy is similar to other developed countries where annual GDP growth rates tend to be low because the economic base is large. Hong Kong's economic development has passed through several phrases in the last five decades with industrialization that began since the 1960s and lasted until the early 1980s when low cost production across the border in Mainland China attracted many labor-intensive manufacturing plants from Hong Kong. Since the 1970s, success in industrialization and exports obviously required reliable banking facilities. The development in the banking sector in Hong Kong is considered to be a pre-requisite to the development of a full-fetched financial center that incorporated expansion in investment and stock markets.

Hong Kong's re-export business was revitalized in the 1980s when exports from Mainland China expanded. The growth in re-export soon gave way to growth in services, as Hong Kong served as a facilitator to industries and businesses in Mainland China. The expansion of the Mainland China economy leads to further economic integration in services and in finance. Hong Kong's economy in future will become more oriented and linked to the economic development in Mainland China.

Another observation from Figure 2.2 is the change in the economic structure of Hong Kong. It can be argued that until the end of the 1980s, the Hong Kong economy was mainly external-driven, and economic activities tended to go more along with the rest of the global economy as industrialization led to domestic export expansion. Hong Kong's GDP growth rates have experienced large changes, and a two-digit growth rate was common. Since the 1990s, economic activities in Hong Kong have increasingly been internal-driven as: 1) the decline in the industrial sector has resulted in a decline of domestic exports; 2) the rise in property development has resulted in the concentration of much investment resources geared to the domestic economy; and 3) increasingly Hong Kong has provided services to Mainland China's growing economy. Other than the exceptional large negative growth rate in 1998, Hong Kong has not been able to reach a GDP growth rate that can exceed a single-digit. In the 26 years between 1962 and 1987, the average real GDP growth rate (in constant 2005 price) is 9.77%. In the 22 years between 1988 and 2009, the average real GDP growth rate (in constant 2005 price) is 4.0%. One can argue that the Hong Kong economy has reached its maturity and full capacity, and further growth can only be gradual. Another interpretation can be that further economic restructuring is needed in order to expand new economic opportunities.

There are great economic differences between Hong Kong and Mainland China at the time of the sovereignty change in 1997. For example, while Hong Kong ranks the freest economy, China ranks below 100 in the world ranking of economic freedom. The capitalistic nature of the Hong Kong economy means property right and ownership are guaranteed, and the private sector takes the lead while the government takes a back seat in economic activities, engaging mainly in infrastructure development, establishment of useful civic institutions and investment in education. The government exercises the "invisible hand" and has intervened appropriately only where necessary. Over the decades before the sovereignty reversion in 1997, examples of government intervention included the import price of rice, supply of fresh water from Guangdong, temporarily assistance provided to banks during crisis periods, and provision of public housing for the needy and so on. The government intervention in the post-1997 years has been controversial, though Hong Kong was faced with hard economic recession, and short-term government policies were needed to alleviate extreme economic hardships. The more controversial examples of government intervention are mostly industry-related, as subsidy has been given to the film industry, and loan guarantees have also been given to small- and medium-sized enterprises during the economic recession in 2002–2003. Due to the fall in the residents in a number of off islands, and instead of promoting infrastructure and revitalizing the economic well-being of residents in the off islands, the SAR government has decided in April 2010 to spend HK$12 billion in subsidizing six private ferry companies that provide ferry services to four off islands.

On the contrary, the socialist nature of the Mainland economy depends a lot on state planning, state ownership, government support and control. Despite the increasing role of the non-state sector since economic reform in 1978, key economic activities in Mainland China have to seek approval and agreement from either the central or provincial government. In short, the post-1997 situation is one in which the sovereignty of a highly developed, most open and freest economy is reverted back to the largest socialist economy in the world. It is true that the Mainland China economy has moved a long way since its economic reform in 1978, but Mainland China will have to take into account the influence of Hong Kong on the rest of China. Equally, Hong Kong will have to change to take account of the new sovereign leadership in Beijing.

After the Sino–British agreement in 1984, the Hong Kong economy was officially turned into a period of "transition" in the remaining 13 years of British rule. In the absence of a post-1997 government, there were numerous uncertainties. For example, Li (2006) has argued that investors in Hong Kong could have considered the year 1997 as a "terminal" date in their investment activities, implying that investors would secure the highest possible returns before July 1997. This necessarily would mean a "short-term investment behavior" sentiment among the investors. A "short-term investment behavior" would probably involve a minimum deployment of capital inputs with an expectation to gain a maximum return in the shortest possible time. Such long-term investment as industrial innovation and research and development activities will not look attractive to investors. On the contrary, maximization of investment returns would also lead investors and businesses to minimize the cost of production. Table 2.2 shows that over the years the large difference in real wage between Hong Kong and different cities and provinces in Mainland China. However, one has to bear in mind that the concept and measurement of wage differs between Hong Kong and Mainland China. Typically, while wages in Hong Kong are gross and largely market determined, the various living and welfare expenses of workers and households in Mainland China have often been subsidized, and their wages reflect simply their net wage earnings.

The combined effect of the "short-term investment behavior" can be seen from various economic outcomes. The rising cost in Hong Kong, for example, coupled with the low labor cost across the border in Shenzhen and other open cities in southern China in the early 1980s, had led a great number of Hong Kong manufacturers to shift their production plants out of Hong Kong, resulting in a so-called "industrial hollowing". Thus, industrial migration to southern China turned out to be the natural outcome of the short-term investment behavior. The "industrial hollowing" hypothesis can be supported by the data. Table 2.3 shows that the service sector in Hong Kong has expanded to become the dominant sector. The share of industry in GDP at factor cost in Hong Kong has fallen drastically from 30.9% in 1980 to less than 15% by 1997. Speculation and property acquisition is another aspect of "short-term investment" behavior. Table 2.4 reports the amount of bank loans given to different economic activities. The percentage share of loans and advances given to manufacturing has fallen from about 10% in 1980 to less than 4% in 2000. The amount of loans and advances given to the property and related sector has occupied the largest share, as the combined share of Building and Construction and Residents (property loans) has exceeded 50% since 1998. Real estate development and property has become the largest user of bank loans and advances. One important implication from Table 2.4 is the growing narrowness or lack of diversification of investment in Hong Kong, as over 50% of bank loans have been provided to one industry.

Another feature of a "short-term investment behavior" is the speculation on stocks and property since investors can liquidate their assets almost instantly should uncertainty arise or shocks emerge. Given the rapid rise of income and consumption and the urge of "prosperity and stability" since the completion of the Sino-British negotiation over the post-1997 Hong Kong in 1984 and the subsequent economic recovery since 1985–1986, many investors and individuals saw the favorable financial prospects and turned to become speculators, leaving behind their manufacturing industries and engaged instead in speculative activities in real estate and stocks. Table 2.5 gives a picture of the "wealth effect" that summarizes the performance of the stock market index and turnover since 1978 and the percentage change in

TABLE 2.2 Annual average real wages of Hong Kong and Mainland China (in 2002 prices, US$)

	Hong Kong†		Mainland*		Provinces (overall)*				Cities (overall)*			
	Overall	Manu	Overall	Manu	Guangdong	Guangxi	Hunan	Fujian	Shanghai	Beijing	Shenzhen	Guangzhou
1990	22,124	15,577	896	868	1,226	894	843	905	1,221	1,111	1,841	1,467
1991	22,063	15,893	851	833	1,222	852	783	880	1,228	1,047	1,890	1,463
1992	23,101	15,897	895	870	1,330	902	834	918	1,411	1,123	2,031	1,582
1993	23,104	16,383	928	922	1,467	945	865	958	1,556	1,316	2,296	1,747
1994	23,524	16,801	673	635	1,056	683	609	725	1,098	970	1,604	1,279
1995	24,032	17,499	719	676	1,079	683	627	766	1,213	1,065	1,679	1,349
1996	23,603	17,613	753	685	1,107	670	619	811	1,294	1,162	1,808	1,433
1997	24,078	18,271	765	702	1,147	669	630	894	1,352	1,304	1,999	1,552
1998	22,730	18,418	893	843	1,222	695	653	1,019	1,440	1,467	2,256	1,710
1999	23,257	19,460	1,011	944	1,370	767	719	1,149	1,713	1,669	2,621	1,962
2000	24,576	20,785	1,130	1,055	1,544	854	786	1,277	1,860	1,897	2,907	2,303
2001	24,816	21,157	1,302	1,171	1,751	1,018	922	1,439	2,128	2,295	3,245	2,652
2002	24,624	21,975	1,500	1,329	2,025	1,238	1,055	1,607	2,352	2,639	3,559	3,090
2003	26,814	22,138	1,676	1,492	2,400	1,428	1,442	1,715	3,295	3,052	3,673	3,408
2004	37,899	24,628	1,841	1,612	2,579	1,554	1,564	1,798	3,553	3,543	3,782	3,682
2005	38,544	23,852	2,094	1,797	2,759	1,746	1,736	1,954	4,058	4,063	3,825	3,998
2006	38,918	24,779	2,425	2,074	3,004	2,070	2,006	2,244	4,941	4,855	4,158	4,310
2007	40,672	22,462	2,880	2,412	3,460	2,479	2,402	2,579	6,009	5,763	4,628	4,835
2008	40,199	23,250	3,490	2,889	4,034	2,950	2,866	3,114	7,134	7,271	5,358	5,643
ARG												
1990–02	0.94	2.93	5.14	4.49	4.97	3.55	2.65	5.47	6.43	8.28	6.43	7.12
2004–08	0.09	0.01	15.87	14.20	11.00	15.70	14.81	12.81	16.82	19.03	7.98	10.66
ANG												
1990–02	5.15	7.18	16.02	15.13	15.94	15.50	13.30	16.62	17.41	19.55	17.41	18.19
2004–08	0.11	0.03	20.05	18.32	14.69	20.81	19.53	16.61	19.97	21.67	11.33	13.99

Notes: † = Compensation of employees/number of person engaged, and real figures are nominal figures deflated by the Consumer Price Index. Statistics of number of persons engaged for 1990–2003 (2004–2008) are compiled based on the Hong Kong Standard Industrial Classification Version 1.1 (Version 2.0). * = Real figures are nominal figures deflated by Consumer Price Index. The average wage of staff and workers refers to the average wage per person in enterprises, institutions and government agencies. ARG and ANG = average annual real and nominal growth, respectively. Manu = manufacturing.

Sources: *Gross Domestic Product*, Hong Kong, various years; *Statistical Yearbook of China*, Beijing, various years, and various provincial statistical yearbooks; and *International Financial Statistics*, Washington DC.

TABLE 2.3 Production-based GDP: Percentage share by economic activity (at factor prices)

Year	GDP at Factor Cost (HK$ Billion)	Agriculture & Fishing	Industry	Services
1980	136.2	0.8	30.9	68.3
1981	167.2	0.7	30.8	68.5
1982	186.4	0.7	29.0	70.3
1983	205.5	0.6	30.8	68.6
1984	244.4	0.5	27.3	68.2
1985	259.4	0.5	25.0	70.5
1986	303.0	0.4	29.5	70.1
1987	376.1	0.4	28.3	71.3
1988	448.8	0.3	26.7	73.0
1989	511.4	0.3	25.8	73.9
1990	574.8	0.3	24.3	75.4
1991	651.7	0.2	22.0	77.8
1992	756.5	0.2	19.9	79.9
1993	859.5	0.2	17.5	82.3
1994	986.6	0.2	15.6	84.2
1995	1,060.5	0.1	15.2	84.7
1996	1,177.5	0.1	14.7	85.2
1997	1,288.0	0.1	14.0	85.9
1998	1,218.3	0.1	14.2	85.7
1999	1,194.8	0.1	13.8	86.1
2000	1,245.0	0.1	13.4	86.5
2001	1,233.1	0.1	12.6	87.3
2002	1,223.2	0.1	11.6	88.3
2003	1,191.8	0.1	10.7	89.2
2004	1,244.8	0.1	10.0	89.9
2005	1,332.8	0.1	9.3	90.6
2006	1,423.3	0.1	8.7	91.2
2007	1,552.0	0.1	7.6	92.3
2008	1,567.9	0.1	7.9	92.0

Source: Census and Statistics Department, Hong Kong.

the price index of property in Hong Kong. The three sets of figures all showed an increase that cumulated to a peak in 1997. After the Asian financial crisis in 1997–1998, the Hang Seng Index remained steady, and it was not until 2007 when the stock market overheated again as the stock turnover increased by 13.31% in 2007. Similarly, property price returned to a positive growth rate since 2004, though the base year differs in the data series.

Another pre-1997 economic aspect that Li (2006) pointed out was the emergence of a wage-price inflation spiral during the 13 transition years between 1984 and 1997, when wage in both the public and private sectors experienced a two-digit increase for a number of years after 1984. Table 2.6 reproduces the relevant data from Li (2006:61),

TABLE 2.4 Percentage share of loans and advances in Hong Kong

Year	Total (HK$ billion)	Manufacturing	Building & Construction	Miscellaneous		Wholesale & Retail
				Total	Residents	
1978	*56.4	12.94	12.28	32.50		30.52
1979	*75.8 (34.9)	12.50	13.04	34.48		29.06
1980	*124.3 (64.0)	10.72	15.45	37.98		25.92
1981	143.4 (15.4)	9.90	23.53	45.75	10.71	12.40
1982	187.3 (30.6)	9.03	26.44	43.76	10.20	10.87
1983	208.9 (11.5)	8.93	22.55	44.26	12.05	12.57
1984	220.9 (5.7)	8.51	21.78	45.21	13.29	12.79
1985	234.9 (6.4)	8.40	17.06	51.31	15.85	12.57
1986	270.7 (15.2)	9.29	12.78	56.96	18.16	12.43
1987	352.9 (30.3)	8.46	11.20	61.13	18.55	12.31
1988	465.5 (32.0)	8.38	12.65	58.10	18.48	12.83
1989	584.6 (25.6)	7.91	16.47	57.48	18.83	10.72
1990	689.4 (17.9)	7.15	15.68	58.93	21.15	10.83
1991	817.1 (18.5)	6.67	15.38	60.43	24.38	9.87
1992	909.9 (11.4)	7.00	15.88	59.83	24.61	9.69
1993	1,075.8 (18.2)	6.85	16.77	59.99	24.92	9.24
1994	1,258.6 (17.0)	6.82	19.79	55.08	23.72	10.92
1995	1,398.2 (11.1)	7.16	18.75	55.59	24.98	11.89
1996	1,637.2 (17.1)	6.57	20.34	55.64	25.77	10.78

(*Continued*)

TABLE 2.4 (*Continued*)

				Miscellaneous		
Year	Total (HK$ billion)	Manufacturing	Building & Construction	Total	Residents	Wholesale & Retail
1997	2,037.3 (24.4)	5.43	21.61	56.74	26.55	10.10
1998	1,957.8 (–3.9)	4.84	21.25	57.74	30.08	9.18
1999	1,819.8 (–7.0)	4.41	21.11	59.39	33.44	7.92
2000	1,861.5 (2.3)	3.96	21.40	58.36	33.65	6.45
2001	1,790.1 (–3.8)	3.98	21.73	59.67	36.14	5.65
2002	1,742.9 (–2.6)	4.05	21.74	59.21	36.82	5.76
2003	1,708.5 (–2.0)	4.69	21.09	59.54	36.07	5.48
2004	1,792.4 (4.9)	5.54	21.56	58.38	34.07	5.53
2005	1,930.3 (7.7)	6.18	23.34	55.77	31.43	5.21
2006	1,974.0 (2.3)	5.22	24.91	55.54	30.13	5.34
2007	2,274.3 (15.2)	5.34	25.43	55.53	27.37	5.11
2008	2,524.1 (11.0)	5.81	27.21	52.25	25.76	6.03
2009	2,499.9 (–0.1)					

Note: * Figures were based on old series. Figures in brackets are annual growth rates. Building and Construction include property development and investment. Residents = professional and private individuals to purchase flats under the 'Home Ownership Scheme' and the 'Private Sector Participation Scheme' and to purchase other residential properties.
Source: Census and Statistics Department, Hong Kong.

TABLE 2.5 The wealth effect

Year	Hang Seng Index	Stock Turnover (HK$ billion) (/GDP)	% Change in Price Index of Private Domestic Premises*
1978	526.91	27.4 (0.32)	
1979	619.71	25.6 (0.23)	
1980	1,121.17	95.7 (0.67)	
1981	1,506.84	106.0 (0.62)	
1982	1,105.79	46.2 (0.24)	
1983	933.03	37.2 (0.17)	
1984	1,008.54	48.8 (0.19)	–12.77
1985	1,567.56	75.8 (0.28)	17.07
1986	1,960.06	123.1 (0.39)	10.42
1987	2,884.88	371.4 (0.96)	22.64
1988	2,556.72	199.5 (0.43)	21.54
1989	2,781.04	299.1 (0.57)	26.58
1990	3,027.47	288.7 (0.50)	11.00
1991	3,471.54	334.1 (0.50)	37.84
1992	5,545.97	700.6 (0.90)	9.71
1993	7,695.99	1,217.2 (1.36)	7.74
1994	9,453.52	1,137.4 (1.13)	21.25
1995	9,098.47	826.8 (0.77)	2.20
1996	11,646.55	1,412.2 (1.18)	–1.41
1997	13,294.70	3,789.0 (2.82)	13.03
1998	9,484.47	1,701.1 (1.32)	–16.28
1999	12,859.93	1,915.9 (1.56)	–11.19
2000	15,838.53	3,047.6 (2.37)	–1.90
2001	12,446.85	1,949.9 (1.54)	–2.75
2002	10,321.22	1,598.9 (1.28)	–12.58
2003	10,346.25	2,545.7 (2.06)	–11.75
2004	12,988.19	3,948.4 (3.06)	5.57
2005	14,402.00	4,498.1 (3.25)	11.33
2006	17,118.31	8,332.6 (5.65)	5.90
2007	23,700.45	21,506.1 (13.31)	11.14
2008	20,606.72	17,600.7 (10.51)	13.65
2009	18,203.01	15,439.5 (9.45)	–13.48

Notes: For Hang Seng Index, 31.7.1964 = 100, figures are monthly averages. * = For 1984–1991 (1992–009), the change is based on index with 1989 = 100 (1999 = 100).

Sources: Census and Statistics Department and Hong Kong Monetary Authority, Hong Kong.

which shows that wage had increased most in Transport, Storage and Communications (experienced a double-digit increase in 5 years between 1982 and 1998), following by Electricity and Gas (4 years). One should note that the large increase in wage has been concentrated in services, especially non-tradable services. Table 2.7 shows the price change followed by the comprehensive Consumer Price Index (CPI) and the Consumer

TABLE 2.6 Wage performances in different Hong Kong industries, 1982–1998

Economic Sectors	Number of 2-Digit Growth (in both nominal and real)
Mining and Quarrying	2 (1986, 1989)
Manufacturing	2 (1986, 1992)
Electricity and Gas	4 (1985, 1989, 1996, 1997)
Wholesale, Retail, Trade, Restaurant and Hotel	1 (1986)
Transport, Storage and Communications	5 (1982, 1984, 1989, 1991, 1994)
Financing, Insurance, Real Estate & Business Services	1 (1993)
Community, Social and Personal Services	1 (1991)

Source: Li (2006:61).

TABLE 2.7 Inflation movements: General versus service sector (Percentages)

	Index A		Index B		Hang Seng Index		Composite Index	
Month/Year	CPI	CSPI	CPI	CSPI	CPI	CSPI	CPI	CSPI
12/92	8.6	9.6	8.5	9.8	10.2	11.3		
12/93	8.1	11.2	9.5	12.2	10.3	12.0		
12/94	6.6	9.7	7.3	9.8	7.9	11.4		
12/95	6.7	8.4	6.5	7.6	6.7	7.9		
12/96	4.8	6.0	5.2	6.8	5.8	7.7	5.2	6.7
12/97	–1.4	–2.5	–1.7	–1.8	–1.8	–0.1	–1.6	–1.4
10/98	–3.1	–1.1	–5.1	–4.1	–4.1	–3.2	–4.2	–2.9
12/99	–2.9	–0.9	–4.9	–2.4	–4.1	–2.5	–4.0	–2.0
12/00	–0.9	0.1	–2.1	0.5	–2.3	0.6	–2.1	0.4
12/01	–6.2	–1.2	–2.6	–0.9	–1.7	–0.6	–3.6	–0.9
12/02	1.0	–2.0	–2.6	–1.4	–2.8	–0.9	–1.5	–1.4
12/03	–1.2	–4.7	–2.1	–3.4	–2.5	–3.6	–1.9	–3.8
12/04	0.5	1.7	0.2	1.9	–0.1	1.6	0.2	1.7
12/05	1.7	0.7	1.9	1.2	1.9	1.8	1.8	1.3
12/06	1.9	0.7	2.3	2.0	2.7	2.1	2.3	1.8
12/07	3.4	–0.8	3.9	2.3	4.0	2.3	3.8	1.6
12/08	1.2	–3.2	2.4	–1.0	2.7	*0.0	2.1	–1.1
12/09	1.7	*–0.0	1.2	0.3	0.9	0.1	1.3	0.1

Notes: * = less than 0.05%. CPI = consumer price index. CSPI = consumer service price index. The CSPI is made up of the service items in the CPI. The different indices record the difference in household monthly income, with Index A showing the lowest income group. For example, the average monthly household expenditure during October 2004 to September 2005 for CPI(A), CPI(B), Hang Seng Index (sometime known as CPI(C)), and the Composite CPI are HK$4,000–HK$15,499, HK$15,500–HK$27,499, HK$27,500–HK$59,999 and HK$4,000–HK$59,999, respectively. The approximate percentage of households covered for the four indices are 50%, 30%, 10% and 90%, respectively.

Source: Hong Kong Coalition of Service Industries, Hong Kong General Chamber of Commerce, and Census and Statistics Department, Hong Kong.

Service Price Index (CSPI). One observation is that when CPI is rising in the 1990s, CSPI tends to rise faster, as many services are non-tradable and a higher inflation is not matched with increase in import supply. Similarly, the CSPI shows a milder fall when compared to the fall in CPI between 1997 and 2002. Prices inflation of services tend to be sticky downwards. The situation has changed since 2003 when the movement of CSPI tends to be weaker than changes in CPI in a number of years.

Another piece of evidence in the high wage-price inflation spiral before 1997 can be seen from Table 2.8 that reproduces the data on the civil service pay adjustments. Large, double-digit civil service pay adjustments occurred in a number of years between the late 1980s to the mid-1990s. Wage adjustment in the private sector tends to follow the change in the civil service sector. However, civil service pay adjustment has been either frozen or dropped since the Asian financial crisis in 1998.

The high inflation was probably the result of the combination of excess demand pull and cost push. Excess demand inflation emerged due to the rising income and the expansion of purchasing power. Cost push inflation appeared as wage increased, and employers had to pass the rising wage to the final consumers. During the transaction years, employment was extremely favorable and unemployment rate was lower than 2% in a number of years. Furthermore, both inflation and speculation were fueled with low interest rate, and the frequent negative real interest rate encouraged investors, including housewives, to speculate. The data on the prices of both real property and stock kept rising, producing nominal wealth appreciation to all asset holders. Wealth appreciation allowed individual to spend more, leading to a booming economy.

Table 2.9 summarizes the performance of a number of macroeconomic variables. Despite the low unemployment due probably to rise in income and demand, a prolonged period of negative interest rate (with inflation rate higher than saving deposit rate) appeared in much of the 1980s and 1990s. Secondly, despite the large increase in the growth rates of re-exports that boosted the large total export to GDP ratio, the rapid fall in domestic exports that began from the late 1980s reconfirmed the "industrial hollowing" hypothesis. The growth in domestic investment has remained low in most years before 1997, confirming a high level of uncertainty and the lack of willingness to engage in long-term investment.

There were signs of economic overheating in 1995 with a drop in the price of real property and the trend of unemployment reversed upwards, as shown in Table 2.9. By 1995, however, speculators come from various parts of the world and massive hot money continued to flow into Hong Kong. The 1997 sovereignty change had now become an opportunity and occasion of massive asset and wealth appreciation. Speculation actually became more severe between 1995 and 1997, as both the stock and property prices entered a one-way street.

The short-term and long-term consumption function in Hong Kong has been discussed in Li (2006:41–47). Using quarterly data for the period 1976Q3 to 2001Q3, Li (2006) shows that the level of real private domestic consumption in Hong Kong followed closely the real GDP trend. When the components of household expenditure are disaggregated into real private domestic consumption in durable goods, non-durable goods, food and services, data observations showed that food has remained stable as a basic component of real private domestic consumption.

TABLE 2.8 Civil service pay adjustment (percentages)

	Salary Band		
Year	Lower	Middle	Upper
1979–1980	16.55	16.16	17.14
1980–1981	18.20	17.38	18.03
1981–1982	15.01	14.95	14.96
1982–1983	5.53	4.74	4.48
1983–1984	11.21	9.93	9.12
1984–1985	10.98	9.12	8.76
Special from 1.1.1986*	2.70	2.70	2.70
1985–1986	7.00	7.00	7.00
1986–1987	7.13	6.40	6.30
1987–1988	9.62	9.93	9.56
1988–1989	14.81	14.81	13.43
1989–1990	15.00	15.00	15.00
1990–1991	10.43	10.43	10.43
1991–1992	11.60	11.60	11.17
1992–1993	10.66	10.66	9.76
1993–1994	9.89	9.89	9.47
1994–1995	10.14	10.14	9.98
1995–1996	7.67	7.67	7.68
1996–1997	6.81	6.81	6.90
1997–1998	5.79	5.79	6.03
1998–1999	0.00	0.00	0.00
1999–2000	0.00	0.00	0.00
2000–2001	0.00	0.00	0.00
2001–2002	2.38	2.38	4.99
2002–2003	–1.58	–1.64	–4.42
2003–2004	–3.00	–3.00	–3.00
2004–2005	–3.00	–3.00	–3.00
2005–2006	0.00	0.00	0.00
2006–2007	0.00	0.00	0.00
2007–2008	4.62	4.62	4.96
2008–2009	5.29	5.29	6.30
2009–2010	0.00	0.00	–5.38

Note: * = Special pay adjustment for non-directorate staff, with effect from 1.1.1986.
Source: Civil Service Bureau, Hong Kong.

The consumption for services has increased rapidly, despite the different periods of economic setback. The consumption of durable and non-durable goods showed a similar trend, and both suffered a large drop in 1997–1998 after the Asian financial crisis.

TABLE 2.9 Hong Kong's macroeconomic indicators

		Growth rate of								
Year	Nominal Per Capita (US$)	Real GDP (2007 Price)	Domestic Investment	Domestic Export	Re-export	Export of Services	Total Export/ GDP Ratio	Unemployment Rate	Inflation Rate	Savings Deposit Rate
1981	5,966	9.4	9.2	18.0	38.8	21.9	70.63	3.9	10.3	11.71
1982	6,113	3.0	1.9	3.2	6.3	14.3	65.19	3.6	9.7	6.54
1983	5,566	5.9	–8.2	25.7	26.9	16.2	74.27	4.5	4.5	7.38
1984	6,179	9.9	2.7	32.1	48.3	21.3	84.92	3.9	9.6	6.59
1985	6,512	0.7	0.1	–5.8	26.1	9.0	84.95	3.2	5.4	3.28
1986	7,405	11.0	6.1	18.6	16.4	17.5	86.62	2.8	3.9	2.50
1987	9,043	13.4	14.2	26.8	49.2	28.4	96.06	1.7	8.7	2.13
1988	10,591	8.4	6.6	11.5	50.7	18.0	105.98	1.4	9.0	3.19
1989	12,091	2.2	3.8	3.0	25.8	14.3	106.39	1.1	12.8	5.79
1990	13,480	3.9	8.2	0.8	19.5	12.0	106.83	1.3	7.5	5.92
1991	15,444	5.7	9.4	2.3	29.2	13.1	110.95	1.8	9.0	4.71
1992	17,930	6.1	22.5	1.3	29.2	15.4	114.89	2.0	9.9	2.32
1993	20,328	6.0	14.6	–4.7	19.2	12.7	112.74	2.0	8.7	1.50
1994	22,458	6.0	22.6	–0.4	15.2	11.8	111.70	1.9	6.5	2.45
1995	23,428	2.3	9.4	4.3	17.4	8.3	120.47	3.2	4.1	4.20
1996	24,702	4.2	13.2	–8.4	6.6	12.5	113.70	2.8	5.8	3.77
1997	27,170	5.1	19.4	–0.4	5.0	0.4	106.66	2.2	5.7	4.08
1998	25,508	–6.0	–14.0	–10.9	–6.9	–8.5	104.25	4.7	0.8	5.19
1999	24,714	2.6	–16.3	–9.5	1.7	5.5	106.50	6.2	–4.5	3.75
2000	25,375	8.0	6.8	6.1	18.1	14.0	119.56	4.9	–3.6	4.47

(*Continued*)

TABLE 2.9 *(Continued)*

Year	Nominal Per Capita (US$)	Growth rate of: Real GDP (2007 Price)	Growth rate of: Domestic Investment	Growth rate of: Domestic Export	Growth rate of: Re-export	Growth rate of: Export of Services	Total Export/ GDP Ratio	Unemployment Rate	Inflation Rate	Savings Deposit Rate
2001	24,811	0.5	–4.1	–15.2	–4.6	1.8	113.99	5.1	–1.9	2.16
2002	24,285	1.8	–14.1	–14.7	7.7	8.4	122.17	7.3	–3.5	0.14
2003	23,558	3.0	-8.5	–7.1	13.4	4.2	141.12	7.9	–6.2	0.03
2004	24,454	8.5	5.1	3.5	16.8	18.5	156.29	6.8	–3.5	0.02
2005	26,093	7.1	5.1	8.0	11.7	15.3	162.75	5.6	–0.1	0.97
2006	27,698	7.0	11.6	–1.1	10.0	14.1	166.81	4.8	–0.3	2.50
2007	29,900	6.4	0.8	–18.9	10.8	16.9	166.36	4.0	2.9	2.10
2008	30,830	2.1	2.7	–16.8	6.0	8.6	168.59	3.6	1.5	0.14
2009	30,088	–2.7	1.8	–36.4	–11.8	–6.6	151.15	5.2	0.2	0.01
Average										
1981–85	6,067	5.78	1.14	14.64	29.28	16.54	75.99	3.82	7.90	7.10
1986–90	10,522	7.78	7.78	12.14	32.35	18.04	100.38	1.66	8.40	3.90
1991–95	19,918	5.22	15.68	0.56	22.04	12.26	118.07	2.18	7.64	3.03
1996–00	25,494	2.78	1.82	–4.62	4.90	3.56	114.15	4.16	0.84	4.25
2001–05	24,640	4.18	–3.30	–3.88	9.00	9.64	139.26	6.54	–3.04	0.66
2006–09	29,629	3.20	4.23	–18.30	3.75	8.25	163.23	4.40	1.08	1.19
1981–90	8,295	6.78	4.46	13.39	30.80	17.29	88.19	2.74	8.15	5.50
1991–00	22,706	4.00	5.86	–2.03	13.47	8.43	116.11	3.17	4.24	3.64
2001–09	26,857	3.74	0.47	–10.29	6.67	9.02	149.91	5.59	–1.09	0.90

Notes: Savings deposit rate is period average figure, percent per annum. Inflation rate is the percentage change of GDP deflator.

Sources: *Hong Kong Annual Digest of Statistics*, Census and Statistics Department, various years; and Hong Kong Monetary Authority.

Li (2006:45) uses the quarterly income and consumption data to estimate the marginal propensity to consume (MPC) and the consumption function for Hong Kong. By using the quarterly data for the period 1979Q3–2001Q3, the long-run MPC can be estimated from the fitted least squares regression of real consumption and real disposable income (real GDP less total tax revenue), while the short-run MPC can be estimated from the year-to-year changes in the two variables. The empirical result shows that Hong Kong's MPC estimates are rather low in the long-run (0.65), and even lower in the short-run (0.57). The consumption of services occupied the largest portion with 0.29 in the long-run, durable and non-durable occupy about 0.10 to 0.16 (10% and 16%, respectively) in the total consumption, while food takes the smallest portion.

A low MPC implies a high marginal propensity to save (MPS = 1 − MPC). A long-run MPS of 0.35 is considered to be high, but is common among East Asian economies where personal thrift is considered as a virtue. The high short-run MPS (0.43 = 1 − 0.57) could be explained by the need to save more, say for property purchase in the sample period. The income multiplier is defined as 1 ÷ MPS. Thus, the short-run (1 ÷ 0.43) income multiplier in Hong Kong is 2.3256, while the long-run income multiplier (1 ÷ 0.35) is 2.8571 for the sample period.

The estimates of Hong Kong's consumption function is shown in Li (2006:47). The empirical result shows that: 1) the overall estimate for total consumption is about twenty percent (0.1863) of current income, and real interest rate has a rather weak inverse relationship with consumption; 2) the real disposable income produces the highest impact on durables (0.4844), followed by food (0.1347) and non-durables (0.1217); 3) despite large domestic expenditure on services, it shows a unitary relationship with current income, meaning that changes in services consumption are close to a one-to-one relationship with changes in disposable income; 4) the interest rate movements probably will not affect food and services consumption, but its negative sign in all the durables and non-durables consumption estimates suggested an inverse relationship between interest rate and consumption; and 5) the weak estimates, however, suggested that interest rate movements did not have much impact on consumption, due probably to the large inflation since the late 1980s, resulting in a negative interest rate in a prolonged period of time in the sample period.

One trend that has been affecting the level of consumption in Hong Kong since the 1980s has been the "push and pull" effect that resulted in cross border consumption in Shenzhen and other cities in the Pearl River Delta region. Though there is clear difference in quality, such as fire safety in public places, the high cost and price of consumption goods and services in Hong Kong has "pushed" Hong Kong residents to travel and consumed across the border in Southern China, while the low cost and price of consumption goods and services has "pulled" household expenditure from Hong Kong. Much of the consumption expenditure, however, has been made on informal activities conducted by the underground economy in Shenzhen and other nearby cities, such as low cost entertainment outlets, fake products, personal services and holiday packages. The lower prices in different types of consumer products, including the acquisition of properties, have attracted Hong Kong people to spend their weekends and leisure time in Shenzhen and nearby cities in the Guangdong Province. These consumption expenditures have direct substitution effect on the aggregate level of consumption in Hong Kong. Namely, the more Hong Kong residents consumed across the border, the less will be consumed locally in Hong Kong. While Shenzhen and other nearby cities have benefited the rise in consumption by Hong Kong travelers, others concerned the social impact of the underground or informal economy in Shenzhen and other cities in the Pearl River Delta.

Over the years, the *Census and Statistics Department* in Hong Kong has published reports giving data on Hong Kong residents traveling to Mainland, particularly to Shenzhen and nearby cities in Guangdong for leisure, entertainment and shopping. For example, the total number of outbound trips to the Mainland by Hong Kong residents between 1990 and 2000 increased at an average rate of 11.6% per year. Hong Kong residents made a total of 50.1 million and 52 million outbound trips to the Mainland for various purposes in 2000 and 2001, respectively. Since Hong Kong residents have invested substantially in Southern China, business travel in 2000 accounted for 32% (or 16.2 million person-trips) of the total travel to Mainland China. The remainder of 68% (or 33.8 million person-trips) referred to personal travel, which has increased by 23% when compared to 1999. The share was quite stable. In 2001, the shares between business travel and personal travel were 31% and 69%, respectively. The April 2001 report pointed out that the major factors accounted for the rise in cross border consumption activities were due to the development of infrastructural links, expansion of facilities at control points, simplified cross-boundary procedures and the availability of goods and services at relatively lower prices.[10]

Personal travel included both package tours and non-package tours, and their consumption expenditure modes included holiday, visits to friends and relatives, recreational, cultural, educational and health-related activities. The distribution of consumption expenditures by broad expenditure group in non-package tours in Guangdong (including Shenzhen) was estimated to compose of lodging and meals (58% and 57% in 2000 and 2001, respectively), followed by entertainment, transportation and other services (31% in both 2000 and 2001) and shopping (11% in 2000 and 12% in 2001).

Table 2.10 shows the consumption expenditure of Hong Kong residents traveling to Mainland China between 2000 and 2009. In the All Persons Travel category, the overall average expenditure per person-trip has dropped since 2000, but has bottomed out in 2005 and revised upwards, though by 2009, the figure (650) is still much lower than in 2000 (870). This trend is true for both average expenditures per person-trip in Guangdong as well as outside Guangdong. The trend is similar in total consumption with a fall until 2003 before it bounced back and continued to increase. Total consumption in the Guangdong Province is much higher than consumption outside the Guangdong Province. Table 2.10 also shows that travel outside the Guangdong Province has become more popular. Between package tours and non-package tours,

---

[10] More recent figures are available from the various survey reports on cross boundary statistics. For example, *Cross-Boundary Statistical Report, Cross-Boundary Travel Survey, Thematic Household Survey, Survey in the PRD Region, and Northbound Southbound* published by the Planning Department, Hong Kong.

TABLE 2.10 Personal expenditure of Hong Kong residents in Mainland China (HK$)

	Average Expenditure Per Person-Trip			Total Consumption (100 million)		
	Overall for the Mainland	Guangdong Province	Outside Guangdong Province	Overall for the Mainland	Guangdong Province	Outside Guangdong Province
			All Personal Travel			
2000	870	640	3,790	293	202	91
2001	770	590	3,140	276	196	80
2002	690	540	2,880	263	193	71
2003	600	480	2,590	204	153	51
2004	620	470	2,940	240	171	68
2005	600	460	2,970	241	174	68
2006	610	470	3,040	263	194	69
2007	620	480	3,100	291	213	78
2008	630	500	3,180	293	218	74
2009*	650	500	3,090	318	233	85
			Package Tours			
2000	2,100	1,050	3,600	64	19	45
2001	1,830	1,010	3,120	60	20	40
2002	1,720	880	3,040	56	18	39
2003	1,470	790	2,680	37	13	25
2004	1,470	680	3,110	47	15	33
2005	1,370	740	3,070	48	19	29
2006	1,290	690	3,070	46	18	28

(*Continued*)

TABLE 2.10 (*Continued*)

	Average Expenditure Per Person-Trip			Total Consumption (100 million)		
	Overall for the Mainland	Guangdong Province	Outside Guangdong Province	Overall for the Mainland	Guangdong Province	Outside Guangdong Province
2007	1,310	760	3,300	58	26	32
2008	1,320	790	3,290	47	22	25
2009*	1,220	760	3,050	52	26	26
			Non-Package Tours			
2000	740	620	3,850	229	183	46
2001	670	560	3,160	216	176	40
2002	590	520	2,710	207	175	32
2003	530	460	2,500	167	141	26
2004	540	460	2,810	192	157	36
2005	530	440	2,900	193	154	39
2006	540	460	3,020	217	175	42
2007	550	460	2,980	233	187	46
2008	570	480	3,120	246	196	50
2009*	600	480	3,110	266	207	59

Note: * figures are subject to revision.
Source: *Hong Kong Monthly Digest of Statistics*, various issues, Census and Statistics Department, Hong Kong.

average expenditure per person-trip is much higher in package tours, but total consumption is much higher in non-package tours. Thus, travelers with package tours tend to be the economical spenders, while non-package tour travelers tend to consume more.

Despite the drop in overall expenditure since 2000 as shown in Table 2.10, the various events since 2003 probably have revived Hong Kong residents' consumption behavior. Firstly, the outbreak of the severe acute respiratory syndrome (SARS) in April and May of 2003 would have discouraged cross-border consumption considerably. Secondly, the issue of visa-free travel to Guangdong, Shanghai and Beijing residents beginning from the third quarter of 2003 has meant that Hong Kong will become attractive to Mainland residents whom come to Hong Kong for holiday and shopping. Economic confidence has recovered by 2004.

On the other hand, the increase in in-bound Mainland tourists since the last quarter of 2003 has revived the various markets in Hong Kong, notably in tourism, restaurants and retails. In other words, while Table 2.10 shows the extent of Hong Kong people travelling to Mainland China, it is more important to examine the increasing number of Mainland tourists flooding to Hong Kong. Many Mainland tourists come to Hong Kong to shop for luxury brands, as the protection of intellectual property rights is strong in Hong Kong. The rising production cost and inflation in Mainland China, together with the revaluation of Renminbi has resulted in the rising prices in Shenzhen and other nearby cities, thereby discouraging cross-border consumption since 2005. The trend of cross-border consumption has been reversed, as the focus has turned away from Hong Kong residents consuming in Mainland China, to the "cash rich" mainland residents consuming in Hong Kong, including brand name products, properties and medical services.

2.5 The Burst of the Bubble

Few would have thought of the accumulation and burst of the bubble, as speculators were all engaged in a "musical chair" game, so long as the speculators passed the bug (the asset they held and transacted, typically real estate) before the music stopped, they would have gained. By 1997, the Hong Kong economy was engaged mostly in such nominal activities as speculation, retail, tourism, and services, while such real economic activities as industries and physical exports have shrunk considerably. The early phrase of the Asian financial crisis that officially began on July 2, 1997, did not seem to affect the sentiment in Hong Kong. Things made a sharp U-turn in early 1998 when the Hong Kong dollar was attacked, coupled with the massive withdrawal of funds from Hong Kong, and expectation was reversed (Li and Wong, 2008). Real GDP dropped by 5% in 1998, while unemployment reached 6.2% and domestic investment dropped by 16.6%, as shown in Table 2.9.

The bubble eventually bursted and various economic difficulties emerged in Hong Kong. The collapse of the large and expanded bubble-like nominal sector could not be rescued nor supported by the weak, fragile and shrinking real sector. In other words, the economic consequences from the collapse of the stock and property markets cannot be sustained by the small and contracted real economy that had undergone "industrial hollowing" and falling domestic export. The nominal sector indicated by both property price and stock price had fell drastically, unemployment had increased rapidly, but new investment was not forthcoming while funds entered Hong Kong previously for speculative purposes departed, resulting in an "investment vacuum", where the departure of previous investment was not matched with entry of new investment. Businesses were faced with difficulty and large and foreign retails shops closed. Li (2006) euphemistically labeled it as a "post-Olympic syndrome" when economic setback appeared after a major event that promoted investment, tourism, employment and construction. Although the stock market revived in 1999, the prolonged recession exposed a structural imbalance in the economy.

The economy of Hong Kong in the first decade (1997–2008) since sovereignty reversion did not enjoy a smooth ride, as the decade was plagued with different kinds of crises one after another and imposed different degrees of economic hardship to the residents in Hong Kong. Li (2006) has argued that the first decade of the post-1997 Hong Kong has experienced the "worst of three worlds" of economic recession, periodic crises and young government. The first crisis began soon after July 1997 with the Hong Kong identity issue when the legal authority in Hong Kong took up the interpretation that mainland children born to Hong Kong parents have the right of abode in Hong Kong, creating a shock in population movement from Mainland China to the territory. Although the issue was eventually solved with the cooperation of the Beijing authority by allowing a daily quota of 150 immigrant families, and other than the dented political image of the government, the practical concern was the possible rapid expansion in the size of the population, the needed employment provision and social consequences of a widening income gap and welfare burden of the government and the tax payers, especially when the government was facing budgetary deficits.

Secondly, there were a number of unpredictable outbursts of deadly health hazards. The "chicken flu" that occurred in a few occasions created health hazard, and business activities fell as people worried about the pandemic. The new government was caught red-handed as rapid and instant policy decisions were needed. A more severe health hazard was the severe acute respiratory syndrome (SARS) that occurred in early 2003, and because of its fast, uncontrollable and invisible spread within the community, the economy was brought to a standstill with low confidence and drastic fall in aggregate consumer demand. The third wave of health hazard of "swine flu" emerged in 2009. Although the swine flu was originated overseas, the Hong Kong authority has taken extensive precautions and did not experience any harsh and detrimental impact.

The SARS health hazard in 2003 was coupled with another political crisis. Article 23 of the Basic Law stipulated that "[T]he Hong Kong SAR shall enact laws on its own to prohibit any act of treason, secession, sedition, subversion against the Central People's Government,...". While the SAR government wanted to pass a law, there was sharp and divided controversy regarding the definition of treason and other potential unintended consequences that would conflict with Hong Kong's other values. The unpopularity of the SAR government reached the freezing point when there was massive demonstration on July 1, 2003, rejecting both the passage of Article 23 and the economic hardship resulting from the SARS health hazard. Following the resignation of top officials in the government, the passage of Article 23 was eventually shelved and withdrawn, thereby avoiding a confrontational political crisis.

Despite economic recovery that began in late 2003 with the favorable economic policies Beijing launched, such as the visa-free travel package, the trading of Renminbi in Hong Kong and the opening of trade to Hong Kong exporters in the first phase of the Closer Economic Partnership Agreement (CEPA), the first Chief Executive, Tung resigned in 2005 before the expiry of his second term, and Donald Tsang, the then Chief Secretary, succeeded Tung to be the second Chief Executive of Hong Kong SAR. "I will get the job done" is the motto of Tsang during his campaign for the Chief Executive post.

The Asian financial crisis that officially started on July 2, 1997, that dragged on till mid-1998 when Hong Kong stock market and property price collapsed and together with speculative attack on the Hong Kong currency, was responsible for the economic recession for the years that followed. Economic slump with high unemployment and low business confidence were the major features resulting from the Asian financial crisis. The September 11, 2001, terrorist attack in New York and Washington DC, and the subsequent Iraq War and the war against terrorism imposed another external crisis and hardship that worked unfavorably to the Hong Kong economy.

Another round of economic crisis emerged in the third quarter of 2008 when the investment lord of New York, Lehman Brothers, declared bankrupt in September following a number of failures and closures in banking, financial and real estates in the US, thereby sending a tsunami-like financial wave to the rest of the world with collapses in financial markets and institutions. The extent of economic hardship in 2008 was compared to the Great Depression of the 1920s. Similar to the 1997 Asian financial crisis, the Hong Kong economy bounced back quickly soon after the closure of Lehman Brothers, despite the protest of those who lost in the purchase of the Mini-bonds issued by Lehman Brothers. By comparing the stock market performance of ten economies in the two financial crises of 1998 and 2008, Wong and Li (2010) concludes that exchange rate stability, such as the linked exchange rate adopted in Hong Kong, is crucial in the period of the two crises. With growing inter-dependence among world financial markets, a sound exchange rate policy and an open, equitable and transparent regulatory financial system is an importance piece of financial infrastructure.

There are a number of economic dilemmas facing both the government and the people. Li (2006) summarizes that despite the economic recovery that Hong Kong enjoyed since 2005, economic restructuring is badly needed but is not forthcoming fast enough to generate employment opportunities and promote economic mobility. The first dilemma is the role of the government. Given that Hong Kong has enjoyed fiscal surplus for years, the post-1997 government was faced with severe fiscal hardship. The fiscal dilemma is whether a policy of easing short-term hardship that is mainly demand-driven with large fiscal expenditure, or the pursuit of a more long-term goal that could be supply-driven and employment creating. The government did mainly a number of fine-tuning activities that eased short-term pain.

The second dilemma is the extent of government intervention. Public outcries, though many were politically motivated and took advantage of the young government, had led the government to be on the defensive, and it has become popular for more direct intervention and even subsidy. The government has to respond, though inappropriately in many cases, to "popular demands". The distinction between "private cost" and "social cost" has increasingly become blurred. Instead of facing up to the financial burden and cost resulting from individuals' private economic and investment decisions made previously, economic failures have imposed various degrees of hardship on the individuals, making them less reluctant to take up their "private cost". Instead, many crisis-affected individuals are prepared to push their "private cost" to the government by making extensive public complains, with the intention that the government would use public funds to rescue them, thereby turning their private loss into social burdens.

Another area of dilemma relates to investment. While the Mainland China market looks promising, there has been more investment from Hong Kong to Mainland China than the reverse. Investment in Hong Kong has also been concentrated in finance and property, and the chances of employment creation are weak. The lack of industries would mean economic mobility through the advancement of industrial skills is not forthcoming. On the contrary, a large number of jobs in such services as retail, restaurants, personal beauty services, office supports, transport and logistics require low skill, and economic mobility through income increase remains low.

In housing and property acquisition, the "home ownership scheme" (HOS) that started in the 1970s had enabled the sandwich class of households to acquire property in the user market. Though there are existing loopholes in the HOS system, the scrap of the HOS in 2001 has removed one of a practical mechanism of wealth creation and accumulation through "forced saving" and the chance of owning property in the private market. Since then, the property sector has become dichotomized into public housing provision for "low income" households and the expensive property in the private market. Since the 2008 financial crisis, there have been revived calls for the reinvigoration of the HOS.

Economic integration with the Mainland China economy, especially with the southern provinces along the Pearl River, gives rise to another consideration. The basic theoretical underpinning is that from the economic resources (land, labor and capital) point of view, the Mainland China economy is said to have "absolute advantage" over Hong Kong. Resource-wise, therefore, Mainland China can do whatever Hong Kong has done. Taking this view, Hong Kong will lose to Mainland China economically. Economic integration becomes only a matter of "fitting" Hong Kong into the development of southern China. The other side looks at the "comparative advantage" of Hong Kong and considers how the various comparative advantages of Hong Kong can be deepened, sharpened and expanded such that the Hong Kong economy progresses along with the Mainland China economy. In other words, the preservation and extension of "comparative advantage" is the only way to help Hong Kong to keep its own distinct position.

2.6 Economic Formalization

Being an open, small and city-state economy, the performance of the Hong Kong economy all along has to "flow" with the rest of the world economy, providing trading and business opportunities for whoever sees Hong Kong a chance to make progress. Similarly, Hong Kong is primarily an immigrant city that attracted forward-looking, progressive and enterprising individuals to settle and work tirelessly to make their business and individual ventures come true. A former Hong Kong Governor once remarked that Hong Kong people are only interested in making money. Given that most of the surrounding areas of Hong Kong experienced prolonged and different extent of difficulty and hardship in much of the last century, given that Hong Kong does not have a large agriculture sector that serves as a shelter or cushion at times of economic difficulties, and given that political liberalization in the form of universal suffrage under the British rule had not been made a reality, the only way to maintain stability has been through economic progress such that individuals can maintain their economic security.

Economic growth not only can enrich people, but also can provide new employment opportunities for others. Jobs are certainly not paid equally, but the level of income inequality can be tolerated so long as there is economic progressive and individuals can see their economic future. Income inequality is seen not as an inter-personal comparison, but is seen as an intra-personal comparison where individuals can compare themselves over time. During the process of economic development, Hong Kong has taken up supply-side economic strategies, focusing on providing export of merchandize goods, export-related services and light manufacturing to the rest of the world. Foreign direct investment in the post-World War II years in the early 1950s provided the initial capital for exports and industrialization, but local investment caught up quickly as local entrepreneurs have learned the skill and experience and geared up to the export market. By the 1970s, the level of local income has caught up considerably, and by the 1990s, the Hong Kong market has gained world attention as a key consumer and retail market and the lack of a sale tax and the good business ethics have made Hong Kong an attractive consumer outlet.

These scenarios provide only the consequences. Economic freedom in Hong Kong has been built over the decades. Around the time of the Second World War in the mid-1940s, the Hong Kong society was not different from other nearby Asian economies. Plagued with numerous economic difficulties, the underground economy in Hong Kong was rampant. Corruption by government officials, use of relationship in getting things done, slumps in much of the local residential areas, poor living conditions, presence of triad societies, hawkers romping around the streets, and visible poverty constituted social history in Hong Kong. In distinguishing from other Asian economies, and partly due to the expanding population that adhered to stability and individual economic drive, Hong Kong has made tremendous improvement in the various social and economic fabrics over the decades, partly out of needs, partly out of indigenous awareness as population increased, and partly out of events that required new developments.

Numerous examples on economic formalization can be suggested over the years, either through the work of the government or through a better and stronger establishment of institutions and organizations. Roadside food stalls have been common before the 1970s, but partly due to health reasons, the emergence of formal restaurants and various fast-food outlets, and lack of public space, roadside food stalls have been eliminated as licenses were withdrawn and not renewed, with only few exceptions. A similar picture can be seen in the restriction and gradual elimination of street hawkers as their disappearance gave way to formal retail shops and restaurants to prosper. By today, the remaining numbers of hawker are restricted to a few locations; say in Mongkok and Yau Ma Tei areas, which have evolved into tourism attractions.

In recent years, especially after the economic recession that resulted from the Asian financial crisis in 1997, some local restaurants in their peak business hours in the evening have illegally occupied open places in the pedestrian walkways or even street areas outside their restaurants. In the Saigon district, for example, some seafront restaurants have gone excessively far by providing mobile sheltering facilities to their patrons during the peak dinning hours, thereby arbitrarily, unilaterally and unfairly taking away the size of the pedestrian walkways. There have also been suggestions, including those from the legislators, to revitalize the presence of hawkers in order to reduce unemployment for the unskilled at the peak of the economic recession in 2001–2003. Examples include the establishment of a hawkers market in the former Kai Tak airport premises. Hawkers whom engaged in informal economic activities compete directly with retail shops that hire workers, pay rents and probably contribute profit tax to the government. Due to poor organization and business, many businesses in the former Kai Tak airport hawkers market ended up in losses and the hawker market closed eventually, putting an end to the false sentiment on the revitalization of hawkers market in modern Hong Kong.

The establishment of the Independent Commission Against Corruption (ICAC) in 1974 is probably an important step in ironing out informal or underground economic activities in whatever form of corruption and briberies in all institutions. To promote a truly law-based, transparent and equitable society with the virtue of the "level playing field", good ethics and freedom from corruption allow all individuals and businesses to be creative, forward-moving and to maximize their full talents and abilities. Other examples of economic formalization include taxi licensing as taxi cabs are the legalized formal public transport. The emergence of modern banking since the 1970s has replaced many informal loan provision circuits among individuals, especially among those low income households, though there are still the presence of loan sharks handled by triad societies.

Over the decades, Hong Kong has removed, minimized and eliminated numerous informal economic activities, giving way to the benefits produced by formal economic activities. Other than the rule of law that forms the back bone of Hong Kong, poverty has been drastically reduced by encouraging investment and creation of job opportunities, and by a low and simple tax regime that fostered entrepreneurship. Though the percentage of young individuals receiving high education in Hong Kong is still below many of the developed countries in the world, illiteracy has been eliminated and education has enriched the skill level of a great of number of individuals. Vocational training, in addition to post-secondary education, such as the Caritas Bianchi College of Careers established in the early 1970s, provided alternative support to human capital development at the middle management levels. Roadside food stalls and hawkers have been illegalized so as to make way for formal businesses in restaurants and retail shops. Pawn shops and underground money exchange between groups of individuals in different localities have been given way to formal banking facilities.

Good law enforcement through the various law enforcing agents, such as the ICAC, police, customs and immigration officials, has reduced, controlled and minimized illegal activities. A number of international laws are adopted in Hong Kong to protect the copy rights, rights of children and ethnic minorities from abuse and discrimination. Social welfare services are expanded to take care of the sick and underprivileged to ensure a minimum level of protection and survival. Complaints against the misconduct in government activities are openly handled by appropriate institutions. For example, the mission of the Audit Commission is to "provide independent, professional and quality audit services to the Legislative Council and public sector organizations in order to help the Government enhance public sector performance and accountability in Hong Kong". Similarly, the mission of the Office of the Ombudsman states that "through independent, objective and impartial investigation, the work of the Office of Ombudsman is to redress grievances and address issues arising from maladministration in the public sector and bring about improvement in the quality and standard of and promote fairness in public administration".

Economic formalization has proceeded along with social development in Hong Kong. The gradual elimination of informal economic activities has been replaced by a system and set of standard practices, and individuals and different economic sectors in Hong Kong are protected by the open and equitable system and practices. Although there is still room for improvement and upgrading, economic formalization has laid the foundation for modern development in Hong Kong, and the emergence of a proper and sound legal system allows all individuals to participate in the economy openly and equally, and that experience radiates to the rest of the world with the message that the system in Hong Kong is reliable and fair for all. This is exactly the spirit and message embodied in the "level playing field" concept in Hong Kong's business development.

Economic freedom and formalization allows a bigger role by professionals, specialized associations and interested groups. Different professional bodies are set to govern the standard and practices in their own fields, associations are established to uphold various interests and liaise with similar bodies elsewhere. Example include religious groups, professions and people with shared interests and needs, non-government organizations, independent bodies, associations on technological advancement, consumer protection and so on. Independent media allows uninterrupted news and information flows. Welfare-related bodies fill up the various social gaps that can enhance the quality of life in Hong Kong. Over the years, the establishment of civic organizations in Hong Kong has flourished, providing an independent layer of trust and standard free from political and government intervention, hassles and harassment. Many civic establishments are not politically motivated and affiliated. Hence, there is an absence of extreme violence and vicious discontent in the society because what stands between the government and the governed are the numerous civic establishments that upheld fairness, equity, transparency and professionalism, thereby ensuring social security and protection.

With economic formalization, economic freedom allows individuals, especially the new generations of young individuals, potentials for their own creative and entrepreneurial development, unrestricted from existing pattern of business and ownerships. In other words, economic freedom allows new comparative advantages to be discovered through individual hardship and ingenuity. With the development of new comparative advantages, individuals will discover new areas of business, and channels through which their wealth can be generated. With individuals actively working for their own interests, the government can simply take the "back seat" and engage more in improving and enlarging the economic capacity of the economy, through improvements in infrastructure, advancement in human capital, attention given to the needy and so on.

2.7 A Free Civic Economy

There is one other crucial advantage of economic formalization and the promotion of civic establishments in Hong Kong. A free civic economy with strong personal ethics, manner and social responsibility minimizes, if not eliminates, conflicts. Economic freedom, coupled with equality in opportunity and transparent rules, laws and regulations, permits individuals to pursue their own business and professional interests. Of course, since economic activities are conducted at different phases in a business cycle, risk and returns to economic activities will differ. When individuals are allowed to maximize their economic endeavors in a free economy, economic security can then be ensured. Since individuals' economic security provide them with the resources to take care of their social needs, the provision of economic security has a positive spillover effect on provision of social welfare. In short, with economic security, individuals can have the ability to look after their own social welfare needs.

Because of variation in risk and returns in economic activities, the outcome of one individual's economic activities will differ from another. Such inequality coexists among individuals, and because returns are based on risk and individual endowment, the unequal outcome can be tolerated. One can thus argue that economic activities produce "relative" outcomes, as some receive or gain more than others. In a free civic economy, individuals know best to maximize their returns. Indeed, most economic activities produce different results and outcomes, individuals come to accept the outcomes that are relative to and different from each other. Such relative outcomes, however unequal, are accepted and tolerated, and stability in a society can naturally be maintained. As such, economic freedom maximizes the relative outcomes of individuals, and since individuals come to accept their outcomes, societal stability is achieved, which in turn produces a virtuous circle as stability encourages and allows more economic activities to take place, and individuals in turn exploit and maximize economic opportunities.

The rule of law is often regarded as a yardstick in a free economy. More importantly, the legal profession provides arbitration or a service that helps to settle an activity that would have absolute outcome of win or lose between the two parties in a law suit. There are societal activities that produce absolute outcomes. Indeed, most non-economic outcomes produce absolute, zero-sum outcomes of win or lose, or even life and death, results. Examples include political elections, religious faith and sports.

All forms of political elections produce a win or lose outcome. In primitive democratic regimes, a political election may result in the death or severe harassment of the loser. In matured democracy, on the contrary, periodic political elections produce a winner and a loser, but there are other choices and chances for the losing individual or party. Similarly, a free civic society permits freedom in political affiliations, and political elections become a personal choice, and democracy provides only an institutional framework for people to exercise their personal choice on political leaders on a periodic basis. Indeed, there are numerous civic, professional and business organizations that handle activities that produce zero-sum outcomes.

A person's choice of religious faith is an absolute outcome. The adoption of one religion does not allow the person to take up another religion simultaneously. Freedom allows individuals to choose their faith on a private basis. Individuals are free to use their own private time and effort in pursuing their spiritual destiny. The Olympics, the World Cup and numerous sport associations, for example, turn various sports into modern battles that allow players to compete, and individuals can show their support to their sport players or teams. This turns an activity with absolute outcome into a personal preference and activity. All forms of sport competition produce absolute outcomes, as there is always only one winning team. Indeed, all kinds of contests produce absolute outcomes as there are winners and losers.

Numerous examples of activities with absolute outcomes can be discussed. The core argument is that in a free civic society, all economic activities produce relative outcomes that allow individuals and groups to perform and coexist in peace and stability. Through the existence of various civic establishments, activities that produce absolute outcomes can largely be personalized. Either choices are given to individuals or absolute outcomes are decided according to civilized and professional rules.

Thus, a major advantage of a free civic economy is that it allows the maximization of relative outcomes, achieves the highest possible degree of stability, and turns activities with absolute outcomes into personal choices or based on agreed and transparent rules and laws. Economic freedom, coupled with a high degree of civic awareness, gives an optimal, if not the best, form of human pursuit and development. Indeed, it basically provides a framework upon which a society can progress through time, though there can be ups and downs resulting from the emergence of new situations and development and the different phases of business cycles.

In short, economic freedom yields a high level of economic relativity, whereby individuals can maximize their economic activities and performance, and at the same time, maintain autonomy in their personal choice on activities that do not produce relative outcomes. Thus, through economic freedom and the organization of a civic society, potential conflicts are minimized, if not eliminated, as individuals are fully engaged to maximize their economic gains and outcomes.

2.8 Conclusion

Can Hong Kong's experience of economic freedom be exported? Of course, one is not referring to Hong Kong as a perfect economy, nor free from problems, challenges and conflicts. Surely, the experiences and practices of economic freedom exercised in Hong Kong can serve as lessons, and provide parallel references and influences to other emerging and developing economies that hope to achieve a higher degree of economic freedom and development. Indeed, this is the main contribution Hong Kong can provide to the economic development of the world. In the meantime, the Hong Kong economy shall not feel complacent, but shall continue to look for areas of improvement and new areas of development in economic freedom so as to make economic freedom more sustainable and comprehensible.

The interesting question is that from a historical point of view Hong Kong actually is no different from other developing economies, other Asian economies and other former British colonies, but how and why Hong Kong can make such a progress and achievement in economic development through the adoption of economic freedom is definitely worth a place and attention in the economic development of the world, providing insightful lessons and ready-made answers.

The various arguments discussed include the paradigm of economism that contains the features of a pro-growth regime, the need to diversify comparative advantage, the indirect role of the government as a promoter, a supporter and a keeper, the attitude on poverty reduction and a pursuit of equality in opportunity. The persistent drive to maintain laissez-faire economic principles, the evergreen spirit of entrepreneurship and individual progress, the continued support of foreign inflow of capital and, at the same time, the appropriate development in various civic establishments domestically have all contributed to the economic success of Hong Kong.

Over the years, Hong Kong has played different roles. The most significant role has been the service provided to Mainland China. After the establishment of the People's Republic of China in 1949 and the closed door policy since the early 1950s, Hong Kong businesses and residents whom shared similar political ideology have been stealthily aiding trade with Mainland China, providing the much needed foreign exchange to China. In the early stage of economic reform in Mainland China since 1978, the Hong Kong residents have served as the supplier of capital fostering numerous economic, business, industrial and infrastructural developments, especially in the Guangdong and other southern provinces. With a gradual consolidation in the foundation of economic reform in Mainland China, Hong Kong once again serves as the reference point to a great number of economic activities in Mainland China. For example, experiences and activities in Hong Kong have definitely been used as a point of reference and comparison in quality control in industrial manufacturing, efficiency in the management of enterprises, estimation of investment potentials and raise of capital in financial markets, and organization of economic resources and provision of welfare.

With rapid economic growth, the attention of economic development in Mainland China that has gradually shifted from a high rate of economic growth to improvement in the quality of life, from an external oriented economy to emphasis in domestic performance, and from the rise in material well-beings to improvement in moral standards and ethic requirements can become the new areas of references. In short, given that Hong Kong has become a matured and advanced economy, and despite the calls that cities in Mainland China may "catch up" with Hong Kong in growth and development terms, Hong Kong's experience and adherence to economic freedom will show clear distinctions from cities in Mainland China.

Despite being the freest economy, the Hong Kong economy is not free from problems and challenges. There are various areas of concerns. One is how to keep and maintain the freest economy as it is. In other words, to uphold the quality and standards in the various economic and civic fabrics will necessarily mean the need to deepen existing activities, ensuring that the future development will be better than the former decades. Given that Hong Kong's sovereignty has been reverted back to Mainland China in 1997 and the various ingredients that the Basic Law has provided, Hong Kong needs at the same time to develop new and enlarge existing advantages as much as possible. This necessarily requires the continued vibrancy of the Hong Kong people. With the continued growth in Mainland China, the Hong Kong economy will definitely become more integrated with the Mainland China economy, enjoying and sharing the fruit of economic success as well as receiving and responding to the various "spill-over" from the consequences of economic reform in Mainland China.

One also needs to take into account the views from the sovereign authority in Beijing, and to a large extent, Hong Kong's economic performance will be judged along with the economic development in the entire Mainland China. Given the vast differences between Mainland China and Hong Kong in numerous dimensions but the urge to integrate fully, a fine skill is needed to steer Hong Kong from the planned nature of economic development in Mainland China, having able to serve but not being absorbed into the vast state-controlled nature of the Mainland China economy. At the time of the Sino–British negotiation over the future of Hong Kong in 1982–1984, the idea of keeping the capitalist system of Hong Kong for 50 years after 1997 will expire in 2047, when authority in Beijing will once again have to decide on the "future" of Hong Kong.

The reason why the Sino–British negotiation over the future of Hong Kong was conducted in 1982 was because businesses began to question about the prospect and security of investment in Hong Kong after 1997. It was exactly 15 years before the historic handover year of 1997 that the issue on future of Hong Kong was raised. If history were to repeat itself, it would be around the year 2032 when businesses in Hong Kong and the British government that oversees the operation of the Basic Law, once again question the sovereign authority in Beijing whether Hong Kong's capitalist market system will be preserved after 2047. To a large extent, this surely will depend on how Hong Kong would then be like, and how Mainland China, as well as the Guangdong province and Shenzhen that is adjacent to Hong Kong, would see the role of Hong Kong in the development of Guangdong and southern China, the position of Hong Kong in the Asia region and in the world economy. There are obviously different possibilities, depending on how both economic as well as non-economic dimensions are being considered. The ultimate challenge to economic freedom is therefore not how much Hong Kong has achieved, but how Hong Kong upholds and embraces economic freedom in the post-1997 years.

3 GDP: Performance, Volatility and Comparison

3.1 Introduction

Economic freedom ensures growth and prosperity, as it allows individuals to conduct their own investment and spending activities; and different outcomes will produce economic fluctuations. Coupled with the global economic climate at various times, changes in investment expectations, in business opportunities, in the size of the economic capacity and in the relevant stage of economic development will generate income volatility. In turn, economic fluctuations become unavoidable and unequal outcomes among individual economic actors are inevitable. Economic freedom provides opportunities for individual economic actors to maximize their returns; and the process itself leads to economic changes and movements in outputs.

Indeed, the practice of economic freedom should best be regarded at the macro-level as a fundamental criterion and infrastructure that provides the base for an economy to produce long-term benefits, and at the micro-level as an attitude or behavior that allows individuals to maximize market opportunities. Together, the economy's productive capacity and efficiency can be expanded and maximized, creating the highest possible amount of job opportunities and market possibilities. The short-term changes, on the contrary, are reflected in the movements of the business cycle and changes in different economic variables, such as inflation, employment and private expenditure. As individuals act differently in the market, their activities generate "waves" that contributes to the ups and downs in the business cycle.

Business cycles are always different from each other in terms of their magnitude, time involved and impact. As such, income volatility differs at different stages of a business cycle. Income changes also differ at different stages of economic development. Statistically, the typical situation of an expanding economy is that the growth rate of GDP is high when the overall level of GDP is rather low. In other words, when the economic base is small, any improvement can easily show a large percentage change in a specified time period. Statistically, the high percentage change in GDP is because of the low denominator in calculating the growth rate. As income rises over time and a high level of GDP is achieved, the economy will reach its full capacity and further expansion becomes difficult. The percentage change over a certain period will become low as a result of economic saturation, and the denominator is already large in calculating the economy's growth rate. In other words, when the economy has nearly reached its full economic potential or capacity, at least in the short-term, the growth rate of GDP tends to be low because of a larger income base that acts as the denominator. Given that economic fluctuations are inevitable, the relevant discussion is whether output changes and volatility has been unstable and destabilized other activities.

This chapter examines the movements of economic growth in Hong Kong, and analyses the fluctuations of the business cycles. This is done by studying the volatility of GDP, GDP components (investment, trade and so on) and key macroeconomic variables as unemployment, money supply and stock market movements. Economic freedom provides a base for economic activities to flourish, but that would also generate fluctuations and volatility in the movement of different variables. The more relevant question is to examine if the fluctuation and volatility movements are stable over time. Data of GDP, GDP components and macroeconomic variables for the pre-1997 and the first decade after the Asian financial crisis are used to study the empirical performance of growth and business cycle volatility. Standard technical methods are applied in the analysis, and the discussion on the technicalities is kept to a bear essential, and the empirical findings are discussed in details to provide useful implications on the Hong Kong economy. In a nutshell, economic freedom produces relativities that are exhibited in growth and business cycle movements.

3.2 GDP Volatility

The Asian financial crisis in 1997–1998 has produced an unprecedented blow to the Hong Kong economy. The drop in the level of GDP and the subsequently economic recession that lasted until 2004 had been more severe than the oil crisis occurred in the early 1970s or the political uncertainty generated during the Sino-British negotiation in 1982–1984. With its open economic nature and the occurrence of the Asian financial crisis, one wonders if income or GDP volatility in the Hong Kong economy would remain high and the growth in income has become unstable. On the contrary, it can be argued that given the continuous structural transformation over the last few decades from secondary industry (mainly manufacturing) to tertiary industry (mainly services), and with the sovereignty reversion in 1997, one would expect that income changes would have become more stable or less volatile.

Numerous literature and empirical studies have discussed the stability of national output or income indicated by the level of GDP. Available international evidences suggest that change in GDP volatility can take place for two reasons. At the micro-level, technological innovations, improvement in efficiency and better use of production inputs can improve firms' ability to respond to demand changes. As a result, firms will have a higher ability to absorb business shocks and smooth out economic fluctuations. For example, studies using experiences from developed countries argued that technological innovation in the 1980s has led to economic structural change that resulted in a decline in volatility in investment and consumption. McConnell and Perez-Quiros (2000) and McConnell *et al.* (1999) used data from the US and showed strong evidence of reduction in the volatility of real GDP growth from the first quarter of 1984. Similarly, Blanchard and Simon (2001) revealed that output volatility for Canada, Australia, Great Britain, France and Germany has declined sharply in the mid-1980s.

The second reason for a reduction in output volatility can be due to the improved performance in both fiscal policy and monetary policy that minimized the negative impact of economic shocks and stabilized economic growth. In Blanchard and Simon (2001:150), for example, the GDP volatility of the US has declined steadily since the 1950s due probably to the rapid decline of government spending volatility after the Korean War, and that the use of inflation targeting in the US since the 1990s by managing closely such monetary variables as the interest rate have improved GDP volatility. In Japan, Blanchard and Simon (2001) point out that although Japan has experienced an increase in the stability of GDP growth in the 1980s, but since the early 1990s, the inability of the monetary policy has resulted in a prolonged liquidity trap and a rebound in GDP volatility throughout the 1990s.[1]

In the case of Hong Kong, three related issues in the volatility of GDP growth can be considered. The three related issues are:

1) Periodic comparisons of GDP volatility: this shows the changes in the performance of GDP volatility over different time periods;
2) Dynamic movement of GDP components and macroeconomic variables: this examines the change of individual GDP components and macroeconomic variables so as to give a better understanding on economic growth; and
3) Correlation between GDP volatility and business cycles: this studies the relationship between economic growth and business cycles, whether they will move together or differ drastically.

The data used in the analysis include GDP, GDP components and other macroeconomic variables. Output or GDP components include private consumption, government consumption, investment or fixed capital formation, imports and exports. Macroeconomic variables chosen in the volatility study include inflation (measured in both the GDP deflator and the Consumer Price Index (CPI)), money supply, employment, wage, stock market and housing price.

The GDP of an economy changes and generally increases over time. A smoothed GDP trend on the original GDP time series can be obtained by using the Hodrick–Prescott (HP) filter (Hodrick and Prescott, 1997; Prescott, 1986). The HP filter can help to produce the smoothed trend series from the original time series, and the business cycle component is the difference between the smoothed trend series and the original series. In other words, the business cycle component is simply the "filtered out" series.

Technically, for the GDP and its components, the original time series is indicated by $\{y_t, t = 1, 2, \ldots, T\}$, and we let $\{\tau_t, t = 1, 2, \ldots, T\}$ be the smoothed trend series, and then the cyclical series of y_t is $c_t = y_t - \tau_t$, indicated by $\{c_t, t = 1, 2, \ldots, T\}$. The

[1] In monetary economics, a liquidity trap is a situation of a stagnant economy with the nominal interest rate close to zero, and the monetary authority is unable to stimulate the economy with traditional monetary policy tools. In such a situation, citizens do not expect a high return on physical or financial investments; instead, they end up keeping or hoarding their assets in short-term cash in bank accounts rather than making long-term investments. This behavior usually further worsens the economic recession.

HP filter is a two-sided linear filter that computes the smoothed trend series (τ) of y by minimizing the variance of y around τ, subject to a penalty that constrains the second difference of τ. Hence, the HP filter effectively helps to compute the smoothed trend series (τ) from the original series (y). This is done by minimizing the variance of the original series around the trend series, and in order to control the smoothness of the trend, the right degree of smoothness will have to be located. In other words, the HP filter chooses τ to minimize:

$$\underset{\tau_t}{\text{Min}} \sum_{t=1}^{T} (y_t - \tau_t)^2, \tag{1}$$

subject to

$$\sum_{t=2}^{T-1} [(\tau_{t+1} - \tau_t) - (\tau_t - \tau_{t-1})]^2 \leq \mu. \tag{2}$$

τ_t is smooth because the trend growth rate does not change much over the period as it is constrained.[2] The constraint shown in Eq. (2) implies that the growth of the trend is limited by the value of μ. The smaller the value of μ, the smoother is the trend path. If the value of μ is zero, suggesting that the constraint is very straight, the trend will effectively become linear. If the series is integrated of order 1 (that is, level non-stationary but difference stationary), a zero value of μ would imply that the business cycle component is not stationary. On the contrary, if the value of μ is very large (that is, when $\mu \to \infty$), there will not be any constraint, and we would have smoothed too little. If so, the smoothed trend is just the original series (that is, $y_t = \tau_t$) and we will not have the business cycle component.

The Lagrangian method is commonly used in calculus to solve optimization problems. Prescott (1986) used the Lagrangian method to solve the minimization problem. The Lagrangian takes the form of an objective function of Eq. (1) less the product of the Lagrangian multiplier (λ) and the constraint indicated by Eq. (2). This is shown as:

$$L = \sum_{t=1}^{T} (y_t - \tau_t)^2 - \lambda \left[\sum_{t=2}^{T-1} (\tau_{t+1} - \tau_t) - (\tau_t - \tau_{t-1})^2 - \mu \right]. \tag{3}$$

Notice that there is a one-to-one correspondence, namely a positive correlation, between λ and μ. One practical problem is to find the right degree of smoothness, namely the value of the Lagrange multiplier (λ) which can be set by using different values, depending on the kind of data. The reason that we have to find a value for λ is because we do not know the correct degree of smoothness for μ. In Prescott (1986), μ is chosen when the Lagrange multiplier λ is 1600.[3] This

---

[2] The growth rate is given by the log difference. Hence, $\tau_{t+1} - \tau_t$ is the growth rate at period $\tau + 1$ and $\tau_t - \tau_{t-1}$ is the growth rate at period t.

[3] If annual and monthly data are used, then $\lambda = 100$ and $\lambda = 14400$, respectively.

shall produce a correct degree of smoothness in the fitted trend. The use of the HP filter effectively eliminates the variations at all frequencies and induce a stationary cyclical component in the series. If the quarterly data of eight years are used in the study, the frequency is 32 quarters. And with $\lambda = 1600$, the HP filter can produce a stationary cyclical component. A frequency of 32 or more quarters implies that a trend analysis can be made as fluctuation is examined over a long period of time.

The quarterly data of various macroeconomic variables are collected. Hong Kong's real GDP, GDP components (private consumption, government consumption, investment, export and import) and GDP deflator for the period from the first quarter of 1973 (1973Q1) to the second quarter of 2006 (2006Q2) are collected. Other macroeconomic variables may provide a shorter quarterly data series. For the Consumer Price Index (CPI), the available quarterly data began from 1980Q4. The quarterly data for money supply that consists of the two definitions of money (M1 and M2) is available from 1976Q3, while the Hang Seng Index (HSI) is available from 1973Q1. The quarterly data for unemployment and real wage are available from 1981Q4 and 1982Q1, respectively. Quarterly data for the price of housing began from 1978Q1. All quarterly data are collected either from the government sources (Census and Statistics Department and Rating and Valuation Department) or the CEIC database. The influence from seasonal factors is taken into account. The quarterly data series is adjusted seasonally by the Census X12 method. Income volatility is considered by examining the performance of the various macroeconomic factors, such as the GDP components, and factors representing the labor market, stock market, real estate market and monetary variables.

Figures 3.1 and 3.2 show the seasonally adjusted real GDP growth and cycle in Hong Kong, respectively, for the period 1973Q1–2006Q2.[4] The seasonally adjusted real GDP growth trend shown in Figure 3.1 suggests that real GDP growth remained volatile in the 1970s and 1980s, due probably to such reasons as the open nature of Hong Kong that followed closely fluctuations in the world economy. The volatility of GDP was severe during the Sino–British negotiation over the political future of Hong Kong in 1982–1984. Economic confidence in Hong Kong returned after the successful conclusion of the Sino–British negotiation, and coupled with the structural change where the Hong Kong economy has increasingly become service oriented, GDP volatility decreased considerably beginning from the late 1980s. However, Hong Kong's GDP growth stability was affected severely by the outbreak of the Asian financial crisis in 1997–1998 and the severe acute respiratory syndrome (SARS) in 2003. The GDP cycle shown in Figure 3.2 gives a similar picture. One comment is that GDP volatility in Hong Kong is asymmetric, meaning that volatility is lower (higher) when GDP is rising (falling).

The analysis will examine the volatility in the growth of GDP, GDP components and macroeconomic variables between the three periods of pre-1985Q4, 1986Q1–1997Q2 and 1997Q3–2006Q2. The beginning date of the first period depends on

[4] Both the performance of the seasonal non-adjusted GDP growth and cycle and the graphical presentation of the growth and cycle performance of the GDP components and other macroeconomic variables are available, but are not included in the text.

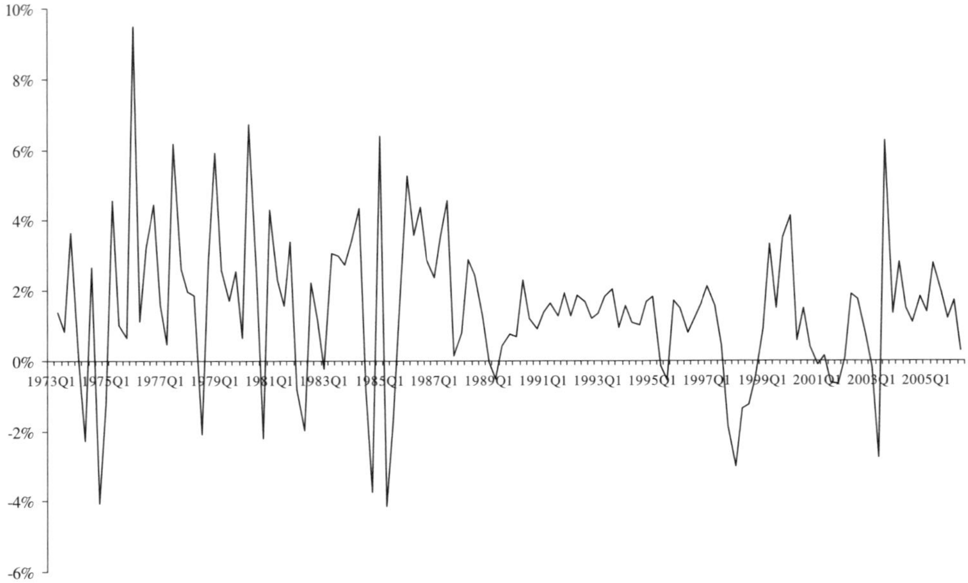

FIGURE 3.1 Seasonally adjusted GDP growth rates: 1973Q1–2006Q2

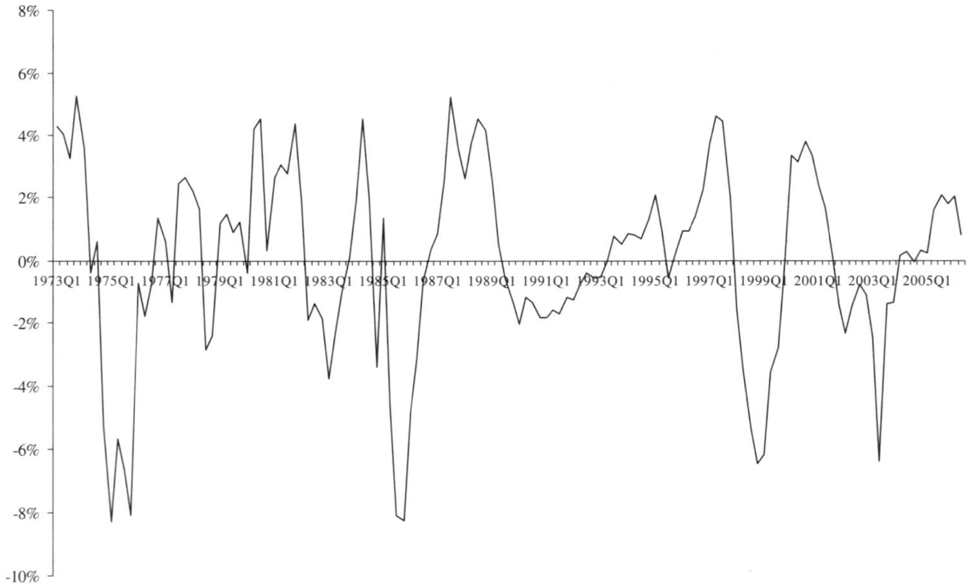

FIGURE 3.2 Seasonally adjusted GDP cycles: 1973Q1–2006Q2

data availability of individual economic variable, but the data of all variables in the first period ends in 1985Q4. The break in 1985Q4 shows the output volatility before the conclusion of the Sino–British negotiation. The second period, 1986Q1–1997Q2, gives the volatility performance in the so-called "transition years" in Hong Kong after the conclusion of the Sino–British negotiation, while the third period, 1997Q3–2006Q2, gives the volatility situation in roughly the first decade after the Asian financial crisis.

Table 3.1 shows the volatility performance indicated by the standard deviations of the growth and cycle of GDP, GDP components and other macroeconomic variables for the entire sample period and the three sub-periods. In general and with the exception of government consumption, the cycle volatility is higher than the growth volatility (with a standard deviation of 3.01% in cycle as compared to 2.14% in growth for GDP). Their differences tend to be larger in those macroeconomic variables that experienced the highest degree of volatility, namely the stock market indicated by the Hang Seng Index (21.77% in cycle as compared to 14.72% in growth), housing price (11.83% in cycle as compared to 6.11% in growth) and unemployment (18.65% in cycle as compared to 10.92% in growth).

TABLE 3.1 Growth and cycle volatility of Hong Kong — Standard deviation (%)

	Whole period		Pre-1985Q4		1986Q1–97Q2		1997Q3–06Q2	
	Gr.	Cy.	Gr.	Cy.	Gr.	Cy.	Gr.	Cy.
GDP	2.14	3.01	2.82	3.65	1.22	2.16	1.86	2.97
GDP components:								
Private consumption	2.57	3.09	3.45	3.82	1.71	2.21	1.91	2.89
Govt. consumption	3.79	3.68	5.17	4.91	2.62	2.29	2.45	3.07
Investment	5.09	7.97	5.51	9.70	3.96	5.93	5.47	7.61
Import	4.44	6.68	5.58	7.48	3.26	5.53	4.01	6.71
Export	3.74	5.88	4.86	6.86	2.51	4.40	3.30	5.91
Macro variables:								
GDP deflator	1.74	2.36	1.64	2.87	0.92	1.63	0.81	2.30
Consumer price index	1.35	1.90	1.10	2.31	0.55	1.25	0.90	2.15
M1	6.00	7.10	4.45	5.43	7.86	7.42	4.46	7.97
M2	3.46	5.16	4.81	8.57	1.83	1.77	1.69	2.95
Hang Seng index	14.72	21.77	18.00	28.61	12.24	14.88	12.18	17.59
Employment	0.74	1.19	0.76	0.93	0.74	1.23	0.72	1.26
Unemployment	10.92	18.65	10.46	16.23	11.56	18.14	10.31	20.47
Wage	1.40	2.33	1.20	2.53	1.47	2.76	1.35	1.66
Housing price	6.11	11.83	5.94	14.84	4.84	9.09	6.02	12.27

Note: Gr. = growth, Cy. = Cycle.

Such a performance in volatility is expected since both stock market and housing market have experienced large fluctuations in the sample period. Although unemployment has remained low, it has experienced sharp changes in various years, thereby producing high volatility. The volatility of employment is much lower than the volatility of unemployment in both growth (0.74% as compared to 10.92%) and cycle (1.19% as compared to 18.65%). This is considered normal as the size of the working labor force is larger than the number of unemployed. Therefore, changes in employment can only have a smaller impact on volatility than changes in unemployment. Among the various GDP components, trade (import and export) and investment showed a higher degree of volatility, thereby reflecting the open nature of the economy.

Between the three sub-periods, there is a reduction in volatility between pre-1985Q4 period and transition years (1986Q1–1997Q2) in both growth (from 2.82% to 1.22%) and cycle (from 3.65% to 2.16%). The three exceptions in growth volatility are M1 (from 4.45% to 7.86%), unemployment (from 10.46% to 11.65%) and wage (from 1.2% to 1.47%). Although the unemployment level has remained low, but the data shows that unemployment growth rate has fluctuated in the second period. For example, the upward revision in unemployment in 1995 should have resulted in a rise in unemployment volatility. On the contrary, employment volatility has improved slightly in the second period (from 0.76% to 0.74%).

As expected and due obviously to the impact of the Asian financial crisis, the volatility of some GDP components and macroeconomic variables has deteriorated in the third period (1997Q3–2006Q2). Among the various GDP components, the volatility of government consumption has dropped (from 2.62% to 2.45%), due probably to the fiscal deficit faced by the government. Among the macroeconomic variables, the cycle volatility provides a more consistent performance. The cycle volatility of most macroeconomic variables deteriorated in the third period. Due to the fall in wage and earning, wage is the only improvement in cycle volatility in the third period (from 2.76% to 1.66%).

To see if the Hong Kong GDP growth volatility is symmetric; that is, volatility is lower (higher) when GDP is falling (rising) or not, we first need to check the stationarity of the time series by applying the unit root test, commonly known as the Dickey–Fuller (DF) and the augmented Dickey–Fuller (ADF) tests (Dickey and Fuller, 1979). The typical ADF test is based on the following formulation:

$$\Delta Y_t = u + \delta T + \alpha Y_{t-1} + \sum_{k=1}^{n} \beta_k \Delta Y_{t-k} + \varepsilon_t, \tag{4}$$

where Δ is the difference operator, Y is the natural logarithm of the time series, T is the time trend, and n is the number of lags necessary to obtain white noise for the error term, ε_t. The lags of ΔY_t are used as the additional regress for the ADF test because they allowed for possible serial correlation in $\{\varepsilon_t\}$. We include the time trend in the unit root test, as this would allow the alternative of the hypothesis to be trend-stationary. In other words, the data used for the analysis are all first difference stationary (namely, the growth rates are stationary while the levels are not), and the growth rates become reliable parameters in the analysis.

3.3 Volatility Clustering and Asymmetry

The two concerns in the study of volatility are volatility clustering and volatility asymmetry. A phenomenon of volatility clustering occurs when a period of high (low) volatility persists or continues for a while after a period of increased (decreased) volatility. A phenomenon of volatility asymmetry occurs in a situation when volatility rises (falls) in periods of falling (rising) growth. For example, volatility in financial markets is likely to rise in a bear market period and fall in a bull market period (Engle and Ng, 1993). As Table 3.1 shows, the standard deviation of GDP growth of Hong Kong was lower when the economy boomed in the early 1990's (1.22), but was higher when the economy was in recession after the Asian financial crisis (1.86). This evidence seems to suggest that the GDP growth volatility of Hong Kong is asymmetric.

To incorporate volatility fluctuation into a model for empirical studies, Engle (1982) has devised the Autoregressive Conditional Heteroskedasticity (ARCH) model that takes into consideration the high persistence of volatility. The ARCH model has further been improved by incorporating a past forecast variance term to become the Generalized Autoregressive Conditional Heteroskedasticity (GARCH) model (Bollerslev, 1986). The GARCH model thus gives the condition on news about volatility from previous period as well as the forecast of variance in the previous period (known as the past forecast variance). This is used to examine if volatility clustering happens in the output growth of Hong Kong.

Neither the ARCH model that examines variance or volatility clustering nor the GARCH model that examines the dependence on forecast variance of previous period can capture volatility asymmetry. The Threshold Generalized Autoregressive Conditional Heteroskedasticity (T-GARCH) model developed by Zakoian (1994) and Glosten *et al.* (1993) is capable of capturing the existence of volatility asymmetry with respect to the direction of real GDP growth. Hamori (2000) further points out that the presence of volatility asymmetry is supported if the empirical estimation from the T-GARCH model provides a better fit than the GARCH model. On the other hand, volatility symmetry is supported if the GARCH model yields a better empirical result.

Theoretically, the ARCH models are designed with the intention to forecast the conditional variance. It is called the "conditional variance" because the variance of the variable is one-period ahead of forecast variance based on past information. By taking the square root of the conditional variance, we come up with conditional standard deviation. On the other hand, the GARCH (p, q) model specifies that the variance of the variable depends upon its own past volatility (p) and past forecast variance (q). Thus, the variance in the current period of the GARCH model depends upon three factors: a) the constant, b) past information about volatility (which is taken to be the squared residual from the previous time period, known as the ARCH term), and c) past forecast variance (known as the GARCH term). Hence the (p) component in the GARCH (p, q) model is referred as the ARCH term, while the (q) component is referred as the GARCH term. This specification effectively suggests that an agent predicts the current period variance by forming a weighted average from past forecast. The ARCH model in fact becomes a special form of GARCH model that contains no lagged forecast variances in the conditional variance equation.

We adopt the Autoregressive Moving Average, ARMA (1, 1), process as the conditional mean equation for the GARCH (1, 1) model and the T-GARCH (1, 1, 1) model. The mean equation, which is the equation that represents the growth rate, is specified as:

$$y_t = c_0 + \alpha y_{t-1} + \beta \varepsilon_{t-1} + \varepsilon_t, \tag{5}$$

where y refers to the growth of the variable. The equation for conditional variance (σ_t^2) is:

$$\sigma_t^2 = c_1 + \chi \varepsilon_{t-1}^2 + \eta \sigma_{t-1}^2 \tag{6}$$

where ε_{t-1}^2 refers to information about volatility from the previous period, measured by the lag of the squared residual from the mean equation (namely, χ, the ARCH term), and σ_{t-1}^2 indicates the last period's forecast variance (namely, η, the GARCH term). The specification for the conditional variance under T-GARCH (with a threshold order equal to 1) is given by:

$$\sigma_t^2 = c_1 + \chi \varepsilon_{t-1}^2 + \eta \sigma_{t-1}^2 + \lambda \mathrm{D}_{t-1} \varepsilon_{t-1}^2 \tag{7}$$

where $D_t = 1$ for $\varepsilon_t < 0$ and $D_t = 0$ otherwise. The T-GARCH conditional variance specification allows the impact of the first lag of the squared residuals to have different effect upon volatility depending upon its sign. The impact of a positive shock, that is when $\varepsilon_{t-1} > 0$, is given by χ, while the impact of a negative shock, that is when $\varepsilon_{t-1} < 0$, is given by $\chi + \lambda$. Thus, a significant λ indicates evidence of asymmetry, with a negative (positive) shock having a greater impact upon volatility if $\lambda > 0$ $(\lambda < 0)$.

Table 3.2 shows the empirical results for both the GARCH and T-GARCH models. First, for the GARCH test on real GDP growth, the coefficient of ARCH term ($\chi = 0.4858$) and GARCH term ($\chi = 0.6162$) are both significant at 1% level, suggesting a presence of volatility clustering. In other words, the prediction of the current period variance is based on the variance forecast of the previous period. For the T-GARCH test, however, the ARCH term ($\chi = 0.1565$) becomes insignificant, while the GARCH term ($\chi = 0.6907$) remains significant. The function of the Schwarz Information Criterion (SIC) is to decide which model produces a better result. The positive coefficient of λ (0.4850) is significant at 5% level, implying that growth volatility is asymmetric and that the negative shock has a greater impact on volatility.

Volatility asymmetry in GDP growth can further be seen from the conditional variance indicated by the standard deviation of the T-GARCH model shown in Figure 3.3.[5] The conditional variance in the whole sample period (1973Q1–2006Q2) provides clear evidence of volatility asymmetry in Hong Kong's GDP growth. The conditional variance indicated by the standard deviation was low during

[5] The conditional standard deviation of the T-GARCH model for all other GDP components and macroeconomics variables are available but not included here.

TABLE 3.2 Tests results of GARCH and T-GARCH models for Hong Kong

	GARCH	T-GARCH	GARCH	T-GARCH	GARCH	T-GARCH
	GDP		Private consumption		Govt. consumption	
c_0	0.0137	0.0122	0.0135	0.0126	0.0155	0.0162
	(0.0000)	(0.0000)	(0.0000)	(0.0000)	(0.0000)	(0.0000)
α	0.5408***	0.5306***	–0.3263	–0.1989	–0.0751	–0.1122
	(0.0784)	(0.0509)	(0.3288)	(0.7490)	(0.8070)	(0.7307)
β	–0.3000	–0.2909	0.2593	0.1826	–0.2941	–0.2833
	(0.3861)	(0.3455)	(0.4620)	(0.7734)	(0.3411)	(0.3813)
c_1	7.70E-06	6.79E-06	2.90E-06	–1.39E-06	0.0001	0.0002
	(0.1962)	(0.1150)	(0.1319)	(0.8290)	(0.2786)	(0.2876)
χ	0.4858*	0.1565	–0.0270*	–0.0538	0.3943***	0.5258***
	(0.0013)	(0.2149)	(0.0075)	(0.1523)	(0.0664)	(0.0689)
η	0.6162*	0.6907*	1.0114*	1.0194*	0.6106*	0.5746*
	(0.0000)	(0.0000)	(0.0000)	(0.0000)	(0.0020)	(0.0060)
λ		0.4850**		0.0536		–0.2601
		(0.0234)		(0.2097)		(0.3277)
SIC	–4.9629	–4.9662#	–4.5617#	–4.5530	–3.7187#	–3.6902
	Investment		Import		Export	
c_0	0.0116	0.0132	0.0228	0.0222	0.0223	0.0180
	(0.0238)	(0.0031)	(0.0000)	(0.0000)	(0.0001)	(0.0035)
α	–0.0521	0.0321	0.4904*	0.5561*	0.6891*	0.7115*
	(0.9297)	(0.9561)	(0.0001)	(0.0000)	(0.0000)	(0.0000)
β	0.1526	0.0690	–0.1953	–0.2428*	–0.2861	–0.3404***
	(0.7909)	(0.9043)	(0.1543)	(0.0273)	(0.1224)	(0.0663)
c_1	0.0013	0.0008	0.0001	–9.46E-05	0.0001	0.0001
	(0.4210)	(0.0448)	(0.0000)	(0.0000)	(0.0829)	(0.0941)
χ	–0.0641**	–0.1848*	0.1141*	–0.1431*	0.2439**	0.0757
	(0.0183)	(0.0052)	(0.0000)	(0.0000)	(0.0247)	(0.5045)
η	0.5625	0.8071*	1.0245*	1.0301*	0.6266*	0.6241*
	(0.3553)	(0.0000)	(0.0000)	(0.0000)	(0.0000)	(0.0000)
λ		0.1139**		0.0518		0.4426
		(0.0490)		(0.2573)		(0.1105)
SIC	–2.9367	–2.9813#	–3.6290#	–3.6148	–3.8856#	–3.8769

(Continued)

the economic boom years of the early 1990s, but was high during years that experienced negative shocks, typically the Asian financial crisis in 1997 and the SARS incidence in 2003.

Among the various GDP components, growth in investment also shows volatility asymmetry (0.1139). All the GDP components have significant ARCH (χ) and

TABLE 3.2 (*Continued*)

	GARCH	T-GARCH	GARCH	T-GARCH	GARCH	T-GARCH
	GDP deflator		Consumer price index		Housing price	
c_0	0.0027	0.0027	0.0172	0.0076	0.0288	0.0188
	(0.7486)	(0.6390)	(0.0382)	(0.4236)	(0.0522)	(0.2079)
α	0.9509*	0.9379*	0.9766*	0.9662*	0.7632*	0.7709*
	(0.0000)	(0.0000)	(0.0000)	(0.0000)	(0.0000)	(0.0000)
β	0.3361*	–0.4729*	–0.4395*	–0.4162*	–0.0705	–0.0746
	(0.0000)	(0.0000)	(0.0000)	(0.0018)	(0.6838)	(0.6266)
c_1	1.17E-06	8.37E-07	1.29E-05	1.25E-05	0.0009	0.0009
	(0.0019)	(0.3440)	(0.0039)	(0.0000)	(0.0530)	(0.0253)
χ	–0.0273*	–0.0046*	0.9764*	0.1267	0.4052**	0.1103
	(0.0002)	(0.0000)	(0.0000)	(0.4254)	(0.0140)	(0.5304)
η	0.9969*	1.0115*	–0.0488	0.0218	0.1253	0.0968
	(0.0000)	(0.0000)	(0.7414)	(0.8230)	(0.6149)	(0.6725)
λ		–0.0632*		1.4887*		0.6520***
		(0.0000)		(0.0018)		(0.0854)
SIC	–6.1295#	–6.1277	–7.4356	–7.4564#	–3.2814	–3.2861#
	M1		M2		Hang Seng index	
c_0	0.0342	0.0298	0.0347	0.0264	0.0280	0.0334
	(0.0000)	(0.0000)	(0.0000)	(0.0099)	(0.0277)	(0.0006)
α	–0.5928	0.5605	0.9514*	0.9571*	0.1270	0.7957*
	(0.2318)	(0.4591)	(0.0000)	(0.0000)	(0.7989)	(0.0000)
β	0.5314	–0.4700	–0.6825*	–0.6966*	–0.0263	–0.8264*
	(0.3369)	(0.5707)	(0.0000)	(0.0000)	(0.9564)	(0.0000)
c_1	0.0014	0.0003	4.28E-05	4.04E-05	0.0113	0.0113
	(0.0008)	(0.1526)	(0.2964)	(0.2945)	(0.0004)	(0.0008)
χ	0.8720*	1.1565**	0.8349*	0.4259***	0.3761*	0.5869**
	(0.0012)	(0.0129)	(0.0004)	(0.0841)	(0.0075)	(0.0466)
η	0.0026	0.5959*	0.3727*	0.4243*	0.0561	–0.3745
	(0.9856)	(0.0000)	(0.0032)	(0.0000)	(0.7535)	(0.2349)
λ		–1.0754**		0.6796***		0.0021
		(0.0287)		(0.0704)		(0.9901)
SIC	–2.8177#	–2.7717	–4.4703#	–4.4537	–1.0114	–1.0293#

(*Continued*)

GARCH (η) terms, implying the presence of volatility clustering. Among the three price variables of the GDP deflator, CPI and housing price, volatility clustering occurs in the GDP deflator (–0.0632), but the T-GARCH estimates are not supported by the SIC. On the contrary, the estimates of CPI (1.4887) and housing price (0.6520) are supported by the SIC. One can conclude that investment growth and general

TABLE 3.2 (*Continued*)

	GARCH	T-GARCH	GARCH	T-GARCH	GARCH	T-GARCH
	Employment		Unemployment		Wage	
c_0	0.0035	0.0039	−0.0151	−0.0076	0.0056	0.0054
	(0.0006)	(0.0003)	(0.3961)	(0.7135)	(0.0138)	(0.0161)
α	0.5153	0.5684	0.5097*	0.4301**	0.7896*	0.7942*
	(0.2346)	(0.1469)	(0.0052)	(0.0205)	(0.0000)	(0.0000)
β	−0.3374	−0.4217	0.0865	0.2842***	−0.6618*	−0.6721*
	(0.4474)	(0.3047)	(0.6256)	(0.0615)	(0.0024)	(0.0019)
c_1	5.36E-06	6.73E-06	−0.0003	0.0004	7.68E-05	7.47E-05
	(0.6151)	(0.4527)	(0.0727)	(0.3863)	(0.0314)	(0.0459)
χ	0.0894	0.0797	0.0716**	0.4229**	0.4352***	0.4079
	(0.3851)	(0.4080)	(0.0411)	(0.0491)	(0.0699)	(0.2423)
η	0.7994*	0.8909*	0.9431*	0.6546*	0.1860	0.1751
	(0.0032)	(0.0000)	(0.0000)	(0.0000)	(0.3910)	(0.4459)
λ		−0.2064		−0.1794		0.1334
		(0.1847)		(0.5162)		(0.7491)
SIC	−6.7646#	−6.7422	−1.6245#	−1.5291	−5.5917#	−5.5451

Notes: *, ** and *** indicate 1%, 5% and 10% level of significance, respectively. SIC is the Schwarz Information Criterion. # indicates the model that SIC chooses. The numbers in the brackets are the *p*-value figures.

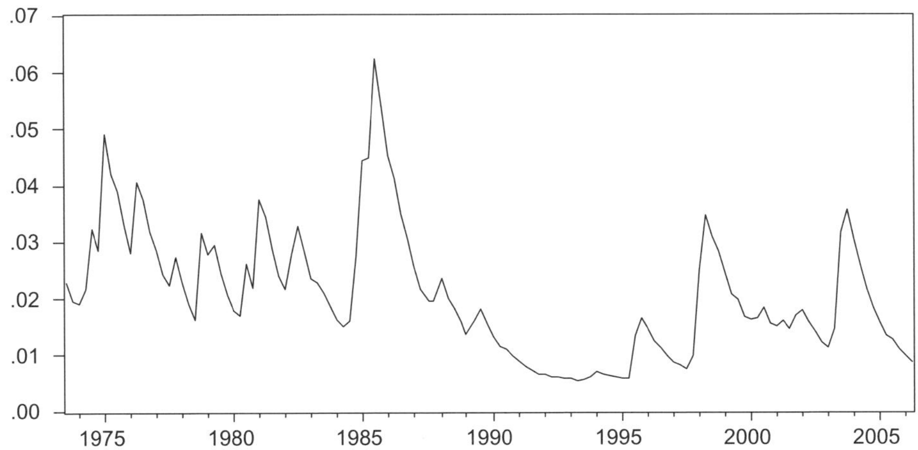

FIGURE 3.3 Conditional standard deviation of GDP growth for Hong Kong

price level are the major variables that lead to asymmetry in GDP growth in the sample period.

For the two monetary variables of M1 and M2, there is also the evidence of volatility clustering, but that M2 depends on the variance forecast of previous period while M1 does not (η = 0.0026, not significant in the case of M1 in the GARCH model). Both the coefficients of λ for M1 (−1.0754) and M2 (0.6796) are significant, but they are not supported by the SIC. It is expected that the Hang Seng Index shows volatility clustering, but its volatility neither depends on the past forecast variance nor be asymmetric. In the labor market, unemployment and wage exhibited volatility clustering. The volatility for both unemployment and employment shows dependency on past forecast variance. All three labor market variables show volatility symmetry.

The growth of all GDP components and the GDP deflator also shows dependency on past forecast variance as their GARCH terms (η) are all statistically significant. Thus, it is not surprising to observe that the variance of current period's GDP growth depends on past forecast variance. The volatility of money market and labor market also has the same type of behavior and that their GARCH terms are significant. However, such observations do not exist in the stock market and housing market as the GARCH terms for Hang Seng Index and housing price are not significant at all.

Finally, we observe strong evidence of volatility asymmetry for GDP growth, because the T-GARCH term (λ = 0.4850) is statistically significant and is supported by the SIC (−0.9662). Further investigations reveal that investment (with λ = 0.1139 and SIC = −2.9813) is the only GDP component that has volatility asymmetry. We can conclude that investment volatility is low when the economy is booming, but investment volatility is high when the economy is in recession. Since investment is always highly correlated with GDP, investment leads to volatility asymmetry in the GDP growth in the Hong Kong economy. We can see that the occurrence of negative shocks have really raised the GDP growth volatility, but volatility fell considerably when the economy recovered.

The volatility for the general price level (the GDP deflator and the CPI) also showed strong asymmetric performance. It also holds in the housing market that the T-GARCH term is significant. However, there is only weak evidence of volatility asymmetry in the money market and there is no such evidence in the labor market and stock market. The volatility of labor market and stock market is thus symmetric, and they are not the factors that lead to volatility asymmetry in Hong Kong's GDP growth.

The volatility performance of all variables in Table 3.2 can conveniently be summarized by using the following two criteria. One criterion is the evidence of volatility clustering (χ) or the dependency on past forecast variance (η), while the other criterion is the evidence of volatility asymmetry (λ). Three performance indicators are applied to each criterion. The three performance indicators for the presence of volatility clustering or the dependency on past forecast variances are:

a) Strong evidence: the χ or η coefficient has at least gained a significance level of 10% in the preferred model;
b) Mixed evidence: the χ or η coefficient is not significant in the preferred model but has at least gained a significance level of 10% in the non-preferred model; and
c) No evidence: the χ or η coefficient is not significant in both models.

The three performance indicators for the evidence of volatility asymmetry are:

a) Strong evidence: the λ coefficient has at least gained a significance level of 10% in the T-GARCH model, which is preferred to the GARCH model;
b) Weak evidence: the λ coefficient has at least gained a significance level of 10% in the T-GARCH model but is not preferred to the AGRCH model; and
c) No evidence: the λ coefficient is not significant in the T-GARCH model.

Table 3.3 summarizes the various GARCH and T-GARCH test performance indicators. The performance of both investment and GDP deflator showed "strong" in all criteria, probably they have influenced GDP volatility importantly. Most variables showed strong performance in evidence for volatility clustering and/or dependency on past forecast variance. The monetary, finance and labor variables showed a weaker performance in the evidence for volatility asymmetry. One can show that demand factors (consumption, investment, import and export) have exhibited stronger volatility performances than supply factors (employment, unemployment and wage) in the sample period.

To conclude, we show that there is an evidence of volatility clustering on GDP growth, that is, a period of high (low) volatility continues for a while after a period with increased (decreased) volatility. As a matter of fact, volatility clustering occurs in all GDP components and other macroeconomics variables, such as GDP deflator, money supply, Hang Seng Index, housing price, real wage and unemployment. In other words, the period of high (low) volatility in financial market, labor market, housing market, price level and money market persists after a period with increased (decreased) volatility.

TABLE 3.3 Summary results of the GARCH and T-GARCH tests for Hong Kong

	Evidence of volatility clustering (χ)	Dependency on past forecast variance (η)	Evidence of volatility asymmetry (λ)
GDP	Mix	Strong	Strong
Private consumption	Strong	Strong	No
Govt. consumption	Strong	Strong	No
Investment	Strong	Strong	Strong
Import	Strong	Strong	Mo
Export	Strong	Strong	No
GDP deflator	Strong	Strong	Strong
Consumer Price Index	Mix	No	Strong
Housing price	Mix	No	Strong
M1	Strong	Mix	Weak
M2	Strong	Strong	Weak
Hang Sang Index	Strong	No	No
Employment	No	Strong	No
Unemployment	Strong	Strong	No
Wage	Strong	No	No

3.4 Business Cycles

The discussion so far relates to the growth of macroeconomic variables. To relate the discussion to business cycle, we examine the cross correlation between output (GDP) and macroeconomic variables. Cross correlation is defined as:

$$\gamma_{xy}(l) = \frac{c_{xy}(l)}{\sqrt{c_{xx}(0)}.\sqrt{c_{yy}(0)}}, \tag{8}$$

where $l = 0, \pm 1, \pm 2, \ldots$ while

$$c_{xy}(l) = \begin{Bmatrix} \sum_{t=1}^{T-1} ((x_t - \bar{x})(y_{t+1} - \bar{y}))/T, l = 0, 1, 2, \ldots \\ \sum_{t=1}^{T+1} ((y_t - \bar{y})(x_{t-1} - \bar{x}))/T, l = 0, -1, -2, \ldots \end{Bmatrix}, \tag{9}$$

and

$$c_{xx}(0) = \sum_{t=0}^{T} (x_t - \bar{x})^2/T, \quad \text{(the variance of the } x \text{ series)}, \tag{10}$$

and

$$c_{yy}(0) = \sum_{t=0}^{T} (y_t - \bar{y})^2/T, \quad \text{(the variance of the } y \text{ series)}. \tag{11}$$

T indicates the time period. Since the cyclical components are stationary, the mean and the variance of the cyclical series do not change over time. Thus, the mean of the cyclical series is equal to zero, while the variance of the cyclical series is a constant. As the cyclical component is equal to the original series minus the trend series, the cyclical component is obtained after the original series are inserted into the Hodrick-Prescott (HP) filter. We then get the business cycles of GDP and all other macroeconomic variables for the sample period. Equation (8) is used to run the cross correlation and obtain the estimated coefficients. To examine how the macroeconomic variables are correlated with GDP, we let GDP be x, and the other macroeconomic variables would then be y in Eq. (8). For instance, if y is investment, we are looking at the cross correlation between investment and GDP.

There are four important implications in the cross correlation analysis.

1. **Cyclical fluctuation:** We compare the cyclical fluctuation of each variable and see which is more volatile than output. This is done by comparing the standard deviation of the cyclical component between the macroeconomics variables and GDP.

2. **Cross correlation estimates:** The cross correlation estimates indicate whether the variable is correlated with the output cycle. This is shown by considering the value of the coefficients. The higher is the value of the coefficient, the higher is the correlation between the macroeconomic variable and GDP. For instance, if the value exceeds two standard error bounds, we can conclude that the variable and GDP are correlated. The value for two standard error bounds would approximately be equal to $\pm 2\sqrt{T}$. Since we have 134 quarters (from 1973Q1–2006Q2) for most of the variables, the critical value for a significant coefficient would then approximately be equal to ±0.1728. The four criteria that are used to decide on the degree of correlation are:
   a) Strong when the value of the correlation coefficient ranges from 0.7 to unity;
   b) Medium when the value of the correlation coefficient ranges between 0.4 and 0.7;
   c) Weak when the value of the correlation coefficient ranges between 0.2 and 0.4; and
   d) No correlation when the value of the coefficient ranges from 0 and 0.2.
3. **Pro- and counter-cyclical:** The results can be used to identify which variables are pro-cyclical (movement following output) and which variables are counter-cyclical (movement against output), provided that the coefficient value is statistically significant (that is, above 0.1728). For instance, a positive sign of the coefficient for cross correlation between consumption and GDP (that is, positive correlation) suggests that consumption is pro-cyclical. On the contrary, if the sign of the coefficient for cross correlation is negative between consumption and GDP (that is, negative correlation) we can conclude that consumption is counter-cyclical.
4. **Lead-lag effects:** The cross correlation results also reveal the lead-lag effect in the economy. We will compare whether the lead value (coefficients of future quarter periods of $\gamma(1)$, $\gamma(2)$ and $\gamma(3)$) is higher than the lag value (coefficients of previous quarter periods of $\gamma(-1)$, $\gamma(-2)$ and $\gamma(-3)$) or vice versa in order to observe the lead-lag effect in a business cycle. For example, if output is highly correlated with the lagged value of money, one can conclude that money leads the cyclical movement of output. In order words, the order of causation in the business cycle goes from money to output. On the contrary, if GDP is more correlated with the lead value of money supply, then GDP leads the cycle of money. But if the contemporaneous correlation (current quarter period at $\gamma(0)$) between the macroeconomic variable and GDP is very high (that is, coefficients exceeded 0.7), one can conclude that the two cycles of GDP and money actually move at the same time.

Table 3.4 displays the results of the cross correlation between GDP and the different GDP components and macroeconomic variables. The discussion can first be made on the GDP components before other macroeconomic variables.

Private consumption: The cyclical movement of private consumption is similar to that of output (GDP). GDP leads the cycle of private consumption in the long-run

TABLE 3.4 Cross correlation with the GDP cycle in the Hong Kong economy

Variables	SD (%)	Cross correlation of GDP with $\gamma(-3)$	$\gamma(-2)$	$\gamma(-1)$	$\gamma(0)$	$\gamma(1)$	$\gamma(2)$	$\gamma(3)$
GDP	3.008	0.330	0.524	0.762	1.000	0.762	0.524	0.330
P-Con	3.089	0.225	0.356	0.510	0.598	0.517	0.413	0.337
G-Con	3.683	0.029	−0.036	−0.057	−0.036	−0.109	−0.039	0.041
Invest	7.976	0.126	0.321	0.519	0.713	0.728	0.641	0.576
Import	6.685	0.235	0.435	0.630	0.705	0.610	0.447	0.231
Export	5.881	0.264	0.465	0.651	0.751	0.585	0.387	0.148
Deflator	2.358	−0.406	−0.285	−0.152	−0.036	0.161	0.276	0.304
CPI	1.896	−0.450	−0.409	−0.310	−0.161	−0.025	0.071	0.145
M1	7.104	0.241	0.309	0.326	0.277	0.237	0.161	0.066
M2	5.156	−0.010	−0.038	−0.043	−0.062	−0.051	−0.008	0.011
HSI	21.765	0.490	0.547	0.587	0.519	0.332	0.197	0.016
Empl	1.193	−0.055	0.129	0.336	0.567	0.638	0.565	0.417
Unempl	18.646	0.155	−0.054	−0.303	−0.565	−0.678	−0.656	−0.573
Wage	2.328	−0.146	−0.167	−0.145	−0.047	0.046	0.135	0.224
HP	11.829	0.035	0.206	0.335	0.405	0.423	0.386	0.305

Notes: All data are seasonally adjusted. SD = standard deviation; P-Con = private consumption; G-Con = government consumption; Invest = investment; CPI = Consumer Price Index; HP = housing price; HSI = Hang Seng Index; Empl = employment; Unempl = unemployment.

as GDP is more correlated with the lead of private consumption (0.517 in $\gamma(1)$ as compared to 0.510 in $\gamma(-1)$ and so on). This finding is in line with the norm that output must be produced before consumption can take place.

Government consumption: Government consumption is uncorrelated, as coefficient estimates are small in most cases, and has fluctuated slightly more than output, since the standard deviation (3.683) is slightly higher than the standard deviation of GDP (3.008). Furthermore, although some coefficients for government consumption are negative, they are not significant at all. There is thus no correlation between GDP and government spending, and that GDP cannot lead government spending, and neither government spending can lead output. This confirms the relative small size of the Hong Kong government, and that short-term government welfare assistance is not growth-promoting.

Investment: Investment is the most volatile variable among the GDP components (standard deviation of 7.976) and is largely correlated with output. It is clear that GDP leads the investment cycle. Investment plays an important role as its stability is definitely preferred, as it leads to a lower volatility in output. A stable source of investment activities is needed in maintaining growth stability in Hong Kong.

Export and import: Both import and export are twice more volatile (with high standard deviation) than output. There is no significant lead-lag effect between import and GDP, they move almost at the same time although the lagged value is slightly higher than the lead value. Export evidently leads the GDP cycle (0.651 in

$\gamma(-1)$ as compared to 0.585 in $\gamma(1)$ and so on). Given the open nature of the Hong Kong economy, changes in exports and imports will have direct impact on growth stability. A rise in export will benefit Hong Kong all the time. Trade and export is still the core economic component in Hong Kong.

Prices: Consistent with basic economic theory, prices are counter-cyclical and lead the business cycle. The evidence is that the lagged values of both GDP deflator and CPI are negative but are more significant than the lead values. Both the deflator and CPI cycles are less volatile than the output cycle (with standard deviations smaller than GDP). In short, severe inflation has to be avoided.

Monetary aggregates: For the monetary aggregates, it is surprising to find that M2 has little to do with the output cycle. The correlations remained close to zero for all the leads and lags. M1 is pro-cyclical (a positive and significant estimate at $\gamma(0)$), which is consistent with economic theory. The difference in the performance between M1 and M2 suggested that M1 and M2 in Hong Kong are obviously two different instruments. In the case of M1, their positive correlation coefficients are significantly different from zero correlation, and GDP is highly correlated with the lagged values of money, since the lag correlation coefficients are higher than the lead correlation coefficients in Table 3.4. Therefore, we conclude that money leads the business cycle and the causation goes from money to output, and, namely, that the high level of M1 in this period will produce a higher level of output in next period.

Hang Seng Index: As for the stock market, the contemporaneous correlation, $\gamma(0)$, between output and stock price index is positive and high (0.519). Thus, the stock market is pro-cyclical, and that output is correlated more with the lagged values of the stock market (with an estimate of 0.587 in $\gamma(-1)$ as compared to 0.332 in $\gamma(1)$ and so on). This shows that the stock market is an important determinant in affecting the Hong Kong economy and it leads the output cycle.

Housing price: The housing or real estate market is another volatile market. The positive correlation between housing price and output is consistent with real estate economic theories that there exists a significant wealth effect between income and demand for property. The housing price is pro-cyclical. In the long-run, GDP leads the real estate cycle, although both the lead and lagged values are significant. This empirical finding suggests that it is the growth of GDP that leads to growth in housing market. An excessive high property price will effectively slow down other economic activities, resulting in a lower growth in GDP.

Labor market: The labor market is less volatile than output. The standard deviation of the employment cycle is just above 1% (1.193). In line with simple labor economics theory, employment is pro-cyclical and unemployment is counter-cyclical. Output is highly correlated with the lead values of both employment and unemployment. It tells us that GDP leads the cycle of labor market, which also exhibits wage rigidity. The correlation between GDP and wage is positive and significant after three quarters, and we find (but not shown here) that the correlation is still significant until the ninth quarter. In other words, increase in output in the Hong Kong economy can lead to wage increase between three to nine quarters. Despite the delay in time, it is true that wage cannot increase without rise in GDP. This sheds lights on the idea of

TABLE 3.5 Summary results of cross correlation in the real business cycle of Hong Kong

Macro variables	Cyclical volatility compared to output	Extent of correlation with output	Pro-/counter-cyclical	Lead/Lag output cycle
P-CON	Similar	High	Pro	Contemporaneous
G-CON	Slightly higher	Non-correlated	Neither	No effect
Investment	>2 times higher	Very high	Pro	Contemporaneous
Import	>2 times higher	Very high	Pro	Contemporaneous
Export	≅2 times higher	Very high	Pro	Contemporaneous
GDP deflator	Lower	Contemporaneously non-correlated	Counter	Lead
CPI	Lower	Contemporaneously non-correlated	Counter	Lead
M1	>2 times higher	Low	Pro	Lead
M2	Higher	Non-correlated	Neither	No effect
HSI	Much higher	High	Pro	Lead
Employment	Lower	High	Pro	Lag
Unemployment	Much higher	High	Counter	Lag
Wage	Lower	Contemporaneously non-correlated	Neither	Lag
HP	Much higher	Medium	Pro	Lag

Notes: P-Con = private consumption; G-Con = government consumption; CPI = Consumer Price Index; HP = housing price; HSI = Hang Seng Index.

a minimum wage in Hong Kong. A high minimum wage would discourage employment, especially when the economy is not expanding.

We can conclude by summarizing all the findings in Table 3.5 under the four categories:

1) The cyclical volatility compared to output;
2) The extent of correlation with output;
3) The nature of pro- or counter-cyclical; and
4) The lead or lag effect to the output cycle.

Cyclical volatility compared to output: With the exception of private consumption and government consumption, the cyclical volatility of other GDP components is either more than or close to two times higher than the GDP cycle. The cyclical volatility for the general price level (both the CPI and GDP deflator) is lower than that of GDP. We find that the money supply cycle is more volatile than the GDP cycle, while the labor market (aggregate unemployment and real wage) has lower cycle volatility. The stock market and housing market are the two most volatile markets in the Hong Kong economy and it is not surprising that their cyclical volatility is much higher than output.

Extent of cross correlation: Cross correlation results showed that government consumption has no correlation with GDP at all. This probably is due to the relative small size of the public sector, and that the total public expenditure to GDP ratio in Hong Kong has, with only a few exceptions in economically recessed years, rarely exceeded 20%. On the contrary, the contemporaneous correlation between GDP and its components is very high. For instance, the correlation value between GDP and consumption is close to 0.6, and it even exceeded 0.7 for export, import and investment. The general price level and real wage are non-correlated contemporaneously with GDP. Money supply does not show strong correlation with GDP. The contemporaneous correlation value between M1 and output is lower than 0.3, this cannot be regarded as high. M2 is non-correlated with GDP. For the remaining macroeconomic variables of Hang Seng Index and the labor market, their cross correlation with output remained high, but the housing market shows a medium high cross correlation with output, suggesting that movements in property market may not generate the same degree of output changes in the sample period. In other words, property market speculation is common.

Pro- or counter-cyclical: In the discussion on whether the macroeconomic variables are pro-cyclical or counter-cyclical to GDP growth, we find that other than government consumption which is non-correlated with GDP, all other GDP components are pro-cyclical. Those macroeconomic variables that show pro-cyclical movement with GDP include the stock price and housing price. This phenomenon is in line with the economics theory that the higher the level of output or income, the more wealthy people become. The positive wealth effect thus leads to the rise of stock price and housing price as a result of an increase in demand. Similarly, the higher (lower) the output is, the higher (lower) the demand is for labor. Thus, aggregate employment is pro-cyclical while aggregate unemployment is counter-cyclical. As expected, we also see that the general price level is counter-cyclical while money supply (only M1 here) is pro-cyclical. Since M2 has no correlation at all with output, it is neither pro-cyclical nor counter-cyclical.

Lead/Lag effect in output cycle: Because of the high contemporaneous correlation or similar lead and lag coefficient values between GDP and its components (except government expenditure), one can argue that the cycles of GDP components are actually moving at the same time with GDP in the Hong Kong economy. The general price level, money supply (M1) and the stock price lead the output cycle. On the other hand, GDP also leads several variables; for example, GDP leads the volatile housing market and the labor market. As for the correlation between real wage and output, although the contemporaneous correlation is insignificant, we find significant correlation coefficients from the third quarters onwards.[6] This suggests that wage

[6] A near zero value in the contemporaneous correlation between wage and output is commonly known as the Dunlop–Tarshis observation (Dunlop, 1938; Tarshis, 1939), which accordingly to Lucas (1976, 1981) whom primarily refuted the classical and Keynesian argument of a strong correlation between wage and employment, and instead pointed out that wage or labor productivity does not display a strong positive correlation with employment (see also Christiano and Eichenbaum, 1992; Sargent, 1987; and McCallum, 1989).

rigidity happens in the Hong Kong labor market, and the change in the output level could affect wage after a minimum of three quarters.

A number of conclusions on the empirical study on GDP growth volatility and business cycle in the Hong Kong economy can be drawn. They are:

1. The Hong Kong GDP has been subjected to seasonal movement since the 1990s, due probably to the high seasonal variation in external trade (export and import), which are highly correlated with output and leads the output cycle.[7] When the seasonal effect is removed, output volatility in the Hong Kong economy has shown significant decline since the early 1990s. It is apparent that growth volatility is asymmetric, in the sense that volatility is higher when there is a negative shock, but when the economy is stable and performed well, volatility is reduced. The implication is that the Hong Kong economy needs to institute additional instruments that would reduce the negative impact of economic shocks.
2. Among the various macroeconomic variables that contribute to output volatility, financial market, which is highly correlated with GDP, has shown a significant decrease in both growth and cycle volatility even in the period of the Asian financial crisis. It appears probably that the improvement in the financial system and appropriate technological innovations in the finance sector can contribute to the reduction in growth volatility in Hong Kong, as stronger and more transparent financial regulations and system can prevent malpractices. The obvious implication is that being an international financial centre where markets participants are not restricted, a stronger and appropriate set of financial regulations and practices will be the only mean to safeguard the financial market and system should shock, disturbances and bubbles occur in the financial world.
3. Monetary growth is less volatile in recent years, and it has little to do with GDP volatility, due probably to the linked exchange rate system and that the lack of effectiveness in the monetary policy (namely, the inability to influence the interest rate in Hong Kong) has led to a fall in correlation between M2 and GDP. This should be seen as a positive contribution by the adoption of the linked exchange rate, as it virtually has safeguarded the economy and minimized the negative impact from economic shocks and financial bubbles. In short, the linked exchange rate has served Hong Kong well.
4. Changes in unemployment have become less volatile, but its cyclical movement has remained volatile and counter-cyclical. The wage-price volatility does not increase output volatility through demand effects.

In a nutshell, we find that as an export-led and small open economy, Hong Kong has been subjected to great seasonal movement and high external shocks, but its ability to absorb shock has been increasing. The fall in GDP in the post-Asian financial crisis years has led to a decline in GDP volatility. Government spending in Hong Kong has not been an important factor in affecting GDP volatility due favorably and

---

[7] For instance, the non-seasonal adjusted data has shown increasing volatility in export, import and GDP.

appropriately to the small size of the government. There is clear evidence that the financial sector in Hong Kong has increasingly become more mature. Given the high correlation between stock price and output in the Hong Kong economy, the declining volatility in Hang Seng Index has helped to reduce GDP volatility in Hong Kong. We also find an interesting observation that Hong Kong's GDP growth is lower when the market is bullish and higher when the market is bearish due to asymmetric growth in investment and general price level.

3.5 Growth Volatility in Asian Economies Compared

The method used to study the output volatility of the Hong Kong economy is extended to examine and compare the output volatility of other Asian economies. As Li and Kwok (2009) show in the study of output volatility among five East Asian economies, the question is whether other Asian economies with similar economic background would show similar performance to that of the Hong Kong economy. For comparison, the four Asian economies, Singapore, South Korea, Japan and Chinese Taipei, share similar economic characteristics, such as a policy of export-led, an improvement in labor productivity due to increasing investment in education, high growth rates and rapid industrialization between the 1960s and 1990s. Similarly, all these four economies have suffered different degree of set back during the Asian financial crisis.

We use a similar technical method to show the breakdown in the standard deviation of growth and cycle volatility, and perform the similar GARCH and T-GARCH tests with conditional variance and cross correlation with output. In particular, we examine whether the output and stock market price volatility in one economy affect other economies, and if there is any volatility spillover among these five Asian economies, and to see how these economies react to each other in a cross-country correlation analysis.

All GDP, GDP components and stock price data for the four other Asian economies (Singapore, South Korea, Japan and Chinese Taipei) are collected from the CEIC Database. Quarterly data are used and the end quarter for all variables is 2006Q2. The quarterly data for the beginning period differed among the four Asian economies. The quarterly data for Chinese Taipei dates back to 1961Q1, but the data for South Korea and Singapore began from 1970Q1 and 1975Q1, respectively. The quarterly GDP data for Japan ranged only from 1980 to 2004. The quarterly data on the stock market price also differed among the four Asian economies. For the Taiwan Capitalization Weighted Stock Index and the Korean Composite Stock Price Index, the periods covered are 1976Q1–2006Q2. For Singapore, the Straits Times Index covered the period of 1985Q1–2006Q2. For Japan, the Nikkei 225 is available for the period of 1949Q3–2006Q2.

Similar to the analysis shown in Fig. 3.1 for the Hong Kong economy, Fig. 3.4 (a) to (d) show the seasonally adjusted GDP growth of the four Asian economies. Both Chinese Taipei and South Korea have shown a decline in output volatility since the early 1990s, but have increased after the outbreak of the Asian financial crisis. South Korea has experienced the largest negative output growth after the Asian financial crisis among the selected Asian economies. Surprisingly, the GDP growth of

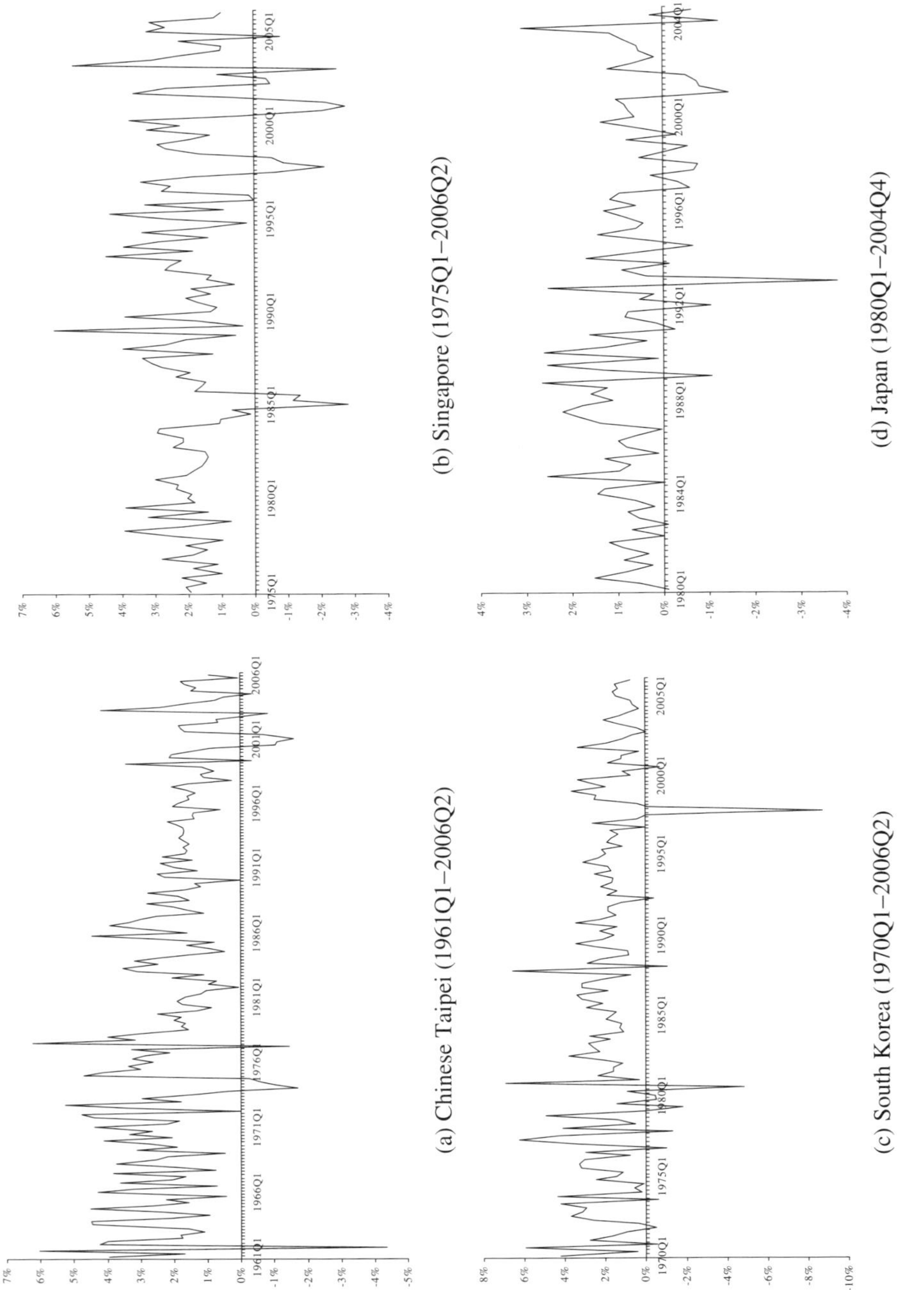

FIGURE 3.4 Seasonally adjusted GDP growths of Asian economies

TABLE 3.6 GDP growth volatility of five Asian economies — Standard deviation (%)

	Whole period	Pre-AFC	Post-AFC	Difference
Chinese Taipei	1.4755	1.4525	1.2117	−0.2408
Singapore	1.5694	1.2890	2.0108	0.7218
South Korea	1.8076	1.7108	1.9265	0.2157
Japan	0.9981	0.9911	0.9258	−0.0653
Hong Kong	2.1367	2.2023	1.8638	−0.3385

Note: AFC = Asian financial crisis. Data are seasonally adjusted. Pre-AFC = Pre-1997Q2; post-AFC = post-1997Q2.
Source: CEIC Database.

Singapore seemed to be more volatile overtime. Japan, though it has developed earlier than the economies of Hong Kong, Singapore, Chinese Taipei and South Korea, has experienced a structural break in the 1980s, but fell into the liquidity trap in the 1990s and output volatility has increased.

The GDP growth volatility of these five Asian economies (including Hong Kong) can better be examined by looking at their standard deviations. For the purpose of comparison, the period of analysis is divided using the Asian financial crisis (AFC) as the historical event date between pre-AFC (pre-1997Q2) and post-AFC (post-1997Q2). Table 3.6 shows the volatility of seasonally adjusted GDP growth for the five Asian economies.

For the volatility of GDP growth based on seasonally adjusted data as shown in Table 3.6, the growth volatility indicated by the standard deviation for Japan in the whole period is most steady, since it has the lowest standard deviation (0.9981) among the five Asian economies. On the contrary, the Hong Kong economy has shown a highest standard deviation in the whole period (2.1367), suggesting that the small open nature of the economy does subject to external shocks. The GDP growth volatility of the other three Asian economies has shown a lower standard deviation than the Hong Kong economy.

However, between the two sub-periods of pre-AFC and post-AFC, the Hong Kong economy has shown a larger decrease in output volatility (−0.3385), followed by Chinese Taipei (−0.2408) and Japan (−0.0653). On the contrary, Singapore has shown a high increase in volatility between the two sub-periods (0.7218), due probably to the pivotal role Singapore has played among the Association of Southeast Asian Nations (ASEAN) that composed of, among others, Indonesia, Philippines and Thailand that had severely been affected by the Asian financial crisis. As for South Korea, the increase in output volatility (0.2157) is due largely to the Asian financial crisis, but had the crisis not happened, the volatility for South Korea's GDP growth would have decreased.

Table 3.7 shows the decompositions of the growth volatility for the GDP components. In the case of Chinese Taipei, there is significant decline in growth volatility for both export and import. In other words, a more stable situation in international trade is the main contributing factor to the lower volatility in output growth in

TABLE 3.7 Growth volatility of GDP components of five Asian economies — Standard deviation (%)

	Whole period	Pre-AFC	Post-AFC	Difference
Chinese Taipei				
Private consumption	1.2217	1.1266	1.0265	–0.1001
Govt. consumption	3.1211	2.8311	3.8667	1.0356
Investment	4.9162	4.8700	4.7167	–0.1533
Import	8.3192	9.1062	4.1114	–4.9948
Export	8.5291	9.3683	3.9818	–5.3865
Singapore				
Private consumption	2.0353	2.0275	2.0570	0.0295
Govt. consumption	9.8198	9.5824	10.4749	0.8925
Investment	6.9183	7.4876	5.1722	–2.3154
Import	3.8546	3.7199	4.1494	0.4295
Export	3.7017	3.7680	3.5342	–0.2338
South Korea				
Private consumption	1.8430	1.2051	2.8458	1.6407
Govt. consumption	1.5364	1.6565	1.0304	–0.6261
Investment	6.2587	6.6898	4.3207	–2.3691
Import	5.7343	5.5506	6.1937	0.6431
Export	4.6020	5.0047	3.2396	–1.7651
Japan				
Private consumption	1.2984	1.3315	1.1340	–0.1975
Govt. consumption	1.3078	1.1202	1.5500	0.4298
Investment	2.0114	2.1430	1.5286	–0.6144
Import	2.6218	2.8143	2.1365	–0.6778
Export	2.2866	2.0080	2.8107	0.8027
Hong Kong				
Private consumption	2.5676	2.7535	1.9111	–0.8424
Govt. consumption	3.7850	4.1409	2.4546	–1.6863
Investment	5.0948	4.8387	5.4664	0.6277
Import	4.4375	4.6037	4.0088	–0.5949
Export	3.7405	3.9058	3.3048	–0.6010

Note: AFC = Asian financial Crisis. Pre-AFC = Pre-1997Q2; post-AFC = post-1997Q2.

Chinese Taipei. There is also a relatively large decline in export volatility in South Korea, but volatility in import growth has increased. Unlike the Hong Kong economy, the volatility of investment for all the other four Asian economies has declined, with Singapore and South Korea gaining a decline of more than 2%.

In the case of private consumption, growth volatility for Hong Kong has improved most, while the Asian financial crisis has reduced private consumption in

South Korea drastically since its growth volatility has increased most by 1.6407. The private consumption volatility for the other three Asian economies has remained more or less unchanged. In the case of government consumption, the notable economy is Singapore whose volatility in government consumption is much higher (9.8198) than all other Asian economies, and it has achieved a high growth volatility with a standard deviation of 10.4749 in the post-AFC period. This obviously suggests that the Singapore government has intervened considerably in the economy.

Table 3.8 shows the volatility for the stock market price in the five Asian economies. The stock market price data have also been seasonally adjusted to get rid of the potential seasonal influence. The stock markets in both Hong Kong and Chinese Taipei have a better performance in absorbing shocks. The volatility of stock market in Japan and Singapore has increased slightly in the post-1997 period. However, the volatility for Japan is the lowest among the five Asian economies for the entire sample period. The stock price volatility performance of South Korea is worst. The volatility has more than doubled, with a standard deviation increased from 8.8945% to 18.3524% between the pre-AFC and post-AFC periods. The Asian financial crisis must have affected South Korea most among the five Asian economies. Clearly, the stock market and financial sector in South Korea are weaker in absorbing shocks.

To see how growth volatility itself is related in each other among the five Asian economies, we employ the same methodology as in the previous sections with GARCH and T-GARCH tests (Eqs. (5), (6) and (7)). First, since stationarity is required to obtain reliable parameter estimates and statistical inference, we similarly apply the ADF test (shown by Eq. (4)) to see whether or not unit root existed in the real growth rate. We know that the Hong Kong data are first difference stationary in previous exercise. For other Asian economies, the ADF tests show that the null hypothesis on the existence of a unit root is rejected in all test models. In other words, the data for the other Asian economies are all first difference stationary and the growth rates used in the volatility tests are reliable parameters. Again, the ARMA (1, 1) process is used as the mean equation for the GARCH (1, 1) and T-GARCH (1, 1, 1) models.

TABLE 3.8 Volatility of stock price for five Asian economies — Standard deviation (%)

	Whole period	Pre-AFC	Post-AFC	Difference
Chinese Taipei	14.4415	15.3034	11.0421	–4.2613
Singapore	11.5390	11.2978	11.9256	0.6278
Korea	12.4674	8.8945	18.3524	9.4579
Japan	8.3099	8.1481	8.6905	0.5424
Hong Kong	14.7206	15.5798	12.1810	–3.3998

Note: Pre-AFC = Pre-1997Q2; post-AFC = post-1997Q2.
Source: CEIC Database.

Table 3.9 shows the GARCH and T-GARCH test results of GDP for the five Asian economies.[8] The growth performances of Singapore and South Korea are similar to that of Hong Kong. Their ARCH terms (χ) are significant in the GARCH (1, 1) tests but not significant in the T-GARCH tests, and the SIC suggests that the T-GARCH test is the better model in explaining growth volatility. Hence, although it seems that volatility clustering occurred to the output growth of Singapore and South Korea, but their output growth is actually asymmetric instead. The positive coefficient of λ in the T-GARCH tests for Singapore and South Korea is significant at 5% and 1%, respectively, suggesting that their growth volatility is asymmetric and the negative shock has a greater impact on their volatility.

Besides volatility asymmetry and similar to Hong Kong, the output growth in Singapore and South Korea also depended on past forecast variance, as the GARCH terms (η) in the tests are all significant at 1%. We also observe that the GDP growth of Chinese Taipei depended on the past forecast variance, but its volatility is not asymmetric. We find strong evidence that volatility clustering appeared in Chinese Taipei, as its ARCH terms are significant for at least 5% level in both models.

For Japan, the results shown in Table 3.9 are completely different. Japan shows no evidence in the dependence on past variance of forecast. The GARCH terms (η) are not significant at all in both models. The ARCH terms (χ) are significant at 1% level for both models, giving an evidence of volatility clustering. Surprisingly, under the T-GARCH test (although not supported by SIC), the coefficient λ is negative and is significant at 1%. This provides the evidence that the growth volatility is asymmetric in Japan. In this case, the output growth volatility would be higher (instead of lower) when the economy is bullish, but lower (not higher) when the economy is bearish.

Table 3.10 summarizes the empirical results of the GARCH and T-GARCH tests on GDP growth for the five Asian economies, while Fig. 3.5 gives the conditional standard deviation of the four Asian economies. Similar to Fig. 3.3 for Hong Kong, Fig. 3.5 shows the conditional standard deviations of the four Asian economies that provide a better understanding in the dynamics of their GDP volatility with results using the preferred model indicated by SIC. The results of Fig. 3.5 reveal that Chinese Taipei shows a strong performance in the growth dynamics, and that the conditional standard deviation has the decreasing trend overtime. The conditional standard deviation was about 4.5% in the early 1960's and it was reduced to slightly above 1% in 2006. There are two periods that the conditional standard deviation was rising: one in the mid-1970 and the other in the post-AFC period. The negative shock brought by the Asian financial crisis actually did not lead to a high increase in the GDP volatility of Chinese Taipei. By contrast, the increase in the output volatility in Chinese Taipei in the mid-1970 is even higher.

Japan also performed very strongly in GDP volatility and that Japan's conditional standard deviation is quite low (below 1.6%) in the whole sample period, except in the early 1990's and in 2004. The liquidity trap that began in Japan in the early 1990's should be the main reason for the rise in output volatility. In 1994, Japan's

[8] The details of GARCH and T-GARCH models test results for the GDP components and stock price of the four Asian economies are not included here.

TABLE 3.9 Tests results of GARCH and T-GARCH models: GDP of five Asian economies

	GARCH	T-GARCH	GARCH	T-GARCH	GARCH	T-GARCH	GARCH	T-GARCH	GARCH	T-GARCH
	Chinese Taipei		Singapore		South Korea		Japan		Hong Kong	
c_0	0.0174	0.0171	0.0203	0.0185	0.0126	0.0187	−0.0046	0.0060	0.0137	0.0122
	(0.0000)	(0.0000)	(0.0000)	(0.0000)	(0.6178)	(0.0000)	(0.9519)	(0.0000)	(0.0000)	(0.0000)
α	0.6146*	0.6225*	0.6566**	0.6457**	1.0067*	−0.0620	0.9942*	0.0509	0.5408***	0.5306***
	(0.0029)	(0.0017)	(0.0154)	(0.0293)	(0.0000)	(0.8210)	(0.0000)	(0.9636)	(0.0784)	(0.0509)
β	−0.4091	−0.4129***	−0.3000	−0.4726	−0.9680*	−0.0015	−0.9710*	0.0343	−0.3000	−0.2909
	(0.1056)	(0.0920)	(0.1142)	(0.1323)	(0.0000)	(0.9957)	(0.0000)	(0.9745)	(0.3861)	(0.3455)
c_1	6.09E-06	5.40E-06	2.92E-05	5.93E-05	3.49E-05	5.15E-05	6.34E-05	3.46E-05	7.70E-06	6.79E-06
	(0.0397)	(0.0638)	(0.0874)	(0.0134)	(0.0150)	(0.0167)	(0.0039)	(0.1501)	(0.1962)	(0.1150)
χ	0.2358*	0.1855**	0.4309*	0.0194	1.2447*	0.3384	0.4822*	0.2763*	0.4858*	0.1565
	(0.0043)	(0.0368)	(0.0062)	(0.8777)	(0.0000)	(0.1855)	(0.0049)	(0.0053)	(0.0013)	(0.2149)
η	0.7399*	0.7480*	0.5191*	0.3621**	0.2085*	0.1494**	−0.0510	0.4929	0.6162*	0.6907*
	(0.0000)	(0.0000)	(0.0000)	(0.0109)	(0.0010)	(0.0200)	(0.7629)	(0.1177)	(0.0000)	(0.0000)
λ		0.1075		0.8566**		1.7725*		−0.3321*		0.4850**
		(0.3825)		(0.0244)		(0.0010)		(0.0052)		(0.0234)
SIC	−5.7822#	−5.7592	−5.4653	−5.4867#	−5.2694	−5.2797#	−6.2446#	−6.2115	−4.9629	−4.9662#

Notes: *, ** and *** indicate 1%, 5% and 10% level of significance, respectively. SIC is the Schwarz Information Criterion. # indicates the preferred model. The numbers in the brackets are the *p*-value figures.

TABLE 3.10 Summary results of volatility clustering and asymmetry: GDP growth of five Asian economies

	Chinese Taipei	Singapore	South Korea	Japan	HK
Evidence for volatility clustering (χ)	Strong	Mix	Mix	Strong	Mix
Dependency on past variance forecast (η)	Strong	Strong	Strong	No	Strong
Evidence for volatility asymmetry (λ)	No	Strong	Strong	Weak	Strong

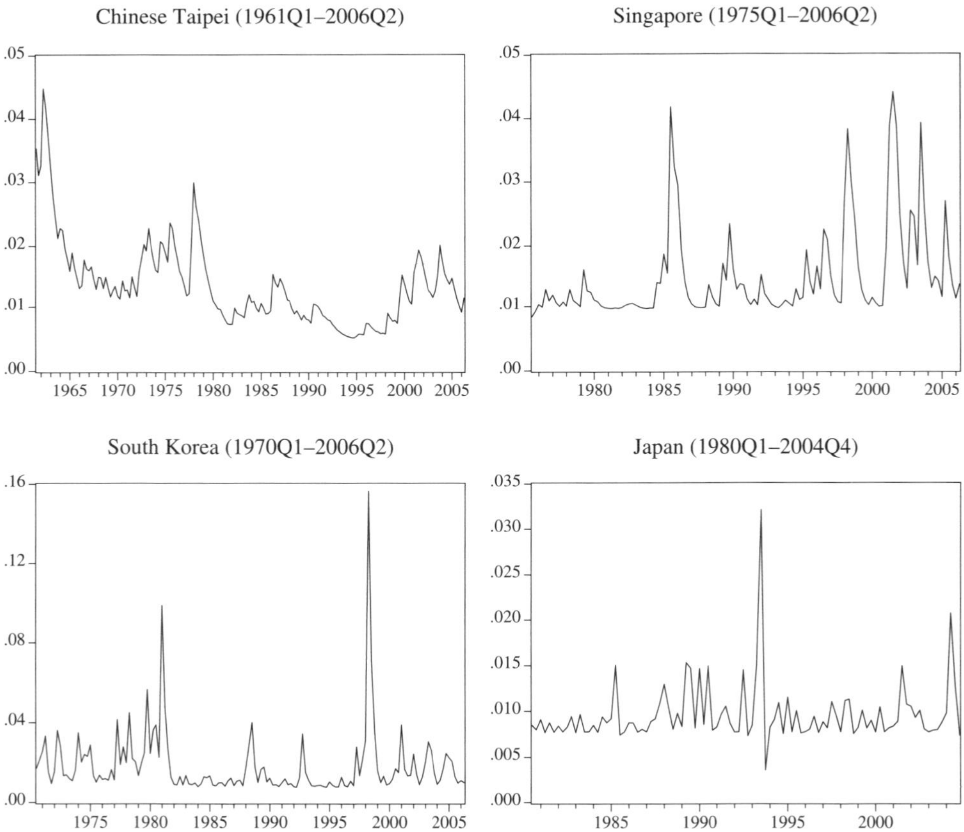

FIGURE 3.5 Conditional standard deviation of GDP growth for the four Asian economies

output volatility even rose to above 3%. The Asian financial crisis did not cause an increase in output volatility for Japan: its conditional standard deviation stayed at around 1% in the post-1997 period, and though the volatility in 2004 increased to 2%, but it soon fell again.

Singapore's output volatility was rather stable in the period of 1975–1985, and the conditional standard deviation was around 1%. But Singapore's output volatility has become more volatile from the mid-1980 to early 1990's. The conditional standard deviation has exceeded 4% and 2% in 1986 and in 1990, respectively. The output volatility of Singapore for the period 1986–1997 is obviously higher than that of the 1975–1985 periods. The negative shock brought by the Asian financial crisis has increased the output volatility of Singapore considerably. The conditional standard deviation of Singapore shown in Fig. 3.5 has risen to above 4% in 1998. It seems that after the Asian financial crisis, the economy of Singapore has become rather unstable and the conditional standard deviation remained high in the entire 2000–2006 period.

The economy of South Korea is the most volatile economy when compared to the other three Asian economies. The trend of conditional standard deviation increased from 1970 to 1981, as it has increased from around 3.7% in 1970 to around 10% in 1981. South Korea did experience a structural break of low output volatility for the period from 1982 to 1997. However, the negative shock brought by the Asian financial crisis has affected South Korea most among the other three Asian economies, and that its conditional standard deviation has risen to around 16% in 1998. The output volatility of South Korea in the period of 2000–2006 is still higher than in the period of 1982–1997 as shown in Fig. 3.5.

The summary results of volatility clustering and volatility asymmetry for the five Asian economies on GDP components and stock market price are shown in Table 3.11. In the case of the Singapore economy, the evidence of variance clustering in government spending suggested that government consumption is a key driver to output growth. There is also a strong evidence on past forecast variance dependency for government spending, investment and export in Singapore. However, neither the GDP components nor the stock market price show asymmetric volatility. There probably can be other variables, such as monetary or labor market variables, which led to volatility asymmetry in Singapore's output growth.

The volatility performance of GDP components and stock market price in South Korea is in line with the performance of its output growth volatility. All GDP components and stock market price have shown evidence of variance clustering and dependency on past forecast variance. With the exception of government spending and export, all other GDP components and stock market price show significant evidence of volatility asymmetry.

Very similar observations are made in the case of Chinese Taipei and that all GDP components showed significance in both the ARCH and GARCH terms, but none of them showed strong evidence of asymmetric growth. It is only export that has the weak evidence of asymmetric volatility. Interestingly, the asymmetric volatility is unusual in Chinese Taipei's stock market. The stock market price of Chinese Taipei produced compelling evidence that its volatility is high when the stock market booms, low when the stock market sinks, since the T-GARCH term is negative but significant.

In the case of Japan, since investment in the only variable that showed strong evidence in asymmetric volatility, one can conclude that investment is the main variable explaining Japan's asymmetric GDP growth. The stock market price may also play a role in Japan's GDP growth asymmetry as it showed weak evidence in asymmetric

TABLE 3.11 Summary results of volatility clustering and asymmetry: GDP components and stock price of five Asian economies

	P-Con	G-Con	Invest	Imp	Exp	Stock
Chinese Taipei						
Evidence for volatility clustering (χ)	Strong	Strong	Strong	Strong	Strong	Strong
Dependency on past forecast variance (η)	Strong	Strong	Strong	Strong	Strong	Strong
Evidence for volatility asymmetry (λ)	No	No	No	No	Weak	Strong
Singapore						
Evidence for volatility clustering (χ)	No	Strong	No	No	No	Strong
Dependency on past forecast variance (η)	No	Strong	Strong	No	Strong	Strong
Evidence for volatility asymmetry (λ)	No	No	No	No	No	No
South Korea						
Evidence for volatility clustering (χ)	Strong	Strong	Mix	Mix	Strong	Strong
Dependency on past forecast variance (η)	Strong	Strong	Strong	Strong	Strong	Strong
Evidence for volatility asymmetry (λ)	Strong	No	Strong	Strong	No	Strong
Japan						
Evidence for volatility clustering (χ)	Strong	Strong	Strong	Strong	No	Strong
Dependency on past forecast variance (η)	No	Weak	No	Strong	No	Strong
Evidence for volatility asymmetry (λ)	No	No	Strong	No	No	Weak
Hong Kong						
Evidence for volatility clustering (χ)	Strong	Strong	Strong	Strong	Strong	Strong
Dependency on past forecast variance (η)	Strong	Strong	Strong	Strong	Strong	No
Evidence for volatility asymmetry (λ)	No	No	Strong	No	No	No

Note: P-Con = private consumption; G-Con = government consumption; Inv = investment; Imp = import; and Exp = export.

volatility. The stock market price and all GDP components, except export, have shown strong evidence of variance clustering, while only import and stock market price have shown strong evidence in dependency on past forecast variance. This helps to explain why the ARCH term in GDP growth is significant while the GARCH term is not. In other words, Japan's output growth exhibited variance clustering but not dependency on past forecast variance.

From the discussion on growth properties, it would be interesting to examine for each of the other four Asian economies the cross correlation of the business cycle between the different GDP components and stock market price, as shown by the Hodrick–Prescott trends in Table 3.12 (Table 3.4 gives the case of Hong Kong). A number of observations can be made. Since all the five Asian economies are export-led, their performance in export dominated their growth and is the main variable for their outstanding development. The export cycles are much more volatile than the output cycle, as indicated by two standard deviations of export and GDP.

Similar to Hong Kong, the import cycles for Singapore and South Korea moved in the same direction with GDP. In Japan, the contemporaneous correlation between import and GDP is also large, and import leads output in the long-run. In Chinese Taipei, output leads imports, and that the higher income level would induce increase in import and vice versa. The private consumption cycles in South Korea, Singapore and Japan moved in the same direction with their output cycle. The private consumption pattern of Chinese Taipei is similar to that of Hong Kong, and although their contemporaneous correlation between GDP and private consumption is large, output leads private consumption in the long-run.

The lack of correlation between government consumption and output is apparent in both Hong Kong and South Korea. In the case of Chinese Taipei, the contemporaneous correlation between GDP and government consumption is also insignificant, while the positive lagged values are weakly significant, which suggests that increases in government spending could raise GDP and vice versa. Surprisingly, government consumption in both Singapore and Japan is counter-cyclical. The contemporaneous and lead coefficient values are significant in Japan, while the lagged coefficients are significant in Singapore. This suggested that the negative growth of GDP in Japan (such as the liquidity trap period of the 1990s) possibly led to increase in government spending in order to boost up the economy, and when output has increased, the Japanese government would play a less important role. On the contrary, the significant lag structure in Singapore suggested that government consumption leads the output cycle. The strong government-directed Singapore economy possible leads to a high effect on GDP when there is a change in government policy. The crowding out effect (government investment displaces private investment) in Singapore may lead to a negative correlation.

The contemporaneous correlation between investment and output is high in Hong Kong (71.3%), Japan (90.6%) and South Korea (78.4%). In the case of Japan and South Korea, the cyclical movement between investment and output is the same. For Chinese Taipei, Singapore and Hong Kong, it is evident that GDP leads the investment cycle in the long-run.

In the stock market, with the exception of Chinese Taipei, the performance for the other four Asian economies is similar and that their stock market price leads the

TABLE 3.12 Cross correlation with the output cycle: Four Asian economies

		Cross correlation of output with						
Variables	SD %	$\gamma(-3)$	$\gamma(-2)$	$\gamma(-1)$	$\gamma(0)$	$\gamma(1)$	$\gamma(2)$	$\gamma(3)$
Chinese Taipei								
GDP	2.089	0.374	0.590	0.794	1.000	0.794	0.590	0.374
P-Con	1.649	0.112	0.291	0.508	0.705	0.692	0.606	0.521
G-Con	3.209	0.280	0.291	0.216	0.125	0.036	−0.046	−0.085
Invest	5.731	0.036	0.132	0.238	0.314	0.282	0.202	0.152
Import	7.715	0.005	0.189	0.410	0.447	0.579	0.477	0.290
Export	8.281	0.314	0.480	0.632	0.705	0.572	0.397	0.166
Stock	24.072	−0.002	0.201	0.390	0.507	0.488	0.420	0.343
Singapore								
GDP	2.556	0.337	0.598	0.832	1.000	0.832	0.598	0.337
P-Con	2.719	0.250	0.432	0.588	0.675	0.586	0.406	0.177
G-Con	7.078	−0.352	−0.308	−0.281	−0.170	−0.046	0.022	0.081
Invest	7.573	0.063	0.216	0.402	0.572	0.613	0.567	0.482
Import	5.704	0.317	0.487	0.665	0.770	0.667	0.435	0.191
Export	5.258	0.375	0.524	0.654	0.721	0.606	0.389	0.146
Stock	15.719	0.361	0.462	0.580	0.554	0.343	0.086	−0.139
South Korea								
GDP	2.270	0.321	0.569	0.753	1.000	0.753	0.569	0.321
P-Con	1.835	0.252	0.478	0.677	0.807	0.675	0.491	0.288
G-Con	1.706	−0.102	−0.112	−0.135	−0.063	−0.097	0.013	0.111
Invest	8.595	0.283	0.513	0.666	0.784	0.665	0.556	0.408
Import	6.957	0.263	0.537	0.742	0.783	0.628	0.452	0.202
Export	7.421	0.211	0.276	0.286	0.260	0.173	0.036	−0.122
Stock	19.728	0.402	0.477	0.501	0.397	0.253	0.022	−0.182
Japan								
GDP	1.275	0.401	0.561	0.736	1.000	0.736	0.561	0.401
P-Con	1.874	0.442	0.568	0.725	0.952	0.747	0.573	0.435
G-Con	1.629	0.019	−0.130	−0.192	−0.221	−0.372	−0.399	−0.376
Invest	3.052	0.463	0.594	0.753	0.906	0.724	0.566	0.388
Import	5.047	0.681	0.727	0.703	0.643	0.479	0.271	0.067
Export	4.028	0.236	0.398	0.543	0.563	0.464	0.300	0.148
Stock	13.709	0.441	0.414	0.325	0.200	0.095	0.009	−0.100

Notes: P-Con = private consumption; G-Con = government consumption; Invest = investment; and Stock = stock market price; SD = standard deviation.

output cycle. Being the regions' financial centers, the stock market price and output correlation is strong in both Hong Kong and Singapore, with a correlation value of over 50%. In the case of Chinese Taipei, it is rather that output leads the stock market cycle.

TABLE 3.13 Cross correlation between Hong Kong and other Asian economies

		Cross correlation of Hong Kong output with						
Output in	SD %	$\gamma(-3)$	$\gamma(-2)$	$\gamma(-1)$	$\gamma(0)$	$\gamma(1)$	$\gamma(2)$	$\gamma(3)$
Hong Kong	3.008	0.330	0.524	0.762	1.000	0.762	0.524	0.330
Chinese Taipei	2.089	0.403	0.547	0.631	0.644	0.506	0.287	0.085
Singapore	2.556	-0.090	0.138	0.305	0.422	0.413	0.350	0.251
South Korea	2.465	0.201	0.340	0.422	0.435	0.289	0.127	0.028
Japan	1.275	-0.127	-0.040	0.022	0.125	0.178	0.198	0.166
		Cross correlation of Hong Kong stock market price with						
Stock price in	SD %	$\gamma(-3)$	$\gamma(-2)$	$\gamma(-1)$	$\gamma(0)$	$\gamma(1)$	$\gamma(2)$	$\gamma(3)$
Hong Kong	21.765	0.339	0.536	0.726	1.000	0.726	0.536	0.339
Chinese Taipei	26.236	−0.230	−0.139	−0.040	0.125	0.153	0.145	0.152
Singapore	15.719	0.114	0.377	0.575	0.752	0.514	0.317	0.096
South Korea	18.190	0.003	0.112	0.206	0.288	0.226	0.221	0.179
Japan	13.694	0.063	0.195	0.315	0.457	0.353	0.295	0.193

Note: The results for the cross correlation coefficients of a restricted sample that show the same starting and ending quarterly data for output (1980Q1–2006Q2, with the exception of Japan that ended in 2004Q4) and stock market price (1985Q1–2006Q2) are similar.

One can further examine the interaction of the growth volatility of the five Asian economies to see if there is any spillover of output growth volatility. The Hong Kong economy is used as the reference point, and the exercise is to see how the macroeconomics performances of other Asian economies are cross-related to Hong Kong. Table 3.13 shows the cross correlation of Hong Kong output and stock market prices with the other Asian economies.

With the output contemporaneous correlation of 0.644, the output of Chinese Taipei is closely related to Hong Kong's output, probably due to Mainland China, which is the common factor in affecting the two economies. But the stock market between Hong Kong and Chinese Taipei is uncorrelated as the coefficients of all leads and lags are statistically insignificant. The output of Singapore and Hong Kong is significantly correlated. On the other hand, the output of Japan shows no correlation with Hong Kong's output, but both Japan and Singapore exhibit a similar movement in the stock market price of Hong Kong. The correlation of the stock market between South Korea and Hong Kong is not that high, in comparing with the correlation in output.

As a whole, the strong correlation of stock market price among Japan, Singapore and Hong Kong showed strong evidence that these three financial markets are dominant in Asia. Their lead-lag effects are not obvious and these three markets move almost at the same time, suggesting that shocks in one market can be contagious to the others in a short time. As for their output, there should be no spillover effect

TABLE 3.14 Cross-economy correlations between same GDP components

	Cross correlation of Hong Kong export with						
Export of	$\gamma(-3)$	$\gamma(-2)$	$\gamma(-1)$	$\gamma(0)$	$\gamma(1)$	$\gamma(2)$	$\gamma(3)$
Chinese Taipei	0.264	0.527	0.695	0.665	0.459	0.139	–0.155
Singapore	0.073	0.269	0.437	0.501	0.474	0.412	0.302
South Korea	0.307	0.520	0.593	0.525	0.330	0.045	–0.210
Japan	–0.419	–0.169	0.084	0.269	0.341	0.323	0.246
	Cross correlation of Hong Kong import with						
Import of	$\gamma(-3)$	$\gamma(-2)$	$\gamma(-1)$	$\gamma(0)$	$\gamma(1)$	$\gamma(2)$	$\gamma(3)$
Chinese Taipei	0.043	0.350	0.567	0.659	0.550	0.322	0.037
Singapore	0.106	0.298	0.460	0.534	0.543	0.473	0.364
South Korea	0.374	0.518	0.526	0.505	0.402	0.240	0.067
Japan	–0.231	–0.055	0.086	0.216	0.301	0.298	0.312
	Cross correlation of Hong Kong investment with						
Investment in	$\gamma(-3)$	$\gamma(-2)$	$\gamma(-1)$	$\gamma(0)$	$\gamma(1)$	$\gamma(2)$	$\gamma(3)$
Chinese Taipei	0.175	0.230	0.279	0.331	0.310	0.210	0.169
Singapore	–0.264	–0.166	–0.020	0.066	0.126	0.221	0.211
South Korea	0.270	0.260	0.172	0.095	0.021	–0.031	–0.136
Japan	0.242	0.360	0.457	0.456	0.423	0.370	0.284
	Cross correlation of Hong Kong private consumption with						
Private in consumption	$\gamma(-3)$	$\gamma(-2)$	$\gamma(-1)$	$\gamma(0)$	$\gamma(1)$	$\gamma(2)$	$\gamma(3)$
Chinese Taipei	0.027	0.063	0.121	0.189	0.232	0.293	0.259
Singapore	0.024	0.137	0.257	0.290	0.269	0.239	0.168
South Korea	0.133	0.154	0.232	0.305	0.266	0.199	0.139
Japan	0.050	0.127	0.146	0.140	0.120	0.099	0.004

Note: Government expenditure is not included in the cross-correlation analysis.

between Japan and Hong Kong. Chinese Taipei and South Korea lead the output cycle of Hong Kong, while Hong Kong leads that of Singapore.

Lastly, the cross-economy correlation coefficients on the GDP components are examined to see how the components themselves are correlated and how they can affect Hong Kong's output cycle. Table 3.14 shows the cross correlation of the same GDP components between Hong Kong and other four Asian economies, while Table 3.15 shows the cross correlations of Hong Kong's output with different GDP components in other Asian economies. With the exception of Japan, the export of all

TABLE 3.15 Cross-economy correlations between different GDP components

	Cross correlation of Hong Kong output with						
Export of	$\gamma(-3)$	$\gamma(-2)$	$\gamma(-1)$	$\gamma(0)$	$\gamma(1)$	$\gamma(2)$	$\gamma(3)$
Hong Kong	0.264	0.465	0.651	0.751	0.585	0.387	0.148
Chinese Taipei	0.403	0.547	0.631	0.644	0.506	0.287	0.085
Singapore	0.094	0.270	0.432	0.496	0.468	0.399	0.280
South Korea	0.384	0.530	0.600	0.537	0.410	0.196	−0.049
Japan	−0.372	−0.222	−0.055	0.063	0.133	0.106	0.045

	Cross correlation of Hong Kong output with						
Import of	$\gamma(-3)$	$\gamma(-2)$	$\gamma(-1)$	$\gamma(0)$	$\gamma(1)$	$\gamma(2)$	$\gamma(3)$
Hong Kong	0.235	0.435	0.630	0.705	0.610	0.447	0.231
Chinese Taipei	0.097	0.361	0.480	0.517	0.473	0.301	0.098
Singapore	0.043	0.230	0.430	0.493	0.459	0.400	0.283
South Korea	0.272	0.413	0.499	0.430	0.318	0.185	0.032
Japan	−0.145	0.042	0.236	0.391	0.447	0.446	0.392

	Cross correlation of Hong Kong output with						
Investment of	$\gamma(-3)$	$\gamma(-2)$	$\gamma(-1)$	$\gamma(0)$	$\gamma(1)$	$\gamma(2)$	$\gamma(3)$
Hong Kong	0.126	0.321	0.519	0.713	0.728	0.641	0.576
Chinese Taipei	0.141	0.219	0.253	0.284	0.210	0.102	0.017
Singapore	−0.319	−0.245	−0.008	0.073	0.106	0.191	0.106
South Korea	0.098	0.144	0.226	0.216	0.177	0.153	0.091
Japan	0.035	0.035	0.136	0.202	0.242	0.294	0.260

	Cross correlation of Hong Kong private consumption with						
Private consumption of	$\gamma(-3)$	$\gamma(-2)$	$\gamma(-1)$	$\gamma(0)$	$\gamma(1)$	$\gamma(2)$	$\gamma(3)$
Hong Kong	0.225	0.356	0.510	0.598	0.517	0.413	0.337
Chinese Taipei	0.048	0.214	0.323	0.413	0.394	0.314	0.237
Singapore	0.030	0.208	0.426	0.497	0.444	0.396	0.289
South Korea	0.129	0.219	0.260	0.278	0.175	0.073	−0.002
Japan	−0.148	−0.061	0.014	0.132	0.191	0.236	0.250

Note: Government expenditure is not included in the cross-correlation analysis.

the other three Asian economies showed strong correlation with Hong Kong's output and export. The insignificant correlation between Japan and Hong Kong is in line with other findings regarding their non-correlated macro-economy. As for the import performance, Japan is also the least correlated with Hong Kong, although the correlation is still statistically significant. Trade in Chinese Taipei has shown very strong correlation with output and trade with Hong Kong, suggesting a strong bilateral trade relationship with Mainland China for both Chinese Taipei and Hong Kong.

In the case of investment, Chinese Taipei has a weak correlation with Hong Kong's output, but there is no correlation with all other Asian economies. However, investment in Chinese Taipei is positively correlated with investment in Hong Kong, probably due to the common factor of the Mainland China economy. Apart from Chinese Taipei, investment in Japan has a significant correlation with investment in Hong Kong, suggesting that Japanese firms would spillover their investment to Hong Kong when they expanded their investment activities.

As for private consumption, it is unlikely that domestic spending can influence consumer spending in other Asian economies. There is no significant relationship between the private consumption of Hong Kong, South Korea and Japan. The private consumption of Japan shows no correlation with Hong Kong's output cycle, but there is weak correlation between Hong Kong and South Korea. However, when looking at the contemporaneous cross correlation in private consumption, there is significant relationship between Hong Kong's private consumption with that of Singapore and Chinese Taipei, due probably to the common consumption trend among Singapore, Chinese Taipei and Hong Kong.

There are several conclusions on the volatility discussion among the five Asian economies. Firstly, other than Hong Kong, Chinese Taipei is another Asian economy that has enjoyed a decline in output volatility, after taking into account of the Asian financial crisis. Chinese Taipei, similar to Hong Kong, also enjoyed a decline in stock market price volatility. In the case of the South Korean economy, the experience of the volatility decline in the earlier decade was severely affected by the Asian financial crisis, and its stock market price volatility has increased tremendously. Singapore has shown no evidence of improvement in absorbing shocks for both output and stock markets. Japan's GDP growth and stock market price are the steadiest among the five economies, with a standard deviation of less than one percent and 10% respectively.

The performance in output growth for Singapore and Korea are similar to that of Hong Kong. The evidence for volatility clustering is mixed, but there is strong evidence that the volatility depended on the past forecast variance and the volatility is higher when the economy is slow. Chinese Taipei performed differently and that there is significant evidence for volatility clustering and the volatility is symmetric. Surprisingly, Japan's volatility of GDP growth does not depend on the past forecast and the volatility is asymmetric in a different direction. Concerning the growth performance of the stock market price, all economies perform differently. One surprising result is that the volatility of the stock market price in Chinese Taipei is higher when the market is bullish and lower when the market is bearish or depressed.

The cross correlation results suggest that the business cycle between Hong Kong and Chinese Taipei is most similar. It is probably because they are both affected by the important common factor of investment and trade with Mainland China. Empirical results support the hypothesis that, with the exception of government consumption, Singapore and Hong Kong share similar characteristics in macroeconomic condition, as their output cycles are highly correlated. Hong Kong's output cycle has a strong correlation with South Korea's GDP cycle. This could probably be due to the strong cross correlation between South Korea's export and Hong Kong's output. Japan's GDP cycle has shown no correlation with the output cycle of Hong Kong, though Japan's investment is the variable that has affected Hong Kong most, and expansion of Japanese business would lead to a spillover effect to Hong Kong and bring positive prospects to the investment atmosphere in Hong Kong.

3.6 Summary Findings and Implications

To minimize technical complications, this section presents the summary and the implications of the various findings on the volatility of GDP, GDP components and other variables. The summary and implications are discussed in three areas that involve GDP volatility, business cycles and Hong Kong's comparison with other four Asian economies.

On Volatility

The GDP growth volatility analysis concentrates on two features. One feature is volatility symmetry where volatility movement of GDP growth and the individual GDP components or macro variables go in the same direction. For example, a low GDP growth volatility co-exists with a fall in the performance of the particular GDP component or macroeconomic variable, and vice versa. The implication of volatility symmetry is that GDP growth and other variables behave consistently and predictably. However, it is often that the relation is asymmetric, depending on the lead-lag relationship between GDP growth and the other component/variable. One possibility concerns investment, and that since changes in investment lead to changes in GDP, their volatility relationship can be asymmetric.

The second feature is volatility clustering, which is a situation where a period of high volatility persists after a period of increased volatility, and vice versa. Volatility clustering is possible when, for example, an increase in GDP growth volatility is due to a fall in investment, but the increase in GDP growth volatility may have impact on other variables, which can prolong the high volatility in GDP growth.

Overall, Hong Kong's GDP growth volatility exhibits the features of asymmetry, where a negative growth tends to have a bigger impact on volatility, and clustering, where situations in the current period are influenced by what has happened in the last period. Among the three sub-periods in the sample, evidences show that Hong Kong's GDP growth volatility tended to stay high before the late 1980s, due probably to the economic uncertainty resulting from the Sino-British negotiation over the post-1997 political future of Hong Kong, but has experienced a period of low volatility in the 1990s when GDP in Hong Kong was rising. However, volatility was negatively affected after the outbreak of the Asian financial crisis in 1997. In short, economic hardships tend to generate more fluctuations that exerted negative impacts on the economy. Policies should aim at macroeconomic stability, implying that short-term changes in policy that are geared to produce purely short-term impact may not be entirely suitable for Hong Kong. On the contrary, seasoned and tested economic policies that are geared to produce long-term effects and stability can minimize economic volatility.

By and large, the performance of individual GDP components followed the movement in GDP growth. The volatility of most GDP components increased in the post-1997 period. One exception is government consumption, probably due to the growing fiscal pressure and the resulting large budget deficit after the Asian financial crisis, its volatility improved marginally in the post-Asian financial crisis period. Export and imports show a higher degree of volatility, due to the open nature of the Hong Kong economy.

The growth performance in investment and the movement of the general price level are the two variables that contributed to the asymmetry in Hong Kong's GDP growth volatility. In other words, investment volatility is low when the economy is booming, but high when the economy is in recession. Since GDP and investment show a close correlation, changes in investment will have lower volatility on GDP when GDP is rising or remained high. On the contrary, when GDP is falling or remained low, movement in investment activities will have a great impact on GDP. The implication is that Hong Kong has to maintain a stable investment growth. The picture is similar in the case of the general price level, and that price stability is needed in minimizing GDP growth volatility.

Other than the general price level, most macroeconomic variables show strong evidence of volatility clustering and/or dependency on past forecast variance, but volatility performance of most macroeconomic variables have deteriorated in the third period. Due to their large fluctuations in the sample period, both stock market and housing price show high volatility. Given that Hong Kong is a world financial center on the one hand, and the dominance of the housing market on the other hand, their price movement will result in greater GDP growth volatility for the Hong Kong economy. The solution to a lower GDP growth volatility will be to diversify Hong Kong's economic structure more so as to maintain a wider economic base, and that sudden shocks in both the stock and housing markets will then exert only a lower or marginal level of volatility on GDP.

The three supply-side economic variables of employment, unemployment and wage showed volatility symmetry. In general, due to their slow movement and delayed response to economic changes, these supply-side variables produced a lower GDP growth volatility than the demand components of private consumption, investment and export and import. Furthermore, due obviously to the difference in volume as the size of the employed is higher than the size of the unemployed, unemployment volatility is higher than employment volatility. The money supply also shows volatility clustering.

On Business Cycle

There are a number of issues in the business cycle analysis. One issue is to examine whether the volatility of individual GDP components and macroeconomic variables is higher or lower than output volatility. The more important issue relates to cross correlations that show whether there is correlation between GDP and other GDP components and macroeconomic variables. Similarly, their relationships can either be pro-cyclical (output following) or counter-cyclical (output leading). The estimates also show the lead-lag effect between GDP and all other variables.

Among the GDP components, the evidence shows that growth in GDP leads changes in private consumption, which is expected. A rise in output that allows more spending to take place, and consumption rises. However, GDP and government consumption are uncorrelated, reflecting the relatively small role of government in Hong Kong. Since total public expenditure as a percent of GDP is low (rarely goes beyond 20%), the Hong Kong economy is largely driven by the private sector. Thus, the more important GDP components are investment and export. Investment is most volatile and largely correlated with output. Changes in output attract more investment, as GDP leads the investment cycle. On the contrary, since trade has been a major ingredient in the Hong Kong economy, export leads the output cycle. Expansion in trade gives rise to expansion in GDP. In short, investment and trade are the most important components in Hong Kong's GDP.

Among the macroeconomic variables, prices are counter-cyclical, suggesting that price rises along with the rise in GDP. Price movements in Hong Kong also lead the business cycle. The money supply of M1 also leads the business cycle, and the causation goes from money to output. This probably is due to the adoption of the linked exchange rate system to the US currency since 1982 that money supply, typically M1, is governed by the level of export that earns the foreign currency before eventually converting back to the Hong Kong currency. Thus, the higher the level of M1 this period produces a higher level of output next period. However, M2 is a very different monetary instrument, and change in M2 has little or no impact on output. The presence of the linked exchange rate has effectively reduced the strength of the monetary instruments in Hong Kong, as such monetary variables as the interest rate in Hong Kong would have to follow the movement of the interest rate in the US, thus resulting in a fall in the effectiveness of M2 in influencing GDP growth in Hong Kong.

The stock market is an important determinant in the Hong Kong economy. Movements in the stock market are pro-cyclical, and the boom in the stock market will affect the output level positively. In the housing market, the rise in GDP leads the housing market cycle. The analysis points to the importance of the stock market and the housing market in Hong Kong, as they both exhibited a wealth effect between income and demand for stock and property in Hong Kong. The good news is that a strong and progressive performance in both the stock and housing markets can determine the income level of Hong Kong. The bad news is that Hong Kong's income and wealth are narrowly dependent on these two markets, and improvement in economic diversity is needed.

In the case of labor and employment, the labor market, as expected, is less volatile, but employment is pro-cyclical and unemployment is counter-cyclical. Naturally, GDP leads the level of employment. There is evidence of wage rigidity, as the correlation between GDP and wage is positively significant between the third and the ninth quarters, meaning that wage increase (decrease) will take place only after three to nine quarters when there is an increase (decrease) in output.

Comparison With Other Asian Economies

The first issue in the comparison of growth volatility between Hong Kong and other four Asian economies include their growth volatility in GDP, GDP components (private consumption, government consumption, investment, export and import), and stock market in the pre- and post-Asian financial crisis periods.

As compared to the other four Asian economies, Hong Kong, obviously due to its very open nature, experienced the highest output volatility for the entire sample period, but has experienced the biggest drop in output volatility between the pre- and post-Asian financial crisis periods, reflecting the severe drop in output during the Asian financial crisis period. The stock markets in Hong Kong and in Chinese Taipei have a better performance in absorbing shocks. On the question of volatility symmetry and clustering among the five Asian economies, the evidence shows that the growth performance of Singapore and South Korea are similar to that of Hong Kong in the sample period, and that negative shocks have a greater impact on their volatility.

Japan: For Japan, although its output volatility has increased since the 1990s, output volatility is most steady among the five Asian economies. Output volatility has dropped in the post-AFC period, and the volatility in the stock market is the lowest among the other Asian economies. The performance of volatility symmetry and clustering in Japan is very different from Hong Kong, Japan shows no evidence of dependence on past variance of forecast and a strong evidence on volatility clustering. One can conclude that the presence of a liquidity trap in Japan in the early 1990s could explain the rise in output volatility.

Singapore: Singapore's output growth has become more volatile overtime, and has shown a high increase in volatility between the pre- and post-AFC periods. Although volatility in investment has declined in the post-AFC period, the volatility of government consumption is much higher than all other Asian economies, due probably to the relatively large government intervention in the economy. The evidence suggests that government consumption is a key element to output growth.

Chinese Taipei: The economy of Chinese Taipei has shown a decrease in output volatility since the Asian financial crisis, and among the GDP components, there is a significant decline in trade volatility, suggesting that export is the factor that contributed to the decline in output volatility. Chinese Taipei exhibited a strong evidence of volatility clustering, and the negative shock brought by the Asian financial crisis did not lead to a rise in output volatility. But the volatility of the stock market in Chinese Taipei remains high when the stock market booms, but stock market volatility is low when the market recesses.

South Korea: The economy of South Korea has experienced the largest negative growth since the Asian financial crisis. Among the GDP components in South Korea, the volatility of both investment and export have declined. Private consumption volatility declined in the post-AFC period, but the stock market volatility performed worst among the five Asian economies.

On the empirical findings of the cross correlation between GDP and GDP components and the stock market in each of the Asian economies, one clear conclusion is that export has dominated the growth of all five Asian economies as their export cycles are more volatile than output cycles, confirming the strong export nature of their economies. The import cycle also moves in the same direction as the output cycle. Private consumption in the Asian economies shows a similar picture, that private consumption cycles in South Korea, Singapore and Japan move in the same direction as output cycle, while output cycle leads private consumption in both Chinese Taipei and Hong Kong.

The role of government is strong in the case of Singapore, but government consumption in Japan in the 1990s aimed to boost up the economy. Similar to Hong Kong, the role of government tends to be smaller in both Chinese Taipei and South Korea. Investment has been at different degrees an important factor in output growth in all five Asian economies. The influence of the stock market in output is strong in Hong Kong and Singapore, reflecting the important position of their financial markets.

When Hong Kong is used as a reference economy, the evidence showed that the output relationship between Hong Kong and Chinese Taipei is close, suggesting that Mainland China is the common factor in their economic activities. Output in Singapore is correlated with output in Hong Kong, but Japan's output is uncorrelated with Hong Kong's output. The strong stock market correlation among Hong Kong, Singapore and Japan ensure that they are the key dominant financial markets in Asia.

In the various cross correlation analysis between Hong Kong and other Asian economies, the evidence showed that with the exception of Japan, the export of Singapore, Chinese Taipei and South Korea are strongly correlated with Hong Kong's export. Japan probably has a very different export structure from Hong Kong. Investment between Hong Kong and Chinese Taipei, again due to the common factor of Mainland China, is correlated. Hong Kong's investment is correlated with investment in Japan, suggesting that Hong Kong is a destination for Japan investment. There a significant relationship in the private consumption among Hong Kong, Chinese Taipei and Singapore, reflecting the similar consumption pattern and trend among these three economies.

3.7 Conclusion

The analysis in this chapter is important in confirming that economic freedom is the fundamental factor in the economic activities of individuals, and their results can generate changes in GDP growth and volatility in business cycles. A number of findings actually confirm the factors that have been successfully conducted in Hong Kong. First is the open nature of the Hong Kong economy, and that volatility is related more to the external factors of trade and investment. This lends further support to the importance of the pro-growth nature of the Hong Kong economy. Secondly, GDP growth does not depend too much on government expenditure, implying that the "private sector takes the driver seat, government takes the back seat" nature of the government is appropriate for the Hong Kong economy. The small role of the government has served the Hong Kong economy well and should be kept and maintained. Extensive government intervention and involvement in industries, services and businesses is highly undesirable. This echoes vividly to the call for the Hong Kong economy to restructure in line with its own comparative advantages.

The sound, strong and improved regulations and practices in the financial sector shall strengthen Hong Kong's financial attractiveness. This should be seen as an improvement in financial infrastructure so as to serve as a base for the long-term development of an international financial center with freedom of capital flows. Such a finding should send a high signal to the financial authority that a strong financial system is a pre-requisite for Hong Kong. In particular, investment is an important contributor to GDP and reduction in growth volatility. Thus, despite the fact that economic development in Mainland China will have a direct impact on Hong Kong's GDP, it would be more appropriate for investors in Mainland China to invest in Hong Kong, rather than encouraging Hong Kong investors to continue investing in Mainland China as in much of the 1980s and 1990s. One has to acknowledge that the tide has turned, and Hong Kong should look for investment inflow from Mainland China to boost up Hong Kong's GDP growth.

Another conclusion from the analysis on the monetary aggregates shows that the linked exchange rate that relates the Hong Kong currency to the US dollar is appropriate, as it does not exert any volatility to GDP growth. Indeed, money supply in Hong Kong does not depend on any specific monetary policy, but on the ability to serve the export community. The higher the level of export, the greater the ability to earn foreign currency, which in turn increases the money supply in Hong Kong. This is seen as advantageous to output volatility in Hong Kong.

The price movements in both the stock and housing markets have imposed negative impacts on GDP volatility, suggesting that economic activities have been too reliant on the two markets. Such a finding is in line with the discussion that economic narrowness in Hong Kong has been due to the over-concentration of activities in the two speculation-prone stocks and property markets. While these two markets provide continued benefits to the economy, the message is that appropriate economic diversification or restructuring is badly needed in Hong Kong so as to widen the economic base as well as to maintain GDP growth volatility.

Regarding the labor sector that examines employment, unemployment and wage movements, the findings show that GDP growth leads employment (that is, employment is pro-cyclical), meaning that output growth generates employment, and not vice versa. Wage increases can only follow after GDP growth has taken place, with a lag of three to four quarters. Such a finding confirms the pro-growth nature of the economy, namely that output growth is paramount, and investment is the important vehicle in output generation. This reaffirms the relevance and importance of supply-side economic strategy. This is particularly so due to the importance of the large private economy, and that demand and private consumption follows output growth and employment generation.

When compared to other Asian economies, Hong Kong has gone through a period of high output volatility, due probably to the Sino-British negotiation on the future of Hong Kong in 1982–1984, and the economic boom in the mid-1990s before the bubble burst after the Asian financial crisis in 1998. Nonetheless, Hong Kong's GDP volatility has dropped more significantly than other Asian economies since 1997, due probably to a number of factors. For example, the rapid fall in GDP and economic recession in the post-AFC years, the small role of the government sector, the open nature of the economy that permits free capital flows, the large Mainland China economy that complemented Hong Kong's growth, the linked exchange rate that provided stability, or at least did not generate additional instability, to the monetary sector.

What all these analyses and findings come to is the confirmation on the advantages of a free economy. While individuals are free to conduct their economic activities, returns and gains are based on self-endowment and efforts of individuals rather than government subsidies and assistance, and the resulting changes in output growth and the resulting movements in business cycles allow the economy to move on with hardship being minimized in time and in depth. Despite the various ups and downs and the emergence of crises in the sample period, output growth and employment generation still hold the key to economic success. In short, while economic freedom serves as a powerful mechanics in the growth engine, a strong supply-side economic strategy is still the instrument that successfully lubricates Hong Kong's engine of growth. Increase in investment, growth in GDP and reduction in output volatility are the ingredients that prosper a pro-growth economy.

Economic and financial crises will come and go and the Mainland China economy will continue to expand. The dual strategy for Hong Kong will be to take advantage of the development of the Mainland China economy and at the same time strengthen its own economic base by restructuring so as to create new comparative advantages, adhering to economic freedom and supply-driven policies as the fundamental infrastructure in economic development. This is the only appropriate strategy for Hong Kong to maximize its future possibilities and minimize the unwanted hardship arising from economic shocks.

4 Total Factor Productivity: Performance of Industries and Sectors

4.1 Introduction

There are literally very little restrictions on investment activities in Hong Kong. Given the available resource endowments and various market potentials, businesses and individual entrepreneurs are free to invest either in manufacturing or financial portfolios. Given a favorable fiscal environment, investment incentives are maximized. Economic freedom is an underlying infrastructure that permits individuals to be creative in all kinds of businesses, limited only by law, ethics, regulations and professional standards. Investment in businesses will result in output expansion and increase in economic growth, which in turn produces more employment opportunities, and output generates end products that lead to a higher standard of living. With economic freedom, the collective societal effort is to ensure that the laws, regulations and standards are high and strong enough to deter and eradicate misconducts, inequalities, victimization, discrimination and favoritism.

Land, labor and capital are three traditional types of economic resources, though entrepreneurship has often been regarded as another resource. Freedom of transactions allows a maximum use of economic resources, thereby guaranteeing a maximum rate of economic growth, employment and output. The availability of economic resources has to be considered dynamically, as the deployment of resources changes over time due to new competition, new resources, technological advancement, different phrase of the business cycle, price differences reflecting supply and demand conditions and so on. Productivity is a convenient term that measures the contribution to growth by both the availability and the combined use of economic resources. Thus, the study of productivity allows one to understand the performance of a major fabric in a free economy.

Using data mainly from the early 1980s, this chapter first studies the productivity performance of the aggregate economy, which then breaks down into different economic sectors and individual industries. The capital and labor data are constructed to examine the contribution by economic resources and the possibility of technological changes. While the Hong Kong economy has enjoyed openness, continued industrial changes, economic restructuring and growth, the situation since the 1980s posed severe challenges from two key aspects. On the one hand, the Sino-British negotiation over the political future of Hong Kong after 1997 dominated the entire domestic economic scene. On the other hand, the opening up of Mainland China since 1978 provided Hong Kong both an opportunity and a challenge. It was an opportunity because Hong Kong has served Mainland China in a number of ways, especially during the early stage of the reform. It was a challenge because the potential size and capacity of the mainland economy could easily catch up, marginalize and replace Hong Kong. The economic chemistry of these two events could be enormous. Business and industries since the 1980s have gone through tough times and pushed the Hong Kong economy to untested and unknown frontiers.

While the productivity analysis of the entire economy shows the trend and contribution to growth by different economic resources, the study on individual economic sectors and industries can help to identify economic strengths and weaknesses, such that new business opportunities can be explored and economic restructuring can be promoted through channeling and switching of resources from low productivity to high productivity activities. The Hong Kong economy survives through comparative advantages, and the spirit of comparative advantage is the exploration of new economic dimensions and channels so as to create new advantages through time. The productivity analysis can actually provide an X-ray on the Hong Kong economic body so that strengths, weaknesses, constraints and potentials can all be made transparent for potential developments.

The discussion on productivity in this chapter should be seen as the beginning of a series of discussion on the texture of economic freedom in Hong Kong, as additional productivity-related analysis on sizes of establishments, human capital, economic efficiency and competition in the subsequent chapters will supplement the understanding of a free Hong Kong economy. Economic freedom serves as an infrastructure for the economy to grow and prosper, but the process of growth does face ups and downs due to the different phrases of the business cycle, and emergence of new situations and competition from "late comers" in economic development. Economic freedom is not a one-time off phenomenon, but requires continued attention to ensure that economic freedom is preserved at the least and expanded or maximized at the most.

4.2 Aggregate Total Factor Productivity

In standard neo-classical production function, economic growth is divided into two distinct parts. One part concerns a movement along the production function (from one point to another point with different combinations of inputs), while the other concerns an upward or outward shift of the function that indicates the achievement of a large productive capacity in the economy.

A movement along the production function can be the result of an increase in output per labor due to capital accumulation (that is, an increase in the capital-labor ratio, commonly known as capital deepening). However, due to the possibility of diminishing returns to capital, the pace at which increase in output per labor can occur at a decreasing rate. This implies that mere movement along the production function through capital accumulation cannot indefinitely bring high economic growth rates.

On the contrary, an upward shift in the production functions, probably brought about by technological progress, can offset the diminishing returns to capital (PECC, 2000). In short, the growth rate of output can be partitioned into two components, with one being associated with factor accumulation and another being associated with technological progress.

Total factor productivity (TFP), as Li (2006) points out, provides a multi-factor concept that aims to capture all efficient changes to factor inputs (capital, labor, technology and other non-measurable factors) shown by the ratio of real factor input to real product output. Although capital is considered as a quantifiable stock, recent empirical work suggests that the more relevant input factor is the flow of capital services in the production period. Schreyer (2003) argues that both capital goods and labor are considered as "carriers" of capital services and labor services that respectively form the actual input in the production process. The rates of return to capital and wage payment to labor are considered as rewards for their services in the defined period.

The analysis on the TFP of an economy using the growth accounting method can begin with the standard primal growth model that incorporates the following neoclassical production function.

$$Y = f(A, K, L), \tag{1}$$

where Y is the total income or output, A is the level of technology, K is the capital stock, and L is the quantity of labor. It can be argued that the standard primal growth model can include various endogenous variables that contribute to TFP. In addition to the analysis of the aggregate economy, the TFP analysis has often been extended to study productivity growth in specific sectors. A faster pace in the change of industrial structure will speed up economic growth. Thus, changes in the productivity growth of different economic sectors can lead to changes in an economy's demand structure that ultimately contribute to increase in income (PECC, 2000).

Differentiating Eq. (1) with respect to time, and after division by Y and the rearrangement of terms, yields:

$$\frac{\dot{Y}}{Y} = g + \left(\frac{F_K K}{Y}\right) \cdot \left(\frac{\dot{K}}{K}\right) + \left(\frac{F_L L}{Y}\right) \cdot \left(\frac{\dot{L}}{L}\right), \tag{2}$$

where F_K and F_L are the marginal products of capital and labor, respectively, and g indicates the part of output growth contributed by technological progress. In other words, the three independent variables on the right hand side of Eq. (2), namely the TFP, capital input and labor input, contribute to output growth (the right hand side dependable variable). The rate of technological progress g can be calculated from Eq. (2) as a residual:

$$g = \frac{\dot{Y}}{Y} - \left(\frac{F_K K}{Y}\right) \cdot \left(\frac{\dot{K}}{K}\right) - \left(\frac{F_L L}{Y}\right) \cdot \left(\frac{\dot{L}}{L}\right). \tag{3}$$

The standard primal estimate of the rate of technological progress can be derived from Eq. (3) as:

$$g = \frac{\dot{Y}}{Y} - \left[S_K \bullet \left(\frac{\dot{K}}{K} \right) + S_L \bullet \left(\frac{\dot{L}}{L} \right) \right], \qquad (4)$$

where $s_K = F_K K/Y$ and $s_L \equiv F_L L/Y$ are the respective shares of capital and labor factors payment in total output. The value g is often described as an estimate of TFP in the growth analysis. A constant return to scale is assumed, meaning that the condition of $S_K + S_L = 1$ must hold if all of the income associated with the output is attributed to either the capital factor or the labor factor.

4.3 An Accounting Approach to Measuring Economy-Wide Productivity

Similar to Li (2006), this section calculates and shows the various data requirements in order to estimate Hong Kong's economy-wide TFP figures.[1] Unless otherwise stated, the data are obtained from materials published by the Census and Statistics Department of Hong Kong. The three other major sources of government publication are the *Gross Domestic Product 2006* (*GDP2006*), various issues of the *Hong Kong Annual Digest of Statistics* (*HKADS*), and the *Quarterly Report of Employment and Vacancies Statistics* (*EVS*). The period covered in the analysis stretches over 25 years, from 1981–2005. Industries in Hong Kong are officially classified under nine categories:

1) Agriculture and fishing;
2) Mining and quarrying;
3) Manufacturing;
4) Electricity, gas and water;
5) Construction;
6) Wholesale, retail, import and export trades, restaurants and hotels;
7) Transport, storage and communications;
8) Financing, insurance, real estate and business services; and
9) Community, social and personal services.

The analysis involves the construction of data for output, capital and labor and the two factor payments shown in the standard primal growth accounting of Eq. (4). Hong Kong's aggregate output can be shown by the production-based GDP (or

---

[1] The sources of data, the choice of variables and the methodology used in constructing the variables and are similar to that in Li (2006, Chapter 3). Most data and variables are updated to 2005. The only exception is the classification of economic sector between tradable and non-tradable, as a slightly different classification is used in this chapter.

GDP at factor cost). Hong Kong's production-based GDP figures since 1980 can be found in *GDP2006*. The GDP deflator figures are used to deflate the nominal production-based GDP figures to obtain the constant and real figures at 1990 prices (*GDP2006*).[2]

The capital stock figures can be constructed from the accumulation of gross investment, defined as:

$$K_t = K_{t-1} + RNI_t, \tag{5}$$

where RNI_t is the real net investment, which is real gross investment less depreciation. The real capital stock figure (K_t) is constructed from the accumulation of real gross investment. Real gross investment consists of real gross domestic fixed capital formation in the private sector and real changes in stocks, both expressed in constant 1990 prices. Gross domestic fixed capital formation is the summation of investment in buildings and construction that should include investment in non-residential buildings, other construction works and real estate developers' margin, all machinery, equipment and computer software in the private sectors.[3] The current price of total gross domestic fixed capital formation is deflated by its respective implicit deflators (*GDP2006*, Table 2) to achieve the real gross domestic fixed capital formation. The current prices and volume indices of changes in inventories are available from *GDP2006* (Table 1). Real changes in inventories are obtained by multiplying current price of change in inventories by volume indices.

In order to locate the benchmark capital stock and the rate of depreciation for gross capital stock, the estimation in this analysis uses the two assumptions in Kim and Lau (1994). First, a depreciation rate of 5% is applied. Second, capital stock is set equal to five times the value of gross fixed capital formation in 1966 (the earliest available year of the gross fixed capital formation figure).

Data on the total number of persons engaged is used to calculate the labor input measured by the total number of labor working hour (L) as follows:

$$L = (l - u)\, h\, (52.14), \tag{6}$$

where L is the total number of working hours, l is the size of registered labor force, u is the number of unemployed people, and h is the median weekly labor working hours per employed worker. There is a total of 52.14 (365/7) weeks in a year. The

---

[2] The aggregate output of the economy is measured by the production-based GDP (value-added) in 1990 prices. The full set of production-based GDP data is available from 1980 onwards (Table 15 and Table 17, *GDP2006*). These figures are then deflated by the implicit GDP deflators (Table 2, *GDP2006*) in order to obtain the real GDP in constant 1990 market prices.

[3] Adjustment is conducted on the data for buildings and construction (*GDP2006*, Table 9) since the data included investment in residential buildings. For the period 1966–2000, the data for investment in residential buildings are available in *GDP2001* (Table 8). For the years of 2001–2005, the investment in residential buildings data are estimated by multiplying the value of building and construction by the average percentage of residential buildings over building and construction from years 1966 to 2000.

data on the registered labor force and the number of the unemployed are available from the different issues of *HKADS*. The data on the total number of people engaged and the mean weekly labor working hours per employed worker are available from the Chinese Economic Information Company (CEIC) Database. It is assumed that the median and the mean weekly labor working hours per employed worker are close to each other.

Since a constant return to scale is assumed, the share of payment of the two factors (capital and labor) sum to unity. The labor share of factor payment can be calculated. The value-added figures of each economic sector are used to calculate the labor factor share. This is done by dividing the compensation of employees by the nominal production-based GDP figures. The value-added figures of individual economic sectors are available from *GDP2006* (Table 16) and the figures consist of compensation of employees and gross operating surplus. The compensation of employees is mainly wage payment to workers, while the gross operating surplus is the return to employers and entrepreneurs, including self-employed workers. The compensation of the self-employed should in theory be included in the compensation of employees; otherwise, an unadjusted figure of compensation of employees would understate the share contributed by the labor factor payment.

The number of self-employed for the period of 1985–2005 can be obtained from *HKADS* and the CEIC Database. The data for the years before 1985 is extrapolated using the assumed ratio of self-employed to the total employed. The unobserved average labor income of the self-employed is assumed to be the same as that of other employees. The estimated labor income of self-employed is then added to the total compensation of employees to derive the adjusted compensation of employees.[4] By deducting the labor share of factor payment from unity, the capital share of factor payment can then be obtained.

Industry-specific deflators are needed to transform nominal output values into real output values for all industries. It is reported in *GDP2006* that since there are additional comprehensive monthly and quarterly economic surveys conducted in recent years, more economic data are available and short-term economic indicators such as the quarterly business receipts of service industries and producer price indices for selected services industries can be compiled. This has enabled the Hong Kong Census and Statistics Department to compile the annual and quarterly GDP by economic activity at constant prices.[5] Figures of annual and quarterly GDP by economic activity at constant 2000 prices are available only for the years from 2000 to 2005.[6]

---

[4] See Eq. (6) and (7) of Chapter 3 in Li (2006:96).

[5] The Census and Statistics Department utilized 4 methods to derive the constant price value-added of economic activities in Hong Kong: (a) single extrapolation of base year value-added by deflated gross output measures; (b) single extrapolation of base year value-added by volume/quantity measures such as trade volume and physical units of outputs; (c) single extrapolation of base year value-added by input indicators, like hours worked; and (d) double indicators methods (*GDP2006*:143).

[6] See Table 18 and Table 19, *GDP2006*. The compilation method, including its limitation for the quarterly constant price value-added of individual economic activities is summarized in *GDP2006* (pp. 144–147).

However, since the series of annual GDP data by economic activity at constant prices shown in *GDP2006* is short, and the various data applicable to the specific calculation formulae are not given in *GDP2006*, the construction for industrial deflators used in the analysis follows the same method in Li (2006:97–99).[7]

The general formula for calculating the industry-specific implicit price deflator is derived from the nominal value added (VA_t) and either the index of industrial production (IIP_t) or the volume index (VO_t). The industries that are dependent on the IIP_t are manufacturing and mining and quarrying. The industries that depended on the VO_t data include agriculture and fishing, construction, and the service industries of retail, restaurants and hotels. A value index (VI_t) can be derived from the following:

$$VI_t = (VA_t / VA_{1990}) \cdot 100, \tag{7}$$

where VA_t and VA_{1990} are the value added in year t and in the base year, 1990, respectively. The implicit price deflator is simply defined by[8]:

$$\text{Implicit price deflator} = VI_t / IIP_t \text{ or } VI_t / VO_t. \tag{8}$$

Due to data variations, adjustments are made to the available data, including:

Electricity, gas and water: data on the consumption of electricity and gas from the Census and Statistics Department and the consumption index are used to replace the data for IIP_t.

Wholesale: the implicit price deflator of retained imports is used as the proxy deflator. The estimate for the value of retained imports and their quantum index for the period 1990–2005 are obtained from the various issues of *Hong Kong Monthly Digest of Statistics*. The difference in the value of imports and re-exports gives the value of retained imports, and the value at current prices can easily be transformed into the value at 1990 prices. The retained import value for the period 1981–1989, however, is estimated from the 1990–2005 data. The implicit price deflator is calculated from the values of retained imports at both the current prices and 1990 prices.

Import and export: the proxy deflator is the weighted average of the deflators for domestic exports, retained imports, and exports and imports of trade-related services.

Transport, storage and communications: The transportation sub-index of the *Hong Kong Composite Consumer Price Index* (*CPI*) is used as the proxy for the land transport deflator. Such transportation sub-index covers fares for ferries, trains, taxis and public transport, motor licenses and insurance, parking fees and tunnel tolls. For water transport, air transport and other transport services, the proxy deflator is the weighted average of the deflators for export and import of transportation services, in which the weights used are their respective nominal shares in the export and import

---

[7] Most of the industry-specific deflators for the years 2001–2005 show only small variations between those available in *GDP2006* and those constructed in this analysis.

[8] Data are collected from the various issues of *Hong Kong Annual Digest of Statistics*, Hong Kong Census and Statistics Department, and the CEIC Database.

of transportation services. The deflator for the storage industry is derived from the rental index for private flatted factories (*HKADS*). The *CPI* miscellaneous index for telephone services (from CEIC Database) is used as the proxy for the communications industry.

Finance, insurance, real estates and business services: The weighted averages of the deflators for export and import of financial services and the deflators for the export and import of insurance industry are used as proxy deflators for the finance industry and the insurance industry, respectively. The implicit price deflator for real estate developers' margins is used as the proxy deflator for the real estate industry. Figures for the real estate developers' margin for years 2002–2005 are calculated by extrapolations, using fixed average ratio of the available data of real estate developers' margin to total building and construction (*GDP2006*); figures for volume indices for years 2002–2005 are calculated from fixed average of volume indices for years 1966–2001 (*GDP2001*). The implicit price deflator for the export of other services is used as the proxy deflator for business services.

Community, personal and social services: For community, personal and social services, the proxy deflator is the Miscellaneous Services Sub-Index of the *CPI*. This covers school fees and education charges, medical services, entertainment expenses, household services, hairdressing, repairs of personal and household goods, subscriptions, and postal and telephone services.

Table 4.1 summarizes the 21 industry-specific price deflators grouped under 19 categories. The industries that show a rapid rise in inflation include construction, electricity, gas and water (EGW), retail, hotel, restaurants, land transport, community, social and personal services (CSP), and real estate. Table 4.2 shows the data of output, capital and labor. Between 1980 and 2005, Hong Kong's production-based real GDP has increased by 276.4%, while capital stock and labor have increased by 390% and 55.9%, respectively.

The aggregate productivity growth estimates for the various periods between 1981 and 2005 are shown in Table 4.3. For the entire period, output, capital and labor have grown by 5.4%, 6.6% and 1.8%, respectively. Hong Kong's output has experienced the fastest growth in the 1986–1990 period (averaging 8.3%), and a higher growth rate of 6.8% in the 1980 decade when compared with the 4.5% in the 1990 decade. The fastest growth rate of the capital stock is in the two periods of early 1980s and early 1990s (1981–1985, 1991–1995), averaging 8.1% in the two subperiods. Labor has experienced the fastest growth rate during 1981–1985, averaging 3.5%, and the lowest growth rate of 0.1% during 1991–1995.

All the average growth rates of output, capital and labor are higher in the 1980s than in the 1990s (6.8%, 7.7% and 2.4%, respectively, for the period 1981–1990, and 4.5, 6.8 and 1.7%, respectively, for the period 1991–2000). The share of payment contributed by labor and capital remains steady over the years. The three components that contribute to income or output growth (namely, TFP, capital input and labor input) are given in the last three columns in Table 4.3.

Figure 4.1 shows the growth of TFP in Hong Kong for the entire sample period of 1981–2005. Hong Kong's average TFP is 1.5% for the full period, but its performance has varied significantly, with a fastest growth rate of 4.1% in 1986–1990, but

TABLE 4.1 Industry-specific implicit price deflators

Year	AF	Mu	MQ	Con	EGW	Who	Reta	Hot	Rest	I/E	Stor	Com	OT	LT	CSP	Fin	Ins	RE	BS
1980	75.4			44.5	36.1			42.3			38.4	54.9	55.7	38.2	36.3	57.7	53.6	52.9	45.7
1981	80.1	67.9	216.0	49.4	43.8	65.2	55.8	46.6		65.5	54.9	65.1	60.7	46.0	42.1	64.0	58.7	58.4	50.6
1982	89.9	68.7	262.4	49.4	56.2	67.6	60.6	50.4		68.5	43.9	68.1	65.6	51.1	46.7	68.2	63.5	51.3	54.8
1983	92.2	73.7	236.9	45.3	70.0	77.1	66.8	57.0	57.9	77.2	38.4	77.6	69.9	56.9	53.6	72.5	67.6	33.5	60.3
1984	86.8	80.7	193.4	45.7	75.0	84.8	72.4	64.0	61.8	86.0	38.1	79.2	74.4	62.7	58.2	77.5	72.8	31.0	65.3
1985	86.4	81.5	241.2	45.6	81.0	80.8	72.8	66.9	63.9	83.6	43.0	88.7	74.8	66.7	62.6	78.2	74.7	31.4	66.1
1986	87.9	83.8	202.3	49.6	91.1	86.2	75.7	72.1	65.5	87.5	44.8	89.6	75.9	69.5	66.6	79.5	77.6	39.2	68.1
1987	86.7	86.9	129.2	63.1	93.7	90.9	80.5	79.6	68.7	91.5	56.2	89.6	80.6	74.8	71.6	82.1	80.5	59.8	73.0
1988	90.6	91.6	108.9	81.0	92.5	96.0	87.6	87.6	75.4	95.5	79.0	89.6	86.1	78.6	79.1	85.4	86.2	83.6	77.5
1989	90.0	97.2	105.6	93.9	91.5	98.0	93.2	93.8	87.1	98.1	101.0	99.9	95.4	88.1	89.6	93.8	92.0	98.4	89.4
1990	100.0	100.0	100.0	100.0	100.0	100.0	100.0	100.0	100.0	100.0	100.0	100.0	100.0	100.0	100.0	100.0	100.0	100.0	100.0
1991	108.9	97.0	104.7	108.2	97.5	103.5	106.3	105.9	112.5	103.2	106.7	109.1	106.1	112.4	110.6	109.2	106.8	111.5	109.2
1992	117.9	97.6	95.1	126.0	102.6	105.8	111.8	113.6	124.4	105.5	115.2	109.1	108.0	120.5	122.1	117.5	113.2	160.0	117.2
1993	133.5	90.9	91.9	143.4	110.5	108.3	117.8	121.4	135.7	107.6	122.9	110.6	108.1	129.9	133.1	127.2	121.8	215.5	127.7
1994	138.2	86.1	116.5	155.0	141.6	109.2	124.5	131.9	146.7	109.3	128.6	112.5	110.9	141.4	149.3	131.0	123.8	247.3	128.6
1995	134.3	82.3	146.9	147.6	147.2	118.2	132.2	139.4	156.7	116.5	120.0	111.9	116.7	152.0	158.7	136.7	131.6	203.6	129.8
1996	138.4	83.5	149.7	161.3	162.6	118.6	138.3	150.3	162.6	117.6	110.5	110.7	111.2	161.4	168.7	144.1	130.0	233.5	132.0
1997	153.1	82.3	131.9	175.5	172.2	117.2	143.5	158.0	169.3	116.5	111.4	106.7	110.1	167.9	173.7	145.5	129.6	239.0	134.1
1998	168.1	79.6	159.9	167.7	178.9	112.0	143.6	142.7	173.3	112.5	92.4	102.9	104.2	174.3	175.9	131.2	128.6	179.7	124.5
1999	151.3	78.4	174.1	163.8	183.5	118.3	134.0	130.1	170.6	116.0	83.8	95.7	103.9	175.2	172.3	138.8	123.2	158.1	116.2
2000	104.6	84.2	137.5	160.4	178.2	124.8	128.5	129.7	169.0	120.0	80.0	90.1	108.9	176.8	173.4	147.6	121.8	139.2	115.8
2001	95.5	77.8	103.8	148.8	177.2	114.6	125.4	126.3	168.6	112.2	75.7	83.5	105.7	177.5	171.8	140.0	121.6	123.4	110.4
2002	111.3	74.2	90.0	139.0	179.4	102.5	123.5	125.4	166.4	103.8	69.3	77.0	104.8	176.2	169.6	140.5	125.2	197.5	104.0
2003	96.7	70.6	84.5	130.0	171.2	99.4	121.4	124.0	164.2	101.3	62.8	63.2	107.8	175.5	163.2	118.4	127.3	165.6	100.3
2004	106.7	68.6	51.0	134.5	172.0	104.8	123.4	131.1	164.5	104.8	64.8	61.7	113.1	176.4	165.9	108.1	128.6	150.7	99.0
2005	100.0	68.6	69.1	146.2	165.3	111.6	124.2	135.8	165.8	109.2	69.2	59.8	118.4	178.7	168.0	122.6	131.9	158.0	98.5

Notes: AF = Agriculture and fishing, Mu = Manufacturing, MQ = Mining and quarrying, Con = Construction, EGW = Electricity, gas and water, Who = Wholesale, Reta = Retail, Hot = Hotels, Rest = Restaurants, I/E = Import and export, Stor = Storage, Com = Communication, OT = Other transport services, air transport and water transport, LT = Land transport, CSP = Community, social and personal services, Fin = Financing, Ins = Insurance, RE = Real estate and BS = Business services.

TABLE 4.2 Aggregate data for productivity accounting

Year	Production-based real GDP (HK$ Million)	Capital stock (HK$ Million)	Number of people employed (Thousand)	Total labor working hours (Million)	Adjusted labor share
1980	296,787	499,371	2,236.1	5,363	0.522
1981	329,707	561,637	2,393.1	5,740	0.519
1982	335,035	612,110	2,407.1	5,773	0.540
1983	354,071	653,007	2,426.7	5,820	0.551
1984	383,623	698,704	2,505.2	6,009	0.544
1985	385,760	738,547	2,543.3	6,365	0.567
1986	434,203	788,239	2,623.6	6,566	0.546
1987	495,812	854,513	2,680.8	6,709	0.519
1988	540,448	927,543	2,725.1	6,820	0.509
1989	549,441	986,973	2,723.1	6,815	0.521
1990	574,848	1,052,792	2,711.5	6,786	0.533
1991	597,657	1,125,303	2,753.7	6,892	0.530
1992	633,119	1,212,174	2,737.6	6,851	0.516
1993	663,612	1,289,986	2,800.1	7,008	0.515
1994	712,039	1,406,119	2,872.8	7,190	0.498
1995	747,132	1,556,362	2,905.1	6,816	0.524
1996	784,274	1,678,993	3,073.4	7,211	0.521
1997	812,728	1,817,564	3,163.6	7,423	0.528
1998	767,376	1,905,463	3,122.0	7,325	0.563
1999	801,173	1,943,154	3,112.1	7,464	0.573
2000	888,786	2,032,398	3,207.3	8,027	0.568
2001	897,092	2,122,082	3,251.3	8,137	0.587
2002	922,304	2,203,371	3,220.2	8,059	0.587
2003	960,257	2,284,648	3,197.4	8,002	0.586
2004	1,040,229	2,365,162	3,276.5	8,200	0.568
2005	1,117,008	2,446,686	3,340.8	8,361	0.554

Source: *Gross Domestic Product 2006*, and *Hong Kong Annual Digest of Statistics*, Census and Statistics Department, Hong Kong.

a lower rate of 2.6% in 2001–2005. Hong Kong did experience high productivity growth in the second half of the 1980s, during which was the period after the conclusion of the Sino-Britain Joint Declaration and restoration of economic stability, but before heavy speculative activities began in the early 1990s. When the economy began to overheat in the 1991–1995 period, productivity fell considerably and a negative growth in TFP was experienced in 1996–2000, especially after the emergence of the Asian financial crisis that hit the economy hard. The output growth experienced in the 1991–1995 period (3.9%) was due probably to expansion in capital (8.1%), while labor contributed to almost nothing to output growth. The political uncertainty during the Sino-British negotiations in 1981–1985 and the Asian financial crisis period, coupled

TABLE 4.3 Hong Kong's productivity accounting: 1981–2005 (Compound annual growth rates)

	Growth rates			Share of payment		Contribution to output by		
	Output	Capital	Labor	Capital	Labor	TFP	Capital	Labor
1981–1985	5.4	8.1	3.5	0.46	0.54	–0.2	3.7	1.9
1986–1990	8.3	7.3	1.3	0.47	0.53	4.1	3.5	0.7
1991–1995	5.4	8.1	0.1	0.48	0.52	1.4	3.9	0.0
1996–2000	3.5	5.5	3.3	0.45	0.55	–0.8	2.5	1.8
2001–2005	4.7	3.8	0.8	0.42	0.58	2.6	1.6	0.5
1981–1990	6.8	7.7	2.4	0.46	0.54	2.0	3.6	1.3
1991–2000	4.5	6.8	1.7	0.47	0.53	0.4	3.2	0.9
1981–2005	5.4	6.6	1.8	0.46	0.54	1.5	3.0	1.0

Note: The sum of the last three columns should equal to the first column. Any difference is the result of rounding off.

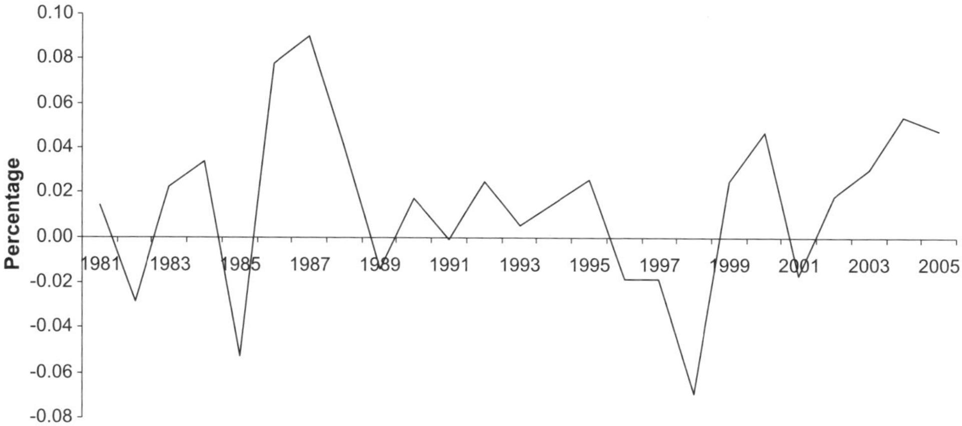

FIGURE 4.1 Hong Kong's total factor productivity growth: 1981–2005

with the so-called "post-Olympic syndrome" that followed Hong Kong's sovereignty conversion in 1996–2000, led to the decline in TFP, from an average annual growth rate of TFP to –0.2% in 1981–1985 to –0.8% in 1996–2000. TFP growth returned to a positive rate of 2.6% in 2001–2005 when the economy began to recover from economic recession after the Asian financial crisis.

4.4 Productivity Growth of Industries

The economy-wide TFP estimates provide an aggregate picture on the growth of TFP, but the disaggregate picture of TFP growth can be seen from the productivity

TABLE 4.4 Percentage share of industries in real GDP at factor cost: 1983–2005

Year	AF	Mu	MQ	Con	EGW	WRTRH	TSC	CSP	FIRB
1983	0.38	17.27	0.04	7.93	2.10	15.38	6.68	16.87	17.19
1984	0.37	18.47	0.04	7.29	2.14	17.48	6.62	16.48	16.14
1985	0.36	17.54	0.04	7.13	2.31	18.60	6.94	17.51	17.75
1986	0.34	18.05	0.04	6.55	2.28	18.04	7.15	16.33	18.34
1987	0.31	18.39	0.04	5.38	2.24	20.19	7.81	14.87	17.99
1988	0.29	17.84	0.04	4.60	2.22	21.46	8.59	14.20	17.90
1989	0.28	17.69	0.04	4.91	2.36	23.07	8.44	14.20	18.03
1990	0.25	16.74	0.04	5.17	2.40	23.65	9.00	14.08	18.95
1991	0.22	16.26	0.04	5.25	2.55	24.94	9.01	14.18	20.77
1992	0.20	15.60	0.03	4.58	2.65	26.55	9.69	14.23	20.04
1993	0.18	14.80	0.03	4.43	2.62	29.02	9.99	14.66	18.90
1994	0.16	13.76	0.03	4.11	2.39	29.13	10.47	14.14	18.91
1995	0.14	13.24	0.03	4.87	2.31	28.49	10.69	14.73	19.98
1996	0.13	12.14	0.03	5.07	2.28	29.80	11.13	14.93	19.96
1997	0.12	11.63	0.03	4.99	2.25	30.21	11.00	15.53	21.55
1998	0.12	11.25	0.02	5.37	2.54	30.61	11.15	17.13	24.26
1999	0.10	10.09	0.02	5.00	2.45	28.34	10.84	17.70	22.99
2000	0.10	9.04	0.02	4.35	2.33	27.65	10.84	16.22	21.94
2001	0.12	8.56	0.02	4.28	2.39	29.19	10.91	17.06	21.77
2002	0.10	7.51	0.02	4.02	2.39	30.49	11.28	16.99	18.61
2003	0.09	6.55	0.01	3.60	2.36	30.00	10.67	16.72	21.05
2004	0.08	6.23	0.01	2.89	2.22	29.81	10.23	15.30	22.18
2005	0.08	5.94	0.01	2.36	2.16	30.10	9.88	13.77	21.07
Aver	0.20	13.24	0.03	4.96	2.34	25.75	9.52	15.56	19.84

Notes: AF = Agriculture and fishing, Mu = Manufacturing, MQ = Mining and quarrying, Con = Construction, EGW = Electricity, gas and water, WRTRH = Wholesale, retail, import and export trades, restaurants and hotels, TSC = Transport, storage and communications, CSP = Community, social and personal services, FIRB = Finance, insurance, real estates and business services, Aver = average.

Source: *Gross Domestic Product 2006*, Census and Statistics Department, Hong Kong.

growth of different industries, and their performance can reflect the changing composition of industrial structure of an economy (PECC, 2000).

Table 4.4 summarizes the economic proportions of the nine industries in Hong Kong for the period of 1983–2005 in terms of percentage share in real GDP at factor cost.[9] The two industries of agriculture and fishing, and mining and quarrying have a negligible percentage share in real GDP. Manufacturing has occupied the largest share of almost 20% in the early 1980s, but has declined constantly to less than

[9] Due to data unavailability of some industries, the discussion of TFP can only begin in 1983 or 1984.

10% since 2000. The percentage shares of the two infrastructure-related industries of electricity, gas and water, and construction have remained low, with little change for the former industry while the latter has decreased from 7.93% in 1983 to 2.36% in 2005. The category of transport, storage and communication shows a different trend with a low share of 6.68% in 1983 but has increased gradually to almost 10% in 2005.

Among the largest three service industries, the percentage share of the industry of wholesale, retail, import and export trades, restaurants and hotels has increased from 15.38% in 1983 to 30.10% in 2005, making it the largest industry in 2005. Finance, insurance, real estate and business services has a share of 17.19% in 1983 (a share similar to manufacturing with 17.27%), and has increased its share modestly to 21.07% in 2005. Community, social and personal services declined from 16.87% in 1983 to 13.77% in 2005. The fourth largest service is transport, storage and communication that has only expanded gradually from 6.68% in 1983 to 9.88% in 2005. These four services occupied a total of 74.82% in real GDP at factor cost in 2005.

Table 4.4 provides a picture on the changing industrial structure in Hong Kong. With rapid growth in manufacturing industries since the 1960s, Hong Kong has experienced a period of "de-industrialization" or "industrial hollowing" beginning from the 1980s when light manufacturing industries began to move to Southern China across the border due to lower cost attraction. The agriculture and fishing industry fell off to less than 0.1% by 2005. The manufacturing industry has declined dramatically, while services have increased its share sharply. The share of finance, insurance, real estate and business services has been leading the increasing trend in Hong Kong.

The TFP calculations based on the eight classifications of industries (mining and quarrying are grouped into agriculture and fishing) in Hong Kong are shown in Table 4.5.

1. **Agriculture, fishing and mining:** The combined industries of agriculture and fishing, and mining and quarrying have experienced negative growth rates in output, capital and labor by an average of –1.0%, –4.9% and –8.5%, respectively, for the entire sample period. Their TFP growth is high in the 1980s. Lacking a strong rural economy, the primary industry has a minimal impact on the Hong Kong economy.
2. **Electricity, gas and water:** The growth rates for output and capital are high at 5.9% and 9.6%, respectively, for the sample period, but the growth rate of labor is negative with –1.7%. Unfortunately, its TFP growth rate has been weak, with only 1.2% in the 1980s, but –4.1% in the 1990s, giving –1.4% for the sample period. The output of electricity, gas and water is contributed mainly from capital, with 7.6% for the entire sample period, while labor's contribution is negative (–0.4%). By and large, this is a capital-intensive sector, and contribution from labor is low. Nevertheless, this is a matured infrastructure industry in the Hong Kong economy and can provide only a steady economic contribution unless there is massive technological breakthrough in energy construction.
3. **Construction:** Other than the two-digit growth rates in capital for the decade 1986–1995, the performance of construction is generally weak, with negative growth rates in output (–0.1%), capital (–0.5%) and labor (–1.9%), and the

TABLE 4.5 Productivity accounting of industry classifications: 1983–2005 (Compound annual growth rates)

		Growth rates			Share of payment		Contribution to output by		
		Output	Capital	Labor	Capital	Labor	TFP	Capital	Labor
Agriculture and fishing, mining and quarrying	1983–1985	1.1	–5.7	–8.3	0.70	0.30	7.6	–4.0	–2.5
	1986–1990	5.0	–12.4	–10.7	0.61	0.39	16.7	–7.5	–4.2
	1991–1995	–4.6	–0.3	–10.8	0.59	0.41	0.0	–0.2	–4.5
	1996–2000	–4.3	–5.2	–10.9	0.65	0.35	3.0	–3.4	–3.9
	2001–2005	–1.2	–0.9	–1.5	0.63	0.37	–0.1	–0.6	–0.5
	1983–1990	3.5	–9.9	–9.8	0.64	0.36	13.4	–6.4	–3.5
	1991–2000	–4.4	–2.8	–10.9	0.62	0.38	1.4	–1.7	–4.2
	1983–2005	–1.0	–4.9	–8.5	0.63	0.37	5.2	–3.1	–3.2
Electricity, gas and water	1983–1985	10.9	28.3	0.0	0.77	0.23	–10.7	21.6	0.0
	1986–1990	9.2	1.9	0.5	0.79	0.21	7.6	1.5	0.1
	1991–1995	4.5	8.6	–1.2	0.76	0.24	–1.7	6.5	–0.3
	1996–2000	3.8	14.8	–7.0	0.81	0.19	–7.0	12.0	–1.3
	2001–2005	3.1	3.4	0.0	0.85	0.15	0.2	2.9	0.0
	1983–1990	9.9	11.1	0.3	0.78	0.22	1.2	8.6	0.1
	1991–2000	4.1	11.6	–4.1	0.79	0.21	–4.1	9.1	–0.9
	1983–2005	5.9	9.6	–1.7	0.80	0.20	–1.4	7.6	–0.4
Construction	1983–1985	1.0	–21.0	–5.5	0.13	0.87	8.6	–2.8	–4.8
	1986–1990	1.6	12.2	0.8	0.09	0.91	–0.3	1.1	0.8
	1991–1995	4.1	16.0	–1.9	0.16	0.84	3.2	2.5	–1.6
	1996–2000	1.2	–5.4	4.6	0.13	0.87	–2.1	–0.7	4.0
	2001–2005	–7.4	–8.4	–8.3	0.07	0.93	0.9	–0.6	–7.7
	1983–1990	1.3	–1.6	–1.6	0.11	0.89	2.9	–0.2	–1.4
	1991–2000	2.7	4.7	1.3	0.14	0.86	0.9	0.7	1.1
	1983–2005	–0.1	–0.5	–1.9	0.11	0.89	1.6	–0.1	–1.6

(*Continued*)

TABLE 4.5 (*Continued*)

		Growth rates			Share of payment		Contribution to output by		
		Output	Capital	Labor	Capital	Labor	TFP	Capital	Labor
Manufacturing	1983–1985	7.9	13.0	1.4	0.29	0.71	3.1	3.8	1.0
	1986–1990	7.3	7.4	–3.3	0.35	0.65	6.8	2.6	–2.2
	1991–1995	0.5	–7.0	–12.1	0.38	0.62	10.7	–2.7	–7.5
	1996–2000	–4.1	4.0	–9.7	0.40	0.60	0.2	1.6	–5.8
	2001–2005	–3.8	–9.8	–5.8	0.35	0.65	3.5	–3.4	–3.8
	1983–1990	7.5	9.5	–2.5	0.33	0.67	6.1	3.1	–1.7
	1991–2000	–1.8	–1.7	–10.9	0.39	0.61	5.5	–0.6	–6.7
	1983–2005	0.9	0.2	–6.6	0.36	0.64	5.1	0.1	–4.3
Wholesale, retail, import and export, restaurants and hotels	1984–1985	14.8	17.7	8.4	0.47	0.53	2.0	8.4	4.4
	1986–1990	13.6	6.7	5.4	0.47	0.53	7.6	3.2	2.9
	1991–1995	9.4	7.9	4.2	0.42	0.58	3.6	3.3	2.4
	1996–2000	2.9	9.1	–0.2	0.41	0.59	–0.7	3.7	–0.1
	2001–2005	6.5	10.5	0.3	0.48	0.52	1.3	5.0	0.2
	1984–1990	14.0	11.8	6.7	0.47	0.53	4.9	5.6	3.5
	1991–2000	6.1	8.5	2.0	0.42	0.58	1.4	3.5	1.2
	1984–2005	8.6	9.3	2.9	0.45	0.55	2.5	4.5	1.6
Finance, insurance real estates and business services	1983–1985	1.3	–8.3	4.7	0.59	0.41	4.3	–4.9	1.9
	1986–1990	9.7	11.2	9.4	0.61	0.39	–0.8	6.8	3.7
	1991–1995	6.5	13.0	8.5	0.64	0.36	–4.9	8.3	3.1
	1996–2000	5.5	1.4	2.8	0.53	0.47	3.4	0.7	1.3
	2001–2005	3.8	–0.6	1.8	0.41	0.59	3.0	-0.2	1.1
	1983–1990	6.5	3.4	7.6	0.60	0.40	1.4	2.1	3.0
	1991–2000	6.0	7.0	5.6	0.58	0.42	–0.4	4.1	2.3
	1983–2005	5.7	4.1	5.5	0.55	0.45	1.0	2.2	2.5

(*Continued*)

TABLE 4.5 (*Continued*)

		Growth rates			Share of payment		Contribution to output by		
		Output	Capital	Labor	Capital	Labor	TFP	Capital	Labor
Transport, storage and communications	1983–1985	6.7	17.0	4.3	0.45	0.55	–3.3	7.7	2.4
	1986–1990	14.1	10.2	6.8	0.52	0.48	5.5	5.3	3.3
	1991–1995	9.1	9.5	5.3	0.51	0.49	1.6	4.8	2.6
	1996–2000	3.8	8.8	0.5	0.47	0.53	–0.6	4.2	0.3
	2001–2005	2.8	7.7	0.8	0.50	0.50	–1.5	3.9	0.4
	1983–1990	11.3	12.7	5.9	0.49	0.51	2.0	6.3	3.0
	1991–2000	6.4	9.2	2.9	0.49	0.51	0.4	4.5	1.5
	1983–2005	7.3	9.3	3.5	0.49	0.51	0.9	4.6	1.8
Community, social and personal services	1983–1985	4.4	15.8	4.0	0.19	0.81	-1.8	3.0	3.3
	1986–1990	3.7	–2.8	2.7	0.17	0.83	1.9	–0.5	2.2
	1991–1995	6.3	9.3	3.8	0.13	0.87	1.8	1.2	3.3
	1996–2000	5.6	0.0	4.6	0.09	0.91	1.4	0.0	4.2
	2001–2005	1.3	–6.3	4.7	0.04	0.96	–3.0	–0.3	4.5
	1983–1990	4.0	3.8	3.2	0.17	0.83	0.7	0.7	2.6
	1991–2000	5.9	4.5	4.2	0.11	0.89	1.7	0.5	3.7
	1983–2005	4.2	1.8	4.0	0.12	0.88	0.5	0.2	3.5

Note: The sum of the last three columns should equal to the first column. Any difference is the result of rounding off.

average TFP growth rate is 1.6% in the sample period. Despite the dominance of the real estate in Hong Kong, the construction industry has remained a weak sector, due to a number of reasons. One reason is the low skill requirement in a large number of construction jobs. As construction is mainly labor intensive, there is a lack of capital input growth over the years, as construction machinery tends to last long, with a low replacement rate. The large supply of competing workers in the industry, coupled with weak organization among construction workers and the need for a middle-man in the liaison of construction work. Given that construction is a matured industry and a rapid growth is unlikely, as it occupied only about 5% of real GDP at factor cost in 2005 (Table 4.4). Nonetheless, the construction industry does provide job opportunities for a large number of low skill workers. Improvement in the construction industry can only come from the supply side, with advancement in skills among workers and the growth of competing workers, especially from immigrant workers.

4. **Manufacturing:** For manufacturing, its low growth rates in both output (0.9%) and capital (0.2%) for the sample period is expected as Hong Kong passed through a process of "de-industrialization" or "industrial hollowing" since the late 1980s, as demonstrated by the large negative labor growth rate (–6.6%). However, the manufacturing industry does not experience any negative TFP growth rate in the sample period and in all sub-periods in Table. 4.5. Indeed, contribution to output growth in the manufacturing industry comes mainly from growth in TFP (5.1% for the sample period). This suggests that what remain in the manufacturing industry after the de-industrialization saga of the 1980s and 1990s are the cream in the industry, and the surviving firms probably have strong technological, financial and skill backup. Over time, the restructuring of these remaining firms can bring new developments in the manufacturing industry. The TFP estimates for manufacturing are generally promising, and the de-industrialization does hurt the manufacturing industry in Hong Kong, but the migration of industries to Southern China can be seen as the removal of uncompetitive industrial plants, giving rooms and potentials for the modern industries to be developed in Hong Kong, thereby upgrading and enlarging competitiveness and comparative advantages in Hong Kong. It will be a matter of time when industrialists and investors will reconsider Hong Kong as an industrial base, especially manufacturing-related industries that enhances the production based in Mainland China.
5. **Wholesale, retail, import and export trade, restaurants and hotels:** This has been an expanding industry and experienced high growth rates in output (8.6%), capital (9.3%) and labor (2.9%) for the sample period. Indeed, the growth rates in the 1980s are much higher than in the 1990s, though the situation improved after the Asian financial crisis in the 2001–2005 years. Other than the Asian financial crisis period of 1996–2000, this industry has experienced a positive TFP growth rate in all other periods, with an average of 2.5% for the sample period. The contribution to output growth comes mainly from capital (4.5% for the sample period). By and large, this industry contains mainly labor-intensive industries, often with low skill requirement. Improvement in service quality can promote the industry, especially in skill requirement, ethic standards and

employment opportunities. Some industries, typically hotels, are tradable services that compete internationally with overseas hotel chains and the various vocation training institutions in Hong Kong with ample training facilities to upgrade the quality of the services. Others, typically local restaurants, wholesale and retail are dominated by SMEs, and vocational training tends to be on the job rather than through formal institutional qualifications. Although employment will vary with the business cycle, wages are unlikely to rise substantially due to strong competition in the labor market, especially those workers released from their former employment in manufacturing industries. Increases in service demand seem to be the long-term viable solution to growth in this sector. Since this sector occupied 25.75% of real GDP at factor cost in 2005 (Table 4.4), rents and wage are the key components in the survival of businesses in this sector. While rents depended a lot on movement in the business cycle, the legislation of a "minimum wage" since May 2011 has to be considered with extreme care, as the adoption of minimum wage usually cannot be reversed. In Hong Kong, a single across-the-board application of a minimum wage does not have much use and advantage, and the resulting rise in total cost, especially among SMEs, can result in a fall in total employment, and even some closures and bankruptcies of business. It will be more appropriate to have different minimum wage or entry wage established for different businesses in this sector. The difference in the minimum or entry wage of different labor intensive services, such as restaurants, retail and hotels, can serve as a market signal for workers to switch from one job to another, thereby promoting labor mobility among workers in the service sector.

6. **Finance, insurance, real estate and business:** This industry has experienced a positive growth rate in all periods in output, capital (except 2001–2005 with –0.6%) and labor. However, despite the high growth rates of output (5.7%), capital (4.1%) and labor (5.5%) for the sample period, the contribution to output growth by TFP is low (1.0% for the sample period), while capital (2.2%) and labor (2.5%) have contributed more. By and large, this industry contains mainly labor-intensive services, though the required human capital and skill level in finance, insurance and business are higher than in real estate and other services. The growth of TFP is expected to be weak as a number of services are related to the nominal economy where mainly financial transactions are involved. This industry involves a large amount of updated information and communication knowledge, the geographical location of Hong Kong has a natural advantage among various key financial centers of New York, London, Tokyo, Singapore, Sydney, Seoul and Taiwan and so on. Other "soft" capital includes the presence of strong regulations, good ethical practices and complete adherence to the rule of laws that protect and promote trust, equity and transparency.
7. **Transport, storage and communications:** This industry has experienced large positive growth rates in output, capital and labor. Capital is the largest contributor to output growth (4.6%), while TFP growth has only a marginal contribution (0.9% for the sample period). While the communications industry may require knowledge and skill in electronics and computing, transport and storage are labor intensive services that do not require a high skill level. Extensive economic integration with Southern China has imposed pressure on the employment level in

this industry, as the demand for jobs may fall if workers do not have alternative employment opportunities when re-export businesses are constrained by the port facilities in various parts across the border. As shown in Table 4.4, this industry occupies about 10% of real GDP at factor cost in 2005, any unfavorable changes in this industry may reduce employment opportunities, especially in cross-border transport if re-export business remains unchanged. Thus, employment in this industry is formidable.

8. **Community, social and personal services:** In the case of community, social and personal services, labor is the major contribution to output growth (3.5% for the sample period), while the contribution by TFP growth is marginal (0.5% for the sample period). This is another labor-intensive service industry, with the output growth (4.2%) for the entire sample period and the growth of labor (4%) is more than twice that of growth in capital (1.8%). Growth in TFP has been low and constant (0.5% for the sample period), other than the early 1980s during the Sino-British negotiation and the post-AFC period of 2001–2005 when a negative TFP growth was experienced. Labor has been the contributing factor to output growth, while contribution by capital is marginal. Despite being the third largest service industry (with real GDP at factor cost of 9.52% in 2005 shown in Table 4.4), expansion in this industry has been slow or even declined in recent years. One reason could be the possibility of employment saturation in this industry, and further expansion is limited. One can see from Table 4.4 that the real GDP at factor cost has risen to slightly more than 10% in 1994 to the peak of 11.15% in 1998 and lasted till 2002 with 11.28%. These large percentages correspond with the recession years after the Asian financial crisis. In other words, a number of community and social services are welfare related, such as social workers, medical personnel and voluntary workers, and that they are in high demand during economic recession, but once unemployment falls and economic hardship is reduced and households can look after their economic needs, demand for social and community services will fall, leading to an overall reduction in real GDP at factor cost. On the contrary, other personal services, such as beauty parlors and health and physical training agents, will face a higher demand when economic recession is over.

The performance of the eight economic industries for the sample period can be seen by their rankings in the share of GDP, output growth and TFP. Table 4.6 shows the summary, as well as an indication on the mode of production, which is judged by examining their share in factor payments. There are several points of discussion when all the industries are analyzed. Firstly, from the share in GDP, Hong Kong's industrial structure has changed from manufacturing in 1983 to wholesale, retail import and export, restaurants and hotels in 2005. Finance, insurance real estate and business services have remained the second most important industry. Together with community, social and personal services, services are the dominant sectors in Hong Kong.

As far as the mode of production is concerned, industries in Hong Kong are largely labor intensive. Both the agriculture, fishing, mining and quarrying sector and the electricity, gas and water industries are small in their overall share in GDP, and

TABLE 4.6 Summary ranking of output growth and total factor productivity

	Share in GDP ranking				Output growth ranking			TFP ranking		
Sectors	1983	2005	Overall	Mode of production	1983–1985	2001–2005	Overall	1983–1985	2001–2005	Overall
AFMQ	8	8	8	K intensive	7	6	7	2	6	1
Manu	1	5	4	L intensive	3	7	6	4	1	2
EGW	7	7	7	K intensive	2	3	3	8	5	8
Cons	5	6	6	L intensive	8	8	7	1	4	4
WRTRH	4	1	1	L intensive	1	1	1	5	3	3
TSC	6	4	5	L intensive	4	4	2	7	7	6
FIRB	2	2	2	K intensive	6	2	4	3	2	5
CSP	3	3	3	L intensive	5	5	5	6	8	7

Notes: AFMQ = Agriculture, fishing, mining and quarrying; Manu = Manufacturing; EGW = Electricity, gas and water; Cons = Construction; WRTRH = Wholesale, retail, import and export trade, restaurants and hotels (Output Growth and TFP Rankings start in 1984); TSC = Transport, storage and communications; FIRB = Finance, insurance, real estate and business services; and CSP = Community, social and personal services. K = capital and L = labor.

cannot make large impact on technology. Finance, insurance, real estate and business services at best are "information intensive". All other major economic sectors are mainly labor intensive. In the output growth ranking, the wholesale, retail, import and export, restaurants and hotels industries have performed consistently, as their output growth has remained high. The weaker industries with low output growth include construction and community, social and personal services. The ranking of TFP growth, however, differs in different years, though the weaker ones include electricity, gas and water, community, social and personal services, and transport, storage and communications.

4.5 Productivity Growth of Economic Sectors

Different economic sectors can commonly be classified into tradable goods, tradable services, non-tradable goods and non-tradable services. By "tradable", it usually means that goods or services can be sold in a distant destination, and that an element of export or import is involved. Because the tradable goods or services can either be exported or imported, tradable goods or services tend to face competition from foreign suppliers. On the contrary, non-tradable goods or services are entirely restricted to the local market, and there is a lack of import substitute. It follows that because of the presence of possible foreign competition, the price of tradable goods or services tend to be more flexible and competitive than non-tradable goods or services. Lacking the presence of foreign substitutes, non-tradable goods or services can rigidly be set at a monopolistic price, which usually is higher than if there is supply from the foreign market.

The classification of economic sectors into tradable and non-tradable goods and services, however, can be problematic.[10] One general "rule of thumb" is that goods or services are regarded as tradable when 10% of the value-added content of the good or service is exported. Given the very open nature and the lack of natural resources and supply of raw materials in the Hong Kong economy, there is literally the presence of a "foreign" component in most goods and services.

A clear cut between tradable and non-tradable goods and/or services can be difficult. For example, the real estate industry in Hong Kong includes the activities of real estate development, leasing, maintenance, brokerage and agency service. Although real estate development is done mainly by local developers, real estate properties in Hong Kong are demanded by foreigners or non-local residents and a large proportion of leasing activities is related to foreign businesses. Equally, businesses that handle the maintenance, brokerage and agency services in real estate that are normally regarded as non-tradable can also be conducted by foreign-owned companies in Hong Kong. In the 2005 *Report on Annual Survey of Building, Construction and Real Estate Sectors* (Census and Statistics Department, Hong Kong), for example, the maintenance, brokerage and agency service together has contributed 22.69% of total value-added in the entire real estate sector, the remaining 77.31% of the total value-added belonged to

---

[10] In line with other studies, the tradable and non-tradable classification in this chapter differs slightly from Li (2006). It is believed that the classification will give a stronger result.

real estate development and leasing. Using the data from the US, Jensen and Kletzer (2005) argue that the real estate and rental sector should remain as tradable. Studies by DeGregorio *et al.* (1994) and Kubota (2000) also regard real estate services as tradable.

The sector classifications in Gonzalez-Soriano (1990) can be used as the basis for distinguishing between the tradable and non-tradable sectors. Construction, public utilities (electricity and gas) and such services as wholesale, retail and land transport are consumed locally and should be regarded as non-tradable economic activities. Community, social and personal services are also regarded as non-tradable, since it is mainly consumed locally. On the contrary, water transport and air transport, communication services, hotel and restaurants are tradable economic activities.

The 21 industries in Hong Kong can now be classified into four sectors as:

1. **Tradable goods sector:** agriculture and fishing; mining and quarrying; and manufacturing;
2. **Tradable services sector:** import and export trade; restaurant and hotel; air and water transport; other transport services, storage and communications; and financing, insurance, and real estate and business services;
3. **Non-tradable goods sector:** construction; electricity, gas and water;
4. **Non-tradable services sector:** wholesale and retail; land transport; community and social and personal services.

Table 4.7 shows the real output and percentage shares of the four sectors. The tradable goods sector that contains mainly manufacturing, together with agriculture and fishing, and mining and quarrying, peaks in the 1980s with a largest percentage share of 29.1% in 1980. However, since 1994 the share of tradable goods in total real output drops from a 2-digit share percentage to single digit percentage. By 2005, its percentage share in real GDP at factor cost amount to only 2.5%, becoming the smallest of the four sectors. The non-tradable goods sector also has experienced a fall in its share in real output from 8.5% in 1980 to the lowest of 4.5% in 2005. For the non-tradable goods sector, construction and electricity, gas and water experiences a slightly decreasing share. Indeed, these two goods sectors occupy a total of 7.3% in the share of real output in 2005, as shown in Table 4.4.

For the two services sectors, the tradable services turns out to be the largest sector in Hong Kong, which has increased from the lowest 32.2% of share in real output in 1983 to the highest percentage share of 59.6% in 1998, before leveling off to 56.2 in 2005. The tradable services sector is now the dominant sector in the Hong Kong economy. Overall, the non-tradable services sector experiences a rather steady share in the sample period, though it has edged below 20% to 18.7% in 2005, making itself the second largest sector in the economy.

Table 4.8 shows the TFP calculations for the tradable and non-tradable sectors. For the entire sample period, all of the four economic sectors have shown a positive average TFP growth. Among the four economic sectors, the tradable services sector has the highest average TFP of 1.8% for the whole period, followed by the non-tradable services sector (1.2%), tradable goods sector (0.6%) and non-tradable goods sector (0.4%). In general, all the four economic sectors have experienced a higher

TABLE 4.7 Real output and percentage share of economic sectors at factor cost

	Tradable goods		Tradable services		Non-tradable goods		Non-tradable services	
	HK$ Million	% Share	HK$ Million	% Share	HK$ Million	% Share	HK$ Million	% Share
1980	86,252.9	29.1	n/a	—	25,342.7	8.5	n/a	—
1981	84,243.6	25.6	n/a	—	30,757.0	9.3	72,245.2	21.9
1982	67,258.2	20.1	n/a	—	33,135.5	9.9	83,104.2	24.8
1983	66,150.4	18.7	113,995.8	32.2	34,161.7	9.6	81,852.1	23.1
1984	78,204.6	20.4	125,222.9	32.6	34,276.7	8.9	88,303.2	23.0
1985	70,082.0	18.2	13,5491.3	35.1	33,748.3	8.7	95,308.1	24.7
1986	74,119.2	17.1	156,347.3	36.0	35,178.1	8.1	100,102.2	23.1
1987	86,467.5	17.4	191,366.9	38.6	36,427.9	7.3	108,397.1	21.9
1988	97,330.6	18.0	219,607.4	40.6	36,694.4	6.8	115,582.5	21.4
1989	104,952.3	19.1	230,869.0	42.0	39,922.1	7.3	119,326.2	21.7
1990	97,900.0	17.0	253,873.0	44.2	43,515.0	7.6	123,722.0	21.5
1991	98227.6	16.4	282,678.2	47.3	46,488.1	7.8	128,962.2	21.6
1992	95,327.3	15.1	304,258.0	48.1	45,344.1	7.2	138,538.8	21.9
1993	82,114.4	12.4	321,635.1	48.5	46,146.0	7.0	147,939.8	22.3
1994	60,866.5	8.5	344,840.7	48.4	46,182.8	6.5	153,419.7	21.5
1995	56,602.0	7.6	384,783.1	51.5	53,607.4	7.2	159,417.1	21.3
1996	50,120.2	6.4	411,756.2	52.5	57,622.3	7.3	169,071.4	21.6
1997	46,258.2	5.7	442,175.9	54.4	58,843.0	7.2	177,647.2	21.9
1998	39,475.4	5.1	457,293.2	59.6	60,649.9	7.9	176,771.6	23.0
1999	35,462.7	4.4	450,373.9	56.2	59,442.0	7.4	188,438.1	23.5
2000	38,847.1	4.4	488,057.3	54.9	59,255.1	6.7	192,617.4	21.7
2001	34,661.4	3.9	506,488.6	56.5	59,390.6	6.6	202,088.7	22.5
2002	29,521.7	3.2	501,141.7	54.3	58,222.5	6.3	204,890.8	22.2
2003	26,713.6	2.8	547,612.4	57.0	56,165.6	5.8	205,492.4	21.4
2004	26,609.6	2.6	597,346.5	57.4	52,322.8	5.0	211,479.7	20.3
2005	28,334.1	2.5	627,649.5	56.2	50,321.8	4.5	208,973.7	18.7

Notes: The percentage shares may not sum to 100 percent due to the ownership of premises, which is excluded in the discussion. n/a: Real figures cannot be calculated due to the lack of data.
Sources: *Gross Domestic Product 2006*, Census and Statistics Department, Hong Kong.

TABLE 4.8 Productivity accounting of economic sectors: 1983–2005 (Compound annual growth rate)

		Growth rates			Share of payment		Contribution to output by		
		Output	Capital	Labor	Capital	Labor	TFP	Capital	Labor
Tradable Goods	1983–1985	1.4	11.2	1.3	0.30	0.70	–2.9	3.4	0.9
	1986–1990	6.9	6.4	–3.4	0.36	0.64	6.8	2.3	–2.2
	1991–1995	–10.4	–6.8	–12.1	0.38	0.62	–0.3	–2.6	–7.5
	1996–2000	–7.3	3.7	–9.7	0.40	0.60	–3.0	1.5	–5.8
	2001–2005	–6.1	–9.5	–5.8	0.35	0.65	1.0	–3.4	–3.7
	1983–1990	4.8	8.2	–1.7	0.34	0.66	3.1	2.8	–1.1
	1991–2000	–8.8	–1.7	–10.9	0.39	0.61	–1.6	–0.7	–6.6
	1983–2005	–3.7	–0.2	–6.7	0.37	0.63	0.6	–0.1	–4.2
Tradable Services	1984–1985	9.0	6.9	9.9	0.51	0.49	0.7	3.5	4.8
	1986–1990	13.4	10.2	8.1	0.54	0.46	4.2	5.5	3.7
	1991–1995	8.7	11.5	6.5	0.54	0.46	–0.5	6.2	3.0
	1996–2000	4.9	5.4	0.6	0.48	0.52	2.0	2.6	0.3
	2001–2005	5.2	5.4	0.8	0.46	0.54	2.2	2.5	0.4
	1984–1990	12.1	9.3	8.6	0.53	0.47	3.2	4.9	4.0
	1991–2000	6.8	8.4	3.5	0.51	0.49	0.8	4.3	1.7
	1984–2005	8.1	8.0	4.5	0.50	0.50	1.8	4.0	2.2

(*Continued*)

TABLE 4.8 (*Continued*)

		Growth rates			Share of payment		Contribution to output by		
		Output	Capital	Labor	Capital	Labor	TFP	Capital	Labor
Non-tradable goods	1983–1985	0.6	10.4	–4.8	0.34	0.66	0.2	3.6	–3.2
	1986–1990	5.2	4.0	0.8	0.34	0.66	3.4	1.3	0.5
	1991–1995	4.3	10.6	–1.8	0.35	0.65	1.7	3.7	–1.2
	1996–2000	2.0	9.8	3.2	0.36	0.64	–3.6	3.5	2.1
	2001–2005	-3.2	1.9	–7.4	0.43	0.57	0.2	0.8	–4.2
	1983–1990	3.5	6.3	–1.3	0.34	0.66	2.2	2.1	–0.9
	1991–2000	3.1	10.2	0.7	0.35	0.65	–0.9	3.6	0.4
	1983–2005	1.8	7.0	–1.8	0.37	0.63	0.4	2.6	–1.2
Non-tradable services	1983–1985	4.7	13.0	3.6	0.28	0.72	–1.6	3.6	2.6
	1986–1990	5.4	0.6	2.2	0.28	0.72	3.6	0.2	1.6
	1991–1995	5.2	5.2	2.2	0.22	0.78	2.4	1.2	1.7
	1996–2000	3.9	4.1	2.7	0.17	0.83	0.9	0.7	2.2
	2001–2005	1.6	1.3	2.8	0.12	0.88	–1.0	0.2	2.5
	1983–1990	5.1	5.1	2.7	0.28	0.72	1.7	1.4	2.0
	1991–2000	4.5	4.7	2.4	0.20	0.80	1.7	0.9	1.9
	1983–2005	4.1	4.1	2.6	0.21	0.79	1.2	0.8	2.1

Notes: The sum of the last three columns should equal to the first column. Any difference is the result of rounding off. Due to data unavailability, the discussion of the tradable services sector began from 1984 onwards.

TFP growth rate in the 1980s than that in the 1990s, and aside from non-tradable services sector, improvements can be seen in the period of 2000–2005 when all the sectors have been striving for recovery after a period of severe economic recession.

The tradable goods sector

The tradable goods sector has experienced the highest TFP growth of 6.8% in the period of 1986–1990, but has encountered a negative growth in TFP in the 1990s, with a large –3.0% in the period of 1996–2000 when the Asian financial crisis occurred, but has recaptured growth and reached a positive 1.0% in the period of 2001–2005. The TFP growth for the entire sample period is small at 0.6%. This surely is a declining sector, as all the growth rates of output (–3.7%), capital (–0.2%) and labor (–6.7%) shows a negative in the sample period. It is probably true to say that the tradable goods sector has remained steady, and will not be a key sector unless new investments emerge to revive the manufacturing sector. The option still opens given the great degree of economic freedom in Hong Kong. In the meantime, it will be appropriate for the existing manufacturing firms to do their best and excel themselves hoping that their effort will in turn attract new investments to the sector. Certainly, one is not thinking of the traditional labor intensive in Hong Kong, but new and emerging industries, such as medical-related engineering, environment friendly industries and so on. The spirit of entrepreneurship will serve as a strong incentive for some individuals and corporations to create new comparative advantages in Hong Kong.

The tradable services sector

The tradable services sector has experienced the highest TFP growth also in the period of 1986–1990 (4.2%). The periods of 1986–1990 (10.2%) and 1991–1995 (11.5%) also saw a large increase in capital growth. The tradable service sector has encountered the lowest average growth of TFP in the period of 1991–1995 (–0.5%). However, this sector has shown a positive TFP growth rate of 2.0% in the period of 1996–2000, during the Asian financial crisis period, and the TFP growth rate further increased to 2.2% in the period 2001–2005, even though the growth of capital remained steady (at 5.4%) while growth in labor has only improved slightly. Such evidence supports the fact that the tradable services sector is the strongest economic sector in Hong Kong. This sector has the highest TFP growth rate of 1.8% for the sample period. With migration of manufacturing to Mainland China, the increase in producer service has helped to expand the tradable service sector. Increasingly, economic resources that were employed in the tradable goods sectors have gradually been restructured into the tradable services sector, especially after the economic recession in 2003. For example, factory buildings have been refurbished into showrooms, art galleries and so on. With time, the tradable services sector will become the favorable sector in the economic restructuring process as more economic resources are geared into businesses in this sector. One potential challenge, however, is the rising competition from nearby economies, especially cities across the border and in other parts of Asia. Nonetheless, competition and challenges from neighboring economies have been a constant factor facing Hong Kong. The appropriate strategy will be to do the best and extend the economy to the highest possible frontier. Economic freedom always serves as a generator of economic opportunities.

The non-tradable goods sector

The non-tradable goods sector has experienced the highest TFP growth in the period of 1986–1990 (3.4%). However, it encountered slow or even negative growth rate of TFP for the remaining periods, with the lowest of –3.6% during the period of the Asian financial crisis. Focus can be drawn to the period of 2001–2005, when this sector reached almost as low as 0.2% growth rate in TFP while the Hong Kong economy has been slowly recovering from recession. Such a low TFP growth rate could be explained by the sharp fall in the growth rates of both capital and labor (from 9.8% to 1.9% and from 3.2% to –7.4%, respectively). In other words, the non-tradable goods sector, which consists of construction and electricity, gas and water, exhibited signs of inefficiency and low productivity, due probably in the case of electricity and gas to over-investment. The non-tradable goods sector has a lowest TFP growth rate of only 0.4% for the whole sample period. Given that this sector is geared to the local economy, output growth is not expected to fare too much, but probably will become static and slow moving. Given that the demand for public utilities, such as electricity and gas, is not expected to rise substantially in the near future, and the possibility of importing from Mainland China, large investment is not expected, unless the need for environmental improvement urges the suppliers to engage and invest in technological advancement.

The non-tradable services sector

The non-tradable services sector has experienced the lowest TFP growth rate (–1.6%) in the period of 1983–1985, but in the following five-year period of 1986–1990, it has encountered a sharp increase of 3.6%, with a big decrease in the growth of capital and labor (capital growth decreased from 13% to 0.6%; labor growth decreased from 3.6% to 2.2%). On the whole, the situation of the non-tradable services sector shares a similar economic trend with the tradable goods sector, characterized by inefficiency, exhibited low marginal products and over-investment. This sector has a negative TFP growth rate (–1.0%) in the post-AFC period of 2001–2005, and a small positive TFP growth rate of 1.2% for the entire sample period. Output growth depends largely on labor, as this sector consists mainly of labor intensive businesses.

4.6 Labor Productivity and Unit Labor Cost

The growth accounting methodology can be extended to study labor productivity and unit labor cost of different industries and economic sectors in Hong Kong.[11]

---

[11] Analysis in this section followed and extended the study in Li (2006).

In theory, the TFP estimates show the long-term development trend of individual industries or sectors, labor productivity and unit labor cost figures can complement the TFP analysis by showing short-term changes in productivity and cost competitiveness.

Labor productivity is indicated by the ratio of real output to the number of people engaged. This effectively gives the average productivity of individual workers. Unit labor cost is indicated by the ratio of the index of average real monthly adjusted compensation per person engaged to the labor productivity index. The year 1990 is used as the base year in the estimation. The unit labor cost shows the short-term competitiveness of labor. The data for the sample period is gathered from the various issues of the *Quarterly Report of Employment* and the *Vacancies and Payroll Statistics* (*EVS*) from the Census and Statistics Department of Hong Kong.

Between labor productivity and labor unit cost, there exists a contemporaneous negative correlation, meaning that the higher the labor productivity, the lower is the unit labor cost, keeping constant the level of compensation or wages paid to workers. The negative correlation relationship can only be broken unless real compensation or wages to workers rises faster than labor productivity. But this would not normally happen as wages paid to workers are rigid in the short-term in most cases and real compensation could not rise faster than labor productivity given the same period of time. There is thus a lead-lag effect in which the rise in labor productivity would cause a rise in unit labor cost after some periods of time.

Before looking at the labor productivity and unit labor cost of different industries and economic sectors, it would be useful to compare the average figures between labor productivity and unit labor cost in the sample period. Table 4.9 reports the average labor productivity growth rates and the average unit labor cost growth rates for the 21 industries and 4 economic sectors in Hong Kong for the period 1981–2005. The industries and economic sectors in Table 4.9 are ranked according to the average growth rates of labor productivity in the sample period. There are a total of 9 industries which experienced an average labor productivity growth rates at or higher than 5%, 11 industries with a growth rate lower than 5%. The real estate industry is the only one with a negative growth rate in labor productivity. The other three low growth industries include restaurants, land transport and community, social and personal services. These are the traditional low-skill and labor intensive service industries.

On the average growth rates in unit labor cost, there are a total of 14 industries that experienced a positive growth rate, with the largest of 8.34% in real estates, followed by insurance (3.62%), mining and quarrying (2.67%), agriculture and fishing (2.62%), finance (2.44%), hotels (1.65%) and business services (1.59%). The remaining seven industries have an average growth rate of less than 1% in unit labor cost. A total of 7 industries (manufacturing, communications, electricity, gas and water, air transport, import and export trades, water transport, and land transport) have experienced a negative average growth rate in unit labor cost. Most of the negative growth rates are small (below 1%), with the exception of electricity, gas and water (–3.61%). Most of these seven industries are competitive or require low skill. One can conclude that other than real estate, the average unit labor cost has not increased too much.

TABLE 4.9 Labor productivity and unit labor cost: Average percentage growth rates

	1981–2005	Labor productivity	Unit labor cost
Industries	Mining and quarrying*	12.74	2.67
	Manufacturing*	8.40	–0.52
	Communications	8.39	–0.05
	Electricity, gas and water*	7.36	–3.61
	Agriculture and fishing	7.20	2.62
	Finance	6.45	2.44
	Air transport	6.12	–0.50
	Other transport	5.15	0.19
	Storage**	5.00	0.69
	Import and export trades*	4.82	–0.05
	Water transport	4.46	–0.57
	Wholesale*	4.33	0.32
	Construction	3.94	0.36
	Hotels	3.61	1.65
	Insurance	3.27	3.62
	Business services	3.16	1.59
	Retail*	2.89	0.89
	Community, social and personal services	1.15	0.50
	Land transport	0.43	–0.06
	Restaurants***	0.34	0.08
	Real estates	–4.32	8.34
Economic sectors	Non-tradable goods	5.16	–1.40
	Tradable services***	3.80	0.46
	Tradable goods	2.77	–0.71
	Non-tradable services*	1.83	0.87

Notes: *, **, *** refer to the sample periods of 1982–2005, 1983–2005 and 1984–2005, respectively.

Indeed, when the average growth rates of labor productivity and unit labor cost are compared, there are 19 industries where the average growth rate in labor productivity is higher than the average growth rate of unit labor cost. There are two exceptions. The average unit labor cost growth rate in insurance (3.62%) has been faster than the average labor productivity growth rate (3.27%), though the difference is small. The difference in real estate is much larger, with 8.34% in the average growth rate in unit labor cost and –4.32% in the average growth rate in labor productivity. Real estate in the only outlier industry, where labor productivity is low and unit labor cost is high, suggesting a high degree of inefficiency and over employment in the real estate industry.

All the four economic sectors shown in Table 4.9 have a positive average growth rate in labor productivity, with the non-tradable goods having the highest of 5.16%, followed by tradable services (3.80%), tradable goods (2.77%) and non-tradable services

(1.83%). The average growth rates in labor productivity are definitely higher than unit labor cost in all four sectors. Two economic sectors have experienced a positive growth in unit labor cost (non-tradable services with 0.87% and tradable services with 0.46%), while tradable services show a negative growth (–0.71%) in unit labor cost, followed by non-tradable goods (–1.40%). On the whole, the unit labor cost has experienced only a mild increase in the sample period. When compared between labor productivity and unit labor cost, it is certain from the four economic sectors that the average growth in labor productivity has exceeded the average growth in unit labor cost.

One can conclude from Table 4.9 that in the twenty five years (1981–2005), labor productivity has risen much faster than unit labor cost. This is true in the majority of industries, with the notable exception of real estate. Efficiency can appropriately be measured by the percentage gap between labor productivity and unit labor cost. A larger gap indicates a more efficient or productive industry. Given the rather low average increase in unit labor cost, Hong Kong industries appear to be quite cost competitive and businesses are cost conscious in their investments.

Under normal circumstances, there exists a contemporaneous negative correlation between labor productivity and unit labor cost. In other words, a rise in labor productivity is matched with a fall in unit labor cost. This relationship can simply be examined by calculating the correlation ratio between labor productivity growth rates and unit labor cost growth rates. Table 4.10 shows the correlation ratios ranked by their negative signs. Among the 21 industries, there are a total of 17 industries with the expected negative correlation ratio. There are seven industries (air transport, hotels, finance, retail, water transport, communications, and business services) with a negative correlation ratio larger than 0.6. These industries face strong foreign competition. The remaining four industries (real estates, community, social and personal services, mining and quarrying and agriculture and fishing) have shown instead a positive correlation ratio, and they are the least exposed to foreign competition. In the two service industry of real estate and community, social and personal services, their unit labor cost has risen along with, or even faster than, labor productivity. The two primary industries (mining and quarrying, and agriculture and fishing) are less important "sunset" industries in Hong Kong. It is likely that their unit labor cost has to rise in order to attract workers into the industry.

Table 4.10 also shows the correlation ratios for the four economic sectors. The non-tradable services sector is the only sector that shows a positive correlation between the growth in labor productivity and the growth in unit labor cost. This is in line with the argument of a lack of foreign competition in this sector. The negative correlation ratio for tradable goods (–0.39) is higher than the other two economic sectors of non-tradable goods (–0.06) and tradable services (–0.05).

To take a closer look at the relationship between labor productivity and unit labor cost, one can examine the trend in the entire sample period. The analysis can be presented in four aspects. First, the level performance (with 1990 = 100) shows the overall trend movement of labor productivity and unit labor cost. This gives the direction of change over time. The alternative as discussed in Table 4.9 is to consider the growth rate of labor productivity and unit labor cost. This magnifies the change in the trend over time.

There are two possibilities to study the contemporaneous correlation between labor productivity and unit labor cost. How fast the change in unit labor cost is when

TABLE 4.10 Correlation of growth rates between labor productivity and unit labor cost

Industries	Ratio	Economic sectors	Ratio
Air transport	−0.90	Tradable goods	−0.39
Hotels	−0.79	Non-tradable goods	−0.06
Finance	−0.77	Tradable services	−0.05
Retail	−0.69	Non-tradable services	0.15
Water transport	−0.64		
Communications	−0.63		
Business services	−0.61		
Insurance	−0.60		
Restaurants	−0.60		
Other transport	−0.59		
Storage	−0.55		
Electricity, gas and water	−0.45		
Import and export trades	−0.43		
Land transport	−0.36		
Manufacturing	−0.35		
Construction	−0.22		
Wholesale	−0.19		
Real estates	0.01		
Community, social and personal services	0.19		
Mining and quarrying	0.25		
Agriculture and fishing	0.54		

there is a change in labor productivity can be examined by showing the contemporaneous trend of labor productivity and the contemporaneous (t), the lag-one period ($t-1$) and lag-two period ($t-2$) trends of the unit labor cost. In other words, when labor productivity changes at contemporaneous time t, the concern is how soon unit labor cost can catch up, whether it is the contemporaneous or at same time period (t), the following time period ($t-1$), or the following two periods ($t-2$). It is unlikely that unit labor cost adjusts to labor productivity contemporaneously. It is more likely that such adjustment takes place at $t-1$, $t-2$ or even longer. Such an analysis is useful in that it can show the time lag in unit labor cost needed for the adjustment. In simple words, how fast unit labor cost catches up with labor productivity? In addition, when looking at the sample period, it is possible that the lag behavior changes in different time periods. For example, it would be $t-1$ in the 1980s, but $t-2$ in the 1990s. These four possibilities (level trend, growth trend, 1-lag unit labor cost trend and 2-lag unit labor cost trend) can be presented as portions (a), (b), (c), and (d), respectively, in a combined figure for the 21 industries and the four economic sectors.

Let's begin with the analysis on economic sectors before proceeding to the individual industries, the four-portion figures can provide a relationship between labor productivity and unit labor cost. Figures 4.2–4.5 show the labor productivity and unit labor cost for the tradable goods sector, tradable services sector, non-tradable

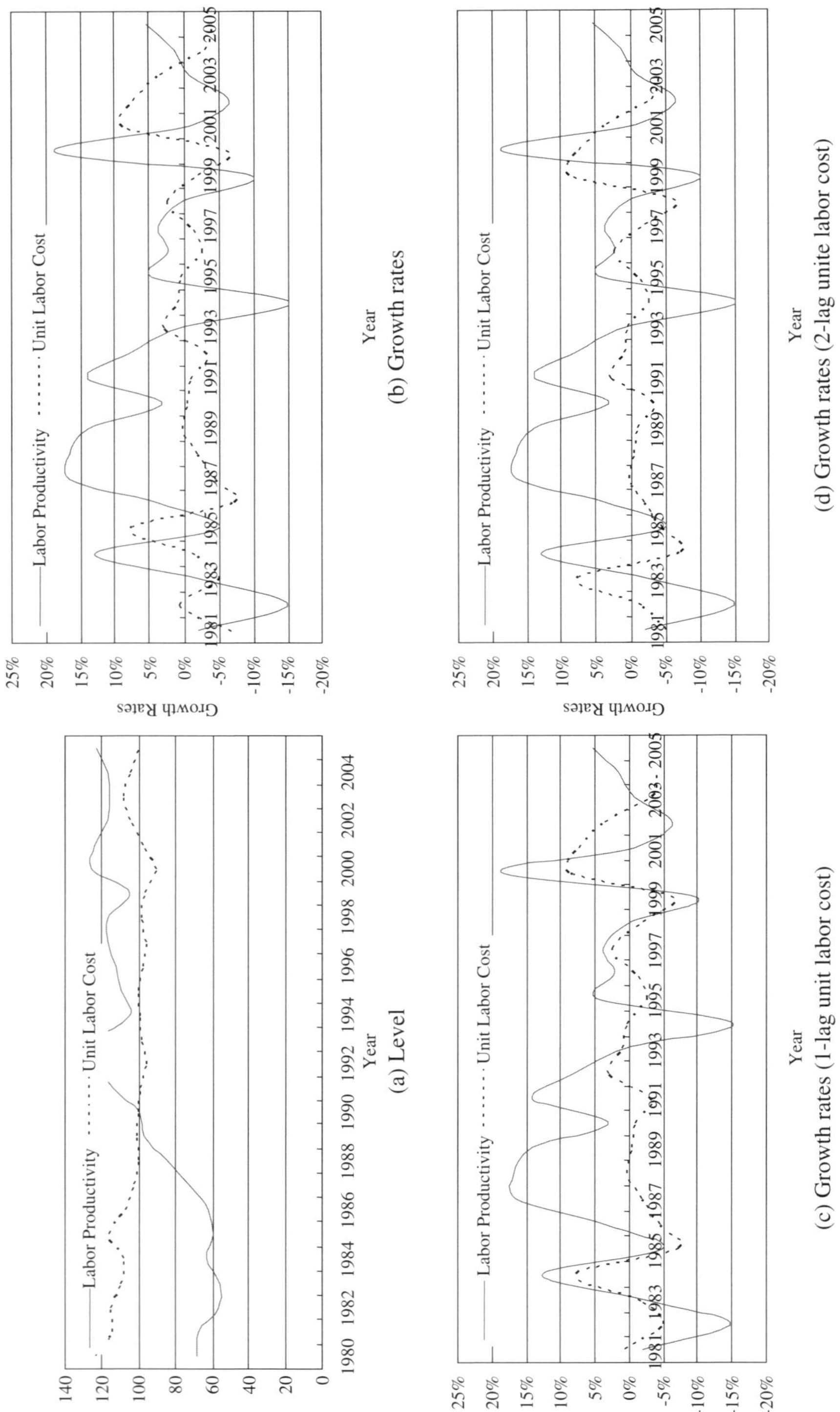

FIGURE 4.2 Labor productivity and unit labor cost: Tradable goods sector

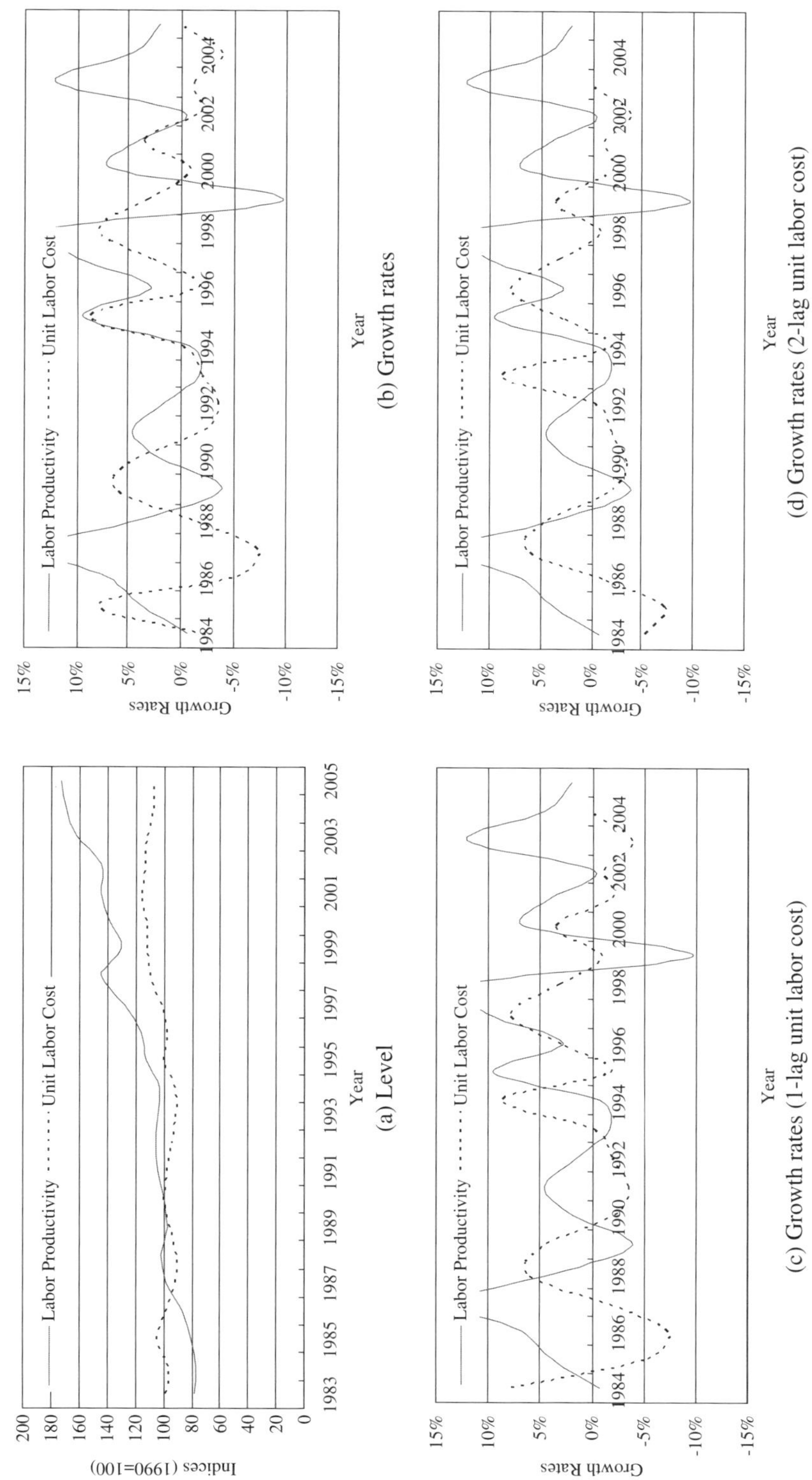

FIGURE 4.3 Labor productivity and unit labor cost: Tradable services sector

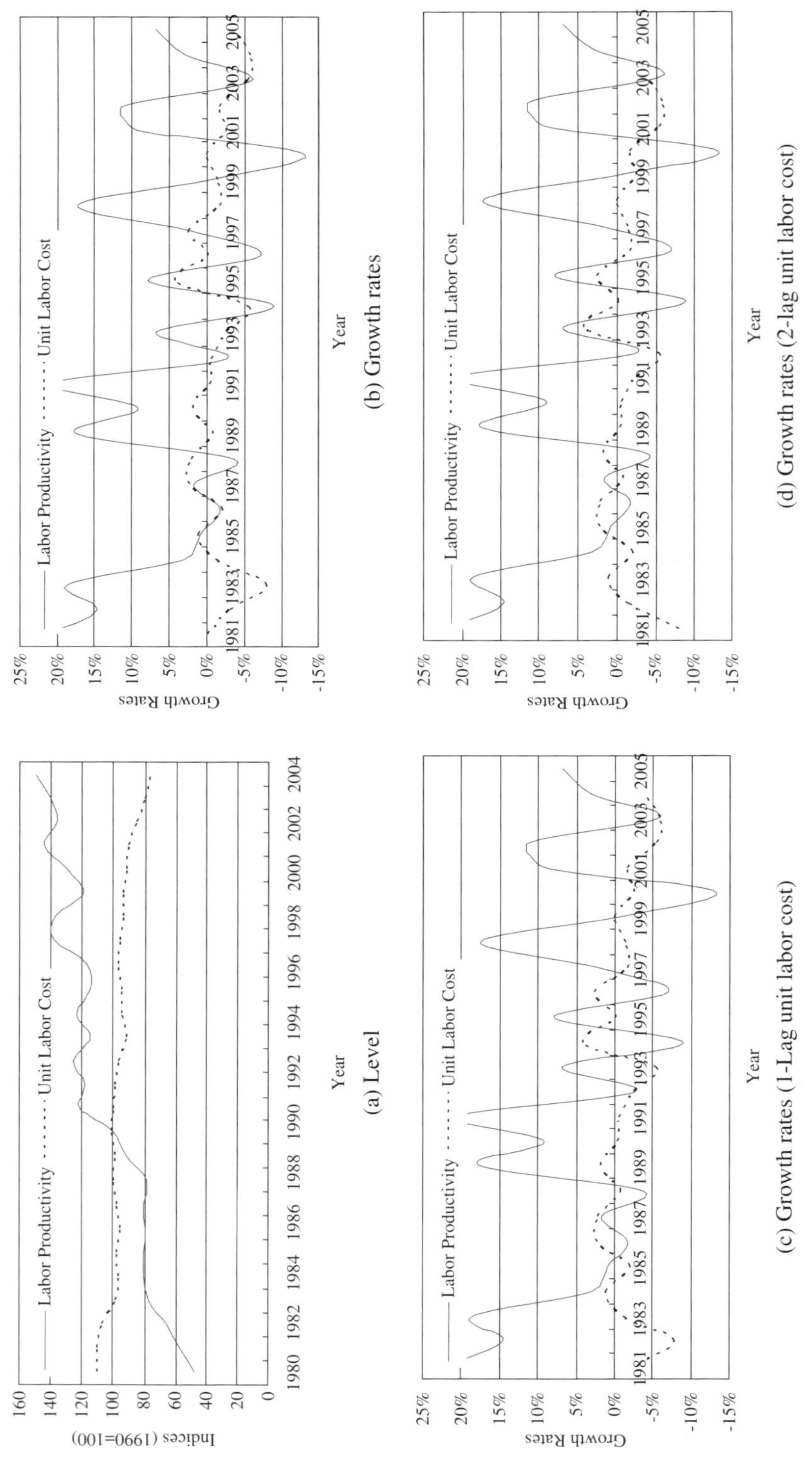

FIGURE 4.4 Labor productivity and unit labor cost: Non-tradable goods sector

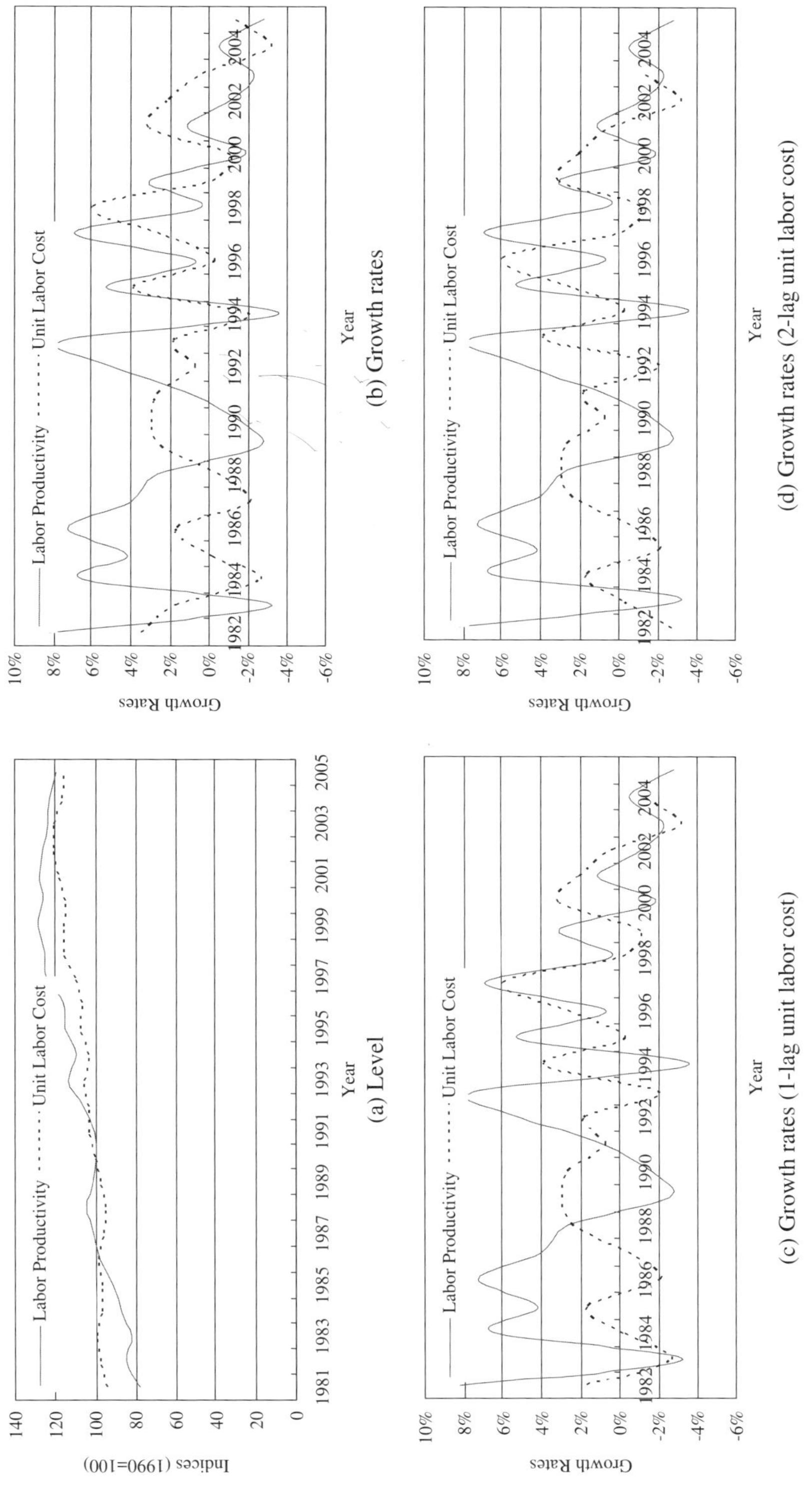

FIGURE 4.5 Labor productivity and unit labor cost: Non-tradable services sector

goods sector, and non-tradable services sector, respectively, for the sample period. The discussion will look at the level trend shown by the (a) portion of the figure, the growth trends shown by the (b), the 1–lag and 2–lag unit labor cost trends of (c) and (d) portions, respectively, of the figure. In most cases, the contemporaneous and 1–lag scenarios are more relevant than the 2-lag scenario.

Figure 4.2: The tradable goods sector

i) The level trend: One clear feature is that labor productivity in this sector has been rising since 1985, while the unit labor cost has been maintained at a stable trend until the late 1990s. As the manufacturing activities began its "sunset" stage from the mid–1980s, demand for industrial workers in Hong Kong has fallen, and the small manufacturing sector suggests that workers who remain in the industries are the more productive and efficient ones. Hence, despite a stable unit labor cost, labor productivity has increased. The high productivity can serve as incentives for further development and attract new investment in this sector.

ii) The growth trend: The growth rate of labor productivity in this sector has fluctuated, especially in early 1980s, early 1990s and late 1990s during the Asian financial crisis periods. The unit labor cost, on the contrary, has shown a more steady growth trend, though there were high growth rates in 1984–1985 and 2000–2002. The growth rate of labor productivity and unit labor cost moves in opposite directions in 1982 and 1987–1993, indicating that the growth in labor productivity in this period was the direct result of the falling unit labor cost. When the unit labor cost is shown using the 1-lag, one can see an overall close correlation or connection between the movement of labor productivity and unit labor cost, especially in 1983–1985, 1996–1998, and 1999–2001 periods. These are the periods when unit labor cost rose and fell together with labor productivity.

Figure 4.3: The tradable services sector

i) The level trend: Labor productivity in this sector has shown an increasing trend from about 80 index points at the beginning of the sample period to over 160 index points at the end of the sample period. On the contrary, the unit labor cost has experienced a stable trend. The tradable services sector does face an internationally competitive price, and growth in the sector must have come from higher productivity.

ii) The growth trend: The two trends have experienced sharp changes in growth rates. Diverging trends in the movement of labor productivity and unit labor cost appeared in the 1985–1992 period, suggesting that the two variables moved in opposite directions. One contemporaneous relationship appeared in the mid–1990s from 1994 to 2002 when the growth rates of labor productivity and unit labor cost moved at the same time. In this period, unit labor cost adjustment is quite contemporaneous. The two 1-lag growth trends do not show any close relationship. But in the case of the 2-lag growth trends, a close relationship occurred in much of the 1980s from 1985–1989. In other words, unit labor cost adjustment was delayed by at least 2 time periods in the 1980s, but the delay has been improved. By the 1990s, the adjustment is contemporaneous, as shown in the (b) portion of Fig. 4.3. In other words, this sector has grown to become more efficient and competitive between the 1980s and 1990s.

Figure 4.4: The non-tradable goods sector

i) The level trend: Labor productivity in this sector has risen by 100 index points (from about 50 to 150 between the beginning and the end of the sample period). The major contribution to the increase in labor productivity comes from electricity, gas and water. The unit labor cost, on the contrary, has mildly been decreasing in the entire sample period.

ii) The growth trend: Labor productivity has shown drastic changes in growth, with sharp increases and decreases in different periods. On the contrary, the growth trend of unit labor cost is much milder. The two contemporaneous trends can be found in the two periods of 1984–1986 and 1993–1996. In these two periods, changes in unit labor cost occurred instantly with growth in labor productivity. In the case of 1-lag, the two trends do not seem to match before 2000, but show some similarity since 2001 or 2002 during the falling period and the rise in growth rates after 2003, though the magnitude of the growth rates differed between the two trends. It seems more appropriate to use the 1-lag trend to explain the post-AFC situation. Unit labor cost adjusts to labor productivity either contemporaneously or lag one time period in the non-tradable goods sector.

Figure 4.5: The non-tradable services sector

i) The level trend: The two trends appear to move together in the same direction. The two trends have risen continuously until the late 1990s when the Asian financial crisis emerged, then leveled off. The magnitude of increase is larger in labor productivity (from about 80 index points in 1980 to over 120 index points in 1999) than in unit labor cost (from about 90 index points in 1980 to about 110 index points in 1999). It can be argued that the increase in the unit labor cost has contributed to the fall in competitiveness in this sector. Since the price and cost of non-tradable services do not face competition from imports, their "monopolistic" nature has contributed to increases in price and cost during economic upturns. The behavior in the price and cost of most non-tradable services tends to be rigid downwards, meaning that they can easily be increased during the boom periods but are reluctant to decrease during recessions.

ii) The growth trend: The two trends have experienced sharp increases and decreases in their growth rates. A dichotomy appears between the two trends at different time periods. Fluctuation of growth rates in labor productivity appears to be higher in the 1980s and 1990s. But its growth rates have become milder since the Asian financial crisis in 1998. On the contrary, the growth rates of unit labor cost has remained mild in the 1980s, but have fluctuated more sharply since the mid–1990s. The period 1993–1994 provided a clear case of contemporaneous adjustment between labor productivity and unit labor cost. Again, this is the period where the economic boom was rapidly building up in Hong Kong. Similarly, the period 1999–2003 has shown another contemporaneous adjustment between labor productivity and unit labor cost. The two 1-lag scenarios appear in 1982–1984 and 1996–1998, when the two trends moved together. In conclusion, unit labor cost in this sector tends to adjust to labor productivity either in the current timer period or lag one time period.

One observation from the four economic sectors is that the unit labor cost adjusts to labor productivity quite quickly, either contemporaneously or lag one time period. The good news is that the Hong Kong economy is efficient and information flow is quick. The bad news is that should any economic shocks occur in Hong Kong, the economy will experience sharp fluctuations, thereby increasing overall economic volatility, as discussed in Chapter 3. Indeed, while the Hong Kong economy is open and free, such a feature can also capture shocks and uncertainties developed or originated elsewhere in the region or in the world economy that can easily contagion or impose both direct and indirect impact on the Hong Kong economy.

The four presentations (level trend, growth trend, 1-lag unit labor cost and 2-lag unit labor cost) can be provided to the individual industries in Hong Kong, though the industries are grouped according to the economic sectors. Figures 4.6–4.8 examine the three industries in the tradable goods sector. Figures 4.9–4.20 show the twelve tradable services industries. The next two figures look at the two industries in the non-tradable goods sector, while the remaining four figures present the four industries in the non-tradable services sector.

The Three Industries in the Tradable Goods Sector

Figure 4.6: Agriculture and fishing

i) The level trend: It shows a rising labor productivity trend that has revised upwards after the Asian financial crisis in 1998. The unit labor cost trend is steady, but it has fluctuated more since 1997, due probably to the different periods of health hazards (for example, chicken flu in 1997–1998 and SARS in 2003). On the whole, labor productivity has risen faster than unit labor cost, suggesting the industry is competitive.

ii) The growth trend: Labor productivity has experienced a positive growth rate from the early 1980s up to the mid–1990s. The labor productivity growth trend has been unsteady since 1997, with a negative larger than ten percent in 1998 and 2002, but it has reached a big jump in year 2000, with a growth rate of 47.04%. The unit labor cost growth rates have also fluctuated more since the early 1990s, with a strong growth of 35.28% in 2000. Probably due to seasonal factors and the small size of the industry, unit labor cost tends to adjust contemporaneously with labor productivity in agriculture and fishing.

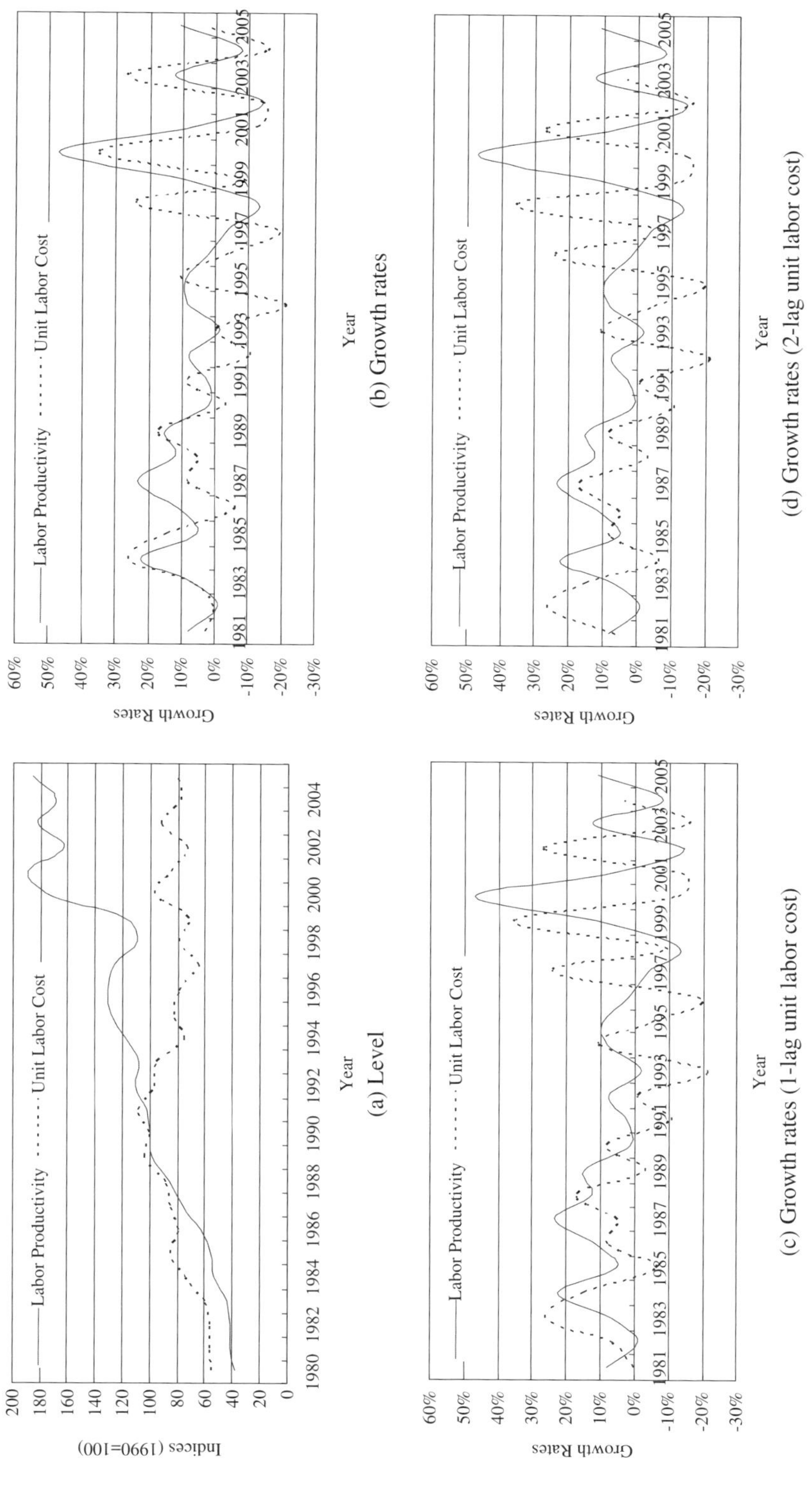

FIGURE 4.6 Labor productivity and unit labor cost: Agriculture and fishing

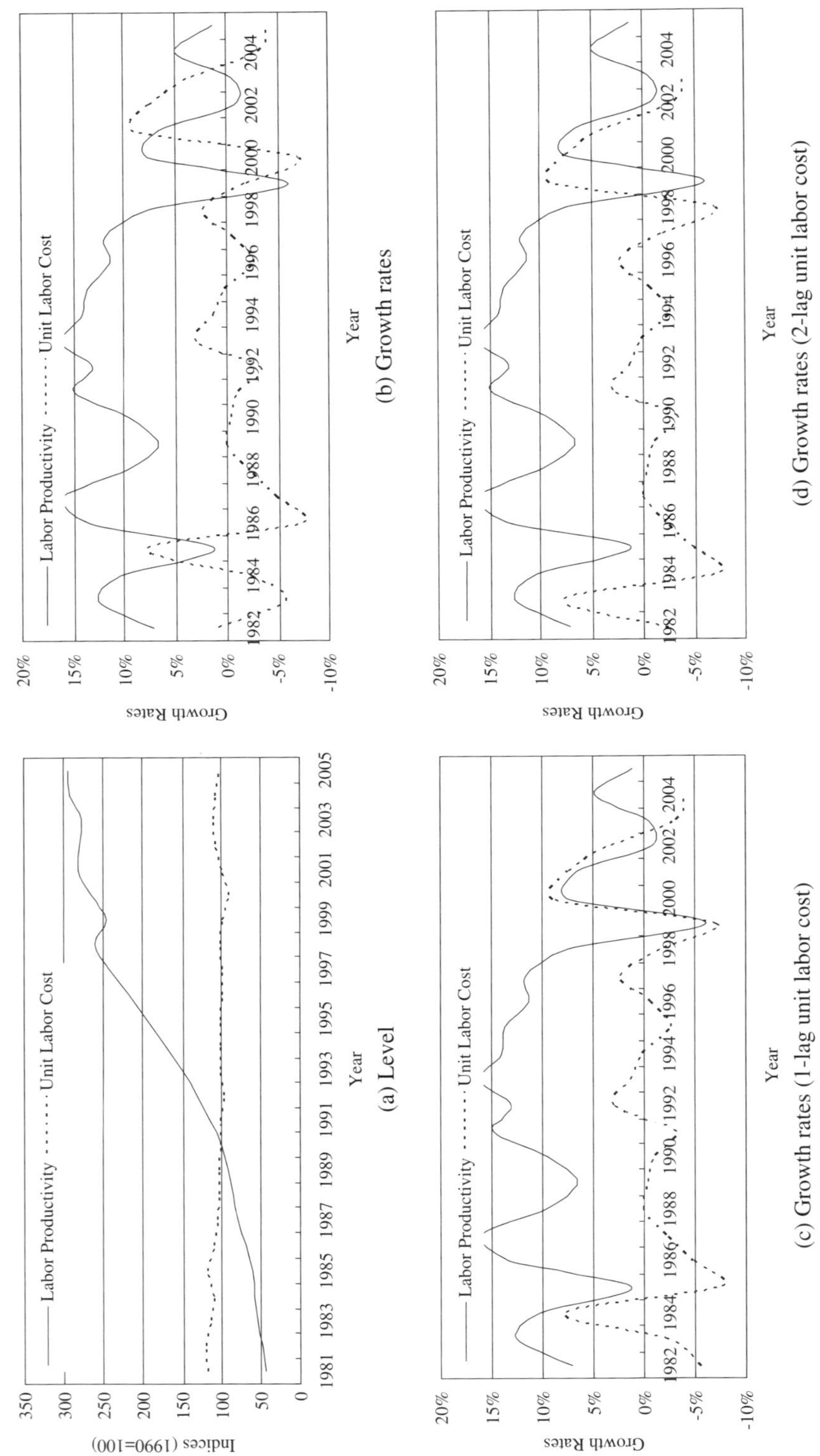

FIGURE 4.7 Labor productivity and unit labor cost: Manufacturing

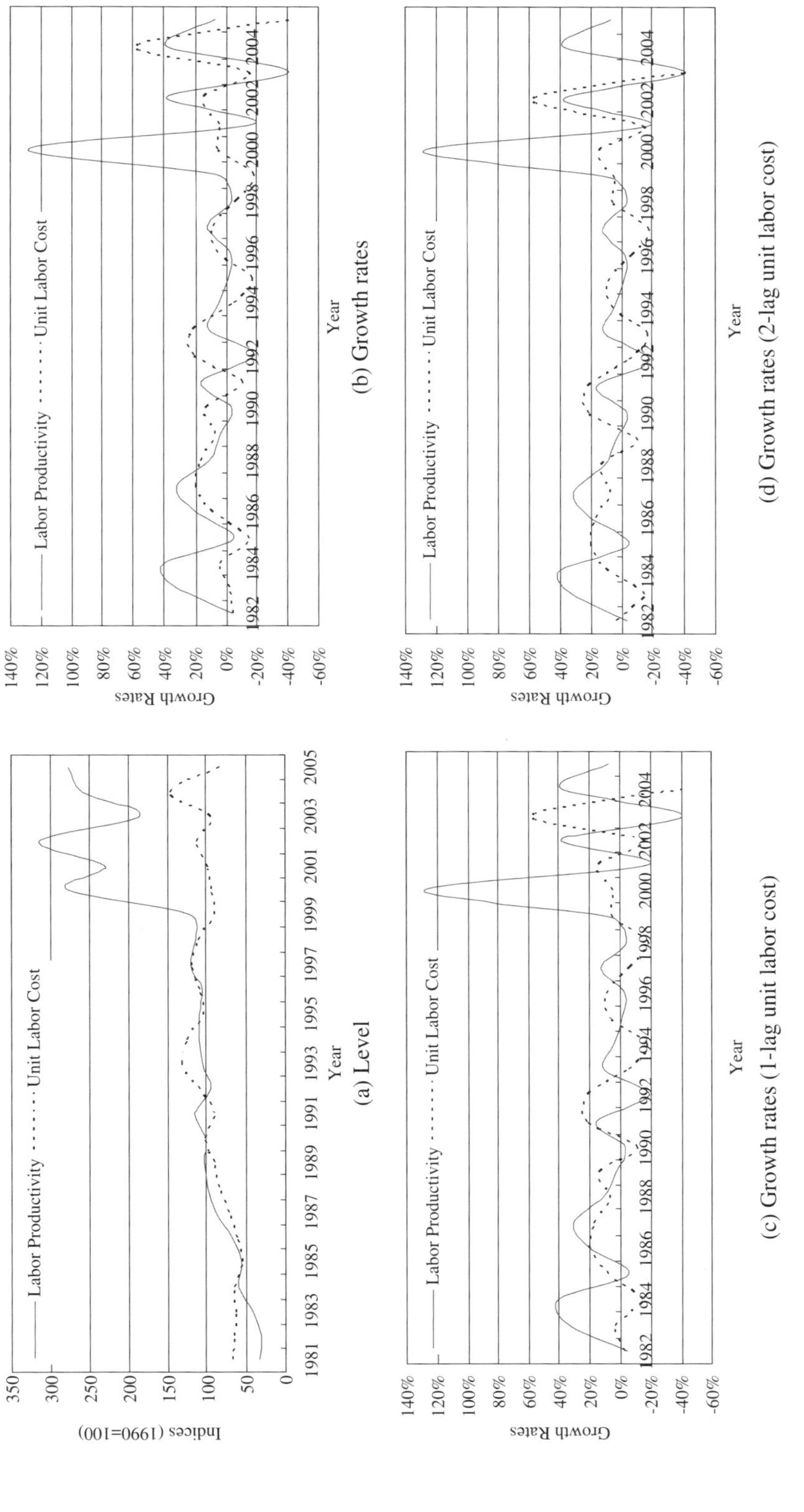

FIGURE 4.8 Labor productivity and unit labor cost: Mining and quarrying

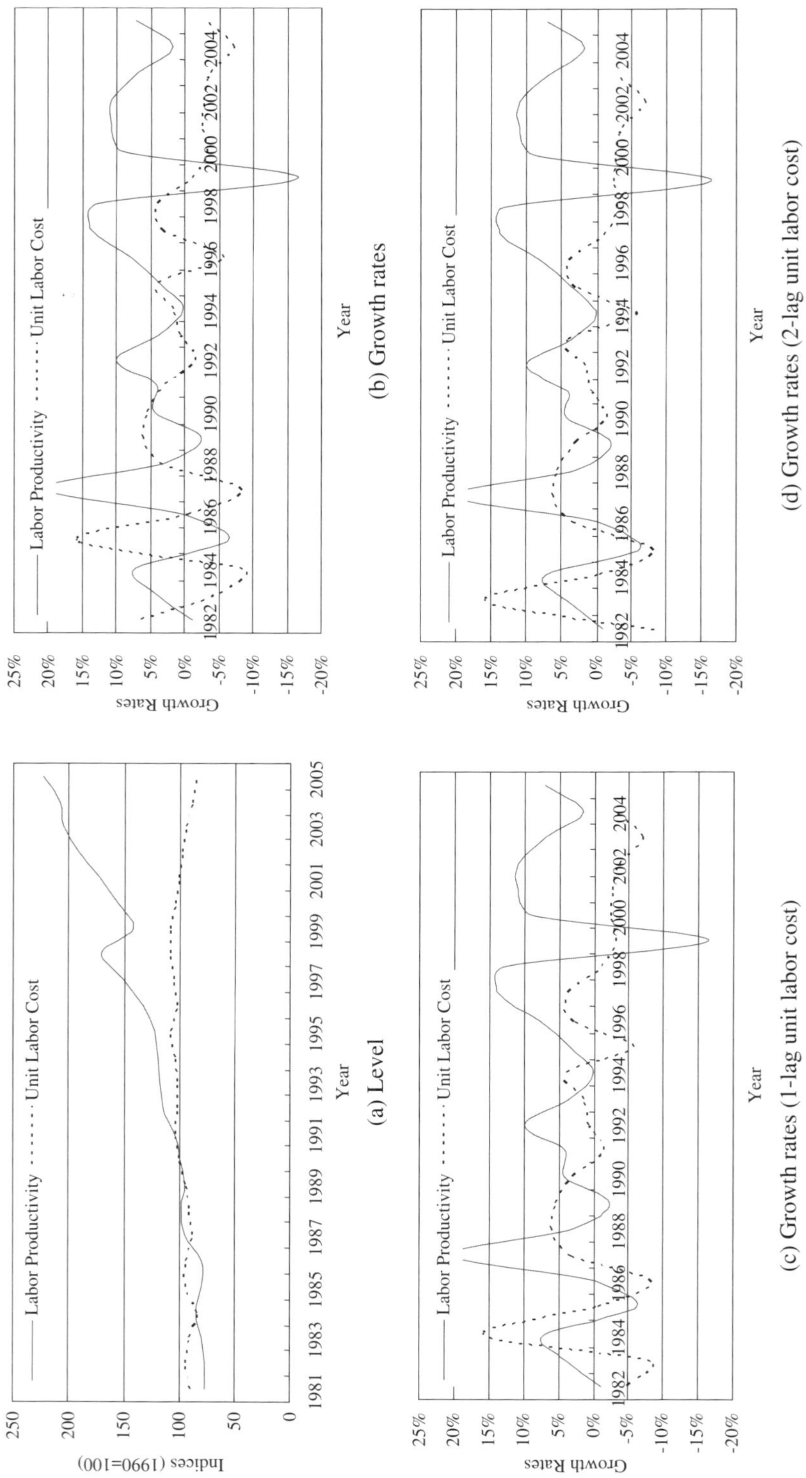

(a) Level

(b) Growth rates

(c) Growth rates (1-lag unit labor cost)

(d) Growth rates (2-lag unit labor cost)

FIGURE 4.9 Labor productivity and unit labor cost: Import and export trades

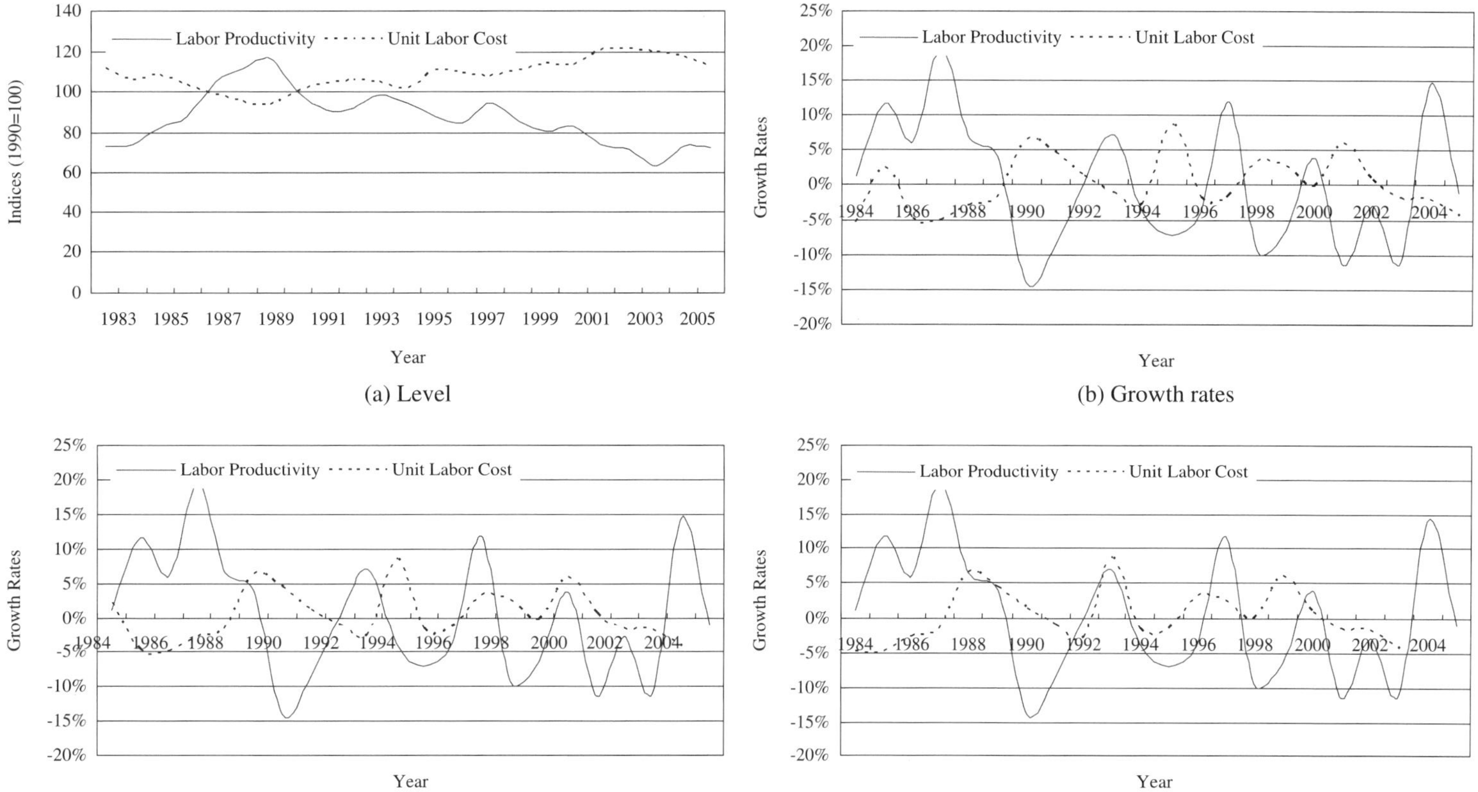

(a) Level

(b) Growth rates

(c) Growth rates (1-lag unit labor cost)

(d) Growth rates (2-lag unit labor cost)

FIGURE 4.10 Labor productivity and unit labor cost: Restaurants

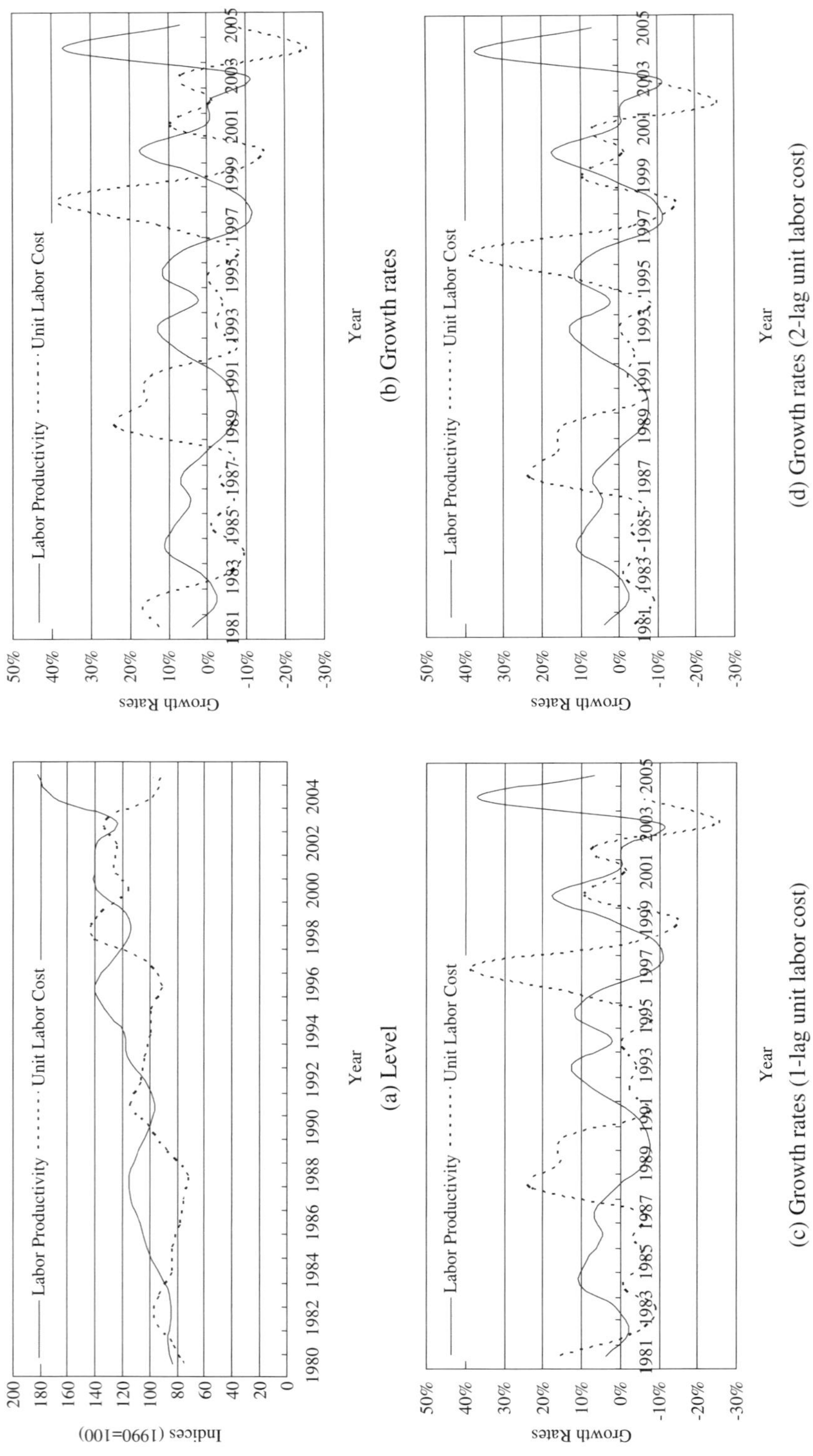

FIGURE 4.11 Labor productivity and unit labor cost: Hotels

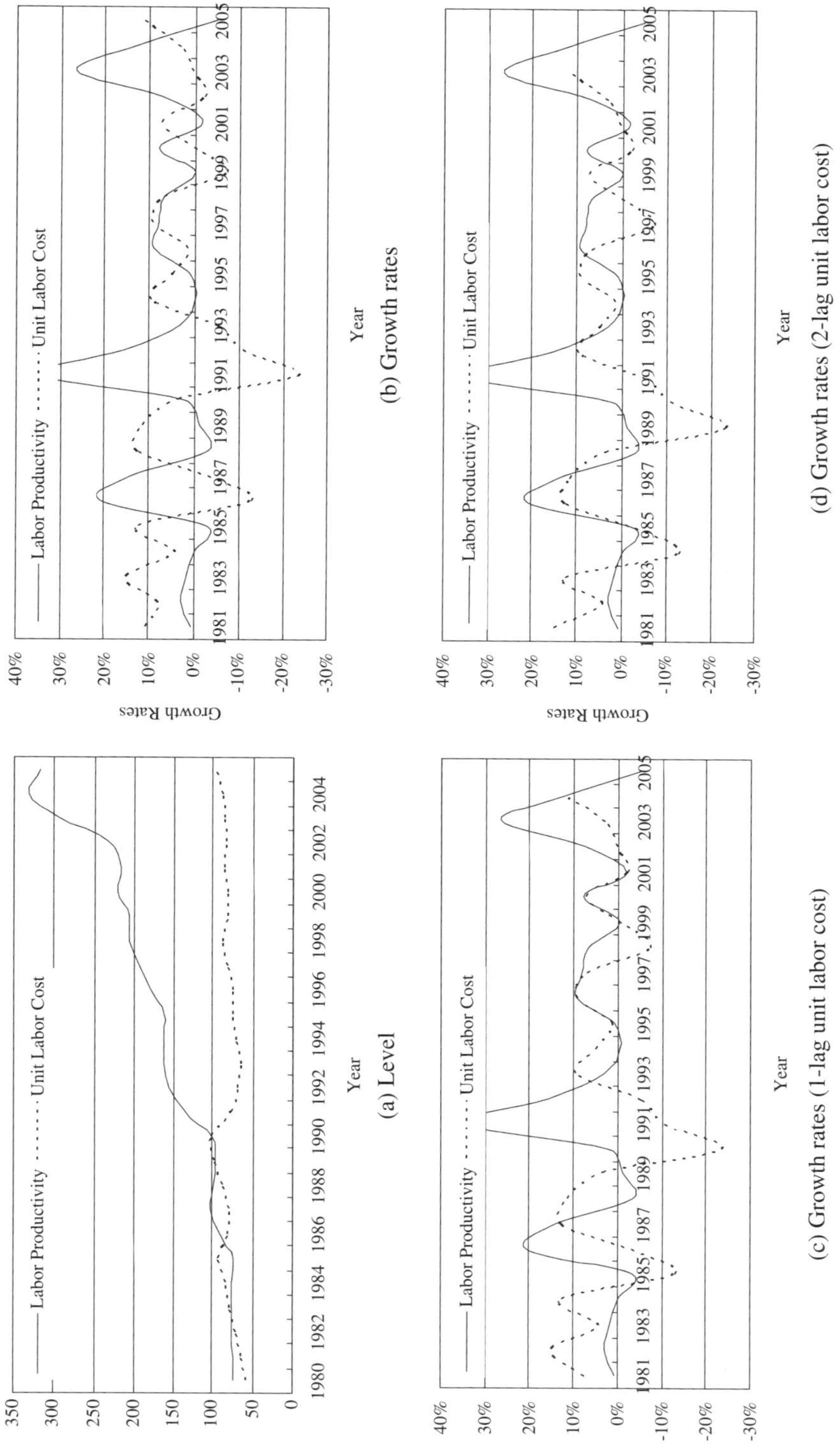

FIGURE 4.12 Labor productivity and unit labor cost: Finance

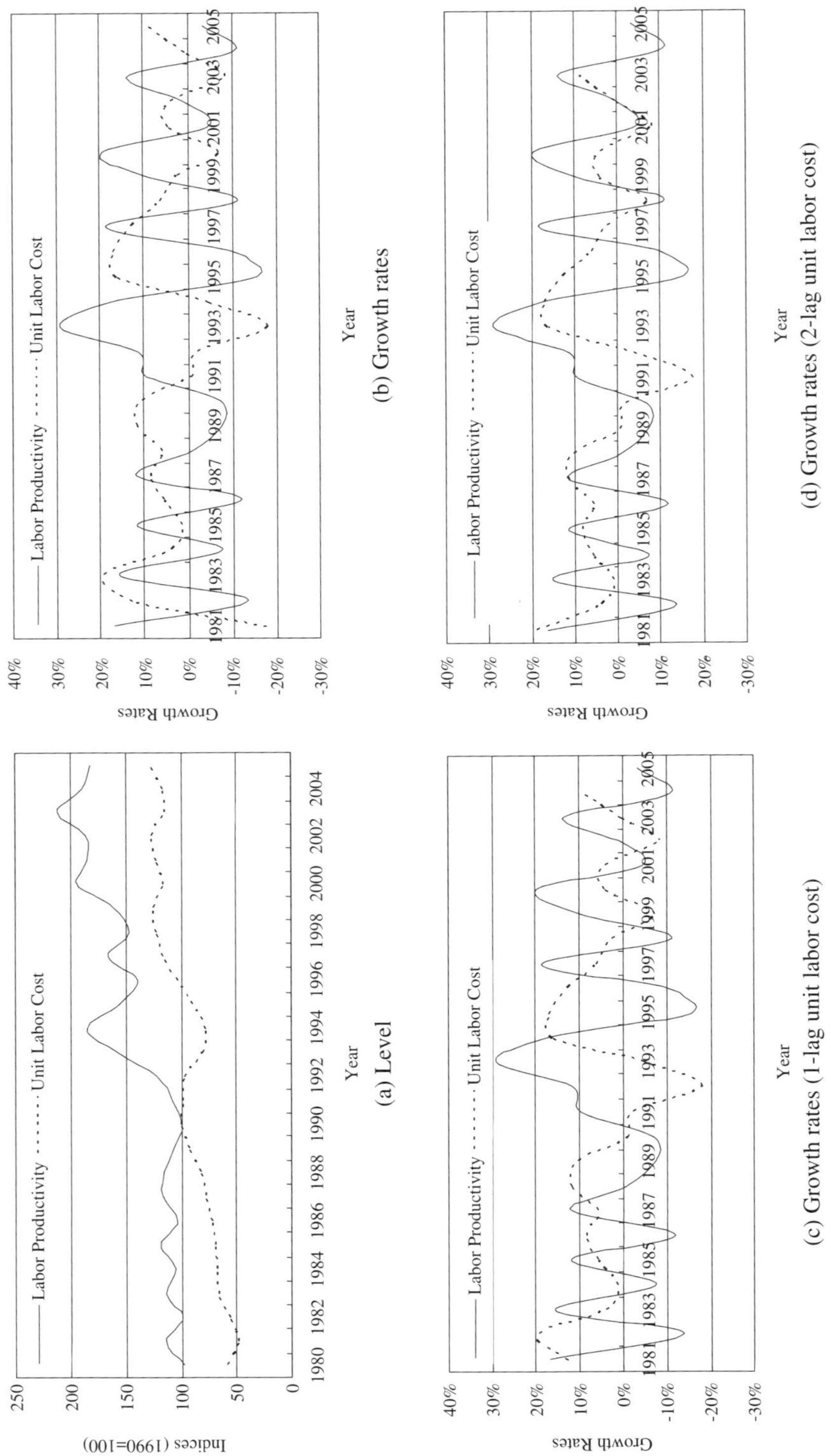

FIGURE 4.13 Labor productivity and unit labor cost: Insurance

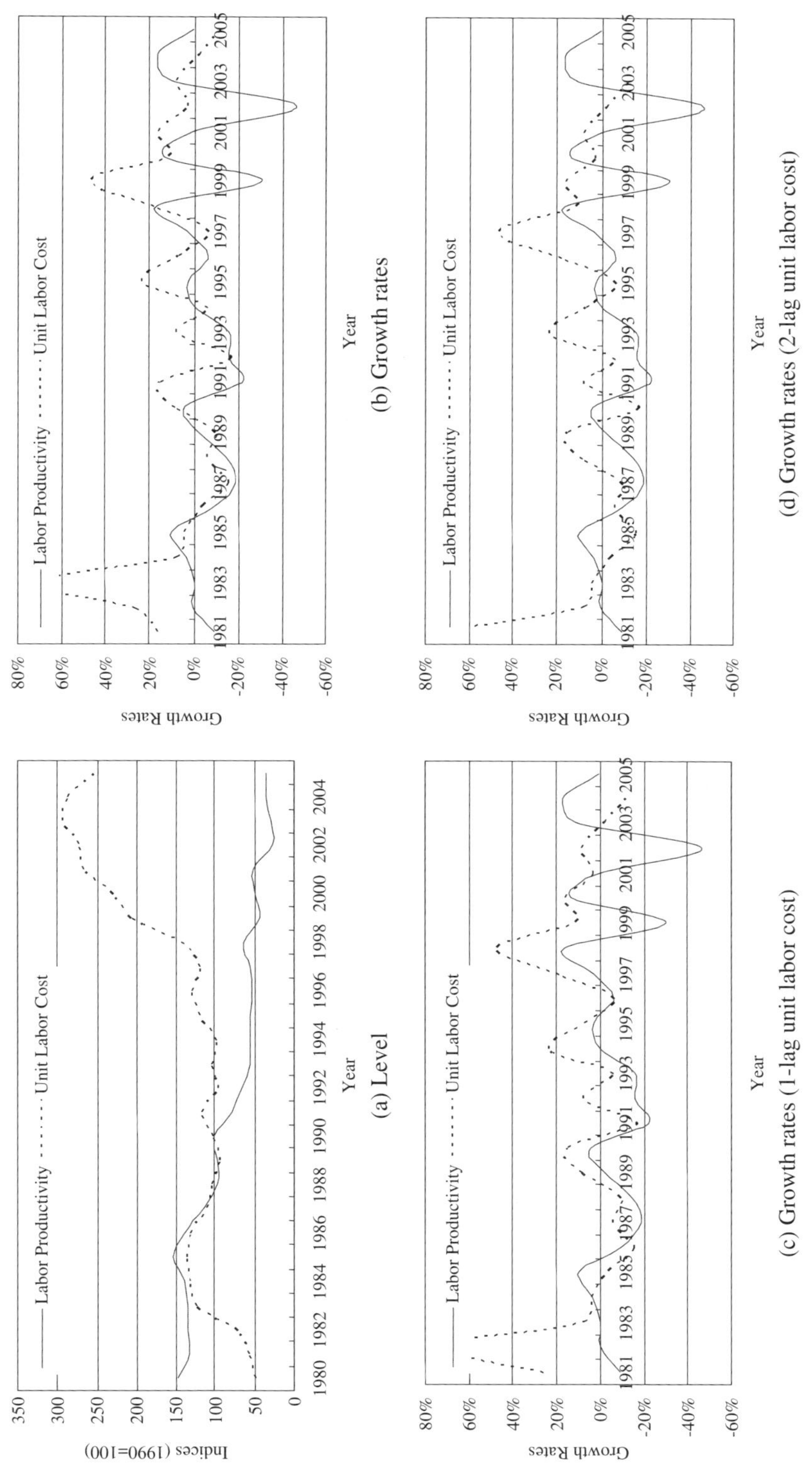

FIGURE 4.14 Labor productivity and unit labor cost: Real estate

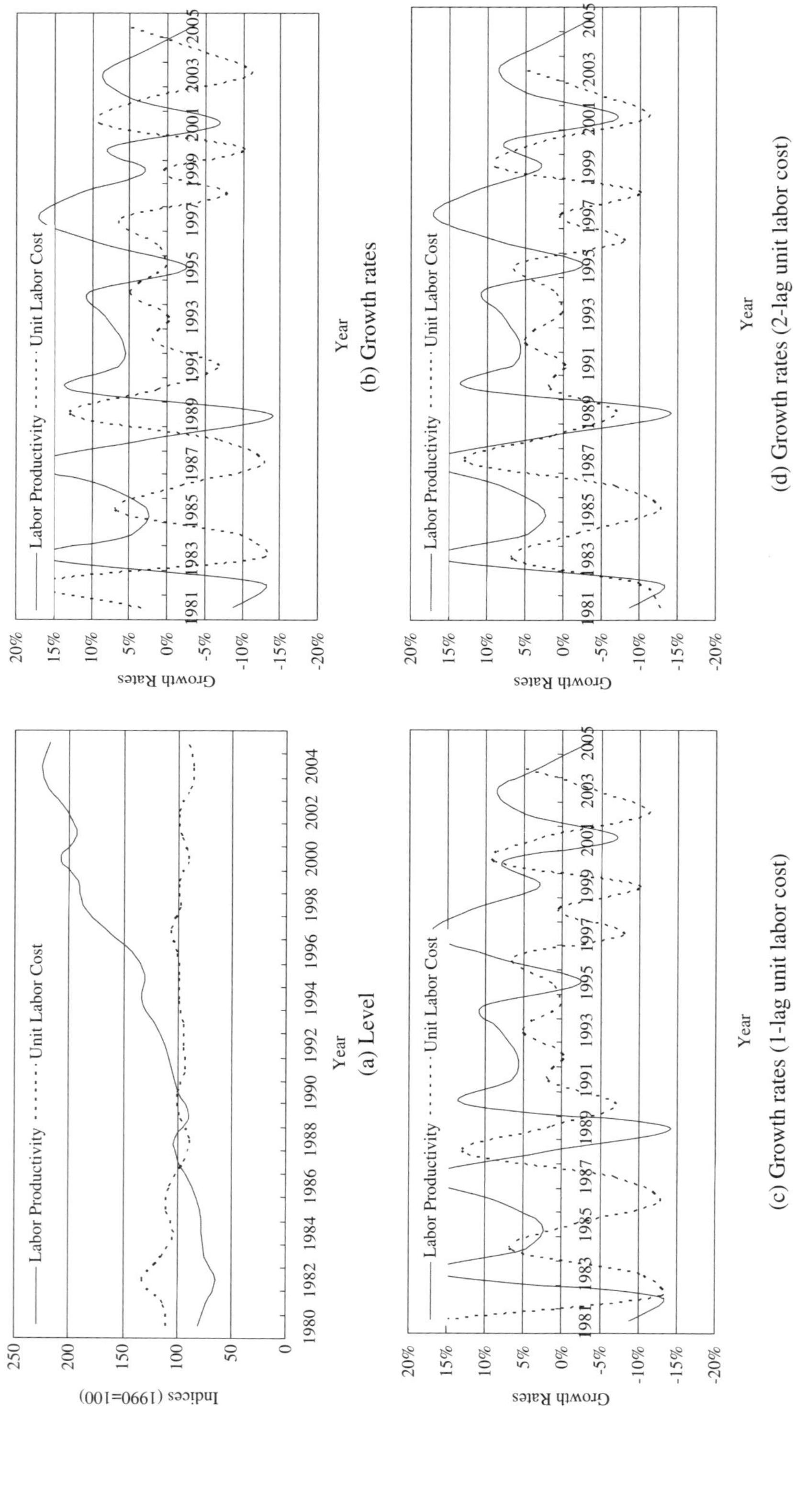

FIGURE 4.15 Labor productivity and unit labor cost: Business services

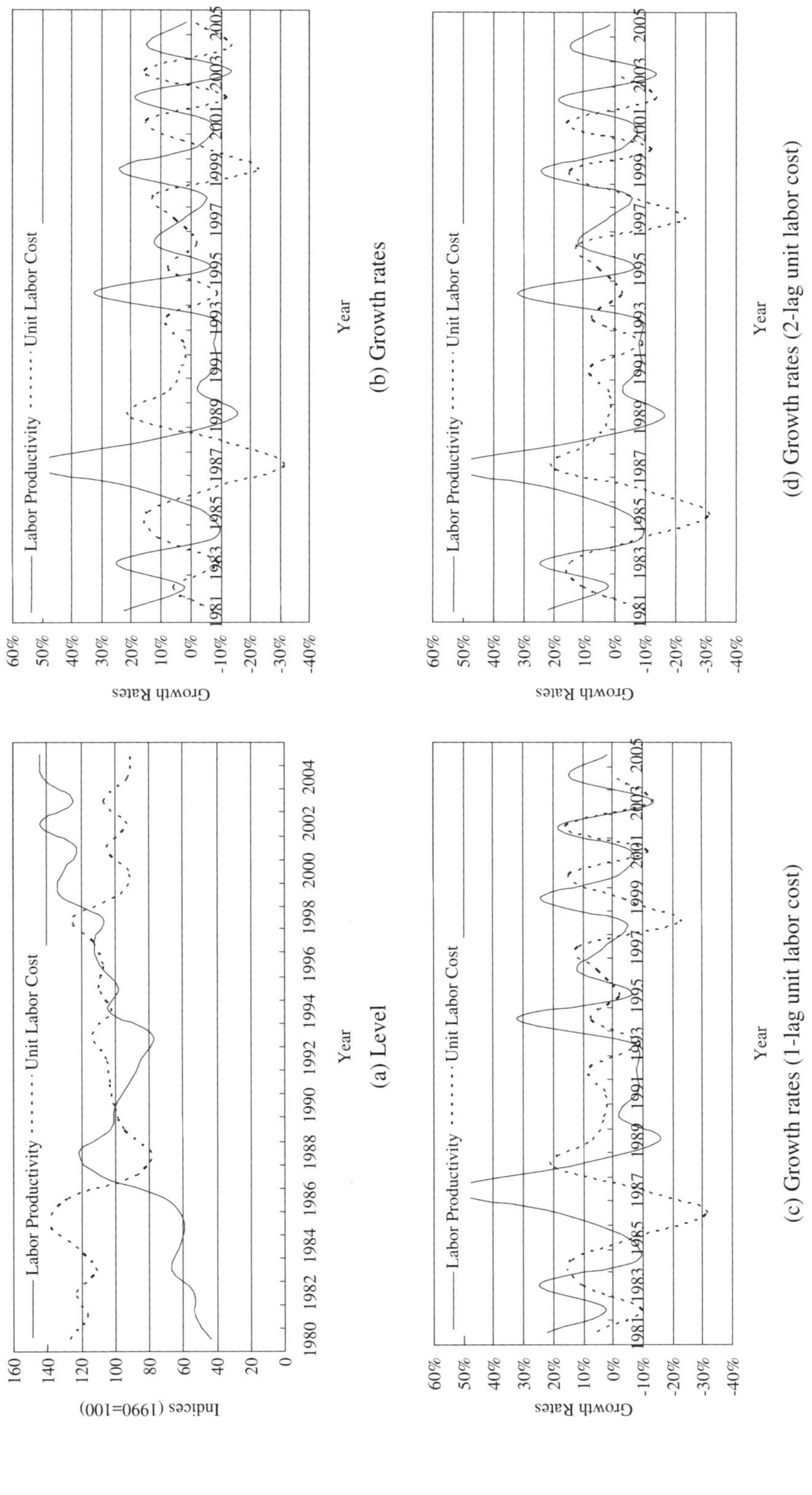

FIGURE 4.16 Labor productivity and unit labor cost: Water transport

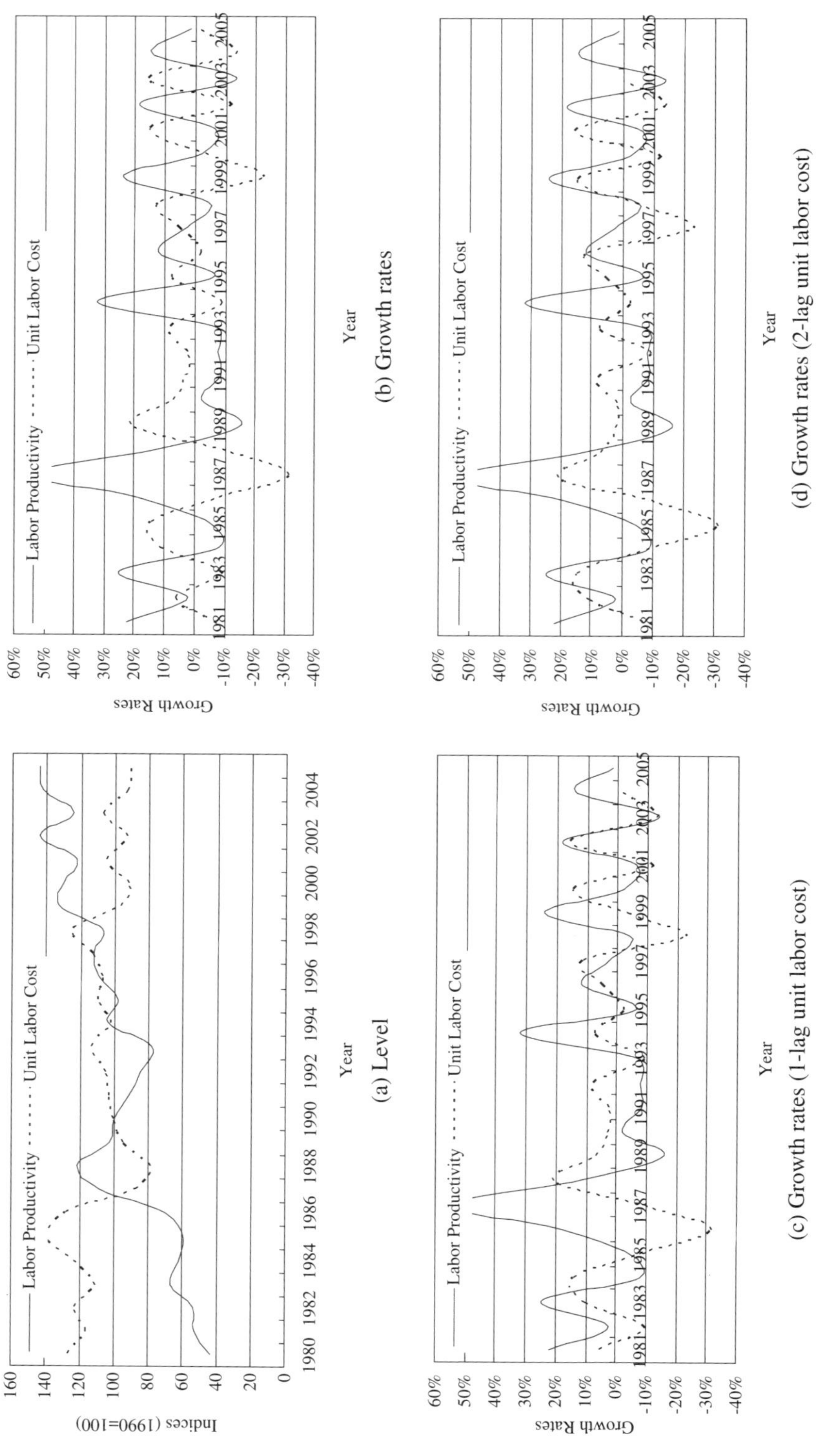

FIGURE 4.17 Labor productivity and unit labor cost: Air transport

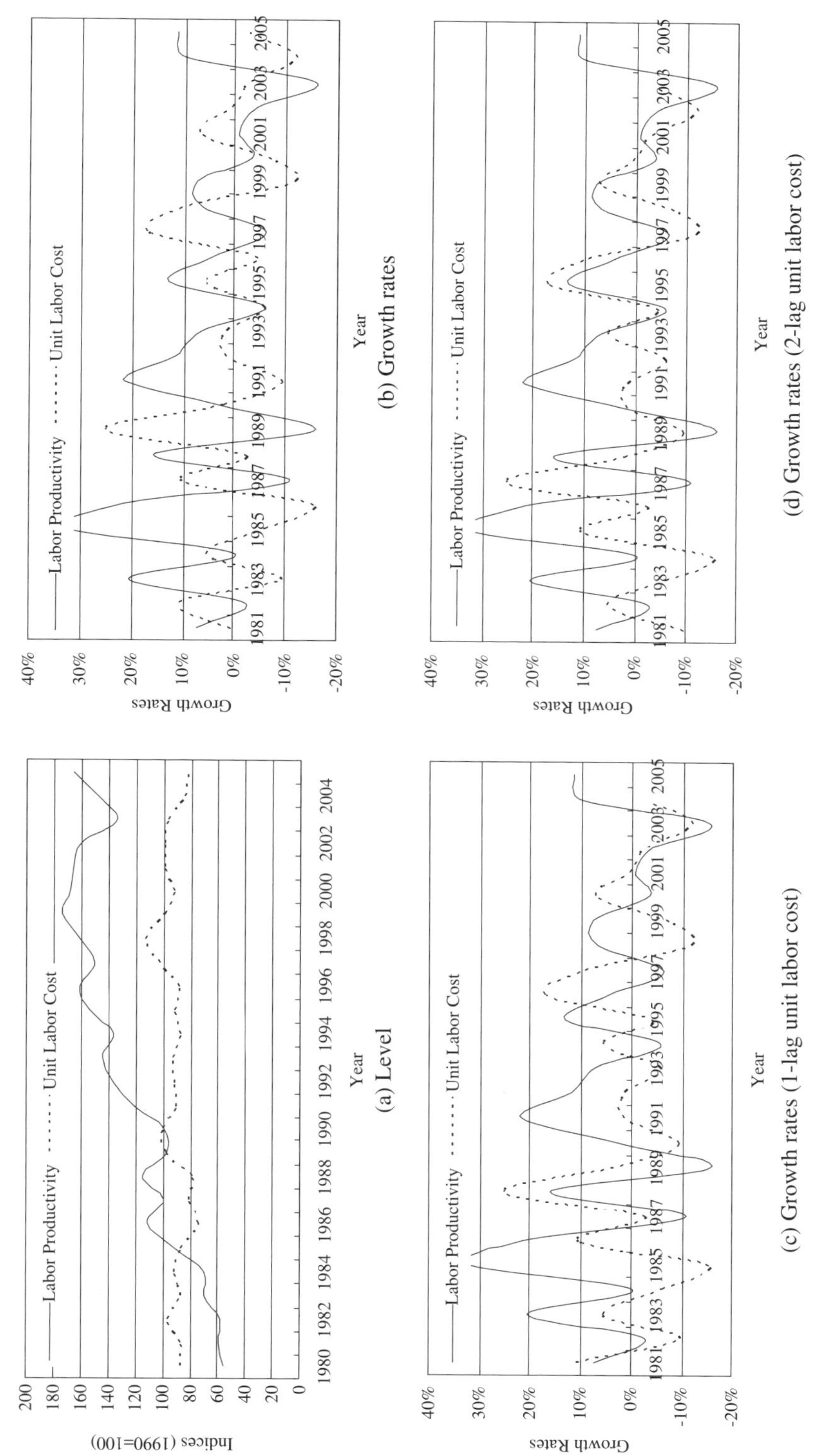

FIGURE 4.18 Labor productivity and unit labor cost: Other transport

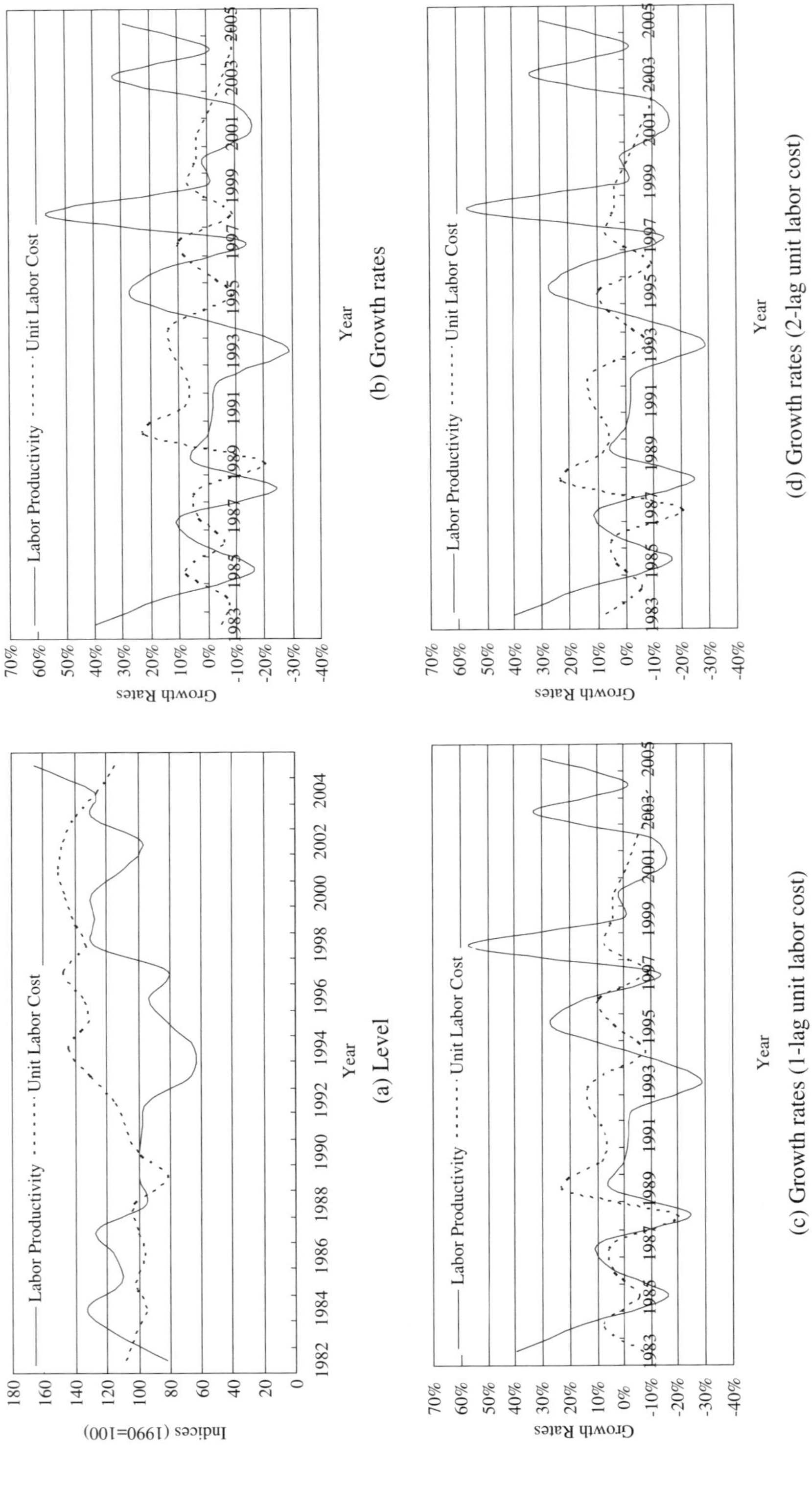

FIGURE 4.19 Labor productivity and unit labor cost: Storage

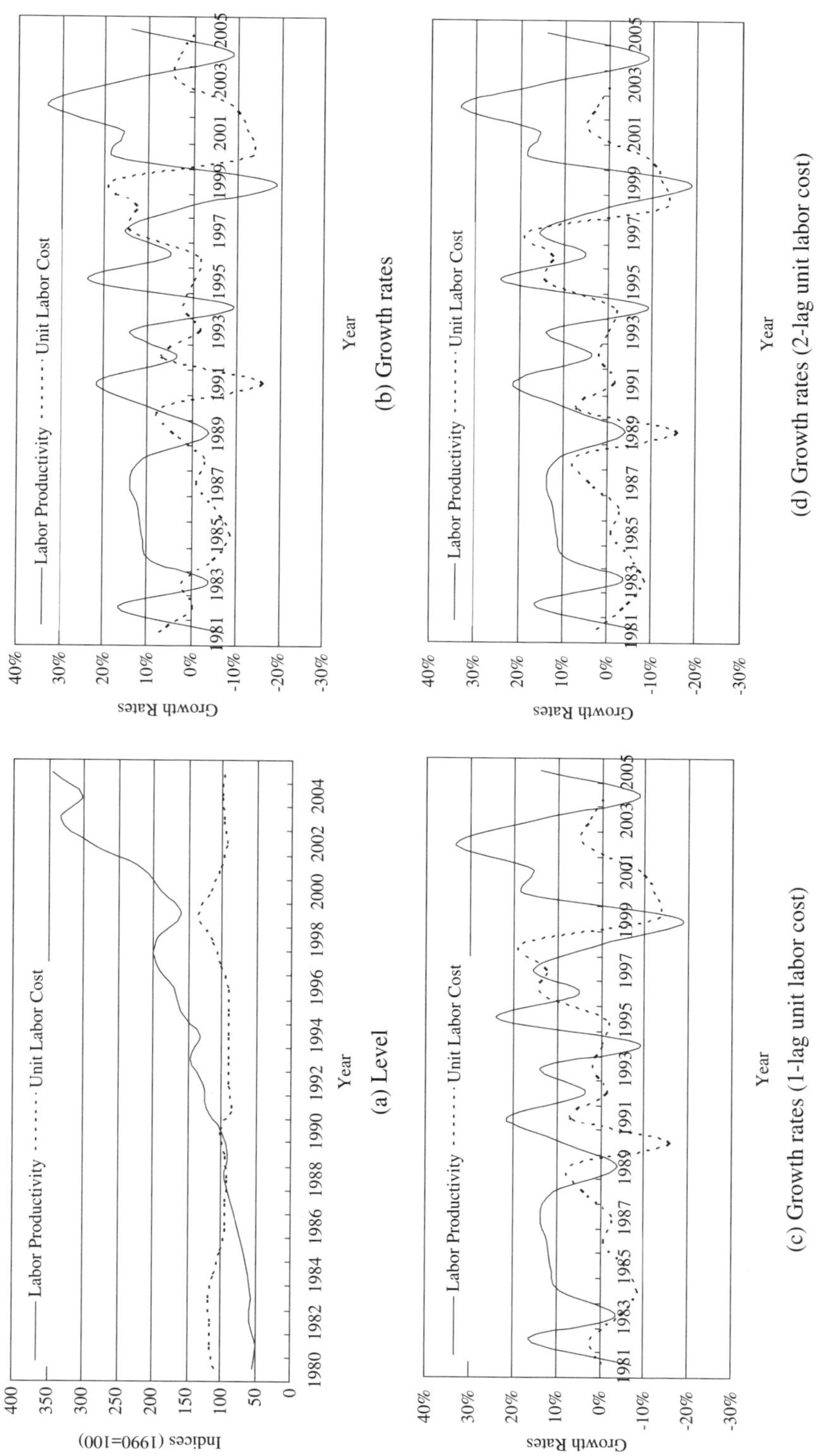

FIGURE 4.20 Labor productivity and unit labor cost: Communications

Figure 4.7: Manufacturing

i) The level trend: Labor productivity has been rising drastically from below 50 index point in 1981 to nearly 300 in 2005, though the pace of increase has slowed since 1998. The rise in labor productivity can be explained partly by the de-industrialization with workers shifted to other industries, and partly by the fact that those workers who have remained in manufacturing are the productive workers. The extremely stable movement in the unit labor cost does reflect the large number of workers having shifted away from manufacturing as industrial migration to Southern China occurred since the mid-1980s. The high labor productivity means that additional investment in the manufacturing sector could help Hong Kong's economic restructuring, though labor-intensive industries that have left Hong Kong are not likely to return. Hong Kong may be suitable for other new industries, such as quality control and testing, research and development, medical-related industries.

ii) The growth trend: Labor productivity has experienced positive growth rates for almost all the years, with the exception for years 1999, 2002, and 2003 during which the labor productivity have reached negative growth rates of –6.08%, –0.80%, and –0.45%, respectively. Its movement has fluctuated more in the 1980s than the 1990s. The unit labor cost, on the other hand, has experienced either low or negative growth rates for all the years in the sample period, with the exception in 1985 (with 7.72%) and in 2001 (with 8.89%). One clear observation is the opposite movements in the performances of the labor productivity and unit labor cost growth rates, especially in the 1980s and 1990s. This suggests that the rise in labor productivity is due to the contemporaneous inverse movement in unit labor cost. But the unit labor cost is adjusted to labor productivity after one time lag.

Figure 4.8: Mining and quarrying

i) The level trend: The two trends showed a similar movement until 1998, when labor productivity increased sharply. This is a very small industrial sector, as Hong Kong has almost exhausted its possession of minerals.

ii) The growth trend: There have been steady but rather narrow ups and downs in both performances of labor productivity and unit labor cost for the mining and quarrying industry. There have been significant decline in labor productivity in 1992 (with –19%), 2001 (with –17.75%), and in 2003 (with –40.96%). The contemporaneous picture seems to explain the two trends better, namely that due to the small size of the industry, unit labor cost adjusts to changes in labor productivity in the same time period.

The Twelve Industries in the Tradable Services Sector

Figure 4.9: Import and export trades

i) The level trend: The labor productivity trend has risen considerably, while the unit labor cost has remained constant in the sample period, suggesting that this is a competitive industry, with easy entry and exit of firms that will utilize every available business opportunity and possibility.

ii) The growth trend: The labor productivity growth rate has experienced a big jump in 1987 (20.51%) and a big fall in 1999 (–16.54%). The unit labor cost has shown high fluctuation in the 1980s and a sharp drop during the Asian financial crisis. The two trends tend to go in opposite directions. This is especially obvious from the early 1980s until the outbreak of the Asian financial crisis. For example, when labor productivity has been increasing at positive growth rates of 7.17% in 1984, 20.51% in 1987, and 10.03% in 1992, unit labor cost has been decreasing at negative growth rates of –8.42%, –8.46%, –1.66%, respectively. One clear observation is that the growth rate of unit labor cost has remained negative since 1998. The 1-lag adjustment seems to work for the two trends.

Figure 4.10: Restaurants

i) The level trend: The restaurant industry probably is a labor intensive industry and contains mostly low-skill workers, and jobs are competitive and salary remains low. This can be seen from the clear decline in labor productivity since the late 1980s. The unit labor cost has marginally edged upwards for about ten years from the late 1980s to the late 1990s, and since the turn of the century, the unit labor cost has remained stagnant. The improvement in the skill level of workers is needed, while industry modernization should be introduced so that distinction can be made between those modern food and beverage business from the traditional Chinese restaurants.

ii) The growth trend: There are large fluctuations in the labor productivity growth rates, and there are more negatives than positive growth rates. The unit labor cost growth trend is no different, though the degree of fluctuation is lower. There is clearly inverse movement in the direction of the two growth trends in the whole sample period. In 1987, for example, labor productivity has experienced a growth rate of 19.73%, while the unit labor cost decreased at the rate of –4.93%. Surprisingly, the 2-lag adjustments tend to show a better match in the movement of the two growth trends, suggesting that unit labor cost takes about two time periods to adjust to changes in labor productivity.

Figure 4.11: Hotels

i) The level trend: The two level trends tend to have moved in opposing directions and a rise (fall) in labor productivity was matched with a fall (rise) in unit labor cost. Hotel is still a labor intensive industry, and the rise in labor productivity is achieved at a lower unit labor cost. The diverging trend (the rise in labor productivity that matches with the fall in unit labor cost) has become severe since 2003, probably as a result of the SARS incident in Hong Kong.

ii) The growth trend: The two divergent level trends are further supported by the two growth trends. The two trends fluctuated a lot in the sample period, with negative growth rates in a number of years. The significant diverging trend (the rise (fall) in labor productivity matched by the fall (rise) in unit labor cost) can be clearly seen, especially in 1997 (when labor productivity was declining at –9.99%, but unit labor cost was growing at 12.41%) and 2004 (when labor productivity was growing at 36.70% while unit labor cost was falling at –25.81%). The observation is that control in unit labor cost is crucial in promoting labor productivity in this industry characterized by labor intensive production technique.

Figure 4.12: Finance

i) The level trend: The finance industry has been regarded as a pillar industry in Hong Kong. Its labor productivity has increased a lot, but the steady trend of the unit labor cost actually reflected that the industry is competitive and that remunerations are mainly commission based that may not show up in the unit labor cost.

ii) The growth trend: The labor productivity growth trend is uneven in the sample period, as sharp growth rates appeared in some years, due probably to the fluctuating nature of the industry that often is subjected to shocks. In the years when there were large growth rates in labor productivity, the unit labor cost experienced a reverse direction with sharp drop in its growth rates. A significant movement in the opposite directions between the two trends occurred in 1986 (with labor productivity rising at 20.67% but unit labor cost declining at –13.04%) and 1991 (with labor productivity rising at 36.00% but unit labor cost declining at –23.80%). A similar pattern occurred in 2003 as well. The unit labor cost adjustment tends to occur after 2-lags. This is quite surprising since finance is a fast moving industry with transactions taking place contemporaneously. The 2-lag probably confirms that the finance industry bases a lot on commissions.

Figure 4.13: Insurance

i) The level trend: The labor productivity trend has increased more rapidly in the 1990s than in the 1980s, while the unit labor cost has risen gradually since the early 1990s. The early 1990s (1990–1994) during the period of economic boom and the built up of the bubble saw the rapid rise in labor productivity.

ii) The growth trend: The pattern of growth rates for labor productivity is extremely unsteady, with the coexistence of large positive and negative growth rates between years, suggesting that the insurance industry is competitive and volatile. The growth trend of the unit labor cost is less volatile. The diverging trend between the two growth rates can obviously be seen in the early 1990s (1990–1994). The labor productivity has experienced positive growth in three consecutive years from 1991, 1992, and 1993 (with 9.51%, 11.32%, and 29.20%, respectively), while the unit labor cost has experienced negative growth in these three years (with –0.96%, –2.08%, and –18.03%, respectively). Meanwhile, when unit labor cost has encountered positive growth in 1995 (16.06%) and 1996 (16.80%), labor productivity has declined at a rate of –15.63% in 1995 and –10.03% in 1996. Similar to the finance industry, the 2-lag appears to suit the adjustment between unit labor cost and labor productivity.

Figure 4.14: Real estates

i) The level trend: The performance in this industry is an exception with labor productivity experienced a continuous fall while the rather stable trend in the unit labor cost turned to a rapid rise since 1998. The continuous fall in labor productivity suggests that the real estate industry has over-expanded and over-invested, probably with a situation of surplus labor or disguised unemployment, implying the presence of a large number of workers whose marginal product is very low, or even negative. The low set up cost can explain the over expansion in real estate business, as rental payment occupies probably the highest portion in total cost, while labor cost depends largely on commission. There is very little skill involved, as some training on the real estate market trends and the appropriate legalities are almost the needed knowledge. The real estate market in Hong Kong does not have an equitable and strong code of practices when it comes to legal charges, floor measurement and the way properties are marketed, and together with ample speculations, real estate agents do profit handsomely especially when the market is on its rising trend, and can sustain a period of low market activities when the market is falling.

ii) The growth trend: A number of negatives appeared in the labor productivity growth trend, and the trend fluctuated more severely since 1997. The growth trend of unit labor cost has shown an opposite movement. For example, when the unit labor cost has risen from 18.45% in 1998 to 47.19% in 1999, the labor productivity growth has declined a lot from 16.35% in 1998 to –30.31% in 1999. The pattern of the two growth series appeared similar after adjusting 1-lag in the unit labor cost.

Figure 4.15: Business services

i) The level trend: The rise in the two trends is gradual and shows similarity in their movement. The overall performance of labor productivity and unit labor cost in this industry is normal, as this is a competitive industry, and the industry moves along with changes in the business cycle in Hong Kong.

ii) The growth trend: Labor productivity has experienced sharp fluctuations, with large negative growth rates when the Hong Kong economy experienced recessionary pressures in 1982 during the Sino-British negotiation, in 1989 with political turmoil in Beijing, and in 1999 after the Asian financial crisis. The unit labor cost growth rates seemed to be steadier with narrower ups and downs, with small negative growth rates in different years in the sample period. The 1-lag in the growth trend of unit labor cost produces an acceptable pattern, suggesting that unit labor cost adjusts to labor productivity after one time period. The ability to keep cost low will be the ticket to success in business services.

Figure 4.16: Water transport

i) The level trend: This industry has performed successfully as the continuous rise in labor productivity is matched with a steady trend in unit labor cost. The development in this industry is steady and drastic changes are not expected, though increased economic integration activities with Mainland China will lead to more expansion in the long-run.

ii) The growth trend: The two growth trends show favorable positive growth rates in most years. The unit labor cost adjustment tends to appear in the 2-lag case, the only exception is the Asian financial crisis years (1997–1998) when the adjustment is more likely to be contemporaneous. This suggests that unit labor cost adjustment is rather long in the water transport industry, but in time of economic crisis, the adjustment becomes more instantaneous, due probably to changes in demand.

Figure 4.17: Air transport

i) The level trend: The trend of air transport should be in line with international prices, cost and development. On the whole, the two trends have been unsteady, with labor productivity rising while unit labor cost edging downwards in a number of years. This could reflect changes in the global economy, especially movement in oil price and changes in air travel.

ii) The growth trend: The two growth trends diverged greatly in the entire sample period. The gaps between the growth rates of the two indices are widest in 1987 when labor productivity has grew by 54.77% while the unit labor cost has declined by –31.76%. The two growth trends tend to go in similar directions in the 2-lag situation, suggesting that unit labor cost is adjusted to labor productivity after two time lags. This reflects possibly that air transport is conducted by large corporations and wage increases tend to be more rigid and delay in cost adjustments is expected.

Figure 4.18: Other transport

i) The level trend: Similar to water transport, the rising trend in labor productivity is matched with a steady trend in unit labor cost.
ii) The growth trend: The growth rates of both labor productivity and unit labor cost fluctuated more in the 1980s than in the 1990s and 2000s. Diverging trends are also more noticeable in the 1980s. The 1-lag adjustment appeared in the 1980s and early 1990s, while the 2-lag adjustment appeared since 1994.

Figure 4.19: Storage

i) The level trend: The performance of the storage industry is exceptional, with labor productivity edging downwards until 1994, but fluctuated since. On the contrary, unit labor cost tended to be stable in much of the 1980s, but increased since 1990 and lasted until 2000, before it edged downwards after the Asian financial crisis. Labor productivity has performed poorly during the economic booms years before 1997. The storage industry can be revived, as increasingly former factory spaces have been converted to storage rooms. The continued expansion in re-export business will keep the storage industry in a favorable situation.
ii) The growth trend: The growth in labor productivity seems to have fluctuated more than the unit labor cost in the whole sample period. The growth rate of labor productivity has remained low from 1984 to 1992. The 1-lag in unit labor cost seems to show a good match between the two trends, suggesting that unit labor cost adjusts to labor productivity after one time period.

Figure 4.20: Communications

i) The level trend: This industry has performed well, as labor productivity has risen steadily and gradually, except a short break in 1998, while the unit labor cost trend is both steady and stable. The low movement in unit labor cost reflects the possibility of low skill requirement among the workers in this industry.
ii) The growth trend: The growth of labor productivity is steady in the 1980s, followed by sharp changes in the 1990s. The growth of unit labor cost is weaker, as a number of years have shown small negative growth rates. The 2-lag situation in unit labor cost seems to provide a better adjustment between labor productivity and unit labor cost.

Among the twelve industries in the tradable services sector, the three industries that showed weak performances include restaurants, real estates and storage. Their labor productivity showed a declining trend, while unit labor cost showed a rising trend. The labor-intensive mode of production is a major feature among these three industries. Similarly, a low level of skill is required in these industries. The real estate industry is the worst performer with continuous decrease in labor productivity and a rapid rise in unit labor cost after 1997. Among the remaining nine industries, the few industries that experienced sharp growth rates in the sample period include insurance and other transport. The best performing industry in labor productivity growth is finance, which has experienced mostly positive growth rates in labor productivity.

The three industries that follow closely the 1-lag adjustment in unit labor cost include business services, other transport and storage. The other three industries that follow closely the 2-lag adjustment in unit labor cost are finance, water transport and communications. In short, there is a high degree of divergence in their performance among the twelve tradable services industries, with finance being the best performing industry and the real estate the worst performing industry in this sector.

The Two Industries in the Non-tradable Goods Sector

Figure 4.21: Construction

i) The level trend: Labor productivity has increased a lot in the entire 1980s, but has remained quite steady since 1992. On the contrary, the unit labor cost trend is very steady.

ii) The growth trend: The labor productivity growth rates have fluctuated a lot with negative growth rates in many years, while the growth rates of unit labor cost have remained steady, mild and low in most years. Indeed, with the exception of period 1984–1988 when the two growth rates decreased contemporaneously, the mild and low unit labor cost growth rates do not seem to match with the labor productivity growth rates. This may reflect the different cycles in the property market, but it is more likely that labor productivity does not have much relationship with unit labor cost in construction industry.

Figure 4.22: Electricity, gas and water

i) The level trend: As a public utility, the water industry is largely controlled by the government, who ensures a stable supply of fresh water from the Guangdong Province. Labor productivity has increased considerably from below 50 index points in 1981 to about 250 index points in 2005. The unit labor cost, however, showed a falling trend. Both electricity and gas are public utilities with private ownership, and they face a strict government control on profit ceilings.

ii) The growth trend: There is a clear diverging pattern between the two. While labor productivity has experienced minor negative growth rates in 1995 and

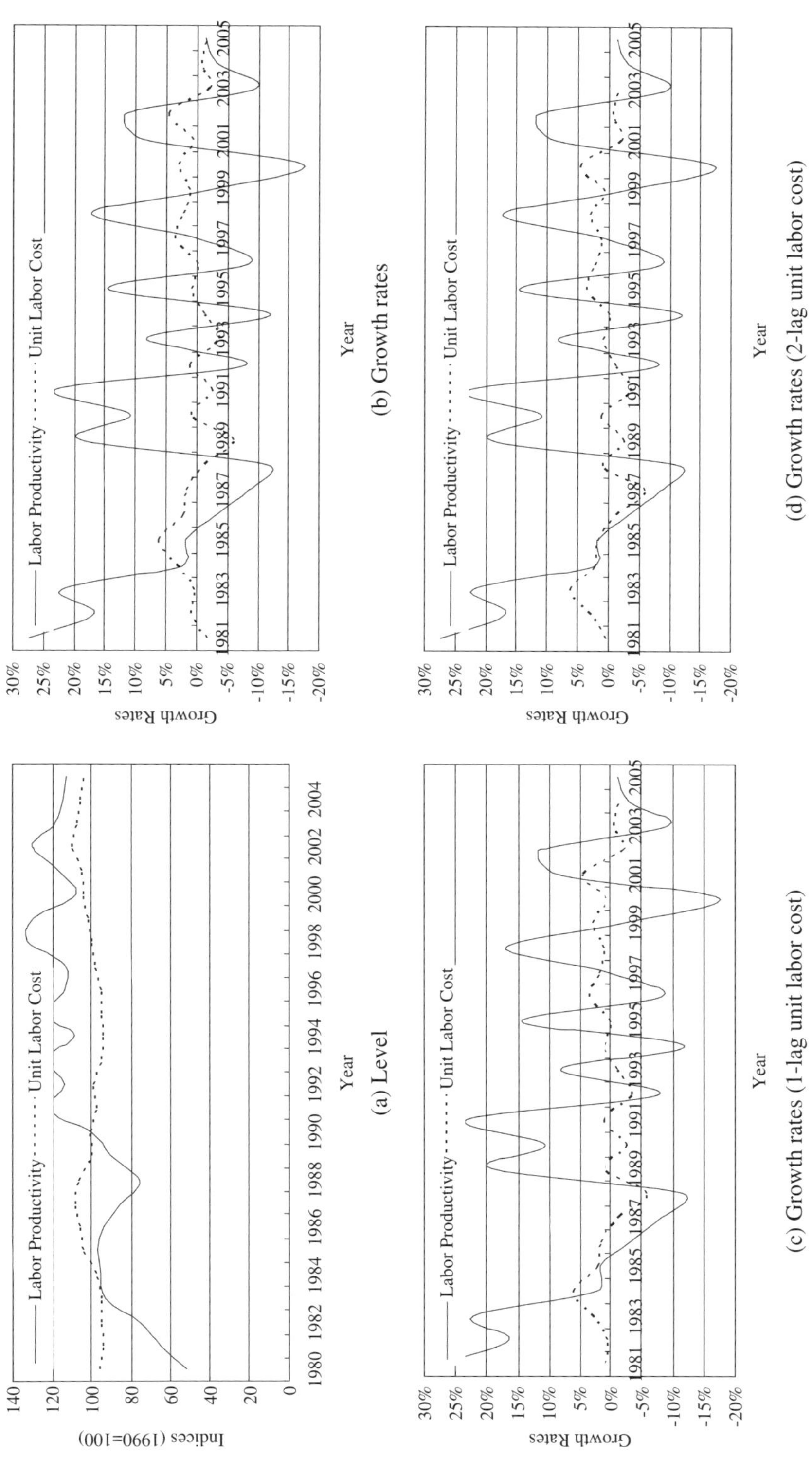

FIGURE 4.21 Labor productivity and unit labor cost: Construction

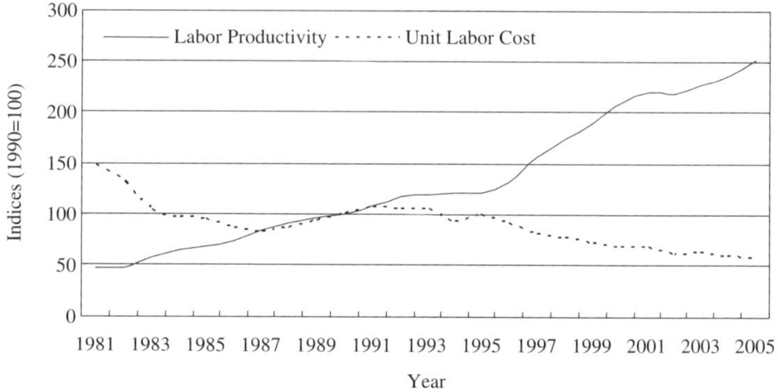

(a) Level

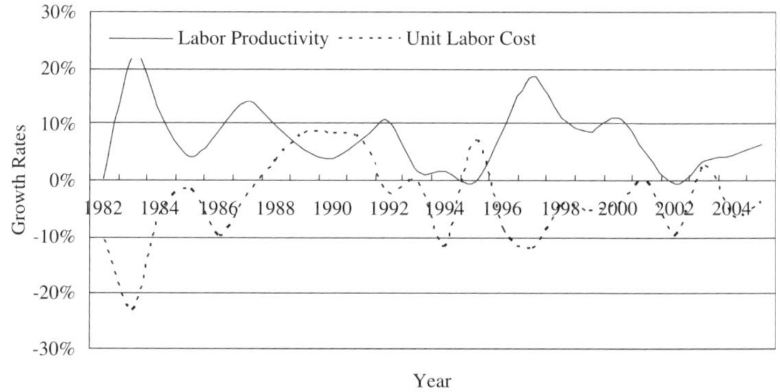

(b) Growth rates

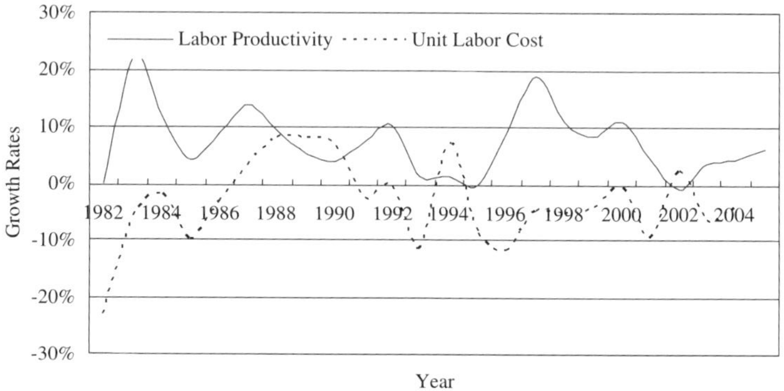

(c) Growth rates (1-lag unit labor cost)

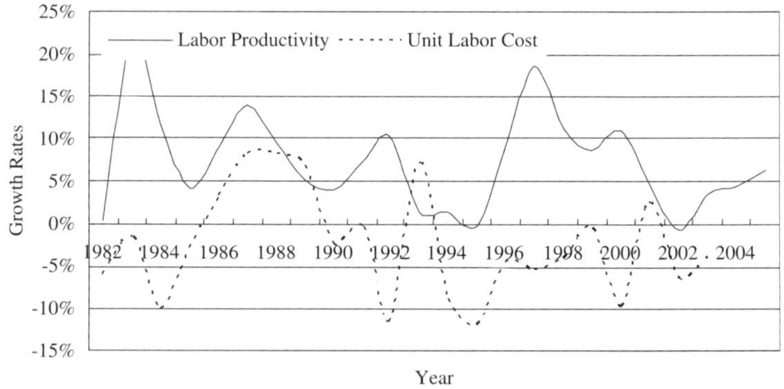

(d) Growth rates (2-lag unit labor cost)

FIGURE 4.22 Labor productivity and unit labor cost: Electricity, gas and water

2002, the unit labor cost has experienced large negative growth rates in a number of years. Most positive growth rates in labor productivity are matched by the negative growth rates in unit labor cost. Controlling unit labor cost enhances labor productivity in these three public utilities. The unit labor cost adjustment with the 2-lag seems to give a better match between unit labor cost and labor productivity

The Four Industries in the Non-Tradable Services Sector

Figure 4.23: Wholesale

i) The level trend: The two indices show a rising trend, with labor productivity rising faster than unit labor cost. The unit labor cost trend is steady and has changed little in the sample period. Indeed, the unit labor cost has declined again since 2003.

ii) The growth trend: The two trends have experienced sharp changes with negative growth rates appeared in various years. Despite the rising trend, the growth performance has not been stable for the wholesale industry; it probably is affected by changes in the business cycle. The industry is also labor intensive with mainly low skill workers. The 1-lag appeared to explain the unit labor cost adjustment to labor productivity.

Figure 4.24: Retail

i) The level trend: The movement of the two indices showed a similar trend. The increases in both trends have been mild, though the two trends moved in opposite directions in 1983, 1987–1988, 1997 and 2003. Overall, the increase in the index has been small in the sample period.

ii) The growth trend: The growth in labor productivity has been unsteady but low with both positive and negative cases. The two growth trends tended to move in opposite directions, for example in 1984, 1987, 1995, 1998 and 2004. In 2005, while labor productivity was growing at 6.64%, the unit labor cost was falling to –1.59%. The unit labor cost adjustment tends to appear after 1-lag.

Figure 4.25: Land transport

i) The level trend: The unit labor cost trend is very steady, basically has remained unchanged in the sample period. On the contrary, the labor productivity trend has experienced a cycle, rising until the early 1990s before it revised downwards since 1994. The land transport industry is again a labor intensive industry, with largely low skill workers. The rise in labor productivity between 1986 and 1994 coexisted with the economic boom in the Hong Kong economy.

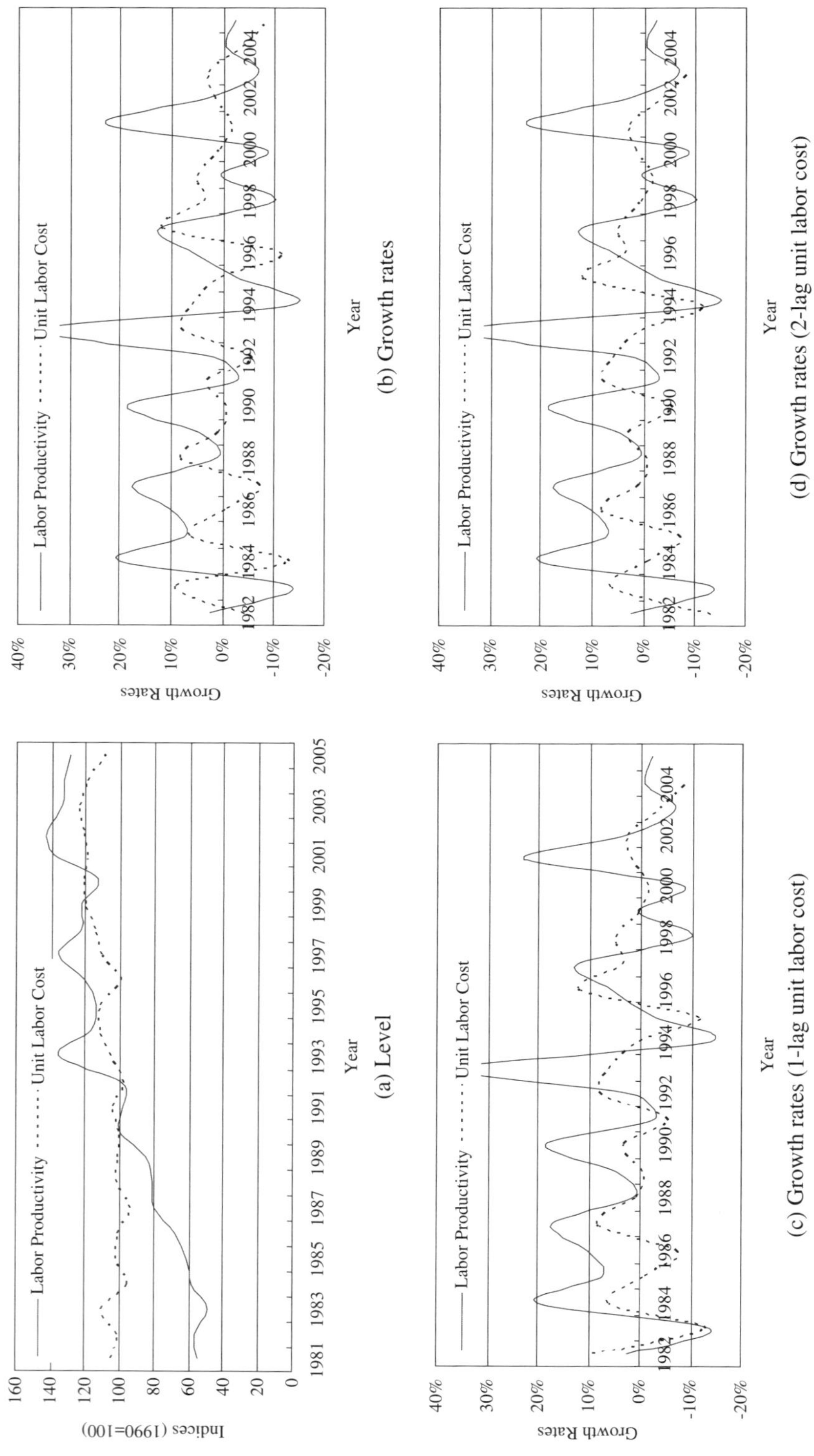

FIGURE 4.23 Labor productivity and unit labor cost: Wholesale

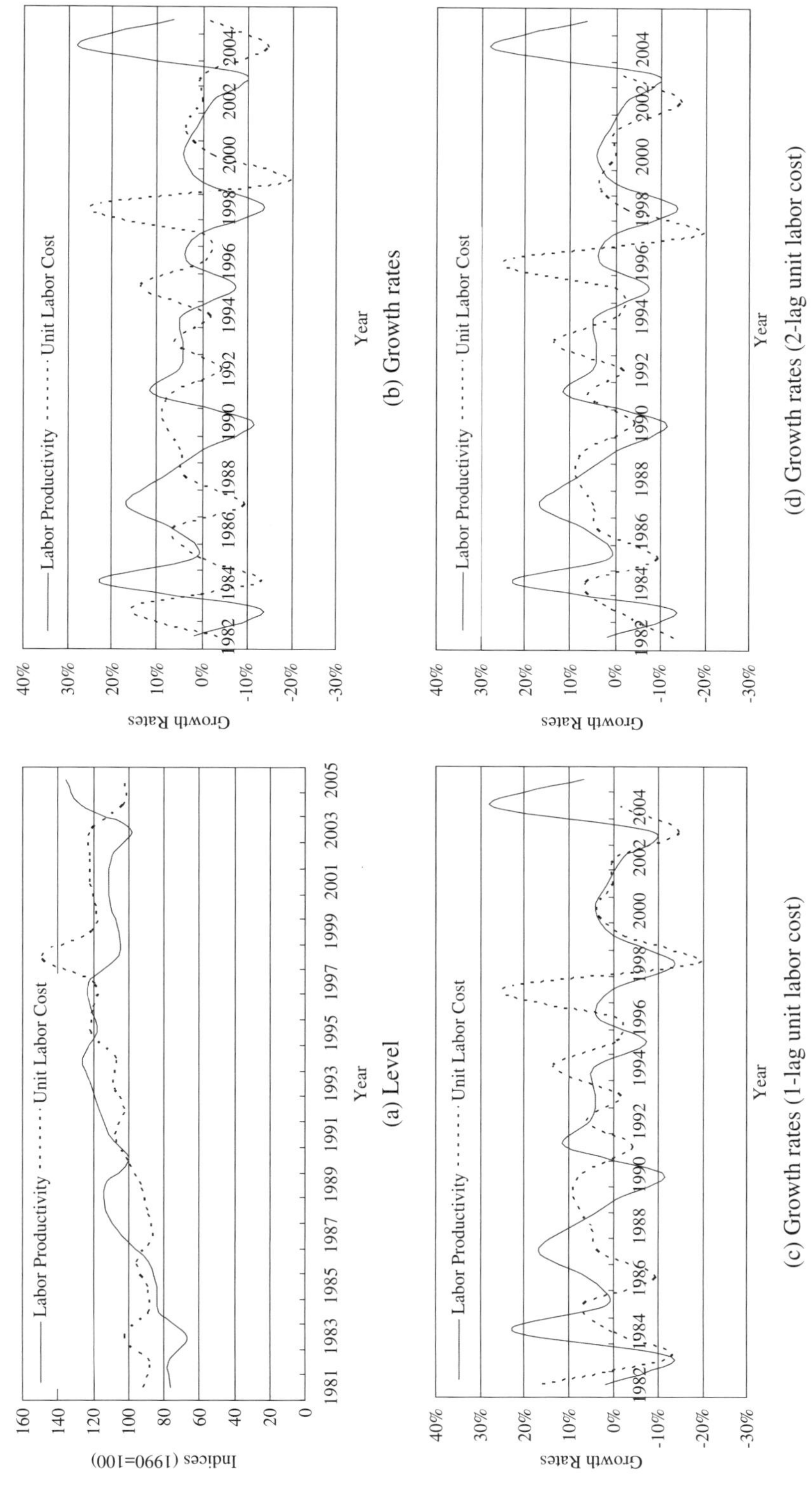

FIGURE 4.24 Labor productivity and unit labor cost: Retail

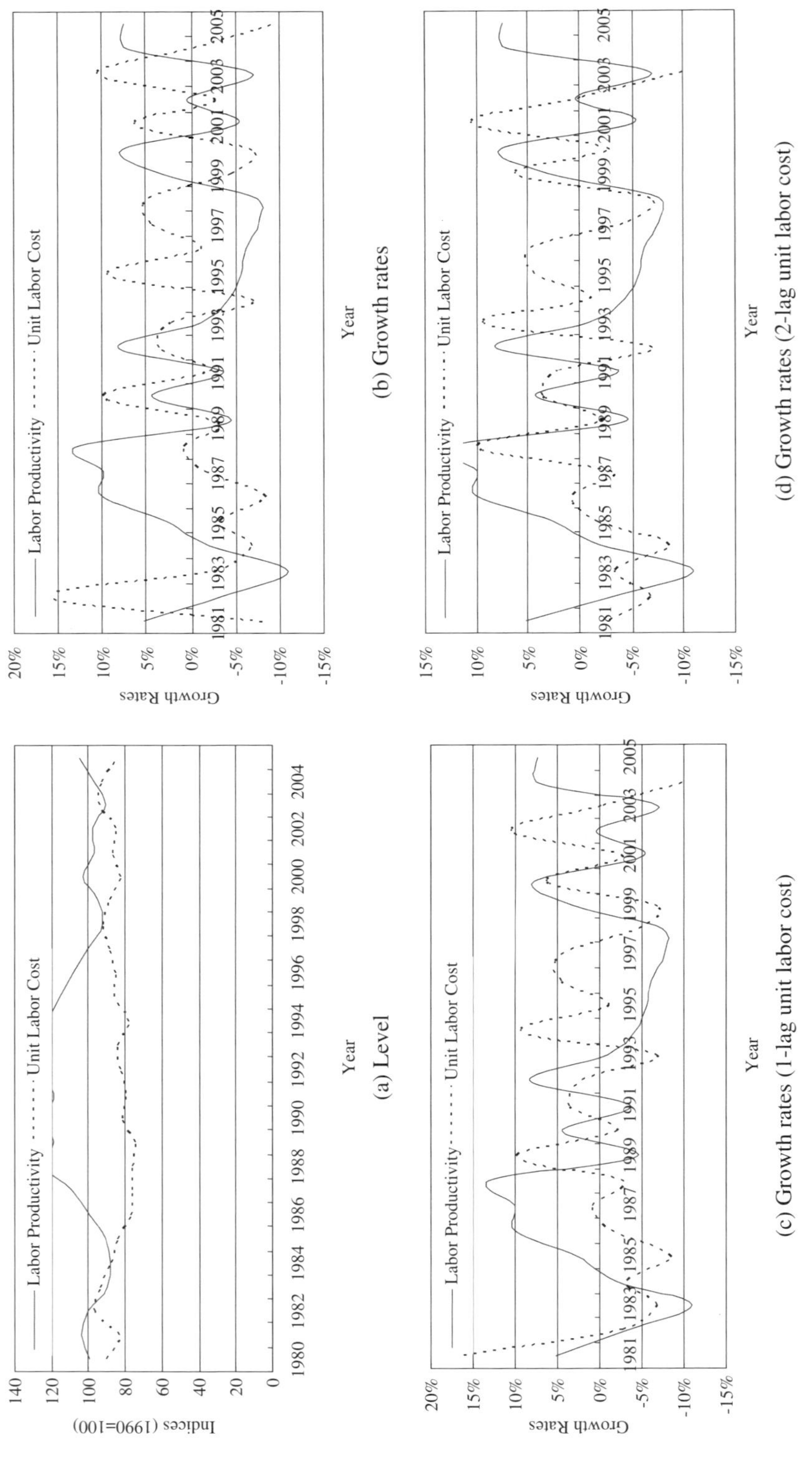

FIGURE 4.25 Labor productivity and unit labor cost: Land transport

ii) The growth trend: The growth trends showed sharp cyclical movements with prolonged positive growth rates in labor productivity in the 1984–1988 periods, but a prolonged negative growth rates in the 1994–1999 periods. The growth trend of unit labor cost is equally volatile. There are more negative than positive growth rates in the two trends. The land transport industry probably was faced with a high degree of volatility. This can be seen from the unit labor cost adjustment, which can either be contemporaneous (1988–1992), 1-lag (1982–1984 and 1999–2003), or 2-lag (1997–1998).

Figure 4.26: Community, social and personal services

i) The level trend: The movement of the two indices is very similar, though labor productivity has risen faster since 1994, but it fell after the Asian financial crisis.
ii) The growth trend: Labor productivity has shown a prolonged period of falling growth rates in 1984–1990, and a prolonged negative growth rates since 1999. The growth rate in unit labor cost has been small, with negative growth rates in several years. This industry is again characterized by the labor-intensive mode of production, contained largely low skilled workers. The unit labor cost adjustment tends to be contemporaneous.

One common feature among these four industries in the non-tradable services sector is that their level trends tended to move in a similar way, though the wholesale industry has a larger index change than the other three, while land transport has an inverted U-shape in the labor productivity level trend in the period from 1986 to 1997. Despite their non-tradable nature, the four industries are mainly labor-intensive, and the low skill level of workers has restricted their growth and expansion, making them more volatile in the different phrases of the business cycle. Equally, there is not much room for technological improvement in these four service industries. One rapid change is the fast emergence of large corporations that have replaced the large number of small business entities. For example, the supermarket industry has absorbed a large number of small retail shops, and shops in public housing estates have been amalgamated by corporations, thereby challenging the very survival of small retails in Hong Kong.

There are a few observations from the performance of the twenty one industries. Firstly, the majority of industries have shown an acceptable performance in that both labor productivity and unit labor cost have risen, but many have shown a reverse trend after the Asian financial crisis. The more problematic and outlier industries include restaurants, real estate, storage and land transport, as their labor productivity indices showed a declining trend. The major feature among these industries probably is over-investment with "surplus labor" or "disguised" unemployment, resulting in low marginal products. Resource diversion away from these industries is recommended, but their highly labor-intensive technique, coupled with the low skill level of workers and the increasing supply of low skill workers through, for example, immigration, it remains difficult for these industries to improve or upgrade. The solution lies in improving both the supply and the quality of the employed in this sector.

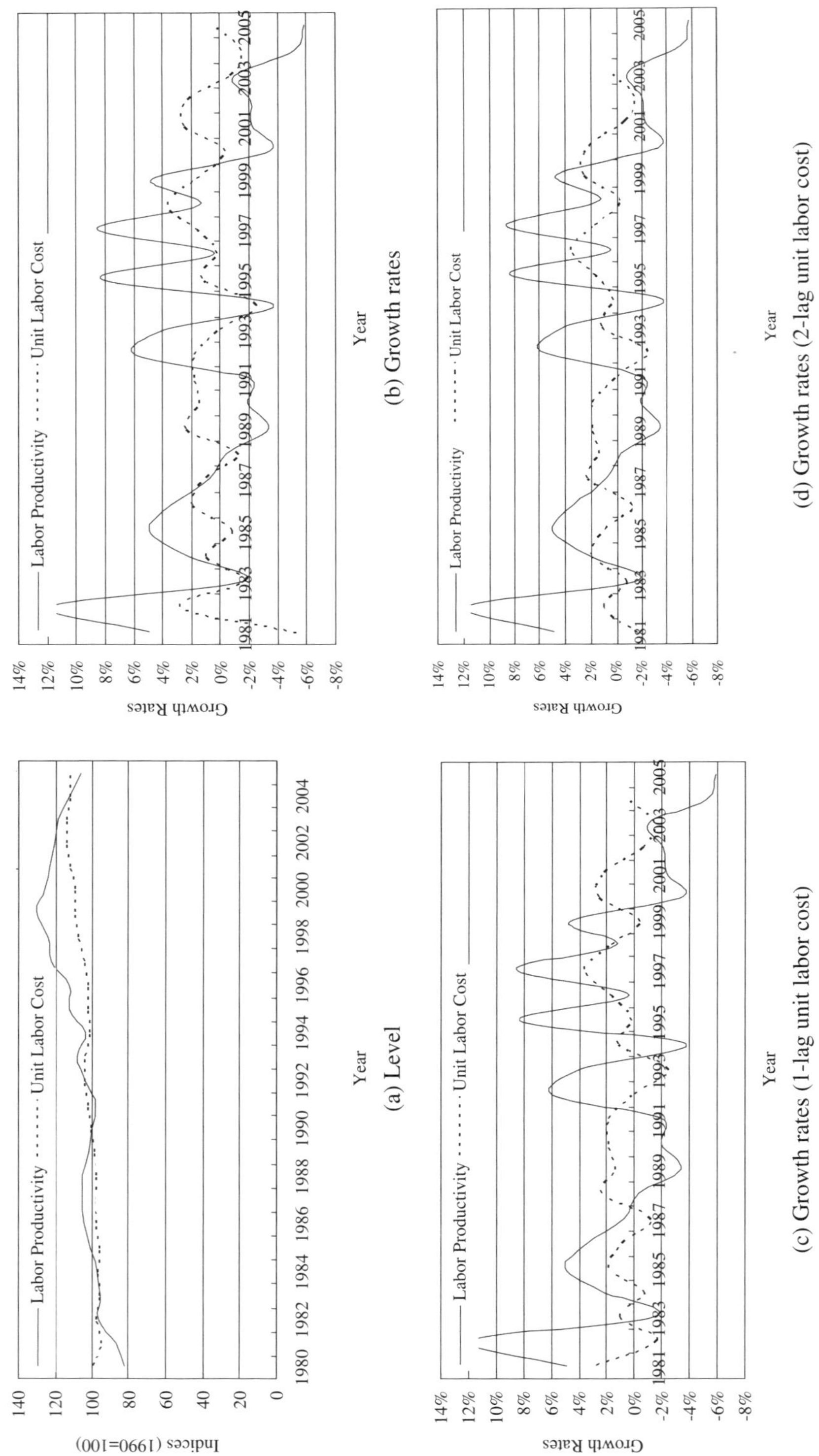

FIGURE 4.26 Labor productivity and unit labor cost: Community, social and personal services

Secondly, manufacturing can be an attractive industry when revived, as labor productivity has been kept at a high level. The more relevant question is the proper mixture of manufacturing industries, rather than the one-sided concentration in the service industry. Labor-intensive, low cost light manufacturing has no future in Hong Kong. The next phrase for Hong Kong's industrial development is the high value-added contemporary industries, such as quality control and testing, and biomedical industries. Thirdly, in a number of industries, the two indices showed that the rise (fall) in labor productivity was matched with the fall (rise) in unit labor cost, indicating that the performance of labor productivity and unit labor cost tended to go in opposite directions. These diverging patterns showed that labor productivity and unit labor cost are negatively correlated with each other, suggesting that increase in labor productivity can be achieved by a lower unit labor cost.

In most industries, there existed a lag of one time period between the growth rates of labor productivity and unit labor cost. The growth in labor productivity in the current year is expected to be followed by growth in unit labor cost after 1 year in most cases. This finding suggests that the next stage of the analysis should examine the causality relationship between the labor productivity and unit labor cost. Namely, whether the direction of causality runs from growth in labor productivity to unit labor cost, or vice versa, or the growth of the two trends are unrelated.

4.7 The Granger Causality Tests

The 1-lag and 2-lag discussion in the previous section assumes that changes in labor productivity will lead to changes in unit labor cost, either in the same time period, or one or two time lags. However, both the correlation and graphical analysis discussed so far do not provide any cause-and-effect relationship between labor productivity and unit labor cost. This section applies the Granger causality tests to examine if statistically one can detect the direction of causality (cause-and-effect relationship) between the two variables. The Granger test involves the estimation of the following regressions:

$$LP_t = c_1 + \sum_{i=1}^{n} \alpha_i LP_{t-i} + \sum_{i=1}^{n} \beta_i LUC_{t-i} + u_{0t} \text{ , and} \tag{9}$$

$$LUC_t = c_1 + \sum_{i=1}^{n} \sigma_i LUC_{t-i} + \sum_{i=1}^{n} \delta_i LP_{t-i} + u_{1t}. \tag{10}$$

LP refers to labor productivity growth and *LUC* refers to unit labor cost growth. It is assumed that the disturbances u_{ot} and u_{it} are uncorrelated. Eq. (9) postulates that current *LP* is related to past values of *LP* itself and *LUC*. Eq. (10) postulates a similar behavior for *LUC*. The variable *LP* is said to be Granger-caused by variable *LUC* if the variable *LUC* contributes to the prediction of variable *LP* in Eq. (9).

The bivariate regressions shown by Eqs. (9) and (10) argue that there is unidirectional causality from *LUC* to *LP* if the estimated coefficients on the lagged *LUC* in Eq. (9) are statistically different from zero as a group (i.e., $\sum \beta_i \neq 0$) and the set of estimated coefficients on the lagged *LP* in Eq. (10) is not statistically different from zero (i.e., $\Sigma\delta_i = 0$). On a similar line of argument, unidirectional causality from *LP* to *LUC* exists if the set of lagged *LUC* coefficients in Eq. (10) is not statistically different from zero (i.e., $\Sigma\beta_i = 0$) and the set of the lagged *LP* coefficients in Eq. (10) is statistically different from zero (i.e., $\Sigma\delta_i \neq 0$). There is bilateral causality when the sets of *LP* and *LUC* coefficients are statistically significantly different from zero in both regressions. In other words, there is independence when the two sets of *LP* and *LUC* coefficients are not statistically significant in both regressions.

In implementing the Granger causality tests, the F-statistics are calculated under the null hypothesis that all the coefficients of β_i and δ_i equal to zero in Eqs. (9) and (10). If the resulting F-statistics are higher than the critical value, the hypothesis of non-Granger causality is rejected. Since stationarity of both the *LP* and *LUC* series is the prerequisite for the Granger causality test, the unit root tests are applied to both *LP* and *LUC* to ensure that both variables are stationary. The unit root tests are performed by estimating the following regressions:

$$\Delta LP_t = \beta_t + \beta_2 t + \sigma LP_{t-1} + \delta_i \sum_{i=1}^{m} \Delta LP_{t-1} + u_t, \quad \text{and} \tag{11}$$

$$\Delta LUC_t = \beta_t + \beta_2 t + \sigma LUC_{t-1} + \delta_i \sum_{i=1}^{m} \Delta LUC_{t-1} + u_t. \tag{12}$$

A constant, or an intercept, and the time trend terms are included in these two regressions. The null hypothesis for both equations is $\sigma = 0$, suggesting that there is a unit root. The situation is non-stationary when there is a unit root problem. The Augmented Dickey–Fuller (1979, 1981) (ADF) tests are applied to Eqs. (11) and (12) to perform the unit root tests. The ADF tests are applied to allow for the possibility of serial correlation in u_t. If the computed absolute value of the τ statistic exceeds the ADF absolute critical τ values either at 1%, 5% or 10% significance level, the null hypothesis that the given time series is stationary is rejected. If, on the other hand, it is less than the critical value, the time series is non-stationary.

Table 4.11 shows the unit root tests of the two series of *LP* and *LUC*. In the case of *LP*, the results of the ADF tests show that aside from the industries of agriculture and fishing, hotels, insurance, communications, community, social and personal services, the time series of all other industries and economic sectors are stationary. In the case of *LUC*, the results of the ADF tests show that the times series of all industries and economic sectors are stationary, with the exception of the construction industry. The Granger causality tests are applied only to those industries (15 industries) and economic sectors which have a stationary time series.

A total of six time lags are conducted in the causality test, but Table 4.12 reports only the results of the causality tests with 1-lag. Table 4.13 shows the summary results and observations. Among the 15 industries, the 1-lag model estimates reveal that the wholesale industry showed causality that runs from labor productivity growth to unit labor cost growth, implying that labor productivity has to rise before wage increase that results in a rise in the unit labor cost can increase. The 4-lag model

TABLE 4.11 Unit root tests results

	LP				LUC			
		ADF critical $|\tau|$ values				ADF critical $|\tau|$ values		
	Computed $|\tau|$	1%	5%	10%	Computed $|\tau|$	1%	5%	10%
The 21 Industries								
Agriculture and fishing	2.1731	4.5326	3.6736	3.2774	7.1510	4.3643	3.6122	3.2431
Mining and quarrying	6.3847	4.4163	3.6220	3.2486	6.5409	4.4163	3.6220	3.2486
Manufacturing	3.4469	4.4163	3.6220	3.2486	3.8484	4.4679	3.6450	3.2615
Electricity, gas and water	4.0883	4.4407	3.6329	3.2547	3.4829	4.4163	3.6220	3.2486
Construction	3.8653	4.5326	3.6736	3.2774	2.4086	4.4526	3.6736	3.2774
Wholesale	4.1600	4.4679	3.6450	3.2615	6.6389	4.4163	3.6220	3.2486
Retail	5.1852	4.4163	3.6220	3.2486	6.9254	4.4163	3.6220	3.2486
Import and export trades	5.2777	4.4983	3.6584	3.2690	3.8415	4.4679	3.6450	3.2615
Restaurants	4.2800	4.4679	3.6450	3.2615	3.8753	4.4679	3.6450	3.2615
Hotels	2.6294	4.5326	3.6736	3.2774	3.4865	4.5926	3.6736	3.2774
Finance	4.1043	4.4407	3.6329	3.2547	3.4231	4.4163	3.6220	3.2486
Insurance	1.6265	4.5326	3.6736	3.2774	3.4513	4.4679	3.6450	3.2615
Real Estates	4.7952	4.4163	3.6220	3.2486	3.4468	4.3943	3.6122	3.2431
Business services	4.3771	4.3943	3.6122	3.2431	4.9541	4.3943	3.6122	3.2431
Land transport	3.3525	4.3943	3.6122	3.2431	3.7263	4.4679	3.6450	3.2615
Water transport	5.7951	4.4163	3.6220	3.2486	7.4283	4.4163	3.6220	3.2486
Air transport	5.0620	4.3943	3.6122	3.2431	4.5390	4.4163	3.6220	3.2486
Other transport	3.7277	4.5326	3.6736	3.2774	5.3622	4.3943	3.6122	3.2431
Storage	5.2141	4.4407	3.6329	3.2567	4.9605	4.4407	3.6329	3.2547
Communications	1.7818	4.4983	3.6584	3.2690	4.0546	4.3943	3.6122	3.2431
Community, social and personal services	2.6176	4.4163	3.6220	3.2486	6.6948	4.3943	3.6122	3.2431
The 4 Economic Sectors								
Tradable goods	4.3037	4.5326	3.6736	3.2774	4.0574	4.4407	3.6329	3.2547
Tradable services	3.7975	4.5716	3.6908	3.2869	4.0200	4.4679	3.6450	3.2615
Non-tradable goods	3.6858	4.5326	3.6736	3.2774	3.7171	4.3943	3.6122	3.2431
Non-tradable services	3.5224	4.4679	3.6450	3.2615	4.3096	4.4163	3.6220	3.2486

TABLE 4.12 Granger causality tests results between labor productivity and unit labor cost (1-lag estimates)

	LP does not cause LUC		LUC does not cause LP	
	F-statistics	P-value	F-statistics	P-value
The 15 Industries				
Mining & quarrying	1.1671	0.2399	1.3212	0.2639
Manufacturing	1.2314	0.2803	0.5078	0.4843
Electricity Gas Water	1.9731	0.1755	1.4975	0.2353
Wholesale	3.6100	0.0720**	2.6657	0.1182
Retail	0.0310	0.8620	0.0324	0.8589
Import & Export	0.5386	0.4715	1.3686	0.2558
Restaurants	2.7737	0.1131	3.8787	0.0645***
Finance	0.0229	0.8813	0.4388	0.5149
Real Estate	1.1507	0.2956	0.1661	0.6877
Business Services	0.1206	0.7319	0.1488	0.7036
Land Transport	0.3634	0.5531	1.3507	0.2582
Water Transport	6.2000	0.0212**	8.9121	0.0071*
Air Transport	1.4665	0.2394	2.7355	0.1130
Other Transport	0.0003	0.9857	0.7991	0.3815
Storage	0.1648	0.6893	0.3056	0.5868
The 4 Economic Sectors				
Tradable goods	4.3292	0.0499**	2.0563	0.1663
Non-tradable goods	1.1083	0.3044	0.0790	0.7814
Tradable services	0.3662	0.5526	0.9541	0.3416
Non-tradable services	0.0457	0.8328	0.3378	0.5676

Note: *, ** and *** indicate significance at 1%, 5% and 10% level, respectively.

reported in Table 4.13 reveals that there is unidirectional causality from labor productivity growth to unit labor cost growth in the mining and quarrying industry. The interpretation is similar to the wholesale industry that labor productivity has to rise before wage can go up, though mining and quarrying is a peripheral industry already.

On the contrary, the restaurants industry shows a reverse causality, suggesting that the rise in unit labor cost requires a rise in labor productivity, such as an increase in overtime work, a better training or improvement in experience. The water transport industry shows a bilateral causality, meaning that both labor productivity and unit labor cost can influent each other. For all remaining industries, although there is no existence in the Granger causality running from labor productivity growth to unit labor cost growth, the hypothesis that unit labor cost growth does not Granger-cause labor productivity growth is also not rejected in all the lag models.

Among the four economic sectors, the 1-lag model revealed that the tradable goods sector shows a unidirectional causality from labor productivity to unit labor cost. All the hypotheses that unit labor cost growth does not Granger-cause labor

TABLE 4.13 Summary result of type of causality between labor productivity and unit labor cost

	Lags	F-statistics	P-value	Decision	Type of Causality
Industries					
Wholesale	1	3.6100	0.0720***	LP Granger-cause LUC	Unidirectional causality from LP to LUC
Restaurants	1	3.8787	0.0645***	LUC Granger-cause LP	Unidirectional causality from LUC to LP
Water transport	1	6.2000	0.0212**	LP Granger-cause LUC	Bilateral causality between LP and LUC
	1	8.9121	0.0071*	LUC Granger-cause LP	
Mining and quarrying	4	3.5469	0.0430**	LP Granger-cause LUC	Unidirectional causality from LP to LUC
Economic sectors					
Tradable goods	1	4.3292	0.0499**	LP Granger-cause LUC	Unidirectional causality from LP to LUC

Note: *, ** and *** indicate significance at 1%, 5% and 10% level, respectively.

productivity growth are accepted for all the industries. In short, there is no unidirectional causality from unit labor cost growth to labor productivity growth. Nonetheless, it would be fair to argue that in a free economy where cost of production is determined largely by market forces, the growth in labor productivity takes precedence to growth in unit labor cost.

4.8 Conclusion

This chapter has covered a number of issues related to the productivity performance of all key industries and economic sectors in Hong Kong using data from the 1980s. Over the years, the economy of Hong Kong has definitely enjoyed maximum advantages from economic freedom. The continued inflow of capital resources has nurtured local capital, and the needed development in technology has fostered development in manufacturing and service industries. Local entrepreneurship has suitably complemented the deployment of resources, and in turn many entrepreneurs have established large corporations that consolidated the Hong Kong economy and served as show cases for other potential businesses. Economic freedom allows individual creativity to the fullest possible extent, both in good and bad economic times.

Economic freedom carries a strong sense of dynamism. Economic growth in different decades depended on the different usage of available resources that give rise to outputs through development in industries and businesses. Thus, the Hong Kong economy has passed through different stages of economic growth and comparative advantages. While behaving like other developing countries before the Second World War, epoch-making changes took place after the end of the Second World War with large inflows of capital resources from North America and European countries on the one hand and from Mainland China after the establishment of the communist regime in 1949 on the other hand. Industrial development began and with economic freedom and openness, Hong Kong products have been supplied to various corners of the world, especially in light manufacturing with labor-intensive techniques. Open trade facilitated the needed banking activities, and the flourish of international banks in the 1960s promoted Hong Kong's status as an international finance center. In many ways, for good and bad alike, the Hong Kong economy "flows" along with changes in the world economy.

With low cost attraction in the 1960s, Hong Kong benefitted as a "late comer" to other developed Asian economies, along with Japan, Singapore, Taiwan and South Korea (Li, 2002). The ultimate aim in economic development is to have more economies enjoying higher growth leading to higher quality of living and reduction of poverty. The developed world will open arms to welcome newly developed economies in Asia and other parts of the world. With the economic reform in Mainland China in 1978, Hong Kong took up a new role of fostering, nurturing and facilitating the development of a market economy in the Special Economic Zones (SEZs) along the coastal cities, the Guangdong Province adjacent to Hong Kong, and numerous regions and Mainland China, providing unqualified financial assistance to industrial and infrastructural developments. The "show case" role of Hong Kong has benefitted the Mainland China economy with invaluable and beyond-measurable consequences, though one has to cherish the hard work and readiness to adopt market economic practices demonstrated by people in Mainland China in the process of market reform.

While economic activities in Mainland China have often used Hong Kong as a reference, the Mainland China economy can be listed by the turn of the century as a new "late comer" in economic advancement, improving growth and livelihood of people through free market activities along with other developed Asian and world economies. Like other key economic events in previous decades, the rapid growth of the Mainland China economy has posed both a challenge and opportunity to the Hong Kong economy. There are surely new uncertainties facing Hong Kong, but turning uncertainties into realities, and challenges into opportunities require uncharted skills, creativity and favorable environments. The fundamentals of a free economy at least will rescue, while at most will help to maximize the pace of economic changes and restructuring, though the role of the government and the new political scenes since 1997 has come under new focus.

While the discussion on the relationship between Hong Kong and Mainland China is reserved in a later chapter, this chapter aims to examine the internal economic abilities and constraints Hong Kong is facing. The data on the numerous industries in Hong Kong since the early 1980s has demonstrated a number of possibilities. Firstly, Hong Kong faces different comparative advantages at different time periods. Due to political challenges, economic shocks and crises, Hong Kong has passed through business cycles, with economic expansions and recessions at different intervals. Secondly, economic bubbles can provide short-term benefits, but can at the same time generate instabilities and volatilities. Lessons can be learned from the estimation of total factor productivity among industries and economic sectors. The difference in the productivity performance can serve as market signals for resources and investments to be rechanneled to high productivity sectors and industries.

In general, the best performer in productivity has been the industries in the tradable services sector, typically because of competition from overseas suppliers. Manufacturing has declined drastically, but there is possibility for the manufacturing industry to revive or restructure into production-related services. Industries in both non-tradable goods and services sectors show a weak performance, especially in the real estate industry, as productivity has remained low with over-investment.

A large number of key services in Hong Kong are based on labor-intensive mode of productivity. While employment in manufacturing industries tends to grow with skills and experience, a large number of employment in services do not require skills, nor can generate skills with the length of employment. For example, young ladies working as sales in fashion shops can secure employment at a young and youthful age, but sale jobs do not have much skill enhancement or training opportunities. People working as sale persons in fashion shops may have low employment sustainability once they age and become uncompetitive to incoming youthful workers, or occurrence of shocks and crisis resulting in the closure of the business. As such, job and employment security is low among workers in a large number of service industries. Economic restructuring with diversity and employment creation can be a solution, but that requires sustainable growth and expansion in investment and availability of suitable resources.

The productivity analysis in this chapter serves a number of functions. Firstly, it concentrates in examining the changing strength in Hong Kong's domestic industries. These changes can provide further implications and discussion on the future development of the Hong Kong economy, and how economic freedom can further be utilized to help Hong Kong to change and face challenges. Secondly, productivity analysis shall lead to related areas of discussions, such as performance of TFP in different size of establishments, human capital, economic efficiency, competition and competitiveness of the Hong Kong economy, and so on. Economic analyses are connected to each other, and analysis in one aspect of the economy can lead to other aspects.

5 Small- and Medium-Sized Enterprises: Diversity and Productivity

5.1 Introduction

The modern stage of industrialization in Hong Kong has commonly been associated with the post-Second World War development, especially since the 1950s with the occurrence of two distinctive events in the investment scene in Hong Kong. Being a free economy with abundant supply of low cost labor then, Hong Kong attracted a considerable amount of foreign investment mainly from Great Britain, USA. and other European countries, where post-war development had resulted in rapid expansion in demand for consumer products, especially in countries in Europe and North America. The establishment of a communist regime under the People Republic of China in 1949 had posted a threat to capitalists and businesses, and hastened their migration to Hong Kong. Many landed in Hong Kong were industrialists who came with large amount of capital for establishing industries in Hong Kong. Indeed, the freedom of capital movements in and out of Hong Kong under the British rule was considered as a perfect shelter away from political harassment and victimization.

Studies by Clayton (1997, 2000 and 2006) have shown that there are two schools of thought on the theory of industrialization in Hong Kong. On the one hand, the "displacement" thesis argues that industrialization that occurred between the 1930s and 1950s was caused by the transfer of capital, skill and machinery from war-torn China. The newly-arrived capital was motivated to invest in industries due to the massive consumer goods needed in Western countries, and Hong Kong industrialists specialized in the sub-contracted production business from overseas manufacturers. The "evolutionary" thesis, on the other hand, argues that the gradual structural change that dates back to the earlier decades has provided the needed business and industrial infrastructure for the inflow of capital anyway. The basis of a free economy is an important element in both debates.

Another key fabric in a free economy in the formation of business is the size of business establishments. Traditionally, both investments from overseas and from Mainland China have been popular and occupied a crucial position in promoting output and employment. Established industrial plants that were geared to supply the overseas markets were mainly conducted by family-owned, small-scale enterprises. The lack of strong welfare support and the will to establish one's own industrial enterprises in a situation supplemented by economic freedom encouraged the flourish of entrepreneurs in Hong Kong. There have been numerous studies on the relevance and importance of entrepreneurship in a market economy (e.g., Baumol,

1990; Vogel, 1989), but a common feature of entrepreneurship in Hong Kong is that many owners of small- and medium-sized businesses (SMEs) are previous employees in their own profession or trade working for other employers. After gaining sufficient expertise, experience and gathered enough market knowledge from their previous employment, they gradually started their own businesses and expanded their connections. Many successful entrepreneurs ended up building their own business empire.

Indeed, throughout much of the free world, entrepreneurs tend to start with SMEs in order to reduce cost and risk. Hong Kong is no exception. Through the creative work of entrepreneurs, SMEs have grown to become the most popular form of business enterprise. However, one should not take it for granted that SMEs are the most productive form of business establishments. Over the years, economic dynamism has shaped the contour of SMEs, with some newly developed while others failed to survive from strong competition. The owners of SMEs themselves also need to position their business dynamically. The conventional wisdom is that SMEs are flexible, and can switch easily to different production lines and businesses; but flexibility also produces a sense of fragility and, especially at a time of crisis and uncertainty, SMEs may not be able to face up to severe economic shocks and waves.

Since the 1980s, SMEs in Hong Kong have been faced with challenges. The political uncertainty issue had resulted in large numbers of entrepreneurs and families migrating to other countries, while the low cost of production across the border after the opening up of Mainland China in 1978 had pushed a large number of manufacturing plants to relocate to Guangdong and other parts of Mainland China. Since 1997, the Asian financial crisis and the subsequent economic recession have imposed unprecedented pressure on the survival or revival of SMEs. Though the Hong Kong government at the peak of the post-AFC recession around 2001 and 2002 had provided indirect support through a guarantee on the provision of bank loans to SMEs, the bulk of SMEs still prefer to conduct their business at their own pace.

Industrial amalgamation has been suggested as a viable alternative form of business establishment that allows for preservation of individual entrepreneurship, flexibility in ownership, contribution of individual expertise, and a stronger business foundation capable of combating the relentless occurrence of economic shocks and crises. In other words, while individual entrepreneurship is an "evergreen" and has formed its roots in the business culture of Hong Kong, business owners may have to examine their business survival and competition realistically and carefully. The entrepreneurial spirit is that individual businesses look after their own interests and the entrepreneurs become their own bosses. To maximize business opportunities and build up business strength, amalgamating with other firms and enterprises may erode the advantage and freedom of being one's own boss, but the enlarged enterprise can stand up to pressures and challenges from changing conditions, thereby minimizes business risk. It is important to consider whether SMEs or large enterprises in Hong Kong are more productive, thus contributing more to economic growth in Hong Kong. Nonetheless, the evergreen nature of SMEs has made it the backbone of economic freedom in Hong Kong, as new business opportunities often begin with SMEs.

The study of SMEs in Hong Kong will provide an essential understanding in the context of a free economy. The study will first look into the nature and characteristics of SMEs to provide an understanding of SMEs in individual manufacturing and service industries in Hong Kong. A good understanding and knowledge on the economics of SMEs, in terms of skill, capital and technology requirement can show the important economic linkage between freedom, entrepreneurship, business and SMEs. The use of economic data on SMEs can show various limitations and potentials of SMEs, while the analysis on the performance of total factor productivity (TFP) growth of SMEs and non-SMEs will further provide insights into the dynamic nature of SMEs in different industries. These findings will be useful for SMEs in individual industries as business investment may change according to the economic directions of SMEs.

The next section discusses the features and characteristics of SMEs in Hong Kong, pointing out their various strengths, limitations and challenges. Section 5.3 will concentrate on the support to SMEs rendered by the government. Section 5.4 presents the statistical realities and the industrial dispersion of SMEs in Hong Kong. The key contribution of this chapter will be Section 5.5 where the TFP analysis discussed in previous chapters will be extended to the performance of TFP among different SMEs in Hong Kong. The last section concludes the chapter.

5.2 Characteristics, Limitations and Challenges

The bulk of industrial business in Hong Kong is conducted by SMEs. Indeed, SMEs in Hong Kong have flourished due largely to the free market economic principle and the traditional high entrepreneurial spirit of the people in Hong Kong. The Support and Consultation Center for SMEs in the Trade and Industry Department in Hong Kong gives a practical definition of SMEs. The definition for a SME is that "manufacturing enterprises with fewer than 100 employees and non-manufacturing enterprises with fewer than 50 employees are regarded as SMEs in Hong Kong". Various studies have examined the nature and characteristics of SMEs among industries in Hong Kong.

There are several common features of SMEs in Hong Kong. Family ownership is popular among SMEs in Hong Kong, as that will provide clear control of the business. In order to maximize profits and minimize production cost, capital finance comes mainly from personal networks or from banks as an alternative. Labor-intensive assembly production and extensive sub-contracting activities are common. A high degree of flexibility is exhibited among SMEs in Hong Kong. The labor intensive mode of production provides flexibility because producers can organize an appropriate labor force at short notice. Sub-contracting also requires a rapid production of a wide variety of products with a minimum level of capital investment. Indeed, sub-contracting activities serve as a market indicator to the SMEs as they actually reflect the direction of growth and expansion in different business activities. Indeed, taking small orders of batch production rather than mass production involves a quick delivery time and business turnover.

However, Storey (1994), Tang (2003) and Tam *et al.* (2005) point out that despite the innovative and uncomplicated organizational structure, SMEs are severely constrained by a lack of funds and physical human resources and experience a lower bargaining power when dealing with large organizations. Secondly, SMEs are less able to undertake research and development (R&D), and benefit less from economies of scale with insufficient production capacity and limited resources in selling and marketing. In short, the growth of SMEs may be constrained by a lack of corporate strategy involving such factors as location, size, and age of the firm.

There are several forms of sub-contracting. The original equipment manufacturing (OEM) refers to a system in which foreign firms provide product specifications, and foreign buyers sell the local made products using the foreign buyers' own brand names. Another form of sub-contracting is the original design manufacturing (ODM) that refers to a situation where the local firm conducts at least some of the product design and production according to the original design supplied by the foreign buyer. Thirdly, the original brand manufacturing (OBM) refers to a situation in which the local firm designs and produces the product using its own brand name. In terms of technology application, computer aided design (CAD), computer aided manufacturing (CAM) and rapid prototyping (RP) technology are commonly used in order to keep to a short product cycle. The studies by Siu and Kirby (1999) and Siu (2005) show that OEM is the more common form of sub-contracting, as OEM can often satisfy the specific requirement of low price and prompt delivery.

The ease of entry is another key feature of SMEs and OEM can by-pass the process of R&D in order to assimilate the manufacturing and design technology (Hobday, 1995). Davis (1996) argued that SMEs in Hong Kong show a combination of "high IQ and low technology". Redding (1993) further argued that SMEs in Hong Kong have specialized themselves as sub-contractors and have built up networking relationship in the form of molecular organizations. Siu (2005) also showed that instead of spending massively on marketing and advertising, SMEs in Hong Kong prefer "word-of-mouth" promotion. The SMEs operating under the OEM mode cannot really generate any impact on the market, and brand name development is severely limited. In sum, many SMEs in Hong Kong are short-sighted, lack long-term plans and market strategies.

There is a common saying among SMEs in Hong Kong that due to the high cost of R&D, the application of high technology by SMEs is uncompetitive and unsustainable when compared to that by large corporations and can end up with loss, while the application of low technology can flourish and be profitable due to its low cost and a quick turnover in business. Beginning from the 1980s when the low cost advantage in Hong Kong has been threatened by the emergence of neighboring "late comer" economies of Indonesia, Thailand, the Philippines and Mainland China, SMEs in Hong Kong had transformed themselves into high value-added, design-intensive manufacturing industries by adopting ODM and OBM strategies (Berger and Lester, 1997). The argument of a lack of R&D activities among SMEs can be challenged by the following evidences. By using experience from the US, Rothman (2007) pointed out that SMEs are most inventive as they are less bureaucratic, more conservative and risk-averse than large corporations. Many SMEs in the US have generated breakthrough discoveries, and are more likely to be among the top 1% of frequently cited patents than large corporations, indicating that SMEs are more effective in producing high value innovations.

The use of information technology (IT) among SMEs has been a concern. There are two surveys conducted by the Census and Statistics Department in Hong Kong on the use and penetration of IT during May and August 2006. These two surveys on households and business establishments are the *Thematic Household Survey Report No. 27: Informational Technology Usage and Penetration* and *Report on 2006 Annual Survey on Informational Technology Usage and Penetration in the Business Sector*. According to these two surveys, the percentage of all establishments using personal computers (PCs) was 60.5% in both 2005 and 2006, while the percentage of establishments having internet connection has increased slightly from 54.7% in 2005 to 55.9% in 2006, suggesting that the use of information technology maintained a steady growth.

In the two surveys, the large establishments are businesses with 100 or more people engaged for the manufacturing sector and 50 or more people engaged for other sectors. The small establishments are those enterprises with less than 10 people engaged regardless of sectors. All other establishments that do not fall in these categories are regarded as medium-sized establishments. In the case of PCs usage, the percentages of large, medium-sized and small establishments using PCs are 99.2%, 85.9% and 56.2%, respectively, in 2006. The corresponding percentages in 2005 are 97.5%, 88.9% and 56.4%, respectively. The large establishments are keener on using PCs. In the usage of internet connections, the percentage of large establishments in 2005 and 2006 are 91.5% and 94.7%, respectively. The same percentages for medium-sized establishments are 83.6% and 80.7%, respectively. The corresponding percentages for small establishments are 50.5% and 51.7%, respectively. In 2006, 17.5% of all establishments have a webpage or website for the provision of information about their products and services. This has increased by 2% when compared to 2005. The percentage continued to be much higher for large establishments (74.7%) than medium-sized establishments (37%) and small establishments (13.5%). These survey figures show that SMEs in Hong Kong do not use much IT for their business. However, given rapid changes in the availability and use of IT, the SMEs need to grasp the most updated and accurate information for their marketing and business strategies. The knowledge in IT is needed for SMEs to promote their products and services. In other words, SMEs have to prepare more for the "e-business".

A high degree of creativity and ingenuity is needed for successful SMEs, as they will have to identify their areas of comparative advantages. In a sense, entrepreneurs in SMEs to start with have to choose a low concentration industry with potentials, and should explore new or infant markets in order to master their own pace and potential of development. SMEs have to be well versed and informed with market characteristics, such as price difference, and formulate with care both short- and long-term business strategies. Innovation and reforms can always keep SMEs abreast of time, making them competitive and trend-leading. Innovation in techniques, craftsmanship, methods, materials and equipment can be used to develop new products. SMEs can improve their existing products in terms of size, model, appearance, variety and color. In other words, adding new features and catering to the need of customers can create new markets.

The development of an efficient and effective management system is another key feature in SMEs. Family-style SMEs may not be conducive to improving managerial efficiency. Corporate governance places emphasis on management integrity and fiduciary duties, with emphasis on such features as objectivity, transparency, benchmarking and accountability. A system of effective corporate governance can delineate the rights and responsibilities of each group of stakeholders and can institute mechanisms of checks and balances.

The SMEs in Hong Kong has undergone a sea change when Mainland China opened up her economy in 1978. The process of de-industrialization in Hong Kong began with the attraction of low production cost across the border in Southern China. The key consideration in producing in Mainland China is the advantage of low cost. In 2003, Mainland China's labor compensation per hour is US$0.8, the same for India is US$1.12, Thailand is US$1.96, South Korea is US$9.99, Japan is US$20.68 and the US is US$21.86. SMEs in Hong Kong gradually gave up their production base in Hong Kong, and set up their production plants in Mainland China, primarily through various local and village-origin connections. The "front shop, back factory" model has been used by a large number of Hong Kong SMEs in their industrial migration to the Pearl River Delta (PRD) region. With the relocation of low-end manufacturing to the PRD region (the back factory), firms in Hong Kong can focus more on high value added activities, such as marketing, financing, design and R&D (the front shop). A "triangular manufacturing" mode of relationship has commonly been established. Foreign buyers place their orders with Hong Kong OEM trading firms, which have established offshore processing factories in PRD. And upon completion, the finished products are shipped directly to the buyers overseas.

However, due to the absence of sufficient and effective industrial regulations and management supervision in many industrial plants in Mainland China, there have been reported incidences of industrial hazards, occupational diseases, overwork, management abuse and unfit use of chemical and other industrial inputs. For example, a total of twelve young workers had jumped to their death due probably to overwork in the first half of 2010 in a large Shenzhen factory complex owned by a Taiwanese company. Other cases include workers in jewelry processing factories have fallen to the victim of silicosis disease due to long working hours cutting and sanding semi-precious stones that generated clouds of dust in the crowded working environment.[1]

5.3 Government and Institutional Support

The importance of SMEs has similarly been studied in a large number of economies, as SMEs can provide sustainable employment to a large workforce. In most cases, SMEs are business enterprises employing a small number of employees, but there is little separation of ownership from control and SMEs usually occupy a relative small market share. An integrated framework of analysis that contains a three-dimension approach has been used by Farhoomand (2005) to summarize a number of SMEs in Hong Kong's manufacturing, utilities and service industries. The first dimension focuses on analysis that looks at SMEs from the macroeconomic viewpoint at the national level, from the sector viewpoint at industry level, and from the microeconomic viewpoint at the enterprise level. At the national level, the analysis involves the role of government in providing support schemes to SMEs. At the sector level, SMEs

[1] *South China Morning Post*, May 27, 2010; *New York Times*, June 18, 2003.

can be found in virtually all kinds of manufacturing and service industries, though their characteristics differ among industries. There are a number of varieties at the enterprise level involving managerial style, organization structure, and strategic goals.

The concerns in the second and third dimensions discussed in Farhoomand (2005) are the lifecycle and the environmental variables, respectively. The lifestyle of SMEs looks at the three phases on the birth, growth and maturity of the SMEs. The birth stage concerns the formation of the organization structure of the SMEs. The growth stage involves the introduction of new products and methods of production, and venture into new markets with new sources of supply. The mature stage relates to the analysis in the forms of corporate entrepreneurship and a more structured organization, involving possible mergers and acquisitions, diversification, contracting, licensing and franchising possibilities.

The third dimension concerns different environmental variables that are grouped under economics (such as population, GDP, economic policies, etc.), technological (such as technical transfer, infrastructure, intellectual property rights, etc.), culture (such as family values, socio-ethnic issues, historical heritage, etc.) and regulatory discussions (such as government incentives, custom requirements, foreign involvement, etc.).

A number of components in the three dimensions of analysis discussed in Farhoomand (2005) hinge on the relevance and importance of economic freedom. The birth, growth and success of SMEs are possible primarily because of economic freedom that allows individual entrepreneurs from different walks of life to start and engage themselves with their own choices and expertise. Through the activities of SMEs, the welfare of individual enterprises, and subsequently the welfare of all enterprises when individual enterprises are summed across different businesses, can be maximized and realized.

The relevance and importance of institutional and government support is the first dimension in Farhoomand (2005). Typically, due to the individualistic and entrepreneurial nature of SMEs, they often obtain market information and establish contacts through independent business associations. For the SMEs in Hong Kong, there are three levels of business associations through which business information and networking can be established. The most general business associations that are catered for all types of business enterprises in Hong Kong include the Hong Kong General Chamber of Commerce, the Chinese General Chamber of Commerce, the Chinese Manufacturers' Association of Hong Kong, and the Federation of Hong Kong Industries. Most of these general business associations share some similarities in supporting business development, fostering positive business attitudes and nurturing business sentiments. They differ in their backgrounds and orientations. For example, there is political difference with one business association being pro-Mainland China, while another caters more to local businesses interests.

The second level relates the business and trade associations geared particularly for SMEs in Hong Kong. The Hong Kong Small and Medium Enterprises Association (HKSMEA), for example, was established in 1996 with the aim to help companies to recover from economic recession and open new opportunities for growth and development. The HKSMEA shows great concerns on copyright infringement and points to the difficulty in securing financial loans, and helps to push for innovative design, assists members in securing funds and conducts seminars and exchange activities. There are other relevant SMEs associations in Hong Kong including the Hong Kong Small and Medium Enterprises General Association, the Hong Kong Promotion Association for Small and Medium Enterprises, the Hong Kong Chamber of Small and Medium Business, and the Hong Kong Association of International Cooperation of Small and Medium Enterprises.

At the third level, there are trade-specific and industry-specific associations. For example, the Textile Council of Hong Kong represents all textile associations and acts as a voice for the industry in all related matters. Similarly, the objectives of the Hong Kong Apparel Society include the promotion of industry unity, share of common interests in the industry, and foster growth and development. There are numerous industry-specific associations that look after the interests of businesses in that industry. SMEs in Hong Kong can also become members of foreign chamber of commerce in Hong Kong, which allow them to have direct contact with overseas businesses. Similarly, different foreign chambers of commerce in Hong Kong also show great interest in welcoming local businesses, especially SMEs, to be their members so as to promote networking and mutual business interests. All key advanced countries in the world have established their chamber of commerce in Hong Kong, serving as a link or bridge between foreign businesses in Hong Kong and the businesses in their home countries. Key examples are the American Chamber of Commerce, the British Chamber of Commerce, the Canadian Chamber of Commerce, the Japan Chamber of Commerce and so on.

The Hong Kong SAR Government has always taken an active role in aiding SMEs in Hong Kong, especially after the economic collapse resulting from the Asian financial crisis. The intention is to maintain a vibrant SMEs sector so as to avoid severe fall in employment through businesses conducted by the SMEs. By and large, the government support provided to SMEs in Hong Kong is mainly indirect that worked through funding schemes, establishment of consultation and support centers in the Trade and Industry Department (TID), Hong Kong Trade Development Council (HKTDC), the Hong Kong Productivity Council (HKPC) and the Hong Kong Science and Technology Parks Corporation (HKSTP). These institutional supports provide a rather comprehensive range of support geared to all SMEs and manufacturing industries.

In response to the economic downfall after the outbreak of the Asian financial crisis in 1997/1998, and at the peak of the economic recession in October 2001, assistance rendered to SMEs was elaborated in the Policy Address by the then Chief Executive, Mr. Tung Chee-hwa. A total of HK$1.9 billion (US$0.24 billion) had been set aside for the establishment of four funding schemes that would help over 100 thousand SMEs to face new development and opportunities in the post-crisis situation. The four funding schemes established in late 2001 included the SME Loan Guarantee Scheme (formerly known as the SME Business Installations and Equipment Loan Guarantee Scheme), the SME Export Marketing Fund, the SME Training Fund and the SME Development Fund.[2] These schemes were further

[2] Support was based on the recommendations of *Report on Support Measures for SMEs* submitted by the SME Committee in June, 2001, that studied the situation facing the SMEs in Hong Kong after the Asian financial crisis.

improved in December 2002 by raising the ceiling of the guarantee, broadening the scope of individual schemes, extending the loan guarantee period, and rationalizing the application procedure. Further changes have been made in January 2005 after a review of the schemes. Although assistance from banks would likely be considered on a case-by-case basis, major banks in Hong Kong regularly report the extent of assistance provided to SMEs.

Within the Trade and Industry Department, the Support and Consultation Centre for SMEs (SUCCESS) have collaborated with various industrial and trade organizations, professional bodies, private enterprises and other government departments to provide SMEs with a comprehensive range of business information advice and facilities. The main business information services provided by SUCCESS include: (1) comprehensive information on starting up business in Hong Kong and the various licensing and certification requirements; (2) a website that contains SME-related information, activities, services and facilities; (3) free access to business electronic databases; (4) collection of reference materials for businesses; (5) regular publication of the "SME Pulse" on issues related to SMEs; and (6) broadening of knowledge and entrepreneurial skills by holding regular seminars, workshops and other activities. In addition, SUCCESS also provides consultation services to SMEs through "Meet the Advisors" business advisory service and the SME Mentorship Program.

The HKTDC has set up the Small and Medium Enterprises Centre to provide comprehensive resources for information, tips, seminars and events, online forums and other activities. The HKPC has also set up the SME Centre with the funding from the Innovation and Technology Fund of the Hong Kong SAR Government to enhance the capabilities and competitiveness of SMEs in Hong Kong. The SME Centre claims to provide a "total solution" service offering customized business solutions and networking opportunities. The HKSTP provides the SME Incubation Program that aims to help technology companies to start their business through reduced office rental and credit allowance, and business support programs comprising management, marketing, investment and general services.

The indirect approach that provides mainly institutional support to SMEs in Hong Kong has been seen as appropriate and is in line with "the private sector takes the driving seat, while the government takes the back seat" mentality of minimum government intervention. Government assistance will unlikely be provided to an individual SME, and due to the diverse nature of SMEs that spread across industries and services, it would indeed be difficult to assist individual SMEs on a case-by-case basis. On the contrary, SMEs in Hong Kong may not necessarily be keen to seek government support through easier provision of loans from banks. In the first instance, SMEs may feel reluctant to disclose detailed accounts to the bank, as many SMEs are family owned and controlled. Disclosing the business accounts to the banks and relevant bodies for scrutiny may prove to be difficult for family-based SMEs or individual entrepreneurs. Secondly, many SMEs are conducting cross border investment, and banks are reluctant to aid such investment since cross border investment in capital machinery and other assets may not be accepted as collaterals by banks in Hong Kong. Thirdly, the open and flexible nature of Hong Kong would always mean that new opportunities may not be far away. In the end, many SMEs do not find the assistance from government too useful, but instead rely on their own way of survival.

Nonetheless, the package offered by the government at least has shown a good will and provided an alternative should SMEs really face their survival problem.

One can regard the two forms of "economic fertilizer" supports from government with financial assistance support from banks, and market information and technical support from institutions as complementing alternatives. The government support will critically be used when SMEs are faced with short-term financial needs and economic shocks. The institutional support, on the contrary, can be seen as an on-going form of indirect "fertilizer" assistance that SMEs can make use of at their own paces and needs.

5.4 Industrial Dispersion of SMEs

In March 2008, there were over 260,000 SMEs in Hong Kong which accounted for over 98% of the total business units and about 50% of total employment amounted to over 1.2 million people (excluding civil service).[3] Business enterprises other than SMEs are regarded as non-SMEs. Table 5.1 shows the distribution of SMEs of major industries in Hong Kong in March 2008. The import and export trade has the largest number of SMEs (90,800), followed by the wholesale and retail, restaurants and hotels (64,808). Together, they accounted for about 60% of the SMEs in Hong Kong and represented over half of the employment in SMEs. The number of SMEs in manufacturing occupies only 5.3% of total, equivalent to 7.27% of total number of people engaged. Given that there are only a handful of electricity and gas companies in Hong Kong, and mining and quarrying is an insignificant industry, construction probably will occupy the majority of the 781 SMEs in Hong Kong. Indeed, construction consists of large number of manual workers, and that explains the higher average number of people engaged (14.21 people).

The various annual survey reports conducted by the Census and Statistics Department in Hong Kong have documented the information on the total number of establishments, number of people engaged and the value-added content of both SMEs and non-SMEs. Although not all industries show the same availability of data, the detailed development of 11 industries in Hong Kong for the period of 1980–2005 can be documented. A summary on the SMEs in the various industries is shown in Table 5.2.

Manufacturing (Figure 5.1)

The Industrial Production and Tourism Statistics Section of the Census and Statistics Department has compiled the *Annual Survey of Industrial Production*. There are a total of eight industry groups in the annual survey, comprising: (1) food, beverages and tobacco; (2) wearing apparel, except knitwear and footwear; (3) textile (including knitting); (4) paper products, printing and publishing; (5) chemicals, rubber,

[3] These figures are best estimates as the *Quarterly Survey of Employment and Vacancies* released by the Census and Statistics Department does not provide a complete coverage of data on total business units and total employment (excluding civil service).

TABLE 5.1 Distribution of SMEs in Hong Kong (as of March 2008)

	Number of SMEs (1)	Number of people engaged[a] (2)	Average number of people engaged (2)/(1)
Total[b]	264,825	1,222,287	4.62
Industry			
Manufacturing	14,069	88,408	6.28
Mining, quarrying, electricity, gas and construction[c]	781	11,100	14.21
Services			
Import and export trade	90,800	410,562	4.52
Wholesale, retail, restaurants and hotels	64,808	301,697	4.66
Financing, insurance, real estate and business services	54,327	206,043	3.79
Community, social and personal services	30,929	147,763	4.78
Transport, storage and communications	9,111	56,714	6.22

Notes: [a]People engaged include: (i) individual proprietors, partners and people having family relationships with any of the proprietors or partners and working in the business unit without regular pay, and those who are actively engaged in the work of the business unit for at least one hour on the survey reference date; (ii) both permanent and temporary full-time salaried employees and working directors of limited companies paid by the business unit, who are either working inside or outside Hong Kong or temporarily absent from work on the survey reference date; and (iii) part-time employees and employees on night or irregular shifts working for at least one hour on the survey reference date. [b]Economic activities not covered include entire sector of agriculture and fishing; construction (besides manual workers at construction sites); hawkers and retail pitches (besides market stalls); taxis, public light buses, goods vehicles, barges, lighters and stevedoring services, self-employed insurance agents with no business registration; public administration, religious organizations, authors and other independent artists, domestic helpers, and miscellaneous recreational and personal services. [c]Business units in the construction sector refer to construction sites, and people engaged refer to manual workers only.
Source: Support and Consultation Centre for SMEs, Trade and Industry Department, Hong Kong.

plastic and non-metallic mineral products; (6) basic metals, fabricated metal products, machinery and equipment; (7) electrical and electronic products; and (8) other miscellaneous manufacturing.

Figure 5.1 shows the performance of SMEs in the manufacturing sector in the number of establishments, the number of persons engaged and the value-added for the period 1979–2005. In the number of establishments, one can see that the SMEs constitute the majority of firms in the manufacturing sector, with an average of 97.5% in the sample period. The proportion of SMEs to total is quite constant over the years, despite the different period of economic cycles in the 1980s and 1990s. There were 51,249 SMEs in 1989, dropped by 73.3% to 13,688 in 2005.

TABLE 5.2 Summary performance of SMEs in eleven industries

Industry/Sector		No. of establishments		People engaged		Value-added (HK$ Million)	
Remarks on SMEs	Year	Total	Percent	Total	Percent	Total	Percent
Manufacturing	1980	39,041	96.0	936,803	54.1	28,331	48.7
Share of value-added is falling,	1990	51,823	97.7	762,599	60.6	92,241	50.4
expansion requires new	2000	18,958	98.4	214,221	58.4	69,753	40.6
techniques, explore new areas.	2005	14,050	97.4	164,248	49.3	47,322	32.9
Transport	1980	26,516	98.0	110,784	57.9	6,691	32.7
Monopolies appear in major	1990	35,505	99.2	173,336	55.7	37,004	34.7
transport modes, not much room	2000	35,069	98.9	292,337	45.7	88,044	29.2
to expand, a matured industry.	2005	33,459	98.9	215,701	44.3	104,208	30.1
Wholesale	1980	9,416	99.5	53,831	92.7	2,430	85.5
Industry consolidating, rise of	1990	18,239	99.6	79,381	92.7	9,027	91.7
large companies likely, becoming	2000	19,481	00.7	67,051	91.9	12,545	85.3
less competitive.	2005	15,971	99.6	60,303	87.9	12,553	82.1
Retail	1980	36,143	99.7	141,485	83.3	5,614	72.3
Rapid growth of large retails,	1990	53,845	99.6	194,723	70.9	20,484	53.4
a falling market share, less	2000	49,173	99.5	193,764	65.3	28,752	43.6
competitive.	2005	46,729	99.3	198,700	54.4	36,090	33.6
Import and Export Trade	1980	15,407	98.4	118,145	76.6	13,105	64.3
Remain flexible, need constant	1990	69,140	99.0	376,157	78.9	85,487	68.7
upgrading to compete, venture	2000	94,197	99.1	490,780	81.0	225,359	67.7
into new areas, instant catch up.	2005	80,369	98.7	469,643	76.3	305,532	68.8

(*Continued*)

TABLE 5.2 *(Continued)*

Industry/Sector		No. of establishments		People engaged		Value-added (HK$ Million)	
Remarks on SMEs	Year	Total	Percent	Total	Percent	Total	Percent
Restaurants	1980	4,216	86.1	119,772	40.7	3,323	53.6
Highly mobile, face strong	1990	8,694	90.4	187,171	48.4	9,883	69.0
competition from non-SMEs,	2000	10,532	91.0	209,040	54.0	25,905	52.2
needs good business ethics.	2005	12,354	92.9	199,286	53.5	22,466	44.3
Hotels and Boarding Houses	1980	732	94.9	19,273	12.7	1,266	6.0
Losing to market leaders and high	1990	1,595	95.7	36,706	12.8	6,693	5.6
quality hotels, need to explore	2000	692	88.3	28,252	6.4	9,648	1.9
new business areas.	2005	775	89.0	27,506	7.5	12,689	2.3
Storage	1980	183	91.8	4,064	54.8	354	57.7
Expanding market, potential	1990	244	88.1	4,706	46.2	1,153	38.8
growth of non-SMEs, severe	2000	260	91.9	4,401	52.9	1,149	66.1
price competition.	2005	283	93.6	4,340	52.0	1,520	54.3
Communications	1980	50	62.0	16,010	2.2	1,730	0.7
Large capital requirement, need	1990	395	94.9	27,131	10.2	10,324	1.4
to be flexible and follow new	2000	1,034	91.4	35,700	16.8	23,979	1.5
developments in IT.	2005	781	91.7	30,802	22.5	21,515	11.1
Financing	1980	1,847	97.9	15,582	77.1	1,568	85.7
Large capital requirement,	1990	3,560	95.4	27,702	45.8	4,978	40.4
becoming uncompetitive, best to	2000	5,012	96.1	47,776	47.7	32,432	34.0
merge and amalgamate with others.	2005	4,680	96.2	47,685	44.6	44,167	27.2
Business Services	1980	1,885	95.5	26,482	47.1	1,958	40.4
Profession-related and knowledge-	1990	11,196	98.0	85,599	51.2	15,562	50.1
based, need to remain flexible and	2000	21,804	98.5	147,005	49.5	41,896	46.5
make quick adjustments.	2005	24,494	98.4	178,089	44.5	52,028	35.6

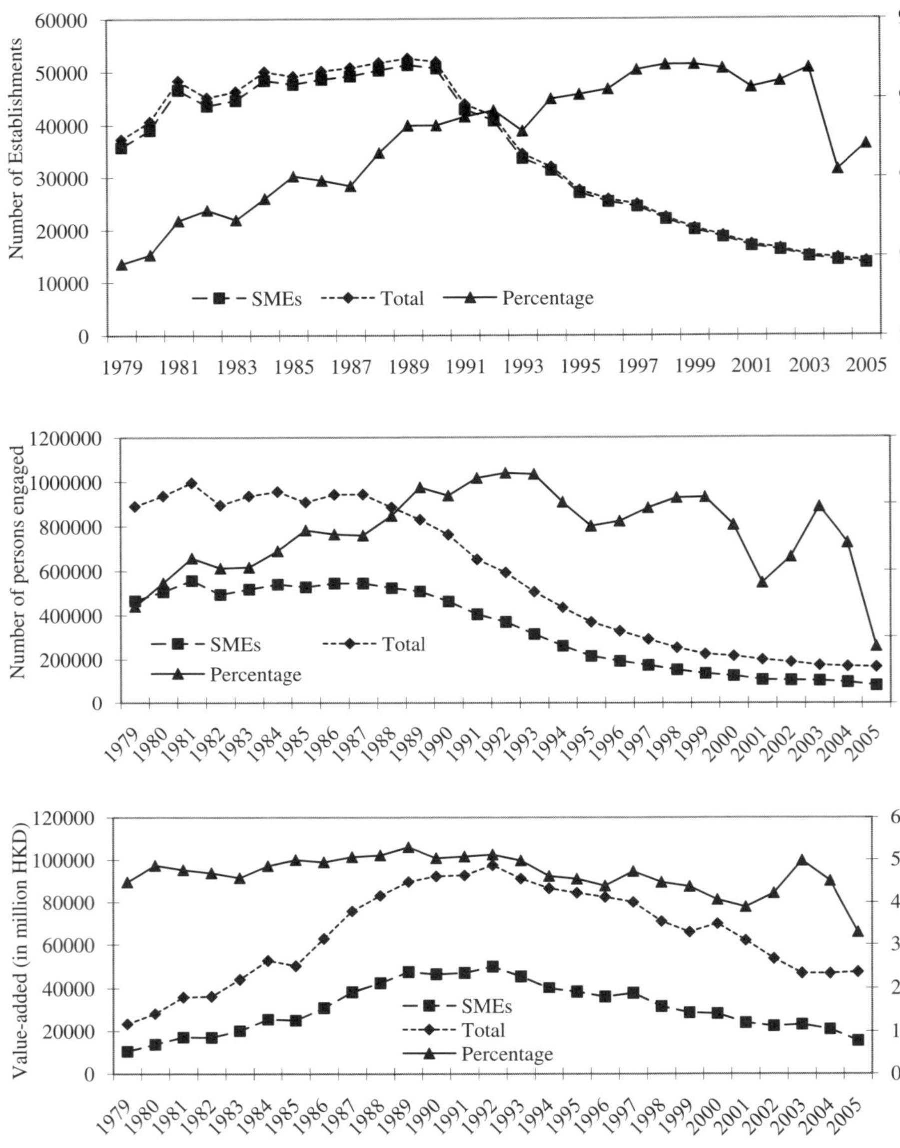

FIGURE 5.1 Performances of SMEs in manufacturing

The average percentage of the number of people engaged in SMEs for the sample period is 57.9%, though the percentage has fluctuated over the years. The rather steady increase in the 1980s, cumulated to the highest percentage of 62.32% in 1992, reflected the historic peak period of SMEs in the manufacturing sector. However, the highest number of persons engaged in the SMEs was in 1981 with 557,518, but the number has fallen to 80,989 in 2005, a drop of 85.47%, reflecting the process of rapid de-industrialization that began since the mid-1980s. The value-added figures incorporated the gross output (net of stock appreciation for work-in-progress, finished products and goods for sale) less immediate consumption. The average percentage for the value-added of the SMEs amounted to 46.7% in the sample period, though the percentage trend fluctuated considerably. The percentage was on an increasing trend in the 1980s, reaching a peak of 62.32% in 1989.

By looking at the three average percentages of 97.5% in the number of establishment, 57.9% in the number of persons engaged and 46.7% in total value-added by SMEs in the sample period, one can conclude that output of SMEs in the manufacturing sector, measured in terms of value-added, has been low. In other words, the non-SMEs that contained the remaining average of 2.5% in the number of establishments employed 42.1% in the number of persons engaged and produced a value-added of 53.3% on average. One possibility would be the unreliability of data since many SMEs under-report their activities, or due to the miscalculation of value-added figures when many SMEs engage in cross-border business.

In conclusion, the manufacturing industry is restructuring with the disappearance of labor intensive production techniques, and is being replaced by the more contemporary manufactures that are related, for example, to health and medical industry and quality control and testing activities. Many of these new adventures will involve high technology and large capital, or gradually shifting to production-related services.

Transport (Figure 5.2)

The report on the *Annual Survey of Transport and Related Services* conducted by the Census and Statistics Department in Hong Kong has provided data on eight groups of transport establishments including: (1) land passenger transport; (2) land freight transport; (3) supporting services to land transport; (4) ocean and coastal water transport; (5) inland water transport; (6) supporting services to water transport; (7) air transport; and (8) services incidental to transport. Figure 5.2 shows the performance of SMEs in transport sector in the number of establishments, the number of people engaged and the value-added for the sample period from 1980 to 2005. The number of establishments in the transport sector has remained quite constant, due probably to the mature nature of the sector. The sector experienced a gradual increase in the number of establishments until 1994, followed by a gradual decline. SMEs are the most common form of transport establishment, with an average percentage share of 97.98% in total number of transport establishments. Many SMEs provide services in land passenger transport and land freight transport are self-employed taxi, van or lorry drivers. Such a one-man business is more flexible in coping changes in the market, and can depart from the business easily.

The number of people engaged from the SMEs averaged 51.87% in the sample period. Such a low percentage is probably due to the large public transport operators of the major underground Mass Transit Railway (MTR), the train that goes to the border (formerly the Kowloon Canton Railway Corporation), the bus companies and the airline companies that take up the remaining percentage of the number of people engaged. Between 1980 and 2005, the number of people engaged in transport SMEs has increased by 48.9% from 64,143 to 95,477 people. In the same period, the

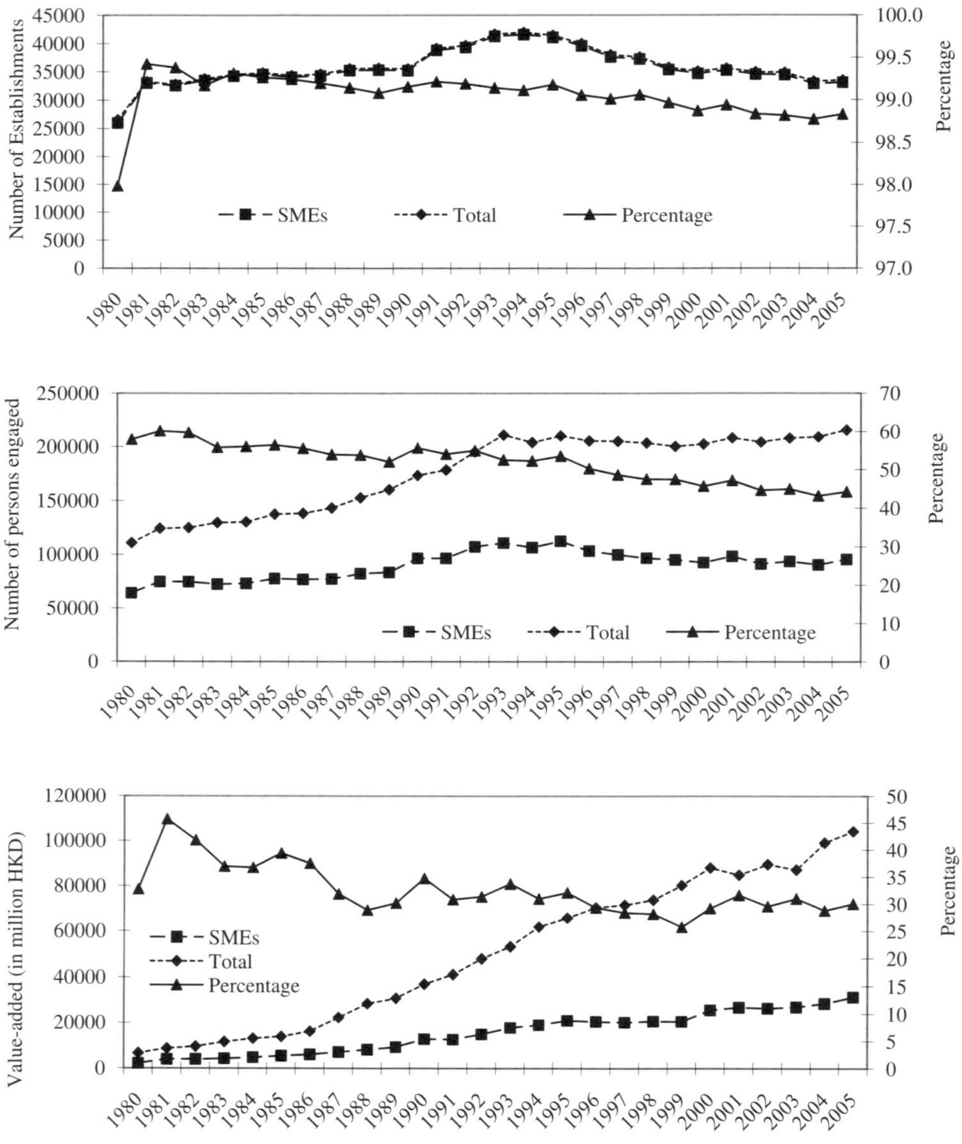

FIGURE 5.2 Performances of SMEs in transport

number of people engaged showed an increase of 94.7%, suggesting that the market leaders in the transport sector have expanded quickly.

The value-added by the SMEs in the transport sector occupied an average of 32.59% between 1980 and 2005. Such a low percentage reflected the continued expansion of the large transport corporations. Due to the "natural monopoly" nature of a number of public transport companies, the magnitude of their operation ensured a large value-added. Given the large needed investment in the public transport system, SMEs that compose mainly of individual suppliers cannot be comparable to large transport corporations.

One can conclude that modern transportation in Hong Kong is supplied by large corporations that operate in a "natural monopoly" situation. Transport is a matured industry, with few expansions. Cross border transport may even decline should Hong Kong's re-export business fails to expand further. On the whole, it would be difficult for SMEs to expand in the transport sector.

Wholesale (Figure 5.3)

The annual report of the *Annual Survey of Wholesale, Retail, Import and Export Trades, Restaurants and Hotels* has provided the operating information of these five industries. For wholesale, retail and import and export trade establishments, their value-added equals to sales and other receipts less income from other sources, textile export quota transfer receipts, total value of purchases of goods for sale and operating expenses, but plus interest payments, textile export quota transfer payments and changes in stocks. The products sold in the wholesale industry include; (1) food, alcoholic drinks and tobacco; (2) fuel; (3) clothing, footwear and allied products; (4) other durable and consumer goods, not else classified; (5) machinery, equipment and parts; (6) transport equipment; (7) raw materials and semi-manufacturers; and (8) general commodities.

Figure 5.3 shows the performance of SMEs in the wholesale industry in terms of number of establishments, number of persons engaged and value-added for the period 1980–2005. The wholesale industry is dominated largely by SMEs, as the percentage of SMEs in the total number of establishments is no less than 99%. The number of wholesale establishments reached a peak in both 1992 and 1996, reflecting the economic boom of the 1990s, but the number of establishments has dropped considerably since 1997. An average of 92% in the number of people engaged has been taken up by SMEs, though the percentage has ranged between 85% and 95% in the sample period. At the peak in 1993, the number of people engaged by SMEs amounted to 83,869 people. By 2005, it has dropped by 36.8% to 53,027 people. The average percent of value added taken up by SMEs amounted to 88.17 percent. The share by SMEs is quite stable since 1997, indicating that expansion in the wholesale industry in Hong Kong is limited.

Although the wholesale industry composes mainly of SMEs, the industry has experienced an expansion of large companies that will provide better coordination and economy of scale. This will impose strong competition to the survival of SMEs.

Retail (Figure 5.4)

The products sold by retail operators include: (1) food, alcoholic drinks and tobacco; (2) fuel; (3) clothing, footwear and allied products; (4) other durable goods and consumer goods not else classified; and (5) transport equipment. Figure 5.4 shows the performance of SMEs in the retail industry. Again, the retail industry is dominated by SMEs, with an average of 99% in the number of establishments in the sample period. The number of SMEs in the retail industry peaked in 1992 with 60,418 establishments.

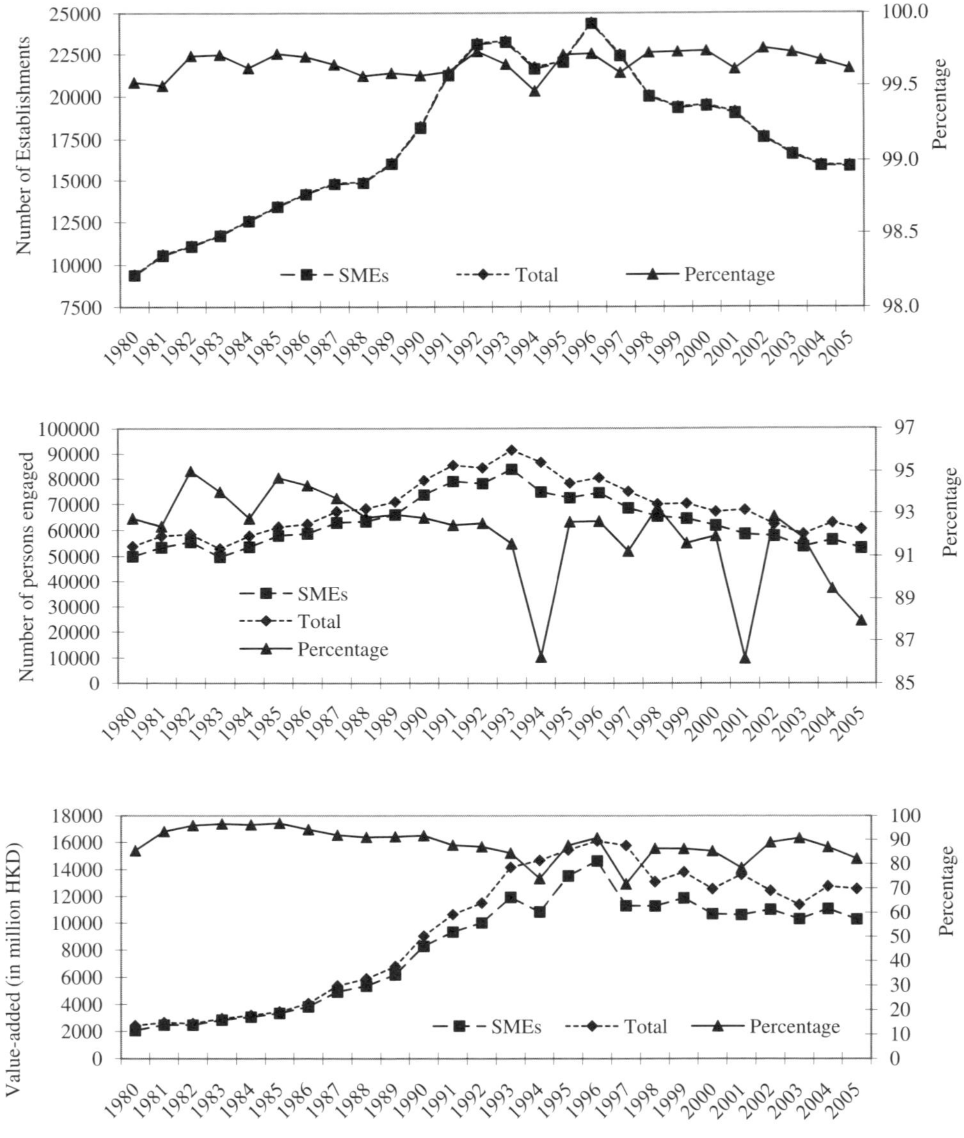

FIGURE 5.3 Performances of SMEs in wholesale

On average, 71.03% of people engaged are taken up by SMEs. Such a percentage is lower than the number of establishments, reflecting that there are a handful of large retailers in Hong Kong. Indeed, the continuous fall in the percentage of people engaged in SME suggests that the large retails have increased their market power, as evidence by the number of new and large shopping malls and brandname chain stores. The average number of people engaged in 1980 was 141,485, reaching a peak in 1997 of 244,255 people, but has fallen since. In value-added, SMEs conducted an

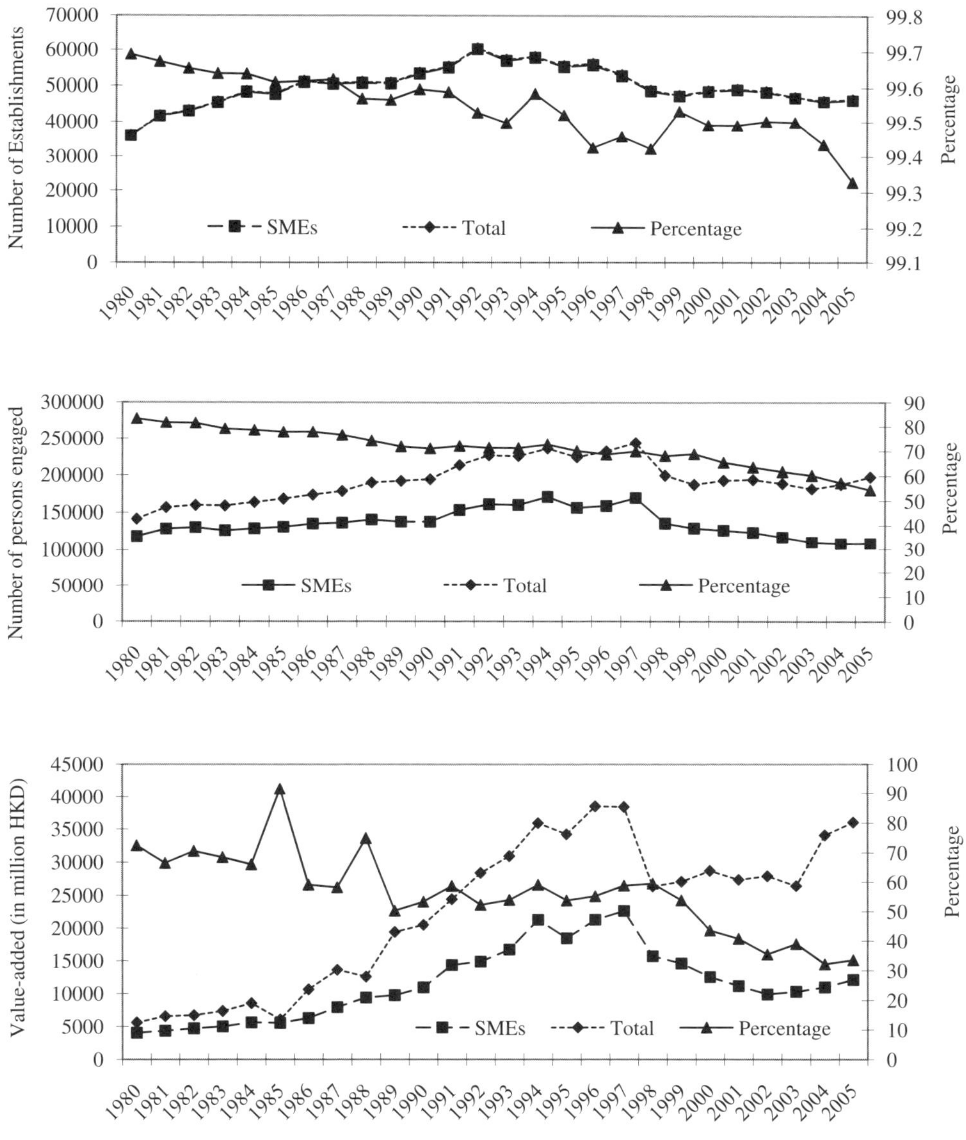

FIGURE 5.4 Performances of SMEs in retail

average of only 56.2%, reflecting the rising competitiveness of large scale retails shops. The disadvantage of SMEs in the retail industry emerged in 1998 when the value-added of SMEs has dropped from 59.52% in 1998 to merely 33.57% in 2005. Small-scale retail businesses are no longer competitive, and the changing consumer behavior in favor of large shopping malls is becoming the rising and dominant trend.

The retail industry experiences a rapid growth of non-SMEs, and the market share of SMEs is falling rapidly, making SMEs very competitive and difficult to survive. With the growth of a "shopping paradise" as more and more foreign brandnames establishing

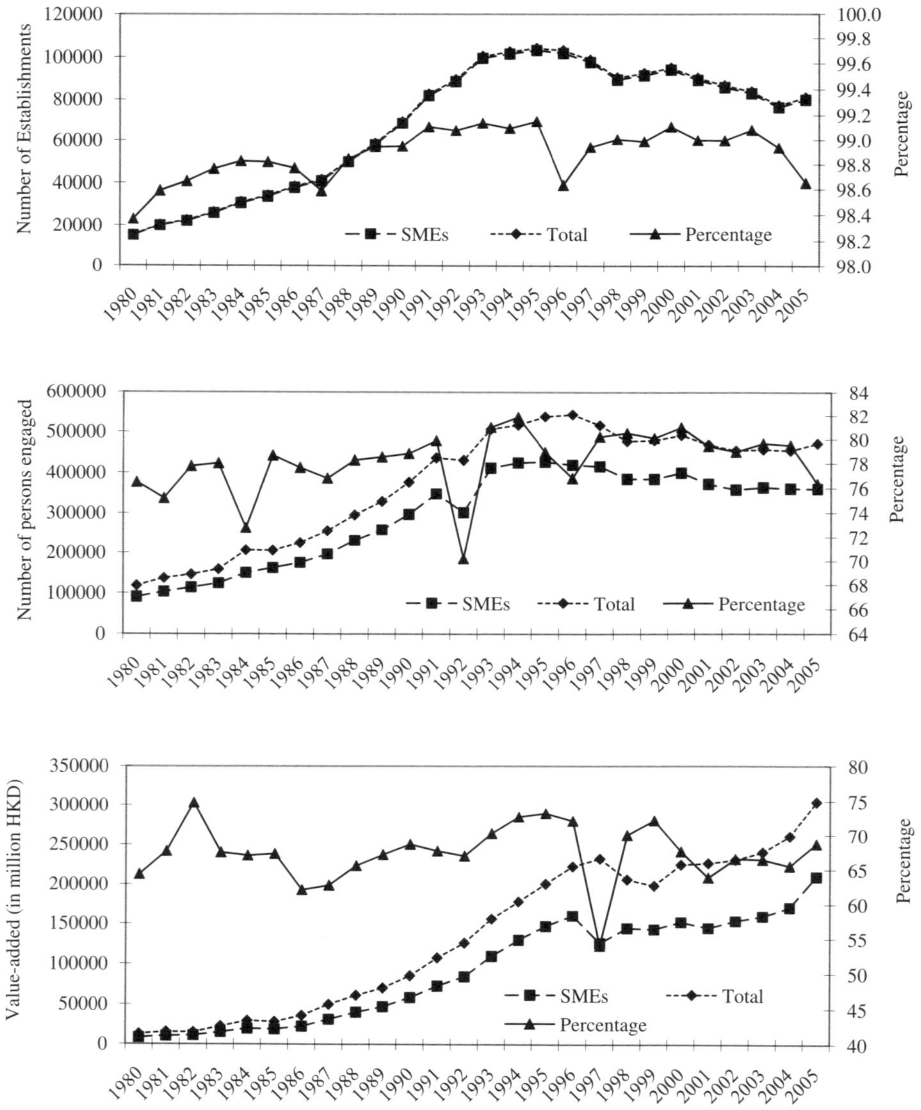

FIGURE 5.5 Performances of SMEs in import and export trade

their presence in Hong Kong, and as rents of retail shops rise, there will be strong competition from the fast growth of non-SMEs in the retail business.

Import and export trade (Figure 5.5)

The products included in the import and export trade are: (1) food, alcoholic drinks and tobacco; (2) fuel; (3) clothing, footwear and allied products; (4) other durable and consumer goods not else classified; (5) machinery, equipment and parts; (6) transport equipment; (7) raw materials and semi-manufactures; and (8) general commodities. The number of enterprises has experienced large changes in the sample period, as shown in Figure 5.5. The number of SMEs in 1980 was 15,158, increased and peaked to 102,629 in 1996 before dropping to only 75,788 in 2004. On average, 98.89% of enterprises are SMEs. SMEs have effectively dominated the import and export trade business.

On average, the SMEs occupied 78.23% of people engaged. The year 1992 that marked the Sino-British negotiation over the political future of Hong Kong has led to a sharp drop in the number of people engaged by SMEs. In 1980, there were a total of 15,407 people engaged in the import and export trade industry, peaked in 1995 with 103,504 people engaged before falling to 80,369 in 2005. The average percentage of value-added taken up by SMEs for the period 1980–2005 is 67.41%. This reflects the strong position of the few large remaining enterprises that took up the remaining 32.59% of value-added on average. Over the sample period, the amount of value-added exhibited an upward trend, except for a sudden decrease in 1997 due obviously to the outbreak of the Asian financial crisis. Between 1980 and 2005, the value-added of SMEs has increased on average by 13.42%. Despite the few large enterprises, SMEs in the import and export trade industry are competitive and showed a promising performance.

A high degree of flexibility is needed in import and export trade. With the changing world demand, SME is the more suitable form of business establishment, and SMEs seem to survive competitively along with non-SMEs in the market.

Restaurants (Figure 5.6)

The kinds of restaurants covered in the analysis include: (1) Chinese restaurants; (2) non-Chinese restaurants; (3) fast-food shops; (4) bars; and (5) eating and drinking places not else classified. The average percentage share of SMEs in the total number of restaurant establishments in the sample period (1980–2005) is 90.98%, implying that the sector composes mainly of SMEs. The pattern of restaurant establishments seems to exhibit a V-shape development with sharp falls followed by a quick recovery. Despite its somewhat erratic pattern, the overall trend showed an upward path, with only 3,629 establishments in 1980, risen to 11,471 establishments in 2005. Eating out has become a common pattern of people's livelihood in Hong Kong, due probably to the small living area at home that cannot provide sufficient gathering space for friends and families, the growing convenience of eating out, and the growing size of the female working force.

As shown in Figure 5.6, the SMEs in the restaurant sector on average occupied 49.85% of total number of persons engaged. The percentage seems to be increasing in the sample period. The two years of 1993 and 2001 showed the two peaks where the number of people engaged in restaurants was highest. In terms of value-added, SMEs in the restaurant sector produced on average 48.66% of value-added. This suggests that small restaurants are not that profitable, probably barely covering the economic cost and owners prefer to stay in the severely competitive restaurant industry than to look for employment. With growing popularity of brandname chain

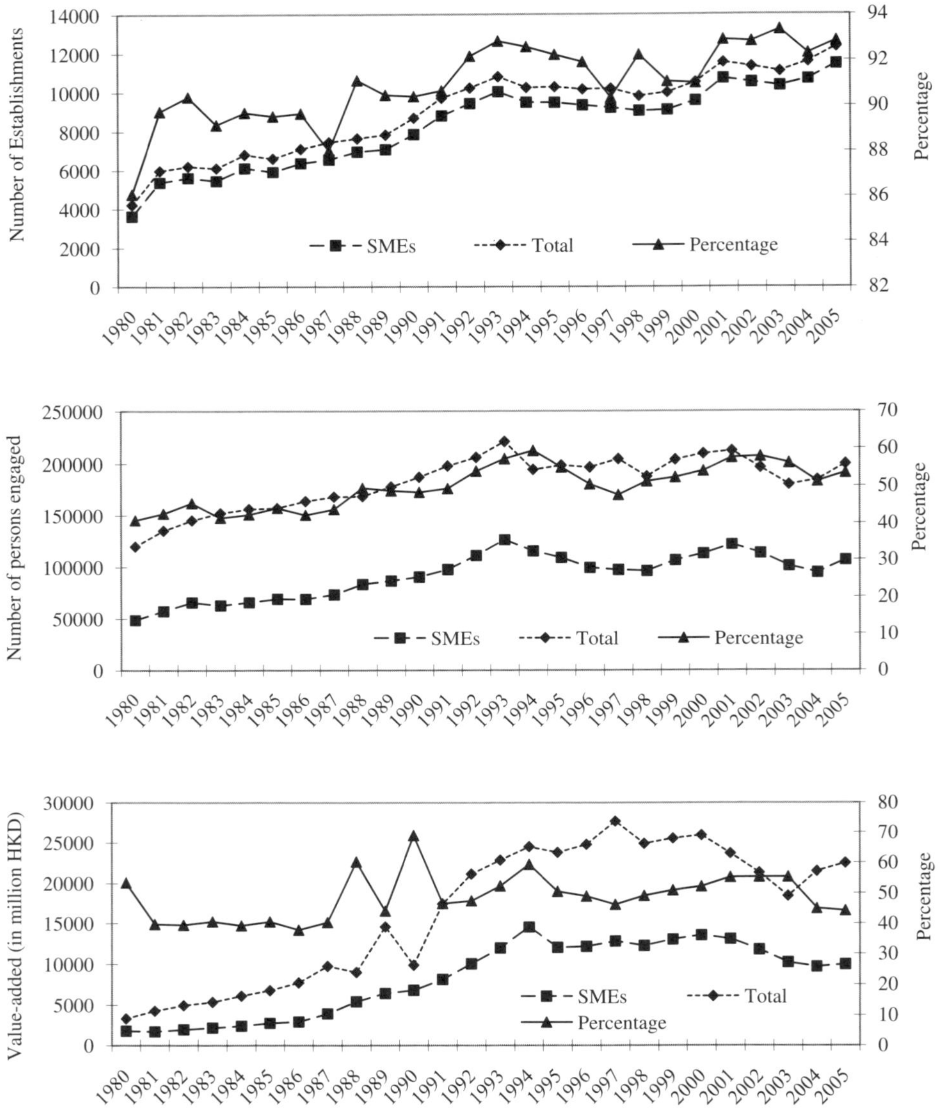

FIGURE 5.6 Performances of SMEs in restaurants

restaurants, franchising and provision of high quality restaurants in modern shopping malls, small restaurants will find it difficult to compete and survive. Indeed, one can see from Figure 5.6 that the value-added of SMEs in the restaurant sector has reached a peak in 1994, and has declined continuously since. Large restaurants are becoming more competitive and are dominating the industry.

The restaurant business is very competitive, and business mobility is high as restaurants can open and close within a short time, depending on rental cost and the economy. SMEs are facing increasing competition from large and well established restaurants.

Hotels and boarding houses (Figure 5.7)

Figure 5.7 shows the number of establishment, people engaged and value-added for the hotel and boarding houses sector. On average, SMEs occupies 93.09% of total number of establishments. There exist a large number of small boarding houses and a small amount of large hotels in Hong Kong. The economic operation of small boarding houses has become difficult since the early 1990s. With the

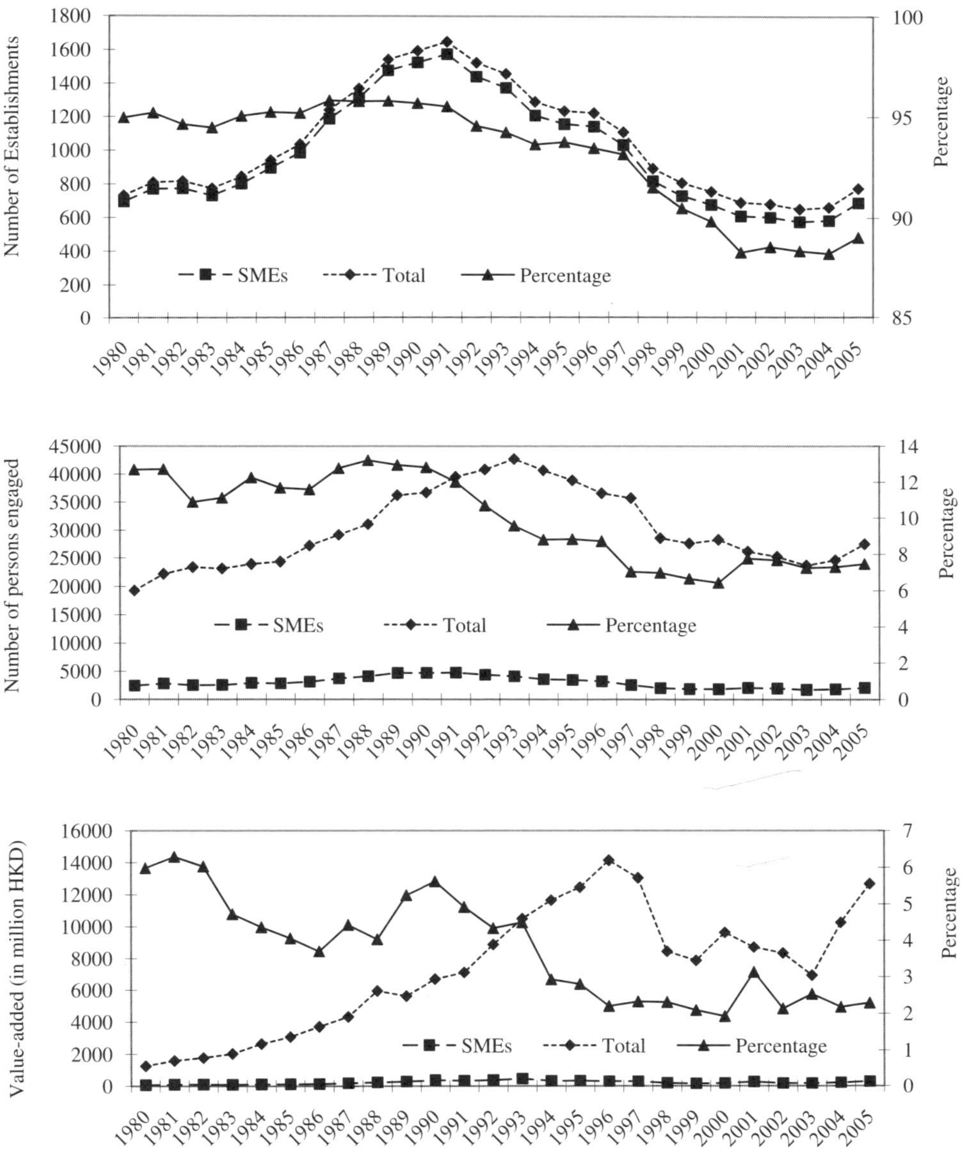

FIGURE 5.7 Performances of SMEs in hotels and boarding houses

introduction of the Individual Visit Scheme for Mainland residents to visit Hong Kong after the outbreak of SARS in 2003, there has been a revival in demand for more economical accommodation, and a rebound on the number of SMEs in this sector appeared in 2003. These economical boarding houses with few facilities and smaller room size are located mainly in the surrounding areas of the central business district, and the advantage of easy transportation makes them attractive to travelers.

From 1980 to 2005, the average percentage of SMEs in total number of establishments in this industry sector is 93.09%. But the average percentage of people engaged in SMEs in this sector is only 9.92%, suggesting that large hotels are the key employers. Indeed, over the sample period of twenty five years, there is an obvious drop in the percentage of people engaged in SMEs, suggesting that large hotels with high quality facilities are gaining competitiveness. The situation in terms of value-added is worse, as SMEs in this sector occupied an average percentage of 3.73% only. This is even lower than the percentage in the number of people engaged. Thus, the bulk of the value-added in hotels and boarding houses come from large hotels.

One observation is that family travels and visits to Hong Kong are much lower than business travels. While the former is for holiday and tends to economize on the cost of accommodation, the latter could either be purely business or business/leisure combined, but the cost of accommodation will likely be paid by the business firms who will go for the up-market hotel accommodation. As for the visa-free travel from nearby cities across the border, accommodation may not be much needed if daily travels and visits become common, given the efficient transport network and system. Family connections in Hong Kong encourage visa-free travels but such visits may not require local accommodation. It has been suggested that economical accommodation should develop outside central business district. For example, the provision of "bed and breakfast" facilities around major tourist attractions, such as the Disney theme park or the Buddha in Lantau Island, can encourage more family travels that are geared purely for holidays rather than business and shopping.

In conclusion, large hotels are the market leaders, due largely to the dominant nature of business travel to Hong Kong, while family travel to Hong Kong plays a secondary importance in the hotel industry. The survival strategy for SMEs will be to explore new areas and potentials in different type of travels.

Storage (Figure 5.8)

The different groups of establishments in the service sector reported in the *Annual Survey of Storage, Communication, Financing, Insurance and Business Services* include: (1) storage; (2) communications; (3) financing (except banking); (4) insurance; and (5) business services and rental of machinery and equipment. Storage refers to the provision of cold storage, general cargo warehouses and other storage services. As shown in Figure 5.8, the average percentage of SMEs in all establishments in the sample period is 91.21%. Such a high percentage may be due to the spatial constraint

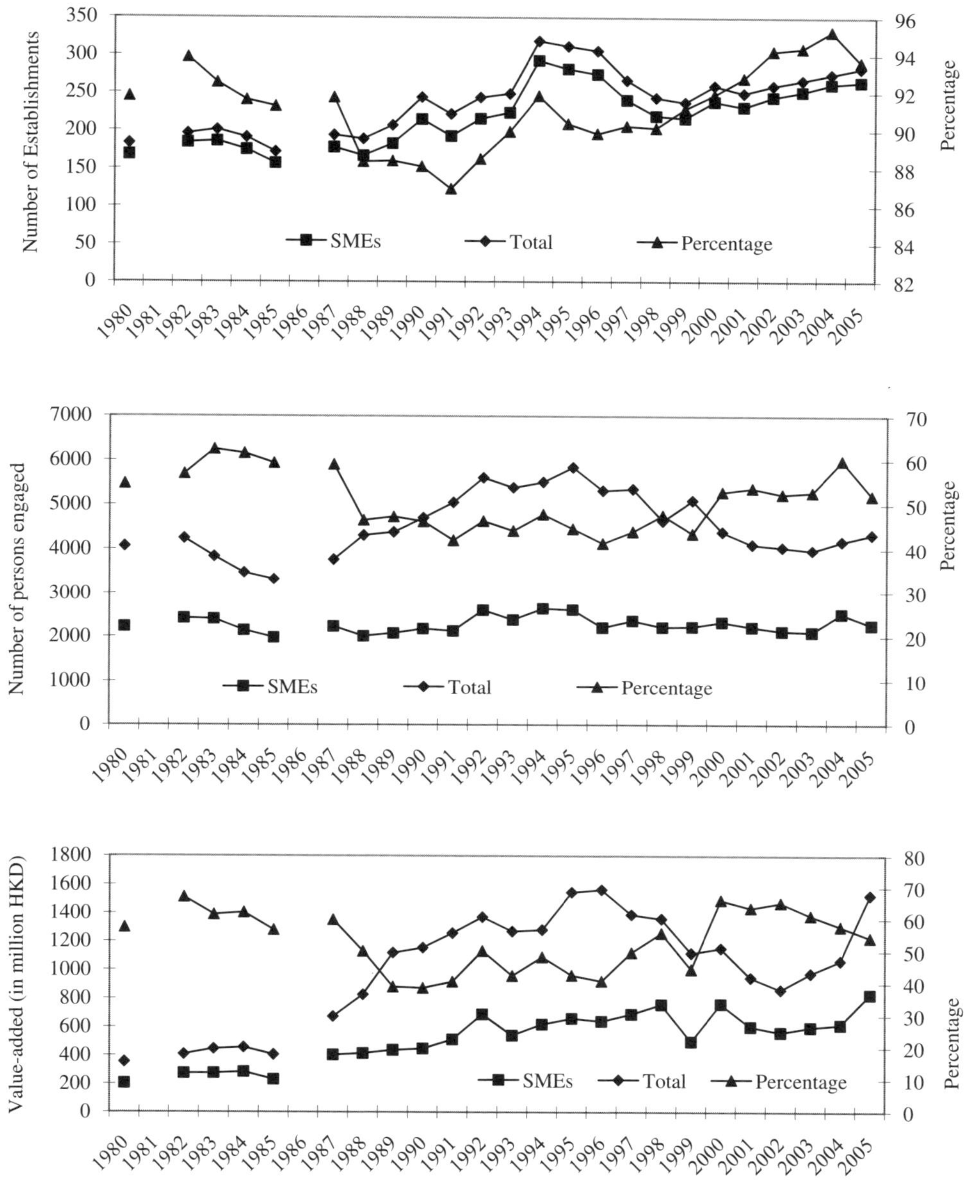

FIGURE 5.8 Performances of SMEs in storage

of the territory, and the high land price limited the development of large storage service. The number of SMEs has expanded between 1980 and 1994, but the number has increased again after the Asian financial crisis. The growing popularity of mini-warehouses for either commercial or personal use and the availability of former factory building spaces which have been restructured to become warehouses have led to the increase since 1998.

However, the average percentage on the number of people engaged in SMEs amounts to only 50.85% in the sample period, though the percentage has remained stable. One observation is that storage facilities do not require too many workers, as the required labor concentrated mainly in on-site management, reception, sales and marketing work. For example, the man-to-firm ratio for SMEs in this sector has not exceeded 14 people in the sample period. The average percentage of value-added occupied by SMEs in the storage sector amounts to 53.24% in the sample period. This percentage is similar to the number of persons engaged. SMEs in the storage sector have grown and become strong and competitive, making use of the resources from unused factory spaces.

Due to the potential of economic restructuring, and the availability of unused factory space, the storage business has expanded; and SMEs are still the dominant form of business establishment, maintaining a steady market share. However, there is a need to watch out for the expansion of non-SMEs when the market becomes more matured and saturated. Price competition will become severe as the market expands.

Communications (Figure 5.9)

Communication is a fast-growing sector in Hong Kong for the past two decades with the advancement in mobile and computer technology. This sector consists of telephone, telegraph, miscellaneous communication services, courier services and radio paging services. In the twenty five years of the sample period, as shown in Figure 5.9, the average percentage of SMEs in total number of establishment is 89.17%, and the percentage has remained very stable. Such a large percentage signals that the Hong Kong market is only capable to allow a small amount of large and leading companies to survive. The number of SMEs has been increasing, reaching a peak in 1989 and 1996. The industry continues to grow after 1998, reaching a new peak in 2001, when the number of establishments experienced a continuous decline. This suggests that the dominance of market leaders has wiped out the fast moving SMEs.

In the case of people engaged, SMEs occupied only an average of 13.49% in the sample period. Over the twenty five years period, there has been an obvious increase in the percentage of people engaged. This small percentage, however, is quite disappointing, taking into account of the fact that 89.17% of establishments are SMEs. One obvious reason is the low labor intensity among communication businesses. Communication services providers are lowering their use of labor so as to maintain a more compact company structure without a fall in the quality of service. Nonetheless, the number of people engaged in communication has increased by 1,855% between 1980 and 2005.

The percentage of value-added taken up by SMEs in this sector is also discouraging as SMEs only provided an average of 2.36% in the sample period. The time series of the SMEs shown in Figure 5.8 is volatile with negative value-added occasionally. Such a low percentage share points strongly to the dominance of large companies in the communication services sector. This industry contains a large number of SMEs that are not very productive. Large market leaders are most important. The survival strategy of SMEs is to remain flexible and catch up with new developments in the market. A high degree of competition is expected.

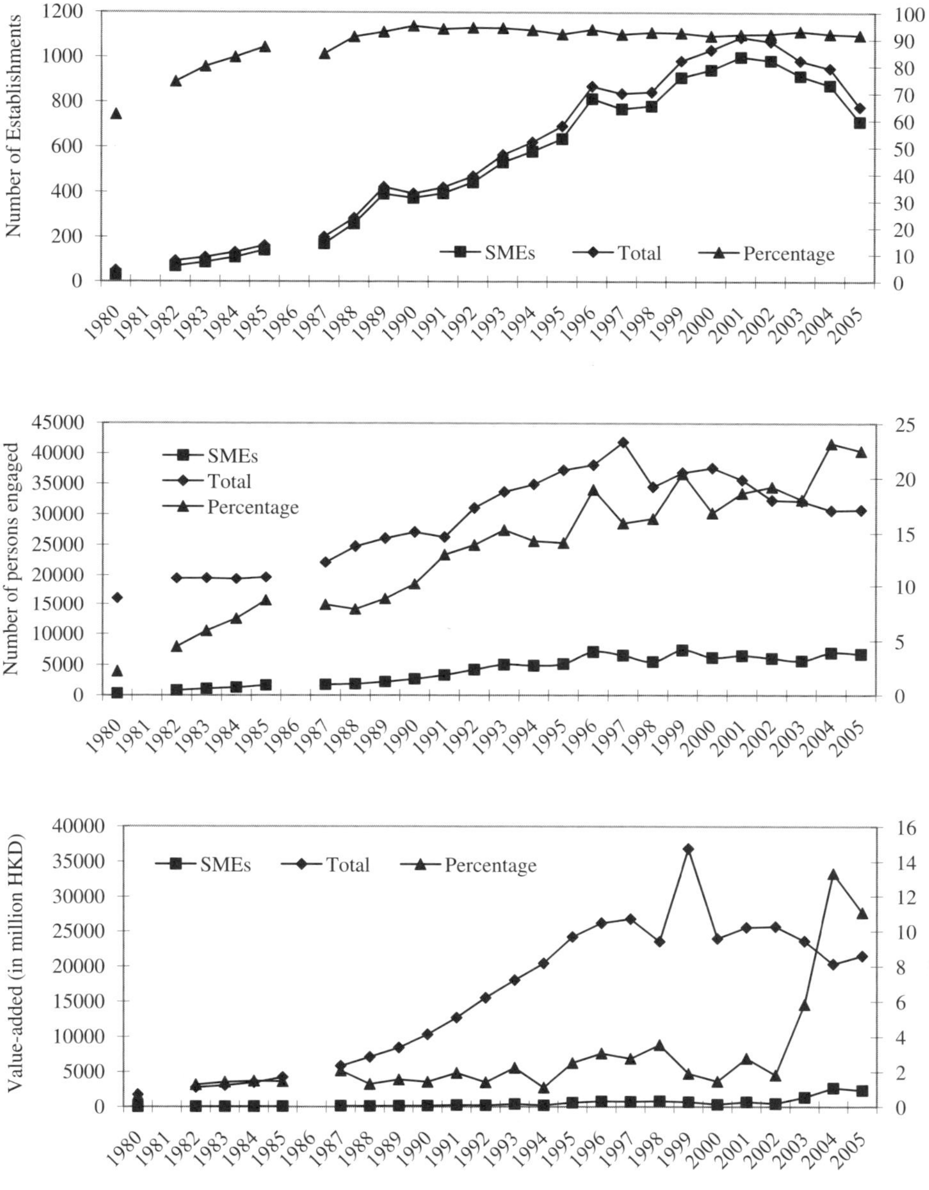

FIGURE 5.9 Performances of SMEs in communications

Financing (except banking) (Figure 5.10)

Although the government has repeatedly stated in its budgets and policy addresses that financial services is one of the four pillar industries in Hong Kong, Hong Kong has become an international financial center for a number of years since the 1980s. This sector includes: (1) investment and holding companies; (2) personal loans,

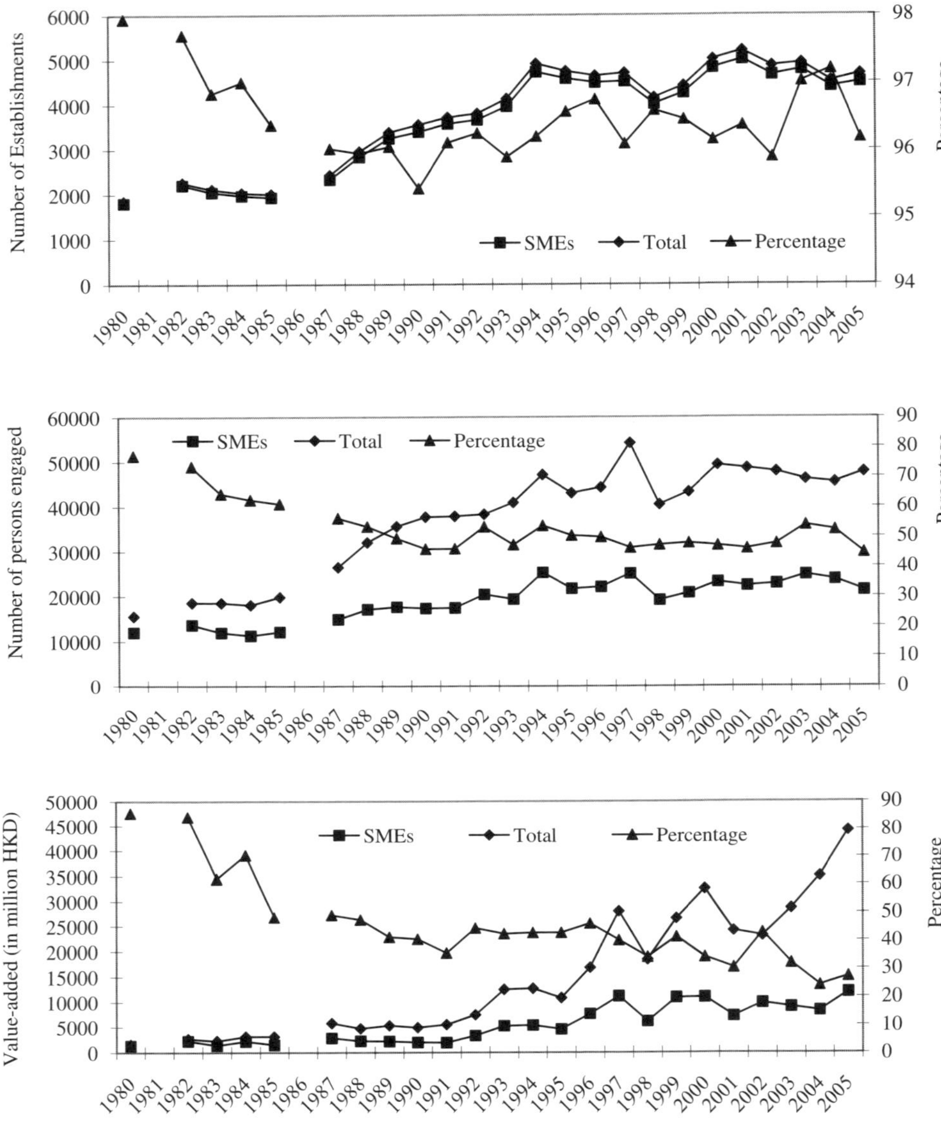

FIGURE 5.10 Performances of SMEs in financing (except banking)

mortgages, installment credit, finance leasing, factoring and bill discounting companies; (3) stock and share companies, commodity futures and gold bullion brokers/dealers, stock, bullion and commodity exchanges, money changers and foreign exchange brokers/dealers; pawnshops, financial institutions and financial services not elsewhere classified.

As shown in Figure 5.10, the average percentage of SMEs in the total number of establishments in the financing sector is 96.46%, and the percentage has not fallen below 95% in the sample period. The number of establishments peaked in 2001, and the percentage increase between 1980 and 2005 is 1,488%. But the people engaged by SMEs on average amounts to only 53.15%, with a gradual decrease from 77.1% in 1980 to 44.6% in 2005, indicating that the growth of employment in large financial companies is faster than growth in SMEs. The performance of SMEs in the average percentage of value-added in the financing sector amounts to only 45.3%. This confirms that the large financial companies are becoming more competitive and advantageous with expanding market share. It will become an obvious trend and outcome as financial companies involve large flows of capital and high level of risk that can only be achievable and provided by large financial companies.

Financing is basically a capital intensive business. Enterprises without a healthy financial position can become uncompetitive. One solution would be for SMEs to strengthen their financial position by merging and amalgamating into larger financial enterprises.

Business services and rental of machinery and equipment (Figure 5.11)

The business service sector includes: (1) rental of machinery and equipment; (2) legal services; (3) accounting, auditing and bookkeeping services; (4) data processing and tabulating services; (5) engineering and technical services not related to construction and real estate activities; (6) miscellaneous business services (business management and consultancy services, employment agency, security and detective services, designing services, secretarial, typing and translation, printing agent, and business services not elsewhere classified); and (7) advertising and related services (public relation services and market research companies).

This diverse sector contains different types of business services. As shown in Figure 5.11, the SMEs hold a large average of 98% of establishments in the sample period, and the percentage has never fallen below 95%. The number of SME establishments has shown an upward trend in the early 1990, but the number returned to an increasing trend since 1998. Many business services are professionals that are governed by their codes of practices, professional businesses tend to be in the form of partnerships that fall under the SMEs classification. The SMEs in this sector on average takes up 50.07% of people engaged, suggesting many business services are small and consist of one-person enterprises.

The global technology of the dot-com stock meltdown in 2000 had led to a fall in the number of people engaged by SMEs. Between 1980 and 2005, the number of people engaged by SMEs has increased by 534% from 12,485 people to 79,174 people. However, when compared to the overall percentage growth (572%) in the number of people engaged, one can conclude that market leaders have expanded faster than SMEs in the sample period. This can be supported by the relatively low percentage of value-added taken up by the SMEs. On average, SMEs occupy 46.67% of value-added in this sector, with the largest peak share of only 55.73% in 1994. The SMEs enjoyed a period of steady growth in value-added between 1980 and 1997, but the development of large companies has performed strongly since.

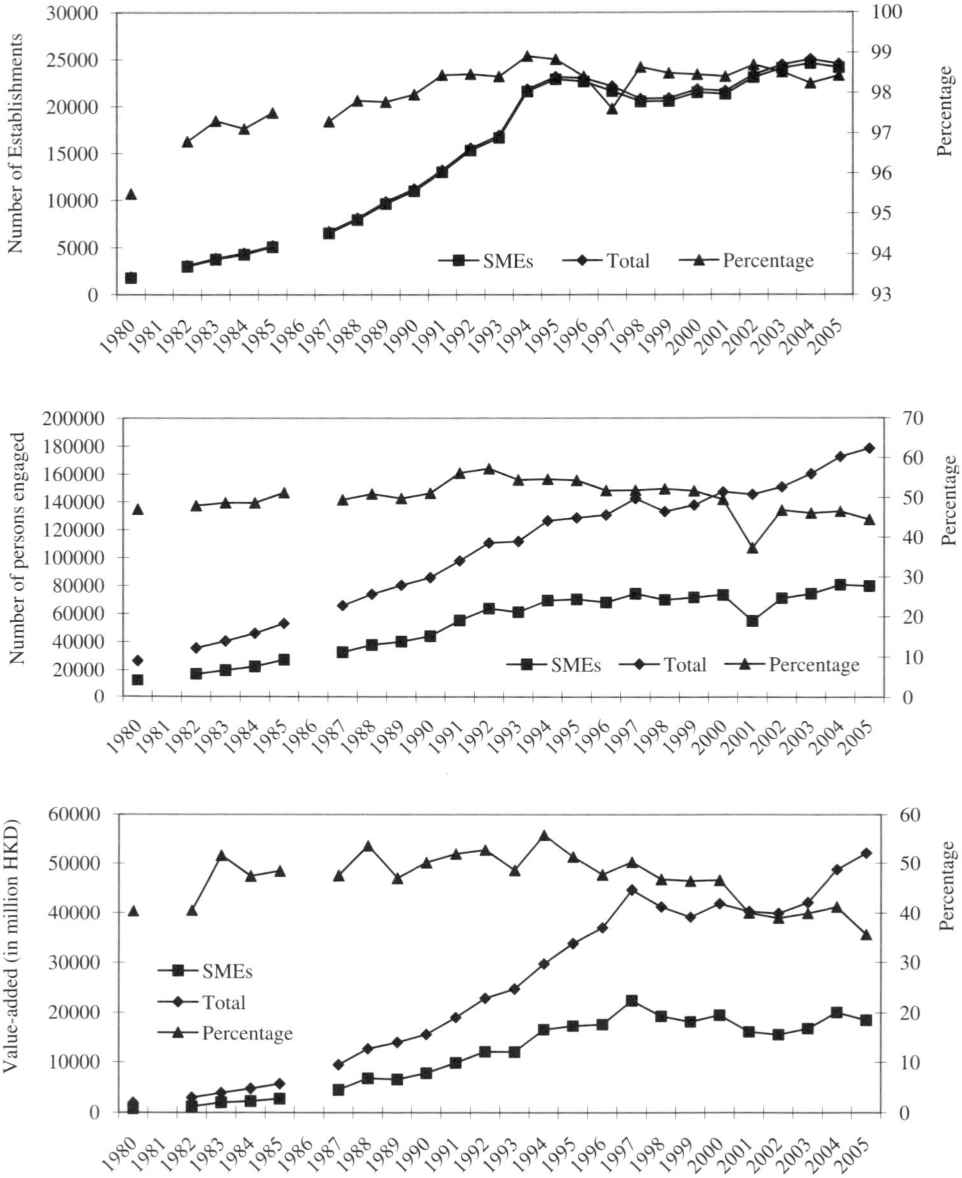

FIGURE 5.11 Performances of SMEs in business services, rental of machinery & equipment

This is a growing and competitive industry. SMEs have the advantage of flexibility and making quick adjustment to changing situations and needs. Much of the business relates to established and matured professions that have stated rules in the form of business establishments. Profession-related SMEs are mainly knowledge-based, but competition can be keen, depending on the stage of the economy. SMEs in many professions have looked for potential expansion in the Mainland China market.

To conclude from the performances of SMEs among the eleven manufacturing and services industries, one can use the data on the percentage of value-added occupied by SMEs in 2005 as a benchmark. One criterion is that those industries whose SMEs exceed 50% of total value-added in 2005 can be categorized as expanding. In this category, SMEs are profitable and can expand their business. The three industries in the expanding category are wholesale, import and export trade, and storage. SMEs are expected to expand in these three industries.

Secondly, those industries with SMEs sharing more than 30% but less than 50% of total value-added in 2005 can be categorized as competitive. There are a total of five industries that fall into this category. The five industries are manufacturing, transport, retail, restaurants, and business services. SMEs in these industries are facing strong competition from non-SMEs; and the needed business strategy can include amalgamation with other similar enterprises to form a stronger and larger enterprise, exploration of new ideas and catching up with the latest development, and/or introduction of improvement in their services. In retails, restaurants and business services, sale services can be improved by learning how to be more courteous and customer-friendly. After-sale services are generally weak in Hong Kong, as repairing activities are minimal and unnecessarily costly with the intention to encourage the customer to buy new products rather than understanding the need of the customers.

The third category consists of SMEs whose scores are less than 30% in total value-added in 2005 can be considered as matured industries. This category contains the remaining three industries (hotels and boarding houses, communications, and financing), and their characteristics are either capital intensive or information intensive. Unless the SMEs amalgamate with similar enterprises to strengthen their survival potential, SMEs will find it difficult to compete with large multinationals and non-SMEs in these three modern industries.

The idea of industrial amalgamation has been suggested for various reasons. In the mid-1980s during the peak of political uncertainty in the Sino-British negotiation and large immigration of Hong Kong people to major Commonwealth countries, business and industrial amalgamation could allow entrepreneurs took their turn to immigrate while having a hold in their business in Hong Kong in case they chose to return to Hong Kong after the needed period of residence in other countries. Today, with the growing popularity of non-SMEs, the challenge from IT, advancement in technology, rapid changing market conditions and periodic economic crises, it will be appropriate for SMEs to consolidate and grow strong in order to contain a higher risk level in their business, the suggestion for businesses to amalgamate into larger business entities can provide a long lasting business opportunities. Similar to mergers and acquisitions, SMEs can amalgamate with other SMEs either vertically (with different lines of businesses) or horizontally (with similar lines of business).

The amalgamation of SMEs certainly provide the advantage of a stronger and larger business enterprises, enjoy scale economies, higher potentials of securing better financial deals and compete with other non-SMEs and multinationals. The legal system in Hong Kong should provide strong lawful backups. One cultural disadvantage is that individual entrepreneurs would have to share their decision making, involving a higher degree of corporate governance, and a more systemic management system. Professional, industrial and trade associations can play the "match making" role of introducing individual SMEs to amalgamate into larger enterprises. Indeed, as the Mainland China economy is growing rapidly, businesses in Mainland China will grow, and SMEs in Hong Kong will soon face strong competition from both SMEs and non-SMEs from Mainland China. It is time to act and protect local businesses before it is too late.

5.5 Total Factor Productivity by Size of Establishments

It has been pointed out that the aggregate growth in TFP is a weighted average of the TFP growth in different industries. Changes in TFP growth in industries will change aggregate growth even if the industrial structure remains unchanged. The growth in TFP of different industries could be due to technological progress within individual industries and/or improvements in the organizational process. Organizational changes would occur when there is an emergence of new firms or mergers of different firms that eventually constitute to TFP growth. Since changes in both industrial structure and productivity growth constitute changes in the growth of the economy, a study on the industry productivity by the size of establishments can provide insights on the directions of factor mobility as well as the direction of economic structural changes.

Following the definitions of SMEs in the Support and Consultation Centre for SMEs in the Hong Kong Trade and Industry Department, the TFP growth of the industrial groups by size of establishments can be calculated using the available data on value-added, number of people engaged and compensation of employees of the SMEs and non-SMEs. Unfortunately, the data for the SMEs and non-SMEs are available only for the five industries of manufacturing, retail, import and export trade, business services and all transport. Nonetheless, the analysis on these five industries can give a clear guideline to the TFP performance between SMEs and non-SMEs in Hong Kong. Implications on other industries and services in Hong Kong can be made.

Data compilation for SMEs and Non-SMEs

First of all, figures of the value-added, number of people engaged and compensation of employees of the SMEs and non-SMEs of the five specific industries for the sample period from 1983 to 2005 are obtained from the various publications of the Census and Statistics Department.[4] The ratios of the three items (namely, value-added, number of people engaged, and compensation of employees) for the SMEs

[4] All data are obtained from reports conducted by Census and Statistics Department, including: *Reports on Annual Survey of Industrial Production* (1983–2005); *Reports on Annual Survey of Wholesale, Retail, Import and Export Trades, Restaurants and Hotels* (1983–2005); *Reports on Annual Surveys of Storage, Communication, Banking, Financing, Insurance and Business Services* (1983–2005), and *Reports on Annual Surveys of Transport and Related Services* (1983–2005).

and non-SMEs for each specific industry are multiplied annually by their respective industry's total nominal value-added, total number of people engaged and total compensation of employees gathered from *GDP2006* and *Quarterly Report of Employment and Vacancies Statistics* (EVS). In this way, the total figures of nominal value-added, total number of people engaged and total compensation of employees can be broken down into SMEs and non-SMEs figures.

As the number of people engaged is available for both SMEs and non-SMEs, their annual labor working hours can then be estimated from the following formula:

$$\text{Annual labor working hours} = \text{Number of people engaged} \times \text{Median of weekly working hours} \times \text{Number of weeks in a year } (365/7 = 52.14). \quad (1)$$

The number of self-employed for SMEs and non-SMEs can then be calculated by multiplying the number of people engaged with the ratio of self-employed. The adjusted compensation of employees for SMEs and non-SMEs can also be calculated by the following formula:

$$\text{Adjusted compensation of employees} = \text{Compensation of employees} + \text{Compensation per employed person} \times \text{Number of self-employed}. \quad (2)$$

Once the data for the adjusted compensation of employees of SMEs and non-SMEs is available, the share of payment of labor for SMEs and non-SMEs can then be calculated by dividing the adjusted compensation of employees by the nominal value-added. As the two factor shares of payment sum to unity, the share of payment of capital for SMEs and non-SMEs can then be derived. With the availability of the share of capital for SMEs and non-SMEs, the capital income for SMEs and non-SMEs can be calculated by multiplying the share of payment of capital by the nominal value-added. The capital stock for SMEs and non-SMEs of a specific industry can be calculated using the following formula:

$$\text{Capital stock} = \text{capital income}/\text{aggregate capital income for all industries} \times \text{total national capital stock}. \quad (3)$$

In this way, all the variables for value-added, capital stock and number of labor working hours, share of payment of labor and share of payment of capital for SMEs and non-SMEs for specific industries can be made available from the method of estimation shown in the last chapter. The five tables from Table 5.3 to Table 5.7 show the total factor productivity analysis of these five industries based on the size of establishments. A discussion on individual industries can be studied and compared.

Manufacturing

As shown in Table 5.3, the manufacturing industry has an average growth rate of 0.9% in output for the whole period, with a stronger performance of a positive

TABLE 5.3 Productivity accounting for manufacturing by size of establishments: 1983–2005 (compound annual growth rates)

		1983–1985	1986–1990	1991–1995	1996–2000	2001–2005	1983–1990	1991–2000	1983–2005
Growth Rates									
Output	Total	7.9	7.3	0.5	–4.1	–3.8	7.5	–1.8	0.9
	SMEs	10.2	7.5	–1.5	–6.2	–7.7	8.5	–3.9	–0.6
	Non-SMEs	5.8	7.1	2.4	–2.4	–1.4	6.6	0.0	2.0
Capital	Total	13.0	7.4	–7.0	4.0	–9.8	9.5	–1.7	0.2
	SMEs	21.7	9.0	–8.8	–0.8	–14.1	13.6	–4.9	–1.1
	Non-SMEs	8.4	6.2	–5.8	6.7	–8.0	7.0	0.3	0.7
Labor	Total	1.4	–3.3	–12.1	–9.7	–5.8	–2.5	–10.9	–6.6
	SMEs	3.1	–2.5	–12.8	–9.6	–9.0	–0.7	–11.2	–7.1
	Non-SMEs	–0.7	–4.5	–11.1	–9.7	–2.0	–5.0	–10.4	–6.1
Share of Payment									
Capital	Total	0.29	0.35	0.38	0.40	0.35	0.33	0.39	0.36
	SMEs	0.23	0.31	0.32	0.32	0.29	0.28	0.32	0.30
	Non-SMEs	0.35	0.40	0.43	0.45	0.39	0.38	0.44	0.41
Labor	Total	0.71	0.65	0.62	0.60	0.65	0.67	0.61	0.64
	SMEs	0.77	0.69	0.68	0.68	0.71	0.72	0.68	0.70
	Non-SMEs	0.65	0.60	0.57	0.55	0.61	0.62	0.56	0.59
Contribution to Output by									
TFP	Total	3.1	6.8	10.7	0.2	3.5	6.1	5.5	5.1
	SMEs	2.7	6.4	10.0	0.5	2.7	5.2	5.3	4.6
	Non-SMEs	3.4	7.4	11.2	–0.1	3.0	7.0	5.7	5.3
Capital	Total	3.8	2.6	–2.7	1.6	–3.4	3.1	–0.6	0.1
Input	SMEs	5.1	2.8	–2.8	–0.3	–4.1	3.8	–1.6	–0.3
	Non-SMEs	2.9	2.5	–2.5	3.0	–3.1	2.7	0.1	0.3
Labor	Total	1.0	–2.2	–7.5	–5.8	–3.8	–1.7	–6.7	–4.3
Input	SMEs	2.4	–1.7	–8.7	–6.5	–6.4	–0.5	–7.6	–5.0
	Non-SMEs	–0.5	–2.7	–6.3	–5.3	–1.3	–3.1	–5.8	–3.6

growth rate (7.5%) in output in the 1980s but a weak performance in output growth rate in the 1990s (–1.8%). The highest growth rate in output (7.9%) happened during the period of Sino-British negotiations (1983–1995) over Hong Kong's sovereignty reversion, while the lowest growth rate in output (–4.1%) occurred in the period of 1996–2000 when the Asian financial crisis hit the Hong Kong economy hard. A mild improvement (–3.8%) was seen in the period of 2001–2005 when the economy was recovering from recession.

When the performances between SMEs and non-SMEs are compared for the sample period, the non-SMEs (2.0%) had a higher average growth rate than the SMEs (–0.6%). Though the non-SMEs performed worse than SMEs did during the Sino-British negations in the early period of the 1980s, the non-SMEs had a better performance during both the Asian financial crisis and SARS periods.

In the TFP performance, the manufacturing industry has an average TFP growth rate of 5.1% in the whole period, with a peak of 10.7% in the early 1990s but dropped to 0.2% in the Asian financial crisis period (1996–2000). Between the two sizes of establishments, the SMEs had a higher average TFP growth rate than the non-SMEs only during the Asian financial crisis period (0.5% for SMEs and –0.1% for non-SMEs). Although the non-SMEs have a higher TFP growth rates in all other periods, their differences in the TFP growth rates are not too large, with 4.6% and 5.3% for the sample period for the SMEs and non-SMEs, respectively. This probably suggests that the SMEs in the manufacturing sector are quite efficient and competitive, but have to prepare for possible strong competition from non-SMEs.

The changing structure in the manufacturing sector can be seen from the contribution to output by the capital inputs. In the 1980s, the performance of SMEs was stronger than non-SMEs, with 5.1% in 1983–1985 and 2.8% in 1986–1990, as compared to 2.9% and 2.5%, respectively, in the two sub-periods in the 1980s. Since the 1990s, however, the situation has been reversed with non-SMEs contributed more than SMEs did. This is probably due to the falling importance of SMEs during the process of de-industrialization in the 1990s, resulting in the non-SMEs having a stronger ability to survive. Thus, non-SMEs provide a stronger performance than SMEs. This gives a clear picture of restructuring in the manufacturing industry in Hong Kong. With the migration of family-owned SMEs to Mainland China since the mid-1980s, it is the larger non-SMEs that can maintain and provide a stronger and competitive back-up financially, technologically and market-wise.

Retail

One can see from Table 5.4 that the retail industry has an average growth rate of 3.7% in output in the sample period, with the highest output growth rate of 6.6% in 1986–1990, and the lowest growth rate of 0.3% in 1996–2000. There is a significant difference in the performance of output growth rates between SMEs (0.4%) and non-SMEs (7.4%) for the sample period. Such a large difference is due to the negative output growth rates experienced by SMEs in three sub-periods of 1983–1985, 1986–1990, and 2001–2005. In short, non-SMEs in the retail sector have experienced much higher output growth than SMEs.

TABLE 5.4 Productivity accounting for retail by size of establishments: 1983–2005 (compound annual growth rates)

		1983–1985	1986–1990	1991–1995	1996–2000	2001–2005	1983–1990	1991–2000	1983–2005
Growth Rates									
Output	Total	4.0	6.6	3.0	0.3	4.9	5.6	1.7	3.7
	SMEs	–0.9	3.8	3.2	–3.8	–0.4	2.0	–0.4	0.4
	Non-SMEs	14.1	10.4	2.8	4.4	8.4	11.8	3.6	7.4
Capital	Total	8.0	–1.2	–2.6	5.6	11.3	2.2	1.4	3.8
	SMEs	2.2	–3.1	0.7	–3.3	5.6	–1.1	–1.3	0.2
	Non-SMEs	22.3	1.8	–7.8	18.0	15.1	9.0	4.3	8.2
Labor	Total	2.7	1.6	–0.2	1.6	0.6	2.0	0.7	1.1
	SMEs	1.0	–0.3	–0.4	0.2	–3.0	0.2	–0.1	–0.6
	Non-SMEs	9.3	7.1	0.4	4.6	6.3	7.9	2.5	5.2
Share of Payment									
Capital	Total	0.44	0.45	0.35	0.26	0.32	0.45	0.30	0.36
	SMEs	0.47	0.48	0.46	0.33	0.29	0.48	0.39	0.40
	Non-SMEs	0.39	0.36	0.22	0.15	0.34	0.37	0.19	0.29
Labor	Total	0.56	0.55	0.65	0.74	0.68	0.55	0.70	0.64
	SMEs	0.53	0.52	0.54	0.67	0.71	0.52	0.61	0.60
	Non-SMEs	0.61	0.64	0.78	0.85	0.66	0.63	0.81	0.71
Contribution to Output by									
TFP	Total	–1.1	6.2	4.1	–2.3	0.8	3.5	0.7	1.6
	SMEs	–2.5	5.4	3.1	–2.9	0.0	2.4	0.2	0.7
	Non-SMEs	–0.3	5.3	4.2	–2.3	-0.9	3.4	0.8	1.4
Capital Input	Total	3.6	–0.5	–0.9	1.4	3.6	1.0	0.4	1.4
	SMEs	1.0	–1.5	0.3	–1.1	1.6	–0.5	–0.5	0.1
	Non-SMEs	8.7	0.6	–1.7	2.8	5.1	3.4	0.8	2.3
Labor Input	Total	1.5	0.9	–0.1	1.2	0.4	1.1	0.5	0.7
	SMEs	0.6	–0.1	–0.2	0.2	–2.1	0.1	–0.1	–0.4
	Non-SMEs	5.7	4.5	0.3	3.9	4.2	5.0	2.0	3.7

The retail industry has an average TFP growth rate of 1.6% for the whole period, with the highest rate of 6.2% during the late 1980s and lowest rate of –2.3% during the late 1990s. When comparing the SMEs with non-SMEs, the non-SMEs (1.4%) have a much better performance in average growth rate of TFP than the SMEs (0.7%). The only period when the TFP growth of SMEs (0.0%) performed better than the non-SMEs (–0.9%) is the post-AFC period of 2001–2005. In all other periods, the TFP growth of non-SMEs has performed better than the SMEs in the retail industry. This suggests that in the retail industry, the SMEs are losing their competitiveness as the larger non-SMEs are dominating the Hong Kong market. Indeed, when examining the contribution to output growth by capital and labor, non-SMEs outperformed SMEs in all periods.

One implication is that small retail shops are getting outdated or faced with locational problems, and consumers are increasingly adopting to patronize large retail supermarkets, chain stores with brandnames and shopping malls in modern residential complexes. Another implication is that the dominance of non-SMEs will erode the needed business and market competition in Hong Kong economy, and that the non-SMEs with their large capital investment and provision of modern stores, supermarkets and shopping malls will turn them into market leaders that will eventually marginalize the individual SMEs. It is true that the retail industry has been restructured since the 1990s, and that individual retail shops are losing to large corporations and brandname chains. This process of restructuring has been facilitated by the emergence of large, multi-functional and modern shopping malls and arcades in business areas and residential complexes. This is particularly true as Hong Kong is rapidly becoming a shopping paradise with loads of shoppers from Mainland China, and the growing market is definitely more advantageous to non-SMEs.

Import and export trades

As shown in Table 5.5, the import and export trade has enjoyed a high average output growth rate of 11.1%, but with much higher rates in the 1980s than the 1990s. Although the non-SMEs have a slightly higher average output growth rate (12.1%) than the SMEs (10.7%) for the sample period, the SMEs have performed better than the non-SMEs in different periods (18.1% for SMEs and 16.6 percent for non-SMEs in 1986–1990; 14.9% for SMEs and 9.9% for non-SMEs in 1991–1995; 7.9% for SMEs and 6.8% for non-SMEs in 2001–2005). The SMEs did perform weaker during the period of Sino-British negotiations (25.1% for non-SMEs and 10.9% for SMEs in 1983–1985), and the Asian financial crisis period (8.3% for non-SMEs and 2.7% for SMEs in 1996–2000).

The whole industry enjoyed an average TFP growth rate of 2.4%, with the highest achievement in the late 1980s (8.1%) and lowest during the Asian financial crisis period in later half of the 1990s (–0.7%). On average, the SMEs performed slightly better than the non-SMEs in the contribution of TFP to output growth (3.7% for non-SMEs and 3.9% for SMEs in period of 1983–1990; 1.1% for non-SMEs and 1.8% for SMEs in the period of 1991–2000; 1.9% for non-SMEs and 2.4% for SMEs in the period of 1983–2005). One interesting observation is that in the case of contribution to output growth by capital input, non-SMEs have performed slightly

TABLE 5.5 Productivity accounting for import and export trade by size of establishments: 1983–2005 (compound annual growth rates)

		1983–1985	1986–1990	1991–1995	1996–2000	2001–2005	1983–1990	1991–2000	1983–2005
Growth Rates									
Output	Total	14.8	17.6	13.4	4.3	7.5	16.5	8.8	11.1
	SMEs	10.9	18.1	14.9	2.7	7.9	15.3	8.6	10.7
	Non-SMEs	25.1	16.6	9.9	8.3	6.8	19.7	9.1	12.1
Capital	Total	20.2	8.4	10.7	10.7	10.4	12.7	10.7	11.3
	SMEs	12.6	9.5	12.3	6.7	12.7	10.7	9.4	10.6
	Non-SMEs	46.3	5.8	6.1	20.8	5.8	19.5	13.2	13.7
Labor	Total	14.6	10.9	8.8	−0.4	0.0	12.3	4.1	5.9
	SMEs	−10.0	28.5	8.8	0.1	−1.1	12.4	4.4	5.8
	Non-SMEs	−11.5	28.3	8.7	−2.5	4.5	11.6	3.0	6.2
Share of Payment									
Capital	Total	0.57	0.55	0.49	0.49	0.55	0.55	0.49	0.52
	SMEs	0.56	0.54	0.50	0.47	0.54	0.55	0.48	0.52
	Non-SMEs	0.57	0.55	0.48	0.50	0.57	0.56	0.49	0.53
Labor	Total	0.43	0.45	0.51	0.51	0.45	0.45	0.51	0.48
	SMEs	0.44	0.46	0.50	0.53	0.46	0.45	0.52	0.48
	Non-SMEs	0.43	0.45	0.52	0.50	0.43	0.44	0.51	0.47
Contribution to Output by									
TFP	Total	−3.0	8.1	3.7	−0.7	1.8	4.1	1.5	2.4
	SMEs	8.1	−0.2	4.4	−0.5	1.6	3.9	1.8	2.4
	Non-SMEs	3.6	0.7	2.5	−1.0	1.5	3.7	1.1	1.9
Capital Input	Total	11.4	4.6	5.3	5.2	5.7	7.0	5.2	5.9
	SMEs	7.1	5.1	6.1	3.1	6.8	5.9	4.6	5.5
	Non-SMEs	26.4	3.2	3.0	10.5	3.3	10.9	6.5	7.3
Labor Input	Total	6.4	4.9	4.4	−0.2	0.0	5.5	2.1	2.8
	SMEs	−4.4	13.1	4.4	0.1	−0.5	5.6	2.3	2.8
	Non-SMEs	−4.9	12.7	4.5	−1.2	2.0	5.1	1.5	2.9

better than SMEs in general. But in the case of contribution to output growth by labor input, the difference between non-SMEs and SMEs is not that great. This suggests that flexibility, mobility and adaptation to changing situations are important in the import and export trade in Hong Kong. SMEs have an advantage as they are flexible and can adjust to market needs easily and efficiently, and can therefore survive along with the non-SMEs.

Business services

The estimates for the business services industry shown in Table 5.6 are that the industry has a high average growth rate in output of 9.8% in the sample period, with the highest output growth rate occurred in period of 1991–1995 and lowest but still positive rate of 6.1% in the period of 2001–2005. The industry's output growth rate could still reach 7.3% during the Asian financial crisis period. The non-SMEs (10.2%) have a slightly higher average output growth rates than the SMEs (9.2%) for the entire period.

With the exception of early 1980s, the business services industry has enjoyed a positive TFP growth in all periods, with an average TFP growth rate of 2.5%. The highest TFP growth rate was seen in the post-AFC period of 2001–2005 (4.0%). Although there is no significant difference in the TFP growth rates between non-SMEs and SMEs (2.6% for non-SMEs and 2.4% for SMEs), their differences can be seen at individual periods, with the non-SMEs experiencing drastic changes in different sub-periods. The performance of TFP growth rates is higher in the 1990s than in the 1980s for both types of establishments. The SMEs have experienced large drop in capital growth in the two periods of 1996–2000 and 2001–2005. Increasingly, the non-SMEs will outperform the SMEs in the business service, reflecting a process of industry consolidation with non-SMEs gradually dominating.

The performance in the contribution to output growth by capital input and labor input has been steady, with positive growth rates in many periods. This industry is a pillar industry in Hong Kong, and its continued expansion has allowed both SMEs and non-SMEs to benefit, though non-SMEs tend to have a stronger performance in difficult times, and can stand against shocks and crises more readily than SMEs.

Transport

The analysis for the transport industry shown in Table 5.7 included figures for land transport, water transport, air transport and all other transport services. The transport industry had an average output growth rate of 7.0%, with the highest rate of 13.5% occurred in the late 1980s period and lowest rate of 3.1% during the recovery period of 2001–2005. Except for the period 2001–2005 when non-SME experienced only 2.8% output growth rate while SMEs enjoyed a growth rate of 3.7%, the non-SMEs on average have a better performance in output growth rate than the SMEs (7.9% for non-SMEs and 5.5% for SMEs).

The whole transport industry has only a low average TFP growth rate of 0.4%, with a higher performance of 1.6% during the 1980s, but slackened to –0.2%

TABLE 5.6 Productivity accounting for business services by size of establishments: 1983–2005 (compound annual growth rates)

		1983–1985	1986–1990	1991–1995	1996–2000	2001–2005	1983–1990	1991–2000	1983–2005
Growth Rates									
Output	Total	14.6	11.5	11.7	7.3	6.1	12.6	9.4	9.8
	SMEs	21.6	12.2	12.2	5.2	0.6	15.7	8.6	9.2
	Non-SMEs	9.2	10.7	11.1	9.3	10.2	10.2	10.2	10.2
Capital	Total	28.3	8.5	11.7	-0.9	2.5	15.5	5.2	8.1
	SMEs	82.1	11.4	14.3	-5.9	–20.0	34.0	3.7	7.1
	Non-SMEs	8.0	5.1	7.7	6.4	14.2	6.2	7.0	8.3
Labor	Total	8.6	10.5	9.7	5.4	2.0	9.8	7.5	7.1
	SMEs	11.0	10.4	11.0	3.4	–0.2	10.6	7.2	6.7
	Non-SMEs	6.2	10.5	8.2	7.6	4.0	8.9	7.9	7.4
Share of Payment									
Capital	Total	0.32	0.35	0.31	0.23	0.14	0.34	0.27	0.27
	SMEs	0.34	0.37	0.36	0.27	0.09	0.36	0.32	0.28
	Non-SMEs	0.29	0.33	0.25	0.20	0.17	0.31	0.22	0.24
Labor	Total	0.68	0.65	0.69	0.77	0.86	0.66	0.73	0.73
	SMEs	0.66	0.63	0.64	0.73	0.91	0.64	0.68	0.72
	Non-SMEs	0.71	0.67	0.75	0.80	0.83	0.69	0.78	0.76
Contribution to Output by									
TFP	Total	–0.3	1.7	1.3	3.3	4.0	0.9	2.6	2.5
	SMEs	–13.8	1.4	-0.1	4.3	2.5	–3.4	2.6	2.4
	Non-SMEs	2.5	2.0	3.1	2.0	4.4	2.1	2.5	2.6
Capital Input	Total	9.0	3.0	3.6	–0.2	0.3	5.3	1.4	2.2
	SMEs	28.3	4.2	5.2	–1.6	–1.8	12.3	1.2	2.0
	Non-SMEs	2.3	1.7	1.9	1.3	2.4	2.0	1.6	2.0
Labor Input	Total	5.8	6.8	6.7	4.1	1.7	6.4	5.5	5.2
	SMEs	7.2	6.5	7.0	2.5	-0.2	6.8	4.9	4.8
	Non-SMEs	4.4	7.1	6.1	6.1	3.3	6.1	6.1	5.6

TABLE 5.7 Productivity accounting for all transport by size of establishments: 1983–2005 (compound annual growth rates)

		1983–1985	1986–1990	1991–1995	1996–2000	2001–2005	1983–1990	1991–2000	1983–2005
Growth Rates									
Output	Total	7.4	13.5	7.2	4.3	3.1	11.2	5.7	7.0
	SMEs	5.3	10.7	5.5	2.3	3.7	8.6	3.9	5.5
	Non-SMEs	8.8	15.2	8.0	5.1	2.8	12.8	6.6	7.9
Capital	Total	16.8	11.7	7.5	12.2	4.7	13.6	9.8	10.0
	SMEs	14.6	4.7	4.1	10.7	6.1	8.3	7.4	7.4
	Non-SMEs	19.5	17.7	9.4	12.9	4.0	18.4	11.1	12.0
Labor	Total	4.8	6.8	4.4	0.6	2.2	6.0	2.5	3.6
	SMEs	2.8	6.5	3.6	-2.6	1.5	5.1	0.5	2.3
	Non-SMEs	7.5	7.2	5.4	3.7	2.7	7.3	4.6	5.1
Share of Payment									
Capital	Total	0.43	0.50	0.48	0.46	0.49	0.48	0.47	0.47
	SMEs	0.54	0.55	0.49	0.44	0.53	0.55	0.46	0.51
	Non-SMEs	0.36	0.48	0.47	0.47	0.46	0.43	0.47	0.46
Labor	Total	0.57	0.50	0.52	0.54	0.51	0.52	0.53	0.53
	SMEs	0.46	0.45	0.51	0.56	0.47	0.45	0.54	0.49
	Non-SMEs	0.64	0.52	0.53	0.53	0.54	0.57	0.53	0.54
Contribution to Output by									
TFP	Total	−2.6	4.3	1.3	−1.7	−0.3	1.6	−0.2	0.4
	SMEs	−4.0	5.2	1.7	−1.0	−0.3	1.8	0.2	0.6
	Non-SMEs	−3.0	3.0	0.8	−2.9	−0.5	0.7	−1.1	−0.4
Capital Input	Total	7.2	5.9	3.6	5.6	2.3	6.4	4.6	4.7
	SMEs	7.9	2.6	2.0	4.7	3.2	4.5	3.4	3.8
	Non-SMEs	7.0	8.5	4.4	6.0	1.9	7.9	5.2	5.5
Labor Input	Total	2.7	3.4	2.3	0.3	1.1	3.2	1.3	1.9
	SMEs	1.3	2.9	1.8	−1.4	0.7	2.3	0.3	1.1
	Non-SMEs	4.8	3.8	2.9	2.0	1.5	4.2	2.4	2.8

during the 1990s. In the TFP growth rates, the SMEs have outperformed the non-SMEs, as the SMEs have enjoyed an average TFP growth rate of 0.6% compared to –0.4% for the non-SMEs. Probably other than the few large corporations in the air, bus and marine transportation, the transport industry contains a large number of individual suppliers and SMEs. In other words, major transportation companies in Hong Kong in underground and over-ground trains, buses and ferries, even though they are privately owned, they are either quasi-monopolies or franchised with control from the government. The more disperse types of land transport are taxi services, coaches and cross-border lorry and coach services. Intra-industry competition varies from one type of transport to another, though inter-industry competition is quite severe, depending on services, price and routes. The non-SMEs performed better than SMEs in the contribution to output growth by both capital input and labor input, suggesting that the large, quasi-monopoly transport companies showed strong performance. There is, however, increasing public pressure for public transport to go green and be environment-friendly and to reduce energy consumption.

The analysis of TFP performance in both SMEs, and non-SMEs among the five industries come to different conclusions. Despite the large number of SMEs that occupy a high percentage of employment, the future outlook of SMEs may not be promising and depending on the nature of the industry in terms of market condition, competition, and capital and labor performances. Even though the SMEs show strong performance in business services, import and export trade and transport, there is no promise if their survival will not be competed away by the growing presence of non-SMEs, especially in situations of a falling market and a rising cost. In the two industries of manufacturing and retail, SMEs have shown a weak performance, losing to the growing dominance of non-SMEs, due to business and economic restructuring in the last decades.

In short, despite the popularity of SMEs in the traditional business of Hong Kong, non-SMEs have a bigger chance of survival, given the strong competition, the possibility of economic and financial crises, and the ability to raise and utilize capital and labor resources. The analysis shows in general that non-SMEs are more productive than SMEs, given their ability in raising capital and the use of advance technology. There is, however, variation among industries, with some, such as import and export trade, still provide a strong survival network for SMEs, while others, such as retail business, the chance for SMEs to expand is slim, as the market is rapidly occupied by non-SMEs and multinationals.

While large non-SME corporations have their own business strategies, the survival of SMEs will have to take a more proactive, forward looking view, and prepare for a stronger strategy before they are being eroded from competition. Industrial amalgamation can be a possible solution, though greater business transparency and information availability are needed among entrepreneurs of SMEs. Business associations and industry bodies can facilitate the "marriage" of different SMEs, encouraging them to re-group into larger enterprises. In a sense, business enterprises in contemporary Hong Kong are in a cross-road situation. While individual entrepreneurship forms the traditional sources of SMEs, the growing size of non-SMEs have competed away many business opportunities from individual entrepreneurs.

Nonetheless, creative and risk-taking individuals with entrepreneurial spirit are still free to start their businesses. There is thus much potential for the survival of SMEs, just that the market conditions have changed. Indeed, other than large capital investment, there is a host of factors that can work favorably to the survival of SMEs. An individual can possess special knowledge on the market potential, source of inputs, needed education and skills, business connections, timing of entry and location advantage attributes. Armed with economic freedom, there are always opportunities for individuals to progress and SMEs to emerge, grow and prosper, though new economic conditions require different kinds of SMEs and business attributes.

5.6 Conclusion

Economic freedom serves as an incentive that promotes growth and prosperity. The spirit of entrepreneurship is strong in a free economy. The establishment of SMEs has become a culture in Hong Kong where individuals learn skills and pick up experiences before engaging in their own entrepreneurial businesses. Data analysis in different industries shows that SMEs behave differently among industries. In other words, while SMEs have been the traditional form of business enterprises, the growing success of non-SMEs in some industries has posed survival challenges to the traditional SMEs. In short, SMEs themselves have to change in light of the changing nature of individual industries. To gain strength and vigor, industrial amalgamation, where industries group together either vertically or horizontally to form large corporations with different expertise, shall give a "2 + 2 = 5" outcome.

Economic freedom is always the breeding ground for entrepreneurship and the establishment of SMEs as the starting form of business entities. There will not be a shortage of supply in the establishment of SMEs in Hong Kong. Indeed, in terms of market knowledge, business dimensions, expertise and skills, SMEs in Hong Kong have gone far and have changed drastically, making advancements in virtually all directions and have become an "evergreen" in the Hong Kong economy. However, SMEs in Hong Kong shall not feel complacent, and the true entrepreneurial spirit is that SMEs will face and make changes according to challenging and evolving situations. Analysis in this chapter has shown the diversity of SMEs and their potentials in different industries, services and businesses.

SMEs in Hong Kong have to be forward looking, taking into account at least the growing Mainland China economy, and the various consequences. Hong Kong has often been regarded or given the chance as the first mover in the Mainland China economy. One possible view is that Hong Kong businesses, including SMEs, have the first advantage to "conquer" the Mainland China market. However, given the huge size of the Mainland China market, and the relative small number of Hong Kong businesses, the opposing view is that the Mainland China market will soon out-grow the businesses from Hong Kong. And in turn, given the extent of economic freedom in Hong Kong, there will be in the long-run growing number of Mainland China businesses coming to Hong Kong. Armed with abundant capital, especially when the renminbi has appreciated substantially, and once the control on the outflow of renminbi was to be relaxed, Hong Kong economy could be "flooded" by businesses from Mainland China. In other words, as economic freedom in Mainland China improves, there can be an "export" of businesses from Mainland China. The future of SMEs in Hong Kong will also be faced with business challenges from Mainland China, with increasing competition in various dimensions, financially, technologically and so on. The positive side is that with the ever growing Mainland China market, the growth in the Mainland China economy will always provide new business opportunities for SMEs in Hong Kong. As such, equipping with advance market information and trends shall become the future assets for SMEs.

6 Knowledge-Based, Human Capital and Freedom

6.1 Introduction

In the broadest possible sense, all world economies are knowledge-based, but the different lies in the kind of knowledge required for different economic environments and different stages of development. In primitive societies, "required" knowledge may be the various survival skills and an ability to organize a tribal or rural economy based on cultural or traditional practices. In modern civilized societies, "required" knowledge incorporates a wide range of skills, qualifications and capabilities. Formal education has been considered as a backbone of knowledge in the contemporary world. The higher the level of educational achievement people in a society have, the higher the level or pool of knowledge available for economic development. This is because an educated or knowledgeable person, in addition to a handsome financial reward in the form of a high wage or earning the person makes, is a "common good" that will generate further positive impact on economic development. The advantage of having an educated or knowledgeable person will radiate to other aspects of development, thereby creating positive spill-over effects to others through numerous social and economic mediums.

The modern economic history of Hong Kong dates back to its period of British colonization 1842–1997. In the early days as a British colony, Hong Kong was used mainly as a free port for trading of merchandize between China, Great Britain and other Asian countries. The provision of modern education was not high in the development agenda then. Over the years, a number of foreign associations, non-governmental organizations and religious bodies came as mercenaries, and subsequently established primary and secondary schools in Hong Kong, using English as a medium of communication. By today, these establishments have been rooted in Hong Kong, as many primary and secondary schools have strong affiliation and association with external institutions. There are also other good quality public schools organized by the government, other local bodies and charitable organizations. Indeed, expenditure on education has become one of the major public policy items in Hong Kong, receiving regular appraisals and periodic assessments.

Language as a medium of instruction in both primary and secondary schools has been a concern for a long time. While the majority of people in Hong Kong are ethnic Chinese, mainly migrated from various provinces in southern China, and since Cantonese is the mother-tongue, the use of Cantonese has been widespread and the use of English was minimal at the time of the British colonization, applicable mainly in the colonial government and foreign business sector. As formal education has gradually been established, and economic development progressed with the rise of income, English has gradually become more important and has ascended to become a major language in business communication. By today, it is essential for young people in Hong Kong to excel in English.

In the education circle, the use of mother-tongue as the medium of language instruction has been debated. The scientific argument is that students who can receive their education through the mother-tongue dialect as a vehicle of language delivery are thought to be more effective in understanding the subject matter. However, as Hong Kong is a free port with trade and exchange being the key activity, the use of English has become more of a necessity and as a symbol of openness than a national prestige or ethnical pride. With the establishment of schools by religious mercenaries in the early days of colonization and the pragmatic need for the use of English in business activities, schools that used English as a medium of instruction have become popular and more attractive. By today, the two languages of Chinese and English and the two Chinese dialects of Mandarin or Putonghua and Cantonese have become the accepted norm of language usage. For pragmatic career development of the younger generation in Hong Kong, the ability to master both Chinese and English has become a must.

Does economic freedom promote education, or education nurture economic freedom? Whatever their direction of causality, economic freedom and education certainly complement and reinforce each other in the process of building up a civilized society. Education, other than serving as the primary purpose of reducing illiteracy, allows individuals to gain greater knowledge and skill, through which an understanding in the complexity of issues and affairs can be made. The more important function of education is to permit intellectual diversity. Through formal education at primary, secondary and tertiary levels, individuals can nurture and discover their areas of interest in knowledge and ability, and eventually can specialize in a certain area of expertise. Thus, education serves as a vehicle through which people are trained for different jobs and professions. And through education, individuals can acquire special knowledge or skills that enable them to make a living and create wealth. With education, individuals can then choose their own work or engage in business.

An educated person or work force in the society can produce numerous immediate and externality effects. The immediate effect of education is to allow individuals to acquire a skill or knowledge for their career development and acquire a decent standard of living. From the point of view of the government's fiscal policy, as more people are educated and armed with recognized qualifications, their ability to survive economically increases, and in turn would rely less on social welfare or government assistance. An educated work force will produce a greater ability to pay income tax, and in turn, a government can then use and channel saved fiscal resources for the benefit of other needy populations.

A more educated workforce usually attracts investment as knowledge and human capital are key inputs to production in the contemporary business world. The rise of investment will certainly lead to higher output, more employment opportunities and development. In addition, an educated workforce will soon produce a cluster effect that allows an economy to excel in one area or another. Also, a better educated population will have spillover effects on non-economic arenas.

Improvements in social awareness, ethic standards and civilized behaviors are products of a more educated society. Furthermore, the advantage of an educated population can be longitudinal; namely, one educated person would like to see more educated people, and one educated person in the current generation would like to see that future generations will be more educated, and so on. From an economic development viewpoint, there are not only multiple advantages in the provision of education, but education always produces a positive sum game as societies can only become more and more educated.

Intuitively, a free economy permits the achievement of the highest possible standard of education development, and an increase in an overall education of a population will result in intellectual diversity that in turn promotes, consolidates, deepens and extends the numerous virtues of freedom. The ultimate advantage of education is its function to free the minds of individuals and allow them to expand infinitely and venture into different dimensions and alternatives in work and life.

In Hong Kong, education at primary, secondary and tertiary levels is supplied by the dual existence of private schools, schools with subvention from the government and public schools run by the government. In tertiary education, although most key universities are funded by the government, there is a tendency to increase self-financed courses as well as a small number of private universities and post-secondary educational institutions. There are also numerous overseas accredited tertiary institutions that liaise with local institutions for post-secondary courses, thereby allowing diversity in the supply of tertiary education.

The dual supply system exists also in other public goods and utilities, such as radio broadcasts and medical services. Although it has been criticized for unfairness in school entry due probably to the "label effect" that distinguishes prestigious schools from the rest, the dual supply system does provide on the one hand a greater choice for parents, and on the other hand, a reduction in the financial burden of the government in shouldering the entire education expenses. Furthermore, due to the desire to improve institutions, different categories of educational institutions in Hong Kong do positively compete among themselves, thereby generating a market force in promoting education quality.

Conventionally, the literacy rate and the percentage of educated population are considered as standard measures of educational achievement in an economy, which can then be compared across different world economies to distinguish the more advanced from the less advanced economies. Economic data on government and non-government expenditures on education and the size of the educated population can provide a measure on the "knowledgeness" of an economy.

The more recent debate on economic development has concentrated on the impact of human capital on productivity and growth. There are a number of ways to measure and quantify human capital. One accepted measurement is the number of schooling years per capita. There are two theoretical frameworks that look at the impact of human capital on growth. Firstly, the theory on the source of growth is typically represented by the aggregate Cobb-Douglas production function that can include human capital as one of the inputs. Neo-classical growth model assumes there are constant return to the three factor inputs of physical capital, human capital and labor. Human capital is embodied in the individual worker and there is no externality to education (Solow, 1957; Mankiw *et al.*, 1992; Tamura, 2006; Baier *et al.*, 2007; Li, 2009). On the contrary, the endogenous growth model argues that human capital does influence an individual's output utility, and that in turn can influence the aggregate output of an economy (Lucas, 1988; Mulligan and Sala-i-Martin, 1995, 1997). The endogenous growth model maintains that there can be external, spill-over effect of individual education within and across different economic utilities. Empirical studies suggest that there are direct and indirect (external) effects of schooling on growth and the effect of human capital varies with different levels of education and on the level of technology of the economy (Gemmell, 1995, 1996; Benhabib and Spiegel, 1994; Barro and Sala-i-Martin, 1995; Barro, 1999).

In the endogenous growth model, a distinction is drawn on the composition of human capital (that is the different levels of primary, secondary and tertiary schoolings) and impact of each schooling level (that is the productivity of each level of schooling). For example, it has been argued that primary and secondary schoolings are important to growth in developing economies where adoption and imitation activities prevail, while tertiary schooling is important for growth in developed economies, where innovation and research and development activities dominate (Aghion *et al.*, 2005; Gemmell, 1996, 1997; Vandebbussche *et al.*, 2006).

This chapter first provides a discussion on a knowledge-based economy, which is often related to the level of education and know-how. Section 6.2 looks at the different definitions of a knowledge-based economy and how other Asia economies consider the relevance and importance of knowledge in their contemporary economic development. Section 6.3 examines the situation in Hong Kong, and how policies in Hong Kong have been instituted to secure a knowledge-based economy. Section 6.4 goes further to examine the level of human capital in Hong Kong; and in relation to the discussion of total factor productivity, the human capital is used as another factor input variable to see how human capital has affected the level of productivity. This shall be the major empirical exercise, as it would examine the contribution of human capital to growth and to productivity in Hong Kong.

Another related and important element is the intellectual property rights (IPR). Section 6.5 discusses the performance and areas of improvements of IPR in Hong Kong. Freedom plays an important part in IPR, both as an engine that encourages creativity and innovation, but Section 6.6 raises a number of concerns in economic freedom. To put the argument in perspective, Section 6.7 argues that economic freedom can serve as a built-in infrastructure to a knowledge-based economy and in the development of IPR. The last section concludes the chapter.

6.2 The Knowledge-Based Economy

The term "knowledge-based economy" (KBE) can be subjected to different interpretations. One common and obvious definition of a KBE is the reference to the use of knowledge to produce economic gains (Drucker, 1969; McGregor, 1988). Knowledge or know-how is considered as an economic resource in growth and development, implying that knowledge and education can be a product, a service or an asset that yields returns. According to Wikipedia,[1] a KBE differs from a traditional economy in several ways. Unlike other economic resources which would deplete when used, knowledge can be shared and grow through application. With information intensity, a transmission of knowledge can be speedy and operate globally at different time zones. There is, however, a difference between KBE and information economy that works through the internet. The internet provides a service that depends solely on mass connectivity, but such service provision may not involve knowledge-based skills. Connectivity through the internet hastens the globalization of information, and goods and services are developed and transacted through electronic networks. One problem in the mass connectivity through internet is the difficulty of applying national laws and taxes, as the abstract nature of economic activities are no longer connected to land, labor and physical capital.

KBEs are "economies in which the proportion of knowledge-intensive jobs is high, the economic weight of information sector is a determining factor, and the share of intangible capital is greater than that of tangible capital in the overall stock of real capital" (Foray, 2004). The development of a KBE can be seen from "an ever-increasing proliferation of jobs in the production, processing, and transfer of knowledge and information". Employment and jobs are increasingly related to knowledge-intensive activities.

Although there are differences between knowledge and research, knowledge has been an essential element in economic development. Knowledge creation through invention and innovation are being delivered through the organization of businesses, the process of production and the actual manufactured products and services. Knowledge can be disseminated through education and media channels. The knowledge "revolution" that emerged since the 1970s has concentrated mostly in informational technology. In the industrialization era in the 18th century in Europe when machines were the key component in the production of physical goods, apprenticeship in manufacturing plants was an effective form of knowledge diffusion. In the modern information age, knowledge is created mostly through formal research and development in laboratories and specialized research centers, but learning conducted through numerous offline and online channels has been an effective way of knowledge distribution and dissemination.

There are three properties of knowledge as an economic good (Foray, 2004). Knowledge is an intangible good. In a globalized world with efficient information flow across the world, knowledge can easily be reproduced or transmitted. Knowledge has a high "social return" and serves as a powerful mechanism in economic growth. On the contrary, because knowledge can be transmitted easily and efficiently, it creates problems on the resource allocation to innovation, invention, research and development (R&D). This leads to the intellectual property right issue. There is high risk to the innovators or inventors when copying, imitating and duplicating of new technology, products and services can easily be conducted. The first property of knowledge is that knowledge is a non-excludable, fluid and portable good. What makes knowledge exclusive is that it is difficult to control.

---

[1] http://en.wikipedia.org/wiki/Knowledge_economy

Once released or leaked openly, knowledge cannot be kept secret as other people will use it to their advantage.

The second property of knowledge as a good is non-rival, meaning that once it is made known, different users of the knowledge can consume it at the same time. It is non-rival because one user's consumption will not deter another user from consuming it. This property is similar to a public good, like radio broadcast. The difference between knowledge and a public good like radio broadcast is that knowledge carries the feature of "infinite expansibility". The same individual can use the knowledge repeatedly, and different users can use the same knowledge without depriving anyone using it.

The third property is that knowledge is a cumulative good. The use of one idea or knowledge gives rise to other new ideas by the user of the knowledge. The existence of these three properties ensures that knowledge is a public good, and the social return of an invention often exceeds the private return. Examples include Thomas A. Edison (1847–1931), known as the "father of electricity age", and Charles K. Kao (born in 1933), known as the "father of fiber optics" and is the Nobel Laureate in Physics in 2009. Their inventions have enormous and long-lasting impact in the development of world economy. The inventions of compass, gunpowder and paper in China are also historical landmarks.

The Organization for Economic Cooperation and Development (OECD) that composes mainly developed countries reported that economies are increasingly based on knowledge and information, and that knowledge is recognized as the driver of productivity and growth (OECD, 1996). Knowledge has been central to economic development, as it is embodied in human beings in the form of human capital and in technology. In the OECD, a KBE implies a strong dependence on the "production, distribution and use of knowledge". The OECD (1996:9) report estimates that over 50% of GDP in the major OECD economies is knowledge-based. The OECD (1996:12) report points out that knowledge can be codified into: know-what, know-why, know-how and know-who. Know-what is related to the factual knowledge. Scientific principles and laws of nature form the basis of know-why. Know-how refers to the skill required in doing something, while know-who involves who knows what and who knows how to do what.

In a fully KBE, investment is attracted to high-technology goods and services, especially information and communication technologies. Such intangible investments as R&D, training of computing and technical expertise have become important, resulting in a high demand for skilled labor and knowledge-based services. Knowledge and technology are considered as external influences on production, and will have to be incorporated into the traditional production function that has often focused only on capital, labor and other production inputs.

The science system that incorporates knowledge production, knowledge transmission and knowledge transfer is important in a KBE. Knowledge production involves the development and provision of new knowledge through typically public and private research institutions, expenditure on R&D and the legal protection on scientific knowledge. Knowledge transmission involves the education and development of human resources. Both the quantity and quality of education institutions, together with the orientation of science, technology and a broad-based education, are crucial in knowledge transmission. Knowledge transfer is the dissemination of knowledge. This involves the application of knowledge by different users. Have knowledge been extensively used by institutions and businesses to increase the value-added content of domestic production? The OECD shows that different measures on knowledge inputs, knowledge outputs, knowledge networks and relationship between knowledge and learning can be constructed as indicators in measuring a knowledge-based economy.

In light of the growing importance of technology, especially information technology, and the emerging process of globalization, the OECD (1999) in a follow up report suggests that the scoreboard that composes of three parts can be used as a benchmark of a KBE. The first part examines investment in intangibles as an indicator for KBE, involving the extent of knowledge-based industries, the role of information and communication technologies, and expenditures on science and technology. The second part focuses on the extent of globalization, especially the trends in international trade, foreign investment, internationalization of technology, and the role of multinational enterprises in the host countries. The third part deals with selected indicators of economic performance and competitiveness, such as productivity and unit labor costs, international trade and output of scientific and technological activities. The extent of knowledge-based across countries can then be compared through these benchmark indicators.

The experience of KBEs in selected Asian countries has been documented in another OECD (2000) report. As summarized in Table 6.1, each of the six Asian countries has engaged in some form of forward plan intended to promote and strengthen their economic capacity in knowledge-based activities. Among the six Asian economies, both South Korea and Singapore are more aggressive and have engaged resources in a number of established activities, Chinese Taipei has also made ambitious plans, while Malaysia and Thailand are still in the initial stage. China is still in the formative stage of a knowledge-based economy. As for the knowledge-based industries, IT, electronics, chemicals and biotechnology are common among the six countries.

6.3 Hong Kong's Performance

A number of education-related policies in Hong Kong since 1997 have resulted in public controversies. Policy proposals and debates included the use of mother tongue in formal education, English language ability test for secondary teachers, the closure of schools due to low student demand as birth rate has dropped, the conversion of a four-degree degree in tertiary institutions, and the potential merge of universities and so on. Although it has been argued that the use of Chinese or Cantonese in formal education could raise students' innate potentials, both parents and business at large have demanded for a higher ability of the English language. The use of English in schools has helped to maintain the international image of Hong Kong. Due to its unpopularity and the confusion over the use of mother-tongue language in secondary schools, the government has tacitly abandoned the mother-tongue policy around 2005 or 2006 and allowed the English language to be used more extensively in secondary schools. Secondary schools are given more freedom to choose their language of instruction.

TABLE 6.1 Knowledge-based strategies and industries in selected Asia economies

National Strategy	Knowledge-Based Industries
South Korea	
Master Plan on Information Production (1996–2000): vision of a creative and knowledge-based society; key initiatives of *Cyber Korea 21*; and promotion strategies. The *Cyber Korea 21* vision includes: information infrastructure; increase productivity and promoting new businesses and jobs through ICT; and design competitive export products.	Semiconductors; telecommunications; software; specialty chemicals; biotechnology; and environmental industry.
Singapore	
The *Industry 21* blueprint: knowledge-based economy driven by services and manufacturing; develop high-valued knowledge-based services; *IT2000: A Vision of an Intelligent Island*: develop a global hub; improving quality of life; revitalize traditional sectors; global connections; enhance individual potentials.	Electronics; information technology; chemicals; and biotechnology.
Chinese Taipei	
The 2000 Plan: a "green Silicon island"; accelerates new inventions; creates new markets; encourages innovations, application of IT technology; and review economic conditions.	Information technology; telecommunications; consumer electronics; aerospace; and biotechnology.
Malaysia	
Industrial Master Plan (1996–2005): investment in high-end manufacturing, cluster-based development, and productivity-driven growth. *Multimedia Super Corridor* (1996): a 20-year timeframe for economic transformation.	Electronics; chemicals; and biotechnology.
Thailand	
IT Policy into the 21st Century: correct social and economic imbalances, invest in information infrastructure, build ICT manpower, and promote good governance.	Information technology; electronics; software; and telecommunications.
China	
Conference in 1999 on knowledge economy and development: interest at both national and local levels; look for broader framework conditions; go beyond ICT to cover software and high-value added services; and develop domestic science and technology base.	Information technology; telecommunications; software; consumer electronics; chemicals; and environment industry.

Source: *Knowledge-based Industries in Asia*, OECD, 2000.

The conversion of the three-year to four-year undergraduate degree studies raised resource implications between universities and secondary schools, and employment opportunities for secondary teachers. With a four-year undergraduate degree program, more resources will have to be provided to tertiary institutions, and less for secondary schools. In the case of the English language test for secondary school teachers, it was originally aimed at quality improvement but the way it was being executed and conducted by high ranking government officials had upset many secondary school teachers, causing embarrassment to those teachers with weak language ability, uncertainty in their employment and the attitude of the parents and school students. Though unsuccessful, the potential merger between two prestigious universities has even become personality driven and cumulated undesirable public controversy. Due to the low birth rate during the economic hardship years, criteria, albeit controversial, are applied by the government to close schools in selected areas.

The more consistent and positive education policy orientation since 1997 has been the "life-long" learning educational approach, which basically aimed to promote adult education for full-time employees by making use of their spare time to upgrade their knowledge, skill and academic ability. Fiscal incentive through tax exemption was given to income spent on course fees. The number of part-time postgraduate and undergraduate courses offered by local as well as overseas education institutions in Hong Kong has expanded considerably. To enlarge the number of post-secondary education and to increase the proportion of population that received post-secondary education, the government has embarked on the provision of associate degrees. Some associate degree admissions are self-funded, but the large number of associate degree places offered by local institutions and their exit alternatives has been the concern of the associate degree graduates, as the number of university degree places are limited and associate degree graduates have to compete for jobs with other graduates.

One potential drawback of the "life-long" approach to higher education is that it could produce a misleading and distorted signal to the younger generation that should they fail to receive higher education at their young age, they would have further chances in their later life. This signal could be self-fulfilling and reduce the drive to study and obtain higher education at the youngest possible age. Such a misleading and distorted signal would delay their education at the young age, thereby lowering the overall education and skill of the young generation, causing an economic "deadweight loss".

The two government reports on KBE published by the Census and Statistics Department (2005, 2009) have acknowledged that modern economic growth relies to a great extent on the creation and distribution of new knowledge, and provided a statistical perspective of Hong Kong as a KBE. Acknowledging the difficulty in the measure of a KBE, the government reports examine four areas of: (1) information and communication technology (ITC); (2) human capital development; (3) innovative system; and 4) business environment.

As far as the ITC area is concerned, as shown in Table 6.2, the reports (Census and Statistics Department, 2005:5–6; 2009:7) indicate that the telecommunication market in Hong Kong has been fully liberalized in 2003; and among the various pioneering development, Hong Kong is the first metropolis since the early 1990s to have the telephone network digitized, and adopted the Code Division Multiple Access

TABLE 6.2 Information and communication technology

Year	No. of public mobile subscriber per 100 population	percentage of people aged 10 and above: having used personal computer	percentage of people aged 10 and above: having used the internet service	Household personal computer penetration rate (%)	Household internet penetration rate (%)
1994	7.6				
1995	11.0				
1996	18.7				
1997	32.7				
1998	44.0			34.5	11.8
1999	60.1				
2000	78.0	43.1	30.3	49.7	36.4
2001	84.7	50.3	43.3	60.6	48.7
2002	92.5	54.0	48.2	62.1	52.5
2003	106.4	56.2	52.2	67.5	60.0
2004	120.0	59.5	56.4	71.1	64.9
2005	125.0	58.8	56.9	70.1	64.6
2006	136.7	62.9	60.8	71.7	67.1
2007	152.3	66.4	64.8	74.2	70.1
2008	162.3	68.2	66.7	74.6	70.9

Source: *Hong Kong as a Knowledge-Based Economy: A Statistical Perspective*, 2005 and 2009, Census and Statistics Department, Hong Kong.

(CDMA) standards in the world. Other statistical supports included the world highest mobile subscriber penetration rate which has reached 162% at the end of 2008. The number of personal computer (PC) per 100 inhabitants has increased from 40 in 2000 to 60 in 2005. For the age group at 10 and above, the number of internet users per 100 people has increased from 30 in 2000 to 57 in 2005 and further to 67 in 2008. Household PC penetration rate has increased from 50% in 2000 to 70% in 2005 and further to 74.6% in 2008. The same pattern of increase applies to the internet penetration rate, which has increased from 36% in 2000 to 65% in 2005 and further to 70.9% in 2008. Hong Kong has indeed become the test-bed for the ITC industry. In the International Telecommunicaion Union report in 2004, Hong Kong ranked second in the world in broadband penetration rate.

The discussion on human capital in the two Census and Statistics Department (2005 and 2009) reports concentrated mainly on the data performance on education. For example, education is the largest government expenditure item in the budget, as it has increased from 19% in the financial years of 1994–1995 to 23% in 2004–2005 and further to 24% in 2008–2009. The percentage of population aged 15 and over with post-secondary education has increased from 13.3% in 1994 to 21.6% in 2004 and further to 24.5% in 2008. There are various discrepancies in the reporting and classifications between the Census and Statistics Department 2005 and 2009 reports. In the 2005 report, the percentage of managers, administrators, professionals and associate professionals in the total employed people aged 15 and above has increased from 25% to 33% between 1994 and 2004. In the 2009 report, the percentage of professionals and associate professionals in the total employed people aged 15 and above has increased from 21% in 1998 to 26.1% in 2008.

A number of indicators can be used in examining the issue of innovation. The two Census and Statistics Department reports (2005 and 2009) show that the level of research and development (R&D) expenditure as a percentage of GDP in Hong Kong is generally lower than other developed economies in Asia, although it has edged up as a percentage of GDP from 0.43% in 1998 to 0.55% in 2001, to 0.69% in 2003 (with 56% of the R&D expenditure conducted in universities), and further to 0.77% in 2007. The R&D activities by business firms have improved over the years. For example, the percentage of business entities that have engaged in at least one innovative activity has expanded considerably from 16% in 2001 to 43% in 2004 but remained steady at 42% in 2007. To nourish and deepen R&D activities, the government has promoted a number of R&D centers with the aim to coordinate R&D activities in various technology-related areas.

In the discussion on business environment, the Census and Statistics Department 2005 report (9–10) raised the standard arguments in the Hong Kong economy, such as the open and external-oriented nature, and the various economic attributes of a low tax regime, transparent common law system, impartial judiciary, robust financial structure and system and infrastructure and so on. The 2005 report concludes that it is difficult to quantify and price knowledge, but Hong Kong has position itself well.

Table 6.3 shows some scattered statistics over different years on both the percentage of population and the percentage of employed people in the various categories of education attainment and work. Although the proportion of population aged 15 and above with post-secondary education has increased from 11.2% in 1991 to 24.5% in 2008, the percentage of population aged 15 and above working as managers, professionals and associate professionals is still below 10%. Table 6.4 shows the gross domestic expenditure on R&D as a ratio of GDP and government expenditure on education. It has not been a tradition for Hong Kong to engage massively in R&D expenditure, as shown in Table 6.4. Equally, government expenditure on education in fiscal year 2008–2009 still lies below 5% of GDP.

One can argue that on the whole the statistics do not show strong support on human capital development and KBE. Being an open economy, however, Hong Kong can also "import" talents and different expertise from overseas sources. Although, it has been popular for foreign companies to send their personnel from their parent companies overseas to work in Hong Kong, or to recruit overseas talents in Hong Kong, it has been noted and argued that other cities are also competing with Hong Kong for the same pool of talented people, professionals and expertise. The statistics shown in Table 6.3 and Table 6.4 only confined to development of human capital at the local level. There are other complications. One concerns the inflow of "one-way permit" legal immigrants from Mainland China since 1997 on a daily quota of 150 households. It is expected that 1.64 million people will settle in

TABLE 6.3 Indicators of human capital in Hong Kong

	1991	1994	1996	1998	2001	2004	2006	2008
Percentage of population aged 15 and above with post-secondary education*	11.2	13.3	15.2	17.4	16.4	21.6	23.0	24.5
Percentage of population aged 15 and above working as professionals/ associate professionals			10.3		12.1		12.6	
Percentage of population aged 15 and above working as managers/ professionals/associate professionals	14.4		17.5		18.3			
Percentage of employed persons aged 15 and above working as professionals/ associate professionals				21.0				26.1
Percentage of employed persons aged 15 and above working as managers/professionals/ associate professionals		25.0				33.0		
Percentage of population aged 15 and above with post-secondary education working as professionals/associate professionals			6.0		6.9		8.2	
Percentage of population aged 15 and above with post-secondary education working as managers/ professionals/associate professionals	6.3		8.9		9.8			

Notes: * = There is minor discrepancy in the reporting in 1991, 1996 and 2001.
Source: *Hong Kong as a Knowledge-based Economy: A Statistical Perspective*, *2005 and 2009*, Census and Statistics Department, Hong Kong.

TABLE 6.4 Government expenditure on R&D and education

Year	Gross domestic expenditure on R&D as a ratio of GDP (percent)	Fiscal Year	Government expenditure on education	
			Billion HK$	Percentage of GDP
1998	0.43	1998–1999	49.2	3.9
1999	0.46	1999–2000	51.1	4.0
2000	0.47	2000–2001	52.2	4.0
2001	0.55	2001–2002	53.1	4.1
2002	0.59	2002–2003	55.6	4.4
2003	0.69	2003–2004	57.3	4.6
2004	0.74	2004–2005	54.5	4.2
2005	0.79	2005–2006	54.3	3.8
2006	0.81	2006–2007	51.9	3.5
2007	0.77	2007–2008	53.8	3.3
		2008–2009	75.9	4.5

Source: *Hong Kong as a Knowledge-based Economy: A Statistical Perspective, 2005 and 2009*, Census and Statistics Department, Hong Kong.

Hong Kong through the "one-way permit".[2] These immigrants are mostly women having married in Mainland China to Hong Kong men with permanent residents, and their families have the right of abode in Hong Kong. Although the daily quota may not be used up entirely, immigrant inflows from this category usually are from backward areas in Mainland China and need to rely on the education system in Hong Kong. The situation could be worse if children with Hong Kong resident status come to Hong Kong at their adult age, and their education and social background may not help them to secure jobs or fit into the social life in Hong Kong, resulting in new and added social problems.

After the outbreak of the severe acute respiratory syndrome (SARS) pandemic in 2003 and the economic recession that followed, the Hong Kong SAR Government since 2005 has allowed legal immigration through an investment of HK$6 million or with useful talents. The idea is to import wealthy or economically able, capable and talented individuals and this has become attractive to various individuals from Mainland China, such as talented sport and art personalities. Nonetheless, the bigger and long-term concern is the aging population and the imbalance between adult males and females.

A statistics released in July 2010 by the Census and Statistics Department showed that Hong Kong's population will increase from around 7 million in 2010 to 8.89 million in 2039, and the elderly is projected to rise from 13% to 28% of total population between 2009 and 2039. Due in part to the growing number of domestic helpers from Southeast Asia mainly, there will be fewer men than women. In 2009,

[2] *South China Morning Post*, July 30, 2010.

there were 889 men to every 1,000 women, and the figure will drop to 744 in 2039. The gap is bigger in the 25–44 age groups with 746 men against every 1,000 women in 2009, but the figure will drop to 631 in 2039. Due to better health care, the median age of people in Hong Kong will rise from 40.7 years in 2009 to 47.6 years in 2039. In addition, the fertility rate is expected to drop from 1,042 births in 2009 to 936 in 2039. Furthermore, 95% of those babies born in Hong Kong whose parents are not Hong Kong residents will leave Hong Kong, though half of these will return before the age of six to receive education in Hong Kong.[3] Repeated calls for the government to have a population policy have been made, as it will have various economic implications on housing, social welfare, health and education support at different levels.

An alternative way to assess the amount of expenditure committed to education is the total public expenditure that includes capital expenses. Total public expenditure on education in Hong Kong has been a major expenditure item. In the financial year 1986–1987, education occupied 17.97% of total public expenditure, the highest among all public expenditure items. Such a percentage share has remained steady and has edged upwards since the early 1990s. By the financial year of 1997–1998, education occupied 20.03% of total public expenditure, but the percentage share has fallen in the following years due probably to the economic hardship resulting from the Asian financial crisis, and the percentage share has maintained at 20.7% in the 2003–2004 financial year. The same percentages for the financial years of 2003–2004 and 2008–2009 are 23% and 24%, respectively.

Additional statistical performance in education attainment from population census can provide a clear picture on the level of human capital and the extent of knowledge-based in the Hong Kong economy. Table 6.5 shows the school attendance rates of different age groups for the two years of 2001 and 2006. For the two youngest age groups, statistics shows a slight decline in school attendance, due probably to the economic hardship suffered by parents as school attendance for these two age groups are mainly non-government funded. This alarming situation could have prompted the government to pay more attention to pre-primary education. In his 2006–2007 Policy Address, the Chief Executive, Mr. Donald Tsang Yam-Kuen pledged to subsidize early childhood education by allocating HK$70 million (about US$8.97 million) as a one-off Capacity Enhancement Grant for kindergartens and vouchers would be provided to parents beginning from the 2007–2008 academic year up to an annual subsidy of HK$13,000 (US$1,667) per student in non-profit-making kindergartens.[4] Despite the good will of the government, criticisms aroused as to why only non-profit-making kindergartens were favored, and why the subsidy was not incorporated into a broader education policy, or it is just another form of uncoordinated government economic intervention?

Table 6.5 shows an increase in school attendance for all the age groups of 12–16 and above, especially the two age groups of 17–18 and 19–24. The economic hardship in the post-AFC years has encouraged young people to gain more education;

---

[3] *South China Morning Post*, July 30, 2010.

[4] *The 2006–2007 Policy Address*, Hong Kong SAR Government, October 11, 2006, Section 43–45.

TABLE 6.5 School attendance rates (percent), 2001 and 2006

	2001			2006		
Age group	Male	Female	Total	Male	Female	Total
<3	8.1	7.7	7.9	7.4	7.6	7.5
3–5	94.6	94.7	94.7	89.9	88.3	89.1
6–11	99.9	99.9	99.9	99.9	99.9	99.9
12–16	96.9	98.0	97.5	98.7	99.1	98.9
17–18	68.0	74.1	71.0	81.1	84.6	82.8
19–24	26.8	26.1	26.4	38.4	36.3	37.3
25+	0.4	0.3	0.3	0.5	0.4	0.4
All	22.1	20.3	21.1	21.2	18.5	19.8

Notes: Attendance rates are the percentage of population attending full-time schools or education institutions in the respective age group. There can be minor reporting error in the two youngest age groups (<3 and 3–5) as the reporting date differed from the attendance date.
Source: 2006 Population by-Census Office, Census and Statistics Department, Hong Kong.

while at the same time there is an increase in the supply of post-secondary educational places. Between the two sexes, it is worth to note in both years that school attendance rates for females is higher than males in the age group of 17–18, but lower in the next age groups of 19–24 and 25+. When the statistics on all age groups is considered, the school attendance rates for all age groups have declined from 21.1% to 19.8% between 2001 and 2006. This could be due to the structural change in population between the two years.

Table 6.6 shows the education attainment for the Hong Kong population aged 15 and above for the two years of 2001 and 2006. A clear improvement is the increase in the percentages of the two post-secondary categories, but the rise was partly substituted by the percentage fall in Sixth Form graduates (namely that Upper Secondary graduates moved on to obtain post-secondary qualifications). Nonetheless, the rise in education attainment in the post-secondary categories can reflect the importance placed on the "life-long" learning policy and the expansion of post-secondary educational places. The percentage fall in the education attainment of pre-primary and primary education shown in Table 6.6 suggests that the population aged 15 and above in Hong Kong has gained more education between 2001 and 2006.

Table 6.7 further shows the age groups of different education attainment categories in 2006. The majority of the population in the 25–34 age group has received an education attainment of upper secondary or above, with 26.66% having first degree or post-graduate education. The education attainment pattern has shifted when one looks at the higher age groups. The education attainment of the 45–55 age groups has concentrated mainly in primary, lower and upper secondary. The last two age groups of 65–74 and 75> showed the lowest education attainment. Table 6.7 also shows that 8.62% of the population aged 25 or above in 2006 has no schooling or pre-primary education attainment, though most belong to the high age groups. On the

TABLE 6.6 Education attainment of population aged 15 and above

Education attainment (Highest level attended)	2001		2006	
	Number	Percent	Number	Percent
No schooling/pre-primary/P1–P5	1,024,829	18.3	928,648	15.7
Primary	1,035,386	18.5	1,017,576	17.2
Lower secondary	949,313	17.0	1,023,044	17.3
Upper secondary	1,353,765	24.2	1,470,377	24.8
Sixth form	483,652	8.6	366,424	6.2
Diploma/certificate/sub-degree course	164,704	2.9	351,346	6.0
Degree course	587,323	10.5	767,256	13.0
Total	5,598,972	100	5,924,671	100

Definitions: No-schooling/Pre-Primary/P1–P5 = people with no schooling, or who have completed Pre-Primary, Primary 1 to Primary 5 education but have not completed or not attended Primary 6 education. Primary = people who have completed Primary 6 to Secondary 2 education but have not completed or not attended Secondary 3 education. Lower Secondary = people who have completed Secondary 3 to Secondary 4 education but have not completed or not attended Secondary 5 education. Upper Secondary = people who have completed Secondary 5 education but have not completed or not attended Sixth Form education, and persons who have completed the "Craft level" are included. Sixth Form = people who have completed Sixth Form education but have not completed or not attended Post-Secondary education. Diploma/Certificate = people who have completed courses in Institute of Vocational Education/former Polytechnics/commercial schools/industrial training courses of Vocational Training Council.
Source: 2006 Population by-Census Office, Census and Statistics Department of Hong Kong.

contrary, 19.52% of population aged 25 or above have received tertiary education attainment (non-degree, first degree and post-graduate).

Table 6.8 gives a comparison of the education attainment of population aged 25 and above between Hong Kong and the US in 2006. Although Hong Kong's population aged 25 and above is equivalent to only 2.63% in the US, the percentage shares in the three categories of education attainment are very different. In the first two levels that reached Upper Secondary in Hong Kong or high school in the US, the percentage share of population aged 25 or above is 80.5% in Hong Kong and 47% in the US. In the two education level of post-secondary but lower than first degree, the percentage shares are 6% and 25.4% for Hong Kong and the US, respectively. In the third category, only 13.5% of population aged 25 and above in Hong Kong received first degree and post-graduate education, the same percentage in the US is 27.6%. Improvement is definitely needed in the general education attainment level in Hong Kong if education attainment is considered to be the basis of a knowledge-based economy.

The job structure in Hong Kong has changed in line with the knowledge-based nature of the economy. Table 6.9 shows the working population by occupation in the four years of 1991, 1996, 2001 and 2006. Several observations can be made. The percentage shares of professionals and associate professionals in 1991 were 3.7% and 10.3%, respectively, but they have increased to 6.1% and 16.1% in 2006. The notable increase is the service and shop sales workers, as its percentage share has increased from 13.2% in 1991

TABLE 6.7 Population aged 25 and above by education attainment, 2006

Age group	No schooling/ Pre-primary	P1–P5	Primary	Lower secondary	Upper secondary	Sixth form	Craft level	Tertiary non-degree	First degree	Post-graduate	Total
25–34	6,856	13,103	68,889	168,069	317,063	78,673	2,625	106,261	238,575	38,172	1,038,286
	(0.66)	(1.26)	(6.63)	(16.19)	(30.54)	(7.58)	(0.25)	(10.23)	(22.98)	(3.68)	(100)
35–44	16,228	44,912	164,742	223,806	391,075	83,907	2,386	92,417	168,886	46,946	1,235,305
	(1.31)	(3.64)	(13.34)	(18.12)	(31.66)	(6.79)	(0.19)	(7.48)	(13.67)	(3.80)	(100)
45–54	39,688	123,805	323,979	210,009	257,989	66,266	1,236	56,309	81,798	23,190	1,184,269
	(3.35)	(10.45)	(27.36)	(17.73)	(21.78)	(14.44)	(0.10)	(4.75)	(6.91)	(1.96)	(100)
55–64	56,169	118,641	188,605	107,967	92,183	34,968	867	24,573	35,478	5,972	665,423
	(8.44)	(17.83)	(28.34)	(16.23)	(13.85)	(5.26)	(0.13)	(3.69)	(5.33)	(0.90)	(100)
65–74	123,328	108,308	106,531	42,862	29,487	16,775	583	14,536	25,765	1,630	469,805
	(26.26)	(23.05)	(22.68)	(9.12)	(6.28)	(3.57)	(0.12)	(3.09)	(5.48)	(0.35)	(100)
75>	186,482	84,575	64,915	18,099	11,153	6,431	123	3,584	6,959	447	382,768
	(48.72)	(22.10)	(16.96)	(4.73)	(2.91)	(1.68)	(0.03)	(0.94)	(1.82)	(0.12)	(100)
Total	428,751	493,344	917,661	770,812	1,098,950	287,020	7,820	297,680	557,461	116,357	4,975,856
	(8.62)	(9.91)	(18.44)	(15.49)	(22.09)	(5.77)	(0.16)	(5.98)	(11.20)	(2.34)	(100)

Note: Refer to Table 6.5 for definitions. Percentage shares are shown in brackets.
Source: Census and Statistics Department, Hong Kong.

TABLE 6.8 Percentage population aged 25 and above by education attainment: The US and Hong Kong

Age group/Sex	Total	25–34	35–44	45–54	55–64	76–74	75>	Male	Female
Hong Kong (2006)									
Population (1,000)	4,976	1,038	1,235	1,184	665	470	383	2,316	2,659
Lower secondary and below (percent)	52.5	24.7	36.4	58.9	70.8	81.1	92.5	51.0	53.7
Upper secondary/Sixth form/Craft level (percent)	28.0	38.4	38.6	27.5	19.2	10.0	4.6	27.2	28.7
Diploma/Certificate (percent)	3.0	4.6	3.7	2.4	2.1	1.8	0.6	3.0	2.9
High Diploma/High certificate/ Non-degree (percent)	3.0	5.6	3.8	2.3	1.6	1.3	0.3	3.4	2.7
First degree (percent)	11.2	23.0	13.7	6.9	5.3	5.5	1.8	12.3	10.2
Post-graduate (percent)	2.3	3.7	3.8	2.0	0.9	0.3	0.1	3.0	1.7
United States of America (2005)									
Population (1,000)	189,362	39,307	43,350	41,960	29,532	18,388	16,825	90,896	98,465
Below high school (percent)	14.8	13.3	11.6	10.9	13.7	22.3	30.2	15.1	14.6
High school (percent)	32.2	28.8	31.7	32.1	32.5	37.2	35.4	32.1	32.2
College and non-degree (percent)	16.8	18.7	16.8	17.6	16.9	14.2	13.0	16.4	17.2
Associate degree (percent)	8.6	9.0	10.0	9.9	8.5	5.7	4.5	7.6	9.5
First degree (percent)	18.1	22.4	20.2	18.7	16.3	12.4	10.5	18.3	17.9
Post-graduate (percent)	9.5	7.9	9.7	10.9	12.1	8.1	6.5	10.6	8.6

Sources: Census and Statistics Department, Hong Kong; Statistical Abstract of the US, US Census Bureau.

TABLE 6.9 Working populations by occupation, 1991, 1996, 2001 and 2006

	1991		1996		2001		2006	
Occupation	Number	percent	Number	percent	Number	percent	Number	percent
Managers and administrators	249,247	9.2	369,323	12.1	349,637	10.7	361,891	10.8
Professionals	99,331	3.7	151,591	5.0	179,825	5.5	205,435	6.1
Associate professionals	279,909	10.3	369,132	12.1	498,671	15.3	542,309	16.1
Clerks	431,651	15.9	512,719	16.8	529,992	16.3	567,964	16.9
Service and shop sales	359,319	13.2	419,721	13.8	488,961	15.0	550,855	16.4
Craft and related workers	397,992	14.7	373,143	12.3	321,000	9.9	286,007	8.5
Plant and machine operators and assemblers	365,826	13.5	259,909	8.5	238,666	7.3	208,409	6.2
Elementary occupations	503,832	18.6	564,682	18.6	635,393	19.5	633,227	18.8
Agricultural, fishery and unclassified	27,996	1.0	23,478	0.8	10,561	0.3	9,639	0.3
Total	2,715,103	100	3,043,698	100	3,252,706	100	3,365,736	100

Source: Census and Statistics Department, Hong Kong.

to 16.4% in 2006. On the contrary, the biggest drop in occupation is plant and machine operators and assemblers, which has halved from 13.5% in 1991 to 6.2% in 2006, reflecting the fall in manufacturing industry.

The large increase in the percentage share in service and shop sales work deserves some discussion, as it has crucial implication on employment, retirement and possible welfare requirement in Hong Kong's long-term fiscal structure. Manufacturing industries, whose employment is manifested in craft and related workers, plant and machine operators and assemblers, are often skill oriented. Workers gain experience and skill through age, earnings tend to rise with experience. In other words, so long as there are manufacturing industries, the employment life of manufacturing workers lasts longer.

In the case of nominal services, especially female shop sales workers, employers tend to hire younger female workers in retail shops and the wage of younger sales is usually lower. In retail shop sales employment, however, there can be limited gain in experience, training or skill advancement with the number of years of employment, and working hours might even be long or inflexible. Thus, a retail shop sales female worker could easily become unemployed when she reaches her middle age, probably before reaching the age of retirement, and since the skill level of these retail shop sales workers remains low, it would be difficult for them to look for alternative employment when these female shop sales workers have come to their middle age. In other words, the life of employment for the female retail shop sales is short and lacks advancement possibility in skills and protection from aging. If they were to become unemployed at a fairly young age and if other job opportunities are not forthcoming, they will end up relying on government welfare.

There should not be any market "discrimination" in age and sex of the employees, but it is natural for employers to choose the more suitable employees in practice. The cumulative consequence of a "worst" case scenario is that a retail shop sales female worker can easily become unemployed by the time the worker reaches the age of late 30s or early 40s. Due to the lack of skills and without further re-training, such a worker would find it difficult to look for alternative employment, unless the economy has been restructured and more job opportunities are forthcoming. Since the wage earnings had not been high for working as a retail shop sales person, a large saving for retirement could not be expected. In the end, the worker would have to rely on social welfare assistance from the government for economic survival at a fairly young age. This creates a burden on the government's long-term fiscal policy.

The primary difference is that quite a large number of service jobs require low education attainment and low skill, and there is limited training possibility or advancement during employment. Job security is low when there are changes in market expectation, or when the job chooses workers with a younger age. Thus, the life employment duration could be shorter in low-skill service jobs. On the contrary, workers in manufacturing industries would usually gain industrial experience, skill, and possibly further training as employment proceeds. As such, workers in manufacturing industries are better equipped; their life employment duration could be longer, lasting for a number of decades. This will have positive implication on the economy, as employment would remain steady and would not need to rely on welfare assistance from the government.

This problem can somewhat be examined in Table 6.10. Other than agriculture and fishery and mining and quarrying which occupied a small percentage share in Hong Kong's GDP, construction has engaged the largest percentage of primary and lower secondary graduates. The traditional low-skill service industries that employed a large number of primary, lower secondary and upper secondary graduates are wholesale, retail, import, exports, restaurants and hotels (WRIRT) and transport, storage and communications (TSC) and community, social and personal services (CSP). Their low education attainment could constraint their life-long employment and could face strong pressure of competition from new workers entering the same job markets. Indeed, WRIRT and TSC together already occupied 65.3% of upper secondary graduates in 2006.

In manufacturing, the percentage share of primary, lower and upper and secondary graduates is lower, but the percentage share of non-degree, first degree and post-graduate is higher than WRIRT and TSC. On the contrary, the service industry of finance, insurance, real estate and business services (FIEB) have occupied the largest percentage share of first degree graduates (24.8%) and post-graduates (7.9%). Other industries that have occupied graduates from tertiary education include electricity, gas and water (EGW) and community, social and personal services (CSP).

Other than the direct comparison between Hong Kong and the US on education attainment in Table 6.8, comparison with other economies can be made in order to see how well the Hong Kong economy is performing. In Table 6.11, comparison on the percentage of populations that has attained upper secondary and tertiary education is shown on a number of selected OECD economies, though the difference in the classification of education, especially among upper secondary education, may differ slightly among economies.

Similar analysis can be studied in the percentage of population that has attained upper secondary education in Table 6.11. The percentage of population that has attained upper secondary education for Hong Kong is 55% in 2006, which is far below the OECD average of 70% in 2007. For the two categories of population percentages in each of the economies, the youngest age group tended to have the highest percentage of educational attainment, but it got lower as the age groups progressed. For Hong Kong, the percentage has declined from 55% to 29% in the case of population that has attained upper secondary education, while the decline in the population attaining tertiary education has dropped from 22% to 10%. In short, the Hong Kong economy needs to deepen its education attainment across all age groups. While changes or improvement for the elder age groups may not be attainable, effort on the younger age groups to improve their education attainment is urgently needed.

A further comparison on the mean years of education among a number of western and Asian economies can be found in Toh and Lee (1995) reported in Table 6.12. Although the position may have changed slightly since 1992, the comparison is still useful. Among the sample of economies in Table 6.2, the economy with the highest mean years of schooling is the US with 12.4 years, followed by other developed countries. Among the Asian economies, Japan topped the ranking, followed by South Korea. The performance of most Asian economies, including Hong Kong, ranked much lower, with increasing gap between advanced European economies and Asian economies.

TABLE 6.10 Education attainment of working population by industry groups: Percentage shares, 2006

Education attainment	AF	MQ	Manu	EGW	Cons	WRIRT	TSC	FIEB	CSP	Total
No schooling/ Pre-primary	26.3	—	1.3	0.8	2.4	1.7	1.2	0.7	2.1	1.6
P1–P5	17.7	—	4.7	3.2	8.7	4.8	5.1	2.2	4.6	4.6
Primary	27.7	5.9	15.3	13.4	24.9	14.1	17.3	7.6	12.4	13.8
Lower secondary	11.4	39.6	16.5	14.0	24.3	18.7	19.6	9.6	15.1	16.4
Upper secondary	11.0	11.8	31.0	25.1	21.2	33.1	32.1	27.2	25.4	28.8
Sixth form	1.1	—	6.7	5.4	4.1	7.3	6.1	8.6	10.1	7.8
Craft level	0.1	—	0.3	0.5	0.4	0.2	0.2	0.2	0.2	0.2
Non-degree	1.1	21.3	8.8	14.5	6.1	7.0	6.5	11.4	8.0	8.1
First degree	2.3	21.3	12.3	15.8	6.3	10.8	9.6	24.8	17.2	14.6
Post-graduate	1.3	—	3.0	7.1	1.8	2.4	2.4	7.9	5.0	4.0
Total	100	100	100	100	100	100	100	100	100	100
Number	7,616	169	325,066	14,335	230,227	916,217	391,285	571,378	905,425	3,361,718
Percentages	0.2	0.0	9.7	0.4	6.8	27.3	11.6	17.0	26.9	100.0

Notes: AF = Agriculture and fishing; MQ = Mining and quarrying; Manu = Manufacturing; EGW = Electricity, gas and water; Cons = Construction; WRIRT = Wholesale, retail, import and export trades, restaurant and hotel; TSC = Transport, storage and communications; FIEB = Financing, insurance, real estate and business services; CSP = Community, social and personal services.
Source: Census and Statistics Department, Hong Kong.

TABLE 6.11 Comparison of education attainments by age groups: 2007

	Attained upper secondary education					Attained tertiary education				
	25–64	25–34	35–44	45–54	55–64	25–64	25–34	35–44	45–54	55–65
Australia	68	81	70	64	54	34	41	34	32	27
Brazil	37	47	37	31	22	10	10	10	10	8
Canada	87	91	90	86	78	48	56	53	45	39
Denmark	75	85	80	71	66	32	40	34	30	24
Finland	81	90	87	81	65	36	39	43	36	28
France	69	83	74	63	53	27	41	29	20	17
Germany	84	85	86	85	81	24	23	26	25	23
Italy	52	68	56	48	34	14	19	14	11	9
Japan*	84	94	94	82	65	41	54	46	41	24
S. Korea	78	97	92	65	39	35	56	40	21	11
Mexico	33	39	37	29	18	16	19	16	15	9
Netherland	73	83	77	71	61	31	37	31	30	26
Poland	86	92	90	86	74	19	30	18	13	12
Sweden	85	91	90	83	74	31	40	31	29	26
Switzerland	86	90	87	85	81	31	35	34	30	26
Turkey	29	38	26	22	16	11	14	10	9	8
UK	68	75	69	66	61	32	37	32	31	25
USA	88	87	88	89	87	40	40	42	40	30
Hong Kong†	55	75	64	41	29	22	37	25	14	10
OECD average	70	79	74	67	56	27	34	29	24	20

Notes: * = The year of reference for the Attained Upper Secondary Education is 2003. † = 2006 data.
Sources: *Education at a Glance 2009*, OECD, Paris; Census and Statistics Department, Hong Kong.

TABLE 6.12 Mean years of schooling compared, 1992

Country/Economy	Total (Years)	Male (Years)	Females (Years)	Females as percentage of male
USA	12.4	12.3	12.5	101.6
Canada	12.2	12.4	12.0	96.8
Australia	12.0	12.1	11.9	98.3
France	12.0	11.9	12.1	101.7
United Kingdom	11.7	11.6	11.8	101.7
Switzerland	11.6	12.0	11.2	93.3
Germany	11.6	12.2	11.1	91.0
Sweden	11.4	11.4	11.4	100.0
Netherlands	11.1	10.9	11.4	104.6
Japan	10.8	10.9	10.7	98.2
New Zealand	10.7	10.5	10.9	103.8
South Korea	9.3	11.6	7.1	61.2
Philippines	7.6	8.0	7.2	90.0
Hong Kong	7.2	8.8	5.5	62.5
Singapore	7.0	7.7	6.3	81.8
Malaysia	5.6	5.9	5.2	88.1
Mainland China	5.0	6.3	3.8	60.3
Burnei Darussalam	5.0	5.5	4.5	81.8
Indonesia	4.1	5.3	3.1	58.5

Source: Toh and Lee (1995).

The other concern in the mean year of schooling is the gender gap, shown in the last column of Table 6.12. Among the selected economies, Sweden is the most equal economy in the mean years of schooling between the two sexes. South Korea is least equal with males (11.6 years) receiving a higher mean years of schooling than females (7.1 years) in 1992, while females (11.4 years) received a higher mean years of schooling than males (10.9 years) in the Netherlands. The gender inequality gap, however, is much higher in South Korea (61.2%) than the Netherlands (104.6%). The gender gap for the Hong Kong is also high (62.5%). In general, the gender gap in the mean years of schooling is higher among Asian economies than Western economies, though improvement would have taken place since 1992.

6.4 Human Capital and Total Factor Productivity

This section extends the analysis in Chapter 4 of total factor productivity (TFP) by incorporating the human capital element in the total factor productivity (TFP) discussion. While the labor variable showed the quantity of input, the quality of labor can be seen from the level of education workers have attained. Recall the TFP analysis in Chapter 4 that the input share payment of capital and labor are estimated. The empirical question is how much the labor share payment in the total factor productivity analysis is due to human capital. The aggregate labor share payment in Hong Kong has increased from 54% in 1981–1985 to 58% in 2001–2005, as shown in Table 4.3 in Chapter 4. To see how much human capital has contributed to output growth, the labor share payment can be decomposed into contribution by raw labor and by human capital. The study by Lui (2006) shows that while physical capital accounted for 48% share in factor payment, raw labor accounted for 12% and human capital accounted for the remaining 40%. This percentage share is similar to the percentage share payments shown in Table 4.3 in Chapter 4, with payment percentage share of 46% in capital and 54% in labor for the period 1981–2005.

To obtain empirically the share of human capital in productivity accounting, Mincer (1994) has adopted the following equation:

$$\ln y_i = C + \alpha_1 S_i + \alpha_2 S_i^2 + \beta_1 E_i + \beta_2 E_i^2 + \varepsilon_i, \tag{1}$$

where S_i represents the number of years of schooling, E_i is the number of years of working experience for individual i, y_i is the earning of the individual, and ε_i is a random error term with zero mean. If both S_i and E_i are equal to zero, then $\ln y_i = C$, suggesting that the expected income of a person who has absolutely no human capital but has to rely solely on raw labor, like a McJob.[5]

To incorporate human capital in the calculation of TFP, Equation (2) in Chapter 4 can be modified to take into account the growth of human capital to become:

$$\dot{Y}/Y = g + \left(\frac{F_K K}{Y}\right)\cdot(\dot{K}/K) + \left(\frac{F_L L}{Y}\right)\cdot(\dot{L}/L) + \left(\frac{F_H H}{Y}\right)\cdot(\dot{H}/H). \tag{2}$$

The standard primal estimate of the rate of technological progress becomes:

$$\hat{g} = \dot{Y}/Y - [s_K \cdot (\dot{K}/K) + s_L \cdot (\dot{L}/L) + s_H \cdot (\dot{H}/H)], \tag{3}$$

where K is capital, L is labor and H is human capital; and $s_K = F_K K/Y$, $s_L = F_L L/Y$ and $s_H = F_H H/Y$ are the respective shares of capital, labor and human capital factors payment in total output, while $\dot{K}/K$, $\dot{L}/L$ and $\dot{H}/H$ are the growth of capital, labor and human capital, respectively. The value $\hat{g}$ is then the growth of TFP.

[5] According to Wikipedia, McJob is a slang for a low-paying, low-prestige job that requires little skill and offers very little chance of intra-company advancement. McJob, the term derives from the name of a popular fastfood restaurant, is often known as contingent work with little training and high staff turnover, and a McJob worker is tightly regulated by managers. Most McJobs appear in the service industry, particularly in fastfood, coffee shops and retail shop sales.

Compiling the human capital stock

The stock of human capital can be expressed by the mean years of schooling for the aggregate economy, as well as for different industry groups. The data used to calculate the mean years of schooling for both the aggregate economy and for different industrial groups can be derived from the tables on "Working Population by Industry (Major Group)" and "Educational Attainment (Highest Level Completed)" in the *Hong Kong Population Census*, which is updated and published every 5 years, for the six census years of 1981, 1986, 1991, 1996, 2001 and 2006.[6]

Data on mean years schooling are rearranged into 6 levels of educational attainment:

Level 1 refers to no schooling, kindergarten or pre-primary level (0–3 years of schooling);
Level 2 refers to primary (4–9 years of schooling);
Level 3 refers to lower secondary (10–12 years of schooling);
Level 4 refers to upper secondary (13–14 years of schooling);
Level 5 refers to matriculation, post secondary, polytechnic, technical institute, or non-degree tertiary courses (15–17 years of schooling); and
Level 6 refers to university or degree tertiary courses (18–24 years of schooling).

The mid-points for the 6 levels of education attainment are 2, 7, 11.5, 14, 16.5 and 21.5 years. The years of schooling for each level of educational attainment can be calculated by multiplying the mid-point intervals of years of schooling by the number of working people. The total years of schooling is obtained by adding up all the years of schooling for each level of educational attainment. The mean years of schooling is then obtained by dividing the total years of schooling by the total number of working people. In other words, the mean years of schooling can be estimated by the following:

$$\sum_{i=6}^{6} x_i y_i \Big/ \sum_{i=1}^{6} x_i, \qquad (4)$$

where x is the number of people in the working population; y is the mid-point interval of the years of schooling; and i is the level of educational attainment.

The procedure above is used to estimate the mean years of schooling for the aggregate Hong Kong economy, as well as the eight industries (they are: (1) manufacturing; (2) construction; (3) wholesale, retail, import and export trade, restaurants and hotels; (4) transport, storage and communications; (5) finance, insurance, real estate and business services; (6) community, social and personal services; (7) electricity, gas and water; and (8) agriculture, mining and quarrying) for the 6 years (1981, 1986, 1991, 1996, 2001 and 2006). Due to the lack of data

---

[6] The sources of data include: *Hong Kong 1981 Census Main Report*, Volume 2: Table C6; *Hong Kong 1986 by-Census Main Report*, Volume 2, Table C12; *Hong Kong 1991 Population Census*, Table C11; *1996 Population By-Census*, Table C11, *2001 Population Census*, Table C119; and *2006 Population Census*, Table C119.

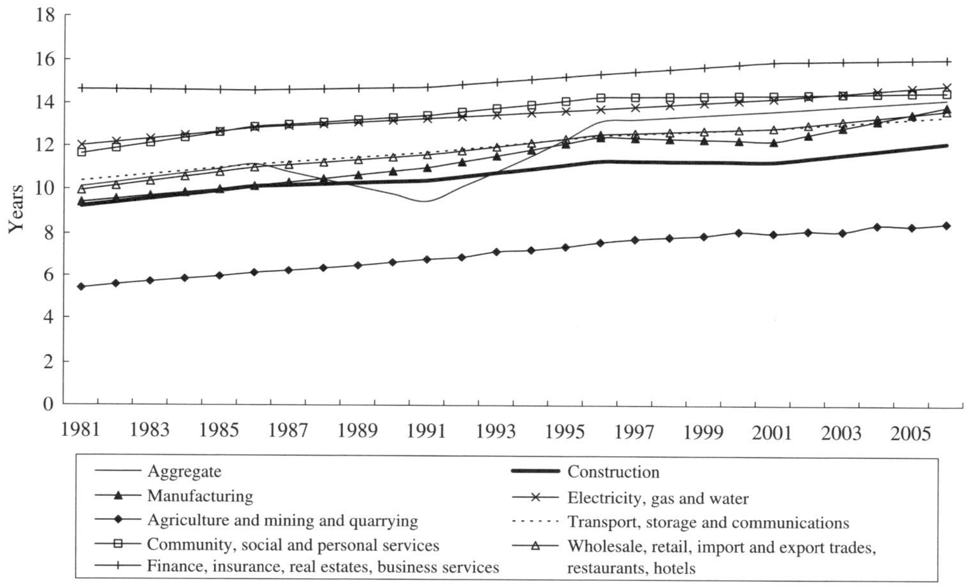

FIGURE 6.1 The mean years of schooling in Hong Kong: 1981–2006

for the two census years of 1991 and 1996, the mean years of schooling for agriculture and fishing, mining and quarrying, and electricity, gas and water are estimated from the four years (1981, 1986, 2001 and 2006) only.

By making use of the data from the six census years, the estimates for all the interval years can be made by using an exponential growth formula to calculate the growth rates of human capital. As a result, the mean years of schooling are obtained for the aggregate economy as well as the industries for all the years from 1980 to 2006. Figure 6.1 presents the mean years of schooling for the aggregate economy as well as the eight industrial groups. There is clearly an increasing trend in the mean years of schooling for the aggregate economy and the various industries in the sample period. Finance, insurance, real estate and business services have the highest mean years of schooling (from 14.6 years in 1981 to 16.1 years in 2006), while agriculture and mining and quarrying has the lowest mean years of schooling (from 5.2 years in 1981 to 8.2 years in 2006). At the aggregate level, the mean years of schooling has increased from 10.1 years in 1981 to 14.2 years in 2006. Hong Kong has experienced a decline in the mean years of schooling in the late 1980s and early 1990s, due probably to the migration of professionals resulting from the uncertain political future. The mean years of schooling reached a peak of 11.1 years in 1986, but fell to the lowest of 9.5 years in 1991 before it gradually revised upwards again.

Other than those comparisons on educational attainment and years of schooling between Hong Kong and other economies, more recent studies have shown a comparison of human capital performance between Hong Kong and Mainland China. Li (2009) and Liu and Li (2006) have estimated the TFP of the Mainland China economy and different regions, and employed an inventory approach to estimate the human capital performance of Mainland China and regions. Although the statistical basis between Mainland China and Hong Kong differed considerably, Figure 6.2 reproduces human capital performance in Mainland China for the period of 1984–2006 in Li (2009:219). The thirty provinces in China are grouped in four geographical regions. The Eastern region consists of the ten coastal provinces of Beijing, Tianjin, Hebei, Shandong, Jiangsu, Shanghai, Zhejiang, Fujian, Guangdong and Hainan. The Western region includes the eleven interior provinces of Inner Mongolia, Xinjiang, Tibet, Qinghai, Gansu, Ningxia, Sichuan (including Chongqing), Guizhou, Yunnan, Guangxi and Shaanxi. The Northeastern region consists of the three provinces of Heilongjiang, Jilin and Liaoning. The Central region composes of the remaining six non-coastal provinces of Shanxi, Henan, Hubei, Hunan, Anhui and Jiangxi.

Due probably to the large population and the low level of education across the country, the level of human capital in Mainland China on average is lower than in Hong Kong, and there is vast difference between the four regions in Mainland China. The Northeast region in Mainland China has the highest level of human capital with about 9 years of schooling, while the national average is about 6 years.

The findings in Figure 6.1 and Figure 6.2 are supported by other studies. Using a similar methodology to that of Li (2009) in estimating the human capital performance of Mainland China, Li *et al.* (2009) have reported the actual years of schooling in

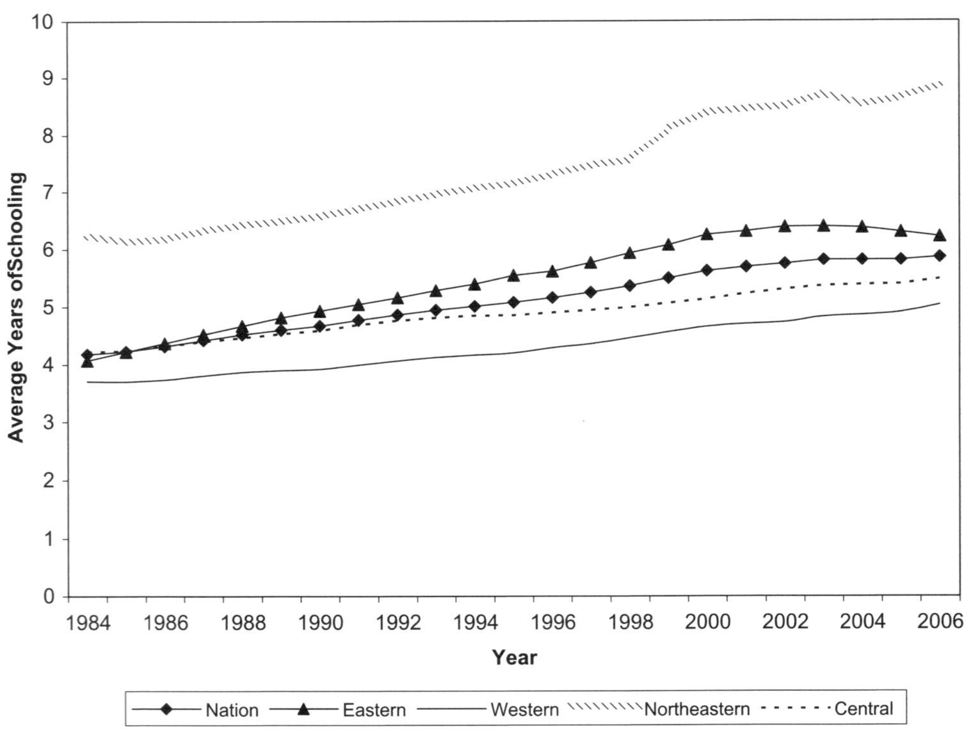

FIGURE 6.2 Human capital of Mainland China: National and regional trends
Source: Li (2009:219).

TABLE 6.13 Human capital measured in average schooling years: East Asia and China

		1985	1990	1995	2000
Li *et al.* (2009)	China				
	National average	4.17	4.62	5.10	6.27
	East	4.26	4.98	5.50	6.74
	Northeast	6.00	6.34	6.91	8.45
	South	3.51	3.96	4.33	5.03
	West	3.94	4.04	4.54	6.05
Barro and Lee (2001)	China	4.15	5.23	5.48	5.74
	Hong Kong	7.51	8.37	9.33	9.47
	Chinese Taipei	6.87	7.44	8.03	8.53
	South Korea	8.03	9.25	10.09	10.46
	Singapore	4.50	5.52	7.82	8.12
	Japan	8.51	9.22	9.44	9.72

Sources: Li *et al.* (2009); Barro and Lee (2001).

Mainland China and regions, and the figures are compared to the study in Barro and Lee (2001), as shown in Table 6.13. When the various regions in Mainland China are compared to the findings in Barro and Lee (2001) in other Asian economies, the human capital performance in the Northeast region of China is similar to that of Chinese Taipei in year 2000. At the national level, Mainland China's human capital performance in year 2000 is lower than all other five East Asian economies.

Share of payment

With the estimated data on human capital expressed by the mean year of schooling, the initial share of labor has to be broken down into the share of raw labor and the share of human capital. The share of raw labor is calculated by dividing the total raw income of all people engaged by the nominal production-based GDP, namely:

$$\text{Share of raw labor} = \frac{\text{Total raw income of all the people engaged}}{\text{Nominal production-based GDP.}} \quad (5)$$

The total raw income is the total value of raw wage of all people engaged in a year, and that is the product of raw hourly wage per person engaged, the median number of weekly working hours, the number of weeks in a year (365/7 = 52.14) and the total number of people engaged (employed and the self-employed), shown as follows:

$$\begin{aligned}&\text{Total raw income of all the people engaged} = \text{Raw hourly wage}\\&\quad\text{per person engaged} \times \text{median no of weekly working hours} \times\\&\quad 52.14 \times \text{total no. of people engaged.}\end{aligned} \quad (6)$$

The raw hourly wage per person engaged is assumed to be HK$15 in 1980 and is growing at an annual exponential growth rate of 2%. The share of human capital is just the difference between the adjusted share of labor (which is the initial figure of the adjusted compensation divided by the nominal production based GDP) and the share of raw labor shown by Equation (5). It is assumed that the three factor payments (capital, raw labor and human capital) sum to unity.

Table 6.14 summarizes the results of the aggregate TFP calculations after incorporating the stock of human capital. The contribution made by human capital to productivity and output growth can easily be seen. The share of human capital has increased steadily from 6% to 41% between the 1981–1985 and 2001–2005 periods. On the other hand, the percentage share of raw labor payment has decreased from about 48% to 16% between the same two periods. This reflects the growing importance of human capital in Hong Kong's productivity estimation.

The contribution to output growth by human capital has performed very differently in different periods. By and large, the contribution to output growth by human capital is low, with only 0.1% for the sample period of 1981–2005. The contribution was weakened severely in the period of 1986–1990 when Hong Kong experienced a great amount of migration to overseas countries due to the political uncertainty generated from the negotiation on the post-1997 future of Hong Kong. As a result, the contribution to output growth by human capital in the 1981–1990 decade was negligible. On the contrary, the economic boom in the first half of the 1990s has seen a significant increase in the contribution to output growth by human capital, with 1.7% for the period 1991–1995, giving an average of 1.3% in the decade of 1991–2000. After the Asian financial crisis in 1998, the economic recession that followed has produced a relatively low contribution to output growth by human capital, with an average of 0.3% in the period of 2001–2005.

With the inclusion of human capital, the impact on economic growth by labor has obviously declined, as one can compare Table 6.14 with Table 4.3 in Chapter 4. For the entire sample period, for example, the contribution to output by labor has changed from 1.0% in Table 4.3 in Chapter 4 to 0.4% in Table 6.14. The contribution to output growth by TFP has also changed slightly as a result of including the human capital variable. For the entire sample period, the contribution to output growth by TFP has actually increased slightly from 1.5% in Table 4.3 to 1.6% in Table 6.14. The overall trend is similar in other sub-periods, with the exception of the 1991–2000 decade, where with the inclusion of human capital the contribution to output growth by TFP has changed from 0.4% (Table 4.3 in Chapter 4) to –0.2% in Table 6.14. This simply indicates that human capital has become an important variable in output growth in the 1991–2000 decade. A somewhat similar picture can be seen in the period of 1991–1995, when the contribution by human capital has become the more important variable than the TFP. This can be seen from the growth rates of human capital in Table 6.14, where the growth rate of human capital is –0.1% in the 1981–1990 decade has increased to 3.3% in the 1991–2000 decade.

Table 6.15 shows the TFP calculations after incorporating the stock of human capital for the eight industrial groups in Hong Kong. One observation is that the growth of human capital is larger than the growth of raw labor for the entire sample period, the 1980s and the 1990s in agriculture and fishing, and mining and quarrying, electricity, gas and water, and manufacturing. The reverse situation, where the growth of raw labor is larger than the growth of human capital in all the three periods

TABLE 6.14 Incorporating human capital in Hong Kong's productivity: 1981–2005 (Compound annual growth rates)

	Growth rates				Share of payment			Contribution to output by			
	Output	Capital	Raw labor	Human capital	Capital	Raw labor	Human capital	TFP	Capital	Raw labor	Human capital
1981–1985	5.4	8.1	3.5	2.0	0.46	0.48	0.06	–0.1	3.7	1.7	0.1
1986–1990	8.3	7.3	1.3	–2.2	0.47	0.29	0.23	4.9	3.5	0.4	–0.5
1991–1995	5.4	8.1	0.1	4.7	0.48	0.17	0.35	–0.2	3.9	0.0	1.7
1996–2000	3.5	5.5	3.3	1.9	0.45	0.14	0.41	–0.2	2.5	0.5	0.8
2001–2005	4.7	3.8	0.8	0.8	0.42	0.16	0.41	2.6	1.6	0.1	0.3
1981–1990	6.8	7.7	2.4	–0.1	0.46	0.39	0.15	2.3	3.6	0.9	0.0
1991–2000	4.5	6.8	1.7	3.3	0.47	0.15	0.38	–0.2	3.2	0.3	1.3
1981–2005	5.4	6.6	1.8	1.4	0.46	0.25	0.29	1.6	3.0	0.4	0.4

Note: The sum of the last three columns should equal to the first column. Any difference is the result of rounding off.

(the sample period, the 1980s and the 1990s) occurred in the service industries of wholesale, retail, import and export trades, restaurants and hotels, finance, insurance, real estates and business services, transport, storage and communications, and community, social and personal services. It is no surprise that when the industries that have higher growth rate in human capital than raw labor, they have also higher contribution to output growth by human capital. This is true in all the production industries and the reverse is true in all the service industries.

Consider the performance of human capital in individual industry shown in Table 6.15, one can see that the factor that contributed to output growth differed among industries. In the case of agriculture and fishing, mining and quarrying, the performance of TFP is unsteady with large TFP growth in 1983–1990 and human capital is another factor contributed to output growth. In the case of electricity, gas and water, apparently capital is the most important factor that contributed to output growth, confirming that this is a rather capital intensive industry. Contribution to output growth by human capital is positive but small. For the construction industry, the TFP and human capital are the two factors that contributed to output growth consistently, while the contribution by capital and raw labor have been unsteady. In the case of manufacturing, TFP and human capital are the two reliable contributing factors in the sample period, suggesting that industrial development in Hong Kong does have a prospective future, and Hong Kong should attract new investment to the manufacturing sector.

In the remaining four services industries (wholesale, retail, export and import trade, restaurants and hotels; financial, insurance, real estates and business services; transport, storage and communications; and community, social and personal services), their contribution to output growth by the four factors are quite even, as there are few negative growth rates among these four service industries. In the case of wholesale, retail, import and export trade, restaurants and hotels, capital is the largest and most important contributing factor (4.0% for the sample period), followed by TFP (3.4% for the sample period). This suggests that despite the labor-intensive nature of this service industry, their development and expansion depends a lot on new investment. The situation is slightly different in the case of finance, insurance, real estate and business services, since the most important factor that contributed to output growth is TFP (2.7% for the sample period), followed by capital (2.2% for the sample period). It is obvious that technical progress and continuous inflow of investment are the two champion factors in the financial sector as a whole.

The inclusion of human capital in the productivity analysis can further be disaggregated into the four economic sectors of tradable goods, tradable services, non-tradable goods and non-tradable services. Table 6.16 shows the TFP calculations for the tradable and non-tradable sectors when the input factor of human capital is added. In the case of the tradable goods sector, the estimates showed that human capital is the factor that has contributed positively to output growth in both the 1991–2000 decade and the entire sample periods, while TFP and capital also contributed positively in the 1983–1990 decade. Once again, this confirms that those who remain in the manufacturing sector are the skillful workers.

The tradable services sector is the best performing economic sector, as all the four input factors have contributed positively to output growth. In the entire sample period, capital contributed mostly with a compound annual growth rate of 4%,

TABLE 6.15 Incorporating human capital in Hong Kong's industries: 1983–2005 (Compound annual growth rates)

		Growth rates				Share of payment			Contribution to output by			
		Output	Capital	Raw labor	Human capital	Capital	Raw labor	Human capital	TFP	Capital	Raw labor	Human capital
Agriculture and fishing, mining and quarrying	1983–1985	1.1	–5.7	–8.3	2.4	0.70	0.38	-0.08	8.4	–4.0	–3.1	-0.2
	1986–1990	5.0	–12.4	–10.7	2.1	0.61	0.27	0.12	15.1	–7.5	–2.8	0.3
	1991–1995	–4.6	–0.3	–10.8	2.3	0.59	0.16	0.26	–3.4	–0.2	–1.7	0.6
	1996–2000	–4.3	–5.2	–10.9	1.1	0.65	0.12	0.23	0.1	–3.4	–1.3	0.3
	2001–2005	–1.2	–0.9	–1.5	1.1	0.63	0.14	0.22	–0.7	–0.6	–0.2	0.2
	1983–1990	3.5	–9.9	–9.8	2.2	0.64	0.31	0.05	12.8	–6.4	–3.0	0.1
	1991–2000	–4.4	–2.8	–10.9	1.7	0.62	0.14	0.25	–1.7	–1.7	–1.5	0.4
	1983–2005	–1.0	–4.9	–8.5	1.8	0.63	0.20	0.17	3.4	–3.1	–1.7	0.3
Electricity, gas and water	1983–1985	10.9	28.3	0.0	1.4	0.77	0.08	0.16	–10.9	21.6	0.0	0.2
	1986–1990	9.2	1.9	0.5	0.8	0.79	0.05	0.17	7.6	1.5	0.0	0.1
	1991–1995	4.5	8.6	–1.2	0.7	0.76	0.03	0.21	–2.1	6.5	0.0	0.2
	1996–2000	3.8	14.8	–7.0	0.7	0.81	0.01	0.17	–8.3	12.0	–0.1	0.1
	2001–2005	3.1	3.4	0.0	0.8	0.85	0.01	0.14	0.1	2.9	0.0	0.1
	1983–1990	9.9	11.1	0.3	1.0	0.78	0.06	0.16	1.1	8.6	0.0	0.2
	1991–2000	4.1	11.6	–4.1	0.7	0.79	0.02	0.19	–5.0	9.1	–0.1	0.1
	1983–2005	5.9	9.6	–1.7	0.8	0.80	0.03	0.17	–1.9	7.6	–0.1	0.1
Construction	1983–1985	1.0	–21.0	–5.5	1.8	0.13	0.23	0.64	3.9	–2.8	–1.3	1.2
	1986–1990	1.6	12.2	0.8	0.8	0.09	0.17	0.74	–0.3	1.1	0.1	0.6
	1991–1995	4.1	16.0	–1.9	1.5	0.16	0.07	0.77	0.6	2.5	–0.1	1.1
	1996–2000	1.2	–5.4	4.6	0.3	0.13	0.06	0.81	1.4	–0.7	0.3	0.3
	2001–2005	–7.4	–8.4	–8.3	1.2	0.07	0.08	0.85	–7.1	–0.6	–0.7	1.0
	1983–1990	1.3	–1.6	–1.6	1.2	0.11	0.19	0.70	1.0	–0.2	–0.3	0.8
	1991–2000	2.7	4.7	1.3	0.9	0.14	0.07	0.79	1.2	0.7	0.1	0.7
	1983–2005	–0.1	–0.5	1.9	1.1	0.11	0.11	0.77	–0.6	–0.1	–0.2	0.8
Manufacturing	1983–1985	7.9	13.0	1.4	1.5	0.29	0.70	0.01	3.1	3.8	1.0	0.0
	1986–1990	7.3	7.4	–3.3	1.6	0.35	0.46	0.19	5.9	2.6	–1.5	0.3
	1991–1995	0.5	–7.0	–12.1	2.3	0.38	0.28	0.34	5.8	–2.7	–3.4	0.8
	1996–2000	–4.1	4.0	–9.7	0.3	0.40	0.20	0.40	–3.8	1.6	–2.0	0.1
	2001–2005	–3.8	–9.8	–5.8	2.0	0.35	0.23	0.42	0.2	–3.4	–1.3	0.8
	1983–1990	7.5	9.5	–2.5	1.6	0.33	0.55	0.12	5.6	3.1	–1.4	0.2
	1991–2000	–1.8	–1.7	–10.9	1.3	0.39	0.24	0.37	1.0	–0.6	–2.6	0.5
	1983–2005	0.9	0.2	–6.6	1.5	0.36	0.35	0.29	2.7	0.1	–2.3	0.5

(*Continued*)

TABLE 6.15 (*Continued*)

		Growth rates				Share of payment			Contribution to output by			
		Output	Capital	Raw labor	Human capital	Capital	Raw labor	Human capital	TFP	Capital	Raw labor	Human capital
Wholesale, retail, import and export trades, restaurants and hotels	1984–1985	14.8	17.7	8.4	2.0	0.49	0.48	0.04	2.1	8.6	4.0	0.1
	1986–1990	13.6	6.7	5.4	1.3	0.53	0.29	0.19	8.3	3.5	1.5	0.2
	1991–1995	9.4	7.9	4.2	1.5	0.45	0.20	0.34	4.5	3.6	0.9	0.5
	1996–2000	2.9	9.1	–0.2	0.7	0.41	0.19	0.40	–1.0	3.7	0.0	0.3
	2001–2005	6.5	10.5	0.3	1.1	0.48	0.19	0.33	1.0	5.0	0.1	0.4
	1984–1990	14.0	11.8	6.7	1.5	0.47	0.38	0.14	5.6	5.6	2.5	0.2
	1991–2000	6.1	8.5	2.0	1.1	0.43	0.20	0.37	1.6	3.6	0.4	0.4
	1984–2005	8.6	9.3	2.9	1.2	0.43	0.28	0.29	3.4	4.0	0.8	0.4
Finance, insurance, real estates and business services	1983–1985	1.3	–8.3	4.7	–0.1	0.59	0.16	0.25	5.5	–4.9	0.8	0.0
	1986–1990	9.7	11.2	9.4	0.2	0.61	0.12	0.27	1.8	6.8	1.1	0.0
	1991–1995	6.5	13.0	8.5	0.7	0.64	0.08	0.28	–2.6	8.3	0.7	0.2
	1996–2000	5.5	1.4	2.8	0.8	0.53	0.08	0.39	4.2	0.7	0.2	0.3
	2001–2005	3.8	–0.6	1.8	0.3	0.41	0.10	0.50	3.7	–0.2	0.2	0.1
	1983–1990	6.5	3.4	7.6	0.1	0.60	0.13	0.26	3.4	2.1	1.0	0.0
	1991–2000	6.0	7.0	5.6	0.7	0.58	0.08	0.34	1.2	4.1	0.4	0.3
	1983–2005	5.7	4.1	5.5	0.4	0.55	0.10	0.35	2.7	2.2	0.6	0.1
Transport, storage and communications	1983–1985	6.7	17.0	4.3	1.4	0.45	0.22	0.33	–2.4	7.7	1.0	0.5
	1986–1990	14.1	10.2	6.8	1.1	0.52	0.15	0.33	7.4	5.3	1.0	0.4
	1991–1995	9.1	9.5	5.3	1.3	0.51	0.10	0.39	3.2	4.8	0.5	0.5
	1996–2000	3.8	8.8	0.5	0.7	0.47	0.09	0.44	–0.7	4.2	0.0	0.3
	2001–2005	2.8	7.7	0.8	0.8	0.50	0.09	0.40	–1.5	3.9	0.1	0.3
	1983–1990	11.3	12.7	5.9	0.8	0.49	0.18	0.33	3.5	6.3	1.0	0.4
	1991–2000	6.4	9.2	2.9	1.2	0.49	0.10	0.41	1.2	4.5	0.3	0.4
	1983–2005	7.3	9.3	3.5	1.0	0.49	0.12	0.38	1.8	4.6	0.4	0.4
Community, social and personal services	1983–1985	4.4	15.8	4.0	2.1	0.19	0.23	0.58	–0.7	3.0	0.9	1.2
	1986–1990	3.7	–2.8	2.7	1.1	0.17	0.16	0.67	3.0	–0.5	0.4	0.7
	1991–1995	6.3	9.3	3.8	1.2	0.13	0.11	0.76	3.8	1.2	0.4	0.9
	1996–2000	5.6	0.0	4.6	0.4	0.09	0.08	0.3	4.9	0.0	0.4	0.3
	2001–2005	1.3	–6.3	4.7	0.2	0.04	0.10	0.86	0.9	–0.3	0.5	0.2
	1983–1990	4.0	3.8	3.2	1.5	0.17	0.19	0.64	1.8	0.7	0.6	0.9
	1991–2000	5.9	4.5	4.2	0.8	0.11	0.09	0.80	4.4	0.5	0.4	0.6
	1983–2005	4.2	1.8	4.0	0.9	0.12	0.13	0.75	2.8	0.2	0.5	0.7

Note: Due to a limitation of data, the estimates for the wholesale, retail, import and export trades, restaurants and hotels started from 1984 onwards.

TABLE 6.16 Incorporating human capital in Hong Kong's economic sectors: 1983–2005 (Compound annual growth rate)

		Growth rates				Share of payment			Contribution to output by			
		Output	Capital	Raw labor	Human capital	Capital	Raw labor	Human capital	TFP	Capital	Raw labor	Human capital
Tradable goods	1983–1985	1.4	11.2	1.3	1.6	0.30	0.69	0.00	−2.9	3.4	0.9	0.0
	1986–1990	6.9	6.4	−3.4	1.7	0.36	0.45	0.19	5.8	2.3	−1.5	0.3
	1991–1995	−10.4	−6.8	−12.1	2.3	0.38	0.28	0.34	−5.2	−2.6	−3.4	0.8
	1996–2000	−7.3	3.7	−9.7	0.3	0.40	0.20	0.40	−6.9	1.5	−2.0	0.1
	2001–2005	−6.1	−9.5	−5.8	1.9	0.35	0.23	0.42	−2.2	−3.4	−1.3	0.8
	1983–1990	4.8	8.2	−1.7	1.6	0.34	0.54	0.12	2.7	2.8	−0.9	0.2
	1991–2000	−8.8	−1.7	−10.9	1.3	0.39	0.24	0.37	−6.0	−0.7	−2.6	0.5
	1983–2005	−3.7	−0.2	−6.7	1.6	0.37	0.34	0.29	−1.8	−0.1	−2.3	0.5
Tradable services	1984–1985	9.0	6.9	9.9	1.0	0.51	0.28	0.21	2.5	3.5	2.8	0.2
	1986–1990	13.4	10.2	8.1	0.9	0.54	0.20	0.27	6.1	5.5	1.6	0.2
	1991–1995	8.7	11.5	6.5	1.3	0.54	0.13	0.33	1.2	6.2	0.9	0.4
	1996–2000	4.9	5.4	0.6	0.9	0.48	0.11	0.40	1.8	2.6	0.1	0.4
	2001–2005	5.2	5.4	0.8	0.8	0.46	0.12	0.42	2.2	2.5	0.1	0.3
	1984–1990	12.1	9.3	8.6	0.9	0.53	0.22	0.25	5.1	4.9	1.9	0.2
	1991–2000	6.8	8.4	3.5	1.1	0.51	0.12	0.37	1.6	4.3	0.4	0.4
	1984–2005	8.1	8.0	4.5	1.0	0.50	0.15	0.34	3.0	4.0	0.7	0.3
Non-tradable goods	1983–1985	0.6	10.4	−4.8	1.9	0.34	0.18	0.48	−3.0	3.6	−0.9	0.9
	1986–1990	5.2	4.0	0.8	0.8	0.34	0.12	0.54	3.3	1.3	0.1	0.5
	1991–1995	4.3	10.6	−1.8	1.4	0.35	0.06	0.59	−0.2	3.7	−0.1	0.8
	1996–2000	2.0	9.8	3.2	0.1	0.36	0.05	0.59	−1.7	3.5	0.2	0.1
	2001–2005	−3.2	1.9	−7.4	1.4	0.43	0.05	0.52	−4.4	0.8	−0.4	0.7
	1983–1990	3.5	6.3	−1.3	1.2	0.34	0.14	0.52	0.9	2.1	−0.2	0.6
	1991–2000	3.1	10.2	0.7	0.7	0.35	0.05	0.59	−1.0	3.6	0.0	0.4
	1983–2005	1.8	7.0	−1.8	1.0	0.37	0.08	0.55	−1.2	2.6	−0.2	0.6
Non-tradable services	1983–1985	4.7	13.0	3.6	2.1	0.28	0.36	0.36	−1.0	3.6	1.3	0.7
	1986–1990	5.4	0.6	2.2	1.2	0.28	0.24	0.48	4.1	0.2	0.5	0.6
	1991–1995	5.2	5.2	2.2	1.4	0.22	0.16	0.62	2.8	1.2	0.3	0.9
	1996–2000	3.9	4.1	2.7	0.6	0.17	0.12	0.72	2.4	0.7	0.3	0.4
	2001–2005	1.6	1.3	2.8	0.7	0.12	0.14	0.74	0.6	0.2	0.4	0.5
	1983–1990	5.1	5.1	2.7	1.5	0.28	0.29	0.43	2.2	1.4	0.8	0.7
	1991–2000	4.5	4.7	2.4	1.0	0.20	0.14	0.67	2.6	0.9	0.3	0.7
	1983–2005	4.1	4.1	2.6	1.1	0.21	0.19	0.60	2.1	0.8	0.5	0.7

Notes: The sum of the last three columns should equal to the first column, any difference is the result of rounding off. The limitation of data leads to estimate for the tradable services sector began from 1984 onwards.

followed closely by TFP with 3%. Surprisingly, human capital (0.3%) contributed least among the four factors. On the contrary, the contribution to output growth by labor (0.7% in the sample period) is highest among the four economic sectors. This suggests that the tradable service sector still contains a considerable amount of labor-intensive activities.

The performance of the non-tradable goods sector has been weak, with a negative growth in TFP (−1.2%) in the sample period. Output growth in the non-tradable sector mainly depended on capital input (2.6%), followed by human capital (0.6%). By and large, given the dominance of services in the Hong Kong economy, both the tradable goods and non-tradable goods sectors have shown a weaker performance in TFP, but a strong performance in human capital.

The performance in the non-tradable service sector is promising, as the four input factors have contributed positively to output growth in the sample period. The positive contribution by TFP and human capital are consistent across the two decades (1983–1990 and 1991–2000) and the entire sample period (1983–2005). Contribution by capital is positive (0.8%), but is lower than capital's contribution to both the tradable services and non-tradable goods sectors. The non-tradable services sector contains mainly non-capital intensive industries.

The tradable goods, tradable services, and non-tradable goods sectors have experienced a higher TFP growth rate in the 1980s than that in the 1990s. In the post-AFC period of 2001–2005, the two services sectors have shown a stronger performance than the tradable goods and non-tradable goods sectors. Human capital has contributed positively in all economic sectors and in all different sample periods, with the two non-tradable sectors showing a higher rate of contribution than the two tradable sectors.

One interesting observation on the contribution to output growth by human capital can be found between the three sub-periods of 1983/1984–1990, 1991–2000 and 2001–2005. Despite the better performance in the two services sectors, the contribution by human capital in the tradable services increased from 0.2% in 1984–1990 to 0.4% in 1991–2000, but declined to 0.3% in 2001–2005. In the case of the non-tradable service sector, the contribution by human capital remained constant at 0.7% in the two decades of 1983–1990 and 1991–2000, but declined to 0.5% in 2001–2005.

On the contrary, the contribution to output growth by human capital for the non-tradable goods sector first declined from 0.6% in 1983–1990 to 0.4% in 1991–2000, but has risen to 0.7% in 2001–2005. The best performer, surprisingly, is the tradable goods sector, where human capital's contribution to output growth has increased in the three periods from 0.2% in 1983–1990, to 0.5% in 1991–2000 and further to 0.8% in 2001–2005 periods. Such evidence once again supports strongly that the tradable goods sector in Hong Kong has good potentials and the manufacturing sector can be revived to become a major economic pillar in Hong Kong.

6.5 Intellectual Property Rights

Knowledge creation is a cumulative process that often builds up from existing knowledge and understanding. The explicit way of knowledge creation can be seen in the forms of innovations, inventions, discoveries and pioneering works and studies. These creations are literally products that are owned by the creator. To preserve the ownership of inventors, innovators and authors, the civilized world have enacted laws that protect the intellectual property right (IPR) of individuals' innovations and inventions. Intellectual property laws are designed to protect different forms of subject matter, and it confers a bundle of exclusive rights in relation to the particular form or manner in which ideas or information are expressed or manifested. The term "intellectual property" denotes the specific legal rights which authors, inventors and other intellectual property holders may exercise. Intellectual property laws and enforcement vary widely from jurisdiction to jurisdiction. There are inter-governmental efforts to harmonize them through international treaties such as the 1994 World Trade Organization (WTO) Agreement on Trade-Related Aspects of Intellectual Property Rights (TRIPs). Violations of IPRs can legally be dealt with by the WTO.

There are three major forms of IPR protections. One form of IPR protection is the patent which is granted to a novel, industrially applicable and non-obvious invention, and the patent gives the holder a right to prevent others from practicing the invention without a license from the inventor for a certain period of time (typically 20 years from the filing data of a patent application). The second form of IPR protection is the copyright that exists among creative and artistic works, such as books, movies, music, paintings, photographs and software. The copyright gives the holder the exclusive right to control reproduction or adaptation of such works for a certain period of time, ranging from 10 to 30 years depending on jurisdiction, or the life of the author plus several decades. The third form of IPR protection is a trademark that distinguishes the products or services of different businesses.

Over the past decades, IPRs have become the forefront of global economic policymaking, as many countries in the 1990s unilaterally strengthened their IPR laws and regulations. It is believed that stronger IPRs protection should increase incentives for innovation and raise returns to international technology transfer. However, it also raises the costs of acquiring new technological products, especially those technology consuming developing countries that rely heavily on imported technology and know-how.

The performance of IPRs among world economies can be compared by examining the *Index of Patent Rights*, developed by Ginarte and Park (1997) using 110 world economies for the sample period 1960–1990. The *Index of Patent Rights* is calculated from the following five categories of patent laws:

(1) Extent of coverage: The seven items covered include pharmaceuticals, chemicals, food, plant and animal varieties, surgical products, micro-organisms, and utility models.

(2) Membership in international agreements: The law provides nondiscriminatory treatment to foreigners, and the three agreements include:

    (a) Paris Convention and various revisions since 1883: In simple terms, the Paris Convention on patent rights extends national treatment to foreign nationals, thereby upholding a nondiscriminatory principle;

    (b) Patent Cooperation Treaty (PCT) of 1970: The PCT provides a simple administrative procedure that allows the filing of a single patent application effective in all member countries; and

(c) International Convention for the Protection of New Varieties of Plans (UPOV) of 1961: The UPOV deals with the rights of the plant breeders similar to that of the patent right, and common standards and scope of protection are required. Countries committed to all three agreements will receive a score of 1.

(3) Protection from restrictions on patent rights: Patent holders have to be protected since they can risk the loss of their patent rights from three possibilities:
(a) "Working" requirements: The "working" requirements refer to the actual production of the invention. If it was economically or financially unviable, the patentee does not have to put the invention into practice. But the patent may require that the invention be manufactured or imported if the patent holder is a foreigner. A country received 1/3 of the score if there is an absence of such "working" requirement.
(b) Compulsory licensing: Compulsory licensing requires the patentees to share the gains from the exploitation of the invention with third parties. This effectively reduces the return to invention that the patentee can appropriate, especially at the beginning when the patent was obtained. A country receives 1/3 of the score if it does not impose compulsory licensing after three to four years from the date the patent was granted; and
(c) Revocation of patents: In the revocation of patents, countries will have to revoke non-working patents in order to obtain a full score. Otherwise, countries that do not revoke patents for non-working will receive a score of 1/3 only. Countries that provide protection to all three possibilities receive a score of 1.

(4) Enforcement mechanisms: the legal enforcement framework includes:
(a) Preliminary injunctions: These are pre-trail actions that make sure individuals do not engage in alleged infringements. The legality is to protect the patentee from infringement;
(b) Contributory infringement pleadings: This refers to actions that cause or results in infringement by others; and
(c) Burden-of-proof reversals: These are procedures that shift the burden-of-proof in infringement cases from the patentee to the alleged infringer.

(5) Duration of protection: For patent rights that normally give a term of 20 years from the date of application, countries will receive a score of 1, or proportionally lower if the protection period is shorter than 20 years. If the patent rights are measured from the date of grant, the protection duration is 17 years.

The *Index of Patent Rights* has been extended by Park and Wagh (2002) to 2000 in the Fraser Institute's 2002 annual report of *Economic Freedom of the World*. By examining the patent rights performance of a large number of world economies, Park and Wagh (2002) report that, among the five categories of patent laws, the largest variation in patent rights comes from Coverage (category 1), Protection (category 3) and Enforcement (category 4). Many developed and developing countries do not find it easy to eliminate compulsory licensing in Enforcement, probably because it is a policy instrument that enables a government to exercise leverage over the direction of technological development. Most countries score high on Duration, as many countries have recently become signatories to international treaties on IPR. There is also relatively less variation in category on Membership. This probably suggests the need to incorporate in future index calculations of new and important patent treaties that have recently entered into force or are about to do so. One example is the Patent Law Treaty of the World Intellectual Property Organization.

As shown in Table 1.1 of Chapter 1, other than the *Economic Freedom of the World*, an annual report of the Fraser Institute in Vancouver, the performance of an economy's IPR has also been incorporated into the yearly *Index of Economic Freedom* conducted by the Heritage Foundation in Washington D.C. Table 6.17 reports at five-year interval from 1960 to 2000 the *Index of Patent Rights* for Hong Kong and selected countries. A number of observations can be made. One observation is that improvements in *Index of Patent Rights* is a long-term process, as countries take years to make changes, due probably to the long legal process needed. Even in countries where changes have occurred, the improvements are small in all cases. Over the four decades between 1960 and 2000 in Table 6.17, all countries have made some improvements, and the improvements accelerated in the 1990s. India is the only selected country in Table 6.17 that its *Index of Patent Rights* has declined between 1960 and 1990. In general, developed or advanced industrialized countries show a higher score than developing countries.

The performance of Hong Kong in the *Index of Patent Rights* also showed an improvement, but the improvement has been small in the four decades between 1960 with a score of 2.04 and 2000 with a score of 2.90. The *Index of Patent Rights* of Hong Kong was below the mean score in the entire 1960s and 1970s, but Hong Kong has attained a score slightly higher than the mean score in the 1980s.

Unfortunately, despite its continued improvement since 1995, Hong Kong's score has slipped below the mean score once again in the two years of 1995 and 2000. When compared to other East Asian economies of Japan, South Korea and Singapore in 1960, Hong Kong's score was slightly lower, since the scores of all these economies were below 3. By 2000, however, the other three East Asian economies have far exceeded Hong Kong in the *Index of Patent Rights*, reaching a score higher than 4, while Hong Kong's score is only 2.9. In other words, Hong Kong's performance in the patent right laws has not improved as rapidly as other economies in the East Asia region. When the five individual categories of patent right laws are considered, as shown in Table 6.17, one can see that Hong Kong has performed poorly in both Enforcement and Protection from restrictions on patent rights. The performance in Coverage has also been weak with a score of 0.57 in 2000. Hong Kong needs more effort in improving its IPR laws.

One criticism of the *Index of Patent Rights* is that it covers mainly laws but not the effectiveness in the actual execution of the patent laws. The improvement suggested in Park and Wagh (2002) is to use the intellectual property component in the *Global Competitiveness Report* (GCR) conducted by the World Economic Forum in Geneva. The estimations in the GCR are based on hard data and surveys of opinions by firms and executives about how patent protections are implemented in different countries. One can argue that the intellectual property component in the GCR covers the entirety of intellectual property, as subjects are asked to rate the intellectual

TABLE 6.17 Index of patent rights, 1960–2000

										Scores in 2000				
Countries	1960	1965	1970	1975	1980	1985	1990	1995	2000	Cov.	Member.	Protect.	Enfor.	Dur.
Australia	2.90	2.90	2.90	2.90	3.23	3.23	3.32	3.86	4.19	0.86	1.00	0.33	1.00	1.00
Brazil	1.64	1.64	1.64	1.51	1.85	1.85	1.85	3.05	3.05	0.71	0.67	0.00	0.67	1.00
Canada	2.76	2.76	2.76	2.76	2.76	2.76	2.76	3.57	3.90	0.57	1.00	0.67	0.67	1.00
Chile	1.98	1.98	2.41	2.41	2.41	2.41	2.41	3.07	3.41	0.86	0.33	1.00	0.33	0.88
China								1.55	2.48	0.14	0.67	0.33	0.33	1.00
France	2.76	3.10	3.24	3.24	3.90	3.90	3.90	4.05	4.05	0.71	1.00	0.33	1.00	1.00
Germany	2.33	2.66	3.09	3.09	3.86	3.71	3.71	3.86	4.52	0.86	1.00	0.67	1.00	1.00
Hong Kong	2.04	2.04	2.04	2.04	2.24	2.57	2.57	2.57	2.90	0.57	0.67	0.33	0.33	1.00
India	1.85	1.85	1.42	1.62	1.62	1.62	1.48	1.51	2.18	0.14	0.67	0.33	0.33	0.70
Indonesia	0.33	0.33	0.33	0.33	0.33	0.33	0.33	1.24	2.27	0.57	0.67	0.00	0.33	0.70
Italy	2.99	3.32	3.32	3.46	3.71	4.05	4.05	4.19	4.33	1.00	1.00	0.33	1.00	1.00
Japan	2.85	3.18	3.32	3.61	3.94	3.94	3.94	3.94	4.19	0.86	1.00	0.33	1.00	1.00
South Korea	2.80	2.80	2.94	2.94	3.28	3.61	3.94	4.20	4.20	0.86	0.67	0.67	1.00	1.00
Mexico	1.70	1.70	1.99	1.99	1.40	1.40	1.63	2.86	2.86	0.86	0.67	0.00	0.33	1.00
New Zealand	2.85	3.18	3.18	3.18	3.32	3.32	3.32	3.86	4.00	1.00	1.00	0.33	0.67	1.00
Singapore	2.37	2.37	2.37	2.37	2.57	2.57	2.57	3.90	4.05	0.71	0.67	1.00	0.67	1.00
Switzerland	2.38	2.71	3.14	3.14	3.80	3.80	3.80	3.91	4.05	0.71	1.00	0.67	0.67	1.00
Thailand	1.51	1.51	1.51	1.51	1.85	1.85	1.85	2.24	2.24	0.57	0.00	0.00	0.67	1.00
USA	3.86	3.86	3.86	3.86	4.19	4.52	4.52	4.86	5.00	1.00	1.00	1.00	1.00	1.00
Max	3.86	3.86	3.86	3.86	4.24	4.52	4.52	4.86	5.00					
Min	0.00	0.00	0.00	0.00	0.00	0.00	0.00	0.00	0.00					
Mean	2.13	2.22	2.27	2.28	2.40	2.44	2.46	2.86	3.22					
Standard deviation	0.71	0.74	0.79	0.79	0.90	0.94	0.95	1.06	0.95					

Notes: Cov. = Coverage; Dur. = Duraton; Enfor. = Enforcement; Member. = Membership in international treaties; and Protect. = Protection from restrictions on patent rights.

Source: Ginarte and Park (1997, Table 1); Park and Wagh (2002, Chapter 2).

property regime of each country, which can cover quite a broad spectrum of issues from patent rights to trademarks to copyrights and to geographic indications. Park and Wagh (2002) show that there is a remarkably high correlation of 0.8 between the *Index of Patent Rights* and the intellectual property component in the GCR for the period from 1995 to 2000, suggesting a relatively strong match between the statutory level of patent protection, indicated by different patent laws, and the perceived levels of protection for intellectual property among practitioners.

The *Global Competitive Index* (GCI) shown in the *Global Competition Report 2009–2010* conducted by the World Economic Forum is based on a total of 12 pillars, and each pillar contains a number of indicators. The pillars and indicators are:

1st pillar: Institution (19 indicators): property rights; intellectual property protection; diversion of public funds; public trust of politicians; judicial independence; favoritism in decision of government officials; wastefulness of government spending; burden of government regulation; efficiency of legal framework in settling disputes; efficiency of legal framework in challenging regulations; transparency of government policymaking; business costs of terrorism; business costs of crime and violence; organized crimes; reliability of police services; ethical behavior of firms; strengthen of auditing and reporting standards; efficacy of corporate boards; and protection of minority shareholders' interests.

2nd pillar: Infrastructure (8 indicators): quality of overall infrastructure; quality of roads; quality of railroad infrastructure; quality of port infrastructure; quality of air transport infrastructure; available seat kilometers; quality of electricity supply; and telephone lines.

3rd pillar: Macroeconomics (5 indicators): government surplus/deficit; national savings rate; inflation; interest rate spread; and government debt.

4th pillar: Health and primary education (11 indicators): business impact of malaria; malaria incidence; business impact of tuberculosis; tuberculosis incidence; business impact of HIV/AIDS; HIV incidence; infant mortality; lift expectancy; quality of primary education; primary enrollment; and education expenditure.

5th pillar: Higher education and training (8 indicators): secondary enrollment; tertiary enrollment; quality of education system; quality of math and science education; quality of management schools; internet access in schools; local availability of research and training services; and extent of staff training.

6th pillar: Goods market efficiency (15 indicators): intensity of local competition; extent of market dominance; effectiveness of anti-monopoly policy; extent and effect of taxation; total tax rate; number of procedures required to start a business; time required to start a business; agricultural policy cost; prevalence of trade barriers; tariff barriers; prevalence of foreign ownership; business impact of rules on foreign direct investment; burden of customs procedures; degree of customer orientation; and buyer sophistication.

7th pillar: Labor market efficiency (9 indicators): cooperation in labor-employer relations; flexibility of wage determination; rigidity of employment; hiring and firing practices; firing costs; pay and productivity; reliance on professional management; brain drain; and female participation in labor force.

8th pillar: Financial market sophistication (9 indicators): financial market sophistication; financing through local equity market; ease of access to loans; venture capital availability; restructure on capital flows; strength of investor protection; soundness of banks; regulation of securities exchanges; and legal rights index.

9th pillar: Technological readiness (8 indicators): availability of latest technologies; firm-level technology absorption; laws relating to ICT; foreign direct investment and technology transfer; mobile telephone subscriptions; internet users; personal computers; and broadband internet subscribers.

10th pillar: Market size (2 indicators): domestic market size index; and foreign market size index.

11th pillar: Business sophistication (9 indicators): local supplier quantity; local supplier quality; state of cluster development; nature of competitive advantage; value chain breadth; control of international distribution; production process sophistication; extent of marketing; and willingness to delegate authority.

12th pillar: Innovation (7 indicators): capacity for innovation; quality of scientific research institutions; company spending on R&D; university-industry collaboration in R&D; government procurement of advanced technological products; availability of scientists and engineers; and utility patents.

The rankings of all indicators are grouped into either "competitive advantage" or "competitive disadvantage". The conclusion in the performance of the 12 pillars are grouped into five stages of development: (1) Factor driven; (2) Transition from factor driven to efficiency driven; (3) Efficiency driven; (4) Transition from efficiency driven to innovation driven; and (5) Innovation driven. Table 6.18 reports the 2009–2010 data performance of Hong Kong and four other Asian economies (Singapore, Japan, South Korea and China) from *The Global Competitiveness Report 2009–2010* conducted by the World Economic Forum. The performance in Table 6.18 shows a number of interesting indicators, including the overall and the 12 pillars rankings out of 133 economies and the score that ranges from 1 (lowest) to 7 (highest), the stage of development (from factor driven to innovation driven), and the number of "competitive advantages" in each of the 12 pillars.

Other than China, which is still regarded as a developing economy, and its stage of development at the Efficiency driven stage is lower than the other four Asian economies which have all gained the advanced Innovation driven stage of development. In terms of the ranking and among the five Asian economies, Singapore ranks highest at 3 out of 133 with a score of 5.5 out of 7, followed by Japan at 8 out of 133 with a score of 5.2 out of 7, while Hong Kong ranks 11 out of 133 with a score of 5.2 out of 7. China has a lower performance, with ranking at 29 out of 133 and a score of 4.7 out of 7. Overall, the ranking performances of all five Asian economies are good, as they are the top 30 most competitive economies in the sample of 133 world economies. In general, the performances of both Hong Kong and Singapore in the 12 pillars are better than the other three economies.

Hong Kong has a total of 4 pillars gaining a top 5 ranking. They are Financial Market Sophistication, Infrastructure, Goods Market Efficiency, and Labor Market Efficiency. The worst two performers are Health and Primary Education and Innovation. Singapore has scored highest among the 133 economies in Institutions, Goods Market Efficiency and Labor Market Efficiency, while Market Size (due obviously to its small economy) and Macroeconomic Stability performed not so well. Among the 12 pillars, Singapore has gained a total of 5 pillars in the top 5 ranking.

TABLE 6.18 Performance of global competitiveness in 2009–2010

	Hong Kong	Singapore	Japan	S. Korea	China
Ranking (out of 133)/Score (1–7)	11/5.2	3/5.5	8/5.4	19/5.0	29/4.7
stage of development	Innovation	Innovation	Innovation	Innovation	Efficiency
Institutions					
Ranking/Score	11/5.6	1/6.1	27/5.3	53/4.2	48/4.4
Ranking of:					
i) Property Rights	8	4	19	48	39
ii) Intellectual Property Protection	23	1	20	41	45
Competitive Advantage (out of 19)	9	17	0	0	2
Infrastructure					
Ranking/Score	2/6.5	4/6.4	13/5.8	17/5.6	46/4.3
Competitive Advantage (out of 8)	7	5	2	3	2
Macroeconomic Stability					
Ranking/Score	16/5.7	35/5.2	97/4.2	11/5.8	8/5.9
Competitive Advantage (out of 5)	0	1	2	1	3
Health & Primary Education					
Ranking/Score0	43/5.8	13/6.2	19/6.1	27/6.0	45/5.7
Competitive Advantage (out of 11)	3	5	6	1	2
Higher Education & Training					
Ranking/Score	31/4.7	5/5.6	23/5.1	16/5.2	61/4.1
Competitive Advantage (out of 8)	0	5	1	3	1

(Continued)

TABLE 6.18 *(Continued)*

	Hong Kong	Singapore	Japan	S. Korea	China
Ranking (out of 133)/Score (1–7)	11/5.2	3/5.5	8/5.4	19/5.0	29/4.7
stage of development	Innovation	Innovation	Innovation	Innovation	Efficiency
Goods Markets Efficiency					
Ranking/Score	2/5.5	1/5.8	17/5.1	36/4.6	42/4.5
Competitive Advantage (out of 16)	10	12	4	2	5
Labor Market Efficiency					
Ranking/Score	4/5.6	1/5.9	12/5.1	84/4.2	32/4.7
Competitive Advantage (out of 9)	6	8	2	0	2
Financial Market Sophistication					
Ranking/Score	1/5.9	2/5.9	40/4.7	58/4.4	81/4.1
Competitive Advantage (out of 9)	8	9	0	0	0
Technological Readiness					
Ranking/Score	9/5.7	6/5.9	25/5.2	15/5.5	79/3.4
Competitive Advantage (out of 8)	1	4	1	5	0
Market Size					
Ranking/Score	27/4.7	39/4.5	3/6.2	12/5.6	2/6.6
Competitive Advantage (out of 2)	1	0	2	2	2
Business Sophistication					
Ranking/Score	15/5.2	14/5.2	1/5.9	21/4.9	38/4.5
Competitive Advantage (out of 9)	2	1	7	2	2
Innovation					
Ranking/Score	28/3.9	8/5.1	4/5.5	11/4.8	26/3.9
Competitive Advantage (out of 7)	0	3	4	4	4

Source: *The Global Competitiveness Report 2009–2010*, World Economic Forum.

Japan has the highest ranking in Business Sophistication, followed closely by Market Size, but the worst performers are Macroeconomic Stability and Financial Market Sophistication. The performance of South Korea is more of an average score, with none of the 12 pillars gaining a top 10 position. Macroeconomic Stability and Innovation are the two best pillars in South Korea, while the worst performers are Labor Market Efficiency and Financial Market Sophistication. In the case of China, the highest ranking is Market Size followed by Macroeconomic Stability, while the worst performance pillars are Financial Market Sophistication and Technological Readiness.

The rankings and scores reflect the number of items that are classified as "competitive advantage" in the 12 pillars. Hong Kong scored no Competitive Advantage in both Macroeconomic Stability and Innovation. Since the Market Size of both Hong Kong and Singapore are much smaller than the other three economies, both Hong Kong and Singapore scored poorly in the Market Size pillar. Hong Kong has long been successful as an international market, and has scored high in the Goods Market Efficiency, Labor Market Efficiency and Financial Market Efficiency. However, it is debatable whether Hong Kong has scored so poorly in Macroeconomic Stability, as Hong Kong does not have much debts, has a healthy fiscal performance, a steady inflation and interest rate similar to other advanced countries. One wonders where the source of macroeconomic instability in Hong Kong is.

While one can use these indicators as reference, one can also find inconsistencies in these scores. For example, as shown in Table 6.18, Hong Kong ranks 1st in Financial Market Efficiency with 8 out of 9 Competitive Advantages. Singapore ranks 2nd, but has gained a total of all 9 Competitive Advantages. All the other three economies of Japan, South Korea and China scored no Competitive Advantage in Financial Market Efficiency. This is debatable, since Japan is one of the major regional and world financial centers, and China is probably the fastest growing financial market in the world.

The two indicators of Property Rights and Intellectual Property Protection are grouped under the first pillar of Institutions. Hong Kong has scored 8th out of a total sample of 133 economies in the ranking of Property Rights, but performed much weaker in Intellectual Property Protection with a ranking of 23rd. These performances are much weaker than Singapore. In short, Hong Kong has much to do in improving IPR protection. Despite the strong IPR laws, for decades before the mid-1980s, the informal or underground economy in Hong Kong has engaged in the production and marketing of fake electronics products, music and movie disks, computer games and other brand name luxury consumer products, such as watches and ladies handbags. The districts of Mongkok and Sham Shui Po in Kowloon and Wanchai in Hong Kong are the popular places where one could shop for fake items of various types. Since the mid-1980s, however, the government had made strong effort to eliminate these hot places, forcing a number of vendors to close down. By today, the illegal sale of fake or IPR-violated products done by causal hawkers in the informal economy, partly due to the continued supply from across the border, are taking place at various night-markets or tourist areas.

Despite the claim that it is difficult in practice to eliminate the source of supply of fake products, and the easiness in selling the product in the informal market, there is a strong and constant need on the part of law enforcement in ironing out both the sources and marketing of IPR-violated products. In the long-run, educating the young on not violating IPR and stronger promotion in ethical standards and personal conducts are needed. Eventually, it also depends on restricting the source of supply across the border. Thus, it seems the promotion of IPR protection is a long-term battle for Hong Kong.

6.6 The Life of Employment

The discussion so far relates to two issues in a knowledge-based economy. One issue is the level of education and the quality of human capital. This issue deals with the percentage of population receiving high level and technical education. It is therefore true to say that a highly educated economy tends to be more developed, produce a higher level of output and earn a higher level of income. In this regard, development in human capital in Hong Kong indicated by the percentage of adult population receiving higher education is still lower than other developed economies.

The second issue relates to the extent of jobs and employment in the services sector that requires extensive knowledge as an input. It is true that the service sector is the dominant economic sector in Hong Kong, but the concern is whether the bulk of jobs in the service sector are that knowledge-based. These two concerns give rise to a number of discussion areas.

A dichotomy exists in the kinds of service jobs in Hong Kong. On the one hand, modern technology-related and producer-related service employment required a high level of technical education. On the other hand, the bulk of employment in numerous "nominal" services requires only low-skills. The concern is that jobs in the "nominal" service sector do not have much chance for upgrading and skill improvement and their earnings remain low. Consequently, job mobility becomes low. Examples include McJobs and various services employment in retail shops, or small businesses catered to some personal services, clerical jobs like messengers, security jobs in real estates and handy works in restaurants. Due to their low-skill requirement, these jobs usually require long-hour of work, and little opportunity for training or upgrading. Often, these jobs take on young people, but they are replenished when employees reach a middle-age. Due to their low-skill and long hours of work, these workers do not have much time and chance for self-study or commit to other life-long learning activities.

In short, the employment-life of these workers in "nominal services" can be short, and upward job mobility is low. By the time these workers have reached their mid-age, they can be vulnerable to job insecurity and can be laid off when there are signs of economic downturn. Consequently, these people will likely seek social welfare when they reach their mid-age, as their low earning could not help them much in savings during their years of employment. Job security is weak to a large number of jobs in the "nominal" service sector. There are various possibilities to rescue such an employment phenomenon among jobs in the "nominal" service sector:

(1) Ethics and conducts: One possibility is to introduce skill promotion in these jobs. In the retail sector, for example, the conduct, quality, ethical standards and

personal courtesy of sales workers can be trained and improved. How to make the customers and those patronizing the shop more comfortable and feel at ease is not an easy task. The very ego the sales person displayed or the lack of courteous behavior when in contact with customers could already damage potential businesses. After-sale service in Hong Kong is weak in general. For example, repairing work done by different electronics brand names is deliberately set to be very costly and difficult so as to discourage repairs on the one hand and encourage more sales in new products on the other hand. Prices of numerous personal services, such as photographic studios, are not sufficiently transparent for their price setting and service to customers. Request for returns or refunds for tailor-made furniture that is found to be unmatched with the original samples upon delivery would normally not be entertained. In short, there is still a large degree of uncivilized, discriminatory and unfair market behavior in various services, and the quality of jobs and attitude of workers in the service sector needs urgent promotion.

Sales behavior in retail shops and repair business in Hong Kong can learn from the experiences of Japan and other economies. In Japan, for example, customers in retail shops are well treated and made those who patronize the shop feel comfortable and at ease, as they emphasize a lot on the quality of services, especially in departmental stores. In other countries, after-sales service and repairing jobs are seen as a way to build up the long-term image of the brand name. These are some examples of areas where workers in the "nominal" service sector can be given more chances of progress and skill enhancement.

(2) Professional and business associations: the related question is how can good practices in personal service jobs be instituted and incorporated into part of the system. There are several possibilities of improvement. One is to establish more or strengthen existing professional and business associations that will impose their own professional ethical norms and standards, such that a higher standard can be instituted. The drawback is that there may be rested interest groups that would delay or defer improvements. Sometimes, it is exactly these professional associations which are reluctant to bring changes for the obvious reason of rested interest and rent seeking, and that improvements will not be introduced. Their monopolistic position is a strong armory in bringing changes and quality enhancement. More transparent checks and balances can be introduced into the various professional and business associations to ensure that their prime interest is the provision of quality service to the public.

(3) Consumer Council: the role and power of the Consumer Council can be strengthened and deepened, as they can help to check and enrich the quality of jobs in the various nominal services sector. The Consumer Council can provide guidelines in the job deployment in a number of services, as they tend to be more impartial and provide trust-worthy assessments. There can be, of course, various problem of a large consumer council. Firstly, the large size of the consumer council would make it less transparent, self-centered and behave ineffectively due to rested interests. There are a large number of consumer products and services, and it would not be possible to allow a single organization to act on behalf of all consumers on all aspects of consumption.

(4) Legal system and government administration: the legal system and the government machinery, such as the Labor and Welfare Bureau, can serve as a useful source to encourage workers to gain skills in their work environment, with the aim to increase the workers' employment capability, and to encourage employers to provide more skill training so as to allow greater job mobility.
(5) Personal drive: ultimately, the workers themselves have to take a more proactive role in upgrading their skills, knowledge and other quality endowments. A strong attitude on personal drive and even entrepreneurship behavior is needed. The drive to take up and steer a person's own career development and life style and not rely on government assistance or welfare is the basic fundamental attitude, which is applicable whether the person is educated or not, and does not matter the kind of job or trade the person is engaging.

When jobs in the KBE are dichotomized into high-skill with high paid jobs in technical and professional employment versus low-skill with low paid jobs in nominal services, the economy should experience an increase in income inequality. Income inequality could be worsened if there is at the same time an increase in the supply of low-skill workers through immigration. Wages in the low-skill jobs will have to remain low if there is competition for low-skill jobs. Income inequality can be improved only when there is greater job mobility among low-skill workers.

Education advancement and increase in knowledge acquisition has become a sure mean to avoid falling into poverty. In the meantime, the amount of low-skill, low paid jobs will not help to improve an economy's overall inequality performance. It is more important in the short-term to avoid poverty deterioration than to argue on the gap in income inequality, which usually depends on a number of factors and takes a long period of time to narrow. In short, the dichotomy in the skill level of workers in a knowledge-based economy does give rise to income inequality.

The economic solution to income inequality in a KBE depends a lot on supply-side economics, including creation of new jobs through investment activities, improvement in personal skills and knowledge through training and education, and improvement in the overall competitiveness of the economy.

6.7 Freedom as a Built-in Infrastructure

What should be the role of economic freedom in a KBE? Consider one remark made by the Hong Kong-based action movie star, Mr. Jackie Chan, at the Boao Forum in Hainan Island, China, on April 20, 2009, that: "I do not know whether it is better to have freedom or to have no freedom. With too much freedom... it can get very chaotic, could end up like that in Taiwan". Although it was claimed that his remark was taken out of context, the remark has immediately drawn numerous attacks from scholars and concerned groups. Scholars from Mainland China accused Mr. Jackie Chan of "turning his back on a system that helped catapults him to where he is now". Another scholar from Mainland China remarked that "To us, Hong Kong is still a free island sitting in between a free world and an authoritarian system, so we want to protect such status".[7] This really underscores the important of economic freedom and its place in the Mainland China economy.

Freedom is no chaos; it is a system that allows individuals to excel their own area of talents, creativity and skills, to use their endowment to maximize rewards and to receive the best they can obtain in the market place. Economic freedom provides a noble system. But, the exercise and practice of economic freedom will have to be confined to transparent rules, regulations, laws, discipline, ethical standards, check and balances and conducts and manners in personal behavior that all individuals have to respect and concur. To make a movie involves creative work, but pirate downloading violates the very IPR that protects individuals' creativity and is a crime, not freedom. The production of milk power to supply to the market is a business activity in a market economy, but to produce and sale toxic milk power is a crime, not freedom.

There is huge conceptual understanding between freedom and chaos. Economic freedom will turn into chaos when individuals misuse and abuse the very system that supported economic freedom and take the law into their own hands. In a KBE, economic freedom serves like another piece of infrastructure in the society that allows individuals to learn whatever their ability can take them to, do whatever their talent can direct them to and think liberally to chart their own path of life. The infrastructure of economic freedom provides a strong and broad base for every individual to perform the best they can, protected by the legal framework and supported by strong ethic behavior and governance. The provision of economic freedom eliminates all kinds of discrimination and rested interest; individuals can entirely have an open mind on whatever ideas they have that can legally and ethically be transformed into goods and services in a market economy.

Freedom or economic freedom in particular is best to be regarded as an infrastructure, similar to the provision of education, health services, transport system, street lighting, and sewage system and so on. It has to be properly instituted, and once instituted, economic freedom can become a "take it for granted" social asset that is utilized, and at the same time respected, by all citizens. Economic freedom then becomes a social and economic statute that stands between individuals and between the government and the governed, ensuring that all individuals and parties can maximize their activities, allowing them to conduct activities in all legal directions, checking that everyone is treated equally and have equal opportunities in reaching their goals.

Rome was not built in one day. Equally, instituting economic freedom is a gradual process that probably requires a "building block" approach. Hong Kong has taken decades to build up its economic free status, and yet there is still more can be done to improve, extend, expand, deepen and perfect the various aspects of economic freedom. For example, further improvements of intellectual property rights are needed, and human capital needs to be strengthened to become a truly knowledge-based economy.

---

[7] *South China Morning Post*, April 21, 2009.

6.8 Conclusion

This chapter begins with the discussion of a KBE, its definitions and characteristics. Performances in other Asian economies are gathered, and the experience in Hong Kong has been elaborated. Despite the constant emphasis on the important of knowledge in its overall economic development, Hong Kong's performance in education achievement and attainment is not as high as other developed countries. More work is needed to boost the percentage of people attaining education, especially in the percentage of young people achieving higher education. Attainment of education and achievement of knowledge requires stability and can be realized only in the long-term perspective. Given a stable and right environment, talents and creativity from the young generation will gradually be nurtured. As such, it will not be advisable for the government official to indulge in making unpredictable and unreasonable policy changes, as it would generate unnecessary instability on the part of the education recipients, and at the same time, giving out confusing messages to the employers.

In short, there is still a long way for Hong Kong to go if Hong Kong wants to become a fully developed knowledge-based economy. The education system must be strengthened, and quality at various levels must be improved. While the "lifelong" learning behavior has been promoted, the emphasis is to have as many young people to receive more education as possible, especially higher education, as that would contribute to increase the level of human capital. At the same time, while high education is the ultimate goal, the equally important ground work is the education at primary and secondary levels. The traditional format of education can also incorporate more realistic and practical fields of learning. For example, the language education focuses on both English and Chinese. One should realize that Hong Kong is surrounded by a number of other Asian languages: Japanese, Korean, Malay, Thai, Vietnamese and so on. Although a lot has been talked about people in Hong Kong working in Mainland China, for the young people in Hong Kong to well prepare in the Asian region, a good ability and diversity in Asian languages is an asset. Despite the business in the private sector that may teach these languages, it would be advisable for the education system in Hong Kong to incorporate the learning of other Asian languages at an early age so that young students can acquire a "lifelong" ability in any Asian language.

This chapter examines the contribution of human capital to productivity, and distinguishes the performance of human capital in different economic sectors and industries. The more important conclusion is that despite the "de-industrialization" in Hong Kong, the manufacturing sector is still strong in maintaining human capital. While services is the key sector in Hong Kong, a more important concern for a number of services, especially those 'nominal' and personal services that require low skill and low education, is the length of employment for those workers doing McJobs and employed in retail sales businesses that provide little social mobility. Some social scientists have suggested the presence of an "M-shape" structure of employment in the service sector, with a dichotomy of highly educated and skilled employers in the top service industries like finance and professions on the one hand, and on the other hand a large number of unskilled and low educated people working for a large number of nominal services, such as retail, restaurant, land transport and so on. The extreme development in earnings and wages in the "M-shape" structure in the two types of services will enhance a greater degree of inequality and promote more social discontent.

A related feature to a KBE is the level and quality of intellectual property rights (IPR). Again, Hong Kong has committed to lot in promoting and securing IPR. Legally, Hong Kong has the required framework and expertise. In the execution of IPR, Hong Kong faces a number of problems, as the IPR-violated products may not be originated in Hong Kong, and the police, customs and immigration officials will have to work hard in order to minimize, if not eradicate, the presence of IPR-violated products on sales in Hong Kong, especially in the informal economy. While education on the relevance and importance of IPR is the long-term solution, short-term solutions should come from both supply and demand sides. While government officials need to make more efforts in eradicating the inflow of IPR-violated products (the supply side), people in Hong Kong, including the tourists, should not patronize shops selling IPR-violated products. The legal solution in the form of heavier fines and imprisonment can also be used.

Indeed, one should distinguish freedom from the abuse of IPR. The presence of IPR is to protect, and at the same time encourage, creativity and innovation. Equally, a free environment is needed for enterprises and individuals to be more creative and innovative. It is true that in most cases that the result of creativity and innovation would be in the form of a machine, a product or a service. Creative ideas and thoughts also need to be intellectually protected. A free civic society can provide the most suitable environment for creative ideas and thoughts. The full extent of liberalism will enable ideas, thoughts, workmanship and talents to be created unhindered. This is another piece of social infrastructure that provides and promotes economic opportunities for the benefit of all. For a full fetched knowledge-based economy, a free civic society is a pre-requisite.

7 Measurement of Economic Efficiency

7.1 Introduction

This chapter extends the discussion on the performance of total factor productivity (TFP), tradable and non-tradable economic sectors and human capital to incorporate economic efficiency analysis on Hong Kong economy. Every economy has a production frontier that shows a maximum possible production capacity. This production frontier intuitively states that given the availability of existing economic resources and the level of technology, there will be a maximum amount of output that the economy can produce. Thus, it would be appropriate to see that the production frontier expands overtime, meaning that more output can be produced as the economic capacity is enlarged.

The analysis so far looks at the expansion of the production frontier through the growth of input factors, namely the quantity of capital and labor used in the production process, and the growth of technology, namely technical advancement that leads to an enlargement of the economy's production capacity. Since a number of non-quantifiable variables, including the growth of technology, cannot be measured, the use of the TFP is just an envelope term that takes into account the contribution of these non-quantifiable factors in the production frontier. This chapter extends a traditional view and shows that in addition to the growth of input factors, the TFP expressed in percentage can be disaggregated into three factors. The economic impact of the TFP can then be seen in much detail when it is disaggregated into the factors of economies of scale, technological advancement and economic efficiency.

Intuitively, economies of scale show the economic benefits derived from a certain combined usage of inputs of capital and labor. In other words, when more of one factor is used *vis-à-vis* another factor, the added use of that factor will either produce a positive result, namely economy of scale, or a negative result, namely diseconomy of scale. Technological advancement represents the improvement in technology. This is important because technology always helps to expand the production frontier. The third factor is known as economic efficiency. The intuitive idea of economic efficiency is that given the production frontier, the question is whether the economy is actually producing at a point on the production frontier (namely at full capacity), or typically at another point below the production frontier (namely below full capacity). The term "inefficiency" is used to show the distance between the actual or realized production and the full or potential production. Economic inefficiency arises if an economy's production is conducted below the production frontier. An improvement in economic efficiency suggests that the economy is moving closer to the production frontier. Thus, an improvement in efficiency could independently increase the level of output, without any changes in inputs and technology.

Although the analysis on efficiency may not be able precisely to factor in the contribution made by economic freedom, one would naturally think that a freer economy can easily contribute to economic efficiency. One can relate to a number of issues that can promote efficiency, or reduce inefficiency. Individual drive and entrepreneurship, for example, promote efficiency in production. A positive attitude to work can promote efficiency as workers may be punctual, more effective and reduce wastage. The adoption of flexible working hours is thought to promote efficiency as workers can somewhat decide on their working hours, which will suit their daily life effectively. Reducing the commuting time to work is another example that can promote efficiency, as workers may not have commuting fatigue by the time they reach their workplace.

Economic efficiency, thus, can be seen from a number of factors: cultural, habitual, and behavioral. The provision of economic freedom can definitely promote economic efficiency, when people are free to establish their businesses at their own choice, free to acquire skills and educational qualification to become more productive, free to choose their ways of life, job opportunities and career path unrestricted by religion or ideology. Economic efficiency can definitely be promoted through the pursuit of economic freedom.

Since this chapter extends the analysis of the previous chapters, the sources and compilation of Hong Kong data used in this chapter, unless otherwise stated, will be the same as those used in the previous chapters. This includes the construction of different macroeconomic variables and the classification of economic sectors.

The following sections set out the technical aspects and report the empirical results of the analysis.[1] Instead of reproducing the detailed the mathematical breakdown of the TFP decomposition that involved a certain amount of understanding in calculus shown in Liu and Li (2008) and Li and Liu (2011), the following section summarizes the mathematical construction. Section 7.3 establishes the empirical methodology by discussing the stochastic frontier model. A major advantage in choosing the stochastic frontier model is that it relaxes a major constraint in the assumption of constant return to scale and allows non-constant return to scale in the production function. Section 7.4 presents the efficiency analysis based on the Hong Kong data, which is similarly classified into four economic sectors as discussed in previous chapters. Section 7.5 reports the similar empirical findings in Mainland China. One should note that the statistical database between Mainland China and Hong Kong is not the same. As such, the empirical results of economic efficiency in Mainland China can only be considered as a trend analysis rather than a direct comparison between Mainland China and Hong Kong. The difference in the empirical results can be used as an intuitive exercise. The last section concludes the chapter.

---

[1]Non-technical readers are advised to skip the two technical sections (Sections 7.2 and 7.3) and go straight to the section that discusses the Hong Kong performance.

7.2 Scale of Economy, Technology and Efficiency

In theory, the TFP discussed in previous chapters gives an overall measure of factors that contribute to economic growth. The assumptions embodied in the standard neo-classical Solow (1957) growth model include: 1) perfect competition in the product market; 2) a constant return to scale, and 3) producers who are operating at an optimal production capacity. These assumptions have been challenged by studies using the output-oriented stochastic frontier production approach which argues that with given sets of factor inputs, deviations between actual and optimal output due to technical inefficiency are possible (Aigner *et al.*, 1977). In the stochastic frontier approach, a non-constant return to scale is possible and the TFP growth can be decomposed into three components of technical progress, technical efficiency change, and scale of economy (Kumbharkar and Lovell, 2000).

Theoretically, technical progress in an economy is the rate of change in its technological level, and is indicated by an outward shift in the economy's entire production possibility frontier with a larger overall production capacity, which is made possible as a result of a greater use of technology and innovation. Technical efficiency change in an economy refers to a movement from a position within the production possibility frontier towards the production frontier. The scale of the economy shows the various input elasticity of physical capital, labor and human capital when there are changes in the combined usage of these inputs level.

The assumption of a constant return scale in the neo-classical Solow growth model is removed in the stochastic frontier analysis. This is because the elasticity of factor inputs provides a measure of the total return to scale, and that a non-constant return to scale can exist as increases or decreases in input could generate positive or negative contributions to productivity change. In the case of an increasing return to scale production, for example, output increases at a higher percentage with respect to an increase in inputs and hence achieves an improvement in productivity. In short, such a decomposition of the TFP growth figures provides a better understanding in the components that drive productivity growth.

For a production function with a single output and a single input, the productivity of the input factor at time t can simply be defined as $\frac{\Upsilon_t}{X_t}$, where Υ_t is the quantity of output and X_t is the quantity of input. Similarly, the TFP for a production function with multiple inputs at time t can be defined as (see the original construction in Liu and Li, 2008; Li and Liu, 2011):

$$TFP_t = \frac{\Upsilon_t}{\Phi_t}, \tag{1}$$

where Φ_t is the aggregate input which is derived from a suitable aggregation method to include inputs, such as capital and labor, with different units of measurement. Taking logarithm and differentiation with respect to time, the growth of *TFP* is defined as:

$$\dot{TFP_t} = \dot{\Upsilon}_t - \dot{\Phi}_t, \tag{2}$$

where $T\dot{F}P_t = \frac{\partial TFP/\partial t}{TFP}$, $\dot{\Upsilon}_t = \frac{\partial \Upsilon/\partial t}{\Upsilon}$, and $\dot{\Phi}_t = \frac{\partial \Phi/\partial t}{\Phi}$. Suppose there are n inputs X_{it} with input price w_{it}, $i = 1, 2,..., n$ at time t. Using Divisia aggregation, the growth of input factors can be defined as (Jorgenson and Griliches, 1967):

$$\dot{\Phi}_t = \sum_i \frac{w_{it} X_{it}}{C_t} \dot{X}_{it}, \tag{3}$$

where $\dot{X}_{it}$ is the growth of input X_{it} and $C_t = \Sigma_t w_{it} X_{it}$ is the total cost. The weight for each input growth, $s_{it} = \frac{w_{it} X_{it}}{C_t}$, is the share of cost of X_{it} to the total cost. Then the growth of TFP is:

$$T\dot{F}P_t = \dot{\Upsilon}_t - \sum_i \frac{w_{it} X_{it}}{C_t} \dot{X}_{it}. \tag{4}$$

The growth of output $\dot{\Upsilon}_t$ in the stochastic frontier production function is defined as:

$$\Upsilon_t = F(X_{1t}, X_{2t},...,X_{nt}, t)e^{-u_t}. \tag{5}$$

The inclusion of t in function F allows for the production function to shift over time, due to technical progress. The last term in Equation (5) measures technical inefficiency. Taking logarithm transformation yields:

$$\log \Upsilon_t = \log F(X_{1t}, X_{2t},..., X_{nt}, t) - u_t. \tag{6}$$

Technical inefficiency occurs when $u_t > 0$ and the level of log Υ_t is less than the level of log F. Taking differentiation with respective to time, the output growth equation becomes:

$$\dot{\Upsilon}_t = \frac{1}{F}\left[\frac{\partial F}{\partial t}\right] - \frac{\partial u}{\partial t} = \frac{1}{F}\left[\sum \frac{\partial F}{\partial X_{it}} \frac{dX_{it}}{dt} + \frac{\partial F}{\partial t}\right] - \frac{\partial u_t}{\partial t}$$
$$= \sum \frac{\partial F}{\partial X_{it}} \frac{X_{it}}{F} \frac{\frac{dX_{it}}{dt}}{X_{it}} + \frac{\frac{\partial F}{\partial t}}{F} - \frac{\partial u_t}{\partial t} = \sum \frac{\partial F}{\partial X_{it}} \frac{X_{it}}{F} \dot{X} + \frac{\frac{\partial F}{\partial t}}{F} - \frac{\partial u_t}{\partial t}. \tag{7}$$

Define technical efficiency (TE) as the ratio of the actual output (Υ_t) and the corresponding stochastic frontier output (F_t):

$$TE_t = \frac{\Upsilon_t}{F_t} = \frac{\exp(\beta_0 + \beta_1 \ln X_{it} + v_t - u_t)}{\exp(\beta_0 + \beta_1 \ln X_{it} + v_t)} = \exp(-u_t) = e^{-u_t}. \tag{8}$$

The growth of the technical efficiency $T\dot{E}_t$ is:

$$T\dot{E}_t = \frac{\frac{\partial TE_t}{\partial t}}{TE_t} = \frac{-e^{-u_t} \frac{\partial u_t}{\partial t}}{e^{-u_t}} = -\frac{\partial u_t}{\partial t}. \tag{9}$$

The technologic progress A_t is defined as:

$$\dot{A}_t = \frac{\frac{\partial F}{\partial t}}{F}. \tag{10}$$

Denote the output elasticity with respect to input X_{it} as:

$$e_{X_{it}} = \frac{\partial F}{\partial X_{it}} \frac{X_{it}}{F}. \tag{11}$$

Then

$$\dot{\Upsilon}_t = \sum_i e_{x_{it}} \dot{X}_{it} + \dot{A}_t + T\dot{E}_t, \quad \text{or} \quad \dot{\Upsilon}_t = e_{X_t} \sum_i \frac{e_{x_{it}}}{e_{X_t}} \dot{X}_{it} + \dot{A}_t + T\dot{E}_t, \tag{12}$$

where $e_{X_t} = \sum_i e_{x_{it}} = \sum_i \frac{\partial F}{\partial X_{it}} \frac{X_{it}}{F}$ is the sum of the output elasticity for all inputs and is a measure of scale economy. When $e_{Xt} > 1$ (= 1, < 1), the production is increasing (constant, decreasing) return to scale.

The measure of output growth does not involve price information. However, the definition of input growth $\dot{\Phi}_t$ includes the price of inputs as $\dot{\Phi}_t = \sum_i \frac{w_{it} X_{it}}{C_t} \dot{X}_{it}$ where w_{it} is the input price. To eliminate the price information, we consider the cost minimization problem of the objective function as $\min_{X_{it}} C_t = \sum_i w_{it} X_{it}$, subject to the constraint of:

$$\Upsilon_t = F(X_{1t}, X_{2t}, \ldots, X_{nt}, t) e^{-u_t}. \tag{13}$$

In the Lagrangian form, the objective function and the constraint are written as:

$$L(X_{it}, \lambda) = \sum_i w_{it} X_{it} + \lambda(\Upsilon_t - F e^{-u_t}), \tag{14}$$

where λ is the Lagrange multiplier. The first-order condition for minimization is $\frac{\partial L}{\partial X_{it}} = 0$ and $\frac{\partial L}{\partial \lambda} = 0$. For $\frac{\partial L}{\partial X_{it}} = 0$,

$$\frac{\partial L}{\partial X_{it}} = w_{it} + \lambda \left(\frac{-\partial F}{\partial X_{it}} e^{-u_t} \right) = 0, \quad \text{and} \quad w_{it} = \lambda \frac{\partial F}{\partial X_{it}} e^{-u_t}. \tag{15}$$

And for $\frac{\partial L}{\partial \lambda} = 0$, $\lambda = \frac{\partial C_t}{\partial \Upsilon_t}$ (λ is an unknown that represents the effect of the change in the parameter Υ in the objective function). By substituting the value $\lambda = \frac{\partial C_t}{\partial \Upsilon_t}$ into w_{it}, we obtain:

$$w_{it} = \frac{\partial C_t}{\partial \Upsilon_t} \frac{\partial F}{\partial X_{it}} e^{-u_t}. \tag{16}$$

Note that $\frac{\partial C_t}{\partial \Upsilon_t}$ is the marginal cost. In the absence of technical inefficiency, the first-order condition is:

$$w_{it}^{*} = \frac{\partial C_t}{\partial \Upsilon_t}\frac{\partial F}{\partial X_{it}}. \tag{17}$$

The marginal cost in production is equal to the marginal revenue in profit optimization and the input price is equal to the marginal revenue of product. The measure of cost efficiency can be defined as:

$$CE_t = \frac{\sum_i w_{it}X_{it}}{\sum_i w_{it}^{*}X_{it}} = e^{-u_{it}}. \tag{18}$$

This implies that:

$$CE_t = TE_t. \tag{19}$$

This shows a dual relationship between the production function frontier and the cost function frontier. Substituting Equation (17) into w_{it} in the input share $s_{it} = \frac{w_{it}X_{it}}{C_t}$, we have:

$$\begin{aligned} s_{it} &= \frac{w_{it}X_{it}}{C_t} = \frac{\partial C_t}{\partial \Upsilon_t}\frac{\partial F}{\partial X_{it}}\frac{X_{it}}{C_t}e^{-u_t} = \frac{\partial C_t}{\partial \Upsilon_t}\frac{\partial F}{\partial X_{it}}\frac{X_{it}}{C_t}\frac{\Upsilon_t}{F_t} \\ &= \frac{\partial C_t}{\partial \Upsilon_t}\frac{\Upsilon_t}{C_t}\frac{\partial F}{\partial X_{it}}\frac{X_{it}}{F_t} = e_{C\Upsilon}e_{X_{it}}, \end{aligned} \tag{20}$$

where $e_{C\Upsilon} = \frac{\partial C_t}{\partial \Upsilon_t}\frac{\Upsilon_t}{C_t}$ refers to the cost elasticity with respect to output, and $e_{X_{it}} = \frac{\partial F}{\partial X_{it}}\frac{X_{it}}{F}$ is denoted previously as the output elasticity with respect to input X_{it}. Note that this scale economy (e_{Xit}) is:

$$\begin{aligned} e_{X_t} &= \sum_i e_{X_{it}} = \sum_i \frac{\partial F}{\partial X_{it}}\frac{X_{it}}{F} = \sum_i \frac{w_{it}}{\frac{\partial C_t}{\partial \Upsilon_t}e^{-u_t}}\frac{X_{it}}{F} \\ &= \sum_i \frac{w_{it}}{\frac{\partial C_t}{\partial \Upsilon_t}}\frac{X_{it}}{\Upsilon_t} = \sum_i \frac{1}{\frac{\partial C_t}{\partial \Upsilon_t}}\frac{w_{it}X_{it}}{\Upsilon_t} \\ &= \sum_i \frac{\frac{C_t}{\Upsilon_t}}{\frac{\partial C_t}{\partial \Upsilon_t}}\frac{w_{it}X_{it}}{C_t} = \frac{\frac{C_t}{\Upsilon_t}}{\frac{\partial C_t}{\partial \Upsilon_t}}\sum_i \frac{w_{it}X_{it}}{C_t} \\ &= \frac{C_t}{\Upsilon_t}\frac{\partial \Upsilon_t}{\partial C_t}\sum_i \frac{w_{it}X_{it}}{C_t} = e_{C\Upsilon}^{-1}\sum_i \frac{w_{it}X_{it}}{C_t} = e_{C\Upsilon}^{-1}. \end{aligned} \tag{21}$$

From Equations (20) and (21), the input share is:

$$s_{it} = \frac{w_{it} X_{it}}{C_t} = e_{CY} e_{X_{it}} = e_{Xt}^{-1} e_{x_{it}} = \frac{e_{X_{it}}}{e_{X_t}} \quad . \tag{22}$$

Substituting Equation (22) into Equation (3), the factor growth without price information becomes:

$$\dot{\Phi}_t = \sum_i \frac{e_{X_{it}}}{e_{X_t}} \dot{X}_{it} . \tag{23}$$

Substituting Equations (23) into (12), the output growth is:

$$\dot{Y}_t = e_{X_t} \dot{\Phi}_t + \dot{A}_t + T\dot{E}_t . \tag{24}$$

By subtracting and adding $\dot{\Phi}_t$ and rearranging terms to consider the unit economies of scale, Equation (24) becomes:

$$\begin{aligned} \dot{Y}_t &= \dot{\Phi}_t + (e_{X_t} - 1)\dot{\Phi}_t + \dot{A}_t + T\dot{E}_t, \quad \text{or} \\ \dot{Y}_t &= \sum_i \frac{e_{X_{it}}}{e_{X_t}} \dot{X}_{it} + (e_{X_t} - 1) \sum_i \frac{e_{X_{it}}}{e_{X_t}} \dot{X}_{it} + \dot{A}_t + T\dot{E}_t . \end{aligned} \tag{25}$$

This shows that output growth is decomposed into four components: weighted sum of input growth, adjusted economies of scale, technical progress, and growth of technical efficiency. It should be noted that the weight $\frac{e_{x_{it}}}{e_{X_t}}$ for each input growth is equal to the cost share of each input. The economies of scale effect $(e_{Xt} - 1)$ is adjusted by the growth of aggregate input $\dot{\Phi}_t$. By using Equation (2), the *TFP* growth is:

$$\begin{aligned} T\dot{F}P_t &= (e_{X_t} - 1)\dot{\Phi}_t + \dot{A}_t + T\dot{E}_t, \quad \text{or} \\ T\dot{F}P_t &= (e_{X_t} - 1) \sum_i \frac{e_{x_i}}{e_{X_t}} \dot{X}_{it} + \dot{A}_t + T\dot{E}_t . \end{aligned} \tag{26}$$

The *TFP* growth can now be decomposed into three components: adjusted economies of scale effect, technical progress, and growth of technical efficiency.

The graphical presentation of a productivity change is shown in Figure 7.1. A productivity change is measured as the ratio of output change to input change. The inputs are measured along the horizontal axis and the outputs are measured along the vertical axis. The production of the economy Z at two periods, t and $t + 1$, are indicated by points Z_t and Z_{t+1}. The movement from Z_t to Z_{t+1} indicates that there has been productivity growth from period t to $t + 1$, and such productivity growth can be indicated by the steeper slope of PF_{t+1} (production function for Z at time $t + 1$) compared with the flatter slope of PF_t (production function for Z at time t).

In Figure 7.1, economy Z is said to have moved closer to the frontier from period F_t to $t + 1$, since the distance between Z_{t+1} and C is smaller than the distance between

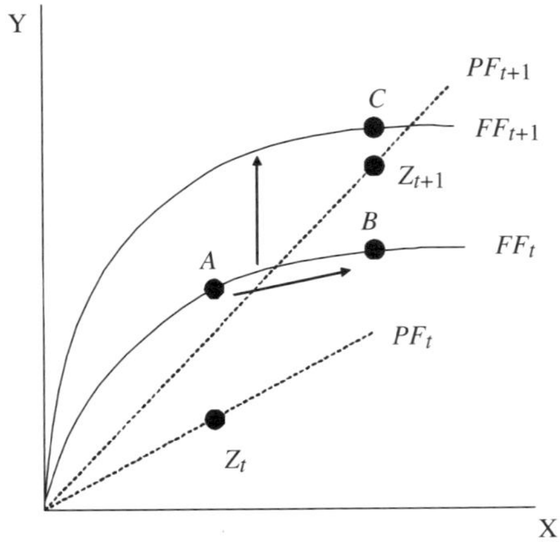

FIGURE 7.1 The decomposition of total factor productivity

Z_t and A, indicating that economy Z is catching up with its production possibility. The scale of economy effect is represented by the movement from point A to point B. Such a movement along the frontier function at period t (FF_t) indicates an increasing returns to scale in the production, in which the total elasticity of output with respect to inputs is greater than one. Under such a condition, an increase in inputs in production generates scale economies and a decrease in inputs in production generates scale diseconomies. On the contrary, a decreasing return to scale in the production means that total elasticity of output with respect to inputs is less than one. Under such a condition, an increase in inputs leads to scale diseconomies and a decrease in inputs leads to scale economies. Finally, the movement from point B to C indicates technical change from time t to $t + 1$. Such a technical advancement is represented by the upward shift of the frontier function at time t (FF_t) to frontier function at time $t + 1$ (FF_{t+1}).

7.3 The Stochastic Frontier Model and Estimation Method

A conventional production function shows how a producer maximizes output from the inputs used. At the same time, the producer allocates the inputs efficiently by minimizing cost, and in turn profit can be maximized. The estimation of the production, cost, and profit functions are based on the assumption that producers are actually operating on the functions. In the estimation of such production functions, error terms are assumed to be symmetrically distributed with zero means and the only source of departure from the estimated function is the statistical noise.

However, Kumbhakar and Lovell (2000) point out that such an estimation technique has raised the question of how conventional microeconomic theory and econometric analysis failed to deal with variation in production efficiency since not all producers are successful in solving their optimization problems. In other words, not all producers are technical, cost and profit efficient. Technical inefficiency happens when producers fail to utilize the minimum inputs required to produce the outputs they choose to produce, given the technology at their disposal. Cost inefficiency happens when producers fail to minimize the expenditure required to produce the desired outputs. Cost inefficiency also happens when producers fail to allocate their inputs in a cost-effective manner even if they are technically efficient. Such misallocation of inputs contributes further to the failure of producers to minimize the expenditure required to produce the desired outputs. This eventually leads to the failure of the producers to maximize the profit from their production activities. Furthermore, even if producers are cost efficient, not all producers are successful in allocating outputs in a revenue-maximizing manner and such output misallocation contributes to the producers' failure to maximize profit. Failure to maximize profits refers to profit inefficiency. In short, the producers' optimization problems (either on production, cost, and profit) have shifted the analysis of production, cost, and profit from the convention production functions to production frontier analysis.

A production frontier is indicated by a given technology and the minimum input bundles required to produce the maximum output. Producers operating on (beneath) their production frontier are technically efficient (inefficient). A cost frontier describes the minimum expenditure required to produce a given bundles of output, given the prices of inputs and the technology. Hence, producers operating on (above) their cost frontier are cost efficient (inefficient). Given the price of outputs, a revenue frontier refers to the maximum revenue which can be achieved from a given bundle of inputs and technology. Thus, producers operating on (beneath) their revenue frontier are revenue efficient (inefficient). Finally, a profit frontier describes the maximum profit which can be achieved from the overall production, given the prices of inputs, output produced and technology. Hence, producers operating on (beneath) their profit frontier are profit efficient (inefficient) (Kumbhakar and Lovell, 2000). The stochastic frontier analysis assumes that deviations from the efficient frontier can be either a realization of inefficiency or a random shock (Farrell, 1957).

The model used for the estimation begins with a production frontier function without the random component as suggested in Aigner *et al.* (1977):

$$y_i = f(x_i\,;\,\beta)\cdot TE_i, \tag{27}$$

where y_i is the observed scalar output, x_i is a vector of inputs, β is a $[k \times 1]$ vector of parameters to be estimated, and TE_i denotes the technical efficiency defined as the ratio of observed output to maximum feasible output (Aigner and Chu, 1968). The output-oriented measure of technical efficiency takes the ratio of the observed output to its corresponding stochastic frontier output, as shown in Equation (8).

Such an output-oriented measure of technical efficiency takes a value between zero and one. Indeed, it measures the output of the i-th firm relative to the stochastic frontier output that could be produced by a fully efficient firm utilizing the same vector of inputs. By estimating the parameters of the stochastic production frontier model, the technical efficiency TE_i can be predicted. If $TE_i = 1$ ($TE_i < 1$), then the firm is fully (not fully) technical efficient. As shown by Equation (8), TE_i can be written as an exponential $TE_i = \exp\{-u_i\}$, where u_i is supposed to measure technical inefficiency and when $u_i \geq 0$, then $TE_i \leq 1$ (Battese *et al.*, 2005). Equation (27) can be written as:

$$y_i = f(x_i\,;\beta) \cdot \exp\{-u_i\}. \tag{28}$$

Since u_i is supposed to measure technical inefficiency, it might also be capturing other random shocks that are either beyond the control of the firm's management or not directly attributable to the underlying technology. These shocks could come from weather changes, economic adversities or plain luck. A stochastic component that describes the random shocks affecting the production process can be added. This is indicated by adding a two-sided error term to the one-sided error term, as in Aigner and Chu (1968). The stochastic production frontier now becomes:

$$y_i = f(x_i\,;\beta)\ TE \cdot \exp\{v_i\},\ \text{or}\ y_i = f(x_i\,;\beta) \cdot \exp\{-u_i\} \cdot \exp\{v_i\}, \tag{29}$$

where $\exp\{v_i\}$ denotes the stochastic component that describes the random shocks. When the production function is expressed in a Cobb-Douglas form, $f(x_i\,;\beta)$ takes a log-linear form, and the stochastic frontier production model can be written as:

$$\ln y_i = \beta_0 + \sum_{j=1}^{k} \beta_j \ln(x_{ji}) + v_i - u_i. \tag{30}$$

The logarithmic production function can further be augmented by incorporating a human capital variable and allow variations in output and substitution elasticity with the different levels of factor inputs. The production function for the economic sector panel data of Hong Kong takes a second-order transcendental logarithmic (translog) form, expressed as:

$$\ln \Upsilon_{it} = \alpha + \beta_K \ln K_{it} + \beta_L \ln L_{it} + \beta_{KK}(\ln K_{it})^2 + \beta_{LL}(\ln L_{it})^2 + \beta_{KL} \ln K_{it} \ln L_{it} + \phi_H H_{it} + \sum \delta_{Tt} DT_t + \sum_s \delta_{Ss} DS_s + v_{it} - u_{it}, \tag{31}$$

where $i = 1,\ldots,$ N, and $t = 1,\ldots,$ T; $\ln \Upsilon_{it}$ is the log of real GDP for i^{th} economic sector at time t, $\ln K_{it}$ is the log of physical capital stock for i^{th} economic sector at time t, $\ln L_{it}$ is the log of total number of labor working hours for i^{th} economic sector at time t, H_{it} is the human capital variable expressed for i^{th} economic sector at time t, DT_t is the dummy variable for the time trend that captures technology changes and the parameter δ_{Tt} can be used to measure the level of technology over time, and DS_s is the dummy variable for economic sectors where $DS = 1$ for tradable goods and tradable services sectors and $DS = 0$ for non-tradable goods and non-tradable services sectors.

The random error, v_{it}, is symmetric and normally distributed with $v_{it} \sim N(0, \sigma^2{}_v)$ and the technical inefficiency term, u_{it}, is assumed to be a non-negative truncated normal random error with the $u_{it} \sim N(\mu, \sigma^2{}_v)$, where μ is the mode of the normal distribution (Kumbhakar and Lovell, 2000).

Technical inefficiency can either be time variant (u_{it}) or time invariant (u_i). In the case of time variant technical inefficiency, u_{it} can be expressed as a monotonic 'decay' function as (Battese and Coelli, 1992):

$$u_{it} = \eta_t \, u_i, \tag{32}$$

where $\eta_t = \exp[-\eta\,(t - T)]$, and η is an unknown scalar parameter for technical inefficiency. u_{it} can either be increasing (if $\eta < 0$), decreasing (if $\eta > 0$) or remained constant (if $\eta = 0$).

The maximum likelihood method is generally used to estimate the parameters in a stochastic frontier production. The minimum-mean-square-error predictor of the technical efficiency of the ith economic sector at the tth time period is shown as (Battese and Coelli, 1988, 1992; Kumbhakar and Lovell, 2000; Coelli, 1996; Battese and Corra, 1977):

$$TE_{it} = E(\exp\{-u_{it}\}|\varepsilon_{it}), \tag{33}$$

where

$$\varepsilon_{it} = v_{it} - u_{it}. \tag{34}$$

Equation (31) is applied to the panel data of the Hong Kong economy to derive the measures of output growth, total factor productivity (*TFP*) change, and their sources. From Eq. (31), the output elasticities for physical capital, labor, and human capital for economic sector i and time t are denoted as follows:

$$e_{k_{it}} = \beta_K + 2\beta_{KK} \ln K_{it} + \beta_{KL} \ln L_{it}, \tag{35}$$

$$e_{L_{it}} = \beta_L + 2\beta_{LL} \ln L_{it} + \beta_{KL} \ln K_{it}, \tag{36}$$

$$e_{H_{it}} = \beta_H \, H_{it}. \tag{37}$$

And the economy of scale is measured as:

$$e_{it} = e_{Kit} + e_{Lit} + e_{Hit}. \tag{38}$$

Using Eqs. (25) and (26), the decomposition of output growth and the TFP growth is shown as follows:

$$\dot{Y} = \frac{e_{K_{it}}}{e_{it}}\dot{K}_{it} + \frac{e_{L_{it}}}{e_{it}}\dot{L}_{it} + \frac{e_{H_{it}}}{e_{it}}\dot{H}_{it} + Scale_{it} + \Delta\delta_{Tt} + T\dot{E}_{it}, \tag{39}$$

and

$$T\dot{F}P = Scale_{it} + \Delta\delta_{Tt} + T\dot{E}_{it}, \tag{40}$$

where $Scale_{it} = (e_{it} - 1)\left(\frac{e_{K_{it}}}{e_{it}}\dot{K}_{it} + \frac{e_{L_{it}}}{e_{it}}\dot{L}_{it} + \frac{e_{H_{it}}}{e_{it}}\dot{H}_{it}\right)$ is a measure of the adjusted economy of scale effect. δ_{Tt} can be estimated from Eq. (31) and $\Delta\delta_{Tt} = \delta_{Tt} - \delta_{Tt-1}$ is a measure of technical progress or the rate of change in technical level. $\dot{TE}_{it}$ refers to the change in technical efficiency and can be estimated from Equations (33) and (34).

7.4 Economic Efficiency in Hong Kong

Although the calculations of variables and various definitions used in the empirical study follow the materials covered in previous chapters, it would be useful to recap some of the key issues. Industries in Hong Kong are officially classified under nine categories: 1) agriculture and fishing; 2) mining and quarrying; 3) manufacturing; 4) electricity, gas and water; 5) construction; 6) wholesale, retail, import and export trades, restaurants and hotels; 7) transport, storage and communications; 8) financing, insurance, real estate and business services; and 9) community, social and personal services. These industries are then re-classified into four economic sectors for the sample period from 1983 to 2005: tradable goods, tradable services, non-tradable goods and non-tradable services.

1. Tradable Goods Sector: agriculture and fishing; mining and quarrying; and manufacturing;
2. Tradable Services Sector: import and export trade; restaurant and hotel; air and water transport; other transport services, storage and communications; and financing, insurance, and real estate and business services;
3. Non-tradable Goods Sector: construction; electricity, gas and water;
4. Non-tradable Services Sector: wholesale and retail; land transport; community and social and personal services.

Hong Kong's output is shown by the production-based GDP (or GDP at factor cost). Industry-specific deflators are used to transform the nominal output values into real output values for all the industries. The real capital stock figures (K_t) are constructed from the accumulation of real gross investment. Figure 7.2 shows the capital stock series for the four economic sectors in Hong Kong over the period 1980–2005. It can be seen that the tradable services sector has the largest level of capital stock. The non-tradable goods sector has the largest growth rate of capital stock (9%), followed by the tradable services sector (7%), non-tradable services sector (6%), and lastly the tradable goods sector (2%).

The labor input is measured as the total number of labor working hours (L). Figure 7.3 shows the labor working hours for the four economic sectors in Hong Kong over the period 1980–2005. For the tradable goods sector, labor has been decreasing significantly from the end of 1980s onwards. In contrast, labor for the tradable services sector has increased significantly over the sample period. Not surprisingly, as the tradable services sector has turned out to be the largest sector in Hong Kong, its labor input has an average annual growth rate of 5%. The non-tradable services sector comes next, with an average annual growth rate of 3%. Both the tradable and non-tradable goods sectors have negative average annual growth rates of –6% and –2% respectively.

Human capital is expressed by the mean years of schooling. Figure 7.4 compares the mean years of schooling of the four economic sectors in Hong Kong over the

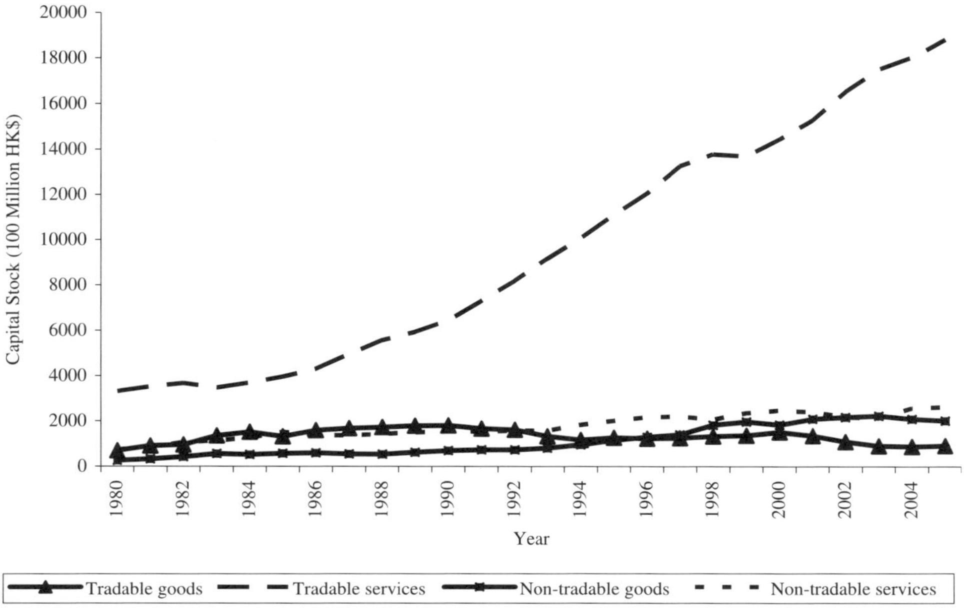

FIGURE 7.2 Capital stock by economic sectors 1980–2005

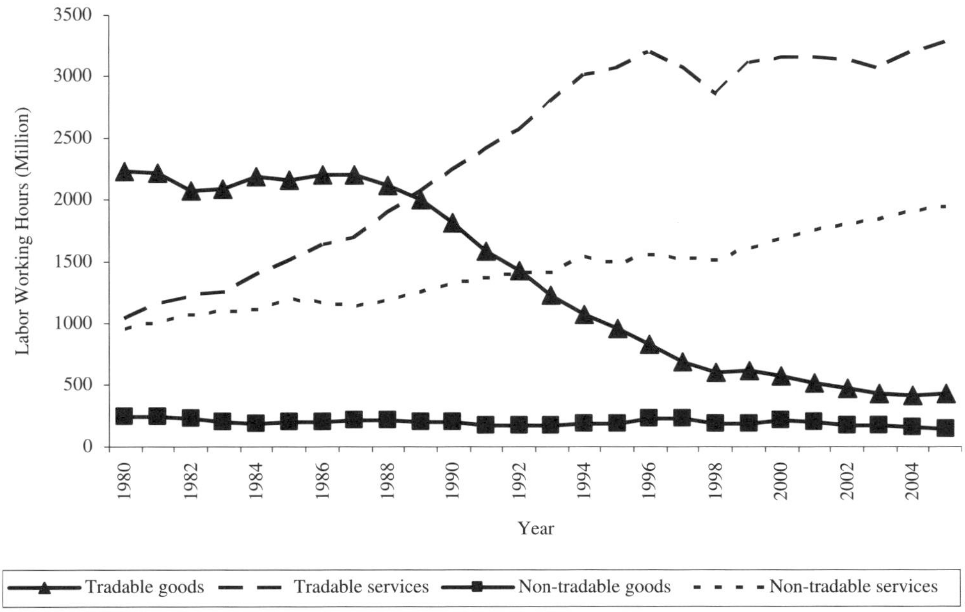

FIGURE 7.3 Number of labor working hours by economic sectors 1980–2005

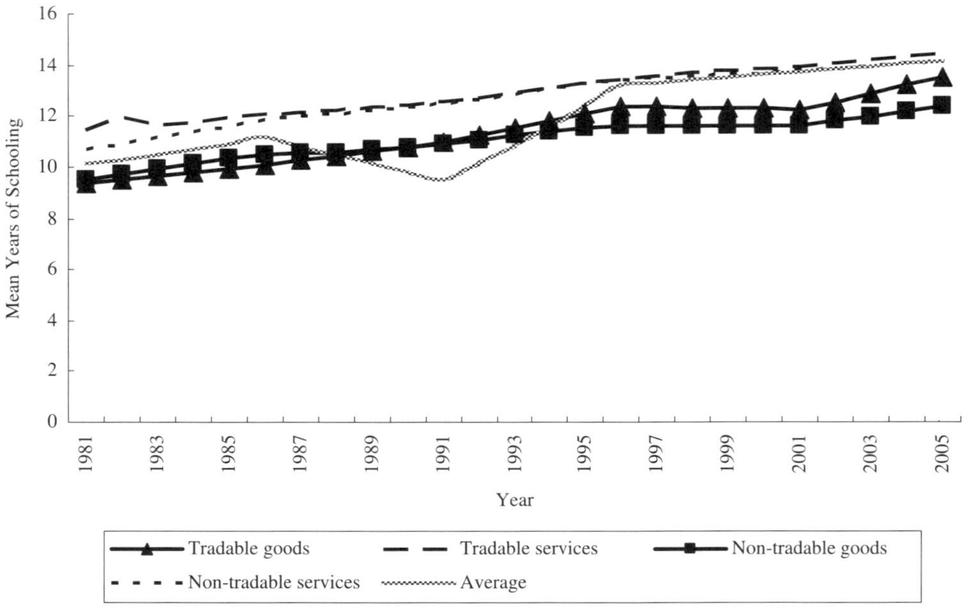

FIGURE 7.4 Mean years of schooling by economic sectors 1981–2005

period 1981–2005. All the industries experienced increasing trends in their mean years of schooling. The tradable services sector has the highest mean years of schooling over the sample period. The non-tradable services sector has the second highest mean years of schooling. The tradable goods sector has overtaken the non-tradable goods sector from 1991 onwards, and so the non-tradable goods sector has the lowest mean years of schooling at the end of the period.

The empirical results in Table 7.1 show the maximum likelihood estimates of the stochastic frontier production for a panel data of the four economic sectors in Hong Kong for the period of 1983–2005, with a total of 92 observations. All the parameters are estimated by using the FRONTIER software. The dependent variable in all the model specifications is log real GDP. There are time trend dummy variables in all the four columns. Columns (1) and (2) contain the results without the dummy variables of economic sectors, while columns (3) and (4) contain the results with the dummy variables of economic sectors. The difference between columns (1) and (3) and that between columns (2) and (4) is the use of the functional form. Columns (1) and (3) contained the results from the basic production function model, while columns (2) and (4) showed the results from the translog specification of the production function model. That is, both columns (2) and (4) allowed variations in output and substitution elasticity with the levels of factor inputs. In other words, they showed production functions with a second-order transcendental logarithmic or translog form.

In the last three rows of Table 7.1, the results of the three sets of model specification tests are shown. The significance levels of all the likelihood-ratio tests of the

TABLE 7.1 Maximum likelihood estimates of the stochastic frontier production: the four economic sectors, 1983–2005

	(1)	(2)	(3)	(4)
lnK	0.4047	−0.3495	0.6405	1.2779
	(0.0300)	(0.4421)	(0.0277)	(0.5807)
lnL	0.7087	0.6433	0.4833	−1.1944
	(0.0313)	(0.5060)	(0.0390)	(0.5017)
lnK*lnK	—	−0.0058	—	−0.0798
	—	(0.0267)	—	(−0.0367)
lnLvlnL	—	−0.1164	—	0.0077
	—	(0.0433)	—	(0.0489)
lnK*lnL	—	0.1385	—	0.1909
	—	(0.0444)	—	(0.0573)
H	0.0641	0.2424	0.1142	−0.0180
	(0.0427)	(0.0792)	(0.0368)	(0.0454)
DS Tradable	—	—	−0.6654	−0.6400
	—	—	(0.0501)	(0.0477)
$\sigma_s^2 \equiv + \sigma_v^2 + \sigma^{2*}$	0.0546	0.1632	0.0062	0.0062
	(0.1205)	(0.0217)	(0.0012)	(0.0009)
$\gamma \equiv \sigma^2 / \sigma_s^2$	0.9324	0.9798	0.3166	0.0000
	(0.0224)	(0.0050)	(0.0507)	(0.0001)
μ	0.4514	0.7998	0.0889	−0.0001
	(0.2802)	(0.1058)	(0.0345)	(0.0245)
η	0.0073	−0.0158	0.0617	0.0217
	(0.0049)	(0.0027)	(0.0098)	(0.0918)
Log Likelihood	105.6346	106.8722	109.9129	102.9867
Log Likelihood Ratio Tests:				
$\beta_{KK,LL,,KL} = 0$	—	2.48	—	−13.84
$\delta_{Tt} = 0$, for all t	64.92	44.60	71.76	41.76
$\delta_{Ss} = 0$, for all s	—	—	8.56	−7.76

Notes: Figures in brackets are the estimated standard errors of the parameters. σ^2 and σ_v^2 are the variance parameter of the inefficiency term u and the random error term v, respectively.

three sets of model specifications are set to be 5%. The first row of model specification test contains the likelihood ratio test for the joint effects of quadratic and interaction terms of the translog specifications. The statistics shown in columns (2) and (4) are insignificant. Therefore, the terms of the translog specifications will be removed from the model. The second set of model specification test contains the likelihood ratio tests for the joint effects of the time trend dummy variable, which indicates technology change. All the statistics in this row show that the technology progress over time is significant. Therefore, the time trend regional dummy variables will not be removed from the model. The last set of model specification test contains the likelihood ratio tests for the joint effects of the economic sectors dummy variable.

The statistic shown in column (3) is significant while the statistic shown in column (4) is not. In all, the basic function of the production model with dummy variables of economic sectors as shown in column (3) gives the preferred model for primary analysis.

The estimates in column (3) of Table 7.1 show that the effects of physical capital, labor and human capital on real GDP are all positive and statistically significant. Amongst the three, the effect of physical capital is predominant in the production functions. The estimated technical inefficiency parameter, η, is positive and statistically significant. This means that the overall technical inefficiency has been decreasing over time. In addition, it can be observed that γ is 0.3166 with the estimated standard error of 0.0507. This estimate means that 31.66% of the variation in the composite error term is due to the inefficiency component. With regard to technical progress, and in addition to the significant joint effects, the estimates of the coefficients of the time trend (δ_t) (shown in Table 7.2) are mostly negative, with the exception of the year 1991, implying that there has been almost no technical progress over the observed period in Hong Kong.

The initial finding is that efficiency has improved in Hong Kong over the sample period, while technological progress has not been catching up. The improvement of

TABLE 7.2 Maximum likelihood estimates of the time trend coefficients (δ_t)

	(1)	(2)	(3)	(4)
1984	0.0437 (0.5795)	0.0260 (0.1516)	−0.0101 (0.3382)	0.0258 (0.3763)
1985	−0.0194 (0.8501)	−0.0444 (0.4742)	−0.1010 (0.7826)	−0.0139 (0.7774)
1986	−0.0112 (0.8565)	−0.0631 (0.5280)	−0.1217 (0.8110)	0.0062 (0.6503)
1987	0.0792 (0.8875)	0.0181 (0.6464)	−0.0580 (0.8283)	0.1036 (0.8406)
1988	0.1059 (0.8946)	0.0385 (0.5266)	−0.0575 (0.8733)	0.1374 (0.5136)
1989	0.1209 (0.8583)	0.0558 (0.5911)	−0.0824 (0.8124)	0.1401 (0.8545)
1990	0.1190 (0.8357)	0.0536 (0.3119)	−0.1193 (0.7415)	0.1366 (0.6631)
1991	0.1872 (0.0800)	0.1537 (0.1109)	0.4663 (0.0884)	0.1525 (0.0714)
1992	0.1759 (0.8514)	0.0987 (0.3956)	−0.1256 (0.8341)	0.2023 (0.8132)
1993	0.1717 (0.7505)	0.0789 (0.5229)	−0.1590 (0.7459)	0.2141 (0.6814)
1994	0.0552 (0.8037)	−0.0536 (0.4861)	−0.3060 (0.7783)	0.1117 (0.7694)
1995	0.0728 (0.8813)	−0.0533 (0.4109)	−0.3388 (0.8684)	0.1194 (0.8070)
1996	0.0196 (0.6402)	−0.1455 (0.4659)	−0.4161 (0.6166)	0.0881 (0.6105)
1997	0.0528 (0.8901)	−0.0954 (0.6379)	−0.4217 (0.8885)	0.1034 (0.6744)
1998	0.0703 (0.5533)	−0.0327 (0.4670)	−0.4535 (0.5486)	0.1058 (0.5098)
1999	−0.0029 (0.8352)	−0.0878 (0.5880)	−0.5445 (0.8332)	0.0249 (0.6633)
2000	0.0035 (0.6264)	−0.0820 (0.3863)	−0.5517 (0.5876)	0.0268 (0.5258)
2001	−0.0136 (0.0930)	−0.0326 (0.1964)	−0.5598 (0.1165)	0.0411 (0.0987)
2002	0.0069 (0.8070)	−0.0315 (0.4301)	−0.5778 (0.8075)	0.0611 (0.6947)
2003	0.0000 (0.7390)	−0.0364 (0.5122)	−0.5916 (0.7417)	0.0811 (0.5977)
2004	−0.0167 (0.8108)	−0.0540 (0.4042)	−0.6264 (0.8067)	0.0612 (0.7646)
2005	−0.0167 (0.3298)	−0.0730 (0.2713)	−0.6438 (0.3812)	0.0686 (0.4874)

Note: Figures in brackets stand for estimated standard errors of the parameters estimates.

efficiency could be due to a number of factors, the uncertainty period that produced a sense of insecurity in the mid-1980s could mean that people have to work harder to ensure a stronger economic situation for the uncertain future, and the economic boom in the mid-1990s leading up to the 1997 crisis, together with massive inflow of "hot money" at the time, could have produced favorable economic attitude that resulted in an improvement in efficiency. The lack of technological progress can be explained easily, as investments were short-term and speculative in nature, while long-term investment in industries has declined. Together with the low level of R&D conducted by private corporations and government, technological progress has suffered considerably. The explanation of service industries often does not require advancement in technology. In short, the environment for technological advancement had been missing. For Hong Kong to regain technological progress, revitalization of industries and restructuring of the economy are needed. The provision of new lands, for example, is badly needed for long-term investment to promote physical capital in Hong Kong.

The empirical results shown in column (3) of Table 7.1 can be used to derive the various estimates according to the respective equations shown previously. These include:

a) the output elasticity with respect to factor input of capital (e_K);
b) the output elasticity with respect to factor input of labor (e_L);
c) the output elasticity with respect to factor input of human capital (e_H);
d) the total returns to scale (e);
e) the adjusted economies of scale effect (*Scale*);
f) the rate of technical progress ($\Delta\delta_{Tt}$); and
g) the growth of technical efficiency (*TE*).

In turn, these estimates are then used to derive the components of output growth ($\dot{y}$) and total factor productivity growth ($\dot{TFP}$). The performance of these measures will vary depending on years and economic sectors.

The cost shares and averages of the weighted input growth components on the four different economic sectors in the sample period are shown in Table 7.3. Columns (1) to (3) show the cost shares of the three factor inputs of physical capital, labor and human capital, while columns (4) to (6) show the weighted input growth for the three inputs. The last column shows the growth of aggregate inputs, and the overall means of these measures are shown in the last row of Table 7.3.

From Table 7.3, it can be seen that the cost share for human capital is the highest with 55.22% on average while the cost share for labor is the lowest with 19.26%; the cost share for physical capital is 25.52%. The last column shows that the growth of aggregate inputs gives an average of 1.53%, with physical capital accounted for the highest contribution of 64.84% (0.99% out of 1.53%), while labor and human capital accounts for −5.75% (−0.09% out of 1.53%), and 40.91% (0.63% out of 1.53%), respectively. This implies that physical capital is the dominant contributor in input growth, although its cost share and growth contribution have been declining over the years.

TABLE 7.3 Cost shares of inputs and input growth: The four economic sectors, 1983–2005

	Cost shares			Input growth			
	$\frac{e_K}{e}$	$\frac{e_L}{e}$	$\frac{e_H}{e}$	$\frac{e_K}{e}\dot{K}$	$\frac{e_L}{e}\dot{L}$	$\frac{e_H}{e}\dot{H}$	$\dot{\Phi}$
Year	(1)	(2)	(3)	(4)	(5)	(6)	(4) + (5) + (6)
1983	0.2744	0.2070	0.5186	—	—	—	—
1984	0.2722	0.2054	0.5224	0.0134	0.0069	0.0081	0.0283
1985	0.2698	0.2036	0.5266	0.0141	0.0080	0.0089	0.0309
1986	0.2675	0.2018	0.5307	0.0149	0.0068	0.0087	0.0304
1987	0.2660	0.2007	0.5332	0.0054	0.0017	0.0053	0.0125
1988	0.2647	0.1997	0.5356	0.0110	0.0074	0.0052	0.0236
1989	0.2632	0.1986	0.5382	0.0210	0.0001	0.0057	0.0268
1990	0.2617	0.1975	0.5408	0.0154	0.0008	0.0056	0.0218
1991	0.2600	0.1962	0.5438	0.0045	−0.0078	0.0066	0.0033
1992	0.2577	0.1945	0.5478	0.0064	−0.0014	0.0089	0.0139
1993	0.2552	0.1926	0.5522	0.0015	−0.0066	0.0099	0.0048
1994	0.2530	0.1909	0.5560	0.0178	0.0061	0.0086	0.0325
1995	0.2507	0.1892	0.5601	0.0287	−0.0071	0.0093	0.0310
1996	0.2485	0.1875	0.5640	0.0152	0.0084	0.0087	0.0323
1997	0.2482	0.1873	0.5645	0.0138	−0.0113	0.0012	0.0036
1998	0.2477	0.1869	0.5653	0.0190	−0.0209	0.0018	0.0000
1999	0.2475	0.1868	0.5657	0.0137	0.0079	0.0007	0.0223
2000	0.2473	0.1866	0.5661	0.0085	0.0067	0.0009	0.0162
2001	0.2469	0.1863	0.5668	0.0035	−0.0088	0.0015	−0.0037
2002	0.2448	0.1847	0.5704	−0.0131	−0.0097	0.0085	−0.0143
2003	0.2431	0.1834	0.5735	−0.0071	−0.0029	0.0074	−0.0026
2004	0.2411	0.1819	0.5769	0.0072	−0.0013	0.0080	0.0139
2005	0.2392	0.1805	0.5803	0.0039	−0.0024	0.0082	0.0098
Mean	0.2552	0.1926	0.5522	0.0099	−0.0009	0.0063	0.0153

Table 7.4 shows the estimates of output elasticity with respect to each input [columns (1) to (3)], total returns to scale and the adjusted economies of scale effect. In the sample period, human capital input in Hong Kong [as shown in column (3)] produces the largest output elasticity with an average value of 1.3896 and its elasticity shows a steady increasing trend. In comparison, physical capital has an average output elasticity of 0.6405 and labor has an average output elasticity of 0.4833. Column (4) shows an increasing trend in the values of total returns to scale that rises from 2.3343 in 1983 to 2.6777 in 2005. Since the total returns to scale is greater than one, the economy of scale will give a positive adjusted economy to scale effect. Columns (5) to (7) show the adjusted economy of scale effect of the three factor inputs. The last column showed that the scale effect has an average value of 2.27%. Physical capital has the highest average value in the adjusted economy of scale with

TABLE 7.4 Output elasticity, economy of scale and adjusted economy of scale effect: The four economic sectors, 1983–2005

	Output elasticities				Adjusted economies of scale effect			
	e_K	e_L	e_H	e	$(e-1)\left(\frac{e_K}{e}\dot{K}\right)$	$(e-1)\left(\frac{e_L}{e}\dot{L}\right)$	$(e-1)\left(\frac{e_H}{e}\dot{H}\right)$	*Scale*
Year	(1)	(2)	(3)	(1) + (2) + (3)	(4)	(5)	(6)	(4) + (5) + (6)
1983	0.6405	0.4833	1.2106	2.3343				
1984	0.6405	0.4833	1.2293	2.3530	0.0181	0.0093	0.0109	0.0383
1985	0.6405	0.4833	1.2503	2.3740	0.0193	0.0110	0.0122	0.0425
1986	0.6405	0.4833	1.2710	2.3947	0.0208	0.0095	0.0121	0.0424
1987	0.6405	0.4833	1.2837	2.4074	0.0077	0.0024	0.0075	0.0175
1988	0.6405	0.4833	1.2961	2.4199	0.0156	0.0105	0.0074	0.0335
1989	0.6405	0.4833	1.3098	2.4335	0.0301	0.0002	0.0082	0.0385
1990	0.6405	0.4833	1.3234	2.4471	0.0223	0.0012	0.0081	0.0316
1991	0.6405	0.4833	1.3395	2.4633	0.0066	–0.0115	0.0097	0.0049
1992	0.6405	0.4833	1.3613	2.4851	0.0096	–0.0021	0.0132	0.0207
1993	0.6405	0.4833	1.3859	2.5096	0.0022	–0.0099	0.0149	0.0072
1994	0.6405	0.4833	1.4074	2.5312	0.0273	0.0094	0.0132	0.0498
1995	0.6405	0.4833	1.4311	2.5548	0.0447	–0.0111	0.0145	0.0482
1996	0.6405	0.4833	1.4534	2.5771	0.0240	0.0132	0.0137	0.0510
1997	0.6405	0.4833	1.4566	2.5804	0.0218	–0.0179	0.0019	0.0057
1998	0.6405	0.4833	1.4615	2.5853	0.0302	–0.0331	0.0029	0.0000
1999	0.6405	0.4833	1.4635	2.5873	0.0217	0.0125	0.0012	0.0354
2000	0.6405	0.4833	1.4662	2.5900	0.0136	0.0107	0.0015	0.0257
2001	0.6405	0.4833	1.4704	2.5941	0.0056	–0.0140	0.0025	–0.0059
2002	0.6405	0.4833	1.4921	2.6159	–0.0212	–0.0156	0.0137	–0.0231
2003	0.6405	0.4833	1.5113	2.6351	–0.0116	–0.0048	0.0122	–0.0043
2004	0.6405	0.4833	1.5323	2.6560	0.0118	–0.0021	0.0133	0.0230
2005	0.6405	0.4833	1.5540	2.6777	0.0065	–0.0039	0.0138	0.0164
Mean	0.6405	0.4833	1.3896	2.5133	0.0149	–0.0016	0.0095	0.0227

Notes: Since the basic function of the production model with dummy variable for economic sectors as shown in column (3) of Table 7.1 is the preferred model for primary analysis, the output elasticities of both physical capital and labor are the same for the four economic sectors during the sample period.

1.49%, while labor has the lowest average value of –0.16% and human capital has an average value of 0.95%. It can be seen that the scale effect is mostly derived from physical capital, which accounts for 65.46% (1.49% out of total value of 2.27%).

Finally, the decomposition of output growth (Υ) and the TFP growth is shown in Table 7.5. Columns (2) to (5) show the four sources of the output growth — growth in inputs ($\dot{\Phi}$), scale effect (*Scale*), rate of technical progress ($\Delta\delta_{Tt}$) and growth

TABLE 7.5 Decomposition of output growth and the TFP growth (1984–2005)

	$\dot{\Upsilon}$	$\dot{\Phi}$	*Scale*	$\Delta\delta_{Tt}$	$\dot{TE}$	$\dot{TFP}$
Year	(1)	(2)	(3)	(4)	(5)	(3) + (4) + (5)
1984	0.0800	0.0283	0.0383	–0.0101	0.0235	0.0517
1985	0.0049	0.0309	0.0425	–0.0909	0.0223	–0.0261
1986	0.0732	0.0304	0.0424	–0.0207	0.0211	0.0428
1987	0.1137	0.0125	0.0175	0.0637	0.0200	0.1013
1988	0.0765	0.0236	0.0335	0.0005	0.0190	0.0529
1989	0.0584	0.0268	0.0385	–0.0249	0.0180	0.0315
1990	0.0334	0.0218	0.0316	–0.0369	0.0170	0.0116
1991	0.6099	0.0033	0.0049	0.5856	0.0161	0.6066
1992	–0.5421	0.0139	0.0207	–0.5920	0.0152	–0.5561
1993	0.1362	0.0048	0.0072	0.1097	0.0144	0.1314
1994	–0.1942	0.0325	0.0498	–0.2901	0.0136	–0.2267
1995	0.0591	0.0310	0.0482	–0.0328	0.0128	0.0282
1996	0.0181	0.0323	0.0510	–0.0772	0.0121	–0.0142
1997	0.0152	0.0036	0.0057	–0.0056	0.0114	0.0116
1998	–0.0211	0.0000	0.0000	–0.0318	0.0108	–0.0211
1999	–0.0230	0.0223	0.0354	–0.0909	0.0102	–0.0453
2000	0.0443	0.0162	0.0257	–0.0073	0.0096	0.0281
2001	–0.0086	–0.0037	–0.0059	–0.0081	0.0090	–0.0049
2002	–0.0469	–0.0143	–0.0231	–0.0180	0.0085	–0.0326
2003	–0.0126	–0.0026	–0.0043	–0.0137	0.0080	–0.0100
2004	0.0097	0.0139	0.0230	–0.0349	0.0076	–0.0042
2005	0.0160	0.0098	0.0164	–0.0174	0.0071	0.0062
Mean	0.0227	0.0153	0.0227	–0.0293	0.0140	0.0074

in technical efficiency ($\dot{TE}$). Column (1) in Table 7.5 shows that the mean of output growth in the sample period is 2.27%. It can be seen that the major contributor to the economic growth is scale effect (*Scale*), which accounts for an average value of 2.27%. Both the input growth and growth in technical efficiency ($\dot{TE}$) are positive, with an average value of 1.53% and 1.40% respectively. It should be noted, however, that input growth shown in column (2) has decreased significantly from 2.83% in 1984 to 0.98% in 2005. However, the contribution from the rate of technical progress ($\Delta\delta_{Tt}$) is negative for many years, with a large mean average value of –2.93%.

Columns (3) to (5) of Table 7.5 show the three sources of TFP growth ($\dot{TFP}$) — scale effect (*Scale*), the rate of technical progress ($\Delta\delta_{Tt}$) and growth in technical efficiency ($\dot{TE}$). The overall mean of the TFP growth is 0.74%. The three components of TFP growth are: 2.27% from the scale effect, –2.93% from technical change, and 1.40% from the growth in technical efficiency. These findings showed that the most important factor for Hong Kong's growth in TFP is scale effect. This means that factor accumulations has contributed mostly to the TFP growth in Hong Kong. On the other hand, the adverse effect from the rate of technical progress reduces the

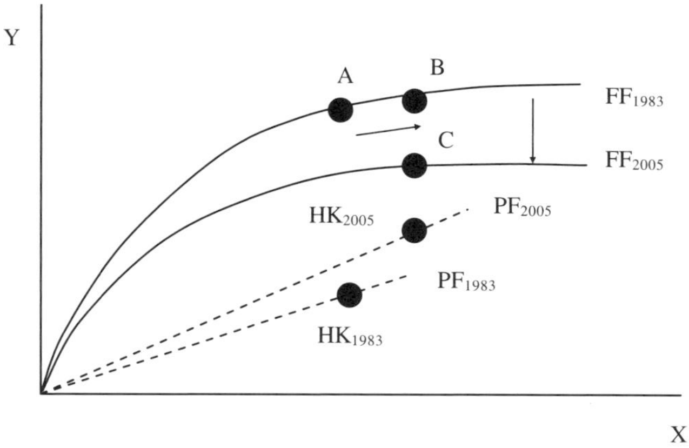

FIGURE 7.5 Decomposition of TFP growth for Hong Kong 1983–2005

potential growth of TFP. In short, technical progress is lacking in the Hong Kong economy.

The decomposition of TFP growth in Hong Kong over the sample period of 1983 to 2005 can be elaborated using Figure 7.5. Total inputs are measured along the horizontal axis, while total outputs are measured along the vertical axis. The production of Hong Kong at two years of 1983 and 2005 are indicated, respectively, by points HK_{1983} and HK_{2005}. Since there has been an average productivity growth of 0.74% from the estimates in Table 7.5, the production function (PF) must have shifted upwards from PF_{1985} to PF_{2005} in Figure 7.5 and the Hong Kong economy is producing at HK_{1983} in 1983 and HK_{2005} in 2005. The increase in productivity growth is indicated by the steeper slope of HK_{2005} compared to the flatter slope of HK_{1983}.

Secondly, the estimates in Table 7.5 show that there is a negative change in technical progress between 1983 and 2005, which is indicated by the downward shift of the production frontier function (FF) from FF_{1983} to FF_{2005}. The negative effect to productivity change as a result of the fall in technical progress in the sample period is represented by the movement from point B to C in Figure 7.5. However, the growth in technical efficiency over the sample period is shown by the difference between the larger distance of HK_{1983} and point A in 1983 and the smaller distance of HK_{2005} and point C in 2005. In other words, due to improvement in technical efficiency, the Hong Kong economy has moved closer to the production frontier between 1983 and 2005, indicating that the Hong Kong economy has been improving its economic efficiency.

The positive effect to productivity growth by the scale of economy (2.27%) in Hong Kong over the sample period is represented theoretically by the movement from point A to point B in Figure 7.5. Such a movement along the frontier function at period 1983 (FF_{1983}) indicates an increasing returns to scale in production, where the total elasticity of output with respect to inputs is greater than one. Under such a condition, an increase in inputs in production generated scale economy and contributed to productivity growth. However, due to the negative effect of technical

TABLE 7.6 Cost shares of inputs and input growth: Economic sectors summary 1983–2005

	Cost shares			Input growth			
	$\frac{e_K}{e}$	$\frac{e_L}{e}$	$\frac{e_H}{e}$	$\frac{e_K}{e}\dot{K}$	$\frac{e_L}{e}\dot{L}$	$\frac{e_H}{e}\dot{H}$	$\dot{\Phi}$
Sectors	(1)	(2)	(3)	(4)	(5)	(6)	(4) + (5) + (6)
TG	0.2632	0.1986	0.5382	–0.0041	–0.0141	0.0083	–0.0099
TS	0.2453	0.1851	0.5696	0.0190	0.0083	0.0055	0.0327
NTG	0.2669	0.2014	0.5318	0.0155	–0.0025	0.0053	0.0183
NTS	0.2471	0.1864	0.5665	0.0094	0.0048	0.0060	0.0203
Mean	0.2556	0.1929	0.5515	0.0099	–0.0009	0.0063	0.0153

Notes: TG = tradable goods sector; TS = tradable services sector; NTG = non-tradable goods sector; NTS = non-tradable services sector.

progress between 1983 and 2005, point C is the eventual point where the Hong Kong economy in 2005 is situated.

To examine the performance of individual economic sector, estimates in column (3) of Table 7.2 are used to fit into the respective equations to derive average estimates for the technical efficiencies and output elasticities of each economic sector in the sample period. Table 7.6 summarizes the cost shares of inputs and input growth for the four economic sectors. In the case of cost shares in physical capital, the non-tradable goods sector has the highest cost share (26.69%), followed by the tradable goods sector (26.32%), the non-tradable services sector (24.71%) and the tradable services sector (24.53%). On the other hand, the tradable services sector has the highest weighted physical capital growth (1.9%), followed by the non-tradable goods sector (1.55%), the non-tradable services sector (0.94%) and the tradable goods sector (–0.41%).

With regard to the other two weighted inputs growth, the tradable services sector has the highest weighted input growth in labor, while the tradable goods sector has the highest weighted input growth in human capital. In all, the tradable services sector has the highest growth in aggregate inputs, with 3.27% shown in the last column in Table 7.6. Physical capital (1.9%) accounts for the largest proportion of input growth. In conclusion, the magnitude in the input growth for the tradable services sector is the highest amongst the four economic sectors in Hong Kong.

Table 7.7 shows the output elasticities and adjusted economies of scale effect of the four economic sectors. Given that the basic function of the production model with the dummy variables for economic sectors shown in column (3) of Table 7.2 is the preferred model for primary analysis, the average output elasticities of both physical capital and labor are the same for the four economic sectors. On the other hand, the tradable services sector has the highest output elasticity of human capital (1.4909) and the non-tradable goods sector has the lowest output elasticity of human capital (1.2787). This shows that the tradable services sector has the highest

TABLE 7.7 Output elasticitics, economies of scale, and adjusted economies of scale effect: Economic sectors summary 1983–2005

	Output elasticities				Adjusted economies of scale effect			
	e_K	e_L	e_H	e	$(e-1)\left(\frac{e_K}{e}\dot{K}\right)$	$(e-1)\left(\frac{e_L}{e}\dot{L}\right)$	$(e-1)\left(\frac{e_H}{e}\dot{H}\right)$	*Scale*
Sectors	(1)	(2)	(3)	(4)	(5)	(6)	(7)	(5) + (6) + (7)
TG	0.6405	0.4833	1.3165	2.4402	–0.0069	–0.0209	0.0121	–0.0158
TS	0.6405	0.4833	1.4909	2.6147	0.0303	0.0128	0.0089	0.0520
NTG	0.6405	0.4833	1.2787	2.4024	0.0220	–0.0038	0.0074	0.0257
NTS	0.6405	0.4833	1.4723	2.5960	0.0149	0.0078	0.0095	0.0322
Mean	0.6405	0.4833	1.3896	2.5133	0.0151	–0.0010	0.0095	0.0235

Note: Same as Table 7.6.

performance in both the total returns to scale and scale effect, while the tradable goods sector has the lowest performance. Again and on average, physical capital accounted for the biggest contribution to scale effect for all the four economic sectors.

Table 7.8 shows the decomposition of output and TFP growth in four economic sectors. The tradable services sector has the highest output growth (7.42%) and highest TFP growth (4.15%), while the tradable goods sector has the lowest output growth (–4.15%) and lowest TFP growth (–3.16%). With regard to the sources of output growth and TFP growth, the tradable services sector has the largest value in input growth (3.27%) as well as scale effect (5.2%), while the non-tradable services sector has the largest value in technical efficiency growth (2.66%). It should be noted that technical progress is measured from the change in time, and as such, it is the same for all the four economic sectors and cannot be used to differentiate the rate of technical progress for different economic sectors.

The performance of technical efficiency levels for the four economic sectors in the sample period can further be explained in Figure 7.6. At the beginning of the sample period, the performance of the non-tradable goods and the tradable goods sectors were above the average in the level of technical efficiency. However, improvement in technical efficiency has been significant in both the non-tradable services and tradable services sectors. The technical efficiency gap among the four economic sectors has narrowed considerably by the end of the sample period. Other than the non-tradable goods sector, which actually has achieved the highest performance in technical efficiency in the sample period, the other three economic sectors have been experiencing significant growth rates in their technical efficiencies. In particular, as Table 7.8 shows, the three sectors of tradable goods, tradable services and non-tradable services were having significant technical efficiency growth rates of 1.35%, 1.88%, and 2.66% respectively. In short, all the four economic sectors have approached closer to full efficiencies over the sample period.

TABLE 7.8 Decomposition of output growth and the TFP growth: Economic sectors summary 1984–2005

	$\dot{\Upsilon}$	$\dot{\Phi}$	*Scale*	$\Delta\delta_{Tt}$	$\dot{TE}$	$\dot{TFP}$
Sectors	(1)	(2)	(3)	(4)	(5)	(3) + (4) + (5)
TG	–0.0415	–0.0099	–0.0158	–0.0293	0.0135	–0.0316
TS	0.0742	0.0327	0.0520	–0.0293	0.0188	0.0415
NTG	0.0174	0.0183	0.0257	–0.0293	0.0028	–0.0008
NTS	0.0498	0.0203	0.0322	–0.0293	0.0266	0.0295
Mean	0.0250	0.0153	0.0235	–0.0293	0.0154	0.0097

Note: Same as Table 7.6.

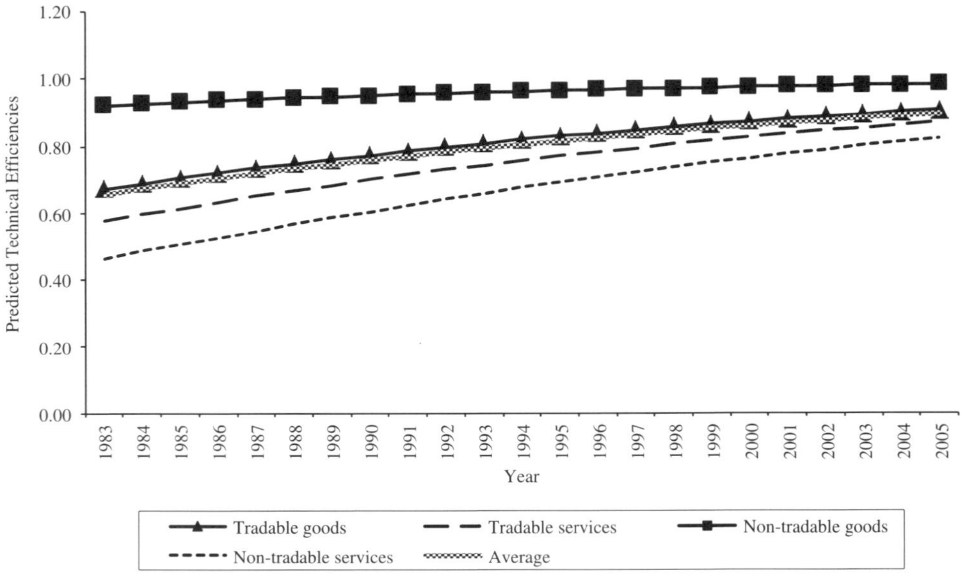

FIGURE 7.6 Predicted technical efficiencies by economic sectors

This section analyzes the output growth and TFP change of the different economic sectors of Hong Kong economy for the year period of 1983–2005. By using the stochastic frontier model, maximum likelihood estimation is applied to an augmented logarithmic production function incorporating human capital in order to work out the productivity change. Four components of output growth are derived from the analysis model, namely weighted sum of input growth, adjusted economies of scale effect, technical progress, and growth of technical efficiency. TFP growth is decomposed into three components of adjusted economies of scale effect, technical progress, and growth of technical efficiency.

Over the entire sample period of 1983–2005, the scale effect contributes the most to the growth in TFP. This means that factor accumulation may contribute mostly to the TFP growth in Hong Kong. In particular, the scale effect is mostly derived from physical capital, while labor reduced the potential economies of scale effect. As such, increased in labor input growth will have significant improvement in the economies of scale effect and hence to productivity change.

The growth of technical efficiency is contributing a positive effect to TFP growth, with its levels approaching near perfect efficiency. In contrast, there is technical decline over the entire period. Adoption of new technology and increase in R&D expenditure will improve technical progress. When the four economic sectors are compared, the tradable services sector has the highest growth in TFP. On the other hand, the tradable goods and non-tradable goods sectors are having negative values in TFP change. Such differences could be explained by the negative scale effects for the tradable goods sector and the low scale effects for the non-tradable goods sector. The empirical findings would suggest that all the economic sectors, particularly the tradable goods and non-tradable goods sectors, should find their ways to improve their scale effects through more effective factor accumulations and to strive for positive technical change through incorporating better technical means in the use of production inputs.

7.5 Comparison With Mainland China

Since 1949 and until 1978, Mainland China has pursued a closed-door economic policy of self-sufficiency with socialist ideology characterized by state-ownership and communes. During the same time period, Hong Kong has practiced an open market capitalist economic system and has earned the status of an international center in finance, trade and investment. In 2005, for example, the total trade flows and the foreign direct investment as a percentage of GDP for Mainland China are 69.5% and 4.1%, respectively. The same percentages for Hong Kong are 385.2% and 34.2%, respectively.[2]

There are also vast differences in institutional performance between Mainland China and Hong Kong. For example, Table 7.9 shows that Mainland China's performances in key institutional indicators are weaker than Hong Kong. Another example is the 2009 rankings produced by the Chinese Academy of Social Sciences on the overall urban competitiveness of 294 cities in the greater China region that comprised of Mainland China, Chinese Taipei, Hong Kong and Macau; Hong Kong is ranked as the most competitive city, followed by Shenzhen, Shanghai, Beijing, Taipei, Guangzhou, Qingdao, Tianjin, Suzhou and Kaohsiung as the top ten most competitive cities. One should note that the location of both Shenzhen and Guangzhou are adjacent to Hong Kong.[3]

Although the Hong Kong economy since 1997 has suffered a series of economic shocks and crisis, including the Asian financial crisis in 1997–1998, the chicken flu that occurred in various years, the severe acute respiratory syndrome

[2] *International Financial Statistics*, IMF (2007).

[3] *Annual Report on Urban Competitiveness*, No. 7 (2009), Blue Book of City Competiveness, Chinese Academy of Social Sciences, Beijing.

TABLE 7.9 Institutional performances: Mainland China and Hong Kong

Institutional establishment (2005)	China	HK
Corruption perception index	3.2	8.3
Voice and accountability	16.8	55.1
Political stability	46.4	73.7
Government effectiveness	47.8	82.5
Regulatory quality	44.5	87.7
Rule of law	40.5	80.0
Control of corruption	36.2	83.7
Property rights protection	30.0	90.0
Regulatory scores	30.0	90.0
Economic freedom (2009)		
Economic Freedom Index	53.2	90.0
Business freedom	51.6	92.7
Trade freedom	71.4	95.0
Fiscal freedom	70.6	93.4
Government size	88.9	93.1
Monetary freedom	72.9	86.2
Investment freedom	30.0	90.0
Financial freedom	30.0	90.0
Property rights	20.0	90.0
Freedom from corruption	35.0	83.0
Labor freedom	61.8	86.3

Sources: *Corruption Index*, Transparency House (2005); *Aggregating Governance Indicators*, World Bank (2005); *Index of Economic Freedom*, Heritage Foundation (2009).

(SARS) in 2003 and the financial tsunami in the US in 2008, a number of agreements on economic cooperation have been made between the central government in Beijing and the Hong Kong SAR Government since the turn of the century. In 2003, a series of Closer Economic Partnership Agreements (CEPA) have been made to lower the import tariff rates of Mainland China for Hong Kong's export in goods and services, and a number of facilitation agreements have also been included. Since 2005, the Beijing government has announced a visa-free travel policy for Mainland residents from major cities and provinces to travel to Hong Kong as tourist visitors. In 2006, led mainly by the Guangdong Province, a regional Pan-Pearl River Delta (Pan-PRD) body has been established that consisted of nine southern provinces and Hong Kong SAR and Macau SAR with the intention to promote regional development and growth. To promote Hong Kong's financial center status, the policy on Qualified Domestic Institutional Investor (QDII) was announced in 2006 permitting mainland capital to come to Hong Kong, but due to the drastic jump and shocks in the financial market in Hong Kong, the policy was shelved in 2007. In spring 2009, Beijing declared that Hong Kong would become the Renminbi trading center.

TABLE 7.10 FDI from Hong Kong and the world to the nine PRD provinces (Actually utilized FDI, US$ million)

	1985			1995			2007		
	HK	World	HK/ World (%)	HK	World	HK/ World (%)	HK	World	HK/ World (%)
Fujian	9.6	11.8	81.6	25.0	403.9	6.2	170.2	406.1	41.9
Guangdong	45.0	51.5	87.4	797.3	1018.0	78.3	830.3	1712.6	48.5
Guangxi	1.3	1.3	100.0	37.2	67.0	55.6	16.0	68.4	23.4
Hainan	2.1	2.1[2]	97.9	56.4	105.5	53.5	n/a	112.0	n/a
Jiangxi	n/a	0.5	n/a	n/a	28.8	n/a	178.9	310.4	57.7
Hunan	n/a	n/a	n/a	32.3	48.8	66.2	157.3	327.1	48.1
Sichuan	n/a	n/a	n/a	n/a	n/a	n/a	n/a	149.3	n/a
Guizhou	n/a	n/a	n/a	n/a	5.7	n/a	n/a	12.7	n/a
Yunnan	n/a	0.2	n/a	n/a	22.5	n/a	15.8	39.5	40.1
9 Provinces*	57.9+	67.3+	86.1+	948.2+	1700.2+	55.8+	1368.7+	3137.9	43.6+
National	95.6	195.6	48.9	2018.5	3752.1	53.8	2770.3	7476.8	37.1

Notes: * = The aggregate figures are based on the available data.
Sources: *China Statistical Yearbook*, and *Statistical Yearbooks* of the nine provinces, various years.

A closer examination on key economic variables showed that provinces closer to Hong Kong have benefitted most from Hong Kong's return to Mainland China through the spillover of investment, trade, cross-border consumption and human capital. For example, at least 43.6% of Hong Kong's total direct investment to Mainland China in 2007 has flowed into the nine provinces in the Pearl River Delta (PRD) region. Table 7.10 shows the inflow of foreign direct investment (FDI) from Hong Kong and from the rest of the world to each of the nine provinces. The FDI from Hong Kong has been the largest share in each province, though Hong Kong's investment funds to Mainland China could have come from elsewhere (Sung, 1991). For the total exports from Mainland China to Hong Kong, the share from the nine provinces amounted to at least 74.6% in 1995, though it has declined to at least 30.4% in 2007. Table 7.11 shows the exports from the nine provinces to Hong Kong and the world.

The knowledge spill over from Hong Kong to Mainland China has also been important. Table 7.12 shows that a total of 218,200 Hong Kong residents are working in China in the third quarter of 2008, equivalent to 6.2% of total employed population in Hong Kong. Table 7.13 shows the number of Hong Kong residents working in several cities in Mainland China in the July–September 2008 period. Of the total Hong Kong residents working in Mainland China, 87.8% are working in the Guangdong province. The two Guangdong cities of Shenzhen and Dongguan occupied a total of 62.9% already. Outside the Guangdong Province, Shanghai is the more popular city, occupying 4.9% of total.

TABLE 7.11 Exports from PRD provinces to Hong Kong and world (US$ million)

	1985			1995			2007		
	HK	World	HK/ World (%)	HK	World	HK/ World (%)	HK	World	HK/ World (%)
Fujian[3]	0.2	0.5	40.3	4.1	9.3	43.9	3.6	49.9	7.2
Guangdong[1]	2.1	3.0	72.1	48.4	55.7	87.0	129.9	369.2	35.2
Guangxi[3]	0.2	0.4	43.6	1.2	2.2	53.3	0.4	5.1	8.2
Hainan[1]	n/a	n/a	n/a	0.4	0.8	53.5	0.4	1.8	23.0
Jiangxi[2]	0.1	0.3	33.2	0.8	1.4	52.5	0.6	5.5	11.3
Hunan[1]	n/a	n/a	n/a	0.3	1.1	31.8	0.8	6.5	12.5
Sichuan[1]	n/a	0.2	n/a	n/a	1.9	n/a	1.5	8.6	17.8
Guizhou	n/a	0.0	n/a	n/a	0.4	n/a	n/a	1.5	n/a
Yunnan[3]	n/a	0.1	n/a	n/a	1.2	n/a	0.4	4.7	9.2
9 Provinces[4]	2.6+	4.5+	57.4+	55.3+	74.1	74.6+	137.8+	452.9	30.4+
National	7.2	27.4	26.3	36.0	148.8	24.2	184.4	1217.8	15.1

Notes: [1] HK is largest export destination in 2007. [2] HK is the second largest export destination in 2007. [3] HK is the third largest export destination in 2007. [4] The aggregate figures are based on the available data.
Sources: Same as Table 7.10. All national data are based on customs statistics, while data for the provinces up till 1998 are from the Ministry of Foreign Trade, Beijing.

TABLE 7.12 Hong Kong residents working in Mainland China

	No. of persons (1,000)	Percent to the total employed persons in HK (%)
Sept to Oct 1995	122.3	4.2
May to June 1998	157.3	5.0
April to June 2001	190.8	5.9
Jan to Mar 2003	238.2	7.4
Jan to Mar 2005	237.5	7.2
July to Sept 2008	218.2	6.2

Source: *Hong Kong Residents Working in the Mainland of China*, Special Topics Report (7–9, 2008), No. 49, February 2009, Census and Statistics Department, Hong Kong.

Table 7.14 summarizes the number of Hong Kong residents working in China in different categories. In the age group category, for example, the middle age group of 40–49 years formed the largest group of 36.7%, which is larger than the percentage of middle age group in Hong Kong (28.2%). For the education attainment, the group with secondary and sixth-form education is the largest group, comprising 48.4%, though it is lower than the percentage of secondary and sixth-form education in Hong Kong (55.8). The groups with post-secondary, both non-degree and

TABLE 7.13 Hong Kong residents working in Mainland China by usual place of work (July–September, 2008)

	No. of people (1,000)	Percent to the total HK residents working in China (%)
Guangdong	191.6	87.8
Shenzhen	75.8	34.7
Dongguan	61.5	28.2
Guangzhou	27.6	12.7
Others	26.7	12.2
Cities outside Guangdong	26.6	12.2
Shanghai	10.7	4.9
Beijing	4.6	2.1
Fujian	4.4	2.0
Others	6.9	3.2

Source: *Hong Kong Residents Working in the Mainland of China,* Special Topics Report (7–9, 2008), No. 49, February 2009, Census and Statistics Department, Hong Kong SAR.

degree, education attainment in Mainland have higher percentage than the percentages in the respective groups in Hong Kong. This implies that labor mobility from Hong Kong to Mainland China is more significant at the high education level than other levels. By industry groups, manufacturing and wholesale/retail services have attracted most persons. Comparing the percentages in the respective groups in Hong Kong, the major gap is in manufacturing. Although only 5.4% of people in Hong Kong are in manufacturing, 41% of Hong Kong residents working in Mainland China are in manufacturing. In terms of occupation, most Hong Kong residents working in Mainland China are managers, administrators, and professionals. The total percentage in these groups is 86.5%, which is much higher than the total percentage of these groups employed in Hong Kong (36.4%). Table 7.14 also shows that 17.1% of Hong Kong residents working in China are employers, while in comparison there are only 3.6% of employers in Hong Kong.

Hong Kong residents working in Mainland China supplements the shortage of human capital in Mainland China. A large proportion of the Hong Kong residents working in China are engaged at the upper end of the occupation hierarchy. For example, the median monthly earning of Hong Kong residents working in Mainland China has reached HK$20,000 (US$2,564), but the median earning in Hong Kong in the same period is HK$10,500 (US$1,346). Knowledge spillover from Hong Kong to Mainland China is an important factor in the economic integration process in the period after sovereignty reversion.

One thing to note is the different basis of data used in both Mainland China and Hong Kong. Since the data used in the study are not entirely comparable, one can only draw some ideas from their efficiency performances intuitively. Nonetheless, since the study is using data over a period of time, the differences in their estimations can still be examined. Such "comparison" can be useful in the context of economic integration between the two economies. The empirical results have drawn heavily

TABLE 7.14 Characteristics of Hong Kong residents working in Mainland China

		No. of people (1,000)	Share to total[1] (%)	Percent of respective group in HK[2] (%)
Age	15–19	NA[3]	NA[3]	1.5
	20–29	24.2	11.1	21.2
	30–39	57.9	26.5	26.3
	40–49	80.0	36.7	28.2
	≧50	55.9	25.6	22.8
Educational Attainment	Pre-primary and Primary	11.3	5.2	12.4
	Secondary and Sixth-form	105.6	48.4	55.8
	Post-secondary: Non-Degree	25.3	11.6	9.7
	Post-secondary: Degree	76.0	34.8	22.1
Industry[4]	Sales and trade	82.5	37.8	32.6
	Finance and business services	24.9	11.4	16.9
	Transportation	8.7	4.0	10.5
	Construction	5.9	2.7	7.8
	Other services	4.6	2.1	26.2
	Manufacturing	91.0	41.7	5.4
Occupation	Managers and administrators	96.4	44.2	10.1
	Professional and associates	92.4	42.3	26.3
	Clerks	10.4	4.8	15.8
	Service and sales workers	2.9	1.3	15.6
	Craft and machine operators	14.9	6.9	13.4
	Elementary jobs and others	1.2	0.7	18.8
Employment status	Employees	168.7	77.3	89.2
	Employers	37.4	17.1	3.6
	Self-employed people	12.1	5.5	6.6
Monthly earning (HK$)	< 5,000	1.1	0.5	13.5
	5,000–9,999	17.1	8.1	31.9
	10,000–14,999	39.7	18.7	19.7
	15,000–19,999	33.0	15.5	10.7
	20,000–29,999	50.0	23.5	11.6
	≧ 30,000	71.6	33.7	12.6

Notes: [1] Share of Hong Kong residents working in China in each group to the total Hong Kong residents working in China. [2] Percent of the employed persons in the respective group in Hong Kong to the total employed persons in Hong Kong. [3] The estimates less than 1000 and statistics are not released due to very large sampling errors. [4] Sales & Trade includes wholesale, retail, import/export trade, restaurants and hotels; Finance & Business Service includes finance, insurance, real estate, business services; Transportation includes transportation, storage, and communications; Other Services includes Community, social and personal services.

Source: *Hong Kong Residents Working in the Mainland of China*, Special Topics Report (July–September, 2008), No. 49, February 2009, Census and Statistics Department, Hong Kong.

from some of the previous studies on the Mainland China economy (Liu and Li, 2008; Li and Liu, 2010; Li *et al.*, 2009).

The stochastic frontier production model is used to analyze the growth attributes of the two economies. In addition to the two physical capital and labor variables, a human capital variable is included in the stochastic frontier production function. The sample periods for Mainland China and Hong Kong are 1986–2006 and 1983–2005, respectively. To determine changes and improvement of efficiency and technical progress for the two economies, the estimates for the period before 1997 are used to compare to the whole sample period. The break point of 1997 is chosen to reflect sovereignty reversion in 1997 and the Asian financial crisis in 1997–1998.

Panel data from Mainland China and Hong Kong are used in the regression exercise. The sources and compilation of the Hong Kong variables are the same as those discussed in previous chapters and sections, which will not be repeated here. The data sources and construction of the different variables (physical capital, labor and human capital) for the thirty provinces in Mainland China updated to 2006 are similar to those used in Li (2003, 2009), Liu and Li (2006) and Li *et al.* (2009).[4]

Table 7.15 presents the maximum likelihood estimates of the stochastic frontier production with the panel data from Mainland China's aggregation of the thirty provinces and Hong Kong's aggregation of the four sectors for the two periods. The first period covered the first sub-sample through 1996 due to the reversion of Hong Kong's sovereignty in 1997 and the Asian financial crisis in 1997–1998, while the second period is the whole sample period. For Mainland China, the first sub-sample period covered 1985–1996 with 360 observations and the whole sample period covered 1985–2006 with 660 observations. For Hong Kong, the first sub-sample period covered 1983–1996 with 56 observations and the whole sample period covered 1983–2005 with 92 observations. The purpose of the selection of these two sample periods is to examine if the two economies have encountered changes in their production efficiencies and frontier functions over time. Because of limited data in the second sub-sample period from 1997 onwards, the estimation was not applied to the second sub-sample period. However, the properties of the estimates for this period can be inferred by comparing the estimations from the first sub-sample period and the whole sample period.

The dependent variables of the models for both periods are the log real GDP. The independent variables, in addition to physical capital, labor, and human capital, included 11 and 21 time dummy variables for the two periods for Mainland China, and 13 and 22 time dummy variables for the two periods in Hong Kong. The last row in Table 7.15 presents the four sets of model specification tests that contained the likelihood-ratio tests for the joint effects of the time dummy variables for the two sample periods. The significance level of the likelihood-ratio tests is set at 5%. The statistics for the two periods in Mainland China and Hong Kong and the significant time dummy variables suggest that technology change over time is significant.

For the pre-1997 period in Mainland China, the effect of physical capital (0.7750) is clearly predominant in the production function. Nevertheless, the effect of labor has kept close to physical capital over time, as indicated by a larger estimate

---

[4] These variables construction methods will not be repeated here.

TABLE 7.15 Maximum likelihood estimates of the stochastic frontier production function

	China		Hong Kong	
	Before 1997 1985–1996	Whole period 1985–2006	Before 1997 1983–1996	Whole period 1983–2005
	(1)	(2)	(3)	(4)
lnK	0.7750	0.4424	0.5393	0.4047
	(0.0381)	(0.0208)	(0.1139)	(0.0300)
lnL	0.1890	0.4320	0.4245	0.7087
	(0.0388)	(0.0239)	(0.0484)	(0.0313)
H	0.0133	0.0386	0.0712	0.0641
	(0.0109)	(0.0064)	(0.1811)	(0.0427)
μ	0.3825	0.8546	0.2750	0.4514
	(0.1838)	(0.1162)	(1.2704)	(0.2802)
η	–0.0361	–0.0223	0.0117	0.0073
	(0.0039)	(0.0017)	(0.0120)	(0.0049)
$\sigma_s^2 = \sigma_v^2 + \sigma_u^2$	0.2031	0.1557	0.0775	0.0546
$\gamma = \sigma_u^2/\sigma_s^2$	0.9880	0.9743	0.9713	0.9324
Log Likelihood	474.4785	771.6274	79.0864	105.6346
Log Likelihood Ratio Test:				
$\delta_t = 0$ for all t	160.76	454.45	37.93	64.92

Notes: Figures in parentheses stand for the standard errors of the estimates. The maximum likelihood estimates of the coefficients of time dummies are not shown in the table.

of labor for the whole sample period of Mainland China (0.4320).[5] The estimated technical inefficiency parameters, η, are negative, meaning that the overall technical inefficiency is increasing over time for both periods. The measure of the variation in inefficiency is indicated by γ, $\gamma = \frac{\sigma_u^2}{\sigma_s^2}$, where σ_s^2 refers to the sum of the variances of the combined error terms (i.e., the variance of the normal random error term, σ_v^2, and the variance of the technical inefficiency term, σ_u^2). The estimates for the two periods suggest that the inefficiency component has shown a greater variation in the composite error term in the pre-1997 period (0.988) than in the whole sample period (0.9743).

In the case of Hong Kong, the effect of physical capital is mildly predominant in the production function in the pre-1997 period, but the effect of labor surpasses that of physical capital in the whole sample period. This implies that the effect of labor has increased in the post-1997 period. The estimated technical inefficiency parameters, η, are positive, suggesting that the overall technical inefficiency is decreasing over

[5]Since the human capital variable is not in logarithm form, its estimates are not comparable with the estimates of the other two inputs. The importance of human capital can be seen from its own elasticity and cost share.

time. The estimates of the variation in inefficiency, γ, show that the inefficiency component has a higher variation in the pre-1997 period (0.9713) than in the whole sample period (0.9324). This implied a mild decrease in the variation since 1997.

The estimates for the sources of output growth ($\dot{Y}$) and total factor productivity growth ($\dot{TFP}$) included the estimates on output elasticity with respect to factor input of capital (e_K), labor (e_L) and human capital (e_H), the returns to scale (e), the adjusted scale effect (*Scale*), the rate of technical progress ($\Delta\delta_t$) and the growth of technical efficiency ($\dot{TE}$).

Table 7.16 shows the overall means of output elasticity with respect to each input and the cost shares of inputs in Mainland China and Hong Kong for the two periods. We first consider the results for the period before 1997. For Mainland China, physical capital has the largest output elasticity with an average value of 0.7750, followed by labor (0.1890) and human capital (0.0650). For Hong Kong, human capital has the largest output elasticity (0.8259), followed by physical capital (0.5393) and labor (0.4245). The differences in the output elasticities between Mainland China and Hong Kong are shown by the differences in returns to scale and cost shares of inputs. The returns to scale in Hong Kong (1.7896) are much higher than that in Mainland China (1.0291), suggesting that the returns to scale are an important factor for the economic growth in Hong Kong. For the cost shares in Mainland China, the share for physical capital (75.31%) is highest, followed by labor (18.37%) and human capital (6.32%). For Hong Kong, the range of the three cost shares is smaller, with human capital the largest (46.11%), followed by physical capital

TABLE 7.16 Output elasticities and cost shares of inputs

	Output elasticities				Cost shares		
	e_K*	e_L*	e_H	e	$\frac{e_K}{e}$	$\frac{e_L}{e}$	$\frac{e_H}{e}$
Pre-1997 period							
China	0.7750	0.1890	0.0650	1.0291	0.7531	0.1837	0.0632
Northeast	0.7750	0.1890	0.0887	1.0527	0.7362	0.1796	0.0842
East	0.7750	0.1890	0.0687	1.0328	0.7504	0.1830	0.0665
South	0.7750	0.1890	0.0525	1.0166	0.7624	0.1860	0.0516
West	0.7750	0.1890	0.0591	1.0232	0.7574	0.1847	0.0578
Hong Kong	0.5393	0.4245	0.8259	1.7897	0.3015	23.74	0.2374
Whole period							
China	0.4424	0.4320	0.2072	1.0817	0.4029	0.3997	0.1911
Northeast	0.4424	0.4320	0.2860	1.1604	0.3812	0.3723	0.2464
East	0.4424	0.4320	0.2219	1.0963	0.4035	0.3941	0.2024
South	0.4424	0.4320	0.1676	1.0420	0.4246	0.4146	0.1608
West	0.4424	0.4320	0.1963	1.0707	0.4123	0.4035	0.1833
Hong Kong	0.4047	0.7087	0.7801	1.8934	0.2139	0.3746	0.4115

Note: * = These estimates are the same for all provinces in China.

(30.15%) and labor (23.74%). In terms of both output elasticity and cost share, physical capital is important for Mainland China and human capital is important in Hong Kong before 1997.

The analysis on the decomposition of TFP can be extended to examine the performance of different regions in Mainland China, as shown in Li *et al.* (2010). The thirty provinces of China are divided according to their economic and geographical similarities into four regions. The East region consists of twelve provinces in the Yellow River Delta and Yangtze River Delta of Beijing, Tianjin, Hebei, Shanghai, Jiangsu, Zhejiang, Shandong, Anhui, Henan, Hubei, Shanxi and Gansu. The South region is composed of nine southern provinces, commonly known as the Pearl River Delta of Fujian, Guangdong, Guangxi, Hainan, Jiangxi, Hunan, Sichuan (including Chongqing), Guizhou and Yunnan. The West region refers to the remote provinces of Mongolia, Tibet, Shaanxi, Qinghai, Ningxia and Xinjiang. The remaining three provinces in North East region are Jilin, Heilongjiang and Liaoning.

For the whole sample period, Table 7.16 shows that the output elasticities for physical capital and labor in Mainland China (0.4424 and 0.4320, respectively) are similar and larger than the elasticity for human capital (0.2072). For Hong Kong, the output elasticities for labor (0.7087) and human capital (0.7801) are similar and larger than the elasticity for physical capital (0.4047). In summary, the output elasticities for labor and human capital in Hong Kong are larger than those in Mainland China; while the elasticity for physical capital for Mainland China and Hong Kong are similar.

By comparing the results from the pre-1997 period and the whole sample period, we can infer the change in the output elasticities for the period since 1997. For Mainland China, the output elasticity for physical capital in the whole sample period (0.4424) is much smaller than that in the pre-1997 period (0.7750). It implies that the output elasticity of physical capital since 1997 has decreased and should be smaller than 0.4424. As for labor and human capital, their output elasticities have increased since 1997 because these two elasticities are larger in the whole sample period than in the pre-1997 period. Therefore, the physical capital has become less important, while labor and human capital have become more important for the period since 1997 in Mainland China. This indicates that diminishing return appeared after the intensive use of physical capital in the pre-1997 period. Among the four regions in Mainland China and for the whole period, the Northeast region shows the largest output elasticity for human capital (0.2860), followed closely by the East region (0.2219), while the South region showed the lowest output elasticity for human capital (0.1676).

For Hong Kong, the output elasticity for labor in the whole sample period (0.7087) is much higher than that in the pre-1997 period (0.4245). This implies that the output elasticity of labor has become higher and labor has become important since 1997 in Hong Kong. However, the elasticities for both physical capital (0.5393) and human capital (0.8259) have shown a mild decrease since 1997 (0.4047 and 0.7801, respectively). Overall, we can conclude that the output elasticities for all three inputs are higher in Hong Kong than in Mainland China since 1997. The returns to scale value in Hong Kong (1.8934) are still much larger than the value in Mainland China (1.0817). Hong Kong consistently has larger returns to scale than Mainland China in the post-1997.

In the whole sample period, Table 7.16 shows that the pattern of the cost share is similar to that of the output elasticity. The cost shares for physical capital and labor in Mainland China (40.29% and 39.97%, respectively) are close and larger than the share of human capital (19.11%). Among the four regions, the South region shows a higher cost share in both capital and labor, but a lowest cost share in human capital. For Hong Kong, the cost shares of labor and human capital (37.46% and 41.15%) are larger than the cost share of physical capital (21.39%). Among the three inputs, Mainland China has a larger share of physical capital than Hong Kong, while Hong Kong has a larger share of human capital than Mainland China.

We can consider the difference in the cost shares between the pre-1997 period and the whole sample period. The cost share for physical capital in Mainland China has declined and the shares for labor and human capital have increased between the first pre-1997 sub-sample period and the whole sample period. For Hong Kong, the cost share for labor has increased and the shares for both physical capital and human capital have decreased between the pre-1997 sub-sample period and the whole sample period. We can conclude that both the cost shares for physical capital and labor are higher in Mainland China than in Hong Kong and the cost share for human capital is higher in Hong Kong than in Mainland China in the second sub-sample period.

Table 7.17 shows the input growth for each input and the adjusted scale effect. In the pre-1997 period, the weighted aggregate input growth in Mainland China is 7.79%, with physical capital accounted for 93.20% (7.26% out of 7.79%), while labor and human capital accounted for 4.88% and 1.93%, respectively. This implies that physical capital is dominant in Mainland China, and a similar picture can be seen from the four regions. The growth of aggregate weighted inputs in Hong Kong show an average of 2.38%, with physical capital accounted for 63% (1.5% out of 2.38%), while labor and human capital accounted for 9% and 27%, respectively. The lower input growth in Hong Kong when compared to Mainland China is mainly caused by the low growth in physical capital, although physical capital is still the main contributor to the input growth in Hong Kong.

For the whole sample period, Table 7.17 shows that the growth of aggregate input in Mainland China has an average of 5.10% and Hong Kong has an average of 1.14%. Both input growth rates are lower than their values in the pre-1997 period. The lower input growth in Mainland China is mainly caused by a lower cost share of physical capital in the whole sample period than in the pre-1997 period. The low input growth in Hong Kong is caused by a low weighted physical capital growth and the negative labor growth (due probably to emigration, see Li (2006)) in the post-1997 years. However, physical capital is still dominating in the weighted input growth for both Mainland China and Hong Kong in the whole sample period. Physical capital accounted for around 80% of Mainland China's input growth (4.06% out of 5.1%) and 70% of Hong Kong's input growth (0.83% out of 1.14%).

Since all the returns to scales shown in Table 7.16 are greater than one, the adjusted scale effect is positive. In the pre-1997 period, Table 7.17 shows that the scale effect is lower in Mainland China (0.24%) than in Hong Kong (1.89%). This difference is mainly caused by the higher returns to scale in Hong Kong than in Mainland China (1.7897 and 1.0291, respectively, shown in Table 7.16). In the whole sample period, the scale effects in Mainland China and Hong Kong are 0.42%

TABLE 7.17 Input growth and adjusted scale effect

	Input growth				Scale effect			
	$\frac{e_K}{e}\dot{K}$	$\frac{e_L}{e}\dot{L}$	$\frac{e_H}{e}\dot{H}$	$\dot{\Phi}$	$(e-1)\left(\frac{e_K}{e}\dot{K}\right)$	$(e-1)\left(\frac{e_L}{e}\dot{L}\right)$	$(e-1)\left(\frac{e_H}{e}\dot{H}\right)$	*Scale*
Pre-1997 period								
China	0.0726	0.0038	0.0015	0.0779	0.0022	0.0001	0.0000	0.0024
Northeast	0.0659	0.0034	0.0013	0.0706	0.0035	0.0002	0.0001	0.0037
East	0.0735	0.0035	0.0016	0.0786	0.0024	0.0001	0.0000	0.0026
South	0.0766	0.0045	0.0011	0.0822	0.0013	0.0001	0.0000	0.0014
West	0.0690	0.0038	0.0017	0.0745	0.0016	0.0001	0.0000	0.0017
Hong Kong	0.0150	0.0022	0.0065	0.0238	0.0120	0.0016	0.0052	0.0189
Whole period								
China	0.0406	0.0067	0.0036	0.0510	0.0034	0.0005	0.0003	0.0042
Northeast	0.0311	0.0034	0.0045	0.0390	0.0050	0.0005	0.0007	0.0062
East	0.0417	0.0059	0.0040	0.0516	0.0040	0.0006	0.0004	0.0050
South	0.0400	0.0086	0.0027	0.0513	0.0017	0.0004	0.0001	0.0022
West	0.0388	0.0072	0.0045	0.0506	0.0027	0.0005	0.0003	0.0036
Hong Kong	0.0083	–0.0017	0.0047	0.0114	0.0074	–0.0018	0.0042	0.0097

and 0.97%, respectively. This gap between the two scale effects in the whole sample period is smaller than the gap in the pre-1997 period. The higher scale effect in Mainland China in the whole sample period is caused by the higher returns to scale (0.42%); the lower scale effect in Hong Kong is caused by the lower input growth (1.14%) in the whole sample period.

Among the four regions in Mainland China, input growth was more rapid in the pre-1997 period than the whole sample period, but the reverse is true in the scale effect. In the pre-1997 sample period, the South region has the highest input growth of 8.22%, but it has caught up by the East region with 5.16% in the whole sample. The success in the East region can be explained by the large increase in the scale effect between the pre-1997 period (0.26%) and the post-1997 sub-sample period that gives a total of 0.5% in the entire sample period.

Finally, the decomposition of output growth and the TFP growth for both Mainland China and Hong Kong for the two periods are shown in Table 7.18. The four sources of the output growth are: growth in inputs ($\dot{\Phi}$), scale effect (*Scale*), rate of technical progress ($\Delta\delta_t$) and growth in technical efficiency (*TE*). In the pre-1997 period, the average economic growth in Mainland China is 9.6%. The major contributor to this high economic growth is input growth (7.79%) and followed by technical progress (3.18%). The adjusted scale effect (0.24%) has only contributed a small fraction to the economic growth. The contribution from technical efficiency is negative in all years with an average of −1.54%. The average TFP growth in Mainland China is 1.88%. Technical progress (3.18%) is the main factor for the TFP growth. The negative contribution from technical efficiency change (−1.51%) significantly reduces the potential growth of TFP in Mainland China.

TABLE 7.18 Decomposition of output growth and the TFP growth: China and Hong Kong

	$\dot{\Upsilon}$	$\dot{\Phi}$	*Scale*	$\Delta\delta_{Tt}$*	$\dot{TE}$	$\dot{TFP}$
Before 1997						
China	0.0960	0.0779	0.0024	0.0318	−0.0154	0.0188
Northeast	0.0841	0.0706	0.0037	0.0318	−0.0218	0.0138
East	0.1010	0.0786	0.0026	0.0318	−0.0125	0.0219
South	0.1048	0.0822	0.0014	0.0318	−0.0104	0.0228
West	0.0790	0.0745	0.0017	0.0318	−0.0283	0.0053
Hong Kong	0.0417	0.0238	0.0189	−0.0050	0.0041	0.0179
Whole period						
China	0.0990	0.0510	0.0042	0.0589	−0.0151	0.0480
Northeast	0.0904	0.0390	0.0062	0.0588	−0.0156	0.0494
East	0.1040	0.0516	0.0050	0.0588	−0.0106	0.0532
South	0.1002	0.0513	0.0022	0.0588	−0.0159	0.0451
West	0.0915	0.0506	0.0036	0.0588	−0.0237	0.0387
Hong Kong	0.0239	0.0114	0.0097	−0.0008	0.0036	0.0126

Note: * = This refers to the time dummy, which is the same for all provinces.

Among the four regions in Mainland China for the whole sample period, the East region shows the highest TFP growth of 5.32%, followed closely by Northeast region (4.94%) and the South region (4.51%). Between the pre-1997 and the whole sample period, all four regions have improved massively in their TFP growth rates. In terms of the fall in efficiency for the whole sample, the West regions performed worst with a drop of 2.37%. On the contrary, the East region has performed least unfavorably with a mild drop of 1.06%.

In the case of Hong Kong, the mean of output growth in the pre-1997 period is 4.17%. The major contributors to Hong Kong's economic growth are input growth (2.38%) and scale effect (1.89%). The small positive value in technical efficiency (0.41%) is offset by the negative value in technology progress (–0.5%). Since the 1980s, the political uncertainty generated by sovereignty reversion, coupled with de-industrialization as manufacturing plants moved to Southern China and the short-term investment behavior could explain the fall in Hong Kong's technical progress in the pre-1997 years. The average TFP growth in Hong Kong is 1.79%, which is close to the TFP growth in Mainland China. However, the major factor for Hong Kong's TFP growth is scale effect (1.89%). A closer examination on the different performances of various TFP components in the pre-1997 period can be seen from the yearly figures (not included in Table 7.18). For example, technical progress has contributed as much as 8.87% and 3.01% to TFP growth in 1987 and 1988, respectively, when the Sino-British Joint Declaration on the political future of Hong Kong was concluded and economic stability was revived. However, it did not improve but instead slackened to negative rates in later periods when the economy overheated in the years before 1997. It can be seen that TFP has reached a peak of 4.96% in 1991 before it fell.

In the whole sample period, Table 7.18 shows that the average economic growth in Mainland China is 9.99%, which is close to its value in the pre-1997 period. However, technical progress (5.89%) has taken up the role of input growth (5.1%) as the major contributor to the economic growth in the whole sample period. The scale effect (0.42%) is still a small positive and the average contribution from technical efficiency remained negative (–1.51%). The TFP growth in the whole sample period is 4.8%, which is much higher than the value in the pre-1997 period (1.88%). This high TFP growth is due largely to technical progress. The economic growth in Hong Kong has an average of 2.39% in the whole sample period. The major contributors to its economic growth are still input growth (1.14%) and scale effect (0.97%). However, these values have fallen to about one-half of those values in the pre-1997 period, and this has led to a lower growth rate in the whole sample period than in the pre-1997 period. The only improvement is the rate of technical progress, with a smaller negative average value of –0.08%. The overall mean of the TFP growth in the whole period is 1.26%. This value is lower than the value in the pre-1997 period and is mainly caused by the lower scale effect. As in the pre-1997 period, the most important factor for Hong Kong's TFP growth in the whole sample period is scale effect.

Comparing the trend economic growth between Mainland China and Hong Kong in the whole sample period, even though a different data base is used for the two economies, Table 7.18 shows that the economic growth in Mainland China is higher than that in Hong Kong since the input growth and technology progress are higher in Mainland China. The technical progress also explained the higher TFP growth in Mainland China than in Hong Kong. Input growth and technical progress have contributed to higher economic growth and TFP growth in Mainland China than in Hong Kong.

In conclusion, Mainland China has experienced increases in output and productivity growth. The empirical results showed that input growth is the main engine to economic growth in Mainland China before 1997. Technical progress is the major contributor to the TFP growth in the whole sample period and significantly contributed to TFP growth after 1997. Technical inefficiency remains and represents a significant drag in Mainland China's productivity growth.

The growth pattern in Hong Kong is different from Mainland China in several ways. The growth in input is the main engine of Hong Kong's economic growth both before and since 1997. The returns to scale in Hong Kong outperformed those in Mainland China for all years in the sample period. Hence, the adjusted scale effect induced by high returns to scale is the major contributor to the productivity growth in Hong Kong. Hong Kong has experienced decreases in output and productivity growth after 1997. The decreases are mainly caused by the low input growth. Unlike Mainland China, Hong Kong has experienced a negative technical progress. Hong Kong should adopt new technology and increase R&D expenditures to improve its technical progress. However, Hong Kong's positive technical efficiency change does contrast sharply with the negative efficiency change in Mainland China. The production methods in Mainland China should be improved in order to improve technical efficiency, while more investment in technology innovation should be made in Hong Kong.

Factor accumulation is important in both Mainland China and Hong Kong as input growth is an important factor for their economic growth. The empirical results show that human capital is a major constraint in Mainland China (Li *et al.* 2009). Continuous investment on education and training is needed. For example, Figure 7.7 shows the human capital in Mainland China, which is measured by the number of schooling years. The human capital with only primary school education has increased

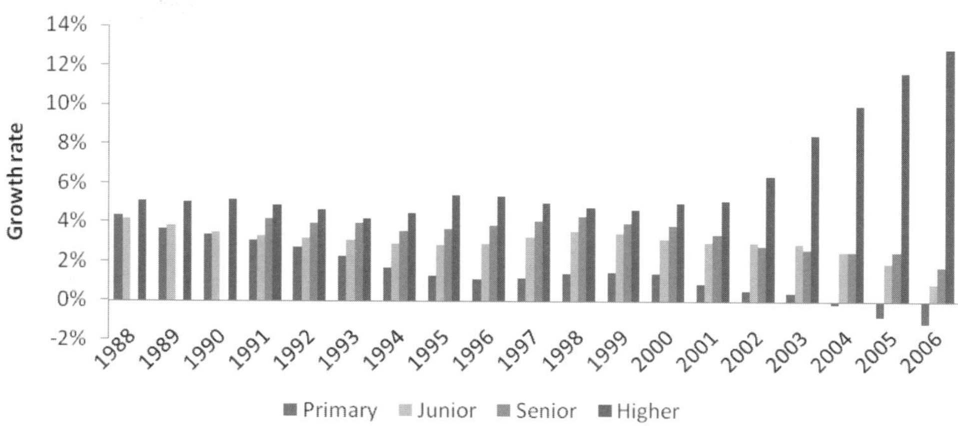

FIGURE 7.7 Growth rates of different educational levels in Mainland China

at an average rate of 0.05% (with negative growth rates in recent years), the same average growth rates for the junior middle school education, the senior middle school education (including vocational secondary school and specialized secondary school) and higher education are 1.54%, 2.08% and 4.64%, respectively, for the whole sample period. While tertiary education has received much attention since economic reform in Mainland China, the weaker section of human capital is the middle range, as seen from the low average growth rates in the human capital with junior middle school and senior middle school education. One other possible explanation for the falling growth rates in the primary and junior education levels could be the one-child policy that may have led to the fall of young population in Mainland China, and fewer children are attending schools.

In the case of Hong Kong, the sample period has reflected a changing situation in the era before and after the sovereignty reversion and Asian financial crisis in 1997. During the period since 1997, the decrease in the physical capital growth and negative labor growth has reduced input growth, and subsequently economic growth and productivity growth in Hong Kong. Political uncertainty before 1997 has resulted in a lack of long-term investment, especially investments related to R&D or large-scale industrial plants. Investment that contributed to technical progress has not been forthcoming after 1997. The Hong Kong economy needs to revert back to a more stable environment that can nurture investment and promote technical progress in the long-term (Li, 2006). However, technical efficiency in Hong Kong has been high, which would give an added advantage when technical progress improves.

The empirical findings can provide implications on the economic integration between Mainland China and Hong Kong. The production capacity in Mainland China has expanded greatly, and the improvement in technical progress is the driving force in productivity growth. Typically, the lack of technical progress in Hong Kong can be complemented by the strong performance in technical progress in Mainland China. Similarly, the poor performance in Mainland China's technical efficiency can be improved by learning from the experience of Hong Kong.

7.6 Conclusion

This chapter has devoted to the discussion of economic efficiency that is closely related to economic freedom. As economic freedom allows individuals and corporations to maximize their activities and returns, improvement in economic efficiency can be achieved through a variety of channels. Although economic efficiency is achieved through mainly cost efficiency, the concept of economic efficiency can have wider implications in culture, governance, business behavior and so on.

The analysis on the total factor productivity discussed in previous chapters has been decomposed into three factors of scale economy, technological progress and technical efficiency. Together with growth of input factors, the analysis can provide further insights to the factors that contributed to growth in Hong Kong. The stochastic frontier approach has been used to examine the empirical performance in Hong Kong. The results which are quite consistent across major industries in Hong Kong showed that the factor that contributed to growth is the economy of scale, followed by a gain in technical efficiency. The sample period of study covered the period of Sino-British negotiation over the political future of Hong Kong, the economic boom years prior to the Asian financial crisis in 1997 and the economic recession years that followed.

The overall picture is that the uncertainty generated from the future of Hong Kong has encouraged short-term investment and speculation which were not technology generating. Traditionally, Hong Kong has not been a strong basis for technological advancement. The amount of R&D activity is rather low, due partly to the lack of funding from government, and partly due to the fact that R&D activities by multinational corporations are not conducted in Hong Kong. It is true to say, however, that some indigenous firms do carried out R&D activities, and government does provide indirect support through institutional assistance to enterprises. Nonetheless, the uncertainty generated from the political future of Hong Kong did delay technological advancement considerably. The post-1997 government did make effort in promoting technological advancement and R&D activities. For example, the establishment of the Science Park has opened up various possibilities, especially in applied technologies that can be used in contemporary industries. Thus, there is possibility for Hong Kong to improve its technological capacity if there are sufficient compliments, such as provision of land for technology-related activities, suitable R&D activities, more government and non-government funding for science, technology and knowledge-based activities.

The good news is that the regression estimations show improvement in efficiency in Hong Kong. This works as a complement, despite the lack of technological progress. People in Hong Kong must have worked more efficiently in different aspects in the 1980s when there was political uncertainty facing the economy, and in the 1990s during the economic boom when people utilized all sorts of opportunities to ensure their economic gains, and after the Asian financial crisis when people in Hong Kong had to struggle for survival in a deep economic recession. The efficiency improvement reflected more the working attitude of the people in Hong Kong, in that when the economy was faced with sequential periods of uncertainties, strong economic upturns with booms and extreme economic recessions with hardship, an economically free regime can always encourage, or pressurize, individuals and businesses to explore new opportunities through hard work, creativity and taking risk.

Indeed, the very open nature of the Hong Kong economy does suggest that there is a high degree of uncertainty, as one never knows when there is economic upturn or downturn, and how long the upturn or the downturn last. An efficient economic performance does ensure the maximization of economic returns, and higher gain in turn provides a greater sense of economic protection and security.

The empirical results also consider the case of Mainland China in a similar sample period. The situation in Mainland China differed from that of Hong Kong considerably. Most importantly, the Mainland China economy was in her early stage of economic openness, and there was massive inflow of capital. Many foreign direct investments that entered Mainland China contained some degree of advancement in technology. Thus, it is quite obvious that growth in factor inputs and technological progress were responsible for economic growth in Mainland China. However, the empirical results show that inefficiency has increased in Mainland China in the sample period. Possible reasons for the fall in efficiency could be a considerably low level of human capital, a low degree of management knowhow, and an immature market economy.

Due to the difference in the sources of data between Mainland China and Hong Kong, it may not be proper to make a direct comparison on efficiency performance between the two economies. Nonetheless, since the analysis is conducted over a period of time, one can draw some conclusions, observations and implications between their performances. One observation is that despite the frequent call for economic integration, there are still vast differences between the two economies. One positive note is that the differences can work positively if they can complement each other.

Now we know that Hong Kong has made improvement in efficiency. A closely related concept to economic efficiency is competition. Indeed, it is the general belief that economic efficiency shall introduce more competition in the economy. Numerous discussions in recent years have focused on the extent of competition in Hong Kong, and whether key businesses and industries in Hong Kong are controlled by large and monopolistic corporations, leaving little room or business opportunities to individual businesses.

8 Competition

8.1 Introduction

The distinction between competitiveness and competition is that the former refers to the performance of an economy while the latter relates closely to the situation in a market or a product. How competitive the Hong Kong economy is when being compared to its neighboring economies is referred to as economic competitiveness. Economic competitiveness gives the overall, aggregate level of comparison between two or more economies. A number of issues are taken into account when an economy's competitiveness is examined. The availability of economic resources, productivity and efficient performance of economic factors, availability of infrastructure, rule of law and civic establishments, quality of human capital, and extent of technological progress can all contribute to economic competitiveness. The various areas of comparative advantages in an economy are counted in competitiveness. In the Mainland China economy, for example, where land is abundant, the development of land-intensive industries, such as motor car manufacturing and assembly, will increase her economic competitiveness. In Hong Kong where economic freedom and the rule of law prevail, the development of financial services and quality control can promote her overall economic competitiveness.

A number of interesting factors have recently been discussed in relation to Hong Kong's overall economic competitiveness. The slogan of "Asia's world city" used by the Hong Kong authorities since 1997 has constantly been challenged when business people previous used to compare Hong Kong with Singapore, and now with Shanghai in the overall business development in general and financial market development in particular. In the tenth anniversary of the sovereignty change in 2007, Hong Kong has once again been discussed as "one of the easiest and most efficient places in the region to open and run a business, buy or rent property, and register and crew a ship". In 2007, the number of foreign consulates in Hong Kong has risen to 52 with new entrants from Eastern Europe, Africa and Asia, confirming the importance of Hong Kong as a regional hub economy.[1] In another report released in 2007, Hong Kong ranks fifth in the world among global commerce cities after London, New York, Tokyo and Chicago, but the drive to improve environmental pollution has been a major drawback.[2]

According to a survey that compares the corruption performance of a total of 13 Asian economies by the Hong Kong-Based Political and Economic Risk Consultancy in 2007, Hong Kong ranked second, after Singapore, as the least

[1] *South China Morning Post*, June 18, 2007.
[2] *South China Morning Post*, June 13, 2007.

corrupt place to do business in Asia. But the survey warned that Hong Kong's "clean" status could be affected by the weak performance in Mainland China, as cross-border business activities increased. Such a warning should pose challenge to law enforcement authorities in Hong Kong. There are other factors that people consider. For example, the composition of population in Hong Kong can also be another factor. The drop in the number of Caucasians in Hong Kong has been seen as a fall in the attractiveness of the Hong Kong economy. In 2001, according to the Census and Statistics Department, non-Chinese composed of 5.1% of total population (amounted to 7.1 million), but in 2006 the percentage of non-Chinese has dropped to 5% of total population (amounted to 6.86 million). However, the use of non-Chinese population in Hong Kong as an indicator has been challenged, as companies are less willing to provide expatriate employment terms. A growing attraction, however, is the number of young, non-Chinese, that travel to Hong Kong seeking for employment opportunities, even on non-expatriate terms. This is partly because an increasing number of foreigners who want to work in an Asia-related environment, as Asia is still the expanding economic region. Hong Kong has become a new attraction, especially for those who intend to do business in Mainland China.

On the question of competition, one is really talking about the openness of the market in allowing different suppliers to compete among themselves. For example, there has been a great concern on the real estate market in Hong Kong as to whether the market is controlled by a few large developers and there is a lack of competition. Another example can relate to a particular product or service, and how competitive the product or service is when competing with other products and service in the same market. Competition has its own virtue as it ensures that the suppliers will do the best in terms of charging the least feasible and supply the most feasible. Consumer welfare is thus maximized.

In a matured civic society, laws on competition have been legislated to protect the welfare interests of consumers. In many world economies, the purpose of competition or antitrust laws is to prevent anti-competitive business practices and seeks to stop unfair business tactics and abuse of market power to gain excess profits at the expense of consumer welfare. The primary objective of competition law is to maintain and encourage competition so as to promote and maximize economic efficiency and consumer welfare. In a sense, competition laws act as civic rules that help to minimize government intervention in business, as the government can get away from lobby by interests groups for intervention. This is particularly relevant for economies with low administrative capacity and/or an immature institutional structure.

The principle objectives of competition laws shall embrace multiple goals, including balances in public interest and in regional development, and diffusion of market power through the promotion of small- and medium-sized enterprises. It has also been argued that competition laws would interface or cross reference with related issues in other markets or business activities. In other words, competition in one market will affect or spill over to another market. The critics warned that it would be contrary to the original aim of the law if the law ended up protecting some enterprises from competition, and inconsistency in the application of the law. On the contrary, using different policies to achieve different goals in the market could balance a wide range of conflicting social, political and economic concerns. Market liberalization and deregulation would be needed to promote efficiency and competition.

While previous chapters have examined the various aspects of economic competitiveness, this chapter concentrates on the extent of competition in the Hong Kong economy. Given its roots in the *laissez faire* economic principles, authorities in Hong Kong have been reluctant to introduce competition laws believing that economic freedom shall provide opportunities to whoever is interested to enter or exit the market. Furthermore, given the diversity and economic openness, businesses and industries in Hong Kong have passed through various stages of competition. In other words, while some matured businesses and industries have undergone severe competition previously and have come to a more stable market situation, other "new" businesses and industries are at the beginning or the early stage of market competition. Competition also depends on the nature of the business, some of which have a natural tendency not to face too much competition for the business to survive. This is usually referred to as the case of "natural monopoly".

All businesses tend to become stronger and larger in order to face up to competition. In the process of competition, those who remain will become stronger and larger, while the weaker competitors would have exited the market. Many businesses become stronger after passing through the competition process, which could have eliminated the weaker competitors. Nonetheless, businesses are reluctant to be restricted by antitrust laws. The reluctance springs from the fact that should a single law on competition be applied to all businesses and industries that are facing a different stage of competition. Or would it be fair to have one law that suits all? Likewise, given the small and efficient economy, it would equally not be practical to have various competition laws that suit different businesses and industries. This chapter examines the need for such a law in Hong Kong by presenting some theoretical debates, making comparison with other world economies in their development of competition laws, and looking at the data to see how concentrated businesses and industries are in Hong Kong. The latter section attempts to provide a practical solution to ensure competition in the economy.

Section 8.2 examines some theoretical debate and provides a literature review on the economics of competition. Section 8.3 looks at the international experience of antitrust legislation, while Section 8.4 discusses the economic data by working out the concentration ratios in order to see how much or little competition exists in different businesses and industries. Before concluding the chapter, Section 8.5 discusses the institutional dimension as an answer to the antitrust legislation in Hong Kong.

8.2 The Theoretical Debates

Over the years, the academic literatures on the economics of competition have been developed with schools of thoughts providing different theories and insights. Beginning with the more traditional school, the following summarized the key debates in different schools. These debates shall shed lights on the debate in Hong Kong.

Classical and neo-classical

First elaborated by the classical Scottish economist Adam Smith (1776) in *The Wealth of Nations*, the concept and form of competition in economics have been debated for centuries. In introductory economics, competition is often regarded as the opposite of monopoly. The assumptions in the theory of perfect competition include a large number of buyers and sellers so that no one can influence the market price, the provision of perfect market information so that every buyer and seller faces the same information, and all suppliers are selling a homogeneous products. On the contrary, the monopoly is the only seller in the market and can dictate the market price.

At the theoretical level, classical economists argue that competition assures allocation efficiency in the use of resources as price is equated with marginal cost of production. As such, competition ensures that resources are geared to their most productive usage, and prices are forced to their lowest possible level. Competition in classical economics is viewed as a force that assures order and stability in an economy. Given the assumption that information on market and production is perfect, all producers know the best production technique to use. As such, producers are making zero economic profits as all producers use the optimal production technique. By forcing the market price to its "natural" level, firms keep their profits as minimum and economic welfare of individuals as maximum. In short, competition is viewed as a price-determining force operating in a free market.

Adam Smith (1776, Book 1, Chapters 7 and 10) concerned very much about the concentration of market power. Pure and perfect competition defines certain business practice and behavior. On the contrary, the monopolists often keep the market under-stocked and do not fully supply the effectual demand and sell their commodities higher than the natural price. Whenever an industry contains a small number of firms, there will be some market power, and hence the possibility of exploiting consumers by making the goods scarcer and getting a higher price. However, there exist natural monopolies where the fixed cost of investment is so large that competition from another supplier is not possible. Examples of natural monopolies usually include utilities, transport and telecommunications. Economies of scale are the main reason for natural monopolies. Hence, the classical economists believe that by imposing price regulations and exercising anti-trust policies, competition policy can make a difference between the potential advantage in the economies of scale, and the drawbacks of consumer exploitation. The classical theory states that in pure competition, producers or entrepreneurs are compensated for their efficiency in resource allocation, but not in their risk-taking. In reality, information is never perfect, and entrepreneurs has to make their decisions in an uncertain environment, and profits are their return.

In distinguishing between the classical and neo-classical debate on competition, McNulty (1968) argues that classical economists view competition as a regulatory force with the price as the instrument. On the contrary, the neo-classical economists argue that competition has never been related systematically to any production technique. The concept of competition has been associated only with exchange in economic activities. Competition occupies a prime position in economics because of the dominance of exchange in all economic activities. Furthermore, the concept of competition has never been related to the cost of production in a systematic way. Although in classical economics, the function of competition is to achieve price minimization to the level of the marginal cost, suggesting that the cost of production regulates price, the classical school cannot provide an answer as to what regulates the cost of production. Thus, it is possible that the optimality of the price and marginal cost equation does not exist, if the marginal cost is needed to be higher than price due to the required production techniques.

The neo-classical economists argue that production and distribution of goods and services in competitive markets maximized social welfare, and new firms can freely enter markets and compete with incumbent firms. The neo-classical synthesis thus discusses allocative, productive and dynamic efficiency. Allocative efficiency, or Pareto efficiency, means resources in an economy in the long-run will go to those who are willing and able to pay for them. This is because rational producers will keep producing and selling, while consumers will keep buying up to the last marginal unit of output. The ultimate outcome is that there is no waste, the wants of people become satisfied and utility is maximized as resources can no longer be reallocated to make anyone better off without making someone else worse off.

Productive efficiency refers to a situation when the economy is making the most it can. Free entry to markets means the economy's resources are deployed to its production frontier. Dynamic efficiency means that producers have to compete constantly with new creation, innovation and research in order to keep their market share (Schumpeter, 1994).

Contrary to allocative, productive and dynamic efficient market models are monopolies, oligopolies and cartels, where the existence of one or a few firms provides no credible threat of entry of competing firms, and prices are raised above the competitive level. The higher price is maintained due to reduction in production, leading to decrease in social welfare by creating a "deadweight loss". Hence, the existences of externalities, barriers to market entry and free-rider problem are the sources of market power. The neo-classical school believes that intervention via competition law is justified when market failures emerge in a *laissez faire* system. Lipsey and Lancaster (1956–1957) discuss the second best option by using the competition law to tame market operation as the "workable competition". The neo-classical school views free market entry as the ultimate tool to deliver allocative, productive and dynamic efficiency. Thus, competition cannot be defined from results (number of firms) but must be defined from the process (ease of market entry).

Knight (1941) points out that competition is simply the freedom of individuals to deal with all other individuals, but McNulty (1968) argues that a fundamental deficiency in the concept of competition is the simplicity that one economic unit tends to affect the economic position of others, but competitors fails to specify how the competing units act in maximizing their net income. In other words, competitors may twist the term of trade to their own advantage, and that the ability to compete among individuals would result in differential growth and profit rates among competing firms in an industry. Competitors who make efforts in improving their term of trade are effectively getting away from competition itself. There is thus a need to distinguish between competition and market structure.

The neo-classical economists (Hayek, 1960; McNulty, 1968) point out that the classical school's dichotomy between competition and monopoly does not take into account the distinction between market structure and business behavior. In market structure, there is a mixture of different degrees of competition. Indeed, firms cannot compete without monopolizing. Equally, competition is featured highly in contemporary business behavior. The very existence of firms means firms have to compete, and it is only in the process of competition that firms can achieve a higher level of production and profit.

Competition has been linked to capitalism. In taking a holistic view on modern capitalism, Veblen (1904) describes market competition as a "dynamic process of rivalry and contention". Instead of focusing on the market structure, Veblen (1921) relates competition to the state of art in industries that incorporate the market structure, method of production, structure of industries and different sectors in the economy. In discussing the transition from the eighteenth century to the nineteen century, Veblen (1904, 1919 and 1921) argues that free competition with an absence of trade and industry restriction through state regulations occurred in the eighteen century. Market competition was effective because the industrial system was loose, and the producers had more or less equal power as the market was diffused, and there were little or no compulsory state restrictions.

With a greater division of labor and technology advancement, outputs have become standardized. With an increasing usage of credits and the exhaustion of new foreign markets as outlets, a major development in the nineteenth century was the separation between industry and business, and the growth of modern enterprises. While the primary goal of industry is actual production, the goal of business is profit and pecuniary gain. Market competition turned to become business competition to ensure the largest net gain in terms of price, and in turn production would depend on market profitability. With difference in the size of capital and technological variation, the gains from market competition are not distributed equally. Veblen (1921) does not equate market competition with market structure as argued in the neo-classical school, and characterizes market competition as a dynamic process in business behavior that takes place at the corporate, industrial, sectoral, national and international levels simultaneously.

Innovation and competition policy

There are two contrasting concepts in competition policy. Firstly, antitrust authorities have been established in order to control the damaging behavior of firms that naturally try to increase their monopoly power through different means like collusive agreements, merger and acquisitions. Innovative firms, especially technological advance firms, tend to exercise monopolistic power in the market. The antitrust authorities need to step in so as to impose a specific state of affairs on firms' behavior. Secondly, competition policy assumes that there is no optimum in market structure and as firms engaged continuously in the process of innovation, the duty of the antitrust authorities is to prevent market disequilibrium, including market failure, from occurring.

Scholars argue that innovation is central to the concept of competition policy because innovation is thought to bring changes in the economic fundamentals.

Innovation often changes the existing industrial structure and lead subsequently to modification in market conditions. Changes in market conditions included changes in cost of production, profitability, relative prices and modification in consumer preferences. Innovation involves a process of researching, learning and selecting with the outcome of generating new options in production. In the process of innovation, firms or production units do not know *ex ante* whether it is profitable to innovate. The uncertainty in the outcome of innovation implies that market equilibrium, and similarly, market structure can be disrupted (Nelson and Winter, 1982; Metcalfe and Ramlogan, 2005).

Instead of the independent action of a single dominant firm, innovations that being about new alternatives produce new forms of coordination among firms and institutions. With innovation, firms can coexist in the market not only for the presence of increasing returns, but each firm in the market presents a different step in the life cycle of the production process (Gaffard and Quéré, 2006). Firms' increasing returns are often regarded as a transitory competitive advantage that do not systematically involve with market failures, and the need for a regulatory intervention is not called for. Competition can play a primary role in the coordination process in that it helps to make the innovation process viable and the derived productivity gain can be realized. As such, competition does not only help to equalize supply and demand in a given market, but also helps both industrial structure and technology adapt to new opportunities created by expanding markets (Richardson, 1975).

The process of innovation can make a firm more fragile as the firm searches for and learns about new economic opportunities. During the innovation process, for example, firms may make horizontal agreements as a mean to compensate for a temporary increase in investment cost. Instead of exercising abusive market power, such agreements can be legitimated by the high expenditure on innovation. Hence, it is essential for the competition authorities to scrutinize the actual cost structure of the firm and to take account of its innovative characteristics in order to estimate the extent to which the antitrust rules can apply.

Due to the *ex ante* inability of firms to secure their investment returns, innovation is often considered as a source of business uncertainty. Antitrust authorities should show forbearance on joint venture among firms, and not as coordination between firms as a case of market imperfection. At the opposite end, however, imperfect competition is a characteristic of all markets. Quéré (2003) states that imperfect competition is normally associated with firm rivalry that would lead to abusive market power and block innovative choices. Metcalfe (1998) distinguishes between good and bad market imperfections, commonly known as the "market imperfection and market failure" dilemma. On the one hand, market imperfection could be innovation enhancing, but on the other hand, innovation could result in market control and make the market less perfect and more concentrated (Gaffard and Quéré, 2006).

Industrial economics and the Austrian school

In static economic analysis, perfect competition is taken to be synonymous to welfare maximization, and measures that increase the intensity of competition is instantly assumed to enhance welfare. The literature on industrial organization, however, tends to emphasize on competition rather than welfare. In the "structure-conduct-performance" (SCP) paradigm, Bain (1956) considers industries that have a high level of concentration would exhibit dominating market power and charge monopolistic prices, which in turn could affect economic performance and ultimately economic welfare. Economic inefficiencies are found in industry structure, with the causation that runs first from structure to conduct and then to economic performance. The SCP paradigm concludes that economic welfare can be increased when monopolistic situations are replaced by competitive circumstances.

Audretsch *et al.* (2001a) argue that the presence of monopoly rent will lead to allocative inefficiency. Monopoly rent induces agents to siphon-off earnings and the resource loss in the process of monopoly rent collection could otherwise be devoted to production. It is argued that the misallocated resources cumulatively can add up to a value in excess of the monopoly rent. In industrial economics, it has been argued that perfect competition is not constantly perceived as a guarantee of welfare maximization, due largely to the presence of externalities and spillovers which reduced investment in innovation. On the contrary, dominant firms do have a dynamic vision on market competition, and they do not necessarily adopt prices that maximize immediate monopoly profits, as that would encourage entry and competition. These firms may end up pursuing long-term goals in conducting non-price strategies, such as research and development, and advertisement.

The earlier group of critics on competition focused on market dynamics. The Austrian school of economics argues that classical economists have misused the term "competition", as it is considered a state of affairs rather than a process. The static model of competition can only explain where the market would end up, but not how it got there. In other words, the attention has focused on the achievement of equilibrium rather than the adjustment process (Herbert and Link, 1982; Audretsch *et al.*, 2001a). The Austrian school argues that although losers incur loses, it is the winners who earn positive economic profits that spur innovation and growth. Successful firms earn temporary monopoly profits as their reward for the innovative activity (Kirzner, 1973; Shackle, 1972). The Austrian school perceives that competition policy would interfere and regulations are needed only when incumbent firms have substantial monopoly power and undertake little innovation, and industries with negligible barriers to entry should be left to operate without constraint. In short, the Austrian school advocates for a *laissez faire* approach to regulation.

Contestable markets

Baumol (1982) argues that all forms of market structure will have to face competition, and pioneers that markets are "contestable" in that market entry is absolutely free, but not costless, and exit is absolutely costless. Market entry is free but can be costly because the new entrant will have to evaluate its profitability level in relation to the incumbent firms' prices. Firms in a contestable market are vulnerable to the "hit-run-entry" in that the entry of new firms can quickly ripped the profit and exited before price changes. Hence, a perfectly competitive market is necessarily contestable, but a perfectly contestable market is not necessarily competitive. This is because firms in a contestable market can take up difference sizes, cannot control the number of firms in the market, and may not produce homogeneous products. Firms in a contestable market have absolute freedom to exit, and the entry risk is minimized if the departing firms can recoup the cost incurred in the entry process. For example, loss can be minimized if the capital owned by the departing firm is reused.

According to Baumol (1982), there are three welfare attributes in a contestable market. Firstly, firms in a contestable market have zero or negative economic profits, since by definition, a contestable market does not offer more than a normal rate of return even if the market is oligopolistic or monopolistic. The reason is that when the contestable market is still profitable, a transient entrant can replicate a profit-making incumbent's output at a similar cost and undercut the price of the incumbent slightly such that profit can still be earned. In short, freedom of entry allows that a transient entrant can choose a price slightly lower than the incumbent's, and the positive economic profit earned by the incumbent firm constituted automatically an earning opportunity for an entrant.

The second welfare attribute in a contestable market is the absence of inefficiency as production is maintained at its equilibrium level, because any deviation from production equilibrium, such as inefficient organization or reduction in cost, constitutes an invitation to entry. Thirdly, no product can be sold at a price less than its marginal cost of production in the long-run equilibrium in a contestable market. It implies that predatory pricing cannot be used as an instrument of unfair competition. Equally, resources allocation in production is optimal.

In relation to antitrust policy, Baumol (1982) argues that when entry is completely free all potential entrants exercise discipline over the incumbents. To avoid new entrants, monopolistic or oligopolistic firms in the contestable market behave virtuously by offering to consumers the benefits brought about by competition. Any deviation from good behavior instantly makes the monopolistic or oligopolistic firms vulnerable to hit-and-run entry. The lack of entry in a contestable market, therefore, can be a sign of virtue, not vice, since all contestable market firms are behaving virtuously, particularly when the cost of entry is negligible.

On the quality of products in the contestable market, Baumol *et al.* (1982) and Rashid (1988) argue that with a significant amount of investment required, firms have to remain in the business for sometime. This requires that firms have to please customers by providing good quality products. The conclusion is that firms in a contestable market are "governed" by good quality products as firms depended on customers. This guarantees good product quality, and that freedom of entry means that existing firms have to be efficient.

8.3 Antitrust Legislation: International Experience

Extensive coverage has been made on the experience of antitrust legislations in different world economies. The factual descriptions and the historical dimensions of antitrust legislations of different world economies, for example, have been covered in the various publications by the *Global Competition Report*. For example, the *Asia Pacific Antitrust Review* (2008) has provided the factual description of antitrust legislations in Australia, Canada, China, India, Japan, Korea, Papua New Guinea and Singapore. The *Antitrust Review of the Americas* (2009) has provided similar evidence on different industries in the United States and other American countries, including Argentina, Brazil, Canada, Colombia, Mexico and Venezuela. The *European Antitrust Review* (2009) has reported the substantive areas in the European Union and covered a total of twenty three countries.

Antitrust legislations and experiences from major world and Asian economies are worth considering, as they can provide useful lessons for Hong Kong. The experiences of individual countries are considered, and their commonalities can be drawn.

The United States of America and Canada

Antitrust laws in the United States contain a body of laws that prohibited anti-competitive behavior of monopoly firms against unfair business practices. Certain practices that are deemed to hurt businesses and/or consumers or violate standard of ethical behavior have been made illegal. The kinds of activities that are subject to the scrutiny of the antitrust laws include: a) price fixing, which is a price agreement between competitors selling the same product or service; b) bid rigging, which is a form of price fixing and market allocation involving an agreement in which one party of the bidders will be designated to win the bid; c) geographical market allocation, which is an agreement between business competitors not to compete within each other's geographical territories; and d) walker process fraud, which is an illegal monopolization behavior by maintaining and enforcing a patent obtained via fraud in the Patent Office.

The three major federal anti-trust laws of the Sherman Antitrust Act of 1890, the Clayton Act of 1914 and the Federal Trade Commission Act of 1914 are handled by the Antitrust Division of the United States Department of Justice (See Table 8.1).

TABLE 8.1 The antitrust laws in the United States

The Sherman Act 1890:
Prohibitions: trusts in restraints of trade; monopoly trade; trust in territories; price fixing; market division; and bid-rigging. Penalties: The maximum criminal penalties are US$100 million for a corporation and US$1 million for an individual, along with up to 10 years of imprisonment. The maximum fine may be increased to twice the amount that the conspirators gained from the illegal acts or twice the money lost by the victims of the crime, if either of those amounts is over US$100 million.
The Clayton Act 1914:
Prohibitions: mergers and acquisitions that may lessen competition substantially; price discrimination; and exclusive dealings.
The Federal Trade Commission Act 1914:
Prohibitions: unfair method of competition; unfair or deceptive acts of practices; and all other prohibitions of the Sherman Act.

Source: *Federal Trade Commission Guide to the Antitrust Law*, Antitrust and Competition Division, United States Federal Trade Commission.

The Sherman Antitrust Act of 1890: This was the first US government action to restrict monopolies and cartels. The Act states that "Every contract, combination in the form of trust or otherwise, or conspiracy, in restraint of trade or commerce among the several states, or with foreign nations, is declared to be illegal", and that "Every person who shall monopolize, or attempt to monopolize, or combine or conspire with other person or persons, to monopolize any part of the trade or commerce among the several States, or with foreign nations, shall be deemed guilty of a felony".

The Clayton Antitrust Act of 1914: This Act was enacted in order to remedy the deficiencies of the Sherman Antitrust Act of 1890. The Clayton Antitrust Act prohibited particular types of conduct not deemed to be in the interest of a competitive market that the Sherman Antitrust did not. The various practices of monopolies and anticompetitive agreements harmful to consumer were outlawed, including:

(a) price discrimination between purchasers that would substantially lessen competition or tend to create a monopoly in any line of commerce;
(b) exclusive dealings in which sales are based on the condition that the buyers do not deal with the competitors of the sellers, or the buyers also purchase another different product that only when these acts will substantially lessen competition;
(c) mergers and acquisitions with the effects of substantially lessen competition; and
(d) any person being a director of two or more competing corporations.

The Federal Trade Commission Act of 1914: This Act prohibited unfair methods of competition in interstate commerce, but carried no criminal penalties. The Act also led to the establishment of the Federal Trade Commission to police any violation of the Act.

Whether the antitrust legislations in the United States have been successful is a subject of concern. Crandall and Winston (2003) have documented a number of cases, including:

(a) The Standard Oil: A case of market power dominance and price fixing.

The Standard Oil refined and marketed crude oil produced in various states and developed transportation and production facilities in the late 1800s and early 1900s. There were complaints about its business practices in relation to negotiation contracts with railroads and in denying other oil companies in accessing pipelines and transportation facilities. The court's decree dissolved Standard Oil into a large number of separate and independent companies. However, the break up of the Standard Oil has little effect on either consumers or on profit, as the alleged market power had already declined considerably from it heydays.

(b) The American Tobacco Company: A case of market power dominance by trust formation.

By 1910, the American Tobacco Company producing regular cigars, smoking tobacco and cigarettes held at least 75% of sales in the United States. The company obtained its dominant market power through the acquisition of firms and aggressive pricing that resulted in selling price below manufacturing cost. The decree led to the division of cigarette production into three separate firms. But the three-firm oligopoly gave rise to a battle for market share through advertising and not price. Dissolving the company did not bring positive effects to the farmers. The three-firm oligopoly earned similar profit levels, and did little to promote meaningful competition to the tobacco industry.

(c) The Aluminum Company of America: A case of restraining trade and monopolizing the industry.

The Aluminum Company of America in 1909 integrated backwards into mining ore and forward into fabricating products. The company was charged with restraining trade and monopolizing the aluminum industry. The company also controlled the Aluminum Limited of Canada, which provided the largest aluminum import into the United States. The decree required the company to give up its Canadian subsidiary and to terminate contracts with chemical firms and participation in collusive agreements. However, the decree did not reduce the company's dominance in the very small market that could support only one supplier anyway. In 1937, the company was again charged with monopolizing the aluminum market, but the final decree also did not bring any effect on the price of aluminum. As the demand for aluminum grew in the 1950s, new firms have entered the market and the company's natural monopoly position could not be maintained, and its market share dropped.

(d) The AT&T: A case of monopolization.

The US Department of Justice brought a monopolization case against AT&T in 1974. The 1982 decree required AT&T to divest its local operating companies, and that created in several regional Bell companies that provide local telephone service, while AT&T retained its long distance operations and a telephone equipment company. The breakup required by the decree did increase long distance telephone competition and the charges for the long distance telephone service fell. A closer examination, however, would show that the intervention by the antitrust authority was unnecessary, because another federal regulatory agency, the Federal Communication Commission, could promulgate that the Bell companies modify their switching facilities to provide greater access to all long distance users.

(e) The Microsoft Antitrust Case: A case of monopoly on personal computer operating system market.

It began in 1991 with an inquiry by the Federal Trade Commission over whether Microsoft was exercising monopoly practices on the personal computer operating system market (Lopatka and Page, 1999, 2001). Investigation by the Department of Justice that began in 1993 resulted in a settlement in which Microsoft consented not to tie other Microsoft products to the sale of Windows but remained free to integrate additional features into its operating system. In the following year when Microsoft introduced and insisted that Internet Explorer was only a feature and not a product added to Windows. In 1998, the

Department of Justice and twenty other states disagreed and filed another civil action against Microsoft, alleging that Microsoft abused its monopoly power in its handling of the operating system sales and web browser sales. Microsoft was alleged that it has restricted the market for competing web browsers.

Microsoft argued that merging Microsoft Windows and Internet Explorer was the result of innovation and competition. The ruling of the court in 2000 concluded that Microsoft has committed monopolization and required Microsoft to break up into two separate units, with one to produce the operating system and the other to produce software components. In 2001, the Department of Justice reached an agreement with Microsoft to settle the case, it required Microsoft to share its application programming interfaces with third-party companies.

The antitrust laws in the US have also been criticized. Rothbard (1998) claims that the only type of monopoly that should be broken up in *laissez faire* capitalism is coercive monopoly, which is referred to the persistent and exclusive control of a vitally needed resource, good or service, such that the community is at the mercy of the controller. In a coercive monopoly, the firm fixes prices and makes production decisions without any concern to competitive market force. Such a coercive monopoly can only exist through government intervention. Along a similar line, the advocates of free market economics claimed that the principles that underlie antitrust laws are that antitrust laws will do more harm than good. Friedman (1999) argues that monopoly practices like predatory pricing does not work in practice and are better defeated by a truly free market than by antitrust laws. Greenspan (1967) also argues that antitrust laws will discourage businesses from innovation.

The critics to antitrust laws held the view that it is better to rely on competition to govern differences in customer treatment than to rely on detailed government intervention in the pricing and services or product delivery (DiLprenzo, 1985). Schumpeter (1994) points out that government monitoring in market creativity and flexibility will only hamper the free business mechanisms. Creativity that brings above-average returns could in turn generate technical and organization innovation. Indeed, entrepreneurs whom created new products and services would gain above-normal returns for a while before competitive forces set in. There is no need for antitrust laws in this sense, as the perfect information in the market will encourage new competitors.

The Canadian situation differs from that of the US considerably. The industrial revolution in Canada had led to industries concentrated in different regions. Regional concentration itself, however, has no danger as long as the barriers to entry are low. Canada's National Policy Tariff Act in 1879 attempted to stimulate the development of Canada's manufacturing sector through protection by high tariff barriers and blocked foreign firms from entering the concentrated Canadian manufacturing markets. Domestic firms cooperated to achieve high price because of such a tariff, and such collusion was not illegal. There was, however, demands for collusion control that led to the first modern antitrust law in Canada in 1889.

Table 8.2 summarizes the main content of the Competition Act of 1889. According to the Competition Act of 1889, private litigants can apply to the Competition Tribunal for a remedial order for reviewable practices, such as refusal to

TABLE 8.2 Canada's Competition Act of 1889

Prohibitions:

(a) Criminal offences (relations with competitors) included price fixing, agreement concerning quantity and quality of product, other conspiracy offences, and bid-rigging.
(b) Criminal offences (relations with customers) included resale price maintenance, price discrimination and predatory pricing.
(c) Reviewable trade practices (merger) included the acquisition of control over or a significant interest in whole or part of a business if it is found that the merger would have lessen or is likely to prevent competition substantially.
(d) Reviewable trade practices (non-merger) included refusal to deal, exclusive dealing, tied selling, market restriction and abuse of dominant position.

Exemptions:

(a) Refusal to supply/deal: due to the purchaser's poor credit rating, or the supplier is satisfied with its existing distribution network;
(b) Predatory pricing: if it is designed to meet competition or keeping existing customers or obtain new clients;
(c) Reviewable trade practices (merger): mergers in respect of public interest are exempted;
(d) Exclusive dealing/market restriction: if the practice is carried out for a reasonable time so as to facilitate new entrants to the market; and
(e) Tied selling: when the conditions relating to exclusive dealing are not met.

Penalties:

Criminal offences punishable by fine up to 10 million Canadian dollars and/or imprisonment of up to 5 years. Non-criminal provisions can force businesses to put an end to some of their practices.

Source: Bériault and Borgers (2008).

deal, tied sales, exclusive dealing and market restrictions. The Competition Tribunal is a mixed quasi-judicial adjudicative body consisting of judicial and lay members.

Headed by the Commissioner of Competition, the Competition Bureau in Canada is the independent agency that protects and promotes competitive market in Canada, making sure that consumers are fully informed. The Competition Bureau is responsible for the administration and enforcement of the Competition Act and other similar acts, including the Consumer Packaging and Labeling Act, the Textile Labeling Act and the Precious Metal Market Act (Bériault and Borgers, 2008). Despite the success brought about by the 1889 Act, there have been frequent calls for reforms and substantial amendments have been made in the 1970s and 1980s. For example, the competition law contrasted with other industry-specific regulations in areas like telecommunication and natural gas (Ross, 2004).

It has been agreed that Canada's antitrust policies have been used as a weapon to flight big companies or to protect domestic firms from international competition. The focus is to make the economy more efficient through the protection and enhancement of competitive market forces. Similarly, the thinking of *laissez-faire* did not support competition laws because concentration and collusion are somewhat inevitable due to economies of scale and that collusion would be unstable anyway. The *laissez-faire* thinkers and the Chicago School respect the power of the market, and argue that unregulated free markets are still the best generators of wealth and prosperity. Free markets will correct competition problems and many market imperfections are only problems of government actions. Furthermore, there could be limitations of the enforcement officials and courts, and even a well-crafted law may be harmful if it is poorly enforced. It is more relevant to examine efficiency than competition, as healthy competition involved a steady flow of entry and exit in the market. Apparently, antitrust policies designed a long time ago may get outdated, as the ever growing pace of deregulation, privatization, globalization, and network externalities would lead to new forms of strategic alliances and joint ventures business.

European countries

In the European Union (EU), competition law regulated the exercise of market power by large companies, governments or economic entities. The EU competition law prohibited control of collusion and other anti-competitive practices by cartels, preventing the abuse of dominant firms in the market. The EU competition law is governed by Articles 81 and 82 of the European Commission Treaty of 1958, which provided the rules on business practices that limit market competitions. Since May 1, 2004, all national competition authorities are empowered to apply the provisions of the European Commission Treaty in order to ensure there is no distortion on competition within EU. Table 8.3 summarizes the main points of the European Commission Treaty of 1958.

TABLE 8.3 The European Commission Treaty 1958

Articles 81 and 82 Prohibitions: Any abuse by one or more dominant firms within part or whole of the EU market on:

(a) Fix purchases, incorporating selling price and other trading conditions;
(b) Limit or control production, markets, technical development or investment;
(c) Share markets or sources of supply;
(d) Give dissimilar conditions to equivalent transactions with other trading parties; and
(e) Making a contract conditional on factors irrelevant to the subject of the contract.

Exemptions:

Apply to agreements that allowed consumers a fair share of the resulting benefit that do not impose restriction or eliminate competition.

Penalties:

Fines up to 10% of their worldwide turnover for firms which make agreements and concerted practices that distort competition within the EU market.

Source: *The European Commission Treaty 1958*, The EU.

Consumer International (2007) has provided consumer welfare analysis on three specific retail markets (paracetamol, printer ink cartridges and petrol) in the EU member states with the intention to identify regulatory barriers to competition and encourage consumers to be proactive in making informed choices in their consumption. In the case of paracetamol, its price is generally cheaper than those branded products such as Panadol, but consumer awareness is low and sales among EU member states tended to be modest. The question is whether a harmonized EU policy on the sale of paracetamol is needed. In the case of printer ink cartridges, there have been a number of cheaper alternatives to the manufacturer's own brand. The market for these alternatives was supposed to be openly competitive, but the take up of these alternatives has been low. For the printer manufacturers, technical tactics are used to secure their market for ink cartridges. In the case of petroleum, the question is cross-border consumption when taxes varied significantly between neighboring EU states, and prices are highest on motorways as inconvenience of seeking alternative petrol stations made petrol stations in the motorways a semi-captive market. Consumer International (2007) pointed to the importance of institutions in competition law enforcement. For example, consumer involvement should be encouraged in setting policy, in monitoring market abuses and in seeking compensation when occurred. The *ex-ante* involvement of individual consumers and consumer organizations has been more successful than the *ex-post* judicial procedures and complaints.

The United Kingdom

The Office of Fair Trading (OFT) in the UK is the consumer and competition authority. It aimed to ensure market works for consumers by encouraging businesses to comply with competition and consumer law, and empowering consumer with knowledge and skills so as to make informed market choices. The competition laws are governed by the Articles 81 and 82 of the European Commission Treaty and Chapters I and II of the Competition Act of 1948. The law firstly prohibited anti-competitive agreements on prices for goods and services, on limiting production, on market carve ups and on consumer discrimination, and secondly prohibited the abuse of a dominant market position including the charge of an excessive high price, refusing to supply to customers with long standing, charging different prices to different customers and making a contract conditional on factors which are irrelevant to the subject of the contract.

In the case of penalties, businesses can be fined up to 10% of their annual world-wide turnover. Small businesses may be immune from financial penalties, but no immunity will be granted to businesses involved in price-fixing agreements. Company directors whose company has breached competition law may receive disqualification orders that will prevent them from getting involved in the company's management for up to 15 years.

Utton (2000) remarks that the introduction of competition policy in the UK took place during the time of the nationalization process and price controls were popular. Heath (1961) and Swann *et al.* (1974) find that competition policy did lead to increase in price competition in the short-run, and there were gains in technical and allocative efficiency together with a reduction in excess capacity in the medium run.

These studies, however, also discovered that information agreements involving pre-notification of price changes were made. Although the law was tightened in the Restrictive Trade Practices Act of 1968, firms still continued with restrictive practices by other means. The authorities in the UK have been hampered by the limited scope for proceeding against firms which have no ostensible agreements but in practice appeared to act together.

Furthermore, it is difficult to access monopoly because the behavior of dominant forms can be varied. Shaw and Simpson (1989) conclude that normal competition processes involving new entry and import growth had greater impact on dominant firm performance than the implementation of the recommendations of the antitrust authorities. The experience in the UK showed that it is easier to monitor restrictive agreements than single firm dominance. Mergers usually involved two firms, but their indirect impacts are more difficult to identify than direct impacts. There have been major proposals for reforming the Competition Act.

Clarke *et al.* (1998) point out a couple of criticisms on the competition policy in the UK. One is that the penalties for the infringing competition policy were too weak to provide effective deterrents. The sanction to companies that have been operating unregistered agreements was just to declare the agreement void and any contract made under it unenforceable. Secondly, the Monopoly and Mergers Commissions have to start from a completely neutral position, and there was no presumption that the referred merger was likely to operate against the public interest. The phraseology of the Competition Act has also been criticized in that it has weighted the scale in favor of those companies wishing to merge.

Belgium and the Netherlands

Both Belgium and the Netherlands are small open economies with similar economic characteristics. Belgium has adopted a new antitrust legislation similar to the EU in 1993, but the Netherlands continued to implement their own antitrust laws until 1998. Konings *et al.* (2001) examine the effect of competition law in these two European countries. Two issues are considered: 1) whether competition law would have an effect on the mark-up of firms; and 2) whether the presence of competition law would lead to lower mark-ups between Belgium and the Netherlands. After the introduction of the competition law in 1993 in Belgium, the mark-up actually increased, instead of decreased, while the mark-up in the Netherlands first declined and then increased again. On average, the mark-up is higher in the Netherlands than in Belgium. The presumption of a decrease in the cost-price margin after the introduction of the competition policy was declined.

There can be a number of explanations on why the competition laws implemented in Belgium did not have an effect on the price-cost margin of Belgium firms. One explanation is that being a small economy, Belgium firms would behave competitively and the existing price system together with competition from imports was sufficient to discipline firms' behavior. The higher price mark-up in the Netherlands suggested that Dutch firms behaved more anti-competitively than Belgium firms, and the Netherlands has been seen as a cartel paradise, thus a tougher competition policy is needed. The experience in the Netherlands pointed to the importance on the behavior of small firms in a dynamic situation in that the relatively modest small market shares upon entry tended to increase in subsequent years, and that new and small firms can become a significant source of innovative activity (Audretsch *et al.*, 2001b).

Australia and New Zealand

There are two key competition authorities in Australia. The National Competition Council (NCC) is a policy advisory body that concerned the development and implementation of competition policy, and advised the government on natural monopolies as to whether such markets can open to competition from third parties. The Australian Competition and Consumer Commission (ACCC) is an independent statutory authority formed in 1995 to administer the Trade Practice Act of 1974 and other similar acts. The major functions of ACCC are to ensure that businesses and individuals comply with fair trading, consumer protection and competition, and regulate national infrastructure industries. Table 8.4 summarizes the major content of the Trade Practice Act of 1974.

In New Zealand, the agency that regulated competition is the Commerce Commission which was set up in 1986 under Section 8 of the Commerce Act. The Commerce Commission ensured that all goods and services are provided at competitive prices. As such, industries are constrained from making excessive profits but shall share their efficiency gains with their customers. Table 8.5 shows the ingredients of the Commerce Act of 1986.

Mainland China and Chinese Taipei

The three government agencies in Mainland China that exercised authority over competition policy are the State Administration of Industry and Commerce (SAIC), the National Development and Reform Commission (NDRC), and the Ministry of Commerce (MOFCOM). In March 2003, MOFCOM was formed from the amalgamation of the Ministry of Foreign Trade and Economic Cooperation (MOFTEC), the State Economic and Trade Commission (SETC) and the relevant sections of the State Development Planning Commission (SDPC) (Bush, 2008).

The first law on competition since economic reform in Mainland China was promulgated by the Standing Committee of the National People's Congress (NPC) that gave rise to the Unfair Competition Law of 1993, which is administered by SAIC, and focused on intellectual property and consumer protection issues. The 1993 Law prohibited business restrictive practices, such as predatory pricing and bid rigging, and ensured fair market competition (Bush, 2008). The second law, the Price Law, was promulgated in 1997 with the objective to strengthen the role of price in rational disposition of resources. The 1997 Price Law is enforced by NDRC, which is a research and policy-making agency that focused on price control policies and prohibited anti-competitive business practices like predatory pricing and price discrimination.

In relation to foreign investment and enterprises, MOFCOM issued in 2003 the Provisional Rules for Mergers and Acquisitions of Domestic Enterprises by Foreign

TABLE 8.4 Australia's Trade Practice Act of 1974

Offences and Prohibitions:

(a) Price fixing and other collusive agreements between competitors;
(b) Market sharing and bid-rigging;
(c) "Third line forcing", refers to tying arrangements in which the supply of goods by one person is conditional upon the acquirer acquiring goods from another person;
(d) Minimum resale price maintenance;
(e) Acquisition of shares and assets;
(f) Misuse of market power;
(g) Exclusive dealing arrangements between suppliers and customers; and
(h) Horizontal and vertical arrangements.

Exemptions:

(a) Applies when price-fixing provisions are for the purpose of joint venture;
(b) Applies to arrangements between competitors ancillary to a wider pro-competitive joint venture agreement.

Consumer Protection Provisions:

(a) Firms ensure the true advertising and promotional materials and accurate public statements and packaging; and
(b) Access to essential infrastructure operated by natural monopoly firms is allowed.

Penalties:

(a) Maximum pecuniary penalties are the greater of an Australia dollar 10 million per contravention, or three times the gain from the contravening conduct, or when the gain cannot be ascertained, 10% of the annual turnover of the group of companies to which the contravening company belongs.
(b) Jail terms for serious cartel conducts have been considered.

Source: Armitage and Hellman (2008).

TABLE 8.5 New Zealand's Commerce Act of 1986

Prohibitions:

(a) Restrictive or anti-competitive trade practices including: substantially lessening competition, exclusion of competitors; price fixing; taking advantage of market power; and resale price maintenance.
(b) Mergers and acquisitions to lessen competition substantially are prohibited.

Exemptions:

(a) Price fixing: applied when there is no substantial lessening of competition, such as joint ventures involving joint purchase or advertising.
(b) Mergers and acquisitions: proposed acquisition will not lead substantially to lessening of competition in the market, or that the benefits enjoyed by the public are found to outweigh the detriments.

Source: *The Commerce Act 1986*, Government of New Zealand.

Investors, with the objectives of encouraging foreign investment in China, introduction of advanced foreign technology and management experiences, realization of proper resources allocation, job opportunities security, maintenance of fair competition and economic security. The latest Anti-Monopoly Law 2007 aimed to restrict monopolistic practices, ensured fair competition, enhanced economic efficiency and maintained the interests of both consumers and the public. Table 8.6 summarizes the major content of the 2007 Law.

In Chinese Taipei, the Executive Yuan is the central authority in charge of the competition policy. The Fair Trade Act of 1992 comes under the duty of the Fair Trade Commission that prepared and formulated the fair trade policy, laws and regulations, and reviewed all fair trade matters related to the 1992 Act, investigated activities of enterprises that violated the Fair Trade Act of 1992. Table 8.7 summarizes the key contents of the 1992 Fair Trade Act in Chinese Taipei.

Japan and South Korea

The Japan Fair Trade Commission (JFTC) is the government's administrative agency set to fulfill the objectives of the Fair Trade (Anti-Monopoly) Act of 1947. As an independent administrative commission, the JFTC exercised its power with no direction

TABLE 8.6 Mainland China's Anti-Monopoly Law of 2007

Prohibitions:

(a) Horizontal and vertical monopoly agreements: prohibited horizontal agreements among competing undertakings on price fixing, limit production or sales volume and market division; vertical agreements include fixing minimum resale price.
(b) Abuse of dominance: prohibited predatory pricing, refusal to deal, exclusive dealing, tying and discrimination.
(c) Merger review: concentrations that included mergers, acquisition of control over other undertakings through equity and asset purchases and contracts should be notified and approved in advance.

Exemptions:

(a) Agreements that can improve technology, promote R&D, increase quality, reduce cost, promote efficiency and contribute to disaster relief or public interest.
(b) Concentrations can be approved if it can be proved that the concentration can result in positive effects on competition that outweighs the negative effects operating in the public interest.

Penalties and Consequences of Contravening Conducts:

(a) Penalties to enterprises that enter monopoly agreements or abuse of dominance include confiscation of illegal gains, fines and orders to cease the offending conduct.
(b) For concentration, corrective measures and fines are imposed to enterprises that violate the provisions.

Source: Bush (2008).

TABLE 8.7 The Fair Trade Act of 1992, Chinese Taipei

Prohibitions:

(a) Against monopolies: prohibited monopolistic enterprises to: i) prevent any other enterprises from competing by unfair means, ether directly or indirectly; ii) fix the price of goods or remuneration for services improperly; iii) make a trading counterpart to give preference treatment with no justification; and iv) abuse its market position.
(b) Against mergers: i) enterprise/s will have one third of the market share after merger; ii) one of the enterprise in the merger has one forth of market share; and iii) sales of the preceding fiscal year of an enterprise in the merger exceeds the threshold amount announced by the competition authority.
(c) Against concerted actions: prohibited any enterprises to have concerted actions.
(d) Against unfair competition: actions that lessened or impeded fair competition include: i) causing another enterprise to discontinue supply, purchase or business transactions with a particular enterprise so as to harm such particular enterprise; ii) treating another enterprise discriminatively with no justification; iii) cause the trading counterparts of its competitors to deal with itself by coercion or any other improper means; iv) causing another enterprise to refrain from price competition by improper means; v) acquiring the secret of production information of trading counterparts or technology of other enterprises by coercion or any other improper means; and vi) limiting the business activities of the trading counterparts by improper means of the requirements of business engagement. It also prohibits any enterprises to make or use false or misleading representations or symbols, and statements.

Exemptions:

(a) A merger may be approved if the overall economic benefit of the merger outweighs the disadvantages results from restricted competition.
(b) Concerted action is exempted if it is beneficial to the economy and in the public interest, including those that unify models of goods so as to reduce cost, improve quality or increase efficiency, joint research on goods or markets so as to upgrade technology, promotes exports or strengthens trade, joint actions to improve operational efficiency or strengthens the competitiveness of small and medium enterprises.

Penalties and Consequences of Contravening Conducts:

Cease or rectify the conduct of the enterprise, punish by fine or imprisonment.

Source: *Fair Trade Act 1992*, Fair Trade Commission, Taipei.

or supervision from any higher organ of the government. Table 8.8 summarized the key contents of the 1947 Act.

There are other competition laws that subsequently supplement the 1947 Act. The Subcontracts Act 1956 regulates the abusive practices of dominant bargaining position, and the late payment or reduced payment of subcontract prices. The Premiums and Representations Act of 1962 regulates the deceptive representations and advertisements regarding quality, contents and prices of goods. It also provides

TABLE 8.8 The 1947 Fair Trade Act of Japan

Prohibitions:

(a) Acts that monopolized the market: entrepreneurs cannot exclude competitors from the market, or restrict business activities of new entrants, and dominant entrepreneurs cannot control the market through acquisition of stock and restrain business activities of other entrepreneurs.

(b) Acts that restrained competition with other entrepreneurs: cartel formation, bid-rigging, participation in international cartel, and activities by trade associations.

(c) Acts that impeded fair competition: refusal to deal, discriminatory pricing and treatment, unjust low price sales (except they are bargain sales or dispose of perishable or seasonal products at low prices), unjust high price purchasing, tie-in-sales, abuse of dominant bargaining position, resale price restriction, dealing on exclusive and restrictive terms, interference with competitor's transactions, and interference with internal operations of competitors.

(d) Business combinations or activities that restrained competition: mergers, divisions, acquisition of business, stockholding, interlocking directorates, excessive concentration of economic power, holding of voting rights by a bank or an insurance company (unless they are approved by JFTC or permitted by law).

Penalties:

(a) Surcharge rates: the amount is calculated by multiplying sales amounts of products or services in questions during the period.

(b) Criminal: imprisonment or monetary fines are imposed.

Source: *For Fair and Free Competition*, 2006, Japan Fair Trade Commission.

for the maximum and total amount of premiums so as to prevent offering of excessive premiums. The Elimination and Prevention of Involvement in Bid Rigging Act of 2002 provides measures to eliminate and prevent involvement in anti-competitive practices like bid-rigging, and punishments are imposed on employees whose acts are harmful to fair bidding.

Criminal accusations are common in Japan. In 1974, criminal accusation was given against a cartel involving twelve oil wholesalers for violations of the Fair Trade Act of 1947. In 1995 and 2005, respectively, criminal accusations were given against bid-rigging cases concerning electric equipment installation work and steel bridge construction projects.

In the case of South Korea, the Korea Fair Trade Commission (KFTC) is a ministerial-level administrative organization that comes under the Prime Minister, and it aimed to promote competition, strengthen the rights of consumers and restrained concentration of economic power. The KFTC also formulated and administered competition policies and functions independently without intervention from another organization (Jung and O'Brien, 2008). Table 8.9 summarizes the major coverage of the Monopoly Regulation and Fair Trade Act of 1980 in South Korea.

TABLE 8.9 The 1980 Monopoly Regulation and Fair Trade in South Korea

Prohibitions:

(a) Against the abuse of market-dominant positions: price abuse, output control, obstruction of competitors' business activities, market entry blockage, and exclusion of competitors and damaging consumer interest. A market-dominant company occurred when the company has a market share of 50% or more, or when the largest three companies with a combined market share of 75% or more.
(b) Against improper cartels: concerted acts and collaborative behaviors, joint engagements in price fixing, territorial or customer allocation or hindrance or restrictions of other companies to restrain competition.
(c) Against distribution and vertical restraints: exclusive dealing, customer or territorial restrain, refusal to deal, discrimination, tying or transactions with conditions, unfair transactions, abuse of superior bargaining position, interference with management and resale price maintenance.

Exemptions:

(a) A company is not presumed to be market-dominant if a company has an annual turnover of less than 1 billion won or a market share of less than 10%.

Penalties:

(a) To market dominant companies: an administrative charge of up to 3% of the annual turnover or up to 1 billion won, or an order against the dominant company to reduce process or to discontinue the infringement.
(b) To improper cartels: order the company to issue a public announcement on the violation, and impose an administrative surcharge of up to 10% of the revenue generated during the relevant period.
(c) To distribution and vertical restraints: minimum resale price maintenance is deemed illegal, apply the "rule of reason" to investigate if vertical restraints can improve economic efficiency or consumer welfare and the extent by which pro-competitive effect outweighs the anti-competitive effect.

Source: Jung and O'Brien (2008).

Singapore and ASEAN

The Competition Commission in Singapore is a statutory body established under the Competition Act of 2004. Besides the task of administering and enforcing the 2004 Act, the Commission aimed to promote the efficient functioning of markets by curbing anti-competitive activities. The duties of the Commission included: a) maintain and enhance efficient market conduct and promote productivity, innovation and competitiveness; b) eliminate and control business practices that have an adverse effect on competition; and c) advise the government and other public authorities on policies in respect of competition. As a statutory body, the Commission has the investigation and adjudication power on anti-competitive activities and to impose

TABLE 8.10 Singapore's Competition Act of 2004

Prohibitions:

(a) Anti-competition agreements: agreements with the objective or effect to prevent, restrict and distort competition.
(b) Abuse of dominant position: the infringing party holds a dominant position in the relevant market.
(c) Control of mergers: mergers with the result of lessening of competition.

Exemptions:

Prohibitions will not apply to merger situations that result in net economic efficiency, are approved by the minister, the Monetary Authority of Singapore or any regulatory authority, are governed by the competition legislation such as energy and telecommunication industries, and are related to public goods.

Source: Lim and Clements (2008).

sanctions (Lim and Clements, 2008). Table 8.10 shows the main points of the 2004 Competition Act.

The Association of Southeast Asian Nations (ASEAN) composed of Indonesia, Malaysia, Philippines, Thailand, Singapore, Cambodia, Myanmar, Laos, Brunei and Vietnam. Among all ASEAN members, only four countries of Thailand, Indonesia, Singapore and Vietnam have implemented competition law. When compared to the economic structure of all ASEAN members, Sivalingam (2006) argues that differences in economic growth and foreign direct investment inflow could explain why these four ASEAN members introduced competition law earlier than the others.

In the case of Thailand, the two laws on competition are the Price Fixing and Anti-Monopoly Act of 1979, and the Thailand Trade Competition Act of 1999. In Indonesia, the legislation on the Prohibition of Monopolistic Practices and Unfair Business Competition was established in 2000. For Vietnam, the Competition Act was established in 2005. Together with Singapore, these four ASEAN countries enacted their competition legislation due to different reasons.

The Thailand Competition Act of 1999 was established due to the International Monetary Fund (IMF) conditionality for financial assistance in the Asian financial crisis in 1997. Similarly, even though the Indonesian government was reluctant to introduce competition legislation initially, the IMF made it a condition that competition law should be introduced in exchange of its financial assistance in the Asian financial crisis in 1997. Despite Singapore's argument of international competitiveness, the US-Singapore Free Trade Agreement in 2003 required Singapore to introduce sound economic policies.

In order to satisfy the demands from a membership into the World Trade Organization (WTO) and the Vietnam–US Bilateral Trade Agreement in 2001, Vietnam enacted its competition legislation is 2005. The Vietnam–US Bilateral Trade Agreement in 2001 required Vietnam to broaden its market-oriented reforms, to reduce barriers of trade, investment and services, and to create fair and transparent rules for the US investors (Vietnam Country Commercial Guide, 2003). It seemed that both Indonesia and Thailand introduced their competition laws while they were suffering from economic and financial distress. At the same time, Singapore and Vietnam introduced their competition legislation with the purpose to promote trade and integration with United States and the world economy.

There are similarities and differences in the objectives of the competition laws among the four ASEAN nations. For Thailand, the objective of the Thailand Competition Act aimed to foster competition so as to ensure fair and free trade within a competitive environment. The attainment of efficient pricing can increase the consumer choice in terms of products and services offered. For Indonesia, the objective of its competition legislation was to create a conductive business climate by preventing restrictive business practices and by creating effective and efficient enterprises. For Singapore, the objective of its 2004 Competition Act was to enhance efficient market conduct and promote productivity, innovation and competitiveness. For Vietnam, the objectives of its Competition Act of 2005 were to promote an equitable market environment, encourage fair competition, prevent restrictive business practices, protect the interests of the state, businesses and consumers, and promote socio-economic development.

Sivalingam (2006) notes that due to different conditions in each of the four ASEAN countries, there are variations in the competition legislation introduced in these four countries. For example, not all of the four countries emphasize on efficient market, productivity and innovation. Indonesia does not focus on efficient markets, while Thailand and Vietnam do not emphasize on productivity and innovation. In the jurisdiction coverage of the competition laws, the Thailand Trade Competition Act did not apply to central, provincial and local administration and state-owned enterprises. Practices of groups of farmers' cooperatives recognized by law and operated by farmers and businesses prescribed by Ministerial Regulation were also exempted from the competition legislation of Thailand. For Indonesia, the competition legislation did not apply to state-owned entities, which included monopolies, small and medium enterprises and cooperatives. For Singapore, the public sector was excluded from complying with the requirements of the Competition Act. The public sector included government authorities and statutory bodies and other semi-regulated industries like telecommunications, media, transportation, energy and waste disposal. In Vietnam, exemptions from competition legislation ranged from government agencies and state-owned enterprises, intellectual property rights, research and development activities, to small and medium enterprises.

In the case of horizontal agreements, the competition legislation in all four ASEAN countries prohibited horizontal agree-ments like price fixing. Thailand's competition legislation prohibits price fixing and geographical market division especially in cases that resulted in monopoly profits gained by parties to the agreement. However, there are still some exemptions. The Trade Competition Commission, the competition authority, was empowered to decide if the horizontal agreements can promote business and if they affect efficiency and consumer welfare adversely. For Indonesia, horizontal agreements like price fixing which caused unfair business competition, predatory pricing, division of market so as to provide exclusive dealership, boycotting, formation of cartels and agreements to control supplies to influence prices were all prohibited. The "rule of reason" criterion did not apply and thus, it appeared that all the horizontal agreements with restrictive practices were illegal *per se*.

The competition legislation in Singapore prohibited horizontal agreements as *per se* illegal within Singapore. However, exemptions are given to those horizontal agreements which will improve production or distribution and promote technical or economic progress. As such, the "rule of reason" criterion will only be applied to those horizontal agreements which are anti-competitive and have a negative net economic benefit. In Vietnam, its competition law provided exemptions for horizontal agreements which can promote research and development, increase the efficiency in production and distribution, increase the business capacity of SMEs, improve the quality of goods and services and increase the international competitiveness of enterprise in Vietnam. In all, horizontal agreements are illegal for all four countries. However, the "rule of reason" criterion can be applied to exemptions for Thailand, Singapore and Vietnam. Only Indonesia does not have provision for enterprises to apply the "rule of reason" criterion.

There have been different arguments concerning vertical restraints. Some argue that vertical restraints may decrease consumer welfare, while others argued that vertical agreements may increase profits, technical and allocative efficiency. Bork (1966) argues that manufacturers may find it profitable to impose vertical restraints when consumers received a net benefit. That is, manufacturers would impose vertical restraints to encourage distributors to supply services and when they can get higher profit by increasing sales. Consumption will then increase when the value of supplied services exceeded the additional charge, which is included by the distributor to pay his expenses. Thus, vertical restraints increased profits from manufacturing when consumers received net benefits from increased services.

With regards to the competition legislation on vertical agreements, there is harmonization in all three ASEAN countries except Singapore. The vertical restraints in Indonesia, Thailand and Vietnam are illegal per se, while the Competition Act in Singapore evaluated the effect of the vertical agreements on a cost-benefit basis. Singapore has adopted a policy which is close to the reasoning raised by Bork (1966) in dealing with vertical restraints.

In situations of abuse by companies in the dominant position, anticompetitive practices of firms of dominant positions such as price fixing and tie-in-sales are considered as illegal *per se* in both Thailand and Indonesia. The Competition Commission of Singapore will consider a dominant firm to be practicing predatory pricing as an abuse if it finds a history record showing that such firm has lowered prices consistently to drive out new entrants. The Competition Act of Singapore has "rule of reason" provision in determining reported cases of abuse of dominant position. Exemptions are given to dominant firms which can show that they are serving a general economic interest or they are efficient. In Vietnam, exemptions are given to enterprises with dominant position whose activities can improve the quality of goods, promote technological innovation or improve consumer welfare. In conclusion, there is harmonization in competition laws in both Thailand and Indonesia in that both countries considered the abuse of dominant practices illegal *per se*. Singapore and Vietnam applied a "rule of reason" to test whether such a type of abuse is illegal.

In relation to mergers, there is no harmonization in competition laws in all the four ASEAN countries. Singapore and Thailand have the "rule of reason" in dealing with the restrictive practices of mergers. Mergers are prohibited if they substantially lessen competition in a relevant market. However, for Singapore, a "rule of reason" is applied in accessing whether the actions of mergers are anti-competitive. Mergers are exempted when they promote innovation, productivity or longer term economic efficiency. For Thailand, mergers may be exempted if such mergers are beneficial to business promotion or they have no serious harm on the economy. In both Vietnam and Indonesia, on the other hand, the anti-competitive effects of mergers are illegal *per se*. However, in Vietnam, enterprises in mergers may still apply for exemption.

Singleton (1997) observes that the exempted activities from competition law of the four ASEAN countries reflected mainly the prevailing conditions in many developing countries, such as low technological bases, small domestic markets, shallow finance, and limited judicial and bureaucratic capabilities. Fox (1991) argues that there should be other laws that address social concerns, and that competition laws just ensured a proper functioning of market supply and demand, and that society's resources are allocated efficiently.

8.4 The Hong Kong Experience

Institutionally, the Hong Kong Consumer Council (HKCC), which is a statutory body established in 1974, is rested with the responsibility to speak for the consumers and is committed to enhance consumer welfare. The HKCC has taken the lead to arouse the general public and government attention to the consequences of monopolistic markets and anti-competitive business behavior in Hong Kong. In the 1990s, for example, the HKCC has launched a series of studies on market concentration and anti-competitive behavior of firms and their impact on consumer welfare in many services in Hong Kong. The studies on the service sector included the markets for bank deposits, supermarkets, gas supply, telecommunications, radio broadcasting and residential property (Consumer Council, 1994a, 1994b, 1996a, 1996b, 1999, 2000, 2003, 2007a, 2007b). Their studies show that there is a low level of market competition and barriers to entry are high.

Supermarkets

The Consumer Council's *Supermarket Industry in Hong Kong* (1994b) reported that supermarkets were first established in the 1950s in Hong Kong, but by the 1980s, the supermarket industry has matured and has been characterized by two dominant supermarket chains that have a combined market share of approximately 70% of total supermarket sales. Although there were two new entrants in the supermarkets in the 1990s, but their business quickly collapsed and exited within a few years. Williams (2007) found that market dominance of the two supermarkets has expanded by 29% between 1993 and 2003.

The Consumer Council report noted that the market position of the two supermarkets will not likely be challenged in the foreseeable future, as there is significant barrier to entry due to the extensive network of outlets of the two big chains, the high start-up cost and high rental cost would naturally inhibit the financial ability of new entrants, especially if the entrant is to have an effective competitive threat to the market dominance of the two supermarkets. The dominant position of the two supermarkets has significant bargaining power over suppliers, including demands for exclusive agreements and choice of products. There is, however, little price competition between the two supermarkets, suggesting a large degree of similarity on items. However, in another report in 2003, the Consumer Council reported that the price of foodstuff in supermarkets has increased substantially during the five-year deflationary period in Hong Kong. The Consumer Council recommended a monitoring system to be established for the supermarket sector so that power is given to investigate the anti-competitive complaints against incumbent firms.

The arguments proposed by the Consumer Council have been debated contrarily. Firstly, it would not be entirely right to compare supermarkets with small retail shops or food stalls in the fresh food market due to the large scale operations of the supermarkets, the kind of services provided, the wider choice of product displayed and the location advantages of the supermarkets. As such, supermarkets are different industry from that of corner retail shops or stalls in the fresh food or wet market. The large share of the two supermarkets could reflect the cost structure rather than a monopolized industry. The concentration of the supermarkets might reflect the need to capture the economies of scale and scope, which can result in an improvement in the quality of the products and price mix that provides a better service to the consumers.

The case of the supermarkets actually brings out another related issue in competition law, namely regulations on cross-sector competition, mergers and acquisitions. The two key supermarkets are related to other businesses in Hong Kong. One supermarket belongs to a conglomerate that has multiple businesses in property development, property management, and chain operation in electrical retail and in drugstore. The other belongs to a conglomerate that runs a network of convenience stores and a competing chain of drugstores. The more relevant concern is the cross-sector competition in case when the same real estate developer allows its own chain of supermarket to be located in the same property estate that may have taken away the consumption choice of the residents and the potential competition from other supermarket operators.

The core question is not so much the freedom for corporations to establish cross-sector businesses, but the extent of market control that the corporation can exercise. Typically, armed with strong property development business, the corporation can use its own new property development in ensuring good locations for its own supermarket chains. Competitors are naturally disadvantaged.

Residential property market

The Consumer Council's report on *How Competitive is the Private Residential Property Market* (1996a) argued that Hong Kong's residential property market is highly concentrated and anti-competitive in the practice of alternating sales, releasing flats in batches and not selling completed units, and recommended that the government should take measure to lower the barriers of entry by making more smaller lots available for auctions and give preference to smaller developers in projects that are controlled by the government.

It has been argued, in addition to the findings in the Consumer Council (1996b) report, that the missing link in Hong Kong's property sales is a standardized method of calculating the saleable areas, the somewhat manipulative manner in which new properties are released to the market, including the release of the property price and the various fees and charges. In addition, there is also the problem of cross-sector business. Property developers also establish property management companies to manage their own residential properties. Residents and consumers thus are not given the chance of having an "independent" property management alternative.

Legal services

The anti-competitive concerns in Hong Kong's legal profession have concentrated on its antiquated practices. There still existed a strict division of the profession into solicitors and barristers, despite the fact that such a tradition has been abandoned in most other major common law jurisdictions (Cheng and Wu, 1998). In relation to the issue on the rights of audience in the higher courts to be extended to qualified solicitors, the Law Society that represented the solicitor profession firmly believed that it is in the interests of court users and the public that higher rights of audience are granted to solicitors. The Law Society of Hong Kong (2006) affirmed that public confidence in the court system would be enhanced by giving more choices, reducing costs as well as raising standards of advocacy. However, the Hong Kong Bar Association (2006) refused to fuse the two branches of the legal practitioners into a single profession or to extend the rights of audience in the higher courts to competent solicitors. From the point of view of the general public and solicitors, the restriction on rights of audience is undoubtedly the attempt to continue the monopoly of barristers in the higher courts.

The two-counsel rule, which is another restrictive practice of tie-in-sales, led to increase in legal expenses. Barristers are divided into Senior Counsel and junior barristers. The two-counsel rule means that a Senior Counsel cannot appear in a court or tribunal without the appearance of a junior barrister. Another tie-in-sales practice of the mandatory intermediation by a solicitor whenever the public needed to use the service of a barrister has also been opposed on the grounds of redundancy and inefficiency (Cheng and Wu, 1998).

The legal profession in Hong Kong has not been plagued by anti-competitive practices by dominant legal firms, but anti-competitive issues have been resulted from its long tradition, restrictions and regulations. Examples of anti-competitive practices in the profession included unreasonable restrictions on the rights to conduct trials in higher courts, the two-counsel rule, mandatory intermediation, admissions criteria not based entirely on competency, scale fees and the lack of price information.

Reform within the legal profession in Hong Kong is needed in order to be in line with international standards. The abolition of mandatory conveyance scale fees, which is an anti-competitive business practice of price fixing, announced by the

Law Society on September 1, 1997, was definitely a positive development and an effective tool to increase competition in the legal services industry in Hong Kong. The abolition of other malpractices of the two-counsel rule and mandatory intermediation and increased transparency on professional practices to the public can undoubtedly increase efficiency in the legal profession (Cheng and Wu, 1998).

Public goods

Over the years, a number of public goods and services are run by the private sector under a monopoly franchise granted by the government. Such a practice follows the *laissez-faire* economic policy to minimize government intervention but at the same time the government acting on behalf of the public can oversee the quality of supply and the price charged. Examples of government franchise included buses, power and telecommunication (Chan, 1997; Liu, 1992; Ure, 1991). In the case of water supply and postal services, the government has taken over the provision and became the monopoly supplier.

There has been pressure on the liberalization in Hong Kong's internal market as drawbacks of monopoly or quasi-monopoly arrangements became apparent. The Hong Kong Legislative Council has been debating franchises and their respective scheme of control arrangements. During the 1990s, the Hong Kong government began liberalizing certain sectors like the telecommunications and banking. In all these liberalized sectors, prices have fallen and service quality improved.

In the banking sector, the Hong Kong Monetary Authority (2002) has undergone a number of market reform and liberalization measures, including full deregulation of savings and current account deposits from July 2001 onwards and full relaxation in 2001 of the one branch policy by allowing foreign banks subjected to the one building condition to open up to three branches to which customers have access.

With regard to public transport, the government may need to comprehensively review the options of introducing more competition into the public transport market and should recognize the inter-relationships among the various modes of transport. From 1997 onwards, all bus routes have operated on a non-exclusive basis and all franchises are no longer subject to a profit control scheme (Leung, 2001).

The improvement in the telecommunication sector has been remarkable since the Office of the Telecommunication Authority actively policed the market and took action on unfair practices. For example, the monopoly of the former Hong Kong Telecom in the supply of local and overseas telephone operator service was abolished. However, by using the case of the Pacific Link Communication Limited acquisition by Hong Kong Telecom CSL in 1997, Chen and Lin (2002) pointed out the potential drawback of the dual roles of the enforcer and the presence of asymmetric information in the sector approach. In particular, the Office of Telecommunication Authority monitored the prices of regulated firms, but at the same time made judgment on complaints over the competition in the telecommunication sector.

Despite various attempts to introduce competition law, Hong Kong does not have a comprehensive competition law, but a number of competition regulations that apply to individual business or industry, such as the telecommunication and broadcasting (Carnabuci and Wang, 2008). The Hong Kong Consumer Council (HKCC) published in November 1996 a report on *Competition Policy: The Key to Hong Kong's Future Success* (1996b) stressed that an effective competition policy required a wide-ranging and proactive approach to promoting competition, and recommended that the government should enact a competition law to cover horizontal and vertical collusive agreements and abuse of dominant position. The competition law recommended by the HKCC should cover prohibitions in price-fixing cartels, bid-rigging, retail price maintenance, exclusive dealership, tie-in sales and long-term contracts, and abuse by undertakings of a dominant position that prevents, restricts or distorts competition. The HKCC recommendations also included the establishment of an independent competition authority with the power to investigate possible breaches of the law.

For decades, the Hong Kong government believed that market forces provide the optimal solutions in the economy and that intervention in the form of competition law would be unnecessary, as such a law would potentially be harmful to the unregulated market operation. In response to the report by HKCC, the Hong Kong government emphasized that the objective of any competition policy has been to promote economic efficiency and the best allocation of resources from the perspective of the society, and a sector-specific approach to the promotion of competition has been adequate. The Competitive Policy Advisory Group (COMPAG) was established in 1997 and a formal policy statement was issued in 1998 promulgating that the Hong Kong government would not introduce an overall law on competition, but would set up a sector-specific competition policy framework.

In June 2006, the Competition Policy Review Committee (CPRC) published a report noting that while Hong Kong is a free and open economy with few market barriers, there is concern about possible cases of anti-competitive conduct, and concluded that a cross-sector competition law should be introduced, and an independent Competition Commission be established. In November 2006, the Commerce and Economic Development Bureau of the Hong Kong SAR Government issued a public discussion paper entitled *Promoting Competition: Maintaining our Economic Drive* (Consumer Council, 2007b). A subsequent report that summarized the response from the public entitled *Public Consultation on the Way Forward for Hong Kong's Competition Policy* indicated that there was a wide support for a cross-sector competition law and a strong regulatory environment for competition. The objective of the law aimed to prohibit conduct that lessened competition substantially. The concern in the business sector, however, is that such a law could lead to higher cost and time-consuming litigations.

In May 2008, the Commerce and Economic Development Bureau issued the *Detailed Proposals for a Competition Law: A Public Consultation Paper*. Table 8.11 shows a summary of a total of 50 proposals grouped under seven sections. A general prohibition on agreement and concerted practices with the purpose or effect of substantially lessening competition is suggested in the 2008 Consultation Paper. Since it is not common to see large scale merger activity in Hong Kong, the proposed competition law should not include regulations on merger activities. Instead of sector-specific laws, the proposed law should cover all economic sectors. However, exemptions could be granted based on specific mechanisms and criteria, as restriction

TABLE 8.11 Summary of the Proposed Competition Law in Hong Kong

Sections (Number of proposals)

I. Purpose of the legislation and definition of key terms (2) — outlined the purpose of the legislation and the definitions of terms;
II. Appointment of a Competition Commission (13) — proposed a new establishment with the power to investigate and determine whether an infringement of the law had taken place, and the authority to apply remedies, penalties, check and balances;
III. Appointment of a Competition Tribunal (7) — forum for the review of decisions by the Competition Commission, made up of judicial officers and experts in economics, commerce or competition law;
IV. Prohibition against anti-competitive conduct (10) — two broad areas of i) participating in agreements and concerted practices that lessen competition substantially, and ii) abusing substantially market power; penalties for infringement would be civil in nature;
V. Right to institute private action (10) — allowed private actions to be brought before the Competition tribunal, actions could either be "follow-on: actions (seek compensation for losses), or "stand-alone" actions (seek a determination by the Tribunal);
VI. Provisions related to application (3) — specific measures that concern the small- and medium-sized enterprises (SMEs), and the question of shared jurisdiction in certain sectors and regulatory bodies; and
VII. Exemptions and exclusions (5) — justification for granting exemptions or exclusions in agreements that carry greater economic benefit than anti-competitive harm or could achieve other important social or public policy objectives.

Source: *Detailed Proposals for a Competition Law — A Public Consultation Paper*, 2008, Commerce and Economic Development Bureau, Hong Kong.

on competition may not necessarily harm economic efficiency or conflict with other aims in the society. For example, government or statutory bodies would naturally be exempted from the prohibition on anti-competitive agreements if it yields economic benefits that outweigh the potential harm. The conduct rule of the competition law applies to "undertakings", which may be defined as individuals, companies or other entities engaging in economic activities. The conduct rules of the competition law should not apply to undertakings entrusted with the operation of services of general economic interest, such as essential public services.

Evidences from Hong Kong suggested that the neo-classical model of competition law is favored, and a sectoral approach to competition policy is emphasized. This can be seen by a number of competition rules being built into legislation regulatory guidelines and codes of conduct for various industries. This included the Consumer Goods Safety Ordinance, Unconscionable Contracts Ordinance, Supply of Services (Implied Terms) Ordinance, Sale of Goods Ordinance, Trade Description Ordinance, and the Competition Provisions in the telecommunications and broadcasting industries. The primary objective of these ordinances and guidelines was to enhance economic efficiency and free flow of trade so as to benefit consumer welfare.

The dynamic forces of competition in the market have been an important consideration. The insight is that business behavior that is being viewed anti-competitive from a static angle should not affect economic efficiency in a dynamic sense. A market that appeared to be monopolistic or the existence of a market-dominating firm is not necessarily competitive if the market is accessible and contestable. This has been noted in the statement on competition policy by COMPAG (2003).

8.5 Industrial Concentration

A practical way to examine the degree of competition in Hong Kong is to consider the industrial concentration ratio in total business receipts of the largest 10, 20 and 50 companies in the industry/business (denoted as CR10, CR20 and CR50, respectively). A selection of industries concentration ratios in Hong Kong, as summarized in Table 8.12, is available in the *Statistics on Sectoral Concentration*, released in June 2007 by the Census and Statistics Department for the two years of 2004 and 2005. A fair amount of detailed concentration ratios are given in five key economic sectors in Hong Kong for the two years of 2004 and 2005.

Usually, concentration is considered as heavy if the largest 10 companies have occupied more than 50% of total business receipts in the industry. The concentration ratios shown in Table 8.12 do review a number of points. In the manufacturing sector, it is clear that the beverage industries, basic metal industries and electrical appliances, housewares and electronic toys are very concentrated, and competition is weak in these sectors. The high concentration in electrical appliances, housewares and electronic toys and basic metal industries could be due to the small number of companies still remaining in Hong Kong. There is a rapid rise in the concentration ratio of the paper and paper products industry between 2004 and 2005. The food industry is less concentrated, since the concentration ratio in both CR20 and CR50 have declined in both years. Textile is least concentrated, and the ratios showed there was a rapid change between 2004 and 2005.

In general, the construction industry is not very concentrated, reflecting the popularity of subcontracting in the industry. The most competitive sector is probably wholesale and retail, import and export trade and restaurants, though the concentration ratios for hotels have increased. For the transport, storage and communications sector, concentration is definitely high in air transport, followed by land transport and telecommunications, storage is the least concentrated in that sector, though there was not much change between the two years. In the finance and real estate sector, banking, insurance and financial and investment companies experienced a similar degree of concentration. Real estate services are competitive. The rental business service is least concentrated.

TABLE 8.12 Hong Kong's concentration ratios of industries in total business receipts

	CR10		CR20		CR50	
Major sectors and industry groups	2004	2005	2004	2005	2004	2005
Manufacturing						
Food	40	41	63	58	81	78
Beverage	99	99				
Textile	20	17	27	31	40	61
Paper and paper products	58	95	79	95	99	95
Basic metal industries	99					
Elect. appliances/houseware/ electronic toys	98	98				
Construction						
Work at sites	54	73	65	80	88	92
Miscellaneous	40	37	47	45	58	57
Decoration, repair & maintenance	12	13	19	18	25	27
Wholesale, Retail, Trade, Rest., Hotels						
Wholesale	11	13	16	19	22	29
Retail	22	22	32	31	44	42
Import and Export	6	8	9	11	15	16
Restaurants	9	9	11	11	14	14
Hotels and boarding houses	36	34	59	55	89	86
Transport, Storage and Communications						
Land passenger transport	72	72	76	76	80	80
Supporting services to land transport	67	83	84	92	91	96
Air transport	96	96	99	98		
Storage	40	39	53	53	76	73
Telecommunications	71	71	86	87	96	96
Miscellaneous telecommunication services	87	86	88	89	91	93
Finance, Insurance, Estate, Bus. Services						
Banking	67	56	74	62	86	72
Finance & investment companies	63	64	78	78	91	92
Real estate	22	25	33	39	53	59
Rental: machinery, equip. business services	14	17	21	24	34	38

Source: *Statistical on Sectoral Concentration*, 2007, Census and Statistical Department, Hong Kong, June.

8.6 A Freedom-Oriented Approach

The dilemma Hong Kong faces is that on the one hand there is a need to ensure equity in competition and market entry to the provision of private goods and services, but on the other hand there is the danger of limiting market potentials, especially for long-term development and economic diversity. There are several considerations one has to take into account when discussing the introduction of a competition law in Hong Kong.

Firstly, given the flexible and open nature of the economy, economic activities in Hong Kong are definitely influenced, if not dominated, by external circumstances. The economic survival of Hong Kong relies much on the dynamics of the external economy. It would therefore be unwise to restrict the consideration only to static situations. Secondly, when introducing antitrust legislations, one has to be careful in distinguishing between whether the legislation would help to promote competition or just to preserve and stylize the current status quo, thereby limiting potential future growth and development. Experiences from developed countries reflect that the antitrust legislations do serve the purpose of limiting market control, but at the same time produced disincentives and imposed restrictions with unintended consequences for future expansion and development of the industry and the market.

An open market must imply that participants are free to enter the market at any time. Individual entrepreneurs and businesses can have different intentions and look at the same market differently. Some may enter the market with detailed knowledge of the market, while others may use the entry as a testing ground. Furthermore, different businesses in Hong Kong are undergoing different stages of competition; while some businesses are competing in their early stage, others have passed the competition "cycle" and have become quite matured. With a simple and small-sized economy, one also has to consider the various market conditions. While some businesses face market saturation, namely that there is little room to expand in business, others are experiencing a young market and competition is expected. Thus, competition is limited if the businesses are faced with market saturation, which occurs when the market has reached its full potential and there is little room for expansion. On the contrary, a young market will invite competition, which will eliminate the weak suppliers even though there is no entry restriction into the market. The process of competition continues so long as the market expands to allow new comers.

For a free economy, an important concern is the ability to generate economic opportunities for the future generation. Hence, antitrust legislation should be seen as an additional instrument that serves as an infrastructure to strengthen economic freedom in Hong Kong, making the economy a more civic and ethically a stronger place for businesses, thereby allowing current and future businesses equal chance and opportunity. Competition is no longer related just to cost, but contains a host of business-cycle affected and market-related conditions. It is true that businesses do exercise different strategies to cope with competition. A line has to be drawn in preserving the market so as to allow new competitors, permitting a level playing field for both existing and future businesses, and imposing effective blockage that guard against market abuse.

A two-tier strategy can be exercised. The first-tier takes care of a number of basic conditions that ensure openness, transparency and efficiency in market competition. A number of general anti-competition conditions, such as price fixing, bid-rigging, cartel, market allocation agreements, price abuse and discrimination, cross-industry controls and so on can be written into law as a general protection to open competition. The first-tier of control should be in line with practices elsewhere, and the legislation should be passed with little controversies. The main purpose of the first-tier strategy is to ensure open competition in a free market economy, but at the same time will not impose unnecessary restriction on potential development and future opportunities. It simply acts as another transparent instrument to ensure equity in the level playing field.

However, while the first-tier strategy shall not be too intensive as to limit future economic opportunities, as market conditions may change, the second-tier strategy is market-related, sector-specific and professional-oriented, allowing different professions, trades and businesses to specify their own conditions, practices and regulations on competition in their own markets. The second-tier strategy could allow flexibility in catering the needs in different markets, trades and businesses. As competition varies across businesses and industries, it would be best to allow participation by people from both inside and outside the business and industries so that consensus can be reached and transparency can be maintained in setting up professional, business and competition standards. It is important for independent individuals and institutions to be incorporated in the decision making process to ensure fairness, transparency and avoid rested interest.

Different trade associations, chambers of commerce, business and professional bodies and workers unions can come up with their own preference in their market competition. The standard set on competition can probably be geared realistically to the special conditions in different businesses. It is likely that professionals, workers and business organizations themselves have a good idea on the extent of competition in their own specific markets. The extra step needed is to formalize and consolidate the kind of competition standards that are accepted by the producers and consumers. An overall standard and requirement on market competition can be reached if enough associations and professional bodies make efforts to come up with their recommendations, which can be turned into standard practices and accepted level of market openness. One advantage in the second-tier strategy is that regular changes and new adjustments resulting from changing conditions can be entertained. The civic way of governing market competition can be a supplement to the detailed legislation on market competition. A strong civic behavior can help to preserve open competition.

However, a full establishment of the second-tier strategy is definitely easier said than done, as rested interests in different professions and trades could lead to delays, controversies, conflict and disagreements in setting standards. It would also take a long time to accomplish, unless a time frame is legally specified. In practice, it is likely that some more efficient and active professions and businesses would produce a set of standards earlier and faster than others. In addition, there is the role of the government in taking an overall view on market competition, ensuring there is consistency and no irregularities existed among different markets in Hong Kong.

In a full fetched market economy in Hong Kong, entry to any market should not be restricted and both local and non-local investors with capital and resources can equally seize the opportunities. New markets can develop from new products. Numerous examples can be found. Health conscious consumers would spend not only in healthy food, but on body building, beauty parlors and different types of beauty-related medical operations. In addition to ensure open market and fairness, professional associations are needed also to ensure quality control, safety standards, standard practices, professional requirements and ethical judgment. For example, it has become popular for beauty–related medical operations to have a good standard, as they are often conducted by private medical personnel, whose qualification, professional standards and practices are important from a social safety and security point of view. Innocent patients can be affected for life if careless operations are conducted by the unqualified medical personnel in the private market. Ultimately, people intended to receive beauty-related operations have to aware of the risk involved and check the quality of the medical operation.

Another example is e-commerce and cyber activities in the internet, where the market can be invisible and the location of participants could even be unknown. New developments in markets will call for new challenges in competition. In the meantime, the focus on antitrust legislation is more likely on the few key businesses and industries in Hong Kong, typically the real estate market, banking, land transport, energy supply and retails.

8.7 Conclusion

Despite the small size of the Hong Kong economy, it has far wider implications and the economic behavior in Hong Kong radiates to nearby and other emerging economies in Asia. Given its diverse economic nature, it has been argued that a single antitrust law that restricts all anti-competitive practices may not be able to take into account the specific requirement of the individual sectors. A sector-specific competition policy framework would seem more beneficial to the Hong Kong economy. An appropriate competition policy in Hong Kong should have the objective of promoting economic efficiency, principally in terms of fostering growth, economic strength and competitiveness. The maintenance and expansion of market opportunities, a positive policy towards private enterprise and competition, a positive policy towards foreign investment, foreign trade and exchange controls, a transparent and fair labor and immigration policies are essential elements to improve the overall competitive environment.

While it is undesirable to have comprehensive antitrust laws, there should be a legal framework strong enough to deter anti-competition activities and behavior. This should be seen more as a legal infrastructure that enriches the legal and economic framework than an instrument of restriction on business development. It has always been easy to criticize the different aspects of the Hong Kong economy, but proposing constructive activities are more important. No economy can be regarded as perfect, but in the free economy of Hong Kong, there is a constant need for improvement so as to make the economy a better place for all.

Since business development is an important aspect in Hong Kong, the building and accumulation of a strong business ethic can help to maintain a high business exposure and maximize future business potentials that will benefit all. While individuals and corporations engaging in businesses are welcome in Hong Kong, it is equally important to ensure a level playing field, such that one market participant would not hinge negatively on the business welfare of all other participants. It would be advancement in civic freedom if businesses themselves adhere to a good ethic in competition, equity and transparency.

Hong Kong is a dynamic economy, and future development must be encouraged. One must not restrict people who have successfully made business gains and wealth in Hong Kong. Equally, there should not be any restrictions on the generation of economic opportunities for future businesses. In other words, success by contemporary businesses should not be discriminated, but they will also have to face competition in future as new businesses emerge. Opportunities have become another source of growth and development. Fair competition can maximize business and economic opportunities.

9 The Finance Sector: Rankings, Development and Challenges

9.1 Introduction

In the *Index of Economic Freedom* released by the Heritage Foundation in January 2011, Hong Kong once again achieves the highest score with an overall score of 89.7, followed closely by Singapore with an overall score of 87.2. Among the ten components, the best performance in Hong Kong is Business Freedom with a score of 98.7, and it is followed by Fiscal Freedom with a score of 93.3. Financial Freedom, along with Trade Freedom, Investment Freedom and Property Rights, achieved a score of 90. Among the top 10 freest economies, the other two economies that have scored 90 in their Financial Freedom are Australia (ranked third) and Denmark (ranked eighth). Although Singapore ranked second in the overall ranking, its score in Financial Freedom is 60, well below that of Hong Kong.

Freedom in financial flows is a key component in economic freedom, as it allows firms and individuals to transfer financial assets and capital funds in and out of the country. The free flows of funds effectively mean that funds are free for investment in the economy, which shall promote economic growth eventually. Obviously, it is encouraging and economically healthy to see more inflows than outflows. But when the economic health lacks soundness, funds will flow out of the country; and the outflow will have other negative implications on the economy. Freedom in the flow of funds can thus provide an indicator on the performance of other economic activities.

The flow of funds enters the country either in the form of physical investment geared to industries, services and infrastructure, or in the form of portfolio investment in securities and equities. The former leads to growth in the real economy where physical outputs and exports are generated, while the latter produces fluctuation in the nominal economy, typically in the security market transactions. Naturally, flows of funds in the security market generate financial volatility that has positive and negative impacts on the economy, depending on the magnitude and content of the volatility.

The need to minimize financial volatility on the one hand, and to maintain fairness and transparency on the other hand, requires the establishment of a set of rules and regulations to impose the standards and practices followed by all players in the financial market. The strong rules and regulations thus form the infrastructure in the financial and investment markets. A regular revival and updating of rules and regulations in line with other world markets helps to strengthen the market status considerably.

There are three key institutions that are responsible for the activities of the financial structure. The Hong Kong Exchange and Clearing Limited (HKEx) itself is a listed company and is charged with the responsibility to ensure sound rules and regulations, practices and ethics in the financial market. The Securities and Futures Commission (SFC) is responsible for regulating the securities and futures markets in Hong Kong. The SFC is an independent non-governmental statutory body outside the civil service and is headed by professionals. The maintenance of Hong Kong as an international financial center and the establishment of financial infrastructure are the responsibility of the Hong Kong Monetary Authority (HKMA). The HKMA is a government authority responsible for the stability in both monetary and financial systems, and reports to the Financial Secretary. The foreign reserve of Hong Kong, known as the Exchange Fund, is managed by the HKMA.

The high degree of financial freedom allows the financial sector in Hong Kong to grow and expand. By today, Hong Kong has achieved the status as an international financial center, at least in the Asian region and shows strong performance when compared to Tokyo and Singapore. Many investors align Hong Kong's financial center status with that of London and New York, though the financial center in Hong Kong is smaller when compared to both London and New York. More recently, Hong Kong has also been compared to the rapid expanding financial center of Shanghai, while some even argue about the fall of Hong Kong.

While comparisons can easily be made, there are a number of historical and contextual issues in financial freedom that have gradually transformed Hong Kong into an international financial center. Factors that relate to the input-side of a financial center involve the availability of expertise and the strength of rules and regulations. Economic openness in Hong Kong has permitted also a free flow of foreign financial professional working in Hong Kong, in addition to those locally trained professional personnel. The extent of foreign involvement from the very beginning has the advantage of foreign recognition of the financial market in Hong Kong. Others have argued that the geographical location of Hong Kong is another advantage, as it provides a convenient time zone to other financial centers, especially between New York and London.

The success and strength of financial freedom can best be seen from the performance at output end. The rest of this chapter will show how the development of the financial system and market in Hong Kong has benefitted from financial freedom. The various ingredients as an international financial center are discussed in the following sections.

9.2 Economic Competitiveness and Financial Centers

Studies on world financial centers tend to be descriptive and comparative (Tschoegl, 2000; Schenk, 2002; Poon, 2003; Grote, 2007). Recent focus has been on the competitive advantages of financial centers (Lee, 2001). The competitive advantages of a financial center can include a number of sustainable factors and the practice of relevant policies and strategies. Examples of competitive factors include such socio-economic factors as medical system, communication network, human resources and quality of life, sound regulations and favorable taxation, strong economic fundamentals and financial structure (Kaufman, 2001; Luxembourg Finance Center, 2007; Corporation of London, 2005; McKinsey & Co., 2007; Dufey and Giddy, 1978; McGahey *et al.*, 1990; Goldberg, 1991; Montes, 1999).

The Corporation of London (2005) has identified London as the best international financial center, and specified a total of fourteen competitiveness factors that an international financial center should possess. These fourteen competitiveness factors are, in the order of importance: (1) skilled personnel, (2) regulatory environment, (3) access to international financial markets, (4) business infrastructure, (5) access to customers, (6) fair and just business environment, (7) government responsiveness, (8) corporate tax regime, (9) cost of operation, (10) professional services, (11) quality of life, (12) culture and language, (13) quality of commercial property and (14) personal tax regime.

Table 9.1 compares the financial market performances in ten world economies in terms of their stock market capitalization, stock market performance, debt securities market, foreign exchange market and derivatives market, and the ranking of banks. To avoid the impact of the 2008 financial crisis, the data in Table 9.1 cover the stable time period in 2006 and 2007. Table 9.1 suggests that based on the performance of stock market capitalization, debt securities market, foreign exchange market turnover and over the counter (OTC) derivatives market turnover, the rankings of the largest five financial centers, in descending order, are New York, London, Tokyo, Singapore and Hong Kong. Among these five financial centers, the best performance of stock market in terms of percentage change in 2006 is Hong Kong, followed by Singapore, New York, London and Tokyo. The biggest market for merger and acquisition activities is still New York, as the transaction amounted to US$1,899 billion for the fiscal year of 2006–2007.

Table 9.2 reports the corporate and personal income tax rates for the ten economies. Among the ten economies, the tax rates for Hong Kong are lowest, followed closely by Singapore. The second group of low-tax economies composes of India, South Korea and Chinese Taipei. The tax rates for USA, Japan and Australia are the highest. The *Global Financial Centers Index* (GFCI) published by the City of London (2007) compared 46 financial centers in the world, and the calculation of the index is based on five aspects of competitiveness, namely People, Business Environment, Market Access, Infrastructure and General Competitiveness. The People aspect included the availability of personnel, education and human capital. The Business Environment aspect concerned the soundness of regulations and tax rates, economic freedom, corruption, and ease of doing business. The Market Access aspect related to the level of securitization, equities and bonds trading. The Infrastructure aspect included the cost of office rental. The General Competitiveness aspect gives an overall competitiveness level of the cities.

Table 9.3 shows the summary on the strengths and weaknesses of the world's top ten financial centers, shown in GFCI. Among the 46 global financial centers, the top ten financial centers are London, New York, Hong Kong, Singapore, Zurich, Frankfurt, Sydney, Chicago, Tokyo and Geneva. Being the world's third largest financial center, London report concludes that Hong Kong is a real contender to be a genuine global financial center. Because of large volume of financial transactions, the traditional weakness of a high cost does not detract financial trading in Hong Kong.

TABLE 9.1 Performance of international financial centers

	USA	UK	Japan	Hong Kong	Singapore	India	China	Chinese Taipei	South Korea	Australia
Stock Market Capitalization										
Total Stocks (US$bn, 6/2007)	18,247	3,867	4,790	683	356	837	2,360	676	909	1,216
Floating Capita* (US$bn, 6/2007)	16,283	3,661	3,611	337	206	263	465	522	598	1,053
Stock Market Performance										
%Change between 31/12/2006 and 13/7/2007	9.5	8	5.9	15.7	22.4	10.8	46.3	21.1	36.8	12.7
%Change in Year 2006	13.6	10.7	6.9	34.2	27.2	46.7	130.4	19.5	4	19
Debt Securities Market — Amount Outstanding (US$bn)										
International Debt Securities (3/2007)	4,211	2,699	151	49	50	21	17	18	91	437
Domestic Debt Securities (12/2006)	22,316	1,238	8,401	51	79	326	1,184	201	1,010	459
Foreign Exchange Market Turnover (US$bn)										
Daily Average (4/2004)	461	753	199	102	125	7	1	8	20	81
Daily Average (4/1998)	351	637	136	79	139	2	0	5	4	47
OTC Derivatives Market Turnover (US$bn)										
Daily Average (4/2004)	599	1,176	185	82	100	4	NA	6	11	73
Daily Average (4/1998)	294	591	121	51	91	1	NA	2	1	32
Total M&A Activity (US$bn, FY 2006–07)	1,899	431	107	26	24	40	61	16	25	157
Ranking of Bank Soundness (125 economies, 2006)	27	1	76	13	21	37	123	100	82	8

Notes:* = The shares used in the calculation of the indices reflect only those shares that are available to investors, not all the company's outstanding shares. OTC = Over the Counter; M&A = merger and acquisition; and FY = fiscal year.

Source: Axiss Australia, Canberra.

TABLE 9.2 Corporate tax and personal income tax rates of ten economies

Economies	Highest combined corporate tax rate (%, 2007)	Highest marginal personal income tax rate (%, 2006)
USA	40.0	35
UK	30.0	40
Japan	40.7	37
Hong Kong	17.5	16
Singapore	20.0	20
China	33.0	45
Chinese Taipei	25.0	40
South Korea	27.4	35
Australia	30.0	45
India	34.0	30

Source: *Corporate Tax Rate Survey 2007*, KPMG; *World Tax Summaries*, PriceWater-houseCoopers.

However, in terms of the difference in the score points, the difference between London [765] and New York [760] is only 5 score points, while the difference in the score points between New York and Hong Kong [684] is a much wider gap of 76 score points. Hence, even though Hong Kong ranked third among the 46 global financial centers, Hong Kong's financial center has a distance to catch up. And between the score points of Hong Kong and Singapore [660], the gap is 24 score points.

The *World Bank Development Indicators* provided the annual data for three financial variables of listed domestic companies, market capitalization and total value of stock traded or stock turnover. The performance of these three financial variables in 2005 for the five economies of the United Kingdom, United States, Hong Kong, Singapore and Japan are compared. When judged by the performance of the three financial variables, the rankings are USA, Japan, United Kingdom, Hong Kong and Singapore. By looking at the magnitude of the financial variables among the five economies, one can see that USA provides the largest financial activities, followed by both Japan and UK, which in turn are much larger than both Hong Kong and Singapore.

There are numerous studies that have documented the economic virtues of Hong Kong as an international financial center. Leung and Unteroberdoerster (2008) argue that the excellent performance of supply-side factors are the key advantages in Hong Kong's status as a financial center, and the special link with Mainland China provides Hong Kong with a first-mover advantage in the growth of financial services in future. The track-record of Hong Kong as Asia's center for cross-border financial transactions has over the decades nurtured a number of supply-side factors, such as skilled labor, strong regulatory framework, and the quality and depth of business services. Professional bodies, such as the Business and Professionals Federation of Hong Kong (2009) also adhere to the various factors that contribute to the financial success in Hong Kong.

TABLE 9.3 The top ten international financial centers

(Ranking) [Score]	Strengths and Weaknesses
London (1) [765]	The performances of most key factors are excellent. London is in the top quartile in over 80% of its instrumental factors, and is especially strong on people, market access and regulation. The main negative comments concern corporate tax rates, transport infrastructure and operational costs.
New York (2) [760]	The performances of most key factors are very strong. New York is also in the top quartile in over 80% of its instrumental factors. People and market access are particular strengths. Regulation is the main negative factor.
Hong Kong (3) [684]	Hong Kong is a thriving regional centre, and performs well in all key competitiveness areas, especially in regulation. The high costs do not detract from overall competitiveness. Hong Kong is a real contender to become a genuinely global financial centre.
Singapore (4) [660]	Most areas are very good and banking regulation is often cited as excellent. It performs well in four of the key competitiveness areas but falls to 9th place on the factor of general competitiveness. Definitely the second Asian centre.
Zurich (5) [656]	A very strong financial centre, especially in private banking and asset management provision. Zurich performs well in three of the key competitiveness areas but loses out slightly in the people factor and in general competitiveness.
Frankfurt (6) [647]	Despite a strong banking focus, Frankfurt suffers from inflexible labor laws and skilled staff shortages. Market access, infrastructure and business environment are strong but Frankfurt falls outside the top ten rankings for people and general competitiveness.
Sydney (7) [639]	A strong national centre with good regulation and offers a good quality of life. Sydney is strong in four of the key competitiveness areas but falls outside the top ten for people, as many financial professionals leave for larger English speaking centers.
Chicago (8) [636]	The number two centre in the US, but being hampered by the same regulatory regime as New York. It scores highly for people but is let down by its infrastructure and market access rankings. Remains a powerful regional and specialist centre.
Tokyo (9) [632]	Does not fare well in terms of regulation and business environment, but the size of the Japanese economy means that Tokyo has good liquidity. It fares poorly on people but has good infrastructure and market access.
Geneva (10) [628]	A strong niche centre similar to Zurich. Private banking and asset management continue to thrive. Strong in business environment and general competitiveness but let down by infrastructure.

Source: *The Global Financial Centers Index*, London, March 2007.

TABLE 9.4 Factors of economic competitiveness

Factors	Sub-Factors: (Total Number)
Economic performance	Domestic Economy: Size (12); Growth (7); Wealth (6); Forecasts (4). International Trade (21). International Investment: Investment (15); Finance (2). Employment (8). Price (4).
Government efficiency	Public Finance (11). Fiscal Policy (14). Institutional Framework: Central bank (6); State Efficiency (9). Business Legislation: Openness (7); Competition & Regulation (11); Labor Regulation (3). Societal Framework: (11).
Business efficiency	Productivity and Efficiency (11). Labor Market: Costs (4); Relations (5); Availability of Skills (13). Finance: Bank Efficiency (10); Stock Market Efficiency (8); Finance Management (3). Management Practices (10). Attitudes and Values (7).
Infrastructure	Basic Infrastructure (23). Technological Infrastructure (21). Scientific Infrastructure (22). Health and Environment (20). Education (15).

Source: *World Competitiveness Yearbook*, IMD, Geneva.

Comparison of economic competitiveness and international financial centers can also be made by using different sources. For example, the performance of four broad groups of factors is considered as relevant and important to economic competitiveness in the *World Competitiveness Yearbook* conducted annually by the Institute of Management Development (IMD) in Geneva, Switzerland. These four factors are Economic Performance, Government Efficiency, Business Efficiency and Infrastructure. Each of these four factors is comprehensively divided into a number of sub-factors and indicators, making a total of 323 indicators in the twenty sub-factor categories within the four factors, as summarized in Table 9.4. Such a wide coverage of factors can provide a comprehensive list of indicator on the economic competitiveness factors and performance of financial variables in different economies.

The *World Competitiveness Yearbook* covered a total of 60 world economies. The ranking ranges from 1 to 60, with 1 being the highest ranking and 60 the lowest ranking. The performance of Hong Kong is compared to four major world financial center economies of United Kingdom, USA, Singapore and Japan. Figures 9.1, 9.2, 9.3, 9.4 and 9.5 show the annual ranking of the four factors in the economic competitiveness of the United Kingdom, United States, Hong Kong, Singapore and Japan over the sample period (1992–2006).

Several observations can be made on these five economies. In the case of the UK as shown in Figure 9.1, most factors reach their peak in 2002 and 2003, followed by a significant drop in the rankings in 2004 and 2005. The rankings pick up in 2006,

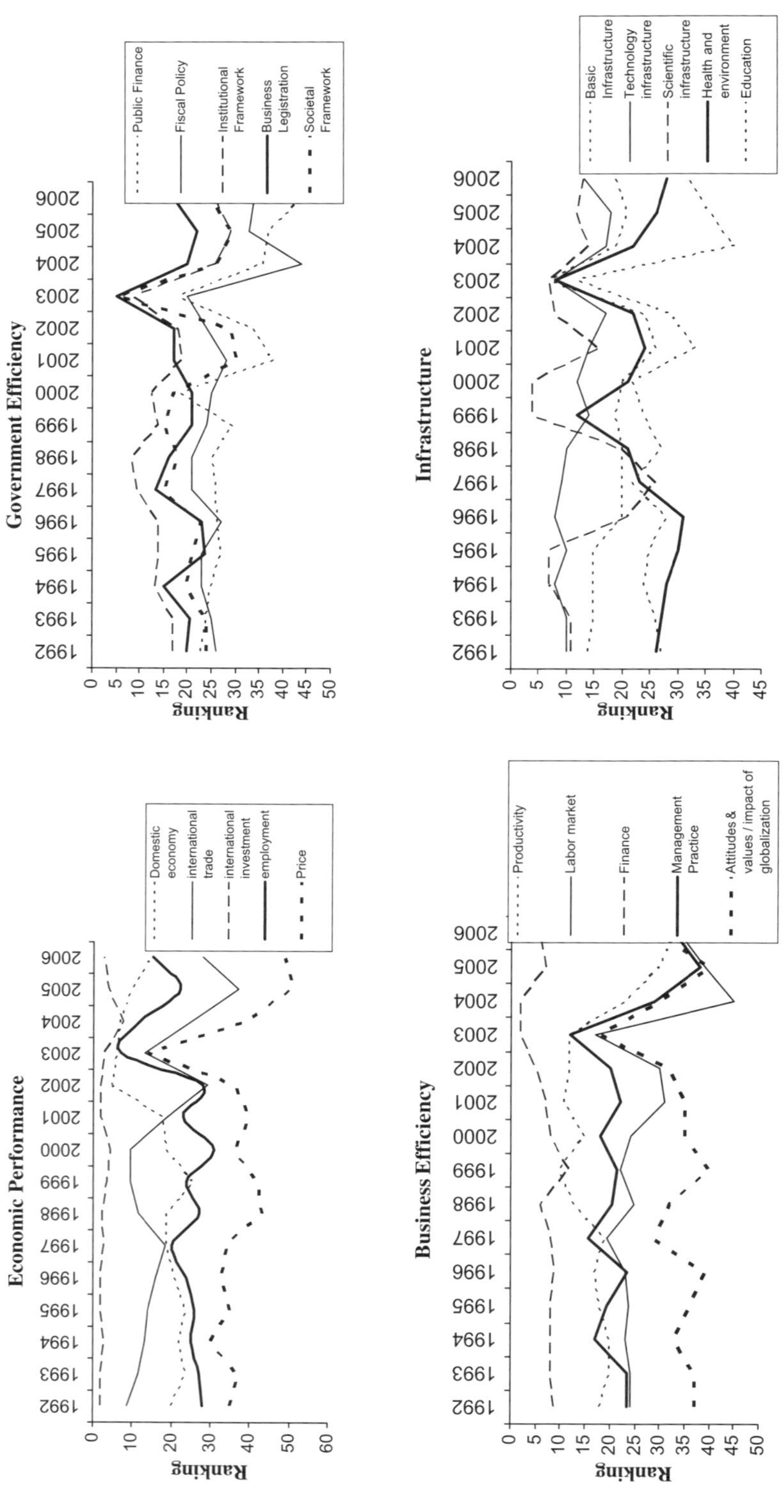

FIGURE 9.1 Ranking of economic competitiveness: United Kingdom

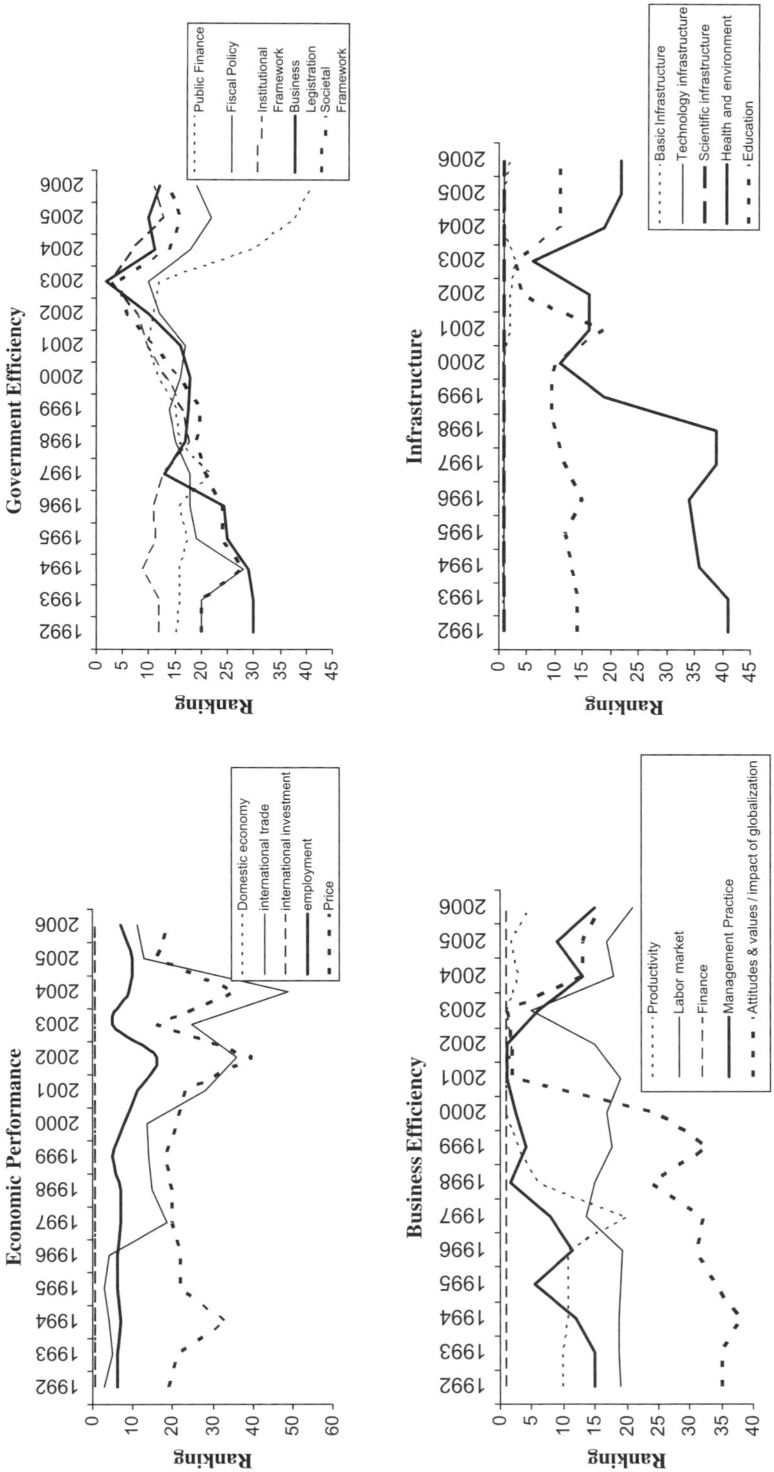

FIGURE 9.2 Ranking of economic competitiveness: United States of America

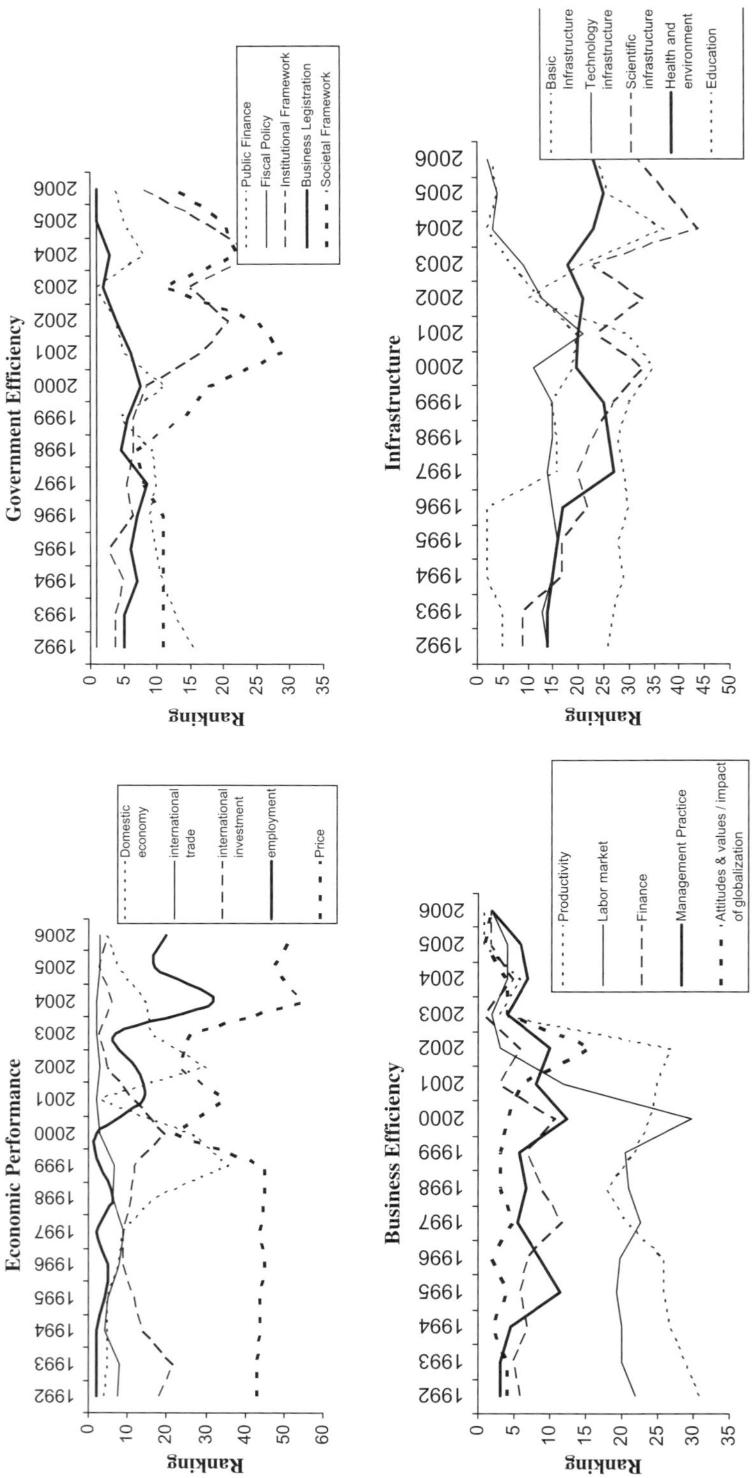

FIGURE 9.3 Ranking of economic competitiveness: Hong Kong

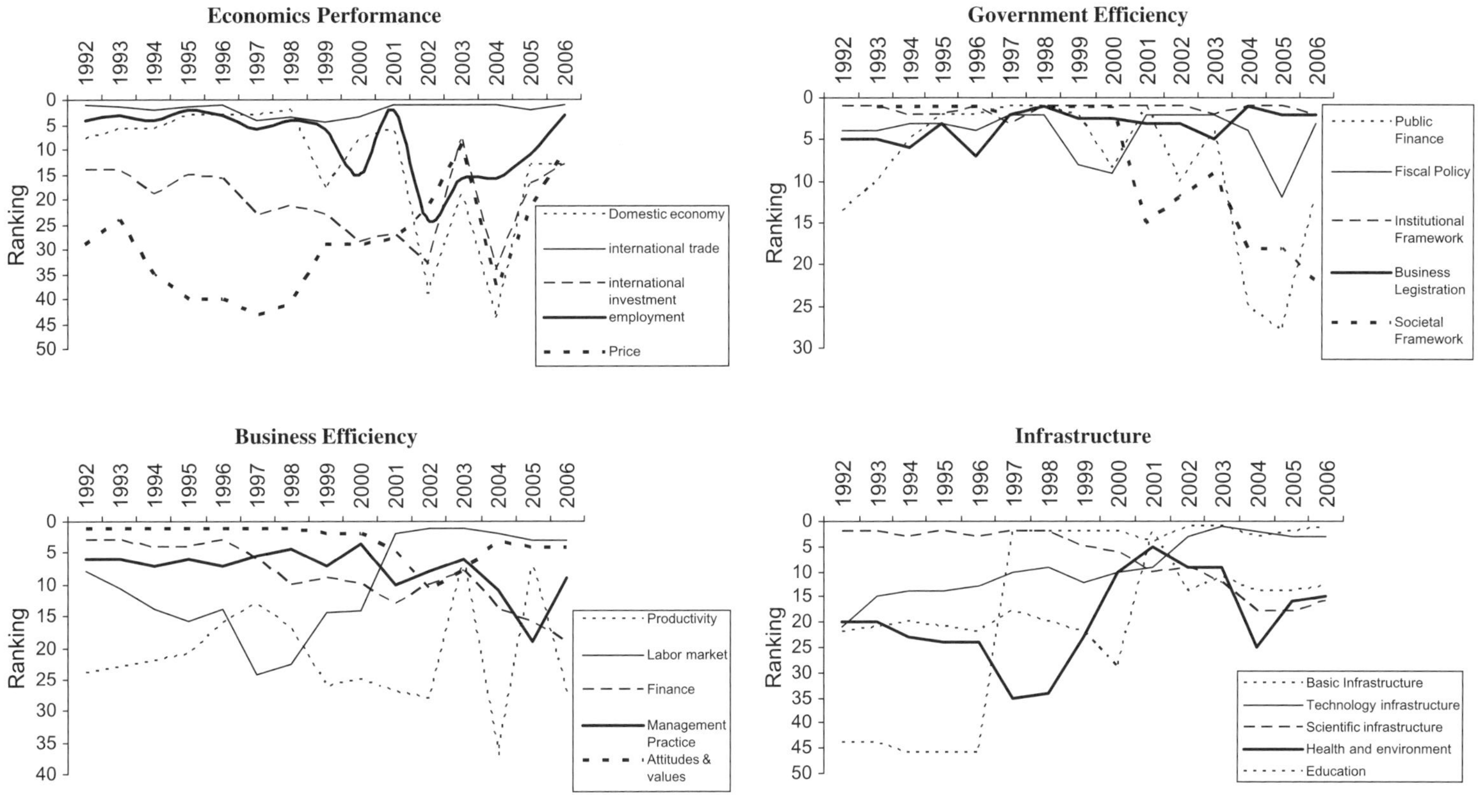

FIGURE 9.4 Ranking of economic competitiveness: Singapore

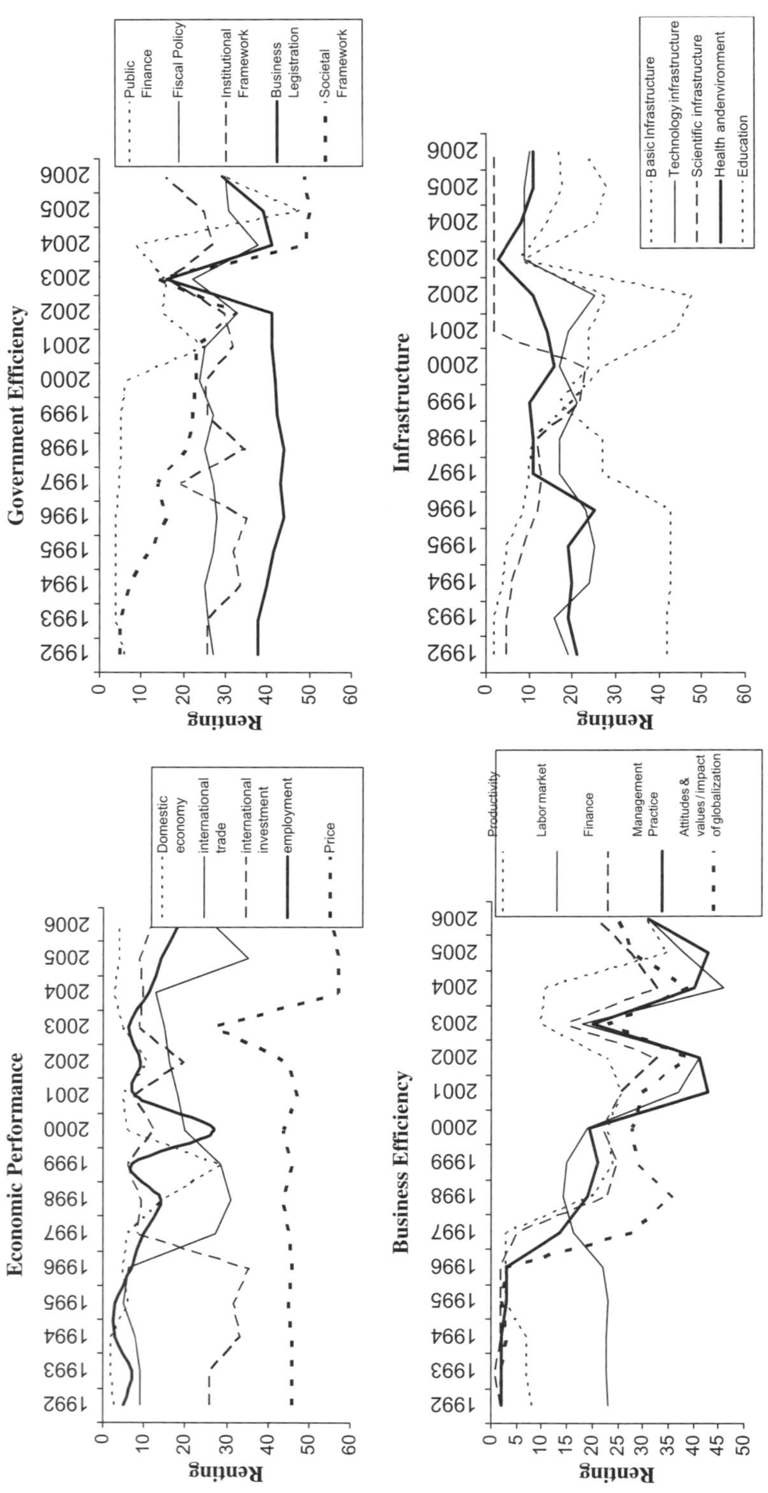

FIGURE 9.5 Ranking of economic competitiveness: Japan

with the exception of Price that reflects a rising cost of living in the UK. Government Efficiency in UK shows a constantly improving trend. In the USA, Figure 9.2 shows a significant improvement in Economic Performance, especially in International Trade between 2004 and 2006. The performance in International Investment is excellent and has been kept at the highest position.

For Hong Kong, as shown in Figure 9.3, the overall Economic Performance is improving, with the exception of Price that reflects the high cost of living and low competitiveness, Government Efficiency in Hong Kong has improved. Similarly, Business Efficiency, productivity and labor market in particular, perform well since 2002 and 2003. Hong Kong experienced a weak performance in Infrastructure, especially in scientific infrastructure, health and environment and education. Similar to Hong Kong, the Singapore economy has gone through a downward movement in a number of indicators in 2003 and 2004, as Figure 9.4 shows, but has recovered quickly since 2005, with the exception of societal framework under Government Efficiency and finance under Business Efficiency. In Japan, as Figure 9.5 shows, the overall Economic Performance presents a slightly downward movement, especially in employment. There have been obvious improvements in Government Efficiency and Business Efficiency since 2004.

The relationship of any two economic variables (X, Y) can be examined by calculating their correlation coefficient from the following equation:

$$\text{Correl}(X,Y) = \frac{\sum (x-\bar{x})(y-\bar{y})}{\sqrt{\sum (x-\bar{x})^2 \sum (y-\bar{y})^2}}, \tag{1}$$

where $\bar{x}$ and $\bar{y}$ are the average values of observations x and y, respectively. The correlation coefficient ranges from 0 to 1, and in general, when the coefficient is larger than 0.5, one can argue that the two variables are correlated. Table 9.5 shows the correlation coefficients between the four factors of economic competitiveness and the stock market turnover (ST) to GDP ratio for the five economies.

In the UK, Table 9.5 shows that among the four factors, Economic Performance showed a relatively high correlation of 0.5890, but Infrastructure shows a negative correlation (−0.5282), suggesting that more attention should be given to the development of economic infrastructure in UK. The stock market turnover to GDP ratio in both the USA and Hong Kong correlated strongly with Business Efficiency (0.8407 and 0.7645, respectively), due probably to their strong management. By contrast, in both Singapore and Japan, their Infrastructure shows strong positive correlation with performance in the stock markets (0.5238 and 0.7699, respectively). However, Tokyo as a financial center ranks lower than others because the stock market turnover to GDP ratio shows a strong negative correlation with Economic Performance (−0.5310) and Government Efficiency (−0.5912), and a weak negative correlation with Business Efficiency (−0.4838).

A rather simple and straight forward econometric analysis can be conducted in order to examine the relationship between the four factors of competitiveness and the financial variable. In the one-equation model given in Equation (2), the independent variables are the ranking of the four economic competitiveness factors of the five

TABLE 9.5 Correlation between finance and economic competitiveness factors, 1992–2006

	ST/GDP	Economic performance	Government efficiency	Infrastructure	Business efficiency
UK					
ST/GDP	1.0000				
Economic performance	0.5890	1.0000			
Government efficiency	0.0507	–0.2551	1.000		
Infrastructure	–0.5282	–0.7630	0.6325	1.000	
Business efficiency	0.3779	0.6932	0.2739	–0.2849	1.0000
USA					
ST/GDP	1.0000				
Economic performance	—	1.0000			
Government efficiency	–0.1775	—	1.0000		
Infrastructure	—	—	—	1.0000	
Business efficiency	0.8407	—	0.0854	—	1.0000
Hong Kong					
ST/GDP	1.0000				
Economic performance	–0.0448	1.0000			
Government efficiency	–0.2255	0.2593	1.0000		
Infrastructure	–0.3655	0.5816	0.1674	1.0000	
Business efficiency	0.7645	–0.2992	0.0521	–0.6161	1.0000
Singapore					
ST/GDP	1.0000				
Economic performance	0.2722	1.0000			
Government efficiency	–0.0098	0.3411	1.0000		
Infrastructure	0.5238	–0.0109	–0.2177	1.0000	
Business efficiency	–0.4191	0.0651	0.1014	–0.4551	1.0000
Japan					
ST/GDP	1.0000				
Economic performance	–0.5310	1.0000			
Government efficiency	–0.5912	0.8263	1.0000		
Infrastructure	0.7699	–0.7995	–0.8870	1.0000	
Business efficiency	–0.4838	0.8325	0.9478	–0.8467	1.0000

Note: ST = stock market turnover. — = shows no correlation since these factors ranked best for the USA in a number of years.

Sources: *World Bank Development Indicators*, The World Bank; and *World Competitiveness Yearbook*, 1992–2006, IMD, Geneva.

economies for the sample period of 1992–2006, while the dependent variables can either be the stock market turnover (ST) to GDP ratio, or the stock market capitalization (MC) to GDP ratio.

$$FV_t = \alpha + \beta_1 \text{ ECON}_t + \beta_2 \text{ GOVT}_t + \beta_3 \text{ BUSE}_t + \beta_4 \text{ INFRA}_t + \varepsilon_t, \qquad (2)$$

where FV_t indicates either the MC/GDP or ST/GDP ratio, $ECON_t$ gives the ranking of Economic Performance, $GOVT_t$ is the ranking of Government Efficiency, $BUSE_t$ indicates the ranking of Business Efficiency, while $INFRA_t$ shows the ranking of Infrastructure. α is the constant term and ε_t is the random error term.

Table 9.6 presents the empirical regression results. As the world's best financial center and when the dependent variable is the ST/GDP ratio, the regression estimates of London in the UK give a high R-square of 0.8906, implying that 89% of the variance can be explained by the four economic competitiveness factors, and the one-equation model is marginally significant with the F-statistics equals to 18.3215 and a probability value (p-value) of 0.0002. However, the regression estimates do not show any significant factor, suggesting that the development of London as a financial center is quite even. When the MC/GDP ratio is used as the dependent variable, however, the regression result shows that Government Efficiency (with coefficient estimate of 0.1704) is a positively significant factor for the London financial center, suggesting that a financial center with an efficient government along with a fair regulatory environment is highly attractive. In other words, financial institutions tend to seek a well-regulated location where the government is capable of keeping a high standard of integrity, transparency and enforcement.

The empirical estimates of New York, as shown in the upper portion of Table 9.6 with ST/GDP as the dependent variable, give a higher R-square and the model is

TABLE 9.6 Impact of economic competitiveness factors on financial centers

	UK	USA	Hong Kong	Singapore	Japan
Dependent Variable: ST/GDP Ratio					
Economic performance β_1	–0.9829	—	0.0097	0.0012	–0.0007
Government efficiency β_2	–6.9845	2.0650	0.3354	–0.0070	–0.0134
Business efficiency β_3	1.2533	13.0451**	0.1243**	-0.0004	0.0187
Infrastructure β_4	–5.9636	—	0.0564	0.0001	0.0425**
R-square	0.8906	0.6153	0.6631	0.0597	0.7008
F-statistics	18.3215	8.7972	4.9209	0.1587	5.8557
Significance of F	0.0002	0.0036	0.0187	0.9545	0.0108
Dependent Variable: MC/GDP Ratio					
Economic performance β_1	0.0654	—	0.0059	0.0309	0.0020
Government efficiency β_2	0.1704*	–1.3418	–0.0514	0.0047	–0.0087
Business efficiency β_3	–0.0883	5.1502**	0.0880**	–0.0605	0.0124
Infrastructure β_4	–0.1778	—	–0.002	0.0141	0.0182
R-square	0.5647	0.7181	0.6179	0.4032	0.3197
F-statistics	3.2429	14.0114	3.6385	1.6887	1.1747
Significance of F	0.0598	0.0007	0.0498	0.2284	0.3787

Notes: ** and * = significant level at 1% and 5%, respectively. The constant term and the standard errors, and the t-statistics and p-values of the coefficients are excluded.

Sources: *World Competitiveness Yearbook*, IMD, Geneva; *World Bank Development Indicator*, The World Bank; and CEIC Database.

significant (with F-statistics = 8.7972). Among the coefficient estimates, Business Efficiency (13.0451) is significant and gives a positive impact on New York's financial center. This is supported by a similar result (5.1502) when the MC/GDP is the dependent variable in the lower portion of Table 9.6. This suggests that a financial center with experienced management and skilled manpower is critical to its development, as they make significant contribution to the training and development in human capital, market exploration and product development (Kaufman, 2001; Lee, 2001). Government Efficiency, though not significant, shows a negative relationship with the performance of the financial center.

The performance of Hong Kong as an international financial center is similar to that of New York. The regression estimates show a high R-square, and that Business Efficiency is the significant factor that has positive relationship with the development of the financial center. This is so in the two results using the ST/GDP and MC/GDP ratios as the dependent variable. A financial center with rich human resources and a high degree of business efficiency is attractive to financial development. Well-versed bankers and financial managers interact with each other for efficient market deals, developing new financial products and exploring new business opportunities. The other three economic competitiveness factors are not significant to the Hong Kong financial center.

The empirical regression estimates for Singapore is not satisfactory as the R-square is below 0.5, and none of the four economic competitiveness factors produce significant relationship with the financial center in Singapore. It suggests that the impact of the four economic competitiveness factors on Singapore's financial center is even. In the case of Japan, the estimates in the upper portion of Table 9.6 where the ST/GDP ratio is the dependent variable, show that Infrastructure is significant and is positively related to the performance of Tokyo as Japan's financial center. This suggests that a financial center equipped with efficient transportation and good communication network is very important, while a clean environment is a key determinant in the success of Japan's financial center. In the other estimates, both the Economic Performance and Government Efficiency show a negative relationship with financial performance.

9.3 Economic Growth and Stock Market Development

The existence of stock markets provide a channel for capital accumulation, through which the generated investment leads to economic growth. One school of thought argues that a well-developed stock market can promote capital mobilization, risk diversification and reduction and the provision of market information will speed up long-term economic growth (Levine, 1991; Greenwood and Smith, 1996; Goodhart, 2004). Goldsmith (1969) claims that financial development can support economic growth, while Patrick (1966) postulates a bi-directional relationship between economic growth and financial development. More recently, Levine and Zervos (1998) show a positive and significant correlation between stock market development and long-term economic growth.

Furthermore, the development of the stock market helps to improve productivity through the process of capital accumulation. Greenwood and Smith (1996) find that the presence of stock markets reduces the cost of saving and investment. Competition in the stock market can lead to an efficient allocation of capital that produces the highest possible return. Obstfeld (1994) claims that stock market openness can improve resource allocation, accelerate growth as well as reduction in international risk. Stock market openness can increase national welfare through increase in consumption. Others argue that stock market liquidity can play a key role in economic growth. This is because the stock market allows savers who invest in long-term profitable projects to liquidate the asset at a convenient time (Bencivenga *et al.*, 1996; Levine, 1991; Hicks, 1969).

Due to its highly liquid nature, stock markets can provide incentives for investors. Kyle (1984) argues that investors can obtain market information on listed corporations, and their investment in the stock market can improve resource allocation and accelerate economic growth. A related argument using the concept in the principle-agent theory deals with the compensation provided to the managers in the corporation listed in the stock market. Jensen and Murphy (1990) note that compensations provided to the managers are linked to stock market performance. This effectively can align the interest of the principles (owners of the listed corporation) and the agents (managers) and produce a positive impact on efficient resource allocation and economic growth. Holmstrom and Tirole (1993) similarly argue that stock markets provide a good measurement in monitoring managerial performance because stock market prices do reflect and include information on the performance of the management.

The economic benefits derived from an active stock market, however, have been opposed by others. Stiglitz (1985) claims that investors make use of movements in the stock price to search for market information. Demirguch-Kunt and Levine (1996) show that the increased liquidity in the stock market may deter economic growth because it reduces saving and encourages speculation. Because investors can easily liquidate their assets in the stock market, shareholders will have little incentive to exert corporate control and monitor the business performance of the corporation, which eventually lead to a governance problem. Similarly, Pagano (1993) points out that high liquidity in the stock market can invite speculation, and the subsequent reduction in savings means a fall in the provision of capital designated for productive investment activities.

It is useful to examine empirically how the stock market has facilitated Hong Kong's economic growth. The stock market in Hong Kong has experienced a period of rapid growth over the last few decades. Total market capitalization of listed companies increased by 1,063% from US$74 billion in 1988 to US$861 billion in 2004. Trading activities also surged rapidly. The value of shares traded increased by 1,809% from US$23 billion in 1988 to US$439 billion in 2004. In the same period, GDP per capita in Hong Kong increased by 130.7% from US$10,366 to US$23,917.[1]

Empirical studies using Hong Kong data for the sample period of 1988–2004 can be conducted to see how activities in the stock market affected the Hong Kong

---

[1] *World Bank Development Indicator*, Online Database, and *Hong Kong Annual Digest of Statistics*, Census and Statistics Department, Hong Kong.

macroeconomy. Three stock market proxy indicators are used as independent variables in the simple regression exercise (Levine and Zevors, 1980; Demirguch-Kunt and Levine, 1996). The first proxy indicator is the stock market size, measured by the total value of shares traded to Gross Domestic Product ratio (TVGDP). This ratio gives the information on the trading amount of firm equity as a share of the Gross Domestic Product. The estimated coefficient (β_1) shows whether the size of the financial market can contribute to the overall economic growth of the Hong Kong economy. A positive value of the estimated coefficient gives a positive relationship with economic growth.

The second proxy indicator in the empirical exercise is the market capitalization to GDP ratio (MCGDP). This ratio reflects the ability in the mobilization of capital and risk diversification. As listed corporations in the stock market raise capital openly, private savings and funds are diverted to the purchase of issued shares. The amount of funds in the economy as a whole will be constrained, and the level of aggregate savings and consumption will have to fall. As such, the overall effect on growth can even be negative. A negative coefficient estimate (β_2) implies that funds are withdrawn from the public, thereby reducing aggregate consumption expenditure, which influences negatively on the economic growth, though this probably is a short-term phenomenon.

The third proxy indicator is the turnover ratio (TV_MC) showing the ratio of the value of total shares traded to market capitalization. The turnover indicator can be interpreted as a proxy for market trading and, in particular, the extent of market speculation. When the market is bullish, a considerable amount of trading activities will be speculative that involves mainly short-term monetary transactions and the capital funds may not be channeled to the production of physical output. The coefficient estimate (β_3) can be negative as it reflects more on short-term speculation than on long-term investment geared for economic growth.

The dependent variables in the regression analysis include the various annual percentage growth rates of GDP and components, namely, GDP, GDP per capita, household consumption, gross capital formation, export of goods and services, import of goods and services, saving deposit and unemployment.[2] The regression of the empirical estimation is specified as follows:

$$\text{GY} = \beta_0 + \beta_1(\text{TVGDP}) + \beta_2(\text{MCGDP}) + \beta_3(\text{TV\_MC}), \tag{3}$$

where GY indicates the proxies of dependent variables. Technical tests have been carried out to ensure that the regressions are sound. The unit root test, commonly known as the Dickey-Fuller test (Dickey and Fuller, 1981), is used to check the stationarity of the time series. The Dickey-Fuller test result shows that some variables in the time series are stationary, while others are not. The unit root test shows that the first difference of variables turns out to be stationary. As such, the regression analysis is conducted using the first difference of the variables. In addition, the Granger

[2] The data are obtained from the *World Bank Development Indicator*, Online Database, and *Hong Kong Annual Digest of Statistics*, Census and Statistics Department, Hong Kong.

TABLE 9.7 The ordinary least square estimates

Dependent variables	Coefficient estimates			
GDP components (annual percent growth rates)	TVGDP (β_1)	MCGDP (β_2)	TV_MC (β_3)	R Square
GDP	0.222 (2.573*)	–0.096 (–2.392*)	–0.531 (–2.543*)	0.367
GDP per capita	0.259 (3.190*)	–0.113 (–2.983*)	–0.607 (–3.095*)	0.467
Consumption	0.192 (–1.566)	–0.093 (–1.639)	–0.452 (–1.524)	0.177
Gross capital formation	0.668 (2.198*)	–0.316 (–2.242*)	–1.447 (–1.971)	0.318
Export	0.467 (3.084*)	–0.219 (–3.120*)	–1.201 (–3.289*)	0.477
Import	–0.004 (–0.024)	0.009 (–0.104)	–0.230 (–0.525)	0.411
Saving deposit	0.024 (0.551)	–0.022 (–1.074)	–0.042 (–0.402)	0.481
Unemployment	–0.004 (–0.108)	0.017 (–0.921)	0.005 (–0.047)	0.676

Notes: The *t*-statistics are shown in parentheses, and * indicates a significance level of 5%.

causality test is used to examine the causal relationship between economic growth and stock market development. The causality results indicate that there is a causal relationship between stock market development and economic growth.[3]

The Ordinary Least Square (OLS) regression results reported in Table 9.7 show that there is a significant relationship between stock market development and growth. The coefficient estimates of total value of shares to GDP ratio (TVGDP) show that a significant relationship with growth in GDP, GDP per capital, gross capital formation and export. One can conclude from the regression result that the size of the financial market indicated by the total value of shares traded contributes to 22% of GDP growth in Hong Kong in the sample period. The gross capital formation (investment) in the financial market contributes most (66.8%) to growth. The R-squares shown in Table 9.7 are relatively low, suggesting that there can be other explanations for the GDP growth in Hong Kong.

The coefficient estimates for both market capitalization to GDP ratio (MCGDP) and stock market turnover to market capitalization ratio (TV_MC) in Table 9.7 are mostly negative. In the case of market capitalization, a mild negative coefficient estimate (–9.6%) on the growth of GDP suggests that private funds that are withdrawn from household consumption when corporations issued shares in the stock exchange have the same implication of an increase in saving, and a lower level of consumption should impose a negative impact on GDP growth. The large negative coefficient estimate of the turnover to market capitalization is interesting. Turnovers in the stock market reflect the amount of trading transactions, which involves nominal monetary transactions, and such transactions can be geared to speculation in a bullish market. Thus, a negative impact on GDP growth is expected, as stock turnovers are short-term transactions that do not have strong impact on real GDP

[3] The results of unit root test and causality test are excluded from the text.

growth. The large negative coefficient estimate (−53.1%) really confirms that stock market speculations are harmful to GDP growth.

9.4 Strengthening Stock Market Competitiveness

The Hong Kong Exchanges and Clearing Limited (HKEx) is responsible for the trading and settlement of securities as well as the provision of fund raising opportunities to companies in the Hong Kong stock market, which consists of the Main Board and the Growth Enterprise Market (GEM). The Main Board aims to help established companies with track records of operating profits to raise capital. The key listing requirements of the Main Board include: (1) A trading record of not less than three consecutive years; (2) A profit level not less than HK$20 million; and (3) An expected market capitalization not less than HK$100 million.

On the contrary, the GEM helps emerging enterprises to raise funds, and the listing requirements are relatively mild; they include: (1) An active business pursuit for two years before listing application; (2) The minimum public float is 20%/25%, or a minimum of HK$1 billion/HK$30 million, for companies of market capitalization over/under HK$4 billion. The major financial products available in the Hong Kong stock market include equities, bonds, warrants, trust and mutual funds as well as equity linked instruments. The HKEx provides an efficient and transparent regulatory framework to facilitate the trading of securities and raising of funds for both institutional and retail investors. All stock trading orders are automatically matched and executed in price and time priority using the Third Generation Automatic Order Matching and Execution System (AMS/3). The three key indices that measure the performance of the securities market in Hong Kong are the Hang Seng Index, the Hang Seng China Enterprises Index (also known as the H-share Index), and the Morgan Stanley Capital International Index.

Hong Kong has experienced different degrees of success in the stock market since 2006. The total market capitalization in the securities market achieved a record high of HK$13,339.9 billion (US$1,710.24 billion), and the stock market turned to become bullish as the Hang Seng Index (HSI) that recorded the stock market movement reached a new historical high of 20,001 points on December 28, 2006. By the end of 2006, the HSI closed at 19,964 points and achieved an annual growth of 34%, while the Hang Seng China Enterprises Index rose by 94% to close at 10,340 points.[4]

In addition, the annual market turnover achieved a new high of HK$8,376.3 billion (US$1,073.88 billion) in 2006, giving an annual growth rate of 85% between 2005 and 2006. There are a total of 62 companies newly listed (56 new companies listed in Main Board, 6 new companies listed in GEM) in 2006, raising a total capital of HK$333.9 billion (US$42.81 billion). Table 9.8 shows the performance of key stock market variables for the selected years between 1999 and 2009. The more significant changes in this period can be seen from Issued Capital and Market Capitalization, which have increased by 361.9% and 227.5% between 1999 and 2009, respectively.

[4] *HKEx Fact Book 2006*, Hong Kong Exchanges and Clearing Limited.

TABLE 9.8 End of year performance in Hong Kong's security market

(HK$ billion)	1999	2000	2002	2004	2006	2008	2009	2010
Listed Companies	708	790	978	1,096	1,173	1,261	1,319	
Domestic*	695	779	968	1,086	1,165	1,251	1,308	
Foreign#	13	11	10	10	8	10	11	
Listed Securities	1,212	1,349	1,586	2,176	3,383	5,831	6,611	
New Listed Firms	38	90	117	70	62	49	73	
Issued Capital	225.9	288.92	387.34	441.06	901.1	980.6	1,043.5	
Market capitalization	4,734.8	4,862.4	3,611.3	6,695.9	13,337.7	10,298.8	17,874.3	
Equity Funds raised	149.7	467.3	110.5	281.8	524.5	427.3	642.1	850.0
IPO	17.14	132.1	52.0	97.2	333.9	66.0	248.2	445.0
SM	132.6	335.2	58.5	184.6	190.7	361.3	393.9	405.0

Notes: * = Included all Mainland China incorporated enterprises with H-shares listed on the Hong Kong Exchange. # = A listed foreign company is incorporated overseas and has a majority of its business outside Hong Kong and Mainland China. IPO = Initial public offers. SM = Secondary market. The 2010 figures are obtained from the "2011 HKEx Annual Media Luncheon" presentation, January 11, 2011. (Exchange rate: US$1 = HK$7.8)

Source: *Hong Kong Exchange Fact Book 2006 and 2009*, Hong Kong Exchanges and Clearing Limited.

Total Equity Fund Raised performed differently over the years, but Listed Securities increased by 445.5% between 1999 and 2009.

Among the members of the World Federation of Exchanges stated in the *Annual Report and Statistics 2006*, Hong Kong in 2006 ranked 4th in total equity raised, ranked 2nd in newly listing of funds raised and ranked 6th in market capitalization. Table 9.9 shows the world top thirty exchanges ranked by the value of market capitalization in 2006. There are a couple of observations. Having ranked 6th, the percentage change of market capitalization between 2005 and 2006 in Hong Kong was 63%. The same percentage for both Shanghai Stock Exchange (221%) and Shenzhen Stock Exchange (97%) was much higher, though they ranked lower at 14th and 26th, respectively. Secondly, there is a clear gap in market capitalization when Hong Kong Stock Exchange is compared to Euronext, as the difference (US$1,993,197 million) is actually larger than Hong Kong's own market capitalization (US$1,714,953 million).

In 2006, there were three Mainland-incorporated banks [Bank of China (BOC), China Merchant Bank (CMB), and Industrial and Commercial Bank of China (ICBC)] listed in Hong Kong's Main Board stock market. The fund raised by ICBC exceeded HK$124.9 billion (US$16 billion), which was regarded as the largest initial public offering (IPO) in the history of the world stock markets. The ICBC was also the first Mainland enterprise concurrently listed in the A-shares in the Shanghai stock market and H-shares in the Hong Kong stock market.

The derivatives market in Hong Kong also performed well in 2006, with a total of 42.91 million futures and options contracts traded, giving a year-on-year increase of 68%. The number of newly listed derivative warrants in 2006 reached a record high of 2,823, with a total issued premium of HK$247.8 billion (US$31.77 billion), giving an annual increase of 68%. Between 2005 and 2006, the total turnover value

TABLE 9.9 Ranking of top 30 exchanges by market capitalization (US$ million)

Ranking/Regions	Exchanges	End 2006	End 2005	% change
1. Americas	NYSE Group	15,421,168	13,632,303	13
2. Asia-Pacific	Tokyo SE	4,614,069	4,572,901	1
3. Americas	Nasdaq	3,865,004	3,603,985	7
4. EAME	London SE	3,794,310	3,058,182	24
5. EAME	Euronext	3,708,150	2,706,804	37
6. Asia-Pacific	Hong Kong SE	1,714,953	1,054,999	63
7. Americas	Toronto SE	1,700,708	1,482,185	15
8. EAME	Deutsche Borse	1,637,610	1,221,106	34
9. EAME	BME Spanish Exchange	1,322,915	959,910	38
10. EAME	Swiss Exchange	1,212,308	935,448	30
11. EAME	OMX Stockholm	1,122,705	802,561	40
12. Asia-Pacific	Australian SE	1,095,858	804,015	36
13. EAME	Borsa Itallana	1,026,504	798,073	29
14. Asia-Pacific	Shanghai SE	917,508	286,190	221
15. Asia-Pacific	Korea Exchange	834,404	718,011	16
16. Asia-Pacific	Bombay SE	818,879	553,074	48
17. Asia-Pacific	National India SE	774,116	515,973	50
18. EAME	JSE South Africa	711,232	549,310	29
19. Americas	Sao Paulo SE	710,247	474,647	50
20. Asia-Pacific	Taiwan SE Corp.	594,659	476,018	25
21. Asia-Pacific	Singapore	384,286	257,341	49
22. Americas	Mexican Exchange	348,345	239,128	46
23. Americas	American SE	282,801	201,403	40
24. EAME	Oslo Bors	279,910	190,952	47
25. Asia-Pacific	Bursa Malaysia	235,581	180,518	31
26. Asia-Pacific	Shenzhen SE	227,947	115,662	97
27. EAME	Athens Exchange	208,256	145,121	44
28. EAME	Wiener Borse	192,770	126,252	53
29. Asia-Pacific	Osaka SE	181,754	191,969	–5
30. Americas	Santiago SE	174,419	136,493	28

Note: EAME = Europe–Africa–Middle East.
Source: *Annual Report and Statistics 2006*, World Federation of Exchanges, London.

of derivative ad equity warrants increased by 109%, giving a value of HK$1,792.8 billion (US$229.8 billion) in 2006.[5]

The turnover of the debt security market in Hong Kong in 2006 amounted to HK$6.25 million (US$0.8 million), a decrease of 40% when compared to 2005. Meanwhile, there were nine Exchange Traded Funds (ETFs) and five Real Estate Investment Trusts (REITs) listed in 2006. The turnover of unit trusts and mutual

[5] *Hong Kong Exchange Fact Book 2006*, Hong Kong Exchanges and Clearing Limited.

funds in 2006 amounted to HK$105.3 million (US$13.5 million), showing an increase of 104% over 2005. The share in the turnover between ETFs and REITs in 2006 was 55% and 45%, respectively. A new product, the Callable Bull/Bear Contracts (CBBC) was first traded in June 2006. There were a total of 24 listed CBBC products, and their total turnover in 2006 was HK$11.3 billion (US$1.45 billion).

In 2010, Hong Kong for the second year in a row is the largest issuer of IPOs globally. The HKEx reported that Hong Kong has also been transformed from being a China offshore listing venue, with IPO funds raised amounted to HK$292 billion in 2007, to become a global listing venue, with a total of IPO funds raised amounting to HK$445 billion in 2010. While the landmark IPOs between 2005 and 2007 are mainly China banks and enterprises, the landmark IPOs in 2009–2010 are international enterprises from US, Russia, France as well as Mainland China. In 2010, the total raised IPO funds in the three stocks markets in Hong Kong (US$57 billion), Shenzhen (US$45.4 billion) and Shanghai (US$28.7 billion) amounted to US$131.1 billion. By comparison, the IPO funds raised by the three key stock markets of NYSE (US$39.1 billion), London (US$15.7 billion) and NSADAQ (US$9.4 billion) amounted to US$64.2 billion.[6]

However, one should not be complacent about the success in Hong Kong's stock market performance as performances can vary over the years, and Hong Kong's stock market faces competition from nearby and other international financial centers. A "Strength–Weakness–Opportunity–Threats" (SWOT) analysis can be conducted to examine the various advantages and disadvantages of the Hong Kong stock market. The result of a SWOT analysis can provide useful information for decision makers to craft an effective and sustainable strategy for the development of the Hong Kong stock market, so that potential opportunities can extensively be explored, while threats can be avoided or contained as far as possible.

In the *Global Financial Center Index* conducted by the City of London in March 2007, Hong Kong ranked third in the world financial centers behind London and New York. Hong Kong is clearly ahead of other Asian markets in most aspects and performed well in regulations, supervision and accounting policy. There is a high degree of transparency in Hong Kong's stock market, as full information disclosure is legally required. In addition to an efficient and responsive government, Hong Kong leads other Asian markets in the areas of competitiveness that considered people, business environment, market access, infrastructure and general competitiveness. The skilled workforce and the low tax regime are additional attractions.

With the rapid growth and maturing of the vast China economy, there are definitely new financial business opportunities for the Hong Kong stock market. Firstly, Hong Kong has a comparative advantage in providing a reliable platform to channel foreign funds into the Mainland economy. Similarly, Hong Kong can provide investment services and financial products for Mainland institutions and individuals.

---

[6] "2011 HKEx Annual Media Luncheon" presentation by Charles Li, Chief Executive of HKEx, January 11, 2011.

For example, the stock market in Hong Kong can serve as a center for Mainland enterprises and investors to raise capital.

With regard to its weaknesses, Hong Kong has high overhead cost. The professional service charge, such as accountancy, business valuation and underwriting, are expensive, the rent and salary levels are high in general. Another weakness is its growing reliance on the support of Mainland enterprises. The tendency in 2006 is that the large China impact, and that the H-shares, red chips and other Mainland enterprises are playing a rapidly and increasingly dominant role in Hong Kong's stock market. By the end of 2006, and out of the 975 listed companies on the Main Board, there were 95 H-shares companies and 86 red chips, which together constituted 48% of market capitalization in the Main Board. There were 17 H-share companies among the 56 companies newly listed on the Mainland Board in 2006.

Being entirely close to the China market, unexpected shocks in Mainland China's finance can send both positive and negative signals to the stock market in Hong Kong. Hong Kong also faces challenges from competition from the Shanghai and Shenzhen stock markets. It has been argued that improvements in these two Mainland markets could diminish the financial center role of Hong Kong. For example, the full convertibility of the Renminbi in the future means that investors can channel funds directly between Mainland and foreign countries, bypassing Hong Kong completely.

By full convertibility, it means there is no restriction in both the inflow and outflow of the Renminbi exchanges for foreign currencies in the current account and capital account of the country's balance of payment. The current account mainly involves the export and import of goods and service trade balance, while the capital account involves capital and portfolio investments. Both accounts form the major components in China's balance of payment. If these two accounts produce a surplus, it will contribute to the country's foreign reserve. As of 2011, the Renminbi is still partially convertible, meaning that there is less restriction in the current account where international trade is conducted. Restriction is applied mainly in the capital account.

The strengths, weaknesses, opportunities and threats of the Hong Kong stock market are summarized in Table 9.10. On balance, there are more strengths and opportunities than weaknesses and threats, but an attitude of complacency should be replaced by a drive to move the securities market forward to a new height and a new chapter. Progress is needed in keeping ahead of other world and regional financial markets, preparing for new challenges and upgrading existing practices and technologies.

To promote the competitiveness of the stock market in Hong Kong, one should look for appropriate strategies that can deepen the work and status of Hong Kong's financial market with the eventual aim to strengthen its long-term position. Several strategies can be suggested, including the pursuit in international diversity, lengthening the trading period, and developing new products.

International diversity: Hong Kong should put more efforts to attract well-established companies from different regions in the world to list in Hong Kong. While Hong Kong can be a convenient market for Mainland companies to list, non-Mainland-based companies should also be attracted to Hong Kong in order to maintain diversity and balance.

TABLE 9.10 Summary of the SWOT analysis of the Hong Kong stock market

Strengths	Weaknesses
1. World standard supervision and accounting policy 2. Sound regulatory framework 3. Information disclosure 4. Full of experienced talents 5. Free follow of capital 6. Simple tax system	1. Over reliance on the support of Mainland enterprises; Need diversity 2. High overhead cost
Opportunities	**Threats**
1. As a platform for Mainland enterprises to raise capital 2. Channel global fund to the Mainland market 3. Provider of financial services and investment products to Mainland	1. Facing competition from Mainland and overseas stock markets as they improve 2. Number of China enterprises raising capital in Hong Kong increased at a declining rate

Lengthen the trading hours: It has been suggested that the trading hours of the Hong Kong stock market can be lengthened to cater for investors' needs. Because of the time convenience between Hong Kong and other stock markets in Asia, US and Europe, and the increasing pace of globalization and the demand for hedge trading, Hong Kong can introduce an evening trading session, say from early evening to around midnight. The Osaka Securities Exchange, for example, has announced on September 18, 2007, that an evening trading session for stock index futures and options would be introduced.[7] Having an evening trading session can produce several advantages. It increases the total amount of stock turnover by providing trading opportunities for investors outside the intra-day periods in both the morning and afternoon sessions. Moreover, it allows investors to respond promptly to companies' financial statements or news announcements after the close of the stock market. The evening trading session can coincide with the daily opening in the major stock markets in Europe, and investors can respond to the activities in the European stock markets.

The odds against the introduction of the evening session are the various related activities as financial transaction take place. For example, there may not be sufficient banking and logistic support in the evening session. As a result, the suggestion of an evening trading session, or even the introduction of a "round-the-clock" trading requires a thorough feasibility study.

It was announced by the HKEx in January 2011 that the extension of trading hours has been approved by the Securities and Futures Commission (SFC). Effective from March 7, 2011, the trading sessions of HKEx securities market will start earlier from 9.30 in the morning to noon and from 1.30 to 4.00 o'clock in the afternoon.

[7] *Hong Kong Economic Times*, September 18, 2007.

This is followed by another extension in March 5, 2012, when the afternoon trading sessions will begin from 1 o'clock in the afternoon.[8] The intention is to expand the trading hours to capture the investors' response to the changing market conditions.

Develop new investment products: Hong Kong can develop new products for the stock market, for example, in the derivatives of commodity and currency. Mainland China is one of the largest consumers of commodities, and the Dalian Commodity Exchange is the third largest global commodity exchange market in 2006 behind the New York Mercantile Exchange and the Chicago Board of Trade. Hong Kong can develop the commodity futures to take advantage of the growing global market. In the case of the currency market, Hong Kong can make use of the rising demand for the Renminbi in the international market, and engage or introduce futures contracts based on US dollar and Renminbi, or Hong Kong dollar and Renminbi.

Table 9.11 compares the trading performance of Hong Kong with other global markets in various financial products in 2006. Hong Kong performed strongly in warrants and Exchange Traded Funds (ETF), followed by equities, as seen from their high growth rates between 2005 and 2006. The performance of bond is

TABLE 9.11 Percentage shares in total trading in equities, warrants, exchange traded fund, bonds and derivatives in 2006

		Percentage shares			
	Total US$ million	Asia-Pacific*	American	EAMA	Hong Kong
Equity	69,829,944	16.11	51.42	31.28	1.19 (79)
Warrants	760,204	7.78	0.32	61.59	30.31 (109)
ETF	2,845,703	2.02	90.08	7.64	0.26 (179)
Bond	13,223,334	0.62	6.54	92.84	0.00 (–43)
Total Number of Contracts (1,000)			Percentage Shares		
Stock options	2,652,512	1.00	77.79	20.53	0.68 (107)
Stock futures	279,730	36.10	0.00	63.86	0.04 (681)
Stock index options	1,282,262	43.91	26.14	29.57	0.38 (46)
Stock index futures	1,375,515	15.79	53.02	29.75	1.44 (47)
Currency options	33,226	—	42.20	57.80	—
Currency futures	158,359	2.00	88.24	9.77	—
Commodity options	102,859	0.04	90.44	9.52	—
Commodity futures	794,164	32.21	44.91	22.88	—

Notes: Figures in parentheses are the percentage change between 2005 and 2006. * = Hong Kong is excluded from Asia-Pacific exchanges. ETF = Exchange Traded Fund. EAMA = Europe–Africa–Middle East market.

Source: *Annual Report and Statistics 2006*, World Federation of Exchange, London.

[8] HKEx News Release, January 24, 2011.

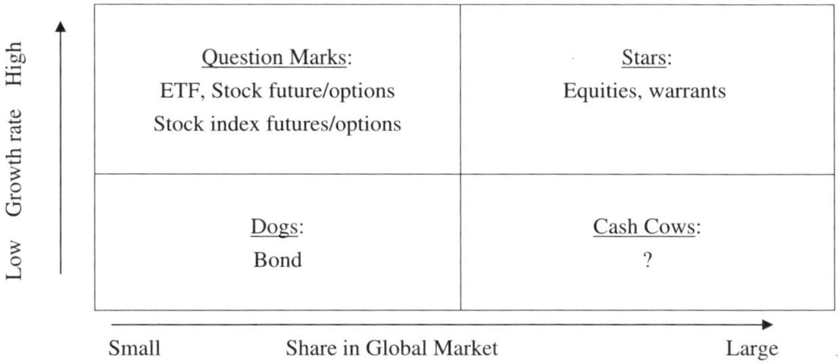

FIGURE 9.6 The Boston matrix for Hong Kong

unsatisfactory. In the derivatives market, though the percentage share in the global market is small, Hong Kong experienced a large percentage growth in stock futures and stock options. The other derivative products of currency options, currency futures, commodity options and commodity futures are absent in the Hong Kong stock market.

The potential development of the Hong Kong stock market can be examined by constructing the Boston Matrix based on the market information shown in Table 9.11. The Boston Matrix shown in Figure 9.6 is originated from the Boston Consulting Group in the early 1970s, classified financial products into four groups of Dogs, Cash Cows, Stars and Question Marks.

Financial products that are classified under Stars are those financial products that experienced a high growth rate and a large global market share. The two products in Hong Kong that come under Stars are equities (global market share of 1.19%, and a growth rate of 79%) and warrants (global market share of 30.31%, and a growth rate of 109%). The large and constant inflow of capital from the Mainland investors to acquire quality equities in the Hong Kong stock market ensured a high growth rate. According to the World Federation of Exchanges, Hong Kong is the second largest trader of warrants in the world, behind the Deutsche Borse Exchange in Germany. There is thus immense potential for the trading of both equities and warrants in the Hong Kong stock market.

Financial products that fall within Questions Marks are those with a performance of a low global market share but a high market growth rate. They include the Exchange Traded Funds (ETFs) (global market share of 0.26%, and a growth rate of 179%), and the four derivative products of stock options, stock futures, stock index options and stock index futures. These four derivative products experience a small global market share, but different degrees of growth rates.

"Dogs" are financial products whose performance shows a low global market share and a low growth rate. Bond trading in Hong Kong falls into this category. The bond market in Hong Kong shows a weak performance, with a global market share close to zero and a negative growth rate (–43%) between 2005 and 2006. One of the reasons in the weak performance of the bond market in Hong Kong is the lack of economies of scale and the small number of market players. Further financial infrastructure establishments are needed in order to promote further development of bond trading in Hong Kong. They include the establishment of a central trading platform and an efficient channel for the information dissemination, the development of derivatives to facilitate risk management, the improvement in the transparency and access of the retail market and an education program to promote and educate potential investors.

Financial products that produced a low growth rate but occupied a large global market share are classified as Cash Cows in the Boston Matrix. In Hong Kong, there is no such financial product that can be classified as Cash Cows.

The construction of the Boston Matrix can help to map a strategy for the further development of the financial market in Hong Kong. Products in the financial market shall probably start from Dogs with low growth rate and low global market, and proceed to become Question Marks that gain high growth rate but low global market. With a prolonged period of high growth rate, the financial product will then move to become Stars with high growth rate and large global market. Once the financial products are fully matured and occupied a major position in the market, their growth rates will slow down, but can capture a large global market. Subsequently, they can become Cash Cows with low growth rate but large global market.

In conclusion, Hong Kong is ahead of other financial market in Asia, but with the challenge from the growing Mainland economy and the rapid pace of globalization, Hong Kong has every need and potential to strengthen its comparative advantage in the financial world. Strategically, Hong Kong should widen its coverage of financial products, keep to the free market principle, improve the regulations where needed, boost market diversity, polish and deepen the various existing strengths.

9.5 The China Factor

Economic development in Mainland China definitely has great impact on the Hong Kong economy. Indeed, Hong Kong has been a major provider of financial capital to the mainland economy since her economic reform in 1978, particularly through the continuous inflow of foreign direct investment from Hong Kong. As an international financial center, Hong Kong's reputable and sound financial structure has been used by mainland enterprises and institutions to raise capital and conduct appropriate financial transactions. As the financial situation in Mainland China matures, Hong Kong in turn will benefit from the vast development in the Mainland economy.

The development of stock markets in Mainland China and Hong Kong can be summarized in the following three features (Sun and Zhang, 2009). Firstly, the stock markets in Mainland China can be seen as the evolution of the great structural change since economic reform in 1978. Prior to the 2005 "reform of non-tradable shares" in Mainland China's capital market, it was noted that about two-third of the shares of listed companies under the two-tier structure were non-tradable. The 2005 capital market reform allowed the gradual float of these non-tradable shares, resulting in a rise in the real market values of the shares. The second characteristic is that the financial markets in Mainland China and Hong Kong are not homogenous. While Mainland China still imposes restrictions on both the inward and outward flows in its

TABLE 9.12 GDP growth and per capita GDP in Hong Kong, Shanghai and Shenzhen

	Hong Kong		Shanghai		Shenzhen	
Year	GDP growth (percent)	Per capita GDP (HK$)	GDP growth (percent)	Per capita GDP (HK$)	GDP growth (percent)	Per capita GDP (HK$)
1990	4.0	148,219	9	5,658	48	6,432
1991	5.7	155,359	18	6,670	38	6,223
1992	6.5	163,998	25	8,285	34	6,962
1993	6.3	171,410	36	11,205	43	7,756
1994	5.6	176,988	30	14,542	40	8,677
1995	3.9	180,323	25	17,404	33	10,542
1996	4.2	179,772	18	20,452	24	12,157
1997	5.1	187,401	16	23,062	24	13,714
1998	–5.5	175,690	10	25,193	18	14,672
1999	4.0	180,977	9	27,374	18	15,752
2000	10.0	197,268	18	28,502	21	17,122
2001	0.6	197,067	9	32,281	13	18,848
2002	1.8	199,804	10	35,329	20	21,935
2003	3.2	206,604	17	39,124	21	25,510
2004	8.6	222,586	21	46,342	19	29,810
2005	7.5	238,284	13	51,486	16	33,598
2006	6.9	253,151	13	57,113	17	44,857

Source: CEIC Database, *Shanghai Statistical Yearbook* and *Shenzhen Statistical Yearbook.*

capital account, Hong Kong is an open market to all investors and issuers and imposed no restrictions on its residents investing in foreign financial markets. Thirdly, with increasing financial integration between Mainland China and Hong Kong, any policy decisions on the financial development in Mainland China has important implications on Hong Kong's status as an international financial center. There is a mutual and bilateral promotion of financial market development between Mainland China and Hong Kong. While Hong Kong has played an important role in the open up of China's capital account and financial market development, Mainland China's rapid economic growth and development in the financial markets have provided Hong Kong with opportunities to fortify its position as a leading international and regional financial center.

Tables 9.12, 9.13 and 9.14, show the GDP, international trade and international investment performances among the three cities of Hong Kong, Shanghai and Shenzhen. Table 9.12 shows that although the GDP growth rates of Shanghai and Shenzhen are much higher than Hong Kong, their GDP per capita are lower. Table 9.13 presents that Hong Kong is a much larger trading economy than that of Shanghai and Shenzhen, though Shanghai is catching up quickly. In international investment, as shown in Table 9.14, although Mainland China has been the largest recipient of foreign direct investment, Hong Kong has performed much stronger on

TABLE 9.13 Performances in trade: Hong Kong, Shanghai and Shenzhen

	Import/GDP			Export/GDP			Total trade/GDP		
	Hong Kong	Shanghai	Shenzhen	Hong Kong	Shanghai	Shenzhen	Hong Kong	Shanghai	Shenzhen
1990	0.76	0.18	0.44	0.76	0.18	0.47	1.52	0.35	0.91
1991	0.87	NA	0.41	0.86	NA	0.42	1.73	NA	0.82
1992	1.00	NA	0.36	0.97	NA	0.38	1.98	NA	0.74
1993	1.06	NA	0.31	1.03	NA	0.31	2.09	NA	0.62
1994	1.17	NA	0.26	1.10	NA	0.29	2.27	NA	0.55
1995	1.34	0.41	0.22	1.21	0.47	0.24	2.55	0.88	0.46
1996	1.33	0.40	0.17	1.21	0.42	0.20	2.54	0.82	0.37
1997	1.33	0.36	0.15	1.20	0.48	0.20	2.53	0.84	0.35
1998	1.24	0.35	0.12	1.17	0.50	0.17	2.42	0.84	0.29
1999	1.16	0.36	0.12	1.13	0.50	0.16	2.29	0.85	0.28
2000	1.26	0.43	0.13	1.20	0.55	0.16	2.46	0.98	0.29
2001	1.19	0.35	0.13	1.12	0.45	0.15	2.30	0.80	0.28
2002	1.20	0.31	0.14	1.16	0.41	0.16	2.36	0.72	0.29
2003	1.30	0.36	0.15	1.25	0.46	0.18	2.55	0.82	0.33
2004	1.40	0.42	0.16	1.34	0.56	0.18	2.74	0.97	0.34
2005	1.43	0.41	0.16	1.39	0.63	0.21	2.82	1.04	0.37
2006	1.50	0.44	0.17	1.42	0.72	0.23	2.92	1.16	0.41

Source: CEIC Database, *Shanghai Statistical Yearbook* and *Shenzhen Statistical Yearbook*.

TABLE 9.14 International investment: Hong Kong, Shanghai and Shenzhen

	FDI inflow/GDP			FDI outflow/GDP		
	Hong Kong	Shanghai	Shenzhen	Hong Kong	Shanghai	Shenzhen
1998	8.85	0.03	0.01	10.18	0.04	N.A.
1999	15.05	0.02	0.01	11.86	0.04	N.A.
2000	36.69	0.02	0.01	35.17	0.03	N.A.
2001	14.28	0.02	0.01	6.81	0.04	N.A.
2002	5.91	0.03	0.01	10.67	0.04	N.A.
2003	8.60	0.03	0.01	3.47	0.04	N.A.
2004	20.52	0.02	0.01	27.57	0.04	N.A.
2005	20.19	0.03	0.01	18.31	0.05	N.A.
2006	N.A.	0.03	0.01	N.A.	0.10	N.A.

Source: CEIC Database, *Shanghai Statistical Yearbook* and *Shenzhen Statistical Yearbook*.

a per capita basis. Moreover, Hong Kong clearly has experienced a bi-lateral flow in investment, as it is active in both inflow and outflow of investment funds.

Using established data, Figure 9.7 displays four economic trends in Mainland China on GDP per capita, fixed asset investment, foreign direct investment and external trade. One common feature among these four macroeconomic variables is that they have all increased considerably, especially since the turn of the century or after Mainland China has gained accession to the World Trade Organization in 2001. Figure 9.8 presents four major financial and monetary flows in the Mainland economy. Money supply has increased rapidly for a continued period, especially M2. The issued shares included the A, B, H and N-shares issued in various stock markets. The number of issued shares is indicated by the left hand axis, while the amount of raised capital is indicated by the right hand axis in Figure 9.8. The loans to sector shows the amount of bank loans lent to different economic sectors. Foreign reserves include gold reserve, reserve and Special Drawing Right in the International Monetary Fund, and foreign exchanges held by the central government. Foreign exchange reserves occupy the largest percentage in total reserve. In 2006, for example, 99.4% of foreign reserves in China were held in foreign exchanges.

Since the early 1980s, capital inflows to Mainland China have been increasing, and most of the inflows have been in the form of foreign direct investment (FDI). The total amount of FDI increased from US$920 billion in 1983 to US$69,468 billion in 2006. Meanwhile, Mainland China's capital outflow has also been rising. The total amount of Mainland China's outward direct investment has risen by 19 times approximately, from US$370 million in 1991 to US$6,953 million in 2005. Mainland China's outward investments are expanding rapidly from Asia to Europe and to the United States.[9] Movements in Mainland China's outward

[9] The more significant cases included: (1) China Construction Bank's 100% acquisition of the share capital of the Bank of America (Asia); (2) the Chinese government's investment in the EU Galileo Project; and (3) the Lenova takeover of IBM's PC division.

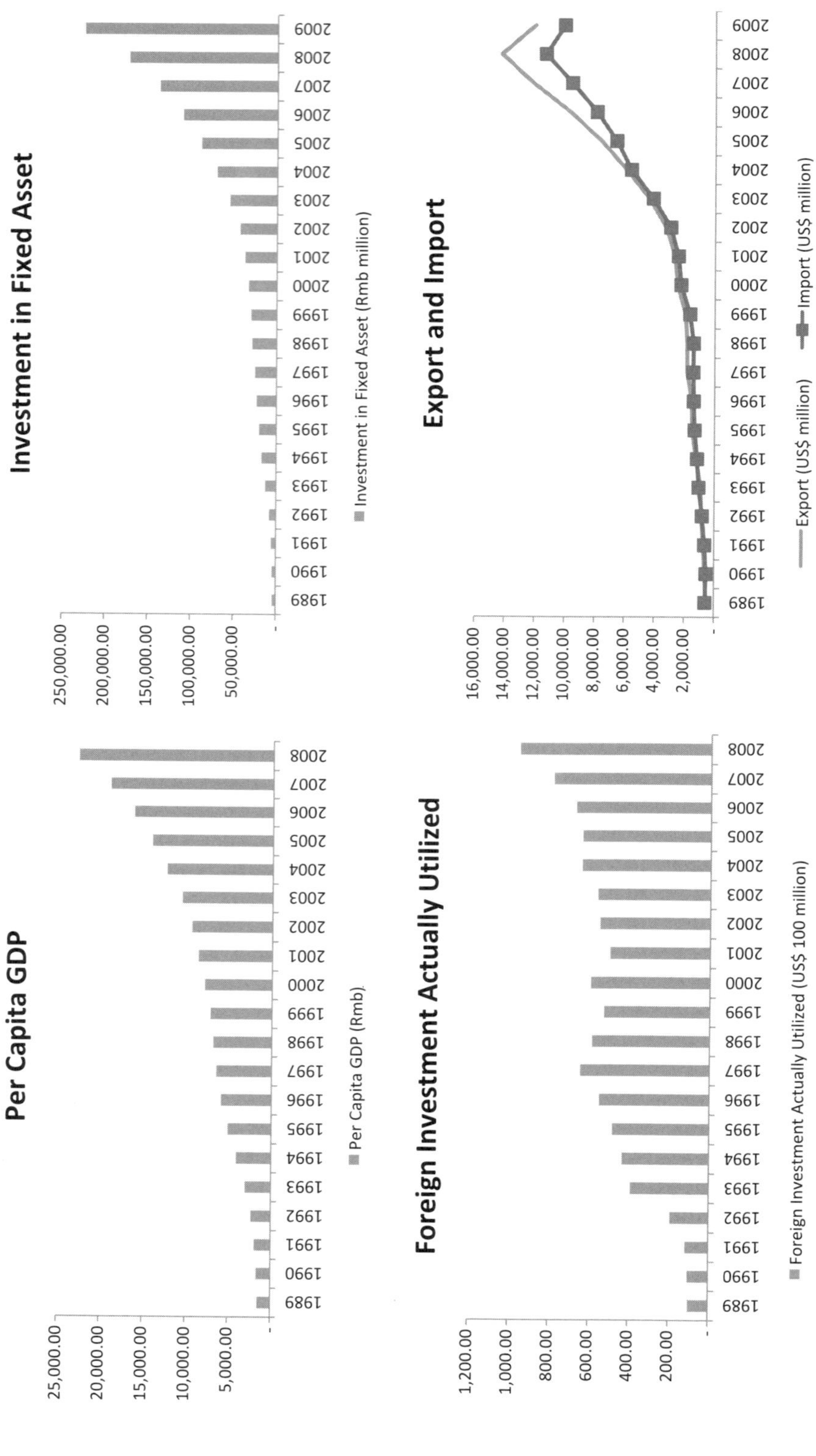

FIGURE 9.7 China's macroeconomic trends

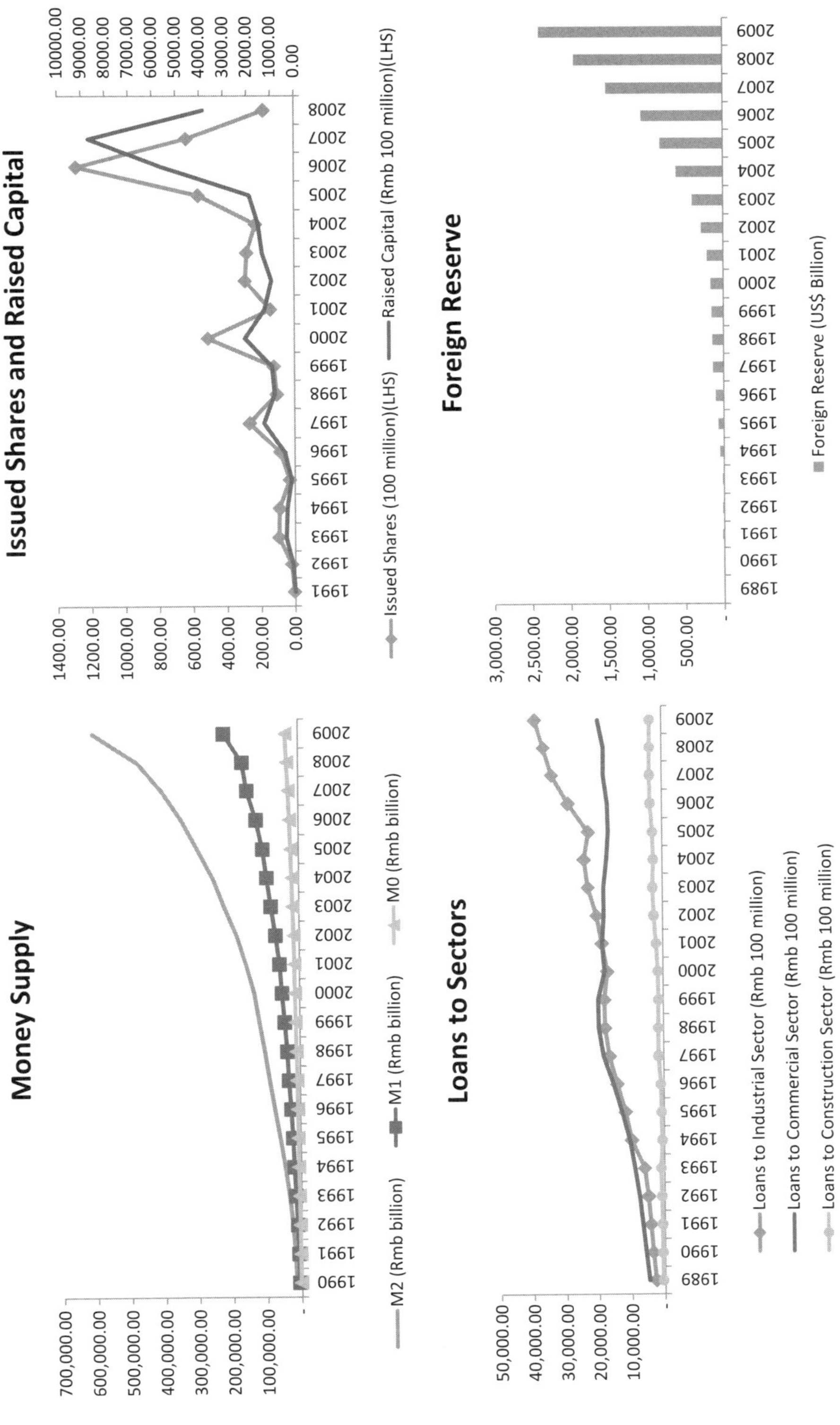

FIGURE 9.8 China's major financial flows

investment have considerably raised her economic influence among the Anglo-American countries.

Other than outward direct investment, Mainland China's use of foreign exchange reserves in acquiring US treasury bonds, especially after the 2008 financial crisis, is another form of capital outflow. There is, however, the possibility of capital flight from Mainland China, as the Renminbi, which is not yet fully convertible, can unofficially and informally be taken out of the country. Capital flights cannot be observed nor recorded easily and the capital flight calculations often are unreliable.

One can make a simple judgment on the magnitude of liquidity or "hot money flows" in the Mainland China economy. For example, in 2008, Mainland China's nominal GDP from established data amounted to Rmb300,670 (100 million), fixed asset investment amounted to Rmb172,828.39 million, capital raised through the stock markets amounted to Rmb3,852.21 (100 million), and bank loans amounted to Rmb303,394.6 million. These three domestic flows items occupied 2.865% of nominal GDP. Foreign direct investment in 2008 amounted to US$923.95 million, while trade surplus amounted to US$2,970.4 million. Foreign reserve was US$1,948.03 billion.

Studies in development economics have shown that developing countries often face a shortage in capital, or the existence of a "capital gap", as domestic savings is insufficient to fund the needed investment, and foreign capital inflows are needed as a substitute to deficient savings (Chenery and Strout, 1966). However, as reported in the Asian Development Bank, the saving rate in Mainland China has been high by world standard and has stayed around 35% to 45% of GDP since the 1990s. As shown in Table 9.15, China's saving gap has disappeared since 1997, as gross domestic saving exceeded gross domestic investment. Since 1997, domestic savings have increasingly exceeded domestic investment, and the difference peaked in 2005. In 2006, although there was a considerable decline in the saving gap, it was expected that considerable portions of domestic savings had been diverted to portfolio investments in the stock markets.

Over the years, the increase in liquidity in the Mainland China economy has produced both benefits and challenges to the Hong Kong financial sector. On the one hand, with the ample supply of financial capital and resources, the mainland economy would now have the ability to finance its own economic development. Secondly, as Mainland China's outward investment increases, Hong Kong will benefit as a recipient as Hong Kong can attract investment from Mainland China. Furthermore, China's overseas financial activities may also use Hong Kong's financial facilities and other forms of infrastructure, thereby positively promoting Hong Kong's businesses.

There are also new challenges. While Hong Kong has fostered the economic and financial development of the mainland economy since the early 1980s, there is every possibility of the "late comer" effect that gives the rapid and vast economic and financial expansion of the Mainland economy, its financial magnitude can easily swamp the small size of the Hong Kong economy, eventually marginalizing Hong Kong. It has also been argued that with the continued financial expansion, the Mainland economy is faced with a situation of excess liquidity, implying a situation with too much cash

TABLE 9.15 Domestic saving and investment in China (US$ million)

	Gross domestic investment	Gross domestic saving	Saving gap (S-I)
1989	633.3	582.8	–50.5
1990	674.7	657.7	–17.0
1991	786.8	769.0	–17.8
1992	1,008.6	972.0	–36.6
1993	1,571.8	1,343.4	–228.4
1994	2,034.1	1,895.6	–138.5
1995	2,547.0	2,404.6	–142.5
1996	2,878.5	2,725.7	–152.8
1997	2,996.8	3,083.2	86.4
1998	3,131.4	3,281.4	150.0
1999	3,295.2	3,404.0	108.9
2000	3,484.3	3,769.9	285.6
2001	3,976.9	4,277.7	300.7
2002	4,556.5	4,864.1	307.6
2003	5,596.3	5,837.3	241.0
2004	6,916.8	7,284.5	367.7
2005	7,956.0	8,695.0	739.0
2006	9,409.9	9,908.4	498.5

Source: Asian Development Bank.

flowing around the economy. An economy that experiences a prolonged period of excess liquidity can easily develop into a financial bubble as holders of excess liquidity will engage in speculative activities.

9.6 Competition From Shanghai

Shanghai was a leading financial center in the Far East ahead of Tokyo and Hong Kong in the early 1940s. When the Shanghai Stock Exchange was established in 1946, there were 24 foreign banks, 200 private lenders, trust companies and financial institutions.[10] After 1949, the Shanghai Stock Exchange was closed as Mainland China adopted the central planning economic system, and the whole financial market in Shanghai was abolished. Since Mainland China's economic reform in 1978, Shenzhen and other Special Economic Zones (SEZs) along the coast of Southern China were the major destinations of Hong Kong investments in the 1980s. Small-scale corporate equity trading reemerged in Shenzhen in the mid-1980s. Financial activities were revitalized in the SEZs and Shanghai has become the designated financial center by the central authority, the Shanghai Stock Exchange was set up in November 1990, while the Shenzhen Stock Exchange opened in 1991 (Li and Wong, 1997; Wong *et al.*, 1997).

[10] *The Banker*, March 2003.

A stock market primarily functions to serve as an intermediary between providers of capital and users of capital. Patrick (1966) suggests that the development of a stock market can either be created from a "demand-following" phenomenon in which the stock market emerged in response to the demand for financial services by the savers and investors, or a "supply-leading" situation in which the stock market is established in advance of the demand for such services. Montes (1999) points out the four types of financial markets based on the performance in intermediation. There can be domestic or foreign providers of capital, and also domestic and foreign users of capital. The four types of financial markets are:

Type 1, from domestic to domestic: the market serves as intermediaries between domestic providers of capital and domestic users of capital;

Type 2, from foreign to domestic: the market serves as intermediaries between foreign providers of capital and domestic users of capital;

Type 3, from domestic to foreign, the market serves as intermediaries between domestic providers of capital and foreign users of capital;

Types 4, from foreign to foreign: the market serves as intermediaries between foreign providers of capital and foreign users of capital.

Since the Shanghai Stock Exchange is geared mainly for the mainland economy, it is classified as Types 1 market where the financial intermediation takes place between domestic providers of capital and domestic users of capital. Because of the presence of foreign capital control in Mainland China, it is difficult for Shanghai to effectively channel capital between foreign providers/users of capital and domestic providers/users of capital. Thus, for the time being, the foreign intermediaries can only play a marginal role in Shanghai's financial sector, though multinational corporations often work through the official channel for their investment in the mainland economy. However, as the mainland China economy further develops, there will be more investment opportunities to foreign investors. The financial intermediary role of Shanghai to transform capital between international and domestic market will increase.

The securities traded on the Shanghai Stock Exchange consisted of stocks, funds, bonds and warrants. The stocks are divided into A-Shares and B-Shares. The A-Shares are designated for domestic investors, while the B-Shares are designated for foreign investors. On February 2001, The China Securities Regulatory Commission (CSRC) has allowed domestic investors to invest in B-shares. By the end of 2006, there were 845 A-shares and 54 B-shares, with a market capitalization of Rmb195,148 billion and Rmb1,346 billion, and an annual turnover of Rmb241,260 billion and Rmb2,942 billion for A-shares and B-shares, respectively. There were a total of 45 newly listed companies in 2006 and their total market capitalization amounted to Rmb217,000 billion.

In Shanghai's fund market, the first open-end fund was issued in September 2001 after the introduction of the closed-end fund in 1998. By the end of 2006, there were 17 funds and 3 Exchange-traded Funds (ETF). The total trading value has increased to Rmb3,375 billion, an increase of 2,400% when compared to the amount of Rmb135 billion in 2001. In the bond market, and by the end of 2006, there were

62 treasury bonds, 67 corporate bonds and 10 convertible bonds listed and traded in the Shanghai Stock Exchange. The bond market has since developed rapidly as the central government has often adopted a contractionary monetary policy by issuing treasury bonds to reduce excess liquidity in the banking system.

The trading of warrants mainly involved the future exchange market and the gold exchange market. In 1995, three future exchanges were established: Shanghai Metal Exchange, Shanghai Cereals and Oils Exchange and Shanghai Commodity Exchange. The copper, petroleum, building materials, agricultural products and chemicals are the main items traded in the markets. Since 1998 when the three exchanges were merged into the Shanghai Futures Exchanges, the development of futures market has been expanded significantly. The Shanghai Gold Exchange (SGE) was set up in October 2002 after the introduction of the Weekly Gold Pricing System and the abolition of the Gold Products Retail License System. However, the development of SGC is still at the early stage, as only 'physical' trading is conducted. The trading of gold futures could be improved after an enhancement of the trading systems and related regulations.

The stock market in Shanghai has been volatile due to optimistic market sentiment and the excessive liquidity in the banking and financial system. For example, the Shanghai Stock Exchange Composite Index climbed to a record high of 6,092 point on October 16, 2007, but it had dropped below 1,000 points in June 2005. The excess liquidity (or so called "cash-rich") is the direct result of a number of favorable inflows of capital and cash and foreign exchange.

Mainland China has enjoyed large trade surplus since the 30% depreciation of the Renminbi in 1994, and has accumulated a significant trade surplus in the current account. In addition, Mainland China has become the largest recipient of foreign capital through foreign direct investment. Mainland China's reluctance as reflected in the slow pace in the appreciation of the Renminbi against the US dollar has meant that the Chinese authority has aggressively been buying the US currency in order to increase the supply of Renminbi, especially after the burst of the US financial crisis in late 2008. For example, it was reported that Mainland China is already the largest foreign holder of US treasuries, and has increased its holding of US government notes and bonds by US$28 billion to a total of US$801.5 billion in May 2009. The total amount of US government notes and bonds held by the Chinese government exceeded US$800 billion, equivalent to 37.6% of Mainland China's US$2.13 trillion foreign exchange reserves.[11] Continued trade surplus has made Mainland China the country with the largest foreign reserve in the world. The increase in the supply of the Renminbi could easily flow into the stock market, as Renminbi holders seek a higher rate of return than from bank deposits. Using data from the CEIC Database, Figure 9.9 shows the composite index trends of both Shanghai and Shenzhen stock markets.

Secondly, a number of mainland banks have raised capital through the initial public offerings in the Hong Kong stock market, though a sizable amount may have stayed in Hong Kong. Since 2005, the amount of capital raised in Hong Kong through the initial public offerings included the Construction Bank of China

---

[11] *China Daily eClips*, Business, July 18, 2009.

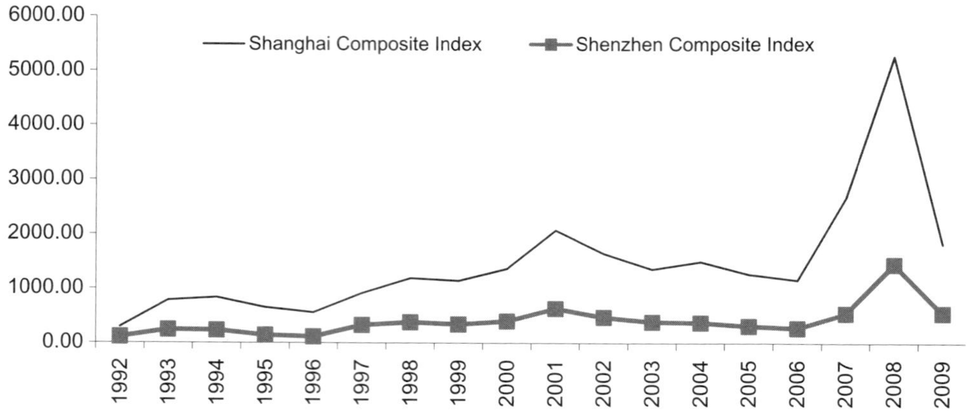

FIGURE 9.9 Composite Index: Shanghai and Shenzhen

(US$80 billion), Industrial and Commercial Bank of China (US$191 billion) and Bank of China (US$112 billion). A simple calculation is that if the required reserve ratio was assumed at 15%, the total amount of US$383 billion newly raised capital divided by the reserve ratio would yield an additional maximum capital of US$2,533.3 billion available for loan.

Thirdly, in speeding up the process of privatization of state-owned enterprises, many state-owned enterprises issued shares that served as a vehicle through which state ownership can be transferred to private ownership. After the launch of the "non-tradable share reform" in April 2005, an enormous volume of state-owned enterprises shares was released into the market. This increased the overall ratio of shares held in the private sector that eventually paved the way for the privatization of state-owned enterprises. As investors can now play a monitoring role in the corporate performance of the enterprises, it is expected that corporate governance and profitability would improve, thereby pushing up the stock prices.

Despite Shanghai's challenge to Hong Kong as Mainland China's key international financial market, some have questioned the historical high performance in the Shanghai Stock Exchange, and whether there is the possibility of a financial bubble. For example, the Shanghai Composite Index has increased over 500% from 1,080 points to 5,552 points in a short period between June 2005 and September 2007. The number of new monthly investor accounts, as shown in Figure 9.10, has increased from 69 in June 2005 to 4,711 in July 2007.

Figure 9.11 shows that the price-to-earnings (PE) ratio, which is a measure of the price paid for a share relative to the income or profit earned per share by the stock issuing firm, has increased significantly from a ratio of 16 in June 2005 to a ratio of 64 in September 2007. It has been argued that the current levels of share prices may have deviated considerably from the underlying economic fundamentals and corporate earnings.

On the contrary, others believe that when looking at other market bubbles, Shanghai has not performed too poorly and there is still room for the Shanghai stock market to grow. For example, during the technology bubble in the late 1990s, the Nasdaq Index increased by over 500% to its peak from January 1995 to January 2000,

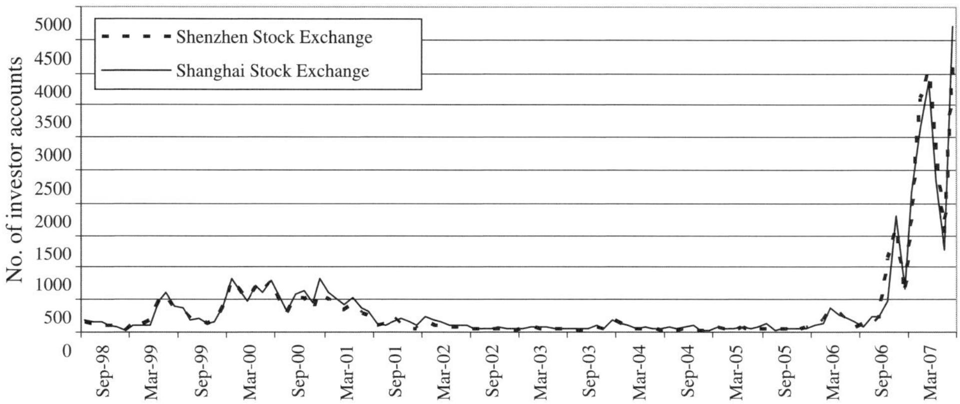

FIGURE 9.10 Number of new investor accounts

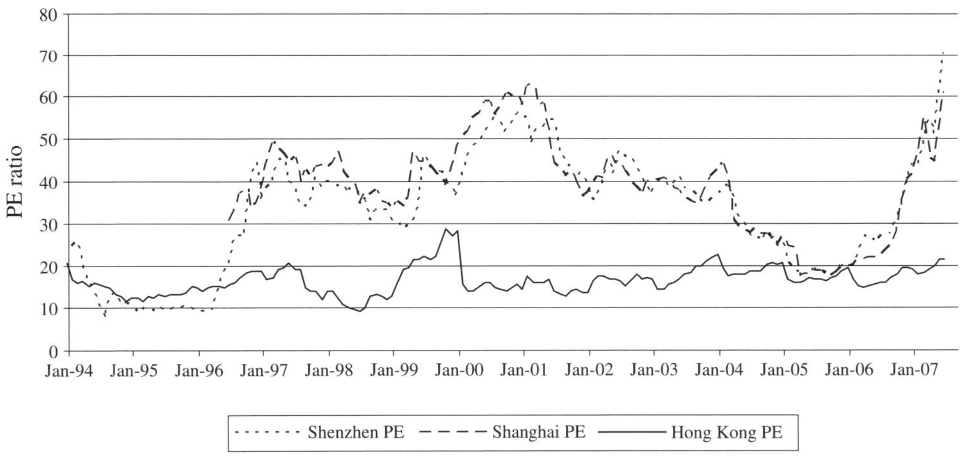

FIGURE 9.11 Comparison of PE ratios: Hong Kong, Shanghai and Shenzhen

and the PE ratio recorded a ratio of 140. During the 1980s bubble in Japan, the Topix Index in the Tokyo exchange increased by 460% from January 1981 to December 1989 and the PE ratio was 71.

Moreover, the stock market in Shanghai has experienced a prolonged bear market, while economic growth has increased by about 70% in the period 2001–2005. The severity of the catch-up in the stock market is thus not surprising, as the strength of the Mainland China economy and the large liquidity in the market can push the stock prices further. Apart from that, it is believed that the central government will adopt aggressive policies to calm speculation and reduce the rising risk in the stock market.

The rise of Shanghai as a financial center has also led to the debate on the possibilities of a merger between the two or even three financial markets of Hong Kong, Shanghai and Shenzhen. Those who favor the merger will question whether Hong Kong can maintain its position as a financial center over the next decade. The advantages of a single, merged China stock market include the possibility of narrowing the regulatory differences and to encourage more cross-border trading and listings. Analysts from the China Securities Regulatory Commission, however, note that it was too soon to talk about the merger of the three stock markets.[12]

According to the *Global Financial Center Index* conducted by the City of London (2007), Hong Kong has all the three prerequisites of a good financial center: talent, quality regulation, and a sound system. Hong Kong's advantages include a good financial system, mature mechanism and sound legal system, efficient government, smooth coordination among different banks, a large pool of financial talents such as fund managers and financial analysts, a mix of cultures, rapid information dissemination and a free flow of capital. Although Hong Kong faces competition from other nearby stock markets, it is unlikely for Hong Kong to lose out to Shanghai in a short period of time. Joseph Yam, the former Chief Executive of the Hong Kong Monetary Authority, remarked that there can be advantages if the two markets are "linked". For example, the overall liquidity would increase, price would become more efficient, market discipline could be promoted, and it would be easier for market players to manage risk.[13]

Whether it is possible for the Shanghai, Shenzhen and Hong Kong exchange markets to merge depends on four criteria: (1) whether the central government will ease its foreign exchange restriction and allow full convertibility of the Renminbi; (2) whether there can be a merge between A-shares and H-shares; (3) how to tackle the issue of different legal systems between Hong Kong and Mainland China, and (4) the ownership issues of stock exchanges. The Hong Kong Exchanges and Clearing Limited (HKEx) is a listed company. Hong Kong and Mainland China use different legal system: Hong Kong applies common law but the mainland uses continental law that makes the merger of the exchanges complicated.

Another possibility would be for the stock markets in Mainland China to exercise acquisition over the Hong Kong Exchanges and Clearing Limited (HKEx). Given the huge amount of liquidity that Mainland China or Shanghai can mobilize, it would be financially feasible for a large portion of shares of the HKEx be acquired by the Shanghai Stock Exchange.[14] For example, Shanghai's GDP in 2009 reached US$218,300 million, increased by 8.2% from 2008, but Hong Kong's GDP amounted to US$210,700 million, an increase of 2.7% from 2008 (Ho, 2010). The possibility of the takeover bid was raised in 2007 when the Hong Kong SAR Government announced on September 7, 2007, the mobilization of HK$2.4 billion through the Exchange Fund to increase the holding of shares issued by the HKEx from 4.5% to 5.88%. The announcement led to the share price of the HKEx to surge by as much as 24.68%.

Armed with the precedence of mobilization of HK$118 billion to purchase stocks to keep the market from crashing in 1998, the Hong Kong SAR Government

---

[12] *South China Morning Post*, September 15, 2007.

[13] *China Daily*, June 29, 2007.

[14] A rule in Hong Kong has been in place that bans anyone from holding more than 5% of the shares issued by the HKEx (*South China Morning Post*, September 11, 2007).

intervened in the stock market in the second time, though the official explanation is that the acquisition could lead to additional cooperation with stock markets in Mainland China. The acquisition by the Hong Kong government has been criticized by analysts as it created a conflict of interest as government policies may have other impact on companies listed in the stock exchange.[15]

With a government holding of 5.88% in HKEx, it would be unlikely for any other stock market to takeover HKEx, thereby ensuring that the HKEx will remain as a Hong Kong financial institution. This might give a stronger signal to mainland investors that Hong Kong has a reliable financial structure, and further financial cooperation can be conducted. Nonetheless, in the spirit of cooperation, the HKEx and the Shanghai Stock Exchange has in January 2009 signed a Closer Cooperation Agreement that the two stock markets will be committed to work more closely with each other to raise funds for the further development of mainland enterprises and mainland economy (Ho, 2010). The 2009 agreement has effectively settled the debate on the competition between the two stock exchanges in Hong Kong and Shanghai, as cooperation has become the ultimate intention and objective.

Indeed, each of the two stock markets has their own characteristics and Mainland China is big enough to have more than one stock exchange. For various reasons, mainland enterprises may prefer to list their shares in the Hong Kong or New York stock exchanges. There are also a few fundamental differences between the two stock markets of Shanghai and Hong Kong. First, the Hong Kong currency is linked to the US dollar and is internationally convertible, while the Renminbi is not fully convertible and is still in the internationalization process.

One has to consider other fundamental conditions of a financial center. Hong Kong has been an international banking center since the 1960s and 1970s before transforming itself into an international financial center. The rise of Hong Kong as an international banking center was due to the need for international trading finance. The rise of the stock market was the result of a "demand-following" and a home-grown need for corporations to raise capital locally. On the contrary, Shanghai's growth as a financial center was regarded as "supply-leading" as its development was the result of a deliberate decision by the central government that Shanghai be designated as a financial center in Mainland China, though historically Shanghai had once flourished as the Far East financial center before 1949.[16]

Another key feature of a stock market viewed by the investors is choice and the provision of alternatives. If all the three stock markets in Shanghai, Shenzhen and Hong Kong were merged into one single but larger stock market, there could be a lower degree of portfolio choice and less market diversity for investors. The attitude and psychology that the rise of Shanghai is equivalent to the fall of Hong Kong is inappropriate. The rise of one financial center should produce a positive sum game, rather than a zero-sum game. In short, given that Shanghai is rising rapidly as a financial center and there is excess liquidity in Mainland China, it would be appropriate for both Hong Kong and Shanghai to develop in a way most suitable to them.

---

[15] *South China Morning Post*, September 11, 2007; *Hong Kong Economic Journal*, September 8, 2007.

[16] *South China Morning Post*, January 19, 2007.

The international nature of the Hong Kong financial market can play a role in supporting the development of stock markets in Mainland China in the regulatory framework and training of personnel. Before the full convertibility of the Renminbi, it would not be advisable for the mainland and Hong Kong stock markets to merge. Nonetheless, Hong Kong needs to improve and expand its activities in order to maintain its status as an international finance center, and there is no room for a complacent attitude.[17]

When Hong Kong's financial market is compared to New York, one can consider the future role of Hong Kong as an international financial center in Mainland China, He *et al.* (2006) show that the financial sector in New York employed twice as many people and generated four times more output than Hong Kong. The greatest difference between the two financial markets is in the securities industry. Hence, the securities industry in Hong Kong has the greatest potential to expand, because the securities industry in Hong Kong could serve the need of fund raisers and investors from Mainland China. As an international financial center, Hong Kong should not only serve to bridge the fund flow between Mainland China and the rest of the world, but should also facilitate a two-way capital flows between Mainland China and Hong Kong.

Other than Shanghai, one should also play close attention to the development in Shenzhen, one of the Special Economic Zones established in the 1980s and is located across the border of Hong Kong and is the first destination that received the bulk of capital investment from Hong Kong. In the thirty years since economic openness in Mainland China in 1978, Shenzhen has developed rapidly. By today, Shenzhen has claimed to be a leading economy in Southern China, especially in the Pearl River Delta. Government officials in Shenzhen have been active in promoting Shenzhen as an industrial, financial and service center. For example, one of the developments in the Pearl River Delta is a plan to turn Qianhai, a newly developed satellite town near Shenzhen, into a service and financial hub that would compete with similar business activities in Hong Kong (Pauly, 2011).

9.7 New Development Areas: The Renminbi and Islamic Finance

While Hong Kong has been the key investor in Mainland China, and over the years, funds from Hong Kong has been invested in Mainland China. The maturity of the mainland economy shall also benefit Hong Kong. The various continuous and large inflows of funds to Mainland China have turned Mainland China into a highly liquid economy. Together with the rapid rise in trade surplus and the pressure for the Renminbi to appreciate, Mainland China needs to find ways to ease the inflow of funds so that the capital account surplus could be reduced and the need for the Renminbi to appreciate is minimized. Mainland China's excess liquidity provides a golden opportunity for business expansions in Hong Kong's financial sector.

---

[17] "Hong Kong and Shanghai Financial Centers", *Comments on Finance*, No. 31, Economic Research Department, Bank of China (HK), April 20, 2009 (in Chinese).

At a different level, the financial sector in Hong Kong also wants to expand its scope so as to nurture a larger and stronger financial sector in future. While internal qualities and standards need to be upgraded, deepened and strengthened, the development of Islamic finance in Hong Kong has been discussed as a new area of expansion. The financial activities among the Muslim countries have been expanding, mainly due to the large revenue from oil and petroleum. The prolonged high energy price has led the oil exporting countries able to amass sizable amount of world wealth, which can be mobilized for various investment activities. However, numerous rules and practices of Islamic finance require the establishment of new laws and regulations that may conflict with existing practices.

Renminbi offshore center

Over the years, Mainland China has been able to attract funds from Hong Kong and overseas for their economic development and growth. Other than the large inflows of foreign direct investments that are geared largely to the industries and exports, another channel aimed to attract foreign capital to Mainland China is the Qualified Foreign Institutional Investment (QFII) launched in 2002. According to the stipulated regulations, QFII are allowed to invest in Renminbi-denominated stocks, otherwise available only to mainland investors. In 2006, a total of 18 foreign institutional investors with a combined quota of US$3 billion were approved, bringing the total number of approved foreign institutional investors to 52 since it was launched in 2002. It is commonly thought that foreign investment quotas will continue to be expanded, and the total allowed for foreign institutional investors could increase from US$8 billion to US$40 billion in the few years after 2006 as the expansion would help to enlarge the role of institutional investors and develop the capital market.[18]

While the QFII ensured both the inflow of foreign capital and stock market transactions in the mainland economy, there is also an institutional set up that related to the systematic and manageable outflow of funds. On April 13, 2006, the People's Bank of China (PBC) announced the Qualified Domestic Institutional Investor (QDII) scheme that allowed financial institutions to invest in offshore markets such as securities and fixed income products. Similar to the QFII, the QDII scheme is a transitional arrangement that offered domestic investors limited opportunities to access foreign markets under the situation where capital is not able to move completely free in and out of the country.

The QDII scheme allowed "mainland financial institutions with foreign exchange to invest in capital markets outside the mainland such as Hong Kong under certain conditions". The China Banking Regulatory Commission (CBRC) in May 2007 widened the QDII scheme by allowing mainland commercial banks to manage on behalf of the overseas wealth of their clients. The QDII scheme also allowed mainland commercial banks to invest in financial products and intermediaries authorized

[18] The number and amount of investment quota given to the qualified foreign institutional investors can be obtained from the State Administration of Foreign Exchange (Safe) in Beijing.

and supervised by the financial regulatory bodies in Hong Kong. The announcement aimed to orderly facilitate the outflow of capital from the mainland without destabilizing the stock markets. The QDII effectively allowed domestic investors to invest in foreign securities markets through qualified commercial banks, qualified securities companies, qualified insurance companies and other assets management institutions approved by the CBRC.[19]

Qualified commercial banks are allowed to collect Renminbi funds from local institutions and individuals, convert them into foreign exchange and conduct investments in overseas fixed income and money market products. Qualified securities institutions are allowed to collect self-owned foreign exchange of local institutions and individuals and allocate funds in overseas investment portfolio including purchase of equities. Qualified insurance companies are allowed to convert Renminbi funds into foreign exchange, and the QDII scheme has effectively expanded the insurance companies' investment options. They are allowed to invest part of their assets in overseas fixed-income products and money-market products.

The role of the Hong Kong SAR Government is to provide to the relevant mainland authorities with information on Hong Kong markets, regulatory framework and legal system, and to reflect to them Hong Kong's capability and its keen desire to participate actively and constructively in the QDII scheme. As at September 27, 2006, 14 commercial banks have been granted a QDII license with a foreign exchange conversion limit ranging from US$500 million to US$2 billion. Only one securities institution has been given a license, and its foreign exchange conversion is limited to US$500 million. No insurance company has been granted a license.

Key leaders in the finance sector in Hong Kong applauded the QDII scheme, as it reflected the importance and capability of Hong Kong's status as an international financial center. In the government press release on May 14, 2007, the former Financial Secretary, Henry Tang, pointed out the several important aspects of the QDII scheme: (1) It enhances Hong Kong as an international financial center, and Hong Kong is able to provide a world class financial services platform for a wide spectrum of financial services to the Mainland; (2) It facilitates the outward mobility of Mainland investors and financial intermediaries that can orderly alleviate Mainland China's external imbalances; (3) It brings more business opportunities to financial intermediaries in Hong Kong, and enhances the co-operation and development between the Mainland and Hong Kong financial institutions. As a whole, the expansion can make best use of Hong Kong's financial platform to facilitate and complement the Mainland's development needs.

The former Chief Executive of the Hong Kong Monetary Authority, Joseph Yam, agrees that the QDII scheme will bring more business to the financial sector as a whole.[20] The Hong Kong Monetary Authority will cooperate with the Mainland authorities in designing the channels to facilitate capital outflow proactively and gradually, while maintaining a high degree of controllability. The former Secretary for Financial Services and the Treasury, Frederick Ma, points out the two key benefits of

---

[19] *Hang Seng Economic Monthly*, September 2006.

[20] "Expansion of QDII Schemes", Hong Kong Monetary Authority, April 26, 2007.

the QDII scheme to Hong Kong are: (1) Mainland funds that are invested in the financial products in Hong Kong will increase the trading volume and liquidity; and (2) Mainland investors can engage in Hong Kong's financial institutions which contain rich international experience and professional knowledge in global investments.[21] Thus, the QDII scheme will enhance the investment returns and diversify the risks of Mainland investors and at the same time strengthen the development of the financial services sector in Hong Kong.

The Financial Services and Treasury Bureau in Hong Kong concluded that the new measures under QDII are the sign of Mainland's recognition of Hong Kong as a financial center with a regulatory regime compatible to international standards.[22] The QDII measures will provide enormous business and employment opportunities to the financial sector and help promote development of both the Mainland and Hong Kong economies. The measures will thus create a win-win situation for the two economies.

An added advantage in the QDII scheme is to allow mainland investors to interact with international financial institutions in Hong Kong, which in turn deepens and widens the financial market, increases its liquidity and stabilizes Hong Kong's financial structure. There was a positive feedback to the new scheme. Sentiment in Hong Kong's stock market was boosted after the announcement of the extension of the range of QDII-approved products to foreign equities, and the Hang Seng Index hit a new record high of 20,995 points on May 17, 2007, amidst hectic trading.

However, the Hong Kong stock market soon became overheated, and the positive sentiment of the QDII scheme was seen as a mean for Mainland investors to invest massively in Hong Kong. This would add to the risk of destabilizing the Hong Kong economy, especially the consequent speculative activities in the stock market and the possibility of building up another financial bubble has to be considered seriously. In Mainland China, there was also the risk that domestic investors were allowed to invest in securities in Hong Kong and overseas markets. Such a risk could be formidable in view of the excess liquidity, and the large amount of Renminbi that could be mobilized in a short time. In short, the situation could be difficult to control, and may eventually do more harm to the stock markets than an orderly outflow of mainland investment.

On August 20, 2007, the State Administration of Foreign Exchange (Safe) further announced a pilot scheme that permitted individuals in Mainland to invest in the Hong Kong securities. Although there are a number of conditions and trading restrictions on derivatives and short-selling, this effectively freed all individuals in Mainland China to invest in Hong Kong with little limits. Under the pilot scheme, Mainland individuals can open foreign exchange accounts at the Tianjin branch of the Bank of China, or other Bank of China outlets that acted as agents for the Tianjin branch, to trade Hong Kong stocks. There will be no limit on the amount of stock purchased. Although no specific dates for the operation of the scheme was

---

[21] "QDII Enhances Hong Kong's Role", Press Release, Hong Kong SAR Government, April 30, 2006.

[22] "FSTB and You: Expansion of QDII Advantageous to the Mainland and Hong Kong", Secretary for Financial Services and the Treasury, May 2007.

announced, it was considered as a positive step towards capital account liberalization. It was argued that the individual investment scheme effectively made the QDII redundant as individuals can buy stocks directly.[23]

On the date of the announcement, the Hang Seng Index in Hong Kong increased by 1,200 points, the historically third largest increase in a single day. Analysts estimated that some of the mainland's foreign exchange reserve that amounted to US$1.33 trillion would come to Hong Kong. Another financial firm estimated that if a 1% of domestic savings were to come to Hong Kong on a daily basis, it would amount to an estimate of additional HK$10 billion to HK$20 billion trading in the stock market in Hong Kong. The lowest amount of turnover in the Hong Kong stock exchange at the time was around HK$ 70 billion.[24] Such a huge magnitude of expansion in the Hong Kong stock market has resulted in a positive sentiment, and much speculation was involved in the stock trading.

The year 2007 marked the 10th anniversary of the sovereignty change of Hong Kong in 1997. Investment sentiments turned bullish, especially in the second half of 2007 after the announcement of the individual investment scheme. Undoubtedly, a considerable amount of stock market trading in both Hong Kong and Mainland China was speculative in nature. Subsequently, Premier Wen Jiabao declared in November 2007 that the QDII and individual investment schemes were to be shelved, ending months of stock market speculations. It was seen as an appropriate move, as the subsequent events in Mainland China turned out to be unfavorable to risk a currency flight.

Mainland China in the early months of 2008 experienced extremely cold weather, and there were prolonged heavy snow falls that imposed hazards to life in a large number of inner provinces. Passengers that attempted to return to their home village in time for the Chinese New Year were severely affected as the snow storm disrupted many train and other transport services. The side-effect of the snow storms was the fall in food supply, and the price of agricultural products increased in subsequent months. In May 2008, the devastating earthquake in the Szechuan province brought prolonged economic hardship to both the central government and Szechuan province. At the same time, Mainland China was in the final stage of the preparation for the Olympics in August 2008. Decisions that generated unintended consequence in a massive outflow of domestic funds would naturally be seen as risky and hazardous in view of the uncertain circumstances.

Retrospectively, the shelving of the two schemes was appropriate as it avoided the risk of large financial outflow in a sensitive time. In many ways, there are loopholes in Mainland China's financial infrastructure. Due to the close proximity between Hong Kong and Shenzhen, for example, an informal money market and underground trading of the Renminbi has remained active. It has been reported in Shenzhen that there are traders operating illegal foreign exchange services in which Renminbi are exchanged for Hong Kong dollars and are deposited in Hong Kong bank accounts. The deposits are then used in Hong Kong to invest in the stock

---

[23] *South China Morning Post*, August 21, 2007.

[24] *Mingpao Daily*, August 21, 2007.

market. One report showed that a rouge bank in Shenzhen handled illegal transactions from all other provinces totaling Rmb4.3 billion (US$581 million) in a period of 18 months.[25] The various experiences suggested that the Renminbi is still a sensitive issue that could generate unwanted risk and unintended consequences if the issue was not handled with care.

The Hong Kong financial sector can serve the Renminbi in two related ways. On the one hand, given the huge liquidity Mainland China has amassed over the years, new channels are needed to ease the pressure on the appreciation of the Renminbi. On the other hand, the Renminbi needs to be internationalized before it can become fully convertible. The internationalization of the Renminbi would primarily mean an increase in acceptability in other parts of the world, including the increased use of Renminbi in trading and clearing. The international nature of Hong Kong's financial center is most suited to help in conducting more business and trading of Renminbi. Secondly, the stable nature of the Hong Kong currency can be an anchor for the internationalization of the Renminbi. In short, Hong Kong is the most suitable candidate in handling the Renminbi business.

Hong Kong's role as a Rennminbi offshore center has first been raised by the former Chief Executive, Tung Chee-hwa, during his duty-report trip to Beijing in July 2003. The State Council in Beijing subsequently on November 19, 2003, approved that from January 2004 individuals travelling from Mainland China to Hong Kong were allowed to use mainland-issued Renminbi-based credit cards in Hong Kong. On December 25, 2003, the Bank of China (Hong Kong) was given the responsibility for the Renminbi clearing activities in Hong Kong. The development of Renminbi business has been rapid. On February 25, 2004, banks in Hong Kong began to conduct Renminbi banking services for individuals in Hong Kong, including Renminbi deposits, exchange of currency, remittance and Renminbi denominated credit cards.

Further development and expansion took place on November 11, 2005, when the Beijing authority agreed to expand Renminbi business in Hong Kong by allowing enterprises to open Renminbi denominated accounts, relaxing the ceiling of currency exchange, and lifting the maximum credit card limit of Rmb100 thousand, and allowing the opening of Renminbi current accounts. Eventually, Renminbi denominated bonds are allowed to be released in Hong Kong on January 10, 2007, though the exercise would be experimental and the bonds issued in Hong Kong will be limited to those mainland institutions with high credit rating. The latest development that began in July 2009 is that the Renminbi will be used as the settlement currency in all cross-border trade.[26] These developments are usually announced or concluded during the duty-report trip to Beijing by the Chief Executive, Donald Tsang Yam-kuen.[27]

Obviously, the decision to engage Hong Kong for Renminbi business will benefit both Hong Kong and Mainland China. Being the Renminbi offshore trading center,

---

[25] *The China Post*, December 10, 2007.

[26] *Mingpao Daily*, January 11, 2007 and December 17, 2008; *South China Morning Post*, January 11, 2007 and June 30, 2009.

[27] *South China Morning Post*, December 17 and 18, 2008.

Hong Kong has become truly Mainland China's international finance center, while Shanghai is the main financial center for Mainland China's domestic economy.[28] Secondly, the Renminbi business helped Hong Kong to diversify its financial activities and business. In many ways, Hong Kong has the monopoly in Renminbi business, as no other financial centers are given the authority. To Mainland China, the Renminbi business in Hong Kong would help to release some of the excess liquidity problem accumulated in Mainland China and is a step towards the internationalization and full convertibility of the Renminbi. Through the Renminbi business, the international nature of the financial sector in Hong Kong can provide useful lessons to the financial system in Mainland China. In the long-run, the conduct of the Renminbi trading activities in Hong Kong can radiate to other financial institutions in Mainland China, thereby promoting their overall standards and qualities. Other long-term possibilities included the de-linking of the Hong Kong currency to the US dollar or even the replacement of the Hong Kong currency by the Renminbi, though financial practices have been governed by the Basic Law in Hong Kong SAR.[29]

Table 9.16 reports the rapid pace of increase in both Renminbi deposits and cumulative trade settlement in Hong Kong. The statistics suggests that Hong Kong

TABLE 9.16 Renminbi deposits and trade settlement in Hong Kong

Deposits (Rmb billion)		Cumulated trade settlement (Rmb billion)	
2/2004	9	9/2009	0.1
12/2004	12	12/2009	3.6
12/2005	23	3/2010	21.9
12/2006	23	6/2010	70.6
12/2007	33	9/2010	197.1
12/2008	56		
12/2009	63		
6/2010	90		
7/2010	104		
8/2010	130		
9/2010	149		
10/2010	217		
11/2010	280		

Sources: *Mingpao Daily*, January 11, 2007; Hong Kong Monetary Authority; Monetary Policy Execution Report (2009Q3–2010Q3), People's Bank of China.

[28] *South China Morning Post*, January 19, 2007; "Hong Kong's Role in the Regionalization and Internationalization of Renminbi", *Comments on Finance*, No. 2, Economic Research Department, Bank of China (HK), January 13, 2009 (in Chinese).

[29] *South China Morning Post*, June 30, 2009.

does fulfill the role of the Renminbi offshore trading center, though the Chief Executive of HKEx, Charles Li, remarked in January 2011 that the Renminbi deposit in Hong Kong is still less than 5% of total Hong Kong deposits, and the cumulative Renminbi trade settlement is less than 1% of Mainland China's total trade, implying that there is still room for expansion.[30]

Table 9.16 also shows that the increase of Renminbi deposits has been slow at the beginning. The idea of an offshore center for the Renminbi actually served the function that the Renminbi which has been transferred to an overseas country could flow back to Mainland China. Over the years, Renminbi has been flowing out of Mainland China through various informal channels. The supply of the Renminbi has been increasing, as one can estimate from the continuous large increase in money supply. The People's Bank of China that served as the "central bank" may estimate the amount of outflow through "capital flight". As an offshore center, overseas holders of Renminbi can sell the Renminbi back to Hong Kong banks, which will eventually be channeled back to Mainland China through the intermediary, namely the Bank of China in Hong Kong.

When individuals and businesses deposited Renminbi in Hong Kong banks, interest will have to be paid out by the banks. However, these Renminbi deposits cannot be lent out as loans, as businesses in Hong Kong do not transact in Renminbi, and banks would not engage in cross-border loans. Thus, unless banks are allowed to transfer Renminbi deposits back to their subsidiaries in Mainland China where they can made loans to mainland businesses, banks in Hong Kong holding Renminbi deposits would not be too profitable. With the permission to use Renminbi in trade settlement, businesses that are conducting mainland trade in Hong Kong can now use their Renminbi deposits freely to settle their trade. Renminbi has effectively become a quasi-official currency in Hong Kong's trade with mainland. With the wider use of Renminbi in Hong Kong, banks can engage themselves more with Renminbi deposits. This relaxation in the use of Renminbi has made the banks in Hong Kong more willing to conduct Renminbi businesses, as reflected in the large increases since 2008 as shown in Table 9.16.

Islamic finance

Islamic finance has been suggested as a new branch of financial activity in Hong Kong, as Islamic banking and finance has increased their presence in an increasing number of non-Islamic countries. In a paper published by the International Monetary Fund, Solé (2007) has documented the various requirements in order to successfully establish Islamic banking and finance activities. Statistically, Solé (2007) reports that there are more than 300 Islamic financial institutions situated in 51 countries, and as many as 250 mutual funds are compiled with Islamic principles.

Despite the growing popularity of Islamic investors from the Gulf region, due obviously to the rising demand by the Muslim population in Western countries and

[30] "2011 HKEx Annual media Luncheon", presentation by Charles Li, Chief Executive, HKEx, January 11, 2011.

the huge amount of wealth cumulated by the oil exporting countries from the high energy price, Solé (2007) warns that conventional commercial banks and financial institutions wanting to expand into Islamic finance need to familiar with and will have to adopt to a number of Islamic-related principles and practices. To begin with, the preaching of the Quran excludes a number of finance-related activities, such as interest, contractual uncertainty, speculation and gambling. Stock market speculations and short selling are not allowed. There are also a number of prohibitive industries and products. Investment related to tobacco, alcohol, pork-related products, leisure and entertainment, casinos and firearms are prohibited. The basic principles of Islamic finance are established by the Shariah and other rulings and jurisprudence issued by qualified Muslim scholars. To minimize risk, an institution intended to offer Islamic products must appoint a Shariah counselor or a Shariah board to ensure that all terms agreed in a contract do compile with Islamic jurisprudence.

Institutions can consult two multilateral institutions. One established in 1990 is the Accounting and Auditing Organization for Islamic Financial Institutions (AAOIFI) that provided the Shariah standards on accounting, auditing and governance issues. The other is the Islamic Finance Service Board (IFSB) that issued standards for the supervision and regulation of Islamic financial institutions. Solé (2007) reiterates the segregation principle that "an important principle behind Islamic finance is the desire to maintain the moral purity of all transactions", meaning that "the funds intended for Shariah-compatible investments should therefore not be mixed with those of non-Islamic investments". The rationale of this principle is that Islamic funds will not mix with other funds that may be involved with "interest, contractual uncertainty and gambling" activities. For conventional banks wishing to engage in Islamic products, the Shariah principle requires that banks must publicize that the Islamic funds will not be mixed with those non-Islamic activities. Effectively, banks will have to establish different capital funds, accounts and reporting system for Islamic fund activities.

In view of the difference in standards and practices, Solé (2007) shows that experiences seem to suggest that banks intended to engage in Islamic finance should phase in gradually through three stages before establishing a full fetch Islamic bank. The initial stage involves the selection and offer of individual Islamic products. This requires the setting up of Islamic windows in order to reach out to the potential clients. An Islamic window can simply be established within a conventional bank, but the conduct of business is based on Shariah-compatible principles and instruments. As Islamic businesses expand, the bank may consider establishing a subsidiary.

The second stage involves the operation of a full-fledged Islamic bank, where financial products are specifically designed to attract Shariah-compliant investors. The third stage is the development of non-bank Islamic financial institutions and the range of Islamic financial products. One concern relating to the legitimacy of establishing an Islamic subsidiary or a full-fledged bank is the potential risk of using or diverting capital from conventional banks to the Islamic bank. The condition therefore is that funds from conventional banks must originate from Islamic compliant sources, otherwise, the initial capital of the subsidiary or the bank may not be accepted under Islamic practices. For example, conventional banks have to transform all loans and deposits into non-interest bearing assets and liabilities, such as cost-plus-financing contracts, or profit-and-loss sharing deposits.

In Asia, both Malaysia and Singapore have been engaged in Islamic finance for decades. Malaysia in particular has introduced Islamic finance since the early 1970s. Solé (2007) argues that Malaysia has evolved into an internationally integrated Islamic finance system that contained both conventional and Islamic financial institutions. The government in Malaysia has instituted deliberate policies to develop Islamic finance, and the Muslim population has helped to attract capital from international investors. Solé (2007) summarizes the development of Islamic finance in Malaysia into four stages: (1) Operating small Islamic institutions; (2) Operating Islamic windows by conventional banks; (3) Converting some conventional banks to Islamic banks; and (4) Introducing other Islamic financial institutions and markets.

The decision for Hong Kong to engage in Islamic finance was formally called for in the Policy Address delivered by the Chief Executive, Donald Tsang Yam-kuen, in October 2007. The Securities and Future Commission (SFC) argued that the introduction of Islamic finance would give new variety to the retail fund market and benefit the asset management industry. The first Islamic retail fund has been approved by the SFC in November 2007, with the intention is to capture a share of Muslim investment worth an estimate of US$700 billion to US$1 trillion.[31] Selective international banks in Hong Kong expressed interest in the government's effect to promote Islamic finance in Hong Kong, though it has been warned that the development of Islamic finance is a long time process, as Hong Kong is just a beginner.[32] While Singapore and Malaysia have developed their Islamic finance much earlier, Islamic finance is an expanding business that can incorporate new players in the market.

Other concerns of Islamic banking included the small number of Muslim residents in Hong Kong, the lack of experience in Islamic finance and the need to have separate laws and regulations governing Islamic finance practices.[33] Another observation is that Islamic finance transactions may fluctuate along with the price of oil and petroleum, which is the key export revenue for most Islamic economies. The ultimate intention, however, is for Hong Kong to diversify its finance and banking activities, thereby providing an additional source of development and business for Hong Kong. While it will take time for Islamic finance to mature in Hong Kong, it does add a new channel in the financial infrastructure of Hong Kong, and with time Islamic finance can develop and grow along with other financial and banking activities in Hong Kong.

9.8 The Financial Crises of 1997 and 2008

Being an open economy, Hong Kong imposes no restrictions on either the inflow or outflow of capital funds. As such, the Hong Kong financial market shall also sneeze

[31] *South China Morning Post*, November 21, 2007.

[32] *South China Morning Post*, July 10, 2008.

[33] *South China Morning Post*, November 21, 2007.

when other world financial markets catch a cold. In the contemporary world where international financial markets have become integrated, international fund managers often used stock investment as an instrument in their portfolio diversification in order to lower unsystematic risk. Within a decade from 1998 to 2008, Hong Kong has experienced two significant financial crises. Although their original causes differed, the financial sector in Hong Kong has suffered considerably in both crises.

Beginning from the early 1990s, the Japanese economy has been weakened by economic recession, and Japanese investment in much of Asia has been less forthcoming. Since the devaluation of the Chinese Renminbi by about 30% in 1994, export trade in Mainland China has turned from a deficit to a surplus. Exports of a number of Asian economies, especially the Southeast Asian countries of Indonesia and Thailand, dropped considerably in 1995 and 1996, but there was no parallel devaluation in their currencies. Other Asian countries, such as South Korea and Indonesia were constrained by their low international reserves. In Hong Kong, despite the reversion of sovereignty to Mainland China on July 1, 1997, the Hong Kong economy was bubble-like with speculative activities in both property and stock markets. The booming economy existed prior to the sovereignty reversion has attracted hot money to Hong Kong in pursuit of speculative gains. The economy of Hong Kong was extremely liquid in 1997.

The 1997 Asian financial crisis (AFC) officially began on July 2 with the devaluation of the Thai currency when the Thai government abandoned the fixed exchange rate system after the exhaustion of the US$30 billion foreign exchange. Towards the last quarter of 1997, situation turned from bad to worse as a number of key financial institutions in Japan and South Korea declared bankrupt. When the Japanese Prime Minister met the President of the United States in November 1997, there were rumors that Japan might have to withdraw funds from the rest of the world to rescue Japan's economic recession.

In response to that rumor, numerous financial institutions in US and Europe had to be prepared by liquidating their assets elsewhere so as to have enough liquid funds should their economies were faced with Japan's withdrawal. This effectively sparked off a wave of fund withdrawals from financial centers in the freer financial markets in Asia. However, Japan acted responsibly and did not withdraw funds massively from the rest of the world. Thus, when the international financial institutions in North America and Europe realized there was no pressure on fund withdrawal from Japan, their funds re-entered the Asian market in 1999, and most Asian financial markets eventually bounced back to a high level. This has effectively created and explained the V-shape performance of most financial markets in Asia between 1997 and 1999 with a sharp drop and a rapid rise within a short time (Li, 2002; Corsetti *et al.*, 1999).

In the meantime, there were a number of related currency and financial crises in different Asian economies, especially in Thailand, Indonesia and South Korea. For example, the Bank of Korea in November 1997 abandoned the fixed exchange rate system and the Korean won fell below 1,000 against the US dollar. The International Monetary Fund (IMF) had to draw up rescue plans for each of the affected economies in Asia. In December 1997, the IMF approved a US$57 billion worth of bailout package to South Korea.

The AFC hit Hong Kong hard in the two related currency and stock market crises. The Hong Kong Hang Seng Index reached a record high of 16,820 points on July 8, 1997. The currency attack began in mid-August 1997 when the Hong Kong Monetary Authority (HKMA) raised interest rate to defend the linked exchange rate system after an extraordinary and rapid drop in the spot and forward exchange rate of the Hong Kong dollar against the US dollar. In October 1997, the speculators again attacked the currency by making block trades of short selling the Hong Kong exchange rate forward contracts. The inter-bank interest rate jumped to 300%. The Hang Seng Index dropped by 30% in the month of October, 1997, and was down by about 4,000 points.

In the meantime, there was herd behavior in the withdrawal of funds from Hong Kong, as the hot money was rapidly disappearing. The prolonged massive withdrawal of funds led to the burst of the financial bubble, as both the property price and stock market plummeted. In early August, 1998, the speculators returned and shorted about HK$29 billion, and the HKMA used the foreign exchange reserve to prevent the Hong Kong currency from depreciation. It was not until August 14, 1998, when the Hong Kong SAR Government intervened by deploying from the reserve fund an amount of HK$80 billion (US$10.34 billion) to acquire a substantial amount of equity portfolio so as to reduce supply and prevented the Hang Seng Index to fall below 7,000 points. On August 25, 1998, the HKMA tightened the supply of Hong Kong dollar and the overnight inter-bank interest rate rose to 15%. The situation was then salvaged and stabilized as the speculators withdrew (Li, 2002, 2006).[34]

There are two schools of thought that explained the AFC (Kaminsky *et al.*, 1998; Krugman 1998a, 1998b; Radelet and Sachs, 1998a, 1998b; Eichengreen *et al.*, 1998a, 1998b). One school proposes the "fundamental-based" hypothesis that viewed the unsustainable deterioration in macroeconomic fundamentals and the poor economic performance as the causes. The other school is the "financial-panic" hypothesis that involved a sudden and substantial arbitrary downward shift in market expectation and confidence. In addition, the spread of herd behavior had also been a factor that induced capital outflow in a financial crisis, and a sudden drop in capital inflow triggered a financial crisis when credit channels are severely squeezed (Chari and Kehoe, 2003; Calvo, 1998). Rigobon (1998) and Pan *et al.* (2000) have pointed out that the behavior of capital flow is a critical factor in the AFC as massive capital outflow would have magnified the crisis. The AFC has shown that a sharp reversal in capital inflow can result in financial and monetary destabilization. Nonetheless, the post-AFC financial recovery has been speedy as stock turnover showed that key financial markets in the Asian region have regained their vitality by 1999 (Li and Kwok, 2009).

The causes of the 2008 financial crisis are entirely different. It probably began with the collapse of the US subprime mortgage industry in March 2007 that led to a worldwide credit crunch as many hedge funds and banks have invested heavily in subprime mortgage backed securities. The Standard and Poor reported on March 13, 2008, that the subprime losses in US may reach US$285 billion. By September 2008, the situation quickly deteriorated when the US Federal Reserve took over the two

[34] Detail information is obtained from *Mingpao Daily*, *South China Morning Post*, and the Hong Kong Monetary Authority.

largest mortgage based security companies. The financial crisis eventually peaked in mid-September 2008 when the Lehman Brothers reported a loss of US$3.9 billion and declared bankruptcy on September 15, 2008, followed by the collapse of Washington Mutual on September 25, 2008. The subsequent financial meltdown in New York swiftly spread to other international financial centers, generating a tsunami-like impact in Europe, Asia and the rest of the world, as there was uncertainty about the bailout plans. The Dow Jones and Standard and Poor's 500 experienced a loss of 22.1% and 18.2% in the weeks after the collapse of Lehman Brothers, respectively. In late November 2008, the Bank of England estimated the world credit loss has evaporated an amount of £1.8 trillion (Sun and Zhang, 2009).

The 2008 financial crisis has demonstrated the importance of international financial inter-dependence, as its contagion effect can spread swiftly to the rest of the world. Various governments began to rescue the crisis by engaging in a "quantity easing" (QE) package that combined financial, monetary and fiscal instruments. The meeting of the G-20 in early April 2009 committed a total of US$1.1 trillion to boost the global economy.[35] The IMF (2009) had proposed various solutions to the global financial crisis, and in *The Turner Review* (Financial Services Authority, 2009), the Financial Services Authority in London identified ways to improve regulatory framework for the financial sector. Others, however, believe that the solution to the 2008 financial crisis could rest with a better use of monetary policy instruments. For example, in assuring the safety of the financial sector, the US President Obama proposed a plan in early 2010 that imposed limits on commercial banks with the aim to make the banks more secure.[36] Schwartz (2009) pointed out that the monetary factors that contributed to the 2008 financial crisis are the expansive monetary policy, flawed financial innovations and collapse of trading.

Among the Asian economies, the impact began in the fourth quarter of 2008 when such Asian economies as South Korea, Taiwan, Singapore and Malaysia that have specialized in advanced manufacturing suffered large drops in their exports.[37] Mainland China also suffered a fall in export by more than 20% in the last quarter of 2008, and a similar large fall in export appeared also in the first quarter of 2009. In a study that looks narrowly at the impact of the 2008 US financial crisis on the financial markets in Mainland China and Hong Kong, Sun and Zhang (2009) argue that although the two financial systems in Mainland China and Hong Kong have little exposure to the securitized products, still there are spillovers from the US financial crisis.

One possible spillover is the loss of confidence, as the fall in the US financial market has resulted in a similar fall in the stock markets in Mainland China and Hong Kong. Between October 31, 2007 and October 31, 2008, for example, the stock markets in Mainland China and Hong Kong have fallen by 71% and 55.5%,

---

[35] *The Times*, April 3, 2009.

[36] *South China Morning Post*, January 23, 2010.

[37] "Why has Asia been Hit so hard by the Global Economic and Financial Crisis?", Presentation by Takatoshi Kato, Deputy Managing Director, International Monetary Fund, May 12, 2009.

respectively. Another spillover is uncertainty in the direction of capital flows, though the uncertainty could work negatively as well as positively. With optimism, one can argue that the resilience nature of the two financial markets might even attract more capital flows from the crisis-affected markets in US and in Europe. And the inflow of capital would have added to the price volatility in the Mainland China and Hong Kong stock markets. Another obvious economic spillover is the fall in export growth resulted from the low economic expectation. A rapid drop in exports would impact negatively on the performance in the two stock markets.

The empirical study on the impact of the US financial crisis on Mainland China and Hong Kong in Sun and Zhang (2009) show that equity returns in Hong Kong have experience higher price and volatility spillovers than in Mainland China from the financial shock in the 2008 crisis in the United States. In addition, the past volatility shocks in the US financial market tended to have a more persistent effect in the Hong Kong financial market than in the mainland financial market. Sun and Zhang (2009) attribute this situation to Hong Kong's status as an international financial center. Another empirical finding is the increasing financial integration between Mainland China and Hong Kong. In the case of Mainland China, the limited exposure to the subprime crisis and that China has suffered less than other Asian economies is due mainly to its lower level of financial openness. A more pragmatic approach towards capital account liberalization is a key issue Mainland China has to face.

Another empirical study by Wong and Li (2010) compares the performance of stock returns in the two financial crises of 1997 and 2008 using data from a total of eleven world economies, including Mainland China and Hong Kong. To see how performance in one financial center influenced on another in a crisis, Wong and Li (2010) examine the time-varying correlation structure between changes in the real exchange rate and relative stock return differentials. The performance in the two crises of 1997 and 2008 are compared using data from eight Asia-Pacific economies (Canada, China, Japan, Hong Kong, Taiwan, South Korea, Singapore and Indonesia) and two key European economies (United Kingdom and Germany). The performance in each of these ten economies is conducted relative to the performance in the United States, which is considered as the "foreign" country in the sample.

To examine the spillover and the impact of one financial market on another in a crisis period, Wong and Li (2010) follow Malliaropulos (1998) to look at the linkage between the expected real stock differential and the transitory components in the real exchange rate. The data for the 11 economies contained the monthly closing price of the stock index, the nominal domestic exchange rate to the US dollar and the Consumer Price Index (CPI) for the period from January 1990 to December 2008. In the case of Mainland China, the data covered the period of June 1994 to December 2008. All data are expressed in the logarithm format. The relative stock prices are measured first by converting the US stock index into home currency, and then deducting it by the stock index of the home economy. The real exchange rate is calculated by adjusting the nominal home exchange rate against the US dollar by the home and US Consumer Price Index (CPI).

According to Wong and Li (2010), the relative stock price between the home economy and foreign economy expressed in the home currency (ρ_t) can be defined as:

$$\rho_t = s_t - s_t^* - e_t, \tag{3}$$

where s_t (s_t^*) is the domestic (foreign) stock price and e_t is the nominal exchange rate, expressing the domestic currency per unit of US dollar. The real exchange rate (q_t) is shown as:

$$q_t = e_t + p_t^* - p_t, \tag{4}$$

where p_t^* (p_t) represents the foreign (domestic) goods price. The expected stock price differential and expected change in real exchange rate are defined, respectively, as:

$$E_{t-1}\Delta\rho_t = E_{t-1}\Delta(s_t - s_t^* - e_t), \tag{5}$$

and

$$E_{t-1}\Delta q_t = E_{t-1}\Delta(e_t + p_t^* - p_t), \tag{6}$$

where E_{t-1} represents the conditional expectations operator given all available information at time $t-1$. From Equation (6), the expected depreciation of the domestic currency against the US dollar equaled to the expected deviation from the relative purchasing power parity (PPP). Rearranging Equation (4) and substituting it into Equation (5), we have:

$$E_{t-1}\Delta\rho_t = E_{t-1}\Delta z_t - E_{t-1}\Delta q_t, \tag{7}$$

where Δz_t is the real stock return differential between the domestic stock and the US stock, and equals to $\Delta(s_t - p_t) - (s_t^* - p_t^*)$. Equation (7) states that the expected stock return differential is equal to the expected real return differential minus the expected real exchange rate.

The real exchange rate in Equation (7) is assumed to contain both the permanent q_t^p and temporary q_t^T components (Huizinga, 1987; Baxter, 1994). The permanent component is specified as a random walk with drift process, while the temporary or transitory component is assumed to follow a stationary first-order autoregressive process. Similarly, Porterba and Summer (1988) and Malliaropulos (1998) assume that the relative stock price contains both the permanent q_t^p and temporary q_t^T components.

Wong and Li (2010) use the dynamic conditional correlation (DCC) model in Engle (2002) to examine the relationship between changes in real exchange rate and stock return differential. The DCC model formulated the conditional correlation as a weighted sum of pass correlations and allowed the conditional correlation matrix time dependent. The estimation of DCC model is conducted by using a three-stage procedure. Firstly, the univariate GARCH (p, q) models with $p = q = 1$ are fitted into the two series, and the estimated standard residuals can then be obtained. The second stage involved the estimation of the intercept parameters of conditional correlation. Finally, the coefficients governing the dynamics of correlation are estimated using the intercept parameters of conditional correlation.[38]

By concentrating only on their empirical findings and excluding the discussion on the various technicalities and regression tests in Wong and Li (2010), Figure 9.12 produces the plots on the log relative stock price (to US) (left axis) and log real exchange rate for the ten economies (right axis). Between the two crises, there were apparent declines in the relative stock price among the Asia Pacific stock markets during the AFC, but there were no significant changes in the European stock markets. In the case of the real exchange rate, the sudden capital outflow would have caused a sharp depreciation in real exchange rate among the Asian economies, especially in South Korea and Indonesia. Consequently, the managed floating exchange regime in Indonesia and Korea were eventually replaced in 1998 by a free-floating exchange rate.

As for the 2008 financial crisis, though there was a clear downturn in the US stock market, the downward movements in the relative stock prices have actually started from early 2008, suggesting that the stock markets in the sample economies have experienced a more severe shock than the price adjustment in the US stock market. Furthermore, the increasing trend in the real exchange rate of the sample economies represented depreciation in their home currency against the US dollar, with the exception of China, Hong Kong and Japan.

Figure 9.13 shows the empirical findings on the conditional correlation between the relative stock return differential and the change in the real exchange rate for the ten economies relative to the performance to the United States in the two financial crises. The empirical results in Wong and Li (2010) are in line with the theoretical argument that all the dynamic correlation structures are negative, implying that a negative correlation between stock return differential and real exchange rate. One other observation from Figure 9.13 is that given a highly integrated world financial market, capital movement has been a major factor in generating stock return fluctuations. Comparison among the sample economies in each of the two financial crises can be discussed.

The 1997 AFC

In the three economies not affected by the AFC, the United Kingdom, Canada and Germany did not experience any significant capital outflow, and their relative stock return differential and real exchange rate movements were less volatile than the Asian economies until the outbreak of another financial crisis in Russia in late 1998.

On the contrary, one can observe in a number of Asian economies the sharp decline in the stock return differential and depreciation in real exchange rate. The collapse in the conditional correlation structure during the AFC period is due

---

[38] The technicalities are shown in Wong and Li (2010).

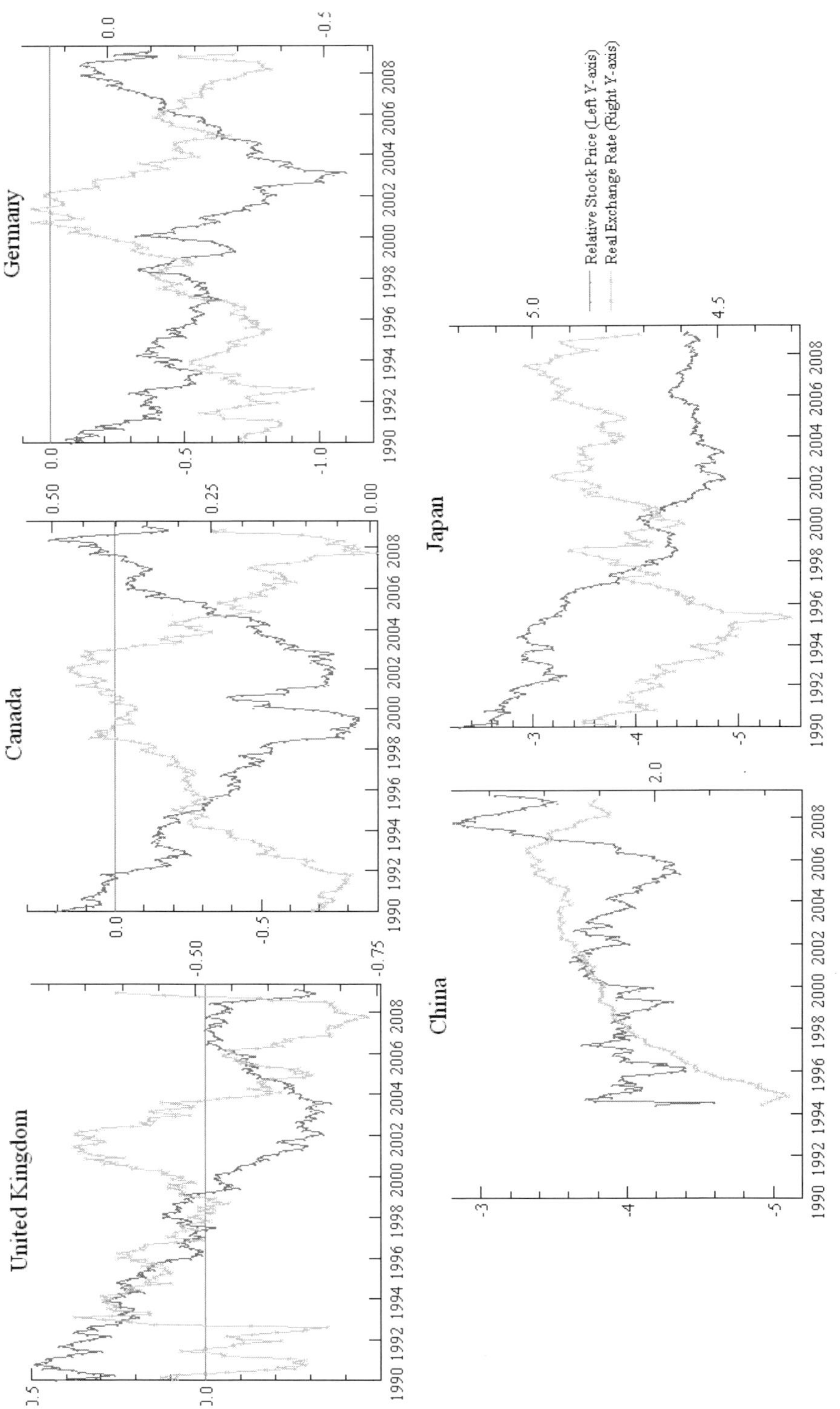

FIGURE 9.12 Time series of log relative stock price and log real exchange rate

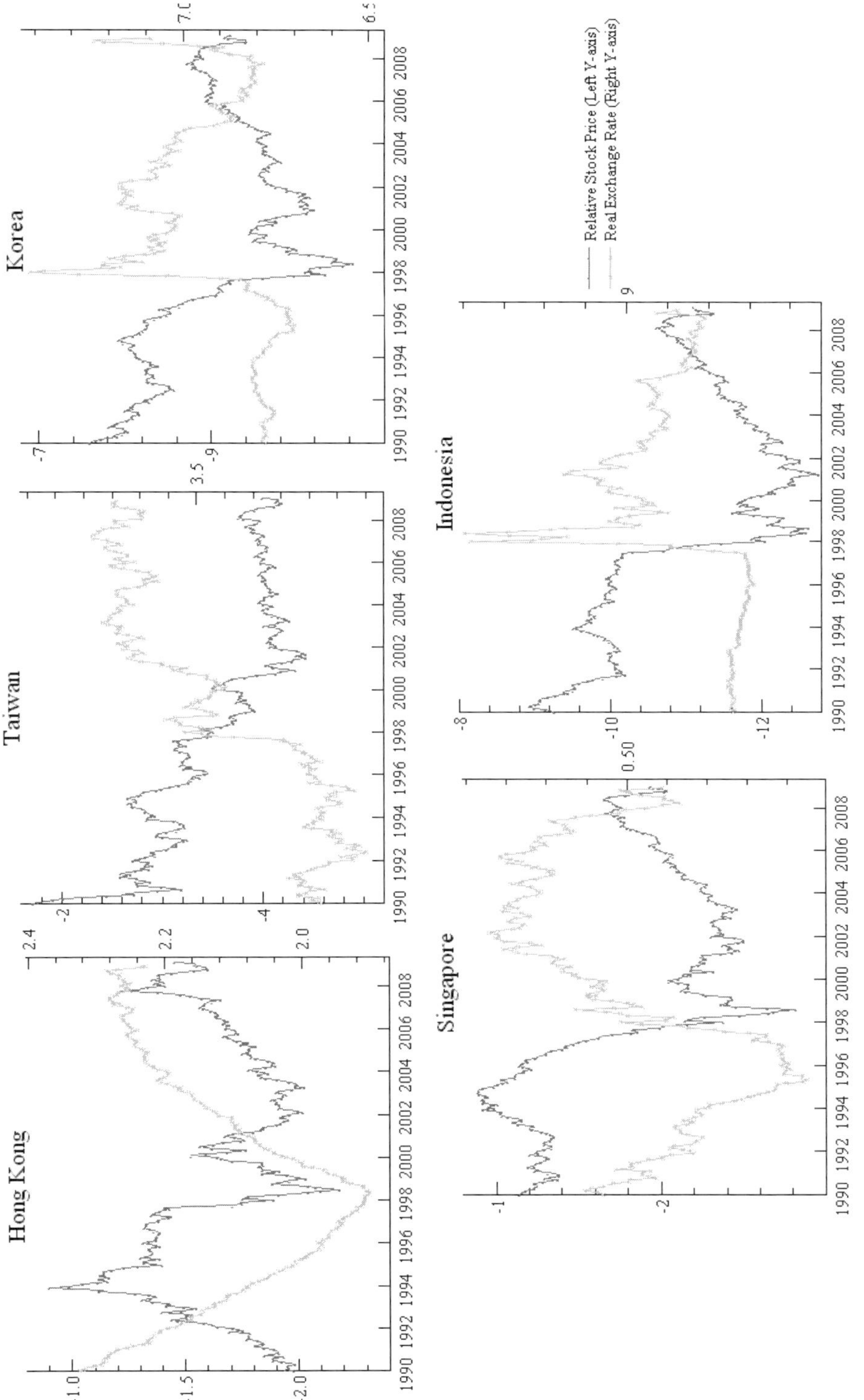

FIGURE 9.12 (*Continued*)

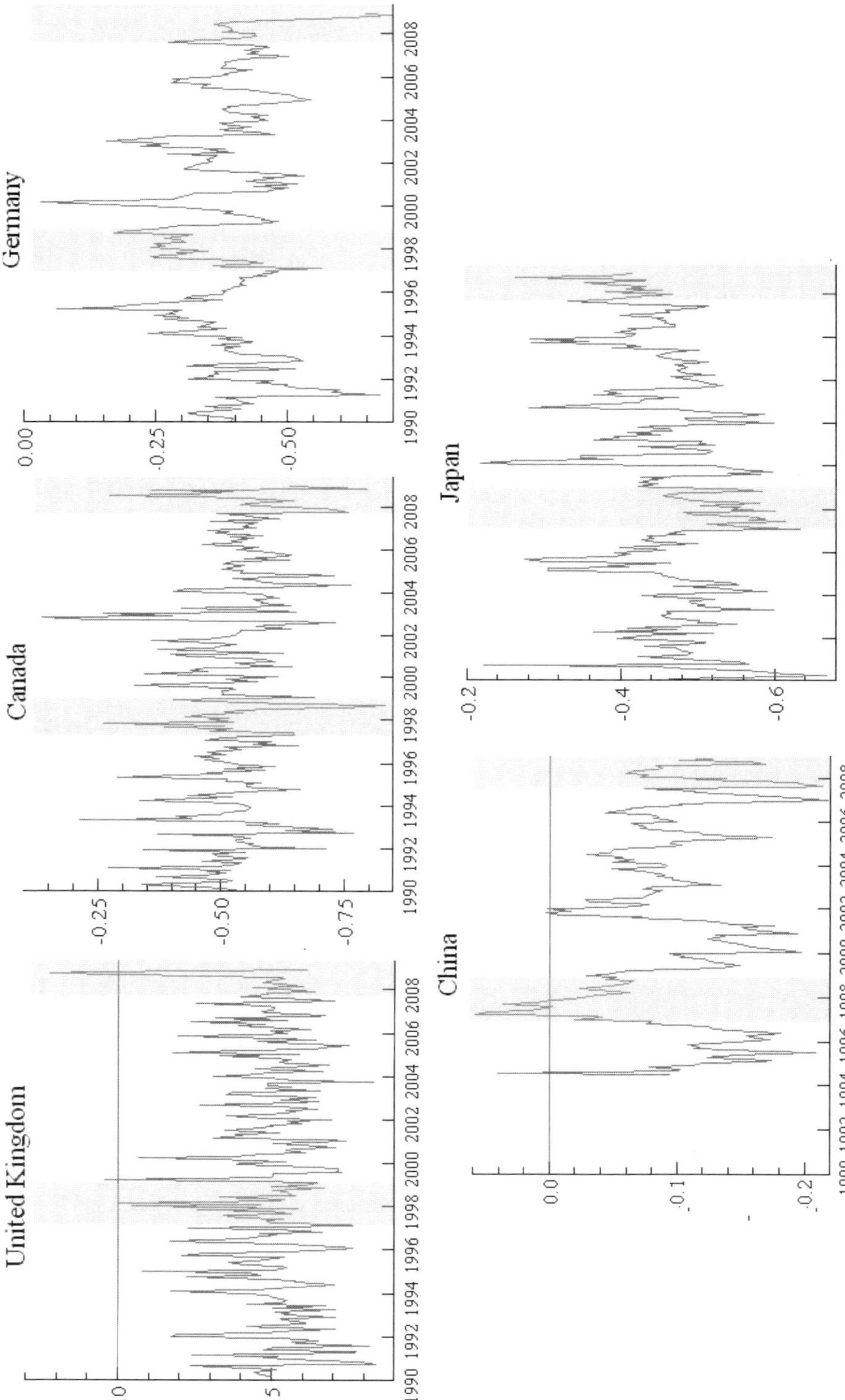

FIGURE 9.13 The dynamic conditional correlation structure between relative stock price differential and change in real exchange rate

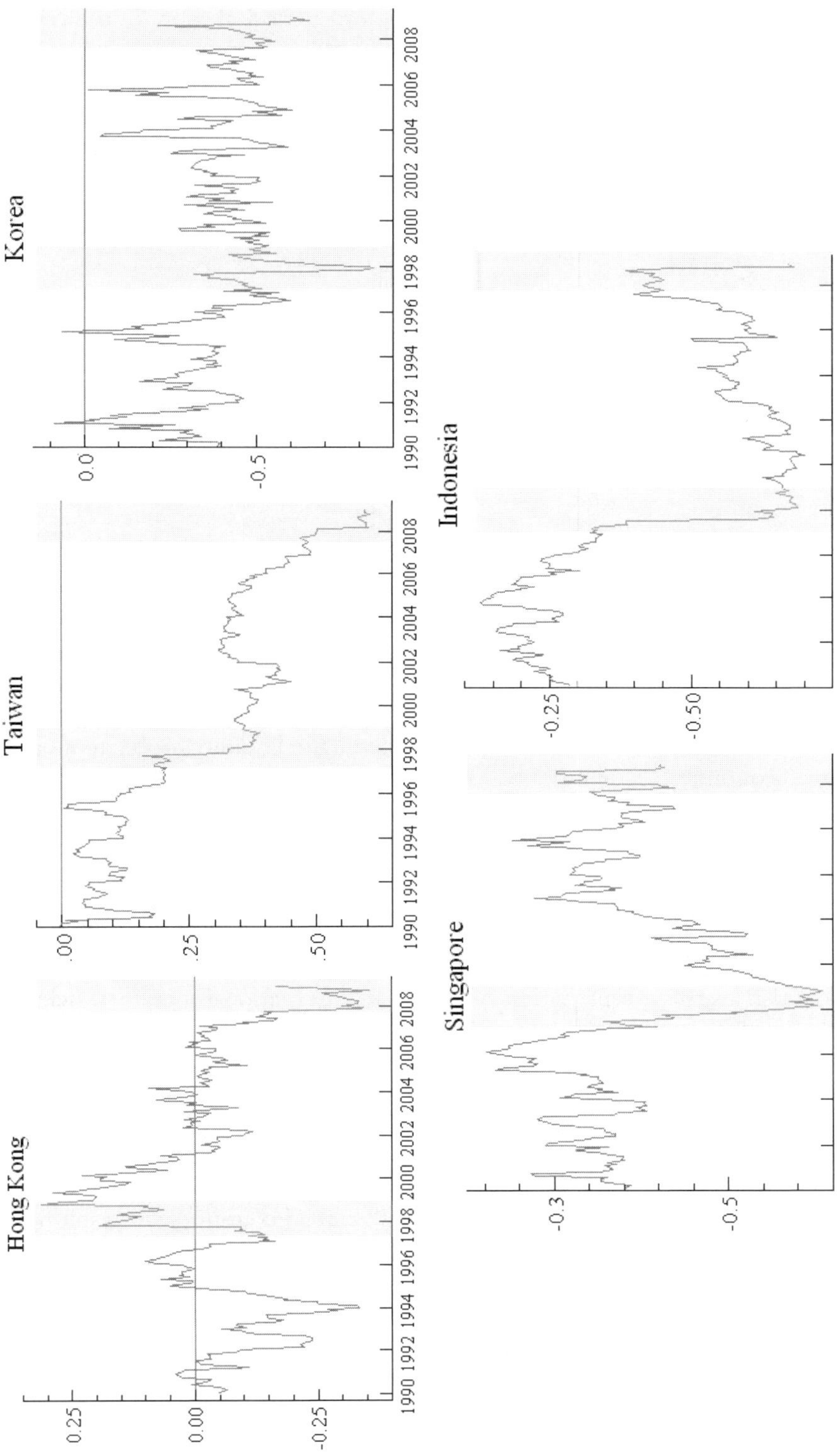

FIGURE 9.13 *(Continued)*

obviously to the massive capital outflow within a short period of time. In the case of Taiwan and Singapore where their floating exchange rate system is permitted to float according to demand and supply, the rapid reversal of capital movement and decline in relative stock price have led to a collapse in their conditional correlation structure. The impact of AFC on South Korea and Indonesia was more serious, as the sudden switch in their exchange rate regime in late 1997 have led to a rise in uncertainty and consequently generated an unfavorable shock in both stock price and exchange rate. Consequently, their decline in the conditional correlation structure was much higher than others.

In the case of Hong Kong, though its currency was attacked during the AFC period, its high CPI had actually resulted in an appreciation of the real exchange rate and, together with the falling stock price, an increase or a positive performance in the conditional correlation. When compared to other Asian countries, Mainland China was less affected during the AFC period, as the fixed exchange rate regime and the non-convertibility of Chinese Renminbi have protected its value from speculative attacks.

The 2008 US crisis

The performance between the Asian and non-Asian economies changed drastically in the 2008 financial crisis. This can be seen by the apparent change in the conditional correlation after the subprime financial crisis appeared in late 2007, and the financial world has changed for the worse upon the bankruptcy of Lehman Brothers in New York on September 15, 2008. Subsequently, the credit and liquidity problem of banks in all sample economies become the major concern.

The 2008 financial crisis has reversed the outcome of the AFC as the economies of United Kingdom, Canada and Germany have been seriously affected in the 2008 crisis, and their sharp decline in conditional correlation primarily suggested a massive capital outflow from their stock markets. However, with a continued deterioration in the US economy and its credit quality, the US dollar actually gained strength against the British pound, Canadian dollar and the Euro. This basically has reflected the situations of risk aversion, repatriation of capital by international investors, deleveraging in the financial market and lack of liquidity in the US economy.

Due to an increase in the volatility of relative stock return differential and real exchange rate, the conditional correlations have changed drastically in most of the ten financial markets, with the exception of Hong Kong, China and Japan. In the case of Mainland China, the appreciation of the Renminbi has caught the world attention since the late 2007. This has attracted massive capital inflows and the stock market index in Mainland China and Hong Kong climbed continuously, resulting in a decline in the conditional correlation of Mainland China and Hong Kong. In the case of Japan, which held the second largest foreign exchange reserves in the world, the strength of the Japanese yen has often served as a currency shelter for other currencies in times of financial crisis.

The change in the conditional correlation among Asian countries is relatively low in the 2008 crisis. This could have reflected that Asian economies, particularly the East Asian economies, have learnt from the disastrous experiences in AFC and have strengthened their monetary system and banking regulation. For instance, since the Hong Kong dollar is pegged to the US dollar and bank deposits in Hong Kong are fully guaranteed, exposure to exchange rate risk was reduced. Hong Kong has introduced timely measures to strengthen the currency board system, including the convertibility undertaking to the linked exchange rate system with the boundaries. Hong Kong is therefore regarded as a suitable region for the disposition of investors and a safe haven for international funds. Similarly, Singapore has adopted a managed floating exchange rate regime that allowed the Singapore currency to fluctuate within an undisclosed band so as to lower the possibility of currency manipulation by speculators. Being the fastest growing economy in the world, the financial crisis in 2008 seemed to have little impact on the Mainland China economy as its economic prospect is relatively optimistic.

One other important observation from Figure 9.13 is that economies with fixed exchange rate regimes, typically Mainland China and Hong Kong, tended to have a stronger guard against financial crisis as their conditional correlation are relatively less volatile. This can be seen by comparing the performance of Mainland China and Hong Kong with South Korea and Indonesia. The deficient free floating exchange regimes in Indonesia and South Korea can be revealed from the 2008 financial crisis because these two economies also experienced a sharp decline in their conditional correlation. By contrast, the exchange rate regimes in Mainland China and Hong Kong definitely have contributed to the stability of the financial system during the 2008 crisis. In short, exchange rate stability can lower the risk of foreign investors and reduce the instability of the financial system so as to alleviate the external financial shocks, especially in those export-oriented economies.

The study in the time varying correlation between relative stock price and real exchange rate by Wong and Li (2010) conclude that an appreciation of the domestic currency would lead to an increase in the domestic stock price relative to the US. In addition, a sharp decline in the conditional correlation structure can be found in the period of financial crises, and large capital outflow is related to a sharp decline in relative stock price. Compared to the AFC, the decline in conditional correlation in the 2008 financial crisis is relative low in a number of Asian economies, suggesting that stronger exchange rate policies and banking regulations have been established since 1997, and their performance have effectively resisted the shocks from the 2008 financial crisis. The financial crisis in 2008 showed little influence on the Mainland China economy and that exchange rate stability is crucial in the period of financial crisis.

With the growing inter-dependence among international financial markets, the lessons from the two financial crises pointed squarely to the importance of a sound exchange rate policy and an open, equitable and transparent regulatory financial system. The G-20 meeting in early April 2009 has rightly pointed to the various needed commitments, such as the establishment of a Financial Stability Board and the greater support in the reporting of financial information, disclosure of illegal tax havens and so on. The Financial Services in London (2009) reported in *The Turner Review* also argued for the need of a systemic approach to examine the various regulatory and supervisory changes. More good practices should be implemented across major financial markets and world economies.

9.9 Conclusion

The discussion on Hong Kong's international financial center has revealed a number of important factors. Financial freedom is the pre-requisite as it involved the freedom of capital flows in and out of the market. The involvement by foreign investors added to the international recognition. Alignment with other international centers in terms of rules and regulations is essential to build up international trust and transparency. In a way, the international financial center is a market for investors, both foreign and local, to "make money", which in turn will facilitate other economic activities that ultimately result in economic growth.

The market turnover has often been regarded only as a necessary condition, but market diversity and a sound financial infrastructure are the necessary and sufficient condition of an international financial center. The historical dimension is also important, as it provided market reliability and confidence. Nonetheless, while the rankings of international financial centers do provide a measurement, it is equally important to regularly improve the indigenous conditions of the market, so that it is dynamically moving along with developments elsewhere.

Armed with decades of macroeconomic stability, Hong Kong has been fortunate to have developed sound financial practices. The status of an international financial center is a dynamic entity that requires constant professional improvements and changes to upgrade the trading and market conditions. Competition from nearby financial markets, such as Singapore, Shanghai and Shenzhen are obvious, but it should be considered positively. Firstly, competition always exists among economies and markets, because investors would like to compare one market with another.

The ranking of international financial centers is itself a comparison of different financial centers. What is more important is the best provision of financial services that Hong Kong provides. It will be up to the investors to decide whether the financial center in Hong Kong is a worthwhile place to conduct their investment activities. Improvements in the supply factors will ensure best performance in the demand-side. Market and product diversity are added factors in attracting investors. All investors will have to diversify their risk and consider spreading their portfolios across different financial markets. Thus, the same investor will invest in more than one financial center, and it would be unlikely that the rise of one financial center will lead to a fall in another. It is more likely that the rise of one financial center will consolidate the position of the more matured financial center. Indeed, it is the rise of financial centers in Zurich, Tokyo, Toronto, Hong Kong and Singapore that echoes the seniority of the financial markets in London and New York.

One also has to recognize that financial activities do generate economic volatilities, as financial market activities by definition fluctuated considerably. The line between investment and speculation is difficult to define. There would thus be spillovers to other economic activities. Typically, financial bubbles, when burst, would create economic hardships as assets and wealth depreciated or evaporated. Financial crisis reflected the evitable downside of financial freedom, but sound regulations, rules, governance, ethic practices and the degree of transparency seem to be the important cushion that absorbs the initial impact of the financial crisis and provides protection to all investors. As a key international financial center, Hong Kong cannot escape from severe financial turmoil elsewhere in the world. Openness, agility and flexibility are the core and evergreen ingredients that Hong Kong's financial center should keep.

At the same time, the extent and experience of financial freedom in Hong Kong is radiating to other emerging economies, as the Hong Kong experience has been learned and acted as a reference point for other fast developing financial centers. It would be beneficial for Hong Kong to see more financial development elsewhere. It is not the competition that Hong Kong should worry; on the contrary it would be the enlargement of economic development, wealth creation and growth in other economies that would benefit Hong Kong in the long-run. New creation in wealth would imply a reduction in poverty, and financial management is a key aspect in wealth management. In short, more financial development elsewhere would imply more financial transactions will be conducted. As the financial pie gets bigger, Hong Kong will definitely benefit. Indeed, this is exactly the long-term goal in financial development that Hong Kong will have to assist the development of other financial markets in Mainland China and other Asian economies. One should consider the growing financial pie rather than how the pie would be distributed.

10 The Linked Exchange Rate, Currency Attacks and Crisis

10.1 Introduction

Monetary freedom is Hong Kong has been rated by the Heritage Foundation in Washington DC to be the best in the world. In the 2011 *Index of Economic Freedom* (IEF), Hong Kong has a score of 87.1, the highest among all world economies. The score of Singapore is close at 86.2 points. No other economies in the top ten freest economies have a score above 86 points. Monetary freedom covered not only monetary policy performance, but inflation and banking practices. In commenting on the score on monetary freedom, the Heritage Foundation concluded that "since the Hong Kong dollar maintains a fixed exchange rate with the US dollar, interest rates and currency movements follow trends in the United States. Hong Kong has efficient clearing and settlement systems". On inflation, the IEF noted that inflation stability is important to monetary freedom, and concluded that "inflation in Hong Kong has been low, averaging 1.6% between 2007 and 2009". The only unfavorable remark made on Hong Kong's monetary freedom is domestic price distortion, as the IEF stated that "the government regulates the prices of public transport and electricity and some residential rents", and as a result, "five points were deducted from Hong Kong's monetary freedom score to account for measures that distort domestic price".

There are two economic policies that all governments in the world can control and manipulate to regulate and stabilize the macroeconomy. One is the fiscal policy that deals with the annual budget and the government expenditure on the economy. In general, fiscal policy is considered more of a short-term influence as government expenditures are committed within the fiscal year and government revenues, through tax payments mainly, are collected annually. It is true that the government can introduce economic stabilization through fiscal instrument, such as tax and expenditures. Very often, the government used fiscal instruments in making commitments to long-term developments. Typically, these are in the capital account of the annual budget, such as the building of infrastructure that has infinite long-term effects on the economy.

The other policy the government exercises is the monetary policy. Monetary instruments available to the government include interest rate, exchange rate and money supply. In most cases, monetary policy is regarded as a policy that influences long-term economic prospects. For example, interest rate changes can influence investments that are geared for industrial outputs. There are also short-term implications of monetary policy. Policies that increase or decrease money supply can affect the level of household consumption and inflation in the short-term. Thus, at a time of low economic activities, the government exercises a low interest rate policy in order to stimulate investment, or increase money supply.

Monetary freedom refers to a situation whereby the government exercises a prudent monetary policy, ensures macroeconomic stability, allows maximal monetary and investment activities in the private sector, and minimizes price intervention so as to avoid unwanted price distortions. During an economically stable time, monetary policy should be exercised with minimal distortions. The role of an effective monetary policy should be one of a "fire fighter" whereby monetary intervention is exercised when needed in an economically turbulent time, but should withdraw once stability is ensured. The proper role of the monetary policy is to respond to and "fine-tune" the activities in the business cycle, and not to generate unnecessary interventions and distortions so as to change the course of the business cycle.

This chapter extends the discussion in the similar chapter in Li (2006, Chapter 5). Instead of looking at the more conventional materials on the demand for money, this chapter expands and extends the discussion on the linked exchange rate system, focusing more on the contemporary debate as to whether the Hong Kong currency should be delinked from the US currency. To add to the debate on the linked exchange rate, this chapter focuses considerably on currency attacks and uses the different episodes to analyze empirically the solutions or early signals that can be used to forecast or prepare for possible currency attacks. Both statistical and econometrics tools are used to come up with a total of four "early signs" of currency attacks in Hong Kong. This however, does not imply that the Hong Kong currency is in danger of attack. On the contrary, the linked exchange rate could have helped to locate the early signs.

One severe impact of the 2008 crisis to the Hong Kong economy is the much politicized mini-bonds incident. Although it is unfortunate to see investors making huge losses in the mini-bonds incidence, the more relevant and wider issue is the stability of the Hong Kong currency and a reliable regulatory structure and system that favors no one but protects everyone. Indeed, one can argue that the 2008 crisis can be turned into an "opportunity" for Hong Kong to engage in a program that will strengthen Hong Kong's status of an international financial center. In financial regulations, for example, Hong Kong can introduce changes that make the Hong Kong system even stronger than the system in other international financial centers. In other words, if used appropriately, the "opportunity" can turn Hong Kong to become a leader as a financial regulator among other international financial and monetary centers.

Before concluding the chapter, it is appropriate to reiterate and examine the role and ingredients of economic freedom in Hong Kong's monetary system, such that lessons can be used as references for other economies. Equally, it is important not to be complacent as the system in Hong Kong also needs to be upgraded, improved, strengthened and perfected. While the economic success in Hong Kong serves as models and references, Hong Kong also needs to prepare for the rainy days and there is always uncertainties, and crises could emerge. Getting prepared is the best a free economy can do. Economy freedom can serve as a recipe or a roadmap, and its success hinges on a number of factors. While well-established institutions can stabilize the system in Hong Kong, institutions have to be checked and balancing instruments have to be placed such that abuse will be minimized, if not eliminated.

10.2 The Linked Exchange Rate System

Hong Kong is a highly external-oriented economy, and the stability of the currency is crucial. The three non-government note-issuing banks in Hong Kong (Hong Kong and Shanghai Banking Corporation, Standard Chartered Bank and Bank of China), when they wanted to conduct fiduciary issues, have to submit US dollar (at HK$7.80 = US$1) to the Hong Kong Monetary Authority's Exchange Fund account in return for the Certificates of Indebtedness, which is required by law as the backing of bank notes issued. Thus the Hong Kong currency notes are fully backed by and convertible into US dollar held by the Exchange Fund. The aggregate balance of the Exchange Fund can show the flow of funds into and out of the Hong Kong currency. Hong Kong has never exercised any form of exchange control.

Hong Kong has experienced different exchange rate regimes (Nugee, 1995). Before the 1970s, the Hong Kong currency was pegged to the British pound sterling, but was fixed to the US dollar since 1972. Due probably to the weakness and the trouble of the British pound sterling in the early 1970s, the Hong Kong currency experienced a free float in November 1974. However, there was a collapse of the floating of the Hong Kong currency due to the heavy pressure of capital outflows in the 1982–1984 Sino-British negotiation over the political future of Hong Kong (Greenwood, 2008). On October 17, 1983, the Hong Kong authority pegged the currency to the US dollar (Latter, 2007a).

The Hong Kong authority effectively adopted a currency board system of an exchange rate linked to the US dollar. One major feature of a currency board system is the full backing of the monetary base (which included bank notes and coins issued, the balance of licensed banks maintained with the Hong Kong Monetary Authority (HKMA), and the outstanding Exchange Fund papers) by the reserve currency, which is the US dollar. The convertibility between the monetary base and the reserve currency is fixed at HK$7.80 to US$1 (Latter, 2007b; HKMA, 2005).

The currency board system requires a rule-based monetary authority that issued base money solely for the exchange of foreign currency, which is known as the reserve currency. The two features of a currency board are that the board has a statutory obligation to assure convertibility of local currency into the foreign currency at a fixed exchange rate; and the issue of local currency is fully backed by the reserve of marketable securities denominated in reserve currency. There are a number of advantages in the currency board mechanism. Williamson (1995) points out the four advantages of assured convertibility, discipline over fiscal policy, certainty of a balance of payment adjustment mechanism, and public confidence.

The most important advantage is the assurance of convertibility based on the 100% reserve coverage. Since the reserve currency assets kept by the currency board is larger than its liabilities, the currency board is able to honor any demand for conversion. Firstly, the removal of uncertainty on the exchange rate helps to reduce the foreign exchange risk faced by traders and investors. Secondly, the currency board system required the exercise of a high degree of macroeconomic discipline and cannot be used to finance fiscal deficit since it is prohibited from buying domestic assets. Thirdly, the currency board exhibited a build-in payment-adjustment mechanism. If the economy experiences a balance of payment deficit, the money supply will drop over time and interest rate rises, thereby attracting capital inflow. In turn, a higher interest rate exerts a deflationary pressure on the economy, leading to an improvement in the current account in the balance of payment. If internal prices are flexible, the lower pressure on aggregate demand will lead to a fall in price and export becomes more competitive. Real output will eventually adjust back to the full employment level with the balance of payment deficit eliminated. Lastly, the currency board maintains public confidence in general and in the financial markets in particular, as the currency board is ruled-based and free from unnecessary intervention.

On the other hand, the three disadvantages of a currency board system included the inability of the monetary policy, the absence of a lender of last resort, and the needed adjustment resulting from the emergence of sudden shocks. In the event of domestic economic difficulty, the currency board does not allow the practice of an active monetary policy, as there is little or no room for the exercise of an autonomous interest rate policy in order to achieve price stability or promote economic growth. One of the traditional roles of a central bank is to act as a lender of last resort. To do so, a currency board regime would violate its basic feature of issuing domestic currency only in exchange for foreign currency rather than against domestic assets. Thirdly, if sudden shocks are triggered by sharp changes in the currencies of close competitors or in the export market, more adjustments on the internal price-cost structure would be required, since the currency board effectively provided a fixed exchange rate. If the various additional adjustments are slow to occur, the economy may experience a longer period of prolonged economic adjustment than if there were an adjustment in the exchange rate.

Despite the official link at US$1 to HK$7.8, the HKMA in April 1992 proposed a "first line of defense". This necessarily meant an intervention on the peg by fixing the exchange rate at US$1 to HK$7.75. In June 1993, the HKMA introduced a Liquidity Adjustment Facility (LAF), which was a discount window that gave the HKMA more power over short-term inter-bank rates. These moves were undesirable since the currency board is a rule-based monetary system and any discretionary action would weaken its credibility.

After the speculative attack on the Hong Kong currency in 1997–1998, the HKMA used the period from April 1, 1999 to August 12, 2000, to convert the Hong Kong dollar in all licensed banks' clearing accounts maintained with the HKMA by one basis point each calendar day. The fixed exchange rate moved, after 500 calendar days, gradually back from US$1: HK$7.75 to US$1: HK$7.8, thus restoring a truly rule-based currency board system. Before 1992, the exchange rate has fluctuated around 7.8, and between 1992 and 1998, much of the exchange rate performance fell below 7.75. The 500-day correction between 1999 and 2000 restored the exchange rate to a steady path of 7.8. The "first line of defense" is a good intention, but its prolonged usage lengthened the 7.8 deviation, making the currency a subject of speculative attack. The adoption of the currency board also comes with the condition that the rate should not be deviated, and has to be restored even if it was temporarily deviated. The currency board framework and the strict adherence to the linked rate are the two inseparable elements. Nonetheless, there have been adjustments and changes since its adoption in 1983 (Greenwood, 2008).

Despite the success of the linked exchange rate system and the currency board that has guaranteed the stability and reliability of the Hong Kong currency, the various crises Hong Kong has experienced since 1997 have prompted many to question the appropriateness of the linked exchange rate, though some discussions are politically motivated. Others criticized the vast amount of foreign currency reserve the Hong Kong government holds in the Exchange Fund managed by HKMA, not understanding that it was exactly because of the large foreign currency reserve that had rescued Hong Kong from crisis and the potential financial collapse since 1997. There is, thus, every reason and the need to have the largest possible foreign currency reserve held in the Exchange Fund. In terms of the size of foreign currency reserve among world economies, Hong Kong has long been ranked third in the world in the 1980s, and probably the top five in the world ranking after the AFC in 1998. Today, Mainland China probably ranks first in the size of foreign reserve in the world, followed by Japan. There is no other reason as not to keep and preserve the largest possible foreign currency reserve Hong Kong holds, as it is not only a world indicator and serves as a cushion in times of financial crisis, the foreign currency reserve is the strength of the Hong Kong dollar.

There have been numerous discussions on the delinking of the Hong Kong dollar to the US dollar. Some have argued the use of a basket of currencies, while others argued the link to the rising Renminbi. Both of these suggestions also carry a number of uncertainties. Despite the various advantages and disadvantages of the linked exchange rate system, the risky question is not the matter of delinking, but what to link the currency with next. In an analogy, it is not the undressing that concerns, the risk lies in what to wear next. In other words, the uncertainty and the risk involved in linking the Hong Kong currency to another currency could be so high that it could destabilize the economy severely, and the delinking itself could generate another crisis. Thus, it is not wise to indulge in such a risky business, especially in a non-crisis time. Perhaps, one could argue retrospectively that the delinking could have taken place during the AFC when a number of other Asian currencies were depreciating. Nonetheless, while there is nothing wrong with the linked exchange rate system, it will be too risky and even a fuss to disturb the system for no worthy reasons.

In the case of linking to a basket of currencies, one would wonder what would be the practical advantages. The US currency will definitely play a major role in the basket of currencies. Similarly, other international currencies, typically the British pound, the Euro and Japanese yen will be included. In addition, since the Renminbi is rising, the inclusion of the Renminbi will be obvious. The question then is the composition of the various currencies in the basket, and whether the rise and fall of one currency will be safeguarded by the performance of another currency in the basket.

The idea of a basket is that since the rise of one world currency will naturally mean the fall of another currency, the basket will therefore minimize exchange rate volatility and can eventually produce stability for the Hong Kong currency. However, the task of adjusting the composition of currencies in the basket itself could generate volatility and uncertainty, and frequent artificial adjustments could lead to human error and wrong judgments resulting in unpredictability and unwanted consequences. Thus, theoretically and conceptually, the advantages gained from the link to a basket of currencies over the existing unilateral link to the US dollar are unclear and unsure. In any case, there is no perfect exchange rate system in the world, and there are always some uncertainties attached to all kinds of exchange rate regimes. The best any economy can do is to find a practical and effective exchange rate regime.

In the case of linking to the rising Renminbi, there are also a number of options. First, the Renminbi is not yet a fully convertible currency. From the outset, it is unwise for the Hong Kong currency, which is a full convertible world currency, to link to Renminbi, which is not yet a fully convertible world currency. Others have argued that the Hong Kong economy shall benefit if the Hong Kong currency is linked to the rising Renminbi. This argument does not reflect the whole truth. As the Renminbi is appreciating, it gains world recognition, and linking to the Renminbi will lead to an appreciating value of the Hong Kong currency. This is true, especially in the case of imports from Mainland China. A depreciating Hong Kong dollar *vis-a-vis* the Renminbi would mean a higher price of imports from Mainland China, leading to a rise in inflation in Hong Kong.

On the contrary, the other part of the truth is that a depreciating Hong Kong dollar *vis-a-vis* the Renminbi would mean cheaper exports to Mainland China, thereby promoting Hong Kong exports of goods and services. Indeed, experiences have shown that when the US dollar was weak, as in much of the 1980s, the Hong Kong currency had become attractive and exports increased as Hong Kong exports became competitive.

Legally, as written in Article 111 of the Basic Law, "the Hong Kong dollar, as the legal tender in the Hong Kong Special Administrative Region, shall continue to circulate". There is also a political dimension in the consideration. Would a separate currency in Hong Kong be useful to Renminbi? One obvious argument is that the Hong Kong currency has been aiding the Renminbi to become an international currency. As Hong Kong has become an offshore Renminbi trading center, the Hong Kong currency, has, for long time, a served as an intermediary between the Renminbi and foreign currencies. While exchanges between Renminbi and foreign currencies are still restricted, exchange with the intermediary, the Hong Kong currency, can greatly facilitate trade and monetary transactions between the Renminbi and foreign currencies. Indeed, the Hong Kong currency has played a significant part in all the gradual steps taken by the mainland authority in the internationalization of the Renminbi. For example, Pauly (2011:53) observed that the Renminbi-dominated bonds issued in Hong Kong served multiple functions of promoting Hong Kong's bond market, aiding the inter-nationalization of the Renminbi and providing funds for infrastructure development in the Mainland economy.

Back in the time before 1978 when the Renminbi was a closed currency, much of the foreign goods entered Mainland China through Hong Kong, and the Hong Kong currency was useful then because it provided hard currency to the Mainland economy to acquire the needed imports. This, of course, is history as the Renminbi now is gaining world attention. Given that all exchange rate regimes in the world economy have suffered from different periodic difficulties, both the Renminbi and the Hong Kong dollar would have no exception. What if the Renminbi were in difficulty in future, suffering from some sort of crisis? For example, what would happen to the value of the Renminbi if there were capital flights from the mainland economy, say when a decision to allow full convertibility of the Renminbi had taken place?

A situation of excess supply of Renminbi could occur, and the value of the Renminbi would drop, resulting in a depreciating pressure. Or if Mainland China's export had fallen due to world economic recession, while there were large demand for import in Mainland China. The fall in export and the simultaneous rise in imports would pressurize the Renminbi to depreciate.

In other words, in a sunny day, there will not be problems with the Renminbi. But, should one be prepared for the rainy day when the Renminbi were to come under severe pressure? Should that extreme scenario happen, the Hong Kong currency can serve as an alternative currency to complement or ease the pressure and problems of the Renminbi. In short, the Hong Kong currency can function as a "back door" or "balancing" currency for the Renminbi. Such a "one country, two currencies" concept shall provide ample practical reason for the existence and preservation of an internationally recognized Hong Kong currency. In any case, despite the rising Renminbi, the Hong Kong currency has been an international matured currency for a much longer period than the Renminbi. While the Renminbi is a contemporary rising and popular currency, the Hong Kong dollar is an internationally tested currency. This probably will remain so until the time when Renminbi becomes fully convertible and faces no uncertainties as a world currency.

After taking into account the pros and cons of linking or delinking the Hong Kong currency to the US dollar, there is no clear answer as to a more superior solution for the Hong Kong currency. And since the current linked exchange rate to the US dollar has done more good than harm, it might as well for Hong Kong to keep the system and let the linked exchange rate system functions to its maximum possible extent.

As there is no perfection in any exchange rate regime in the world, different currencies would have problems at different time periods, due to economic fluctuations and non-economic incidents. The Hong Kong currency is no exception. As a comparison to other world currencies, Li (2006) has reported from the Bank of International Settlement (BIS) that in April 2001, for example, the percentage share (in 200% since two currencies are involved in each transaction) of average daily turnover for the US dollar was 90.4%. For the Hong Kong currency, the share was 2.3%. While the US dollar ranked highest in the global foreign exchange market turnover in April 2001, the Hong Kong currency ranked ninth, following sequentially the US dollar, Euro, Japanese yen, Pound sterling, Swiss franc, Canadian dollar, Australian dollar and Swedish krona.

Indeed, the Hong Kong dollar has also experienced difficult times, and since 1983 when the linked exchange rate system was instituted, the Hong Kong currency has been attacked and faced with different degrees of uncertainties and challenges. Since Hong Kong has no exchange controls, and monetary transactions are not restricted, the massive inflow of capital would boost the economy, but a massive outflow in a short period of time could lead to crisis. It would then be useful to consider the stability of the Hong Kong currency, and what can be learned from previous crises. More importantly, can there be pre-conditions that one can aware of in predicting the possible occurrence of financial crisis and currency attacks?

10.3 Three Episodes of Currency Attacks

Financial crisis involving massive outflows of capital can lead to currency crisis and attacks. In analyzing the Asian financial crisis (AFC), Glick and Ross (1999) and Fratzher (2003) argue that a major feature in the AFC is the extent of financial attack clusters, as financial inter-dependence allowed the contagion effect to spread. Calvo (1998) concludes that a sudden drop in capital flows may generate financial crisis, as credit channels are severely affected. Rigobon (1998) suggests that the behavior of capital flows is important during the onset of a currency crisis, as optimistic expectation induced by high economic growth caused massive capital inflows in the short-term, but financial market overreactions can magnify the crisis. Bekaert and Harvey (1999) point out that speculation can improve the liquidity of the stock market, but the degree of destruction can equally be high when speculators withdrew capital.

Azman-Saini (2006) and other newspaper reports show that hedge funds have been used as an additional instrument in attacking the Asian stock and currency markets during the AFC. Other studies that are relevant to the Hong Kong experience discussed the linkage between the stock, derivative and exchange rate markets at the time of currency attacks. Hau and Rey (2006), for example, develop a theoretical model to examine the correlation between exchange rates, stock prices and capital flows. There are also different definitions of speculative currency attacks. Frankel and Rose (1996) define currency crisis in developing countries as a devaluation by at least 25%, or by at least 10% over the previous year. Eichengreen *et al.* (1996) propose that speculative attacks are said to have occurred when the speculative pressure index, which consists of weighted average in changes in exchange rate, foreign reserve and interest rate, exceeded 25%. Kumar *et al.* (2003) define a crisis by a large interest rate differential adjusted movement in the financial market.

Under the linked exchange rate system, the Hong Kong Monetary Authority (HKMA) exercised a currency board refinement mechanism that involved currency intervention once the exchange rate has reached the strong-side or weak-side of the Convertibility Undertaking Rate. As such, the spot exchange rate in Hong Kong can no longer reflect the actual fluctuation in the market. An alternative would be to consider the movements of forward exchange rate as that can give the best unbiased forecast of future spot rate (Cornell, 1977; Bilson, 1979). Li and Wong (2008) note that since currency attacks usually result in the speculation of either currency depreciation or appreciation, speculative currency attack can be defined by a movement greater than 1 in the standard deviation in the value of the daily exchange rate difference between the 3-month forward rate and the spot rate.

Between 1986 and 2008, Hong Kong has experienced three episodes of currency attacks in 1988 when there was a prolonged weakness in the US currency, in 1998 at the peak of the AFC when speculators used the stock, derivative and foreign exchange markets to attack the Hong Kong currency, and in 2007 when there was pressure on the appreciation of the Renminbi. Table 10.1 summarizes the key events in the three episodes of currency attacks in Hong Kong. The first episode occurred in the period from January 1986 to end of 1990 when the prolonged weak US currency coincided with high inflation in Mainland China. The US recession that began in the mid-

TABLE 10.1 The chronology of the three episodes of currency attacks

First episode: Weak US dollar	
1987	The US current account peaked, leading to a significant capital outflows and sharp depreciation of the US dollar against major foreign currencies.
16/10/1987	The stock markets all over the world experienced a collapse. The Hang Seng Index fell sharply, closing at 3,362.39 points.
20/10/1987	The Hong Kong stock market closed trading for 4 days, shocked all investors.
26/10/1987	Largest one-day decline in Hang Seng Index occurred after the 4-days closure.
29/10/1987	Hong Kong government loaned the exchange reserve to the Hong Kong Futures Guarantee Corporation Ltd. to finance the settlement of obligations to clearing members of the Hong Kong Futures Exchange Company.
21/11/1987 24/11/1987	The US President Ronald Reagan proposed a specific policy to eliminate the twin fiscal and trade deficits. The exchange rate dropped further. Foreign exchange market participants wondered if the deficit elimination policy would be effective and whether the economy would recess.
9/12/1987	The US government put pressure on the Hong Kong Government for abandoning the linked exchange rate mechanism. There was massive inflow of capital for the speculation of the appreciation of the Hong Kong dollar.
12/12/1987	The Hong Kong government emphasized that the linked exchange rate mechanism will not be abandoned.
22/12/1987	The Hong Kong Association of Banks announced that they may exercise a negative interest rate so as to restrain the speculative activity on the HK dollar.
23/12/1987	The US dollar climbed back and the pressure on the appreciation of the Hong Kong dollar was alleviated.
1987–1988	The Hong Kong government removed the interest rate ceiling and floor, enabled the interest rate free to adjust in supporting the linked exchange rate.
7/1988	The HKMA arranged for the Hong Kong & Shanghai Banking Corporation to manage the Clearing House of the Hong Kong Association of Banks.
Second episode: Asian financial crisis (AFC)	
5–7/1997	The AFC started with the attack of the Thai Baht when the US$30 billion worth of foreign exchange exhausted, the Thailand government abandoned the fixed exchange rate system.
8/7/1997	The Hong Kong Hang Seng Index reached a record high at 16,820 points.
14/8/1997 15/8/1997	An extraordinary and rapid drop in the spot and forward exchange rate in the HK dollar against the US dollar. The HKMA raised interest rate to defend the linked exchange rate.
10/1997	The Hang Seng Index dropped by 30% in this month.

(*Continued*)

TABLE 10.1 (*Continued*)

11–12/1997	Speculators shifted their attention to Latin America and South Korea. The Bank of Korea abandoned the fixed exchange rate system, allowing the Won to fall below 1,000 against the US dollar. The IMF approved a US$57 billion worth of bailout package to South Korea.
6/1998	The HKMA proposed the publication of the forecast change in the aggregate foreign exchange balance, with the intention to enhance the transparency of the linked exchange rate mechanism and facilitate a more efficient interest rate adjustment in the money market.
8/1998	Speculators shorted HK$29 billion, while HKMA used the foreign exchange reserve to prevent the Hong Kong dollar from depreciation. On the two days of 6 and 7/8/1998, speculators shorted about HK$20 billion.
14/8/1998	The Hong Kong government's intervention on the stock market by deploying HK$80 billion, the Hang Seng Index was up by 584 points, or 8.3%. The constituent stock, HSBC, increased by 4.6%.
25/8/1998	To increase the cost of speculation, the HKMA tightened the supply of Hong Kong dollar and the overnight interbank interest rate rose to 15%.
26/8/1998	The open interest of the September Hang Seng Index futures contract increased to 73 thousand. The normal total open interest contracts were 45 thousand. It reached a record high of 131 thousand in August.
28/8/1998	It was the futures clearing date, probably the final battle between the speculators and the government. The Hang Seng Index fell slightly, by 93 points, but the turnover was a record high of HK$79 billion.
5/9/1998	The HKMA introduced 7 specific measures to strengthen the currency board arrangements and lower the possibility of manipulation by currency speculators: 1) provide a clear convertibility to all licensed banks in Hong Kong to convert HK$ in their clearing accounts into US$ at fixed exchange rate of HK$7.75 to US$1; 2) abandon the bid rate of the Liquidity Adjustment Facility; 3) determine Discount Window with the base rate from time to time; 4) remove the restriction on repeated borrowing overnight Hong Kong dollar; 5) issue new exchange fund paper only when there is an inflow of funds; 6) offer different discount rates in accordance with different percentage of thresholds of Exchange Funds paper holdings; and 7) restrict on repeated borrowing on debt securities.
Third episode: Expectation on Renminbi	
18/5/2007	The HKMA refined the convertibility undertaking to the linked exchange rate mechanism with the boundaries between 7.75 and 7.85.
1/7/2007	Sustained inflow of hot money to speculate on the appreciation of Renminbi.
24/7/2007	The HKMA intervened in the Hong Kong exchange rate. The inter-bank interest rate increased to above 7%.
17/8/2007	The Hang Seng Index was highly volatile, dropped almost 1,200 points to close at 20,761 points.

(*Continued*)

TABLE 10.1 (*Continued*)

19/8/2007	The implementation of QDII scheme and the proposed "through train" scheme caused a quick recovery of the Hang Seng Index.
23/10/2007	The HKMA bought about HK$775 million worth of US$ as the Hong Kong interest rate was significantly higher than that of the US, and the exchange rate was closed to the strong side of the Convertibility Undertaking.
26/10/2007	Equity related demand for HK dollars caused a further strength of HK dollars.
30/10/2007	The Hang Seng Index and Hang Seng Chinese Enterprises Index rose to record high of 31,638 and 20,400 points, respectively.
31/10/2007	The HKMA undertook a series of strong side Convertibility Undertaking operations and purchased approximately US$1 million against HK dollar.

Sources: News reports from *Mingpao Daily*, *South China Morning Post*, and the Hong Kong Monetary Authority.

1980s has resulted in a period of prolonged weakness in the US exchange rate. Subsequently, the US Federal Reserve adopted a low interest rate policy in order to stimulate the US economy. Under the linked exchange rate system, Hong Kong had to follow the US and pursued a similarly low interest rate policy. Simultaneously, inflation in Hong Kong remained high due partly to the persistent high inflation rate in Mainland China and partly to the excess demand resulting from the economic recovery in Hong Kong after the successful conclusion of the Sino-British negotiation in late 1984. There was a large amount of capital inflow in 1987–1988, mainly in the Hong Kong dollar deposits. The Hong Kong authority had to buy US dollar and sell Hong Kong dollar in the market. Nugee (1995) reports that the Hong Kong government purchased a total of US$2.7 billion and US$3.1 billion in 1987 and 1988, respectively, in order to rescue the linked exchange rate.

The pressure to unpack the link increased. It was rumored that the linked exchange rate system would be abandoned, though the then British Hong Kong government emphasized otherwise. Hong Kong experienced a massive inflow of hot money that challenged the linked exchange rate system. On December 22, 1987, the Hong Kong Association of Banks announced the imposition of a negative interest rate. A negative interest rate policy would mean that large Hong Kong dollar depositors would face a loss as certain charges would be levied on their deposits, and at the same time, no interest payment would be given to the deposits. It was such a vigorous determination that deterred the speculators and the negative interest rate was not imposed in the end.

The second episode of currency attack covered the four years in the Asian financial crisis (AFC) period from January 1996 to end of 2000. The outbreak of the AFC resulted in the depreciation of a number of Asian currencies in late 1997. The US dollar maintained strong in much of the 1990s. It was thus another opportunity for speculators to attack the Hong Kong currency. Between July and October 1997, the Hong Kong Hang Seng Index dropped by 30% from the peak of 16,820 points. Between October 1997 and August 1998, speculators borrowed heavily and dumped the Hong Kong dollar in the market, thus creating an excess supply shock.

The Hong Kong inter-bank interest rate jumped to 300%, but it was in vain as speculators used New York and Melbourne to facilitate their hedging activities in Hong Kong.

Speculators were reaping huge profits from holding short positions in the Hong Kong dollar denominated forward, index futures and equity markets. Speculative attacks on the Hong Kong currency was made as there were block trade of short selling of Hong Kong exchange rate forward contracts. International speculators mobilized hedge funds and their block trade caused high fluctuations in the stock and currency markets (Asman-Saini, 2006). The real attack came in August 1998 when speculators shorted a total of HK$49 billion (US$6.28 billion), though the HKMA used the foreign exchange reserve to prevent the currency from depreciating. It was in August 1998 when eventually the government of Hong Kong Special Administrative Region (HKSAR) intervened by deploying HK$80 billion (US$10.34 billion) from the Exchange Fund to purchase portfolio of stocks that reduced the supply in the market, prevented the Hang Seng Index to dive below 7,000 points from the peak of 16,820 in July 1997, and eventually defeated the speculators.

Such a historical act of government intervention and the unprecedented deployment of government reserve drove speculators away, defended the peg and restored currency stability. However, it has also been criticized that the Hong Kong SAR Government has abandoned the non-interventionist economic policy, and the government's bulk purchase of stocks gave rise to questions of disposal. In early September 1998, the HKMA listed a total of seven specific measures to strengthen the currency board arrangements that lowered the possibility of currency manipulation by the speculators. Most analysts tended to agree that the intervention by the government in purchasing the equities from the stock market was an "one-time" off event as Hong Kong was facing a severe and abnormal financial crisis, and effective instruments were needed to rescue the economy and restore stability at all cost. This, however, is acceptable even though the intervention may have deviated from the norm in stable times.

Several observations can be made from comparing the first two episodes of currency attacks. The Hong Kong currency would be prone to attack in situations of either a prolonged period of strong US currency or a continued period of weak US currency. The large reserve turned out to be the only guarantee to the stability of the Hong Kong currency, because it has the advantage that it would be costly for speculators to mobilize an equivalent huge amount of funds in order to attack the Hong Kong currency. A closer monitor on large currency transactions in and out of Hong Kong and a more transparent financial system would serve as warning signals on future attacks and could provide further currency stability. The Hong Kong authority has to keep a constant watch on the movement of other Asian currencies, ensuring that changes in their value would not spill over to the Hong Kong currency. This necessarily required more cooperation and understanding among key Asian currencies in the region. Improvements in banking regulations, such as the Basle II in 2005 involving a stronger requirement in the capital asset ratio (CAR) of banks has been instituted as a further check to reduce currency crisis.

Mainland China's trade surplus has expanded after the Renminbi devaluated by 30% in January 1994, its growing reserve has added pressure on the revaluation of the Renminbi. In April 2006, Beijing signaled that qualified domestic individual investors (QDII) would soon be allowed to invest in fixed income and money market products in Hong Kong, and the scheme expanded to include investment in stocks in May 2007. This led to the speculation that the Renminbi may become fully convertible and mainland authority would have opened its currency market. In response to these incidents, the stock market in Hong Kong turned bullish and climbed continuously for a few months until a contrary announcement was made by Premier Wen in Beijing in November 2007 that the decision to allow QDII investment to Hong Kong needed further investigation and was shelved. By October 2007, attention has been drawn to the potential impact on the Hong Kong dollar resulting from the possible change in Mainland China's exchange rate system. The Hong Kong dollar reached the strong-side convertibility region within a week. There was a significant interest rate premium for the HK dollar over the US dollar. The HKMA brought about HK$775 million (US$99.35 million) worth of US dollars to maintain monetary stability.

There is a need to investigate on currency attacks in Hong Kong. The three episodes could serve as scenario cases for elaboration. The intention is to see if there can be initial signs of currency attacks, and what the Hong Kong government should look for and identify potential risk factors. Currency attacks should be studied using dynamic models as financial markets and transactions change rapidly. Through such a study, one hopes to identify some conditions of prevention, so that future attacks can be avoided. The following section shows the technical study by Li and Wong (2008) that analyzes the different episodes of currency attacks and came up with a total of four conditions which can help to predict and prevent future currency attacks.[1]

10.4 Signals of Currency Attack: An Empirical Analysis

One can technically study the movement in Hong Kong's capital flows during the three currency crisis periods and identify the features in the period prior to and during the currency attack. The dynamic conditional correlation model developed by Engle (2002) and Tse and Tsui (2002) is used in Li and Wong (2008) to examine the time varying correlation structure between the Hang Seng Index (HSI) returns, the HSI futures (HSIF) returns and the exchange rate forwards premium. In practice, the expectation of market participants played an important role on the stock and foreign exchange markets. The HSI futures (HSIF) returns and the exchange rate forwards premium are relevant and useful factors in studying currency crisis and currency attacks.

The data collected from DataStream included the daily closing price of the HSI, HSIF and the three-month Hong Kong to US dollar exchange rate forward contracts for the period January 1986 to September 2008. The HSI is a capitalization-weighted market index. As of June 2008, there are 43 HSI constituent stocks,

---

[1] Non-technical readers can concentrate on the discussion, results and findings of the analysis, and skip the technical presentation.

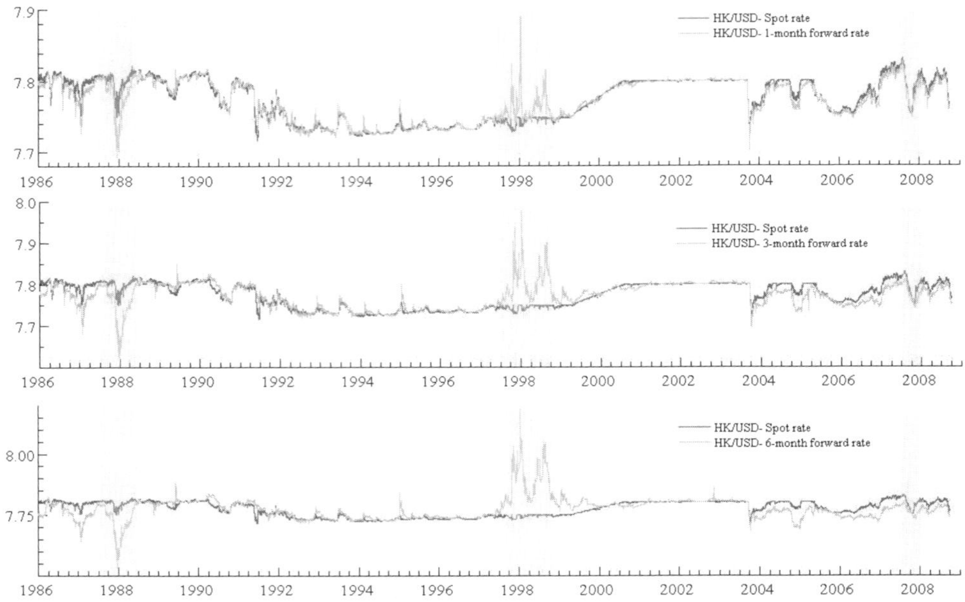

FIGURE 10.1 The spot exchange rate and 1-month, 3-month, and 6-month exchange rate forwards

composing the most representative companies in Hong Kong and Mainland China. However, since the HSIF data are not available until late 1989, only the last two episodes of currency attack in 1997–1998 and 2007–2008 are analyzed empirically. However, all three currency attacks are analyzed statistically.

Figure 10.1 shows the HK dollar to US dollar spot exchange rate against the 1-month, 3-month and 6-month forward rates. The movement of these various rates can reflect the investors' expectation in different time domains. When compared to the spot rate, the forward exchange rate contained additional information on expectation, including the presence of premium (discount) when the forward rate is lower (higher) than the spot rate. One observation is that a large difference in the two rates can be seen during the various currency attack periods. The daily returns of both HSI (HSI returns) and of HSI futures (HSIF returns) are defined by the formula $y_t = \ln(P_t/P_{t-1})$, where P_t is the daily closing price. The HSI and HSIF are shown in Figures 10.2(a) and 10.2(b), while their daily returns are shown in Figures 10.2(c) and 10.2(d), respectively. One can observe that Hong Kong has experienced a sharp decline in both the HSI and HSIF in late 2007 due probably to the announcement in shelving the qualified domestic individual investment (QDII) scheme and the outbreak of the US subprime mortgage crisis.

Table 10.2 shows the HSI returns, HSIF returns and the 30-days exponential moving average of the daily difference between 3-month forward exchange rate and spot rate (3MEMA30). The Skewness and Excess Kurtosis estimates are used to indicate the extent of speculation in the stock market. The results indicated that a high

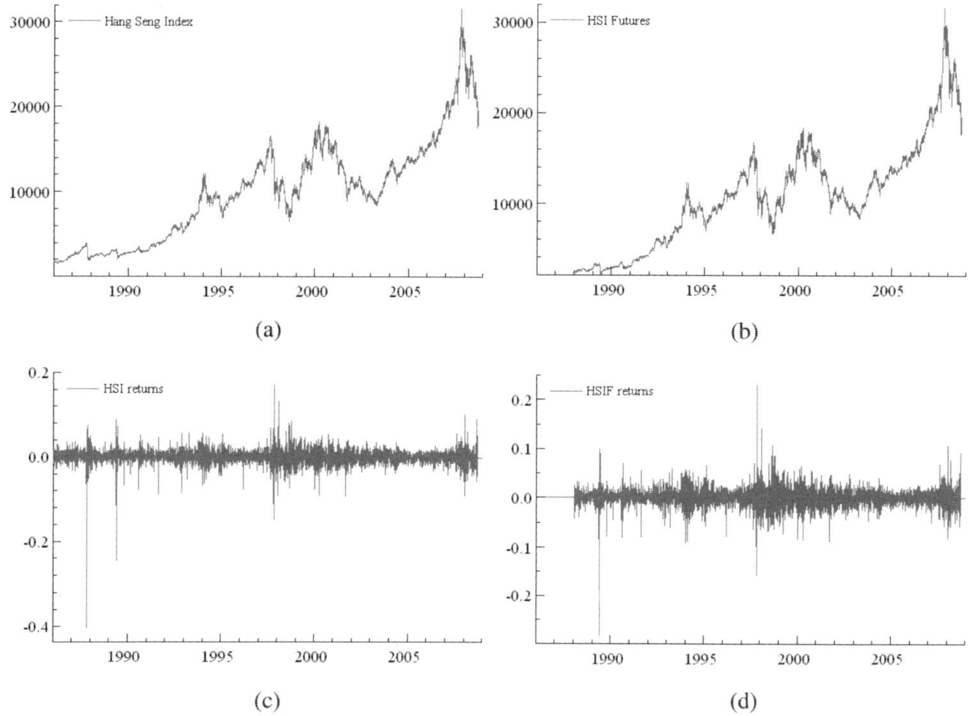

FIGURE 10.2 The Hang Seng index and Hang Seng index futures

TABLE 10.2 Descriptive statistics of HSI returns, HSIF returns and 3MEMA30

Statistics	HSI returns	HSIF returns	3MEMA30[a]
Mean	0.0004	0.0004	0.0003
Standard Deviation	0.016	0.018	0.0227
Skewness	−0.7542	−0.5586	1.6268
Excess Kurtosis	19.422	21.65	9.8659
Minimum	−0.2452	−0.2822	−0.1185
Maximum	0.1725	0.2298	0.1248
Normality test χ^2	10340**	12553**	1456.3**

Notes: [a] = 30-days exponential averaged value. ** = significance level at 1%.

level of speculation is common in the Hong Kong stock market. The Excess Kurtosis of all three series is larger than 3, and the Chi-square tests for normality are statistically significant at 1%. The null hypothesis of normality can be rejected. All series contain the property of a thick tail and non-normal distribution.

In order to see if there is a relationship between the movement of the stock and foreign exchange markets, Li and Wong (2008) apply the dynamic conditional correlation GARCH (DCC-GARCH) model to study the time varying structure between the HSI returns and the Hong Kong exchange rate. In addition, as the open interest contracts can provide information about the position of market participants on HSIF, the open interest contracts, together with the estimated conditional correlations, are used to examine the probability of speculative currency attack by using the logistic (logit) regression model.

Technically and due to the large fluctuation in the exchange rate forward contracts, disturbance can affect the accuracy of the financial attack signal. The exponential moving average (EMA) method is adopted to smooth the exchange rate difference series by applying the weighting factors that decrease exponentially. The 30-days data are weighted exponentially, and the degree of weighting, α, can be expressed as $\alpha = \frac{2}{N+1}$, where N denotes the number of time periods. The conventional EMA formula is:

$$EMA = \frac{\sum_{t=1}^{T} (1-\alpha)^{t-1} P_t}{\sum_{t=1}^{T} (1-\alpha)^{t-1}}, \quad (1)$$

where P_t represents the daily data of the variable. The weighting factor on each data point ensured that the influence of the previous data decreases exponentially.

The following technical procedures are used in Li and Wong (2008) to estimate the DCC-GARCH model. Each of the data series is first fitted into the univariate GARCH models to obtain the estimated standard residuals. The intercept parameters of conditional correlation are then estimated. Finally, the coefficients governing the dynamics of correlation are estimated using the intercept parameters of conditional correlation.[2] The ARCH model in Engle (1982) allows the conditional means and variance to change over time, namely:

$$y_t \,|\Omega_{t-1} \sim (x_t\beta,\, h_t),$$
$$h_t = w_0 + \alpha_1 u_{t-1}^2. \quad (2)$$

It is assumed that $x_t\,\beta$ is the mean of y_t, which is a linear combination of lagged variables included in the information set (Ω_{t-1}) with a vector (β) of unknown parameters. The GARCH model in Bollerslev (1986) is used to estimate the univariate GARCH specification as it allows a longer memory and a more flexible structure. The variance equation of the GARCH (p, q) process can be defined as:

$$h_t = w_0 + \sum_{i=1}^{q} \alpha_i u_{t-1}^2 + \sum_{i=1}^{p} \beta_i h_{t-i}, \quad (3)$$

where $w_0 > 0$, $\alpha_i \geq 0$ and $\beta_i \geq 0$ ($\forall i$). The GARCH (p, q) process permits an autoregressive moving average component in the heteroscedastic variance.

[2] Non-technical readers can skip the econometrics and concentrate on the findings and interpretations. The detailed econometrics presentation is shown in Li and Wong (2008).

Studies have shown that a negative shock to a financial time series is likely to cause higher volatility than a positive shock of the same magnitude (Black, 1976; Christie, 1982; French *et al.*, 1987; Nelson, 1991; Schwert, 1990; Engle and Ng, 1993). In order to catch the asymmetric response, Glosten *et al.* (1993) (GJR) introduce the following model for conditional variance:

$$h_t = w_0 + \alpha_1 u_{t-1}^2 + \beta_1 \sigma_{t-1}^2 + \gamma_1 u_{t-1}^2 I_{t-1}, \quad (4)$$

where $I_{t-1} = 1$ if $u_{t-1} > 0$ and $I_{t-1} = 0$ otherwise. The existence of the asymmetry effect will be found if γ_1 is greater than zero, and α_1 must be non-negative. Equation (4) is a modified GARCH model with the addition of a dummy variable, I_{t-1}. The dynamic conditional correlation (DCC) model is used to examine the dynamic correlation of the exchange rates difference, HSI returns and HSIF returns.

Li and Wong (2008) further argue that the logit regression is a widely used multivariate statistical parametric model for estimating the probability of occurrence for a certain event, such as the probability of currency attack using a series of independent or explanatory variables. The logit model becomes:

$$L[p_t(x_{it})] = \beta_0 + \beta_1 X_{1t} + \beta_2 X_{2t} + \cdots + \beta_i X_{it} + \varepsilon_t. \quad (5)$$

The *i*th coefficient, β_i, represents the influences of a certain unitary variation of X_{it} on the odds, other explanatory variables being constant.

The dynamic conditional correlation estimation process consists of fitting the univariate GARCH specifications to each data series, as shown in Table 10.3. All the coefficient of parameters is statistically significant at 5% level. The three parameters ω, α and β are the GARCH parameters from Equation (3), while γ shows the asymmetry parameter in Equation (4). The asymmetric effect is a common feature in financial markets. Table 10.3 shows that both γ_H and γ_F are significant. H, F, and E represented the estimates for HSI returns, HSI futures returns and exchange rate difference, respectively.

In the HSI returns, bad news can generate a higher level of fluctuation than good news. The coefficient of asymmetry of the exchange rate difference (γ_E) is statistically insignificant. This implied that both good news and bad news generated symmetric effect in the 3-month exchange rate forward premium. Figure 10.3(a) plots the volatility news impact curves of the HSI and HSI futures. The curves highlight the asymmetry response to news of HSI and HSI futures. The Y-axis in the figures represented volatility at time $t-1$, while the X-axis showed the returns of the assets (HSI, HSIF and 3MEMA30). It is clear that the HSI news impact curve has a higher magnitude than the HSI futures news impact curve as the news impact curve of HSI is above the news impact curve of HSIF. Figure 10.3(b) shows the 3-month exchange rate difference, and that both good news and bad news generated the same impact. For the HSI and HSIF, any bad news would trigger a sharp decline in the Hong Kong stock market.

The low unconditional correlation between the exchange rate difference and both the HSI and HSI futures is a concern. Li and Wong (2008) apply the Engle and Sheppard (2001) test for constant conditional correlation prior to the estimation of the Engle (2002) DCC-model and Tse and Tsui (2002) DCC-model. In Table 10.4,

TABLE 10.3 The univariate GARCH models

	ω_H	α_H	β_H	γ_H	ω_F	α_F	β_F	γ_F	ω_E	α_E	β_E	γ_E
GARCH (1,1) with Gaussian Distribution												
Coefficients	0.0008	0.1005	0.8837	—	0.0009	0.0835	0.9030	—	0.0005	1.6629	–0.6625	—
Std. Error	(0.0002)	(0.0151)	(0.0160)	—	(0.0002)	(0.0138)	(0.0148)	—	(0.0000)	(0.0407)	(0.0408)	—
GJR (1,1) with Gaussian Distribution												
Coefficients	0.0006	0.0462	0.8782	0.1007	0.0006	0.0393	0.8963	0.0895	0.0005	1.6650	–0.6624	–0.0034#
Std. Error	(0.0002)	(0.0095)	(0.0154)	(0.0243)	(0.0002)	(0.0085)	(0.0142)	(0.0242)	(0.0000)	(0.0413)	(0.0408)	(0.0045)
GJR (1,1) with Student Distribution												
Coefficients	0.0006	0.0462	0.8782	0.1007	0.0006	0.0393	0.8963	0.0895	0.0005	1.6650	–0.6624	-0.0034#
Std. Error	(0.0002)	(0.0095)	(0.0154)	(0.0243)	(0.0002)	(0.0085)	(0.0142)	(0.0242)	(0.0000)	(0.0413)	(0.0408)	(0.0045)
GARCH (1,1) with Student Distribution												
Coefficients	0.0008	0.1005	0.8837	—	0.0009	0.0835	0.9030	—	0.0005	1.6629	–0.6625	—
Std. Error	(0.0002)	(0.0151)	(0.0160)	—	(0.0002)	(0.0138)	(0.0148)	—	(0.0000)	(0.0407)	(0.0408)	—

Notes: The subscripts of H, F, and E represent the estimates for HSI returns, HSI futures returns and exchange rate difference, respectively. Figures in parenthesis give the standard error of the coefficients. # represents 5% insignificance level. GJR = Glosten *et al.* (1993).

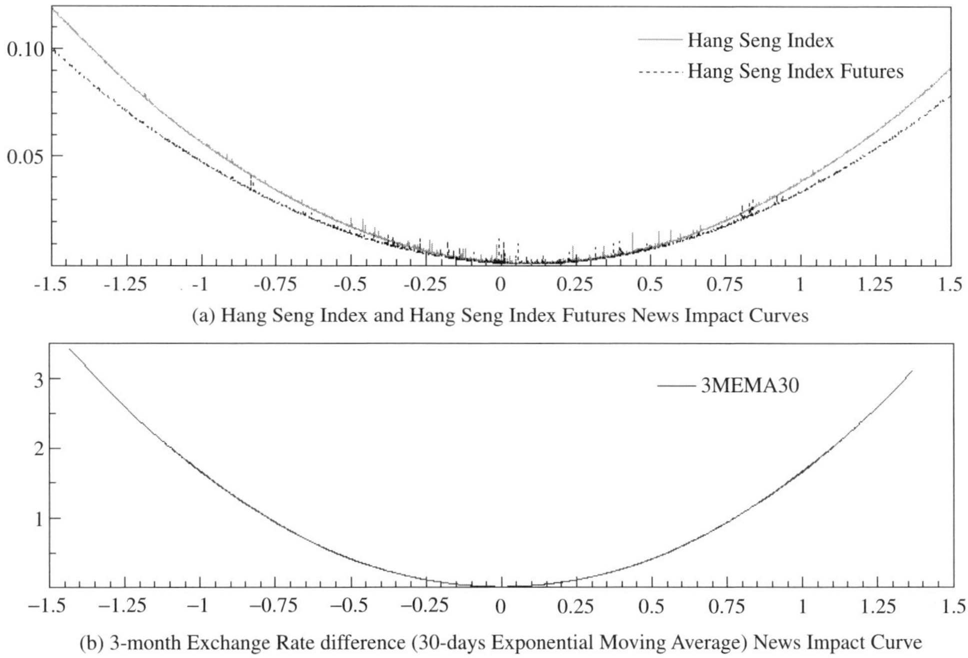

FIGURE 10.3 The news impact curves for HSI, HSI futures, and exchange rate difference

TABLE 10.4 The DCC-GARCH models

	Engle DCC-model			Tse & Tsui DCC-model		
Models/Parameters	α_D	β_D	df	α_D	β_D	df
DCC (1,1)	0.0097	0.9880	—	0.0049#	0.9859	—
	(0.0025)	(0.0040)	—	(0.0050)	(0.0156)	—
GJR-DCC (1,1)	0.0091	0.9907	—	0.0042#	0.9882	—
	(0.0023)	(0.0030)	—	(0.0029)	(0.0086)	—
GJR-Student-DCC (1,1)	0.0078	0.9904	9.5979	0.0041	0.9899	9.1391
	(0.0015)	(0.0020)	(0.5529)	(0.0010)	(0.0025)	(0.5015)
Student-DCC (1,1)	0.0076	0.9904	9.4287	0.0043	0.9893	9.0768
	(0.0014)	(0.0021)	(0.5283)	(0.0010)	(0.0025)	(0.4921)

Notes: DCC = Dynamic conditional correlation; GJR = Glosten *et al.* (1993); Student = Student t distribution. df is the degree of freedom. # represents statistical insignificant at 5%.

Li and Wong (2008) show that the coefficients of the Engle DCC-model parameters are all statistically significant, suggesting that the conditional correlation is not constant over time. The estimated value of α_D in the Tse and Tsui DCC-model is not significant under the Gaussian distribution, but becomes significant under the Student distribution. All the estimates of alphas (α_D) in the models without student represent Gaussian distribution. The estimated value of the degree of freedom (df) of student distribution is 9.0768, which is statistically significant at 1% level. The result matched with the finding of normality Chi-square test shown in Table 10.2. Since a better conditional correlation structure can be obtained if the model is correctly specified, Li and Wong (2008) further compare the two DCC-models using four different criteria and found that the results from the Engle GJR-Student-DCC (1, 1) model are preferred.

The correlation structure between HSI and HSI futures, as shown in Figure 10.4, demonstrates that there is a high degree of positive correlation between the two series. It is clear that changes in the correlation structure have occurred, due possibly to changes in the expectation of market participants. An unfavorable announcement by government or about the constituent stocks would generate a sharp decline in the HSI futures. Because of the 15 minutes lag in the closing time between stock market and futures market in Hong Kong, it is feasible to have a sharp deviation between HSI and HSI futures.

Figure 10.5 shows the two correlation structures of the exchange rate difference to HSI and to HSI futures. Normally, the two correlation structures should have the same pattern. But divergence is possible due to the expectation of market participants. One can note from Figure 10.5 that the conditional correlation dropped to –0.1 in the three currency attack periods of October 1997, July 1998 and October 2007. The fact that a massive capital outflow in late 1997 and mid-1998 has yielded a sharp discount in the 3-month forward rate that resulted in a decline in both HSI and HSI futures. On the contrary, the capital inflow of October 2007 that caused the rise in the 3-month forward rate premium, HSI and HSI futures have generated a decline in the correlation structure. A low correlation between exchange rate difference and HSI, and between exchange rate difference and HSI futures can serve as an early sign of a currency attack. This implies that a sustained decrease in the conditional correlation can be observed prior to currency attacks.

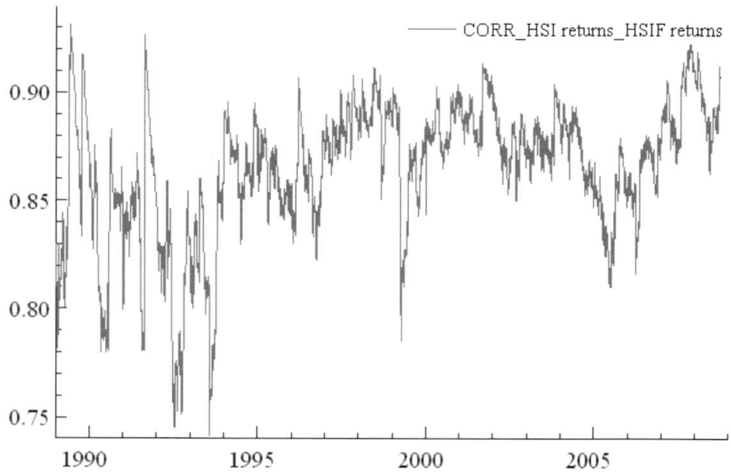

FIGURE 10.4 The estimated conditional correlation of HIS returns and HSIF return

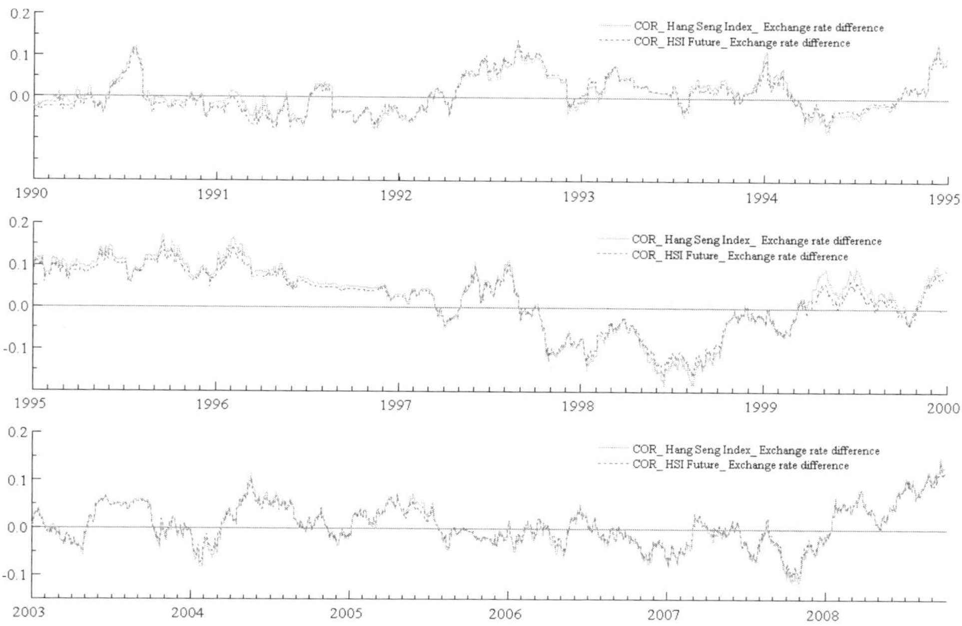

FIGURE 10.5 The estimated conditional correlation of exchange rate difference to HSI returns and HSIF return

The empirical estimation in Figure 10.5 shows that the declining correlation trend is caused by massive capital movement and relatively low correlation between exchange rate difference to HSI returns and to HSIF returns in the currency attack periods. The large difference between forward and spot exchange rates serves as another signal for an imminent currency attack. Figure 10.6 summarizes the difference between the smoothed 3-month and 1-month exchange rate difference. The smoothed 1-month exchange rate difference is used for comparison as it is the closest series to spot exchange rate.

Under normal circumstances, the exchange rate difference curves move around the zero line, which is the equality line between forward rate and spot rate. A significant deviation can clearly be seen before each episode of currency attack in Figure 10.6. For example, the exchange rate forward premium was particularly high in late 1987, when the currency speculation was for the Hong Kong dollar to delink and appreciate (Figure 10.6(a)). In Figure 10.6(c), there is a sharp discount in late 1997 and 1998, when the currency attack was for the Hong Kong dollar to delink and depreciate. One can also note that the non-zero duration generally lasted for a few months, or even longer, before the currency crisis, but could certainly have emerged before the crisis started. For example, we can see that there are over one and half years of deviation between 1MEMA30 and 3MEMA30 before the 1987 crisis, and over half year deviation before the 1997 currency attack and 2007 currency speculation. Indeed, it has lasted longer than a year between 1987 and 1988 and between 2006 and 2007. One can also note that a deviation period of approximately 8 months has appeared before the first attack in October 1997.

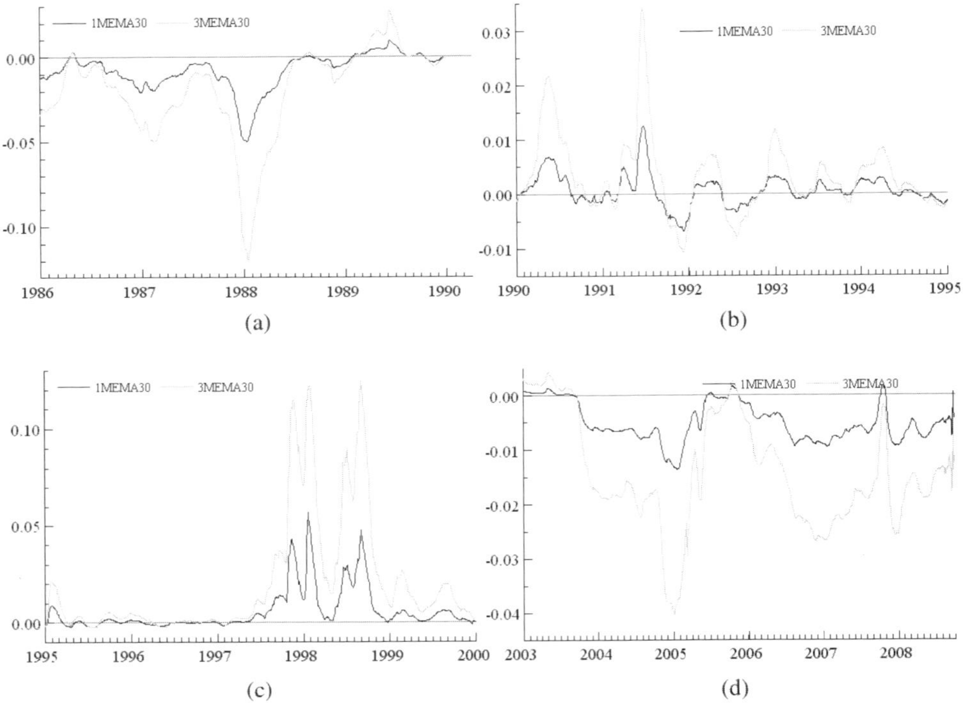

FIGURE 10.6 The exponential moving average of 1-month and 3-month exchange rate difference

Li and Wong (2008) use the conventional logit model to study the interrelationship between stock market, futures market and exchange rate market, and to predict the probability of the occurrence of currency crisis. To determine the importance of the parameters in different markets, a total of four models are used in the estimation of Equation (5), as shown in Table 10.5. Model A consists only of the foreign exchange market variable. The parameter FDP is the difference between 3-month and 1-month forward rate multiplied by the probability of the occurrence, which is indicated by the number of day dispersal.

The coefficient of FDP (74.443) is statistically significant at 1% level, suggesting that FDP is positively related to the currency crisis. The FDP variable showed the difference between 3-month and 1-month forward rates multiplied by probability of the occurrence of number of day dispersal. The regression estimate implies that the longer the number of day dispersals, the higher the possibility of being attacked. This matches with the finding that a large and prolonged difference between forward and spot rate will increase the probability of currency attack in Hong Kong. In general, the 1-month and 3-month forward exchange rates should have the same movement over time, but a sharp difference can lead to market uncertainty and provide valuable information about the future expectation of market participants at the current situation.

Models B and C include the variable CHED, which is the first difference of conditional correlation between HSI and exchange rate difference. The variable CHED

TABLE 10.5 The estimates of the logistic models

Parameters	Model A	Model B	Model C	Model D
Constant	−3.231	−3.327	−2.921	−2.756
	(0.000)	(0.000)	(0.000)	(0.000)
FDP	74.443	69.616	67.969	66.264
	(0.000)	(0.000)	(0.000)	(0.000)
CHED		−60.730	−35.891#	−47.180
		(0.004)	(0.104)	(0.043)
CHFE			−44.964	−53.202
			(0.000)	(0.000)
HSIP				0.007
				(0.000)
Open Interest (HSIF)				−0.587
				(0.048)
AIC	0.534	0.488	0.426	[0.419]
log-likelihood	−1581.848	−1314.321	−1147.126	[−034.602]

Notes: FDP gives the difference between 3-month and 1-month forward rates multiplied by probability of the occurrence of number of day dispersal; CHED is the first difference of conditional correlation between HSI and exchange rate difference; CHFE is the conditional correlation between HSI futures and exchange rate difference; HSIP is the Hang Seng Index premium; Open Interest (HSIF) is the 30-days differenced open interest contracts of index futures. () and [ ] denote, respectively, the *p*-value of the coefficients and the best result in each criterion. # represents insignificance level of 5%.

indicates the changes of conditional correlation. In Figure 10.5, we can see that the conditional correlation clearly declined before and during crisis (for example, from late-1997 to mid-1998, and late-2007). The use of the first difference serves as the transformation needed to avoid the potential problem of multicollinearity. In Table 10.5, the conditional correlation of exchange rate difference to HSI return is significant with a negative sign (−60.73), suggesting that the probability of currency crisis occurrence is negatively related to the change in conditional correlation between exchange rate difference and HSI return. This provides a robust result that the decrease in the correlation would increase the possibility of currency attack.

In Model C, the coefficient estimate of CHFE (−44.964), which is the conditional correlation between HSI futures and exchange rate difference, is statistically significant, suggesting that the conditional correlation between exchange rate difference and HSI futures is negatively related to currency attack. This CHFE variable can provide the information that a decrease in the conditional correlation can lead to the possibility of a currency attack.

The HSI premium (HSIP) is the difference between HSI and HSI futures, noting also that the positive (negative) excess return of HSI futures can be considered as a premium (discount). The daily changes in the HSI premium virtually reflect the expectation on the HSI futures. Figure 10.7 illustrates the HSI premium, and the presence of sharp volatility appears in different periods. The HSI premium also shows large fluctuations in the AFC period. Note that a sharp decline in the HSI premium

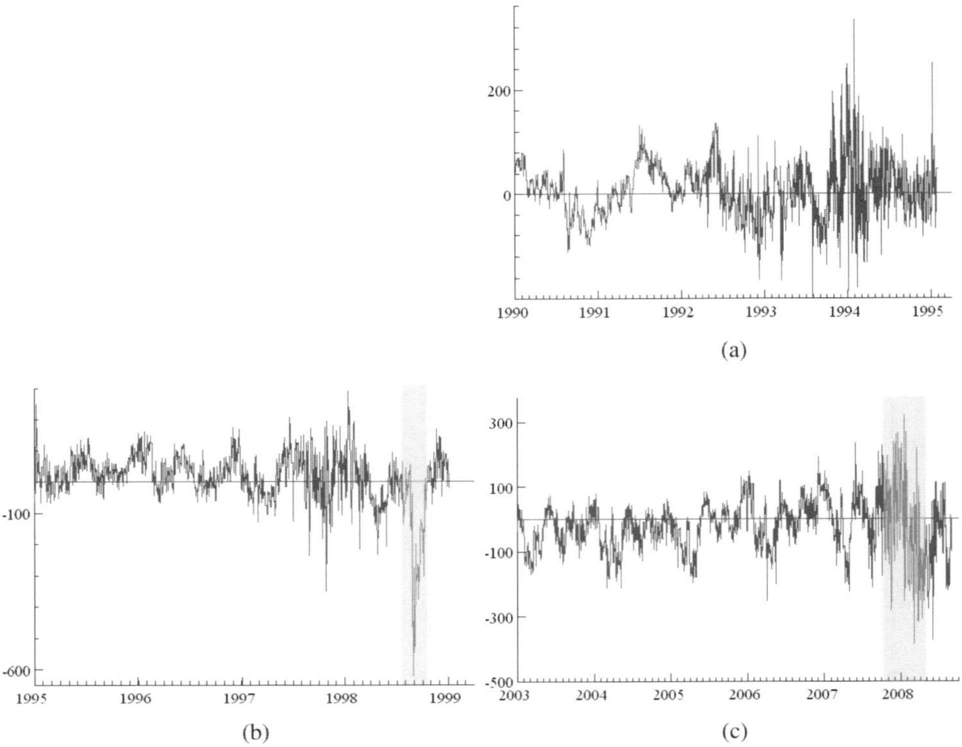

FIGURE 10.7 The Hang Seng index premium

can be seen in August 1998 when the government tackled the currency attack from speculators. In addition, a significant volatility can also be found in late 2007.

The open interest of HSI futures is the number of unexpired open interest contracts. Theoretically, futures contract is an instrument for investors to manage portfolio risk. In general, the open interest of futures contracts should not show any trend. However, an obvious and positive trend that started from March 1998 can be found in Figure 10.8, when speculators quickly accumulated a block of open interest contracts over a few months. By August 1998, speculators closed those futures contracts and exchange rate forward contracts simultaneously, causing a sharp collapse in the open interest, HSI, HSI futures and the exchange rate.

The estimates of Model D in Table 10.5 show that the HSI premium and open interest of futures are related to the currency attacks as their coefficient are statistically significant. The negative sign of the coefficient of open interest (–0.587) provides another crucial clue that when speculators closed their long position of the open interest contracts in turn could cause a serious decline in the HSI, HSI futures and exchange rate. This relationship would be apparent if there are only few participants in the market, and action by any trader could lead to serious market fluctuations.

Li and Wong (2008) use the log likelihood and Akaike information criteria (AIC) to measure the efficiency of the models. Both criteria show that Model D in

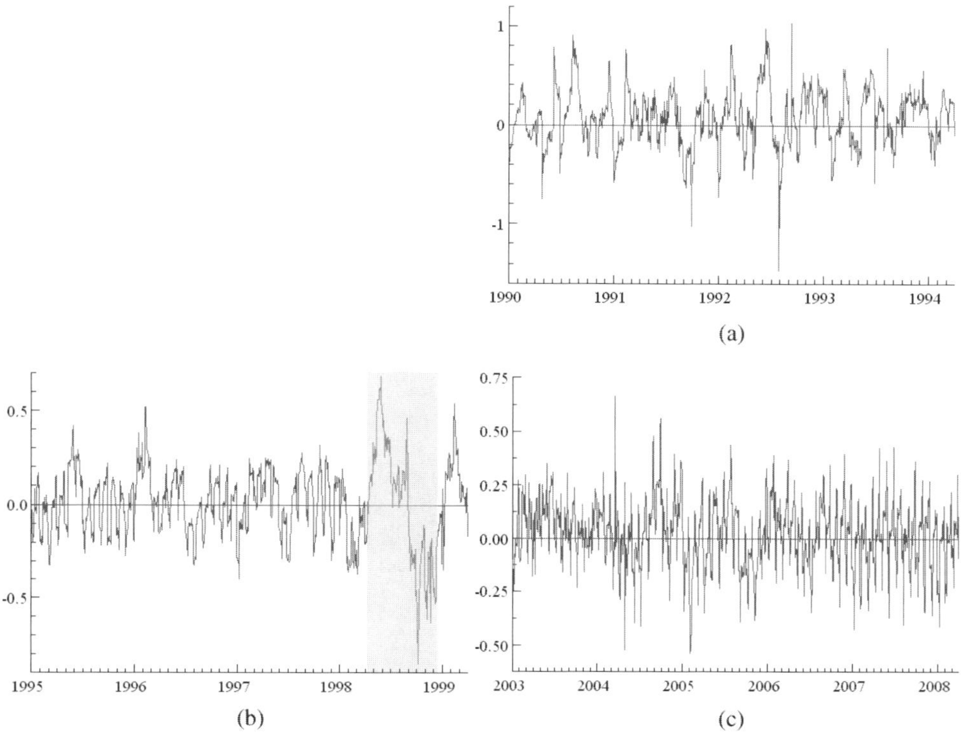

FIGURE 10.8 The open interest contract of HSI futures

Table 10.5 is the best model that can provide reliable prediction for currency attacks. Figure 10.9 shows the estimated probabilities of Model D in different currency attacks periods. The calculated mean and standard deviation of the estimated probability in Model D is 0.1588 and 0.2703, respectively. The data on exchange rate difference showed that over 85% of the daily probability is lower than the mean. Indeed, currency attack is not a familiar and long lasting phenomenon in any economy. Prior attention can thus be given when the estimated probability is higher than the mean. Based on the estimated results of the logistic model (Model D), one can note that currency attacks can be imminent when the estimated probability of speculative currency attack is greater than the mean (15.88%) plus 1 standard deviation (27.03%), which is equivalent to a probability of or higher than 43%.

The empirical study on currency attack has shown that the relationship between HSI return, HSI futures returns and exchange rate difference is significant during the three episodes of currency attacks in Hong Kong. An unusual movement of exchange rate difference and strategic disposition by the speculators can be identified. The speculators took advantage of the record high level in the HSI in all three episodes, especially when retail investors looked for large returns by selling their overvalued stocks. The estimations show that information can generate impacts on conditional volatility and conditional correlation. Chari and Patrick (2003) point out that information can heighten the uncertainty of individuals and the volatility of

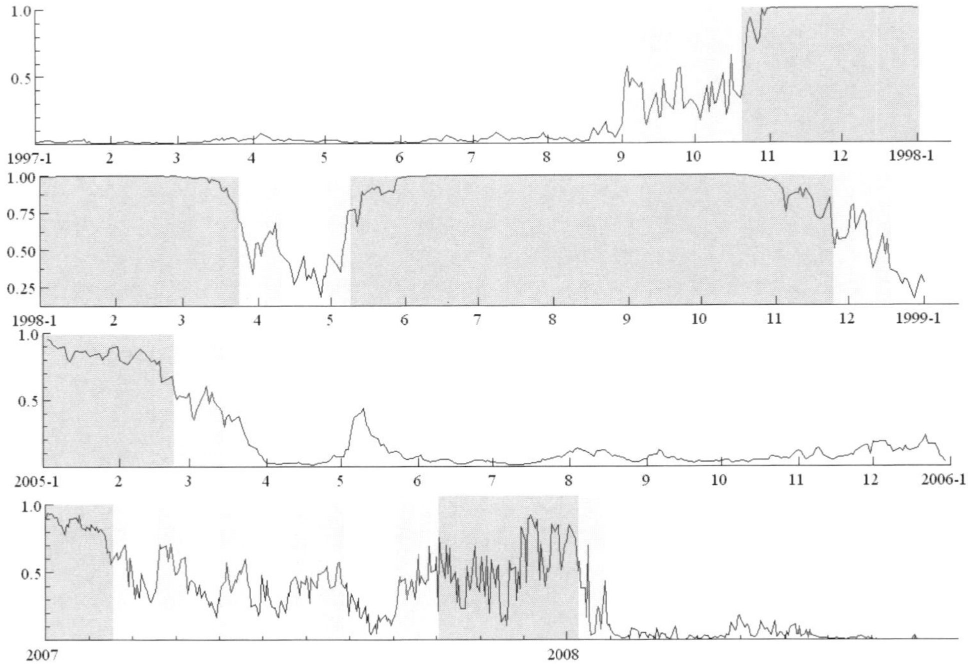

FIGURE 10.9 The estimated probabilities of currency attacks occurrence by logit model

Note: Lighter (darker) shades are the estimated probability of speculative attacks lie between 1 and 2 (greater than 2) standard deviations.

the markets because the time needed to access the information is different among individuals.

In conclusion, the Li and Wong (2008) study shows a total of four major factors that can provide information or signals to potential currency attacks in Hong Kong. They are:

1) Figure 10.5: The first signal would be **large drop in the conditional correlation between HSI and exchange rate differences** either prior to or during the period of currency attack. It implies that an abrupt decline of HSI could be accompanied by capital outflow during currency attacks.
2) Figure 10.6: The second signal shows that there existed a **prolonged non-zero deviation between the 3-month and 1-month exchange rate forward premium or exchange rate forward discount before the currency attack**. The two cases when premium occurred are shown in the first episode and the third episode, while the case of discount can be seen clearly in the second episode. A potential currency attack could be imminent when there is a prolonged period, say three quarters, of non-zero deviation in the 3-month and 1-month forward exchange rates.
3) Figure 10.7: **The high fluctuation in the HSI premium can provide a signal to an imminent currency attack**, as shown by the AFC in mid-1998 (second

episode) and in late 2007 (third episode). Negative news in the market may lead to a downward revision in market expectation, and the subsequent loss in market confidence can result in capital outflow. The chaos generated from the global market shocks could highly affect the expectation of market participants, and hence the magnitude of the HSI premium would increase.

4) Figure 10.8: The fourth signal appeared when **a rapid accumulation of open interest of HSI futures was faced with an equally rapid closure within a short time**. The market normally cannot afford a massive volume of open interest contracts in a short time. The monetary authority can counteract the accumulation by raising the deposit of futures contracts, as that can raise the cost of speculation.

The results of the logit model showed that the prediction criterion for currency attack is the mean of probability plus 1 standard deviation. For example, if the mean is 50% and 1 standard deviation is 25%, then the high probability to currency attacks is 75%. Notable signs can be identified prior to currency attacks and closer observations with timely and appropriate actions can deter speculators in attacking the Hong Kong currency. One other lesson from the empirical study is that despite Hong Kong's high ranking as an international financial center (Cheung and Yeung, 2007), capital funds coming to Hong Kong are mainly short-term with the intention to make speculative gains through activities in the stock market, derivatives market and foreign exchange market. This result is in line with the information given in Table 10.2 that a high level of speculation is common in the Hong Kong stock market.

The situation in late 2008 has turned for the worse as the closure of Lehman Brothers on September 15, 2008 in New York sparked a sea change in the financial world. The credit and liquidity of banks have become the major concern. Following an unfound rumor about the financial stability of the Bank of East Asia on September 24, 2008, the Hong Kong SAR Government has decided to provide a stronger support to the banking sector by declaring on October 14, 2008, the provision of a fully bank deposit guarantee until 2010, from the previous level of 10% only.

Inflow of capital shown by the large demand for Hong Kong dollar took place after the announcement as the spot exchange rate frequently reached the strong-side of the Convertibility Undertaking Rate. In order to maintain liquidity in the banking system, the HKMA had to at multiple occasions inject large capital to balance the Hong Kong dollar. Though the HIBOR rate is lowered, one concern is that the exchange rate is still strong even after the injection. The situation in the financial economy would remain difficult as unexpected shocks that imposed financial burden on banks in Hong Kong would also impose pressure on foreign exchange reserve, thereby reducing the ability to defend any speculative attacks on the Hong Kong dollar. The HKMA would have to monitor the market closely for potential currency attacks.

Indeed, even though the world financial crisis that occurred in late 2008 was not targeted to attack the Hong Kong currency, its impact to the financial sector in Hong Kong was equally devastating and provided useful lessons for Hong Kong on how to strengthen, deepen and consolidate a number of financial and monetary regulations, rules and practices. One should bear in mind that a free economy provided ample opportunities for both inflow and outflow of capital, but in practice, financial sustainability rested on a sound, international, transparent and rule-based monetary and financial system that provides a level-playing field indiscriminately on all market participants. The continuous improvement and maturity of the financial and monetary institution is the most effective guarantee for Hong Kong.

10.5 Financial and Monetary Lessons From the 2008 Crisis

Most analysts agree that the 2008 financial crisis began with the collapse of the US subprime mortgage industry in March 2007. The crisis peaked in mid-September 2008 with the collapse of Lehman Brothers and Merrill Lynch was sold to the Bank of America. The situation deteriorated when the US Federal Reserve took over the two largest mortgage based security companies. Other international financial centers soon experienced severe credit crunches as banks and hedge funds have invested heavily in subprime mortgage backed securities. The first rescue came on October 3, 2009, when President George W. Bush announced that the US government would create a US$700 billion worth of bailout program to purchase failing bank assets.

The immediate dilemma facing the United States and the world economy is the extent of economic recession that followed. Some have argued that world economic recession would be similar to the Great Depression in the 1920s and the United States would experience the worst recession since the Second World War. Some economically weaker European countries, such as Iceland, Greece, and Portugal soon faced extreme financial difficulties. The economic choice is simply one between soft landing and hard landing. A hard landing solution would allow economic recession to take its course, but unemployment and foreclosures of real estates could be suicidal politically. A soft landing approach would avoid the rising unemployment and limited foreclosures in the real estate market. This would necessitate more government involvement and financial intervention with the idea of preventing wealth or asset to depreciate drastically. More importantly, the interest rate will stay low for a rather long period of time to avoid foreclosures and further stimulate other investments.

The United States has engaged in a series of monetary intervention through a "quantity easing" (QE) strategy. The first stage, QE1, lasted from December 2008 to March 2009, injected US$1.7 trillion into the financial system through the buying of treasury and asset-backed bonds to help large financial institutions to avoid a further worsening of the crisis. With an economic contraction of 4.1% in GDP and a peak unemployment rate of 10.1%, economic recession in the United States lasted for 18 months, much shorter than the Great Depression's duration of 43 months. With the intention to stimulates growth and reduce unemployment, the Federal Reserve in November 2010 launched the second round of quantity easing, QE2, that involved the purchase by the Fed an additional US$600 billion worth of US treasuries in the following 18 months. The Federal Reserve Chairman Ben Bernanke explained in the *Washington Post* the theoretical base of QE2 to include "the lowering of mortgage rates to spur the property market, lowering corporate borrowing to spur investment, and pushing higher the stock market to boost the wealth effects and confidence and spur consumption".[3] It has been argued that the success of QE1 was partially accredited to the global consensus and cooperation, but QE2 is seen more of a unilateral desire by the United States, while other developed countries do not follow.

There are a number of lessons from the 2008 financial crisis. Other than the concern on economic recession, the other debate is the need to distinguish between the financial fundamentals and the monetary fundamentals in the crisis. The financial fundamentals may involve in how the market had been conducted and behaved, and the ethics of financial agents and market participants. The monetary fundamentals, on the contrary, concerned the underlying monetary conditions that allowed the financial market and agents operated in the way it had. Typically, the conduct of a monetary policy could have direct impact on financial activities. For example, a lower interest rate would stimulate borrowing and investment in the stock market. The level of interest rate is a monetary policy decision, while the amount of borrowing and investment transactions in the stock market is a decision taken in the financial market.

Both international financial institutions and individual governments have made huge efforts in rescuing financial and economic collapses. On the financial front, for example, *The Turner Review* conducted by the Financial Services Authority (2009) in London identified ways to improve regulatory framework for the financial sector. The International Monetary Fund (2009) and the *Squam Lake Report* (French *et al.*, 2010) proposed various solutions to the global financial crisis. The meeting of the Group of Twenty (G20) industrialized and emerging market economies in early April 2009 committed a total of US$1.1 trillion to boost the global economy.[4] The subsequent G20 summit meeting in September 2009 proposed strong policy response to counter global economic crisis and agreed to continue strengthening regulation of the international financial system that included the protection of consumers, depositors, and investors from abusive market practices, and encouraged the resumption of lending to households and businesses.

These proposals have concentrated mostly in correcting the financial fundamentals that addressed financial market infrastructure (financial regulations, behavior of banks, professional ethics, remuneration of CEOs and division between traditional banking and i-banking) and product composition (financial innovations, level of risk and soundness of sale agents). There are a number of issues and areas of improvement in the financial sector that has been highlighted since the outbreak of the 2008 financial crisis.

In the case of i-banking, the concern is whether the commercial banks that involved traditionally with loans and deposits should also engage in investment businesses. Most i-banks have their investment sections within the banks, and information flows become automatic. This involves a secrecy or privacy issue, because after having access to the financial information of the depositors and clients, agents in the

---

[3] "The Impact of QE2", *Economic Review*, Bank of China (Hong Kong) Limited, October 2010.

[4] *The Times*, April 3, 2009.

investment section of the i-bank can easily call up and convince the client for the sale of investment portfolios. There is thus the possibility of information misuse, and whether banks have the right and obligation to release the financial information of their clients to their investment section within the same i-banks. A related issue is the ethical standard of the agents in the i-banks. If agents in the investment section of the i-banks have to fulfill their sale quotas, they may approach and convince the depositors with the intention to fulfill the quota, rather than understanding and seeing to the need of the clients.

To correct the possible abuse of information and the low ethical standard of the investment agent in the i-bank, we need to separate the traditional banking activity from the investment activities in the i-banks. In other words, there should not be any free flow of financial information from the banks to the investment sections without the agreement from the clients or depositors themselves. Or, the investment section should be separated from the banking section, so that depositors whom want to invest would approach the investment companies independently. In Hong Kong, the situation on how investment products are sold has improved since the 2008 crisis. The correction has taken place when the depositors decided to invest, the depositors can have a cool off period to rethink carefully before finally committing, and there will be a senior bank official to seek further clarification from the depositors, ensuring that the depositors' decision in the investment is *bona-fide*, and further detailed information on the kind of investment is provided and explained to the depositors. However, such an improvement is short of the possibility of information abuse.

The coverage and effectiveness of regulations on the way banks conduct their investment activities is another concern. In general, the debate has been between on the one hand a freer system and more room is given to banks to ensure their good behavior, and on the other hand more regulations to protect the investors to avoid possible abuse and misuse of information by bank personnel. On the whole, the system in the United States provided a freer atmosphere for their banks to conduct investment activities, while European banks tended to face more regulations. The choice depended on how one considers the role of the regulations. Are regulations stumbling blocks that restrict the market? Or regulations can serve as guidelines and references that stand between the banks and the investors, thereby protecting the investors rather than restricting the market? The attitude in the post-2008 financial world is that new financial regulations are needed to protect the investors. The United States proposed in January 2010 to make the "financial system safer" by imposing limits on commercial banks.[5] The "too big to fail" argument has now led to the discussion on the appropriate size of commercial banks and the formula in calculating the remuneration provided to the chief executive officers (CEOs) of banks.

The third issue has to do with the risk of the financial products. Are there too many financial products in the market? Would some of the existing financial products have low market worthiness? What should be the criteria for the finanical institutions to approve their financial products? For example, would financial derivatives that are built on other financial products be allowed? Should the financial products be fully supported by some form of assets? Who can provide accurate information on the riskiness of the

[5] *South China Morning Post*, January 23, 2010.

financial products? There are rating agencies that rate financial companies. Can the risk of financial products be rated? The fundamental question is the degree of investment trust-worthiness on the financial products. If a financial product has a risk rating attached, investors will have better information on their financial portfolio.

The next concern is to develop a system of risk rating for financial products. Who should bear the cost for the provision of the service? Should the rating be done by professional companies paid by the investors? Do we trust the professional companies to provide valid ratings? If it was done by the government, would it be right for the taxpayers to foot the expenses? Like any other ratings, the rating should be conducted on a regular basis. These are questions that would be included in the debate on whether a system of risk rating be developed. On the other hand, would the companies that provide the investment products like their products be risk rated? Nonetheless, a risk rating system will serve as a "report card" on the financial investment products.

The discussion has surrounded the need to institute a system that provides a regularly risk rating to existing financial products, as this can ensure a more transparent portfolio to the investors. The contrary argument is that a system or risk rating works more like an index that provided information on financial products. One can argue that a risk rating index would itself generate market uncertainty, as the more risky financial products would have a poorer rating, though the counter argument would be for the risky products to improve their performance. A more realistic problem is the funding of the rating system. While the investors are the beneficiary of the rating system, would they be willing to pay for the information? Given the large number of financial products and derivatives, it would be costly to have all the market information available for constructing the rating system.

The 2008 financial crisis, however, has demonstrated not only the importance of international financial fundamentals and inter-dependence, but the relevance of monetary fundamentals that related to such questions as the role of monetary policy, the level and movement of interest rate and the response to business cycles. Few scholars have examined the monetary fundamentals of the 2008 crisis. Schwartz (2009) points out the relevance of a sound monetary policy and that the expansive monetary policy, the flawed financial innovations and the collapse of trading are the three factors that contributed to the 2008 financial crisis in the United States. Taylor and Williams (2009) examine the various interest rate performances across some OECD countries in the period of 2007 and 2008 and discussed the emergence of a "black swan" in the money market prior to the September 2008 crisis, while Taylor (2008, 2009a, 2009b) explains the financial crisis by looking at monetary liquidity.

A conceptual understanding on basic monetary economics can help to analyze the monetary aspects of a financial crisis. The basic Keynesian economics model argued that demand for investment (I) is negatively related to the level of interest rate (r). A fall in interest rate ($r\downarrow$) provided a market signal to investors and the resulting increase in investment ($I\uparrow$) would eventually lead to a rise in output ($Y\uparrow$). The Keynesian chain of relationship is that investment, and subsequently output, will rise when interest rate falls, namely $r\downarrow \rightarrow I\uparrow \rightarrow Y\uparrow$. The "New Keynesian" has extended the interest rate–output relationship by taking into account the lag effect of interest rate on output (e.g., Carlin and Soskice, 2005).

However, Keynes' theoretical interest rate and output relationship has subsequently been corrected by new situations. For example, the financial repression school (McKinnon, 1973; Shaw, 1973) has argued that government intervention in bank loans and interest rate policy often ended up with distortions in the opportunity cost of loans. Financial liberalization advocates suggested that Keynes' interest rate to output relationship should be considered in two separate relationships between interest rate and investment ($r \rightarrow I$), and between investment and output ($I \rightarrow Y$). Secondly, the concept of investment has also changed. A large number of financial innovations, such as stocks, bonds and derivatives, have been developed over the last decades, and many financial investments are no longer related to the real economy, but speculative with a high degree of risk.

The simple Keynes' $r \rightarrow I \rightarrow Y$ relationship will have to be re-examined. A lower interest rate (r) will surely encourage investment (I), but whether (I) can positively impact on output (Y) would depend on the productivity and profitability of (I). Difference in cost of borrowing can yield different investment returns. Since the interest rate is in theory the cost of money, a low borrowing cost allowed investment with low productivity to gain access to loans and funds. Hence, the low borrowing cost permitted low return investments to secure loans. Nonetheless, one can conceptually group or scale investments into productive investment (PI) that leads to increase in real output, and unproductive investment (UI) that may increase the monetary flows, but may not increase real output as loans can possibly be geared to speculative or low-productivity activities.

At a persistently low interest rate, money becomes cheap and investors are naturally encouraged to borrow. To compete, banks and financial institutions would impose an easier requirement on profitability and return on investment projects. Thus, the increase of unproductive investment would only enlarge the money supply (m) that ended up with higher inflation (π) with little or without corresponding increase in real output. Thus, the chain of relationship in the case of unproductive investment becomes $r\downarrow \rightarrow UI\uparrow \rightarrow m\uparrow \rightarrow \pi\uparrow$.

One can extend the Keynesian interest rate–output relationship to the possibility of a "low interest rate trap" hypothesis. Figure 10.10 hypothetically stylizes the steps and economic responses in an interest rate smoothing policy. When interest rate fell and investors could fully anticipate the next round of interest rate movement, it would be rational for investors to act when the interest rate had fallen to its lowest possible level (Lucas, 1973, 1981; Muth, 1961; Sargent and Wallace, 1975; Modigliani, 1977). Thus, the initial fall in the interest rate may not lead to much economic adjustment, and that anticipated monetary policy changes could only add "monetary noise" in the real sector (Barro, 1976).

The downward interest rate trend in an interest rate smoothing policy can be shown by the arrow "a" in Figure 10.10. When investors fully anticipated and recognized that the pattern of interest rate would fall further, the initial fall in interest rate might not have generated the expected rise in investment. As such, policy makers would have thought that further drop in interest rate was needed in order to stimulate investment. Knowing this, investors would have a further incentive to wait for further rate cuts. It was only when the interest rate had subsequently reached a very low level, say point "b" in Figure 10.10 that investors would decide to borrow

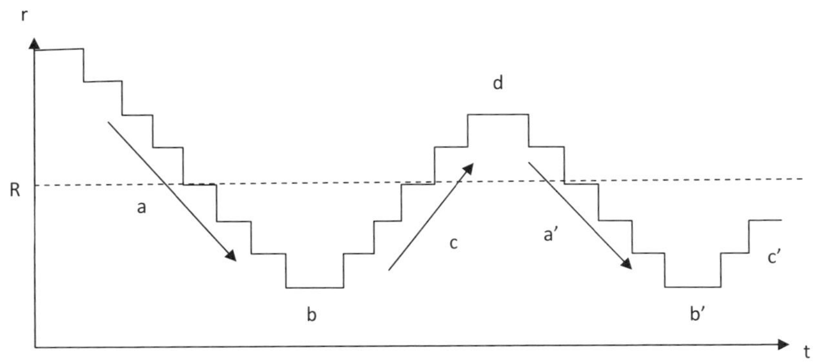

FIGURE 10.10 The "low interest rate trap"

extensively. The extremely low interest rate now encouraged investment, including those unproductive, low-return and speculation varieties.

With a loose loan policy and after a time lag, however, the rapid increase in investment could soon produce signs of overheating, and the subsequent rise in inflation would call for a policy reversal, as indicated by the arrow "c" in Figure 10.10. It was even possible that the initial reversal in interest rate would lead to a rise in investment as investors anticipated the end of a low interest regime and a higher cost of borrowing was expected to come.

As the movement of interest rate revised further upwards, fall in investment might soon lower economic activities. Furthermore, those who had borrowed at the lowest interest rate at "b" might now face a repayment problem. By the time the stepwise interest rate reached a high level at "d", potential economic slowdown emerged and the monetary authority would have to revise the interest rate downward. And a new round of stepwise downward movement in interest rate policy was repeated and investors would similarly repeat their behavior, as shown by the sequence of a′, b′ and c′ in Figure 10.10.

When investors could fully anticipate the interest rate movements, some fragile investors could have waited until the interest rate reached the lowest possible level, where low-return, unproductiveor risky investments were encouraged. For example, home ownership was encouraged as the subsequent low interest rate that meant to encourage home ownership had resulted in a rise in property price. It could have turned out that as property price increased the demand for property also increased as home buyers now feared that the property price would rise further. Some home buyers might not have the full financial creditability, but were prepared to take risk and hedge against the rising property price. Studies on the US economy have shown that banks had over extended their credits in the housing bubble between 2000 and 2007 (Shiller, 2008). At a persistently low interest rate, the rise in the demand for home ownership led to a rise in property price, and more home buyers entered the market before the property price went higher, thus generated a self-fulfilling prophecy of a rising property demand and price spiral.

Fragile or low productivity investments were encouraged at the lowest interest rate if these investments were largely speculative in nature and failed to contribute to real output and employment and these fragile investment would face repayment difficulty once the interest rate revised upwards. The threat of economic recession at a higher rate of interest would discourage the monetary authority from keeping a high interest rate for too long, and instead would prefer to maintain a prolonged period of low interest rate that eventually encouraged more speculation and promoted only the nominal financial economy.

In other words, the economy is "trapped" at the lowest interest rate level at points b and b′ and so on, as on the one hand the investors had got used to the low interest rate and on the other hand the monetary authority found it difficult to maintain a higher level of interest rate for long, say at point d in Figure 10.10. And at a low interest rate, speculation could not be discouraged and together with loose financial regulations and a strong consumption based economic behavior, economic shallowness cumulated to form the roots of a financial bubble. The stepwise interest rate smoothing policy was an unsustainable form of monetary policy, as the persistent and prolonged low interest rate policy helped more to fuel financial instability than to build up sustainable economic capacity.

The solution to the "low interest rate trap" hypothesis can be found from the monetarist school. A policy of stable money supply has been the monetarists answer to money and inflation fluctuations (Friedman, 1968; Dorn and Schwartz, 1987). Similarly, could a stable interest rate provide a more stable investment environment and avoid unnecessary economic fluctuations and unwanted speculations? There are a number of flaws in an interest rate smoothing policy. Firstly, despite the low interest rate that fueled speculation and low return investment and the full anticipation on the part of the investors, investment became "government-led" and business cycles simply responded to the government's interest rate smoothing policy.

On the contrary, for the private sector and investors to take a lead in the business cycle, a stable and considerably high "interest rate anchor", as indicated by *R* and the dotted horizontal line in Figure 10.10, for example, is necessary. It would be appropriate for the policy makers to decide on an interest rate anchor such that the adoption of a steady interest rate would allow the business cycle to develop, evolve around or respond to the interest rate rather than changing the interest rate ostensibly to suit the business cycle. With an interest rate anchor, investment will take place according to profitability, rather than borrowing opportunities. Another role an interest rate anchor can definitely play is to "screen out" unproductive investment, thus channeling the limited funds to the high return investments.

Inflation normally is treated as a short-term phenomenon, while the interest rate is aimed at influencing long-term activities. Is it then desirable to use a long-term economic variable to solve a short-term economic phenomenon? Demand management through fiscal adjustment can be the more suitable alternative short-term variable to correct inflation, while such a long-term variable as the interest rate serves typically to promote long-term investment that increases output in the real economy. The adoption of a low interest rate regime could eventually foster the establishment of risky financial products, encourage misconduct in financial practice, promote nominal bubble economy, distort household economic behavior between saving and consumption, allow financial agents to exploit the loose credit and loan policy, and radiate financial instability to other world economies.

The interest rate smoothing policy may have a further contagion effect, as the interest rate chosen by the government will often be adopted subsequently by other world economies. Thus, the sequence of activities described in Figure 10.10 will be "exported" to other world economies, leading to a domino effect across the world should financial instability arises. A stable interest rate anchor would rescue the world economy from potential instability resulting from poor investment and excessive speculations.

Written in simple language, the stylized analysis related the discussion and attention back to the problem of monetary policy uncertainties (Friedman, 1968; Poole, 1970; Romer and Romer, 1989; Brainard, 1967). Similar to Friedman's (1948, 1960) idea of a steady money supply in controlling inflation, the unintended consequences of a possible "low interest rate trap" in monetary economics can be solved by applying a stable and steady interest rate policy.

The discussion on the "low interest rate trap" does highlight an important monetary phenomenon. To start with, it does encourage low-return investment and speculation. Investors with full anticipation on the movement of the interest rate would react accordingly, resulting in a business cycle that builds around the policy decided by the policy makers. The economy is trapped in low interest rate regimes, as upward revision would soon become recessionary. One should advocate for an effective but steady interest rate anchor such that it allows the business cycle to run its own course. The government would then at most need to fine tune the interest rate anchor should the business cycle deviates from trend.

The lesson from the discussion of the "low interest rate trap" hypothesis is simply that the original intention of keeping a low interest rate regime, especially if it is kept for a prolonged period of time, could lead to an economic situation whereby a prolonged low interest rate would lead to low productivity investments, while a high interest rate would result in economic recession. The economy is effectively "trapped" in a low interest rate regime, with a coexistence of low productivity investment and low output growth.

10.6 The Mini-Bonds Incident

Headquartered in New York, the Lehman Brothers was founded in 1850 and has grown to become the world's fourth largest investment bank and a leader in equity and fixed income sales, asset management, private equity and so on. On September 15, 2008, Lehman Brothers Holdings Inc. filed a petition for bankruptcy, which was regarded as the biggest bankruptcy proceeding in history, and it assets were immediately frozen. An approximate amount of HK$13.9 billion of unlisted credit-linked notes, commonly known as mini-bonds, have been sold to retail investors in Hong Kong (SFC, 2008).

The closure of Lehman Brothers has led immediately to a financial crisis in Hong Kong, as a total of 43,700 investors had much of their investments "evaporated", because they were holding derivatives that were issued or guaranteed by the subsidiary of Lehman Brothers in Hong Kong but had lost most of their value. Most of these derivatives were complex and credit-linked accumulators or "mini-bonds", which were marketed as a proxy investment by financial companies and banks.[6] By early 2010, the number of investors whom had reached a settlement deal with their banks reached 24,471 (56%). This involved a total of 16 banks and three brokers who agreed to repay a combined HK$6.3 billion.[7]

According to the Securities and Futures Commission (SFC) (2008:33), mini-bonds are credit-linked notes (CLNs) arranged by a Hong Kong subsidiary of Lehman Brothers Holdings. These CLNs are structured debt instruments under which payments of interest and principal or both are affected by, amount other things, the occurrence of credit events that included situations where an entity in the basket of reference entitles (such as HSBC, Hutchison Whampoa, DBS Group Holdings Ltd., Swire Pacific Ltd., Sun Hung Kai Properties Ltd., Goldman Sachs Group Inc. and Morgan Stanley) become insolvent or failed to repay loans, etc. The SFC also pointed out that the risks associated with mini-bonds have been set out in some details in the prospectuses that provided general warnings to investors in plain language.

The "mini-bonds saga" soon developed into a political case and frequent demonstrations were organized, with some vocal politicians and legislators openly supporting those investors who had lost in their investment attempting to seek or recover full compensation either from the banks, the approval authorities or the government. The debate and social sentiment was divided. On the one hand, some argued that investments are private activities, and nobody except themselves should bear their risk. Pushing their accountability and loss to a third party and seek compensations through political channels and influences was unacceptable. It would be a poor precedence if losses from investment were compensated, and Hong Kong would have lost its creditability as a financial and investment center. The ultimate legal accountability should rest with Lehman Brothers, and despite its closure, investors should look to its legal procedures for compensation. This would take years for the legalities to be sorted out, but it is the rule of law that Hong Kong cherished.

On the other hand, the argument related to the way the banks sold their mini-bonds, and questions arose as to whether there was misconduct and unethical behavior on the part of the sales agent and the banks. The accusation went further, and whether the approving and supervisory authorities in Hong Kong had done their proper duty in screening the market risk and financial validity of the mini-bonds before they were released in the financial market. There were cases, such as retired and aging depositors whom were not educated and knew nothing of the mini-bonds, were molested or misled by the bank agents to invest in the mini-bonds. The final political argument was that if there were misconducts in the approval, supervisory and screening process, it would ultimately be the government who should be responsible and should,therefore, simply provide full compensation to the investors.

Politically, the mini-bonds saga had demonstrated a clear challenge to the governance of the "young" government in Hong Kong. While there were organized demonstrations and the investors were simply looking narrowly into their investment loss and the wish to claim full compensation, the government was faced with a

[6] *South China Morning Post*, January 9, 2009.

[7] *South China Morning Post*, February 10, 2010.

number of more severe issues, including how to minimize the investment loss, how to prevent the economy from severe recession, how to restructure the financial and monetary authorizes and how to stabilize the Hong Kong currency and avoid another currency attack. In short, it could be another crisis whose impact could even be larger than the Asian financial crisis in 1997/1998.

To stabilize the currency and ease the uncertainty on the part of the depositors, the Hong Kong government declared a precautionary measure on October 14, 2008, that the government would 100% guarantee all bank deposits in local and foreign currencies that was amounted to HK$6 trillion for two years until the end of 2010 from the existing guarantee of HK$100,000 per depositor. Deposit protection was earlier applied in Australia and New Zealand. However, even though the asset of the Exchange Fund in August 2008 amounted only to HK$1.4 trillion, it was expected that the probability of a bank collapse was low, as the average capital adequacy ratio of Hong Kong banks was 14%, while the international standard was only 8%.[8]

Secondly, given the already close-to-zero saving deposit rates, the economic impact of a further interest rate cut was marginal. The prime lending rate that stood at 5% remained unchanged when the US cut its rates further in mid-December 2008, indicating that Hong Kong has kept to a certain level of monetary fundamental despite the financial crisis.[9] Indeed, key bankers in Hong Kong agreed to the need to restore good banking behavior: maintain a strong deposit base and capital ratio, and adopt a prudent lending approach. As compared to the Asian financial crisis in 1997 when the interbank interest rate shot up to 300%, the 2008 crisis was much less severe as the interbank interest rate remained below 2%.[10]

Another debate resulting from the 2008 financial crisis was whether the two regulatory and supervisory bodies in Hong Kong, namely the Hong Kong Monetary Authority (HKMA) that regulated banking activities and the Securities and Futures Commission (SFC) that regulated the securities business, should be merged into a single regulatory authority, arguing that a single regulator for investment product approval and financial behavior might help to prevent a repeat of similar fiascos in future. While there are advantages in having a single monetary and financial regulator, it was pointed out that countries with a single regulator also suffered. A report by an adviser to the HKMA made shortly before the September 2008 financial crisis suggested a total of six recommendations: 1) the HKMA should cooperate more with the SFC with a view to forming a "mega-regulator" in the long-run; 2) consider the strengthening the HKMA's power of sanction and investigation; 3) raise the limit of deposit protection scheme without increasing the premium; 4) ensure banks have appropriate oversight and control of their business operations on the Mainland; 5) follow Basel Committee recommendations on dealing with the subprime mortgage crisis and revise the liquidity regime; and 6) reduce the current three-tier banking system of licensed banks, restricted-license banks and deposit-taking companies to two tiers with banks and other deposit takers.[11]

---

[8] *South China Morning Post*, October 15, 2008.

[9] *South China Morning Post*, December 18, 2008.

[10] *South China Morning Post*, December 17, 2008.

[11] *South China Morning Post*, July 18, 2008.

Other suggestions to improve the post-2008 financial system included the proposal to set up a financial dispute resolution center to handle investment claims up to HK$500,000 against banks, brokers and asset management companies. Similar centers have been established in the United States, Australia, Singapore and the United Kingdom. It was announced that the HK$0.5 million cap on claims was sufficient to cover 80% of the roughly 2,000 investor complains the HKMA received in a typical year. For the first three years, the dispute resolution center would have an annual budget of HK$55 million to be funded by the government and the two regulating authorities of HKMA and SFC, but financial institutions would have to contribute after that. Critics argued that, other than the mini-bonds, the number of complaints were not high, and that the claim might be too low for the mini-bond losers.[12]

Following in early 2009 the unsteady and unstable stock price changes of the Hong Kong and Shanghai Banking Corporation (HSBC) as a result of the bank's poor performance in the mortgage business in the United States, a single sell order during the last few seconds of the auction session on March 10, 2009, had sent the HSBC shares down by an additional 12.47%. The 10-minute closing auction introduced in May 2008, aimed at matching international practices, has resulted in some stocks swinging 20% to 30% during the final minutes of the trading session. The session that is held after the normal trading close at 1600 hours allowed traders to input tender prices. The closing price of the stock is determined by the number of matching orders. The Hong Kong Exchange and Clearning Limited (HKEx), with the approval from SFC, proposed on June 22, 2009, the introduction of a price fluctuation cap of 2% either way in order to tighten the system in the closing session.[13]

There are two separate lines of investigation. One related to the bankruptcy of Lehman Brothers and its subsidiary in Hong Kong, and involved a prolonged legal investigation for the claims on the frozen assets. The other line of investigation related to the consolidation on the rules and regulations in relation to the two supervisory bodies in Hong Kong, namely the SFC and HKMA. While on-going investigation on the various complaints by the investors was being conducted, both the SFC and HKMA have come up with their own investigation, providing the public with in-depth information on mini-bonds and recommendations on the way Hong Kong should go forward to improve the financial system.

The SFC (2008) report, though some sections have been removed due to sensitivity of information, examined the regulatory structure for financial supervision, impact of the failure of Lehman Brothers Holdings Inc. in Hong Kong, the nature of complaints and recommendations. The SFC (2008) report produced a number of recommendations, including Hong Kong's regulatory structure, regulation relating to point of sale and a review on the structure of banking organizations where banks used their general bank deposit channels to help sell investment products, product documentation, definition of professional investors, disclosure of commission received by the intermediary, an after-sale cooling off period, dispute resolution and education provided to investors.

---

[12] *South China Morning Post*, February 10, 2010.

[13] *South China Morning Post*, March 11, 2009; *Hong Kong Economic Journal*, March 11, 2009.

The HKMA (2009) report related particularly to the issue concerning the distribution of structured products connected to Lehman Group Companies. In the overview of the report, the HKMA specified a "disclosure-based" approach in investor protection. The policy objective to enable investors to make informed investment decisions was complemented by the regulatory regime governing the conduct of regulated persons in the sales and distribution processes. The report also clarified the division of responsibilities between the SFC and the HKMA and explained how the HKMA carried out its supervisory responsibilities. Recommendations covered measures that could strength the protection of investors, simplify the supervisory framework of sales and distribution process and provide a cost-effective alternative dispute resolution mechanism.

10.7 Relating to Economic Freedom

There is no doubt that the mini-bonds incident has reflected the inadequacies in Hong Kong's regulatory system, but it is equally important to see that changes are made and introduced speedily in an appropriate time in order to fix the loopholes in the system. While there is no such thing as a perfect financial system, the desire to improve and strengthen the system is the best a free economy can do. Indeed, in economic freedom, so as in monetary and financial freedom, what is relevant is not the person in charge or the type of government, but a sound and transparent system that benefit all and do not favor any individual.

The establishment of a matured financial system will not be influenced nor manipulated by a single individual, nor will the system lean to the benefit of certain groups of individuals. The system shall serve as an intermediary, a civic monument, an infrastructure and a reference framework that works for all. And it will be up to the individuals to make free use of the system for their own benefits. In the process, private investment decisions remained private and individuals would have to be accountable and bear the consequences of all their investment ventures. Indeed, the mini-bonds incident has provided an "opportunity" to strengthen and consolidate the financial system in Hong Kong.

In many ways, because freedom in Hong Kong is not constrained by any individual, but is protected by a system, there is a need to regularly improve and perfect the system at all means and occasions. Similarly, people in Hong Kong look more to the effective functioning of the financial and monetary systems than to the charisma of an individual leader or government official. The influence of personality does not have a role in the daily functioning of a free economy. Equally, it is such a system-led economy that is cherished and served as a lesson for other emerging economies attempting to rise up in the ladder of economic freedom.

The 2008 financial crisis in the United States and mini-bonds incident did provide various other lessons to Hong Kong in relation to its status as the freest economy. Firstly, while the financial system in Hong Kong has so far been developed along with other key financial centers and practices, differences in the regulatory frameworks in US and European Union (EU) countries should be studied in order to decide on a more comprehensive and embracive framework. The regulatory and supervisory bodies in Hong Kong could seize such an opportunity to introduce and legalize a stronger and comprehensive regulatory framework that could even supersede that in US and in EU. A program of financial regulatory reform can be introduced, with the aim on the one hand to gather the strength and on the other hand improve the weaknesses of each financial center. A multi-level program could examine the regulatory framework on the various market participants:

1) Investors: this is the demand side. While investments are welcome, behavior of investors have to be regulated so as not to unduly harm the market. The idea is to ensure unnecessary spillover effects from one investor to another;
2) Banking institutions: this is the supply side. As pointed out in the SFC (2008) report, the way banking institutions make use of the depositors' information have to be checked, and how banks approach depositors in selling the investment products have to be regulated;
3) Difference between local and foreign institutions: this is to eliminate unnecessary protectionist measures, and there should be no discrimination between local and foreign institutions. However, it would be better for the regulatory body in Hong Kong to acquire better information on the business activities of foreign institutions in order to avoid or locate potential crisis;
4) Difference between local and foreign financial products and categories: this involves the risk rating of financial products in order to provide reliable market information to the investors;
5) Ethics of sale agents: this involves the entire sale strategy by the agents, and regulations should provide some basic and compulsory steps for all agents to follow. Working closely with professional associations can help to draft out steps that a sale agent should follow, and these steps would be made known to potential investors so that the sale process is made as structured as possible;
6) Provision of market information and transparency in trading: there are numerous channels through which investors can gather the market information. Regulations should not discourage the provision of market information, but to encourage the dissemination of accurate, unbiased and reliable market information on financial products and innovation. This could involves the need to educate the public and the various market information suppliers to see if there is rested interest in the provision of information; and
7) Legality and structure of regulatory institutions: the regulators also need to be regulated. There should be system checks in the regulatory framework, as this will be an effective way to protect the public interest. Hence, while there can be a debate between the supervisory and regulatory work of the HKMA and SFC, the appropriate debate is how to strengthen their capability. The discussion as to whether a merge could take place will then be made within the framework of capability strengthening.

Such a program of reform shall make Hong Kong a leader among other international financial centers. Armed with a regulatory framework more comprehensive than that of US and EU, investors will find Hong Kong a more secured and consolidated financial center, investment business could subsequently expand and diversify. A stronger regulatory framework serves as the intermediary between the market and individual investors. In the long-run, the financial system in Hong Kong would also become a strong reference point to other international financial centers, providing successful financial freedom lessons to other economies.

Reliable institutions play a "policing" role in economic freedom, as they often provide rules and regulations to market participants while at the same time they are monitored by market participants. The check and balance function of institutions serve as a pillar in economic freedom. The early stage in the development as an international financial center in Hong Kong is the emergence of an international banking center, where financial transactions were conducted by reliable banking institutions. Over the decades, Hong Kong also experienced bank failures, but since all banks in Hong Kong are private corporations, the government plays a supervisory role and acts as a "fire fighter" should crises emerged. The mini-bonds incident also highlighted the role of the banking institutions as carriers of investment activities.

As private corporations, banking institutions differed from other business enterprises. If a chain store closed down or a cinema faced with business difficulties, the government does not need to get involved. Unlike other private enterprises, modern banks do have a social dimension or a social responsibility. Because bank deposits come from different strata of individuals, financial trouble in one bank will probably have a negative spillover or externality effect on other banks and depositors. And since different banks have their own financial strengths and depositors may choose their banks for different reasons, the herb behavior could easily be developed if banking difficulties were not handled with extreme care. Experiences suggested that herb behavior in banking and financial activities could easily develop into a crisis that would have devastating impact on the rest of the economy, including the stability of the currency. In many ways, it is such a social function of banks that required more stringent regulations to be exercised on all banking activities.

As banks in Hong Kong are all private corporations, there is indeed an absence of rested interest between the government and banking institutions, though the larger banks might have a greater voice as the government might need their cooperation. On the contrary, banks in Hong Kong should also see their social role, and implement their business policies accordingly. For example, some large banks imposed a charge on small depositors, claiming that servicing the large number of small depositors would push up their operation cost. With their difference in the size of operations, market competition will eventually help banks to decide on their business concentrations. The relevant issue to the depositors is the availability of choice in choosing their banks.

10.8 Conclusion

Economic freedom does not mean all individuals can do whatever they want. Other than the rule of law that protected individuals' legal rights and the strong ethics that prescribed individuals' interactions with one another, economic freedom has to be "organized" such that individuals' freedom can mutually be respected, and the rules and regulations are transparent and fair to all. In monetary freedom, Hong Kong is blessed with the establishment of a matured system such that it cannot be manipulated by any single individual, and the system acted as an intermediary between the public at large and the governing authorities. All reliable monetary systems contained strong and respectable monetary institutions that objectively set, and periodically revise, upgrade and update the required rules and regulations in line with the need of the contemporary world. In this respect, Hong Kong has done its utmost in preserving an international sound and effective monetary system, as it on the one hand allowed the domestic economy to function to its maximum extent and on the other hand attended to the timely need of the international community.

The monetary system in Hong Kong has largely been influenced by the exchange rate system. There is no perfection in any single exchange rate regime, and all regimes suffer some form of difficulties at different times. Given that there is no single exchange rate regime that fits all economies at all times, the concern is to identify an effective regime so as to provide the highest possible extent of macroeconomic stability. The Hong Kong economy is no different from other economies, and despite the past changes in Hong Kong exchange rate regimes, the linked exchange rate has served Hong Kong appropriately, providing the needed macroeconomic stability at different turbulent times.

Since its adoption, the linked exchange rate has often been debated, arguing for its advantages and drawbacks, but in view of a lack of good alternative, it is still appropriate for Hong Kong to continue to adapt to the linked exchange rate. Nonetheless, there have been three episodes of currency attacks in Hong Kong's linked exchange rate, with different magnitude in each episode. Empirical findings showed that there are early signs of currency attacks in Hong Kong. The Hong Kong authorities can easily track the path of future currency attacks by following the movement of different monetary variables, including the Hang Seng Index and the Hang Seng Index Futures, the forward markets and future contracts.

The financial crisis in 2008 has generated a number of lessons. One conclusion is that there can be a distinction between financial causes and monetary causes in a financial crisis. While many analyses have focused on the financial front, which is the more urgent issue, there is still a need to examine the monetary fundamentals of the 2008 crisis. In particular, interest rate movements can have unexpected and unintended consequences, and that a prolonged low interest rate regime allowed investors to engage in speculative varieties, resulting in unwanted economic bubbles and financial crises.

While the 2008 financial crisis did not lead to currency attack in Hong Kong, the mini-bonds incident has provided the Hong Kong authorities ample opportunities to reflect on the strength of the monetary system, especially in the supervisory role of the two institutions (Hong Kong Monetary Authority and Securities and Futures Commission). Being an international financial center, the monetary tools in Hong Kong have to be strong to guide against attacks. Indeed, Hong Kong can exercise the opportunity to expand and consolidate the various practices, rules and regulations.

Monetary freedom perhaps is the best representative aspect of economic freedom in Hong Kong. In fulfilling the dual function of protecting the domestic economy on the one hand and concurring with international standards on the other hand,

Hong Kong's monetary system has stood against time. The best Hong Kong can do is to provide an efficient and effective system, meet changes as situations require and favor no one but allow fair participation by everyone.

As the Mainland China is growing ever so rapidly, it has been known that in aggregate GDP terms, the Mainland China economy has surpassed Japan to become the number two largest economy in the world, following the United States. The picture on GDP per capita is different. Nonetheless, Hong Kong has gained from the growing Mainland China economy, but at the same time, Hong Kong also is faced with challenges from the growing Mainland China economy. As Hong Kong is a free economy, there is no restriction on monetary transactions. That has been a blessing, especially in the formation of the Renminbi business, but the free monetary system could also be abused if illegal transactions and money laundering are rampant. The cost to monetary freedom is therefore the constant maintenance of a sound system.

11 Positive Non-intervention: Practices and Challenges

11.1 Introduction

In the *Index of Economic Freedom 2011*, the two scores under fiscal freedom and government size should give an indication on the performance of the government in the economy. For fiscal freedom, the level of taxation and the annual budget surplus or deficit, and the size of the public debt are reflected in the degree of fiscal freedom. Normally, credits on fiscal freedom are given to a lower tax rate regime, a budget surplus and the non-existence of public debt. These are indicators shown by a non-interventionist government. Similarly, a higher score is given to a smaller, less interventionist and more efficient government. The two scores can be condensed into a single indicator since fiscal policy is managed by the government and the government's expenses, revenue generation and economic involvements are all shown in the annual budget. Similar indicators and principles are applied in other measures on economic freedom, including the Fraser Institute in Vancouver and the Cato Institute in Washington DC.

In the *Index of Economic Freedom 2011*, Hong Kong scored 93.3 in fiscal freedom. Among the top 10 freest economies (Hong Kong, Singapore, Australia, New Zealand, Switzerland, Canada, Ireland, Denmark, United States and Bahrain), Hong Kong's score ranks second after Bahrain, whose score is 99.8. Singapore's score is 91.1. The score of all other seven economies in the top 10 freest economies are below 90 with Denmark having the lowest score of only 43.2. In government size, Hong Kong scores 89.6, while Singapore has a higher score of 91.3, followed by Bahrain with a score of 80.2. The scores of all other seven economies are lower than 80 and Denmark has a score of only 19.5. The "visible hand" is strong in Denmark where the government has interfered heavily in the economy, probably in the form of high tax and large welfare subsidy expenditures that "crowded out" private economic decisions.

In commenting on these two scores, the *Index of Economic Freedom 2011* recorded that Hong Kong has the lowest effective tax rates in the world and excise duties on beer and wine were removed in 2008. Sound fiscal management has been an asset in Hong Kong in coping with the global downturn. Total government expenditure has maintained below 20% of GDP. However, when compared to the score of government spending in 2010, the 2011 score is 4.1 point lower, due probably to the discretionary stimulus measures that amounted to an estimate of 5% of GDP taken since 2008. Although it is understandable that the government would have to commit more spending during the crisis time, there is a lack of distinction on fiscal behavior between crisis and non-crisis periods. Nonetheless, the government has tried to maintain a balanced budget with little public debt and fiscal deficit appeared only in occasional years.

The various basic features of fiscal policy in Hong Kong included a low tax regime, with individual income tax either progressively from 2% to 17% or a flat rate of about 15% and corporate income tax is about 16.5%, and a small public sector usually measured in terms of the total public expenditure to GDP ratio which only occasionally goes beyond 20%. This is low by world standard, and Hong Kong has been labeled as a tax heaven for international business. In their *Free to Choose*, Milton Friedman and Rose Friedman (1979) remark that the Hong Kong economy is the best example of a free market economy.

The simple economic virtue is that with low tax rates, business activities are maximized, meaning that the "economic pie" will be maintained at the highest possible level. The business-friendly nature of economic policies facilitated business transactions and economic growth can be maximized. With the achievement of the largest "economic pie", individual income can be maximized, and economic security of individuals can be achieved. Individuals then can take care of their private and social needs. This in turn reduces the need for social welfare, and the government can then have more resources either to take care of the truly needy individuals or indulge in economic capacity building for the future development of the economy, such as infrastructure building, education to improve human capital and so on.

Coupled with economic freedom, the simple taxation system has provided a fiscal structure that aided the Hong Kong economy to flourish since the end of the Second World War. The doctrine of *laissez-faire* has formed the basis of economic freedom and prosperity. The term "positive non-intervention" coined by the former Financial Secretary (1961–1971), Sir John Cowperthwaite, merely reflects the economic role of the government and the importance of the private sector in conducting economic activities. Since the 1960s, the term "positive non-intervention" has been used as a framework for the government not to interfere with activities in the private sector. The term relates purely to economics and does not carry any ideological weight.

Despite its practical success, though vagueness at times, the economic policy of "positive non-intervention" has been challenged since Hong Kong's sovereignty reversion in 1997. Article 107 of the Basic Law states that the annual budget in Hong Kong "shall follow the principle of keeping expenditures within the limits of revenues", while Article 108 states that Hong Kong will follow "the low tax policy previously pursued as reference, enact laws on its own concerning types of taxes, tax rates, tax reductions, allowances and exemptions". Typically, the economic situations and various policies practiced before 1997 have been written into the articles in the Basic Law.

However, it is true that since 1997, there has been increasing amount of government intervention in the economy, some interventions were due to the financial crisis that required short-term adjustments and other interventions were involved with numerous welfare expenses given in the form of "caring the society" that primarily crowded out investment decisions and interfered with the economic decision of individuals. There has been a lack of open, transparent and standard criteria in economic intervention and subsidy provision. For example, a total of

HK$50 million and HK$300 million were given to subsidize the movie industry in the 2003 and 2007 fiscal years, respectively.[1] While there were official explanations to the subsidy pointing out the importance of the movie industry in Hong Kong and its relationship with similar industries in Mainland China, the critics pointed to the growing problem of cronyism.

With growing government intervention in the economy, the debate is whether the economic policy of "positive non-intervention" is still relevant in Hong Kong, or how to interpret the policy given the changing situation, apolitically. Strong welfare subsidy and government intervention killed off individual incentives, making individuals reliant, dependent and turned more to government welfare, which eventually would self-fulfill the need for more government assistance. The situation is close to that described by Hayek (1944) in his Nobel-winning book, *The Road to Serfdom*. There is a need to clarify the virtue of economic security in Hong Kong, as the creation of jobs has been the conventional economic wisdom. Teaching a person how to fish is better than giving the person a fish.

This chapter studies the economic policy of Hong Kong, with emphasis on the situation in post-1997. The chapter examined some crucial public finance theories. Features of the fiscal policy of Hong Kong would be elaborated. The latter sections in this chapter would examine the economic policy of "positive non-intervention", with emphasis on its origins, how it has been practiced, what are the post-1997 political challenges and how should the policy of "positive non-intervention" be interpreted in light of the changing situations and the growing Mainland China economy. Some materials are based on the similar chapter in Li (2006, Chapter 4), but the content has been restructured, expanded and updated to incorporate the more important issues and arguments.

11.2 Pubic Finance: Built-in Stabilizer and the Laffer Curve

The government in any economy behaves similarly to that of an individual, whose budget expenditure is always constrained by revenue income. Thus, while most people are keen to see an increase in government expenditure, it would be more important to understand the revenue side of the equation, as it is always easier to spend than to earn. In public finance, fiscal policy is used to maintain macroeconomic stability by the government. Through annual revenues and expenses, the government stabilized the economy by exercising typically an expansionary policy when the economy was experiencing a downward trend to rescue income from falling too drastically, but a contraction policy when the economy overheated so as to minimize the negative impact of inflation.

The ability to exercise an expansionary or contraction fiscal policy depended a lot on the fiscal income and the length of the economic cycle. The government typically saves in an economic upturn when income is rising by running a fiscal

[1] *The Standard*, March 8, 2007.

surplus, and a contraction fiscal policy is exercised to reduce the amount of fiscal expenditure so as to avoid economic overheating. A larger fiscal reserve can then be achieved, indicating an increase in public wealth. The large reserve should not be politically interpreted, because the reserve will be needed in case of economic downturn. Hence, it is a misconception that a rising reserve means that the government can spend more. On the contrary, a larger reserve will serve as a cushion for the economy in a downturn situation. However, what often happened in an economic upturn was that instead of exercising a fiscal contraction, the government eased the various fiscal components in a way that the enlarged fiscal expenditures were accompanied by a reduction in revenue or the ability to tax. Such had happened since the mid-1980s when the rising income in Hong Kong was accompanied by rising government expenditures, leading to overheating in the 1990s.

At a time of economic downturn, it would be appropriate for the government to exercise an expansionary fiscal policy that could result in a fiscal deficit. In Hong Kong, budgetary deficits would typically be financed through the rundown of fiscal reserves. In some advanced economies, the financing of fiscal deficit comes considerably from the issue of government bonds. In a small open economy like Hong Kong in which the government does not normally issue bonds nor borrow from overseas or from the world community, the ability to raise revenue is crucial in determining the size of a budget deficit. In a severe economic recession lasting for a number of years, a prolonged expansionary fiscal policy could soon exhaust the fiscal reserve. In a capitalist market economy of Hong Kong where the private sector dominates and the government plays a secondary role in economic activities, it is advisable to exercise a contraction fiscal policy in an economic upturn but a balanced budget otherwise so as to avoid severe deficits and drastic reduction in fiscal reserve.

In a business cycle where the economy experiences ups and downs, pursuing a balanced budget requires the presence of an adjustable or flexible fiscal structure such that government's revenue can steadily be maintained despite the changing economic and business conditions. This necessarily means that the fiscal structure should contain a range of revenue sources such that the drop in revenue from one source can be compensated by a rise in another. Since there are always social agents calling for more government expenditures for re-distributive purposes, the fiscal constraint in fact clearly rests on the revenue side. The government's ability to maintain a stable revenue source is the more crucial element in a balanced budget. In a comprehensive fiscal framework, there should be enough effective fiscal instruments so that the government can levy sufficient revenue in economically good as well as bad times.

Economic theory says that the automatic or built-in income-stabilizer regulates changes in individuals' income. Individuals' income will be checked by a progressive tax system where a higher income tax rate is imposed when income rises, but individuals pay a lower tax when their income falls. The individual will be entitled to receive transfer payment, or welfare, from government assistance in case of economic hardship. A progressive income tax system that raises additional tax as income rises limits the rise in individual net income as gross income rises, and vice versa in the case of a fall in income. At the aggregate level, the automatic income-stabilizer reduces part of the income fluctuation in the economy, but could not eliminate the fluctuation in income entirely. Discretionary fiscal policy that includes public expenditures and changes in tax rates are the principal weapons of income stabilization in the fiscal framework.

The same economic concept of an automatic income stabilizer can be discussed in the context of government revenue. A taxation system that provides an automatic revenue-stabilizing effect to the government is one in which government's revenue rises as domestic income rises but would not face a drastic reduction in revenue when household income falls. Income tax revenue rises in an economic upturn because individual incomes have gone up and there are more individuals with higher incomes. The problem of collecting sufficient income tax revenue arises in an economic downturn. When income falls and there are less high-income individuals, the government tax revenue will likewise fall. But its fall could partly be rescued by a sufficient large pool of tax-paying individuals even though each individual household is contributing a smaller income tax. Such an automatic revenue stabilizer would serve as a backup support to government income tax revenue.

There is limit to every government's fiscal ability. To maintain macroeconomic stability, the fiscal policy is an instrument that regulates the economy, taking more from the public in good times, but giving back more to the public in the bad times. Faced with crisis and economic downturns, the government would have to run down its fiscal reserve to rescue the immediate problems. Thus, a fiscal policy is not a discrete, one-time affair that can be dealt with on an annual basis. A budgetary surplus does not necessarily mean immediate higher government expenditure so as to exhaust the surplus. A budgetary deficit does not necessarily mean a collapse of the government or an inability to stabilize the economy. Rather, a surplus allows the government to increase reserve that will be used to rescue the economy in a downturn.

Another related public finance theory is the role of government in income redistribution. In economies where income equality is seen as an important social goal and various distributive policies are pursed, governments tend to impose a high and progressive tax so that a high tax is imposed on the high income earners while the low income earners pay a lower tax. A general misconception is that a higher tax rate leads to higher tax revenue, so that the government can have more to re-distribute. Similarly, a lower tax rate does lead to a fall in revenue, as a lower level of revenue will be received. Such a misconception considers only the static situation, not the dynamic situation on the disincentive impact of a higher tax rate.

A tax system consists of the number of taxable items or the tax base, the tax rate imposed on each item, tax inefficiency (how much tax is loss through under-reporting and the timing in the collection of tax) and the tax population (the population pool that pays tax). A government can control the number of tax items and the tax rates. Tax inefficiency is the extent of tax avoidance. There is a possibility of under-reporting of income by individuals and corporations, the government can make regular checks and inspections to minimize tax avoidance. However, the government cannot control the tax population, as this has to do with the number of individuals working and the amount of income individuals are earning. A high tax rate on income would discourage individuals to work, and a large number of tax items reduced both the incentive and ability to consume. Similarly, in the case of business or corporate tax, business enterprises may choose not to invest or relocate their base of investment overseas to avoid high tax. The tax population (the pool of tax-paying individuals and enterprises) is important in defining the success of a tax system, as all individual persons and enterprises will make their economic decisions accordingly.

One should note that the number of individuals or business corporations subject to tax payment changes as tax rate changes. In general, a high tax normally exerts a disincentive effect. High-salaried professionals will consider ways to reduce tax payment, including the possibility of working overseas. Similarly, a high profit tax discourages businesses investment or pushes businesses to consider investing overseas or migrating. In either case, a rise in the tax rate may lead to a reduction in tax revenue. On the contrary, a reduction in salary and profit tax rates lead to higher tax revenue as a lower tax attracts more workers to engage in employment and more businesses to engage in investment.

The economic behavior on tax response is theoretically captured by the Laffer curve (Samuelson and Nordhaus, 1989: 795). The Laffer curve shows the changing relationship between tax rates and tax revenues. In essence, the Laffer curve argues that there is an optimal tax rate that produces maximal revenue. If the imposed tax rate is higher than the optimal tax rate, then a reduction in tax rate can lead to higher tax revenue. The theoretical cone-shaped Laffer curve is shown in Figure 11.1, with the total tax revenue and tax rate indicated by the vertical and horizontal axis, respectively. When the tax rate is low, a rise in tax rate will be accompanied by a rise in total tax revenue. This is true up to the certain optimal tax rate, which is shown by the highest point on the curve, and thereafter, a rise in tax rate would reduce total tax revenue. If the tax rate is below the optimum, tax rate and tax revenue will move in the same direction. Beyond the optimum tax rate, a rise in tax rate will lead to a fall in tax revenue.

The argument behind the Laffer curve is simply that the willingness of tax payment by individuals and households declines, and disincentives set in once they consider the tax rate is too high. Further employment or business productivity is discouraged. Thus, when tax rates are very high, individuals and businesses will "prefer"

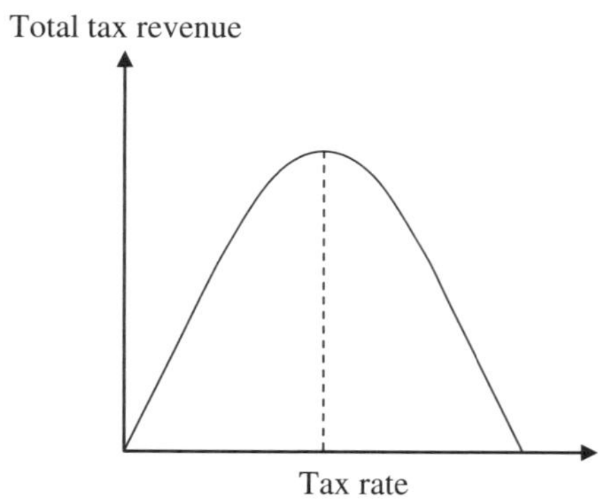

FIGURE 11.1 The Laffer curve

to work less and produce less. Businesses prefer to invest abroad to places where tax rates are moderate or low. Countries in North America and in the European Union tend to have higher tax rates than Asian countries, investment have been coming to Asia economies as a result. It has been argued that the fiscal drawbacks in the advanced countries have aided economic development in East Asia, as investment have been relocated to Asia economies to enjoy the low tax (Li, 2002). Consequently, the higher is the tax rate, the more disincentives it is to employment and business, and lower tax revenue will eventually be collected. It is good to identify the optimal tax rate empirically so as to maximize tax revenue and not to impose undue disincentives to employment and business.

11.3 Revenue and Expenditure Performances

Hong Kong's fiscal policy has conventionally been used as an instrument in promoting economic growth. Its emphasis has been pro-business and the key role played by the private sector. Hong Kong can claim to have a relatively efficient and small government sector, as this can be seen from the simple and low taxation system. The simple tax implies that there are only a handful number of major tax items, and the low tax means that the tax rates are mostly acceptable to businesses and individuals. While the fiscal structure allows various social welfare supports, the pursuit of income equity has not been a target in Hong Kong's fiscal budgets. Individuals are economically rewarded by their own endowments rather than by an elaborative and structured re-distributive policy. Government expenditures on education and training are means for individuals to enrich their endowments, which in turn permit them to gain economic security. Individuals are encouraged to achieve a better economic endowment, and "free lunches" are rarely provided in normal circumstances.

A balanced budgetary performance is inscribed in the Basic Law, the constitution for Hong Kong SAR. At the time when the Basic Law was being drafted in the mid-1980s, Hong Kong was experiencing a situation of continued budgetary surplus. The Hong Kong SAR Government, however, experienced a situation of fiscal deficit after the Asian financial crisis in 1997/98. Debate arises, however, on whether a balanced budget should be pursued on an annual basis or over a business cycle. Experiences show that Hong Kong tends to have budget surpluses more than budget deficits in non-crisis situations. Hence, it is appropriate to assume that the pursuit of a balanced budget is considered over a business cycle.

Due to the economic recession resulting from the Asian financial crisis, the government declared a "structural" deficiency in fiscal policy in 2001. There are a number of structural deficiencies. One is that revenue from land sales accounted for a considerable amount of government revenue before the burst of the economic bubble in 1998. This was due to the high property price, and the high land auction price acted as a "tax" on property transactions. The collapse of the property market in 1998, however, led eventually to the developers forcing the government to stop selling land in 2001, thus revenue from land sales was affected. Secondly, beginning from the early 1990s when Donald Tsang was the Financial Secretary in the then British Hong Kong government, an expansionary fiscal policy was pursued in a time of economic boom, enlarging a number of fiscal expenditures, including welfare-related items. A related deficiency has been the cumulative large amount of income tax exemption made since the early 1990s that had resulted in a large number of income earners fallen out of the tax net, especially in the post-Asian financial crisis recession that led to a severe reduction in income. The large increase in personal tax exemption of 163.4% between 1991 and 1998 (risen from HK$41,000 in 1991–1992 to HK$108,000 in 1998–1999) has enabled a large number of individuals falling outside the tax net, especially when income has been revising downwards since 1998. This has led to the debate on the narrow tax base and the inability to raise tax revenue in the recession years after the outbreak of the Asian financial crisis.

During the recession period from 1998 to 2005, Hong Kong has experienced unprecedentedly large budget deficits in a number of years. A number of suggestions have been made, such as the sale of government bonds and the introduction of the goods and sales tax (GST), but in fear of further economic deterioration and uncertainty, most suggestions were not taken up. The situation deteriorated further in 2003 when economic recession coexisted with the outbreak of a health hazard, namely the severe acute respiratory syndrome (SARS), and the government took harsh but unpopular measures of raising the tax rates.

It has been discussed and debated for some time even before 2003 that the government had attempted to pass the legislative work of the National Security Bill to implement Article 23 of the Basic Law. Article 23 says that Hong Kong SAR "shall enact laws on its own to prohibit any act of treason, secession, sedition, subversion against the Central People's Government, or theft of state secrets, to prohibit foreign political organizations and bodies from conducting political activities in the Region, and to prohibit political organizations or bodies of the Region from establishing ties with foreign political organizations or bodies." In obvious fear that the interpretation of different terms in Article 23 would differ between Hong Kong and Mainland China, and the possible erosion of autonomy and the rule of law in Hong Kong, there was severe political opposition to the passage of the National Security Bill. Public sentiment was at its lowest point after more than 500,000 people took to the streets on July 1, 2003, to express their opposition to the National Security Bill. The situation climaxed when two senior government officials, Regina Ip Lau Suk-yee, the Secretary for Security, and Antony Leung, the Financial Secretary, resigned in mid-July 2003.

Despite the numerous suggestions made on improving Hong Kong's fiscal policy, the inactions or misjudged actions on the part of the government could have itself to blame. Typically, fiscal policy decisions often defied public finance economics. For example, rising government expenditures were made in times of economic booms; policies tended to concentrate more in solving short-term economic ills and made little difference between policies in crisis and non-crisis times. The extent of government intervention has been unprecedented. For example, section 133 in the 2011–2012 budget delivered on February 23, 2011, stated that the government would earmark HK$110 million "to provide after-school homework guidance for students from low-income families and help them with their studies". One wondered why the government thought that students needed after-school homework guidance, let alone students from high-income or low-income families. It would be the government's role to provide a sound and first class education system for the students, but it is an individual decision whether a student would need after-school homework guidance. Not all students would require homework guidance, and different students require different forms of homework guidance. How much the government should interfere in the individual life of students and their parents, in the name of caring?

Despite the intention on "caring", there have been different degrees of public acceptance in the provision of short-term welfare care and economic intervention. On the one hand, the "free lunch" recipients criticized that the provision is not enough and always argued for more. On the other hand, other critics preferred the government to spend more for the building up of the future economy. As more short-term welfare provisions were given despite the economic recovery since 2007, the public viewed that the government lacked economic insights. The discontent exploded unexpectedly right after the delivery of the budget of 2011–2012. Section 177 stipulated that "a one-off injection of HK$6,000 into the Mandatory Provident Fund (MPF) account of all MPF members and members of the occupational retirement schemes..." This immediately sparked public anger because not all individuals have an MPF account. The government was in a dilemma situation and sought help from the pro-China legislators. Within the same week, the Financial Secretary had to find ways to sort out who should be entitled for the HK$6,000, and how the assistance would be allotted to the individuals.

Indeed, for a responsive government with strong sense of governance and creditability, an effective way to deal with the situation could be to declare openly a mistake made and remove section 177 entirely without influencing other aspects of the budget, though the government would face some loss of creditability. Hong Kong has a long history of prudent fiscal policy, and it is rare for the government to deliver a policy without some prior estimation on how it would be conducted. In Macau SAR across the other side of the Pearl River, the Macau SAR Government for years has made massive fiscal surplus from its gambling revenue and has been dishing out cash to its people for a number of years, though the media speculated that it was instrumental in reducing the amount and size of demonstrations thought to embarrass the Macau government. The indigenous population in Macau is less than one million, while the population of Hong Kong exceeded 6 million.

The incident sparked by section 177 in the 2011–2012 budget drew the conclusion that government intervention is becoming excessive, but it has not been acceptable, thankful nor popular, and that the people of Hong Kong prefers higher paid jobs and employment opportunities than short-term welfare assistance. The creditability of the government depended a lot on good governance. The conventional wisdom of Hong Kong's fiscal policy has always concentrated on job creation and investment promotion. The government should withdraw its "visible hand".

The structure of Hong Kong's fiscal policy consists of government revenues and expenditures. Government revenue consists of operating revenue and capital revenue. Operating revenue is further divided into direct taxes, indirect taxes and other revenue. Direct taxes include profit tax, personal assessment, income tax and property tax. Indirect taxes include bets and sweeps tax, hotel accommodation tax, air passenger departure tax, duties, general tax, motor vehicle taxes, royalties and concessions, tax-loaded fees, and entertainment tax. Other revenue includes fines, forfeitures and penalties, properties and investment, loans, reimbursements, contributions and other receipts, utilities, fees and charges and investment income.

Capital revenue composes of three categories of indirect taxes, other revenue and funds. Indirect taxes in the capital revenue account include estate duty and taxi concessions. Other revenue includes land transactions, recovery from Housing Authority and others. Funds included Capital Works Reserve Fund, Capital Investment Fund, Loan Fund, Civil Service Pension Reserve Fund, Innovation and Technology Fund and Lotteries Fund. Capital Works Reserve Fund composed of land premium and others (such as proceeds of bond issues). Table 11.1 shows the major categories of government revenue for the fiscal years of 1981–2009.

The largest source of government revenue came from operating revenue. Direct tax occupied the largest portion of government revenue. Other than 1981–1982, the percentage of government revenue deriving from direct tax had ranged from the lowest of 32.5% in 1997–1998 to the highest of 46.2% in 2008–2009. Percentage fluctuations tended to be larger in the post-1997 years than the pre-1997 years, reflecting a higher degree of economic volatility since 1997. Indeed, during the decade of 1987–1996, the government has received about 40% of its revenue from direct tax. Between 1997 and 2000, however, contribution from direct tax has dropped, due probably to the economic recession. The large percentage increase in 2001–2002 (44.3%) was due more to the fall in total revenue than to a rise in direct tax revenue.

In the case of indirect tax, its percentage share has increased slowly since the 1980s to the highest in 1992–1993 with 30.1%, but has leveled off to below 20% in the two recession years of 1998–1999 and 1999–2000, then edged up again to about 25% in more recent years. The financial crisis of 2008 obviously showed a poor performance as government revenue experienced a drop of 11.69%. The agreement made during the Sino-British negotiation in the 1980s between the pre-1997 British Hong Kong government and the Chinese authority on the amount of land sold per year before 1997 and that half of the revenue would be given to the Land Fund which would become part of the revenue to the Hong Kong SAR Government in 1997–1998 was indicated by the large increase of 7.4% in the indirect tax in the capital revenue in 1997–1998.

Revenue from funds in the capital revenue account has shown a steady increase in percentage share. The Capital Works Reserve Fund is the largest and steady contributor. The revenue from the sale of land is included in the land premium under the Capital Works reserve Fund. The large fluctuation in property price and the price from land sale has led some to argue that the land sale policy should be reformed to ensure a steadier source of government revenue from the sale of land. In the 2005–2006 budget, the land premium as a percentage of total government revenue was 11.9%, the same percentages for the 2006–2007, 2007–2008, 2008–2009 and 2009–2010 budget years were 12.8%, 17.4%, 5.3% and 12.4%, respectively. This confirms that land sale produced an unsteady source of government revenue.

Government expenditures are also divided into operating expenditures and capital expenditures. Operating expenditures included recurrent expenditure (such as personal emoluments, pensions, and departmental expenses), subventions (such as education,

TABLE 11.1 Distribution of government revenue

Fiscal year	Revenue (HK$ Million)	Operating revenue (%)			Capital revenue (%)	
		Direct tax	Indirect iax	Other revenue	Indirect and other	Funds
1981–1982	35,847	29.5	16.6	20.9	28.7	4.3
1982–1983	32,268	36.7	16.2	24.2	18.0	4.9
1983–1984	32,813	34.8	22.9	25.3	9.6	7.4
1984–1985	38,511	35.1	21.6	22.7	15.0	5.6
1985–1986	43,695	38.0	25.3	20.1	10.9	5.6
1986–1987	48,603	38.6	26.7	20.9	4.1	9.7
1987–1988	60,877	40.7	27.0	20.3	1.7	10.2
1988–1989	72,659	41.4	25.6	22.0	2.0	9.5
1989–1990	82,430	40.7	24.7	23.7	1.2	9.8
1990–1991	89,524	40.6	27.7	22.7	1.5	7.7
1991–1992	114,700	39.1	28.8	19.2	1.3	11.5
1992–1993	135,311	40.7	30.1	17.3	1.1	10.7
1993–1994	166,601	39.3	28.3	16.3	1.0	13.6
1994–1995	174,999	42.5	24.1	17.5	1.5	13.7
1995–1996	180,045	43.0	23.2	17.5	1.0	14.9
1996–1997	208,358	40.3	26.1	15.6	1.3	16.6
1997–1998	281,226	32.5	23.2	17.0	7.4	19.6
1998–1999	216,115	35.0	17.7	20.1	1.0	16.5
1999–2000	232,995	28.7	18.7	27.8	1.1	23.4
2000–2001	225,060	32.8	22.6	20.7	5.3	17.6
2001–2002	175,560	44.3	25.8	16.1	1.6	10.8
2002–2003	177,489	41.1	22.1	23.1	1.1	11.3
2003–2004	207,338	38.3	24.4	21.0	1.6	14.2
2004–2005	263,591	36.7	22.1	12.6	1.4	27.3
2005–2006	247,035	45.2	25.2	12.4	1.9	15.3
2006–2007	288,014	40.0	25.1	16.3	1.5	17.1
2007–2008	358,465	37.3	26.8	13.0	2.4	20.6
2008–2009	316,562	46.2	22.8	20.0	1.3	9.8
2009–2010	318,442	38.7	26.5	17.3	2.2	15.3
2010–2011†	374,761					
2011–2012*	375,016					

Note: †, * = revised estimate and estimate, respectively, from the 2011–2012 budget. *Source*: Census and Statistics Department, Hong Kong.

health, social welfare, university and vocational training and other operating expenditure), and non-recurrent expenditures. Capital expenditure included plant, equipment and works, subventions, debt repayment and funds. Table 11.2 shows the summary of government expenditures for the fiscal years 1981–2009.

TABLE 11.2 Distribution of government expenditure

Fiscal year	Expenditure (HK$ Mil.)	Operating expenditure (%) Recurrent	Subvention	Non-recurrent	Capital expenditure (%)
1981–1982	30,808	40.0	12.9	2.2	44.9
1982–1983	33,060	46.0	16.0	1.1	36.9
1983–1984	35,346	48.0	16.8	0.7	34.6
1984–1985	36,087	52.6	19.4	0.6	27.4
1985–1986	40,845	51.7	19.7	1.6	27.0
1986–1987	42,704	52.4	21.7	1.0	23.1
1987–1988	48,375	52.6	21.3	1.2	24.9
1988–1989	56,592	51.9	21.0	1.4	25.7
1989–1990	71,367	48.8	19.9	1.6	29.7
1990–1991	85,557	49.8	20.7	1.3	28.2
1991–1992	92,191	51.6	25.1	1.0	22.3
1992–1993	113,332	43.9	28.1	3.0	25.0
1993–1994	147,438	38.1	25.1	2.6	34.2
1994–1995	164,155	38.4	26.1	0.4	35.0
1995–1996	183,158	38.4	27.3	0.9	33.4
1996–1997	182,680	43.0	30.8	0.6	25.6
1997–1998	194,360	44.2	32.6	5.8	17.4
1998–1999	239,356	39.1	29.5	5.5	25.9
1999–2000	223,043	44.6	33.3	0.9	21.1
2000–2001	232,893	46.5	32.7	0.9	19.8
2001–2002	238,890	48.3	33.6	1.3	16.8
2002–2003	239,177	49.0	33.8	1.0	16.3
2003–2004	247,466	47.4	32.3	2.4	17.9
2004–2005	242,235	47.9	31.5	1.9	18.7
2005–2006	233,071	48.1	32.2	2.3	17.4
2006–2007	226,863	49.6	33.0	2.0	15.4
2007–2008	234,815	51.2	33.7	2.3	12.8
2008–2009	312,412	41.2	26.8	13.9	18.1
2009–2010	289,025	46.0	29.6	4.5	19.9
2010–2011†	303,490				
2011–2012*	371,116				

Note: †, * = revised estimate and estimate, respectively, from the 2011–2012 budget. *Source*: Census and Statistics Department, Hong Kong.

Table 11.2 shows that recurrent expenditure occupied the largest share, with the highest share exceeding 50% in the mid-1980s, and the four years that went below 40% were the fiscal years of 1993–1994, 1994–1995, 1995–1996 and 1998–1999 in the sample period. The percentage share of operating expenditure on subventions has also been rising steadily from below 20% in the early 1980s to over 30% in the entire recession period after the Asian financial crisis. The non-recurrent expenditure item has been unimportant, but the large expenditure in the 2008 fiscal year could be due to the government's assistance provided to the natural disaster victims in Mainland China. However, the percentage share in capital expenditure has been falling steadily from the highest of 44.9% in 1981 to below 20% since 1999. Although the percentages showed a decreasing trend, in absolute terms the government's capital expenditure, especially on plant, equipment and works and subventions varied over the years, depending on the need of the time.

Operating expenditure composed of personal emoluments, personnel related expenses, pensions, departmental expenses and other charges. In nominal terms, all these items have expanded over the years. For example, personal emoluments increased from HK$5,977 million in 1981 to HK$50,497 in 2000. The percentage increases in the two periods (1981–1990 and 1990–2000) were 292% and 115%, respectively. The same percentage increases for personnel related expenses in the two fiscal years were 469% and 113%, respectively, and for pensions were 323% and 269%, respectively. The same percentage increases for departmental expenses were, respectively, −14% and 184%. Other charges have also expanded a lot. Government expenditure on subvention is a major indicator on the extent of involvement in the economy. This included expenditures on education, health, social welfare, universities and polytechnics, Vocational Training Council and miscellaneous.

The most comprehensive figure that indicates the level of government's annual total expenditure is the total public expenditure, which is total government expenditure plus the expenditure of other public bodies. Table 11.3 shows the total public expenditure by functions. The last column on the total public expenditure to the GDP ratio gives an indicator on the size of the public sector in Hong Kong. In normal times, the size of the public sector rarely goes beyond 18% of GDP. During the recession years from 1998 to 2005, the ratio has slightly exceeded 20%. The public sector in Hong Kong is small by international standard.

Various themes can be identified from the fiscal practice of the Hong Kong government. Infrastructure development has also been considered as an instrument in widening the economic base and facilitating business transactions. Urban constructions and building of public utilities have been initiated by the government, while private organizations have sometimes been incorporated in the financing of public projects. Once supplied, infrastructures and public utilities are common goods that can last for a long period of time. Government's provision of infrastructure attracted least criticism as it has a twin advantage of reducing households' "survival cost" and business production cost.

The theme of "investing for the future" has regularly been featured in a number of budget speeches. Government expenditure on education is a major aspect of "investing in future". A better educated workforce raises the quality of human capital that in turn serves as a complement to investment. A more productive workforce will receive a high wage payment and can easily seek employment in the market. On the one hand, a high wage received by workers based on productivity increase enables the government to have a higher level of revenue from each income tax payer. On the other hand, a higher level of employment will enlarge the government's income tax

TABLE 11.3 Total public expenditure by function

		Percentage share in TPE										
Fiscal Year	TPE	CEA	Econ	Edu	Env	Hth	Hous	Infra	Sec	SW	Su	TPE/GDP
1986	47.9	4.37	5.60	17.97	3.32	9.11	12.07	13.71	15.55	5.36	12.94	15.3
1987	53.6	4.47	5.93	17.65	3.26	9.28	13.11	13.55	15.08	5.33	12.34	13.9
1988	64.8	4.32	5.79	18.02	3.13	8.75	15.05	13.32	14.81	5.37	11.42	14.2
1989	81.9	4.12	5.31	16.37	3.86	8.85	14.12	16.74	14.09	5.33	11.20	15.5
1990	95.2	4.39	5.71	17.41	4.76	9.70	13.04	12.11	14.54	5.58	12.77	16.2
1991	108.0	3.71	5.70	18.02	5.08	9.90	11.64	12.78	13.79	5.87	13.51	15.9
1992	123.5	3.56	6.17	17.96	5.12	10.04	10.47	13.80	13.19	5.91	12.98	15.6
1993	155.2	3.16	8.11	16.39	4.45	11.89	10.70	14.54	11.16	5.91	13.70	17.0
1994	166.0	3.27	4.80	17.42	4.93	11.64	11.87	15.42	11.43	6.60	12.61	16.1
1995	191.3	3.21	5.01	17.58	5.24	12.69	9.97	13.60	11.43	7.39	13.88	17.5
1996	211.2	3.60	5.49	17.84	5.43	11.91	11.48	10.57	11.53	8.49	13.56	17.4
1997	234.8	3.46	7.27	20.03	5.57	11.92	10.50	9.02	10.12	9.25	12.87	17.5
1998	266.5	3.24	8.04	18.19	5.01	11.78	14.58	8.68	9.43	9.90	11.15	20.8
1999	269.5	3.39	4.55	18.67	4.64	11.84	17.02	8.51	9.60	10.25	11.53	21.6
2000	267.5	3.09	4.67	19.22	4.24	12.24	15.93	8.53	10.00	10.53	11.56	20.8
2001	269.4	3.10	5.10	19.40	4.10	12.70	11.90	9.30	10.20	11.20	13.00	21.1
2002	263.5	3.10	5.20	20.80	4.30	12.60	9.10	9.30	10.30	12.30	13.00	21.6
2003	279.2	3.00	5.60	20.70	4.00	12.40	10.00	9.40	9.80	12.20	12.90	21.6

(*Continued*)

TABLE 11.3 (*Continued*)

Fiscal Year	TPE	Percentage share in TPE										TPE/GDP
		CEA	Econ	Edu	Env	Hth	Hous	Infra	Sec	SW	Su	
2004	263.2	2.95	6.35	20.69	3.87	12.23	6.82	13.77	9.70	12.65	10.95	20.4
2005	251.5	3.10	6.79	21.57	3.85	12.57	6.12	12.87	9.86	13.22	10.04	18.2
2006	244.9	3.28	5.66	21.21	4.16	13.12	5.99	11.91	10.26	13.70	10.72	16.6
2007	252.5	3.25	5.37	21.32	4.77	13.32	5.68	10.45	11.08	13.81	10.95	15.6
2008	331.0	11.66	7.55	22.66	3.74	11.09	5.26	8.83	8.46	11.86	8.89	19.7
2009	310.3	4.56	6.07	18.94	4.39	12.46	5.58	15.28	9.61	13.20	9.92	19.1
2010[s]	323.8	4.70	5.54	19.10	4.73	12.31	5.58	14.90	10.11	12.64	10.39	18.5
2011*	339.3	6.27	11.99	17.46	4.78	11.48	5.02	13.87	8.12	11.69	9.32	21.0

Notes: TPE = Total public expenditure (HK$ billion), CEA = Community and external affairs, Econ = Economic, Env = Environment, H^{th} = Health, Hous = Housing, Infra = Infrastructure, Sec = Security, SW = Social welfare, Su = Support, GDP = Gross Domestic Product. †, * = revised estimate and estimate, respectively, from the 2011–2012 budget.

Sources: Financial Services and Treasury Bureau, Hong Kong, *The 2010–2011 Budget*, February 23, 2011.

pool. In the long-run, investing in education produces a good return to both the individual and the government.

While the workforce has become more educated and productive and does not need government assistance, the government can channel the saved resources to the new pool of needy individuals as there are always new entrants of individuals into the society needing government assistance. In short, economic security enables individuals to look after their own economic well-being, and the government can concentrate on helping other needy individuals. The needy individuals who need help today may become economically secured tomorrow, but there are always new flows of individuals who need government help tomorrow. In other words, there is always a stock of needy people who need government help, but the flow involves the movement of individuals entering and exiting the government assistance net.

Table 11.3 shows that education is the largest recipient of total public expenditure. With the exception of 1989, total public expenditure on education has exceeded 17% in the 1986–2010 fiscal years, reached 20% for a number of years since the turn of the century. However, the percentage increase has been gradual. From the lowest of 16.37% in 1989 to the highest of 22% in 2005, the increase is less than 6% over the 17 years.

Total public expenditure on social welfare has increased drastically and has become the second largest public expenditure item. Table 11.3 shows that from a lowest of 5.33% in 1987, it has increased to a share of 13.7 in 2006, an increase of 8.37% in 19 fiscal years. The rapid increase was due to the introduction of a more comprehensive social welfare assistance scheme in 1993, (between 1993 and 1998, for example, total public expenditure on social welfare has increased from 5.91% to 9.90%, an increase of 4% in 6 years) and the economic downturn in the late 1990s (between 1999 and 2002, the percentage has increased from 10.25% to 12.3%, an increase of 2% in 3 to 4 years) had led to increased dependence on government welfare assistance.

The third largest public expenditure item is health, but the increase has been slow. Between 1988 and 2005, for example, the increase was about 4%. The Hospital Authority in Hong Kong is a statutory body established on December 1, 1990, to take over the management of all the 38 public hospitals and institutions and a total staff of 37,000. The Hospital Authority reported that Hong Kong's health service expenditure as percentage of GDP is lower than 4% in 2000, and is much lower than other developed countries. Japan is about 7%, while the United Kingdom is above 6%. However, the missing part in the calculation is the contribution by the private medical services in different economies. In the United Kingdom, for example, where most medical services are provided by the government or the public sector, private provision of medical services has remained weak. In other words, comparison of supply has to be made in both public sector and private sector provisions.

Total public expenditure on housing has fallen considerably, especially since 2001 when the government declared the end of the Home Ownership Scheme due to the collapse of the property market after the Asian financial crisis and pressure from the developers. However, despite the rapidly rising property market since 2007 due probably to economic recovery and the "cash rich" buyers from Mainland China, there have been calls from the public for the government to reintroduce a similar scheme that can help the sandwich class of citizens in Hong Kong. Total public expenditure on infrastructure has also declined, especially in the recession years after the Asian financial crisis. But the need to build the bridge linking Hong Kong, Macau and Zhuhai in west Guangdong, together with the West Kowloon development and the new railway linking Hong Kong to Guangzhou and other highway networks have boosted expenditure on infrastructure.

The Hong Kong economy has experienced a prolonged economic boom in the 1980s and 1990s. The strong economic scene has enabled the government, on the one hand, to commit large expenditures and, on the other hand, increased individual tax exemptions. Indeed, the buoyant fiscal performance has reflected Hong Kong's "prosperity and stability" in the two decades of 1980–2000. As Table 11.4 shows, Hong Kong has experienced large fiscal surplus in a number of years in the 1980s and 1990s, and the fiscal reserve kept increasing, though the outbreak of the Asian financial crisis and the subsequent burst of the economic bubble has led to a U-turn. The buoyant fiscal performance can be seen from the increasing fiscal reserve. In 1981, for example, the closing fiscal reserve to total government expenditure ratio is only 0.81. By 1996, this ratio has increased to 1.17. The inclusion of the Land Fund has enlarged the fiscal reserve tremendously. By 2000, this ratio has increased to 1.85. After the three historical large fiscal deficits in 2001–2003, fiscal reserve rebounded and increased again since 2004.

One can also observe that the fiscal surpluses are extraordinary large in the two fiscal years of 1997–1998 and 2007–2008. Obviously, the year 1997 was the year of sovereignty reversion and the year 2007 was the first decade of sovereignty reversion. It can be anticipated that the business cycle in Hong Kong will be determined by the political and historical factors, namely that the economy will boom in future years of 2017, 2027, 2037 and so on in every tenth anniversary of the sovereignty reversion. However, optimism aside, the two years of 1997 and 2007 were followed by severe economic downturn in their following year. The fiscal year of 1998–1999 experienced a large deficit due to the beginning of the economic recession. The fiscal year of 2008–2009 experienced the smallest fiscal surplus in the sample period, due probably to the 2008 financial crisis in the United States. If there was such a trend, it would help the government in predicting the movement of the business cycle and formulate its fiscal policy accordingly.

The large fiscal reserve has also been subjected to criticism. At the peak of the recession after the Asian financial crisis, some civic leaders even suggested that the fiscal reserve should be returned to the public. Since Hong Kong does not have public debts, and public borrowing is not a common event, thus financing the deficit through the drawdown of fiscal reserve seemed to be the most effective means of financing fiscal deficits. The next question is how large should the fiscal reserve be? At the peak of the recession, fiscal reserve is large enough to maintain about 15 to 18 months of government expenditure. Public finance theory does not specify the optimal size of reserve, but a larger reserve is always better as it is an indicator of the fiscal health of the government. As prolonged fiscal deficit is feasible if the recession persisted, it would be fair to maintain a minimum fiscal reserve equivalent to about 24 months of government expenditure. Again, one has to bear in mind that government expenditures vary between months and between different periods in the business

TABLE 11.4 Government fiscal balances (HK$ million)

Fiscal year	Expenditure	Revenue	Surplus (deficit)	Reserve balance
1981–1982	30,808	35,847	5,039	25,099
1982–1983	33,060	32,268	(792)	24,306
1983–1984	35,346	32,813	(2,533)	21,773
1984–1985	36,087	38,511	2,424	24,197
1985–1986	40,845	43,695	2,850	27,048
1986–1987	42,740	48,603	5,899	32,947
1987–1988	48,357	60,877	12,502	45,448
1988–1989	56,592	72,659	16,066	61,515
1989–1990	71,367	82,430	11,064	72,257
1990–1991	85,557	89,524	3,967	76,546
1991–1992	92,191	114,700	22,509	99,054
1992–1993	113,332	135,311	21,979	121,033
1993–1994	147,438	166,602	19,164	140,197
1994–1995	164,155	174,998	10,843	151,040
1995–1996	183,158	180,045	(3,113)	147,927
1996–1997	182,680	208,358	25,678	173,605
1997–1998	194,360	281,226	86,866	457,543
1998–1999	239,356	216,115	(23,241)	434,302
1999–2000	223,043	232,995	9,952	444,254
2000–2001	232,893	225,060	(7,833)	430,278
2001–2002	238,890	175,560	(63.331)	372,503
2002–2003	239,177	177,489	(61,688)	311,402
2003–2004	247,466	207,338	(40,128)	275,343
2004–2005	242,235	263,591	21,356	295,981
2005–2006	233,071	247,035	13,964	310,663
2006–2007	226,863	288,014	58,601	369,264
2007–2008	234,815	358,465	123,650	492,914
2008–2009	312,412	316,562	1,450	494,364
2009–2010	289,025	318,442	25,917	520,281
2010–2011†	303,490	374,761	71,271	591,552
2011–2012*	371,116	375,016	3,900	595,452

Notes: The reserve balance for the 1997/1998 fiscal year included the net worth of HK$197,072 million from the Land Fund on July 1, 1997. In 2000, a provision of HK$6,143 million was made for the fall in the market value of Exchange Fund investments. Expenditures figures exclude "Transfers between the General Revenue Account and Funds". Figures for 2009–2010 are subject to audit by the Director of Audit. †, * = revised estimate and estimate, respectively, from the 2011–2012 budget.
Source: Census and Statistics Department, Hong Kong.

circle. An economic recession would obviously require more government expenditure than a non-crisis economy.

In practice, the amount of fiscal reserve equivalent to the number of months of government expenditure has varied over the years. Fiscal reserve exceeded 25 months of government expenditure in 1997–1998, but due to the severe economic recession and the unprecedented large fiscal deficit, fiscal reserve has slide down to 13 months of government expenditure in 2003–2004. It bounced back to around 25 months in 2007–2008, but leveled off to around 18 months in 2011–2012. The Financial Secretary, John C. Tsang, has forecasted that the fiscal reserves "were projected to fall to some 15 months of government expenditure by the end of 2014–2015".[2]

By judging at the depth and length of economic recession that lasted from 1998 to 2005, a period of 15 months is quite a short period of time. Such a level of reserve is regarded as low when one considers the previous fiscal performances in Hong Kong, as a low fiscal reserve would make the government vulnerable to external shocks and might have difficulty in ensuring needed macroeconomic stability. Indeed, the government might end up creating crisis and generate instability on its own should its reserve was to fall below 12 months of government expenditure, as businesses and investors might lose confidence in the economy.

Conventionally, the fiscal policy in Hong Kong has been regarded as conservative. When estimating budgetary revenues and expenditures for the coming fiscal year, the government tended to exercise a high degree of prudence. It means that in revenue estimation, the government tended to minimize revenue inflow. In expenditure estimation, the government tended to maximize the amount to be spent. Fiscal conservatism implied that the government at the end of the fiscal year did not spend as much as it estimated, and its actual revenue was higher than the estimated revenue. In the end, there is a greater chance to end up with a fiscal surplus.

Actual expenditure being lower than the estimated expenditure could arise due to delay in projects, change in plans or price changes. Actual revenue being larger than the estimated revenue could arise due to increase in economic prosperity, that prosperous businesses and the rise in income and earning permitted the government to collect larger revenue than estimated. In an economic upturn, it often happened when the actual revenue exceeded the estimated revenue. On the contrary, in an economic downturn, actual expenditure exceeded estimated expenditure, because the rise in unemployment turned more people to seek for government assistance, and in turn the government's revenue declined.

The deviation or discrepancy between the estimated and actual figures for the period 1981–2007 are shown in Table 11.5, where positive figures represented a situation in which actual figures exceeded estimated figures, and negative figures represented the reverse. In the revenue figures, there are a considerable number of years with large positive percentages, implying that the estimated revenue figures have been conservative. There are only a few years with negative percentages; mostly corresponding to economically difficult times (for example 1982–1983, 1998–1999 and 2002–2003). The mean deviation for total revenue is 5.02% (4.66% for the 1981–2000 sample period in Li (2006, Table 4.7)), suggesting that on average total revenue is underestimated by about 5%. Between the mean deviation of the operating revenue and capital revenue, the former (6.30) has a much lower mean deviation

[2] *The Financial Secretary Invites Your Views*, The 2011–2012 budget consultation paper presented to the Legislative Council, November 29, 2010.

than the latter (14.5). This suggested that operating revenue was easier to estimate than capital revenue. Indeed, the standard deviation for capital revenue is much higher than the other two.

The estimates of fiscal revenues are on average more conservative than the estimates of fiscal expenditures. The deviations of total expenditure in Table 11.5 contained only two double-digit entries in 1993 and 1994 fiscal years, but a considerable number of small single-digit negative entries, suggesting a situation of

TABLE 11.5 Discrepancy between actual and preliminary budget items (%)

Fiscal year	Total revenue	Operating revenue	Capital revenue	Total expenditure	Operating expenditure	Capital expenditure
1981–1982	9.27	14.19	–0.73	20.01	10.59	13.76
1982–1983	–17.23	–1.71	–69.49	–7.38	6.65	–31.34
1983–1984	1.66	–5.29	35.70	–0.26	–2.96	4.85
1984–1985	6.02	0.38	27.74	–3.32	–2.78	–4.74
1985–1986	17.72	7.65	68.45	6.21	0.49	21.70
1986–1987	17.92	8.82	74.77	7.40	1.46	27.18
1987–1988	24.15	15.37	88.35	8.20	1.46	28.49
1988–1989	15.96	17.62	3.18	1.86	–0.56	8.84
1989–1990	6.87	7.16	4.44	3.22	–0.11	10.59
1990–1991	1.02	–0.53	16.54	–6.34	–4.02	–12.26
1991–1992	10.37	7.45	30.13	–9.86	–0.79	–41.56
1992–1993	5.71	6.78	–2.27	–1.56	2.02	–12.30
1993–1994	7.57	4.54	23.33	10.16	–1.15	31.87
1994–1995	–4.71	–2.87	–14.42	11.05	–1.75	34.77
1995–1996	–5.31	–4.01	–12.06	7.33	–2.16	26.21
1996–1997	5.55	6.13	2.93	–0.58	–3.07	6.64
1997–1998	14.84	13.49	18.46	–4.05	2.24	–33.94
1998–1999	–26.13	13.88	–81.23	2.64	–1.53	14.60
1999–2000	10.82	10.61	11.46	–4.41	–5.79	0.74
2000–2001	–8.96	–0.43	–36.14	–4.64	–4.98	–3.25
2001–2002	0.56	0.30	8.60	–1.47	0.40	–66.10
2002–2003	–15.99	–7.83	–78.89	–7.44	–3.62	–82.09
2003–2004	–0.50	3.03	–62.03	–5.28	–2.22	–79.27
2004–2005	15.22	14.42	74.86	–7.27	–7.21	–14.40
2005–2006	7.22	7.60	–6.97	–7.54	–7.47	–16.71
2006–2007	10.28	10.27	10.62	–7.26	–7.19	–15.75
2007–2008	25.56	23.02	256.12	–3.75	–3.63	–14.33
Mean	5.02	6.30	14.50	–0.16	–1.40	–7.33
S.D.	12.31	7.69	65.42	7.30	4.02	32.03
Median	6.87	7.16	8.60	1.56	–1.75	3.25

Note: S.D. = standard deviation.

Sources: *Hong Kong Annual Digest of Statistics*, various editions, Census and Statistics Department, Hong Kong; *The Budget*, Speech by the Financial Secretary, various editions.

mild underestimation in many fiscal years. This is true with operating expenditure, where there are more negative deviations than positive deviations, especially since the 1990s. The estimates for capital expenditure are poorer, as there are a large number of double digit negative estimates. This showed that fiscal prudence in operating expenditure was not as strong as in operating revenue estimations, especially during economically difficult times. The mean deviation for total expenditure is –0.16% (1.78% for 1981–2000 in Li (2006, Table 4.7)), but the same figure for operating expenditure is –1.4%. In the case of capital expenditure, the mean deviation is larger at –7.33%, implying that there can be large variations in estimating capital expenditures.

Overall, the Hong Kong government is said to have exercised a higher degree of fiscal prudence in revenues than in expenditures. One can conclude that more fiscal prudence is needed in estimating operating expenditure. In a sense, every government faces difficulty in estimating expenditure. There is a distinction between the number of expenditure items and the amount spent on each item. While the government can control the number of expenditure items, how much expenditure is committed on each item may deviate from government estimation. In social welfare expenditure, for example, the number of needy individuals turning up for welfare assistance may far exceed the estimated number, even though each is entitled to a fixed amount of financial assistance. This is particularly true in an economically difficult time when more individuals failed to achieve economic security and have to rely on government's provision of social security. As such, the actual welfare expenditure will deviate a lot from the estimated expenditure.

11.4 Features of the Tax Structure

In the government's General Revenue Account, the direct tax under operating revenue as shown in Table 11.1 formed the largest proportion of fiscal revenue. Direct tax composed of four main categories of profit tax, salaries tax, personal assessment and property tax. Over the eleven fiscal years of 1991–2001, profit tax has contributed an average of 59.2% of direct tax, while salary tax together with personal assessment and property tax have contributed an average of 38.8% and 2%, respectively.

Salary tax is imposed on all Hong Kong residents on income arising in Hong Kong. There are various tax bands and marginal tax rates. Payment of salary tax is determined according to the taxpayer's net chargeable income, which is computed by deducting from gross income the various personal exemptions and allowances and charitable donations. The standard salary tax rate represented the overall tax rate on salaries, such that the amount of tax charged under the progressive tax structure governed by the various tax bands and marginal tax rates did not exceed the amount charged at the standard tax rate.

In the case of profit tax, persons, including corporations, partnerships, trustees and bodies of persons carrying on any trade, profession or business in Hong Kong are chargeable to tax on all profits, excluding profits arising from the sale of capital assets. There is no distinction between residents and non-residents. There are different tax rates applied to corporations and unincorporated businesses.

The effective tax rate is the actual tax rate charged. The effective profit tax rate for corporate business and the standard tax rate for salary are 16.5% and 15%, respectively. In the 1997–1998 fiscal budget, economic buoyancy has led the government to provide a ten percent exemption under the Tax Exemption (1997 Tax Year) Order. The 1997 Tax Act said that any person who is chargeable to salaries tax, property tax or profit tax for the 1997–1998 assessment year shall be exempted from payment of an amount equivalent to ten percent of the tax to which the person is so charged. The effective tax rates for profit and salary in the budget of 1997–1998 were 14.85% and 13.5%, respectively.

Hong Kong's tax structure has been regarded as simple and low. It is simple in the sense that it can be calculated easily, and the salary tax rates and bands are simple (as shown in Table 11.6). It is low because the various tax rates are low by world standard. Over the last two decades of the 1980s and 1990s, the standard tax rate did not exceed 17% and has been kept at 15% for a long period of time. Profit tax has experienced some minor changes over the years, but the highest was 18.5% (as shown in Table 11.7). The difference between standard tax rate and profit tax has been small, reaching 2.5% only in the two fiscal years of 1992 and 1993, while in most years the difference is 1.5%.

Personal assessment, which is really a pre-payment of the following fiscal year's tax, is the more debatable issue. It has been argued that it is not fair as salary of the following fiscal year has not been earned, yet it is subject to tax. Because of possible salary changes in the following year, personal assessment becomes inaccurate. Others argued that the government may have to impose a higher tax rate if only salary in the

TABLE 11.6 Salary tax rates and bands, 1981–2008

Fiscal year	Increment (HK$ thousand)	Tax rates progression (%)
1981/82–1984/85	10, 10, 10, 10, Remainder	5, 10, 15, 20, 25.
1985/86–1986/87	10, 10, 10, 20, Remainder	5, 10, 15, 20, 25.
1987/88	10, 10, 20, 20, Remainder	5, 10, 15, 20, 25.
1988/89–1989/90	10, 10, 10, 10, 10, 10, 10, Remainder	3, 6, 9, 12, 15, 18, 21, 25.
1990/91	10, 10, 10, 10, 10, 10, 10, Remainder	2, 4, 9, 12, 15, 18, 21, 25.
1991/92–1992/93	20, 20, 20, Remainder	2, 9, 17, 25.
1993/94	20, 30, 30, Remainder	2, 9, 17, 25.
1994/95–1996/97	20, 30, 30, Remainder	2, 9, 17, 20.
1997/98	30, 30, 30, Remainder	2, 8, 14, 20.
1998/99–2000/01	35, 35, 35, Remainder	2, 7, 12, 17.
2003/04	32.5, 32.5, 32.5, Remainder	2, 7.5, 13, 18.5
2004/05–2005/06	30, 30, 30, Remainder	2, 8, 14, 20
2006/07	30, 30, 30, Remainder	2. 7, 13, 19
2007/08	35, 35, 35, Remainder	2, 7, 12, 17
2008/09	40, 40, 40, Remainder	2, 7, 12, 17

Source: Inland Revenue Department, Hong Kong.

TABLE 11.7 Percentage tax rates in Hong Kong, 1981–2008

Fiscal year	Standard tax rate	Profit tax rate for corporations	Fiscal year	Standard tax rate	Profit tax rate for corporations
1981–1982	15.0	16.5	1994–1995	15.0	16.5
1982–1983	15.0	16.5	1995–1996	15.0	16.5
1983–1984	15.0	16.5	1996–1997	15.0	16.5
1984–1985	17.0	18.5	1997–1998	15.0	16.5
1985–1986	17.0	18.5	1998–1999	15.0	16.0
1986–1987	17.0	18.5	1999–2000	15.0	16.0
1987–1988	16.5	18.0	2000–2001	15.0	16.0
1988–1989	15.5	17.0	2003–2004	15.5	17.5
1989–1990	15.0	16.5	2004–2005	16.0	17.5
1990–1991	15.0	16.5	2005–2006	16.0	17.5
1991–1992	15.0	16.5	2006–2007	16.0	17.5
1992–1993	15.0	17.5	2007–2008	16.0	17.5
1993–1994	15.0	17.5	2008–2009	15.0	16.5

Notes: Standard tax rate is applicable to salary, property and profit of unincorporated businesses. In the 1997 fiscal year, a ten percent tax rebate was given out. The effective standard tax rate was 13.5%, while the effective profit tax rate was 14.85%.
Source: Inland Revenue Department, Hong Kong.

current fiscal year is taxed. In fact, when income tax payments are rolled over a number of years, personal assessment canceled out each other, as what you pay for the following year will cancel out from the deduction of tax payment made last year. There is, thus, little support for dropping the personal assessment.

Both the revenue elasticity and expenditure elasticity, which is defined as the proportionate (or percentage) change in tax revenue or government expenditure with respect to a proportionate change in GDP, have been discussed in Li (2006). For government expenditure, the elasticity ratio suggested that a certain percentage of government expenditure was needed for a one percent change in GDP. If the elasticity ratio was larger/smaller than unity, it meant that government expenditure has to be more/less than 1% for every 1% increase in GDP. In fiscal revenue, the elasticity ratio showed the percentage change in revenue collected by the government for every 1% increase in GDP. If the elasticity ratio for revenue is larger/smaller than unity, the government would collect more/less than the one percent increase in GDP.

The logarithm (ln) regression equation for calculating tax revenue or government expenditure elasticity is:

$$\ln (x_t) = \alpha + \beta \ln (y_t) + \varepsilon_t, \tag{1}$$

where x represented either tax revenue or government expenditure and y is GDP. The estimated coefficient, β, represented either the revenue or expenditure elasticity.

Regression analysis can also be supplemented by the following estimation of the buoyancy ratio of tax revenue or government expenditure:

$$x_t = \mu + \gamma\, y_t + \varepsilon_t. \quad (2)$$

The buoyancy ratio (or the marginal propensity), represented by γ, is the ratio of a change in tax revenue over a change in GDP. If the buoyancy ratio is larger/smaller than unity, it meant that for every dollar change in GDP, expenditure or revenue would change by more/less than the change in GDP.

Table 11.8 reproduced the empirical estimates in Li (2006). The elasticity estimate has been updated to include the impact of the Asian financial crisis and the

TABLE 11.8 Fiscal elasticity and buoyancy

	Elasticity†		Buoyancy†
Fiscal expenditure	1986–2000	1994–2006	1986–2000
Total public expenditure	1.2224	1.3626	0.2164
Total government expenditure	1.2173	0.9980	0.1875
Total operating expenditure	1.2225	1.8557	0.1452
Total capital expenditure	1.1704	1.6144	0.0423
Community and external	0.9757	0.0515	0.0064
Economic	1.2369	0.6462	0.0131
Education	1.2660	0.6635	0.0415
Environment	1.5391	0.4862	0.0117
Health	1.4763	0.0901	0.0283
Housing	1.2038	1.4032	0.0299
Infrastructure	0.9282	1.5930	0.0171
Security	0.8820	0.4659	0.0181
Social Welfare	1.6920	2.1018	0.0239
Support	1.2295	0.0406	0.0263
Fiscal revenue	1981–2000	1989–2006	1981–2000
Total government revenue	1.0421	1.1358	0.1866
Total operating revenue	1.0496	0.9940	0.1441
Total capital revenue	1.0348	1.9010	0.0425
Profit tax revenue	1.0234	1.0672	0.0381
Salary tax revenue	1.2490	1.0783	0.0230
Direct tax revenue	1.0563	1.0458	0.0647
Indirect tax revenue	1.0989	0.9872	0.0411
Non-tax revenue*	0.9676	1.2738	0.0383

Note: * = non-tax operating revenue, land transactions and funds. † = the 1986–2000 results are reproduced from Li (2006, Table 4.10).

Source: Census and Statistics Department, Hong Kong.

economic recession that followed. The extended sample periods for the elasticity estimates for fiscal expenditure and fiscal revenue are 1994–2006 and 1989–2006, respectively. These two sample periods can incorporate the economic situation that covered the entire post-Asian financial crisis recession years.

The estimates in Li (2006, Table 4.10) using the sample periods of 1986–2000 for fiscal expenditure and 1981–2000 for fiscal revenue remained the same. Various observations on the original sample have been made in Li (2006). As far as fiscal expenditures are concerned, the overall elasticity ratio is 1.2224, and most of the expenditure items are greater than 1.2, suggesting a one percent change in GDP required a 1.2% change in fiscal expenditures. Three of the four total expenditure items in Table 11.8 exceeded 1.2, implying that the government has been keen to commit fiscal expenditures in the two decades of the 1980s and 1990s. Total capital expenditure was closest to unity with an elasticity ratio of 1.1704. Capital expenditures are more in line with the change in domestic income.

On individual expenditure items, social welfare has the highest elasticity ratio of 1.6920, suggesting that for a one percent change in GDP, government expenditure on social welfare has to increase by 1.69%. Comparing with other expenditure elasticity estimates, one can conclude that the government has committed more fiscal resources on social welfare than other items in the past two decades. A similar argument went to health, as its elasticity ratio is the third highest. For every 1% change in GDP, government expenditure on health has to increase by 1.4763%. Although the elasticity estimate for expenditure on environment is high (1.5391), it should be examined in line with infrastructure (0.9282), and the average of the two gives an elasticity ratio of 1.234. The elasticity ratio for infrastructure is below unity, meaning that for every 1% change in GDP, government has only committed 0.9282% change in infrastructure expenditure. Government should spend more on infrastructure. Most other major expenditure items have an elasticity estimate of 1.2.

In the case of buoyancy estimates for the various fiscal expenditure items, the highest estimate is total public expenditure (0.2164). For every dollar change in GDP, public expenditure will change by twenty-one cents. The buoyancy estimate for total government expenditure (0.1875) is the sum of total operating expenditure (0.1452) and total capital expenditure (0.0423). The low capital expenditure, as also reflected in the estimates for infrastructure, suggesting that the government can engage more in economic capacity building so as to provide and produce more economic opportunities for businesses and individuals. On the buoyancy estimates of individual expenditure items, the buoyancy ratio for education (0.0415) was highest, followed by housing (0.0299). Both education and housing are high-expense items. Other than the estimate of support (0.0263), social welfare and health are the other two items with large buoyancy ratios.

As far as fiscal revenues are concerned, the original sample period (1981–2000) in Li (2006) showed that the elasticity estimates of the three total revenue items were close to unity, suggesting that the revenue system in Hong Kong was an optimal one, and that a one percent change in GDP gave a one percent change in revenue. On individual tax items, salaries tax has the highest elasticity estimate of 1.2490. This showed that a proportionate change (either up or down) in GDP would bring a larger proportionate change in salaries tax. One interpretation is that the government is relying proportionately larger on salary tax. Alternatively, the government should broaden the tax base, either in the case of salary tax by changing the tax rate, tax bands and/or lower the exemption level, or introduce new revenue items. The relative low elasticity estimate for the non-tax revenue (0.9676) suggested that the government can raise more revenue from non-tax sources.

Looking at the various buoyancy ratios under revenues, the buoyancy ratio for total capital revenue (0.0425) is lower than the other two total revenue items (0.1866 and 0.1441). This suggested that there is room for government to levy additional revenue from capital items. In the individual tax revenue items, the buoyancy ratio of direct tax revenue is highest (0.0647), suggesting that the government is relying heavily on direct tax revenue. On the contrary, the low buoyancy ratio of salary tax revenue (0.023) showed that the government is taxing only a small number of salary earners and for every dollar change in GDP, salary tax contribution is small.

One last observation is to consider the buoyancy ratios between the various total expenditure and total revenue figures. The buoyancy ratio of total government expenditure (0.1875) is similar to total government revenue (0.1866). Similarly, the two ratios for total operating expenditure (0.1452) and total operating revenue (0.1441) are close, so as the ratios for total capital expenditure (0.0423) and total capital revenue (0.0425). The major difference is the buoyancy ratio of total public expenditure (0.2164) and total government expenditure (0.1875). Their difference (0.0289) suggested that for every dollar change in GDP, the government is having a bigger change in total public expenditure than total government expenditure. It would be right, therefore, for the government to reduce the size of public expenditure so that the buoyancy ratio will be reduced to 0.2 or lower.

The estimates in Li (2006, Table 4.10) can be considered as the situation in a non-crisis time period. The estimates for the elasticity ratios using the more recent sample period that covered the recession years (1998–2005) are also shown in Table 11.8. As far as the fiscal expenditures elasticity ratios are concerned, there are some differences when compared with the original sample (1986–2000). While the elasticity for total government expenditure remained close to unity (0.998), the other three total expenditure items are higher than those in the original sample (1986–2000), with an elasticity estimate of 1.3626 for total public expenditure. This simply reflected the large government expenditure during the recession years, with a highest elasticity estimate of 1.8557 for total operating expenditure. For individual expenditure items, the government has spent most in social welfare (2.1018), and other than housing and infrastructure whose elasticity estimates are higher than unity, all other expenditure items showed an elasticity estimate less than unity. One simple suggestion is that the government is proportionately spending less than changes in GDP in the sample period 1994–2006, but the estimates have to be read with care since income has fallen during the recession years of 1998–2005 and drastic government expenditure would be needed if the government were to rescue the recession entirely on its own. Thus, the less than unity elasticity estimates reflected more the situation of the recession.

The situation for the elasticity estimates of fiscal revenue is similar between the two sample periods shown in Table 11.8. Virtually all the elasticity estimates are close to unity. Since the government's ability to collect income tax has fallen in the recession years, the elasticity estimate for salary revenue is 1.0783, lower than the same estimate for the 1981–2000 sample of 1.249. The implication is that the tax structure in Hong Kong is optimal, and drastic changes are not expected in different business cycles.

There are various lessons on can learn from the fiscal performance of the last two decades. There is clear distinction in the expenditure side between a normal and non-crisis situation and a crisis and recession situation. The government needed to adjust their expenditure policies between normal times and crisis times. In a normal time period, elasticity estimates in Table 11.8 showed that total public expenditure has deviated from total government expenditure, probably in the areas of social welfare and health. Capital expenditure, especially infrastructure, could be expanded to raise the economic capacity of Hong Kong. On the revenue side, the areas the government could examine closer included salaries tax, non-tax revenue and capital revenue. Generous exemption policies would reduce the government's tax ability, while more revenue could be generated from capital items. Decision on the changes in the fiscal structure has to take into account of other considerations, such as the impact on the business sector or social responsibility of tax payers. Nonetheless, a vigorous fiscal strategy is needed in order to correct and maintain a fiscal framework that has made Hong Kong a success.

In a crisis time period, the government naturally has committed more expenditure on short-term items, as typically indicated by the large expenditure in welfare assistance. This is acceptable provided that it is fiscal management in an economic crisis, but the policy has to be adjusted back to a normal situation once the economic crisis is over, and more fiscal resources should be geared to promote the long-term development of the economy. The elasticity estimates for fiscal revenue do not change much in the two sample periods, indicating that the tax structure in Hong Kong is optimal.

The optimal tax discussed under the Laffer curve can be estimated by using actual empirical data. One can calculate the change in revenue per one percentage change in tax rate, and the ratio of change in revenue-adjusted GDP and change in tax rate. Rather than the use of tax revenue, tax revenue adjusted (or normalized) for tax change can be calculated and empirically estimated. In the following calculation, profit tax revenues are normalized to the tax rate of 16%, which are the 2000–2001 fiscal year tax rates.[3] The salary tax revenue is normalized to the tax rate of 15%, which is also the 2000–2001 fiscal year rates. The profit tax rate for corporations and the nominal GDP at factor cost (production based estimates, extracted from *Estimates of Gross Domestic Product 2000*, Census and Statistics Department, Hong Kong) are used for the calculation of the effect of tax rate change on tax revenue.[4]

The impact of GDP growth on revenue changes has to be neutralized by adjusting tax revenue for GDP growth. The tax revenue is subsequently divided by the

[3]Tax revenue is first divided by the corresponding tax rate of that year and multiplied by 16%.
[4]Tax rates and tax revenues are obtained, respectively, from the Inland Revenue Department and the Finance Bureau, Hong Kong.

GDP of the corresponding year and then multiplied by the GDP in year 2005.[5] These adjusted tax revenues are differenced, and years with increase or decrease in tax rate are noted. For those years that a change in tax rate has occurred, the change in the adjusted revenue per one percent point decrease (increase) in tax rate is calculated. The effect of a change in tax rate on tax revenue can be seen from the average of the revenue-adjusted GDP in those years with negative (positive) change in tax rate. Table 11.9 shows the level of production-based GDP, profit tax revenue and salary tax revenue for the period 1980–2006. Tables 11.10 and 11.11 show the impact on GDP-adjusted revenue resulting from a change in profit tax and salary tax, respectively. Since 1980, there are only few years with an increase or decrease in tax rate.

The change in GDP-adjusted revenue per 1% change in tax rate is shown in Table 11.12. The result of the 1980–2000 sample is similar to that in Li (2006, Table 4.13). Due to the change in tax rates in 2003 and 2004, an extended and new sample period of 1980–2005 is included in Table 11.12. One major difference is that the fiscal year 1998 was the beginning of the recession and GDP was falling. Indeed, statistics showed that the revenue adjusted for GDP growth decreased a lot in 1998 (–3,790 shown in Table 11.11). In 2003–2004, however, it was the tail end of the

TABLE 11.9 Production based GDP, profit and salary tax revenues (HK$ million)

Fiscal year	Production based GDP	Profit tax revenue	Salary tax revenue	Fiscal year	Production based GDP	Profit tax revenue	Salary tax revenue
1980–1981	136,237	5,495	1,490	1994–95	986,597	47,430	23,624
1981–1982	167,182	6,895	1,688	1995–96	1,060,548	46,706	26,258
1982–1983	186,446	7,852	2,356	1996–97	1,177,519	50,063	28,709
1983–1984	205,541	6,939	3,399	1997–98	1,287,967	55,347	30,159
1984–1985	244,370	8,290	4,159	1998–99	1,218,263	45,252	25,063
1985–1986	259,353	10,149	5,406	1999–00	1,194,772	37,699	24,832
1986–1987	302,961	10,836	6,588	2000–01	1,245,059	42,969	26,303
1987–1988	376,061	15,441	7,940	2001–02	1,233,059	44,376	28,635
1988–1989	448,847	19,407	8,546	2002–03	1,223,153	38,800	29,733
1989–1990	511,415	21,231	10,451	2003–04	1,191,807	48,770	27,977
1990–1991	574,848	21,241	13,107	2004–05	1,244,798	58,640	33,991
1991–1992	651,683	25,203	17,417	2005–06	1,333,830	69,797	37,494
1992–1993	756,524	32,248	20,200	2006–07	1,424,446	71,919	38,586
1993–1994	859,509	39,858	22,505				

Source: Finance Bureau and Inland Revenue Department, Hong Kong.

[5]These exercises are similar to those in Li (2006, Tables 4.11, 4.12 and 4.13), the difference in the figures are due to the use of a more recent base year of 2005 instead of 2000 in Li (2006).

TABLE 11.10 Impact on revenue from a change in profit tax (HK$ million)

Fiscal year	Revenue adjusted for tax-change*	Revenue adjusted for GDP growth#	Change in tax rate (%)(A)	Change in GDP-adjusted revenue (B)	(B)/(A)
1980–1981	5,328	53,579			
1981–1982	6,686	54,969		1,211	
1982–1983	7,614	56,131		1,162	
1983–1984	6,729	44,996		−11,135	
1984–1985	7,170	45,215	2.00	219	109
1985–1986	8,778	52,156		6,941	
1986–1987	9,372	47,671		−4,485	
1987–1988	13,725	54,726	−0.50	7,054	14,109
1988–1989	18,265	57,628	−1.00	2,902	2,902
1989–1990	20,588	55,331	−0.50	−2,297	−4,594
1990–1991	20,597	49,249		−6,082	
1991–1992	24,439	51,545		2,297	
1992–1993	29,484	56,814	1.00	5,268	5,268
1993–1994	36,442	61,807		4,993	
1994–1995	45,993	64,075	−1.00	2,268	2,268
1995–1996	45,291	58,697		−5,378	
1996–1997	48,546	56,666		−2,031	
1997–1998	59,633	57,275	-1.65	609	369
1998–1999	45,252	49,508	1.15	−7,767	−6,754
1999–2000	37,699	42,055		−7,452	
2000–2001	42,969	45,999		3,944	
2001–2002	44,376	47,966		1,967	
2002–2003	38,800	42,279		−5,688	
2003–2004	44,590	54,541	1.50	12,262	8,175
2004–2005	53,613	62,786		8,245	
2005–2006	63,814	69,797		7,011	

Notes: According to the Tax Exemption Order (1997), any person who is chargeable to Salaries Tax, Property Tax or Profits Tax for the 1997/1998 assessment year shall be exempted by 10% of the chargeable tax. * = to calculate the profits tax revenue adjusted for tax change, the tax rate is normalized at 16%. This is calculated by dividing the revenue by its corresponding tax rate and multiplying it by 16%. # = to calculate the profits tax revenue adjusted for GDP growth, the revenue is divided by its corresponding GDP and multiply it by the GDP in year 2005.
Source: Finance Bureau and Inland Revenue Department, Hong Kong.

economic recession, and the revenue adjusted for GDP growth had increased considerably (5,106 as shown in Table 11.11). This explained the large differences in the two cases of tax increase in Table 11.12.

The analysis based on the 1980–2000 period is the same as in Li (2006). In the case of profit tax, a decrease in the tax rate brought higher revenue (3,011) than a tax rate increase (–459). In the case of salary tax, a decrease in the tax rate brought

TABLE 11.11 Impact on revenue from a change in salary tax (HK$ million)

Fiscal year	Revenue adjusted for tax-change*	Revenue adjusted for GDP growth	Change in tax rate (%) (A)	Change in GDP-adjusted revenue (B)	(B)/(A)
1980–1981	1,490	14,577			
1981–1982	1,688	13,457		–1,120	
1982–1983	2,356	16,842		3,385	
1983–1984	3,399	22,041		5,199	
1984–1985	3,670	22,684	2.00	643	321
1985–1986	4,770	27,782		5,098	
1986–1987	5,813	28,983		1,201	
1987–1988	7,218	28,141	–0.50	–842	–1,684
1988–1989	8,270	25,377	–1.00	–2,764	–2,764
1989–1990	10,451	27,237	–0.50	1,806	3,720
1990–1991	13,107	30,390		3,153	
1991–1992	17,417	35,621		5,232	
1992–1993	20,200	35,588		–33	
1993–1994	22,505	34,898		–690	
1994–1995	23,624	31,915		–2,984	
1995–1996	26,258	32,999		1,085	
1996–1997	28,709	32,496		–504	
1997–1998	33,510	31,210	-1.50	–1,286	–857
1998–1999	25,063	27,420	1.50	–3,790	–2,526
1999–2000	24,831	27,700		280	
2000–2001	26,303	28,158		458	
2001–2002	28,635	30,952		2,794	
2002–2003	29,733	32,399		1,448	
2003–2004	27,074	31,287	0.50	–1,112	–2,224
2004–2005	31,866	36,394	0.50	5,106	10,213
2005–2006	35,151	37,494		1,100	
2006–2007	36,174	36,104		–1,390	

Notes: According to the Tax Exemption Order (1997), any person who is chargeable to Salaries Tax, Property Tax or Profits Tax for the 1997/1998 assessment year shall be exempted by 10% of the chargeable tax. * = to calculate the profits tax revenue adjusted for tax change, the tax rate is normalized at 15%. This is calculated by dividing the revenue by its corresponding tax rate and multiplying it by 15%. # = to calculate the profits tax revenue adjusted for GDP growth, the revenue is divided by its corresponding GDP and multiply it by the GDP in year 2005.

Source: Finance Bureau and Inland Revenue Department, Hong Kong.

a smaller fall (–396) than a tax rate increase (–1,102). The conclusion is that there is room for a decrease in profit tax, while the salary tax is at its optimal rate, with both a higher or lower rate would produce a fall in tax revenue.

When the increase in the tax rates of 2003 and 2004 are included in the 1980–2005 sample periods, the conclusion for profit tax revenue is still the same, and

TABLE 11.12 Effect of tax rate change on tax revenue

Change in GDP-adjusted revenue per 1% change in tax rate	1980–2000		1980–2005	
	HK$ Million	Number of sample years	HK$ Million	Number of sample years
Profit Tax				
Decrease	3,011	5 (1987–1989, 1994, 1997)	3,011	5
Increase	–459	3 (1984, 1992, 1998)	1,700	4 (+ 2003)
Salary Tax				
Decrease	–396	4 (1987–1989, 1997)	–396	4
Increase	–1,102	2 (1984, 1998)	1,446	4 (+ 2003, 2004)

Source: Finance Bureau and Inland Revenue Department, Hong Kong.

that a decrease in profit tax rate brought larger revenue (3,011) than an increase in the profit tax rate (1,700). In the case of salary tax, due to the large increase in GDP in 2004, an increase in salary tax rate in 2003 and 2004 brought a much larger salary tax revenue (1,446) than the estimate in 1980–2000. This is exceptional, due probably to the large difference in the revenue (GDP adjusted) between 1998 and 2004. The drop in revenue in 1998 has pulled the estimate down in the 1980–2000 sample years, while the increase in revenue in 2003 and 2004 has pulled the estimate up in the 1980–2005 sample years.

One interpretation, according to the Laffer curve, can be that the optimal salary tax rate has been reached. Despite the small number of tax changes in the sample period, one can conclude that the tax rate in Hong Kong is elastic, that a decrease a profit tax can produce larger revenue for the government. The related argument is that the tax rates of 16% for profit tax and 15% for salary tax in Hong Kong are optimal tax rates. These two tax rates should be applied in order to obtain the maximum revenue for the government. In short, a low and simple tax regime has served Hong Kong well.

Other than the Sino-British negotiation years of 1982–1984 and the subsequently short-lived economic recession of 1985 and 1986, the Hong Kong economy experienced expansion at least in nominal terms for the entire 1987–1998 period. Economic growth was matched with speculation in stocks and properties. It was a period of wealth appreciation in the name of "prosperity and stability".

Instead of pursing a contraction fiscal policy at a time of economic boom in the period 1987–1997, Hong Kong had in fact pursued an expansionary fiscal policy, with features of creating more expenditure items and spending more on each fiscal item. There are a number of theoretically unfound economic arguments used by the then Financial Secretary, Donald Tsang Yum-kuen. The continued rise in domestic income and wealth appreciation enabled the government to cumulate fiscal surplus. In an economic boom, the sound economic policy would be to reduce government spending so as not to "add more fuel to the fire" that would result in inflation and erosion of economic competitiveness, and at the same time, allow the private sector to do more for economic growth.

Instead, the prolonged fiscal surplus provided an opportunity for the government to embark on a "wealth reimbursement" program that were to "return wealth" to the citizens in different forms of fiscal concession and government expenditures. Secondly, the large annual percentage growth rates in government expenditures were needed to cover the large inflation rates. In other words, fiscal expansions have to take care of both inflation growth and real expenditure growth, thus together they required the government to make relative large nominal growth rates, though the large expenditures were sustained by the economic buoyancy of the 1980s and 1990s.

Soon after the Asian financial crisis and the subsequent burst of the property bubble and the downfall of the economy, Hong Kong's fiscal direction was reversed. Fiscal deficit appeared as early as 1995, deteriorated drastically in 1998 and prolonged since 2000. The budget for the fiscal year 2001–2002 saw the unprecedented large deficit exceeding HK$60 billion (see Table 11.4). Various major revenue sources, such as profit tax, salaries tax, personal assessment and property tax, land premium, stamp duty on property and stock transactions exhibited a declining trend, and growth in government revenue fell behind income growth.[6] The unprecedented large deficit and its rapid pace of increase have caused society-wide alarm and concern, and various sectors were debating on its solution and the consequences.

During the recession years (1998–2005), the government had difficulty in committing more expenditure due already to the unprecedented large deficits, and the government was reluctant to widen the tax base, even on a temporary basis. Nonetheless, fiscal policies were geared mainly to solving short-term economic ills in order to avoid further economic deterioration. Fiscal prudence was somewhat restored in the peak of the recession years when Antony Leung was the Financial Secretary. For example, although it was unpopular, tax rates were increased in 2003 and 2004, and tax exemption was reduced in two consecutive years. However, the fiscal situation improved after Antony Leung has stepped down in the summer of 2003 and his successor, Henry Tang Yin-yen, engaged in a more innovative fiscal policy by the introduction of government bonds in solving the fiscal deficit. At the same time, economic recovery occurred and, despite the rise in profit tax rates in 2003 and salary tax rates in both 2003 and 2004, fiscal surplus reappeared in 2004. It was thought that the 0.5% increase in salary tax in 2004 was not needed, even though the decision was made in 2003.

However, when Donald Tsang Yum-kuen took up the leadership as the Chief Executive after the abrupt resignation of Tung Chee Hwa in March 2005, and the subsequent appointment of John C. Tsang as the Financial Secretary in 2007,

---

[6] *The 2002–2003 Budget-Background Information for the Financial Secretary's Consultations with Legco Members*, December 2001, Charts 8–9, and *The 2003–2004 Budget — Information Pack for the Financial Secretary's Consultations with LegCo Members*, October 2002, Charts 16–17.

economic recovery returned. The government should re-orientate the fiscal policy in favor of long-term growth activities and reduce the need for solving short-term welfare. Quite the contrary, the fiscal sentiment has still remained in a crisis situation and concentrated mostly in the provision of short-term welfare assistance. The sentiment has extended from "wealth reimbursement" to "caring for the society" elaborated in a number of Policy Addresses by Donald Tsang Yum-kuen and fiscal budgets by John C. Tsang. In other words, there was no change in the fiscal mindset between a crisis-oriented and a non-crisis-oriented policy.

Fiscal concessions since the mid-1990s have affected both the structural budget and the cyclical budget. In the structural budget, various discretionary policy items were added. On the revenue side, reduction in tax burden was given to tax rate concessions (e.g., lowering of tax bands) and increase in tax exemptions. In the 1993/1994 budget, for example, transport concessions were given to the disabled and elderly.[7] On the expenditure side, new expenditure items (e.g., environmental protection, establishment of the Hospital Authority) were made. In the cyclical budget, the government would have to spend at a rate higher than the inflation rate in order to make some change in real growth. Thus, more was given to each fiscal expenditure item. In short, fiscal expansion occurred in two directions: additional fiscal items and additional expenses on each item. But tax exemption occurred in the number of tax exemptions and increase in the level of exemption.

Tax exemption has been used as a concession in the structural budget. Consider Table 11.13 that summarizes the tax payment situation of a single individual without any deduction or allowances given. In 1991, there were four tax bands. The individual had to pay 2% of tax for an annual income from HK$41,001 to HK$61,000, pay 9% if the annual income has increased from to HK$61,001 to HK$81,000, pay 17% for income from HK$81,001 to HK$101,000 and 25% if the annual income range was above HK$101,001. The alternative is to estimate the tax payment from the standard rate without deductions and allowances. The individual will be charged with the lower of the two methods of tax calculations. In reality, the individual may be entitled to various deductions and allowances, but shall not pay more than the standard rate.

In 1992, the four tax bands remained the same, but the individual would have to start paying tax from a higher income of HK$46,001. The increase in tax exemption from HK$41,000 to HK$46,000 showed a percentage change of 12.2%. In 1993, the four tax bands were the same, but the tax exemption had gone up to HK$56,000. Namely, the individual's annual income below HK$56,000 did not need to pay any income tax. Between 1991 and 1993, the tax exemption has increased by a cumulative 36.6%. In other words, the government would receive 36.6% less of tax from the individual. In 1993, the individual was paying an income tax of HK$29,200, equivalent to 13.3% of annual income. In 1994, tax exemption again increased to HK$72,000, a cumulative change of 75.6%. Between 1993 and 1994, the individual's tax payment was reduced by 25.3%.

The exemption from tax kept increasing. By 1998, the amount of tax exemption increased to HK$108,000, and the individual was paying a tax amount of HK$8,540,

[7] *The 1993–1994 Budget*, Speech by the Financial Secretary, March 3, 1993, p. 32.

TABLE 11.13 Tax exemptions and reductions on income earned by a single person

Fiscal year	Tax bands (%) Tax paying annual income (HK$)	Tax paid (% of income)	Cumulative percentage change in Tax reduction	Cumulative percentage change in Basic allowance
1991	2, 9, 17, 25			
	41,000, 61,000, 81,000, 101,000			
1992	2, 9, 17, 25			
	46,000, 66,000, 86,000, 106,000			12.2
1993	2, 9, 17, 25	29,200		
	56,000, 76,000, 106,000, 136,000	(13.3)		36.6
1994	2, 9, 17, 20	21,800	–25.3	
	72,000, 92,000, 122,000, 152,000	(9.9)		75.6
1995	2, 9, 17, 20	20,400	–30.1	
	79,000, 99,000, 129,000, 159,000	(9.3)		92.7
1996	2, 9, 17, 20	18,200	–37.7	
	90,000, 110,000, 140,000, 170,000	(8.3)		119.5
1997	2, 8, 14, 20	13,200	–54.8	
	100,000, 130,000, 160,000, 190,000	(6.0)		143.9
1998	2, 7, 12, 17	8,540	–70.8	
	108,000, 143,000, 178,000, 213,000	(3.9)		163.4
2003	2, 7.5, 13, 18.5	10,735	–63.2	
	104,000, 136,500, 169,000, 201,500	(4.9)		153.7
2004	2, 8, 14, 20	13,200	–54.8	
	100,000, 130,000, 160,000, 190,000	(6.0)		143.9
2005	2, 8, 14, 20	13,200	–54.8	
	100,000, 130,000, 160,000, 190,000	(6.0)		143.9
2006	2, 7, 13, 19	12,300	–57.9	
	100,000, 130,000, 160,000, 190,000	(5.6)		143.9
2007	2, 7, 12, 17	9,900	–66.1	
	100,000, 135,000, 170,000, 205,000	(4.5)		143.9
2008	2, 7, 12, 17	7,440	–74.5	
	108,000, 148,000, 188,000, 228,000	(3.4)		163.4

Note: The estimates of the 1990s were based on the first $220,000 income of a single person.

Sources: Budget Speeches, various years; The Budget Background Information for the Financial Secretary's Consultations with Legislative Council Members, various years.

merely 3.9% of the annual income. The cumulative change in the basic allowance had risen to 163.4%. This is exactly where the narrow tax began. Tax exemption has been generous since 1991. Due to a high inflation in much of the 1990s, the real reduction in tax payment should be higher than those shown in Table 11.13. The 1998 situation remained the same until 2002.

Between 2003 and 2005, tax exemption was reduced by two consecutive amounts from HK$104,000 in 2003 to HK$100,000 in 2004, and the same situation remained until 2007. The cumulative percentage change has been reduced to 143.9%, and the individual would have to pay more tax, amounting to HK$13,200, equivalent to 6% of annual income. The situation was reversed in 2008 and the individual tax exemption was increased to HK$108,000. The individual needed to pay only an amount of HK$7,440 in income tax, equivalent to only 3.4% of the annual income.

One can consider the magnitude of the tax exemption of HK$108,000 by comparing the mean or medium income in Hong Kong. According to the Census and Statistics Department, the median monthly wage in 2009 was HK$11,500, making an annual median wage earning of HK$148,000.[8] Using the information in Table 11.13, all individuals earning the median income in Hong Kong literally paid only 2% of income tax. This explained the T-shape nature of the salary tax, implying that the bulk of salary tax was shouldered by the high income earners. Those with a median income or below virtually paid very little or no salary tax. The unintended consequence is that during the economic recession, many more people's earning has fallen and as they fell out of the tax net, the government would have difficulty in collecting tax. In other words, there is an absence of an automatic built-in stabilizer in the salary tax system.

When tax exemptions were provided to individuals, the government faced the consequence of a large number of individuals dropping out from the tax net, especially when income had fallen after the Asian financial crisis. A phenomenon in Hong Kong's salary tax structure is its narrowness. Effectively, the large increase in tax exemption has shifted from one of a V-shape salary tax structure, in which low income earners are contributing to tax, while the high income individuals contributed the bulk of the salary tax, to a T-shape structure, in which the few high income earners shouldered a large portion of salary tax revenue. This certainly is an unstable and unhealthy structure, especially at a time when income has fallen, and there would even be fewer high income earners but a lot more low income earners would drop out from the tax net. In turn, as income fell and unemployment rose, government welfare expenditures would simply have to go up, a situation described as "fiscal crisis" (O'Connor, 1973) with falling revenue and rising expenditure, resulting in a deepening of fiscal deficit.

The increasing dependence on high income earners for the salary tax revenue can be considered in Table 11.14, though most figures are provisional assessments except 1997. In 1997, the ratio of tax paying to non-tax paying working populations is 1:1.38. The 2% of population paying the standard tax rate contributed 43.9% of salaries tax. The top 100,000 tax paying population shouldered 54.8% of salary tax, and the top 500,000 (0.5 million) tax paying working population shouldered 90.3% of salaries tax. In other words, the 0.5 million tax paying population in Hong Kong shouldered the fiscal expenditures for over 6 million people in Hong Kong. This brings out the narrowness of the T-shape tax structure.

[8] *2009 Report on Annual Earnings and Hours Survey*, Census and Statistics Department, Hong Kong, March 2010.

TABLE 11.14 The T-shape salary tax structure

			Paying standard tax of 15%		% of salary tax paid by 100,000 tax-paying population
Fiscal year	Tax-paying population	Non-tax paying working population	% of working population	% of salary tax	1st, 2nd, 3rd, 4th, 5th, Rest
1997	1,330,000	1,830,000	2.0	43.9	54.8, 16.8, 8.3, 6.7, 3.7, 9.7
1998	1,150,000	2,000,000	0.3	19.5	62.4, 15.1, 7.3, 5.6, 3.4, 6.2
2001	1,200,000	2,000,000	0.3	20.0	61.4, 16.1, 7.8, 5.0, 2.5, 7.0
2002	1,200,000	2,000,000	0.4	23.0	62.1, 17.5, 8.6, 4.9, 2.9, 4.0
2003	1,245,000	1,955,000	2.2*	30.0	59.2, 17.4, 9.5, 4.7, 4.4, 2.0
2004	1,260,000	2,040,000	1.27†	35.8	57.0, 8.0, 10.0, 6.1, 3.4, 5.5
2005	1,220,000	2,150,000	1.40†	38.8	58.2, 16.3, 10.0, 6.6, 3.5, 5.4
2006	1,260,000	2,240,000	1.00†	35.8	59.6, 16.0, 9.3, 5.6, 3.6, 5.9

Notes: With the exception of the actual revenue figures in 1997, others are based on provisional assessments. * The standard rate at 15.5%. † The standard rate at 16%.
Source: *Budget Background Information for the Financial Secretary's Consultations with Legislative Council Members*, various years.

The situation has deteriorated since 1997. By 2003, because of the economic downfall and the number of high income earners have dropped, the estimate on the percentage of working population paying the standard tax rate is 2.2%, and they shouldered 30% of the salary tax. But the top 500,000 tax paying working population shouldered 98% of the salary tax in 2003. By the 2006 fiscal year, the percentage of population paying standard tax rate has been reduced to 1%, implying that there are more people with lower earnings, and the ratio of tax paying to non-tax paying populations has increased to 1:1.7. The richest 500,000 tax paying population shouldered 94.1% of total salary tax. In other words, the salaries tax base is getting narrower.

As compared to the salaries tax structure, profit tax showed a slightly less extreme case. In Table 11.15, the most profitable 2,500 corporations (4.9% of total) with assessable profit no less than 10 million in Hong Kong contributed 78.8% of profit tax in 1999. In 2000, the most profitable 2,800 corporations (5.4% of total) were responsible for 79.7% of profit tax. In 2001, the most profitable 2,500 firms (4.9%) contributed 78.7% of profit tax. By 2005, corporations with assessable profit no less than 10 million (3,900 corporations, 7.8% of total) contributed 81.9% of profit tax. On the contrary, about 70% of least profitable firms contributed less than 5% of total profit tax in all three years. The majority of small corporations and business in Hong Kong ended up paying little or no tax.

The traditional "simple and low" fiscal framework in Hong Kong is its high degree of clarity. The consistency in fiscal clarity and simplicity has became rooted in the Hong Kong economy and accepted by the international community when foreign

TABLE 11.15 The profit tax structure

	Fiscal year 1999			Fiscal year 2000			Fiscal year 2001		
	Corporations			Corporations			Corporations		
Assessable profits (HK$ million)	Number	% of total	% of total tax yield	Number	% of total	% of total tax yield	Number	% of total	% of total tax yield
> 50	500	1.0	59.9	600	1.1	60.6	500	1.0	59.6
> 30 to 50	300	0.6	5.9	400	0.8	6.3	300	0.6	6.1
> 20 to 30	500	1.0	5.1	500	1.0	5.0	500	1.0	5.0
> 10 to 20	1,200	2.3	7.9	1,300	2.5	7.8	1,200	2.3	8.0
> 7.5 to 10	800	1.5	3.1	800	1.5	3.1	800	1.5	3.2
> 5 to 7.5	1,400	2.7	3.8	1,500	2.9	3.7	1,300	2.5	3.5
> 3 to 5	2,300	4.5	4.1	2,400	4.5	3.9	2,300	4.4	4.1
> 2 to 3	2,500	4.8	2.7	2,500	4.7	2.6	2,400	4.6	2.8
> 1 to 2	5,200	10.1	3.4	5,400	10.2	3.1	5,400	10.3	3.5
< 1	36,900	71.5	4.1	37,400	70.8	3.9	37,600	71.8	4.2
	Fiscal year 2003			Fiscal year 2004			Fiscal year 2005		
> 50	600	1	60.3	800	1.2	63.8	800	1.1	64.7
> 30 to 50	400	0.7	6.5	500	0.8	6.1	500	0.7	5.4
> 20 to 30	500	0.9	5.0	600	0.9	4.8	700	1.0	4.4
> 10 to 20	1,500	2.6	8.1	1,700	2.7	7.1	1,900	2.7	7.4
> 7.5 to 10	900	1.6	2.9	1,000	1.6	2.7	1,100	1.6	2.7
> 5 to 7.5	1,600	2.8	3.7	1,800	2.8	3.4	2,000	2.8	3.3
> 3 to 5	2,700	4.7	4.0	3,100	4.9	3.6	3,300	4.7	3.6
> 2 to 3	2,700	4.7	2.5	3,100	4.9	2.3	3,300	4.7	2.3
> 1 to 2	6,000	10.4	3.2	6,700	10.5	2.9	7,000	10.0	2.8
< 1	40,900	70.8	3.8	44,400	69.7	3.3	49,600	70.7	3.4

Source: Budget Background Information for the Financial Secretary's Consultations with Legislative Council Members, various years.

investments come to Hong Kong. As elaborated elsewhere, domestic macroeconomic stability attracted investment that in turn boosted domestic growth and so on. The rising income, wealth appreciation, the booming economy and the expansion of the fiscal surplus did allow the pre-1998 Hong Kong authority room to venture into various "uncharted" areas of fiscal expansion.

In the 1998 budget, for example, most of the increase in tax concessions exceeded the 1997 inflation rate. Individual's basic allowance and allowance for the first two children increased by 8% and 11.1%, respectively. Dependent parent and grand-parents allowances increased by 11.1%, but additional allowances increased by

275% in both cases. Dependent siblings' allowance increased by 11.1%, while single parent allowance increased by 44%. Disabled dependent allowance and training deductions increased by 140% and 50%, respectively. Other salaries tax concessions included a deduction of up to HK$100,000 per year for mortgage interest payments, HK$60,000 per year or elderly residential care expenses, and HK$12,000 per year for retirement contribution. In sum, 99% of salaries tax payers have experienced a reduction in tax burden as a result of the various salaries tax concessions given in the 1998 budget.

In the case of profit tax, the 1998 budget also provided numerous concessions. For example, it allowed a 100% write off for capital expenditure on plant and machinery, while depreciation allowance for commercial building increased from 2% to 4%. The write off of refurbishment expenditure was extended to all businesses. It was estimated that for a business with a net profit of HK$100 million, the payable tax for a trading/retail business would be reduced by 16%, for a banking/financial business by 14.8%, and for an insurance company by 25.5%. With a net profit of HK$50 million, a manufacturing business would have saved 40.5% from profit tax.[9] One can argue that 1998 was as an exceptional year as the authority was trying to rescue the economy from the Asian financial crisis, and Hong Kong's large fiscal surplus and reserve meant that its fiscal health was able to allow additional concessions. Others argued, however, that Hong Kong was experiencing a process of "welfarization", in which the fiscal instruments have been extended beyond simple and fundamental areas, such as basic, children and parent allowances, to various welfare-related allowances that have interfered with the life of private individuals whom should be making their own economic decisions and choice.

11.5 The Welfare Burden

The formalized welfare system in Hong Kong was first introduced in 1971 under the Public Assistance (PA) scheme that consisted of three types of welfare payments. The basic scale rates of payments were meant to meet essential needs and a sliding scale of assistance was adopted depending on the number of members in a household. The basic scale rates were reviewed periodically to take account of inflation as reflected in the PA Index of Prices. Special supplements were given to meet the specific needs of special groups, including old age, disability, child and long-term supplements. The third type was special grants intended to defray special expenses on individual cases, such as the cost of accommodation, need for education expenses, funeral and so on.

All other resources available to the households were taken into account for assessing the living standard of PA households. The PA payment would simply "top up" the household's net available resources. The provision of "disregarded income" was introduced in 1978 with the idea of encouraging self-help. Certain categories of people (disabled, elderly and single parents) who were receiving earnings at the same

[9] *The 2002–2003 Budget- Background Information for the Financial Secretary's Consultations with Legco Members*, December 2001.

time would have a portion of their income disregarded for the purpose of eligibility for PA. This would provide incentive for them to remain in work, and the level of disregarded income was set at 75% of the PA basic rate for a single person. In 1988, the disregarded income provision was extended to able-bodied people in regular employment.

In addition to periodic adjustments due to inflation, the PA scheme also introduced "real improvements" to ensure that the PA payment also covered other needs according to circumstances. This was done in two ways: a general increase in the number of PA recipients, and specific increases for specific categories of recipients. In other words, there was a dual enlargement in both the number of PA recipients and the amount given to each recipient.

Since July 1993, the Public Assistance (PA) scheme was replaced by the Comprehensive Social Security Assistant (CSSA) scheme with the intention to provide a safety net for individuals or families who are unable to support themselves financially. The CSSA covered seven categories of cases. The three non-able-bodied categories included old age, permanent disabled and temporary disabled/ill health. The three able-bodied categories are single parent family, low earnings and unemployment. The category of Others included all the remaining un-categorized cases. Similar to the PA scheme, the CSSA provided cash assistance to bring the income earnings of affected individuals and families up to a level to meet the basic and essential needs.

The 1993 CSSA scheme was more relaxed and provided a larger coverage than the PA scheme. First, the new scheme obviated the need for recipients to apply for benefits under the previous PA scheme and the Special Needs Allowance (SNA) scheme. There was a real increase from 4% to 37% in the level of benefits for different categories, and the sliding scale for family members was abolished. Thirdly, the permissible limit of absence from Hong Kong was relaxed from 45 days for all recipients to 180 days a year for the elderly and disabled and to 60 days for all other categories.

The CSSA payments are also categorized into three types, namely the standard rates, supplements and special grants. The standard rates are grants paid according to individual circumstances. Supplements included the long-term supplement and the single parent supplement. Long-term supplement is granted to those twelve months or longer recipients of CSSA for the replacement of durable goods. Effective from June 1999, long-term supplement is payable to the non-able-bodied adults and children only. Single parent supplement is payable to single parent family facing special difficulties in bringing up a family. Special grants are monthly grants, which are used to cover regular recognized expenses, and household monthly grants, which are used to cover rent allowance, telephone charge allowance, and water and sewage charge allowance.

All CSSA recipients are eligible for free medical treatment at public hospitals and clinics. The old age CSSA recipients pay nothing for their drugs, medical expenditures on wheelchairs and pace-makers. Other services available to the old age included home care service teams, community centers and social centers. Since many of the services and daily supplements are also provided free of charge, the CSSA payments are indeed the *net income* received.

Three conditions governed the eligibility for CSSA assistance. The residence requirement insisted that the applicant must be a Hong Kong resident with a minimum of one year's residence, though the Director of Social Welfare has discretion. Financial tests included both the income test and asset tests conducted on a household basis. There is no income threshold, but the household's income must be insufficient to meet its total monthly needs. Capital assets included cash, savings, investments, real property and other readily realizable assets held by the household. The value of an owner-occupied home is disregarded, though there are exceptions. A household will not be eligible for assistance if the total capital asset exceeded the prescribed limit. For a single able-bodied adult and a single non-able-bodied adult, the current asset limits are HK$24,000 and HK$37,000, respectively. The criterion is more complicated for a family, as variation exists between the presence of non-able-bodied and able-bodied persons as well as difference between the first and other family members. For each able-bodied adult, the asset requirement is HK$16,000 up to a maximum of HK$64,000 for four or more able-bodied persons. For non-able-bodied adult, the capital asset requirement is HK$37,000 for the first member and HK$18,000 for each additional member. The third condition involved a person aged 15–59 in normal health has to give good reasons for not available for work.

Table 11.16 summarized the aggregate number and characteristics of CSSA cases for the period 1980–2006.[10] There are several observations one can make. The overall picture showed that the situation has deteriorated rapidly since the early 1990s, as shown by the double digit percentage growth rates. Looking at the total number of cases, the 1980–1992 decade experienced a growth rate of 4.7%, as compared to 13.3% in the 1993–2002 decade. The turning point in most categories was in 1992 and 1993 when the percentage increased drastically as a result of the introduction of the CSSA. The experience in the mid-1980s was good as some of the categories (temporary disable/ill health, low earning and unemployment) showed a percentage decline, due largely to the revision and the expansionary nature of the Hong Kong economy.

Although old age occupied the largest percentage share, a number of able-bodied cases have caught up over the years. For example, single parent family has increased its share from 6.4% in 1993 to 12.4% in 2002, and unemployment showed a similar picture with an increase from 4.0% in 1993 to 15.2% in 2002. The number of total CSSA cases has increased by 191.8% between 1993 and 2002, giving the average annual increase of 13.3%. By August 2004, the number of CSSA cases has increased to 295,494, with 64% and 34% claimed by the non-able-bodied and able-bodied categories, respectively. The remaining two percent belonged to the others category.

Between the increase in non-able-bodied and able-bodied cases, able-bodied cases have increased much faster, as shown by the rising percentage share over the years from 11.8% in 1980 to 34.1% in 2004. The number of non-able-bodied CSSA cases has increased by 130.2% over 1993 and 2002, giving an average annual increase of 9.9%, which is more than twice when compared to the decade of 1980–1992. Old

[10]Detailed breakdown of the categories can be found in Li (2006, Table 4.19) or from the data sources.

TABLE 11.16 Number of CSSA cases and percentage shares

Year	Total cases	% increase	% Share		
			Non-able-bodied	Able-bodied	Others
1980–1981	45,664		85.4	11.8	2.8
1981–1982	46,734	2.3	86.8	10.0	3.2
1982–1983	50,111	7.2	86.3	9.6	4.1
1983–1984	54,712	9.2	84.4	10.6	5.0
1984–1985	59,167	8.1	83.7	10.2	5.7
1985–1986	62,858	6.2	84.1	11.7	4.2
1986–1987	62,991	0.2	84.6	11.8	3.6
1987–1988	63,196	0.3	85.5	11.1	3.4
1988–1989	64,180	0.2	86.2	10.3	3.5
1989–1990	65,684	2.3	86.5	10.0	3.4
1990–1991	66,383	1.1	87.0	10.0	3.0
1991–1992	71,294	7.4	86.5	10.4	3.1
1992–1993	79,675	11.8	85.7	10.8	3.3
1993–1994	91,362	14.7	84.8	11.9	3.3
1994–1995	104,807	14.7	84.7	11.3	4.0
1995–1996	129,245	23.3	80.7	14.5	4.8
1996–1997	159,837	23.7	77.4	18.4	4.2
1997–1998	186,932	17.0	76.2	19.8	4.0
1998–1999	227,454	21.7	71.1	27.4	1.5
1999–2000	230,681	1.4	71.7	26.7	1.7
2000–2001	228,060	−1.1	72.9	25.4	1.7
2001–2002	241,673	6.0	71.0	27.5	1.6
2002–2003	266,571	10.3	67.2	31.6	1.5
2003–2004	290,206	8.9	63.7	34.8	1.5
2004–2005	295,694	1.9	64.2	34.1	1.7
2005–2006	298,011	0.8	64.9	33.4	1.8
2006–2007	295,333	−0.9	66.0	32.0	2.0

Sources: *Statistics on the Comprehensive Social Security Assistance Scheme*, January 2004, p. 3, *CSSA Monthly Key Statistics, August 2004, Number of CSSA Cases by Nature of Case, 1980–2003*, Social Welfare Department; *Hong Kong Monthly Digest of Statistics*, Census and Statistics Department, July, 2007, Hong Kong.

age has increased most in the non-able-bodied category with a periodic increase of 145.1% and an average annual increase of 10.69% in the period 1993–2002. All able-bodied categories have increased drastically, with a periodic increase of 674.8% and an average annual increase of 28.1% between 1993 and 2002, which is considered as extremely large when compared to the same percentage (4.7%) in the 1980–1992 decade. The performance for unemployment is the worse, as its periodic and average annual increases are 1,002.4% and 34.67%, respectively, in the period 1993–2002. Thus, even though it is the non-able-bodied category that required more assistance, it is the able-bodied category that has grown most.

Despite the detailed breakdown, the clear message from Table 11.16 is that the welfare provided to the abled-bodied category has increased to about one third of all welfare expenditures since 2002. This occurred despite the low percentage increased since 1999 (except 2002). The CSSA introduced in 1993 has led to drastic increase in welfare expenses by the government. In 1983 and 1984 when the economy was facing difficult times due to the Sino-British negotiation over the future of Hong Kong, the percentage increase in the total number of cases was still below 10%. In 1995 and 1996, on the contrary when the economy was booming, the percentage increases were over 23% in both years.

When the Hong Kong economy was overheated in the mid-1990s, welfare applications should fall, as happened in the mid-1980s. For example, unemployment in 1994 was extremely low, yet there was an increase of 32.4% in 1994, followed by another 81.2% increase in 1995. Although low earnings have a small percentage share, its percentage increase exceeded 70% in 1995 and 1996. In other words, the high percentage increase in the mid-1990s showed that the "welfare net" — both the amount of individual assistance and number of applications — has been widened considerably. There was a clear trend between the performance of able-bodied and non-able-bodies categories. The share of non-able-bodied category dropped from 84.8% in 1993 gradually to 63.7% in 2003. On the contrary, the share of able-bodied category has tripled from 11.9% in 1993 to 31.6% in 2002. There is indeed a need to re-examine the role of welfare expenditures in Hong Kong, as there is a clear case of resource distortion from the trend figures presented in Table 11.16.

Welfare assistance is increasingly given to the able-bodied categories. Each CSSA case may contain a number of eligible members or recipients. In 2002, for example, 93.6% of CSSA cases have eligible members. Table 11.17 further produced a picture of welfare deepening in Hong Kong. By August 2004, an overall of 7.8% of resident population in Hong Kong was receiving CSSA payments, compared to 3.5 in percent 1996. Although old age (60 or over) formed the bulk of the CSSA recipients (equivalent to 17.2% of resident population in 2003), it percentage share has declined from 58.2% in 1993 to 36% in 2006. Both the young (below 15) and adult age population (15–59) have increased their percentage share. The young age group has expanded from 3.7% of resident population in 1996 to 13.3% in 2003. A number of observations deserved some attention. One is the aging of the Hong Kong population. Although it is necessary to take care of the old and aging, but one crucial consideration is the amount of resources geared to the welfare of the aging, and whether resources would be more productive in nurturing the young whom would have years ahead to contribute to the economy. Aging may not entirely be the responsibility of the government, as many retirees and aging people are strong and secured economically.

Secondly, the adult age population (15–59) receiving CSSA payment as a percent of resident population has more than doubled from 1.6% in 1996 to 4.7% in 2003. The large and increasing number of CSSA recipients was putting a lot of burden on

TABLE 11.17 Number of CSSA recipients by age, 1993–2006

Year		Below	15–59	60 or over	Total/Overall
1993	No. of recipients	19,612	30,992	70,456	121.000
	% of total	16.2	25.6	58.2	100.0
1994	No. of recipients	20,257	32,886	71,902	125,045
	% of total	16.2	26.3	57.5	100.0
1995	No. of recipients	31,348	50,679	92,128	174,155
	% of total	18.0	29.1	52.9	100.0
1996	No. of recipients	44,453	69,919	109,012	223,384
	% of total	19.9	31.3	48.8	100.0
	% of resident population	3.7	1.6	11.7	3.5
1997	No. of recipients	57,694	94,007	130,922	282,263
	% of total	20.4	33.3	46.3	100.0
	% of resident population	5.0	2.1	13.8	4.3
1998	No. of recipients	84,064	136,410	148,149	368,623
	% of total	22.8	37.0	40.2	100.0
	% of resident population	7.3	3.1	15.3	5.6
1999	No. of recipients	84,964	138,741	152,802	376,507
	% of total	22.6	36.8	40.6	100.0
	% of resident population	7.5	3.1	15.6	5.7
2000	No. of recipients	81,014	130,704	153,467	365,185
	% of total	22.2	35.8	42.0	100.0
	% of resident population	7.3	2.8	15.4	5.4
2001	No. of recipients	88,978	148,536	159,954	397,468
	% of total	22.4	37.4	40.2	100.0
	% of resident population	8.1	3.2	15.8	5.9
2002	No. of recipients	106,680	189,736	170,452	466,868
	% of total	22.9	40.6	36.5	100.0
	% of resident population	9.9	4.1	16.6	6.9
2003	No. of recipients	118,864	224,339	179,253	522,456
	% of total	22.8	42.9	34.3	100.0
	% of resident population	13.3	4.7	17.2	7.6
2004	No. of recipients	121,762	235,447	184,808	542,017
	% of total	22.5	43.4	34.1	100.0
2005	No. of recipients	116,777	235,494	187,692	539,963
	% of total	21.6	43.6	34.8	100.0
2006	No. of recipients	107,970	225,865	187,776	521,611
	% of total	20.7	43.3	36.0	100.0

Sources: *Statistics on the Comprehensive Social Security Assistance Scheme*, pp. 4–5, January 2004, and *CSSA Monthly Key Statistics*, August 2004, Social Welfare Department; *Hong Kong Monthly Digest of Statistics*, Census and Statistics Department, Hong Kong, July 2007.

the annual fiscal budget, which is shown in Table 11.17. The rising number of the young adults receiving social welfare should ring a bell on a number of issues. Is the education system effective in schooling the young? Are there rising job opportunities? Is the government over protecting the young, turning them into too dependent on government assistance? Should a policy that encourages job opportunity be a better alternative than simply the provision of welfare?

As shown in Table 11.18, the nominal and real GDP between 1980 and 2006 fiscal years have increased by 929.21% and 267.83%, respectively. By comparison, the total expenditure on welfare has far exceeded the percentage of GDP increased. Between 1980 and 2006 fiscal years, total welfare expenditure has increased by 7,823.5%, about 7 folds more than the increase in nominal GDP. In percentage of total recurrent expenditure, it has increased from 2.1% in 1983 fiscal year to 9.5% in 2005 fiscal year.

Table 11.18 provided a drastic picture when looking simply at the amount given out over the two decades of 1980s and 1990s. The speed of increase in nominal terms really throws light on the sustainability of the current welfare system. Their pace of increase in even faster than the rise in Hong Kong's nominal GDP over the two decades. The total welfare expenditure doubled in three years from HK$222.6 million in 1980–1981 to HK$486.6 million in 1983–1984. It more or less doubled again by 1990–1991 when the welfare expenditure reached HK$960.1 million. It took seven years this time, probably due to the strong economic recovery since 1985. But the 1990–1991 expenditure was doubled again in 1993–1994 to HK$2,443.4 million. It took only three years this round. The mid-1990s was an economic booming time, yet it took only two years from the 1993–1994 expenditure to double again in 1995–1996 with HK$4,831.1 million, due obviously to the introduction of the CSSA scheme.

And in the next two years (1997–1998), welfare expenditure was doubled to HK$9,441.3 million, due obviously to the economic hardship brought about by the Asian financial crisis. With the exception in 2000–2002 when there was a small decrease in these two fiscal years, the overall rising trend was alarming. The welfare expenditure doubled again between 1996–1997 and 2001–2002. Thus, in the 22 years between 1980–1981 and 2001–2002, total welfare expenditure had doubled six times. Between 2001–2002 and 2006–2007, welfare expenditure has risen by 22.4%. These percentage increases excluded the additional assistance given in each recent fiscal budgets and Policy Addresses.

The fast increase in welfare in Hong Kong has taken place in two directions: increased payment for each case, and rapid increase in the number of cases and recipients over the years. The pace or speed in which the magnitude of increase is certainly unprecedented, or may even be unparallel on an international scale. No government can afford to double its welfare expenditure in two or three years, as it imposed severe constraints and burdened the fiscal ability tremendously. Welfare expenditure in Hong Kong expanded in both economic good and bad times.

In the duration of stay on CSSA, the end of 2002 figures showed that old age recipients tended to stay long, with 54.2% staying longer than five years. Surprisingly, quite a considerable amount of able-bodied recipients stayed longer than three years. For example, 52.5% and 45.5% of single parent family and low earnings stayed longer

TABLE 11.18 CSSA expenditures

	Annual GDP (HK$ Million)				
Year	Current price	Constant 2005 price	Total PA/CSSA (HK$ million)	% of total recurrent expenditure	Average monthly range (HK$)
1980–1981	143,402	401,392	222.6		
1981–1982	172 965	439,078	291.3		
1982–1983	195,408	452,174	407.8		
1983–1984	216,383	478,942	486.6	2.1	
1984–1985	260,761	526,382	583.4	2.2	
1985–1986	276,823	530,147	625.6	2.2	
1986–1987	319,232	588,657	678.4	2.1	
1987–1988	393,541	667,571	706.0	2.0	
1988–1989	465,245	723,945	779.3	1.9	
1989–1990	536,268	740,032	854.8	1.7	
1990–1991	598,950	768,882	960.1	1.6	
1991–1992	690,324	812,666	1,135.8	1.6	
1992–1993	805,082	862,181	1,408.5	1.7	
1993–1994	927,996	914,285	2,443.4	2.6	2,258–9,857
1994–1995	1,047,470	969,265	3,426.8	3.2	2,459–10,974
1995–1996	1,115,739	991,492	4,831.1	4.0	2,736–12,709
1996–1997	1,229,481	1,033,065	7,127.8	5.3	3,045–15,134
1997–1998	1,365,024	1,085,300	9,441.3	6.3	3,312–16,347
1998–1999	1,292,764	1,019,895	13,028.7	7.9	3,702–16,835
1999–2000	1,266,668	1,045,963	13,623.4	7.8	3,746–14,535
2000–2001	1,317,650	1,129,132	13,559.8	7.4	3,854–14,638
2001–2002	1,299,218	1,134,746	14,404.6	7.4	3,778–14,368
2002–2003	1,277,314	1,155,637	16,130.8	8.2	3,751–14,228
2003–2004#	1,234,761	1,190,376	17,306.2	8.8	3,623–13,483
2004–2005	1,291,902	1,291,139	17,631.0	9.2	3,503–13,430
2005–2006	1,382,590	1,383,049	17,766.3	9.5	3,477–13,646
2006–2007*	1,475,910	1,476,430	17,637.7	9.2	3,487–13,771
% Growth	929.21	267.83	7,823.5		

Sources: Statistics on the Comprehensive Social Security Assistance Scheme, Social Welfare Department; Data on Gross Domestic Product, Implicit Price Deflator and Per Capita GDP, Census and Statistics Department, Hong Kong.
Note: The monthly range depends on the number of eligible members. The 2004/2005 figure is the budgeted total. By August 2004, the actual expenditure made is HK$7.7 billion, equivalent to 43% of the total amount budgeted. Before 1993/1994, the figures were Public Assistance (PA) payments. # = CSSA payment rates have been reduced with effect from 1.6.2003 and 1.10.2003, and not a single payment schedule was adopted throughout 2003/2004. * = revised estimates.

than three years, respectively. Unemployment was the only category that showed a tendency of short stay, with 59.3% stayed less than 2 years. This suggested that unemployment recipients were eager to exit the CSSA scheme once employed. Both old age and permanent disability showed the longest median stay of 5.4 years in 2002, while unemployment showed a lowest of 1.3 years. The overall median duration of stay has increased from 2.4 years in 1995 to 4.4 years in 2002.[11]

The CSSA rates have been adjusted by the Social Security Assistance Index of Prices (SSAIP). Because of deflation since 1999, the combined effect on the standard rates by March 2002 had overshoot by 11%. The government decided to cut the standard rate on June 2003, but the cut was to be implemented in two phrases on October 2003 (by 5.7%) and October 2004 (by 5.4%) for the old age, disabled and sick recipients. Welfare advocates have criticized the move, and urged that the government should increase the standard rates when inflation returns.

Out of the total of 466,868 CSSA recipients at the end of 2002, 97.9% of the total CSSA recipients reported that their country of original was Mainland China, including those born in Hong Kong. Those CSSA recipients whose country of origin was not Hong Kong included recipients from Europe, India, Indonesia, Malaysia, Nepal, Pakistan, Philippine, Thailand and Vietnam. Similarly, 65.8% of the total CSSA recipients in 2002 were not born in Hong Kong, and 14.9% of total had less than seven years of residence in Hong Kong. Table 11.19 showed the new arrival CSSA recipients having resided less than seven years in Hong Kong.

It is clear from Table 11.19 that the percentage share of both new arrival of CSSA recipients and cases have increased over the years and peaked in 2003 and 2004, but has subsided in 2006 when the economy regained a strong growth. In the four fiscal years from 1999–00 to 2002–03, the estimated total CSSA expenditure on new arrival recipients were 13,623, 13,560, 14,405 and 16,131 (HK$ million), equivalent to 10.8%, 11.3%, 12.0% and 12.6% of total CSSA expenditure, respectively.[12] There are reported cases of fraud through hotline, post and email. The average number of reported cases of fraud in the five fiscal years of 1999–2000 to 2003–2004 was 3,216, with an increase of 87.6% between fiscal years of 1999–2000 and 2003–2004. The actual number of fraud cases, however, was much smaller. The average actual number of fraud cases for the four fiscal years of 2000–2001 and 2003–2004 were 346.25 cases, involving a total of HK$74.4 million. By August 2004 in the 2004–2005 fiscal year, the actual number of fraud cases amounted to 302 cases, involving a total of HK$16.3 million.

A reasonable question is to compare if the CSSA recipients are doing better or worse than a similar household in the lowest 15% and lowest 25% of the income bracket in Hong Kong. Table 11.20 showed a rough comparison of average monthly earnings between CSSA recipients and households whose incomes were in the lowest two categories of 15% and 25%. The data on the two fiscal years of 2003–2004 and 2006–2007 are shown. On average, CSSA recipients in 2004 were better off by 108.6% and 46% over the lowest 15% and lowest 25% income households, respectively. However, by 2006–2007 when the economy had picked up considerably,

[11] *Statistics on the Comprehensive Social Security Assistance Scheme*, Social Welfare Department, Hong Kong, January 2004, pp. 9–10.

[12] *Statistics on the Comprehensive Social Security Assistance Scheme*, Social Welfare Department, Hong Kong, January 2004, p. 75.

TABLE 11.19 CSSA recipients with less than 7 years of residence in Hong Kong

	CSSA recipients		CSSA cases	
Month/Year	No. of new arrival	% of total	No. of new arrival	% of total
1/1999	43,218	11.5	23,140	10.1
12/1999	46,198	12.3	24,265	10.7
12/2000	48,824	13.4	24,615	11.0
12/2001	58,576	14.7	29,124	12.2
12/2002	69,345	14.9	36,023	13.7
12/2003	71,927	13.8	40,510	14.2
12/2004	72,816	13.3	41,571	14.3
12/2005	60,178	11.1	37,454	12.8
12/2006	47,732	9.2	31,952	11.0

Source: *Statistics on the Comprehensive Social Security Assistance Scheme*, various years, Social Welfare Department, Hong Kong.

TABLE 11.20 Comparison of CSSA Payments with Non-CSSA Household Incomes

	2003–2004			2006–2007		
		% Difference with non-CSSA households in income group*			% Difference with non-CSSA households in income group*	
No. of household member	CSSA payment* (HK$) (monthly average)	Lowest 15%	Lowest 25%	CSSA payment* (HK$) (monthly average)	Lowest 15%	Lowest 25%
1	3,623	+201.9	+113.1	3,487	+87.8	+12.7
2	5,982	+139.3	–75.9	5,798	+8.1	–18.9
3	7,831	+66.6	–28.4	7,809	–14.0	–33.1
4	9,178	+43.3	–14.7	9,236	–13.6	–31.6
5	10,827	+50.4	–20.3	10,968	–2.9	–23.7
6 or above	13,483	+49.8	–23.7	13,771	+12.9	–8.2
Average	8,487	+108.6	–46.0	8,512	+1.2	–21.2

Source: Social Welfare Department, Hong Kong.
Notes: For CSSA households, figures refer only to number of household members eligible for CSSA. CSSA payments refer to situations when CSSA households do not have income other than CSSA payment. CSSA payment rates had been reduced with effect from June 1 and October 1, 2003 and not a single payment schedule was adopted throughout 2003–2004 fiscal year.

CSSA recipients were worse than the lowest 25% income households by 21.2% on average. In terms of the CSSA payment, the CSSA households with 3 or less members/4 or more members in 2006–07 are receiving slightly less/more than in 2003–2004.

There are several issues one can discuss after examining these materials provided mainly by the Social Welfare Department. The primary question is one of economic responsibility and the avoidance of "rent seeking" activities by individuals on government expenditures. Should the government be responsible for all the expenses of the economically weak individuals and households? There are existing channels and instruments available in the society for every individual and household to progress. All young individuals, for example, are entitled to have the school education available in Hong Kong, and if a young person does well in school and academically, his or her economic future would better be secured as job opportunities become available. On the contrary, if a young individual failed to learn and did poorly in receiving school education, the young person would face a low level of individual potential and endowment, which probably would result in doing a low-paid job and face unemployment possibilities. If the young person is given the opportunity but failed to utilize it fully, who is to be responsible? Economic security can ensure social security. If an individual failed to achieve economic security, his or her social security cannot be maintained. If the government were to provide economic and social security to such an individual, the individual would end up relying on government assistance. As such, there should be a clearer line drawn between the economic responsibility of an individual and the government.

While the government has to spend to provide a safety net for all needy individuals, the government needs to have income and revenue to do so. Equally, there are other urgent and demanding issues that every government has to look into. Every fiscal policy has to consider the global economic scenario. While "investing in future" involved expenditure on items that can generate more income and jobs, welfare expenditure is transfer income, which does not have an investment content. The proactive nature of every government is to ensure that individuals have every opportunity to progress so that in turn they can encourage other individuals to get out of poverty. There is thus a distinction between government economic responsibility and private economic responsibility. Similarly, one has to be clear on the distinction between social cost and private cost. An individual has a life time to seek economic security through the achievement of academic qualification, business and entrepreneurial activities. While the government has to look after the sick and the old, seeking government assistance should be considered as the last resort, especially by able-bodied individuals.

The CSSA scheme is meant to provide a basic need, and the scheme should not be treated as a "bail out" for those economically weak individuals. No government can "underwrite" an individual's economic hardship. A loose welfare system does not only defeat its purpose, it backfires on the other successful individuals and other areas of government expenditures. While the government should help the economically weak individuals, it does not naturally mean that the economically successful individuals have to be penalized. Given the small and open nature of the Hong Kong economy, a heavily committed welfare system can easily over-burden the budget when its revenues slackened in a recessed economy. Secondly, by its very nature, social welfare can never be "enough", and the true nature of "basic need" provision is just the provision of the "minimum" or the "survival" level. All able-bodied individuals should try every mean to seek a higher level of economic security.

The experiences of other advanced countries showed that there are stringent requirements and qualifications for social welfare assistance. For example, welfare payments are tax-tided. Namely, an adult individual may entitle for welfare payment only if the adult individual has previously paid income tax. The idea is that the adult individual can only get back what he/she has contributed to the society through tax payment made previously, and that the individual has to work and pay tax during his/her working life time. Since the society does not economically owe any individual, a minimum, bare-survival level could be given if there was no record of tax payment previously. For a young individual or a school-leaver, the condition could be the amount of tax paid by his/her parents.

Residence requirement can be used as another criterion. To avoid the abuse of social responsibility, new arrivals may not be entitled to welfare payment within a period of time. The idea is to ensure that the new immigrants take care of their private responsibility and are economically secured so that the government would not be burdened by their individual private decisions. One other suggestion in the provision of assistance has a time limit. Recipients are given assistance for, say, the first six months, but new evidence for welfare need has to be provided. The welfare system is constructed to help those needy individuals, not as a mean for individuals to shirk their private responsibility on their own economic security. Other experiences showed that a cap can be imposed, either on the amount given to each individual or on the number of individuals. A combination on different conditions can be introduced to have a more effective and fiscal-sound welfare expenditure formula. It would become fiscally uncontrollable for the government if both the entitlement and the number of entitlement rise continuously.

An extensive CSSA scheme can be economically unsustainable, given the narrow tax base and the fall in revenue during economic recession. It in reality underwrites the economic ills of all individuals, mixes the distinction between private and social responsibility, and burdens the fiscal budget making it unable to self-correct through the balance in revenue and expenditure. As such, the government has no choice but to raise tax. Given the low tax regime in Hong Kong, new tax items have to be explored, which will have a negative multiplier effect on expenditure, income and jobs. An unsustainable, expensive and extensive social welfare scheme could produce a vicious circle of heavy government commitment on welfare, adding disincentives to successful individuals and sending a poor signal to the investors. Ultimately, it would even raise unemployment that required more welfare assistance.

It is true that governments have to assist and help the economically weak individuals and household, but the strategy is to introduce a virtuous circle and not a vicious circle. A virtuous circle encourages incentives and attracts more inward investment. Virtuous circles provide pro-active solutions. Economically weak individuals can be helped through the active process of employment. On the contrary, a vicious circle would be to encourage economically weak individuals to depend on government subsidies, and would blur the responsibility on the part of the individuals to secure the appropriate endowment in the form of knowledge, skill, education and experience.

A revision in the welfare policy is urgently needed in Hong Kong. For example, other than looking at the eligibility criteria, an effective system that is constructed along with the Mandatory Provident Fund (MPF) can be introduced, bearing in mind that the growing aging population in Hong Kong will require more government expenditures eventually. While welfare advocates always urged for more, it has to be debated on both the theoretical level (on economic responsibility division) and practical level (the actual fiscal burden), with the aim to iron out the needy individuals from those trying to shirk their private responsibility and intend to get a "free ride". In short, it is easy to "rent seek" the government and hold the government at random for economic ills. It is common for welfare advocates to dichotomize the issue of poor and rich, as if the presence of poverty is the responsibility of the government. It is fair to say that welfare advocates have to do their part in ensuring that the government is looking after the needy, but welfare advocates should not sentimentalize the issue of welfare assistance, without looking or properly educating the public the revenue side of the budget, which usually has other more global objectives than the single welfare objective.

There is not such thing as a perfect budget, and there are always some sections of the population dissatisfied with the budget. Likewise, it is feasible to pick one aspect that contradicted with another aspect in a budget. The truth is whether one is taking a global view on the budget that looked at the overall direction or a local view that concerned only a couple of items in the budget. A successful budget is one that leads the economy to a higher stage of economic activity, ensures growth and stability, provides opportunity for investors, encourages individuals to seek their economic security through job and employment, balances income with expenditure, initializes economic virtuous circles and draws clear distinctions between private and social responsibilities. No budget can be successful if it only focuses on its expenditure side and pays no attention to its ability to earn revenues. In a democratic system in which social welfare concerns are well represented, and while all welfare advocates always speak for more welfare expenditures, the public also has the right to exercise their judgment on the extensity and intensity of welfare assistance. After all, welfare assistance is funded out of tax-payers' money. Economically weak individuals need government assistance, but it was not the government whom produced economically weak individuals.

11.6 Widening the Tax Base

Despite the growing fiscal deficit since 2000, the government has been slow in taking appropriate actions. If prolonged economic recovery re-appeared, the fiscal deficit could be short-lived and deficit-removing actions might not be necessary. The debate as to the way to tackle the deficit has been divided. On the one hand, the social welfare advocates argued for "demand-driven" policies and fiscal expansion that focused on helping the needy and encouraged the authority to increase spending. The economic growth advocates, on the other hand, suggested "supply-driven" policies and urged the authority to invest more in future and create employment opportunities. Economic security must take precedence over social security, as a bigger economic pie will have more to share. Much of the debate, unfortunately, has focused on re-distributive issues, which concerned short-term impacts on aggregate demand.

When Donald Tsang Yam-kuen was the Financial Secretary before he stepped down to become the Chief Secretary in 2001, he once laid out seven revenue principles: (1) raise sufficient revenue to meet known spending commitments; (2) maintain adequate fiscal reserves to cushion against uncertainties; (3) maintain a low, simple and predictable tax regime; (4) maintain a rigorous user pay system for fees and charges; (5) combat tax evasion and minimize tax avoidance; (6) provide concessions where needed; and (7) avoid fueling inflation.[13]

Donald Tsang Yum-kuen favored privatization of public utilities, such as the corporatization of the Mass Transit Railway (MTR), as a mean of enlarging government revenues to pay for the deficit. Corporatization or privatization has been regarded as an instrument of reducing government involvement in industries, and private involvement and ownership is said to achieve efficiency. Corporatization of public utilities has severely been debated. On the one hand, corporatizing public utilities reduced government intervention. The utility industry became a business entity responsible for its own cost. On the other hand, corporatization reduced the needed government protection, especially in the area of price control and the exercise of monopoly pricing could be disadvantageous to consumer welfare. One also has to take into account of the investment implications in the process of corporatization. Corporatization is simply a switch of investment funds from the private sector to the government, while the ownership is switched from the government to the private sector. This should help the government to solve its fiscal deficit, but may not lead to new investment or building of new utilities. On the contrary, if the investment funds were deployed on new infrastructure project, the income multiplier resulting from the investment could be larger.

The incoming Financial Secretary, Antony Leung, did not take up the corporatization issue immediately. In his first budget speech on March 2002, the economic role of the government was said to include: (1) the maintenance of an institutional framework conducive to market development; (2) the provision of infrastructure not supplied by the private sector; (3) the provision of resources required to raise the quality of human capital; (4) the intention to secure more favorable market access; and (5) consider taking appropriate measures to secure projects beneficial to Hong Kong.[14]

There were no measures to tackle the fiscal deficit in the financial year of 2002–03, except to dip further into reserves. There were even relief measures of HK$6.4 billion that included concession on property rates and a waiver on water and sewage charge for a year. One fiscal action was to cut civil service pay by 4.75% from October 2002, and the cut in salaries would save the government HK$56 billion annually. The boundary facilities improvement tax (land-departure tax) was proposed for the 2003–2004 budget. The operating deficit before investment income on fiscal reserves was projected to expand from 4% to 5% of GDP between 2001–02 and 2002–03. The 2002–03 budget projected that the fiscal reserves would be reduced to equal to 12 months of government expenditure in 2006, namely, from

[13]*The 1999–2000 Budget Background Information for the Financial Secretary's Consultations with Legco Members*, November 1998, Chart V.

[14]*The 2002–2003 Budget Speech*, March 6, 2002, Section 42.

HK$325.6 billion in 2002 to an estimate of HK$271.2 billion in 2006, giving a difference estimate of HK$54.4 billion for the government to maneuver.[15]

The 2003–2004 budget speech on March 5, 2003, was equally mild and lack of action in tackling the deficit.[16] The one effective instrument used in the budget of 2003–2004 was the rise in salaries tax and profit tax rates to 16% and 17.5%, respectively. The level of basic allowance or tax exemption was revised downwards from HK$108,000 to HK$100,000 in two equal phases. Other tax increase included motor vehicles first registration tax and air passenger departure tax. The government also planned to securitize a total of HK$112 billion worth of assets over the next five years in order to make up the revenue shortage.

On the question of tax allowance, some have suggested that individual allowance should be reduced to HK$84,000, or no higher than the average or median wage in Hong Kong. One should not be alarmed by the fall in individual allowance and jumped to the conclusion that Hong Kong is taxing the poor. To readjust the T-shape tax structure back to a V-shape, it is necessary to widen the tax net so that the government can have inflow of revenue in both economic good and bad times. If a person earns less than HK$84,000 a year, the person's tax will be really low or probably children and other exemption would have removed the person from tax payment. Thus "poor" households effectively do not pay tax. On the other hand, it would likely be the young (for example, graduates and school leavers) who are earning HK$84,000 a year to pay some tax. For them to pay tax is reasonable as they have received years of education from the society. Furthermore, the "low" income level of the younger generation would only be "temporary", because when they have gathered more skill or better experienced, their income will rise further. Hence, the young generation should not and would not be permanently burdened by the tax payment at a lower individual tax allowance. One can think of other similar examples.

On the contrary, the fiscal advantage of a lower individual exemption is that when income is falling or the economy is in recession, the government still can levy some revenue from each of the "low" income earners so as to stabilize revenue income, as argued under the fiscal automatic stabilizer. A lower individual allowance, therefore, can serve as an automatic revenue stabilizer for the government in economic poor time. As the experience of the recession years have shown, the government's revenue source had severely been cut once income fell, as many original income tax payers have now fallen out of the income tax revenue net. Thus, the government collected tax from high income earners only, but was constrained with revenue receipts in an economic downturn, as happened after the burst of the economic bubble in 1998.

In the 2003–2004 budget speech, various causes of the fiscal deficit were discussed. These included the impact of cyclical economic adjustment, outward shift of economic activities, rigidity of pay adjustment, population ageing, and decrease in government revenue and so on. Despite the pledge to reduce total public expenditure to less than 20% of GDP, there is no sign of any reduction in government

[15] *The 2002–2003 Budget Speech*, March 6, 2002, Section 62.

[16] *The 2003–2004 Budget Speech*, March 5, 2003.

expenditures in both the 2002–2003 and 2003–2004 budgets. Budget deficit is enlarged by the fall in revenue on the one hand, and the continuous rise in expenditure on the other hand. This is made worse at a time of low economic performance when the public, especially some political opportunists, pressured the government to spend more in order to rescue the various economic ills.

Upon the sudden resignation of the Financial Secretary, Antony Leung, in summer 2003, many believed that his replacement, Henry Tang Ying-yen, will be more business-like in solving the deficit problem. Even though Henry Tang Ying-yen in his maiden 2004–2005 budget speech pointed out that the Hong Kong community needed a "respite" in order to recover from the economic hardship, he re-defined the fiscal role within the concept of "market leads, government facilitates" and brought in new structural directions in solving the fiscal deficit. One revenue gimmick was the introduction of a personalized vehicle registration mark scheme that allowed vehicle owners to choose their preferred registration marks in an open bidding exercise. Secondly, the government at last decided to issue government bonds to fund infrastructure and other investment projects. The proposal was a bond issue not exceeding HK$20 billion (US$2.564 billion) in 2004–2005.

Although Henry Tang Ying-yen pledged to reduce deficit and restored equilibrium by 2008–2009, one other highlight was the optimistic comments made on the goods and services tax (GST) as a long-term instrument in broadening the tax base. Despite the problems encountered in the implementation of GST and the impact on low-income families, a GST of 5% would generate an estimate of HK$20 to HK$30 billion revenue for the government in a full year. As announced in his 2004–2005 budget speech, the Hong Kong SAR Government would set up an internal committee to conduct a detailed and comprehensive study on the implementation of a GST.

The different strategies adopted by the three financial secretaries since the burst of the economic bubble suggested that the government faced a dilemma in rescuing its deficit. If the government responded to popular public pressure by adopting a policy of fiscal expansion, the government would find it difficult to reduce budget deficit, unless economic recovery was forthcoming. The worst scenario would be that fiscal expenditures were used to rescue failed private activities due to economic shocks or uncertain circumstances. For example, the government reimbursed chicken farmers when there was an outbreak of chicken flu in a number of years since 1997. The farmers demanded compensation from the government even though it was primarily a private business. Negative equity holders whom suffered loss in their investment in real estates also demanded assistance from the government. The sudden deterioration in the number of atypical pneumonia cases, commonly known as severe acute respiratory syndrome (SARS), in early 2003 led to a downfall in tourism, restaurants and retail business. There was pressure again for the government to financially assist these businesses.

If not careful, an expansionary fiscal policy could soon develop into a situation of government underwriting private losses. On the contrary, a firm and vigorous fiscal policy that aimed to reduce the deficit first would produce an image of an effective fiscal framework. A reduction in government expenditure may even "crowd in" private investment, as the kind of goods and services not supplied by the government may now be supplied by the private sector. This should encourage more private investment. Secondly, the cut in deficit through cut in spending would not lead to additional fall in fiscal reserve, which is often an indicator of foreign investment attraction. Furthermore, it has not been a common practice for the government to "rescue" the economy, as the role and impact of the government on the economy has always been limited. It is always easier to tackle the deficit when it was small, but drastic and unpleasant actions were needed once the deficit had become too large or beyond the ability of the current generation to tackle. Indeed, it is probably true to argue that the Hong Kong economy could revive once the fiscal deficit was eliminated.

Despite its contemporary nature of the debate, the goods and sales tax (GST) was first discussed in 1986 when the then Financial Secretary, John Brembridge, suggested the introduction of the GST as a solution to the narrow tax base. In 1991, the suggestion by the succeeding Financial Secretary, Piers Jacobs, was to levy on goods at the wholesale level. However, in March 1999, Donald Tsang Yam-kuen, the Financial Secretary at the time of the sovereignty change in 1997, argued that the timing was not right for the introduction of GST despite signs of prolong budget deficits.[17]

In February 2002, a Task Force on the Review of Public Finances was established to identify the nature of the operating deficit. Concurrently, an Advisory Committee on New Broad-based Taxes was established to consider the introduction of new types of broad-based taxes. The Task Force reported in 2002 that Hong Kong faced an ongoing and persistent structural deficit, and priority should be given to the control of government expenditures. The more controversial issue considered by the Advisory Committee was the introduction of the goods and service tax (GST). The more convincing argument is that sales tax was fair and worked like a "consumers pay" system, as the more one consumed the more one would have to pay tax. Others, including the International Monetary Fund (Zee *et al*, 2001), supported the introduction by arguing that GST was common practice around the world, and given sufficient time for preparation, Hong Kong could introduce a GST and should not deviate from the international norm. A study on the tax base by KPMG Consultancy (2001) raised a number of tax principles and tax possibilities. Other than the GST, the more popular tax possibilities included green tax on environmental pollution, boundary facilities improvement tax (land-departure tax) at the border and capital gain tax. In its report in March 2001, the Advisory Committee (2001) pointed out the pros and cons on each new tax possibility and left the decision to the introduction of GST to the Financial Secretary. In conclusion, the Task Force identified that operating deficit in Hong Kong was structural and a broad-based tax system was required. Cyclical deficits would be regarded as 'self-healing' when the economy experienced an up-turn.

There are four important elements in considering an economy's tax base: the number of taxable items, tax rates (both average and marginal rates), tax inefficiency and size of the tax-paying population. The tax structure composes of direct tax, indirect tax and other revenues. The greater the number of taxable items in each

---

[17] *South China Morning Post*, December 6, 2006.

category, the broader the tax base. It will thus be right to introduce new taxable items. Tax neutrality and fairness are some of the governing principles that needed to be considered when new tax items are introduced. One other principle is the "willingness to pay", especially in indirect tax. By "willingness", it means that the tax payer will feel comfortable, or even obliged, to pay, while the tax can be collected quickly and efficiently. Individuals who bet and consume alcohol are quite willing to pay tax. Tax on capital gains has a high degree of "willingness", as individuals are more willing to pay tax on capital earnings than on income. Tax rates are arbitrary, but a higher tax rate always imposes disincentive on the payer. Tax inefficiency concerns the extent of tax evasion and avoidance on the part of tax payers, and the number of agents involved in the process of tax collection.

The tax-paying population is an important element because it has direct impact on the size of the total revenue. How disincentive a tax increase is can also be seen from the change in the tax population. When tax exemptions are introduced, how much revenue will fall also depended on the size of the tax-paying population in that particular category of tax population. One feature that distinguished the tax-paying population and other elements (tax rate, tax efficiency and taxable items) is that the government may not be able to control the size of the tax-paying population, especially involving businesses and investors whom always have a choice. An unfavorable investment climate or a high profit tax, for example, will discourage investors and the fall in business activities reduced the number of businesses paying profit tax. The tax elasticity concept argued that a rise in the tax rate may not result in a rise in tax revenue. This is exactly because the rise in tax produced a disincentive effect and the tax-paying population for that category could have fallen. On the contrary, it is perfectly feasible for a rise in tax revenue as the tax rate falls because the tax-paying population has risen. The revenue raised from any particular tax is the product of the tax rate, tax inefficiency and tax-paying population. These four elements can be used as criteria in judging the various tax proposals.

In the information pack on the 2005–2006 Budget, the Financial Secretary, Henry Tang Ying-yen, listed seven suggestions on new tax items.[18] They were the goods and sales tax, estate duty, capital gains tax, world-wide tax, duty on alcoholic beverages, green tax and tunnel tolls. The introduction of the GST can increase the number of taxable items, but to decide on the tax rate may prove to be problematic. Consumers certainly are unwilling to pay tax on every item they consume. A high sales tax discourages local demand as well as complicates the amount of tourist expenditure in Hong Kong. A low sales tax may impose a high administrative cost and tax efficiency is low as the number of agents involved in the process is large.

There are two major problems in the GST. One key problem of a GST is that the kind of exemption given to particular groups of citizens or goods could have a re-distributive purpose that would be subjected to debate or discretion. Who should be exempted? Which good should be treated differently? Who make these decisions? This will unnecessarily lead to controversy of fairness and social uneasiness as who

---

[18]*The 2005–2006 Budget: Information Pack for The Financial Secretary's Consultation*, November 2004.

should be helped more or otherwise. The government machinery has to be set up to deal with the distributive nature of the sales tax.

Economic freedom on consumption is the major sacrifice people in Hong Kong have to make when a GST is introduced. Being the freest economy in the world, it is highly unwise to learn the experience from other "less free" market economies. Despite the existence of a GST in a number of developed market economies whose economic freedom ranked lower than Hong Kong, experience showed that those economies that have GST also have high salary tax or corporate tax rates and a more frequent occurrence of fiscal deficit. This is related more to the size of the government or the public sector than the need to raise tax. For example, a more comprehensive welfare system and the need to pay for the defense would require a much larger public sector than one that existed in Hong Kong. Comparing merely the taxation structure without comparing the size of the public sector would not be appropriate. Indeed, the case for the introduction of GST should be reversed, and that Hong Kong's experience should be learned by other high tax economies on how a government can manage to excel with a low and simply tax system and structure.

Unintended consequences can also be observed from overseas experiences after the introduction of a sales tax. In retail, for example, business would be clustered around the sales period, typically after Christmas, as price would be lower and more attractive. In some countries, rents from retail shops can be reduced when retail businesses in the off-peak months slackened. Furthermore, despite the discussion on structural deficit, experience in Hong Kong showed that budget deficits were always temporary and would last only for a few years. The GST, once introduced, will become permanent. The estimated amount of revenue from GST (about HK$20 to HK$30 billion) is not that large and could effectively be collected through other items and channels.

While the government was discussing on the GST as a mean to widen the tax base, estate duty was removed. Although the amount of revenue generated from estate duty would be small, it would not be controversial and has little impact on total government revenue, but it might be worth keeping as an additional source of revenue. World-wide tax is worth considering as a long-term objective, but it involved a huge administrative organization. The green tax is good in theory, but the problem rested with the choice. Plastic bags and car tires are not environmental friendly, but there is a lack of substitute. Foam boxes and plastic utensils are wasting natural resources and should be taxed. But it is usually the working population that consumed lunch boxes made of foam materials and wooden chopsticks. Such a tax may raise their cost of living. There is a lot of wastage in all "fast food" outlets. The green tax can actually be incorporated or grouped into the category of cigarette and alcoholic beverages. The capital gain tax is an effective tax as it is levied on "earnings". People will be willing to pay and tax collection will also be efficient too.

Bearing in mind that there would be no "perfect" tax, one could start from the easiest, least costly, least hurting and most willing to pay. The debate on the introduction of the GST became heated in 2006, but then the pressure on widening the tax base was lessoned as the budget has returned to a surplus situation. In July 2006, a 9-month consultation on GST was formally launched, amidst controversies and opposition. In October 19, 2006, the Legislative Council passed a non-binding motion rejecting the GST. On December 5, 2006, the Financial Secretary, Henry Tang Ying-yen announced that the government would stop advocating a GST altogether, arguing again that it was not the right timing, though the rating agencies warned of possible revenue instability.[19]

Li (2006) suggested a total of four strategies that can either singly or in combination be used to tackle potential fiscal deficit resulting from economic recessions. Though no single strategy can eliminate the budget deficit overnight, each of these four strategies can help to reduce the fiscal burden. It is possible that the determination to eliminate the fiscal deficit and the employment of effective instruments itself already could produce stimulating incentives, and send clear messages to investors.

Firstly, the issue of government bonds in the financial year of 2004–2005 showed a structurally correct direction as it could alleviate short-term fiscal ills. In the intertemporal theory in economics, government bonds are used for capital projects and large infrastructure expenditures. Because these projects benefitted the "future" generation mostly, government bonds, if used correctly, primarily engaged future funds for the activities that benefitted the future generation. If capital expenditures are funded by government bonds, there is less pressure on the recurrent expenditures on the "current" generation. The issue of government bonds has other advantages. It would avoid the need to run down the fiscal reserves, and an economy that saves and borrows at the same time is a better strategy than simply running down its reserve savings. While government bonds shifted the repayment burden to later years, current fiscal reserves does not need to experience a large fall. With a low interest rate policy that has lasted for a long period of time and commercial banks lacked diversification in their lending portfolio, the issue of government bonds could absorb the surplus funds in the banks. Furthermore, the issue of bonds can be used as an instrument in expanding the security market in Hong Kong, thereby making Hong Kong a more comprehensive financial trading center.[20]

There are arguments against the issue of government bonds. Although the pre-1997 government has experience in issuing short-term bonds, Hong Kong has prided to be an economy with no debt. The appearance of government bonds may lead, though unlikely for a small amount of bond issues, to a downgrade of Hong Kong's status in international rankings by international agencies. While the issue of bonds has its theoretical backup, it could serve as "the thin end of a wedge", making Hong Kong's economy gradually dependent on government bonds to finance the

---

[19] *South China Morning Post*, December 6, 2006.

[20] In the 2005–2006 budget consultation paper, it was released that the HK$20 billion issued in July 2004 to institutional and retail investors included institutional notes of HK$9.75 billion (US$1.25 billion) denominated in US dollars and the rest of HK$10.25 billion of institutional notes and retail bonds were denominated in Hong Kong currency. The bond floatation in July 2004 set a number of records, including the largest dual currency offering available to both institutional and retail investors. *The 2005–2006 Budget: Information Pack for the Financial Secretary's Consultation*, November 2004.

fiscal deficits and expenditures. The amount of government bonds issued could be small by international standards and demand may not be forthcoming, especially Hong Kong lacks a mature bond-trading market and the transaction cost could be high. World experiences suggested that economies that started using debts for fiscal finance usually ended up with higher debts over time.

The second strategy could adopt an "equal burden sharing" attitude, where the shouldering of the fiscal deficit is shared and spread across the economy. This effectively meant a contraction in the fiscal policy with an increase in existing taxes and reduction in all existing expenditures. Given the handsome tax concessions provided in various fiscal budgets before 1998, the contraction in the fiscal policy would be acceptable. An "across the board" fiscal contraction avoided the unnecessary debates on re-distributive issues of who should experience a greater or lesser share in the deficit burden. Indeed, re-distributive issues of who should have more or less among different sectors in the economy arise when the government pursues a "partial" fiscal contraction. In re-distributive issues, welfare receivers would be reluctant to see their transfer income reduced. Businesses are equally reluctant to pay higher profit tax, especially at a time when retail level is low. Excessive engagement in re-distributive issues could spill-over to undesirable social and political debates.

Theoretically, the contraction in the fiscal policy, especially at a time of economic hardship, would have a "multiplier in reverse" impact on the falling income and consumption. In Hong Kong where the government plays a minor role, the more relevant debate is how much the government should shoulder the burden of an economic downfall. At a public expenditure to GDP ratio of about 20% (see Table 11.3), many argued that the government should trim its public expenditure to below 20% of GDP. There is thus very little the government could do to revive the economy on a short-term basis, the bulk of economic revival must come from the private sector. On the contrary, investment confidence could be revised upwards had the government manage to eliminate its budget deficit within a reasonable time frame. A financially sound government can prove to be an investment attraction in itself, especially in a small open economy such as Hong Kong.

The third strategy is to identify new revenue sources. In addition to the introduction of new tax items, such as the GST or land-departure tax, the government can look for new non-tax revenue channels. One suggestion is the privatization of a number of remote and isolated islands around Hong Kong. Privatization contracts need not be perpetual, but can be for a number of decades, say 50 years. Provided such basic infrastructure as water, electricity and gas, and pier facilities are installed by the government and various environmental requirements are met, private owners can develop these islands either for private usage or for tourist attractions.

The fourth strategy is the reduction of government involvement in public utilities, a so-called "anti-crowding out" strategy. A reduction in government expenditure in public goods and services may invite additional or new investment expenditure by the private sector. The largest three functional expenditure items are health, education and housing. Engaging more private involvement in these functional areas would save the government's purse, and encourage additional investment by the private sector.

By the end of 2004, the Hong Kong has begun to recover. Land sales in the second half of 2004 were promising. Optimists considered that the fiscal deficit could be over in the 2005–2006 fiscal year. As an interim strategy, the government could extend the size of indirect tax by incorporating some of the unpopular items. In a way, Hong Kong does have a GST on a few selected products, such as alcohol and cigarette and motor vehicles, through the system of indirect tax. A "green tax" or tax on environmental unfriendly products can be included in the indirect tax category, thereby expanding the indirect tax revenue.

11.7 Crisis Versus Non-Crisis Policies

The first decade of the post-1997 Hong Kong economy has been characterized by three features (Li, 2006): (1) a young government that ruled a matured market economy, and the lack of experience in governance led to unnecessary challenges with disruptive consequences; (2) a crisis-prone economy that had undergone numerous severe, unprecedented and mass-scale crises that required immediate actions and solutions and deployment of government resources to ameliorate short-term economic ills; and (3) a prolonged economic recession as a result of the burst of the financial bubble and the exposure of structural defects in the economy.

The combination of these three features has led to various policy reorientations. Typically, economic policies have become short-term in order to avoid further economic deterioration. Numerous short-term subsidies and rebates to households and welfare assistance to the needy have been provided in the annual Policy Address in November and the fiscal budget in February. Examples of subsidies and additional welfare assistance from every budget in recent years can be found. The list included the reduction of hotel accommodation tax and air passenger departure tax in the 1998–1999 budget, the reduction of merchant shipping registration and related fees in the 1999–2000 budget, the establishment of a training fund to subsidize small- and medium-sized enterprises (SMEs) in the 2001–2002 budget, the removal of business registration fee and the water and sewage charges for domestic households in the 2002–2003 budget, the establishment of the Film Guarantee Fund to help the ailing film industry and the re-employment training program for the displaced middle-age workers in the 2003–2004 budget, the extension of about 11,600 temporary jobs in the public sector and the establishment of the SME export marketing and development fund in the 2005–2006 budget, the strengthening of home care services for the elderly and the rehabilitation day services for discharged disabled and psychiatric patients in the 2006–2007 budget, the support given to unemployed and low-income people who resided in remote areas to work across districts and provided children from a disadvantaged background with more development opportunities in the 2007–2008 budget, and the provision of electricity charge subsidy in the 2008–2009 budget.

In an economic crisis, it is understandable that the additional government provisions are needed to avoid economic hardships. Policies geared to combat economic crisis tended to be short lived, one-time off and temporary. These are considered largely as demand-driven policies that led purely to increased government expenditure to ensure that the aggregate consumption level would not fall too much and hurt the general standard of living of the public, particularly the economically weaker households. As the examples have shown, quite a number of short-term welfare assistance is provided under the theme of "caring" for the various population groups. These are additional welfare expenses on top of the formal welfare CSSA system. Of course, other policies also benefitted the non-CSSA recipients.

The prolonged economic recession and the frequent deployment of short-term assistance that are mainly demand-driven generated other problems. One problem is the extent of economic distortion resulting from the continuous provision of additional welfare. A "prolonged short-term" actually would become "long-term". As more resources are geared for repeated short-term consumption, less resource would then be devoted to long-term development and capacity building. In the "long-run", the economy becomes weaker, as economic capacity is constrained. The second problem is the growing reliance on government assistance that killed individual incentives for growth and development. The combination of these two problems would lead to economic structural rigidity and distortion at the expense of long-term efficiency and competitiveness of the Hong Kong economy.

In the non-crisis periods on the contrary, more resources should be devoted to long-term development that enhances growth and competitiveness. The obvious examples since 1997 included the Disney Theme Park that provided long-term attraction to the tourism industry in Hong Kong, and the science park in Tai Po that permitted industries to engage more in research and development activities that can widen the economic base and provide more alternatives to investors in Hong Kong. The new airport at Chek Lap Kok that opened soon after the time of the sovereignty change is another example that enhances long-term transport capacity for the Hong Kong economy.

Long-term policies that are geared to promote infrastructure, economic capacity, technological advancement and resource productivity are considered as supply-driven strategies. The ultimate aim is to create more job opportunities, attract investments, and improve the skill levels of workers. These are long-term strategies that may not have immediate results, but will strengthen the economic base against future economic shocks and crisis. Due to the crisis nature of the economy since 1998, there are fewer supply-driven strategies found in the annual budgets. For example, the building of Route 10 highway that connected North Lantau and Yuen Long in the 1999–2000 budget, the initiative to encourage product design activities in the 2004–2005 budget, the establishment of the language fund to raise the linguistic proficiency of university students in the 2006–2007 budget, the provision of WIFI networks in government venues for free usage in the 2007–2008 budget, and the development of the West Kowloon Cultural District in the 2008–2009 budget.

Economic capacity building has for decades been a major long-term goal. The idea is to build up Hong Kong's economic capacity that can absorb as much available investment as possible. Education and training enhance the capacity of human capital. The reclamation of land can enlarge Hong Kong's much needed land resources, while infrastructure provisions have enabled the expansion of economic activities and can benefit a large number of industries, businesses and individuals. In short, the increase in factors of production can ensure an increase in economic capacity, and fiscal policy should assist the supply-side of the economy. With the availability or supply of more factor resources, the economy can expand naturally according to market conditions when demand rises, and the expansion of the economic pie will automatically take care of demand, income and distribution. It is through such a government-business relationship that, on the one hand, the government can improve economic capacity and, on the other hand, the businesses can make use of the resource capacity to invest and promote growth and development.

The focus on capacity building can encourage investment that can provide economic security to individuals. In turn, the higher the level of economic security, the less the need for government support of social security. The fiscal equation, on the one hand, would experience a rise in revenue through tax from greater employment and aggregate demand and, on the other hand, a reduction in the need on social welfare on the current generation. In the end, the government can recover from the deficit, or have more to spend on the needy individuals.

Thus, while most transfer payments are regarded as "terminal" expenditures, most budgetary items could be used as "intermediate" means to build up economic capacity and generate further investment activities. Indeed, a capacity-building oriented fiscal policy could itself be deficit-reducing, as expanded economic capacity would eventually attract investment and help economic revival. On the contrary, a fiscal policy that features highly terminal transfer payments could stimulate domestic demand temporarily, but in theory transfer payments have a weak multiplier effect and a low economic impact.

While education has been emphasized for a number of years and research and development in technology will take a number of years to mature, the government could concentrate on the development of more land resources. Given the advance development and maturity of the Hong Kong economy, additional land resources could provide additional business opportunities. Additional land reclamation, for example, on the north Lantau Island along the Airport Railway, and along the coastline of Castle Peak Bay on the other side of the North Lantau Highway could create a new business district, like that of Tsimshatsui and Central. With the new airport, telecommunication and logistics related industries can establish their business offices and create a clustering effect of business activities.

Another example is the development of marine-related industry, such as the private luxurious boat industry. Hong Kong can become a dominant center for luxurious boat and yacht industry in Southern China. The West Lamma Channel that lied between the west of Hong Kong island and east of Lantau Island, with the Cheung Chau and Lamma Island guarding the south, could provide a natural sea enclosure for the development of yacht and boat racing activities, while back up industries can be developed in the three southeast islands of the Lantau Island, namely Cheung Chau, Hei Ling Chau and Lamma Island. Allowing competition among the suppliers and making boating activities a popular household leisure could encourage the new development of a cluster of industries. Another area for the similar development of marine-related industries would be the Sai Kung area, especially if some of the remote islands can be privatized or open to tourism, leisure industries would then flourish. The sea east of Sai Kung provides a natural marine ground, spreading all the way out to Jin Island or Bluff Island with larger Sharp Island and Kau Sai Chau in the middle.

Property development and residential areas can put more emphasis on quality and size. The establishment of roof gardens and the installation of energy saving devices are examples that could be applied to new apartment buildings. Addition land reclamation can take place in the Tolo Harbor, such that low-rise residential area inter-mingled with waterways so as to create quality living and space. The example is the city of Amsterdam in the Netherlands where waterways are used to divide roads and residential buildings.

These are some examples of capacity building that can enrich the land and natural resources of Hong Kong, though their feasibility needs to be investigated from various dimensions. It is clear that Hong Kong is not short of possibilities. In fact, one can argue that it is strategically a good timing if the government can engage more in capacity building. Given the administrative and planning delays, by the time these large land reclamation infrastructure projects and the subsequent development of clustering industries would obviously take a few years or a decade before economic impacts can be realized. But, with the new capacity, the Hong Kong economy would have moved to a new stage of the economic development.

Following the 2004 Policy Address, the Lantau Development Task force was set up with the intention to consider the economic and infrastructure development in Lantau Island in view of the new airport, the Disney Theme Park in the Penny Bay opened in September 2005 and the proposed Hong Kong-Zhuhai-Macao Bridge that would land in the northwest shore of the Lantau Island.[21] The Concept Plan for Lantau has come up with four themes of development. One theme is economic infrastructure and tourism that would include the establishment of the cross boundary transport hub, a logistics park, a leisure and entertainment center, a new theme park, a golf resort and other resort facilities. The second theme is to maximize the creation potential of country parks that would include a comprehensive network of heritage trails and eco-trails, and high quality-camping sites. The third theme of conservation included the implementation of country and marine parks. These plans and suggestions could form another step in widening the economic base of Hong Kong.

There is thus a need to make a distinction in the government's policy orientation between crisis times and non-crisis times. To begin with, government officials need to have a clear mind in setting appropriate policy priorities. The Hong Kong economy has recovered since 2005, and income growth has been restored. It would be time for the Hong Kong economy to engage more on long-term capacity building, and resources should gradually be geared away from purely welfare provisions that were meant for alleviating short-term economic ills, and concentrate more to enhance investment and job opportunities and diversify the economic base.

Such a distinction in policy orientation between crisis and non-crisis times has not been sufficiently seen in government policies, both in the Policy Address by the Chief Executive and the annual budget by the Financial Secretary. For example, there was an one-off grant of HK$6,000 into the Mutual Provident Fund (MPF) account of individuals in Hong Kong, and an on-off grant of HK$3,000 to the recipients of old age allowance and so on in the 2009–2010 budget, amidst strong economic

[21]Details of the Lantau Development Task Force can be found in the government website at: www.info.gov.hk/planning/lantau.

growth and the looming property price. In further supporting job seekers in the 2010–2011 budget, a cash incentive of HK$5,000 will be payable to each person who has worked for a continuous period of three months after receiving intensive employment counseling and job matching services. Critics have argued that there are insufficient jobs for the young job seekers and there are regional mismatch of jobs. The long-term solution would be to create jobs in the more distant regions, especially the northern section of the New Territories where youth unemployment is heaviest.

The demand-driven, short-term welfare provision and the lack of sensitivity on the need of the economy exploded right after the Financial Secretary, John C. Tsang, delivered his annual budget on February 23, 2011. Section 177 of the 2011–2012 Budget provided another one-off injection of HK$6,000 into the account of all MPF scheme members and others covered by the Employment Ordinance of Hong Kong. Despite its goodwill, the public did not welcome such a policy decision, and the government was embarrassed as it has to made last minute amendment. The problem could be dealt with in a political matured manner by removing section 177 completely and could leave the rest of the sections intact. In Hong Kong, there has been precedence of making changes to the budget after the speech was delivered. In the mid-1980s, for example, the higher tax imposed on cigarettes was removed after the then Financial Secretary, Piers Jacobs, delivered the speech, fearing that there could be more cross-border trafficking.

Given the resilient nature of the people in Hong Kong, and the free, open market system that individuals would prefer to conduct their economic activities, a "welfare for the sake of welfare" approach has been proved to be inappropriate in Hong Kong. The self-drive, business-like, entrepreneurial attitude of people in Hong Kong prefers to exercise their ingenuity in establishing their own affairs and to "catch their own fish". All the government needs to do is to provide a suitable and competitive environment with suitable supplies of manpower and macroeconomic stability. In short, there is thus a need to re-orientate government policies in view of the changing economic scene. At the same time, the public also needs to aware that economic policies differ in different time periods, and a distinction has to be made between policies applicable in crisis and non-crisis times. Short-term welfare expenses are needed during a crisis time, but it could have been misinterpreted as a permanent policy of the government, and that repeated injection of short-term welfare was thought as an instrument for "caring" of the society. In a non-crisis time, people look for economic opportunities as a way to make progress.

11.8 The Art of Non-Intervention

Since the early colonial days, Hong Kong has been designated as a free port that served trade and economic exchanges between Mainland China, regions in Asia and the rest of the world. The economic policy adopted by the colonial government has been the *laissez-faire* policy that required least or non-intervention from the government, and the bulk of the business activities are left to the private sector. Indeed, welfare assistance was non-existed and government assistance to industries was conducted gradually through infrastructure development. This has served Hong Kong well as businesses were encouraged to flourish. Life was always tough for the low income earners, but the abundance of economic opportunities and the resilient nature of immigrant arrivals to Hong Kong required individuals to rely more on themselves and economic progress was made according to their ability and endowment.

Over the decades and years, Hong Kong has been regarded as model of a *laissez-faire* economy with a high degree of freedom. *Laissez-faire* implied a policy of economic liberalism and non-intervention by the government. There is a high degree of privatization in Hong Kong, there were no tariffs, no control on capital movement and the government has kept regulations to a required minimum, and a stable structure of low tax is maintained (Riedel, 1974; Chow and Papanek, 1981).

Being a Scot and probably a follower of Adam Smith, John J. Cowperthwaite became the Financial Secretary for the 1961–1971 decade in Hong Kong. The policy of "positive non-interventionism" practiced by Cowperthwaite has since been considered as the blue print for the fiscal policy in Hong Kong. The "non-intervention" part suggested that *laissez-faire* capitalism will remain, while the "positive" element suggested that the government would take up a positive role in coordinating various economic policies. This included the co-ordination in the provision of infrastructures, transaction cost in economic activities and maintenance of macroeconomic stability.

Positive non-interventionism has served Hong Kong well, as demonstrated by the economic results. For example, it was reported that half of the population lived in acute poverty in the early 1960s, but a decade later, poverty was reduced to 16% of the population, as Hong Kong turned to become the manufacturing workshop of the world. In the 1961–1971 decade, industrial wage doubled and exports expanded to about 13% annually.[22]

However, as Li (2006) pointed out, "positive non-interventionism" was a convenient terminology but did not have a strong conceptual support. One could equally argue that Hong Kong's government has practiced "positive interventionism" since the Second World War. The "intervention" part suggested that the Hong Kong government has in various occasions involved in the economic decision process, especially in market failure cases, provision of public goods and in crisis periods. It is "positive" because in normal circumstances, the government would not intervene in private economic activities, and would prefer not to provide subsidies to any industries in its "hands-off" policy. It was seen as proper and fair, as the subsidy of one industry or business would simultaneously encourage the same demand from another industry or business. In short, intervention was conducted "positively" so that *laissez-faire* market liberalism and other aspects of economic freedom are kept to a maximum. Latter (2007c) argued that the government of Hong Kong has often faced with complications in deciding on a "hands on" or "hands off" economic policy.

There are, indeed, a number of examples of "positive intervention" by the government in Hong Kong. The Hong Kong government since the end of the Second World War has regulated the price of rice. Since it is a major staple food, the unstable price of rice has been controlled so as to avoid instability even in peacetime. The large influx of refugees in the early 1950s led to problems in housing

[22] *South China Morning Post*, January 28, 2006.

and education. A low-cost public housing policy was adopted in 1970s as a mean to provide housing shelter for the low-income groups. The oil crisis in 1973 led to the breakdown of the international monetary system, and the Hong Kong dollar was forced to float in 1974. The Hong Kong authority engaged in the process of purchasing and selling foreign exchange in order to avoid erratic exchange rate fluctuations.

In the financial sector, the government has intervened when there were problems of bank runs. For example, the monetary crisis in 1983 led to the closure of three banks: the Hang Lung Bank, the Overseas Trust Bank and the Hong Kong Industrial and Commercial Bank. The government acquired these banks temporarily but their ownership was later reverted back to private corporations (Jao, 1988). In the 1970s when the export of Hong Kong was threatened by protectionism from Western nations, the government set up a committee in 1977 to promote economic diversification. Government "intervention" occurred in three major economic areas: development of new towns, protectionism on exports and crisis in the international monetary system. It would be more accurate to argue that the Hong Kong government has positively been interfering with the economy to ensure a fair play in the market and maintain macroeconomic stability in various occasions.

There have been regular calls and debates for government intervention over the decades. In the early 1980s, for example, when the other three East Asian economies of South Korea, Singapore and Taiwan were heavily engaged in the development of the electronics industry, calls were made then to the Hong Kong government to provide more resources for the development of the electronics industry. The argument then was that Hong Kong might lag behind the development of other neighboring economies. The statistics showed that Hong Kong's input into research and development has increased only from 0.47% of GDP (HK$6.2 billion) to 0.79% of GDP (HK$11 billion) between 2000 and 2005, but this is a far cry when compared to neighboring economies, Mainland China spent 1.34% of GDP, Taiwan 2.52% of GDP, South Korea 2.85% of GDP and Singapore 2.36% of GDP.[23] Academics also talked about the "limits of *laissez-faire*" when it comes to innovation policy (Fuller, 2010).

However, the Hong Kong colonial government at various times had stood firm on "positive non-interventionism" and avoided the provision of subsidy to individual industry, fearing more would be needed for other industries. Given the small nature of the government size and public spending, it would not be appropriate for the government to involve in individual industries. Positive non-interventionism was then defined as "an economic policy whereby business decisions are left to the private sector. The government will generally not intervene — through subsidies and direct provision of services, for example, — and when it does, it does so only in ways that will make the economy more efficient, effective and fair".[24]

Looking back, was it a wrong decision not to subsidize the electronics industry in the 1980s? Evidence could speak for itself. In terms of GDP per capita today, Hong Kong's GDP per capita today is probably higher than that in Taiwan and

---

[23] *China Daily Hong Kong Edition*, September 5, 2007.

[24] *South China Morning Post*, September 17, 2006.

South Korea, and similar to Singapore. Furthermore, competition has led the electronics industry to new destinations in Mainland China, Malaysia and other Southeast Asian countries. In the meantime, Hong Kong has expanded to other areas of economic development since the 1980s.

Some have argued that situations have changed since sovereignty reversion in 1997. Hong Kong now is part of Mainland China, but it remained debatable whether economic policy in Hong Kong should take a 180 degree turn from "non-intervention" to "intervention". One basic question or attitude is whether economic development in Hong Kong should be fitted and aligned into the overall development in Mainland China and welded completely into the overall Mainland China economy, thereby evaporating the "Hong Kong advantage" gradually, or whether Hong Kong should make use and take advantage of the economic development in Mainland China for the betterment of the Hong Kong economy, while keeping and even deepening Hong Kong's position. There is a subtle difference in the two views, and economic outcomes can be very different.

It is true that the Hong Kong economy has undergone financial crisis and economic recession, and central government since 1997 has aided Hong Kong in various times. Indeed, in an article in 2009 entitled "The Story of a New Policy" reported that since 2003 Beijing's policy on Hong Kong SAR has changed from "non-interfering" to "positively interfering or intervening", especially in political issues.[25]

Indeed, there are a number of examples in the years after 1997 that the Hong Kong SAR government has intervened in individual businesses and industries. One example was the assistance given to the small- and medium-sized enterprises (SMEs) that began soon after the outbreak of the Asian financial crisis in 1998, though the various relief packages to avoid severe declines in employment in different industries. For example, immediate after the 2008 financial crisis, the rescue plan released by the Chief Executive in December included a HK$100 billion backing for various businesses.[26]

Other typical relief measures in recent years included the one-off tax reduction, exemption of rates, payment of rents for public housing estate tenants and an extra month payment of social welfare disability allowances, transport subsidies provided to youths attempting to find jobs in the central and major business districts and subsidies to households for their electricity bill payment.[27] Some relief measures do interfere with the private lives of individuals and their choice in their economic decisions. For example, assistance was given to children attending kindergarten school organized by the government but not privately run kindergarten schools. Why children attending different types of kindergarten schools are treated differently? Section 133 of the 2010–2011 Budget stated that "many parents of low-income families want their children to receive homework guidance after school" and HK$110 million would be earmarked "to provide after-school homework guidance

---

[25]Cheng (2009).

[26]*South China Morning Post*, November 11, 2008, and December 9, 2009.

[27]Press release on "Economy", Information Services Department, Hong Kong SAR, May 27, 2009.

for students from low-income families and help them with their studies."[28] Why the government assumed that after-school tutoring was needed for children from low-income families? Is there something wrong with the education provided to children from low-income families? Why the government is stigmatizing children from low-income families as children who needed assistance in their after-school studies? Helping with low-income families is one thing, but not to the extent of interfering with individual decision making.

Critics have been arguing that taxation can be more relaxed when the pressure on the government's revenue income has been eased due to economic recovery and recovery from the stock market and property market.[29] Other more controversial examples of subsidizing individual businesses and industries included the subsidy given to the film making industry, the tourism industry and loss-making ferry companies that provided six ferry services to off-islands. In the film industry, the government's direct investment would be limited to small and medium local production and capped at 30% of the production cost.[30] Why direct investments are provided to the small and medium film-making companies and not jewelry companies, restaurants and so on? Where is the line that divided assistance from interfering or intervening?

The government's own financial watch dog, the Audit Commission, reported annually how government funds could have been misused, misallocated or wasted. In 2008–2009, for example, it reported that 81% of animal management budget was spent rounding up stray dogs and cats, some newly build bridges and subways were underutilized, the Hong Kong Chinese Orchestra spent over HK$2 million on drums and tickets for its own concerts to give away, and 78% of post offices are loss-making and so on.[31] The government audit reports served as effective checks on the use of government funds, and identified departments and government units specified in the annual report would have to make improvements accordingly.

Since the economic recovery in 2005, the government has identified in various Policy Addresses and budget speeches a number of pillar industries and sectors for development. The four economic sectors are trade, tourism, logistics and finance, while the six economic pillars are education, medical services, environmental industries, innovation and technology, culture and creative industries, and food safety and product testing.[32] These specifications are welcome by the public at large as they basically identified the new comparative advantages for the Hong Kong economy.

It has been argued that identifications of potential advantages are within the bounds of positive non-intervention. The recent term used by the former Financial Secretary, Henry Tang Ying-yen, is "big market, small government". There is, however, a subtle difference. Similar to the term "market leads, government facilitates" that adhered to the principle of intervening in business matters when needed.[33]

[28] *The 2011–2012 Budget*, February 23, 2011, Hong Kong.
[29] *South China Morning Post*, July 16, 2007.
[30] *South China Morning Post*, November 29, 2009, and February 22, 2010; *Mingpao Daily*, April 20, 2010; *The Standard*, March 8, 2007.
[31] *South China Morning Post*, April 22, 2010.
[32] *South China Morning Post*, July 6, 2009.
[33] *South China Morning Post*, September 17, 2006.

"Small government" directly implied keeping government expenditure and the size of the civil service under control, but can still intervene and may deviate from the free market economy. The lack of a good explanation for government intervention in specific industry has led critics to accuse the government of cronyism and favoritism, and served as a poor precedence to request from other businesses that might have rested interests in seeking subsidies from the government.

The debate on "positive non-intervention" was highlighted when the Chief Executive, Donald Tsang Yum-kuen, remarked in September 2006 that Hong Kong "no longer has a policy of positive non-intervention" after a summit to discuss the opportunities presented to Hong Kong by the Mainland China's 11th Five-Year Plan. A total of 33 individuals from the business and academic sectors were invited in September 2006 to attend the government's Economic Summit on China's 11th Five-Year Plan and the development of Hong Kong, though critics questions the summit's exclusivity.[34] It was argued that the change of direction was needed as Hong Kong's economy has become "marginalized" by the rapid growth in Mainland China, and a position in Mainland China's five-year plan might help to rescue Hong Kong. In the 2009 budget speech, the Financial Secretary, John C. Tsang, elaborated that "the government will act as a more proactive market facilitator in economic development when necessary. It is necessary for Hong Kong to reposition itself in the national plan. The past practice of enterprises moving ahead of the government may not always suit the development trend. The government will play an increasingly important role as a 'champion'".[35]

The Chief Executive, Donald Tsang Yum-kuen, further elaborated the "big market, small government" mentality to mean that the government "responds to the needs of the market and do its best to support and promote economic development within the limits of a small government". Various members from the Executive Council and Legislative Council have either supported or criticized the remark. The Executive Council convener, Leung Chun-ying, raised the issue of the government's role in view of the rapid changes in the mainland and asked if Hong Kong should review its experience and cope with the new environment with new thinking, raising the fundamental question on the structure and functions of the government. Another Executive Council member, Bernard Chen, held the view that Hong Kong is entering a period of pragmatic intervention but "we still need defenders of *laissez-faire*". The former Secretary for Security, Regina Ip Lau Suk-yee, remarked that the principle of positive non-intervention "had become obsolete and was in need of change". Another Legislative Council member, Audrey Eu Yuet-mee, queried the Chief Executive's interpretation as it would "mean that the government does intend to intervene in the private sector without telling us when, how or under what circumstances", and that intervention could lead to cronyism and political favoritism once it moves away from a level playing field.[36]

[34]*Our Way Forward — Action Agenda on China's 11th Five-Year Plan and the Development of Hong Kong*, Economic Summit, Hong Kong SAR Government, January 22, 2007a.
[35]*South China Morning Post*, September 11 and 13, 2006; January 17, 2007; April 7 and December 5, 2009.
[36]*South China Morning Post*, September 6, 12, 13 and 24, 2006, and October 24, 2008. *The Standard*, September 14 and 19, 2006, and March 16, 2007.

In an article entitled "The End of the Hong Kong Experiment" published in The *Wall Street Journal* on October 6, 2006, Milton Friedman, the 1976 Nobel-Prize-winning economist, made a direct comment that it was wrong and "sadly unsurprising" for Hong Kong to give up the *laissez-faire* policy that had led to its continued prosperity since the end of the Second World War. Abandoning the non-intervention policy would "result in an overzealous government that could cause many "imperfections" in the city's economy". A key ingredient in the *laissez-faire* policy is the market ability that self-eliminates imperfections long before the government gets around to it. Friedman noted that there has been strong pressure for Hong Kong to move away from *laissez-faire* since Mainland China's resumption of sovereignty, but remarked that abandoning the long-cherished free market philosophy "would make Hong Kong move into China's direction faster than the other way round". Edmund Phelps, the 2006 Nobel Prize-winning economist, concurred with Friedman's remarks and added that "it would be a pity if the tiger hanged its stripes and became a model of corporatism and reckless interventionism".[37]

A politicized economic policy could deviate from its original intention and different agents with rested interest would interpret the politicized policy differently, and the lack of consensus may itself does harm to the however well-intended policy. Since the mainland economy is a young and a much larger market than the much saturated market in Hong Kong, businesses in Hong Kong certainly may prefer to see policies that can orientate them to the mainland market. However, economic policies should not be influenced by personalities. Effective policies should be kept as they ultimately serve the interest of everyone in the economy.

11.9 The Dividing Line: Private Cost Versus Social Cost

Economic policies should not be politically oriented, as its intention is to promote economic growth and development that shall benefit all. However, economic policies in practice have been used for political ends. In political elections, it is easier to advocate for welfare-oriented policies and large government expenditures on welfare and subsidies. Everyone likes to have a "Santa-Claus" whom could endlessly provide Christmas presents. It is thus politically appealing for politicians to argue for more welfare as if the government is all-powerful in providing assistance. In economic terms, welfare provisions imply that individuals are shifting their survival cost burden to the society, thereby pushing the burden of their private cost to the enlarging social cost. In a strong welfare economy, it would be the government whom provided everything to an individual: housing, education, health, employment and so on.

On the contrary, in a capitalist, *laissez-faire* free market economy, it is the individuals whom are free to decide on their economic choice, and as such individuals are supposed to have taken up their own private responsibilities. Thus, it would be the individuals whom have to bear their own private cost in investment, housing, health,

[37]"The End of the Hong Kong Experiment", *The Wall Street Journal*, October 6, 2006; *The Standard*, October 17 and 23, 2006; *South China Morning Post*, September 27, 2006.

education and so on. In political terms, classical economists would argue for a supply-driven economic policy that encouraged the creation of jobs, and business prosperity that permitted full employment. Once individuals have achieved economic security, they would have the resources to take care of their social and welfare needs. The government will serve only as a facilitator, leaving much room for individuals to make economic progress. In other words, when individuals take up their own private cost, less is needed for government assistance and welfare, and this reduces the high social cost subsequently. The government will be more efficient and may even have more resources for construction that benefit the long-term development of the society.

There are, however, grey economic areas commonly known as market failures that involve the government because there are decisions that require macroeconomic decisions that shall affect the stability of the economy as a whole. These grey economic areas include the emergence of economic and financial crisis when there are shocks that require short-term quick-fix in order to avoid further deterioration, the provision of infrastructure that provide avenues for long-term development, the provision of public goods that may require high fixed cost and the economically weak individuals whom need welfare assistance in their economic and social survival.

In an economic or financial crisis, there is definitely the need for the government to exercise a quick-fix to avoid further economic and social deterioration, and provide policy alternatives for economic revivals so that the economy can get back to its own path of development. In Hong Kong, there have been periodic crises, either in such individual sectors as banking crises or trade protectionism, in such natural problems as water shortage, in such political unrest as demonstrations, in such external problems as the oil crisis and financial crisis, and in such health hazards as the avian flu and the severe and acute respiratory syndrome (SARS) pandemics.

In the provision of infrastructure, such as bridges, reservoirs, tunnels, highways, high speed trains and airports, there are various social and economic dimensions that the government has to consider. One dimension is the involvement of a large fixed cost that may not be profitable for a long time. Private investors may not be interested, and the involvement of the government could facilitate and speed up the construction. The other dimension is the price charged after the construction of the infrastructure. Would a private supplier charge a monopoly price if there is a lack of alternative? This involves decisions on economic sustainability and fairness to the users. The ultimate objective is to avoid unnecessary high price that burdens the public at large. If the government is involved, either as the sole investor or in an investment consortium with private enterprises, the government will have to take into account the affordability of the public.

In the case of public goods provision, the government involvement can be controversial. There are so-called social capital goods that have the excludability problem, such as parks, cultural centers, museums, radio broadcast, cemetery, police and security, post office, fire service and prisons, street lighting, and sewage and so on. These social capital goods are mostly supplied by the government entirely, but can impose a charge on users in some cases. A number of public goods in Hong Kong are supplied on a private basis, or there are dual supplies by both private and public organizations. The media, transports, electricity and gas, education, health and housing

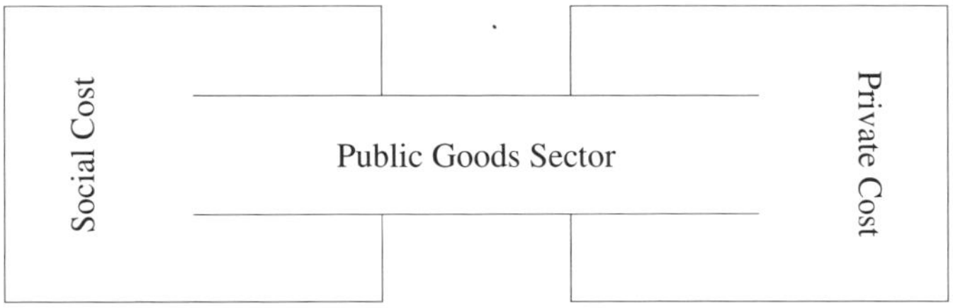

FIGURE 11.2 Distinguishing between social and private cost

in Hong Kong all experienced a dual supply system of both private provision and public provision. There are two major advantages in the dual supply system. One obviously reduced the need for government supply, as private provisions helped to reduce government expenses. The other advantage is that the public can have a choice. Since the kind of medical service one receives, the kind of kindergarten and schools one prefers to send their children to, and the kind of living conditions and location are very personal, it is best to allow individuals to have a choice in their selection of public goods. Hong Kong citizens are used to the dual supply system, and individuals can have a choice, while the bottom line is that there are also public provisions individuals can turn to.

Consider the situation shown in Figure 11.2. On the one hand, there are private decisions, such as investment in stocks, holiday destinations, consumption behavior, marriage and family bearing and so on that involved only private costs. Individuals will have to pay for all these activities and bear the economic outcome and responsibilities. On the other hand, there are a host of macroeconomic activities conducted by the government, such as crisis management, infrastructure construction, and government administration and so on. These social costs are shouldered by the taxpayers.

Complication arises when public goods are involved. A number of public goods that benefit the private individual but the cost are shifted to or born by the government. In education, health and housing, the social costs are acceptable because they produce a more healthy and productive workforce that benefit the society at large. Social cost given to welfare is acceptable so long as the insecure individuals do require assistance, and not taking advantage of the system.

The *laissez-faire* policy in Hong Kong can be summarized in Figure 11.2 and that the bulk of individuals will take care of their private decisions and bear their private cost. The government takes a back seat, serves as a facilitator in economic development and acts as a fire-fighter in time of economic crisis, conducts the appropriate infrastructure development and manages the public sector in order to produce economic efficiency and productivity, maintains macroeconomic stability and engages long-term development to create new comparative advantages. Government administrators are truly 'civil servants' that served the civic aspect of the society. The more controversial area is the provision of public goods, and how much provision of social cost should the government bears. And whether in the process of public goods provision the government has unnecessarily stepped into the private decisions of individuals, unnecessarily shouldering the social cost that are supposed to be taken care of by the individuals.

Consider some examples. It is true that the government shall provide education to all the young school children, and provided that the education system is sound, then whether an individual school student required after-school academic tutoring shall be the decision of individual student. For the needy, the provision of welfare is necessary, but whether a child in a welfare-assisted family needed to attend piano class shall become the decision of the assisted family. How much the government should decide on the needs of every individual, and shoulder the private cost? Getting married and deciding to have a family is a private decision, and individuals should have the economic mean to do so. However, when a man in Hong Kong got married in Mainland China and decided to have children is a private decision. But if the man does not have the economic means to raise the family when the family comes to Hong Kong, welfare assistance will have to be provided. Even though the society should shoulder the welfare burden of needy families, the question is whether it is acceptable for the married man to pass his own private cost to the society and let the tax payers shoulder the social cost of raising his family. Similarly, the aging population is growing in Hong Kong, but many aging people have wealth and may not need welfare assistance. Caring should be given to those who need, but shall not assume the same for all aging population.

The line that divides intervention from non-intervention is the distinction between private cost and social cost. Non-intervention implied that private individuals shall shoulder their own private cost. Intervention stepped in when the individual passes on his or her private cost to the public and let the taxpayers to shoulder the social cost, or the government engages its expenditures that interfere with the economic decisions of the individuals, and have voluntarily incorporated the private cost into social cost, thereby enlarging the fiscal burden of the government. In short, individuals should not be allowed to "rent seek" the social cost and hold the government at random.

In between, there are grey areas, and to minimize the social cost and allow maximum economic freedom, the Hong Kong system allowed dual supply in a number of public goods to ensure choice, minimize unnecessary government expenditure and at the same time ensure a social tolerable minimum level so that no individuals shall fall below a certain standard.

It is worth to clarify more on welfare assistance. In the provision of welfare, the demanders always wanted more, and there are always reasons that more should be given to the needy demanders. It is rare for anyone to advocate for less welfare provision. What involved here are both a fiscal measurement as well as a social measurement. The fiscal measurement is probably the income and expenditure equation. Criteria used can include the percentage growth rates, the size of public expenditure as a proportion of GDP, investment for the future and so on. How much the government should help is indeed the more relevant question. By definition and by its very nature, welfare assistance can never be enough. One should note that the government itself does not have wealth, and every expenditure the government makes must come from revenue, which can either be derived from past saving (reserve), current income (budgetary revenue) or future income/saving (borrowing).

In order to create wealth for the individuals, a sustainable fiscal strategy is one in which government expenditures are geared as much as possible to future investments and not to current consumption.

The government's social responsibility is to ensure that everyone in the society has equal opportunity in enriching their endowment. Whether an individual has fully utilized and benefited from the government's social provisions depends a lot on the individual. There is thus an involvement of private responsibility. For example, while education provision is made available, and if a young person does not progress in learning, and becomes unemployed when the person leaves school, the question is who should then be responsible for the person's economic welfare? Since the education opportunity is provided (social responsibility), but if the young individual does not make effective use of the education provided (private responsibility), should the government take the entire social and economic responsibility for the person?

The practical question is to what extent the government should shoulder the social responsibility of a private act. And if government assistance is provided, what will be the benchmark? Should government assistance be the entire amount, half, or one quarter of the total private cost. If the government does not financially bail out loss-making firms, should the government bail out economically unsuccessful individuals? Should a young person be aware that an uneducated worker will face economic insecurity in future and should a retire person be informed that the cost of living after retirement depends to a large extent on the person's life-time saving?

It is true that there are always non-able individuals who have nowhere to turn to except the government, but it is equally true that the government should not be held entirely responsible for economic failures of the individuals. At best, the government assistance can only help minimally. This explains why fiscal expenditures have to be geared to future investment, while the government's social responsibility is to ensure that maximum economic potentials and opportunities are available. Individuals are dominantly responsible for their own economic performance. Seen in this light, the government's social welfare expenditure should best be equivalent to only some portion of the entire private cost.

11.10 A Crisis-Contained Fiscal Structure

Since Hong Kong's sovereignty reversion in 1997, there are a number of features that occurred repeatedly in the fiscal policy. One is the emergence of crises that forced the government to take drastic and short-term actions in order to alleviate the worsening situation. As the government attempted to address the short-term economic ills, less attention and resources were devoted to long-term development of the economy. A somewhat unintended consequence is that the prolonged and repeated "short-term" activities turned eventually to become "long-term" overtime, and that short-term assistances had become "permanent" and were included in many policy addresses and annual budgets. The public has gradually come to take it for granted that the government will feed them with assistance in both good and bad times.

The second feature is that the various crises have generated uncertainty and instability in government revenue, resulting in the emergence of shape swings between large deficits and large surpluses within a few years. Thus, in one year the government was faced with rising deficits and drew down reserves, while in another year within a short time, the rapid recovery in the stock and property markets has enabled the government to revenue large surpluses. Instead of paving the way for more long-term strategies that shall build up the economic capacity of Hong Kong, the presence and occurrence of fiscal extreme changes have unfortunately amplified the call for assistance and more government welfare-related expenses, in addition to the normal expenditure committed under the social welfare items. Furthermore, once the fiscal reserve has fallen, the government may not have the political will and support and become reluctant to increase the size of the fiscal reserve to its higher level even though there is fiscal surplus, as the government would bow to public pressure of more expenditure and welfare.

Since 1997 and due to the emergence of crises, the government has adopted a somewhat unstructured approach to provide assistance and subsidies to households. One unintended consequence is that this may gradually have cultivated and nurtured a more reliant, subsidy-dependent and welfare-sweetened economy. As a result, those who would like to receive welfare complained that there was not enough, while those who would like to know what the government's intention also disagreed with the ad hoc provision of assistance. Some even argued that the government's approach to welfare is personality driven. In short, the government's provision of short-term assistance is getting the worse of two worlds.

Taking into account of the post-1997 features, uncultivated behavior and unintended consequences, there is a need to formulate an appropriate approach and strategy to Hong Kong's fiscal policy. Firstly, there is a need to distinguish between the need for current consumption, especially welfare to the needy, and the need to steer the economy for long-term development. Secondly, there is the possibility of economic shocks and crises that would destabilize government's revenue and expenditure. Thirdly, a fiscal policy has to be formulated and structured into a transparent system whereby everyone knows the rules and should not be personality-driven.

One possibility would be to create a "crisis fund" within the existing fiscal structure. The "crisis fund" could be created from devoting a portion of the fiscal reserve, and its funding would be adjusted according to changes in the size of the reserve resulted from changing economic conditions. The "crisis fund" would then be used entirely for the management of various crises to assist and replenish the economic losses resulting from economic hardships. Thus, all future assistance due to sharp economic changes will be catered for from the "crisis fund". In a non-crisis period, the "crisis fund" can simply cumulate and grow. The larger it grows, the more it has for the future use in helping the needy should crises occur.

With an item specifically addressed to crisis expenditures, the annual fiscal budget could then return to its normal functions of promoting long-term development, creating new comparative advantages, enable more business-friendly policies to attract new investment that can diversify and expand the existing economic capacity of the Hong Kong economy. The creation of the "crisis fund" within the existing fiscal framework can have the advantage of maintaining fiscal stability on the one hand, and have sufficient funds for crisis management when needed on the other hand. By letting crisis management as a separate fiscal item, resources can then be geared for other meaningful purposes, while at the same time there is financial insurance should economic and financial crisis emerges. In other words, financial crisis will automatically be contained and incorporated within the existing fiscal structure, and the budget will have ready funds to deal with expenditures arising from crises, shocks and uncertainties. As such, fiscal stability can be maintained and deepened.

11.11 Conclusion

Fiscal policy has always been a controversial subject, as non-economic considerations often enter into fiscal decisions. One problem is the ever changing economic conditions that the government has to address. While economic development and growth are long-term and required consistent policies, sudden economic and other shocks may steer the government's fiscal framework to short-term ends. It does require leadership, skill and vision in the government in gearing the fiscal policy appropriately. While it is easy to demand for more government expenditure and assistance here and there, one need to bear in mind that every item of expenditure the government made has to be matched with an equivalent amount of revenue elsewhere. Thus, it would be appropriate to think of the revenue side than on the expenditure side of the equation.

The budget has to be balanced eventually, and what the government spends must equal to government earning somewhere. In Hong Kong, the government has no choice but to balance the budget, either annually or over the business cycle. While the budget can be used to facilitate private economic activities, to enrich capacity building and to amass social capital and wealth, the budget does play a re-distribute role among the different sectors of the society. The budget thus has two alternative roles of growth-promoting or welfare-redistribution. Care should be exercised in whether the budget should be presented and discussed as a whole, or merits should be conducted on each individual item in the budget.

The Hong Kong experience showed that in general fiscal policy is growth-promoting. Bearing in mind that there is always a certain degree of inequality, a budget should be seen on its entirety so long as it does promote growth in an upswing of the economic cycle or prevent possible recession in an economic downturn. A popular demand on the part of the government is always that the government should not cut its expenditures, nor raise revenues. One can often hear people accusing the government by saying "it is not enough", or "the government should do more here and there". From the welfare point of view, government expenditures can never be enough. From the government's point of view, expenditures must be balanced with revenues. The government must earn before it spends and will end up with deficits if the government reduces its revenue capability in an economic upswing and engages in excessive spending in an economic downturn.

While everyone concerns the overall economic picture in Hong Kong, it is not surprising that individuals take a micro view and concentrate often on the discussion of individual items in a budget. Individuals will often react and voice their opinion based on the individual items of the budget. Individual public opinion obviously concentrates on the individual fiscal items, emphasizing often the re-distributive role of the government instead. Discussion on re-distribution is never "Pareto optimal" and is often socially divisive, as one's welfare gain becomes a burden on another.

While the government should welcome public opinions, the question is whether the government is simply responding to public opinions or taking a lead in the formation of public opinions, however pleasant or unpleasant the outcomes could be. Typically, given the diversity of views in the society, government will hear opposing views on any issue. As such, while the government is listening to public opinions, ultimately the government has to form its own policy by adopting a more proactive strategy. A leading government would provide a well-thought and well-coordinated policy before presenting and explaining it to the public, with the intention to convince the public that the government has been acting on a *bona-fide* basis for the public. In other words, what the government has to win is public support, rather than avoiding public criticisms.

The public should understand the limited role of the government in an open economy, and it would be devastating for the government to "underwrite" or "bail out" individual economic activities. In an economic prosperous time, some individuals will gain more than others. Equally, in an economic difficult time, some individuals will face more difficulties than others. Within its own financial limits, the best the government can do is to ensure no one would fall below the survival line, but should not provide guarantee to individual private economic activities.

Hong Kong's fiscal policy is in a sense standing on a crossroad. A re-structuring of the budgetary performance could impose short-term economic unpleasantness, and many active political opportunists would certainly make use of the occasion to politicize government activities, generating uneasy sentiments. On the contrary, what most weak governments in many developing countries experienced is fiscal deterioration at a time of economic downturn, and the severe deficit reduced fiscal creditability. In Hong Kong where government borrowing is uncommon, a decline in fiscal reserve adds extra pressure on the Hong Kong currency, and the economy-wide risk that the currency faces is certainly not a comforting sign.

Hong Kong should also have learned a lesson of tax concessions at a time of a booming economy. While the various fiscal items could provide an income stabilizer to businesses and individuals, the government should also maintain a number of revenue stabilizing mechanisms in economically bad times. Fiscal prudence has proved to be a high-handed strategy for the open economy of Hong Kong, regardless of the different stages in the economic cycle. People in Hong Kong should realize that the government does not and cannot bail out individuals' economic hardships. Equally, a fiscally sound government is itself an attraction and a base for economic recovery. Fiscal politicization would weaken the economic structure and distort economic resources. While individuals have to give their priority in solving the fiscal problem, the government has to show sufficient vigor and determination in their policy decisions.

Fiscal freedom is a major pillar of economic freedom. It showed the important role of the government in nourishing individual freedom, and how the exercise of economic freedom among individuals is regulated and maintained in a civilized and responsible manner, providing a level playing field to all economic agents and individuals. Economic benefits are maximized under economic freedom, and individuals can achieve the highest possible level, given the difference in endowments. Economic relativities are exercised to the largest extent, allowing individuals to make use of the market opportunities, legally, ethically and responsibly.

As a facilitator, the government in normal times should prepare for long-term development, create new comparative advantages and deal with market failures, but in crisis time should prepare for policy that can fix the situation quickly so as to avoid further economic deteriorations. In the provision of public goods, the government could allow the private sector to enter into the supply chain, as that can minimize public spending and maximizing private sector engagement. Of course, a good standard has to be maintained and should allow no sacrifice on qualities. Indeed, a higher standard could even be achieved when private supply is competing with public provision, and vice versa.

Clarification on "positive non-intervention" can be built on the understanding and distinction between private cost and social cost. The private sector should bear the private cost, and should avoid "rent seeking" and shift the cost burden to the government. The decision to intervene economically has to depend on whether doing so will let private cost to be shouldered by the government and increase the social cost. The art of non-intervention is to ensure there is no spilt over of private cost into social cost.

The government has to exercise care and made judgment in areas of market failures in the form of infrastructure construction, crisis management, provision of public goods and welfare provision to the truly needy individuals. Other than welfare expenditures that are purely current consumption, a number of public good provisions do enhance the long-term competitiveness of the economy. Such a distinction should provide a clearer understanding on the "positive non-intervention" economic policy that has been adopted in Hong Kong for decades. Since the *laissez-faire* policy has brought success and prosperity to Hong Kong, there is no reason politically to artificially change the policy, as that shall introduce economic uncertainties and imperfections to Hong Kong.

Indeed, there are ample opportunities for the fiscal policy in Hong Kong to make progress. Instead of lingering on "public opinions", the government can be more proactive and innovative in designing policies suitable for the future development. Instead of making short-term immediate commitments, activities can be tailor-made into various themes to improve and promote economic development. Themes can be used to cluster a number of activities. The theme of city development, for example, can involve a number of activities on road safety, signpost and neon light arrangements and removals, cleaning of streets prior to the rainy season, rats control, illegal occupation of pavement, and so on. All these can enhance city development and a clean and better looking of Hong Kong streets. Similar examples can easily be considered. Themes can also gather public support and the results can boost the image of the government.

It is true that, whether rightly or wrongly, welfare provision has been expanded in the post-1997 period, partly because of the frequent emergence of crises, and partly because of a changed behavior towards government assistance, and partly because of shape changes in government revenues. There is a need to structure a more stable fiscal framework. One effective suggestion is to contain crisis management within the existing fiscal structure by the establishment of a "crisis fund" such that the government will allocate a sum to the fund for crisis management, while the fund can grow in non-crisis times. This can provide the sudden need for expenditures, while at the same time resources can be given to activities that can help to promote long-term development. In a free economy, fiscal freedom requires transparent, non-personality-driven policy that benefits all and looks after both the current and future generations.

12 Land, Property and Housing

12.1 Introduction

Land is regarded as a form of natural resources in economics, and land has been treated differently in different economic freedom regimes. In some free economies, land can be bought and sold privately, and individuals can buy land for their own usage. In other free economies, especially land-constrained economies, the state becomes the owner of all land in the territory, but the government will allot, distribute and sell land for different usages: residential, commercial, industrial and open woodland. In this case, land is purchased or leased from the government for a period that lasts for decades. As such, individuals do not have the ownership right, but have the use right in the acquired land. In either case, individuals and corporations and institutions are free to acquire land for private usage. Rental arrangements are also very common in free economies. Individuals can acquire land resources through rental from the owners.

The three terms of real estate, housing and properties could mean the same, but would convey different implications between usage and ownership, between necessities and non-necessities, and between investment and speculation. Housing is the term that conveys the provision of an essential, basic and necessity good. Housing could simply provide a shelter to individuals, a basic human need and exclude luxurious considerations. Many governments in free economies pursue a housing policy for the needy and ensure a basic living environment for all.

Both properties and real estate imply freedom of ownership. In both cases, they carry an element of investment. The owners can either reside in their purchased property or rent it out to collect rental income. The term real estate could give a broader coverage and implies a large piece of land property or a collection of housing properties that could spread over different locations. In most cases, properties and real estates are long-term investments that will generate cumulative returns over the years or decades. In some cases, real estates could be a piece of raw farmland or undeveloped land kept for future development. The ownership of properties and real estates are considered as wealth of an individual or a business corporation, as they provide either a stream of services (by living in the property) or a stream of income (rental income). The wealth from the ownership is realized when the property or real estate is sold in the market. Over time and given a stable economic environment, there would be an asset appreciation to the property.

It is more difficult to distinguish between investment and speculation. Normally, properties are acquired as a form of long-term investment and as a generator of wealth over time. However, property speculation occurs when property prices are changing very rapidly, due to rapid rise in demand, lack of market regulations, manipulation by the developers or existence of large number of speculators, people may decide to buy and sell properties in a short period of time with the intention to rip the windfall gains from the transaction. Speculation is a risky activity, involving possible gains and losses. The more speculative the property market becomes, the higher is the risk involved in speculation. Thus asset can either appreciate or depreciate in speculation. Individuals could face severe losses when the property depreciates, because individual speculators would not know how the other speculators would behave.

In extreme situations, vicious property speculation would result in financial bubbles, when enough speculators suddenly departed from the market and their rapid sales of assets would pull the market price down, causing asset depreciations. As such, property price could no longer be sustainable in the market, and price would have to fall sharply in order to correct the market distortion resulting from the bubble. One can think of property speculation as a game of "musical chair". When the music stops, the person who eventually holds the property will have to bear the possible gain or loss at the end of the speculation. If the timing coincided with a financial bubble, that individual could suffer loss from the fall in property price.

While speculation could provide windfall gains to the speculators, speculations can have various detrimental economic effects. Property speculation has a redistributive effect, as the rapid rise of property price served like a tax on non-property holders. The rising property price would raise inflation that leads to deterioration in the living standard of the fixed income earners. The eventual burst of the property bubble can lead to numerous economic and financial ills, including prolonged economic recession with rising unemployment and unattractive to investment.

In some matured free economies, property sale practices and the use of fiscal constrains would deter people from vicious speculations in order to protect the majority of property holders who are non-speculators. Property becomes more of a long-term investment with gradual asset appreciation so as to provide a more equal opportunity to all potential property buyers. A strong social and business ethical standards and a set of market rules are needed to be instituted in order to protect all participants in the property market. Thus, to avoid unwanted social discontent, many governments in matured free economies have passed laws and legislations that imposed standardized practices and regulations in property market transactions so as to ensure a steady supply, stable price and a healthy form of property investment but strictly discouraged speculations. Although this could have been criticized as interventionist, it is thought that a healthy, speculation-free and steady property market would serve as an economic instrument, or an infrastructure, that would open up other economic opportunities. Such a policy is considered as a compromise between housing as a necessity, property as an investment and speculators thirsts.

While property can be a mean of wealth acquisition, the market shall function to permit an equal and fair access to buyers of different age groups at different times. The reason is simply that since property mortgage usually occupies a big chunk of an individual's income, the rising speculative property price could mean that more of an individual's income is geared to pay for the property mortgage. With a low affordability ratio, individuals will have less to spend on other items. Thus, it follows that the high, rising and speculative nature of property price would take up a bigger chunk of the individual's resources, and that less resources would be available for the individuals' other aspects of consumption. As individuals have less to spend on other activities, other businesses might face difficulty in their survival. Eventually, economic growth could be constrained if the property market is too powerful and absorbed much of financial resources at the expense of development in other business activities.

Property ownership is a useful channel of wealth generation, as once the mortgage payment period has been completed and the steady economic development would lead to asset appreciation, property owners would see their wealth expands. There is thus an economic dilemma. Should there be more speculation and a faster rise of property price so as to allow a more rapid pace of wealth accumulation and asset appreciation? Or should the property market price be more stable so as to allow more young income earners a higher ability to enter into the property market? The decision involves not only a redistributive aspect in income and wealth, but a host of related economic activities.

Economic freedom does not evolve in a vacuum. To preserve freedom involves the availability of opportunities and chances for everyone to participate in all markets. Transparent rules and regulations and an equitable system will serve as an appropriate mechanism that stands between all transacting parties: buyers, owners, developers, financiers, intermediaries, current and future generations. Like any other economic sectors, the prosperity of the property sector hinges importantly on all market participants and property-related sectors. Equally, the property sector is the one economic sector that can have a balancing impact on other economic sectors. A dominant property sector could "price-out" other economic activities, as high rents discourage businesses on the one hand and high property price reduces affordability and buyers' large mortgage payment further reduces their purchasing power, resulting in lower level of private consumption and businesses on the other hand.

Among the three conventional factors of production of land, labor and capital, land is immobile. Many free economies are constrained by land resources. The property sector does exercise an economic "power" that controls and influences a major and necessity aspect in everyone's life. Economic freedom allows individual ownership of land and property, but a matured free economy would institute a transparent, equitable and long-lasting system that allows equal opportunities in both the ownership and usage of land resources, and that land and property owners and developers shall not hold the economy hostage in their own development and businesses.

The property sector in Hong Kong has been prosperous; permitting a large number of individuals and corporations to achieve large wealth, but periodic speculations since the 1980s have raised property prices tremendously. Properties in Hong Kong have become least affordable among all major world cities in a recent international survey.[1] Activities and developments in the property sector in Hong Kong thus hold a key to the success in the future development of Hong Kong, including the path of economic freedom.

The understanding of economic freedom will not be complete without examining land and property development in Hong Kong. While property is a major

---

[1] *South China Morning Post*, April 20, 2010.

economic sector in Hong Kong, many have argued that it is still far from being a matured economic sector, as its development has raised a number of controversies, including the economic role of the property sector. This chapter first discusses the issue of land in Hong Kong, looking at its supply mechanism and the role of the government. The chapter goes on to examine the performance of the property sector, outlining its special features and the causes of speculation and property bubble.

There is no perfection in the development of an economic sector, but various improvements can be made to Hong Kong's property sector. The last section in this chapter touches on the need for a comprehensive policy that consists of improvements in sale practice that brings fairness and equity to both buyers and sellers, current and future property owners, in the supply of land that reflects the role and commitment on the part of the government in bringing a stable property market and in the provision of housing in the user market.

12.2 Land as a Resource

The population in Hong Kong has been growing rapidly in recent decades. The Hong Kong population in 1975 was close to 4.43 million, increased by 23 percent to 5.47 million by the end of 1985. By 1997, Hong Kong's population reached 6.32 million, an increase of 42.66 percent in the two decades between 1975 and 1997. Due to a number of possible reasons, such as the severe economic recession after the Asian financial crisis in 1997, health threats from the spread of avian flu and the severe acute respiratory syndrome (SARS) in 2003, the population of Hong Kong has fallen short of forecast. In the 2006 population by-census, the population in Hong Kong reached 6.9 million, making an increase of 9.19 percent between 1997 and 2006. In terms of the population spread between the different areas in Hong Kong, 51.9 percent of people in Hong Kong resided in the New Territories, followed by the Kowloon Peninsula with 29.8 percent and the Hong Kong Island with 18.2 percent in 2005. The Hong Kong population is also aging, with the median age increased from 34 years in 1996 to 39 years in 2006.[2]

Land in Hong Kong has been a scarce resource and rapid urbanization in the last few decades has led to high population concentration. The approximate area of Hong Kong in 2005 is 1,104 square kilometers, with the Hong Kong Island and adjacent islands occupying 7.34 percent, the Kowloon Peninsula occupying 4.26 percent, while the New Territories (mainland and islands) occupying the majority of 88.41 percent. Over a century period between 1887 and 2005, land reclamation has provided a total of 68 square kilometers in Hong Kong.[3]

The small area of Hong Kong is often restricted by its mountainous nature. Table 12.1 shows that in 2005 only 23.84 percent of the total area in Hong Kong is

---

[2] *Hong Kong 1986, Hong Kong 1997* and *Hong Kong 2005*, Information Services Department, and Hong Kong 2006 Population By-Census, Census and Statistics Department, Hong Kong.

[3] *Hong Kong 2005*, Information Services Department, and *Planning Statistics*, Planning Department, Hong Kong. Different sources of government statistics reported a slightly different figure for the approximate total area of land in Hong Kong.

TABLE 12.1 Land use in Hong Kong

	1996	1997	1998	1999	2000	2001	2002	2003	2004	2005	2006	2007	2008	2009
Total Area (square kilometers)	1,095	1,096	1,097	1,098	1,099	1,100	1,103	1,108	1,107	1,108	1,108	1,108	1,108	1,108
Developed land (% of total area)	15.99	16.05	16.32	16.75	20.93	21.36	21.66	21.95	23.68	23.84	23.29	23.38	23.56	23.74
Residential	5.30	5.29	5.38	5.46	6.10	6.18	6.17	6.05	6.96	7.04	6.77	6.77	6.77	6.86
Commercial	0.18	0.18	0.18	0.18	0.27	0.27	0.27	0.27	0.27	0.27	0.27	0.27	0.36	0.36
Industrial	1.00	1.00	1.00	1.00	1.73	1.73	1.72	1.90	2.26	2.26	2.17	2.17	2.26	2.26
Government, institution, community	1.64	1.73	1.82	1.91	1.82	1.82	1.90	1.90	2.08	2.08	2.17	2.17	2.17	2.17
Transportation	2.47	2.65	2.83	3.01	4.46	4.45	4.53	4.69	4.79	4.87	4.96	5.14	5.14	5.23
Open space	1.46	1.46	1.55	1.55	1.82	1.82	1.81	1.81	1.90	1.99	1.99	2.08	2.17	2.17
Vacant land	3.93	3.74	3.65	2.46	2.46	2.82	2.99	2.80	2.62	2.35	1.81	1.71	1.53	1.44
Other urban & built up areas				1.18	2.27	2.27	2.27	2.53	2.80	2.98	3.16	3.07	3.16	3.25
Non-developed land (% of total area)	84.02	83.94	83.69	83.24	79.07	78.54	78.33	78.07	76.32	76.17	76.71	76.62	76.44	76.26
Agriculture land	7.03	7.03	6.84	6.65	6.37	6.18	6.07	6.41	6.59	6.59	6.14	6.05	6.14	6.14
Woodland/shrub land/grassland	67.49	67.43	67.37	67.30	67.42	67.18	67.00	66.88	66.03	65.70	66.70	66.70	66.52	66.34
Wetland	0.00	0.00	0.00	0.00	0.55	0.55	0.54	0.90	0.45	0.45	0.45	0.45	0.45	0.45
Barren land	4.02	4.01	4.01	4.01	2.18	2.18	2.18	1.35	0.81	0.81	0.81	0.81	0.72	0.72
Water area	2.37	2.37	2.37	2.37	2.55	2.55	2.54	2.53	2.44	2.62	2.62	2.62	2.62	2.62
Temporary structures & other uses*	3.11	3.10	3.10	2.91										

Notes:* = These classifications are unavailable after 2000. The figure for the total area in 2004 (1,107) is slightly larger than the figure of 1,104 reported in *Hong Kong 2005*, Informational Services Department, Hong Kong, due probably to definitional difference in different categories.

Source: *Planning Statistics*, Planning Department, Hong Kong.

developed land, and that land used for residential purpose is about seven percent of total, while land used for commercial and industrial purposes amounts to only 2.53 percent. On the contrary, about 76 percent of total land area in Hong Kong is non-developed, especially in the form of woodland that has occupied about 66 percent of total land area in Hong Kong. Despite the large population increase in the last three decades, land usage as shown in Table 12.1 has not been changed significantly. Government statistics reported that the overall population density in 2005 was 6,420 people per square kilometer.[4] The concentration ratio would be much higher if it only the residential areas are taken into account.

As a British colony before July 1997, all land in Hong Kong was owned by the Crown, and the British Hong Kong Government could sell and grant leasehold interests for terms of 75, 99 or 999 years, though the practice was standardized to 75 years in the urban areas of Hong Kong Island and Kowloon Peninsula in recent decades. After sovereignty reversion on July 1, 1997, all land within the Hong Kong Special Administrative Region (SAR) has become state property. The Hong Kong SAR Government will be responsible to the management, use and development of the land. Land in Hong Kong is either leased or granted to individuals, legal persons or organizations for use and development. Land leases are renewable at a reassessed annual rent. The provision stated in Annex III of the Joint Declaration, which was the outcome of the Sino-British negotiation over the sovereignty reversion of Hong Kong in 1982–1984, was that beginning from May 1985, land grants in the entire Hong Kong territory would be made for terms that will not expire after June 30, 2047. Grants were made at a premium and a nominal rent that lasted until June 30, 1997, when sovereignty of Hong Kong was reverted to the People Republic of China. Leases will also be extended to June 2047, or for a term of fifty years, with the exception of leases for special purposes. After July 1997, an annual rent equivalent to three percent of the property's ratable value will be applied to grants and leases.[5]

A Sino-British Land Commission was established under the Sino-British Joint Declaration that oversaw the supply of land before July 1997. Other than land granted to the Hong Kong Housing Authority for public rental housing purpose, the Sino-British Land Commission limited the annual land grants to not more than fifty hectares, though the limit could be increased. The land premium income obtained from land transaction was shared equally between the pre-July 1997 British Hong Kong Government and the post-July 1997 Hong Kong Special Administrative Region (SAR) Government. The share of the premium obtained before June 1997 was turned over to the new Hong Kong SAR Government on July 1, 1997.[6]

Table 12.2 showed the actual amount of land disposed by the government in the twenty fiscal years period from 1985–1986 to 2005–2006. One observation is that land supply in Hong Kong has been cyclical and unsteady, and its pace has probably moved along with the economic cycles. A low supply in 1985–1986 was due to the economic downturn during the Sino-British negotiation over the political future of

---

[4] *Hong Kong 2005*, Information Services Department, Hong Kong.

[5] *Hong Kong 1986, 1995, 1997*, Information Services Department, Hong Kong.

[6] *Hong Kong 1995*, Information Services Department, Hong Kong.

TABLE 12.2 Land disposure and premium

Financial year (from April to March)	Actual amount disposed (square meters)	Total premium (HK$ Million)	Total premium/ total govt. revenue (%)	Total premium/ GDP (%)
1985–1986	191,444	2,844	6.90	1.02
1986–1987	272,043	3,878	8.84	1.16
1987–1988	271,169	4,430	7.96	1.08
1988–1989	593,734	13,027	19.80	2.69
1989–1990	265,992	7,801	10.49	1.41
1990–1991	276,889	4,890	5.91	0.79
1991–1992	315,764	14,519	4.31	2.02
1992–1993	296,817	14,993	12.41	1.80
1993–1994	197,207	16,467	11.44	1.72
1994–1995	265,901	16,713	11.06	1.57
1995–1996	925,139	23,398	15.27	2.06
1996–1997	156,648	17,977	10.34	1.42
1997–1998	341,212	32,250	14.10	2.36
1998–1999*	194,969	10,085	5.63	0.79
1999–2000	276,316	11,394	7.03	0.89
2000–2001	235,260	14,617	8.18	1.11
2001–2002	85,695	2,690	1.72	0.21
2002–2003	53,909	3,765	2.55	0.30
2003–2004*	27,236	891	0.30	0.07
2004–2005	70,291	20,406	8.89	1.56
2005–2006	32,952	10,673	5.21	0.76
2006–2007	77,929	13,342	5.83	0.89
2007–2008	114,643	27,232	8.89	1.65
2008–2009	24,547	814	0.30	0.05
2009–2010	59,652	14,466	5.77	0.87

Notes: GDP = sum of quarterly Gross Domestic Product figures of the financial year. * = land sales were suspended from 6/1998 to 3/1999 and from 11/ 2002 to 12/2003.
Sources: Planning Department, Lands Department, Census and Statistics Department, and Information Services Department, Hong Kong.

Hong Kong. A similarly low land supply in 1993–1994 actually followed a long period of high land supply between the financial years of 1988–1989 and 1992–1993. The low supply in the financial years of 1996–1997 and 1998–1999 was the reaction to the Asian financial crisis, and the collapse of the property market that led to the suspension of land sales in June 1998 for the remainder of the financial year until March 1999. The low land disposal since the 2002–2003 financial year was due to the outbreak of the severe acute respiratory syndrome (SARS) in 2003, and the continuation of the low property market expectation resulted in a package of measures that suspended all land sales between November 2002 and end of 2003. Public confidence in the property market returned in 2004.

Land sales in Hong Kong are commonly conducted through auction and tender. It has been debated as to the pros and cons of the way auction is conducted. Open or public auction is seen to be fair and the land goes to the highest bidder. On the contrary, open public auction bidding allowed bidders to have multiple bids and possible collusion can be formed between developers. As the price of land provided a strong indicator to the property price, open bidding often ended up with a very high land price. Since the resumption of land sales in 2004 and the subsequent recovery of the property price, some analysts have observed in open auctions that individual large developer might have bided up the price in the open auction in an attempt to push up the final price in the auction. The developer would then make use of the higher eventual price in the open auction as an evidence of high land price and increase the price in the next release of new properties.

On the contrary, land sales through tender or sealed bid allowed the government to normally choose the average bidder. The advantage of a sealed bid method is that land price tended to be lower as bidders will not have the chance to bid more than once and do not have instant information on how other bidders bid in an open auction. The usual practice in a sealed bid is that the government discloses the bid from all bidders after the land sale is finalized. The disadvantage of the sealed bid is that the government may exercise an unfair discrepancy in choosing the developer from all bidders. Open public auction is the more common method used in Hong Kong, and is favored by the developers, as they can bid for their preferred land lots and the high land price can be passed on to the property price.

The study by Wu (1986) summarized the advantages of public auction and second-price sealed bid. A public auction enabled the most efficient firm to outbid other firms, and it guaranteed efficiency in resource allocation. Another advantage of a public auction is its simplicity of the system. The government is protected against charges of favoritism since all admitted bidders present in the auction room are free to bid. In a sealed bidding, the government needed extra effort in ensuring transparency. Since land lots are put into auction sequentially, bidders have full knowledge of how many land lots are available for bidding. In the case of sealed bid, Wu (1986) argued that the government is protected when there is only one bidder. A sealed bid is less sensational than a public auction as it would attract less attention and publicity. Developers have less opportunity for creating headlines by bidding high prices and can create an illusionary effect in the primary or new sales in the property market for flats. In a sealed bid, the chance of collusion among bidders is reduced, and unfair competition is prevented as firms in a public auction may deliberately outbid others to exclude them.

Another study by Vickrey (1961) argued that land tender is awarded to the firm with the highest bid price, but the price payable is that specified in the second highest bid. Under the assumption of an absence in collusion, bidders have no incentive to hide their maximum price preference and willingness to pay. In a second-price sealed-bid auction where each bidder submits a sealed bid to the government, Vickrey (1961) elaborated the "demand revealing mechanism" and argued that in a second-price sealed-bid auction, the highest bidder will win but pay the second-highest bid price for the land.

The government in Hong Kong announces for each financial year a Land Sale Program that includes details on public land auction and tenders. Instead of fixing the total amount of land to be supplied, the policy on land provision has changed since April 1999. The policy instituted an additional "Application List" procedure, and that developers can submit application for a certain piece of land for development and the government will then select from the applied list for public land auction. Such a procedure effectively ensures that the land so selected will meet market demand, and that the auction price will be determined by market forces. After the repeated land sale suspension between November 2002 and December 2003, the new supply of land can only be triggered from the "Application List".[7]

Land supply can alternatively be secured through redevelopment under the Urban Renewal Authority, though the pace of land redevelopment is usually slow as the process of negotiation over compensations and clearance of occupants take time. By and large, redevelopment of land usage is market driven, and is usually responsive to the need of resource reallocation and redeployment. Typically, due to increasing cost of production in Hong Kong since the 1980s and the opening up of the Mainland China market, a large number of light manufacturing plants in Hong Kong have migrated to Southern China, where labor cost is lower and land supply is abundant. Flatted factory space and buildings in the conventional industrial areas in Hong Kong have increasingly been re-zoned and turned into offices and other commercial usages.

Table 12.2 provided the statistics of total premium the government received from land sales in different financial years. For the entire decade of the 1991–2001 financial years, the total premium has remained high, especially in 1997–1998 at the time of sovereignty handover and the economy was at the peak of economic overheating before the burst of the financial and property bubble. The high total premium received in the 1990s reflected the booming economy. The land price has increased tremendously during the last two to three decades in Hong Kong. Although land from different areas in Hong Kong would fetch different price, the average premium per square meter would give an indicator on the rising price of land over the years. For example, the average premium for one square meter, as calculated from Table 12.2, was HK$14,855 in 1985–1986. By 2005–2006, the average land price has gone up to HK$323,895 per square meter, an increase of 2,080 percent in the two decades of 1995–2005.

The simple economic theory of demand and supply suggested that the high land price has been due to rising demand for land. This is true, but not the whole truth. The other part of the truth is that the high land price has become an instrument of income distribution that worked in favor of the government, land owners and property developers, as the high land price would lead to high property price. Industrialist, investors in physical manufacturing plants and land users would argue that the high land price has eroded Hong Kong's economic competitiveness, as land has always been the essential economic resource. It is clear that the sale and supply of land through the "Application List" method where selected land lots by the developers are to be auctioned will purely be demand- or market-driven, but land price will remain

[7] *Hong Kong 1999*, and *2002*, Information Services Department, Hong Kong.

and be kept high, and that in turn ensures high property price. The "Application List" method only provides land supply when specific land lots are wanted by the developers, and that is not the same as the provision of a steady supply of land, where "steady" would imply a supply of different types of land for residential and other purposes regularly.

Another argument in the land supply and the high land price in Hong Kong is that land premium occupies a large percentage of total government revenue. As column (4) of Table 12.2 showed, the total premium to total government revenue ratio has exceeded ten percent in much of the 1988–1998 decade, with the highest of 15.27 percent in 1995–1996. In the recession years since 1998, the ratio has remained low. In policy terms, it is advisable for the government to have a steady revenue income from annual land premium, but the high percentage would make government revenue dependent on land premium. There is no magic figure in relation to the percentage of government revenue derived from land premium, but a steady range of 7 to 10 percent should be acceptable and could provide a steady, but not dependent, revenue source to the government.

On the contrary, the last column in Table 12.2 suggested that the total premium to Gross Domestic Product (GDP) ratio, other than the four financial years of 1988–1989, 1991–1992, 1995–1996 and 1997–1998, has remained lower than 1.5 percent in most years. Due to the small size of government and the high level of GDP in Hong Kong, one can conclude that the total premium from land sales has a minor effect on Hong Kong's GDP. This contrasts with some advocates who believed that land sales served as a crucial factor in both the government revenue and Hong Kong's GDP.

The conclusion from the discussion in Table 12.2 is that land price has increased tremendously, due probably to the unsteady land supply and the high demand. Although total premium has played a role in the level of total government revenue, land premium has not been important to the overall GDP in Hong Kong. The more appropriate economic policy will be to ensure a steady land supply every year, so that total premium will become a steady and a more stable source of government revenue. As an economic resource, it would be unwise for the price of land to be too high or fluctuates fiercely as it will produce an undesirable redistributive effect, destabilize and erode Hong Kong's economic competitiveness in terms of high land price and high production cost, and produce a picture of inconsistency in resource allocation.

There is thus a need to re-examine the land policy. The fact shown in Table 12.1 is that much land in Hong Kong has not been developed, as only 23.74 percent of total land is considered as developed land in 2009. There is an unparalleled trend between land usage and expansion in population, and while population has increased rapidly in the last decades, land supply and development has been lacking behind.

A gradual and orderly expansion of land development is needed. A strategy can start with the greater use of open space and vacant land that made up 3.61 percent of total land in 2009. In the non-developed land category shown in Table 12.1, the only other possibility is the open up of woodland, shrub land and grassland. The third possibility is land reclamation from the sea. In the case of the Disney theme park, for example, it took the government about two years to reclaim the entire Penny Bay in time for the construction of the Disney theme park. In a press release in 2000 and 2003 that corresponded with stage 1 and stage 2 of the reclamation of Penny Bay for the Disney theme park, a total of HK$3.98 billion and HK$1.005 billion were the contracted cost in stage 1 and stage 2 respectively. Stage 1 involved the work on dredging about 200 hectares of land, construction of 1,800/1,200 meters of permanent/temporary seawall, access road and water supply, installation of geotechnical instruments and earth embankment and so on. The work in stage 2 involved the reclamation of about 60 hectares of land, construction of 1,600 meters of permanent sloping seawall and so on.[8] Land reclamation seems to be the most promising channel in the increase of land supply and development as the government can have full control on the size of reclamation and the cost of reclamation can also be estimated quite accurately.

The development of woodland, shrub land and grassland probably requires complex administrative procedures, such as re-zoning, construction of basic infrastructure including sewage, geological testing and urban planning. There will also be obvious opposition from the environmentalists and "green protectionists" whom would not like to see further urban development in Hong Kong. The argument in "green protectionism" concerned only the preservation of non-developed land, but does not take into account the urgent need resulting from the rising population and increasing property price. Indeed, there can be a positive correlation between green protection and the rising property price. The demand for housing rises as population rises, but the preservation of the non-developed land would mean that the supply of residential housing lacks behind demand, and property and housing price will rise eventually, benefitting only the developers as property price rises further.

Urban redevelopment serves as another alternative to land supply, but it usually is slow as the administrative and legal procedure is complicated and time consuming, involving a number of parties, each of which will have their own self-interest. Negotiation on compensation will take times and can be costly. Similarly, much land in the New Territories is often controlled by the original residents from the "villages", and redevelopment would require a lengthy and costly process of compensation negotiation.

All of these alternatives on increase in land supply do help to alleviate the shortage of developed land in Hong Kong. The strategy will have to take into account the cost of development, the time factor, the size and location and the concern of environmental preservation. Land reclamation seems to be the most convenient form of increase in land supply among all alternatives. A reduction in the percentage of woodland, shrub land and grassland may have to occur at a faster pace. Eventually, it is only through the increased supply of developed land that can serve other aspects of economic development in Hong Kong, including a more stable and affordable property price.

12.3 Economics of the Property Sector

One can analyze the economics of the property sector in Hong Kong by examining the relevant Gross Domestic Product (GDP) components classified under different

[8] Press release, Information Service Department, Hong Kong, May 15, 2000, and April 17, 2003.

economic activities. The economic activities classified under GDP at factor cost include: a) agriculture and fishing, b) mining and quarrying, c) manufacturing, d) electricity, gas and water, e) construction and f) services. Services in turn are divided into: a) wholesale and retail, import and export trades, and restaurant and hotels, b) transport, storage and communications, c) financing, insurance, real estate and business services, and d) community, social and personal services, and ownership of premises.[9]

The three board property-related economic activities included construction, real estate and ownership of premises. Construction included economic activities undertaken by contractors for the construction of buildings and other structural facilities. Real estate included establishments engaged in real estate maintenance management, brokerage and agency, and leasing, as well as those engaged in private development projects on property intended for sale or lease. Ownership of premises consisted of leasing services provided by residential owner-occupiers to themselves, owner-occupied premises of government and private non-profit institutions, and leasing services provided to tenants by owners of premise in individual capacity.

Figure 12.1 showed the proportion of these property-related activities in relation to the level of GDP at factor cost for the period of 1980–2004. Construction has been the economically weakest section among the three types of property-related activities, occupying 7.3 percent in 1981, maintained slightly above 5 percent in the second half of the 1990s, and by 2004, its share as a percentage of GDP at factor cost has dropped to 3.2 percent. Although real estate activities maintained at above 10 percent in 1980–1982 and 1994, its share of GDP at factor cost maintained at

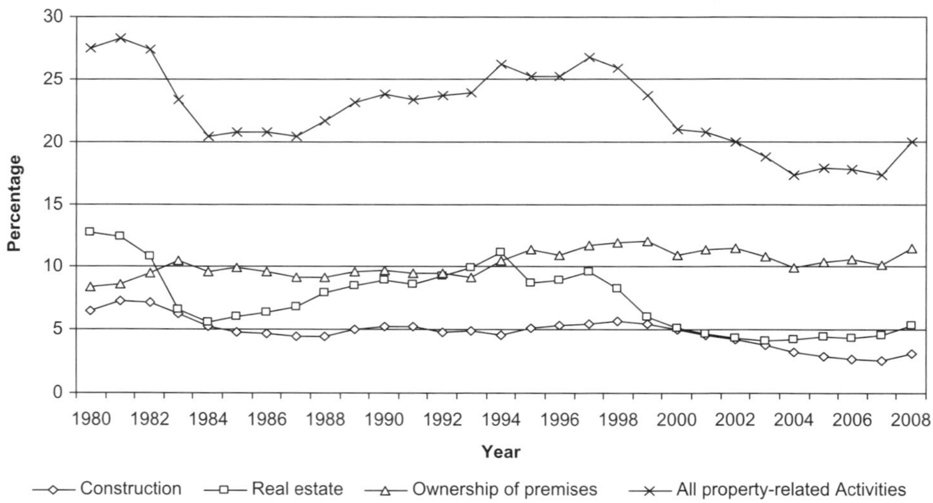

FIGURE 12.1 Property-related economic activities measured as percentage of GDP at factor cost

Source: *Gross Domestic Product*, Census and Statistics Department, Hong Kong.

9 *Gross Domestic Product*, Census and Statistics Department, Hong Kong, various years.

between 5 and 10 percent, but has dropped below 5 percent since 2001. The shape drop in 1984 was due to the confidence crisis in the 1982–1984 Sino-British negotiation, while the two peaks in 1994 (11.1 percent) and 1997 (9.6 percent) could be explained by the property boom, but the continuous fall since 1998 was the result of the property collapse after the Asian financial crisis. The share of construction and real estate together is less than 10 percent of GDP at factor cost, suggesting that competition is high in these two types of economic activities.

On the contrary, the share of ownership of premises as a percentage of GDP at factor cost has remained below 10 percent in most years before 1994, but has edged up to as high as 12.1 percent in 1999 before leveled off to 10.2 percent in 2004. This suggested that the activity of ownership of premises has expanded and would remain steady in the entire economic recession period of 1998–2004.

The sum of the three property-related activities occupied 27.6 percent of GDP at factor cost in 1980, but has dropped considerably in 1984 before it increased gradually to the peak of 26.8 percent in 1997. The Asian financial crisis that led to the burst of the property bubble has resulted in the shrinkage in property-related activities to only 17.6 percent of GDP at factor cost in 2004, the lowest percentage share in the entire observation period as shown in Figure 12.1. The revival of the property sector since 2004, however, could lead to a rise again in percentage share of GDP at factor cost.

The size and impact of the property sector in the financial market can be seen from the share of market capitalization of listed property developers. Figure 12.2 showed the share of property sector capitalization in total market capitalization based on monthly data between early 1985 and mid-2007. The percentage share ranged between twenty to thirty percent in much of the late 1980s and the 1990s, reaching

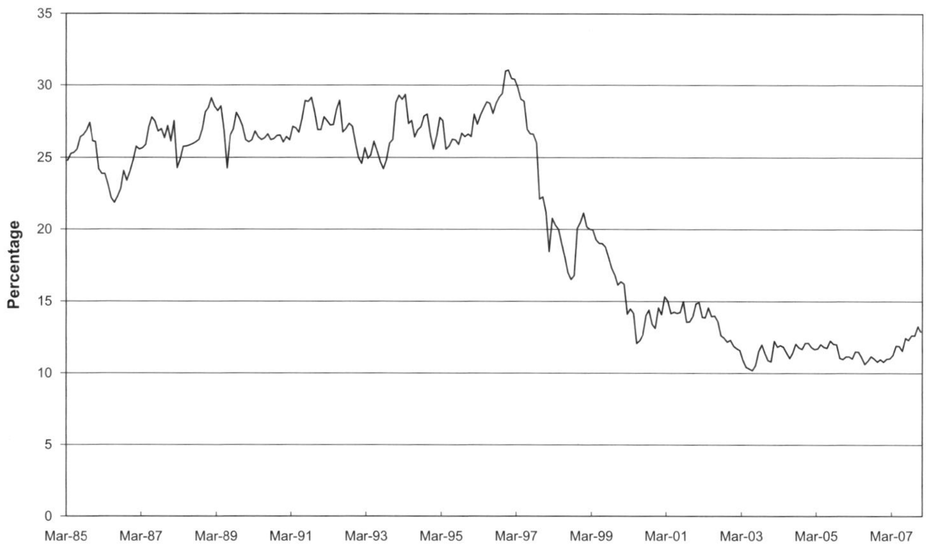

FIGURE 12.2 Share of property sector capitalization to total market capitalization

Source: CEIC Database.

TABLE 12.3 Property-related bank loans (HK$ Million)

Year	(1) HOS/PPS	(2) ORP	(3) BCD	(1+2+3) PRL	Total loans	PRL/total loans (%)
1990	13,664	133,688	108,112	255,464	690,228	37.0
1991	19,077	180,113	125,704	324,894	817,077	39.8
1992	21,628	202,630	144,533	368,791	909,912	40.5
1993	34,886	233,145	180,439	448,470	1,075,777	41.7
1994	39,939	258,557	249,112	547,608	1,258,589	43.5
1995	47,494	301,715	262,199	611,408	1,398,193	43.7
1996	50,620	371,270	333,032	754,922	1,637,191	46.1
1997	60,399	480,401	440,296	981,096	2,037,278	48.2
1998	74,227	515,431	416,226	1,005,884	1,960,371	51.3
1999	76,189	532,370	384,127	992,686	1,819,792	54.5
2000	90,524	535,761	398,365	1,024,650	1,861,465	55.0
2001	107,187	539,723	388,921	1,035,831	1,790,063	57.9
2002	99,214	542,431	378,879	1,020,524	1,743,009	58.5
2003	86,849	529,389	360,412	976,650	1,708,521	57.2
2004	76,548	534,188	386,488	997,224	1,792,395	55.6
2005	67,603	539,192	450,569	1,057,364	1,930,316	54.8
2006	59,763	535,022	491,783	1,086,568	1,974,022	55.0
2007	58,410	564,127	578,244	1,200,781	2,274,284	52.8
2008	57,174	592,980	686,793	1,336,947	2,524,085	53.0

Notes: HOS = home ownership scheme; PPS = private participation scheme; ORP = other residential properties, BCD = building, construction, property development and investment; and PRL = property-related loans.

Source: *Annual Digest of Statistics*, Census and Statistics Department, Hong Kong.

a peak of 31.05 percent in December 1996 before it fell to the lowest of 10.2 percent in June 2003. By and large, the burst of the property bubble since the Asian financial crisis and the various new developments in Hong Kong's stock market has resulted in a smaller role of the property sector in the stock market of Hong Kong.

The commercial banks in Hong Kong have also assisted the business of the property market favorably. Table 12.3 showed the percentage share of property-related loans to total bank loans for the period 1990–2008. The percentage share has been rising since 1990 (37 percent) and peaked in 2002 (58.5 percent) before it leveled down marginally to about 55 percent in 2005. This reflected on the one hand the dominance of the property sector in the Hong Kong economy, and on the other hand, economic narrowness as bank loans which are regarded as a major form of domestic investment formation has over-concentrated in just one economic sector. Total bank loans in Table 12.3 have increased by 265.69 percent between 1990 and 2008, while total property-related bank loans have increased by 423.34 percent in the same period. All the three categories indicated by the first three columns in Table 12.3 have experienced an increase of over three hundred percent in the observation period.

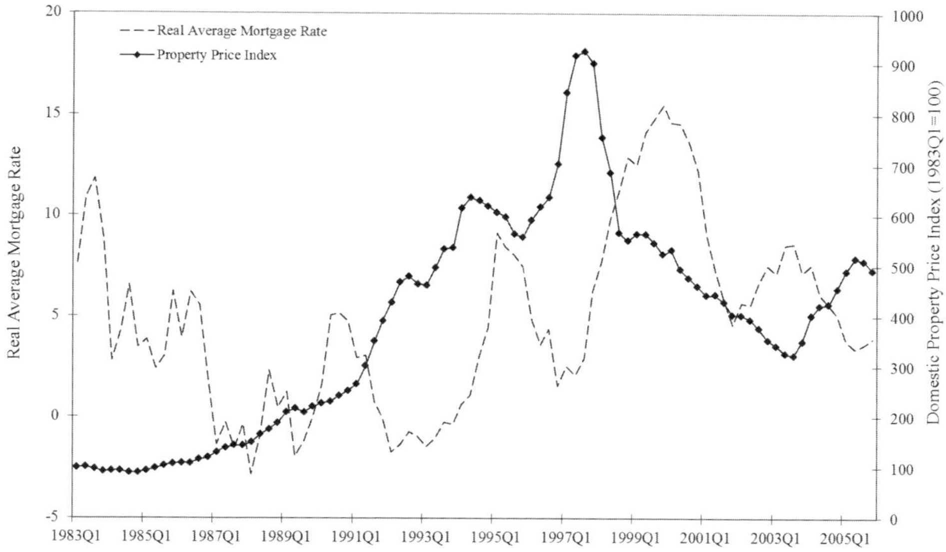

FIGURE 12.3 Real average mortgage rates and property price index

Source: Hong Kong Monetary Authority and Census and Statistics Department, Hong Kong, and CEIC Database.

Due to the presence of the Linked Exchange Rate system that linked the Hong Kong currency to the US dollar, the Hong Kong interest rate has to follow that of the interest rate in the United States. In much of the 1980s and 1990s when a higher inflation rate existed in Hong Kong but a low nominal interest rate in the United States, Hong Kong has experienced a negative real interest rate. The real interest rate showed the difference between the inflation rate (indicated by the Consumer Price Index (CPI)) and the nominal interest or deposit rate. A negative interest rate occurs when the inflation rate exceeds the nominal interest or deposit rate. One expects borrowing to increase in a situation of low or negative real interest rate, meaning that bank loans are cheap and demand for bank loans would rise.

Figure 12.3 showed the real average mortgage rate and the property price index. The mortgage rate usually moves along with the prime rate. At a time of a property boom/recession, the mortgage rate would be 1 or 2 percent point higher/lower than the prime rate. The trend movement of the real average mortgage rate shown in Figure 12.3 could help to explain the rapid rise of the property price. Since the early 1990s, the real average mortgage rate has declined to a negative in various periods (1987Q1–1988Q1, 1989Q1–1989Q2, and 1991Q4–1993Q4). There is a clear opposite movements between the real average mortgage rate and the property price index, when a fall of the former is met by a rise in the latter, say in 1983–1989, 1990–1992, 1995–1997 and 2003–2005 periods. In much of the sample time period, the real average mortgage rate remained below 5 percent, suggesting that the cost of taking the mortgage was low. The property price kept rising until the burst of the property bubble that began in early 1998, when the real average mortgage rate exceeded 10 percent in the period of 1998Q3–2000Q4.

Indeed, the Hong Kong economy has experienced a negative interest rate for much of the 1980s and 1990s. For the different five-year periods of 1981–1985, 1986–1990, 1991–1995, 1996–2000 and 2000–2004, the average inflation rates were, respectively, 7.94 percent, 8.40 percent, 7.32 percent, –0.06 percent and –3.96 percent. The average saving deposit rates for these same periods, respectively, were 7.10 percent, 3.90 percent, 3.03 percent, 4.25 percent and 1.36 percent. In other words, for the entire period of 1980–1995, especially in the decade of 1986–1995, Hong Kong has experienced on average a negative interest rate, which would have fueled borrowing and speculative activities in stocks and property.

12.4 Property Market Performance

The average price of private properties in the Hong Kong Island, the Kowloon Peninsula and the New Territories are shown, respectively, in Figures 12.4, 12.5 and 12.6. In general, property price is the Hong Kong Island is highest. Property price clearly has risen a lot since the early 1990s, cumulated to a bubble that burst after the Asian financial crisis in late 1997, but reached the lowest at the time of the severe acute respiratory syndrome (SARS) in 2003, though the 2003 price was still higher than the pre-bubble years in the 1980s, especially for the large units (≥70 square meters). By 2004, property price has recovered and has since experienced a rapid increase in price. Property developers and traders tended to use the unrealistically high peak price in the property bubble in 1997 as a reference point and assumed that future property price can even be higher without an understanding that the economic fundamentals before and after sovereignty reversion in 1997 has changed.

Among the six property classifications in Figure 12.4, both the Home Ownership Scheme (HOS) and the Private Sector Participation Scheme (PPS) are properties sold by the government to the sandwich class. In terms of the unit size, the HOS/PPS units did overlap with the small/medium property units. Hence, in a booming market, the HOS/PPS provided an alternative to home buyers, especially those in the sandwich class. After the burst of the property bubble and the drastic fall in GDP in 1998, HOS/PPS units became popular as the price was much lower. Private property developers saw that the policy on HOS/PPS as a source of market intervention by the government. The two schemes were stopped in 2002 after developers urged the government to restrict supply due to overlaps between the size of the property under HOS and PPS and the small/medium property units (< 40 square meters). After 2004, there were no additional HOS/PPS flats completed as the government decided against to act as a property developer for the sandwich income households. The remaining HOS/PPS units were scheduled to be put up for sale towards the end of 2006 when the property market recovered. Such a strategy proposed by the developers did cut the government supply considerably, and property buyers have to purchase from the private market.

The two portions in Figure 12.4 showed a similar trend movement among the small and large units, and there is a difference in the price per square meter on the vertical axis. One can see that the price per square meter is higher the larger the unit. The price is about twice as much between a small/medium unit and the largest unit over 160 square meters. Since 2004, there has been a sharp increase in the large units

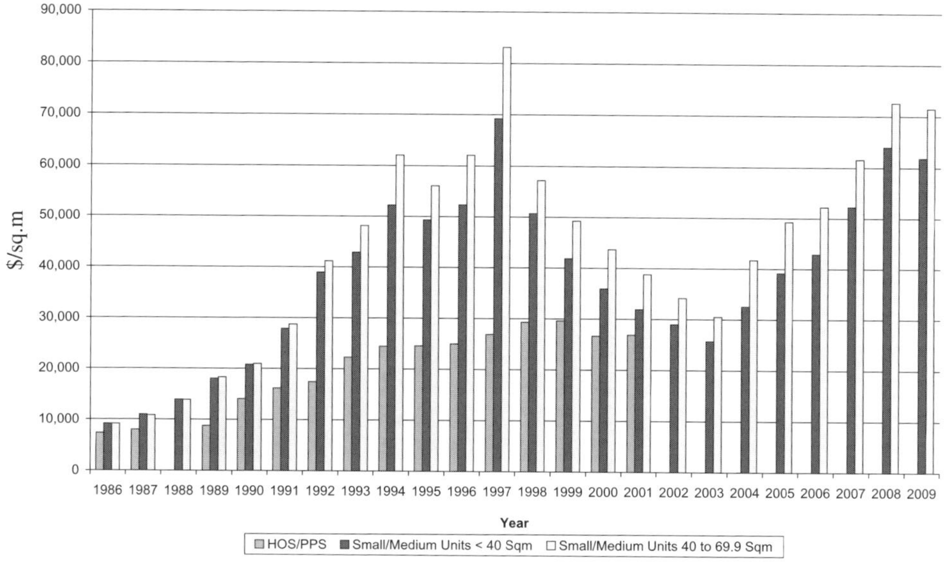

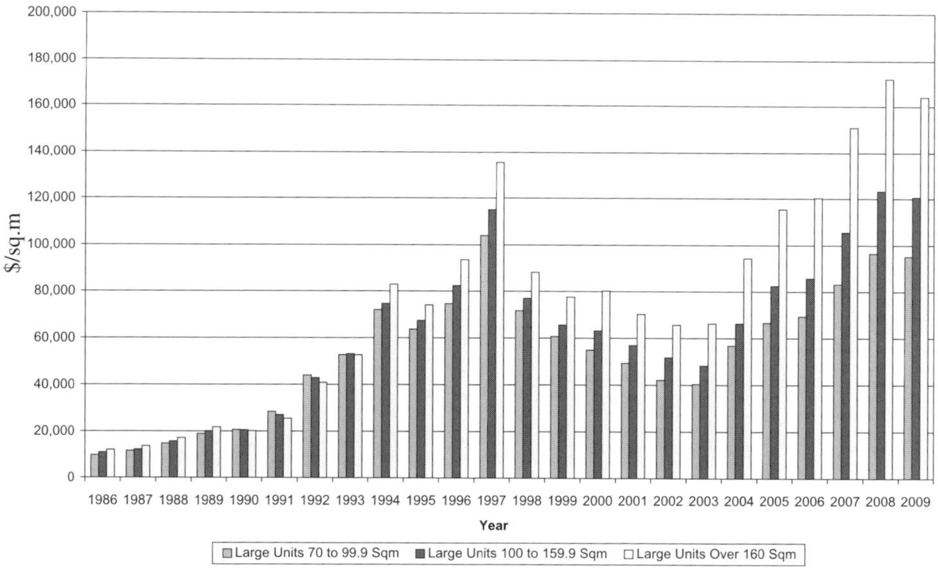

FIGURE 12.4 Average property price: Hong Kong island

Sources: Census and Statistics Department, and Housing Authority, Hong Kong.

with over 160 square meters, and these are the most luxurious units in Hong Kong. Though with a different magnitude, a similar picture can be seen in the price movements in properties in the Kowloon peninsula and the New Territories, as shown by the two portions in each of Figure 12.5 and Figure 12.6.

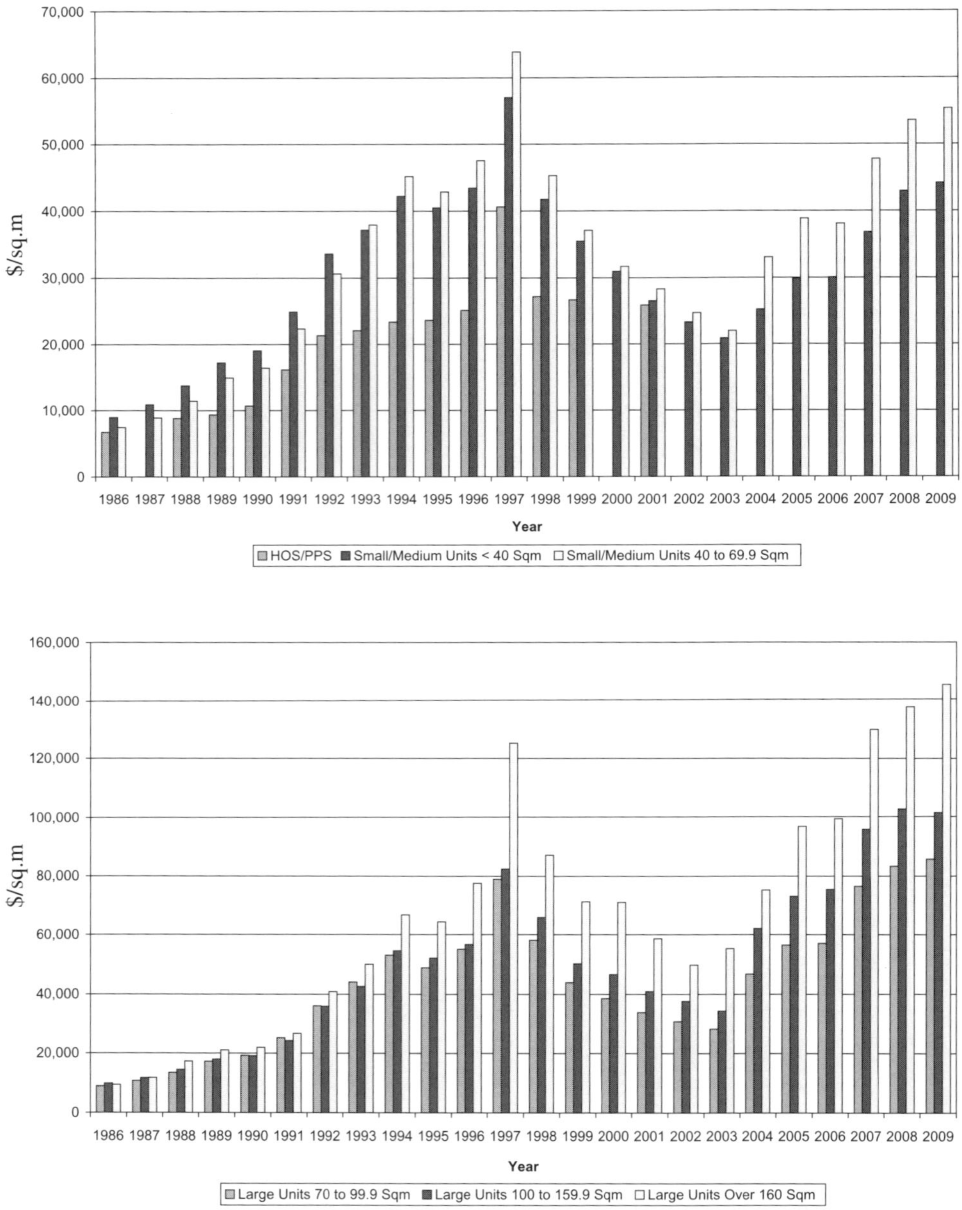

FIGURE 12.5 Average property price: Kowloon Peninsula

Source: Same as Figure 12.4.

Table 12.4 showed the price movements of domestic properties in different periods for the three regions in Hong Kong. The three periods of 1990–1997, 1997–2005 and 2005–2009 represent roughly the bubble years, the financial crisis and post-crisis periods, respectively. One can see that properties in Hong Kong Island

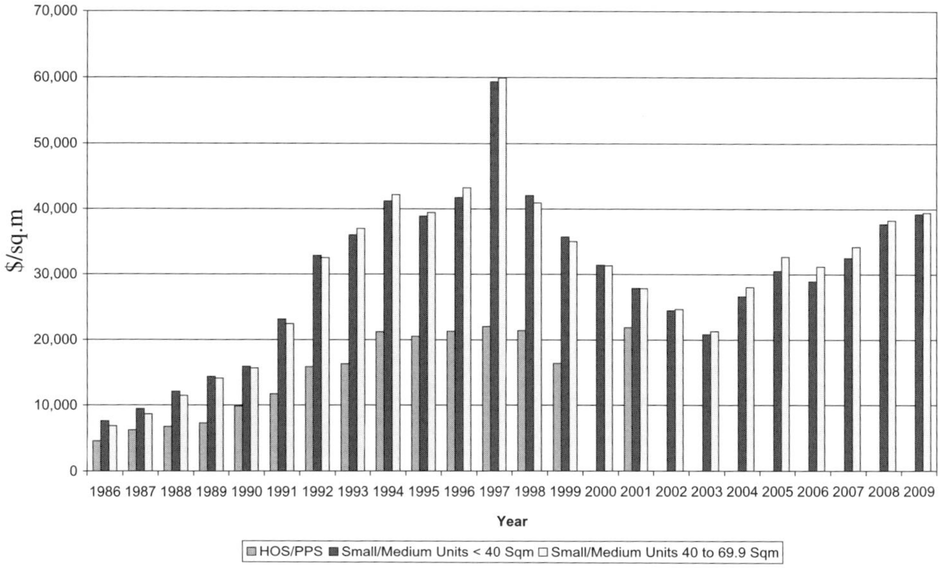

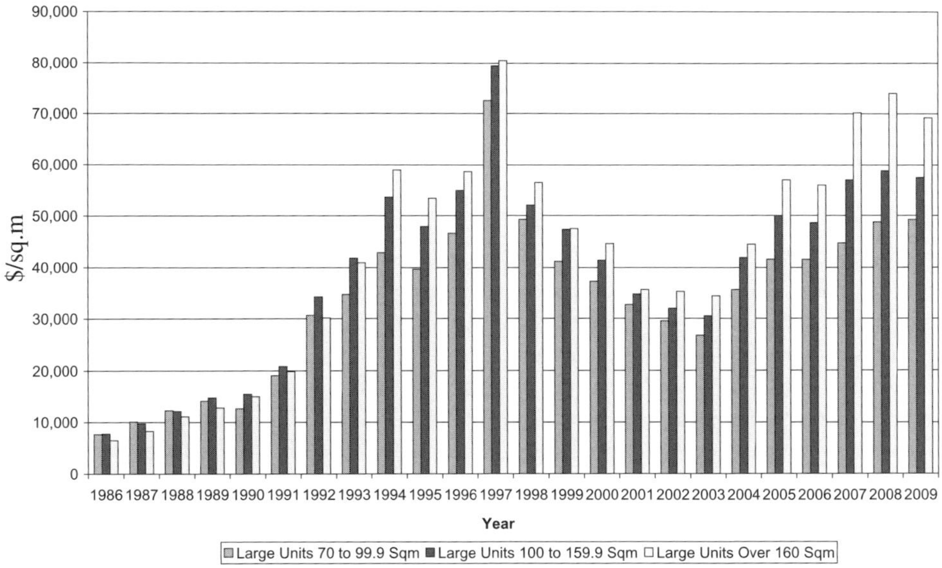

FIGURE 12.6 Average property price: The New Territories

Source: Same as Figure 12.4.

has increased most, especially in the large units, fallen least in the financial crisis years, and bounced back much faster than the other two regions.

During the peak in 1997, as Table 12.4 showed, the price difference between the three regions can be clearly seen. The percentage change in the price of Home Ownership Scheme (HOS) and Private Sector Participation Scheme (PPS) was much

TABLE 12.4 Price movement of private domestic properties

% Change in Price	Hong Kong	Kowloon	New Territories
1990–1997			
Smaller than 70 Sq m	264.9	241.2	277.8
Larger than or equal to 70 Sq m	477.7	375.0	438.5
Average	371.3	308.1	358.2
1997–2005			
Smaller than 70 Sq m	–42.0	–43.1	–47.0
Larger than or equal to 70 Sq m	–35.0	–21.0	–38.5
Average	–38.5	–32.1	–42.7
2005–2009			
Smaller than 70 Sq m	50.7	44.7	24.5
Larger than or equal to 70 Sq m	43.7	46.8	18.3
Average	47.2	45.8	21.4
Price Peak in 1997, HK$/Sq m			
Smaller than 70 Sq m	76,183	60,452	59,611
Larger than or equal to 70 Sq m	135,544	95,463	80,549
Average	105,864	77,958	70,080

Sources: *Hong Kong Monthly Digest of Statistics*, Census and Statistics Department, and Hong Kong Housing Authority, Hong Kong.

smaller. By 1997, the price of HOS/PPS was approximately 1.8 times lower than the price of private small/medium units (< 70 square meters). This gap, however, has narrowed considerably after the Asian financial crisis in 1997, and competition between the two types of supplies increased.

Figure 12.7 showed the overall number of private property completions, take-up and vacancy units for the period 1980–2009. The most noticeable trend is the rising number of vacancy units since the early 1990s, and the gap between completions and vacancy units expanded since around 1995. The number of completions has increased after the Asian financial crisis in 1998, but has declined since 2005. The number of vacancy units has remained high and peaked in 2003. The number of take-up units has remained unsteady over the years, and fluctuated independently from the number of completions. On the whole, the newly take-up showed a declining trend.

Figure 12.8 showed the performance of the vacancy ratios in the period of 1990–2009. The vacancy for private residential units was kept under 40,000 units before 1997, but the vacancy level soared above 60,000 units in 1999–2003. The vacancy ratio rose from 4.5 percent in 1998 to 6.8 percent in 2003. As a percentage of the stock, the vacancy ratio for the large property units (≥70 square meters) has been higher than the small/medium property size (<70 square meters), with the former kept rising since 1993 (4.2 percent), though leveled off somewhat in 1997

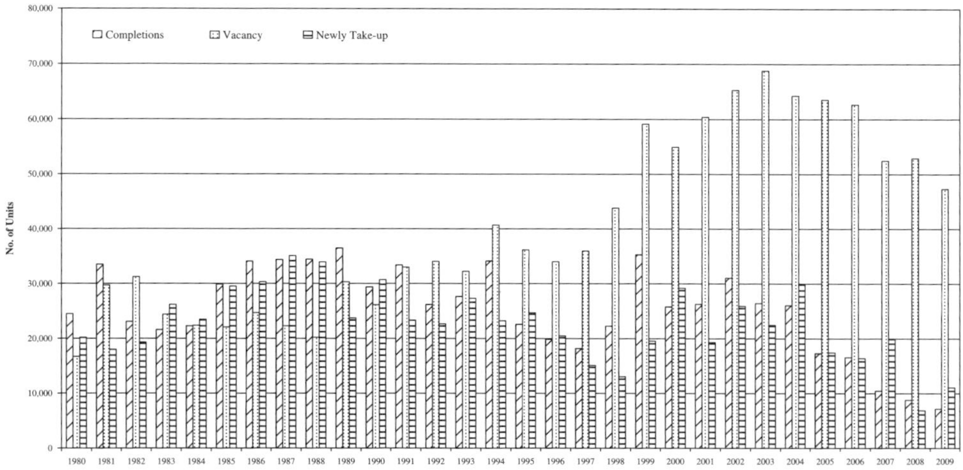

FIGURE 12.7 Private property completions, take-up and vacancy: overall

Notes: Newly Take-up figures are arrived by adding the completions in that year to the vacancy figures at the beginning of the year, subtracting the demolition and the year-end vacancy figures of the year.
Source: *Hong Kong Property Review*, Rating and Valuation Department, Hong Kong.

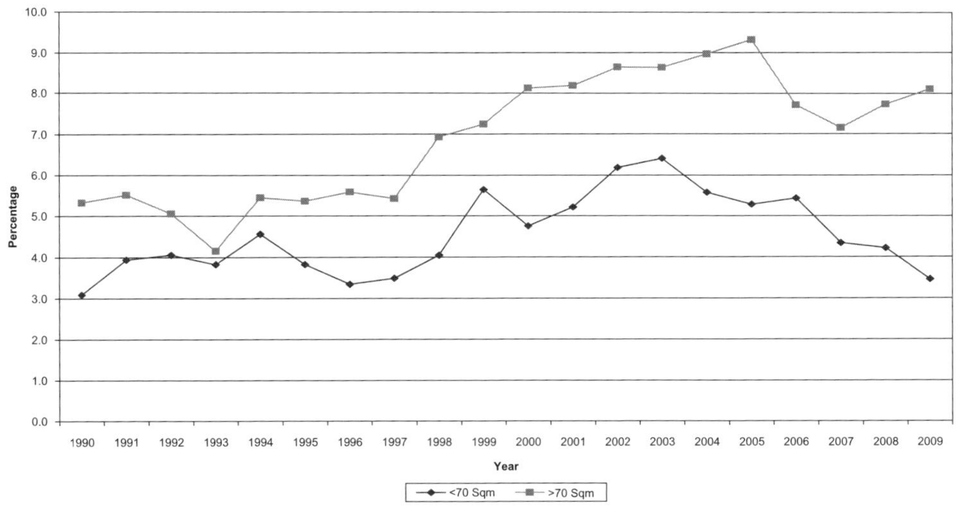

FIGURE 12.8 Private property vacancy ratios by class (Percentage of stock)

Source: Same as Figure 12.7.

(5.4 percent), and then accelerated even after 2003 when the vacancy ratio for the smaller property size declined.

By 2005, the vacancy ratio for the larger property size is 9.3 percent. The vacancy ratio for the smaller property size showed an unsteady trend. It was 3.1 percent in

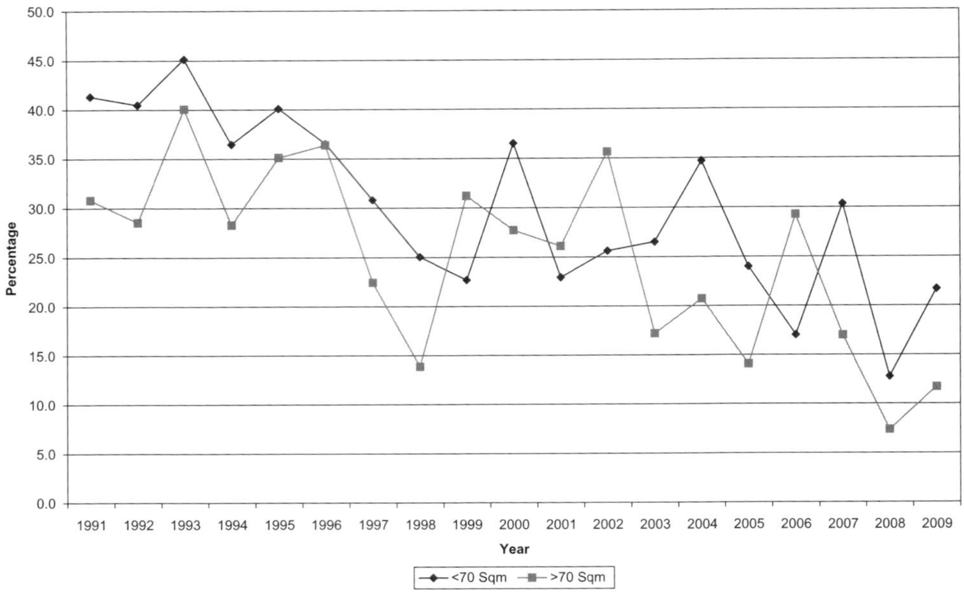

FIGURE 12.9 Private property take-up ratios by class (Percentage of stock)

Note: Take-up ratio is the percentage of the newly take-up to the completion in the year and the vacancy figures at the beginning of the year.
Source: Same as Figure 12.7.

1990, reached a peak of 4.6 percent in 1994, leveled off to 3.3 percent in 1996, and then reached a peak of 5.6 percent in 1999 and another in 2003 with 6.2 percent, before it leveled off to 5.3 percent in 2005. The vacancy ratio gap between the two classes of property has widened. The vacancy ratio for the larger units fell between 2005 and 2007, but has been on a rising trend since 2007.

Figure 12.9 showed the performance of the take-up ratios in the period of 1990–2009. The newly take-up ratio measures the percentage of net increase in the occupied floor space in the year to the completion in that year and the vacancy figures at the beginning of the year. Starting from 1988, the newly take-up ratio has shown a downward trend, and experienced the lowest ratio in 1998 (22.4 percent). The period of 1988 and 1997 was the time of heavy speculative activities in the residential property market. Speculators held their residential property and just waited for the price to boom. The take-up ratio for the large property units is generally lower.

By 2005, the take-up ratios for the larger and smaller property sizes are 14.1 percent and 24 percent, respectively. The take up ratios fell considerably between 2004 and 2005. The take-up ratio for small/medium units decreased from 41.3 percent in 1990 to 24 percent in 2005, and the two percentages for the large units are 30.8 percent in 1990 and 14.1 percent in 2005. Figure 12.9 showed that the newly take-up ratios of the two classes of properties have reached a new low in 2008.

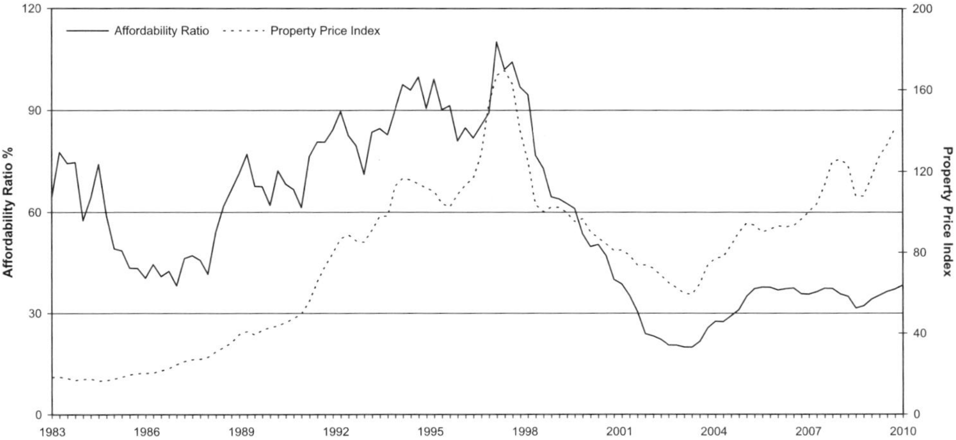

FIGURE 12.10 Affordability ratios and property price index

Notes: The affordability ratio is based on 70 percent financing of a 20-year mortgage. The average private property price is estimated by applying the average price for a property unit of <70 sqm. The property price index is 1999 = 100.

Sources: *Hong Kong Monthly Digest of Statistics*, Census and Statistics Department, and *Economic Report*, Finance Services Bureau, Hong Kong.

The affordability ratio, defined as the ratio of monthly mortgage payment and the median monthly household income, measures the financial ability of the property buyer. The ratio is arrived by dividing the monthly mortgage payment by the median household income based on seventy percent financing of a twenty-year mortgage and the average property of small/medium residential units (<70 square meters). The quarterly data are available from *Hong Kong Monthly Digest of Statistics*, Census and Statistics Department, and *Economic Report*, Finance Services Bureau, Hong Kong. The affordability ratios and the property price index are shown in Figure 12.10. From the lowest affordability ratio of 40.46 in the first quarter of 1986, it climbed to the peak of 110.17 in the second quarter of 1997 before it slide down to 25.79 in the first quarter of 2003. By the end of 2005, the affordability ratio was restored to 47.04. Since 2005, the affordability ratio has remained flat, and probably has fallen again in 2008 in the US financial crisis.

12.5 Demand and Speculation

In estimating the demand for property in Hong Kong, Li (2006) has considered a total of six determinants of demand: income, price, interest rate, Hang Seng Index, number of persons engaged and government expenditure on housing. The level of income showed the economic ability of individual buyers, and that income and demand for property will move in the same direction. Property price should correlate negatively with demand for property, and that a rise in price will lead to a fall in property demand, and vice versa. The interest rate is the opportunity cost of borrowing, and it should have a negative relationship with the demand for property. The Hang Seng Index can be another variable as investment in stocks is an alternative to investment in property. Thus, their relationship is expected to be an inverse one; namely a rise in Hang Seng Index would discourage property demand. The business sentiment in the property market is indicated by the number of persons engaged in the real estate industry. The government also supplied residential housing through the various schemes. Public expenditure on residential housing should show a negative correlation to property demand as government supplies are considered as substitutes.

Li (2006) used quarterly data for the sample period 1986Q1–2003Q4 to study the following demand function:

$$q_t = \beta_0 + \beta_1 y_t + \beta_2 \, price_t + \beta_3 prime_t + \beta_4 \, hsi_t + \beta_5 \, person_t + \beta_6 \, govex_t + \beta_7 \, D97_t + \beta_8 \, q_{t-1} + \varepsilon_t, \tag{1}$$

where the subscript t represents time period (quarterly); q_t is the value of assignments of building units that included all property transactions (residential, factory, retail shops and offices); y_t is real GDP in constant 2000 prices; $price_t$ is the weighted composite price index for four kinds of private property (namely residential units, offices, flatted factories, and retail shops, with 1979Q4 = 100); $prime_t$ is real prime interest rate; hsi_t is the quarterly average of Hang Seng Index; $person_t$ is the number of persons engaged in the real estate industry; $govex_t$ is the public expenditure on residential housing; and ε_t is the random error term. β_0 is the intercept. $D97_t$ is a dummy variable which is defined as 1 for all periods from the third quarter of 1997 onwards, and 0 otherwise. The inclusion of the dummy variable marked the structural change before and after the burst of the property bubble. The lagged dependent variable, q_{t-1}, can be considered as an expectation proxy.[10]

The empirical study in Li (2006) was applied to the four types of properties (private residential, offices, factory and retail shops). The price index variable in Equation (1) was decomposed into two variables. One variable is the weighted price of the type of property in question, say private residential, and the other variable is the sum of the weighted price index of the other three types of properties (offices, factory and retail shop). Such a construction in turn is applied to other three types of properties. This construction effectively produced the following four equations.

For private residential properties:

$$q_t = \beta_0 + \beta_1 y_t + \beta_2 \, price\_r_t + \beta_3 \, price\_ofs_t + \beta_4 \, prime_t + \beta_5 \, hsi_t + \beta_6 \, person_t + \beta_7 \, govex_t + \beta_8 \, D97_t + \beta_9 \, q_{t-1} + \varepsilon. \tag{2}$$

For offices:

$$q_t = \beta_0 + \beta_1 y_t + \beta_2 \, price\_o_t + \beta_3 \, price\_rfs_t + \beta_4 \, prime_t + \beta_5 \, hsi_t + \beta_6 \, person_t + \beta_7 \, govex_t + \beta_8 \, D97_t + \beta_9 \, q_{t-1} + \varepsilon. \tag{3}$$

[10] Refer to Li (2006, Section 6.3) for the definition and construction of variables and the sources of data. Although the analysis has not been updated to a more recent time period, it is expected that the conclusion from the empirical findings are similar.

TABLE 12.5 Estimation of the property demand function, 1986Q2–2003Q4

Explanatory variables	(1)	(2)	(3)	(4)	(5)
Intercept	–0.0161	–0.0189	–0.0142	–0.0268	–0.0269
	(–0.45)	(–0.53)	(–0.39)	(–0.74)	(–0.76)
Real GDP	1.4374	1.6772	1.4671	1.9601	1.6465
	(0.88)	(1.01)	(0.89)	(1.19)	(1.02)
Price Index (All Properties)	2.5180				
	*(5.01)				
Price Index (Residential)		2.1009			
		*(3.44)			
Price Index (Offices)			–0.1382		
			(0.31)		
Price Index (Factory)				–0.2633	
				(–0.52)	
Price Index (Retail Shop)					1.4125
					†(2.22)
Price Index (OFS)		0.4022			
		(0.67)			
Price Index (RFS)			2.7183		
			*(3.83)		
Price Index (ROS)				2.6076	
				*(4.93)	
Price Index (ROF)					1.1427
					(1.54)
Prime Interest Rate	0.0080	0.0061	0.0072	0.0030	0.0037
	(0.57)	(0.42)	(0.50)	(0.21)	(0.26)
Hang Seng Index	–0.1074	–0.1459	–0.1171	–0.1934	–0.1550
	(–0.48)	(–0.64)	(–0.52)	(–0.85)	(–0.70)
No. of Persons Engaged	0.2557	0.1059	0.1832	0.1047	0.5764
	(0.39)	(0.15)	(0.27)	(0.16)	(0.86)
Public Expenditure	–0.3465	–0.3402	–0.3324	–0.3214	–0.1934
	(–1.55)	(–1.51)	(–1.48)	(–1.45)	(–0.83)
1997 Dummy Variable	0.0235	0.0253	0.0210	0.0255	0.0234
	(0.48)	(0.51)	(0.42)	(0.52)	(0.48)
Lagged Dependent Variable	–0.3832	–0.3977	–0.3981	–0.4069	–0.4127
	*(–3.94)	*(–4.03)	*(–3.95)	*(–4.16)	*(–4.22)
Adjusted R^2	0.4366	0.4307	0.4314	0.4466	0.4528
Durban–Watson Statistic	2.143	2.252	2.191	2.287	2.015

Notes: Figures in parentheses are the *t*–statistics. * and † represent the 1 percent and 5 percent level of significance, respectively.

For factories:

$$q_t = \beta_0 + \beta_1 y_t + \beta_2\, price\_f_t + \beta_3\, price\_ros_t + \beta_4\, prime_t + \beta_5\, hsi_t + \beta_6\, person_t + \beta_7\, govex_t + \beta_8\, D97_t + \beta_9\, q_{t-1} + \varepsilon. \quad (4)$$

For retail shops:

$$q_t = \beta_0 + \beta_1 y_t + \beta_2\, price\_s_t + \beta_3\, price\_rof_t + \beta_4\, prime_t + \beta_5\, hsi_t + \beta_6\, person_t + \beta_7\, govex_t + \beta_8\, D97_t + \beta_9\, q_{t-1} + \varepsilon. \quad (5)$$

The notations r, o, f, and s used in the price variables in Equations (2) to (5) represented private residential units, offices, flatted factories, and retail shops respectively. For example, in Equation (2) the first price variable, $price\_r_t$, indicated the weighted price index of residential units (r), and the second price variable $price\_ofs_t$ is the weighted sum of price indexes for offices (o), flatted factories (f), and retail shops (s), collectively.

The empirical findings in Li (2006), reproduced in Table 12.5, can be summarized as follows:

1. All estimates of real GDP are positive but statistically insignificant, suggesting that income had not been a crucial factor in the demand for property.
2. The price of all properties was a dominant factor, as the estimate is high and significant (2.5180).
3. The coefficient estimate for the price ofS private residential property is large and significant (2.1009), meaning that both price and demand moved in the same direction, which contradicted the inverse relationship between price and demand.
4. The coefficient estimates for the price of offices and factory units are not significant but negative, suggesting that their price and demand are inversely related, which is in line with the normal demand behavior. The price of offices and factory were not important in the overall demand function.
5. The estimated coefficient for retail shop is positive and significant (1.4125). The price changes in private residential properties and retail shops were the most important factor in the demand function.
6. The expectation proxy, as indicated by the lagged dependent variable, shows a significant estimate in all equations, though their sign may not be meaningful since the level of demand was the total property value transacted.
7. The coefficient estimates for other variables are mostly insignificant. The coefficient estimates in all five equations for the prime interest rate are low, positive and insignificant. This was due obviously to the high inflation experienced in the pre-1997 period and the prime interest rates at various times were negative. The positive sign of all coefficients showed that an increase in the (negative) real interest rate had encouraged demand.
8. The coefficient estimates for the Hang Seng Index produced a negative sign, which is in line with the fact that property demand and Hang Seng Index are substitutes and their relationship should be an inverse one, but all estimates are weak and statistically insignificant.
9. The coefficient estimates for the number of person engaged and total public expenditure on housing are insignificant, though their signs are correct. The conclusion is that all these four variables (prime interest rate, Hang Seng Index, number of persons engaged in real estate and public expenditure on housing) did not impose significant influence on the demand for property. The estimates of the dummy variable are also insignificant.

The conclusion from the estimates on the demand for property in Hong Kong is that price is the dominant factor. And within the price of different property types, prices of private residential properties and retail shops are most important. Furthermore, their relationship showed a positive one. Namely, when the price of private residential properties and retail shops rose, demand increased. This could provide a strong indicator on the so-called "upward sloping demand curve" and the presence of speculative activities. The estimated coefficient for private residential property gave a large positive coefficient (2.1009), followed by retail shop (1.4125). The demand for private residential property had reacted strongly to changes in its price. The higher was the price of private residential property, the larger would be the demand, indicating a possible "property price trap", in which buyers were driven to buy in anticipation of a higher price at a later time.

The empirical estimation of the property demand function produced a strong conclusion that the price of private residential property was the most important determinant in the property demand. There were excessive speculative activities that eventually helped to build up the bubble. Li (2006, Section 6.4) argued that a major element has to do with the marketing strategy of the developers, and the way speculators reacted to market sentiments. Overall, developers practiced a "limited supply" strategy, in which buyers experienced a sense of loss if they did not buy before a new price was imposed on the next round of supplies.

In the "limited supply" strategy, the developer released a small number of new apartments, and at the same time announced the percentage price increase in the next round of supply. Buyers thus rushed to buy up the initial supply. When the second round of limited supply was released, price did go up by some percentages. Developers could then state publicly that price would increase further in their next round. Buyers who were unable to buy or missed in the first round would be tempted to buy in the second round before it was too late. The price difference between the different rounds of supply did reflect the quality difference of the supply. Usually, the lower floors in the apartments or apartments with a poorer view were released at a lower price, while the better "quality" apartments were released later at a higher price.

Imagine that the first round of apartment sales fell into the hands of the speculators, whom could re-sell the property knowing for sure that price would go up later. The "high demand–high price" relationship could be elaborated by considering an upward-sloping demand schedule, in which more was demand as price rose because the economic psychological behavior is that the price would go up further in future supply. The limited supply of new apartments released by the developers and the subsequent increase in price in the next round could produce a series of equilibrium points that actually chased an upward-sloping demand curve of real estate consumers.

As first argued in Li (2006), Figure 12.11 captured the concept of the upward-sloping demand curve. In Figure 12.11, the first round of supply (Q_1) is sold at (P_1), but the second round of the limited supply (Q_2) will be sold at a higher price (P_2), and so on. Joining up these intersection points chases an upward sloping demand curve (DD), not a supply curve.[11] More would be demanded as price rises, and the

[11] This is known as the identification problem in the supply and demand analysis (Greene 1991).

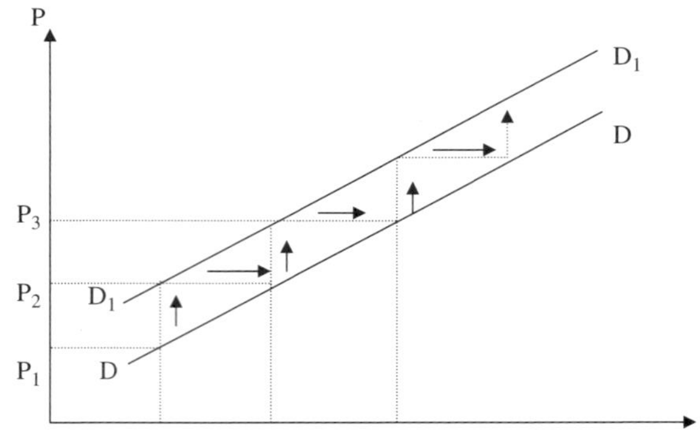

FIGURE 12.11 The upward-sloping property price spiral

rising price is further fueled by the presence of speculation. The rising price of the new release leads to price and asset appreciation in the secondary market. The activities of property speculators effectively pushed up the price, resulting in an upward shift of the upward-sloping demand curve to the line D_1D_1 in Figure 12.11. The consequence is that the speculator bought the property at P_1 and sold it at P_2. The difference P_2–P_1 is the speculator gain. Similarly, at Q_2, speculator gained P_3–P_2.

Assuming at quantity Q_1, the speculators managed to purchase the property at price P_1, and sell at P_2. Realizing the speculative gain, developers expected the price in the next round of supply (Q_2) equals to P_2. When the new supply again fell into the hands of the speculators, the price become P_3, which in turn become the price indicator to the developers in the third round of new supply (Q_3). The combined activity of the developers and speculators produced an upward spiral of accelerated property price, as shown by the arrows in Figure 12.11.[12]

In theory, speculation can help to redistribute income and distort efficiency. The government earned because of the high land price. Developers gained because they enjoyed a rising price. Speculators gained because they could rip a quick cash return. Owners of existing property gained because of asset appreciation. Commercial banks gained because the actual mortgage interest they received would be much higher than the interest stated in the mortgage agreement if the property was transacted or sold before the maturity of the mortgage agreement. Two groups of individuals faced a lost: the fixed income earners, especially when the rate of wage increase is not keeping up with the increase in property price, and those who cannot afford the initial down payment. The "deadweight loss" is that the high property price has eroded the competitiveness of the Hong Kong economy, and the prolonged speculation cumulated to the economic bubble. Secondly, a property-dominant economy

---

[12] The conventional explanation in the theory of demand is that the upward sloping demand curve is flatter than the upward sloping supply curve. When price is above equilibrium, excess demand emerges when price rises, which in turn leads to a larger excess demand and price rises further. This explanation produces a price escalation spiral, but it does not incorporate the speculative element in the analysis.

is unhealthy and may even be unsustainable as a lack of expansion in other sectors could reduce the business of other sectors and that in turn restricted economic growth.

An earlier study conducted by the International Monetary Fund has also shown that the Hong Kong property market was prone to speculative bubbles. The IMF study by Kalra *et al.* (2000) reported that at the peak of the property boom in mid-1997, property prices have exceeded the development of the fundamental factors by about forty to forty-five percent. Another study by Peng (2002) pointed out that about half of the property price fluctuation was attributed to changes in the fundamental variables since the early 1990s, but the other half was explained by the bubble and its cumulated effect when it burst. The study by Chan *et al.* (2001) concluded that property bubbles exploded most sharply between 1990–1992 and 1995–1997. Ho (2000) employed causality techniques and showed that causality ran from property prices to speculation in the residential property market. A number of papers published in the *Quarterly Bulletin* of the Hong Kong Monetary Authority have touched on the property market in Hong Kong. Gerlach (2002) looked at the role of bank lending and property prices in Hong Kong and concluded that bank lending appeared to be driven by the rise in property demand in the sense that banks enabled but not propagated the run-up to the property bubble.

Another study by Kwok (2006) pointed out that there are two main approaches to study property price. The determinants approach suggested that the various demand-side determinants in the property price could include real income, mortgage cost or the real interest rate, and equity price. Supply-side determinants could include unemployment rate, construction cost, housing completion, population growth, land sale, transaction volume and money supply (Longbottom and Nellis, 1981; Sutton, 2002; Berg, 2002; Chen and Patel, 1998; Hui *et al.*, 2003, Leung and Wong, 2004; Ganesan and Tse, 1997, 1999; Tse, 1998; and Raftery and Tse, 2001). The second approach is the use of causality relationship to see which determinant would have a unidirectional or bidirectional relationship with property price (Granger, 1969). By using Hong Kong's annual and quarterly data for the periods 1978–2005 and 1993–2005, respectively, Kwok (2006) showed that a bidirectional relationship existed between GDP, consumption, investment or unemployment and the property price, but a unidirectional causality relationship existed between the best lending rate or the number of households and the property price.

Other studies, for example, included discussions on the distinction between the wealth effect and credit price effect. Kapopoulos and Siokis (2005) pointed out that the wealth effect occurred when unanticipated gains in asset price raised the demand for property, while the credit price effect occurred when the rise in property price led to a rise in the value of the collateral, and that in turn made it easier for households to borrow, resulting in a possible rise in the demand for property. Property price and the demand for different classes of property are interconnected. When the wealth of households expanded, households living in a smaller size property situated in low quality locations would move up market to larger size property in good locations. Haurin *et al.* (2003) considered the forward ripple effect in Hong Kong in property boom years, but Kwok (2006) claimed that a reverse ripple effect is possible in economic recession. Giuliodori (2004) summarized the various effect of property price on monetary and macroeconomic variables. For example, the so-called Tobin's *q* theory (Tobin 1998) would argue that investment in property will increase when the housing prices and construction costs ratio exceeded unity. The two studies by Kwok (2006) and Peng (2002) used the basic concept in the asset pricing model to examine the excessive increase in residential property price and the extent of the property price bubble in Hong Kong.

In a perfect capital market with no speculative activity in the property market, property price should equal to the present value of the infinite stream of the rental income from the property. Speculation in the property market emerged when property price (P) deviated from the present value of the rental income (R). One can estimate the present value of the rental income by assuming that it is the present value of rental income (R) discounted by real best lending rate (r) at time t, expressed as:

$$P_t = R_t / r_t. \tag{6}$$

Equation (6) can be used to produce a rent-to-price ratio function for empirical estimation, shown as follows:

$$R_t / P_t = \beta_0 + \beta_1 r_t + \varepsilon_t, \tag{7}$$

where R_t is the per-square-meter rental income of residential units, P_t is per-square-meter price of residential units (market price), r_t is prime interest rate which is the quarterly average of nominal prime interest rate (the best lending rate) released by the Hong Kong and Shanghai Banking Corporation Limited (HSBC), and ε_t is the random error term, all at time t.

Equation (7) is used to estimate both the residential and commercial properties in Hong Kong. The quarterly data set that covered the period from March 1982 to December 2005 (1982Q1 – 2005Q4) can be obtained from the Census and Statistics Department, and data on price and rental income of properties can be found in the *Hong Kong Property Review*, Rating and Valuation Department, Hong Kong. For the residential property market, the estimation work is conducted for the entire Hong Kong as well as the three regions of Hong Kong Island, Kowloon peninsula and New Territories. For all the regions, the property price index and rental index are used since the actual dollar price data are not available. For the three regions, the actual dollar price and rental income of residential units are used. Class B of domestic residential premises that ranged from 40 to 69.9 square meters is selected for the regression estimation.

For the commercial property, the regression work is conducted for all commercial properties in the entire Hong Kong and separately for the Central District in Hong Kong Island and Tsim Sha Tsui district in Kowloon. Data for three different categories (Grades A, B and C) of commercial property are used for the Central and Tsim Sha Tsui districts. According to the Rating and Valuation Department, the three grades (A, B and C) of commercial office property are classified under different qualitative criteria. Grade A commercial properties are modern with high quality finishes, grade B commercial properties have ordinary design with good quality finishes, while grade C commercial properties are plain with basic finishes.[13]

The market price and rental income data are used in the regression estimation of Equation (7). With the estimated rent-to-price ratio ($R_t/\hat{}P_t$), a fundamental price ($\hat{P}_t$) can be generated using the following equation:

$$\hat{P}_t = \mathrm{R}_t/(R_t/\hat{}P_t). \tag{8}$$

According to the asset pricing model, the fundamental price is the sum of the discounted present value of the net future rental income a residential property unit provides. In laymen terms, the fundamental price can be regarded as the "user-market" or the "equilibrium market" price that reflected the stream of rental income the property earns.

Property speculation would push the market price up, and the extent of price deviation between the market price and fundamental price could give an indication of property speculation. Property is under-priced when the market price is below the fundamental price. Conversely, property is over-priced when the market price is far above the fundamental price. One can argue that a property bubble could emerge when the property market has experienced a prolonged and severe period of over-price. A property bubble existed when the market price is far above the fundamental price. Such a price distortion could be due to market frictions and economic shocks. Typically, rental incomes from property tended to show a steady trend and adjusted at a much slower pace than market price, due probably to the restriction by the time length of the contract lease. Hence, a reasonable deviation between the market price and fundamental price can be expected.

Table 12.6 reported the regression estimation results of Equation (7) for both residential property and commercial property sectors. One general observation is that the goodness of fit measure, indicated by the R-square ratios are low, especially in the commercial properties, indicating that the prime rate and rental income are not powerful in explaining the property price in Hong Kong. In other words, there are other determinants that could appropriately explain the rising property price in Hong Kong. Using Equation (8), the coefficient estimates shown in Table 12.6 are used to construct a fundamental price series for the four residential property sectors (entire Hong Kong and the three regions) and three commercial property sectors (entire Hong Kong and the three different grades in Central and Tsim Sha Tsui districts). The various fundamental price series constructed from Equation (8) are mapped with the market price.

Figure 12.12 plotted the two price series (fundamental price and the actual market price) for the entire residential property market in Hong Kong. One can see that property price in Hong Kong had been under-priced in much of the 1980s when the fundamental price was higher than the actual market price, but the early 1990s saw the turning point and the two price series reversed, and cumulated ultimately into a

---

[13] For detailed classification of commercial properties, refer to *Hong Kong Property Review*, Rating and Valuation Department, Hong Kong.

TABLE 12.6 Regression results of the rent-to-price ratio regression (1982Q1–2005Q4)

Residential Property (Dependent Variable: Rent-to-Price Ratio)				
	Entire HK	Hong Kong Island	Kowloon Peninsula	New Territories
Constant	0.3332 (0.0786)	3.3319 (0.6938)	2.8027 (0.8591)	3.3320 (0.9280)
Prime Rate	0.0495 (0.0089)	0.4129 (0.0789)	0.5458 (0.0977)	0.3022 (0.1125)
Size (%) and [date of maximum under-price]	41 [9/1985]	38 [9/1985]	41 [9/1985]	46 [12/1987]
Size (%) and [date of maximum over-price]	81 [6/1997)	84 [3/1998]	116 [6/1997)	114 [9/1997)
R-square	0.2462	0.2256	0.2492	0.0774

Commercial Property (Dependent Variable: Rent-to-Price Ratio)							
		Central			Tsim Sha Tsui		
	Entire HK	Grade A	Grade B	Grade C	Grade A	Grade B	Grade C
Constant	0.9402 (0.1017)	4.1983 (0.7847)	6.5254 (0.8286)	6.1780 (0.8548)	3.0438 (0.8027)	4.9578 (0.7613)	8.6413 (0.7278)
Prime Rate	0.0186 (0.0117)	0.3561 (0.0904)	0.1368 (0.0954)	0.2843 (0.0984)	0.4917 (0.0924)	0.3552 (0.0877)	0.0868 (0.0838)
Size (%) [date of maximum under-price]	33 [3/1986]	50 [9/1986]	54 [6/2003]	42 [9/2001]	43 [6/1985]	38 [12/2001]	30 [3/2002]
Size (%) [date of maximum over-price]	67 [6/1997]	96 [3/1997]	132 [6/2004]	85 [12/2005]	93 [12/1996]	72 [9/1997]	88 [9/2005]
R-square	0.0263	0.1431	0.0216	0.0823	0.2333	0.1501	0.0114

Notes: Standard error figures are given in parentheses. The month and year that corresponded to the peaks are shown in square brackets.

property bubble. For the whole residential market, the under-price period emerged between 1985 and 1989, while the over-price period can be found since the early 1990s and peaked in June 1997 with 81 percent, as shown in Table 12.6. The under-price regime returned between late 2001 and late 2003, but the residential property market experienced over-price again since 2004.

Figures 12.13, 12.14 and 12.15 reported a similar picture of price deviation between fundamental price and actual market price for the residential market in the three regions of Hong Kong Island, Kowloon peninsula and New Territories, respectively. The three regions showed a similar trend. The magnitude of the under-pricing and over-pricing between the 1980s and 1990s are reported in Table 12.6. Among the three regions, the peak of under-pricing occurred in 1985 and 1987. The peak of the under-pricing for both Hong Kong Island and Kowloon occurred in September 1985, with 38 percent and 41 percent, respectively. The under-price peak of the New Territories came later in December 1987 with 46 percent.

The extent of over-pricing was more serious, as reported in Table 12.6. The over-price peak for the whole Hong Kong came in June 1997 with 81 percent. Among the three regions, the peak of the over-price occurred between June 1997 and March 1998. Residential property in Kowloon was most over-priced with 116 percent, followed closely by the New Territories with 114 percent. Residential property in Hong Kong Island experienced a maximum of 84 percent over-pricing in March 1998. Figure 12.16 summarized the extent of actual market price deviation from the fundamental price in the residential property market of the entire Hong Kong and the three regions.

A similar exercise is conducted for commercial properties in the entire Hong Kong (Figure 12.17) and for the three grades of offices in the Central district in

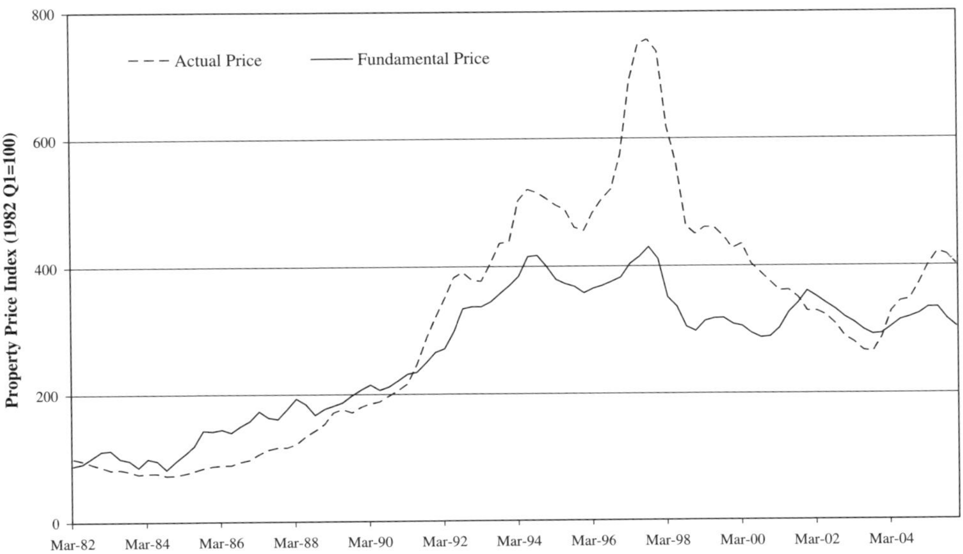

FIGURE 12.12 Actual and fundamental price of residential properties

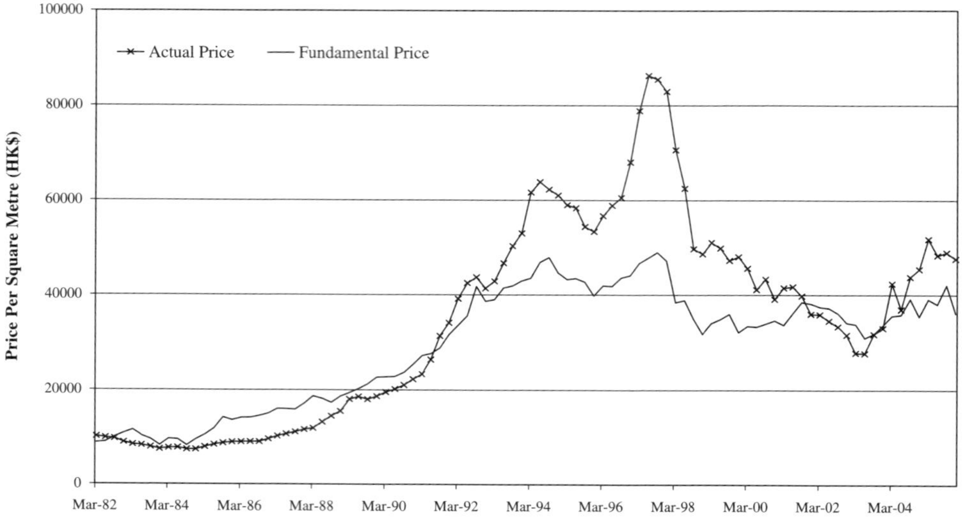

FIGURE 12.13 Actual and fundamental price of residential properties: Hong Kong Island

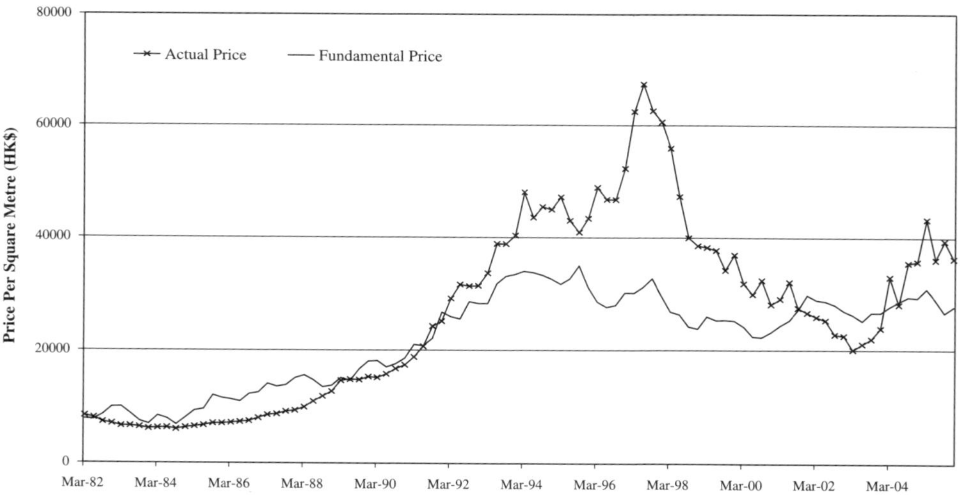

FIGURE 12.14 Actual and fundamental price of residential properties: Kowloon

Hong Kong Island and the Tsim Sha Tsui area in Kowloon (Figures 12.18–12.23). For the entire commercial property market in Hong Kong, as reported in Table 12.6, the peak of the under-price came in March 1986 with 33 percent, while the peak of the over-price came in June 1997. The under-price and over-price peaks among the different grades of commercial property in Central and Tsim Sha Tsui differed considerably. While grade A commercial property followed the property bubble, grades

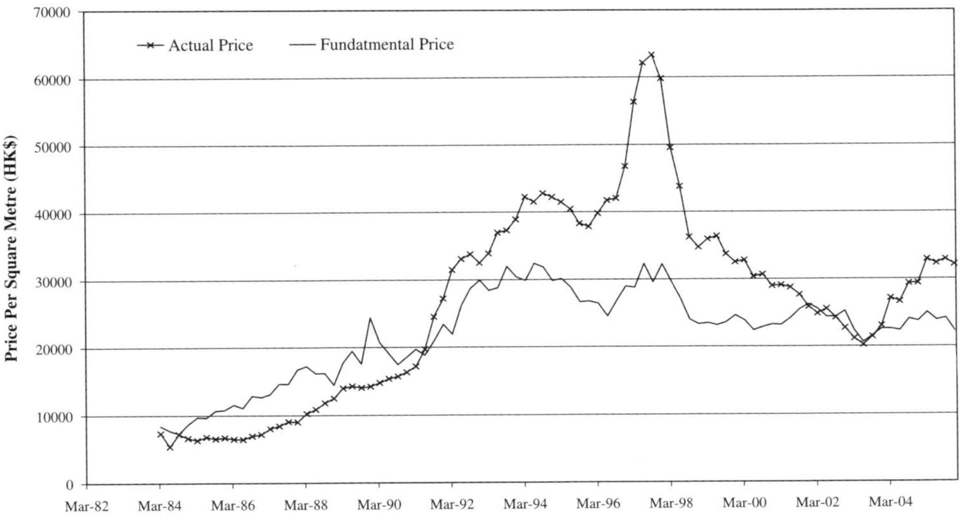

FIGURE 12.15 Actual and fundamental price of residential properties: New Territories

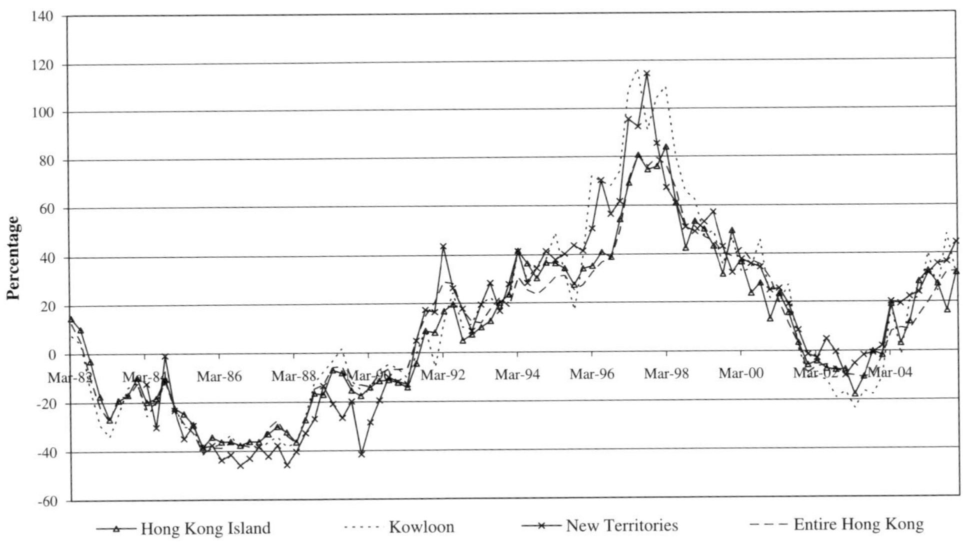

FIGURE 12.16 Percentage price deviations in residential property market

B and C commercial properties suffered more in the post-Asian financial crisis years, as their under-price peaks occurred between December 2001 and June 2003. Grade B commercial property in the Central District was most over-priced in June 2004 with 132 percent.

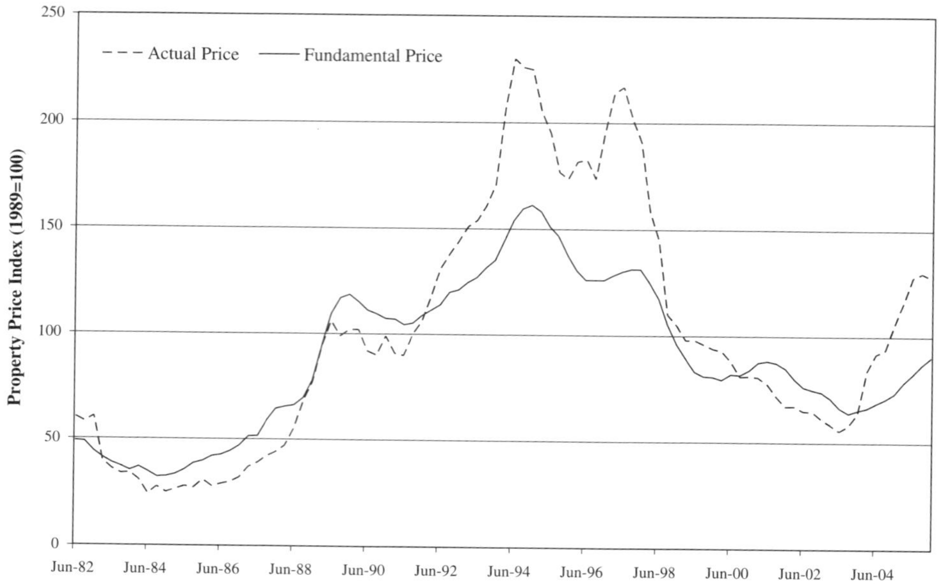

FIGURE 12.17 Actual and fundamental price of commercial properties

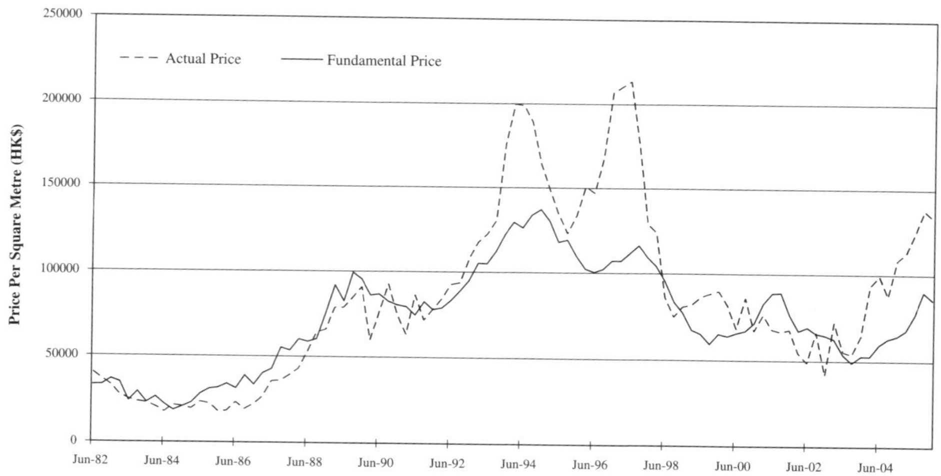

FIGURE 12.18 Actual and fundamental price of commercial property (A): central

12.6 A Three-Dimension Policy

From the property price index shown in Figure 12.10, one can see that the property market recovered in 2005, and other than a short period of downfall in 2008 due probably to the US financial crisis and the mini-bond incidence as a result of the closure of Lehman Brothers in New York, the property price in Hong Kong has

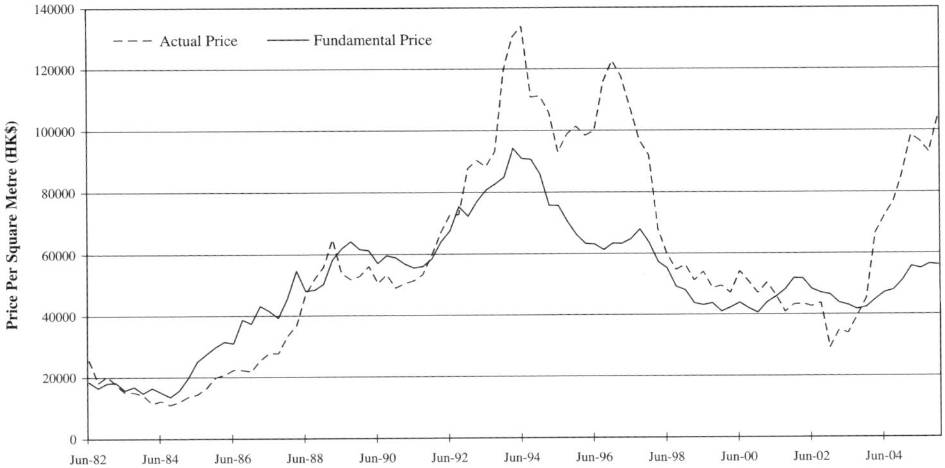

FIGURE 12.19 Actual and fundamental price of commercial property (A): Tsim Sha Tsui

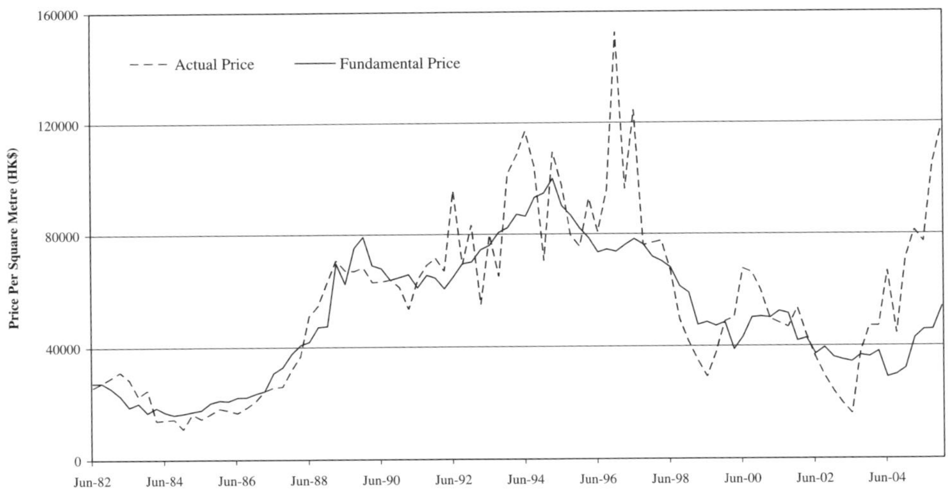

FIGURE 12.20 Actual and fundamental price of commercial property (B): central

kept rising and become overheated after 2009. The concern of a real estate bubble soon emerged. By February 2011, the Financial Secretary, John C. Tsang, remarked that the overall property price has surpassed the peak in 1997.[14] A consultancy firm in US surveyed in early 2010 that "Hong Kong homes are the least affordable among the world's major cities". The survey showed that people in Hong Kong pay more than 10 times their annual income to buy a flat, which is the

[14] *South China Morning Post*, April 14, 2011.

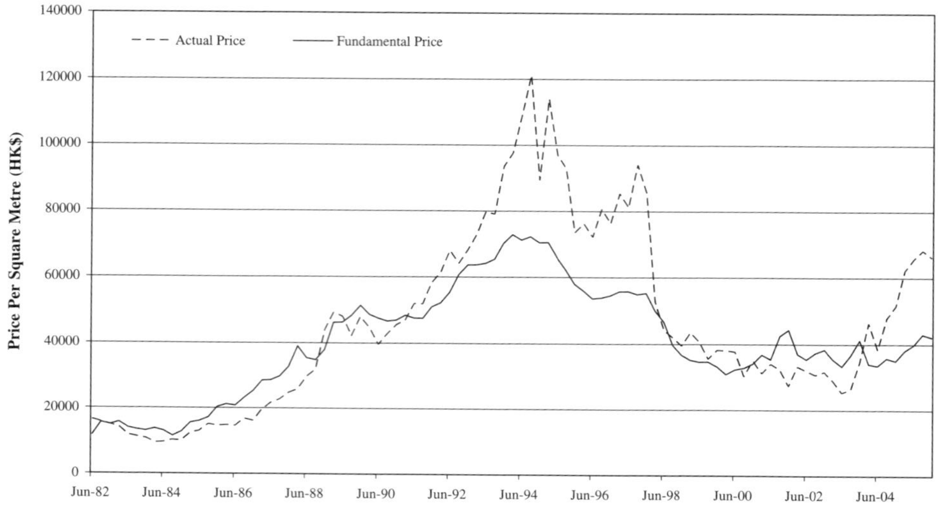

FIGURE 12.21 Actual and fundamental price of commercial property (B): Tsim Sha Tsui

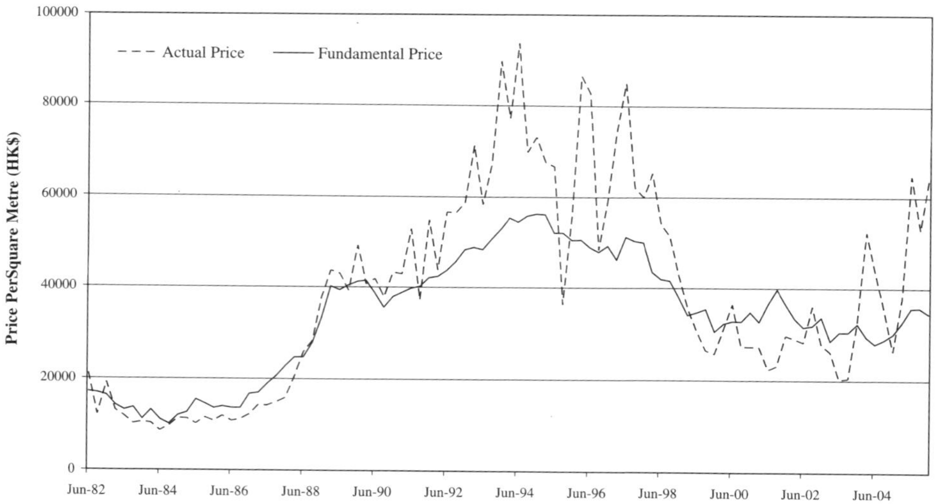

FIGURE 12.22 Actual and fundamental price of commercial property (C): central

highest in the survey that covered 272 world metropolitan cities.[15] The concern has also been captured in an International Monetary Fund report by Ahuja and Porter (2010), though the study based on the situation in 2009–2010 came to a different conclusion that "house prices do not appear to be out of line with

[15] *South China Morning Post*, April 20, 2010.

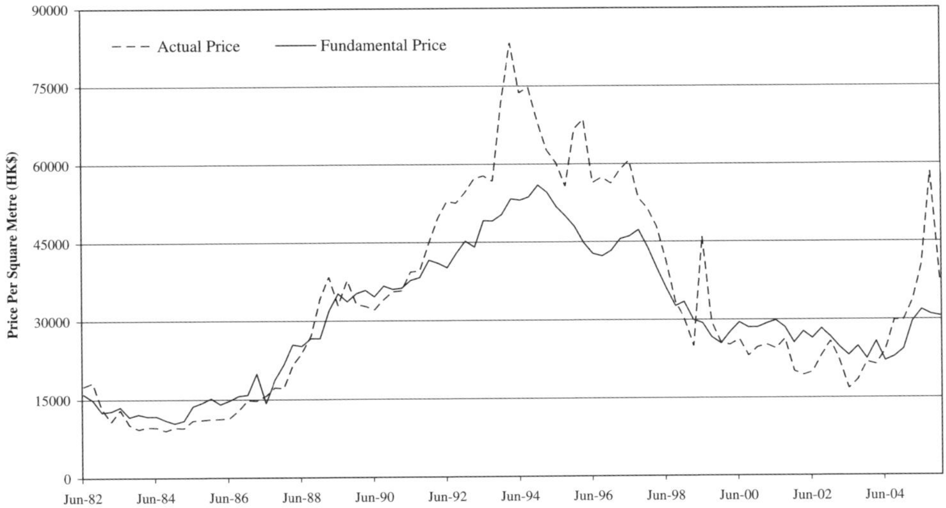

FIGURE 12.23 Actual and fundamental price of commercial property (C): Tsim Sha Tsui

fundamentals in Hong Kong SAR although prices are rising rapidly", and that "low interest rate and improving growth prospects, as well as a tight supply… means that house price growth will continue to be strong".

Other than the reasons of a prolong low interest rate policy and a tight supply shown in the study by Ahuju and Porter (2010), the situation on the demand for property in Hong Kong has changed and is different from the last property bubble prior to the 1997 Asian financial crisis. Economic recovery since 2005 has led to a revival for the property demand, but by 2009, property speculation returned for various reasons. One possible change is that properties in Hong Kong have become very much an export good, and especially the high price luxurious houses and apartments. The open nature of the Hong Kong economy does not impose restrictions on property demand by non-local residents. Any legal person can own a piece of property in Hong Kong.

At the peak of economic recession after the Asian financial crisis, the government introduced in October 2003 the Capital Investment Entrant Scheme (CIES) that allowed immigration with capital investment to reside in Hong Kong with a threshold of investment no less than HK$6.5 million. It thus turned out to be attractive for new immigrants to purchase properties in Hong Kong. However, since October 2010, at the peak of the property price, the CIES was revised and the threshold of investment for admission to Hong Kong has been raised to HK$10 million, and real estate is suspended as a class of Permissible Investment Asset (PIA).[16]

[16] Between October 2003 and October 2010, around 8,200 investors with 15,500 dependents have been admitted to Hong Kong, bringing in around HK$58 billion of investment. Information on the CIES can be found in the Immigration Department, Hong Kong SAR Government website.

The Chief Executive, Donald Tsang Yum-kuen, explained that such home purchases from the CEIS accounted for 42 percent of the total investment under the CIES in the first three quarters of 2010.[17]

Secondly and since around 2008, an increasing number of "cash-rich" residents from Mainland China have come to purchase property in Hong Kong as an investment and a way to get rid of their cash in Mainland China. Despite the fact that Renminbi is not a full convertible currency and there are official restrictions on the outflow of the Renminbi, there are numerous channels where residents from Mainland China can transfer their cash to Hong Kong. After the three decades of economic reform in China, the emergence of a new class of "cash rich" residents whom come to invest and speculate on real estates in Hong Kong, especially on the luxurious apartments and houses. This has resulted in a rapid deviation from the economic fundamentals in Hong Kong. In a sense, the new supply of luxurious apartments in Hong Kong could effectively be consumed by the cash rich residents from Mainland China, and the rising price has exerted a spilt-over effect on properties in the user market in the local economy, leading to a continued rise in property price, and speculators see their chance and enter the market for speculative gains. Hence, Hong Kong property prices will keep rising so long as Hong Kong is attractive to the rich residents from Mainland China.

Another area of debate is the mechanism through which new properties are sold in the market and the method of properties transaction. Other than the debate on the method of land sales, there has also been complaint on the lack of standards and fair practices in the way the size of properties are measured, the way developers promote new developments and the accuracy of the information provided. The "near-monopoly" pricing strategy by the developers on new developments has led to the possibility of market manipulation by the developers.

In economics, the problem is known as information asymmetry when one party to a transaction has more or better information than the other party. The buyer in a new development is basically at the mercy of the developer, as it is the developer who holds all the information, and there is a lack of rules and regulation regarding the disclosure of information to the buyer. For example, the developer may not accurately report the exact size of the usable areas and provide only the gross areas that can include such common areas as the lift lobby, garden and other open areas. The price of new property has sometimes been provided on an individual and selective basis to the potential buyer, and not a general price list for public consumption. There are instances where the developer gave false information on the number of apartments or properties sold in the same block or development site. Other cases included the collusion between the developer and buyers to give a false price of the luxury apartment or penthouse in order to boost up market sentiment. The police raided the offices of a developer as investigation was conducted by the government involving the sale of luxury flats that sold for as much as HK$88,000 (US$12,282) per square foot, and the sale announcement sparked accusation of market manipulation.[18]

[17] Press release "CE tackles property market concerns in Policy Address", Hong Kong, October 13, 2010.

[18] *South China Morning Post*, August 13, 2010.

In short, the public has often questioned the reliability of the information disclosed by the developer.

Over the years, the government has adopted an "appeasement policy" on the behavior of property developers and real estate agents, arguing that maintaining a market-driven property market is paramount, and "verbal warnings" are given to developers should their unscrupulous practices in the sales of new and incomplete apartments and houses have become excessive. The reluctance on the part of the government in introducing more stringent regulations has led to a general consensus that there may be collusion between the government and property developers.

The Estate Agents Authority (EAA) has regularly issued practice circulars to real estate practitioners on a need basis to remind them the relevant laws and regulations and to provide them with guidelines on conduct and practice. As a civic institution, the EAA "strives to promote the standard of services of the estate agency trade and encourages open, fair and honest property transactions". Between 2004 and 2006, for example, the EAA has issued five Practice Circulars related to first sales. On October 24, 2006, the EAA issued a Practice Circular on the guidelines in ten areas that estate agency practitioners should follow when dealing with first sales of residential properties. The ten areas included the guidelines on the price lists, deposits, authorization for advertising, accuracy of advertisement, representations by agents, publication of sales information, obtaining potential purchases' identity cards, number of agents at sales sites, maintaining order at sales sites, and compliance with laws, rules and regulations when conducting sales activities in the vicinity of sales sites. Under the Estate Agents ordinance, disciplinary sanctions included admonishment, reprimand, attachment or variations of conditions to a license, fine amounting to HK$300,000, suspension of a license for 2 years and revocation of a license in extreme cases.[19]

The developers also have their own Real Estate Developers Association (REDA) of Hong Kong that obviously acted to preserve and defend their own interest and can influence government policy decisions, despite continued public dissatisfaction on the way property transactions are being handled in terms of information accuracy, sales method and monopolistic power in price setting. Nonetheless, the rapid rise in property price has led to huge public reaction and forced the government to act. It was reported that private residential property prices had increased by 20 percent year-on-year between the third quarter of 2009 and 2010, and that property price has gained an accumulated increase of 7.2 percent in the first two months of 2011.[20] The way the developers manipulated the luxurious housing market has led to public discontent. For example, the developers' tactics included conducting sales at mid-night, selling flats on a batch by batch basis and disclosing the price list until the last minute.[21] Realizing their poor public image, the property developers through the REDA in early August 2010 hired an international public relations firm to conduct a wide-ranging survey on the property sector in Hong Kong, after a series of

---

[19] Press release, Estate Agents Authority, Hong Kong, October 24, 2006.

[20] *South China Morning Post*, April 14, 2011.

[21] *South China Morning Post*, April 13, 2010.

controversies on property sale practices.[22] In subsequent rules released on fairer flat sales by the government, REDA flashed their "power" by openly declared that REDA was "unhappy that the government made the announcements before reaching consensus with REDA".[23]

Seen from the various recent Policy Addresses by the Chief Executive and the budget speech by the Financial Secretary, one can identify that the government has pursued a gradualist and building-block approach to correct the distortion in the property market. For example, the Chief Executive announced in his Policy Address on October 13, 2010, a series of short, medium and long-term housing strategies. The Financial Secretary and other key officials have subsequently made a number of clustered announcements that were meant to introduce transparency and fairness into the various aspects of trade in the property market. The gradualist and building-block approach is meant to introduce the regulations piece by piece so as to minimize its impact on the property market and avoid sharp price adjustments that may spill over to other economic activities. It is true that given the strong power of the property sector in Hong Kong, and the degree of sensitivity it carried in various economic aspects, it would be wise for the government to introduce over a period of time a cluster of policies that could stabilize the property sector.

On the contrary, others worried if the regulations are just piecemeal, lip-service serving only as response to sweeten public dissatisfaction and may not have sufficient force on the developers.[24] For the establishment of a stable property sector and in order to provide a level playing field to all suppliers and demanders of properties, the regulations and practices have to be introduced on a more permanent and standardized basis and legislations are needed in order to transform the good practices into a well-recognized and respected system. It is important for Hong Kong to have a fair, equal opportunity, crystal clear economic system that would not be personality driven, nor influenced by individual events.

Many of the rules and policies introduced in 2010 can broadly be grouped into three related dimensions of sale practices, land supply and housing provisions in Hong Kong. These dimensions have effectively defined a new policy on sales practice, land supply and housing provision.

Sales practices

Property sales covered a range of issues, but the removal of the information asymmetry problem is seen as most paramount. Beginning from April 2010, a total of 12 proposals were announced on improving the transparency of sales and the avoidance of market manipulations, including the issue of a price list and a sale brochure three days in advance of sales. Another proposal included allowing the prospective buyers to take measures in show flats that would include all external walls

[22] *South China Morning Post*, August 1, 2010.
[23] *South China Morning Post*, April 13, 2010.
[24] *South China Morning Post*, July 26, 2010.

and the developers would have to provide accurate information in show-flats. Another rule required developers to provide the address and location of development in promotional materials that often showed only an idealized picture. Another rule stated that developers are required to comply with the consent scheme when uncompleted flats are for sale. In addition, developers will have to disclose of sales information on all canceled deals within five working days after a preliminary agreement for purchase is terminated, and secondly, the developer must state the estimated date of completion of a development five days after signing the agreement to sell a unit.[25]

The foremost important issue disclosed in the Policy Addressed delivered in October 2010 was to introduce legislations that regulate the sale of first-hand flats, including the use of saleable floor area as the basis for listing the price per square foot. From mid-August 2010, and in order to curb property speculation, purchasers of first-hand uncompleted flats will not be allowed to re-sell, sub-sell or transfer the benefits of the agreements for sale and purchase before completion of the transaction. A penalty equivalent to 10% of the total purchase price will be forfeited if buyers cancel the transactions.[26]

The Consumer Council on August 26, 2010, called for improvements in information dissemination to the public in the residential property market and put forward a number of recommendations.[27] There should be clear guidelines regarding pre-launch activities of first-hand properties. Developers and sales agents are refrained from releasing non-official "intentional prices" or the use of imprecise terms relating to the potential price of flats before the official announcement of flat sales. There should be an upper limit to the number of "private sales". Thirdly, prospective buyers must be given sufficient time for viewing the show-flats. There should also be controls over unreliable and deceptive representations. The Consumer Council proposed an online "Property Market Information Platform" that provides the public with comprehensive property market information on first-hand private residential properties. This, of course, assumes that developers are willing and prepared to provide the information efficiently. In the provision for sales brochures and price lists, the Consumer Council recommended that price lists and sales brochures be available at sales offices for distribution and the time gap between the sale of flats and the release of the transaction records be shortened. Lastly, the Consumer Council recommended that the existing mechanism on handling complaints should be strengthened.

Financial instruments have also been used to fight property speculation. A capital gain tax has been imposed in November 2010, amounting to 15 percent if a home was resold within six months.[28] It has been argued that Hong Kong's capital gain tax

---

[25] *South China Morning China Post*, April 13, 16 and 22, 2010; *The Standard*, April 22, 2010; and *Sing Tao Daily*, April 22, 2010.

[26] "Measures stabilize property market", Information Service Department, Hong Kong, August 13, 2010.

[27] *Mingpao Daily*, July 28, 2010. Press release, Consumer Council, Hong Kong, July 26, 2010.

[28] "Amendment to the Stamp Duty Ordinance to curb speculation in residential properties", Transport and Housing Bureau, Hong Kong, November 19, 2010.

on property speculation can learn from overseas countries, where the capital gain tax can be used more effectively in dealing with speculations. For example, the tax could be exempted if the property purchased is the household's principal residence. In other words, the tax is imposed on the second ownership of property. However, there can be a number of variations. Properties could be purchased using a company's name, or by a non-resident. As such, it could be easier and simpler to have a single capital gain tax rate.

On August 13, 2010, the Hong Kong Monetary Authority (HKMA) announced its aim to prevent excessive mortgage lending by issuing a circular to banks requiring them to implement a set of prudential measures for residential mortgage loans. The content of the circular included: a) applying a maximum loan-to-value ratio of 60 percent to properties valued at or above HK$12 million. The 70 percent loan-to-value ratio for properties valued below HK$12 million continued to apply, and the maximum loan amount is capped at HK$7.2 million; b) lowering the maximum loan-to-value ratio for properties not intended to be occupied by the owners to 60 percent, and mortgage applicants have to declare whether they intend to occupy the mortgage property; and c) standardizing the limit on debt servicing ratios of mortgage applicants to 50 percent, instead of a range between 50 percent and 60 percent. At the same time, the Mortgage Corporation also revised mortgage insurance that aimed at discouraging speculations.[29]

Land supply

A number of related and clustered announcements have been made in 2010 and 2011 in order to increase the supply of land and construction of properties. These announcements included the increase in "government-initiated" land sales arrangements in addition to the existing method of Application List system, new land reclamation near the airport in the Tung Chung area, and allowing variations in urban re-developments.

Firstly, in his 2010 Policy Address the Chief Executive, Donald Tsang Yum-kuen, declared the establishment of a land reserve to ensure sufficient land provision for an annual average of some 20,000 private residential flats in the following 10 years. The intention of conducting more "government-initiated" land sales arrangements, in addition to the Application List system that allowed developers to choose from the land list for public auction, was announced in August 2010. By April 2011, the government announced the sales of 9 residential sites, and that land sales will be conducted on a more regular basis. In other words, the government would be taking a more active role in land sales to stabilize supply, though the Application List system that had put the government in a very passive role still exists should developers want to apply a specified plot of land for auction.[30]

---

[29] "More property controls announced", Information Services Department, Hong Kong, August 13, 2010. *South China Morning Post*, April 14, 2011.

[30] "More property controls announced", Information Services Department, Hong Kong, August 13, 2010. *South China Morning Post and Mingpao Daily*, April 14, 2011.

The Secretary for Development, Carrie Lam Cheng Yuet-ngor, agreed that the two-pronged arrangement of proactively selling land and maintaining the Application List can stabilize and sustain the Government's land policy.[31] However, others have argued that many of the new land plots put up for sales are small and may not have much influence on property price, though the small land plots could provide more opportunities for small developers. The more effective instrument in land supply is the land price and the method of land sales through open auctioning.

New measures in urban renewal and redevelopment have been considered. While it is a timely and costly process to convince the residents and owners for urban redevelopment, the Urban Renewal Authority (URA) on April 18, 2011, decided to take up the role of a facilitator in redevelopment.[32] As a facilitator, the URA would help to band together a joint sale of owners of old buildings to investors or developers with the objective to release the occupied land for redevelopment and achieve sufficient financial returns to the occupiers of the old buildings. Owners of the old building, of course, have to comply with a number of conditions before the URA steps in to act as a facilitator. Nonetheless, this is seen as a positive sign in the speeding up of urban renewal and redevelopment that eventually would increase supply of private residential properties.

In addition to the determination to tackle the problem of building dilapidation and unauthorized building works as the major obstacle to urban redevelopment and renewal, the Chief Executive also discussed the re-zoning of about 30 hectares of land designated probably for industrial usage to residential usage.[33]

Housing

The two government bureaus currently involved in land deployment and provision of housing are the Development Bureau and the Transport and Housing Bureau. In addition, the Housing Authority, which was established as a statutory body in April 1972 under the Housing Ordinance, is rested with the responsibility to determine and implement public housing programs. Major duties included planning and building public housing, managing public rental housing estates, interim housing estates and transit centers. In 1978, in order to provide more home ownership opportunities to the sandwich class residents, the Home Ownership Scheme (HOS) was introduced as a kind of subsidized housing sold at discounted prices. Other subsidized home ownership schemes, such as Private Sector Participation Scheme and the Tenants Purchase Scheme, were introduced by the Housing Authority. Since 1978, over 433,000 subsidized flats have been sold to households in the low and middle income groups at discounted prices.

Other than the Housing Authority, there is the Hong Kong Housing Society which is an independent and non-profit oriented organization that provides rental

---

[31] Information Services Department, Hong Kong, April 16, 2011.

[32] "URA: Facilitator role in redevelopment", Urban Renewal Authority, Hong Kong, April 18, 2011.

[33] Press release "CE tackles property market concerns in Policy Address", Information Services Department, Hong Kong, October 13, 2010.

estates, rural public housing, flat-for-sale, sandwich class housing and senior citizen residences. As of March 2006, the Housing Society's management portfolio contained rental estates, managed properties, Tenants Purchase scheme estates, and estates of the Housing Authority, non-domestic premises and car parking spaces.

However, as discussed fully in Li (2006, Section 6.6), the HOS scheme was discontinued in 2002 at the peak of the property market recession after the Asian financial crisis and the pressure from the developers. Li (2006) attributed to the problem of 'supply overlap' and the ease of re-sale by the occupiers in the private market, even though some conditions have to be satisfied before re-sale. The loophole of the HOS scheme is the difference in the price of flats when compared to the residential properties of similar size in the private market. Thus, in an economic recession, the privatized HOS flats would become attractive as they were sold at a much cheaper price than a flat with a similar size in the private residential market supplied by the developers. In other words, the HOS flats sold in the secondary market would not be rechanneled back to the government. The HOS occupiers actually purchased the HOS flats at a discounted price but sold the flats at the market price in the secondary market, pocketing the price difference themselves.

The rapid rise in property prices since 2009 has led to the discussion in the revitalization of the HOS for household in the sandwich class. Opinions on the revitalization of HOS have been divided as to whether the system practiced before 2002 should be adopted, or a new system of housing assistance to the sandwich class be constructed. The government reacted first by announcing in March 2010 the sale of the remaining 4,000 HOS flats and the 374 flats under the Hong Kong Housing Society's sandwich class scheme, and issued in June 2010 public consultation document to solicit views on subsidizing home ownership.

The discussion on the revitalization of the HOS and the provision of subsidized housing for domestic users has led to a renewed strategy on housing stated by the Chief Executive in the 2010–2011 Policy Address (Sections 11 to 49).[34] The Chief Executive put forward three government policies on housing. They are: 1) helping the low-income group by providing public rental housing (PRH); 2) promote land supply instead of participation in subsidized housing; and 3) provide quality infrastructure for the healthy and sustainable development of the property market.

On PRH, the 2010–2011 Policy Address ensured that an adequate supply of land to produce about 15,000 flats each year so that the average waiting time of three years will be maintained. Instead of providing direct subsidies, the Chief Executive offered the "My Home Purchase Plan", which is a relief measure to give sandwich class home buyers time to save up. In collaboration with the Hong Kong Housing Society, the government shall provide land to HKHS to build small and medium "no-frills" flats for lease to eligible applicants at prevailing market rent. Should the tenant choose to buy the rental or another flat at prevailing market price or a flat in the private market, the tenant will receive a subsidy for use as down payment equivalent to half of the net rental payment they made during the tenancy period. Given that the

---

[34] *Sharing Prosperity for a Caring Society*, the 2010–2011 Policy Address, Hong Kong, October 13, 2010.

tenancy period is up to five years, the tenant will get 50 percent of their net rental payment back for the purchase of their flat or another flat. The plan contains a total of some 5,000 flats in different sites, with the first project providing 1,000 such flats in 2014.

Despite the various suggestions in the Policy Address, public pressure on the revival of the HOS has been growing in 2011. The more relevant public concern is how to improve the HOS system and remove the loopholes of 'supply overlap' between the provision of HOS housing and the provision from the private market. To remove the 'supply overlap', Li (2006) has suggested that the government will have to go one step further to ensure that HOS housing will remain with the government, and the tenants have to sell back to the government should they want to exit the HOS market. This has two main advantages. Tenants exiting from the HOS will sell the flat back to the government so that the government can resale it to another needy family. Thus, HOS will always be used to help sandwich families and will not compete with supply from the private market. Secondly, households taking up the HOS will have their wealth built up as the HOS is their property that can be liquidated to acquire property in the private market should they choose to do so.

Another concern is the pricing of the HOS, both at the time of purchase by the household and the time the housing is selling the flat back to the government. There can be a number of possibilities. When the government sells the HOS to the household, the price alternatives can include the cost of production, the average market price, some adjusted price from the private market, or a discount of the price in the private market. When the household decides to exit from the HOS and sells it back to the government, the price alternatives can include the production cost adjusted by inflation, or some discounted price from the private market. Ultimately, a system has to be established so that the households can decide if HOS would provide a more suitable alternative of property acquisition than the private market, bearing in mind that the provision of HOS flats are meant to help sandwich households to acquire their property, and allow them to build up their asset wealth for their future purchase should they decide to acquire properties in the private market.

Much discussion has also been made on the appropriate number of HOS to be supplied. Again, a number of criteria can be applied in deciding on the quantity to be supplied, though it would ultimately have to be worked out by a trial and error process. Decisions could initially be based on the rate of population growth, or on a percentage based on the number of young graduates, or on a percentage based on the number of public housing occupants, or just on an annual quantity to be adjusted over the years.

The provision of HOS can have wider societal implications. For example, high technology or energy-saving provisions could be used in the new buildings, as such would make Hong Kong more environmental friendly. The size of HOS can also be enlarged to provide better living conditions to households. A better living environment in terms of the size of the HOS could lead to other benefits. For example, children can have more space for their private studies, families may spend more time together in a larger living space, and young couples may be more prepared to live with their parents and so on. In other words, the revived HOS scheme can be used to achieve other long-term desirable social goals. It therefore would positively produce "a stone killing more than one bird" consequence for the Hong Kong economy.

Although the 2010–2011 Policy Address did not revive the HOS scheme, it is possible that the next Chief Executive after 2012 will have to make a more decisive policy on the HOS policy. In respond to the public pressure, the Director of Housing in the Hong Kong SAR Government remarked in late June, 2011, that there would not be instant solution to the heated property market even if the HOS scheme was revived as "it would take seven years to get the first flat on sale". Professional surveyors queried the length of time involved and proposed that a maximum of four years would probably be the appropriate time.[35]

Nonetheless, the key message from the policy principles discussed in the 2010–2011 Policy Address is the importance of a reliable, open and transparent system on land supply, property sales and housing provision. The property market does fluctuate with the business cycle, and demand changes according to circumstances. A government policy on land sales and housing should be proactive and not reactive. The establishment and nurture of open and transparent system should serve as a level playing field to all market participants. In Hong Kong, it is always the system that shall stand between the various parties in business transactions. A steady supply of land through regular land sales, an improved system of sales practices and a policy that distinguishes the role of housing as a necessity from a speculation vehicle can serve to stabilize the housing demand.

A well-established system should avoid a piecemeal approach that reacts only to market sentiments. Nonetheless, the policy stated in the 2011–2012 Policy Address should best be regarded as a starting point as more policies are needed to be written into law so as to strength and improve the land deployment and housing provision system. Improvements can further be made, for example, in sale practices, method of land sales and the land premium as a source of fiscal revenue and so on.

12.7 Conclusion

Individual freedom in property transactions and land acquisition is probably a major component in the investment freedom. Perhaps, it would be appropriate to have a separate measurement within the economic freedom index to show how activities in the land and property sector will improve an economy's freedom performance. It is the outcome of economic stability that depended considerably on the distribution and utilization of land and property transactions. There are numerous developing economies with abundance of land, but the land resource is not contributing to economic growth. Instead of making productive use of land resources, wars and civic unrests are common in poor countries, delaying and distorting the advantages gained from productive use of land resources. And the armed military fighting only adds to more economic losses, as the land could alternatively be used in a peaceful manner in aiding human development, industrial expansion and economic growth to create virtuous economic cycles that will benefit all. For decades, Hong Kong has enjoyed

[35] *South China Morning Post*, June 28, 2011.

peaceful development, and civic unrest is rare, thereby allowing maximum potentials in economic development.

In free economies where property rights are clearly defined, the usage and/or ownership rights of land and property by individuals is wealth creating, allowing individuals to gain economic security and avoid the need for social welfare and government assistance. However, while the rights of wealth holders have to be protected, there should also be channels through which wealth will be created for the future generation through land acquisition and property ownership. Thus, economic freedom will encourage the establishment of institution and development of a sound property transaction system that will give ample opportunities for property ownership for both the current holders and future would-be holders of property.

Property ownership can provide residential services as well as a stream of future income. The market price of properties is therefore sensitive in realizing the level or size of future income from property ownership. Like any other manufactured goods, property price fluctuates depending on demand and supply conditions. However, sharp and rapid fluctuation in property price may create economic volatility that would destabilize investment, consumption and ultimately economic growth. Developers obviously want the property price to rise in one direction, property holders would like to see their wealth expand as property appreciates. In Hong Kong, land sales provide a handsome source of fiscal revenue to the government. Would-be owners could only minimize their other expenses in order to save up for the initial down-payment. There is thus in everyone's interest to have the property price to rise as much as possible.

The contrary is that a dominating property sector would erode economic competitiveness, making Hong Kong a costly place to do business. If resources were mostly geared to the property sector, there would be less room for other businesses to prosper. There can thus be a lack of economic balance between the various parties involved in property development and transactions. The question is how to define in Hong Kong a balance that will: a) allow property to create wealth for the owners; b) keep a steady pace of property development for the would-be property owners; c) provide sufficient housing for the needy; d) maximize economic activities and businesses without hindrance from changes in property price; and e) impose no hardship to government's fiscal policy.

There is no single instrument or solution that can make everyone happy, since all property transactions involve rested interests in a number of parties. A comprehensive policy or strategy is needed in order to stabilize the property sector and market. From the market point of view, sale practices will have to be fair, transparent and equitable to current and future buyers. To the developers, their rested interests have to be compromised with the need to maintain overall economic competitiveness and price stability, to ensure equal opportunities available to both large and small developers, and to adhere to good practices and professional judgment and honesty in ethical standards. To the property owners in Hong Kong, there has to be an understanding that property price can go up and down, and while wealth can be created through property acquisition, gradual asset appreciation is a long-term affair. On the contrary, speculation is risky and can lead to heavy losses. The government can pledge for a stable property sector to maximize employment opportunities and maintain a low rate of inflation by exercising a number of policy instruments, such as a stable supply of land, a steady rise in the price of land, and a provision of housing as necessities.

An analogy in the relationship between the sea and the ocean liner can be used in the relationship between the property sector and the economy. While a calm sea (the property sector) would allow the ocean liner (the economy) to travel afar to reach different destinations (economic achievements), but a roaring sea could destabilize and sink the ocean liner. The development of the property sector in Hong Kong is lacking behind the experience of other matured free economies, as property speculations have occurred repeatedly. Although there is no perfection in a property trading system, it would be wise to maintain, promote and improve competitiveness and confidence.

Economic freedom can provide benefits and advantages to an economy consistently because there are well-established rules, regulations, practices and ethical standards that are acceptable and respected by all market participants without influence from personalities. In other words, there should be a clear-defined system that stands between all parties in a property transaction, each party should aware of their potentials and responsibilities, and no single party could have an upper hand. The system should also protect the future generations, allowing equal opportunities and possibilities for all would-be owners of properties in future. Having high property prices and excessive speculations will surely increase the wealth of the current generation, as their property assets keep appreciating, but that will not be sufficient or long-lasting as chances of wealth creations would equally have to be made available to the future generations. This necessitates the establishment of a sound trading system in the property sector.

13 Inequality, Poverty and Economic Opportunity

13.1 Introduction

The basis of economic freedom is the permission for individuals to excel in their own business, profession and trade, using their amassed endowments, talents, skills and wealth. Given the difference in the individual endowments, economic outcomes are bound to differ among individuals. Differences in economic outcome naturally produce economic inequalities among individuals. Indeed, economic freedom permits and expects diversity in economic outcomes. If the tax system is well-publicized and transparent, individuals should know the amount of tax they have to contribute to the society. However, the more relevant concern in economic freedom is not how much an individual has achieved, but how the society can create diverse economic channels through which individuals can benefit from their marketable endowments.

In all societies, there are bound to have individuals who have economic and social survival difficulties. These are commonly known as "the poor" who need economic and welfare assistance for their survival. While economic freedom allows individuals to flourish in their business and trade, the society shall provide a safety net to ensure that no single person will fall below, and at the same time, institute instruments that deter the abuse of the safety net. Poverty should therefore be seen as a flow, rather than a stock, of individuals in the society. The concept of a flow relates to the number of individuals entering and exiting the poverty pool at any time, while the concept of a stock concerns the actual number of individuals in the poverty pool. Very often, policy makers consider the static actual number at any time, but the more relevant concern should be the dynamic flow of the numbers entering and exiting the poverty pool. Economic policies should, therefore, concern more on the flow so as to prevent as many individuals as possible entering into, and simultaneously helping individuals departing from, the poverty pool. In other words, the dynamic policy concern is to minimize the number of poor people in the poverty pool. The poverty situation improves when the number of entrants is falling faster than the number of exits.

An answer to poverty in a free economy rests in a creation of economic opportunities. Despite differences in rewards and wage payments among individuals and the presence of economic inequality, the starting point to alleviate poverty is job availability and business opportunities. In simple terms, all working-age individuals must have something to do to ensure their economic security and survival. Once economically surviving and independent, they can make their own progress in various businesses, trades and professions, and need not to rely on welfare assistance. Economic opportunity is not a free good, but is a scarcity factor that needs to be created and expanded, depending on a number of circumstantial conditions, such as the cost of production, macroeconomic stability, investment attraction, laws on property rights and so on. Economic development arises due to increasing availability of opportunities through typically investment activities, and economic freedom provides an environment for economic opportunity to flourish. One can even argue further that economic opportunity is the fifth factor of production in economics, in addition to the four conventional factors of production of land, labor, capital and entrepreneurship.

In the different stages of development since the end of the Second World War, the Hong Kong economy had mainly practiced supply-side economic policies that became attractive to foreign and subsequently local investments. The different stages of development in light or labor-intensive industrial manufacturing, banking center, re-export trade, services and financial centers have provided numerous economic opportunities for jobs, professional and business development. Job security seems to be the most important economic activity in the different stages of economic development in Hong Kong and businesses flourished because individuals can freely start their own trade once sufficient skill and knowledge is achieved.

As the economy flourished, income inequality is generated, and the contrast could have increased through decades of development. Income inequality tends to become more severe in times of economic recession, for example, when many high-earning individuals lost their jobs and/or secured only lower paid jobs. Thus, there are less high-income earners and more low-income earners, producing deterioration in the ratio between the high- and low-income earners. In the meantime, there is an increasing need to help the needy individuals through welfare assistance. The aim is to ensure that the needy individuals can also survive economically, and that there is equality in economic opportunity. Given the need for welfare assistance, the common objective is to ensure, secure and create more economic opportunities so that welfare-assisted individuals can have something to do, either working for employment or starting a business.

This chapter relates economic freedom to economic opportunities, knowing that there is always some degree of economic inequality, and the need to exercise appropriate policy to reduce the poverty pool in Hong Kong. While inequality is an everlasting problem, poverty reduction is a long process and poverty can only be minimized but not eliminated. The appropriate policy should be to examine the dynamics of poverty, rather than looking at the quantity of poverty all the time. The chapter also suggests the need to understand the economic survival cost, instead of the cost of living, as an alternative measure to look at the poverty line. Lastly, the creation and expansion of economic opportunity, and the pursuit of equality in opportunity, are still best methods to reduce poverty.

13.2 Inequality

The problem of inequality could be as old as the history of human beings, and emerges so long as differences can be found between two human beings. Thus, one can argue that inequality is a perpetual problem that exists along with the existence of human beings. Inequality cannot be eliminated, but the best humans can do is to generate less of it. Inequality due to religion, race, sex, social class, geographical region and political affiliation can be a life-time phenomenon. Very often, inequality is an attitude problem that people psychologically hold the view that one person is better or superior than another. The presence of inequality has also been used as a political instrument for various ends. Such life-time inequality can only be eradicated by a freer society that can institute law on equality, civic rules and ethical manner and behavior. Income inequality is a less stringent form of inequality because it can be improved through hard work, gains in skills, achievements in new qualifications and other forms of marketable endowments.

Indeed, income inequality has always been a socio-economic dilemma. On the one hand, less is preferred. On the other hand, income inequality is maintained by the economic system. Through education, different types of professions and experts are created, and people with good or high education will be rewarded economically more than less educated individuals. Hence, while the society needs more educated people, education itself brings income inequality. How small is a difference, there is still a difference in earnings made between an educated person with a sound professional skill and an unskilled uneducated labor worker. In that sense, income inequality is inevitable. The relevant solution is to have as many individuals receiving as much education as possible, so that all individuals will become experts in their professions.

On the contrary, the issue of income inequality has often been discussed by political activists as a political capital. Since there are always more low-income earners than high-income earners in all economies, it is politically appealing to raise that issue in a political platform as an instrument to gain support from the low-income earners. One popular political yardstick is a promise of more redistribution policies in favor of the low-income earners by more government spending and higher taxation, yet these were the policy words normally said before an election. There is no guarantee that such a policy would be delivered after an election, as political circumstances could change and/or economic circumstances may not be favorable to further increase tax rates without leading to more economic disincentives. Among the different factors of production of land, labor and capital, capital is most mobile and can leave the country within a short time if the investor finds it more attractive to invest elsewhere. Labor is less mobile due to immigration constraints. Thus, an unfavorable tax policy could easily drive investment out of the country, leaving the workers behind and that would result in higher unemployment. Redistribution is more of a short-term instrument and often generates economic disincentives or even leads to economic recession, while the longer term concern is job creation, employment opportunity and economic security.

Income inequality can be seen from a relative or an absolute point of view. A relative viewpoint in income inequality is that the performance of one individual is compared to another individual in their income earnings (Li, 2002). The income of a rich person P is compared to the income of a poor person Q. This probably gives only a snapshot and static measurement in a particular point in time that the earning difference of the two persons is recorded. Such a static, inter-personal measure of income difference is captured by the Gini coefficient that records the income earning of all individuals classified into different quintiles at a particular year in time. The Gini coefficient usually shows a ratio from 0 to 1, the closer the ratio is to 0, the more equal the society is; and the closer it is to 1, the more unequal the society becomes.

Such a measure is quite simple and does not take any other issues into account, e.g., the size and age population, stage of economic development, stage of the business cycle, competitive nature of the economy, level of industrialization, amount of job opportunities and availability of social mobility.

Very often, it does not help one to understand the entirety of income inequality if only inter-personal measure of income inequality is used. This is because there are always some high earning, rich people and some low earning, poor individuals in the society at any time. The Gini coefficient merely shows the aggregate picture in the various income quintiles. It definitely may not be the same rich person or the same poor person counted in the same quintile in the Gini coefficient measurement over different periods of time. In other words, the same person will change his earning ability and income, and will be counted in a different section or income quintile in the Gini coefficient measurement over the years.

Consider a scenario such that a young person today is receiving a low earning and is positioned in the lower quintile of the income scale in the economy. In five-year time, this person would have gained some work experience and even some additional qualifications, and by ten-year time, this person would receive a much higher income and would move into a higher quintile in the income ladder. As such, this person will not be counted in the low quintile of the income ladder anymore. In other words, the person has made improvement in his/her income over time. Indeed, even if two individuals today started out with the same earnings, their earning performance will surely differ in five-year or ten-year time. This cannot be explained simply by income inequality. Furthermore, in every year, there will appear another group of young people who do not have much experience or qualification and will occupy positions in the low-income ladder in the economy. From a dynamic point of view, there will always be new entrants of people with low-income earnings. This reflects the reality of the earning ladder for all individuals. Referring to such an economic trend as income inequality may not be appropriate, because static or snapshot inequality measures unfortunately do not reflect such an economic phenomenon of mobility or individuals climbing up their earnings ladder through time.

An alternative measure of inequality is to consider the absolute, intra-personal measure of income inequality. In a developing economy with rising opportunities, the earning of an individual is expected to increase over time. As the person is getting better off economically and with the rise in earnings, the person is able to ensure his or her own economic and social security. Typically, a young person would experience a period of low earning, but with time and gain in experience, skill and knowledge, the person's earning will rise. How much the earning rises depended on the market demand. While the earning of one individual is rising, the earnings of other individuals presumably are also rising at different rate and pace. As such, it should not matter to one individual if the earning of another individual is rising at the same time. Over time, the individual is comparing with his/her own earning, and however much the individual has earned additionally, there is still someone who earns more and another person who earn less than the individual. In other words, so long as the individual is getting better off economically over time, it is possible that other individuals may get more or less better off at the same time. To the single individual, the absolute, intra-personal comparison is a more relevant measure than the relative, inter-personal comparison (Li, 2002).

Short of better alternatives in statistical measurement, the Gini coefficient (Gini, 1912) shows income inequality in a numerical ratio, while the Lorenz curve (Lorenz, 1905) shows income inequality in a graphical form. The formula used by many economies to work out the Gini coefficient ($\mathcal{g}$) is:

$$\mathcal{g} = \sum_{j=1}^{n} X_j Y_{j+1} - \sum_{j=1}^{n} X_{j+1} Y_j, \quad (1)$$

where X_j and Y_j are the cumulative percentage of population and household incomes, respectively, and n is the number of income groups and Σ stands for summation. The basic idea of the Gini coefficient is to show the percentage of population over the percentage of income received. Thus, in a particular period of time, the closer the Gini coefficient is to zero, the more equal income is distributed, and the more unequal income is distributed if it is closer to one.

The Gini coefficient and the Lorenz curve can be seen from Figure 13.1, with the horizontal axis showing the cumulative share of household population, while the vertical axis showed the cumulative share of household income. The diagonal line, or the forty-five degree line, is the line of perfect equality, with, for example, 10% of population receiving 10% of income, 50% of population receiving 50% of income, and so on. The further is the Lorenz curve deviates from the forty-five degree line the higher is the level of inequality. The Gini coefficient is simply the ratio of the difference between the line of perfect equality and the Lorenz curve (area A) to the triangular region underneath the diagonal perfect equality line (area A + area B).

In statistical measures, household incomes are typically broken down into various quintiles, the lowest 20% of income, the lowest 40%, 60% and so on. Such a break down is thought to be more appropriate as it takes into account the various sections of populations and income earners. The Gini coefficient has also been worked out for the income of various sectors, such as urban and rural sectors, property sector, industrial

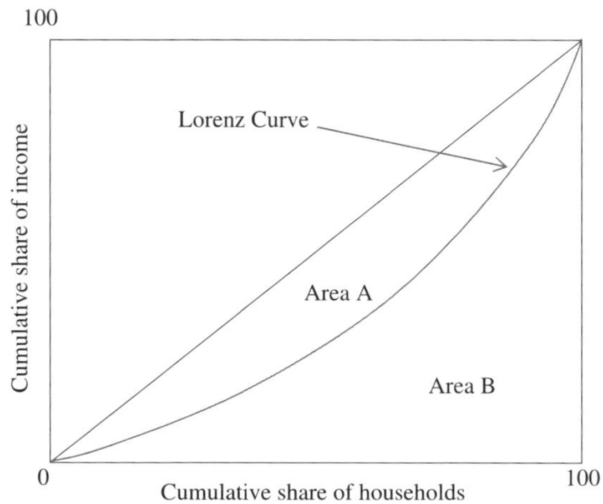

FIGURE 13.1 Gini coefficient and the Lorenz curve

TABLE 13.1 Gini coefficients in Hong Kong

	Original monthly household income	Post-tax post-social transfer monthly household income	Post-tax post-social transfer monthly household per capita income
1981	0.451		
1986	0.453		
1991	0.476		
1996	0.518	0.466	0.427
2001	0.525	0.470	0.421
2006	0.533	0.475	0.427

Source: Census and Statistics Department, Hong Kong.

and manufacturing sector, age and sex groups and so on. There are other studies that provide different measures of income inequality that conveys a similar message.

There are can be a number of ways the Gini coefficients have been reported. Table 13.1 shows the Gini coefficient for Hong Kong in three different measures. The "gross" measure of Gini coefficient is just the original monthly household income that has increased from 0.451 in 1981 to 0.533 in 2006, an increase of 0.082 in the sample period. Such a gross measure does not take into account other relevant factors in incomes. One can conclude that income distribution has become more diverse and income inequality has increased in the period. The increase was mild in the 1980s when the 1981 and 1986 Gini coefficients are almost the same, but the increase in inequality has been drastic in the 1990s. The Hong Kong economy in much of the 1990s experienced both an economic boom and bubble that burst after the Asian financial crisis in 1997–1998. The increase since 1996 has been mild because of the economic recession in the years between 1998 and 2005.

However, the second column of Table 13.1 shows the "net" measure of Gini coefficients when the post-tax and post-social transfers are taken into account. The post-tax income is probably the net income a household received after the payment of salary tax, while post-transfer referred to those who have received welfare assistance or some form of financial transfer that showed the net income. In the net income term, the Gini coefficients are much more stable and constant in the decade between 1996 and 2006, and the increase has been milder. Furthermore, when the Gini coefficients shown in last column of Table 13.1 are measured on a per capita income basis that took into account the size of the working population in Hong Kong, the Gini coefficients in the 1996–2006 decade have remained basically unchanged, and are considerably lower than the "gross" measures shown in the first column.

The level of GDP per capita can be an economic indicator worth considering along with the Gini coefficient ratio, especially when one is comparing income among advanced and developing countries. Table 13.2 shows the 2008 performance of Gini coefficient and GDP per capita for a number of Asian economies. One observation is that economies with low Gini coefficient are the advanced economies with higher GDP per capita, though Vietnam, Lao PDR and India could be the exception. On

TABLE 13.2 Gini coefficients and GDP per capita, 2008

	Gini coefficients	GDP per capita (US$)
Japan	0.249	34,312
South Korea	0.316	19,751
Canada	0.326	43,485
Switzerland	0.337	58,084
Indonesia	0.343	1,925
Vietnam	0.344	818
Lao PDR	0.346	656
Australia	0.352	43,312
United Kingdom	0.360	45,575
New Zealand	0.362	30,256
India	0.368	978
United States	0.408	45,845
Cambodia	0.417	600
Thailand	0.420	3,737
Singapore	0.425	35,163
Hong Kong	0.434	29,650
Philippines	0.455	1,625
Malaysia	0.492	6,948

Sources: *World Income Inequality Database*, various years, World Bank; *International Financial Statistics*, various issues, International Monetary Fund.

the contrary, economies with high Gini coefficients tend to have lower GDP per capita. Table 13.2 shows that when compared to other Asian economies, Hong Kong's Gini coefficient is higher than Japan and South Korea and is similar to Singapore (see Li, 2002, Chapter 3).

On the relationship between income inequality and economic development, the empirical study by Li and Zhou (2010) using data from advanced economies grouped under the Organization for Economic Cooperation and Development (OECD) and other developing countries (non-OECD) shows that advanced countries tend to have lower income inequality, higher GDP per capita and a lower rate of growth since their economies have advanced to a more saturated stage. Table 13.3 summarizes the average performance of Gini coefficients, GDP per capital and GDP growth rates for the 30 OECD and 45 non-OECD countries using data for the period from 1962 to 2003. The minimum, maximum and mean values are shown, together with the statistics on the standard deviation. There is a huge contrast when comparing the performance of Gini coefficients and GDP per capita. For the three values of minimum, maximum and mean, the Gini coefficients of OECD countries are lower than the non-OECD countries. On the contrary, OECD countries are higher than non-OECD countries in GDP per capita. This suggested that countries with higher GDP per capita tend to have a lower Gini coefficient ratio. GDP per capita is an important factor in reducing the Gini coefficient ratio. The mean value of Gini coefficient for OECD countries is 0.343, but the same value for non-OECD countries is 0.445. In

TABLE 13.3 World Gini coefficients and GDP: 1962–2003

	Gini	GDP per capita (US$)	GDP growth
30 advanced OECD countries			
Minimum	0.178	2,028.78	–19.29
Maximum	0.580	63,419.40	12.49
Mean	0.343	18,658.44	2.53
Standard deviation	7.70	8,009.19	3.80
45 non-OECD developing countries			
Minimum	0.207	561.52	–21.60
Maximum	0.637	33,401.80	16.47
Mean	0.445	7,167.09	1.73
Standard deviation	10.45	5,723.07	5.55

Source: Li and Zhou (2010).

the GDP growth rates, Table 13.3 also shows that OECD countries tend to have a smaller growth gap (from –19.09 to 12.49%) than non-OECD countries (from –21.6 to 16.47%). The mean of GDP growth rate is higher for OECD countries too. The conclusion from the Li and Zhou (2010) study is that steady growth in GDP and increase in GDP per capita can help to alleviate the poverty and inequality problem.

The contrast in the performance between rich and poor countries shown in Table 13.3 has led to studies that shall not only concern the inequality, but individual "capability" that relates to personal heterogeneities, environmental diversities, social variations, relational differences and distribution within a family (Sen, 1991–1993, 1997). Analysis on inequality have also been extended to the study of human development, or the behavior of top income earners over a long historic period of time (Krishnakumar, 2007; Krushnakumar and Ballon, 2008; Krushnakumar and Negar, 2008; Atkinson *et al.*, 2011). For example, the United Nations Development Program (UNDP) estimated the annual Human Development Index (HDI) for all world economies. Although the HDI has also been extended to other related estimations, such as gender development, the basic HDI consisted of the measurement on three life dimensions of healthy life (indicated by life expectancy), education (indicated by mean years and expected years of schooling) and decent living standards (indicated by GDP per capita). In the 2010 HDI, the 169 countries are classified into four categories of Very High Human Development (42 economies), High Human development (43 economies), Medium Human Development (42 economies) and Low Human Development (42 economies). The top five economies in descending order are Norway, Australia, New Zealand, United States and Ireland. Hong Kong ranked 21st, and the other two Asian economies that ranked higher than Hong Kong are Japan and South Korea, which ranked 11th and 12th, respectively. The other remaining Asian economy in the first category is Singapore (ranked 27th). Both China (ranked 89th) and India (ranked 119th) are in the third category of Medium Human

Development. There is no single Asian economy in the 42 Low Human Development economies.

In short, given the perpetual nature of inequality, it is more appropriate to focus on aspects that can improve the capability of individuals so that they have stronger survival ability in the economy, rather than simply redistributive policies on transfer payments that are often short-lived, unsustainable and produced a low income multiplier effect. The HDI does not focus on inequality, but on individual capabilities that help in their own development. The HDI basically echoes on the importance of growth and development that can provide more economic opportunities for individuals to progress, and rather than merely income inequality, it is equality in opportunity that is seen to be more appropriate for human development.

13.3 System-Driven Versus Santa Claus

The World Bank has consistently worked on the issue of poverty. The *Global Monitoring Report* (World Bank, 2011a) showed by 2015 that worldwide extreme poverty with people living on less than US$1.25 a day is estimated to drop to 14.4% (883 million) of world population.[1] The same extreme poverty rate in the world was 52% in 1981, dropped to 42% in 1990, and further decreased to 25% in 2005. The World Bank report noted that the decline in poverty since the 1980s has varied across regions, with East Asia and Pacific region probably led by Mainland China's rapid growth has made huge improvement. Between 1981 and 2005, and using the US$1.25 a day poverty line at 2005 prices, poverty in the East Asia and Pacific region has fallen from 78% to 17%. On the contrary, the number of poor people living in the Sub-Saharan Africa has doubled, with an increase from 11% to 27% in the same period. Although the number of poor remained almost the same due largely to population growth, the poverty rate in South Asia, Latin America and the Caribbean, Middle East and North Africa has fallen in the same period. When a US$2 a day (at 2005 prices) is used as a poverty line, the percentage of world population has fallen from 70% in 1981 to 47% in 2005. Due to the rise in world population, the percentage in 2005 has remained about 2.5 billion people. To reduce world poverty, the World Bank has asked developing countries to specify Poverty Reduction Strategy Papers (PRSPs) on ways to combat against poverty in their countries.

Poverty can be considered both in absolute terms and in relative terms. Absolute poverty implies insufficient provision in basic human needs in goods and services. The essential element in absolute poverty is the inability to satisfy or secure a minimum subsistence that includes a bundle of goods and services regarded as essential to the physical need of an individual or a household. The absolute approach adopted by countries including the United States took into account of physical needs rather than social needs. The official poverty line would specify a set of income thresholds adjusted for different sizes of households to reflect the necessary purchasing power to meet the basic needs. The World Bank has specified that for high-income economies, including Hong Kong, the poverty line is US$14.4 per day per person.

[1] *Poverty at a Glance*, World Bank (2011b).

The same specification of the poverty line for other low income economies is much lower. In Eastern Europe and Latin America, the poverty line is US$4 and US$2 per day per person, respectively.

Poverty can alternatively be seen in relative terms. Relative poverty takes into account the lack of resources in obtaining needed diets and in participating customary activities and amenities in the society. The usual measurement of relative poverty is to compare one person's income to a portion of the medium income in the society. In major European countries, a household whose equivalent income is below the threshold of 60% of the national equivalent medium income is considered as living in poverty.

There are other similar approaches to define poverty. For example, the budget standard method extends the absolute approach to incorporate other socially determined needs. Another method is the income proxy method that uses a behavioral approach in determining a proportion of expenditure on necessities based on the consumption patterns of the comparable segments of the society. One can determine that a household spending more than a certain percent of income on necessities are considered as poor. However, determining and quantifying the essential needs involved inevitably controversies in subjective value-judgment, and often considered as interventionist in the private life of households. For example, the Community Care Fund in 2011 recommended a total of 10 plans to alleviate poverty, including a HK$165.9 million study tour scheme for 240,000 poor pupils, with each obtaining a maximum funding of HK$3,000.[2] Such recommendation immediately sparked public controversy as to whether a study tour is considered as a necessity for the poor pupils. Questions are being asked on how far a poor pupil can travel with a subsidy funding of HK$3,000 (US$385), and are there not provisions of information and education programs through other forms of media that pupils can learn about other parts of the world, and whether the poor pupils taking the fund could be stigmatized and have other unfavorable consequences.

While the Comprehensive Social Security Assistance (CSSA) scheme has taken care of welfare expenditure on the needy individuals, the harsh economic recession emerged after the Asian financial crisis in 1997/1998 and the resulting rise in income inequality has prompted the government to look into the problem of poverty in Hong Kong. The Commission on Poverty was established by the Hong Kong SAR Government in February 2005 to study poverty arising from the rising unemployment of unskilled workers, intergeneration poverty, disadvantaged groups and the elderly. With the theme of "From Welfare to Self-Reliance", the Commission lasted until June 2007 and came up with the *Report of the Commission on Poverty*.[3] The major focus of the Commission included the understanding of poverty, making of immediate improvements and identifying directions for future work. The work programs included the unemployed and working poor, children and youth, the elderly and a district-based approach.

Table 13.4 shows the percentage of population in the four categories of poverty for the six years from 2001 to 2006, noting that the early sample years are recession years, and economic recovery returned only in 2005. Thus, the six sample years

---

[2] *South China Morning Post*, April 24, 2011.

TABLE 13.4 Poverty in Hong Kong — Percentage of population

Categories of poverty	2001	2002	2003	2004	2005	2006
Workless households	7.1	8.8	9.8	9.2	9.0	8.9
Households income below average CSSA payment	13.8	15.0	14.8	13.7	12.4	11.2
Single parents income below average CSSA payment	1.0	1.2	1.0	1.1	1.1	1.0
Unemployed persons	5.1	7.3	8.0	6.8	5.6	4.8

Source: Census and Statistics Department, Hong Kong.

reflect more the situation in recession years. Among the four categories of poverty in Hong Kong, the worst performer was the household whose income was below the average Comprehensive Social Security Assistance (CSSA) payment. Low income, probably due to a large number of unskilled workers, is the major cause of poverty in Hong Kong. However, the percentage has declined in both 2005 and 2006, reflecting the change in situation as a result of economic recovery.

Workless households composed of young school leavers who suffered from lack of skill, lack of experience and lack of knowledge, especially if they live in high unemployment districts and are far from central business districts. This category of poverty has edged upwards from 7.1% in 2001, reaching a peak when Hong Kong experienced the health hazard of severe acute respiratory syndrome (SARS) in 2003, but remained high at 8.9% in 2006. Unemployed persons formed a much smaller category of poor population in Hong Kong, dropping to 4.8% in 2006, indicating that poverty resulting from unemployment has mainly been temporary, and they will depart from the poverty pool once economic recovery returned. Single parent household whose income is below the average of CSSA payment is about 1% of the population. The situation needs to be attended to but is not regarded as serious.

Table 13.5 reported the categories of poverty according to the 18 districts in Hong Kong for the three sample years of 2001, 2004 and 2006. In general, districts in the Hong Kong Island are the best performers. Despite the general belief that districts in the New Territories are poorer, Yuen Long is the poorest district in the New Territories. Table 13.5 shows that the poorest districts are in the Kowloon peninsula, namely Kowloon City and Sham Shui Po, where a large amount of new immigrants resided. The three worst performers in 2006 were Yuen Long with 17%, Tuen Mun with 15.8% and the North with 14.7% of population with income below the average CSSA payment.

In addition to reduction of poverty through the district network, the Commission on Poverty also recommended the establishment of non-profit making social enterprises that could pursue both business and social objectives and purposes. Following the report by the Commission on Poverty, the Chief Executive announced in his Policy Address in October 2010 the establishment of a Community Care Fund (CCF).

The innovative aspect of the CCF is to seek donations from private corporates an amount of HK$5 billion (US$0.64 billion). With the matching fund from the government, the CCF will have a total fund of HK$10 billion (US$1.28 billion).

TABLE 13.5 Poverty by district — Percentage of population

	Workless households			Income below CSSA			Single parent below CSSA			Unemployed persons		
Districts	2001	2004	2006	2001	2004	2006	2001	2004	2006	2001	2004	2006
Central & Western	4.9	7.3	5.8	7.7	8.1	5.9	*	*	*	2.9	3.4	2.2
Wan Chai	6.0	8.0	8.9	7.5	7.7	7.9	*	*	*	2.9	3.0	2.4
Eastern	5.2	7.2	6.6	9.6	9.4	7.1	0.7	0.6	0.5	3.6	5.0	3.5
Southern	5.5	5.6	6.6	9.8	9.9	7.5	*	*	*	4.0	4.8	3.6
Yau Tsim Mong	10.0	11.0	9.2	15.8	12.9	10.3	*	*	*	5.6	6.8	4.0
Sham Shui Po	10.3	11.8	11.7	17.4	16.4	13.2	1.0	1.4	0.8	6.7	7.6	5.8
Kowloon City	7.3	8.3	8.8	11.4	10.2	8.6	*	0.9	*	4.6	5.5	3.9
Wong Tai Sin	6.7	10.3	9.6	14.0	15.0	11.6	1.0	1.0	1.1	5.4	7.9	5.4
Kwun Tong	8.4	10.7	9.9	16.5	13.8	11.1	1.2	1.3	0.7	6.0	8.3	5.2
Kwai Tsing	7.5	10.8	9.1	16.5	15.8	11.9	1.4	1.5	1.4	6.3	9.0	6.5
Tsuen Wan	6.2	7.9	7.9	10.2	11.0	8.9	*	*	*	4.6	6.1	4.3
Tuen Mun	6.9	9.7	9.8	16.2	18.5	15.8	1.6	1.9	1.9	6.1	8.4	5.6
Yuen Long	8.6	11.3	12.1	18.1	19.6	17.0	1.4	2.0	1.9	6.3	8.1	5.6
North	9.6	10.9	9.6	19.6	17.5	14.7	1.2	1.3	1.4	6.1	8.2	5.9
Tai Po	6.1	9.2	8.8	14.5	15.7	12.9	1.2	1.4	1.2	4.8	7.7	5.2
Sha Tin	6.0	7.3	7.4	12.3	11.7	9.8	1.0	1.0	0.8	4.5	8.1	4.8
Sai Kung	5.1	7.3	6.6	11.5	11.6	9.1	*	1.0	0.9	4.1	5.8	4.3
Islands	9.6	8.3	9.6	13.6	15.1	14.4	*	*	*	6.9	6.6	4.9
Overall	7.1	9.2	8.9	13.8	13.7	11.2	1.0	1.1	1.0	5.1	6.8	4.8

Source: Census and Statistics Department, Hong Kong.

Note: * = Figures of small magnitude are suppressed owing to large sampling error.

However, by the time the CCF was to be implemented, the economy has reached a high growth rate again. It was reported that the growth rate of GDP in the first quarter of 2011 reached 7.2%, marking the fifth consecutive quarter of growth above the average annual growth over the past decade. Inflation has been edging up fast in early 2011 also. At the same time, the lawmakers have approved HK$5 billion government funding for the CCF. Such an increase in expenditure would simple pour oil on the gradually overheating economy.[4] Again, in an echo to the soundness of fiscal policy, it is a wrong timing as a rapid rise in income should not be accompanied by further fiscal expansion so as to fuel the rise of inflation. Knowing that the government is prepared to spend more on welfare and subsidies, suppliers and retailers would likely to increase price in an already booming economy with low unemployment and rising GDP. Thus, further fiscal expenditure would fuel inflation.

The optimism from the business sector unfortunately did not materialize, and it was report in May 2011 that corporate donation amounted only to HK$1.8 billion (US$0.23 billion) with cash received amounted to only HK$680 million (US$87.28 million), far short of the target of HK$5 billion. In May 2011, the CCF has made a total of 10 suggestions in its supposedly first round of activities, including a HK$165.9 million (US$21,27 million) on study tour scheme for 240,000 poor pupils and a HK$192.78 million (US$24.72 million) project to pay for the lunches of 51,000 primary pupils. The appropriateness of the suggestions has again been challenged as to whether the community will have to intervene into the private life of the poor individuals. Others commented that there are far too many charity funds in Hong Kong that have been lending a helping hand to the needy individuals already.[5]

The incident of CCF has clearly demonstrated an important issue in the approach to deal with the poverty problem. In Hong Kong, the poor population has theoretically been taken care of by the social welfare system, known as the Comprehensive Social Security Assistance (CSSA) system that classified the economically needy individuals into four categories shown in Table 13.4. It is true that welfare assistance can never be sufficient, as the choice facing the government and the public at large is whether to provide the needy with a "fish" or educating the needy on "how to fish". There have been complaints by welfare advocates that the CSSA system does not give enough, does not cover all the needy individuals, does not cover such non-survival goods as piano lessons and after class private tutoring, and does not catch up with current needs and so on.

Equally, there have been cases of abuses of the CSSA system where people with wealth have cheated the system, or couples pretended to be separated so as to qualify for single-parent family assistance, or the high amount of financial assistance has discouraged households to seek employment. On the contrary, there are cases that those entitled for welfare are not aware of the benefits from the CSSA, or the needy individuals are physically unable to complete the process of application, or their low level of knowledge and literacy have deterred them from applying, or they just refuse

---

[4] Press releases, "Economic Situation in First Quarter of 2011", Hong Kong SAR Government, May 13, 2011. *China Daily Hong Kong Edition*, May 14, 2011.

[5] *South China Morning Post*, April 24, May 7 and May 10, 2011. *China Daily Hong Kong Edition*, May 6, 2011.

to receive CSSA, preferring to make their own living through hard work than to rely on the government for welfare.

In other words, there is always some loopholes in any welfare system. There can be a coverage problem, a lack of financial funding or a change in circumstances, and individuals reluctant or unaware of their welfare benefits. While the government is making provisions through the CSSA to help the poor, needy individuals should also have to make their way to the appropriate government agents to seek help and receive their entitled assistance. In any case, it is crucial to have a system that looks after the needs of the economically insecure individuals. What the government and the public can do is to make regular improvements to the system so as to perfect its coverage, amount of assistance and special cases due to abrupt changes and shocks in the economy. A regularly improved system will provide an open, transparent and equal set of rules and standards applicable to all potential recipients. A rule-based welfare system can be long-lasting, fairer and less controversial and preferable to a Santa Claus, personality driven system that could only contain *ad hoc* circles of influences.

It might be due to the sharp changes in the business cycles that required additional short-term assistance or due to the personality favors of certain high-ranking officials, assistance given to the poor and the needy individuals should not be structured in an *ad hoc*, irregular and personality-driven basis. All additional assistances should be incorporated into the formal and standardized CSSA system. *Ad hoc*, unstructured announcements and decisions on additional welfare assistances could serve like the work of the legendary Santa Claus in Christmas where one person is dishing out the niceties to the needy individuals in Hong Kong either in late February in the annual budget or in October in the Policy Address.The Community Care Fund (CCF) is an example of assistances given to the needy individuals in addition to what they are getting through the CSSA system. What the CCF could have done is to suggest ways to help the needy individuals through the improvement of the CSSA system, so that the improvements and suggestions could be incorporated into a long term welfare policy.

In Hong Kong where transparent and standardized economic systems stand between the public and the government authority, it would be appropriate for any government official and interested parties aiming to help the needy individuals work through the system, rather than establishing their own circles of influence and work outside the already established and structured welfare system, resulting in a situation where a formal CSSA system coexisted with a number of *ad hoc* welfare channels that served a similar purpose. A rule-based, transparent, improvable system is far more superior to *ad hoc* circles of influences and controls introduced and manipulated at different times. Helping the poor and needy individual through a reasonable and effective welfare system is a noble social goal in itself.

13.4 Poverty: Stock Versus Flow

However one defines poverty, solutions to the elimination of poverty can be seen from a dynamic viewpoint, distinguishing the stock and the flow of the poor population. The stock represented the actual quantity at a particular point in time. Today, the economy consists of a certain amount of population with difficulty in their economic survival. The stock or the poverty pool consists of the aggregate quantity and the various divisions of unemployed, elderly, single parent and low wage earners. The flow, on the contrary, showed the channels through which more economic unsecured individuals and households would enter the poverty pool, and similarly, avenues and means through which those in the poverty pool could leave the pool and maintain economic security on their own independent efforts. Of course, there would be some weak individuals whom would stay longer in the poverty pool than others.

A policy that merely aimed to help the number of individuals in the poverty pool is only part of the answer. To make the reduction of poverty a sustainable process, it would be necessary to know the channels through which poverty is created, and means through which individuals could achieve economic security. In other words, a policy will have to minimize the number of entry to the poverty pool and to maximize the number of exits from the poverty pool. The poverty problem is alleviated over a period of time when the number of entrants is lower than the number of exits in the poverty pool.

The poverty pool can conceptually be illustrated in Figure 13.2. The number of individuals in the poverty pool constituted the stock, while the "enter and exit"channels represented the flow. The next question is what channels through which individuals will fall into the poverty pool, and what means through which individuals can exit from the poverty pool. The more important policy is to control the flow, while a good welfare system will take care of the stock.

In Figure 13.2, there are four possible channels through which individuals would fall into the poverty pool. The four channels through which the poverty pool would be enlarged are economic recession, number of school leavers, incapable elderly and immigration. Similarly, there are four possibilities through which individuals could depart from the poverty pool, they are: attainment in education, pursuit of vocational training, economic recovery and economic restructuring.

On the entry side of the poverty flow, economic recession is probably the most important channel. Economic recession usually comes with rising unemployment, and unfavorable economic climate comes with a fall in investment activities. The fall in employment, income and demand would surely reverse the movement of the income multiplier, resulting in more people losing their jobs, income and saving.

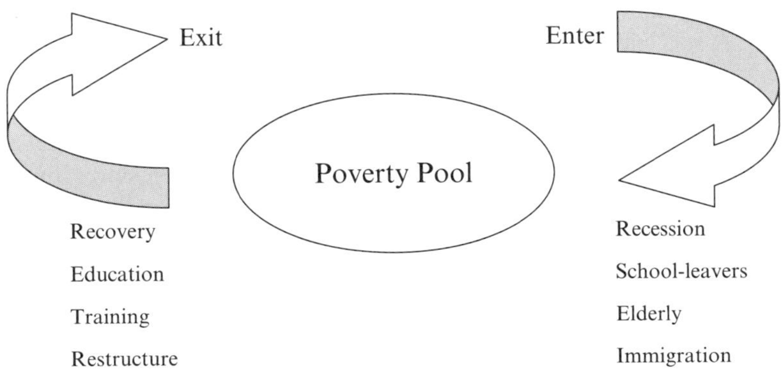

FIGURE 13.2 The stock and flow in the poverty pool

Eventually, there would be more people entering into the poverty pool, feeling economically insecure and needing welfare assistance. A second channel is the number of young people who are transitory between the end of their education, but without work experience and before being absorbed eventually into employment. Young school-leavers with low education and without working experience are a potential group of people easily absorbed into the poverty pool. The third group of potential entrants is the elderly. The elderly are individuals who have retired and have completed their career or working experience. Thus, many elderly are economically secured and do not fall into the poverty pool. What one concerns here is the group of elderly with low savings and their pre-retirement work had mainly been related in unskilled job employment. The worst is that group of elderly whom have no family to turn to. There is thus a need to distinguish between the economically able from the economically incapable elderly individuals and households. Lastly, Figure 13.2 suggests that an immigration policy that were to open up to economically weaker individuals coming to become Hong Kong residents would easily enlarge the poverty pool. Unqualified immigrants could exploit the welfare system, thereby imposing additional fiscal burden to the taxpayers in Hong Kong.

To minimize the number of entrants to the flow, policies will have to gear to the four possibilities of economic recession that would result in new unemployment and fall in earnings, unemployed school leavers or young persons whom have no job experience, elderly whom are both economically unsecured and have no family to turn to, and unqualified immigration policies that would allow individuals coming to reside in Hong Kong and rely on welfare assistance. In many ways, the policies that minimize the entry to the poverty pool would probably turn out to be the same set of policies that helped poor individuals to exit from the poverty pool. In an economic recovery when investment activities increased, the overall demand for workers rises and more job opportunities would become available, thereby pulling workers out from the poverty pool. This explains why a free and business-friendly economic policy is important in alleviating poverty and promoting economic opportunity. There is thus a need for Hong Kong to maintain macroeconomic stability, promote needed infrastructure in order to attract investment and stimulate employment, and engage in policies that are consistent to economic growth.

Education is a sure ticket to get away from poverty, and the higher the level of education an individual obtains, the more likely it is for the individual to acquire and secure jobs. A successful education policy, however, has two dimensions. One obvious deals with the supply side that relates to the education system that outlines the structure, the needed funding and the relevance of the curricula at all levels. The other dimension deals with the demand side that relates to the quality and eagerness of students to learn and receive education. However sufficiently funded, well designed curricula and professionally trained teachers would serve little purpose if the young population in Hong Kong were not prepared to learn and work hard for a higher academic qualification. There is thus a need to promote and orientate the young people in Hong Kong that education in modern society has become a necessity.

Training and re-training in different vocations and skills have been popular among individuals who want to make further progress in their work-related skills or young school-leavers who are weak in academic skills but are prepared to gain vocational skills. Training obviously fulfills the supply side of the equation, while job availability deals with the demand side of the equation. Hence, ultimately, it is the creation of job opportunity that matters. As vocational training concerned more with the practical aspect in a business entity, vocational jobs often fulfilled the middle-management positions in businesses.

While economic recovery often provided short-term policies to ensure that the recession has bottomed out, economic restructuring takes a longer time perspective to accomplish, but required resource reallocation so that the economy would be growth-generating. This may involve a number of coordinated policies on the various factors of production. In Hong Kong, there can easily be a number of suggestions on economic restructuring such that resources can better be used for employment and growth. From an economic policy point of view, economic restructuring, for example, can be organized under various themes so as to cluster together a number of policies to generate economies of scale in policy outcomes.

One theme could be the promotion of a better urban face in Hong Kong. This could include the removal of sewage blockage in every spring in preparation for the rainy season in the summer to avoid flooding in urban streets as well as remote places. A large number of temporary workers can be employed to clean up the streets and remove sewage blockages. Another suggestion is the reduction of noise pollution in all road junctions as there is a 24 hours round the clock beeping noise in all major road junctions in Hong Kong in order to help the blind to cross the roads. One improvement would be to install a remote control on the traffic light post in each road junction, and blind people are also provided with a synchronized remote control that would help them to cross the road when needed. In Hong Kong, it is quite common for shops and restaurants to occupy portions of the street as their business venues, and that has reduced the public space for the pedestrians. On every Sunday, there are thousands of housemaids whom colonized parks and public spaces in Central, Causeway Bay and other open areas for their own entertainment and leisure since Sunday is their day off. Stronger regulations and implementation of relevant policies are needed to clean up these undesirable occupations.

Another theme can be the improvement in the transportation structure and system in Hong Kong. Possibilities could include the change to left-hand drive in order to synchronize with the traffic system in Mainland China. This required a lot of preparations on road signs, planning of traffic routes, training driving lessons and importation of cars and so on. A large number of employment on painting, installation prior to and removal after the shift to left-hand drive would definitely be generated. Secondly, the major urban bus transport system in a great number of European cities relied on the use of electric bus. There can be a number of improvements in Hong Kong. Electric buses are smaller in size, and are space efficient on roads and less polluting to the environment. Along the northern coastal line of the Hong Kong Island, for example, the tram company and the bus company could work together on the possibility of electric buses. A more efficient use of the minibus system can also provide more employment to drivers.

Other suggestions included the organization of boat racing in Hong Kong. As Hong Kong is surrounded by sea, it would be advantageous to organize regularly international boat racing activities that could boost tourism and related industries in boat repairs and production. In property development, green technology can be introduced to provide a better environment. Land in the border areas, much of the Lantau Island and other smaller islands could further be developed and restructured to provide more business, jobs and economic opportunities. Hence, a number of restructuring possibilities can be pursued so as to promote better living and improve economic competitiveness.

In conclusion, poverty is a flow that involved different economically weak individuals getting in and out of the poverty pool. It would be more appropriate to consider policies that on the one hand minimizes the number of entrants, and on the other hand, maximizes the number of departures. A successful policy on poverty is to alleviate the number of poor individuals in the pool, not just thinking of providing more and additional assistance to the same pool of economically weak individuals.

13.5 Mobility

The availability of economic opportunities allows individuals to earn more and move up to a higher earning ladder. Mobility shows how individuals have moved possibly from a low to high income quintile over a period of time. In a sense, statistics on income mobility recorded a group of individuals in the same earning group, but did not chase the earning path of the same individual over time. Nonetheless, it would be an alternative and probably an improved measurement to the Gini coefficient. In a period when economic development is progressive, one expects an upward movement of mobility, as jobs are forthcoming and individuals have ample opportunities for new jobs, and wage rises as demand for workers rises too. On the contrary, downward mobility is possible and occurred usually in a period of economic recession or when development is saturated. When jobs are not forthcoming and wages are falling in an economic recession, earnings of individuals would revise downwards, and it would become possible for individuals to make a lower earning or accepting a lower paid job when unemployment rises. Downward mobility could lead more individuals to work for a lower paid job, and there could be an increase in the number of households in the poverty pool.

The performances of economic mobility in Hong Kong have been empirically conducted by the Hong Kong Institute of Economics and Business Strategy at the University of Hong Kong in two studies that have contributed to the Commission on Poverty report in 2006. The two sequential studies by Siu (2001) and Vere (2006) examined the earnings mobility and intergenerational earnings mobility in Hong Kong over the period 1991–2005, covering the three periods of pre-Asian financial crisis of 1991–1997, Asian financial crisis years of 1997–1998 and the post-crisis recession period of 1998–2005. Economic recovery began in late 2005. It would be interesting to see how economic mobility has performed in the extreme periods of boom and recession. Presumably, earning mobility increased in a period of economic boom, thereby improving inequality, and decreased in a period of recession, thereby leading to deterioration in income inequality.

The essence of the two studies can be summarized in the following two tables, noting that the percentages may not come to 100% due to rounding up. Table 13.6

TABLE 13.6 Overall earning mobility rates: All employed people

(%)	1991–1996	1996–2001	2001–2005
Upward	24.2	23.2	19.9
No Change	49.4	55.9	62.2
Downward	26.4	20.9	16.9

Sources: Siu (2001) and Vere (2006).

gives a summary picture on the mobility of all workers for the three periods. The findings in Siu (2001) and Vere (2006) show that there is upward mobility in each of the three periods, but the overall upward mobility has declined in each of the three periods. In 1991–1996 when the economy was booming, 24.2% of all workers experienced a rise in their earnings and had moved up to a higher quintile. The same percentage dropped to 23.2 during the Asian financial crisis period, and further dropped to 19.9% in the recession years 2001–2005.

The drop in upward mobility means the percentage that remained No Change has increased from 49.4% in 1991–1996 to 62.2% in the recession period 2001–2005. However, it is interesting to note that downward mobility is higher in the boom years (1991–1996), with a percentage (26.4%) higher than the upward mobility (24.2%). This surprising result could probably owe to the rapidly changing economic structure that turned out to be unsustainable when speculation was rampant in the boom years of 1991–1996. The rapid hollowing of industries in Hong Kong could have displaced a number of skilled industrial workers, turning them to work in services. In the latter two periods when the economy faced the outbreak and consequences of the Asian financial crisis, the downward mobility fortunately was lower than the upward mobility. The two studies have also provided a breakdown of the percentages into male and female workers, different age groups, different industries and occupations. To examine the intergenerational poverty, the two studies compare the lifetime earnings between the father and the child in different quintiles.

Table 13.7 closely examines the mobility of different quintiles in four separate periods: the decade of 1991–2000, the Asian financial crisis period of 1996–2001, the economic recession decade of 1996–2005, and the post-Asian financial crisis period of 2001–2005. One observation in all four periods is that upward mobility tended to be higher than downward mobility in the lowest three quintiles of Bottom, 2nd and 3rd quintiles, but the reverse is true when it came to the 4th and Top quintiles, as downward mobility tended to be higher than upward mobility. This meant that the top income earners in Hong Kong were more vulnerable to earning mobility, but it was quite safe for low income earners to climb upwards in the earning ladder. Typically, upward mobility tended to be high from the Bottom quintile to the 4th quintiles, but the upward mobility from the 4th quintile to Top quintile dropped significantly in all periods. On the contrary, the percentage of downward mobility tended to be higher at the 4th and Top quintiles, thereby confirming the vulnerability of high earners in Hong Kong.

Among the different periods, the decade 1991–2002 showed a better performance in general, though the upward mobility for the 4th quintiles was best in the

TABLE 13.7 Earning mobility rates by quintile group: All workers

	Bottom	2nd	3rd	4th	Top	Down	No Change	Up
Quintiles in 1991	Quintiles in 2000 (%)							
Bottom	42.4	24.6	17.5	10.9	4.6	—	42.4	57.6
2nd	25.0	32.5	23.1	14.8	4.7	25.0	32.5	42.6
3rd	16.2	26.1	25.4	23.3	8.9	42.3	25.4	32.2
4th	11.9	11.6	22.9	31.5	22.1	46.4	31.5	22.1
Top	4.5	5.2	11.1	19.6	59.7	40.4	59.7	—
Quintiles in 1996	Quintiles in 2001 (%)							
Bottom	66.6	25.4	6.1	1.8	0.0	—	66.6	33.3
2nd	17.9	49.5	25.4	6.6	0.7	17.9	49.5	32.7
3rd	8.3	23.0	40.9	24.5	3.3	31.3	40.9	27.8
4th	2.7	7.0	18.6	51.1	20.7	28.3	51.1	20.7
Top	1.4	1.9	4.3	19.7	72.8	27.3	72.8	—
Quintiles in 1996	Quintiles in 2005 (%)							
Bottom	58.4	26.5	10.4	4.5	0.30	—	58.4	41.6
2nd	24.9	33.9	27.1	11.9	2.2	24.9	33.9	41.2
3rd	15.7	22.8	25.8	28.1	7.6	38.5	25.8	35.8
4th	8.5	10.7	17.1	38.8	25.0	36.3	38.8	25.0
Top	3.4	4.7	5.4	18.1	68.4	31.6	68.4	—
Quintiles in 2001	Quintiles in 2005 (%)							
Bottom	74.4	21.8	3.0	0.8	0.1	—	74.4	25.7
2nd	22.1	49.7	22.1	6.0	0.1	22.1	49.7	28.2
3rd	9.3	16.4	48.5	24.7	1.2	25.7	48.5	25.9
4th	4.8	7.1	10.4	59.7	18.0	22.3	59.7	18.0
Top	1.5	1.6	1.6	9.1	86.2	13.8	86.2	—

Sources: Siu (2001) and Vere (2006).

1996–2006 decade (25%). The upward mobility for the Bottom and 2nd quintiles has fallen considerably since 1996. The downward mobility is severe for the 3rd and 4th quintiles, especially in the first period. In general, the No Change situation is highest in 2001–2005. Since 1996, the No Change for the Bottom and 2nd quintiles have remained high, confirming that economic recession has made it difficult for low income earners to climb high in the earning ladder.

The overall conclusion from Table 13.7 is that No Change was still the majority of income earners since 1991, the percentage of upward mobility for the Bottom and 2nd quintiles were higher than the downward mobility. The downward mobility was high in the 4th and Top quintiles. Upward mobility has been dampened by the economic recession. The results shown in Table 13.7 echo the need for greater economic opportunities and creation of jobs and employment through increase in investment preferably in physical economic sectors.

13.6 Minimum Wage

The statutory minimum wage came into force in Hong Kong on May 1, 2011, and the initial statutory minimum wage rate is HK$28 (US$3.59) per hour. The issue of minimum wage has been debated for a number of years in Hong Kong, but as expected the debate has been divisive, with the labor unions and welfare groups advocating for the need for a minimum wage to improve the earnings of workers, while the employers claimed that flexibility is needed given the open nature of the Hong Kong economy, where businesses can be very fluid and the largest portion of cost is the payment of rents. The lack of job creation and the slow in upward mobility since the economic recession years have prompted the needed for a minimum wage legislation.

Simple economics theories argued that minimum wage legislation could lead to higher unemployment, because for the minimum wage to be effective, it must be higher than the equilibrium wage where supply of labor meets the demand for labor. A minimum wage higher than the equilibrium wage does protect those who remain in employment, but the overall demand for labor will fall. It is likely that those good quality workers will remain employed. But those unemployed may take the legal risk and undercut the minimum wage in order to secure their jobs. Thus, law enforcement has to be strong to make the minimum wage a viable policy.

The need for the minimum wage arises due to a number of changing circumstances. Job or employment security is decreasing, as unemployment remains fairly high and the increase in job availability has not been forthcoming, especially for unskilled jobs. Over the years, immigration through the family-reunion policy has led to an increase in the supply of low skill laborers. There is thus an increase in the supply of unskilled workers without visible increase in demand, and the market may even force the wage to go down, and the minimum wage is thought to act as a protection so that the excess supply will not pull the wage down. This is the dichotomy Hong Kong is experiencing, with economic recovery and rise of GDP on the one hand, but the rise in supply of unskilled workers and a slow increase in the amount of unskilled jobs would steer the economic welfare of unskilled workers to an opposite direction from the rise in GDP. The long term solution would still be the creation of more jobs, including more low skill jobs and a control in the supply of unskilled laborers.

A number of complications have arisen at the time of the implementation of the minimum wage in May 2011. For example, whether lunch time should be included as part of the working hour has been a concern for some workers. This conflict arises in such businesses as restaurants when the working hours would be divided into two short time periods in the morning/early afternoon and in the evening. Although it is argued that the implementation will take time to get used to, but the diversity of businesses may require a large number of regulations that will intervene with private business decisions. At the beginning of the implementation, there would be a lack of clarity in the use of minimum wage. For example, if a worker is getting a monthly payment of more than HK$5,376 per month (48-hours per week for 4 weeks, with HK$28 per hour), the worker would be getting more than the minimum wage, and should such issues as lunch payment and travel time payment arise? Strictly speaking, the minimum wage is applicable mainly to workers paid on an hourly basis, and not jobs with monthly payment higher than HK$5,376 per month. Nonetheless, the minimum wage can further be improved so that it can provide the protection of a minimum wage but at the same time serves as an indicator on market conditions.

Given the large degree of flexibility and openness in the economy, Hong Kong often has to subject to the changes in economic activities elsewhere. Hong Kong businesses have to respond quickly to changes in the world situation, both favorably and unfavorably. The economic situation in Mainland China, for example, does impose a high degree of dynamism in the Hong Kong economy. In the early 1980s when Mainland China opened up and pursued economic reform, capital from Hong Kong to Mainland China was a one-way street. By 2010, however, the mainland residents have sent their cash to Hong Kong, purchasing luxurious properties that caused property price to sky rocket. The flow of funds changed to a two-way street.

In all matured free economies, wage payment is an indicator of market demand. Wage rises when there is either an increase in productivity or an increase in demand or a fall in supply for that type of workers and jobs. A flat, rigid and across-the-board minimum wage can be adjusted to serve a better purpose. Given that workers' wage tended to increase with experience and productivity, but would be influenced by the stage of the business cycle and the level of skill required, it would be preferable and more meaningful to have the "entry wage" that shows the wage for a new entry into the different types of work. It is even better if the "entry wage" is shown among different industries or services. For example, if entry wage for unskilled jobs in restaurants is lower than entry wage in construction, workers will have the incentive to move from working in restaurants to construction. If sufficient workers leave the restaurants, the employers will have to push the wage up so as to attract workers to stay. Such a simple example shows that the minimum "entry wage" in different jobs can serve additionally as an indicator on market wage so that workers can be informed of their market value. This information shall be useful for workers' mobility and the chance of gaining a higher earning. The relevant government department that concerned with labor and employment issues could provide the information on the entry wage of different workers easily. The "entry wage" concept would serve not only as a minimum wage for workers, but would additionally provide them with information on the wages of other jobs so that they have a chance to change and move to higher paid jobs.

13.7 Economic Survival Cost

Ultimately, poverty is a matter of economic survival. The absolute approach to poverty is concerned with the actual amount of economic resources needed for an individual to survive. Such a measurement is related to the actual needs. On the contrary, the relative approach relates economic survival to a number of socially comparable factors that would go beyond the bare essentials of life and could have intervened in the private life of an individual. Socially comparable factors often involve subjective value judgments that depended a lot on individual orientations, standards and political preferences and personality influence. Between the two approaches, the absolute approach to poverty can be standardized and be made fairer to all welfare recipients. Indeed, the absolute approach could serve as a system that stands between the decision of the policy makers, the welfare recipients and the public at large, ensuring that there is no favoritism, personality or ideology influences. When situation changes, the criteria and conditions imposed on whoever qualifies for poverty assistance would be applied across the board objectively so as to minimize unnecessary social tensions and disagreements.

There are a number of economics jargons that can reflect the level of economic standards. The Consumer Price Index (CPI) typically looks at the price level based on the price change of a bundle of goods. One can improve the cost of living measure by narrowing down to an essential and basic needs of households to reflect the economic "survival cost" of households. Such a "survival cost" measure shows the bottom line or the minimum living cost that a household will have to pay for survival economically. The minimum living cost incorporated only the bare essential necessities that include food, clothing, housing, transport and medical services. Anyone who is situated above the survival level will probably not fall into the poverty pool.

One can use a disaggregated approach by using the relevant "survival" factors to empirically study the concept of economic survival cost. The construction of a price-to-wage ratio in different essential consumption items, for example, could be an alternative to CPI because it could help to determine households' economic affordability, especially the low earning households. A low economic survival cost would enable individuals to satisfy their economic needs easier, and any economic surplus could then be accumulated into future wealth. Individual wealth accumulation would begin with savings of economic or earning surplus. With savings, households could depart from poverty.

Secondly, a lower survival cost would enable individuals to improve their quality of life, as residual earnings could then be used for non-essential items, such as piano lessons for their children. Further improvement in consumer spending could reduce social exclusion resulting from low earning. Thirdly, a low survival cost could promote growth as all individuals have more to spend and diversity in the choice of consumption would allow more industries and services to prosper and develop, thus generating a virtuous economic business cycle. Eventually, the flow of poverty would be minimized as businesses prospered and job opportunities created. The study by Wong and Lee (2002) has discussed the "basic living protection line" that advocated for the earning of a basic living by households. The "minimum living cost" (MLC) has been constructed in South Korea to estimate the amount of necessary expenditure by households.

The statistics used to construct the CPI is based on nine categories of goods and services that include: 1) food; 2) housing; 3) electricity, gas and water; 4) alcoholic drinks and tobacco; 5) clothing and footwear; 6) durable goods; 7) miscellaneous goods; 8) transport and 9) miscellaneous services.

Food: This category consisted of both meals brought away from home and meals taken at home. Their expenditure ratio is approximately 3:2. Since the bulk of food supply in Hong Kong comes from Mainland China, the price of food has obviously been affected by the upward trend of the Renminbi. The appreciation of the Renminbi has begun in 2006. The spot exchange rate between Renminbi and Hong Kong dollar has appreciated by 3.69% between December 2005 and December 2006, and by 6.7% in the ten years between December 1996 and December 2006. There are a total of nine categories of food imported from Mainland China, they included: 1) live animals; 2) meat and meat preparation; 3) dairy products and birds' eggs; 4) fish and aquatic preparations; 5) cereals and cereal preparations; 6) vegetables and fruits; 7) sugar, sugar preparations and honey; 8) coffee, tea, cocoa and spices; and 9) beverages. In 2005, for example, the percentage of individual items imported from Mainland China ranged between the lowest of 12.1% (fish and aquatic preparations) and the highest of 80.7% (live animals), giving an average of 34.4% among the nine categories of food imports from Mainland China.

Housing: Housing is divided into three classifications in official statistics: 1) rent for both private and public housing included rates and government rent; 2) management fees and other housing charges, and 3) materials for house maintenance. The cost of housing occupied about 30% of total household expenditure. Under the Housing Ordinance, the statutory median rent-to-income ratio has been capped at 10%. There have been several shots of waiving the rental payments in public housings by the government since 1998.

Electricity, Gas and Water: The four items used in the calculation of the CPI are: 1) electricity; 2) Towngas; 3) liquefied petroleum gas (LPG) and other fuel, and 4) water and sewage charge. Water and sewage charges have remained constant for many years. However, the accumulated increase in petroleum price has lifted the price of fuel-related items. In the 2008–2009 budget, the government provided electricity subsidies to all households up to a maximum of HK$1,800, costing an estimate of HK$4.3 billion.[6]

Alcoholic Drinks and Tobacco: Expenditure on Chinese wines, foreign wines, beer and cigarettes are definitely not daily necessities. Yet, it is often that low income individuals consumed alcoholic drinks and tobacco. For example, when examining the various quintile expenditure groups in 2004–2005, the expenditure share of alcoholic drinks and tobacco in the first quintile expenditure group was 1.6%, but the same percentage share for the fourth quintile expenditure groups was 0.2%. Nonetheless, this entire category does not constitute a necessity in the economic survival expenditure of individuals.

Clothing and Footwear: The 12 items under this category are divided according to men, women, children and infants. It would be difficult to separate the basic needs from luxurious items of clothing and footwear in the data. One survey from the Friends of the Earth in Hong Kong in 2004 founded that 86% of interviewees confessed their indulgence in non-necessity shopping. A similar survey on "green consumption" in March 2005 showed that 44% of interviewees dumped brand new clothes.

Durable Goods: The nine items grouped under this category included: 1) furniture; 2) home appliances; 3) electricity and gas; 4) video and sound equipment; 5) computers and telecommunications equipment; 6) tableware and kitchen utensils; 7) watches, clocks, cameras and optical goods; 8) travel and sports goods; and 9) other durable goods. Since many durable goods need not be frequently updated by the households, this category will be excluded from the calculation of survival cost estimation.

---

[6] *The 2008–2009 Budget*, Section 148, Hong Kong.

Miscellaneous Goods: The eleven items grouped under this category included: 1) proprietary medicines and supplies; 2) newspapers; 3) books and periodicals; 4) stationery; 5) soft furnishings; 6) cosmetics and personal care products; 7) household cleansing tools and supplies; 8) jewelry; 9) toys and hobbies; 10) purchase of textbooks and 11) other household goods. Other than household cleaning tools and supplies, and textbooks, the other items can be excluded from survival cost estimation.

Transport: The eleven items in this category include: 1) purchases and repairs of motor vehicles; 2) motor fuel; 3) motor licenses, insurance, instructors' fees, parking fees and tunnel tolls; 4) bus fares; 5) tram fares; 6) public light bus fares; 7) taxi fares; 8) mass transit railway (MTR) and railway fares; 9) ferry fares; 10) local transport; and 11) inbound and outbound transport fees. The various forms of public transport and expenditure on inbound and outbound transport are included in the survival cost estimation.

Miscellaneous Services: Some services included in this category are cinema entertainment, package tours, expenses on parties, other entertainment and holiday expenses, beauty treatment and fitness services, photographic and photo-printing services. These services are not considered necessities for survival. However, the cost on education, medical services, household services and hair-dressing, repairs, telephone and communication services are considered as necessities for survival needs.

Based on the items and the categories used in calculating the CPI, Table 13.8 reclassifies the items between necessities and non-necessities according to the survival cost concept. The non-necessities contained goods that are not counted as relevant for economic survival in the nine categories. Thus, the more relevant estimates are the expenditure on necessities. Table 13.8 shows the amount of household expenditure made in the three Household Expenditure Surveys (HESs). The first observation from Table 13.8 is that households spent 83.5% of their expenditures on necessities in 1994–1995, but this percentage has increased to 85.41% in 1999–2000, and has increased further to 87.98% in 2004–2005. This simply meant that the economic survival cost for households in Hong Kong has gone up by 5.36% between the decade of 1994–1995 and 2004–2005. On the contrary, the cost on non-necessities has dropped, meaning that the quality of life in Hong Kong has gone down, and households have to pay more for their economic survival.

Among the nine expenditure categories, Table 13.8 shows that expenditure on food has gone down from 36.49% in 1994–1995 to 31.32% in 2004–2005. Another item that experienced a downward shift in household expenditure is clothing and footwear, down from 5.12% to 2.81% between 1994–1995 and 2004–2005. On the contrary, household expenditure on housing has gone up most from 25.26% to 30.53% between 1994–1995 and 2004–2005. This meant that households on average have to spend an extra 20.86% on their housing. The increase in 1994–1995 and 1999–2000 is more rapid than in 2004–2005, reflecting the consequence of the property bubble in the pre-Asian financial crisis period. Other items that showed an increase in household expenditures included electricity, gas and water, transport and miscellaneous services.

The findings in Table 13.8 can further be reconfirmed by the data in Table 13.9 on the percentage share of total household expenditure in the various Household

TABLE 13.8 Percentage shares of necessities and non-necessities in the consumption bundle for calculating CPI (A)

	1994–1995		1999–2000		2004–2005	
	Necessity	Non-necessity	Necessity	Non-necessity	Necessity	Non-necessity
Food	36.49	0.81	31.11	0.77	31.32	0.78
Housing	25.26	0.08	29.09	0.04	30.53	0.01
Electricity, gas & water	3.37	0.00	3.99	0.00	4.84	0.00
Alcoholic drinks & tobacco	0.00	2.06	0.00	1.50	0.00	1.35
Clothing & footwear	5.12	0.00	3.36	0.00	2.81	0.00
Durable goods	0.00	4.34	0.00	4.96	0.00	4.01
Miscellaneous goods	0.95	5.08	0.98	4.27	0.95	3.73
Transport	6.68	0.49	7.48	0.75	7.56	0.51
Miscellaneous services	5.63	3.64	9.40	2.30	9.97	1.63
Total	83.50	16.50	85.41	14.59	87.98	12.02

Notes: The compilation of CPI (A), CPI (B) and CPI (C) is based on the expenditure patterns of households in the relatively low, medium and high expenditure ranges respectively, while the Composite CPI is compiled based on the overall expenditure pattern of all households taken together to reflect the impact of consumer price changes on the household sector as a whole. The CPI (A), CPI (B) and CPI (C) respectively cover some 50%, 30% and 10% of households in Hong Kong. The monthly household expenditures (in HK$) of these three groups in the base period (i.e., October 2004–September 2005) were $4,000–$15,499, $15,500–$27,499 and $27,500–$59,999 respectively. The expense for water and sewage charges was included under housing in the surveys before 1994–1995.

Sources: *Household Expenditure Survey*, Census and Statistics Department, various issues; author's calculations.

TABLE 13.9 Percentage shares of selected items in total household expenditure

	1979–1980	1984–1985	1989–1990	1994–1995	1999–2000	2004–2005
Housing	20.1	20.6	25.6	31.0	32.2	30.6
Food	38.3	38.3	34.2	29.4	25.7	25.8
Medical supplies & services	2.8	3.0	2.4	2.2	2.7	2.9
Fuel & light	2.8	2.8	2.4	2.4	2.9	3.4
Transport	6.4	7.2	7.6	7.9	9.2	9.5

Source: *Household Expenditure Survey*, Census and Statistics Department, various issues.

Expenditure Survey (HES). From the data on HES, housing share has increased by more than 5% between 1979–1980 and 1989–1990, and a further increase of 5% between 1989–1990 and 1994–1995. However, due to the post-Asian financial crisis recession, the percentage share on housing edged further up to 32.2% in 1999–2000 before it leveled off to 30.6% in 2004–2005. Similar to Table 13.8, food expenditure in total household expenditure has dropped considerably between 1978–1980 and 2004–2005.

Household expenditures on both medical supplies and services and fuel and light have dropped in the 1980s, but have revived upwards in the 1990s. Expenditure on transport has shown a gradual increase. These statistics are also supported by Wong and Lee (2002) whom argued that income elasticity of expenditure on housing is lower than food for poor households in Hong Kong. Housing is a more essential "necessity" than food for low-income households. This echoed strongly the argument for supporting the provision of public housing and the revival of the Home Ownership Scheme (HOS) that catered for the housing of the sandwich class. The argument is that once housing cost has become reasonable, households can improve their purchasing power, and that allow them to improve their quality of life and at the same time their additional consumption would allow other businesses to prosper, and would eventually help to diversify the economic base.

Table 13.10 provides further evidence on the survival cost using the data on the price of various fuels, forms of transport and nominal wage index obtained from the Census and Statistics Department. The data covered the two decades from 1985 to 2005. The first decade of 1985–1995 was the booming period with rapid rise in wages and earnings, while the prices of public utilities were kept steady. In the second decade of 1995–2005, the economy experienced an unprecedented economic recession with decrease in wages and earnings. The economic difference in the two decades can also be seen from the relative prices of public utilities.

In the first decade of 1985–1995, the relative prices of utilities and nominal wage have experienced a fall. This is expected since nominal wages had moved faster than price changes in utilities. The reverse is true in the second decade of 1995–2005, with the largest increase in Towngas, LPG, tram, public light bus, taxi and the underground mass transit railway. The tram operated only along the northern coast on the Hong Kong Island and may not affect the total level of transport much, while water is controlled by the government and the sewage charges have increased for

TABLE 13.10 Percentage change of relative prices of fuels and transport

% Change	Electricity	LPG	Towngas	Water & Sewage Charges
1985–2005	–52.22	–21.06	–14.28	14.72
1985–1995	–52.06	–39.26	–39.06	28.18
1995–2005	–0.33	29.95	40.66	–10.50

	Bus	Tram	Light Bus	Taxi	MTR	Ferry	Train	Light Rail
1985–2005	–4.15	14.42	–4.02	–2.10	–15.40	–23.72	–23.95	*3.25
1985–1995	–3.31	–23.34	–9.75	–9.47	–19.29	–23.25	–22.89	
1995–2005	–0.86	49.26	6.35	8.14	4.82	–0.06	–1.37	3.67

Notes: LPG = liquefied petroleum gas; MTR = mass transit railway; Light Rail began operation in Tuen Mun and Yuen Long in 1988. * = 1990–2005.
Source: *Consumer Price Index*, various issues, Census and Statistics Department, Hong Kong.

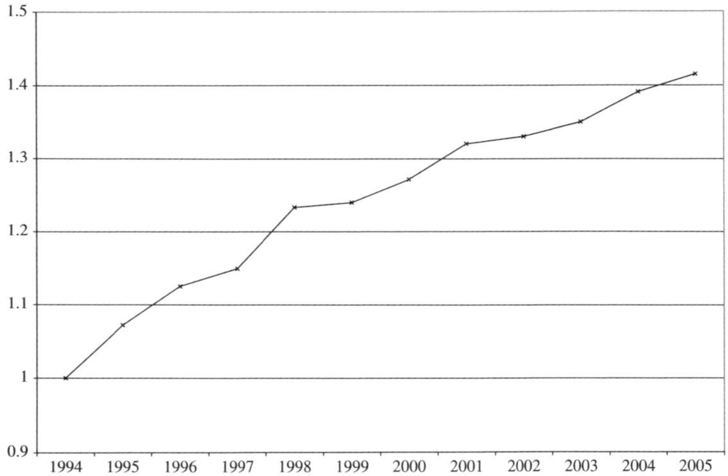

FIGURE 13.3 Relative price of textbooks (1994 = 1)

environmental purposes. The picture shown in Table 13.10 concludes that households' quality of life has been falling in the decade of 1995–2005 due to the fall in wages and earnings and the price increase in public utilities.

The relative price calculations can further be extended to two other survival essentials for most households in Hong Kong. Figure 13.3 and Figure 13.4 shows the relative prices of textbooks and medical services, respectively. The relative price refers to the price of textbooks and medical services to nominal wages, and the data are obtained from the CPI compiled by the Census and Statistics Department. The relative price of textbooks has increased by four-folded in the sample period, and the trend kept on rising. There are a number of factors that led to increase in the price of textbooks. One would be the increase in paper and printing cost. The other cost

FIGURE 13.4 Relative price of medical services (1985 = 1)

increases included overheads and rents. Due to the fall in the number of students and a lower birth rate, the textbook market has been shrinking, leading to a higher average fixed cost and a falling demand. There could be other solutions, including the decision not to change the syllabi over a longer period of time, so that the same textbook could be used for several years by different students. This shall also be environmental friendly too. Another suggestion is to separate the teaching materials into different components so that students can choose to buy only the essential materials, or spend less on the supplements.

The relative price of medical service has increased by 19.88% between 1985 and 2005. When the sample period is divided into two sub-periods, one can see that the pace of increase was much faster in the 1995–2005 decade. Reasons for the increase in the cost of medical services included the lack of supply of medical personnel, high rents for private medical premises and clinics. Even though fiscal expenditure on health has been increasing, there is an urgent need to develop mandatory medical insurance in Hong Kong so that private individuals would gradually have medical insurance coverage as an alternative to dependence on government health provision.

There are altogether fourteen items under private consumption expenditure. They included: 1) food and non-alcoholic beverages; 2) alcoholic beverages; 3) tobacco; 4) clothing, footwear and other personal effects; 5) rates, water and housing maintenance charges; 6) fuel and light; 7) furniture, furnishings and household equipment; 8) household operation; 9) personal care; 10) medical care and health expenses; 11) transport and communication; 12) recreation and entertainment;

TABLE 13.11 Price growth rates (%): 1982–2004

	Accumulated increase	Average growth rate
Food and non-alcoholic beverages	106	6.22
Alcoholic beverages	203	9.67
Tobacco	684	18.72
Clothing, footwear and other personal effects	131	7.23
Rates, water and housing maintenance charges	151	7.97
Fuel and light	83	5.18
Furniture, furnishings and household equipment	27	2.01
Household operation	196	9.45
Personal care	127	7.06
Medical care and health expenses	324	12.79
Transport and communication	74	4.74
Recreation and entertainment	169	8.59
Education	891	21.07
Other services	193	9.38
Nominal wage	259	11.24

Source: *Gross Domestic Product 2005*, Census and Statistics Department, Hong Kong.

13) education; and 14) other services. Table 13.11 compares the price change for the fourteen household expenditure items and the change in nominal wage in the period that covered the economic boom and the post-Asian financial crisis recession years. Other than tobacco which is highly a socially undesirable good, nominal wage increase has been quite high. But on the basis of average growth rates, households needed to spend more on medical care and education.

Lastly, one can examine the increase in household expenditure on different consumption categories. The expenditure-based GDP estimates provided the useful data of consumption expenditure by commodity groups in the domestic market. The data included current market prices, percentage distribution and volume indices. Total private expenditure can be calculated from the product of price and volume indices:

$$PCE_{it} = P_{it} \cdot V_{it}, \qquad (1)$$

where PCE shows the private consumption expenditure in current market prices for item i at time t, and P is price and V is quantity that used the volume indices as the proxy.

Table 13.12 shows both the accumulated growth and average growth rate for the fourteen components in private consumption expenditure for the whole sample (1966–2004) and four sub-sample periods (1966–1976, 1976–1986, 1986–1996 and 1996–2004). For the whole sample period, the private consumption expenditure for education has increased most by 2,423% in accumulated growth, while household expenditures on furniture, furnishings and household equipment had increased least by 196% in accumulated growth. With the exception of furniture, furnishings and household equipment that recorded an average growth rate of 3.06%, all other categories showed an average growth rate of more than 5%.

TABLE 13.12 Private consumption expenditure growth rates

	1966–2004		1966–1976		1976–1986		1986–1996		1996–2004	
	Ac.G	Av.G	Ac.G	Av.G	Ac.G	Av.G	Ac.G	Av.G	Ac.G	Av.G
Food and non-alcoholic beverages	684	5.89	122	8.32	97	7.03	95	6.91	–8	–1.08
Alcoholic beverages	578	5.46	60	4.81	134	8.85	118	8.09	–17	–2.25
Tobacco	2,324	9.26	62	4.97	324	15.55	196	11.45	19	2.19
Clothing, footwear and other personal effects	542	5.30	78	5.92	117	8.04	95	6.90	–15	–1.94
Rates, water and housing maintenance charges	573	5.44	48	3.99	131	8.75	139	9.11	–18	–2.41
Fuel and light	749	6.12	93	6.79	140	9.13	53	4.33	20	2.32
Furniture, furnishings & household equipment	196	3.06	71	5.53	67	5.25	35	3.06	–23	–3.27
Household operation	1,645	8.27	162	10.10	211	12.02	117	8.04	–1	–0.13
Personal care	701	5.95	89	6.56	146	9.41	76	5.81	–2	–0.23
Medical care and health expenses	1,391	7.79	83	6.24	185	11.02	131	8.72	24	2.73
Transport and communication	483	5.02	60	4.82	175	10.65	90	6.64	–30	–4.44
Recreation and entertainment	782	6.23	79	5.99	128	8.58	137	8.99	–9	–1.11
Education	2,423	9.38	46	3.87	209	11.95	362	16.53	21	2.41
Other services	1,083	7.10	98	7.09	159	10.00	138	9.05	–3	–0.42

Notes: Ac.G = accumulated growth rates, Av.G = Average growth rates.
Source: *Gross Domestic Product 2005*, Census and Statistics Department, Hong Kong.

The performance is very different in the sub-sample periods. In the post-Asian financial crisis recession years (1996–2004) when a number of private consumption expenditures have experienced a negative growth, medical care and health expenses have experienced a highest growth with an average of 2.73% per annum. On the other hand, transport and communication experienced a largest drop in private consumption expenditure, with an average fall of –4.44% per annum. Among the four sub-sample periods, the decade 1976–1986 showed the best performance in the growth of private consumption expenditure.

In the three decades before the Asian financial crisis (1966–1976, 1976–1986 and 1986–1996), the growth of private consumption expenditure has varied among the different categories. The categories that showed a declining trend included food and non-alcoholic beverages, furniture, furnishing and household equipment. The categories that showed a rising trend included alcoholic beverages, tobacco, rates and water and housing maintenance charges, medical care and health expenses, recreation and entertainment, education and other services.

There are other considerations in the economic survival concept. Other than the low income earners and although one should not assume that all elderly are faced with economic survival difficulties, the elderly population in Hong Kong is growing, increasing from 13% of population in 2009 to a projected 28% in 2039. The average household size in Hong Kong has been falling from 3.5 persons in 1994–1995 to 3.1 persons in 2004–2005, as shown in the 2004–2005 Household Expenditure Survey conducted by the Census and Statistics Department. There is also an increasing trend of mainland mothers delivering babies in Hong Kong. It is projected that mainland mothers and their children will form a considerable portion of the population in Hong Kong. With a projected number of 2.78 million new births over the three decades from 2009 to 2039, it is estimated that half of the new born will be from mainland mothers. In addition, the one-way permit immigration will bring to Hong Kong another 1.64 million people, mainly of mainland women joining their local husbands.[7]

Income inequality is not the worst kind of inequality because it can be improved and minimized. An effective way to reduce income inequality is reduction in poverty and an effective way to reduce poverty is to nurture economic opportunities and reduce economic survival cost that consisted mainly of necessities, typically food, housing, transport, medical services, clothing and basic household appliances. To minimize survival cost is to maximize purchasing power of individuals. With higher ability to consume, individuals can improve their quality of life and through economic security, social security can also be ensured. This is the ultimate value of economic freedom, as it opens up channels through which individuals can explore their opportunities and take charge of their economic life.

13.8 Economic Opportunity

Supply-side economic strategy has been the hallmark of Hong Kong's economic success since the 1950s. Hong Kong has experienced an economic structural change

[7] *South China Morning Post*, July 30, 2010.

since the opening up of Mainland China in 1978, as the rise of the service sector coincided with the decline of manufacturing industries. The post-Asian financial crisis economic recession has hit the economy hard, and drastic measures tended to be short-term and mainly demand-driven that called for more private and public spending as a way to "buy out" the recession. By 2010, the Hong Kong economy is booming with mainland tourists and inflow of Renminbi as Hong Kong has become the first offshore Renminbi center.

Hong Kong's economic freedom has attracted foreign capital, and the inflow of mainland capital is definitely making use of Hong Kong's financial freedom in property acquisition and investment. Despite Hong Kong's openness, successful supply-side strategies involved a focus on domestic and internal improvements. The ideology behind a supply-side strategy is the drive to prepare oneself so that a better job could be accomplished when opportunity arises. The creation of economic opportunity would not come from the demand-side, namely how much investment and jobs are attracted, but on the supply-side, namely how well prepared an economy is in attracting investment and jobs.

How well an economy is prepared has wider implications. The inflow of foreign investment, the volume of exports, the level of consumption, the amount of bank loans, the rate of industrial output growth and the price level are considered as outcome-based factors in development. Economic opportunity arises so long as there is a greater availability of resources. When the quantity of these outcome-based factors is expanded, more jobs would be created, and income would subsequently rise and more opportunities would be created. Studies on globalization and growth have argued that total economic welfare would increase when countries practiced economic openness, and empirical studies have used a large number of outcome-based factors to explain growth and globalization (Feldstein, 2000; Hausmann *et al.*, 2005; Sala-i-Martin, 1997; Iradian, 2005; Barro, 2000; Li *et al.*, 1998; Bruno and Easterly, 1998). However, it is still debatable as to why developing economies with similar endowments, economic openness and foreign investment have differed considerably in their development outcomes.

Economic opportunity would go beyond outcome-based *ex-post* factors of investment, consumption, bank loans and price, but would involve a number of *ex-ante* factors that concern, for example, the entrepreneurial spirit of individuals, infrastructure complementary to economic development, ethical and moral standards in business and social behavior, civic establishments that ensure qualities and uphold standards, and non-discrimination and equality in opportunities. Some of these *ex-ante* factors are cultural, others can be nurtured through education, policies and family and social values. Entrepreneurial attitude arises from an individual's preference on self-reliance and personal creativity, and taking up business activities as a challenge and venture into uncharted business activities. A low and simple tax structure, a competitive business environment and a clean and business-friendly administration could facilitate the entrepreneurial attitude greatly.

Appropriate infrastructural development, including research and development facilities, would provide another set of *ex-ante* factors that promote long-term development and open up numerous economic opportunities. Other than low labor cost and availability of human capital, infrastructure facilities would be the hardware needed to attract long-lasting investments. The reliability of banks could also be another *ex-ante* factor, as financial security is needed in all kinds of transactions. Sound banking and monetary policies could help to nurture enterprise spirits. The establishment of professional associations and civic organizations would enhance standards, judgment and qualities in different trades, such that personality and political influences would be eradicated. There is also a need to nurture transparency, non-discrimination and ethical requirements. The constant improvements in medical facilities and hygiene standards, for example, could ensure personal health and eliminate diseases, and a healthier population would have more energy in promoting growth and development. Some societal rules, business practice and behavior, such as the opening hours of businesses, could also be considered as *ex ante* factors that would ensure the success of *ex-post* factors.

There is thus a host of "home grown" factors that would proactively shape the economic opportunity set. In many ways, these "home grown" *ex ante* factors would define the initial conditions of development. Thus, the better the "home grown" conditions are, the higher the chance of creating economic opportunities. A number of home grown or *ex ante* indicators could be aggregated and used to define the accessibility of economic opportunities. For example:

1) Education accessibility that would look at the pupil-teacher ratio and percentage of secondary school/university graduates that could define the opportunity to receive education in an economy.
2) Health accessibility could be seen by the number of hospital beds per 1,000 people and by the indicators on diseases and medical personnel are other useful factors.
3) Business accessibility would concentrate on the corporate tax rate, assistance given to small- and medium-sized enterprises, development of entrepreneurship and government policy.
4) Finance accessibility would look at the condition on bank credit provisions and interest rate advantage that help to promote and nurture businesses.
5) Informal economy activities would involve the existence of black markets, extent of underground economy, illegal trafficking, corruption and other so-called underground activities. These activities could provide a sense of public safety.
6) Access to infrastructure could be measured by the mileage of roads, vehicles per capita, mode of public transport, and government policy on public work projects.
7) Social stability could be seen from crime rate, political violence and demonstrations, extent of civic unrest, reliability of the rule of law and so on.
8) Geographical access could provide information on land lock or coastal countries and territorial size of countries.
9) Cultural access would deal with religion, foreign language used, and other aspects of personal freedom and mutual respect.

While it has been popular to deploy policies that would improve the *ex-post* factors, it would be equally important to deploy policies that would improve the various *ex ante* factors in order to promote economic opportunities. Paradoxically, the home grown *ex ante* factors could be used to symbolize the health of an individual. It is only when a person is equipped with a strong healthy could the person work more efficiently and effectively. In other words, given that a good health is an *ex ante* condition, the work the person subsequently does become an *ex post* outcome.

The first lesson in economics theory is the scarcity of factors of production that would include labor, land, capital and entrepreneurship. Economic opportunity could be considered as the fifth scare production factor. If economies do not develop and improve their *ex ante* factors, the economic outcome would become less favorable. For example, countries which plagued with constant war and civic unrest, despite their abundance in land resources, are effectively scarifying their economic opportunities, driving them away to other more business-friendly economies. Equally, a strong welfare state with heavy redistributive policies or high wage would push their domestic investments away to other economies, thereby effectively throwing away the economic opportunities. In short, the outcome-based analysis could only consider the *ex-post* situation and economic consequences. Analysis on the input side of economic development is needed so that a better understanding of *ex ante* factors could help to steer economic policies in the direction that promote and nurture economic opportunities for further growth and development.

13.9 Conclusion

Economic freedom allows individuals to prosper to their fullest possible extent. But due to various differences in endowment and stages of economic cycles, not all individuals can enjoy the same economic outcome. Some will have higher rewards than others, but the resulting inequality could be acceptable so long as the instituted policies are opportunity-generating, and individuals have more chances to prosper and can move up in economic mobility. Those with low personal endowments are faced with difficulty in economic survival. In all free economies, individual diversity would result in a section of the population requiring welfare assistance for their survival and maintenance of basic needs in their standard of living.

Economically free economies will have to set aside resources ready to help the economic weak households so as to enable them to seek improvement in their endowments. Financial assistance given to the needy individuals should provide short-term aid, but not intended to make them dependent and reliant for long-term welfare, but encourage them to seek employment once the market conditions improve. Poverty should be seen from a dynamic point of view, meaning that policies should minimize the number of entries to and maximize the number of exits from the poverty pool. Similar to the understanding of inequality when the possibility of mobility would make intra-personal comparison more meaningful, the household receiving welfare aid may differ, even though the number of needy individuals in the poverty pool remains the same.

Overall, the gains brought about by economic freedom certainly exceed the financial resources needed to improve inequality and poverty. One has to bear in mind that the greater the number of individuals departing from the poverty pool, the higher the ability for individuals to improve their quality of life, and the less resource is needed to aid the poor. That in turns frees the resources for some other activities. A virtual economic circle can thus be generated.

Ultimately, the reduction of poverty is more relevant than to politicize the extent of inequality. Similarly, the relevant policy is to minimize the number of new poor entering into and maximize the number of departure from the poverty pool. The availability of economic opportunity is the key consideration in the reduction of both inequality and poverty. The discussion in this chapter relates to two types of factors that can expand economic opportunities. One set of factors is known as the *ex post* factors that are outcome-based and are concerned with the amount of available resources, such as the level of foreign direct investment, the amount of bank loans, the number of graduates and so on. These factors are the outcome of numerous input factors, and their expansion could provide more economic opportunities for jobs and employment. Less attention has been given to *ex ante* factors, many of which are home grown and have served as input factors. Business-friendly policies, attitude towards business, personal drive and creativity, ethical and moral practice, religious and cultural settings, availability of suitable infrastructure, public safety and a number of other related factors are actually the "first level" of unquantifiable intuitive factors that governed the size and sustainability of the *ex post* factors. Empirical study using world data by Li and Zhou (2010) and Zhou and Li (2011), for example, showed that such domestic factors as corruption, health expenses and education are more important than such external or openness factors as trade and external connectivity in promoting growth, especially those developing economies at low level of GDP. Improvements in domestic or indigenous factors have to be home grown, and their improvement is reflected in the outcome-based factors, such as the amount of foreign investment and exports. For economic opportunities to flourish, policy should aim at improvements in both home grown factors and outcome-based factors. That should be the long-term solution to reduction of inequality and poverty.

14 Economic Integration With Mainland China

14.1 Introduction

Hong Kong has been part of Mainland China geographically and historically. The colonization of Hong Kong by the British government in 1842 has since turned Hong Kong into a free port, allowing free trade and movement of lawful merchandize. There have certainly been high-handed controls by the British colonial administration, but the rule of law and social disciplines that were introduced over the decades have turned Hong Kong into an international trading place. However, the territories of Hong Kong have been regarded as too small, lacking adequate agriculture land, self-insufficient and unsustainable in terms of basic needs, and cannot survive without the vital supplies from Mainland China.

Despite the previous attempts to ensure adequate fresh water supply within the territory, for example, the bulk of fresh water supply and virtually all essential live stocks are supplied from Mainland China through various official agreements between Hong Kong and the Guangdong government, thereby providing life stability to the growing population in Hong Kong. Since colonization and other than the short period of Japanese occupation at the peak of the Second World War, Hong Kong has been regarded as a more stable place than Mainland China, which has undergone revolutions, ideological conflicts, famines and periods of civic unrest. Over the years, immigrants from Mainland China have settled in Hong Kong, making use of the stability and freedom in Hong Kong to work on their personal drive and success.

Historically, the Hong Kong economy has always been "walking on two legs", with one leg always attached to the changing situations and incidents in Mainland China and the other leg is related to the external world, serving foreign investors their business desires that eventually benefitted Hong Kong. The exercise of these two legs has over the years shaped the economic structure of Hong Kong, permitting Hong Kong to ride from one stage of development and growth to another. The first turning point in post-World War II development has been the establishment of the People's Republic of China in 1949 that had ideologically drawn a political line between socialist China and capitalist Hong Kong. The closed door policy in Mainland China since 1949 has forced Hong Kong to look for development alternatives. Despite the lack of self-sufficiency, Hong Kong turned to industrialization, exploiting the combined advantages of its own supply of low-skilled labor, inflow of capital from capitalists fleeing from Mainland China, post-World War II economic aids and investments from the Western world and the growing demand of manufactured goods in North America and Europe. Although history cannot be re-written, it could have been argued to some extent that Hong Kong's post-World War II development has benefitted from the trade embargo imposed on Mainland China after 1949, because those foreign investments that had landed in Hong Kong could have gone to or remained in Mainland China.

Indeed, the Hong Kong economy has gathered strength since the 1950s, as immigrants coming to Hong Kong peaked during the Cultural Revolution in 1966–1967 when socially undesirable and unstable practices were exercised in Mainland China. In the meantime, the inflow of capital, coupled with appropriate economic policies and infrastructure constructions, had aided industrialization in Hong Kong. By the 1970s, Hong Kong has gained the recognition as a "dragon" economy along with Japan, Singapore, Chinese Taipei (Taiwan) and South Korea in East Asia. By 1979, all trade preferential agreements between Hong Kong and the major markets in North America and Europe were removed, and exports from Hong Kong would no longer receive a tariff-free status (Li, 2002). Hong Kong has become an advanced and matured economy, and by the 1980s, Hong Kong's GDP per capita has caught up with that of key European countries.

The second turning point occurred in 1978 when China's late Premier Deng Xiaoping declared an open door policy that pursued economic reform and pragmatism. Economic reform in Mainland China attracted much investment from Hong Kong, from international institutions such as the World Bank, from foreign businesses and governments. While investment from international institutions have concentrated on Mainland China's infrastructure and institutional development, foreign investment focused more on light industries. The establishment of the different Special Economic Zones (SEZs) along the coastal provinces in Mainland China in the early 1980s was designated to attract foreign investment to promote light manufacturing for exports. Quite a considerable amount of investment from Hong Kong in the early 1980s came from persons who are ethnically affiliated to villages, localities and provinces in Mainland China. The role of "overseas Chinese" in providing investment has been important in the early stage of China's economic reform.

Economic reform in Mainland China has led to change in Hong Kong's economic structure by, on the one hand, hollowing out the manufacturing sector as many industries have migrated to Mainland China making use of its low cost and, on the other hand, developing rapidly new producer services that served mainly the businesses in Mainland China. For example, the number of headquarters has grown rapidly, as Hong Kong is becoming a gateway to corporate businesses in Mainland China. Hong Kong's affiliation to the western world and its language advantage, for example, has attracted foreigners to come to Hong Kong as a stepping stone to their investment in Mainland China.

The 1982–1984 Sino-British negotiation over the sovereignty reversion of Hong Kong in July 1997 was another turning point, as the change in economic structure was coupled with migration of Hong Kong people and adoption of a short-term investment behavior aimed at quick returns. With increases in wage and inflation, and fueled with speculation in properties and stocks, the Hong Kong economy boomed prior to 1997, but burst in 1998 after the outbreak of Asian financial crisis, and subsequently entered a period of unprecedented recession that lasted from 1998 to 2005. The post-1997 Hong Kong economy that experienced economic recession and periodic crises was faced with sharp contrast in the Mainland China economy where it experienced a two-digit growth rate for years and its growing industrial capacity has turned Mainland China as the "factory of the world". With a devaluation of the Renminbi by 30% in 1994, Mainland China has since been experiencing a growing trade surplus and has held the largest foreign reserve in the world. The Renminbi has been under severe pressure to appreciate since the turn of the new century, while the official rate has been revaluating gradually by about 6% annually.

Unfortunately and due to various economic and non-economic reasons, the Hong Kong economy was slow to restructure after the Asian financial crisis, as the growing Mainland China economy has become the more attractive destination for investment and trade, taking away Hong Kong's potential opportunities. The rapid growing Mainland China economy poses a number of competitive challenges to the Hong Kong economy, and the producer services that Hong Kong provides to Mainland China prior to 1997 are gradually losing their competitive edge as close substitutes are gradually being developed across the border. Unprecedentedly, and despite the reversion of sovereignty, a trade agreement between Mainland China and Hong Kong in the form of Closer Economic Partnership Agreement (CEPA) was made in 2005, allowing tariff-free status to Hong Kong exports to Mainland China, though Hong Kong may not be producing those goods for export. Since 1995, visa-free travels have also been granted in different stages, allowing more Mainland citizens from coastal cities and provinces to enter Hong Kong for visiting and short-term purpose. While the Hong Kong stock market has provided ample opportunities for Mainland banks and enterprises to raise capital from Hong Kong, and as a step in the internationalization of the Renminbi, Beijing also allowed Hong Kong to become the first offshore Renminbi trading center, and by 2011, Renminbi has become the settlement currency for trade between Mainland China and Hong Kong. One can see that a major factor in the economic integration is for Hong Kong to aid the further development of the mainland economy.

The Hong Kong economy is facing new problems. While the Mainland China market is large and Hong Kong has the proximity advantage, yet the considerable difference in cost of production and living expenses has attracted people from Hong Kong to consume and spend across the border in Shenzhen and other cities in the Pearl River Delta area. Although it was the informal economic sector (restaurants, fake products, messages and other personal services, tailoring, bars and karaoke entertainment) that are being patronized mostly, many Hong Kong people have developed their consumption preference across the border. This was particularly severe in the recession years when cross border entertainments were cheaper than similar consumption patterns in Hong Kong, thereby absorbing the much needed consumption expenditures in Hong Kong in the recession years.

Hong Kong will have to keep pace with the ultra-rapid changes in the Mainland China economy. While people in Hong Kong are committing their consumption expenditures across the border, and many are working and having their families in Mainland China, and some retired people have chosen to retire in Mainland as the cost of living is lower, the rapid growth is the Mainland economy has reversed the trend, as it has become very popular for mainland citizens to visit Hong Kong for shopping, properties and delivery of babies. Since the permission on visa-free travel to Hong Kong, mainland tourists have poured to Hong Kong, though there are reported incidents of poor quality in tourism services. Consumption expenditure by mainland tourists has outpaced the expenditure made by Hong Kong people when visiting mainland destinations. The "cash rich" mainland tourists are "big spenders" when shopping in Hong Kong, firstly for brand name products, but soon shop up large number of properties in Hong Kong, resulting in massive increase in rents in popular tourist areas and in luxurious properties. By 2011, the property price has exceeded that of the previous peak in 1997 prior to the burst of the Asian financial crisis.

The visa-free travel has its dark side. Rich parents from Mainland China travel to Hong Kong to deliver their children in hospitals in Hong Kong, though some may have come to avoid the one-child policy [in Mainland China] if they are having a second child. Well-organized agents have been active in placing pregnant women for their delivery in Hong Kong hospitals. Such an incident has aroused public outcry in Hong Kong in 2011 as medical resources are being constrained. Moreover, babies born in Hong Kong are Hong Kong citizens, and there is no guarantee if these babies born to mainland mothers will return to Hong Kong and seek welfare assistance. There are still a number of attractions in Hong Kong that encourage mainland residents to gain permanent residence in Hong Kong.

There is the formation of a new political economy in Hong Kong. The economic rise of Mainland China and the inflow of Renminbi that provided a new form of capital fund, the mainland people coming to Hong Kong either through birth or family reunion or business immigration are providing a new economic force to the future of Hong Kong. These new comers will help to shape the economic future of Hong Kong, and although a number of questions remain unanswered until a later time, one thing certain is that this could be history repeating itself, that those have made their way to Hong Kong are the more energetic sector of population from Mainland China, willing to come to Hong Kong and get prepared for a different path of life and development from that in Mainland China. A greater degree of freedom and the international exposure that Hong Kong possesses can provide the appropriate environment for a new generation of enterprising citizens. With their new identity in Hong Kong, the chance of holding a Hong Kong identity card and the possibility of a Hong Kong passport, these new immigrants and those born in Hong Kong may have to give up their household affiliation in Mainland China. Hong Kong will become their home.

In any case, one is talking about Mainland China as the potential second largest economy in the world in the not too distant future. The gigantic Mainland China economy, or even the economy of Guangdong province, can easily absorb the Hong Kong economy. There has been talk of marginalization of the Hong Kong economy, implying that the economic status of Hong Kong no longer plays a prominent role in the economic development of Mainland China. Indeed, prior to the time of the sovereignty reversion in 1997, the economic future of Hong Kong has been debated. Should Hong Kong be absorbed into the Mainland China economy or maintain its own special features and keep to its own comparative advantages? There are two sides of the argument. The "pro-Mainland" or "zero-sum" school holds a more complacent view and argues that given the huge mainland economy, Hong Kong can easily be taken care of and can survive by just serving and moving along with the mainland economy. Large businesses in Hong Kong have already looked to the mainland economy for their future development and market, and the Hong Kong economy is quite saturated with little chance of drastic development. The Hong Kong market is too small when compared to the mainland market. Thus it is easy for Hong Kong to hide under the wing of the mainland economy.

The "pro-Hong Kong" or "positive-sum" school looks to economic restructuring and advocates that under the "one country, two systems" framework, it will be to the benefit of the motherland if Hong Kong plays its economic part and serves the mainland economy by creating more comparative advantages that can lead to economic new heights. Hong Kong has to explore its own new advantages, and try to produce a performance better than that under the British rule. With a convertible currency linked to the US dollar, a well maintained infrastructure, international connections, a structured domestic system with civic establishments and an English-speaking population, Hong Kong has all the ingredients to excel to the next stage of advanced economic development. Therefore, the mainland economy should be seen as an advantage to the next phase of development in the Hong Kong economy. Despite the political difference, the "self-rule" should leave Hong Kong with sufficient autonomy to conduct its own economic affairs that promote Hong Kong and at the same time aid development in Mainland China, especially the Pearl River Delta region.

There are of course other complications, as one has to consider some of the dynamic situations in Mainland China, Guangdong province or even Shenzhen region, and Hong Kong itself. Different political and party leaders in Beijing and Guangdong would place different emphasis on the economic integration between mainland and Hong Kong, and between Guangdong and Hong Kong. There is also the political implication between Beijing and Guangdong. Would the Guangdong-Shenzhen-Hong Kong economic annex be seen differently in Beijing? Or Beijing prefers Hong Kong to be different from Guangdong and other cities in southern China? For example, there has been a subtle discussion in addressing Hong Kong as the "dragon head" in the economic development of southern China. Both Guangzhou and Shenzhen would also like to act as "dragon heads" for other cities in other provinces in southern China. Both Guangzhou and Shenzhen have been claiming to lead the Pearl River Delta through their publicized materials.[1]

In many ways, economic integration between Mainland China and Hong Kong has always been taken place, the more relevant concern is economic cooperation and how can the international status of Hong Kong be used as reference point in promoting the mainland economy. Given the brief historical background, this chapter examines the issue and the dynamic implications of economic integration between Mainland China and Hong Kong.

---

[1] *Nanfang Daily*, Guangzhou, China, November 30, 2005; *South China Morning Post*, November 14, 2008; January 9, 2009; *China Daily*, February 16, 2009.

14.2 Comparison of Advantages

One preliminary consideration that has sometimes been overlooked is the different stages of economic development between Mainland China and Hong Kong. Hong Kong is much more economically advanced than Mainland China, especially in terms of per capita GDP, level of infrastructure, social and civic fabrics and so on. Only a few cities in Mainland China, typically Shenzhen, Shanghai, Beijing and Guangzhou whose per capita GDP is closer to that of Hong Kong, while a large number of cities in Mainland China are still developing (Li, 2006). There is a need to understand what one is comparing. Typically, because of its matured or advanced nature, GDP in Hong Kong will grow at a lower rate than Mainland China. Mainland China starts at a lower economic base, and its high growth rate simply reflects the rapid economic catch up. Indeed, the rapid economic rise of Mainland China should be seen as a blessing to Hong Kong, as Hong Kong will benefit from a more-developed and more-advanced mainland economy.

Other than the high growth rate in the mainland economy, one has to look at the various statistics with care. Given the economic diversity, there will be different aspects of development. For example, one expects more public expenditure or investment expenditure on infrastructure development in Mainland China than in Hong Kong, simple because infrastructure development within Hong Kong has reached quite a high stage, though there is need for more physical infrastructure that integrates the two economies, such as railways and highway connections. Thus, when statistics that compares expenditure on infrastructure development between Hong Kong and Mainland China, the low expenditure on infrastructure in Hong Kong simple reflects the different stage of infrastructure development and not that Hong Kong is performing worse than the mainland economy in terms of infrastructure provision.

Indeed, the kind of additional infrastructure needed in Hong Kong differs from that in Mainland China. For example, to strength the shipping industry and turning Hong Kong into a trade hub, Hong Kong is urged to develop and strengthen its maritime industry that involves not only the shipping business, but development in the human capital in shipping and maritime industry, registration center for ships, financial center for raising funds for the shipping business, maritime insurance and maritime arbitration.[2] Secondly, integrating the Hong Kong economy with the Mainland or Guangdong economy requires new infrastructure developments. One is the railway link between Hong Kong and the Shenzhen airport. The railway link is meant to strength the economic ties between Hong Kong, Shenzhen and all cities on the eastern coast of the Pearl River. The second major infrastructure is the Zhuhai Bridge that links Hong Kong with the cities in the western coast of the Pearl River cities of Macau SAR and Zhuhai. The long-term benefit to Hong Kong is that cities in the western part of Guangdong province (such as Jiangmen, Kaiping, Taishan, Enping, Zhaoqing and Yangchun), the western provinces of the Pearl River Delta (namely the provinces of Hainan, Guangxi, Guizhou, Yunnan and Sichuan) and the western provinces in Mainland China (such as Tibet and Qinghai) can have a direct

---

[2] *Mingpao Daily*, *Hong Kong Economic Journal*, and *South China Morning Post*, April 22, 2009.

land connection to Hong Kong, thereby opening up numerous economic and businesses for both Hong Kong and western cities of Guangdong.

By distance, cities in west and southwest provinces of Mainland China are closer to Hong Kong than to metropolitan cities of Shanghai and Beijing. A good land infrastructure will open up future economic development.[3] A further possibility is the land link to Southeast Asian countries of Vietnam and Laos when they follow the path of Mainland China to take up rapid economic reforms. The road network is an important infrastructure link for travel of goods and people. It is perfectly feasible to travel on road from Hong Kong to Beijing, and from Hong Kong to Singapore if the highway networks are well connected and the road safety standards are unified.

The pursuit of economic development is to promote growth and better living standards. After the end of World War II, the Asian "dragon" economies of Japan, South Korea, Hong Kong, Taiwan and Singapore have caught up in their drive to economic development through investments and inflow of capital and industrialization. Their rise in GDP per capita, which is a usual aggregate measure of economic advancement, has qualified them as developed or advanced or industrialized economies. Their GDP per capita, economic freedom, export and competitiveness have been raised to the world level, catching up with other advanced countries in Europe. However, the economic rise of one economy does not necessary mean the economic fall of another economy. World economic development is more of a positive-sum game (namely all economies benefit) than a zero-sum game (namely, one benefits at the expense of another). It is indeed a human intention to turn all world economies into developed and matured countries so that poverty and inequality are minimized if not eradicated. When the East Asian economies have risen in the 1970s and 1980s, they in turned aided other Asian economies to develop through investment and trade, thus enabling nearby economies to benefit.

Economic reform is Mainland China since 1978 has reduced poverty to a large extent, especially along the coastal provinces that turned a large number of individuals into economic able households. While the economic catch up will lift the mainland economy into a higher level of development, the mainland economy still faces a host of socio-economic problems, such as health care, retirement, property rights and usage of land, and the eradication of informal or underground and rent-seeking economic activities (Wu, 2005). Economic development should therefore be seen as a dynamic, on-going process with gradual improvements over the decades. While the availability of hardware is important in the mainland economy, improvement and advancement in software is needed in the promotion of economic maturity. Nonetheless, economic catch up will mean that the mainland economy will gradually be accepted into the world economy. This can be seen in the increase in the position of various world rankings. Thus, there is no surprise to see that the ranking of the mainland economy is getting closer to Hong Kong. In individual industry or service, it is possible for Mainland China to perform better than Hong Kong. In turn, Hong Kong needs to look for new alternatives and economic advantages to stay competitive.

---

[3] *South China Morning Post*, December 19, 2007 and July 30, 2008.

It is no secret that Hong Kong has been the key financier and facilitator in the early stage of economic reform in Mainland China. It can also be argued that history has repeated itself. Hong Kong's economic success since the 1950s has been the continuous inflow of capital from overseas as well as from Mainland China after the revolution in 1949. After 1978 and out of patriotism of the motherland, those capitalists who flee to Hong Kong from Mainland China after 1949 are sending their capital back to Mainland China for economic development. In addition, the low cost of production in Mainland China has pulled, while the high cost of production in Hong Kong in the 1980s has pushed capital to Mainland China. China's economic reform has emerged at a time that coincided with a number of economic and political events, including the Sino-British negotiation over the post-1997 Hong Kong. The late Premier Deng Xiaoping's famous 1978 motto that "it does not matter whether it is a black cat or a white cat so long as it catches mice" has opened up a chapter of stable development that has attracted Hong Kong patriots and other investors to begin investing in Mainland China.

Thus, it is Mainland China which is receiving inflow of capital after 1978. In the 1980s when the Hong Kong economy was at its peak of development, the outflow of investment was regarded as a mean to aid the mainland economy. However, there is the opportunity cost in investment outflow, as investments that had departed from Hong Kong meant that there would be a decline in investment in Hong Kong. Although the stage of development is different, with Hong Kong being a matured and advanced economy and Mainland China is a fast developing economy, the pace of development has taken place on a reverse direction. With its advanced status, like any other advanced economies, Hong Kong experienced a slower pace of growth and development since the 1980s as investment that had left Hong Kong to Mainland China had not been replenished from elsewhere. On the contrary, the rapid pace of the mainland economy has enjoyed a prolonged, close to a two-digit growth for over three decades since the early 1980s. In short, investment from Hong Kong was one-way out, while investment to Mainland China was one-way in.

Despite the difference in the stage of development at the time of sovereignty reversion in July 1997, Hong Kong has shown sign of investment fatigue, as investment from Hong Kong to Mainland China has reached its limits. For example, by the turn of the century while Hong Kong investments focused on small-scale light manufacturing, Guangdong and other rapidly emerging provinces in Mainland China have increasingly look to large-scale investment and high-tech production. After Hong Kong's sovereignty reversion in 1997, "what Hong Kong can do that Mainland China cannot?" was a popular question that challenged investment from Hong Kong. With the growth of the industrial capacity in Mainland China, there is indeed a change in the relationship between Hong Kong and Mainland China. From the resources point of view, the tiny economy of Hong Kong cannot be compared with the vast Mainland China economy. With its vast supply in the three factors of production (land, labor and capital), the economy of Mainland China is said to have "absolute advantage" over the Hong Kong economy, meaning that "whatever Hong Kong does, Mainland China can do, possibly even better".

Hence, while resource-wise Hong Kong is economically losing to Mainland China on an absolute scale, economic integration with the mainland economy should best be considered on the basis of comparative advantages. Indeed, Hong Kong has always exceled in comparative advantages. In previous episodes of economic development, Hong Kong has specialized in different areas of comparative advantages in the supply of different exports and services to the world market at different times. The importance of dynamic comparative advantage has been argued in the paradigm of economism in Li (2002). While an economy is currently adhering to some comparative advantages, the concept of dynamic comparative advantages suggests that the economy will have to develop new comparative advantages at the same time. This is because the comparative advantages of today may not be the comparative advantages of tomorrow. To development the comparative advantages of tomorrow, the economy has to start discovering new comparative advantages today. The success of the Asian "dragon" economies, as reported in Li (2002), strongly adhered to the desire to explore new comparative advantages in order to lengthen their economic competitiveness, either through government initiatives on research and development expenditures on relevant technology, or appropriate institutional establishments to provide the needed connections and manpower, or setting up of a "business-academic-government" link to see to the need to pass appropriate laws and business commitments.

In many ways, there has always been economic integration between the mainland economy and the Hong Kong economy. Hong Kong has been economically serving the mainland in terms of trade, capital flows and a window to the outside world. On the contrary, the mainland economy has constantly been supplying Hong Kong with basic food materials, keeping stable the price of life necessities in Hong Kong. The sphere of economic integration has been enlarged since sovereignty reversion in 1997. All channels of integration have been expanded, extended, multiplied and have become a two-way traffic.

In the flow of funds, though there is still continued investment from Hong Kong to Mainland China, funds from Mainland China to Hong Kong has expanded tremendously, especially portfolio investment in the stock market and the real estate market. A trade agreement, known as the Closer Economic Partnership Agreement (CEPA), has first been concluded in 2005, allowing tariff-free exports from Hong Kong. While people complain about cross-border consumption, visa-free travel since 2005 has boosted mainland tourists to Hong Kong. There are increasing opportunities for mainland professionals and experts to work in Hong Kong. Human capital has increasingly become a two-way flow.

There are limitations that are yet to be eased in the process of integration. Hong Kong is still a market capitalist economy, and the government takes a backseat in businesses. This contrasts sharply with situations in mainland where the government takes a lead in the path and direction of economic development and business ventures. For example, foreign businesses intending to investment in Mainland China have to approach the central or provincial governments directly for the type of investment and industries. Very often, agreements from central or provincial governments are needed for large scale foreign investments. In Hong Kong, there is the well-established business and banking system that caters for foreign investors, and rules and regulations have been instituted so as to produce a level playing field for all investors, and personality issues are not involved. Many obstacles in economic integration arise from the various differences in the economic structure and system between Mainland China and Hong Kong.

14.3 The Complement — Competitive Model

The economy of Hong Kong has often served as a reference point in Mainland China's economic reform and economic opening since 1978. While investment from Hong Kong has been the key economic factor, especially in Guangdong and various cities in southern China, it has become natural and taken for granted that economic activities in the mainland economy will look to the practice in Hong Kong as a guideline. Be it television entertainment shows, construction of housing estates, management practices in business entities and so on, economic and business decision makers in Mainland China usually look to, imitate or transfer their practices from Hong Kong. Serving as a reference point to other emerging economies is not unique to Hong Kong. Indeed, Hong Kong did the same and learned from other more matured and advanced economies at the time when Hong Kong was rapidly developing after the end of the Second World War. The western advanced economies then have served as reference point for the development of the Hong Kong economy. Nonetheless, given that Hong Kong is the more matured economy, practices and 'ways of doing things' can be learned by entities in other emerging economies. This reflects the "complement" role of the Hong Kong economy in the process of integration with Mainland China. The "look to Hong Kong" attitude has remained strong in various economic development aspects, and likewise, practices and the way of doing things in Hong Kong has often been referred by organizations and institutions in Mainland China. For example, the large local government debts and the ever growing fiscal deficit in the mainland economy in 2011 has led to some discussion on learning from Hong Kong's structure of fiscal balance and tax system.[4]

Over the years, Hong Kong investments in Mainland China have helped to develop the mainland economy considerably, especially in manufacturing. As economic situations in Mainland China improves, and the transfer of various practices from Hong Kong to Mainland China have served their purposes. It has come to the possibilities that aspects of economic activities, typically in light manufacturing, have exceled and have performed better than the similar activities in Hong Kong. The process of de-industrialization in Hong Kong typically suggests that Hong Kong's advantage in light manufacturing has been captured by similar production in the mainland economy. As the mainland economy improves, there will come to a situation in which the economic ability in Mainland China can compete with Hong Kong, and can absorb Hong Kong's advantage completely. This forms the "competitive" element in the Mainland — Hong Kong economic relationship.

Li (2006, section 8.6) has illustrated the "complement — competitive" relationship in the process of economic integration between Mainland China and Hong Kong.

---

[4] More than 20% of prefecture governments are facing a debt ratio higher than 100%, for example. On behalf of local governments, the Ministry of Finance will issue a bond amounts to Rmb 46.6 billion in August, 2011. *China Daily eClips*, July 28, 2011.

As compared to Hong Kong in resource terms, Mainland China has abundant land, labor and capital. Mainland China is said to have "absolute advantage" over Hong Kong, and what Hong Kong does economically can also be done in Mainland China. For Hong Kong to survive, Hong Kong has to look for, expand and extend additional "comparative advantages". Namely, Hong Kong's economic excellence will have to depend on and explore areas where Hong Kong has done better than Mainland China, or excel in areas where Mainland China's performance is weaker.

Hong Kong will perform well in "complement" areas, but suffer in "competitive" areas of development in the process of economic integration with Mainland China. The related concern is how Hong Kong should position itself in "competitive" areas. In other words, Hong Kong needs an economic strategy that would prolong Hong Kong's economic survival in the rapidly rising mainland economy.

The competitive-complement relationship can conceptually be elaborated as follows. Consider the four-quadrant Figure 14.1 (same as Figure 8.6 in Li (2006)), where the vertical axis is labeled as the international standard (IS), and the horizontal axis indicates the number of industries (IND). Industries [in Mainland China] that have attained the international standard will be situated in the north-east quadrant of the figure, while industries that are below and/or working towards the international standard are shown in the south-west quadrant of the figure. Both the southeast and northwest quadrants in Figure 14.1 are redundant.

The Complement Curve drawn in the south-west quadrant of Figure 14.1 represents the various manufacturing and service industries that are below international standard (IS). The farther an industry is below the horizontal line, the lower is the standard of the industry. The number of these industries and their distance from the international standard is represented by area A in Figure 14.1. These industries will still need Hong Kong as a reference point in their development process to become standardized industries, and their further development complements the Hong Kong economy. The Competitive Curve drawn in the north-east quadrant of Figure 14.1 presents industries that have achieved international standard. The farther above the horizontal axis, the more successful and competitive the industry

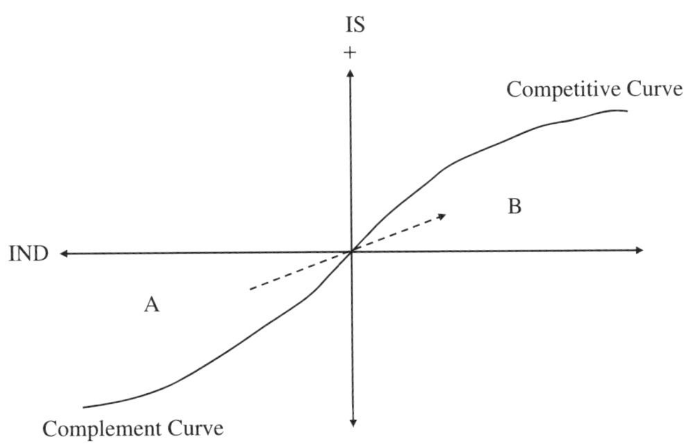

FIGURE 14.1 The complement — Competitive model

is. These internationalized, standardized and mature industries, indicated by area B, will compete with the corresponding industries in Hong Kong.

The "gain-loss" position of Hong Kong in the complement-competitive relationship can be seen from a simple measure on the size between areas A and B. Hong Kong remains better off if area A is larger than area B. On the contrary, Hong Kong loses out to mainland if area B is larger than area A. The complement area A is economically favorable to Hong Kong, while the competitive area B hurts the Hong Kong economy. Such a direct comparison between the two areas can only give a static indication. The dynamic situation is more important and complicated. Once an industry in Mainland China improves and catches up with the international standard, the industry is effectively moving along the Complement Curve in area A to the Competitive Curve in area B. The dynamic scenario is indicated by the broken line arrow from area A to area B. Over the years and as the industry matures, it moves from a position in area A along the Complement Curve to a position in area B along the Competitive Curve.

The outcome of the dynamic scenario may not be favorable to the Hong Kong economy. Assuming the economic structure in Hong Kong remains static and unchanged, the simple consequence is that as more industries in Mainland China shift from being complement to Hong Kong (area A) to being competitive to Hong Kong (area B), area A will then shrink and the Complement Curve will get closer and closer to the horizontal line. At the same time, more mainland industries will become competitive to Hong Kong, and the Competitive Curve shifts upwards, enlarging area B considerably. Conceptually, the shrinkage of the complement area (area A), coupled with the enlargement of the competitive area (area B), is definitely unfavorable to the long-term survival and competitiveness of the Hong Kong economy.

The strategy that Hong Kong (government, businesses, institutions, professionals and individuals) chooses has to turn the "curse" into a "blessing". A "two-leg" strategy will be appropriate for Hong Kong. On the one hand, the prolonging or even an enlargement of the complement area will create appropriate industries that will attract business and industries back to Hong Kong. On the other hand, it would be appropriate for industries in the "competitive" area to use other services in Hong Kong. Examples include the expansion of producer services for mainland businesses. Put in simple terms, one is to enlarge area A, while the other is to encourage industries in area B to use Hong Kong for their business.

How to enlarge area A, or prevent area A from shrinkage? An industry in the mainland economy will typically travel from a point situated at the end of the Complement Curve, which is well below the international standard measured by the vertical axis, to a point nearer to the origin as the industry develops or improves. As the entire mainland economy develops and matures, more and more industries will emerge. The newly emerged industries (manufacturing and services) usually begin from an infant stage with low and diverse standards, and their improvement may need to look to lessons from Hong Kong. Such a development is seen to improve the complement between Hong Kong and Mainland. As more mainland industries that need to improve their standards, the greater the chance is for the Hong Kong economy. This is reflected in the outward movement of the Complement Curve, which will probably shift downwards, thereby creating a larger area A. Hence, the "first leg" of the strategy is to promote and explore new industries in mainland, Guangdong and the Pearl River Delta, as their emergence required assistance from Hong Kong's experience.

A number of examples on complements can be identified in both manufacturing and services industries. The large urbanization drive in the Pearl River Delta region, for example, suggests that various new urban related industries will emerge. Hong Kong has experienced decades of urbanization, and Hong Kong can transfer the urbanization experience through the activities of various related businesses. Another example is Mainland China's accession to the World Trade Organization and the standards required in such industries as banking and finance will provide complement opportunities for Hong Kong businesses. If national banks in China have to become commercially viable and economically competitive, Hong Kong banks will have the first mover advantage. When Mainland China opens up its domestic banking market for foreign banks, banks from Hong Kong can capture the market earlier than other foreign banks. In mid-2003 when both the Mainland authority and Hong Kong government announced the relaxation of travel permits from various provinces, a large increase in Mainland tourists to Hong Kong was expected. One attraction is the consumption of such genuine products as cosmetics, medicine, gold and jewelry and other high valued added consumer items. Since 2007 or so when toxic milk power was discovered in Mainland China, mainland residents traveled to Hong kong to stock up milk power for their new born. Hence the lower the trust-worthiness of consumer products in Mainland China are, the more mainland tourists will buy these products in Hong Kong. The retail industry in Hong Kong will gain.

A major element in the expansion of the Complement Curve is the "pull effect", and that businesses and industries in Hong Kong excel when their corresponding businesses and industries in Guangdong or Mainland China have not reached a certain standard. As the mainland economy is rapidly developing, distortions and imperfections in their process of development push them to look for benchmarks, and Hong Kong will naturally become the first destination for such benchmark reference. Hence, Hong Kong's own strategy would need to maintain really excellent standard and quality in virtually various aspects of economic activities. The eradication of fake products, for example, provided reliability in high value-added products, and this "pulled" consumers from Mainland China to shop in Hong Kong. The pursuance of good quality and the maintenance of international standards is the new comparative advantage in the retail sector of Hong Kong. The implication for such a new comparative advantage to flourish is that Hong Kong's government, public and private institutions have to embark on a drive to deepen standards, practices and rules and regulations of various industries, professions and businesses so as to perfect Hong Kong's systems and structures.

The other "leg" in the complement — competitive strategy is to attract those winning industries in mainland to use related services in Hong Kong. As much of the light manufacturing have migrated to Guangdong and the Pearl River Delta region, for example, and realistically it would be unlikely for these manufactures to return to Hong Kong. The development of light manufacturing in southern China is quite matured. This suggests that the mainland economy will probably advance beyond light manufacturing. The appropriate strategy for Hong Kong would be to attract these successful manufacturing to use Hong Kong for their various related activities. Typical examples are shipping, insurance, marketing and design, quality testing and legal services.

One should note that as industries move from area A to area B in Figure 14.1, area B will expand and the Competitive Curve will shift upwards. Such a movement, however, is restricted to the industries that are common in both Hong Kong and Mainland China. There are, indeed, the developments of other industries in Mainland China that do not have parallels in Hong Kong. For example, motor vehicle production will not be counted in area B, as Hong Kong does not possess the production of motor vehicles. Therefore, expansion in these industries can equally provide economic opportunities for Hong Kong businesses.

The complement — competitive model does at least provide a conceptual framework of analysis in the economic integration between Mainland China and Hong Kong, and at most provides a strategic path for the Hong Kong economy in the economic integration with the mainland economy. There are indeed a great number of new comparative advantages that Hong Kong can develop. While the Competitive Curve and area B showed the areas that mainland has excelled over Hong Kong, on the contrary, Hong Kong should explore and aim to enlarge area A, the complement area. The proposed Hong Kong-Macau-Zhuhai Bridge in the longer time perspective opens up the western part of the Guangdong and the western provinces in Mainland China, which has been lacking behind to that of Shenzhen, Guangzhou and other cities in eastern provinces. The new bridge will definitely bring Hong Kong steps closer to the economic development in western provinces, and their further open up of the market will fall within the complement area of Hong Kong.

The "western" development concept includes the western provinces in Mainland China, typically the four provinces of Guangxi, Hunan, Yunan and Sichuan. Hong Kong has the advantage to complement the economic development of these provinces so long as these provinces are closer, both by land and by air, to Hong Kong than to Shanghai or to Beijing. Although these four provinces are economically much weaker than Guangdong and Shanghai, Hong Kong should consider their long-term potential in markets and manufacture outputs. Establishing better infrastructural partnerships and relationships with these provinces, such as the building of a road and rail network, will be the first steps that will enrich Hong Kong's complement area with these provinces in the longer perspective.

Equally, one shall not be too pessimistic in the competitive areas. In order to attract Guangdong and mainland businesses to use Hong Kong for their related business activities, Hong Kong have to do more by making better connections, promotions and contacts with coastal cities east of the Pearl River, as well as the three provinces of Fujian, Jiangxi and Zhejiang. While they can be closer to Shanghai and Xiamen, Hong Kong still offers an excellent alternative. Competitiveness suggests the availability of better alternatives and choice, and surely there will be some Mainland businesses that will choose Hong Kong over other cities for their transactions.

Also, one should not consider "competitiveness" between different Chinese cities too narrow-mindedly. After all, these cities are part of the same country, and prosperity is Beijing or Shanghai should be seen as a sign of strong economic development. Ultimately, one has to accept that for a large country such as Mainland

China, the emergence of other mega cities means that the mainland economy has expanded. The larger the economic pie, the more there is to share. The stronger is the mainland economy, the more likely for Hong Kong, and other cities, to share the newly created business and economic opportunities. How much other cities in Mainland China have grown and expanded should reflect more on the strength of the mainland economy that will benefit Hong Kong than how much Hong Kong will lose, if at all, to other growing Chinese cities.

The proper mindset for Hong Kong would be to consider a "two-way" traffic in investment activities and resource utilization. In the summer of 2003, Hong Kong has been suggested to become the first offshore center for the trading of Renminbi. In early 2004, discussion on economic integration has been extended to the mutual recognition of academic and professional qualifications. It would be beneficial to both Hong Kong and mainland should there be a greater degree of flexibility in the mobility of human resource. Given mobility of human capital and resources, skilled workers in Hong Kong may find jobs in Guangdong while mainland professionals can choose to work in Hong Kong. Nonetheless, while Hong Kong is drifting along with the mainland economy, Hong Kong should also conduct indigenous and endogenous changes so as to raise its overall economic competitiveness and economic capacity.

14.4 Statistical Performance: Mainland, Guangdong and Hong Kong

One should not think of economic integration or cooperation between Mainland China and Hong Kong as a new topic. Indeed, integration has been an on-going process, though the features of economic integration differed at different historical times. While the Guangdong province has been the constant supplier of fresh water, basic food and livestock to residents in Hong Kong, Hong Kong has aided Guangdong and the mainland economy in various occasions and historical times. Prior to economic reform in 1978, and despite its closed door policy, Hong Kong has served as a trading post for mainland exports and currencies. After economic reform in 1978, overseas investments by overseas Chinese from Hong Kong and elsewhere have enabled the Guangdong and mainland economy to receive investment funds. Hong Kong has provided a pivotal role in the early stages of economic reform in Mainland China, and served as a key economic driver to the Guangdong economy, especially along the coastal cities.

By the 1990s, the development of financial markets in Shenzhen and Shanghai had been following the development path of the financial market in Hong Kong. Since 2005, the authority in Beijing attempted to incorporate Hong Kong's development into its Five-Year Plan, though despite its various economic setbacks and crises, the advanced nature of the Hong Kong economy differs from the developing nature of the mainland economy considerably. Given the large differences between Mainland China and Hong Kong in their economic systems, operations and practices, Hong Kong would have to make substantial changes if Hong Kong were to fit into the economic plans. For example, while some have complained that infrastructure expenditure in Hong Kong has not been caught up with Mainland China, the misunderstanding is that the level of infrastructure development in Hong Kong has already achieved a high level. It would not be appropriate to compare simply on the sheer amount of expenditure on infrastructure without distinguishing between the stage of development between mainland and Hong Kong. Another example can be found in the difference in attracting foreign investment. In Mainland China, both the central or local government has been active in soliciting foreign investments. Official entourages are often organized to encourage foreign firms to invest in Mainland China. In Hong Kong, foreign investments are free to enter or exit, and the government hardly gets involved in making overseas entourages to lure foreign investors to Hong Kong. The free market system and the fiscal incentives are the established and functional systems that operate effectively for all foreign investors.

Mainland — Hong Kong

A statistical review can provide a picture on the extent of economic integration among the three economies of Mainland China, Guangdong province and Hong Kong.[5] Beginning with the macroeconomic performances between Mainland China and Hong Kong, Figure 14.2 shows that the real GDP growth rates between Mainland China and Hong Kong has undergone quite a similar trend, rising and falling at similar time periods though the magnitude of the change differed. This is particularly so in the 1980s, but since the early 1990s, Mainland China has achieved a much higher real growth rate than Hong Kong, reflecting both the matured nature

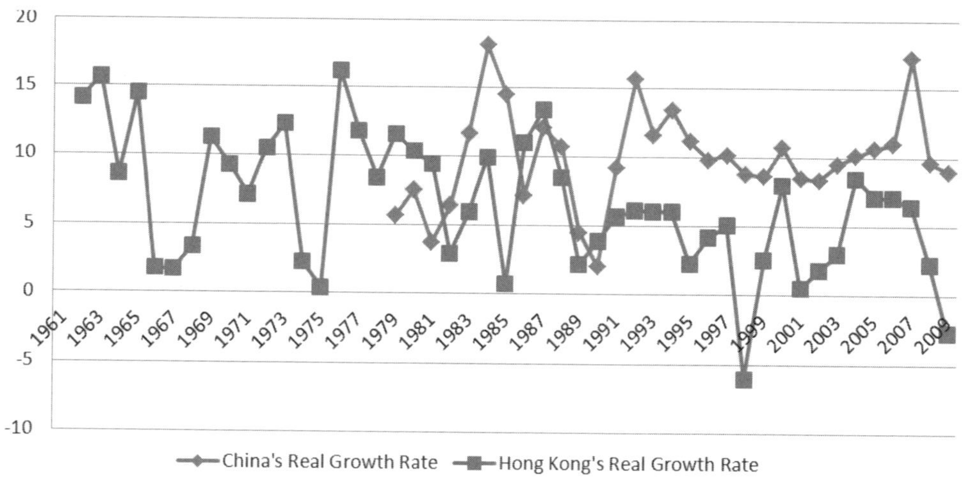

FIGURE 14.2 Performance of real GDP growth rates: Mainland China and Hong Kong

Note: Base year = 2005.

Source: Statistical Yearbook of China; Hong Kong Statistics; and CEIC.

[5] Due to possible data revisions over the years and the different methods in the calculations, data appeared in this chapter may be different from that in Li (2006, Chapter 8).

of the Hong Kong economy with large GDP per capita and the developing nature of the Mainland China with low GDP per capita.

There can be further empirical investigation as to the causality relationship between Mainland China and Hong Kong. Namely, which economy has caused the other in the overall economic trend, or which economy leads in the overall trend? It would be fair to say that it was the Hong Kong economy that led the Mainland China economy in the latter's early stage of economic reform in the entire 1980s, since Hong Kong investment had been the major driver of economic growth then. However, beginning from the early 1990s, probably since 1994 when the Renminbi had devalued by about 30%, and followed by rising level of trade surplus and foreign direct investment. The Mainland China economy in the 1990s had been transformed into a "production-based" economy with rising output, export and productivity that would have created its own economic trend. One could even argue that the rising Mainland China economy since its accession to the World Trade Organization in 2001 had developed its own trend, and would have led or deviated away from the Hong Kong economy since 2005 when the "visa free" policy and the talk of Hong Kong being a "Renminbi offshore centre" has resulted in large inflow of Renminbi into Hong Kong, giving rise to GDP growth, as well as such related problems as the rise in property price and urban congestion. In short, the "lead-led" economic relationship between Mainland China and Hong Kong may have changed over the years.

There are typically two types of investments entering the mainland economy. Portfolio investments relate to the flow of capital funds that enter the financial market for investments in stocks and bonds. Portfolio investments usually make use of the investment climate in the mainland economy and are very mobile and can enter and exit within a short period of time. When the investment climate is favorable, portfolio investments tend to come at a quick pace, but can equally be withdrawn easily when the investment climate becomes unfavorable. One expects to see much fluctuation in portfolio investments. The other form of investment is the foreign direct investments (FDI) that enter the mainland economy in the form of physical investments in the manufacture of industrial goods and in production of service goods. FDI are less mobile and may not be withdrawn easily because they tend to have a long period of commitment once the production plants are built. A major aspect of FDI has been to boost exports of industrial goods from Mainland China.

Table 14.1 reports the amount of outward portfolio investment from Hong Kong to the rest of world and to Mainland China. Hong Kong's portfolio investment to Mainland China has increased by 1,711% between 2001 and 2009, and the share of total to the world has increased from 4% to over 18% in the same period. The growing maturity of the stock markets in Mainland China has attracted portfolio investments from Hong Kong.

The economic role of Hong Kong can further be seen in Figure 14.3 which shows the amount of actual foreign direct investment (FDI) in Mainland China. Hong Kong's FDI to Mainland China has been significant until the mid-1990s. The economic recession in Hong Kong after the Asian financial crisis in 1997 has reduced Hong Kong's FDI to Mainland China while FDI from foreign countries has been rising continuously. However, FDI from Hong Kong has been revived upwards since 2006. By 2009, FDI from Hong Kong has once again exceeded that of FDI from overseas countries.

TABLE 14.1 Total outward portfolio investment from Hong Kong (US$ million)

Year	Total to World	To Mainland China Amount	To Mainland China % of Total	Year	Total to World	To Mainland China Amount	To Mainland China % of Total
2001	205,600	8,416	4.09	2006	580,514	98,646	16.99
2002	244,068	8,194	3.35	2007	778,530	165,710	21.28
2003	334,912	19,676	5.87	2008	557,121	102,848	18.46
2004	400,863	28,126	7.02	2009	811,430	152,378	18.78
2005	436,570	41,299	9.46				

Source: Coordinated Portfolio Investment Survey, International Monetary Fund, June 2011.

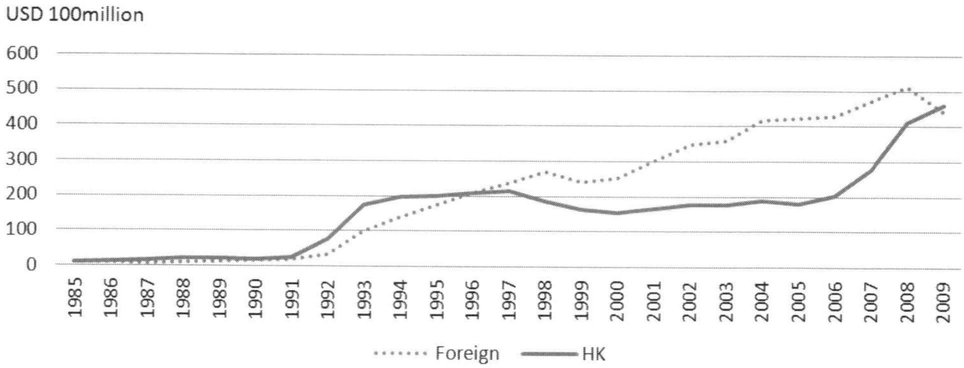

FIGURE 14.3 Actual foreign direct investments in Mainland China

Source: Statistical Yearbook of China, various issues.

The impact of FDI to Mainland China can be seen from the ratio between FDI inflow and China's GDP, as shown in Table 14.2. The actual FDI from Hong Kong (HKDI) shows a higher GDP ratio between 1986 and 1995, equalized in 1996, but fell below the non-HKDI/GDP ratio between 1997 and 2008. On an aggregate basis, the total FDI to GDP ratio reached a peak in 1994 at 6.04%, but the ratio has declined since due probably to the rising level of GDP in Mainland China. By 2009, the ratio is below 2, suggesting that Mainland China's GDP has grown faster and larger than the growth in FDI.

How the Hong Kong financial market has aided investment in Mainland China can also be seen from Table 14.3 that reports the total amount of initial public offerings (IPOs) issued by mainland companies in the Hong Kong stock market and the largest five IPOs in the decade of 2000–2010. The year 2005 saw the largest amount of IPOs raised in Hong Kong by mainland companies with a total of HK$42,353.36 (100 million). Mainland banking and insurance companies are the largest issuers of IPOs in Hong Kong. The stock market in Hong Kong has indeed served as a key player in raising capital for mainland companies. For the 11 years from 2000 to 2010, the total amount of IPO raised from the Hong Kong stock market by mainland companies summed to HK$147,664.64 (100 million).

TABLE 14.2 Mainland China's actual foreign direct investment to GDP ratios

Year	FDI/GDP	HKDI/ GDP	Non-HKDI/ GDP	Year	FDI/GDP	HKDI/ GDP	Non-HKDI/ GDP
1985	0.64	0.31	0.33	1998	4.46	1.82	2.64
1986	0.75	0.45	0.31	1999	3.72	1.51	2.21
1987	0.71	0.49	0.22	2000	3.40	1.29	2.10
1988	0.79	0.52	0.27	2001	3.54	1.26	2.28
1989	0.75	0.46	0.29	2002	3.63	1.23	2.40
1990	0.89	0.49	0.40	2003	3.26	1.08	2.18
1991	1.07	0.61	0.46	2004	3.14	0.98	2.16
1992	2.25	1.58	0.68	2005	2.67	0.80	1.88
1993	4.49	2.84	1.64	2006	2.32	0.75	1.58
1994	6.04	3.54	2.49	2007	2.14	0.79	1.35
1995	5.15	2.77	2.38	2008	2.04	0.91	1.14
1996	4.87	2.44	2.44	2009	1.81	0.92	0.88
1997	4.75	2.26	2.49				

Notes: Foreign direct and other investments actually used are reported for 1985–1986 and 1991–2009; Hong Kong and Macau direct and other investments actually used are reported for 1986; Hong Kong and Macau direct investments actually used are reported for 1987–1990; Hong Kong direct and other investments actually used are reported for 1985 and 1991–2009; foreign direct and other investments actually used (non-Hong Kong and Macau) are reported for 1986; foreign direct investments actually used (non-Hong Kong and Macau) are reported for 1987–1990; and foreign direct and other investments actually used (non-Hong Kong) are reported for 1985 and 1991–2009.
Source: Statistical Yearbook of China, various years.

While discussion has concentrated on how Hong Kong has aided the mainland economy, it is necessary to point out that Mainland China has also increased its outflow of foreign direct investment to the rest of the world. The United Nations Conference on Trade and Development (UNCTAD) pointed out that Mainland China will continue to be one of the top world destinations for inward foreign direct investment, but Mainland China in 2010 is the world's 5th largest outbound direct investment, following the United States, Germany, France and Hong Kong.[6] Table 14.4 reports the total amount of Mainland China's outward investment to the rest of the world. The data shows a rapid increase of outward investment from Mainland China, especially since 2005. With the rapid rise in its outward investment, Mainland China is in turn aiding the economic development in other countries. Dong *et al.* (2011) has shown that countries in Asia and Africa are the major recipients of outward investment from Mainland China. By 2009, for example, 75.5% of Mainland China's cumulative overseas direct investment went to Asia, followed by Latin America with 12.5%.[7]

[6] *China Daily eClips*, July 27, 2011.

[7] *China Daily eClips*, July 27, 2011.

TABLE 14.3 Mainland companies raising IPO in Hong Kong: Largest 5 companies

Year/Total (HK$100 million)		1	2	3	4	5
2000	Name	PetroChina Co.	China Petroleum	Tong Ren Tang	Hua Lien Intl.	Goldpoly New Ene.
31,191.03	Market Cap.	23,268.51	7,868.78	28.84	10.41	9.45
	% of Total	74.6	25.23	0.09	0.03	0.03
2001	Name	CNOOC Ltd.	Aluminum Corp	ENN Energy Hold.	Travelsky Tech	Kingdee Intl SFT
9,822.48	Market Cap.	7,781.37	1,464.86	276.19	137.53	114.80
	% of Total	79.22	14.91	2.81	1.4	1.17
2002	Name	China Telecom	China Oilfield	BYD Co. Ltd — H	Hainan Leilan	Sino Drago New E
5,805.37	Market Cap.	4,111.36	812.65	736.67	36.2	20.37
	% of Total	70.82	14.00	12.69	0.62	0.35
2003	Name	China Life INS	PICC Property	Zijin Mining	Great Wall Mot	Wumart Stores
10,317.67	Market Cap.	6,400.05	1,501.92	1,307.32	322.01	250.1
	% of Total	62.03	14.56	12.67	3.12	2.42
2004	Name	Ping An Insurance	Tencent Holdings	Weichai Power	Shandong Weig.	China Shipping
10,982.06	Market Cap.	4,952.91	3,730.76	829.86	477.18	401.18
	% of Total	45.1	33.97	7.56	4.34	3.65

(*Continued*)

TABLE 14.3 (*Continued*)

Year/Total (HK$100 million)		1	2	3	4	5
2005	Name	China Construction Bank	China Shenhua	Bank of Communication	Dongfeng Motor	China Cosco Hold.
42,353.36	Market Cap.	15,645.33	7,258.99	3,889.01	1,328.61	854.39
	% of Total	36.94	17.14	9.18	3.14	2.02
2006	Name	Bank of China	China Coal Ene.	China Com Cons.	China Natl BDG	Zhaojin Mining
16,825.51	Market Cap.	10,293.85	1,643.98	979.93	845.49	452.97
	% of Total	61.18	9.77	5.82	5.03	2.69
2007	Name	China CITIC Bank	China Rail GR.	Country Garden	Alibaba.com	Fosun Intl
8,216.18	Market Cap.	2,523.19	847.22	667.97	549.45	408.41
	% of Total	30.71	10.31	8.13	6.69	4.97
2008	Name	Want Want China	China Rail CN	Renhe Commercial	China Shanshui	Maoye Intl Hold.
2,782.50	Market Cap.	918.78	754.02	325.68	266.11	202.94
	% of Total	33.02	27.10	11.70	9.56	7.29
2009	Name	Evergrande Real	BBMG Corp.	Longfor Property	Sinopharm	China Longyuan
5,140.35	Market Cap.	879.00	640.32	618.61	545.40	504.59
	% of Total	17.10	12.46	12.04	10.61	9.82
2010	Name	Chongqing Rural	China Rongsheng	Zhongsheng Group	China Zhengtong	Springland Inter.
4,228.13	Market Cap.	419.43	333.2	313.75	206.00	185.75
	% of Total	9.92	7.88	7.42	4.87	4.39

Source: Bloomberg, August 18, 2011.

TABLE 14.4 Mainland China's outflow of foreign direct investment

Year	US$ Million	Year	US$ Million	Year	US$ Million
1983	93	1992	4,000	2001	6,884
1984	134	1993	4,400	2002	2,518
1985	629	1994	2,000	2003	2,855
1986	450	1995	2,000	2004	5,498
1987	645	1996	2,114	2005	12,261
1988	850	1997	2,563	2006	21,160
1989	780	1998	2,634	2007	22,469
1990	830	1999	1,775	2008	52,150
1991	913	2000	916	2009	48,000

Source: United Nations Conference on Trade and Development (UNCTAD).

TABLE 14.5 Direct investment from Mainland China to Hong Kong (HK$ Billion)

Year	Inward direct investment at year end	% Change	Inflow during the year	% Change	Year	Inward direct investment at year end	% Change	Inflow during the year	% Change
1998	213.7		20.2		2004	1,020.1	32.5	62.0	63.2
1999	814.8	281.3	38.6	91.1	2005	1,271.9	24.7	72.9	17.6
2000	1,112.2	36.5	110.7	186.8	2006	2,024.3	59.2	108.7	49.1
2001	958.1	−13.9	38.5	−65.2	2007	3,737.4	84.6	104.2	−4.1
2002	594.6	−37.9	31.7	−17.7	2008	2,311.4	−38.2	179.7	72.5
2003	770.1	29.5	38.0	19.1	2009	2,644.5	14.4	192.3	7.0

Source: Hong Kong Annual Digest of Statistics, Hong Kong, various years.

In the case of mainland's investment in Hong Kong, there is increasingly a two-way relationship in the flow of foreign direct investment between Mainland China and Hong Kong. Table 14.5 shows that the amount of mainland investment in Hong Kong has increased steadily since 2003. Like other sources of foreign investment, mainland investment will create new comparative advantages for businesses in Hong Kong. The various businesses advantages in Hong Kong must have attracted mainland investment. Indeed, mainland investment to Hong Kong will form a new wave of investment activities in Hong Kong.

Similarly, since the visa-free policy in 2003, mainland visitors have been pouring into Hong Kong, and are keen to commit consumption spending in Hong Kong. Table 14.6 shows the number of mainland visitors and the amount spent by overnight in-town and same-day in-town visitors. The data shows drastic changes in the decade of 1998–2009. Between 1998 and 2009, the number of mainland visitors has increased by 572.13%. Total expenditure has also increased by 597%, while per capita spending has increased by 20.64% in the same period. Spending by overnight in-town visitors is much high than same-day in-town visitors at a ratio of 3.28 to 1

TABLE 14.6 Mainland China visitor arrivals and expenditure in Hong Kong

			Expenditure by Visitors (HK$)							
Year	Visitor arrivals	% Change	Overnight In-town $ million	% Change	Same-day In-town $ million	% Change	Total $ million	% Change	Per capita spending	% Change
1998	2,671,628		11,314		662		11,976		5,487	
1999	3,206,452	20.0	10,455	–7.6	737	11.3	11,192	–6.5	4,370	–20.4
2000	3,785,845	18.1	13,235	26.6	1,219	65.4	14,454	29.1	4,831	10.5
2001	4,448,583	17.5	15,823	19.6	1,610	32.1	17,433	20.6	5,169	7.0
2002	6,825,199	53.4	26,065	64.7	1,996	24.0	28,061	61.0	5,639	9.1
2003	8,467,211	24.1	29,800	14.3	3,578	79.3	33,378	18.9	5,235	–7.2
2004	12,245,862	44.6	33,941	13.9	4,642	29.7	38,583	15.6	4,355	–16.8
2005	12,541,400	2.4	36,570	7.7	5,627	21.2	42,197	9.4	4,554	4.6
2006	13,591,342	8.4	39,679	8.5	7,926	40.9	47,605	12.8	4,705	3.3
2007	15,485,789	13.9	47,215	19.0	11,712	47.8	58,927	23.8	5,193	10.4
2008	16,862,003	8.9	53,243	12.8	15,994	36.6	69,237	17.5	5,676	9.3
2009	17,956,731	6.5	63,970	20.1	19,504	21.9	83,474	20.6	6,620	16.6

Source: Hong Kong Annual Digest of Statistics, Hong Kong, various years.

in 2009. It is expected that Hong Kong is an attractive destination for mainland visitors, especially those coming for short-term stay.

The economic performances between Hong Kong and other major cities in mainland are shown in Table 14.7. Shanghai and Beijing show the largest level in GDP, but Hong Kong has a much larger GDP per capita than all other cities in mainland, reflecting the different stages of economic advancement between Hong Kong and other mainland cities. Table 14.7 also shows that the industrial output of Hong Kong is much lower than many mainland cities. Table 14.8 shows the port capabilities of Hong Kong and other key mainland cities. Hong Kong has performed strongly in container seaports capability in 2009, but its capability in seaports is lower than six other cities in mainland. Finally, Table 14.9 reports the ranking of the top 10 world container ports for the period 1995–2010. Hong Kong has been ranked first before 2005, but its position has dropped to third since 2007, and other mainland cities of Shanghai, Shenzhen, Ningbo and Guangzhou have become very competitive.

TABLE 14.7 Income and industrial output of 10 largest cities in 2009

	Gross domestic product		Industrial output	
Cities	RMB 10,000	Per Capita (RMB)	Cities	RMB 10,000
Shanghai	150,464,500	78,989	Shanghai	240,912,649
Beijing	121,530,000	70,452	Suzhou	202,844,954
Guangzhou	91,382,135	89,082	Shenzhen	154,162,429
Shenzhen	82,013,176	92,772	Tianjin	130,836,313
Suzhou	77,402,000	122,565	Foshan	117,796,240
Tianjin	75,218,500	62,574	Guangzhou	113,767,645
Chongqing	65,300,100	22,920	Beijing	110,391,291
Hangzhou	50,875,530	63,333	Wuxi	108,415,288
Wuxi	49,917,200	107,365	Hangzhou	93,907,333
Hong Kong	14,394,402	205,530	Hong Kong	15,555,050

Sources: Report on 2009 Annual Survey of Industrial Production, Hong Kong; *Statistical Yearbook of China*, various years; various provincial statistical yearbooks.

Table 14.8 Cargos handled by Top 10 seaports and container seaports in 2009

Seaports	Through put (million tons)	Seaports	Through put (million tons)	Container seaports	Through put (1,000 TEUs)	Container seaports	Through put (1,000 TEUs)
Shanghai	505	Qinghuadao	244	Shanghai	25,002	Qingdao	10,260
Tianjin	381	Hong Kong	243	Hong Kong	20,983	Tianjin	8,700
Ningbo	372	Dalian	204	Shenzhen	18,250	Xiamen	4,680
Guangzhou	364	Shenzhen	187	Guangzhou	11,190	Dalian	4,552
Qingdao	274	Xiamen	111	Ningbo	10,502	Lianyungang	3,021

Sources: AAPA World Ports Rankings 2009.

TABLE 14.9 Top 10 world container ports, 1995–2010

Year	1st	2nd	3rd	4th	5th	6th	7th	8th	9th	10th
1995	Hong Kong	Singapore	Kaohsiung	Rotterdam	Busan	Hamburg	Long Beach	Yokohama	Los Angeles	Antwerp
1996	Hong Kong	Singapore	Kaohsiung	Rotterdam	Busan	Hamburg	Long Beach	Los Angeles	Antwerp	Yokohama
1997	Hong Kong	Singapore	Kaohsiung	Rotterdam	Busan	Long Beach	Hamburg	Antwerp	Los Angeles	Dubai
1998	Singapore	Hong Kong	Kaohsiung	Rotterdam	Busan	Long Beach	Hamburg	Los Angeles	Antwerp	Shanghai
1999	Hong Kong	Singapore	Kaohsiung	Busan	Rotterdam	Long Beach	Shanghai	Los Angeles	Hamburg	Antwerp
2000	Hong Kong	Singapore	Busan	Kaohsiung	Rotterdam	Shanghai	Los Angeles	Long Beach	Hamburg	Antwerp
2001	Hong Kong	Singapore	Busan	Kaohsiung	Shanghai	Rotterdam	Los Angeles	Shenzhen	Hamburg	Long Beach
2002	Hong Kong	Singapore	Busan	Shanghai	Kaohsiung	Shenzhen	Los Angeles	Los Angeles	Hamburg	Long Beach
2003	Hong Kong	Singapore	Shanghai	Shenzhen	Busan	Kaohsiung	Rotterdam	Rotterdam	Hamburg	Antwerp
2004	Hong Kong	Singapore	Shanghai	Shenzhen	Busan	Kaohsiung	Los Angeles	Los Angels	Hamburg	Dubai
2005	Singapore	Hong Kong	Shanghai	Shenzhen	Busan	Kaohsiung	Rotterdam	Hamburg	Dubai	Los Angeles
2006	Singapore	Hong Kong	Shanghai	Shenzhen	Busan	Kaohsiung	Rotterdam	Dubai	Hamburg	Los Angeles
2007	Singapore	Shanghai	Hong Kong	Shenzhen	Busan	Rotterdam	Dubai	Kaohsiung	Hamburg	Qingdao
2008	Singapore	Shanghai	Hong Kong	Shenzhen	Busan	Dubai	Guangzhou	Ningbo	Rotterdam	Qingdao
2009	Singapore	Shanghai	Hong Kong	Shenzhen	Busan	Guangzhou	Dubai	Ningbo	Qingdao	Rotterdam
2010	Shanghai	Singapore	Hong Kong	Shenzhen	Busan	Ningbo	Guangzhou	Qingdao	Dubai	Rotterdam

Source: Marine Department, Hong Kong.

Guangdong — Hong Kong

The territory of Hong Kong is historically and geographically part of the province of Guangdong, which has for decades been supplying basic food and livestock to people in Hong Kong through the border in Lo Wu. Hence, when the late Premier Deng Xiaoping declared economic reform in 1978 and the opening up of coastal cities and Special Economic Zones (SEZs), cities in Guangdong thus became the "early birds" to receive foreign direct investment from Hong Kong. Table 14.10 compares the

TABLE 14.10 GDP of Hong Kong, Guangdong and Shenzhen

	Hong Kong		Guangdong		Shenzhen	
Year	HK$ billion	% Change	Rmb 100 million	% Change	Rmb 100 million	% Change
1978	85.7		185.85			
1979	112.5	31.27	209.34	12.64	1.9	
1980	143.4	27.47	249.65	19.26	2.7	42.11
1981	173.0	20.64	290.36	16.31	5.0	85.19
1982	195.4	12.95	339.92	17.07	8.3	66.00
1983	216.4	10.75	368.75	8.48	13.1	57.83
1984	260.8	20.52	458.74	24.40	23.4	78.63
1985	276.8	6.13	577.38	25.86	39.0	66.67
1986	319.2	15.32	667.53	15.61	41.6	6.67
1987	393.5	23.28	846.69	26.84	55.9	34.38
1988	465.2	18.22	1,155.37	36.46	87.0	55.64
1989	536.3	15.28	1,381.39	19.56	115.7	32.99
1990	599.0	11.69	1,559.03	12.86	171.7	48.40
1991	690.3	15.24	1,893.30	21.44	236.7	37.86
1992	805.1	16.63	2,447.54	29.27	317.3	34.05
1993	928.0	15.27	3,469.28	41.75	453.1	42.80
1994	1,047.5	12.88	4,619.02	33.14	634.7	40.08
1995	1,115.7	6.51	5,933.05	28.45	842.5	32.74
1996	1,229.5	10.20	6,834.97	15.20	1,048.4	24.44
1997	1,365.0	11.02	7,774.53	13.75	1,297.4	23.75
1998	1,292.8	–5.29	8,530.88	9.73	1,534.7	18.29
1999	1,266.7	–2.02	9,250.68	8.44	1,804.0	17.55
2000	1,317.7	4.03	10,741.25	16.11	2,187.5	21.26
2001	1,299.2	–1.40	12,039.25	12.08	2,482.5	13.49
2002	1,277.3	–1.69	13,502.42	12.15	2,969.5	19.62
2003	1,234.8	–3.33	15,844.64	17.35	3,585.7	20.75
2004	1,291.9	4.62	18,864.62	19.06	4,282.1	19.42
2005	1,382.6	7.02	22,557.37	19.58	4,950.9	15.62
2006	1,475.4	6.71	26,587.76	17.87	5,813.6	17.43
2007	1,615.6	9.50	31,777.01	19.52	6,801.6	16.99
2008	1,677.0	3.80	36,796.71	15.80	7,786.8	14.48
2009	1,622.3	–3.26	39,482.56	7.30	8,201.3	5.32

Note: GDP figures are production based at current price. GDP growth rates are the log difference figures.
Sources: *Guangdong Statistical Yearbook*, *Shenzhen Statistical Yearbook*, *Hong Kong Annual Digest of Statistics*, various years.

GDP and GDP growth rates of Hong Kong, Guangdong and Shenzhen. Bearing in mind the different in the stage of economic development between Hong Kong on the one hand and Guangdong and Shenzhen on the other hand. Data in Table 14.10 shows that both Guangdong and Shenzhen since economic reform in 1978 have experienced rapid growth in GDP. Hong Kong being a more advanced economy has shown a lower growth rate, especially since 1998 after the Asian financial crisis.

Table 14.11 summarizes the data on inward foreign direct investment to Guangdong province. The growth rates of FDI to Guangdong have been large with two-digits in many years. A negative growth rate was experienced only in the two years of 1987 and 2005. Hong Kong has occupied a major position in Guangdong's FDI, as it exceeded 60% in all years before 2000. The year 2004 saw the lowest share of 25.17%, but since then the percentage has been increasing, reaching 60.8% in 2009. Guangdong's FDI from non-Hong Kong sources have also been high, but the growth rates remained unsteady.

Table 14.12 reports the foreign direct investment injected to the four biggest cities in Guangdong in the two decades (1990–2009). Other than the three years of 1998, 2002 and 2004, the FDI of the four cities from Hong Kong has exceeded FDI from non-Hong Kong sources, reflecting the favorable investment conditions in these four cities, and the commitment of FDI from Hong Kong investors. Similarly, the FDI/GDP ratios of Guangdong and the four cities are shown in Table 14.13. Given that Hong Kong has contributed more to FDI in Guangdong and the four cities in many years, the HKDI/GDP ratios are generally higher than the non-HKDI/GDP ratios.

The distribution of FDI among the three economic sectors of agriculture, industry and services in Guangdong and the four cities is given in Table 14.14. It is clear that industry is the largest recipient of FDI in Guangdong, followed by services, and FDI in agriculture is least. The same picture is true in the case of the four cities. However, percentage growth rates of FDI in all economic sectors have fluctuated considerably over the years, reflecting the volatile nature of FDI in Guangdong. Changes in government policies and competition among cities in Guangdong may have contributed to the unsteady changes in percentage growth rates.

The manufacturing sector in Hong Kong has been contracting since the early 1990s. Table 14.15 compares the four key manufacturing industries between Hong Kong and Guangdong. As compared to Li (2006, Table 8.12), the key industries in Hong Kong has changed. Electronics and toys production have given way to the rise of food industry and paper products, printing and publishing industry in Hong Kong.

As shown in Table 14.15, the fall in the output value of textile and wearing apparel industry in Hong Kong is matched with the rise in the same industries in Guangdong. The output values of food and paper product, printing and publishing in Hong Kong has been steady, as shown in Table 14.15, but the output values of these two industries are expanding rapidly in Guangdong.

Table 14.16 further shows the output pattern of industries in Guangdong. Gross industrial output value in Guangdong has increased by seven-fold between 1998 and 2009. The output values of the three traditional industries have increased, but their percentages shares have decreased. The rising industries in Guangdong in

TABLE 14.11 Guangdong's foregin direct investment actually used

			Hong Kong				Non-Hong Kong	
Year	US$10,000 (1)	% Change	US$10,000	% Change	% of (1)	% of Country	US$10,000	% Change
1985	51,529		45,020		87.37	47.11	6,509	
1986	64,392	24.96	60,310	33.96	93.66	45.39	4,082	–37.29
1987	59,396	–7.76	50,267	–16.65	84.63	31.45	9,129	123.64
1988	91,906	54.73	80,308	59.76	87.38	38.33	11,598	27.05
1989	115,644	25.83	91,462	13.89	79.09	44.02	24,182	108.50
1990	145,984	26.24	98,501	7.70	67.47	51.48	47,483	96.36
1991	182,286	24.87	135,657	37.72	74.42	52.60	46,629	–1.80
1992	355,150	94.83	303,879	124.01	85.56	39.43	51,271	9.96
1993	749,805	111.12	652,954	114.87	87.08	37.43	96,851	88.90
1994	939,708	25.33	776,763	18.96	82.66	39.19	162,945	68.24
1995	1,018,028	8.33	797,268	2.64	78.31	39.50	220,760	35.48
1996	1,162,362	14.18	838,660	5.19	72.15	40.22	323,702	46.63
1997	1,171,083	0.75	843,192	0.54	72.00	40.87	327,891	1.29
1998	1,202,005	2.64	812,946	–3.59	67.63	43.92	389,059	18.65
1999	1,220,300	1.52	733,892	–9.72	60.14	44.85	486,408	25.02
2000	1,223,720	0.28	744,826	1.49	60.87	48.05	478,894	–1.54
2001	1,297,240	6.01	708,675	–4.85	54.63	42.39	588,565	22.90
2002	1,311,071	1.07	697,885	–1.52	53.23	39.07	613,186	4.18
2003	1,557,779	18.82	864,593	23.89	55.50	48.85	693,186	13.05
2004	1,991,158	27.82	501,219	–42.03	25.17	26.38	1,489,939	114.94
2005	1,236,391	–37.91	582,361	16.19	47.10	32.45	654,030	–56.10
2006	1,451,065	17.36	680,946	16.93	46.93	33.66	770,119	17.75
2007	1,712,603	18.02	830,295	21.93	48.48	29.97	882,308	14.57
2008	1,916,703	11.92	1,054,412	26.99	55.01	25.69	862,291	–2.27
2009	1,953,460	1.92	1,187,737	12.64	60.80	25.78	765,723	–11.20

Notes: Hong Kong and Macau direct investment actually used for 1985–87; non-Hong Kong and Macau direct inverstment actually used for 1985–87.
Source: *Guangdong Statistical Yearbook*, various issues.

TABLE 14.12 Total Foreign direct investment in four cities (Guangzhou, Zhuhai, Shenzhen, Dongguan)

Hong Kong						Non-Hong Kong					
Year	US$ 10,000	% Change	Year	US$10,000	% Change	Year	US$ 10,000	% Change	Year	US$ 10,000	% Change
1990	53,351		2000	505,073	36.84	1990	33,670		2000	349,537	–7.36
1991	69,759	30.75	2001	491,238	–2.74	1991	39,686	17.87	2001	447,917	28.15
1992	136,529	95.72	2002	490,989	–0.05	1992	43,573	9.79	2002	619,291	38.26
1993	302,546	121.6	2003	618,796	26.03	1993	91,974	111.08	2003	261,914	–57.71
1994	373,043	23.3	2004	303,781	–50.91	1994	111,446	21.17	2004	315,046	20.29
1995	360,566	–3.24	2005	475,397	56.49	1995	148,599	33.34	2005	289,798	–8.01
1996	406,446	12.72	2006	576,234	21.21	1996	198,602	33.65	2006	515,982	78.05
1997	465,877	14.62	2007	665,958	15.57	1997	220,521	11.04	2007	343,418	–33.44
1998	444,308	–4.63	2008	653,079	–1.93	1998	246,301	11.69	2008	471,106	37.18
1999	369,085	–16.93	2009	710,120	8.73	1999	377,293	53.18	2009	460,642	–2.22

Sources: Guangzhou Statistical Yearbook, Zhuhai Statistical Yearbook, Shenzhen Statistics and Information Yearbook, Statistical Yearbook of Dongguan, various issues.

TABLE 14.13 Foreign direct investment-to-GDP ratios: Guangdong and the four cities

	Guangdong Province			Guangzhou+Zhuhai+ Shenzhen+Dongguan		
Year	FDI/GDP	HKDI/GDP	Non-HKDI/GDP	FDI/GDP	HKDI/GDP	Non-HKDI/GDP
1985	2.62	2.29	0.33			
1986	3.33	3.12	0.21			
1987	2.61	2.21	0.40			
1988	2.96	2.59	0.37			
1989	3.15	2.49	0.66			
1990	4.48	3.02	1.46	6.97	4.27	2.70
1991	5.13	3.81	1.31	7.66	4.88	2.78
1992	8.00	6.85	1.16	9.78	7.41	2.37
1993	12.45	10.84	1.63	15.80	12.11	3.68
1994	17.53	14.49	3.11	21.94	16.89	5.05
1995	14.33	11.22	3.22	17.50	12.39	5.11
1996	14.14	10.20	4.13	17.67	11.87	5.80
1997	12.49	8.99	3.72	17.21	11.68	5.53
1998	11.67	7.89	4.07	15.25	9.81	5.44
1999	10.92	6.57	4.76	14.74	7.29	7.45
2000	9.43	5.74	4.10	12.13	7.17	4.96
2001	8.92	4.87	4.57	11.63	6.08	5.55
2002	8.04	4.28	4.31	11.83	5.23	6.60
2003	8.14	4.52	3.62	7.86	5.52	2.34
2004	8.74	2.20	6.54	4.62	2.27	2.35
2005	4.49	2.11	2.38	4.85	3.01	1.84
2006	4.35	2.04	2.31	5.70	3.01	2.69
2007	4.10	1.99	2.11	4.26	2.81	1.45
2008	3.62	1.99	1.63	3.76	2.18	1.57
2009	3.38	2.05	1.32	3.61	2.19	1.42

Notes: For Guangdong province, figures for Hong Kong and Macau direct investments actually used are for 1985–1987, and figures for non-Hong Kong and Macau foreign direct investments actually used are for 1985–1987. For Shenzhen and Dongguan, data used are foreign capital actually used, Hong Kong and Macau capital actually used, and non-Hong Kong and Macau foreign capital actually used.
Sources: Guangzhou Statistical Yearbook, Zhuhai Statistical Yearbook, Shenzhen Statistics and Information Yearbook, Statistical Yearbook of Dongguan, various issues.

terms of percentage shares are motor vehicle, electronic information and electric equipment and special purpose equipment. Table 14.16 clearly shows the rapid changing industrial structure in Guangdong with expansions in the key and new industries.

The containerized cargo business is divided into direct service, trans-shipment and river trade. The performance of the container industry between Hong Kong and

TABLE 14.14 Composition of actual foreign capital in Guangdong and four cities

	Guangdong						Guangzhou+Zhuhai+Dongguan+Shenzhen					
	Agriculture		Industry		Service		Agriculture		Industry		Service	
Year	US$ 10,000	% Change	US$ 10,000	% Change	US$ 10,000	% Change	US$ 10,000	% Change	US$ 10,000	% Change	US$ 10,000	% Change
1988	2,181		77,154		12,571							
1989	2,205	1.10	97,613	26.52	15,826	25.89						
1990	1,324	−39.95	126,068	29.15	18,592	17.48	14,908		61,067		25,305	
1991	1,614	21.90	157,374	24.83	23,298	25.31	486	−96.74	73,056	19.63	30,135	19.09
1992	3,620	124.29	302,300	92.09	49,230	111.31	332	−31.69	132,404	81.24	47,023	56.04
1993	3,388	−6.41	563,321	86.35	183,096	271.92	186	−43.98	244,207	84.44	137,835	193.12
1994	6,890	103.36	694,459	23.28	238,359	30.18	1,723	826.34	322,907	32.23	158,916	15.29
1995	8,376	21.57	745,628	7.37	264,024	10.77	1,863	8.13	360,748	11.72	146,553	−7.78
1996	15,673	87.12	881,019	18.16	265,670	0.62	2,242	20.34	424,173	17.58	178,633	21.89
1997	17,526	11.82	849,094	−3.62	304,463	14.60	2,820	25.78	496,169	16.97	185,777	4.00
1998	17,243	−1.61	859,620	1.24	325,142	6.79	3,482	23.48	450,381	−9.23	235,571	26.8
1999	20,983	21.69	866,133	0.76	333,184	2.47	2,195	−36.96	549,474	22.00	194,709	−17.35
2000	14,451	−31.13	870,751	0.53	338,518	1.60	2,909	32.53	531,193	−3.33	251,915	29.38
2001	17,937	24.12	1,164,149	33.69	303,440	−10.36	5,665	94.74	717,226	35.02	203,774	−19.11
2002	15,866	−11.55	1,277,607	9.75	365,473	20.44	812	−85.67	772,657	7.73	266,699	30.88
2003	17,866	12.61	1,113,213	−12.87	426,700	16.75	3,791	366.87	697,560	−9.72	179,017	−32.88
2004	13,029	−27.07	772,881	−30.57	215,248	−49.56	2,944	−22.34	561,743	−19.47	171,272	−4.33
2005	7,720	−40.75	971,493	25.70	257,178	19.48	1,243	−57.78	686,856	22.27	222,509	29.92
2006	11,539	49.47	1,085,424	11.73	354,102	37.69	1,334	7.32	617,045	−10.16	273,767	23.04
2007	18,295	58.55	1,071,066	−1.32	623,242	76.01	849	−36.36	588,600	-4.61	418,958	53.03
2008	20,832	13.87	1,183,000	10.45	712,871	14.38	526	−38.04	608,589	3.40	515,054	22.94
2009	23,922	14.83	1,171,662	−0.96	757,876	6.31	8,153	1,450.00	624,474	2.61	538,141	4.48

Notes: Agriculture = Farming, forestry, animal husbandry, fishery. Industry = Mining and quarrying, manufacturing, electricity, gas and water production, construction. Services = Geological prospecting, water conservancy, transport, storage, post and telecommunications, wholesale and retail sales and catering trades, finance and insurance, real estate trade, social services, health care, sports and social welfare, education, culture and arts, radio and television, scientific research and poly-technical services, government agencies, party agencies and social organizations, and others.

Sources: *Guangdong Statistical Yearbook, Zhuhai Statistical Yearbook, Shenzhen Statistics and Information Yearbook, Dongguan Statistical Yearbook*, various years.

TABLE 14.15 Output value of the four key manufacturing industry: Hong Kong and Guangdong

	Textile		Wearing Apparel		Food		Paper Products, Printing & Publishing	
Year	Hong Kong	Guangdong	Hong Kong	Guangdong	Hong Kong	Guangdong	Hong Kong	Guangdong
1996	3,235	33,340	3,627	34,066	1,461	34,655	3,712	20,718
1997	3,333	37,058	3,145	36,217	1,314	38,518	3,978	23,031
1998	2,535	40,455	2,586	48,656	1,424	49,426	3,416	31,487
1999	2,336	41,734	2,153	46,565	1,504	48,779	2,946	31,195
2000	2,277	44,940	2,501	51,197	1,435	49,344	3,327	36,977
2001	2,623	54,928	2,651	56,738	1,552	55,500	3,373	42,420
2002	2,248	62,062	2,320	61,926	1,579	61,602	3,182	48,956
2003	2,175	73,844	2,340	72,013	1,355	50,677	3,039	63,479
2004	2,043	86,207	2,309	86,207	1,360	92,613	3,035	74,188
2005	2,133	105,813	1,739	105,813	1,347	109,128	3,084	99,795
2006	1,888	124,065	1,380	109,257	1,569	128,282	3,060	119,639
2007	1,650	152,394	1,035	152,394	1,750	175,862	3,336	155,736
2008	1,227	195,848	1,061	195,848	1,851	251,208	3,234	221,658

Notes: The output values of Hong Kong are in HK$ 10 million at 1990 price. The output values of Guangdong have been transformed into HK$ million by using the mid-year exchange rate obtained from the yearbooks. The Hong Kong statistics are based on the Standard Industrialization Classifications Version 1.1. The industry classification between Hong Kong and Guangdong may differ.

Sources: *Report on Annual Survey of Industrial Production, Hong Kong, various years; Guangdong Statistical Yearbook*, various years

TABLE 14.16 Gross industrial output value of designated-size enterprises in Guangdong (Rmb 100 million)

			Three Key Industries			Three Traditional Industries			Three New Industries		
Year		Gross Output	EI	EESPE	PC	TG	FB	BM	LP	MV	Med
1998	Value	9,738.6	1,599.0	1,229.0	832.0	1,164.0	772.0	567.0			
	%	100.00	16.42	12.62	8.54	11.95	7.93	5.82			
1999	Value	10,538.2	1,950.0	1,292.0	947.0	1,144.0	779.0	591.0			
	%	100.00	18.50	12.26	8.99	10.86	7.39	5.61			
2000	Value	12,480.9	2,418.4	1,626.1	1,355.5	1,226.6	799.1	618.0	387.7	309.7	183.9
	%	100.00	19.38	13.03	10.86	9.83	6.40	4.95	3.11	2.48	1.47
2001	Value	14,035.4	3,109.9	1,833.4	1,430.1	1,246.2	866.7	649.6	425.6	406.7	207.8
	%	100.00	22.20	13.10	10.10	8.90	6.10	4.60	3.00	2.90	1.50
2002	Value	16,378.6	4,164.4	2,077.2	1,552.5	1,372.7	707.7	707.7	476.5	488.0	214.7
	%	100.00	25.43	12.68	9.47	8.38	4.32	4.32	2.91	2.98	1.31
2003	Value	21,513.5	5,932.2	3,033.0	2,044.7	1,593.9	1,161.8	852.0	538.4	751.2	246.6
	%	100	27.57	14.1	9.5	7.41	5.4	3.96	2.5	3.49	1.15
2004	Value	26,720.9	7,454.3	3,831.3	2,449.9	1,839.5	1,538.9	1,070.0	633.2	1,002.7	239.8
	%	100	27.90	14.34	9.17	6.88	5.76	4.00	2.37	3.75	0.9
2005	Value	35,942.7	9,831.3	5,256.8	3,274.9	2,150.4	1,635.7	1,286.4	839.9	1,359.7	286.8
	%	100	27.35	14.63	9.11	5.98	4.55	3.58	2.34	3.78	0.8
2006	Value	44,674.8	11,891.1	6,617.8	4,127.9	2,535.0	1,869.1	1,722.1	1,021.4	1,846.5	372.1
	%	100	26.62	14.81	9.24	5.67	4.18	3.85	2.29	4.13	0.83
2007	Value	55,252.9	13,377.3	8,502.3	5,049.7	3,043.9	2,375.0	2,213.6	1,310.6	2,574.5	432.1
	%	100	24.21	15.39	9.14	5.51	4.3	4.01	2.37	4.66	0.78
2008	Value	65,424.6	15,373.8	9,647.9	6,119.8	3,626.4	2,985.7	2,804.7	1,705.9	2,930.1	498.7
	%	100	23.5	14.75	9.35	5.54	4.56	4.29	2.61	4.48	0.76
2009	Value	68,275.8	15,721.8	9,742.4	5,983.3	4,002.9	3,306.5	3,009.1	1,640.9	3,564.1	618.0
	%	100	23.03	14.27	8.76	5.86	4.84	4.41	2.4	5.22	0.91

Notes: The data covers the industrial enterprises above-designated size (wholly state-owned enterprises and non-state owned enterprises with annual sales revenue above Rmb 5 million). EI = Electronic information; EESPE = Electric equipement and special purpose equipment; PC = Petroleum and chemicals; TG = Textile and garments; FB = Food and beverages; BM = Building materilas; LP = Logging and papermaking; MV = Motor vechicle; and Med = Medicine.

Source: *Guangdong Statistical Yearbook*, Guangzhou.

Guangdong is shown in Table 14.17. There are a total of 8 container ports in Guangdong, with Guangzhou being the largest, followed closely by the newer Yantain and Chiwan ports. The Shanghai Container Terminal (SCT) began to operate since 1998, but its business has catch up rapidly, though since 2007, the data in SCT included the other two smaller ports of Shekou and Mawan. The remaining two container ports are Zhanjiang and Shantou. The container port of Hong Kong has remained strong due strongly to the presence of complement facilities, such as banking, and efficient operation, though high cost in Hong Kong has been a disadvantage. Attracted by lower cost, Hong Kong businesses have been active in investing in container ports in the Guangdong province.

There are a number of conclusions from various economic statistics presented on the Mainland China — Guangdong — Hong Kong link. One is that the mainland economy has grown a lot in the past three decades, and that Hong Kong has acted as a "growth engine". Investments from Hong Kong have served as the 'hardware' to the post-reform economic development, while cross-border references on various economic practices and the way a market economy works functions as the 'software' that lubricate Mainland China's "growth engine". The "one-way" flow of funds from Hong Kong to Mainland China would mean a loss of investment opportunities in Hong Kong. This would mean a reduction in economic activities and employment in Hong Kong, leading to structural rigidities in the Hong Kong economy.

However, as the mainland economy becomes more developed and the rise in income and wage in Mainland China would erode its cost advantage. At the same time, economic growth in Mainland China has permitted and encouraged the outflow of investment. The flow of funds thus becomes a "two-way traffic", and further increase in investment from Mainland China is expected. The "baby sitting" role of Hong Kong in fostering the early stage of post-reform economic development in Mainland China has come to fruition. Investment from Mainland China to Hong Kong would have somewhat compensated the previous loss of Hong Kong investment to Mainland China.

14.5 Zero-sum or Positive-sum

Sovereignty reversion involved only a one-time historical permanent change, but the "two systems" is the long-term concern. Indeed, the decision on the "one country, two systems" reflected exactly the vast systemic difference between Mainland China and Hong Kong. Economically, Hong Kong is a free market capitalist economy with the government takes a "back seat", handles mainly cases where markets "failed" to operate and rarely involved directly in businesses. Investments are free to enter and exit, and foreign direct investment involving a direct decision from the government is infrequent. Hong Kong is considered more as a developed, matured and modern economy, characterized by well-established civic systems that produced reliable and effective governance. Being a city economy, Hong Kong has achieved world standards in a number of areas, though improvements are still needed and complacency is not cherished. The free nature of the Hong Kong economy opens up to economic participants, and other than the need to fulfill legal requirements, Hong Kong does not impose restrictions nor pursue protectionist policy on foreign goods, individuals and businesses.

TABLE 14.17 Container throughput in Hong Kong and Guangdong ports (thousand TEUs)

Year	Hong Kong	Guangdong	Guangzhou	Zhanjiang	Shantou	Shekou	Chiwan	Mawan	Yantian	SCT
1987	2,837									
1988	3,413									
1989	3,705	144.6	112.8	3.5	2.1	18.4	7.7			
1990	4,204	154.1	109.4	5.7	5.3	17.9	15.9			
1991	5,202	244.0	164.7	9.7	15.7	29.5	21.1	3.3		
1992	6,723	278.0	180.4	11.9	28.1	23.6	30.9	3.0		
1993	7,723	319.9	187.6	17.7	55.0	26.0	33.1	0.6		
1994	9,453	378.9	220.7	25.4	55.3	31.6	45.9	0.0		
1995	10,515	539.5	246.0	30.0	69.7	23.2	64.8	0.0	105.7	
1996	11,104	1,178.9	557.5	29.5	90.0	47.9	97.8	2.7	353.5	
1997	14,386	1,736.3	687.3	43.7	74.2	75.7	210.2	6.8	638.4	
1998	14,582	2,876.9	841.4	33.5	63.4	142.0	273.2	27.5	1,038.1	457.9
1999	16,211	4,297.5	1,177.0	49.4	115.4	276.0	481.5	36.1	1,588.1	574.1
2000	18,098	5,577.4	1,429.8	74.8	114.4	325.2	643.8	121.5	2,147.4	720.3
2001	17,826	6,962.8	1,737.8	85.3	158.4	430.2	901.2	146.9	2,752.3	750.7
2002	19,144	9,922.3	2,192.8	104.9	206.2	600.8	154.4	228.9	4,181.5	883.6
2003	20,449	13,323.4	2,769.1	129.2	222.8	871.8	2,236.0	301.1	5,258.2	1,535.3
2004	21,984	17,057.2	3,304.0	167.2	284.7	1,150.3	3,428.0	340.6	6,259.5	2,122.9
2005	22,602	21,425.4	4,682.6	177.8	368.3	1,368.0	4,170.1	386.2	7,355.5	2,447.6
2006	23,539	25,773.4	6,656.3	203.6	443.3	1,505.4	5,261.9	423.6	8,295.6	2,362.0
2007	23,998	31,228.5	9,258.9	272.0	593.9	N/A	6,003.0	N/A	10,016.1	3,056.7
2008	24,494	33,421.1	11,001.4	284.1	719.3	N/A	5,912.6	N/A	9,683.5	3,810.8
2009	21,040	30,502.2	11,199.9	231.6	820.6	N/A	4,766.2	N/A	8,579.0	3,335.6

Notes: TEU = 20-foot equivalent unit (based on a standardized container size of 20ft × 18ft × 18ft). Guangdong is the sum of Guangzhou Port, Zhanjiang Port, Shantou Port, Shekou Port, Chiwan Port, Mawan Port, Yantian Port and SCT Port (Shanghai Container Terminal). Since 2007, the total value of containers handled by Shekou and Yantian are included in SCT Port.

Sources: *Guangdong Statistical Yearbook and Hong Kong Annual Digest Statistics*, various years.

Contrary to Hong Kong, Mainland China pursues Five-Year Plans, even though a market economy has been adopted after economic reform in 1978. Both central and local governments often take a "driver seat" and are involved in decisions on foreign investments and other aspects of economic development. Nonetheless, the mainland economy has expanded a lot, with an average close to a two-digit real growth rate for three decades or more. Since the early 1990s, industrial expansion has been rapid, and the boom in exports in manufactures has turned Mainland China into the "workshop of the world". Exports further expanded upon becoming a member of the World Trade Organization (WTO) in 2001. By 2010, Mainland China has gone far, as it has the largest reserve in the world with prolonged trade surplus and has been attractive in foreign direct investment. Rapid urbanization and industrialization has brought uncertainties in the mainland economy, including the falling growth in agricultural outputs, emergence of labor shortage, and an ever rising fiscal deficit. Regional differences have also been a concern in the mainland economy, with the rich coastal regions contrasting sharply with the remote, underdeveloped poor interior provinces.

The rise in the mainland economy has also coincided with Hong Kong's prolonged economic recession after the Asian financial crisis in 1998. Economic recession that hit Hong Kong hard lasted literally from 1998 to 2004. While other Asian economies have recovered faster than Hong Kong after 1998, the key constraint Hong Kong faced was the economic structural rigidity, with finance and real estate being the key sectors that had fallen hard after the Asian financial crisis. Economic restructuring took a longer time to emerge, and short-term rescues were needed.

Since the turn of the century and coupled with the prolonged economic recession in Hong Kong, the rise of the mainland economy has led to heated debate on the role and position of Hong Kong economy in the context of the growing mainland economy and the policy that the Hong Kong government should adopt. Some pessimists believe that Hong Kong's era of economic growth is coming to an end, and nearby cities of Shenzhen, Guangzhou and Shanghai would overtake Hong Kong. The restructure advocates, on the contrary, hold the view that Hong Kong is still aiding the economic development in the mainland economy, and Hong Kong should at the same time do more for itself. These diverse views can be consolidated into two schools of thought: the "zero-sum" school and the "positive-sum" school.

The "zero-sum" school argues and expects the economy of Hong Kong to decline and Hong Kong will soon be absorbed into the gigantic mainland economy. Since sovereignty revision in 1997, "zero-sum" advocates belief that the rise of Shanghai will eventually take over Hong Kong's advantage, and given the vast development in Shanghai, Hong Kong will lose to Shanghai. Contrasts are often made to the growing financial and industrial development in Shanghai on the one hand, and on the other hand, the somewhat small financial sector and the shrinking industrial sector in Hong Kong. It has been argued that the lack of structural change and economic progress in Hong Kong will result in the "marginalization" of the economy, and will become a periphery to the mass mainland economy. With an expanding mainland economy and a shrinking Hong Kong economy, Hong Kong would soon lose its usefulness to Mainland China, or could even become an economic burden to the mainland economy if Hong Kong's economy keeps declining. For example, a former mainland official in charge of Hong Kong and Macau Affairs, Lu Ping remarked in 2007 that "Hong Kong had missed many opportunities over the past 10 years" and suggested that what Hong Kong need is "long-term strategic planning".[8]

These "zero-sum" advocates basically adopt an "absolute advantage" approach and that the mainland economy has an "absolute advantage" over the Hong Kong economy in virtually all economic aspects. They further hold the view that the economic rise of Mainland China would naturally imply a fall in the Hong Kong economy. The fast growing Guangdong and Shenzhen economies, for example, have led to some arguing ambitiously that their economic ability will help them to become a financial center, an education hub and a service center that could eventually marginalize the Hong Kong economy. For example, it was reported that the Shenzhen government has planned to make Shenzhen five times bigger that its present capacity as a restructuring strategy to increase its competitiveness and bring in more high-tech enterprises.[9]

In the *Blue Book on Urban Competitiveness* survey by the Chinese Academy of Social Sciences, it has been pointed out in the 2010 survey that although Hong Kong still ranked the highest in the overall competitiveness among 294 cities in Mainland China, Hong Kong is losing to Shanghai in economic scale, innovation and government departments, while Beijing ranked highest in living environment.[10] Similarly, studies also tend to compare the successful development of different regions in Mainland China. Typically, the Pearl River Delta adjacent to Hong Kong has been compared with the Yangtze River Delta where Shanghai plays a leading economic role. Comparisons are often made on an absolute, zero-sum basis.[11]

At a time when Hong Kong was faced with prolonged economic recession and a lack of economic restructuring, the "zero-sum" school seemed to have an upper hand in their argument, especially when the central authority in Beijing began to lend support to the Hong Kong economy since 2004 by providing various "advantages" to the Hong Kong economy, including the Closer Economic Partnership Agreement (CEPA) that opened up the mainland market to Hong Kong exports and businesses, the visa-free travel policy for mainland residents to visit Hong Kong, the establishment of a regional body that aligns Hong Kong's development with other southern provinces and incorporating Hong Kong subsequently into Mainland China's 11th Five-Year Plan in 2006. The various economic "gift" Beijing provided to Hong Kong was seen more as a sign of weakness and unsustainability on the part of the Hong Kong economy, and Hong Kong's economic survival would eventually have to depend on Beijing's continued support. A sense of inability, reliance and dependence was created, and Beijing's economic involvement in the Hong Kong economy was considered as a rescue and a recipe. There are other related economic debates within the "zero-sum" school, such as the linked exchange rate and eventual replacement of the Hong Kong currency by Renminbi. The growing welfare assistance can also be

---

[8] *South China Morning Post*, May 23, 2007.

[9] *China Daily*, June 5, 2009.

[10] *South China Morning Post*, April 27, 2010.

[11] *South China Morning Post*, May 24, 2007.

seen as steps towards an economic structure similar to the mainland where subsidies are often given to households. In short, the prolonged economic recession in Hong Kong has served as the instrument for the "zero-sum" advocates to conclude that the Hong Kong has become weaker and needed support.

There are two missing assumptions in the "zero-sum" school of thought. One is the flexible economic structure Hong Kong possesses. It is true that the economic recession was hard hit and previous economic recessions were short-lived, and the Hong Kong economy has been crisis-prone. Economic restructuring was forthcoming at a slow pace, but recovery and revival become possible once Hong Kong has regained its vitality. For example, flatted factory spaces were considered as a burden and an obstacles in the restructuring, as labor-intensive manufacturing would no longer be profitable in Hong Kong. Over the decade, however, many flatted factories have been rebuilt or restructured into office space, commercial areas and even shopping malls. Economic growth picks up once again, as seen from the rise in GDP and a fall in unemployment. When compared to previous economic crises before 1997, Hong Kong would take time to recover and restructure the economy. Previously, it was the attraction of foreign investment that rescued economic recessions, and Hong Kong would have to stand on its own feet. The difference in the experience since 1997, especially in 2005 and 2008, is that policies that led to economic recovery have been consulted with the authority in Beijing. The overall theme is for Hong Kong to further aid economic development in Mainland China, and Hong Kong is given the "first mover advantage" in serving, for example, as a Renminbi offshore center and aiding regional development. Seen economically, these initiatives do provide new opportunities for Hong Kong, and should produce positive economic results.

The other missing assumption is the needed distinction between Hong Kong being a developed economy and Mainland China being a developing economy. Given their difference, the required development trends should be different. For example, the massive investment in infrastructure in Mainland China does not mean Hong Kong is falling behind. The fact is that Hong Kong's infrastructural development has comparatively reached a higher stage than that in Mainland China. Similar arguments can be used for expenditure on education, health and welfare. The rise in major cities in Mainland China and rapid urbanization may mean there will be more modern cities in Mainland China. New metropolis in Mainland China symbolizes a rising mainland economy. Being one of the largest countries in the world geographically and a population equivalent to about one-quarter of the world's population, Mainland China should develop more modern cities and metropolis, with modern living and quality of life. It would be naive to assume that Hong Kong would therefore decline and become uncompetitive. On the contrary, one should welcome the growing maturity of the mainland economy, and would catch up with economic development in Hong Kong.

The "positive-sum" school looks to the comparative advantages between Hong Kong and the mainland economy and advocates a "two-legs" strategy. On the one hand, given Hong Kong's various advantages, Hong Kong can play a crucial role in furthering the development of the mainland economy. On the other hand, Hong Kong should structure its own path of development and similar to previous experiences,

Hong Kong should develop new areas of advantages that can create more businesses and job opportunities. Economic restructuring takes time and there is full of uncertainties, as new economic and business ventures will explore into uncharted areas. In many ways, economic development is like "crossing the river through touching the stones", as one could never know the outcome without trying. Economic integration with the mainland economy is seen as an instrument and opportunity, but Hong Kong needs to do its "homework" in making stronger preparations.

The "positive-sum" advocates basically take up the 'supply-driven' economic approach, believing that ultimately Hong Kong can and should create its own economic strength. The problem facing the "positive-sum" school is the lack of alignment of government policies. For "positive-sum" to be created, economic policies adopted by the Hong Kong government should have a long-term perspective that looks to new possibilities and open up new areas. On the contrary, the "crises-prone" nature of the Hong Kong economy has led the government to look for short-term solution, easing current economic pains and giving out welfare assistance repeatedly. While the economically weaker section of the population welcome the continued welfare assistance, they also complained and wanted more, but the economically stronger section of the population fell a lack of long-term vision of the Hong Kong economy. Ultimately, the small and open nature of the Hong Kong economy does not allow Hong Kong to become a strong welfare state. People in Hong Kong must "learn how to fish" and should not expect the provision of free fish or lunches and prolonged government subsidies. The policy makers should see the difference between policies adopted in a crisis situation and policies needed in a non-crisis situation.

Furthermore, economic crises have led to a different and somewhat distorted attitude. As the Hong Kong authority has been providing short-term assistance, it has come to the point that the provision of government assistance has become an expectation. It has become popular for people in Hong Kong to look to the government as a solution, and complained to the government when their expectation is not met. Such a "dependence" attitude would not be helpful to economic restructuring, and could even be self-fulfilling. One has to bear in mind that Hong Kong's success has been based on a "level playing field" and the small role of the government. It must be the private sector that drives the economy, the government can only provide a supportive role, creating business-friendly conditions, correcting areas of market-failures and projecting long-term possibilities. It would be suicidal for Hong Kong to become a welfare state and robs creativities and opportunities in Hong Kong's economic development.

Nonetheless, it is within this debate that economic integration with the mainland economy is being fostered. Even though Hong Kong is guarded by the "one country, two systems" policy, both Beijing and Hong Kong leaders have expressed their views on how the Hong Kong economy should be drafted, and how Hong Kong can aid the further development of Mainland China, and in turn, how the next phrase of economic development in Mainland China has provided opportunities for Hong Kong. In some sense, there are two areas of royalty under the "one country, two systems" framework: the country and the system, and embarrassments may arise and arm twisting tactics would be required if an issue leads to a royalty conflict between the country and the system.

Different political leaders have over the years expressed their concern of the development in Hong Kong. For example, in his regular duty visits with President Hu Jintao, after the 2008 financial crisis, the Chief Executive, Donald Tsang Yam-kuen, would seek help from President Hu Jintao "to shore up Hong Kong's shrinking economy", and "win-win" proposals designed "to benefit the long-term economic development of both Hong Kong and the mainland" have been submitted.[12] In another occasion when the Chief Executive met with the tourism chief in Beijing, the central government was asked to expand the Individual Visit Scheme and travel permits as a way to help the Hong Kong economy. Tourism was under threat when direct flights from the mainland to Taiwan were resumed. The Chief Executive also used his duty visits to Beijing to raise such issues as measures to ease the various difficulties and challenges facing Hong Kong businesses in mainland, especially in the Pearl River Delta region.[13]

Ever since sovereignty reversion in 1997, Beijing leaders in numerous occasions and at various times have urged Hong Kong to do a better job and not be too reliant on support from Beijing. Many Beijing leaders have shown confidence in the Hong Kong economy in lifting itself from post-Asian financial crisis economic recession. For example, in December 2005, Premier Wen Jiabao commented on the economic improvement in Hong Kong, but there is still the "deep-rooted conflict" unsolved. In 2007, both President Hu Jintao and Premier Wen Jiabao in different occasions conveyed a "four-point" wish to Chief Executive on improvement work in innovation, knowledge-based, human capital and environment.[14] Since the 2008 financial crisis, Premier Wen Jiabao assured Hong Kong that Beijing will make an all-out effort to help Hong Kong by outlining five policy methods that included provision of contingency plans to handle risk resulting from financial crisis, engaging and speeding up the infrastructure bridge project linking Hong Kong with Macau and Zhuhai, ensuring stable supply of food to avoid inflation, extending the individual traveler scheme and providing Hong Kong's small- and medium-sized enterprises operating in Mainland China.[15]

Acknowledging Hong Kong's economic narrowness and over-concentration on finance, Premier Wen Jiabao made five suggestions on the restructuring of the Hong Kong economy. The five suggestions are: 1) extend Hong Kong's comparative advantage, consolidation work should concentrate on promoting Hong Kong as an financial, shipping and trading center; 2) consolidate and expand the industries Hong Kong are good at, especially in services; 3) cooperate in the Pearl River Delta regional development, capture and use the mainland market for Hong Kong's advantage; 4) develop an embracive attitude and preserve Hong Kong's prosperity and stability and guided by the Basic Law, Hong Kong can develop democracy gradually; and 5) improve people's livelihood and promote education.[16]

---

[12] *South China Morning Post*, December 9, 2008.

[13] *South China Morning Post*, December 19, 2008.

[14] *Mingpao*, October 30, 2008; November 24, 2007; *South China Morning Post*, November 24, 2007.

[15] *South China Morning Post*, October 30, 2008.

[16] *Hong Kong Economic Journal*, March 15, 2010; *South China Morning Post*, March 15, 2010.

However, it has not been clear as what Premier Wen's "deep rooted conflict" was referring to. Would it be a political conflict in the path to democracy, or a social conflict in referring to more assistance to the poor, or a reference to the weakness of the government administration? Critics, however, showed concern about Premier Wen's extensive involvement in the Hong Kong economy. Allen Lee Peng Fei, the founding member of Liberal Party of Hong Kong, and a former member of the Legislative Council of Hong Kong, remarked that there is a "second power center" in Hong Kong, and the "one country, two systems" has been given new interpretation.[17]

Other key leaders in Beijing have also spoke positively about developments in Hong Kong. Echoing Premier Wen, the Party Secretary of Guangdong, Wang Yang, remarked also that financial development in any cities in Guangdong could not replace Hong Kong's role as an international financial center, and that speeding up in constructing the Hong Kong-Zhuhai bridge should be an advantage.[18] In his visit to Hong Kong, Vice Premier Li Keqiang, who is tipped to succeed Premier Wen Jiabao as the next Premier, confirmed that the central government will actively support the growth of Hong Kong as the offshore Renminbi center, and increasingly cross-border trade between Hong Kong and mainland will have to be settled in Renminbi. The Renminbi Qualified Foreign Institutional Investor (RQFII) will be allowed to invest in the mainland security market restricted to an initial size of Rmb 20 billion. More mainland financial institutions and enterprises will be allowed to issue Renminbi bonds in Hong Kong. Vice Premier Li reiterated that "Hong Kong has played an irreplaceable role in Mainland China's economic reform, opening up the modernization drive, while the mainland has been providing firm and concrete support for Hong Kong's prosperity and stability".[19] This clearly brings a "positive-sum" message leading to a "win-win" outcome.

Other than the speeches, reports and remarks of individual leaders, a total of three arrangements have been made with the mainland authorities. At the peak of the economic recession in Hong Kong in 2003, the initial phrase of the Closer Economic Partnership Agreement (CEPA) was concluded with the aim to opening up the mainland market for Hong Kong exports, the later phrase of CEPA introduced the open up of services for Hong Kong businesses. The need for more regional cooperation has been incorporated in the Pan-Pearl River Delta (pan-PRD) development that includes the nine southern provinces, Hong Kong SAR and Macau SAR. The pan-PRD is commonly known as the "9 + 2", and it aims primarily to foster more regional cooperation and uses Hong Kong's economic advantages to help other southern provinces. While CEPA is an agreement on the open up of the mainland market, and the pan-PRD is an agreement on regional cooperation, Hong Kong has been drafted into mainland's 11th Five-Year Plan in 2006.

---

[17] *Mingpao*, March 17, 2010.

[18] *Mingpao*, July 23, 2008.

[19] *China Radio International*, August 17, 2011; Hong Kong SAR Government Information Office, August 17, 2011; Xinhua News, August 17, 2011.

14.6 The Closer Economic Partnership Agreement

The Closer Economic Partnership Agreement (CEPA) that was first concluded in 2003 at the peak of economic recession in Hong Kong resulting from the outbreak of the health hazard of severe acute respiratory syndrome (SARS) was aimed to open up the mainland market for Hong Kong exports of goods and services. The first phrase of CEPA concluded on June 23, 2003, was subsequently supported by various supplements. Li (2006, Section 7.8) has outlined the key components, benefits and the different phrases of the CEPAs.[20] The Hong Kong government website has also provided relevant information on the content of the CEPAs and the estimated benefits in terms of employment creation.

The various phrases of CEPA has adopted a "building block" approach, basically contained two aspects of trade concessions; namely on trade in goods and trade and services. Trade facilitation forms the third element in the CEPA agreements. The first CEPA agreement contained twenty three articles in six chapters and became effective from January 2004. The objectives of the agreement, as specified in Article 1, are to strengthen trade and investment cooperation between the mainland and Hong Kong and to promote joint development through the reduction in tariff and non-tariff barriers, the liberalization of trade in services through the elimination of discriminatory measures, and the promotion of trade and investment facilitation. The objectives are embedded in the five principles stated in Article 2 of the agreement. Obviously, CEPA is abided by the "one country, two systems" principle. The contents of the agreement are consistent with the rule of the World Trade Organization (WTO). The third principle is the achievement of mutual benefits, complementarity and joint prosperity for both economies. The agreement accords with the structural needs of both economies and the need to adjust and upgrade the two economic regimes. Despite Mainland China's accession to the WTO, however, Article 4 referred to China's WTO accession and specifically says that "Articles 15 and 16 of the Protocol on the Accession of the People's Republic of China to the WTO and paragraph 242 of the Report of the Working Party on the Accession of China will not be applicable to trade between the Mainland and Hong Kong." This presumably means that the various conditions of China's WTO accession given to other countries do not apply to Hong Kong.

As far as trade in goods is concerned, Mainland China since January 2004 would not impose tariff on a total of 374 imports of goods of Hong Kong origin, and the list of imported goods was expanded in January 2006. Neither non-tariff barriers nor anti-dumping measures are imposed on either side. These 374 goods can be classified under eleven categories: plastic articles, paper articles, textiles and clothing, chemical products, pharmaceutical products, electrical and electronics, clocks and watches, cosmetics, jewelry, metal products and others.

The CEPA II expanded the list of export to another 713 goods (consists of 529 existing tariff codes and 184 planned tariff codes) that are classified under nine categories of food, medicine, marine products, chemicals, rubber, leather, textile, metal products and electronics. Although Hong Kong at the time of the agreement may

---

[20] This section summarizes and expands the materials from Li (2006, Section 7.8).

not have export in some of the goods specified in the list, the inclusion can encourage new investments in the relevant industries. The import tariffs imposed on these CEPA II goods that ranged from a few percent to over 50% were removed in 2005.

The other concern is the rule of origin. The 2003 CEPA concluded that a 25% "local content" is required. The rule of origin is a critical issue in the export of goods, as any part of Hong Kong export goods may be imported or produced elsewhere and assembled in Hong Kong. Annex 2 and 3 of the CEPA suggested that the negotiation is not an easy one as it also involved the two Custom authorities. Although Hong Kong does not prefer to have the rule of origin, there are other considerations from the mainland side. One is the tariff difference; some of the no-tariff concession given to the goods exported from Hong Kong may not enjoy the same treatment if Mainland China imported the same product from other countries. If there is no rule of origin, Hong Kong companies will import from overseas countries and export the same goods to Mainland China, thus bypassing the tariff.

Few will disagree with the economic benefits that a bilateral trade agreement will bring to the two economies. Hong Kong businesses believed that CEPA gave Hong Kong firms a head start.[21] The Commerce, Industry and Technology Bureau in the government reported in June 2007 that the number of jobs created for Hong Kong residents for the three categories of trade in goods, trade in services and individual visa scheme in the three consecutive years of 2004, 2005 and 2006 amounted to a total of 34,938.[22]

Article 11 of CEPA stated that the two economies will "progressively reduce or eliminate existing restrictive measures against services and service suppliers." A total of 17 service sectors in Hong Kong will benefit from the increase in access to the Mainland market. The two common features that apply to a large number of service sectors are the permission for Hong Kong investors to set up wholly-owned enterprises (WOE) in Mainland China. The list of market access for services is extended to 18 service sectors in CEPA II. Preferential treatment is granted to 8 new areas, and further liberalization is provided to 11 of the 18 service sectors. One qualifying requirement is the criterion on "Hong Kong companies". The criteria in general are that Hong Kong companies must be registered in Hong Kong, must engage in the same nature of business, must pay profit tax of Hong Kong, must have operated substantively for a minimum of three years in Hong Kong, must own or rent business premises in Hong Kong, and must employ in Hong Kong 50% or more of its total staff.

Since most of the service sectors, especially the professional sectors, in Mainland China need to catch up either in international standards and practices or in market competitiveness, the Hong Kong service industries can have a bigger role in the free trade agreements. In professional services, clearly a large number of professional companies will invest in the mainland market. Legal firms, accountancy firms and management consultancy firms can explore the mainland market through their

---

[21] *C-biz.org*, August 3, 2003.

[22] *Impact on the Hong Kong Economy*, Legislative Council Panel on Commerce and Trade, Mainland and Hong Kong Closer Economic Partnership Arrangement, Commerce, Industry and Technology Bureau, Hong Kong, June 2007.

professional institutions. However, one has to watch out for the continued protectionist policy practiced by the legal and accountancy professions. These professional bodies could have a strong influence in allowing the number of qualified lawyers and accountants whom can practice in Mainland China. Table 14.18 reproduces the information on the market access for services under CEPA concluded in 2003, though updates are made in the subsequent supplements to CEPA.

Advantages to the service industries in Hong Kong can mainly be condensed into three areas. One is clearly the expanded business opportunities, especially in cases where Hong Kong companies can capture the mainland market. Related to these opportunities are the possibilities of job employment in the mainland. With the wholly-owned enterprises status, it is likely that Hong Kong companies in various service industries will employ Hong Kong trained workers and professionals, at least in the short-run, to work in their mainland offices and branches. The new employment opportunity will then create other economic effects in Hong Kong. One other foreseeable consequence in the standardization of the services sector in the mainland economy will be a rise in wages, prices and asset values, thereby narrowing the cost gap between Hong Kong and Mainland. The third area will be an expansion of two-way investment activities.

Trade and investment facilitation involves a greater degree of transparency, standards conformance and exchange of information, especially in cross-border issues. Cooperation will be conducted in trade and investment promotion, custom clearance, quarantine and inspection of commodities, food safety and quality assurance, electronic commerce, transparency in law and regulations, small- and medium-sized enterprises and Chinese medicine and medical products.

A major theme in this part of cooperation and facilitation concerned a number of institutional arrangements and contacts between Hong Kong and mainland institutions. Medical standards, transfer of relevant information in food safety, custom clearance and so on require understanding and cooperation between the relevant government institutions. The idea is that a greater understanding will promote efficiency in handling trade and related issues when problems arise. The severe acute respiratory syndrome (SARS) outbreak in the spring of 2003, for example, demonstrated a poor linkage among medical institutions between mainland and Hong Kong. Various cross-border activities need further facilitation as economic integration speeds up, and institutional cooperation increases efficiency in the facilitation process.

The conclusion of the CEPA is seen as the major step in the economic integration of the two economies, as bilateral trade agreements are meant to create a "win-win" situation. While the mainland market has become more open, it will be up to Hong Kong companies to make their investment decisions. As such, one should look at the CEPA as a piece of trade infrastructure that will open up opportunities for both economies for a long period of time. The Deutsche Bank (2003) report estimated that under the zero-tariff situation, a fully implemented CEPA will bring an extra 0.4% of GDP growth in Hong Kong annually, and the number of job created ranged from five to ten thousand. The improvement in economic growth can arise from various channels. These included the savings of tariff payment by exporters, the increase in the volume of exports, the increase in investment in the CEPA-related sectors and the resulting increase in consumer spending. On the services sector in Hong

TABLE 14.18 Service sector market access

	Under CEPA
Sector	Summary of market access for Hong Kong companies
Management Consulting	Can establish WOEs in Mainland.
Convention & Exhibition Services	Can supply convention services on a wholly-owned basis.
Advertising	Can establish WOEs in Mainland.
Accounting Services	Qualified (Chinese Certified Public Accountants) Hong Kong accountants can practice in the Mainland and are treated on par. The Temporary Auditing Business Permit for Hong Kong accounting firms is extended to 1 year.
Real Estate & Construction	Can engage in high standard real estate projects and provide services that are excluded in China's WTO commitments on a wholly-owned basis. Can establish WOEs 3 years ahead of China's WTO timetable. Exempt from foreign investment restrictions when undertaking joint construction projects.
Medical & Dental	HK-Mainland joint venture hospitals can employ Hong Kong permanent residents, whom can sit for qualification examinations. Qualified Hong Kong doctors can serve for a maximum of 3 years.
Distribution Services	Can establish WOEs in various supply distribution services, can establish WOE trading companies 1 year ahead of China WTO's timetable. Entry requirement for WOEs are lowered. WOEs in retails can be set up in all cities at prefecture level in the Mainland and at county level in Guangdong, up to 30 outlets in the sale of motor vehicles.
Logistics	Can establish WOEs in Mainland in a number of logistics-related businesses.
Freight Forwarding	Can establish WOEs, capital requirements will be the same as Mainland enterprises.
Storage & Warehousing	Can establish WOEs 1 year ahead of China's WTO timetable, capital requirements will be the same as Mainland enterprises.
Transport	Road transport: can establish WOEs, 1 year ahead of China's WTO timetable, allow direct road freight to all provinces. Maritime transport: can establish WOEs in various shipping related businesses.
Tourism	Can construct, renovate and operate hotel and restaurants on a wholly-owned basis 2 years ahead of China's WTO timetable. Geographical restrictions lifted for joint venture travel agencies.
Audiovisual Services	Can establish majority ownership joint ventures to distribute audiovisual products and to construct and/or renovate cinema theatres. Can import Hong Kong-produced motion pictures excluded from the foreign film import quota.

(*Continued*)

TABLE 14.18 (*Continued*)

	Under CEPA
Legal Services	Minimum residency requirement is reduced to 2 months each year, further waived for offices located in Shenzhen and Guangzhou. Hong Kong practitioners can work for Mainland law firms. Hong Kong permanent residents can sit for Mainland legal qualifications. Hong Kong law representative firms can run business in association with Mainland law firms except in the form of partnership.
Banking	Hong Kong banks and finance companies will have a lower asset requirement and minimum prior business operation requirement, and requirement for setting up a representative office is removed.
Securities	The Hong Kong Exchanges and Clearing Limited can set up a representative office in Beijing. Hong Kong professionals can apply to practice in the Mainland.
Insurance	Can practice in the Mainland without prior approval once appropriate qualifications are obtained. Companies can enter the Mainland through mergers subjects to China's WTO commitments. The maximum limit of capital participation in a Mainland insurance company is raised to 15%.
Legal Services	Consultant permit not required for HK lawyers.
Accounting, Auditing	HK accountant should obtain relevant Mainland qualifications.
Medical, Dental	Can open clinics in Mainland with conditions.
Information Technology	Can apply for qualification certification.
Audiovisual Services	Can establishing WOEs.
Construction	Can apply to undertake construction project.
Distribution Services	Can establish WOEs in retail and wholesale. Conditions imposed on retails of motor vehicles.
Banking Service	Mainland branches of HK banks can conduct insurance business.
Securities & Futures	Can set up joint ventures not exceeding 49% shareholding.
Transport Services	Can establish WOEs.
Freight Forwarding	Can set up branch offices.
Airport services	Allow joint venture or WOEs for small and medium airports. Can supply 7 types of ground services.
Individual-owned Stores	Can set up individual-owned stores.
Professional/technical Qualification Exams.	Allow to take the 30 qualification examinations for professionals and technicians.
Cultural Entertainment	Can set up performing venues and branches.
Trade Mark Agency	Can conduct trade mark agency business.
Job Referral Agency	Can set up WOEs, with minimum registered capital of US$125,000.
Job Intermediary	Joint ventures allowed, minimum registered capital required, shareholding not exceed 70%.
Patent Agency	Allow to take the relevant qualification.

Note: WOEs = wholly-owned enterprises.

Source: Closer Economic Partnership Agreement, Hong Kong, June 29, 2003.

Kong, the Deutsche Bank (2003) concluded that distribution and retail, road transport, tourism, and banking are the likely winners in the CEPA concessions. Other analysts, for example, Morgan Stanley (2003) concluded that CEPA will bring only limited overall economic benefit, as "privileged opportunities do not guarantee success and profitability". The rule of origin and the definition of Hong Kong companies are the two issues that will shape the "competitive landscape" of the CEPA.

Through the various CEPA supplements, trade concessions have increased to 1,600 goods and over 40 services. During his visit to Hong Kong in August 2011, Vice Premier Li Keqiang announced that the further easing of restrictions in service trade will be one of the agenda in the conclusion of the eighth supplement of CEPA.[23] The new emphasis in the service sector is the insurance industry, shipping and air communication, tourism, energy supplies, medical and educational services.

14.7 Pan-Pearl River Delta Region

While the CEPA is a trade agreement between Mainland China and Hong Kong in 2003, another issue in Mainland China has been developing. The development of the western provinces in Mainland China has been given prominent attention in the mid-1990s, as the growing imbalance between the coastal and inner provinces has led to Premier Zhu Rongji to focus on investment in western remote provinces. Some of the western provinces are closer to the southern provinces. Another line of concern is the rising Yangtze River Delta region, and it has come to the attention of provincial leaders to promote regional development. Traditionally, there has been a lack of cooperation among and between provinces, resulting in a lack of cross-provincial development, the usage of resources could not promote economies of scale, there is duplication in development among provinces and excess demands exist along with excess supply of goods and materials between provinces. Coastal provinces have been attractive to foreign investment, and labor migration to coastal provinces has slowed down development in remote areas.

The Guangdong province has been the hotbed of light manufacturing since economic reform in 1978 and has become the major exporting province. As Shanghai was designated for economic development since the early 1990s, say in the financial and banking sector, it created some sense of regional competition between Shanghai leading the Yangtze River Delta region and Guangdong leading the Pearl River Delta region. The sense of regional competition has generated positive response as Guangdong began to reconsider its role and influence in the southern region.

The Guangdong province has several economic advantages, other than the strong export status resulting from investments in light manufacturing. Guangdong is the most prosperous region, and is economically more open than other provinces. Guangdong is situated north of Hong Kong and has enjoyed all the economic advantages from Hong Kong even before economic reform in 1978. Through the tributaries of the Pearl River, Guangdong can reach out to different southern provinces. There is thus a lot Guangdong can do in promoting regional development.

---

[23] Government Information Bureau, Hong Kong, August 17, 2011.

The Pan-Pearl River Delta Cooperation and Development Forum (Forum), held in Hong Kong in early June 2004, brought together the two Special Administrative Regions (SAR) of Hong Kong and Macau and nine southern Mainland provinces (Guangdong, Fujian, Jiangxi, Hunan, Guangxi, Hainan, Sichuan including Chongqing, Guizhou and Yunnan). It is commonly known as the "Pan-PRD" or "9 + 2". The eleven economic entities signed a framework agreement that establishes closer economic cooperation, thus giving rise to the largest formation of economic cooperation initiatives in southern China. The agreement on economic cooperation is based on four fundamental principles of voluntary participation, market orientation, open and fair market and breakdown of barriers. The Forum will be held once a year to enhance cooperation and maximize the benefits from the regional alliance. The nine provinces composed of one fifth of Mainland China's total land area, one third of its population and 250 million labor force, one third of GDP, 27% of value-added industrial output and 43% of exports (Morgan Stanley, 2004).

A total of ten areas of cooperation are identified, as summarized in Table 14.19. The agreement provided a framework that opened up cooperation activities among the various provinces and the two Special Administrative Regions. Several observations can be made from the ten cooperation areas. One observation is that cooperation on the input side of the production process included a better input quality or standard and an improvement in the monitoring system. Secondly, there is an

TABLE 14.19 The ten areas of Pan-PRD cooperation

Industry	Nature of cooperation
Infrastructure	Energy: West-East electricity transmission; coal & natural gas extraction & provision. Transport: integrate & consolidate expressways, railways, air & sea transport. Pipelines: oil & gas.
Industry & Investment	Concentrate on environment & system changes, cooperate in technology.
Commerce & Trade	Eliminate barriers, establish disciplines, & implement CEPA.
Tourism	Regional strategy on tourism development, e-business, remove cross-provincial travel barriers.
Agriculture	Rationalize purchase arrangements, improve agricultural technology & food safety.
Labor	Improve market conditions, increase mobility, training & recognition of qualifications
Science, Education & Culture	Cooperate in academic research, share information.
Information Technology	Establish e-business standards.
Environment Protection	Develop environmental-friendly production, prevent pollution, sustainable growth promotion.
Public Health	Disease prevention, improve reporting system.

Source: *Pan-PRD Regional Cooperation and Development Forum*, Hong Kong, June 1, 2004.

element of specialization in resource supply, and that the resource rich provinces should assist the resource weak provinces. It followed that the current system is one that lacks mutual cooperation among provinces. The agreement enforced that provinces must from now on cooperate with neighboring provinces.

The first "kick off" emerged in the subsequent Pan-PRD Regional Economic and Trade Cooperation Symposium held in Guangzhou in mid-July 2004. Investment contracts totaling Rmb 292.6 billion was successfully signed, with seven largest government projects (totaled Rmb 120.2 billion) in expressways, railways, water transport, electricity, technology, labor and food supply. The remaining Rmb 172.4 composed of 840 enterprises contracts focusing on energy, property, tourism, agriculture and environment (Morgan Stanley, 2004). Cooperation in the input side of the production process will in the long-run promote production capacity and productivity of industries in the non-coastal provinces in southern China. Economic specialization enabled the non-coastal provinces to concentrate more on infrastructure and resources development. The political blessing from Beijing implied that provinces in southern China can now develop their full potential, and will become a growth region parallel to that of the Yangtze River Delta.

The nine provinces in southern China, together with Hong Kong and Macau, have their regional and geo-economic advantages. Typical examples include Guangdong which has established itself in export-oriented manufacturing and absorbed much support from Hong Kong and Macau. Fujian contains Xiamen Special Economic Zone (SEZ) that is a major navigation hub in southeast China. The southern province of Yunnan is located next to the mainland of Southeast Asia containing Vietnam, Cambodia, Laos, Thailand and other Association of Southeast Asian Nations (ASEAN) members. The supply of natural resources is the comparative advantage of the non-coastal provinces. Hunan and Guangxi, for example, are rich in timber, while Jiangxi is rich in copper production. There are numerous tourism spots in all the non-coastal provinces.

Table 14.20 shows an updated 2009 economic overview of the nine provinces (including Chongqing) and the two Special Administrative Regions. The data on population, GDP, wage, domestic and foreign investment, and export are compared. The Guangdong province has the largest population, and all the nine provinces have a population growth rate higher than 6%, including Sichuan when Chongqing is included. Guangdong obviously has the large GDP and GDP per capita among the nine provinces, but GDP per capita of Macau and Hong Kong have far exceeded all the nine provinces. The GDP growth in eight provinces other than Guangdong has exceeded 10% between 2008 and 2009. As a proportion of GDP, agriculture in Hainan and Guangxi has the largest share. Both Chongqing (52.8%) and Jiangxi (51.2%) are the two provinces with the largest share in industry, followed closely by Guangdong (49.2%), Fujian (49.1%) and Sichuan (47.4%). Both Hong Kong and Macau obviously are strong performers in services, as their shares in GDP are 92% and 88.3%, respectively. Among the nine provinces, both Guangdong (45.7%) and Fujian (45.3%) are the strongest performers in services.

Other than Guangdong, the average monthly wages of all other eight provinces are below Rmb 3,000. Hong Kong of course has the highest monthly wage, but

TABLE 14.20 Economic overview of the Pan-PRD region in 2009

Provinces	Guangdong	Guangxi	Hainan	Fujian	Jiangxi	Hunan
Population (10 thousand)	9,638	4,856	864	3,627	4,432	6,406
Nature Growth Rate	7.26	8.53	8.96	6.20	7.89	6.11
GDP (Rmb 100 million)	39,482.56	7,759.16	1,654.21	12,236.53	7,655.18	13,059.69
% growth, 2008–2009	9.7	13.9	11.7	12.3	13.1	13.7
Agriculture, % of GDP	5.1	18.8	27.9	9.7	14.4	15.1
Industry, % of GDP	49.2	43.6	26.8	49.1	51.2	43.5
Services, % of GDP	45.7	37.6	45.3	41.3	34.4	41.4
GDP per capita (Rmb)	41,166	16,045	19,254	33,840	17,335	20,428
Average Monthly Wage (Rmb)	3,039	2,777	2,066	2,364	2,014	2,211
% growth, 2008–2009	9.6	10.2	13.9	11.0	17.3	9.9
Fixed Asset Investment (Rmb 100 million)	12,933.12	5,237.24	988.32	6,231.2	6,643.14	7,703.38
% growth, 2008–2009	18.99	39.42	40.1	19.65	39.99	39.2
Foreign Investment in Foreign Funded Enterprises (US$ 100 million)	1,987.81	120.82	117.58	562.03	194.74	124.19
% growth, 2008–2009	10.06	10.47	4.02	4.03	12.77	5.77
Export(Rmb 100 million)	35,895,489	837,537	130,863	5,331,911	736,849	549,203
% growth, 2008–2009	−11.51	13.99	−17.55	−6.44	−4.64	−34.72

(Continued)

TABLE 14.20 (*Continued*)

Provinces	Guizhou	Yunnan	Sichuan	Chongging	Macau	Hong Kong
Population (10 thousand)	3,798	4,571	8,185	2,859	54	700
Nature Growth Rate	6.96	6.08	2.72	3.7	−1.4	0.37
GDP (Rmb 100 million)	3,912.68	6,169.75	14,151.28	6,530.01	1,448.8	14,383.7
% growth, 2008–2009	11.4	12.1	14.5	14.9	−2.4	−2.6
Agriculture, % of GDP	14.1	17.3	15.8	9.3	0.0	0.05
Industry, % of GDP	37.7	41.9	47.4	52.8	15.7	7.98
Services, % of GDP	48.2	40.8	36.7	37.9	88.3	92.0
GDP per capita (Rmb)	10,309	13,539	17,339	22,920	266,197	205,373
Average Monthly Wage (Rmb)	2,286	2,180	2,346	2,541	7,272	9,365
% growth, 2008–2009	14.4	12.3	13.8	14.5	6.25	0.00
Fixed Asset Investment (Rmb 100 million)	2,412.02	4,526.37	11,371.87	5,214.28		
% growth, 2008–2009	29.37	31.74	59.54	31.03		
Foreign Investment in Foreign Funded Enterprises at Year-end (US$ 100 million)	15.85	68.21	213.67	120.46		
% growth, 2008–2009	11.75	23.24	9.00	19.84		
Export (Rmb 100 million)	135,661	451,325	1,416,945	428,007	66	21,757
% growth, 2008–2009	−28.63	−9.45	7.90	−25.2	−51.9	−12.57

Notes: The GDP are calculated in current price. The production-based GDP figures of Hong Kong and Macau are calculated using 2008 data. The median wage figures are used for Hong Kong and Macau and are converted to Reminbi.

Sources: *Guangdong Statistical Yearbook*, *Guangxi Statistical Yearbook*, *Hainan Statistical Yearbook*, *Fujian Statistical Yearbook*, *Jiangxi Statistical Yearbook*, *Hunan Statistical Yearbook*, *Guizhou Statistical Yearbook*, *Yunnan Statistical Yearbook*, *Sichuan Statistical Yearbook*, *Chongqing Statistical Yearbook*, *Zhongguo Tong Ji Chu Ban She*, Beijing; Census and Statistics Department of Macao; Census and Statistics Department, Hong Kong; and CEIC.

there was no growth rate in 2008–2009. In the case of fixed asset investment, again Guangdong has performed strongest, but a number of provinces except Guangdong and Fujian have shown a growth rate in fixed asset investment close to or above 40% in 2008–2009.The growth rate of fixed asset investment in Chongqing was exceptionally high at 59.54% in 2008–2009. In terms of foreign investment in foreign funded enterprises, Guangdong is way ahead of other eight provinces. Guangdong definitely has absorbed far more foreign resources than other provinces. The three provinces of Guizhou, Yunnan and Hunan are least favorable to foreign investments. Guangdong is the strongest exporting province, way ahead of other eight provinces, followed by Sichuan whose performance is less than half of what Guangdong exported in 2008–2009.

The strong performance of Guangdong could be an envy of other southern provinces. Table 14.21 shows the key industries in each of the provinces and Hong Kong and Macau. Industries in the three provinces of Fujian, Sichuan and Hunan are less concentrated, while the smallest economies of Hong Kong and Macau showed the highest concentration ratio. Despite the regional relationship, Table 14.21 shows that industrial production among the provinces and the two SARs are quite different. For example, Guangdong and Fujian have a similar industrial structure with key production in electronics. Guangxi and Chongqing concentrate more on transport equipment. Hainan and Guizhou have specialized in electric power and petroleum. The four provinces of Hunan, Jiangxi, Yunnan and Sichuan are more raw materials, resources and agricultural oriented. Macau mainly focuses on apparel, while Hong Kong excels in metals and machinery.

Guangdong is definitely leading the development of the southern provinces. Guangdong always sees itself as the pioneer in economic reform, absorbing much of investment from Hong Kong since 1978. In 2008 when Mainland China celebrated its 30 years of economic reform, Guangdong acknowledged its own significance and considered itself as pivotal in making further reform, leading development in the pan-PRD region, gateway to Southeast Asia, and a world-class base on advanced manufacturing and modern services. In 2008, the Guangdong authority has come up with *The Outline of the Plan for the Reform and Development of the Pearl River Delta (2008–2020)*[24] (Outline) that contained a total of 10 dimensions of ambitious development. They include: 1) build a modern industrial system that would accelerate the development of hi-tech industries; 2) strengthen an independent innovation that would develop core technologies; 3) promotion of infrastructure modernization; 4) coordination of urban and rural development to enhance infrastructure and public services; 5) coordinate regional development between the two banks of the Pearl River; 6) enhance resource conservation and environmental protection; 7) expedite the development of social undertakings by perfecting education, medical and housing; 8) creation of new system and advantages; 9) further open up by engaging more with Hong Kong, Macau, Taiwan and the PRD region; and 10) strengthen organization and leadership.

---

[24] *The Outline of the Plan for the Reform and Development of the Pearl River Delta (2008–2020)*, National Development and Reform Commission, State Council, Beijing, December 2008.

TABLE 14.21 The largest five industries in the Pan-PRD region in 2009

Provinces	Industries (percent of total industrial output) [5-industry concentration ratio]
Guangdong [50.34]	Electronics & telecommunication equipment (23.03), Electric equipment & machinery (10.79), Manufacture of transport equipment (6.09), Production & supply of electric power & heat power (5.67), Metal products (4.77).
Guangxi [55.86]	Transport equipment (14.75), Farm & sideline products processing (12.84), Smelting & pressing of ferrous metals (11.50), Production & supply of electric power, steam & hot water (10.83), Nonmetal mineral products (5.94).
Hainan [65.17]	Processing of petroleum, coking & nuclear fuel (35.50), Production & supply of electric power & heat power (9.02), Processing of agriculture & related product (7.74), Manufacture of transport equipment (6.64), Raw chemical materials & products (6.28).
Fujian [36.20]	Electric & telecommunication equipment (10.22), Leather, fur, down & related products (7.26), Nonmetal mineral products (6.50), Production & supply of electric power, steam & hot water (6.37), Garments & other fiber products (5.84).
Jiangxi [45.61]	Smelting & pressing of non-ferrous Metals (16.95), Manufacture of non-metallic mineral products (7.45), Manufacture of raw chemical materials & chemical (7.26), Smelting & pressing of ferrous metals (7.06), Manufacture of electrical machinery & equipment (6.89).
Hunan [38.20]	Raw chemical materials & products (8.24), Manufacture & processing of non-ferrous Metals (8.22), Processing of food from agricultural products (7.61), Manufacture of special purpose machinery (7.58), Manufacture & processing of ferrous metals (6.56).
Guizhou [60.58]	Electric power, gas & tap water production & supply (24.31), Mining & quarrying (12.74), Smelting & pressing of ferrous metals (9.63), Raw chemical materials & products (8.27), Tobacco processing (5.64).
Yunnan [64.16]	Tobacco processing (17.48), Smelting & pressing of non-ferrous metals (14.67), Production & supply of electric power, steam & hot water (11.75), Smelting & pressing of ferrous metals (11.17), Processing of petroleum, coking & nuclear Fuel (9.09).
Sichuan [36.11]	Farm byproducts processing (8.49), Smelting & pressing of ferrous metals (7.69), Raw chemical materials & products (6.89), Nonmetal mineral products (6.68), Ordinary machinery manufacturing (6.36).
Chongqing [55.48]	Transport equipment (34.30), Raw chemical materials & products (5.74), Production & supply of electric power, steam & hot water (5.45), Electric equipment & machinery (5.19), Manufacture of general purpose machinery (4.80).
Macau [74.50]	Apparel, dress & dyeing of fur (42.96), Textiles (11.43), Production & supply of electric power, steam & hot water (10.02), Manufacture of other non-metallic mineral products (5.77), Manufacture of food products & beverages (4.31).
Hong Kong [86.63]	Basic metals, fabricated metal products, machinery & equipment (39.53), Paper, printing, publishing & allied industries (18.32), Food, beverages and tobacco (13.45), Chemical, rubber, plastic and non-metallic mineral products (8.37), Textiles (6.95).

Source: Same as Table 14.20.

The foreword of the Outline specifically pointed out that the Outline covered the nine Guangdong cities (Guangzhou, Shenzhen, Zhuhai, Foshan, Jiangmen, Dongguan, Zhongshan, Huizhou and Zhaoqing) as the focus of development that will radiate to the other cities in the pan-Pearl River region, including Hong Kong and Macau. Despite the Outline was being scrutinized by the National Development and Reform Commission, the focus of the nine cities in Guangdong as the core area of development was considered to be too narrow and even biased, and other cities in the pan-PRD region were considered as periphery. It seems to have played down the contribution by other provinces in regional cooperation. It is expected that billions of Renminbi would be spent on various kinds of investment. In any case, the Outline produced mainly a draft of future development, but many saw that as an ambition of Guangdong in leading other provinces, rather than seeing each province as equal in development in the pan-PRD region.

There are certain areas and cases of economic complementary among the "9 + 2" entities. The industrial provinces can complement the resource-based provinces. Provinces that concentrate on consumer products complement with provinces that are oriented to heavy industries. Traditionally, the light manufacturing in coastal regions are complement by the heavy industries in non-coastal provinces, large state ownership in the non-coastal provinces versus foreign-funded enterprises in coastal provinces, and suppliers of capital versus supplier of labor in the pan-PRD region ensure economic cooperation and integration. Economic integration clearly permits both economies of scale and scope and specialization to function to their fullest extent. Morgan Stanley (2004) had come up with various concerns in the integration of the pan-PRD region. Provinces and cities are vastly different from each other in terms of stage of development. At the time of the pan-PRD agreement, there are various restrictions and barriers that are difficult to remove at the operational level. Bureaucracy at custom points, for example, can discourage inter-provincial trade. Much discussion is given to infrastructure. For example, there are promises in the June 2004 conference in Hong Kong that the pan-PRD region would need 30,000 km of highways and main roads, compared to 19,000 km currently, and railway coverage would increase to 29,000 km by 2020 from 19,000 km in 2003. In the meantime, transport bottlenecks and infrastructure shortage can lead to divergence in cost and delay.

The attitude Hong Kong should take is one of open-mindedness. Similar to CEPA through which a new framework of export is open to Hong Kong businesses, the pan-PRD is another infrastructure framework that provided both "challenges and opportunities" at the regional level. These economic frameworks could work both ways in that Hong Kong businesses are allowed to invest in other provinces, and overtime provincial businesses would be allowed to come to operate in Hong Kong. These challenges and opportunities actually reflect the importance on the strategy Hong Kong pursues. While demand-side activities can bring short-term recovery to the Hong Kong economy, it is the long-term economic capacity and supply-side economics that can give sustainability to the Hong Kong economy. Both the CEPA agreements and pan-PRD are two-way means, not ends, for Hong Kong to interact with the Mainland economy, how much benefits Hong Kong businesses can gain depend largely on Hong Kong's own economic efforts.

Studies that examine the benefits from the CEPA agreement and the pan-PRD development have been positive. For example, Sung (2004) distinguished the reallocative effects and the growth effects in the pan-PRD development. Reallocative effects are the income and employment benefits generated by Hong Kong's PRD-related exports. It was reported that income generated by PRD-related exports/employment accounted for 24.8/23% of Hong Kong's GDP/employment in 2002. However, Sung (2004) also pointed out that Hong Kong's PRD-related entrépot services, which accounted for 60% of PRD-related exports, are expected to grow at a slower rate or even decline, as cargo diversion to other ports in Guangdong will reduce the amount of PRD-related entrépot trade. Growth in other PRD-related services, such as travel services, will have to grow faster in order to compensate for the possible decline in the entrépot trade. As such, the long-term growth effect is difficult to quantify. However, Sung (2004) noted that Hong Kong's investment in mainland would raise the return to capital that in turn would stimulate investment in Hong Kong and raise Hong Kong's growth rate by as much as 1.5%. In general, the upgrading of Hong Kong firms and businesses in various directions and dimensions is a "big plus" to Hong Kong's long-term growth.

Scholars in the Hong Kong Institute of Asia Pacific Studies (Institute) located at the Chinese University of Hong Kong, under the director of Yue-man Yeung, have produced numerous studies on regional cooperation within the pan-PRD region. Though most studies are reported in Chinese, the Institute over the years has produced various occasional papers that summarized a large number of studies on regional cooperation through the discipline of economic geography (for example, Yeung, 1997; Yeung and Chu, 1998, 2000; Yeung and Sung, 1996; Yeung and Shen, 2004, 2008). These studies are useful in providing descriptive and practical suggestions on the possibilities of cooperation, and advocate the "positive-sum" nature of regional cooperation.

Both the business sector and the government have also been active in promoting pan-PRD cooperation. For example, the Hong Kong Pearl River Delta Foundation (Foundation) was founded in 2002 to "acts as a catalyst to accelerate the repositioning of Hong Kong as the business and lifestyle hub of the Pearl River Delta". In repositioning Hong Kong as the PRD's business and lifestyle hub, the Foundation urged to enhance cross-border mobility, build the Zhuhai Bridge as soon as possible and upgrade education and training programs.[25]

The Greater Pearl River Delta Business Council (Council), under the chairmanship of Victor Kwok-king Fung, has regularly produced reports for the government in the Hong Kong — PRD issues. In response to the Guangdong government's Outline in 2008, the Council set up an ad hoc group and reported in September 2009. The Council's report put forward 47 specific policy recommendations under seven headings. The recommendations covered 14 aspects, including healthcare services, environmental protection, education, transportation, social services, professional services, entry of small- and medium-sized enterprises to the mainland market, upgrading and transformation of manufacturing industries, innovative technology,

[25] "Repositioning Hong Kong as the Pearl River Delta's Business and Lifestyle Hub", Hong Kong Pearl River Delta Foundation, November 7, 2002.

culture, creativity and testing and certification. The four sub-groups in the Council has studied a number of studies in the areas of cross-border passenger and cargo flow, joint investment and trade promotion, development of services and human capital and sustainable development.[26]

It was reported in March 2009 that the Hong Kong and Guangdong governments formulated the "Framework Agreement on Hong Kong/Guangdong Co-operation" in the areas of infrastructure, industrial collaboration, environmental protection, education and quality of life. The Council recommended to the Hong Kong government that both Hong Kong and Guangdong "could jointly submit concrete proposals to the Central Authorities with a view to elevating Hong Kong-Guangdong cooperation to the level of national strategy and having relevant proposals incorporated into the National 12th Five-year Plan". It is argued that genuine cooperation under the premise of reciprocity will generate contribution to Mainland China.[27]

There have also been numerous suggestions on the possibilities of cooperation between Hong Kong and Guangdong. For example, the Pan-PRD Consultancy Group of the Central Policy Unit in the Hong Kong government has also suggested numerous channels of cooperation. The Chief Executive has repeatedly noted the importance of regional cooperation in a number of Policy Address speeches. For example, in the 2009–2010 Policy Address, the Chief Executive, Donald Tsang Yum-kuen, said that the development of service industries in the Mainland economy will set a clear direction for Hong Kong in the PRD region.[28] The research arm of the Bank of China in Hong Kong has regularly also made various suggestions. Typical examples include finance, logistics, and travel and cross-border facilitation.[29] Other concerns include the use of border land between Hong Kong and Shenzhen, and new land developments in and near Macau. The border industrial zone and an education hub have been suggested as alternatives in the newly developed land at the border.[30] For example, the Qianhai Bay, which is an area near BaoAn situated south of the Shenzhen BaoAn International Airport, has been designated for development in Mainland China's 12th Five-year Plan. In his 2010–2011 Policy Address, the Chief Executive pointed out that the State Council in Beijing has set clear objectives and directions for the development of Qianhai Bay in August 2009. The Qianhai Bay is meant to be another fast-developing region in west Shenzhen, and should offer ample opportunities for Hong Kong businesses. The 2010–2011 Policy Address stated that the Hong Kong government will "work with the Shenzhen authorities to encourage the trades in Hong Kong to seize the opportunities arising from the development of Qianhai Bay".[31]

---

[26] "Study Report in Response to the Outline of the Plan for the Reform and Development of the Pearl River Delta", September 2009; and "Hong Kong's Role and Positioning in the Economic Development of the Nation — Recommendation Report", September, 2010, Greater Pearl River Delta Business Council, Hong Kong.

[27] Press release, Hong Kong government, February 23, 2010.

[28] 2009–2010 Policy Address, Hong Kong.

[29] *Wen Wei Pao*, March 3, 2008.

[30] *South China Morning Post*, November 14, 2008.

[31] 2010–2011 Policy Address, Hong Kong.

In addition, individual provinces in southern China have also approached Hong Kong government and businesses for the various possibilities of cooperation and development. Individual provinces have established offices in Hong Kong so as to balance Hong Kong's economic cooperation relationship with Guangdong. While Guangdong has been a major beneficiary of Hong Kong investment since economic reform in 1978, Hong Kong has been active in securing opportunities in regional development, and got involved with developments in new areas to create "win-win" outcomes. On the one hand, Hong Kong can extend its existing advantages in the regional cooperation. On the other hand, it is probable that Hong Kong expands its new advantages through regional cooperation with Guangdong and other provinces in the PRD region. Indeed, one can even conjecture that Hong Kong can also serve the western provinces of Mainland China, as well as building up infrastructural and business connections with countries in Southeast Asia that are adjacent to the southern provinces of Mainland China, typically the so called "Indo China" countries of Vietnam, Laos, Cambodia and beyond.

14.8 The Five-Year Plan

The Five-Year Plans have been the traditional economic instrument in hardcore socialist countries to steer the economy in strict directions and markets were all controlled and manipulated. In socialist countries, central planning was the order of the day and economic freedom did not have a place. After 1949, the People's Republic of China has taken up a series of successive Five-Year Plans in organizing the centrally directed economic activities, concentrated on mainly heavy industries and production was organized according to a commune system. Wu (2005) pointed out that the two major problems of central planning are the high cost of obtaining all needed information in planning all economic activities, and the high incentive cost as the central plan integrated interests of the whole society and did not allow differences in value judgments. However, since economic reform in 1978, the essence of central planning has been moderated considerably. The method of formulation of the central plan has been modified to incorporate on-going social and economic changes. Since the sixth Five-Year Plan in 1980–1985, for example, central planning was retitled as the Five-Year Plan for Economic and Social Development.

Instead of directives, the planning process has become more open and standardized. The Five-year Plan was renamed as the Five-Year program since the 11th plan period in 2006–2010. The World Wild Fund in China pointed out that: 1) plan formulation has put forward development strategies instead of setting growth targets, and policies are made to meet the needs of governance reform and provision of public goods; 2) the plan has become more comprehensive, focusing on consistency and complementarity; 3) de-centralized decision making has been promoted to give local governments more autonomy in the formulation of local plans; 4) the planning process has been changed from a closed one to an open one, with a high degree of transparency and public participation; and 4) the planning process and procedures are increasingly becoming standardized.[32]

---

[32] "The 12th Five- Year Plan", World Wide Fund, China, 2008.

Economic planning has never been considered in Hong Kong. The free market has helped and brought success to the Hong Kong economy, making Hong Kong an envy of the world. The international community will never expect Hong Kong to take up central planning. However, Hong Kong does engage in long-term "plans" in the various economic and social spheres. A long-term infrastructure program is needed for a growing population and achievement of economic efficiency. A long-term agreement with Guangdong on the supply of fresh water has been in place for decades. The various long-term programs are translated into policies in Hong Kong that mostly look into the public sector in order to promote a more efficient private sector. Plans or programs directed to the private or business sectors are rare.

As the sovereign authority of Hong Kong, Mainland China can have the obligation and right to include Hong Kong in its Five-Year Plan. As the freest economy, it would be alarming to introduce central planning in Hong Kong. This has become a conflict between the royalty to the sovereign state and royalty to the "two systems". There has to be a compromise. Firstly, the nature of economic planning has changed considerably, and has drastically downplayed the original "central planning" aspect. Secondly, the sections that are relevant to Hong Kong should be meant as an indication of Hong Kong's economic achievement and direction of development, and should not be seen as a strict recipe for Hong Kong's future development. Thus, the idea is that it would be necessary for the central authority in Beijing to recognize and support Hong Kong's development and success. However, it does not mean that Hong Kong should only do what is written in the Five-Year Plan. The content should be seen more as a recognition and support than as a directive.

Hong Kong has been aiding the economic development in Mainland China, but of course, the mainland economy has achieved a lot on its own. The mainland economy and Hong Kong economy should increasingly be seen as partners in development, and influence each other on a bi-lateral, positive-sum basis. In other words, while the mainland economy can still be the investment target for Hong Kong businesses, increasingly Hong Kong will become the investment destination of mainland businesses. Hong Kong can definitely gain the share of the economic success of the mainland economy. To this end, it would be advantageous for Hong Kong to be included flexibly in the Five-Year Plan, so that Hong Kong can sail economically closer with the development in the mainland economy, taking every possible first business opportunity. Secondly, the Hong Kong economy is faced with structural rigidity in the post-economic recession years, and while it will take years to revise its economic structure, connecting and integrating economically closer with mainland businesses would definitely be seen as an advantage and opportunity in helping to revise and widen the Hong Kong economy.

Provided that Beijing is not using the Five-Year Plan as an instrument in deviating from the "one country, two systems" framework, it is wise to allow Hong Kong to share the economic success of the mainland economy. While Hong Kong is still a reference point for activities in the mainland economy, Hong Kong should also appear to be attractive for investment from mainland. Although Hong Kong's capital return has increased as a result of investment in Mainland China (Sung, 2004), the loss of investment in Hong Kong has probably resulted in the loss in jobs and a rise in unemployment in the short-run. Now that the mainland economy has grown to new heights, Hong Kong should in turn become the first destination of outward investment from Mainland China. New investment in Hong Kong could promote more jobs and opportunities.

Critics have warned and worried about the suitability of including Hong Kong in mainland's economic plans, fearing that the autonomous nature of Hong Kong's system will be compromised or eroded. The assumption of such an argument rests with the ability for the Hong Kong economy to make progress on its own. In other words, would the "leaning on mainland" be the only economic policy that Hong Kong depends, or the "two-legs" strategy would be more appropriate and effective with one leg involving the growing mainland economy and the other leg involving domestic progress through investment and job creation. While Hong Kong is gaining the benefit from the growing mainland economy, Hong Kong needs to restructure its own economy. Involving in the mainland economy should be seen more as a mean, while restructuring and promoting the Hong Kong economy is the ultimately end.

The Chief Executive, Tsang Yam-kuen, saw the advantage and need for Hong Kong to get attention in Mainland China's Five-Year Plan. In his various duty visits to Beijing, the Chief Executive has urged the central authority to engage Hong Kong in an early stage in their economic plan.[33] Perhaps, Beijing would be surprised to see the great initiative on the part of Hong Kong's Chief Executive in clamoring a position in the Five-Year Plan. An Economic Summit on "China's 11th Five-Year Plan and the Development of Hong Kong" was organized in early 2007 at the high official level, and key leaders in Hong Kong are grouped into four focus groups on: 1) trade and business; 2) financial services; 3) maritime, logistics and infrastructure; and 4) professional services, information and technology and tourism.[34]

In the 11th Five-Year Plan (2006–2010), Hong Kong's status was mentioned and endorsed by the National's People's Congress in 2006, but the content barely reiterated the support for Hong Kong in maintaining its position as an international financial, trade and logistics center. It would be unfortunate if policy makers in Hong Kong read the 11th Five-Year Plan only to interpret that those reiterations were all that Hong Kong could do or allowed to do. The 11th Five-Year Plan showed a similar level of support to both Hong Kong and Macau. In the case of Hong Kong, it is stated that Mainland China will unswervingly implement the principle of "one country, two systems", under which the people of Hong Kong shall administer Hong Kong with a high degree of autonomy and fully support Hong Kong in maintaining long-term prosperity and stability. Hong Kong's position as an international financial, trade and shipping center will be supported. Hong Kong shall develop its own industries with local advantages and new areas of growth shall be fostered.[35] The wordings in the 11th Five-Year Plan basically reconfirmed the economic position of Hong Kong, and in no way aimed to restrict Hong Kong's development. Hong Kong is free to conduct its own economic affairs, should not be limited to the current advantages and is urged to expand its economic scope at all directions possible.

---

[33] *South China Morning Post*, November 23, 2007; and December 5, 2009.

[34] Action agenda on "China's 11th Five-Year Plan and the Development of Hong Kong", Hong Kong, January 22, 2007.

[35] *The National 11th Five-Year Plan*, Beijing, March 2006.

The Hong Kong government has been active in getting involved in the 12th Five-Year Plan (2011–2015). The Constitutional and Mainland Affairs Bureau in Hong Kong announced on March 17, 2011, that a chapter in the National 12th Five-Year Plan will be dedicated to Hong Kong and Macau, the two Special Administrative Regions of Mainland China. The dedicated chapter shall elaborate on the "significant functions and positioning of Hong Kong in the development strategy of the country". The overall strategy for Hong Kong, according to the Chief Executive, is "the strong support for maintaining the long-term prosperity and stability of Hong Kong" and "enables Hong Kong to decide… our development directions, policies and measures that complement the overall national development strategies".

There are three major areas in the dedicated chapter: a) support Hong Kong in consolidating and enhancing its competitive advantages, including consolidating and enhancing Hong Kong's position as an international financial, trade and shipping center, and develop an offshore Renminbi business center and an international asset management center; b) support for Hong Kong in nurturing emerging industries and developing the six industries where Hong Kong enjoys clear advantages; c) support for deepening the economic cooperation between the Mainland and Hong Kong, continuing the implementation of CEPA and confirming the significant functions and positioning of the Hong Kong — Guangdong cooperation, including the establishment of a financial cooperation zone and a world-class metropolitan cluster with Hong Kong's financial system taking the lead, and opening up the Guangdong service industries for Hong Kong on a pilot basis and extending the pilot scheme to other regions.[36]

One can summarize these three major areas as the support on Hong Kong's comparative advantages, on Hong Kong in furthering its advantages through cooperation and on Hong Kong in leading the region in various businesses and services. In short, it is not a central plan directed to Hong Kong, but a confirmation on the role of Hong Kong in its economic development, its contribution to the country and its leading role in regional cooperation. The content of the National 12th Five-Year Plan allowed Hong Kong to have a firm economic role in national development, both contributing to and gaining from economic advances of the mainland economy. Armed with the advantages from the national plan, Hong Kong shall have ample opportunity to engage and expand its own economic advantages.[37]

The three features of the National 12th Five-Year Plan have also been incorporated importantly into the 2010–2011 Policy Address.[38] To reaffirm Beijing's support on Hong Kong's role in national development, the Vice Premier, Li Keqiang in his visit to Hong Kong in August 2011 specified once again a total of 6 measures in supporting the economic development of Hong Kong. They are: 1) expand services and trade between Hong Kong and Mainland China, and further open up of services for Hong Kong businesses in medical services, legal service, construction

[36] Press release, "Chapter in National Five-Year Plan dedicated to Hong Kong and Macao", Constitutional and Mainland Affairs Bureau, Hong Kong, March 16, 2011.

[37] The research division of the Bank of China in Hong Kong has regularly reported on the content and analysis of the National Five-Year Plan.

[38] 2010–2011 Policy Address by Chief Executive, October 13, 2010.

industry, tourism and disease control; 2) promote Hong Kong's international financial center, permitting a greater capital flow between mainland and Hong Kong; 3) promoting Hong Kong as the fully Renminbi offshore center, including the open up of the mainland stock for foreign investment with a limit of Rmb 20 billion, issuing Renminbi treasury bills in Hong Kong; 4) supporting Hong Kong's further involvement in international and regional economic cooperation; 5) promoting Hong Kong in attracting investment, information and training services; and 6) supporting Hong Kong in regional development.[39]

There are a few implications on the measures announced by Vice Premier Li Keqiang. In the financial area, cross-border trade settlement in Renminbi will be extended from 20 cities to the entire mainland economy. In a country's balance of payment, there are two major accounts. The trade balance account shows the balance in exports and imports of goods and services. A trade surplus will appear in the trade balance positively. The other account is the capital account that records the entry and exit of capital funds. Portfolio investment and foreign direct investment will be recorded in the capital account. Cross-border trade settlement deals with the trade account. The open up of a currency, or full convertibility, implies freedom of currency movement in both trade and capital accounts. By allowing Hong Kong to be the offshore Renminbi trading center and the permission for the use of Renminbi in the two-way investment, Mainland China has basically decided to open up its capital account for Hong Kong investors. Renminbi will largely be allowed to enter and exit Hong Kong freely. This necessarily means a decrease in the control of capital flow from mainland to Hong Kong. This shall be seen as an experiment in the steps leading to the open up and full convertibility of the Renminbi. Secondly, Hong Kong is allowed to be more active in international and regional economic cooperation. Although this has not been featured extensively, one implication is that Hong Kong can participate more fully in economic cooperation within other domains, such as the Asia Pacific Economic Cooperation (APEC). Although Hong Kong is a member of APEC, permission from Beijing is needed if Hong Kong wanted to host the APEC in any particular year in future. APEC members are allowed to take turn to host the APEC on an annual basis. Since the ministerial meeting of the World Trade Organization (WTO) in Hong Kong in 2005, Hong Kong has not been active in regional and international activities.

14.9 Exporting Freedom?

In many ways, the essence of the three Mainland China — Hong Kong agreements (Five-Year Plan, CEPA and Pan-PRD) has a similar theme. Hong Kong is destined to aid the economic development of Mainland China at various levels. The CEPA encourages firms, especially services and professionals, to start business in Mainland China, thereby transferring the various 'software' in management, professional standards and ethics, and market disciplines to businesses in mainland. The pan-PRD aims to involve Hong Kong in regional development, especially in urbanization,

---

[39] Various new and press releases in Hong Kong, August 17, 2011; *South China Morning Post*, August 18, 2011.

removal of informal economic activities and alignment in the quality of life. The Five-Year Plan provides a framework through which economic involvement are conducted at the national level, such as the Renminbi offshore center.

Despite the rapid growth of the mainland economy since the early 1980s, the role of Hong Kong in fostering and facilitating growth and development in Mainland China has not changed; it only differed in dimensions and directions. Since Mainland China's economic reform, one can argue that Hong Kong's aid typically in the form of direct and portfolio investment is the 'hardware' that provided visible and quantifiable assistance to the mainland economy.

Obviously, the cross-border activities have expanded far beyond simply investments. When Shenzhen first opened up as mainland's Special Economic Zone, Hong Kong people have been patronizing the various activities in both the formal and informal sectors. With the rising value of Renminbi and the wealth of the people in Mainland China, the table has turned. The visa-free travel policy has allowed mainland residents to come to Hong Kong for their visit and travel. With the greater degree of market openness, Hong Kong industries and services are allowed to set up either joint-venture or wholly-owned enterprises in mainland. The greater integration of people, businesses and investment have allowed mainland residents to learn and know more about Hong Kong, its various ways of life, systemic differences and advantages, ethical standards and professional practices. Of course, Hong Kong residents are also finding ways to learn and understand more about the motherland. In short, Hong Kong has provided lessons of freedom to mainland residents, allowing them to know more about what a civic free society, though not perfect, is like. The lessons on economic freedom serve as the 'software' in the economic integration between the mainland economy and Hong Kong.

The "one country, two systems" and the "one country, two currencies" frameworks provide ample alternatives and opportunities for further reform in Mainland China, as it is unique in the world economy. No other country in the world would have complementary alternatives in their path of reform, development and growth. Hong Kong is destined to aid development in Mainland China, and while the various agreements on integration related mainly to the mainland economy, Hong Kong equally needs to know more about the mainland, needs to upgrade and uplift its development and drive to civic freedom, including political freedom in the course of time. The Hong Kong economy is not and will not be a periphery to the mainland economy, and will not be marginalized in the process of development in the mainland economy. The further growth and development in Mainland China will not lead to a diminishing role of Hong Kong. The benefit to the mainland economy from the various "comparative advantages" Hong Kong processes outweighs the disadvantages arising from the "absolute disadvantage" position of Hong Kong in the national context.

Armed with economic freedom and its further promotion, Hong Kong's survival is not only ensured, but serves as references and lessons and practices for the future development of Mainland China. The growth of the mainland economy should be considered as a stimulant to the further development of freedom in Hong Kong. A stronger civic free economy and a more diversified Hong Kong can better serve the mainland economy. In growth terms, the mainland economy will outgrow Hong Kong, given the enormous size difference and diversity. Thus, one expects Shanghai and other key cities in Mainland China to grow faster than Hong Kong in various dimensions. A more economically matured Mainland China will serve the international community more effectively, and Hong Kong will have a greater role and usefulness in the process. Economic freedom is the insurance policy for Hong Kong. To continue to enjoy the insurance policy, Hong Kong has to do more, promote and deepen the various aspects of economic freedom. The different aspects of economic integration with the mainland economy encourage Hong Kong to serve as the conveyor or messenger of freedom and at the same time need to engage in a process of self-assessment in the road to freedom.

Indeed, Hong Kong has exported freedom and provided lessons and showed the context of economic freedom to other neighboring and emerging economies. While some have argued about the substitution effect on the loss investment in Hong Kong as a result of funds invested in Mainland China, evidences show that a more economically successful mainland economy will in turn serve Hong Kong, enriching Hong Kong in various aspects of development. Being a small, flexible and relative efficient economy, the economic success of Hong Kong usually flows with economic situations in other parts of the world. At the same time, major blows of economic crisis in other parts of the world also affect Hong Kong considerably, especially the key trading economies.

15 The Free Civic Model

15.1 Introduction

People who are concerned about Hong Kong, such as the late Professor Milton Friedman, remark that Hong Kong has experienced many kinds of freedom except political freedom. Western observers probably are referring to a system of full political democracy and universal suffrage with a "one person one vote" in periodic elections. As a British colony, free political elections were absent, but partial direct election began since the mid-1980s. Instead, the presence of an effective and efficient government was considered appropriate in conducting economic and social affairs. The British governors in Hong Kong were mostly Sinologists and held the view that Hong Kong should remain as an economic-oriented territory. This has an advantage of administrative convenience and efficiency. British Sinologists played a major part in the 1982–1984 Sino-British negotiation and the drafting of the Basic Law over the political future of post-1997 Hong Kong. Lord David Wilson of Tillyorn (Hong Kong Governor, April 1987–July 1992) and the late Sir Percy Cradock (British Ambassador to the People's Republic of China, 1978–1983), for example, strongly believed that steering up public political elections in Hong Kong would displease the central government in Beijing. Political changes and participation in elections in Hong Kong have been infrequent until the last British governor, Christopher Francis Patten (Hong Kong Governor, July 1992–June 1997) who took up a professional politician approach, advocated more democracy and considered political change as a cushion in ensuring Hong Kong's status.

Much intellectual discussion has concentrated on the difference between democracy and freedom. One interpretation is that democracy provides political freedom, typically being exercised through periodic free elections. Universal suffrage in a "one person one vote" system would appear to be fair, open, equal and transparent. In the post-1997 Hong Kong, although for administrative reasons, voters are required to register for the right to vote, that effectively has reduced the voting population considerably as the registered population would surely be substantially smaller than the total population, thereby removing the right to vote for the unregistered portion of the population. Political freedom is important as it allows people to choose their political leaders periodically.

However, the results of any political election and the performance of the elected leader usually appeared in an *ex post* situation, namely that the successful candidate or elected leader could not be judged before the leaders take office. In all political elections, the performance of the elected leader could only be seen after being elected to the office, and how good the achievement or relevant the work was done would only be seen after the elected leader was in office. In other words, the success of any political election could only be judged on an *ex post* basis. The result of any election could never be judged on an *ex ante* basis.

In a political matured country with full universal suffrage, democracy and periodic political elections serve to ensure that elected leaders perform according to their promises and statements made in their manifestos. Hence, although elections have never been judged on an *ex ante* basis, voters can always choose on an *ex post* basis in the next election to re-elect the same person for the second time or remove and choose a new candidate. Democracy and political freedom thus allow the voters to monitor the performance of the elected leaders. The presence of different political parties provide a choice for the voters in political freedom, though in modern economies, political elections are expensive and often require mobilization of large financial resources.

Freedom is a broader concept and covers all kinds of freedom. In a wholly free society, political freedom is only one aspect of freedom. One feature of political election, though it is an exercise of democracy, is the extent of divisiveness between voters, parties, ethnics and a host of other issues. Changes in the society may go along political lines rather than due to genuine needs. Secondly, political election always carries an "absolute outcome", with one party winning and another losing. In democratic but political immature societies, the loser in a so-called democratic election may not be willing to give up political power and authority, and elections might end up in *coup d'états*, or the military junta may interfere to remove a certain elected leader, belittling the very fundamental principle of democracy. Hence, democracy as a form of political freedom in politically immature societies might also be abused.

In politically matured societies, victors and losers in an election would respect the election system and accept the election outcome. The loser in an election would return to a normal and professional life and would not have any personal political repercussions. Voters are free to choose their political candidates. The "absolute outcome" of an election could then be softened into a "relative outcome" when voters are free to exercise their political right in future elections. In other words, voters are also free to vote out the candidate in the next round of election.

Other than political freedom, the presence and exercise of other aspects of freedom would act as a buffer to guard against political abuse or abuse of administrative power by the leader. The presence of a large number of professional associations, unions and ethnic-oriented associations, religious bodies, chambers of commerce, civic institutions and establishments will provide and define the standards, qualities and practices of various civic behaviors and ethical requirements. Civic freedom can be seen as the totality of individual freedom, as the presence of institutions could serve as a bridge, buffer or cushion between the ruler and the ruled. The presence of civic institutions thus provides a balance between the interests of the leaders and the public at large. While political leaders would steer the society in a certain direction, the civic institutions shall ensure that other voices are heard, standards are set and other societal interests are served. Since civic institutions tend to be apolitical and focus more on the professional standards and practices, various qualities concerning professional judgments can then be ensured. Civic institutions can therefore act as intermediaries that serve the people better, providing qualitative performance in a large number of civic activities.

As the freest economy, Hong Kong has a short history of political democracy, but all kinds of civic institutions have extensively been established over the years, and many civic institutions have earned their trust of the public and have served the society well as a guard against politics and other forms of coercion and victimization. A high degree of fair and equal participation can be seen, though there is still room for improvements in ensuring that civic development advances along with economic development. Political movements and activities have been increased, especially since sovereignty reversion in 1997; the danger of an over-politicized Hong Kong could hopefully be safeguarded by the strong presence of impartiality among civic institutions. Civic freedom in Hong Kong would be hurt if civic institutions had become politically oriented, thereby serving only sections of the public with rested interest. While political changes are taking place along with civic development, civic freedom in Hong Kong is the ultimate form of freedom, and it can be maintained only if civic establishments remain apolitical and professionally oriented.

The following sections will elaborate on the free civic model that incorporates political organizations. The Hong Kong experience in civic establishments and political changes are discussed in the latter sections. Civic freedom is the ultimate form of individual freedom, as civic establishments serve as the "go-between" between the state and the people. The sophisticated form of civic development can ensure individual protection.

15.2 Political Freedom Versus Civic Freedom

The relationship between political freedom and civic freedom can broadly be discussed from the three scenarios shown in Figure 15.1. In all the three scenarios, the top section represents the state (the ruler) that composes of the government and the different branches of the administration whose main function is to rule the territory. The bottom portion of the three scenarios shows the people that represents the public and the mass population (the ruled). In between the state and the people, the political system and the civic system will serve different functions. The arrows indicate the two-way connections. The political system consists mainly of political parties, pressure groups and labor unions. The civic system consists of a host of civic institutions that range from professional associations (lawyers, accountants, medical doctors, surveyors, engineers, etc.), chambers of commerce that represent different types of trades and businesses, functional establishments (anti-corruption commissions, religious bodies, sports associations, ethnical associations, youth clubs, environmental groups, charities, etc.), academic institutions and think tanks and to other establishments serving different public interests.

Scenario (a) in Figure 15.1 shows a situation in which the political system and civic system are independent from each other, though there can be connections between the two systems as indicated by the horizontal arrows. In scenario (a), freedom between the two systems is of parallel importance, each will exercise its own influence but both serve as intermediaries between the state and the people. The political system exercises democracy and political freedom through periodic elections

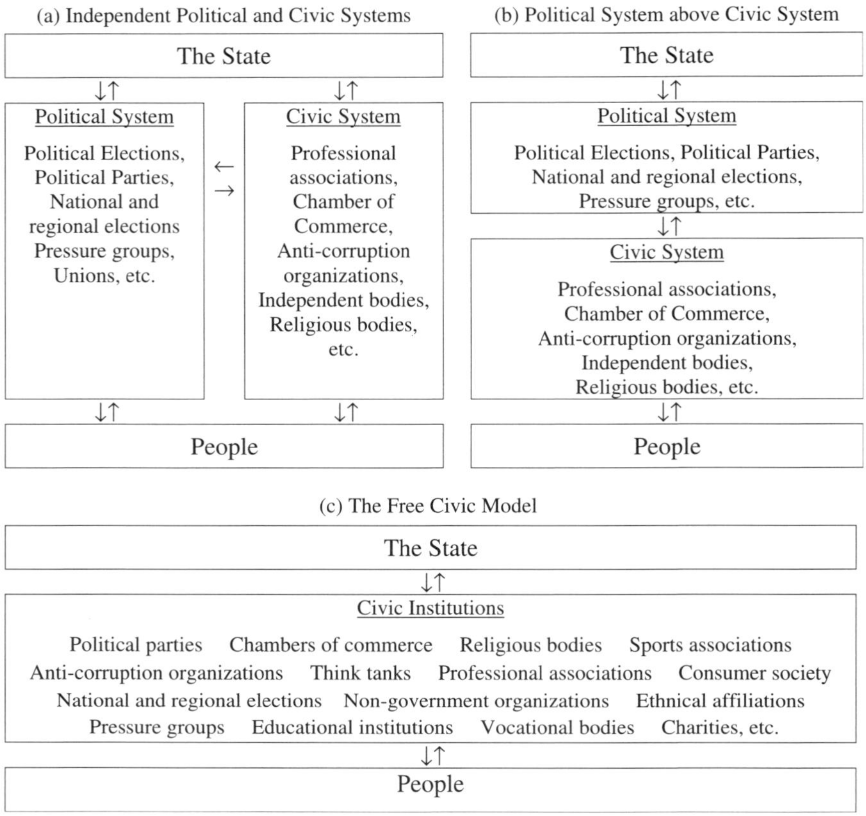

FIGURE 15.1 Scenarios of political system and civic system

independently, while the civic system takes care of other professional and civic-related activities that aim to maintain civic standards and freedom.

Scenario (b) in Figure 15.1 shows a slightly different priority between the political and civic system. The emphasis is given to political freedom, and the political system is considered to be more important than other civic-related activities. While civic-related activities are largely non-political and involve mainly professional associations, the political system is considered to be superior to the civic system, although politicians have other professional relationships in the civic system. For example, many politicians come from the legal background, or members of the cabinet compose of professionals from different walks of life. In scenario (b), activities tend to be more politics-oriented and government decisions shall be sensitive to political orientations. Decisions on public policy tend to have a strong political favor; and political goals are considered prior to civic goals.

The free civic system shown in scenario (c) of Figure 15.1 does not make a distinction between the political system and the civic system. Since political freedom is one aspect of civic freedom, political activities are incorporated into the civic system and become another civic activity. Party politics and periodic elections are part of a broader spectrum of civic-related activities. Political organizations are considered as another form of civic institutions, and they all contribute to the society at different pace and dimension. Indeed, political and civic organizations together can become a stronger institutional body that acts as a check and balance on the activities and decisions of the government and its administration.

There are a number of advantages in the free civic model elaborated in Figure 15.1(c). One clear advantage is the removal of the unintended consequences of divisiveness in political activities. Extreme political acts and views that might hurt the stability of the economy and society can be avoided, bringing a higher degree of social harmony conducive to employment, business development and economic advancement. Secondly, political institutions also need time to gain experience and become mature. Developing and maturing along with other civic institutions allow political institutions and activities to integrate more with other civic developments, rather than sharpening the need for political activities. This can avoid the urge to make political decisions for the sake of political demands, which often are fragmented and characterized by rested interests.

Thirdly, civic institutions are less likely to be politics-oriented and can adhere more to professional standards and strong ethical requirements. The public at large can be more ready to listen to professional and impartial opinions than politics-oriented, or even biased, ideas. The civic system that incorporates political changes provides equality and balance between different political divisions and affiliations, as other civic institutions provide sound approaches and judgments in dealing with societal problems. In short, political changes are diluted with other changes in civic activities and behavior, thereby making political changes a more acceptable and gradual process of civic development. There is of course no perfection in the civic system. The relevant concern is that the achievement of freedom is also an on-going process. Civic freedom is a mean that has to be improved along with other aspects of human development. The achievement of civic freedom requires a building block approach with on-going and dynamic changes. With constant changes and improvements, civic freedom can only move in a forward direction.

15.3 The Civic Society

According to Wikipedia, a civic society is "composed of the totality of voluntary civic and social organizations and institutions that form the basis of a functioning society as opposed to the force-backed structures of a state (regardless of that state's political system) and commercial institutions". A similar concept is known as a "stakeholder society" where public services are run not by the government, but by groups of people who benefit from the activities and nurture civic virtues. The study by Cohen and Arato (1997) discusses the "general economy" that is fair, accountable, equitable, democratic and justice-oriented. On the question of a civic society, numerous other research studies have been conducted within the disciplines of political science and sociology. In a free economy, a healthy development of civic society and institutions can help to fill the gap or act as a buffer zone between the government, individual and businesses.

Examples of civic institutions provided by Wikipedia include: (1) non-governmental organizations (NGOs); (2) private voluntary organizations (PVOs); (3) non-profit organizations (NPOs); (4) community-based organizations; (5) intermediary organizations for the voluntary and non-profit sector; (6) community foundations; (7) community leadership development programs; (8) civic clubs; (9) trade unions; (10) gender, cultural, and religious groups; (11) charities; (12) social and sports clubs; (13) cooperatives; (14) environmental groups; (15) professional associations; (16) academia; (17) businesses; (18) policy institutions; (19) consumer organizations; (18) the media; (19) citizens' militia; (20) religious organizations; (21) civic groups; (22) community organizations; and (23) clubs.

Professional associations

Professional associations probably have formed the largest group of civic institutions in Hong Kong. Shafer and Owsen (2003) point out that "the most basic functions of any professional association are the self-regulation of its members and the support of individual professional members". An efficient and transparent system of self-regulation of any profession is an important feature in a free economy, as professional associations can set standards that avoid close monitoring by the bureaucrats. As professional institutions promote effective standards and development in line with other aspects in the development of economy, these associations effectively have served not only their own profession but also the public at large.

All professional associations carry a code of ethics and conducts by which all members are vowed to abide, covering the quality of professional work, personal integrity and responsibility to the society. The goals of professional association compose of reputation and mission. Founded in 2001, for example, the Hong Kong Coalition of Professional Services (HKCPS) stated that Hong Kong professionals could make great contribution to national development and the growth of Hong Kong through their professional skills, codes of ethics, conducts of professional services, and the experience of international practices in professional service provision. In addition, a series of professional qualification examinations that acted as an entry barrier to the industry is also considered as a tool to safeguard the quality of services in accountancy, for example. A unique punishment mechanism in each profession has been placed to ensure that professional members could lose their right to practice if they lost their membership. Medical associations and lawyers are common examples.

Professional ethics is about the conduct of behavior and practice when professionals carry out their professional work. The institutionalization of codes of conduct and codes of practice is common with many professional bodies for their members to observe. These codes are indeed a formalization of past experience into a set of rules, and members accept adherence to these rules, including restrictions that apply. The codes are usually concerned with the issues, including honesty, adherence to confidentiality agreements, handling of human subjects, impartiality in professional consulting, accountability and resolution of conflicts of interest. Professional ethics also concerns with matters such as professional indemnity. Given certain variations in cultural group, profession and discipline, there is an existence of some universal ethical principles. A code of ethics has functional significance: (1) it defines the ideals and responsibilities of the profession; (2) its regulatory effect protects both clients and professionals; (3) it improves the profile of the profession; (4) it acts as a motivation and inspiration of practitioners; (5) it provides guidance on acceptable conduct; (6) it raises awareness and consciousness of issues; and (7) it improves quality and consistency.

The HKCPA comprises a total of ten high-level professions in Hong Kong. The Hong Kong Institute of Certified Public Accountants (HKICPA) is incorporated by the Professional Accountants Ordinances in 1973, and is the only statutory licensing body of accountants in Hong Kong responsible for regulation of the accountancy profession. Its mission is to serve the accountancy profession and the public through an efficient and transparent system of self-regulation and effective professional development. The HKICPA provides necessary training to become a Certified Public Accountant (CPA).

Renamed in 1972, the Hong Kong Institute of Architects (HKIA) was founded in 1956 as the Hong Kong Society of Architects. It aims at raising the standard of architecture and the standard of professional service provided by its members. It serves as an advisory role to the government and the building industry by applying the collective expertise of members.

The Hong Kong Bar Association (HKBA) was founded in 1949 as the professional organization of barristers in Hong Kong. It sets out rules and regulations and takes proper actions on all matters affecting the legal profession and the administration of justice.

The Hong Kong Dental Association Limited (HKDA) was renamed in 1973 from the Hong Kong Dental Society established in 1950. It aims at representing the dental profession in the formulation of dental policy and in international and mainland dental organizations as a regional dental association, setting the standard of ethics of the profession and reviewing legislation in relation to dentistry in Hong Kong.

The Hong Kong Institution of Engineers (HKIE) was founded in 1947, formerly known as the Engineering Society of Hong Kong before 1975. It aims at promoting the advancement of engineering and facilitating the exchange of knowledge and ideas, providing a broad range of services to members, assisting them in developing their careers and to play a full role in contributing to society, maintaining a high standard of the profession and raising the standing and visibility of engineers.

The Law Society of Hong Kong (HKLS) is a professional association for practicing solicitors in Hong Kong incorporated in 1907 as a company limited by guarantee. It aims at promoting high standards of work and ethical practice in the profession, ensuring compliance with laws and rules affecting solicitors, guiding solicitors on matters relating to professional practice matters and helping them to develop their practices, presenting the views of the profession to the government and other organizations, and providing services to its members.

The Hong Kong Institute of Landscape Architects (HKILA) was founded in 1998 as the professional body for those engaged in the practice of landscape architecture in Hong Kong. It aims at promoting the highest standard in landscape architecture and management. It promotes design excellence by organizing annual design awards and encouraging the participation of landscape architects in major design competition schemes and large scale development projects.

The Hong Kong Medical Association (HKMA) was founded in 1920 and was formerly called the Hong Kong Chinese Medical Association. It aims at maintaining and improving standards of medical practice in Hong Kong and fostering friendly relations both professionally and socially amongst all registered doctors in Hong Kong. It represents the medical profession both locally and internationally and maintains a close link with international counterparts for exchanges views and experience in policy and professional matters. The Hong Kong Institute of Planners was officially started in 1978. In 1991, it became a statutory body with the enactment of the Hong Kong Institute of Planners Incorporation Ordinance 1991 by the Legislative Council. It represents the planning profession in Hong Kong. It aims at promoting and safeguarding development and the environment in Hong Kong in the best interests of the community, raising the status and safeguarding the interests of the town planning profession, promoting the community's awareness of the contribution of town planning and education and research in town planning.

The Hong Kong Institute of Surveyors (HKIS) was established in 1984 as the only professional organization representing the surveying profession in Hong Kong. Its work includes setting standards for professional services and performance, establishing codes of ethics, determining requirements for admission as professional surveyors, and encouraging members to upgrade skills through continuing professional development.

Other reputable professional institutions include Hong Kong Confederation of Insurance Brokers (HKCIB), Professional Insurance Brokers Association (PIBA), Association of Chartered Certified Accountants (ACCA), Association for Investment Management and Research (AIMR), British Institute of Architectural Technologists — Hong Kong Centre (BIAT), Chartered Institute of Building (Hong Kong), Chartered Institute of Marketing (CIM) Hong Kong Branch, Hong Kong Association of Accounting Technicians (HKAAT), Hong Kong Institute of Company Secretaries (HKICS), Hong Kong Institute of Housing, Hong Kong Institute of Real Estate Administration, Hong Kong International Arbitration Centre (HKIAC), Hong Kong Physiotherapy Association, Hong Kong Securities Institute (HKSI), Institute of Clerks of Works (ICW), Institution of Incorporated Engineers (IIE), Institute of Linguists, Hong Kong Institute of Marketing, Pharmaceutical Society of Hong Kong, City and Guilds International Limited, Hong Kong Institution of Textile and Apparel (HKITA), Hong Kong Physiotherapists' Union, Hong Kong Council of Social Services, Hong Kong Social Workers' General Union, Hong Kong Social Workers Association, Hong Kong Journalists Association and Hong Kong Institute of Construction Managers.

In the business sector, there are a large number of chambers of commerce. Founded in 1861, the Hong Kong General Chamber of Commerce is the oldest and largest business organization in Hong Kong. It acts as the members' voice in advising the government on matters affecting businesses and the economy, providing members with business information and opportunities, and facilitating networking through a variety of activities. Other larger local chambers include the Chinese

General Chamber of Commerce. Virtually all foreign businesses have established their chamber of commerce in Hong Kong. These foreign chambers of commerce serve as a bridge between local businesses and businesses from respective countries. Key examples include the American Chamber of Commerce, Canadian Chamber of Commerce, British Chamber of Commerce, Japan Chamber of Commerce, French Chamber, Australia Chamber of Commerce and many others.

Voluntary welfare organizations, green groups and trade unions

Welfare organizations:

Voluntary welfare organizations have occupied a major role in Hong Kong's welfare provision. In the early period of the colony, basic welfare provision was mainly left to Chinese civic groups and religious organizations. Wealthy businessmen and foreign missionaries provided a lot of support. Due to the various civil wars in China at different time periods, a large number of refugees had settled down in Hong Kong. Voluntary welfare activities began with the support of overseas organizations and aid agencies. It was only since 1970s that the government became the main welfare financier. The Po Leung Kuk and Tung Wah Group of Hospitals are two large local organizations founded in early colonial years that still operate until now. Founded in 1878 with the aim of caring for the young and protecting the innocent, the Po Leung Kuk has over the century gradually evolved into a more diversified organization responding to the social and economic changes. The Tung Wah Hospital was constructed and started to provide service in 1872. In 1911 and 1929, Kwong Wah Hospital and Tung Wah Eastern Hospital were built and commenced operation, respectively. These three hospitals were amalgamated into the Tung Wah Group of Hospitals under one Board of Directors. The Tung Wah Group of Hospitals has now developed into a well-established charitable organization with medical and health services, education services and community services.

Other key welfare organizations include the Community Chest, which is an independent, non-profit making organization founded in 1968 to raise funds for all social welfare agencies. The Lion Clubs International District 303 — Hong Kong and Macau District is an international service organization founded by a small group of local business club members in Chicago, USA, in 1917. The Hong Kong and Macau District was formed in 1960–1961 to encourage service minded people to serve their community without personal reward or gain and to serve by giving sympathy to others in distress, aid to the weak and the needy. The Salvation Army (Hong Kong and Macau Command) is an international Christian and charitable organization commenced its services in Hong Kong in 1930 by the invitation of the government. It provided comprehensive services to meet the needs of body, soul and mind, including religious services, social services, education services, emergency relief work, recycling program and lodging services. The Hong Kong Red Cross was established in 1950 with the mission of protecting human life, caring for the health of the vulnerable, and respecting human dignity. It provided blood transfusion service, camp service, first aid and health courses, disasters relief and development. Established in 1960, the Samaritan Befrienders Hong Kong is a local voluntary agency run by volunteer workers. Its mission is to befriend, on humanitarian grounds, people who are facing difficulties or are lonely and depressed, helping them to regain confidence in life.

Green groups:

Due to the need to protect the environment, the green groups have become strong pressure groups in many economies. In Hong Kong, a number of debates on the "green" issue have turned political (Yip and Loh, 2008). The macroeconomic concern is that while most people and the government would adhere to a green environment, one has to remember that Hong Kong is a highly populated metropolis, and the welfare and economic survival of the population takes precedence over other issues. Environmental protection is needed to ensure a clean, livable and sustainable environment, but equally, one should not take up the environmental protection excessively at the expense of ensuring welfare development and employment growth for everyone in Hong Kong. One has to watch out for "green protectionism" that advocates the need of conservation at the expense of improvement in employment opportunities and provision in economic security. The green groups often act as pressure groups, including the World Wide Fund that has the mission to conserve the world's biological diversity and the sustainable use of renewable natural resources, the Green Power that concerns local environmental problems, the Friends of the Earth which dedicates to protecting the environment locally and regionally by engaging government, business and society in promoting solutions to create environmentally sustainable public policies, business practices and life-styles, and the Conservancy Association which dedicates to the protection of the environment and the conservation of natural and cultural heritages.

Trade unions:

A trade union is an intermediary agent that serves as a bridge between the workers and business or government organizations. They are usually independent non-government organizations (NGOs) which focus on labor concerns and promote workers' rights and democratic labor movements. Their underlying principles usually included labor rights, freedom of association, and right to collective bargaining, elimination of forced labor and child labor, and abolition of discrimination at work, gender consciousness and active participation by employees. To help workers become truly empowered, the trade unions would provide workers with access to information, tools, and engage in strategies to help organizing labor movements in a changing society, in an attempt to improve workers' livelihood in the long-run. Another feature of trade unions in Hong Kong is that, rather than formally declaring themselves as labor parties; the corresponding groups indeed monitor and actively take part in public policy making process.

In Hong Kong, there is a strong tie between trade unions and political views and orientations. For example, the Hong Kong Confederation of Trade Unions is pro-democracy while the Hong Kong Federation of Trade Unions is pro-China and raising the public awareness of patriotism is one of their missions. However, the opposing political view does not mean that there is a disagreement between the two main camps of activists in fighting for the interests of workers. Sector-wide trade unions included the Hong Kong Confederation of Trade Unions (HKCTU), which was founded in 1990, that brought together democratic and independent trade unions committed to fighting for the rights and interests of workers. At present, it has about 180,000 members and 87 affiliates, engaging in a wide range of activities, including industry and workplace organizing, public campaigns, lobbying, workers' education, legal assistance for workers, legal representation in labor disputes, and retraining for unemployed workers. It campaigns for universal suffrage and the realization of genuine democratic rights.

The Hong Kong Federation of Trade Unions (HKFTU) was founded in 1948 with initially 22 affiliated unions and membership of 20,000. As of March 2008, it has 176 affiliated unions and 49 associated unions, representing about 300,000 people from all walks of life. Its mission is in guiding labor movements and developing organization of workers, raising the public awareness of patriotism, fighting for workers' interests and improving their livelihood, and taking part in public policy making process. Established in 1984, the Federation of Hong Kong and Kowloon Labor Unions (FLU) has become a federation of 64 affiliated unions and 10 sponsoring associations with membership exceeding 40,000. Its mission is "banding together the working class, striving for reasonable rights, participating in democratic reform, promoting prosperity of society".

Other influential unions are the Hong Kong Social Workers' General Union, which was established in 1980 with the mission to solidify the workers, to fight for their rights, to improve their services, and to support justice. It concerned the impact on workers' entry and advancement opportunities resulting from the contraction on resources, fights for the deserved treatment, lobbies and negotiates with the government in various activities for workers' rights. Trainings are provided to improve the standard of workers' profession. It also concerned democratic development, people's livelihood, freedom and justice of the society. The Hong Kong Construction Industry Employees General Union (HKCIEGU) was established at 1986, uniting 18 subsidiary groups in the construction industry. In recent years after the burst of property bubble in 1997, HKCIEGU has gained much exposure in the newspapers because of the serious unemployment problem and frequent disputes between workers and contractors in industry.

Policy institutions and advocacy groups

Policy institutions exist to ensure that the government policies can be improved. Since 1997, there has been a growing trend in the development of public policy organizations and advocacy groups formed mostly by a group of academics, researchers, business people, unionists and key community personalities. While they are mostly non-profit making, policy institutions provide research outcomes supposedly as input to government policy making. In constructing a public policy, the government often listened to the views and research findings of policy and advocacy groups.

However, there are a number of observations among the numerous policy institutions and advocacy groups established in Hong Kong in recent years. Many are still in their infant stage with a short history of development, fragmented and not organized as a full fetched corporate. The organizers and office bearers in many policy institutions have strong ties with key personalities in Hong Kong, such as the second generation of business tycoons. Most policy institutions and advocacy groups are visibly affiliated to certain political groups, parties or even individual personalities or leaders. Consequently, even though they have proposed views and opinions, their impartiality has often been queried. Many considered themselves as "think tanks" for the post-1997 government, providing viable options to public policies.

Since 2006, the *Think Tank Index* conducted by McGann (2011) at the University of Pennsylvania in the United States has created a process for ranking think tanks around the world, using worldwide surveys from 1,500 scholars, policy makers, journalists and regional and subject area experts. In the 2010 index, all 6,480 think tanks in the world were contacted. The construction of the *Think Tank Index* provided recognition to the leading public policy think tanks in the world and "highlight the important contributions these organizations are making to governments and civil societies around the world" (McGann, 2011:5). The ranking provided a close examination on the think tanks in the world as well as in each major region. According to the 2010 *Think Tank Index*, Hong Kong has a total of 27 think tanks, while China has 425 think tanks. Singapore has 6 think tanks. Japan and South Korea have has 52 and 35 think tanks, respectively.

A total of 75 think tanks have been nominated as the leading think tanks in the world, including the Adam Smith Institute, Chatham House (Royal Institute of International Affairs) and Human Rights Watch in the United Kingdom, and the Brookings Institutions, Cato Institute, Heritage Foundation and the Peterson Institute for International Economics in the United States, and the Fraser Institute in Canada. Think tanks from China, Japan, South Korea and Singapore have been included in the top 75 think tanks. On the regional basis, among the top 25 think tanks in Asia, the only think tank from Hong Kong is the Hong Kong Centre for Economic Research (HKCER) in the University of Hong Kong, which ranked 14th in the Asia region behind thank tanks from China, Japan, India, Indonesia, Australia and South Korea. It can be seen that despite Hong Kong's strong civic development, there is much room for think tanks to develop into an impartial, visible, regional and global institution.

The recently developed policy institutions and advocacy groups in Hong Kong included the Bauhinia Foundation Research Centre, which is a non-profit-making research center founded in 2006 to focus on Hong Kong's long-term competitiveness and its socio-economic wellbeing. The Savantas Policy Institute is a think-tank founded in 2006 by a Hong Kong group studying or working in the US. Its core vision is Hong Kong's transformation into a knowledge-based economy with quality democracy. It emphasizes on the importance of knowledge, science and technology-based innovation, the impact of globalization in economic growth, and greater understanding of democratic ideals, values and culture. The SynergyNet is an intellectual and political network established in 2002 by a group of intellectuals and professionals from the academic, business, social service and political sectors firmly rooted in Hong Kong. It aims to synergize various forces in society, to rearticulate public opinion and to push for rational social dialogues that lead to institutional reforms, policy renewals and vision building, to respond to the challenges brought by the principle of "self-governing" in Hong Kong. Civic Exchange is an independent Hong Kong-based public policy think-tank established in 2000. Its mission is to promote civic education amongst members of the community and to conduct related research and publicize the results in order to provide objective and balanced information to the public concerning economic, social and environmental issues. The Lion Rock Institute was founded in 2004 with a concern for the future of Hong Kong. The Institute aims at having a direct and demonstrable impact on government policy, educating policy makers, active political participants and the general public on the benefit of adopting free market values, and promoting Hong Kong's best free market practices to the world.

The One Country Two Systems Research Institute is a privately-funded research institute founded in 1990 by individuals of social standing who were concerned with the wellbeing of Hong Kong. In almost a decade before 1997 handover, the institute focused on public policy on issues related to the transition of Hong Kong and on the implementation of the Basic Law. Since the establishment of the HKSAR, the institute has been focusing researches on social and economic issues and the economic and cooperative relationship between Hong Kong and its neighboring areas, particularly, Mainland China. The Hong Kong Policy Research Institute Limited was formed in 1995 by people from various businesses, professional and academic backgrounds, including individuals from different political parties. The Institute is committed to harnessing its resources to assist Hong Kong and its neighboring governments to cope with the changes facing Hong Kong and to enhancing regional cooperation and communication between Hong Kong and its neighbors. The Hong Kong Human Rights Monitor is a local independent organization founded in 1995 which aims to promote better human rights protection in Hong Kong both in terms of law and in practical daily life. It is concerned about the issues such as police authority, public service broadcasting, gender and racial discrimination, freedoms of assembly, association, and expression.

The Association for the Advancement of Feminism was established in 1984 with the mission of eliminating discrimination against women in the economic, sexual, cultural, social and legal areas, fighting for women's rights and welfare to ensure the free development of women's personality, potential and opportunities in social participation, promoting for the conscience in order to motivate the advancement of feminism and achieve equality for both sexes. The Association gives comments on public policies, researches on related issues, develops resources and provides legal consultation service. The Justice and Peace Commission of the Hong Kong Catholic Diocese were set up officially by the Catholic Diocese in 1977. It consists of Catholics appointed by the Bishop of the Hong Kong Catholic Diocese. It analyzes social policies that affect people's livelihood, involves in social movements against injustice, advocates for and promotes human rights, promotes social awareness within the church, concerns and studies about Chinese affairs, and publishes materials on various issues. The Hong Kong Alliance in Support of Patriotic Democratic Movements of China was established in 1989 with the purpose of supporting patriotic democratic movements in China. It has become the largest grassroots pro-democracy advocacy group in Hong Kong which is comprised members with different background.

There are other policy institutions that regularly offer opinions on public policies and the path of political development in Hong Kong. For example, the Business and Professionals Federation (BPF) in Hong Kong is headed by Sir David Akers-Jones, a former Chief Secretary and Acting Governor from 1985 to 1987. The vision of the BPF is to "reinforce Hong Kong's role in China and globally as a great world city", and the mission statement states that research is conducted to promote policy initiatives, aiming to serve the long-term interest of Hong Kong.

Government subventions

Over the years, there are a number of societies, councils and commissions initiated by legislations or ordinances in Hong Kong, but are operating independently with the government subvention. Having positioned outside the main executive and administrative structure of the government, these subvention bodies played a significant role in economic and civic development of Hong Kong. Important subvention bodies include the Independent Commission Against Corruption (ICAC), which is an anti-corruption organization established in 1974 working entirely independent and separated from any department of the government including the police. Its mission is to fight corruption in the community through effective law enforcement, education and prevention to help Hong Kong to gain a fair, just, stable and prosperous society. Within January to September 2008, for example, there were 2,549 reports of corruption received by the Commission, while 246 people were prosecuted, 242 people were convicted, 35 people were cautioned and 60 government servants were recommended for disciplinary or administrative action.

The Hong Kong Consumer Council was established in 1974 at a time of inflationary prices and widespread public concern about profiteering. About 95 percent of the Council's funds are from the government. The Council discharges its responsibilities and functions in accordance with the Consumer Council Ordinance enacted in 1977. It protects and promotes the interests of consumers of goods and services and purchasers, mortgagors or lessees of immovable property. It answers consumer enquiries and handles complaints promptly, mediates disputes between consumers and service suppliers, conducts researches, surveys and product testing to produce and publish information and results, provides a regular outlet of information, advice and viewpoints on all matters affecting the interest of consumers, monitors trade practices and liaises with industry body to safeguard consumer interests, and research on consumer policy and launches consumer education campaign or related activities.

The Hong Kong Productivity Council (HKPC) is a multi-disciplinary organization established by statute in 1967 to promote increased productivity and the use of more efficient methods throughout Hong Kong's business sectors. Its mission is to promote productivity excellence through the provision of integrated support across the value chain of Hong Kong firms in order to achieve a more effective utilization of resources, to enhance the value-added content of products and services and to increase international competitiveness. The Council and its subsidiary companies provide a multitude of services to around 3,000 clients each year. Its operation is supported by income from its services and a government subvention in balance.

The Office of Ombudsman was established in 1989 to serve the community of Hong Kong by redressing grievances and addressing issues of maladministration in the public sector. Through independent, objective and impartial investigation, the Ombudsman aims to bring about improvement in the quality and standard of and promote fairness in public administration, thus to ensure that Hong Kong is served by a fair and efficient public administration which is committed to accountability, openness and quality of service.

The Hong Kong Trade Development Council (HKTDC) was established in 1966 as an international marketing arm for Hong Kong-based traders, manufacturers and service providers. With more than 40 offices worldwide, including 11 in the Chinese mainland, the Council promotes Hong Kong as a platform for doing business with China and Asia. Its mission is to create and facilitate opportunities in international trade for Hong Kong companies, especially small- and medium-sized enterprises (SMEs), and to promote a positive image of Hong Kong. It develops and diversifies markets for Hong Kong companies, promotes Hong Kong's products and services in world markets and Hong Kong's leading role as an international business hub for services and information, enhances Hong Kong's position as the pre-eminent international business city of China and Hong Kong's standing as a partner and platform for global business and supporter of free trade. It organizes trade fairs and business missions to connect companies with opportunities in Hong Kong and Mainland China, while providing information via trade publications, research reports and online. High charges on the services provided by the HKTDC had been a complaint by the users.

The Hong Kong Housing Society (HKSA) is a non-governmental organization founded in 1948 and endeavored to provide affordable housing and related services for the people of Hong Kong. The introduction of professional housing management expertise to manage the rental estates, the development of sandwich class housing and senior citizen housing, the implementation of various loan schemes for the government, the participation in urban renewal and the assistance to building management and maintenance of old private buildings are the activities performed by HKSA.

In addition, there exist a large number of charitable organizations, religious affiliation, ethnical bodies and voluntary and education institutions that provide numerous civic activities in Hong Kong, aiming to provide a better livelihood with no interference or intervention from the government.

Political parties

There is no legislation for political parties in Hong Kong. Political parties can be registered either under the Societies Ordinance or the Company Ordinance. Hong Kong has a multi-party system, and no single political party can control the Legislative Council. Ideologically, political parties in Hong Kong are divided more strongly between pro-democracy and pro-China camps than between businesses capitalism and social welfare pursuits. Although there is only one political party formed by businesses, professionals and other businesses can affiliate to both pro-democracy and pro-China political parties. Likewise, some pro-China political parties also claimed to have adhered to "democracy", while some pro-democracy political parties are very welfare oriented or even anti-business. There are thus two lines of division among political parties in Hong Kong between pro-democracy and pro-China, and between pro-business and pro-welfare. Despite the increasing number of political parties, the number of membership in each political party is considerably low, reflecting the apolitical nature of Hong Kong people, though many have shown their preference to different political parties.

Most political parties in Hong Kong are relatively young and have been established since the 1980s. The Hong Kong Association for Democracy and People's Livelihood, for example, was established in 1986 with the vision to achieve democracy and prosperity in China as well as a high degree of autonomy for "Hong Kong people ruling Hong Kong". Its mission is to motivate democracy and improving people livelihood. As of March 2008, it has 110 members. The Democratic Alliance for the Betterment and Progress of Hong Kong (DAB) was established in 1992 with 56 founding members. Its target is to build up a better community, achieving an affluent economy and making Hong Kong a peaceful and contented society. As of October 2008, it has 12,002 members.

The Liberal Party was founded in 1993 by a group of business and professional people, some of whom have been active politicians for some time already. Its vision is to build a caring society that would create wealth by maintaining the values of a free market, and to protect the freedom and lifestyle of the Hong Kong people. In April 2008, it has 1,000 members. The Democratic Party was established in 1994 with the aim to "further unite the democratic forces in Hong Kong to shoulder the responsibility for the future of Hong Kong", and pursue "a high degree of autonomy and an open and democratic government of Hong Kong". In November 2008, it has 688 members. The Frontier was established in 1996, with the aim at striving for the implementation of democratic self-government in Hong Kong and "one-country, two systems", fighting and maintaining basic civil rights and motivating pro-democracy movement and citizens' participation. In October 2008, it has 130 members, but on November 23, 2008, the Frontier had merged with the Hong Kong Democratic Party, though the motion to have it disbanded was not passed. Nonetheless, its society registration was cancelled in late 2009.

Since sovereignty reversion in 1997, more political parties have been established. The Civic Act-Up, for example, was established in 2003 by a group of relatively young activists to challenge the existing pro-government District Council elections. Its work included pressing for universal suffrage for the Chief Executive and Legislative Council, improvement on urban design and transportation, paying special attention to youth, women and ethnic-minority issues, and extending anti-discrimination laws to the areas of age, sexual orientation and race.

In 2006, two political parties were formed. The League of Social Democrats was founded by people from different constituencies including councilors, social activists, and grass-root citizens. It has labeled itself as an opposition party against the uneven wealth situation resulted from the collusion of the government and business. In October 2008, it has 700 members. The Civic Party was established in 2006 with the aim at promoting democracy and social justice. It is committed to making economic success in Hong Kong, improving the quality of life and better opportunities, sustainable development, healthy environment and rich cultural life. In its own website, the Civic Party aspires to be a "governing party", thinks constructively and acts responsibly, not to oppose for the sake of opposition and try to develop proposals which enable people to have a real alternative. In February 2008, it has 300 members.

The most recently established political party is the New People's Party formed in early 2011 by a handful of former senior civil servants. The party affiliates more with the pro-government camp and considered the DAB as a "partner". The political platform of the New People's Party adheres to universal suffrage, economic diversification and reduction in the wealth gap. One of its co-founder, Regina Ip Lau Suk-yee, the former Secretary for Security in the Hong Kong SAR Government, formed the Savantas Policy Institute in 2006, which probably has become the "think tank" of the party.

15.4 Civic Deepening

Given the freedom of association in Hong Kong, the formation of more political parties and policy institution are expected, thereby reflecting plurality and diversity in Hong Kong. There are, however, other considerations. One is the financial funding and sources of financial back up of political parties and policy institutions. If the funding comes from some particular groups of individuals or organizations, the concern is whether the political parties and policy institutions would serve as instruments in furthering ideological, political and policy ends in Hong Kong. In other words, the *bona fide* nature of the parties and institutions has to be carefully examined, if the sources of funding have not been disclosed transparently.

Secondly, the personality issue in many existing and newly established institutions is another concern. In numerous civic institutions in Hong Kong, key office bearers are appointed by the government or the Chief Executive. This is supposed to give a balanced view and open participation. The concern, however, is whether these appointments are transparent, impartial and appointees are "suitably" selected, or their choice of office bearers are connected to family members or second generation of business tycoons, or people with close relationship with political leaders. For example, one common feature in government appointments has been the extensive use of top business personalities in non-business organizations, or appointment of personalities with different backgrounds such that the appointee might not have a good knowledge on the work of the institution to which the person is appointed. Thus, while open participation is a virtue, the concern is the appropriateness of the appointee and the possibility of biasedness and human error.

In other civic institutions, many elected key office bearers also come from individuals with backgrounds that are either connected to wealthy families, former civil servants and business tycoons or closely related to political parties. The establishment of various civic institutions is meant to permit capable men and women to openly, equitably and transparently engage in civic affairs so as to bring the society to a higher stage of development. Of course, capable men and women should also include people with strong connections. Nonetheless, it would turn into a case of cronyism or become a "private club" if key members of civic institutions are all connected to the upper echelon or the ruling elites of the society, thereby forming another arm of control, rather than diversity in civic development with participation of people from all walks of life and all spectrum of the society.

The human factor and governance can be detrimental if not handled fairly and impartially. The virtue of diversity could become the vice of fragmentation. With numerous individuals and interested groups forming their own organizations attempting to influence the society in one way or another, the danger is a deliberate lack of consensus among these individuals and organizations. The emergence of different divergent and uncompromised views would produce civic fragmentation, in that each individual or organization is unwilling and reluctant to compromise with each other for their goals and interests, producing obstacles in the path to social and economic progress. One proposed view would viciously be opposed by another, generating ultimately a "loss-loss" outcome in detrimental political arguments and flights.

The warning is that a politically fragmented civic society would be costly in that the lack of social harmony would send unpleasant signals to investors, and the potential loss in business and investment would ultimately, gradually, undesirably and indirectly reflect in the long-term loss of employment and economic opportunities. The unintended consequence would therefore be a loss of economic competitiveness and erosion of stability, threatening the very core principle of survival in Hong Kong.

A strong sense of civic behavior and attitude is needed in Hong Kong. For example, even though there are regular street demonstrations in Hong Kong over numerous social, political, economic, ethnical and business issues, and press freedom in Hong Kong does permit demonstrations to be reported in the media. One has to have a clear and unbiased civic mind in judging whether the demonstrations are instruments exercised orderly in a civic society to show people's concerns, or minorities with grievances and self-interests intended to disrupt stability, producing a posture for media to report and defy the very basic structure of the rule of law that Hong Kong is built on. Thus, while the exercise of freedom and civic right is highly treasured, abusing freedom and civic right by rent-seeking the very civic system Hong Kong processes should not be tolerated.

In short, there is a bilateral causality relationship between freedom and civic liberty in Hong Kong. Over the decades, freedom in Hong Kong has nurtured a high degree of civic diversity. Indeed, the high level of civic freedom in Hong Kong has played a core role in promoting and preserving all kinds of individual freedom, and civic diversity should be seen and applied positively as a mean to widen freedom and protection of individual rights. The duality of civic diversity, however, could be social fragmentation with individuals having uncompromising political and ideological views and demands, ready to sacrifice the overall wellbeing of people's livelihood for the sake of their extreme views and behaviors and ideologies. As such, the blessing of civic diversity and liberty would turn the society into a curse of political flights and social deterioration, resulting in economic losses that could not be rescued.

The achievement of a free civic society has not been easy, but to maintain, extend and expand the free civic society could equally be challenging, if not difficult. Leaders and people involved in the promotion and maintenance of a free civic Hong Kong needs to have a strong sense of devotion, selflessness, and broadmindedness. A self-center and rested-interest behavior in decision making has no place in a free civic Hong Kong society. While a fair standard has to be maintained, giving chances to others in civic activities is opportunity promoting that would benefit and harmonize the society in the long-term perspective. Although there will always be a personality issue in all levels of decision making, a system of check and balance should carefully be instituted so as to eliminate abuse, favoritism and distortion. Indeed, while Hong Kong has achieved a free civic society, one should not be complacent, as various improvements can still be made to ultimately ensure that a truly "level playing field" can be applied to all levels of civic activities and decisions, free of discrimination, victimization, favoritism, cronyism and unfair judgments.

At the same time, both government organizations and non-government civic institutions should also take a lead in reassessing their own civic governance and performance, and identify areas of governance improvement and best practices. In tertiary institutions, for example, while there is annual funding allocated to research among the academic university institutions, the concern is whether academic freedom has been uphold, or whether research funding has been blocked down by a heavy administrative machinery that only serves its own interest. The fairness and openness of research funding could be improved in all possible aspects, such as the installation of an appeal mechanism in the allocation process. Circles of influence can easily be formed among academics, the concern is whether there are channels through which academic freedom can be checked and protected to avoid the downsides of cartel formation among academics. The concern is to ensure that there were no "invisible hands" and "invisible mouths" in academic institutions that favored some and alienated others. While human errors are difficult to identify, the pursuance of strong civic governance at the leadership can deter potential abuse in management in organizations.

The answer to all these concerns relate to the probability of "civic deepening". How to encourage people to do more civic activities, and how to do better in all civic activities? There is thus more to be done, as civic development and the promotion of civic freedom is a process that contains numerous individual acts. A lot has been done, but there is more to be done. Civic deepening requires a constant and continuous improvement in all dimensions of civic activities. The emergence and appearance of civic inadequacies serve to remind that more is yet to be done. One aspect of civic achievement today could mean further civic development in other dimension is needed tomorrow. There is no perfection in a civic society, but only progress in civic development.

Civic deepening hinges a lot on "civic responsibilities" among individuals, professionals, business entities and associations and government officials and leaders. Civic responsibilities can be promoted through education, ethical behavior and identification of good practices or role models at all levels and sectors. While individuals and households should act responsibly in the civic society, business entities should also play their part in ensuring civic fairness while profits are made, professional association would ensure the quality and standard in their practices. The government would deliver responsible policies so as to ensure civic equity and social balances.

15.5 Politics and 2047

The political structure of the government in Hong Kong is mainly composed of the legislature, the executive and the district organizations. The Legislative Council (Legco) is the ultimate law-making body. Colonial bureaucrats had dominated the seats in the Legco in the colonial days, but since the 1950s a number of unofficial members, known as the "hongs" whom had close business ties with the British, were appointed into Legco by the Governor. It was only since the beginning of the twentieth century that Chinese businessmen were appointed as unofficial members (King, 1975). By the 1960s, over 90 percent of appointed unofficial Legco members were Chinese citizens from wealthy families or with industrial background. Before the Sino-British negotiation in 1982–1984, although only the upper echelon in the Hong Kong society was represented, the Legco served to mediate between the colonial government and the local Chinese society. It was only after the conclusion of the Sino-British Joint Declaration in 1984 that the British Hong Kong Government began to introduce elections to Legco, making fundamental changes to its composition.

In the elections of 1985 and 1988, 24 and 26 were elected members in the Legco that composed of 57 members and 59 members, respectively. Among the 24 (26 in 1998) members, 12 (14 in 1988) were elected by functional constituencies (FCs) and 12 were elected members by Electoral College formed by the district board (DBs), Urban Council (UCs) and Regional Council (RCs). The FCs seats were tailor-made for designated business and professional associations. Both the FCs and the Electoral College were under heavy influence from the government, ensuring that pro-government members were always in the majority. Ma (2007) noted that from 1985 to 1991, only one government bill was withdrawn for reconsideration, though the Legislative Council (Power and Privileges) Ordinance was passed shortly after the introduction of elected members which granted special investigation powers to Legco to summon government officials to give evidence.

The introduction of directly elected seats into Legco in 1991 led to the rise of party politics. The United Democrats of Hong Kong (UDHK), the largest pro-democracy party that become the Democratic Party in 1994, won 12 of the 18 directly elected seats. Together with other pro-democracy groups, the democrats made up about one-third of the 60-members Legco in 1991–95. The Legco started to play a much more important role in influencing government policy, and overseeing government administration.

Another political change after the 1991 election is the appointment of a deputy president in Legco to replace the governor to preside over Legco meetings. In the 1995 election, the appointed seats were abolished, but 9 new constituencies were included into the FCs. The voting age was lowered to 18, and the qualified voting population increased to 2.7 million. After the 1995 election, the democrats held about half of the Legco seats, and Legco members were allowed to elect the president. Ma (2007) also noted that after the 1991 direct election, the Legco changed from a "policy-questioning legislature" to a "policy-influencing legislature". The more effective institutional mechanisms included the budgetary power and private members' bills.

After the direct election in 1991, there appeared a clear political divide in the Legco. On the one side, there were the democrats who pushed for progressive democratic reforms and emphasized human rights and autonomy from China, but at the same time were generally in favor of more welfare reforms for the grassroots. The other side was the conservative pro-business bloc, which was generally cautious about rapid democratization, attempted to maintain a good relationships with the Chinese government and abhorred strong welfare. The Legco in 1991–1992 election resembled a two-party legislature, with the politically and economically conservative pro-government bloc controlling a majority of about 35 votes, and the politically and socially more progressive democrats occupying some 20 seats in Legco. However, the political pattern became more complicated in Legco from 1993 to 1997 during the last governorship of Chris Patten. On the issues of democratization and civil rights, the democrats became allies of the government, but on social class issues the government remained pro-business and gained the support of pro-business members when the democrats and other pro-grassroots members pushed for more grassroots benefits (Ma, 2007).

However, Legco's influence on government policy was weakened by the institutional changes after 1997. For example, bills proposed by Legco members cannot involve public expenditure commitments, and bills must first go to the Legco president for approval. Ma (2007) observed that the Legco president only allowed 10 members' bills out of a total of 29 members' bills between 1997 and 2004. Electoral rules were changed after 1997. The "nine new constituencies" added in 1995 by Chris Patten were redefined and the seats were allocated to various business sectors. The Election Committee (EC), which was composed of district board members in 1995, was redefined to include 400 members weighted in favor of major business and professional groups. The voting method also changed from "the single transferable vote" (STV) to "block vote" in 1997, which enabled each voter in the EC to vote for ten candidates without indicating their preferences. The ten candidates with the most votes would be elected. As the result, as Ma (2007) noted, a power bloc that controlled half of the seats could monopolize the seats in the Election Committee. Furthermore, for the directly elected seats, proportional representation (PR) was used after 1997 to replace the first-past-the-post system adopted in 1995 which was tailor-made for the more popular democrats. Consequently, the democrats had little success in the redefined functional constituencies and pro-government Legco members became the majority after 1997. The changes also brought many independents to Legco. In the two periods of 1998–2000 and 2000–2004, for example, about one-fourth of Legco members were independents.

The Provisional Legislative Council was set up in 1996 by the People's Republic of China (PRC) to serve as a provisional legislature of Hong Kong. It took charges of the Hong Kong legislature until the first Legislative Council formed in 1998. A total of 60 provisional Legco members were elected by the 400 member Selection Committee, which also elected the first Chief Executive of the Hong Kong SAR Government (Lui, 2007).

The Chief Executive (known as the Governor before the sovereignty reversion in 1997) and the members of Executive Council (Execo) are the leaders in the administrative structure composed of government departments and civil servants. The Chief Executive is the head of the Hong Kong Special Administrative Region (HKSAR) of the People's Republic of China. He leads the Government of the HKSAR and has powers and functions to decide on government policies, issue executive orders, and implement the Basic Law and other laws. The Chief Secretary for Administration, the Financial Secretary and the Secretary for Justice are the prior advisors to the Chief Executive. They are also the official members of Executive Council. The Chief Secretary for Administration leads a hundred and eighty thousands strong civil servants under the direction of Chief Executive, and assists the Chief Executive in supervising the policy bureaus as directed and plays a key role in ensuring harmonization in policy formulation and implementation. The Financial Secretary is responsible for financial policy, while the Secretary for Justice is the legal advisor of the Hong Kong SAR Government (Luo and Chen, 2002).

The Chief Executive is required by the Basic Law to consult Executive Council before making important policy decisions, introducing bills to the Legislative Council, making subordinate legislation or dissolving the Legislative Council. In the constitution of the Execo, the Chief Executive can still exercise his authority. Executive Council members are appointed by the Chief Executive from among the principal officials of the executive authorities, members of the Legislative Council and public figures. The removal of members and the matters put before the council are also decided by the Chief Executive. Collective decisions on all issues will be taken in its normal weekly meeting. If the Chief Executive does not accept the majority opinion, he has to give specific reasons in record. The Execo advises upon all principal legislation before it is introduced into the Legco. It also has the power to make subsidiary legislation under a number of ordinances passed by the Legco (Information Services Department, 2008).

The Execo is the most important advisory committee to the Chief Executive, as major policy changes must be approved by the Execo before being introduced into the Legco. Before 1992, almost all Execo members had the experience in Legco. As a result, the Execo and Legco worked together in a harmonious partnership to formulate and ratify policy decisions (Miners, 1998). Although the 1984 Green Paper proposed the possibility that some Execo members should be elected by the Legco, but nothing further came after this proposal. In 1986, two elected members of Legco were appointed to the Execo. The late Sir Edward Youde, Governor from 1982 to 1986, was the first to demand that unofficial members should be bound by the rule of collective responsibility (Miners, 1998).

For many years, there were only three senior secretaries served in the Execo as ex-officio members. After the adoption of the Accountability System for Principal Officials (ASPO) in July 2002, principal officials have also been appointed to serve concurrently in the Execo as official members. This change diluted the influence of non-official members. In November 2005, eight additional non-official members were appointed by the Chief Executive, bringing the total number of non-official members to 15. These changes have restored the influence of the non-official members. The ASPO aimed at resolving the mismatch between the senior civil servants and bureau secretaries, and allowing the Chief Executive to form his own governing team without the restriction of having to choose from inside the civil service. This new system applies to the three senior secretaries and 11 bureau secretaries (Li, 2007).

The Chief Executive, Donald Tsang Yum-kuen, revamped the government structure in July 2007. In order to rationalize the distribution of responsibilities between policy bureaus and to help optimize the synergy and enable the government to sharpen the focus on important and complex issues, the number of policy bureaus expanded from 11 to 12 and duties of the eight existing bureaus were reorganized. The Development Bureau was created to deal with matters related to planning, land use, buildings, urban renewal and development-related heritage conservation. The Home Affairs Bureau was given the added responsibility of looking after social enterprise and the legal aid service. The matters concerning human tights and access to information were transferred to the Constitutional and Mainland Affairs Bureau (Chan and Ng, 2007). The first batch of eight Under Secretaries and nine Political Assistants were appointed on May 20 and May 22, 2007 respectively. Their salaries and nationalities were requested to be disclosed by the Legco members.

The Urban Council was established in 1935 to take charge of public hygiene. With the emergence of new towns like Tsuen Wan, Tuen Mun and Shatin, the colonial government reformed the Urban Council in August 1972. The Urban Council was financially independent and was the only council with elected members in Hong Kong before 1980s. Due to the increasing demand of the services in the New Territories, Regional Council was established in 1986. There were at least two political reasons for the government to set up a new council instead of expanding the Urban Council. Firstly, the Urban Council was the only organization with elected members with actual authority, and its further expansion in authority could be a threat and challenge to the Legco and the government. Secondly, the Heung Yee Kuk and some district board members requested not to expand the Urban Council but to establish a new independent council (Luo and Chen, 2002).

After the establishment in July 1997 of the Provisional Urban Council and Provisional Regional Council, the Hong Kong SAR government reviewed the effectiveness of district organizations, especially following the outbreak of the H5N1 (chicken flu) health hazards in 1997 and 1998. Subsequently, the responsibility of food safety and public hygiene was passed to a specific department and a policy bureau, while the responsibility of recreational and cultural works was passed to a new department. At the end of 1999, the two provisional councils were dismissed (Luo and Chen, 2002).

The other district organization for the New Territories is the Heung Yee Kuk which was established by the villagers in New Territories in 1926 because of the announcement of compensation ordinance in turning the agricultural land into residential land. It aimed at upholding the interests and benefits of the villagers and negotiating with the government. In 1959, the Heung Yee Kuk became a statutory body under the Heung Yee Kuk Ordinance. The ordinance defined Heung Yee Kuk's authorities in three aspects: 1) implement the duties given by the government; 2) advance the understanding and cooperation between the government and residents in New Territories; and 3) give opinions to the government on the development of

New Territories (Luo and Chen, 2002). In 2002, the election of village representatives was brought to the Court of Final Appeal, as elected representatives will have to be consistent with the Bill of Rights and Sex Discrimination Ordinance. As a result, the government established a set of new arrangements for village representative elections in 2003 to ensure that the elections were open and fair, and the native villagers cannot dominate the elections (Home Affairs Department, 2008).

The call for more political freedom and democracy leading to universal suffrage has been a concern in the post-1997 Hong Kong (Ng, 2008). The basis of further political freedom and universal suffrage has largely been stated in the Basic Law. In the case of the Chief Executive election, Article 45 of the Basic law states that "... The ultimate aim is the selection of the Chief Executive by universal suffrage upon nomination by a broadly representative nominating committee in accordance with democratic procedures." Annex I of the Basic Law described the "Method for the Selection of the Chief Executive of the Hong Kong SAR". In particular, Clause 7 in Annex I gives that "If there is a need to amend the method for selecting the Chief Executive for the terms subsequent to the year 2007, such amendments must be made with the endorsement of a two-thirds majority of all the members of the Legislative Council and the consent of the Chief Executive, and they shall be reported to the Standing Committee of the National People's Congress for approval".

In the case of the Legco election, Article 68 of the Basic Law states that "The method for forming the Legislative Council shall be specified in the light of the actual situation in the Hong Kong Special Administrative Region and in accordance with the principle of gradual and orderly progress. The ultimate aim is the election of all the members of the Legislative Council by universal suffrage". Similarly, the method for the formation of the Legislative Council and its voting procedures subsequent to the year 2007 given in Annex II of the Basic Law states that "With regard to the method of forming the Legislative Council of the Hong Kong Special Administrative Region and its procedures for voting on bills and motions after 2007, if there is a need to amend the provisions of this Annex, such amendments must be made with the endorsement of a two-thirds majority of all the members of the Council and the consent of the Chief Executive, and they shall be reported to the Standing Committee of the National People's Congress for the record".

These additional rooms for the exercise of more political freedom given in the Basic Law on elections after 2007 has led to increased and heated discussions on universal suffrage and the "voting procedure subsequent to the year 2007". Due to popular demands and public calls for a solution to direct election for the Chief Executive and members of the Legco after 2007, the Constitutional Development Task Force was officially established in January 2004 with the objective to locate a constitutional balance and formulate a proposed package which would be acceptable to all parties so that constitutional development of Hong Kong could be carried forward (Central Policy Unit, 2005). For the selecting of the Chief Executive in 2007 and forming of the Legislative Council in 2008, the Task Force collected the views from the public and formulated a proposed package in October 2005. The main proposed items are: 1) the number of members of the Election Committee that elect the Chief Executive shall be increased from 800 to 1,600; 2) all District Council members, to be increased from 42 to 529, are proposed to be the members of the Election Committee; and 3) the number of seats in the Legislative Council will be increased from 60 to 70, 35 are returned by geographical constituencies through direct elections and 35 returned by functional constituencies. All the newly added functional constituency seats will be returned through election by District Council members among themselves.

For the timetable on universal suffrage, the Task Force however gave no suggestions in the proposed package other than those made on April 26, 2004, in the Decision of the Standing Committee of the National People's Congress (NPCSC) (Constitutional and Mainland Affairs Bureau, 2004). The Decision of the NPCSC stipulated that the third term election of the Chief Executive in 2007 shall not be conducted by means of universal suffrage and the fourth term election of the all Legislative Council members in 2008 shall not be conducted by means universal suffrage. However, this proposed package was vetoed in the Legislative Council.

The Green Paper on Constitutional Development was published soon after the third term of Hong Kong SAR government was formed in July 2007. The publication was followed by a period of public consultation that ended on October 10, 2007, and the report was subsequently published in December. In the report, the government concluded that implementing universal suffrage for the Chief Executive in 2012 is the expectation of more than half of the public. However, the report also stated that implementing universal suffrage for the Chief Executive first by no later than 2017 would stand a better chance of being accepted by the majority in the community. Also, implementing universal suffrage first for the Chief Executive, then followed by universal suffrage for all members of Legco was the emerged consensus. Subsequently, the Chief Executive, Donald Tsang Yum-kuen, requested the NPCSC to confirm that the two methods for selecting the Chief Executive and members of Legco (Constitutional and Mainland Affairs Bureau, 2007).

The NPCSC subsequently adopted a Decision on December 26, 2007, making clear that appropriate amendments would be made to the specific method for selecting the fourth Chief Executive and the specific method for forming the fifth term of the Legco in 2012. In addition, the election of the fifth Chief Executive in 2017 may be implemented by the method of universal suffrage. Following the universal suffrage on the election of the Chief Executive, the election of the Legco may subsequently be implemented by the method of electing all the members by universal suffrage (NPCSC, 2007). Thus, the Task Group on Constitutional Development of the Commission on Strategic Development was set up in February 2008 with the aim to study feasible options for electing the Chief Executive and forming the Legco in 2012 within the framework given by the NPCSC. In short, the political roadmap is that universal suffrage in the election of the Chief Executive may be introduced as early as 2017. If that was done, universal suffrage for the election of all Legco members would subsequently follow. Thus, the 2017 election becomes crucial in Hong Kong's political freedom, and obviously the situation and the needed changes prior to the 2017 election would become sensitive to the political map of Hong Kong.

The change in Hong Kong's political scene after the sovereignty reversion in 1997 is clearly the emergence of two lines of political divisions. One political division is between pro-China and pro-democracy, and the other conventional line is between capitalist market economy and welfare oriented interventionist economy. As a result, there could be various combinations between the two ideological lines of political divisions. There are other complications. For example, while universal suffrage has been discussed, there is also attack on the validity of the functional constituencies, it is possible that a voter with a professional background would end up with two votes, with one based on geographical constituency and another based on functional constituency. While some have suggested the possibility of a bicameral system that produces an upper house and a lower house in the political structure (Business and Professional Federation, 2006), others argue for the advantages of the functional constituencies and prefer to see a unicameral system similar to that in Mainland China.

It is true that Hong Kong is politically facing the two political alternatives. The pro-China camp tends to assimilate the Hong Kong economy to that of the mainland economy, with typically more government intervention and strong welfare provision, making Hong Kong people more reliant on and ready to seek help from the government. One argument is that people in the pro-China camp tend to anticipate on an *ex ante* basis what Beijing would do, and then draft the policies to suit what Beijing would prefer them to do. Others would believe that the pro-China camp is carrying out the instructions from Beijing on how Hong Kong should be governed. In other words, people in the pro-China camp prefer to think about Hong Kong in the wider Mainland China context, and may not give priority to the actual situation in Hong Kong.

Although the Hong Kong economy suffered considerably since 1998 as a result of the Asian financial crisis, and there was the need of economic rescue by the government. There should be a clear distinction in the role of the government between crisis and non-crisis times. In the crisis time, the government should be more pro-active and carry out short-term policies aiming to rescue the economy from falling further. In the non-crisis time, however, the government should take a back seat once the economy has recovered and leave the private sector to do more. In many ways, the government is exercising a crisis-mentality in a non-crisis time, and short-term, one time off economic assistance continued, leading to the criticism that government interventions have 'crowded out' individual incentives and business activities. The consequence is that the government is becoming more and more involved and intervention becomes frequent, while the private sector is having less economic opportunities, and individuals become more and more dependent on government intervention.

The mainland's attitude on Hong Kong has also been divided. One school of thought will view Hong Kong's return as an end of British colonialism and by the return of Hong Kong's sovereignty, people's livelihood in Hong Kong will have to assimilate to the situation in the motherland as much as possible. The colonial history of Hong Kong was a deviation from the overall socialist development in the mainland, and people in Hong Kong should not take any more advantage from its British connection. The "one country" should come first before the "two systems". The other more pragmatic school of thought, on the contrary, will consider the position of Hong Kong in the regional and world economy and see that through the return of sovereignty, Hong Kong can be more useful in the overall modernization and reform of the China economy. Hong Kong would be encouraged to develop as much as possible so that Hong Kong would have a bright performance. The "two systems" is meant to aid the development of the "one country".

There are various surmises as to how Beijing wants Hong Kong to be. Of course, Hong Kong is part of the motherland, but officially is enjoying the "one country two systems" status until 2047 (see for example, Pepper, 2008). It has been reported that Beijing has intervened in Hong Kong affairs since 2003, and that leaders in the National People Congress has warned people in Hong Kong not to "messing around" with politics, but should focus on economic development instead.[1] For the first time, Hong Kong's economic development has been stated in China's 11th Five Year Plan.[2] Other discussions included the probable extent of directives and instruction the authority in Beijing has given to the Hong Kong SAR Government in carrying out various economic policies, and the need for Hong Kong people to be patriotic to the motherland. On the contrary, though probably depending on different leaders at different times, one hears regularly that leaders in Beijing talked openly on how Hong Kong should find its own path of development. The first Chief Executive, Tung Chee-hwa, is a local businessman, while the second Chief Executive, Tsang Yum-kuen, has been a key government official in both the pre- and post-1997 government. Would Beijing place an ideological strong person as the third Chief Executive in 2012, though the person shall have to be elected locally?[3]

The business sector in Hong Kong tends to be passive, though the big corporates are clearly pro-government. For obvious business interests, big corporates are naturally more interested in the large and growing Mainland China market than the small and saturated Hong Kong market. However, there are other considerations Beijing might have in considering the role of Hong Kong. Regional discrepancies and rivalries could be one consideration. Differences in economic development between south, east and north of Mainland China may lead to other considerations. Even within the Guangdong province itself, economic differences between east and west Guangdong could be one consideration. Would the rapid growth and ambitious expansion of Shenzhen, for example, be a concern to the Guangdong government as well as other cities in the province? The role Hong Kong plays can be a crucial pivot in the overall political development in Mainland China.

As Hong Kong has often acted as a reference point for development in Mainland China, Hong Kong has also been a place where problems and inadequacies that occurred in Mainland China were unfolded. The disclosure of the source of various fake products, toxic milk power and other property right violated productions have often been first reported in the Hong Kong media. While visa-free travel has since

[1] *Mingpao Daily*, August 19, 2008; *South China Morning Post*, March 14, 2007.

[2] *South China Morning Post*, December 5, 2009.

[3] By the summer of 2011, the three candidates that have shown interest in running the Chief Executive post in 2012 are Henry Tang Ying-yen, (Chief Secretary for Administration of the Hong Kong SAR Government), Rita Fan Hsu Lai-tai, (former President of the Legislative Council from 1998 to 2004), and Leung Chun-ying, (Convener of the Non-official Members of the Executive Council).

2003 been given to more and more mainland residents to visit Hong Kong, mainland pregnant women have made use of the Hong Kong medical services and have their babies born in Hong Kong, as that could escape the one-child policy in mainland as well as the attainment of a Hong Kong residence for the new born. Women married to Hong Kong men could also come to Hong Kong for social welfare assistance. The various welfare provisions in Hong Kong given to mainland residents suggest that Hong Kong is shouldering part of the social welfare inadequacies in mainland. The status as a Hong Kong resident has been attractive to mainland residents. Other than the daily quota of immigration on the basis of family reunion, a number of mainland celebrity figures and rich persons have been immigrating to Hong Kong, making using of Hong Kong's free status and openness in further their economic activities and travel necessities. In other words, Hong Kong does serve a number of civic functions for the motherland.

The democrats in Hong Kong have made numerous attempts to seek for more political freedom and universal suffrage at the earliest possible date. Many democrats, however, are pro-welfare and also urge more government expenditures and intervention. Thus, other than the call for democracy, the economic policy on welfare provision among many democrats in Hong Kong is similar to the view of those in the pro-China camp. Indeed, there have been more calls for government intervention and how the government could help the needy than calls for more individual drive in both normal and difficult times and to maintain innovative and creative in business activities.

The year 2047 is another longer term concern as the fifty years of the "one country two systems" expires. The pro-China camp would argue that with political and economic alignment in the fifty years in 1997–2047, Hong Kong would be so mainland-like and totally integrated that there would remain only "one country one system". The true color of people adhering to this view would show themselves when 2047 draws nearer. The "one country two systems" is a political decision, and in theory, Hong Kong's Basic Law shall expire upon 2047 and does not have the "two systems" status anymore. In other words, the year 1997 was a change or reversion of sovereignty, while 2047 is the change of Hong Kong's system.

Looking at the experience of 1997 when talks on the political future of Hong Kong began in 1982, 15 years before the actual transition in 1997. If history were to repeat itself, the question of 2047 may come early in about 2032, when Hong Kong residents, local businesses, foreign businesses and foreign governments, including the government in United Kingdom whom was the other party in the Sino-British Joint Declaration in 1984, would ask the question whether the "one country two systems" will still apply. Would it be terminated or extended or some form of compromise shall appear? The Beijing authority would have to make a deliberate decision on the economic system in Hong Kong.

Equally, the view and attitude of the residents in Hong Kong in 2032 or 2047 will be an important factor. Despite the numerous immigrants from mainland to Hong Kong after 1997, their intention of achieving a Hong Kong resident status would be at the minimal to enjoy a free and stable Hong Kong economy. In many ways, history could have repeated itself in terms of the immigration to Hong Kong.

While the post-Second World War immigrants from mainland to Hong Kong tried to escape the economic hardship in mainland and made use of the freer Hong Kong for their business drive, immigrants from mainland to Hong Kong after 1997 might have the same intention and attitude. Even though some have made use of the sound welfare assistance in Hong Kong, many, especially their second generation, would look to Hong Kong's freedom as a base to further their economic achievement in Hong Kong and in mainland. The removal of the "two systems" framework would evaporate their hard effort of coming to Hong Kong if Hong Kong were having the same system as that of mainland.

In many ways, the 50 years from 1997 to 2047 would be the "transition" in the economic system, and political changes within this period would be sensitive to the long-term survival of Hong Kong, and economic volatility would be high when compared to the pre-1997 decades when Hong Kong was focused entirely on economic development and business achievement. If the 2047 question was to emerge in 2032, for example, Hong Kong's economic stability would once again be tested. Would the experience be similar to the situation in the 1990s with people from Hong Kong immigrating to popular western destinations? Would the threat of instability lead to another unwanted economic recession? And would instability also spill over to other key economic fundamentals, such as currency stability, property price and stock market development? Would there be a Hong Kong border at all? The various economic, political, legal and social security issues that are provided and protected by the Basic Law would re-emerge upon the expiration of the "one country two systems".

The political scene in Hong Kong is facing both a short-term issue and a long-term issue. While to secure more political freedom and universal suffrage in the election of the Chief Executive and Legco members is a short-term issue, the long-term perspective is whether the system in Hong Kong shall expire. The two issues are, of course, closely linked. Politicians would argue that the more political freedom Hong Kong possesses, the more likely that the Hong Kong system would be kept.

In conclusion, while civic freedom in Hong Kong is an important element of freedom, civic deepening in terms of promoting greater civic development is needed to turn Hong Kong into a stronger civic society, with promising economic achievement, social security, respect to civic behavior backed by the rule of law and other core societal values. In fact, it is indeed the constant progress in civic development that makes Hong Kong valuable to Mainland China. Hong Kong so far has served as a reference point to economic development in Mainland China, but in the long-run Hong Kong will serve as a showcase to the rest of the world that Hong Kong has done just as good, if not better, after 1997 when Hong Kong's sovereignty was reverted to China. China will earn an invaluable credit if history were to show that Hong Kong had a brighter chapter of development after 1997 than before 1997.

15.6 Absolute Versus Relative

The core advantage in the promotion of civic freedom is to turn a number of activities that have absolute outcomes into either activity with relative outcome or individualized and become private decisions. Economic activities often produce a relative outcome, typically with one individual or party getting more while the other is getting less. In the discussion on inequality and poverty, the concern is that so long as the economy is growing and all individuals inter-temporarily and intra-personally getting better off, it does not matter that much if inter-personally there is inequality between any two individuals. In other words, economic activities complement each other, though rewards to different individuals in a transaction differ. The relative nature of economic activities have for long been overlooked or misinterpreted or polarized into two opposing forces. Economic growth and development allows individuals to get better off regardless of what the others are getting in absolute terms. Of course, individuals can get worse off in times of economic recessions and crises. But so long as economic opportunities are expanding continuously, all individuals will have equal chances of getting better off economically.

A high level of civic development and freedom serves as a social infrastructure to economic activities. Civic freedom, however, has a greater role to play in a large number of non-economic activities that carry an absolute outcome. There are at least two major types of non-economic activities with absolute outcomes. One type of activity comes with one party winning while the other party losing, such as political elections and sport games. The other type of activities does not have a competitive nature, but individuals are not encouraged to have a second chance, such as religious faith, marriage and formation of a family.

How to turn an absolute victor-loser outcome into a "relative" game? In political elections, individual freedom in the form of democracy does provide a chance for both candidates and voters to have a second chance, thereby demanding results from the victor on the one hand, and allowing the voters to elect again in future elections. Periodic elections can also provide a fix term of office for each victor, and the elected candidate would have a fixed period of time to do the best the candidate can for the benefit of the territory. The provision of periodic elections encourage the victor to do his/her best, and at the same time lessen the damage to the society should the elected candidate did not perform. In a politically matured economy, the choice of parties and candidates becomes a free personal decision, though there could be political campaigns but the individuals are protected from coercion and injustice in elections.

Modern sport games are being organized into clubs, associations and world events such as the Olympics and the World Cup, though there are a lot of commercial businesses involved in popular sport games, with players ripping huge returns from the business of the games. All sports contain absolute outcomes, but civic arrangements and business organizations allowed sport games to be conducted in an organized manner, and individuals are free to choose their sport celebrities and clubs and associations all over the world. The media has provided plenty of free publicity on individual players and sport associations and clubs. Indeed, sport celebrities are ripping huge gains largely because they are 'free riding' the publicity provided free by the international media. Indeed, sports news has become a daily affair, and the results of different games and players are fully reported. Nonetheless, the individuals are free to choose their sport games, thereby individualizing and privatizing the absolute outcome of sports.

Religious faith is often an activity with an absolute outcome. Once chosen, it often becomes a life-time affair. But in a free civic society, the choice of individual faith is free. Men and women are free to choose their religion, and are free to conduct their religious activities at their own pace, space and time. Individuals' choice of faith should not be influenced or imposed by the state, an association or any individual. Civic freedom allows religious plurality, where individuals can go their own ways in their religious orientation and pursuits. Thus, true civic freedom would see the individualization of activities with absolute outcomes. Other examples can equally be discussed within the framework of civic freedom and individualization of activities. In short, civic freedom is seen as a solution to a number of societal problems, especially problems with absolute outcomes where parties involved were faced with a zero-sum game, with one party winning at the expense of the losing party.

Civic freedom is a mechanism, through which individual freedom could be exercised extensively, and activities that have absolute outcomes would be turned into activities that provide personal choices, and their outcome would become relative. Economic relativity would allow individuals exercise their freedom and made personal choices independently.

15.7 Conclusion

While the majority of people in Hong Kong long for more political freedom and expect universal suffrage will soon become a reality, many agree that the democracy process should be orderly, gradual and acceptable to all parties, and that political change is taking place maturely along with other aspects of civic development. The free civic model seems to serve Hong Kong well in that political freedom is incorporated into the wider aspect of civic freedom. All along, due to the slowness in the advancement of universal suffrage and political freedom, civic institutions have served as a check and balance in ensuring administrative efficiency and fairness between the government and the public at large.

However, it does not imply that the free civic model is a perfect system, although it does have the advantage that extreme and disrupting political acts and unwanted social divisiveness were avoided. There could be other inadequacies in the free civic model and improvements have to be made in various areas. Personality could be one possible problem, as individual background and personal orientations could bias their views and decisions. While openness and transparency could serve as a safeguard in civic activities, the process of check and balance should be given equal emphasis.

Civic freedom permits individual choices to be exercised, thereby reducing human conflicts as activities with absolute outcomes could be smoothened. The experience of civic development in Hong Kong can be regarded as a show case for other economies, and lessons can be learned. Examples include the gradual establishments of useful and impactful civic institutions that introduce quality and standards among various professions, thereby providing guiding lights in the process of development, and at the same time serving as a bridge or turnpike through which the relationship between the ruler and the ruled can be ameliorated. Social conflict can be reduced, if not minimized, and provision of individual choices allows individuals to exercise their freedom to the fullest possible extent.

There is also the possibility of a "civic multiplier" whereby one aspect of civic development will lead to another area of civic development, and similarly with the multiplying effect of individual freedom. Ultimately, a matured civic society is one in which freedom are protected by institutions, regulations, ethics, practices and standards, though there should also be constant improvements and advancements in institutions and standards. There is no perfection in a civic society, but a process of civic deepening can ensure a high degree of human protection, institutional transparency and effective administration.

While politics is often divisive, cronyism, ideology, people with rested interest and with family or business affiliations can also lead to civic unfairness, favoritism, victimization and alienation in the promotion of a civic society. Although human errors are inevitable, there is a need to ensure at all levels that it is the capable people that are recruited in different levels of leadership. People do have their own opinions, but a truly civic society will produce equal opportunity for all. Indeed, the process of obtaining and maintaining an all-round civic society is opportunity-generating already. Economic freedom is a key element in civic freedom, as economic activities are relative in outcomes and opportunity-producing. Increase in economic opportunities can in turn facilitate the promotion of civic freedom and, ultimately, civic development.

The build-up and strengthening of a civic system is equally important in promotion civic development. A well-functioning system should be respected and agreed by all participants, though constant improvement in a system shall normally be required. It would take time for a well-functioning system to be developed, as people with rested interest definitely would prefer to establish their favored system. A well-functioning system should be fair to all and should not be personality driven. In short, there is no perfection in a civic society, but only improvements and advancements in all stages and dimensions of a civic society.

16 The Economic Freedom Path of Hong Kong

16.1 The Evergreen

It has not been easy to fully understand the ingredients of the economic freedom in Hong Kong, given its dynamic nature. One is not referring to a "perfect" economy, but constant improvements and changes are necessary. The question is whether changes are proceeding in a beneficial direction. Other than the measurement of GDP and GDP per capita, the quality of life has been a useful alternative indicator. The quality of life or an index of happiness is mainly nominal. The root that provides a number of quantifiable factors, such as GDP growth, quality of life and index of happiness, is the depth and width of economic freedom being practiced in a particular economy. Economic opportunity should be considered as another factor of production, in addition to land, labor, capital and sometimes entrepreneurship. Economic freedom has shown to be a wealth-generating instrument.

The study of Hong Kong's economic freedom is dissected into five sequential elements. The first element is the necessary theoretical and conceptual background. The first two chapters have outlined the major conceptual arguments and how Hong Kong performed. The next few chapters have given the contextual nature of economic freedom. There are a number of technical discussions on Hong Kong's GDP, volatility and business cycles, making comparison with neighboring economies where possible. This is important as the texture of economic freedom could show the economic elements through which the free economy is built upon. The contextual elements can be numerous, and each of the five chapters (Chapters 3, 4, 5, 6 and 7) has dwelled into a separate texture in economic freedom. The analyses on productivity, knowledge-based performance and efficiency, together with discussion on the performance of small- and medium-sized enterprises, have dwelled on mainly the domestic issues. The discussions on these five chapters are not exhaustive, as more contextual materials can certainly be covered and discussed.

The next five chapters (Chapters 8, 9, 10, 11 and 12) are related to the various policy components in economic freedom. The appropriate deployment of policy that upholds economic freedom is a task that requires not only skills, but vision, broad-mindedness, support and collaboration between the public and government. Analyses on the components include the discussion on competition, which is a business-related policy, and performance on the financial, monetary and fiscal sectors have provided the macroeconomic scenarios of economic freedom. Policy on housing and land and performance in the real estate market is another critical component in economic freedom, as property often occupies the largest chunk of an individual's wealth.

Lastly, policies cannot be executed successfully without suitable prior conditions and environments. The three chapters (Chapters 13, 14 and 15) that ventured into the non-economic elements of economic freedom have discussed the few conditional factors that served as lubricant to the engine of economic freedom. The issue of inequality and poverty has always been a sensitive issue all over the world, as there can be ideological division involved. The changing nature on the way these issues are being handled deserves a careful analysis. Economic freedom is also conditional on the extent of civic freedom. While Hong Kong is civically free, deepening of civic freedom, including political freedom, should best be conducted in the course of development. Although there has always been ideological division in Hong Kong, political tolerance has been high as stability has been become the more fundamental issue. Nonetheless, it is economic growth and the provision of economic opportunities that have been viewed as the dearer form of activities in Hong Kong. Economic integration with the mainland economy has been an on-going activity in Hong Kong, but politics aside, the exploration of mutual advantages seem to be the best outcome for both economies.

A lot has been discussed in the analysis on Hong Kong's economic freedom. There are several concluding messages. Economic freedom has functioned similar to an infrastructure that has helped the economy to grow, expand and prosper. The benefits from economic freedom have been pursued at all cost, and periodic difficulties have not dented the drive to economic freedom. By today, economic freedom has become an "economic culture", but continued progress is still required as new challenges emerge. The different economic cycles have reinforced the various texture of economic freedom. Since the economic reform in Mainland China and despite the reversion in political sovereignty in 1997, Hong Kong's economic freedom has also aided the reform and modernization of the Mainland China economy, as Hong Kong has often been used as a reference point to development in the mainland economy. Indeed, being the second generation successful market economies, other emerging economies in Asia and elsewhere has closely been examining the lessons of Hong Kong. Hong Kong's economic freedom has indeed radiated to neighboring economies. Being a city economy without a backup sector, the only choice for Hong Kong is to move forward by combining the success from previous experiences and the advantage of new situations.

One should certainly not hold a "great Hong Kong" attitude. Being part of the greater motherland of Mainland China, residents of Hong Kong could exercise their patriotism by sharing the experience and virtue of economic development and freedom with their counterparts in the mainland economy. After all, to be fair to the people of Hong Kong, Britain's colonization of Hong Kong at the end of the Opium War in 1842 was the weakness of the Qing Dynasty. Hong Kong has since been used as an "immigrant" city, where residents came mainly from Mainland China at different historical time. Although immigrants tended to work harder and drive their own economic destiny, conditions in Hong Kong are often imposed by external conditions and forces. Hong Kong residents are used to response to hardships, but through periodic hardships, new economic outcomes and channels of survivals have been developed.

The attraction of economic freedom in contemporary Hong Kong can be seen by the growing number of able immigrants whom would consider Hong Kong as a breeding ground for their personal drive and the number of young educated entering Hong Kong to develop their professional careers. Increasingly, there are immigrants and educated coming to Hong Kong from places other than Mainland China. Economic revitalization in the form of restructuring and the pursuit of supply-driven policies should be the next task in enhancing growth, stability and prosperity.

Economic expansion in the mainland economy is a plus to Hong Kong. Other than the emergence of many non-economic jargons that are being used to compare Hong Kong with different cities in Mainland China and Asia, it is the results and outcomes that count importantly. For example, it was some years back when foreign traveler visited Hong Kong complained about the standard of English among taxi drivers. There was a campaign to encourage taxi drivers to pick up more English knowledge, as that would enhance Hong Kong's image. The situation has changed and improvements have been made. Hong Kong taxis have been ranked the third best in the world after London and New York in a survey conducted by Hotel.com released on August 25, 2011. Other than English, cleanliness of the taxis and the drivers' knowledge of the city have been praised. This is a typical example of Hong Kong's spirit of economic freedom: mistakes were learned but improvements and progress are subsequently made.

Economic freedom is an evergreen that will only lead Hong Kong to a new economic height. While Hong Kong has been flowing with the world economy in the past, and especially since the 1950s, developments in the mainland economy will make the Hong Kong economy to flow with the rest of the world as well as the rise of Mainland China. As such Hong Kong will not lose.

16.2 Stability and Prosperity

These two creative words were used extensively and repeatedly during the 1982–1984 Sino-British negotiation by the British negotiation team, including Prime Minister Margaret Fletcher that Hong Kong should be kept socially stable and economically prosperous in the transition period before and after the sovereignty reversion in 1997. The intention is to ensure that the living standard and economic wealth in Hong Kong would be maintained in the post-1997 era. Leaders from Beijing have also pledged in various occasions and at various times that Mainland China will ensure stability and prosperity in Hong Kong.

Being a city economy, Hong Kong does not have a large rural economy that could serve as an economic cushion should instability occur. Social stability is therefore a requirement, as any sign of instability or unrest would create chaos given the large population and the lack of alternatives. At the beginning of the Sino-British negotiation in 1982 when political uncertainty was not ensured, for example, Hong Kong residents simply began to hoard food and basic necessities. The supermarkets were hollowed and left only with empty shelves overnight. Equally, residents in Hong Kong are well aware that Hong Kong does not have choices, stay or depart are the two clear alternatives. Thus, Hong Kong residents have come to accept that stability is a common good, and civic unrest is unwelcome as instability would have a high price.

During the Sino-British negotiation over the future of Hong Kong, stability was pursued for various reasons. One was that residents in Hong Kong began to migrate to other western countries at a rapid pace beginning from the mid-1980s. The fear of creating a human resource vacuum in Hong Kong was real. There were numerous economic expansions in the 1980s, including the establishment of new universities. Mass migration would certainly constrain the supply of needed expertise. Surely it is the skilled and professionals who were the most likely migrants. The United Kingdom was reluctant to take up migrants from Hong Kong, as it would affect her domestic economy considerably. Hence, the purpose of maintaining stability was to encourage Hong Kong residents to remain in Hong Kong. One way to maintain stability was to boost the Hong Kong economy, typically through the rapid rise in wage and other economic incentives. Vacant positions were quickly filled up by other aspiring young workers. Thus, rising wage and job mobility became the key attraction, though the rising cost could somewhat have eroded Hong Kong's competitiveness.

The drive to stability has led to an increasing degree of social acceptance and harmony. Other than the presence of divergent political views, residents in Hong Kong have individualized a number of activities that could have a large degree of social diversity. Religious freedom in Hong Kong, for example, has permitted individuals to pursue their personal faith. Social awareness has been increasing in issues related to health and environmental pollution. In other words, stability is considered as a "common good", that the presence of differences is allowed provided stability is maintained.

The intention of pursing prosperity is to enrich the people of Hong Kong as much as possible, as high income and wealth appreciation were the incentive for residents to stay or even returned to Hong Kong after they have migrated. Given the short-term investment behavior prior to 1997, speculation in stocks and real estates was a major mean to wealth appreciation. In the process, the economic structure of Hong Kong was narrowing, as wealth was concentrated in the stock and property markets. Speculation behaved like participants in a game of 'musical chair' where speculators (participants) passed the bucket (stocks and properties) until the music stops. Each time the bucket (stocks and properties) was passed from one person to another in the musical chair game, the person would have gained (from speculation). When the music stopped, namely when the market collapsed, the last person holding the stock or property would suffer for the loss. In the entire process, the person who managed to pass on the stock or property would have gained. Thus, speculation became the wealth generation engine that favored virtually everyone, until the market collapsed, say in 1998 at the peak of the Asian financial crisis. As shown by the metaphor of the "musical chair" game, the acts of speculation would generate more gainers than losers. In other words, the risk of speculation in Hong Kong is low, and that the capital return from speculation would be higher than for capital to engage in other forms of investment activities.

It is true that speculation has become a "profession" in Hong Kong, where the wealthy speculators remained quiet when the market was down, but reemerged once the market became bullish. The presence and activities of speculators do generate economic fluctuations, making the economy unnecessarily volatile, though it is exactly such periodic volatility that provided them with a chance and opportunity to make capital gains through speculations. Indeed, the popularity in daily radio shows, for example, talking about the detailed trading in the stock markets, and the large among of newspaper advertisements on the real estate sector in Hong Kong have no doubt provided "information" on these markets, thereby leading, or misleading, individuals to indulge in speculations.

After 1997 and the economic slaughter resulting from the Asian financial crisis, the Hong Kong economy was exposed to structural rigidity. Though still stable, prosperity could not be maintained at a pace or scale similar to that prior to 1997. There is a growing social force containing the generation born after the 1980s, popularly known as the "post-1980s" generation. The pre-1997 phenomenon of "rising wage and ample economic mobility" was no longer viable after 1997. With high unemployment and the lack of investment to replenish the de-industrialized economy, it has taken a decade or more to gradually recover, while economic restructuring is still yet to be completed. Wage will not be rising rapidly, and there is a lack of new job provisions, let alone mobility. The "post-1980s" generation would have to understand that the economic scene has changed, and that their job security and mobility would show a different experience from those in the pre-1980s generation.

While many from the "post-1980s" generation have complained to the government, sought social welfare and become vocal socially and politically, there is still the economic freedom that allows them to venture into new economic areas. History might have repeated itself, though amid the more saturated economy as compared to previous decades, the "post-1980s" generation would be the generation that should assimilate more to the generation of 1950s and 1960s in Hong Kong when they had to make the best from their own efforts and ingenuity than to the generation of the 1970s and 1980s when many faced with the somewhat artificial "economic prosperity" resulting from political uncertainty.

The pursuit of prosperity in the post-1997 era requires a different path and dimension. In many ways, after the economic recession years, the Hong Kong economy needs new investment and restructuring, allowing new jobs, industries and businesses to emerge and prosper. Hong Kong should look for ways to attract new investment both locally, from Mainland China and from foreign countries. Hong Kong needs to revitalize its attraction in investment, and the "post-1980s" generation will have to foster the new Hong Kong economy. Thus, "wealth does not fall from heaven", but the high degree of economic freedom in Hong Kong is the best piece of infrastructure for the younger generation to work their way out. In short, to pursue prosperity, Hong Kong requires the creation of more job opportunities and new investment activities.

Hence, while the Hong Kong economy has excessively focused on property development and the stock market where wealth could still be generated, there is a need to diversify, restructure and widen the economic base, even faced with high cost.

In many ways, Hong Kong has excelled in post-World War II development, Hong Kong has passed through its industrialization stage successfully in the 1960s, Hong Kong has become a key international financial center since 1970s, Hong Kong has fostered Mainland China's economic reform since the 1980s, and Hong Kong has gone through periodic crises originated mostly from major trading partners. Hong Kong has done a lot through opportunities provided by foreign entities, and continuous domestic improvement has reinforced Hong Kong's attractiveness. The rising mainland economy should be a blessing for the next phrase of economic development in Hong Kong. In a way, the Hong Kong economy is competing with its own successful past. Economic freedom is an effective bridge that shall link Hong Kong's past success to future new economic heights. How to sharpen "economic freedom" in the face of uncertainty?

Hong Kong is an open place for businesses to make gains and profits, and Hong Kong residents also gain in the process. In addition to the need to attract investment from Mainland China, Hong Kong needs new attractions from foreign investments, other than portfolio investments in the stock market. New services and industries have to be encouraged, explored and promoted. Taking the "supply-side" or "supply-driven" approach in development, thoughts to diversify and restructure the economy could begin with the greater utilization of available resources. Hong Kong is surrounded by sea and a free movement of human resources. Skill is another key resource in Hong Kong. How can the skill and knowledge of residents in Hong Kong be used more extensively and effectively? Due to the "lack" of land, businesses and industries that do not need large land space should have a good chance in Hong Kong. Think along these lines, people with strong entrepreneurial mentality would soon be able to figure out new possibilities, opportunities and business ventures in Hong Kong.

Hong Kong does not discriminate foreign businesses. Under CEPA, for example, Hong Kong is free to export to Mainland China, and many items under CEPA could be produced in Hong Kong. Hence, a "made in Hong Kong" export label could stand a good chance in the mainland market. The mainland economy is rapidly becoming a consumption-driven economy, with people having higher income ready to consume. The mainland market should therefore be large enough to compensate for the "high cost" in Hong Kong. Hence, foreign investments can prosper by enjoying the large mainland market through production in Hong Kong. Being the offshore Renminbi center, the Hong Kong currency has effectively been made convertible to the Renminbi, and since the Hong Kong currency is linked to the US dollar, there will effectively be no restriction on the flow of Renminbi through Hong Kong. Such a new arrangement should facilitate greatly those foreign investments in Hong Kong that aimed at the mainland market.

In short, it is when the Hong Kong economy is fully restructured that prosperity could truly be restored. Along the way, one expects various social and political demands, but the intention to maintain stability would hopefully not obstruct the path of economic growth, advancement in development and pursuit of freedom. Residents of Hong Kong, whatever generation they come from, should be more constructive, taking more initiative in businesses, be courageous in venturing into new areas of development, flexing their ingenious muscles to explore the best possibilities.

With economic freedom, Hong Kong is a land of promised success. Stability is a social virtue. Prosperity is the bait to personal growth.

16.3 Road to Freedom, Not Serfdom

Freedom is an interesting human behavior, as one may have to be careful if one aspect of freedom leads to more or less freedom. In exercising economic freedom, there is a subtle difference whether one is to preserve and perpetuate freedom or one is giving up freedom. Economic freedom allows individuals to work for their own best. This is a universal truth, but in reality not all individuals can work for their best. There are people who are not sufficiently equipped with the needed knowledge, ability, skill, opportunity and resources to progress. Doing one's best could also be constrained by the business cycle, business environment and stage of economic development. It is more likely that opportunities are not there for all individuals to do their best, and some individuals prefer to look for an easy way out.

When a person is unable to look after his/her own economic welfare responsibly, it would be the time for the person to shift his/her responsibility and look for a way out. Shifting or shedding individual responsibility and pushing the individual's private cost to the society, which would bear the entire social cost, could be an easy alternative. Institutionally, it would be the government that the "ability lacking" individuals could freely turn to. The welfare system is supposed to cater to help the needy individuals. There is always some individuals facing economic difficulties at any particular point in time, and the provision of welfare by the government on a temporary basis is required in all market economies. Such an institutional arrangement shall not interfere with individual freedom.

The role of the government and the extent of government involvement or intervention are sensitive to economic freedom. It would be easy for individuals to shed their own private cost and seek assistance from the government. Although it would be the duty of the government to aid the needy, the government would compose of bureaucrats and administrators. When individuals seek government assistance, it would expand the work of the government and more bureaucrats would have to be employed. When the size of the government expanded, its work would also have to expand and that would relate to other aspects of our daily life. Thus, the more we asked from the government, the more the government would have to work on our daily activities. This is where individual economic freedom would begin to fade. When the government decided on our daily economic life, and though it might be the taxpayer's money which would pay for the government's expenses, we might end up with less choices and alternatives because the government would have made the economic decision for us.

As more and more daily economic decisions are being conducted by the various governmental bodies, individuals in turn would have less freedom in their own hands. Eventually, the government decision would soon intervene into our daily life, controlling things we would do and leaving us with little alternatives. The situation could easily come to a stage where the government bodies began to control, decide and even manipulate the different aspects of our daily economic life. It is when the bureaucrats started to control that would begin to limit our freedom. Even though the government might be freely elected, the more we asked from the government, the more we were effectively handing out our freedom to the government.

There could be other complications. Government bureaucrats might not be experts, but they have the power to make the decisions. Government bureaucrats might have their own views or political ideologies and other rested interests that might not work to the overall benefit of the economy. Bureaucrats might form their own power groups, and political play between the conflicting groups of bureaucrats might hurt the overall interest of the society. Government officials might not have the full information on what individuals wanted. In any case, there are always diverged wants from the public, and how the government could satisfy all the wants of the public would be questionable. Value judgments may differ among individuals and between the public and the government. Standardization usually could mean that difference in value judgment was sacrificed. Furthermore, when one group of individuals secured government assistance, other groups would complaint. Thus, government would have to involve more to cater for different interest groups. Eventually, the size of government would expand at its own pace. The more we asked from the government, the more we would be controlled, and the more government involvement and intervention there would be. The government would become the biggest decision maker and controller, and individual freedom would then be eroded.

There could also be the fiscal complication. The government is not a production engine. Like any individual, the government's expenditure here must be matched with revenue there. To do so, it would be typical for the government to levy high tax as a mean of redistribution to help the needy, but the levy of tax would also be a mean to maintain their power and control. With larger fiscal revenue, the government could have more to spend, creating and reasserting their own economic power. On the contrary, the high tax would be disincentive, and unfriendly to businesses. The subsequent fall in business would lead to a decrease in investment, output and eventually employment. The higher rate of unemployment would mean there would be more economically "unable" individuals, and to ensure their economic survival, these individuals eventually would have to turn to the government. The size of the government then grows and expands further, reinforcing itself and involving or interfering more in different aspects of our freedom. At the extreme, the disincentive impact resulting from the large redistribution policy and government intervention could discourage businesses and drive capital out of the economy, creating more unemployment and dependence on the government. The government would soon develop into total control of the economy, and individuals would totally dependent on government assistance and aid.

The above scenario may be extreme. The message is exactly one delivered in Hayek's master piece *The Road to Serfdom* (1944). Simply put, as soon as we started asking from the government for economic assistance, the government would have to appear useful, responsible and try to help in the first instance. This probably has to do with the expectation we have from the government. But when the government decided to help some, one consequence would be that those being helped complained that the assistance was inadequate. The other consequence would be that those who did not receive help complained and expected the government to help.

Thus the government was facing the worse of two worlds. To satisfy the demand for assistance from more interest groups, the government would then have to provide more help to all groups. Eventually, intervention breeds intervention at the expense of individual decision, choice, alternative and freedom.

There would always be some sections of the society that needed help, and it would always be the psychology that needy individuals should be assisted. Welfare-oriented politicians would also take the advantage to gain their "political capital". Asking would always be easier than providing, especially when the opportunistic politicians and activists would not need to shoulder the fiscal burden. The question is how much and to what extent the government can help and intervene? For those who need government assistance, the short-term benefit from government assistance would certainly outweigh the harm it would do to everyone's long-term freedom. For those who would not need government assistance, the long-term erosion of economic freedom would be the concern. The problem would be how to find out the true number of "those who need". In Hong Kong, for example, there have been calls to aid the elderly, and there are cases of elderly living on their own and so on. It is true that some elderly would need help. Equally, one would find that the elderly people would often queue up outside banks for application forms for new shares. Many elderly people would spend their time daily in front of the television screen in the local banks to check on the price of their stocks. There are complaints that poor families would live in squatter housing and cramped apartments with limited space. They might need help. But they were equally reluctant to move to distance places, because the cramped living space was situated nearer to the transport network that would provide convenience to their daily work routine. The number of such examples could certainly be extended. In addition, there were also cases of welfare abuse, where retired government officials claimed social welfare, and couples pretended to have divorced in order to claim social welfare.

Where can one draw a line of helping and not helping? What is the line between assistance and intervention? Assistance is provided when the needy individual comes forth to seek for the assistance. Even the needy individuals can have the freedom to seek or not to seek social welfare, depending on whether the individual would like to shift his/her private cost to the public. The needy might prefer to work harder on the job market, or would not feel obliged to seek assistance. Intervention occurs when the government began to dictate to an individual what to do. Indeed, if the government decided to aid the needy families, the assistance should be enough for the families to decide on what and how to spend. It would be possible that the needy families could have misused their assistance. The question then would be how much the government could do to "rescue" families, to take up the private cost of individuals? This is where the importance of a comprehensive policy and a well-established system come in. There would always be loopholes, but if the welfare policy and system were sufficiently transparent and comprehensive, the needy families and individuals would aware of their assistance as well as their obligations. In other words, while the society is shouldering their private cost, there is always a limit to all forms of assistance.

It is true that help should be provided to needy individuals, but the society should not cherish the unable. On the contrary, and other than those physically disabled, resources should best be geared to expand the able group so that the enlarged "economic pie" could provide more opportunities, ensuring jobs, employment and businesses for all individuals with different skills, knowledge, endowments and abilities indiscriminately. In other words, resources should be deployed in such a way as to turn the unable and weak into capable individuals. It is the equality of opportunity that should be cherished. Together with a reliable civic and economic system, the path of economic freedom in Hong Kong is the ability to generate new economic opportunities to help others to prosper.

References

Ahuja, A and N Porter (2010). Are housing prices rising too fast in Hong Kong SAR? Asia and Pacific Department, Working Paper, WP/10/273, International Monetary Fund, Washington DC, December.

Agenbor, PR, JS Bhandari and RP Flood (1992). Speculative attacks and models of balance of payment crisis. *IMF Staff Paper*, 29, 357–394.

Aghion, P, L Boustan, C Hoxby and J Vandenbussche (2005). *Exploiting States' Mistakes to Identify the Causal Impact of Higher Education in Growth*. Cambridge, MA: Harvard University Press.

Aigner, DJ and SF Chu (1968). On estimating the industry production function. *American Economic Review*, 58(4), 826–839.

Aigner, DJ, CAK Lovell and P Schmidt (1977). Formulation and estimation of stochastic frontier function models. *Journal of Econometrics*, 6, 21–37.

Akhter, SH (2004). Is globalization what it's cracked up to be? Economic freedom, corruption and human development. *Journal of World Business*, 39, 283–295.

Ali, AA and WM Crain (2002). Institutional distortions, economic freedom and growth. *Cato Journal*, 21(3), 415–426.

Alon, I and G Chase (2005). Religious freedom and economic prosperity. *Cato Journal*, 25(2), 399–406.

Armitage, P and W Hellmann (2008). Australia overview. In *The Asia Pacific Antitrust Review*. Global Competition Review, London: Law Business Research Ltd.

Atkinson, AB, T Piketty and E Saez (2011). Top incomes in the long run of history. *Journal of Economic Literature*, 49(1), 3–71.

Audretsch, DB, WJ Baumol and AE Burke (2001a). Competition policy in dynamic markets. *Industrial Journal of Industrial Organization*, 19, 613–634.

Audretsch, DB, GV Leeuwen, B Menkveld and R Thurik (2001b). Market dynamics in The Netherlands: Competition policy and the role of small firms. *International Journal of Industrial Organization*, 19, 795–821.

Ayal, EB and G Karras (1998). Components of economic freedom and growth: An empirical study. *Journal of Developing Areas*, 32(3), 327–338.

Azman-Saini, WNW (2006). Hedge funds, exchange rates and causality: Evidence from Thailand and Malaysia. Munich Personal RePEc Archive Paper, No. 716.

Baier, SL, GP Dwyer Jr. and R Tamura (2007). How important are capital and total factor productivity for economic growth? *Economic Inquiry*, 44(1), 23–49.

Bain, JS (1956). *Barriers to New Competition*. Cambridge, MA: Harvard University Press.

Barro, RJ (1976). Rational expectations and the role of monetary policy. *Journal of Monetary Economics*, 2, 1–32.

Barro, RJ (1999). Human capital and growth in cross-country regressions. *Swedish Economic Policy Review*, 6, 237–277.

Barro, RJ (2000). Inequality and growth in a panel of countries. *Journal of Economic Growth*, 5, 5–32.

Barro, RJ and DB Gordon (1983). Rules, discretion and reputation in a model of monetary policy. *Journal of Monetary Economics*, 12, 101–122.

Barro, RJ and JW Lee (2001). International data on educational attainment: Updates and implications. *Oxford Economics Papers*, 3, 541–563.
Barro, RJ and X Sala-i-Martin (1995). Capital mobility in neoclassical models of growth. *American Economic Review*, 85(1), 103–115.
Battese, GE and TJ Coelli (1988). Prediction of firm-level technical efficiencies with a generalised frontier production function and panel data. *Journal of Econometrics*, 38, 387–399.
Battese, GE and TJ Coelli (1992). Frontier production functions, technical efficiency and panel data: With application to paddy farmers in India. *Journal of Productivity Analysis*, 3(1), 153–169.
Battese, GE and GS Corra (1977). Estimation of a production frontier model: With application to the pastoral zone of Eastern Australia. *Australian Journal of Agricultural Economics*, 21(3), 169–179.
Battese, GE, TJ Coellie, CJ O'Donnell and DSP Rao (2005). *An Introduction to Efficiency and Productivity Analysis.* New York: Springer.
Baumol, WJ (1982). An uprising in the theory of industry structure. *American Economic Review*, 72(1), 1–15.
Baumol, WJ (1990). Entrepreneurship: Productive, unproductive and destructive. *Journal of Political Economy*, 98, 893–921.
Baumol, WJ, JC Panzar and RD Willig (1982). *Contestable Markets and the Theory of Industrial Structure.* New York: Harcourt, Brace and Jovanovich.
Baxter, M (1994). Real exchange rates and real interest differentials: Have we missed the business-cycle relationship? *Journal of Monetary Economics*, 33, 5–37.
Beach, WW and T Kane (2008). Methodology: measuring the 10 economic freedoms. In Kim, R, EJ Feulner and MA O'Grady (eds.), *Index of Economic Freedom*, Chapter 4, The Heritage Foundation and Dow Jones & Company, Inc., Washington DC.
Bekaert, G and CR Harvey (2000). Foreign speculators and emerging equity markets. *Journal of Finance*, 55(2), 565–613.
Bencivenga, VR, B Smith and RM Starr (1996). Equity markets, transaction costs and capital accumulation: An illustration. *The World Bank Economic Review*, 10, 241–265.
Benhabid, J and MM Spiegel (1994). The role of human capital in economic development: Evidence from aggregate cross-country data. *Journal of Monetary Economics*, 34, 143–173.
Berg, L (2002). Prices on the second-hand market for Swedish family houses: Correlation, causation and determinants. *European Journal of Housing Policy*, 2(1), 1–24.
Bergh, A (2006). Explaining welfare state survival: The role of economic freedom and globalization. Ratio Working Paper No. 101, University of Lund, Sweden.
Berggren, N (2003). The benefits of economic freedom: A survey. *The Independent Review*, 193–211.
Berger, S and RK Lester (eds.) (1997). *Made by Hong Kong*. Oxford, UK: Oxford University Press.
Bériault, Y and O Borgers (2008). Canada: Overview. In *Antitrust Review of the Americas.* Global Competition Review.
Bernanke, BS and AS Blinder (1992). The federal funds rate and the channels of monetary transmission. *American Economic Review*, 82(4), 901–921.
Bernanke, BS and FS Mishkin (1997). Inflation targeting: A new framework for monetary policy? *Journal of Economic Perspectives*, 11, 97–116.
Bettelheim, C (1988). Economic reform in China. *Journal of Economic Studies*, 15–49.
Bilson, JFO (1979). Recent developments in monetary models of exchange rate determination. *IMF Staff Papers*, 26(2), 201–223.
Bjornskov, C and MJ Foss (2008). Economic freedom and entrepreneurial activity: Some cross-country evidence. *Public Choice*, 134, 307–328.

Black, F (1976). *Studies in Stock Price Volatility Changes.* Proceedings of the 1976 Business Meeting of the Business and Economics Statistics Section, American Statistical Association, 177–181.

Blanchard, O and S Fischer (1989). *Lectures in Macroeconomics.* Cambridge, MA: MIT Press.

Blanchard, O and J Simon (2001). The long and large decline in US output volatility. *Brookings Papers on Economic Activity*, 1, 135–174.

Blinder, AS and R Reis (2005). *Understanding the Greenspan Standard, Economic Symposium on The Greenspan Era: Lessons for the Future.* Federal Reserve Bank of Kansas City, Jackson Hole, WY.

Bollerslev, T (1986). Generalized autorregressive conditional heteroskedasticity. *Journal of Econometrics*, 31, 307–327.

Boockmann, B and A Dreher (2003). The contribution of the IMF and the World Bank to economic freedom. *European Journal of Political Economy*, 19(3), 633–649.

Bork, RH (1966). The rule of reason and the per se concept: Price fixing and market division (Part 2). *Yale Law Journal*, 75, 397–405.

Brainard, W (1967). Uncertainty and the effectiveness of policy. *American Economic Review*, 57(2), 411–425.

Bruno, M and W Easterly (1998). Inflation crises and long-run growth. *Journal of Monetary Economics*, 41(1), 3–26.

Bryant, R, P Hooper and C Mann (1993). *Evaluating Policy Regimes: New Research in Empirical Macroeconomics.* Washington, DC: Brookings Institution.

Bullard, J and K Mitra (2006). Determinacy, learnability and monetary policy inertia. *Journal of Money, Credit and Banking*, 39(5), 1177–1212.

Bush, N (2008). Implementing China's new anti-monopoly law. *The Asia-Pacific Antitrust Review.* Global Competition Review.

Business and Professional Federation of Hong Kong (2009). *Hong Kong 2020 — The Big Picture: Financial Services.* Hong Kong SAR.

Butler, E (2007). *Adam Smith — A Primer.* London: The Institute of Economic Affairs.

Caldwell, B (1997). Socialism and war: Essays, documents, reviews. In *The Collected Works of F. A. Hayek*, Volume 10. Chicago: The University of Chicago Press.

Calvo, G, (1998). Capital flows and capital-market crises: The simple economics of sudden stops. *Applied Economics*, 1, 35–54.

Caplin, A and J Leahy (1996). Monetary policy as a process of search. *American Economic Review*, 86(4), 689–702.

Carlin, W and D Soskice (2005). The 3-equation new Keynesian model — A graphical exposition. Working Paper, University College London and CEPR.

Carlsson, F and S Lundström (2002). Economic freedom and growth: Decomposing the effects. *Public Choice*, 112, 335–344.

Carnabuci, C and M Wang (2008). Hong Kong's competition law and other initiatives. *The Asia Pacific Antitrust Review.* Global Competition Review.

Cecchetti, S (1996). Practical issues in monetary policy targeting. *Federal Reserve Bank of Cleveland Economic Review*, 32(1), 2–15.

Cecchetti, SG, H Genberg, J Lipsky and S Wadhwani (2000). *Asset Prices and Central Bank Policy.* Geneva Reports on the World Economy 2, International Center for Monetary and Banking Studies, Geneva.

Census and Statistics Department, various years. *Estimates of Gross Domestic Product.* Hong Kong.

Census and Statistics Department, various years. *Hong Kong Annual Digest of Statistics.* Hong Kong.

Census and Statistics Department, various years. *Hong Kong Population Census Reports.* Hong Kong.

Census and Statistics Department, various issues. *Hong Kong Monthly Digest of Statistics.* Hong Kong.

Census and Statistics Department, various years. *Quarterly Report of Employment and Vacancies Statistics.* Hong Kong.

Census and Statistics Department, various years. *Quarterly Report of Wage and Payroll Statistics.* Hong Kong.

Census and Statistics Department (1983–2005). *Report on Annual Survey of Industrial Production.* Industrial Production and Tourism Statistics Section, Hong Kong.

Census and Statistics Department (1983–2005). *Report on Annual Survey of Storage, Communication, Banking, Financing, Insurance and Business Services.* Business Services Statistics Section. Hong Kong.

Census and Statistics Department (1983–2005). *Report on Annual Survey of Transport and Related Services.* Logistics and Producer Prices Statistics Section. Hong Kong.

Census and Statistics Department (1983–2005). *Report on Annual Survey of Wholesale, Retail, Import and Export Trades, Restaurants and Hotels.* Distribution Services Statistics Section. Hong Kong.

Census and Statistics Department (2005). *Hong Kong as a Knowledge-Based Economy: A Statistics Perspective.* Science and Technology Section. Hong Kong.

Census and Statistics Department (2005). *Annual Survey of Building, Construction and Real Estate Sectors.* Hong Kong.

Census and Statistics Department (2007). *Statistics on Sectoral Concentration.* Hong Kong.

Census and Statistics Department (2009). *Hong Kong Residents Working in the Mainland of China.* Special Topics Report (7–9, 2008), No. 49. Hong Kong.

Census and Statistics Department (2009). *Hong Kong as a Knowledge-based Economy: A Statistics Perspective.* Science and Technology Section. Hong Kong.

Census and Statistics Department (2010). *2009 Report on Annual Earnings and Hours Survey.* Census and Statistics Department, Hong Kong, March.

Central Policy Unit (2008). *Term of References of Task Group on Constitutional Development of the Commission on Strategic Development.* Hong Kong, September.

Chan, HL, SK Lee and KY Woo (2001). Detecting rational bubbles in the residential housing market in Hong Kong. *Economic Modelling*, 18, 61–73.

Chan, ML (1997). Why regulate bus services? *HKCER Letters.* Hong Kong Center for Economic Research, University of Hong Kong, 44.

Chari, VV and PJ Kehoe (2003). Hot money. *Journal of Political Economy*, 111(6), 1262–1292.

Chen, EKY (1979). *Hyper-Growth in Asian Economies.* London: Macmillan.

Chen, EKY and K-W Li (1994). Manufactured Export Expansion in Hong Kong and Asia-Pacific Regional Cooperation. In Yang, S-C (ed.), *Manufactured Exports of East Asia Industrializing Economies.* Armonk: M.E. Sharpe, 103–134.

Chen, EKY and K-W Li (1997). Industrial policy in a laissez-faire economy: The case of Hong Kong. In Seiichi Masuyama, Donna Vanbenbrink and Chia-Siow Yue (eds.), *Industrial Policies in East Asia.* Singapore: Institute of Southeast Asian Studies, 91–120.

Chen, EKY and P Lin (2002). Competition policy under laissez-faireism: Market power and its treatment in Hong Kong. *Review of Industrial Organization*, 21, 145–166.

Chen, MC and K Patel (1998). Housing price dynamics and granger causality: An analysis of Taipei new dwelling market. *Journal of Asian Real Estate Society*, 1(1), 101–126.

Chen, M-R and W Galenson (1969). *The Chinese Economy Under Communism.* Chicago: Aldine Publishing Company.

Chenery, HB and AM Strout (1966). Foreign assistance and economic development. *American Economic Review*, 56, 149–179.

Cheng, J (2009). The story of a new policy. *The Quarterly Online Journal About Issues Related to Hong Kong and China.* Hong Kong Economic Journal, July.

Cheng, KL and C Wu (1998). *Competition Policy and the Regulation of Business.* Hong Kong: City University of Hong Kong Press.
Cheng, TY (1982). *The Economy of Hong Kong.* Hong Kong: Far East Publications.
Cheung, L, C Leung and WS Peng (2001). The property market and the macroeconomy. *Hong Kong Monetary Authority Quarterly Bulletin*, 40–49.
Cheung, L and V Yeung (2007). Measuring the position of Hong Kong as an international financial center. *Hong Kong Monetary Authority Quarterly Bulletin*, 5–12.
China Statistical Yearbook, various years. Beijing.
Chinese Academy of Social Sciences (2009). *Annual Report on Urban Competitiveness*, No. 7, Blue Book of City Competiveness, Beijing.
Chou, KR (1966). *The Hong Kong Economy: A Miracle of Growth.* Hong Kong: Academic Publications.
Chow, SC and GF Papanek (1981). Laissez-faire, growth and equity — Hong Kong. *Economic Journal*, 91, 466–485.
Christiano, LJ and M Eichenbaum (1992). Current real-business-cycle theories and aggregate labor-market fluctuations. *American Economic Review*, 82(3), 430–450.
Christie, A (1982). The stochastic behavior of common stock variance: Value, leverage and interest rate effects. *Journal of Financial Economics*, 10, 407–432.
City of London (2007). *The Global Financial Centers Index.* London, March.
Clarke, R, S Davies and N Driffield (1998). *Monopoly Policy in the UK: Assessing the Evidence.* Cheltenham: Edward Elgar.
Clayton, D (1997). *Imperialism Revisited: Political and Economic Relations Between Britain and China, 1950–1954.* London: Macmillan.
Clayton, D (2000). Industrialization and institutional change in Hong Kong, 1842–1960. In Latham, AJH and H Kawakatsu (eds.), *Asia Pacific Dynamism 1550–2000.* London: Routledge, 149–169.
Clayton, D (2006). Labour-intensive industrialization in Hong Kong, 1950–1970: A note on sources and methods. *Asia Pacific Business Review*, 12(3), 375–388.
Coelli, TJ (1996). *A Guide to FRONTIER Version 4.1: A Computer Program for Stochastic Frontier Production and Cost Production Estimation.* CEPA Working Paper 96/07, University of New England, Armidale, Australia.
Cohen, J and A Arato (1997). *Civic Society and Political Theory.* Cambridge, MA: MIT Press.
Cole, JH (2003). The contribution of economic freedom to world economic growth, 1980–1999. *Cato Journal*, 23(2), 189–198.
Commerce and Economic Development Bureau (2008). *Detailed Proposals for a Competition Law: A Public Consultation Paper.* Hong Kong SAR Government, May.
Competitive Policy Advisory Group (COMPAG) (2003). *Guidelines to Maintain a Competitive Environment and Define and Tackle Anti-competitive Practices.* Hong Kong SAR Government.
Constitutional and Mainland Affairs Bureau (2007). *The Fifth Report of the Constitutional Development Task Force.* Hong Kong SAR.
Constitutional and Mainland Affairs Bureau (2008). *Report on Public Consultation on Green Paper on Constitutional Development.* Hong Kong SAR, September.
Consumer Council (1994a). *Are Hong Kong Depositors Fairly Treated?* Hong Kong Consumer Council.
Consumer Council (1994b). *Report on the Supermarket Industry in Hong Kong.* Hong Kong Consumer Council.
Consumer Council (1996a). *How Competitive is the Private Residential Property Market?* Hong Kong Consumer Council.

Consumer Council (1996b). *Competition Policy: The Key to Hong Kong's Future Success.* Hong Kong Consumer Council.

Consumer Council (1999). *Hong Kong Banking Sector Consultancy Study.* Hong Kong Consumer Council.

Consumer Council (2000). *A Study of Motor Gasoline, Diesel and LPG Markets in Hong Kong: Findings and Recommendations.* Hong Kong Consumer Council.

Consumer Council (2003). *Competition in the Foodstuffs and Household Necessities Retailing Sector Findings and Recommendations.* Hong Kong Consumer Council.

Consumer Council (2007a). *Impact of Branch Closures and Fee Increases of Banks on Disadvantage Consumers.* Hong Kong Consumer Council.

Consumer Council (2007b). *Promoting Competition — Maintaining Our Economic Drive.* Hong Kong Consumer Council.

Consumer International (2007). *Consumers and Competition: A Consumer Welfare Analysis of Three Retail Markets in 14 EU Member States.* London.

Cornell, B (1977). Spot rates, forward rates and exchange market efficiency. *Journal of Financial Economics*, 5, 55–65.

Corporation of London (2005). *The Competitive Position of London as a Global Financial Centre*, November.

Corsetti, G, P Prsenti and N Roubini (1999). What caused the Asian currency and financial crisis? *Japan and the World Economy*, 11, 305–373.

Crandall, RW and C Winston (2003). Does antitrust policy improve consumer welfare: Assessing the evidence. *Journal of Economic Perspectives*, 17(4), 3–26.

Cukierman, A (1992). *Central Bank Strategies, Credibility and Independence.* Cambridge, MA: MIT Press.

Davidson, SR (2001). Economic and political freedom as determinants of the 1997–1998 financial crisis. Working Paper Series 290228, Social Science Research Network Electronic Paper Collection, November.

Davis, H (1996). High IQ and low technology: Hong Kong's key to success. *Long Range Planning*, 29, 648–690.

DeGregorio, J, A Giovannini and HC Wolf (1994). International evidence on tradables and nontradables inflation. *European Economic Review*, 38, 1225–1244.

Deininger, K and L Squire (1996). A new data set measuring income inequality. *The World Bank Economic Review*, 10(3), 565–592.

Demirguch-Kunt, A and R Levine (1996). Stock market development and financial intermediaries: Stylized facts. *The World Bank Economic Review*, 10, 291–321.

Deutsche Bank (2003). *CEPA: Gateway for China — Hong Kong Integration.* Asia Pacific Equity Research, July.

Dickey, DA and WA Fuller (1979). Distribution of the estimators for autoregressive time-series with a unit root. *Journal of the American Statistical Association*, 74(366), 427–431.

Dickey, DA and WA Fuller (1981). Likelihood ratio statistics for autoregressive time series with unit root. *Econometrica*, 49, 1057–1072.

DiLorenzo, TL (1985). The origins of antitrust: An interest-group perspective. *International Review of Law and Economics*, 5(1), 73–90.

Dorn, J and AJ Schwartz (eds.), (1987). *In Search of Stable Money.* Chicago: University of Chicago Press.

Doyle, M (2006). On the optimality of delay in monetary policy as a process of search. Working Paper No. 06006, Department of Economics, Iowa State University.

Drucker, P (1969). *The Age of Discontinuity: Guidelines to Our Changing Society.* New York: Harper and Row.

Dufey, G and I Giddy (1978). *The International Money Market.* New Jersey: Prentice-Hall.

Dunlop, JT (1938). The movement of real and money wage rates. *Economic Journal*, 48, 413–434.

Easton, ST and MA Walker (1997). Income, growth and economic freedom. *American Economic Review*. Papers and Proceedings, 87(2), 328–332.

Economic Freedom of the World (2007). The Fraser Institute, Vancouver.

Eichengreen, B, AK Rose and C Wyplosz (1994). Speculative attacks on pegged exchange rates: An empirical exploration. *National Bureau of Economic Research Working Paper*, No. 4898.

Eichengreen, B, AK Rose and C Wyplosz (1995). Exchange market mayhem: The antecedents and aftermath of speculative attacks. *Economic Policy*, 21, 249–312.

Eichengreen, B, AK Rose and C Wyplosz (1996). Contagious currency crisis. *National Bureau of Economic Research*, Working Paper, No. 5681, July.

Eichengreen, B, AK Rose and C Wyplosz (1998a). Contagious currency crises: First tests. *Scandinavian Journal of Economics*, 4, 463–484.

Eichengreen, B, T Ito, M Kawai and R Portes (1998b). Recent currency crisis in Asia. *Journal of the Japanese and International Economies*, 12, 535–542.

Endacott, GB (1964). *A History of Hong Kong*. Oxford, UK: Oxford University Press.

Engle, RF (1982). Autoregressive conditional heteroskedasticity with estimates of the variance of the UK inflation. *Econometrica*, 50, 98–1008.

Engle, RF (2002). Dynamic conditional correlation — A simple class of multivariate GARCH models. *Journal of Business and Economics Statistics*, 20, 339–350.

Engle, RF and VK Ng (1993). Measuring, and testing the impact of news on volatility. *Journal of Finance*, 48, 1749–1778.

Engle, RF and K Sheppard (2001). Theoretical and empirical properties of dynamic conditional correlation multivariate GARCH. National Bureau of Economic Research, Working Paper, No. 8554, MA: Cambridge.

Farrell MJ (1957). The measurement of productive efficiency. *Journal of the Royal Statistical Society*. Series A, General, 120, Part 3, 253–281.

Fair Trade Act (1992). Fair Trade Commission, Taipei.

Farhoomand, A (ed.) (2005). *Small Business Management and Entrepreneurship in Hong Kong: A Case Book*. Hong Kong: Hong Kong University Press.

Farr, WK, RA Lord and JL Wolfenbarger (1998). Economic freedom, political freedom and economic well-being: A causality analysis. *Cato Journal*, 18(2), 247–262.

Federal Trade Commission Guide to the Antitrust Law. Antitrust and Competition Division, United States Federal Trade Commission, Washington DC.

Feldstein, M (2000). Aspects of global economic integration: Outlook for the future. National Bureau of Economic Research, Working Paper, No. 7899, MA: Cambridge.

Fidrmuc, J (2003). Economic freedom, democracy and growth during post-communist transition. *European Journal of Political Economy*, 19, 583–604.

Financial Services Authority (2009). *The Turner Review: A Regulatory Response to the Global Banking Crisis*. London, March.

Fischer, S (1990). Rules versus discretion. In Friedman, BM and FH Hahn (eds.), *Handbook of Monetary Economics*. Amsterdam: North-Holland, 1155–1184.

Foray, D (2004). *Economics of Knowledge*. Cambridge, MA: MIT Press.

Fox, EM (1991). Competition policy and Eastern Europe: The Bulfarian project as a case study. *Antitrust Law Journal*, 60, 243–275.

Frankel, J AK Rose (1996). Currency crashes in emerging markets: An empirical treatment. *Journal of International Economics*, 41(3–4), 351–366.

Fratzcher, M (2003). On currency crises and contagion. *Journal of International Money and Finance*, 8, 109–129.

French, KR, GW Schwert and RF Stambaugh (1987). Expected stock returns and volatility. *Journal of Financial Economics*, 19, 3–29.

French, KR, MN Baily, JY Campbell, JH Cochrane, DW Diamond, D Duffie, AK Kashyap, FS Mishkin, RG Rajan, DS Scharfstein, RJ Shiller, HS Shin, MJ Slaughter, JC Stein and RM Stulz (2010). *The Squam Lake Report: Fixing the Financial System*. Princeton: Princeton University Press.

Friedman, M (1948). A monetary and fiscal framework for economic stability. *American Economic Review*, 38, 245–264.

Friedman, M (1960). *A Program for Monetary Stability*. New York: Fordham.

Friedman, M (1962). *Capitalism and Freedom*. Chicago: University of Chicago Press.

Friedman, M (1968). The role of monetary policy. *American Economic Review*, 58, 1–17.

Friedman, M (1981). *The Invisible Hand in Economics and Politics*. Singapore: Institute of Southeast Asia Studies.

Friedman, M (1982). Monetary policy: Theory and practice. *Journal of Money, Credit and Banking*, 14(1), 98–118.

Friedman, M (1991). *Economic Freedom, Human Freedom, Political Freedom*. The Smith Center, California State University, November.

Friedman, M (1993). *Why Government is the Problem?* Hoover Institution, Stanford University.

Friedman, M (1999). *Individual Liberty, Free Markets and Peace*. Cato Policy Report, 21(2).

Friedman, M and R Friedman (1979). *Free to Choose*. New York: Harcourt Brace Jovanovich Publishers.

Frisch, H (1977). Inflation theory 1963–1975: A "second generation" survey. *Journal Economic Literature*, 15(4), 1289–1317.

Fuller, DB (ed.) (2010). *Innovation Policy and the Limits of Laissez-faire*. Hampshire: Palgrave Macmillan.

Gaffard, J-L and M Quéré (2006). What's the aim for competition policy: Optimizing market structure or encouraging innovative behaviors? *Journal of Evolutionary Economics*, 16, 175–187.

Gallup, JL, JD Sachs and AD Mellinger (1999). Geography and economic development. In *Annual World Bank Conference on Development Economics 1998*. Washington DC: World Bank, pp. 127–170.

Ganesan, S and YC Tse (1997). Causal relationship between construction flows and GDP: Evidence from Hong Kong. *Construction Management and Economics*, 15(4), 371–376.

Ganesan, S and YC Tse (1999). Matching housing supply and demand: an empirical study of Hong Kong's market. *Construction Management and Economics*, 17(5), 625–633.

Gemmell, N (1995). Endogenous growth, the solow model and human capital. *Economics of Planning*, 28, 169–193.

Gemmell, N (1996). Evaluating the impacts of human capital stocks and accumulation in economic growth: Some new evidence. *Oxford Bulletin of Economics and Statistics*, 58, 9–28.

Gemmell, N (1997). *Externalities to Higher Education: A Review of the New Growth Literature*. National Committee of Inquiry into Higher Education, Report No. 8, University of Leeds.

Gerlach, S (2002). Bank lending and property prices in Hong Kong. *Hong Kong Monetary Authority Quarterly Bulletin*, 1–10.

Ginarte, JC and WG Park (1997). Determinants of patent rights: A cross-national study. *Research Policy*, 26, 283–301.

Gini, C (1912). *Variability and Mutability*. C Cuppini, Bologna (in Italian).

Giuliodori, M (2004). Monetary policy shocks and the role of house prices across european countries. Working Paper, No. 15, De Nederlandsche Bank, November.

Glick, R and AK Rose (1999). Contagion and trade: Why are currency crises regional? *Journal of International Money and Finance*, 18, 613–687.

Global Competition Review (2008). *The Asia Pacific Antitrust Review*. Global Competition Review.

Global Competition Review (2009). *The Antitrust Review of the Americas*. Global Competition Review.

Global Competition Review (2009). *The European Antitrust Review*. Global Competition Review.

Glosten, LR, R Jagannathan and D Runkle (1993). On the relation between the expected value, and the volatility of the nominal excess return on stocks. *Journal of Finance*, 48, 1779–1801.

Goldberg, M (1991). Asia Pacific international financial centres. *International Journal of Bank Marketing*, 9(5), 4–10.

Goldsmith, RW (1969). *Financial Structure and Development*. New Haven: Yale University Press.

Gonzalez-Soriano, MC (1990). Classifying the economy into traded or non-traded sectors. *Journal of Philippine Development*, 17(2), 231–248.

Goodfriend, M (2005). Inflation targeting for the United States. In Bernanke, BS and M Woodford (eds.), *The Inflation Targeting Debate*. Cambridge, MA: National Bureau of Economic Research, 311–337.

Goodhart, CAE (1996). Why do the monetary authorities smooth interest rates, LSE Financial Markets Group, Special Paper, No. 81.

Goodhart, CAE (2004). *Financial Development and Growth: Explaining the Links*. Basingstoke: Palgrave Macmillan.

Goodstadt, LF (2004). The rise and fall of social, economic and political reforms in Hong Kong 1930–1955. *Journal of the Royal Asiatic Society Hong Kong Branch*, 44, 57–81.

Goodstadt, LF (2006a). Government without statistics: Policy-making in Hong Kong 1925–1985, with special reference to economic and financial management. Working Paper, No. 6/2006, Hong Kong Institute of Monetary Research, April.

Goodstadt, LF (2006b). Dangerous business models: Bankers, bureaucrats and Hong Kong's economic transformation 1948–1986. Hong Kong Institute for Monetary Research, Working Paper, No. 8/2006, June.

Goodstadt, LF (2007). *Profits, Politics and Panics: Hong Kong's Banks and the Making of a Miracle Economy, 1935–1985*. Hong Kong: Hong Kong University Press.

Government of Indonesia (1999). *Law No. 5, Concerning the Prohibition of Monopolistic Practices and Unfair Business Competition*. Government of Indonesia.

Government of Singapore (2004). *The Competition Act 2004*. Government of Singapore.

Government of Thailand (1979). *Price Fixing and Anti-Monopoly Act of 1979*. Government of Thailand.

Government of Thailand (1999). *Thailand Trade and Competition Act, 1999*. Government of Thailand.

Government of Vietnam (2004). *The Vietnam Act of Vietnam*. Government of Vietnam.

Graeff, P and G Mehlkop (2003). The impact of economic freedom on corruption: Different patterns for rich and poor countries. *European Journal of Political Economy*, 19, 605–620.

Granger, CWJ (1969). Investigating causal relations by econometric models and cross-spectral methods. *Econometrica*, 2(2), 111–120.

Greenspan, A (1967). Antitrust. In Ayn Rand. *Capitalism the Unknown Ideal*. Chapter 4, London: Signet Book.

Greenwood, J (2008). *Hong Kong's Link to the US Dollar: Origins and Evolution*. Hong Kong: Hong Kong University Press.

Greenwood, J and B Smith (1996). Financial markets in development and the development of financial markets. *Journal of Economic Dynamics and Control*, 21, 145–181.

Grote, MH (2007). Foreign banks' attraction to the financial centre Frankfurt — A "U"-shaped relationship. Working Paper, Department of Finance, University of Frankfurt, April.

Grubel, HG (1998). Economic freedom and human welfare: Some empirical findings. *Cato Journal*, 18(2), 287–304.
Gwartney, JD and R Lawson (2003). The concept and measurement of economic freedom. *European Journal of Political Economy*, 19(3), 405–430.
Gwartney, JD, RA Lawson and W Block (1996). *Economic Freedom in the World: 1975–1995*. The Fraser Institute, Vancouver.
Gwartney, JD, RA Lawson and RG Holcombe (1999). Economic freedom and the environment for economic growth. *Journal of Institutional and Theoretical Economics*, 155(4), 643–653.
Gwartney, JD, RA Lawson and D Samida (2000). *Economic Freedom of the World: 2000 Annual Report*. The Fraser Institute, Vancouver.
Gwartney, JD, RA Lawson, RS Sobel and PT Leeson (2007). *Economic Freedom of the World*. The Fraser Institute, Vancouver.
Haan, J de and CLJ Siermann (1998). Further evidence on the relationship between economic freedom and economic growth. *Public Choice*, 95, 363–380.
Haan, J de and J-E Sturm (2000). On the relationship between economic freedom and economic growth. *European Journal of Political Economy*, 16(2), 215–241.
Haan, J de and J-E Sturm (2003). Does more democracy lead to greater economic freedom? New evidence for developing countries. *European Journal of Political Economy*, 19, 547–563.
Hamori, S (2000). Volatility of real GDP: Some evidence from the United States, the United Kingdom and Japan. *Japan and the World Economy*, 12, 143–152.
Hanke, SH and SJK Walters (1997). Economic freedom, prosperity and equality: A survey. *Cato Journal*, 17(2), 1–23.
Hau, H and H Rey (2006). Exchange rates, equity prices and capital flows. *Review of Financial Studies*, 19(1), 273–317.
Haurin, DR, LS Ho and G Wong (2003). *Short Run Housing Market Dynamics: An Application to Hong Kong*. Economics Department Working Paper, Lingnan University, Hong Kong, January.
Hausmann, R, L Pritchett and D Rodrik (2005). Growth accelerations. *Journal of Economic Growth*, 10, 303–329.
Hayek, FA (1944). *The Road to Serfdom*. London: George Routledge & Sons.
Hayek, FA (1960). *The Constitution of Liberty*. Chicago: University of Chicago Press.
Hayek, FA (1991). *Economic Freedom*. London: Institute of Economic Affairs.
He, D, I Young and P Lim (2006). Financial sector output and employment in Hong Kong and New York city. *Hong Kong Monetary Authority Quarterly Bulletin*, 22–29.
Heath, JB (1961). Restrictive practices and after. *Manchester School of Economic and Social Studies*, 29, 173–202.
Heckelman, JC and M D Stroup (2000). Which economic freedoms contribute to growth? *KYKLOS*, 53(4), 527–544.
Herbert, R and A Link (1982). *The Entrepreneur*. New York: Praeger.
Heritage Foundation, various years. *Index of Economic Freedom*. The Heritage Foundation and Dow Jones & Company, Inc., Washington DC.
Hicks, JA (1969). *A Theory of Economic History*. Oxford: Clarendon Press.
Ho, L-S (2010). Hong Kong — Economy. In *The Far East and Australasia*, 42nd Edition, November. London: Rouledge, 292–300.
Ho, WKO (2000). Modelling speculative activity in the Hong Kong residential property market. The Applied Regional Science Conference. *RURDS*, 12(2), 138–148.
Hobday, M (1995). East Asian latecomer firms: Learning the technology of electronics. *World Development*, 23, 1171–1193.

Hodrick, RJ and EC Prescott (1997). Postwar US business cycles: An empirical investigation. *Journal of Money, Credit and Banking*, 29, 1–18 (Manuscript, Carnegie Mellon University, 1980).

Holmstrom, B and J Tirole (1993). Market liquidity and performance monitoring. *Journal of Political Economy*, 101, 678–709.

Home Affairs Department (2008). *Village Representative Elections*. Hong Kong, September.

Hong Kong Bar Association (2006). *Submissions on Higher Rights of Audience*. Hong Kong Bar Association.

Hong Kong Monetary Authority (2002). *Further Development and Reform of the Banking Sector*. Hong Kong Monetary Authority.

Hong Kong Monetary Authority (2005). *Hong Kong's Linked Exchange Rate System*. Background Brief No. 1, Hong Kong Monetary Authority.

Hong Kong Monetary Authority (2009). *Report of the Hong Kong Monetary Authority on Issues Concerning the Distribution of Structured Products Connected to Lehman Group Companies*. Hong Kong Monetary Authority, January.

Hong Kong SAR Government, various years. *Budget-Background Information for the Financial Secretary's Consultations with Legco Members*. Hong Kong.

Hong Kong SAR Government, various years. *Budget Speeches*. Hong Kong.

Hong Kong SAR Government (2007a). *Our Way Forward — Action Agenda on China's 11th Five-Year Plan and the Development of Hong Kong*. Economic Summit, Hong Kong, January 22.

Hong Kong SAR Government (2007b). *Report of the Commission on Poverty*. Hong Kong, June.

Hong Kong Stock Exchange (2007, 2009). *Hong Kong Exchange Fact Book*. Hong Kong.

Hsia, R (1984). *The Entrepot Trade of Hong Kong with Special Reference to Taiwan and the Chinese Mainland*. Taipei: Chug Hua Institute for Economic Research, June.

Hui, E, W Seabrooke and J Wong (2003). The impact of interest rates upon housing prices: An empirical study of Hong Kong's market. *Property Management*, 21(2), 153–170.

Huizinga, J (1987). *An Empirical Investigation of the Long-run Behavior of Real Exchange Rates*. Carnegie-Rochester Conference Series on Public Policy, 27, 149–214.

Humphrey, TM (1976). Interest rates, expectations, and Wicksellian policy rule. *Atlantic Economic Journal*, 4(1), 9–20.

Information Services Department (2008). *Government Structure*. Hong Kong, May.

Information Services Department, *Hong Kong*, various years. Information Services Department, Hong Kong.

Institute for Management Development (2006). *World Competitiveness Yearbook — Country Rankings*. Geneva.

International Monetary Fund (2007). *International Financial Statistics*. Washington DC: International Monetary Fund.

International Monetary Fund (2009). *Global Financial Stability Report: Responding to the Financial Crisis and Measuring Systemic Risks*. Washington DC, April.

Iradian, G (2005). Inequality, poverty, and growth: Cross-country evidence. Working Paper, No. 05/28, International Monetary Fund, Washington DC.

Japan Fair Trade Commission (2006). *For Fair and Free Competition*. Tokyo.

Jao, YC (1974). *Banking and Currency in Hong Kong: A Study of Postwar Financial Development*. London: Macmillan Press.

Jao, YC (1988). *Hong Kong's Banking System in Transition: Problems, Prospects and Policies*. Hong Kong: Chinese Banks Association.

Jao, YC (1997). *Hong Kong as an International Financial Centre: Evolution, Prospects and Policies*. Hong Kong: City University of Hong Kong Press.

Jeanne, O (1997). Are currency crises self-fulfilling? A test. *Journal of International Economics*, 43, 263–286.

Jensen, JB and LG Kletzer (2005). Tradable services: Understanding the scope and impact of services outsourcing. Institute for International Economics, Working Paper Series, No. WP 05–9, September.

Jensen, MC and KJ Murphy (1990). Performance pay and top-management incentives. *Journal of Political Economy*, 98, 225–264.

Jorgenson, DW and Z Griliches (1967). The explanation of productivity change. *Review of Economic Studies*, 34, 249–283.

Judd, JP and GD Rudebusch (1998). Taylor's rule and the Fed: 1970–1997. *Federal Reserve Bank of San Francisco Economic Review*, (3), 3–16.

Jung, K-T and TJ O'Brien (2008). Korea: Overview. In *The Asia-Pacific Antitrust Review*. Global Competitive Review.

Kaminsky, GL (1999). Currency and banking crises: The early warnings of distress. IMF Working Papers, No. 99/178.

Kaminsky, G, S Lizondo and C Reinhart (1998). Leading indicators of currency crises. *IMF Staff Papers*, 45(1), 1–48.

Kapopoulos, P and F Siokis (2005). Stock and real estate prices in Greece: Wealth versus "Credit-price" effect. *Applied Economics Letters*, 12(2), 125–128.

Kaufman, GG (2001). Emerging economies and international financial centres. *Review of Pacific Basin Financial Markets and Policies*, 4(4), 365–377.

Keynes, JM (1936). *The General Theory of Employment, Interest and Money*. New York: Harcourt, Brace and World.

Kim, J-II and LJ Lau (1994). The sources of economic growth of the east Asian newly industrialized countries. *Journal of the Japanese and International Economies*, 8(3), 235–271.

King, A (1975). Administrative absorption of politics in Hong Kong: Emphasis on the grassroot level. *Asian Survey*, 15(5), 422–439.

Kirzner, IM (1973). *Competition and Entrepreneurship*. Chicago: University of Chicago Press.

Knight, FH (1941). Freedom: Its meaning. *Ethics*, 52(1), 86–109.

Kohli, U (2007). Terms-of-trade changes, real GDP, and real value added in the open economy: Reassessing Hong Kong's growth performance. *Asia-Pacific Journal of Accounting and Economics*, 14(2), 87–109.

Konings, J, PV Cayseele and F Warzyndski (2001). The dynamics of industrial mark-ups in two small open economies: Does national competition policy matter? *International Journal of Industrial Organization*, 19, 841–859.

KPMG Consultancy (2001). *Tax Base Study for the Hong Kong Government Advisory Committee on New Broad-Based Taxes*. KPMG, Australia, July.

KPMG Consultancy (2007). *Corporate Tax Rate Survey 2007*. KPMG, Australia.

Krishnakumar, J (2007). Going beyond functionings to capabilities: An econometric model to explain and estimate capabilities. *Journal of Human Development*, 8(1), 39–63.

Krishnakumar, J and P Ballon (2008). Estimating basic capabilities: A structural equation model approach applied to Bolivian data. *World Development*, 36(6), 992–1010.

Krishnakumar, J and AL Nagar (2008). On exact statistical properties of multidimensional indices based on principal components, factor analysis, MIMIC and structural equation models. *Social Indicators Research*, 87, 481–496.

Krueger, AB (2003). Introduction. In *The Wealth of Nations*. New York: Bantam Dell.

Krugman, P (1979). A model of balance of payments crises. *Journal Money, Credit and Banking*, 11(3), 311–325.

Krugman, P (1998a). *What Happened to Asia?* Cambridge, MA: Massachusetts Institute of Technology.

Krugman, P (1998b). *Fire Sale FDI*. Cambridge, MA: Massachusetts Institute of Technology.

Kubota, T (2000). *Real Exchange Rate and the Productivity Growth Rates Using Panel Data.* The Doctoral Program in Policy and Planning Sciences, The University of Tsukuba, Japan.

Kumar, M, U Moorthy and W Perraudin (2003). Predicting emerging market currency crashes. *Journal of Empirical Finance*, 10, 427–454.

Kumbhakar, S and KCA Lovell (2000). *Stochastic Frontier Analysis.* New York: Cambridge University Press.

Kwok, M-L (2006). *Housing Price Dynamics in Hong Kong: How Much Can Fundamentals Explain Housing Price?* All China Economics International Conference, APEC Study Center, City University of Hong Kong, December.

Kydland, F and EC Prescott (1977). Rules rather than discretion: The inconsistency of optimal plans. *Journal of Political Economy*, 85(3), 473–491.

Kyle, AS (1984). Market structure, information, futures markets, and price formation. In Gary, GS, A Schmitz and AH Sarris (eds.), *International Agricultural Trade: Advanced Reading in Price Formation, Market Structure, and Price Instability.* Boulder: Westview.

Latter, T (2007a). *Hong Kong's Money: The History, Logic and Operation of the Currency Peg.* Hong Kong: Hong Kong University Press.

Latter, T (2007b). Rules versus discretion in managing the Hong Kong dollar, 1983–2006. Hong Kong Institute for Monetary Research Working Paper No. 2/2007.

Latter, T (2007c). *Hands On or Hands off? The Nature and Process of Economic Policy in Hong Kong.* Hong Kong: Hong Kong University Press.

Lau, S-K (ed.) (1993). *The Politics of Hong Kong in Transition.* Hong Kong: Wide Angle Press (in Chinese).

Lau, S-K (1994). Public attitudes towards political leadership in Hong Kong: The formation of political leaders. *Asian Survey*, 35(3), 243–257.

Law Society of Hong Kong (2006). *Response by the Law Society to the Chief Justice's Consultation Paper on Solicitors' Rights of Audience.* The Law Society of Hong Kong.

Lee, HL (2001). *Financial Centers Today and Tomorrow: A Singapore Perspective.* International Monetary Conference, Singapore, 1–6.

Leung, A (2001). Does Hong Kong need competition legislation? *Financial Times*, July 31, 2001.

Leung, C and O Unteroberdoerster (2008). *Hong Kong SAR as a Financial Center in Asia: Trends and Implications.* Working Paper WP/08/57, Asia and Pacific Department, Washington DC: International Monetary Fund, March.

Leung, CK and KS Wong (2004). The construction and related industries in a changing socio-economic environment: The case of Hong Kong. *International Real Estate Review*, 17(1), 139–172.

Levine, R (1991). Stock markets, growth, and tax policy. *Journal of Finance*, 46, 1445–1465.

Levine, R and S Zervos (1998). Stock markets, banks, and economic growth. *American Economic Review*, 88, 537–558.

Li, H, L Squire and H-F Zou (1998). Explaining international and intertemporal variations in income inequality. *Economic Journal*, 108, 26–43.

Li, K-W (1991). Positive adjustment against protectionism: The case of textile and clothing industry in Hong Kong. *The Developing Economies*, 29(3), 197–209.

Li, K-W (2002). *Capitalist Development and Economism in East Asia: The Rise of Hong Kong, Singapore, Taiwan and South Korea.* London: Routledge.

Li, K-W (2003). China's capital and productivity measurement using financial resources. Center Discussion Paper, No. 851, Economic Growth Center, Yale University, February.

Li, K-W (2006). *The Hong Kong Economy: Recovery and Restructuring.* Singapore: McGraw-Hill Education (Asia).

Li, K-W (2009). China's total factor productivity estimates by region, investment sources and ownership. *Economic Systems*, 33, 213–230.

Li, K-W and M-L Kwok (2009). Output volatility of five crisis-affected east Asia economies. *Japan and the World Economy*, 21(2), 172–182.

Li, K-W and T Liu (2011). Economic and productivity growth decomposition: An application to post-reform China. *Economic Modelling*, 28, 366–373.

Li, K-W and DKT Wong (2008). *The Three Episodes of Currency Attacks in Hong Kong's Linked Exchange Rate*. The 4th Asia Pacific Economic Association Conference, Central University of Finance and Economics, Beijing, December 13–14.

Li, K-W and K-F Wong (1997). The stock markets in China. In Li K-W (ed.), *Financing China Trade and Investment*. Westport: Praeger, 215–238.

Li, K-W, L Yun and GCS Lui (2009). Economic performance of human capital in post-reform China. *The Chinese Economic*, 42(1), 40–61.

Li, K-W, T Liu, HHK Lam and L Wang (2010). Productivity growth among Chinese Mainland Regions and Hong Kong. In Yuan, Z (ed.), *The World Economy in Financial Crisis*. Shanghai Forum Series (2009), Shanghai People's Publisher, 160–187.

Li, K-W and X Zhou (2010). Openness, domestic performance and growth. *Economics Letters*, 107, 13–16.

Li, P-K (2007). The Executive. In Leung, W-M, P L-T Lui, W Wong and I Holiday (eds.), *Contemporary Hong Kong Politics: Governance in the Post-1997 Era*. Hong Kong: Hong Kong University Press, 23–37.

Lim, CK and S Clements (2008). Singapore: Competition law update. *The Asia-Pacific Antitrust Review*. Global Competition Review.

Lion Rock Institute (2007). *Sir Cowperthwaite (1915–2006)*. Hong Kong: Lion Rock Institute.

Lipsey, RG and K Lancaster (1956–1957). The general theory of second best. *Review of Economic Studies*, 24, 11–32.

Liu, PW (1992). Regulating monopolies in utilities and telecommunications by price cap. *HKCER Letters*. Hong Kong Center for Economic Research, University of Hong Kong, 12.

Liu, S-Y (2009). *A Brief History of Hong Kong*. Hong Kong: Joint Publishing Co. Ltd. (in Chinese).

Liu, T and K-W Li (2006). Disparity in factor contributions between coastal and inner provinces in post-reform China. *China Economic Review*, 17, 449–470.

Liu, T and K-W Li (2008). Revisiting Solow's decomposition of economic and productivity growth. Ball State University, Ball State University Working Paper, ECWP200805.

Lo, CP (1992). *Hong Kong*. London: Belhaven Press.

Longbottom, JA, JG Nellis (1981). An empirical analysis of the determinants of house prices in the United Kingdom. *Urban Studies*, 18(1), 9–21.

Lopatka, J and W Page (1999). Antitrust on internet time: Microsoft and the law and economics of exclusion. *Supreme Court Economic Review*, 7, 157–231.

Lopatka, J. and W Page (2001). Who suffered antitrust injury in the Microsoft case? *George Washington Law Review*, 69, 829–859.

Lorenz, MO (1905). Methods of measuring the concentration of wealth. *Quarterly Publication*. American Statistical Association, June.

Lowe, P and L Ellis (1997). The smoothing of official interest rates. In Lowe, P (ed.), *Monetary Policy and Inflation Targeting*. Reserve Bank of Australia.

Lucas, RE Jr. (1973). Some international evidence on output-inflation tradeoffs. *American Economic Review*, 326–334.

Lucas, RE Jr. (1976). Econometric policy evaluations: A critique. In Brunner K and AH Meltzer (eds.), *The Phillips Curve and Labor Markets*, Carnegie-Rochester Conference Series on Public Policy, 1, Amsterdam: North Holland, 19–46.

Lucas, RE Jr. (1981). *Studies in Business-Cycle Theory*. Cambridge, MA: MIT Press.
Lucas, RE Jr. (1988). On the mechanics of economic development. *Journal of Monetary Economics*, 22, 3–42.
Lui, P L-T (2007). The Legislature. In Lam, W-M, P L-T Lui, W Wong and I Holiday (eds.), *Contemporary Hong Kong Politics: Governance in the Post-1997 Era*. Hong Kong: Hong Kong University Press, 39–57.
Lui, T-M F (2006). Some views on the Hong Kong economy. *Hong Kong Journal*, (2), April.
Luo, Y and Z Chen (2002). *Political Administrative Structure of HKSAR*. Hong Kong: Joint Publishing (in Chinese).
Lundström, S (2005). The effect of democracy on different categories of economic freedom. *European Journal of Political Economy*, 21(4), 967–980.
Luxembourg Finance Centre (2007). *Promises and Benefits*, July 20.
Ma, N (2007). *Political Development in Hong Kong: State, Political Society and Civic Society*. Hong Kong: Hong Kong University Press, 97–133.
Malliaropulos, D (1998). International stock return differentials and real exchange rate changes. *Journal of International Money and Finance*, 17, 493–511.
Mankiw, NG, D Romer and DN Weil (1992). A contribution to the empirics of economic growth. *Quarterly Journal of Economics*, 107, 407–437.
Mankiw, GN (2002). US Monetary Policy during the 1990s. In Frankel, F and P Orszag, (eds.), *American Economic Policy in the 1990s*. Cambridge, MA: MIT Press.
McCallum, B (1988). Robustness properties of a rule for monetary policy. *Carnegie Rochester Conference Series on Public Policy*, 29, 173–203.
McCallum, B (1989). *Monetary Economics: Theory and Policy*. New York: Macmillan.
McConnell, MM and G Perez-Quiros (2000). Output fluctuations in the United States: What has changed since the early 1980s? *American Economic Review*, 90(5), 1464–1476.
McConnell, MM, PC Mosser and G Perez-Quiros (1999). A decomposition of the increased stability of GDP growth. *Current Issues in Economics and Finance*. Federal Reserve Bank of New York, 5(13), 1–6.
McGahey, R, M Malloy, K Kazanas and M Jacobs (1990). *Financial Services, Financial Center: Public Policy and the Competition for Markets, Firms and Jobs*. Boulder: Westview Press.
McGann, JG (2011). *The Global "Go-To Think Tanks" 2010*. Final United Nations University Edition, International Relations Program, University of Pennsylvania, January.
McGregor, EB Jr. (1988). The public sector human resources puzzle: Strategic management of a strategic resource. *Public Administration Review*, 48(6), 941–950.
McKinnon, DJ (1973). *Money and Capital in Economic Development*. Washington DC: Brookings Institution.
McKinsey & Co., (2007). *Sustaining New York's and the US's Global Financial Services Leadership*. The City of New York Office, New York.
McNulty, PJ (1968). Economic theory and the meaning of competition. *Quarterly Journal of Economics*, 82(4), 639–656.
Menzies, G (2002). *1421 The Year China Discovered the World*. London: Bantam Books.
Mehra, YP and BD Minton (2007). A Taylor rule and the Greenspan era. *Economic Quarterly*, 93(3), 229–250.
Metcalfe, JS (1998). *Evolutionary Economics and Creative Destruction*. London: Routledge.
Metcalfe, JS and R Ramlogan (2005). Competition and the regulation of economic development. *Quarterly Review of Economics and Finance*, 45, 215–235.
Miller, M, P Weller and L Zhang (2002). Moral hazard and the US stock market: Analysing the "Greenspan Put". *Economic Journal*, 112(478), C171–186.
Mincer, J (1994). *Schooling, Experience and Earnings*. New York: Columbia University Press.

Miners, N (1998). *Institutional Change and the Political Transition in Hong Kong*. London: Macmillan, 139–157.

Modigliani, F (1977). The monetarist controversy or should we forsake stabilization policies? *American Economic Review*, 67, 1–19.

Montes, MF (1999). Tokyo, Hong Kong and Singapore as competing financial centres. *Journal of Asian Business*, 18(1), 153–168.

Morgan, S (2003). CEPA open the gate for more support from Beijing. *Inside Asia Pacific Equity Research*. Hong Kong, November.

Morgan, S (2004). Pan-Pearl River delta: From diversity to cooperation. *Greater China Economics Equity Research*. Hong Kong, September.

Morris, S and HS Shin (1998). Unique equilibrium in a model of self-fulfilling currency attacks. *American Economic Review*, 88(3), 587–597.

Mulligan, CB and X Sala-i-Martin (1995). Measuring aggregate human capital. NBER Working Paper, No. 5016, MA: Cambridge, February.

Mulligan, CB and X Sala-i-Martin (1997). A labor-income-based measure of the value of human capital: An application to the states of the United States. *Japan and the World Economy*, 9, 159–197.

Muth, JF (1961). Rational expectations and the theory of price movements. *Econometrica*, 29, 315–335.

National People Congress Standing Committee (NOCSC) (2007). *Issue Relating to the Methods for Selecting the Chief Executive and the Forming of the Legislative Council of the HKSAR in the Year 2012 and on Issues Relating to Universal Suffrage*. Beijing.

Nelson, D (1991). Conditional heteroskedasticity in asset returns: A new approach. *Econometrica*, 59(2), 347–370.

Nelson, MA and RD Singh (1998). Democracy, economic freedom, fiscal policy, and growth in LDCs: A fresh look. *Economic Development and Cultural Change*, 46(4), 677–696.

Nelson, R and S Winter (1982). *An Evolutionary Theory of Economic Change*. Cambridge, MA: Belknap Press of Harvard University Press.

Ng, M (2008). Democratization of Hong Kong SAR: A pro-democracy view. In Ming, KC (ed.), *China's Hong Kong Transformed: Retrospect and Prospects Beyond the First Decade*. Hong Kong: City University of Hong Kong Press, 59–96.

Nugee, J (1995). A brief history of the exchange fund. *Quarterly Bulletin*. Hong Kong Monetary Authority, 1–17.

Obstfeld, M (1994). Risk-taking, global diversification, and growth. *American Economic Review*, 84, 1310–1329.

Obstfeld, M (1996). Models of currency crises with self-fulfilling features. *European Economic Review*, 40, 1037–1047.

O'Connor, J (1973). *The Fiscal Crisis of the State*. New York: St. Martin's Press.

OECD (1996). *The Knowledge-Based Economy*. Paris: OECD.

OECD (1999). Knowledge-based industries and services. In *OECD Science, Technology and Industry Scoreboard 1999 — Benchmarking Knowledge-Based Economies*. Paris: OECD, Chapter 2.2.

OECD (2000). *Knowledge-Based Industries in Asia*. Paris: OECD.

Pacific Economic Cooperation Council (PECC) (2000). *Productivity Growth and Industrial Structure in the Pacific Region*. Japan Committee for Pacific Economic Outlook, Pacific Economic Outlook Structure Project, PECC.

Pagono, M (1993). Financial markets and growth: An overview. *European Economic Review*, 37, 613–622.

Paldam, M (2003). Economic freedom and the success of the Asian tigers: An essay on controversy. *European Journal of Political Economy*, 19(3), 453–477.

Pan, MS, RCW Fok and YA Liu (2001). Dynamic linkages between exchange rates and stock prices: Evidence from Pacific Rim countries. Working Paper, College of Business, Shippensburg University.

Park, WG and S Wagh (2002). Index of patent rights. In James, G and R Lawson (eds.), *Economic Freedom of the World: 2002 Annual Report*. Chapter 2, Vancouver: The Fraser Institute.

Patrick, HT (1966). Financial development and economic growth in underdeveloped countries. *Economic Development and Cultural Change*, 14, 174–189.

Pauly, LW (2011). *Hong Kong's International Financial Centre: Retrospect and Prospect*. Hong Kong Savantas Policy Institute, February.

Peacock, A (1997). *The Political Economy of Economic Freedom*. Cheltenham: Edward Elgar.

Peng, WS (2002). What drives property price in Hong Kong? *Hong Kong Monetary Authority Quarterly Bulletin*, 19–33.

Pepper, S (2008). Two systems becoming one: The 2047 timetable. In Ming, KC (ed.) *China's Hong Kong Transformed: Retrospect and Prospects Beyond the First Decade*. Hong Kong: City University of Hong Kong Press, 113–154.

Perkins, D (1988). Reforming China's economic system. *Journal of Economic Literature*, 26(2), 601–645.

Persson, T and G Tabellini (eds.) (1990). *Macroeconomic Policy, Credibility and Politics*. Switzerland: Harwood Academic.

Pitlik, H and S Wirth (2003). Do crisis promote the extent of economic liberalization: An empirical test. *European Journal of Political Economy*, 19, 565–581.

Planning Department, *Planning Statistics*, various issues. Planning Department, Hong Kong.

Poole, W (1970). Optimal choice of monetary policy instruments in a simple stochastic macro model. *Quarterly Journal of Economics*, 84(2), 197–216.

Poole, W (1978). The theory of monetary policy under uncertainty. In Teigen, R (ed.), *Readings in Money, National Income and Stabilization Policy*. London: Irwin.

Poon, JPH (2003). Hierarchical tendencies of capital markets among international financial centers. *Growth and Change*, 34(2), 135–136.

Poterba, JM and LH Summers (1988). Mean reversion in stock prices: Evidence and implications. *Journal of Financial Economics*, 22, 27–59.

Prescott, EC (1986). Theory ahead of business cycle measurement. *Quarterly Review, Federal Reserve Bank of Minneapolis*, 9–22.

Provincial Statistical Yearbooks, various years. Provinces of Mainland China.

Quéré, M (2003). Increasing returns and competition: Learning from a Marshallian perspective. In Arena R and M Quéré (eds.), *The Economics of Alfred Marshall: Revisiting Marshall's Legacy*. London: Palgrave, 182–201.

Rabushka, A (1987). *The New China: Comparative Economic Development in Mainland China, Taiwan and Hong Kong*. Boulder: Westview Press.

Radelet, S and J Sachs (1998a). *The East Asian Financial Crisis: Diagnosis, Remedies, Prospects*. Cambridge, MA: Harvard Institute for International Development.

Radelet, S and J Sachs (1998b). *The Onset of the East Asian Financial Crisis*. Cambridge, MA: Harvard Institute for International Development.

Raftery, J and YC Tse (2001). The effects of money supply on construction flows. *Construction Management and Economics*, 19(1), 9–17.

Rangvid, JA (2001). Second generation models of currency crises. *Journal of Economic Surveys*, 15, 613–646.

Rashid, S (1988). Quality in contestable markets: A historical problem? *Quarterly Journal of Economics*, 103(1), 245–249.

Rating and Valuation Department, various issues. *Hong Kong Property Review*. Rating and Valuation Department, Hong Kong.

Redding, SG (1993). *The Spirit of Chinese Capitalism.* Berlin: W. de Gruyter.

Richardson, GB (1975). Adam Smith on competition and increasing returns. In Skinner A and Wilson T (eds.), *Essays on Adam Smith.* Oxford, UK: Oxford University Press.

Riedel, J (1974). *The Industrialization of Hong Kong.* Kiel: Kiel Institute of World Economy.

Riedel, J (1988). Economic development in East Asia: Doing what comes naturally? In Hughes, H (ed.), *Achieving Industrialization in East Asia.* Cambridge, UK: Cambridge University Press, 1–38.

Rigobon, R (1998). *Information Speculative Attacks: Good News is No News.* Cambridge, MA: Massachusetts Institute of Technology.

Romer, CD and DH Romer (1989). Does monetary policy matter? A new test in the spirit of Friedman and Schwartz. In Blanchard, OJ and S Fischer (eds.), *NBER Macroeconomics Annual.* Cambridge, MA: MIT Press, 121–169.

Ross, TW (2004). Viewpoint: Canadian competition policy progress and prospects. *Canadian Journal of Economics*, 37(2), 243–268.

Rothbard, MN (1998). *The Ethics of Liberty. Part III: The State versus Liberty.* New York: New York University Press.

Rothman, A (2007). Reinventing China: In search of an innovative economy. *CLSA Quarterly*, February.

Sala-i-Martin, X (1997). I just ran 2 million regressions. *American Economic Review*, 87(2), 178–183.

Samuelson, PA and WD Nordhaus (1989). *Economics*, 13th Ed., New York: McGraw Hill.

Sanchez-Robles, B and MB Calvo (2002). Foreign direct investment, economic freedom and growth: New evidence from Latin America. Economics, Working Paper, No. 4/03, University of Cantabria, Spain, November.

Sargent, TJ (1987). *Macroeconomic Theory*, 2nd Ed., New York: Academic Press.

Sargent, T and N Wallace (1975). "Rational" expectations, the optimal monetary instrument, and the optimal money supply rule. *Journal of Political Economy*, 241–254.

Securities and Futures Commission (2008). *Issues Raised by the Lehmans Minibonds Crisis: Report to the Financial Secretary.* Hong Kong, December.

Schenk, CR (2002). Banks and the emergence of Hong Kong as an international financial center. *Journal of International Financial Markets, Institutions and Money*, 12, 321–340.

Schreyer, P (2003). Capital stocks, capital services and multi-factor productivity measures. *OECD Economic Studies*, 37(2), 163–184.

Schumpeter, JA (1994). *Capitalism, Socialism and Democracy.* London: Allen and Unwin.

Schwartz, AJ (2009). Origins of the financial market crisis of 2008. *Cato Journal*, 29(1), 19–23.

Schwert, GW (1990). Stock volatility and the crash of 87. *Review of Financial Studies*, 3, 77–102.

Scully, GW (2002). Economic freedom, government policy and the trade-off between equity and growth. *Public Choice*, 113, 77–96.

Sen, AK (1987). *On Ethics and Economics.* Oxford: Basil Blackwell.

Sen, AK (1991). The nature of inequality. In Arrow, K (ed.), *Issues in Contemporary Economics.* Volume 1, Market and Welfare, London: Macmillan Academic and Professional, 3–21.

Sen, AK (1992). *Inequality Reexamined.* Cambridge, MA: Harvard University Press.

Sen, AK (1993). Capability and well-being. In Nussbaum, M and AK Sen (eds.), *The Quality of Life.* Oxford: Claredon Press, 30–53.

Sen, AK (1994). Markets and the freedom to choose. In Horst, S (ed.), *The Ethical Foundations of the Market Economy.* Tübingen: JCB Mohr, 123–138.

Sen, AK (1997). From income inequality to economic inequality. *Southern Economic Journal*, 64(2), 384–401.

Shackle, GLK (1972). Marginalism: The harvest. *History of Political Economy*, 4, 587–602.

Shafer, WE and D Owsen (2003). The role of professional associations. *The CPA Journal*, 15–16.

Shaw, ES (1973). *Financial Deepening in Economic Development*. New York: Oxford University Press.

Shaw, R and P Simpson (1989). *The Monopolies Commission and the Market Process*. London: Institute for Fiscal Studies.

Shiller, RJ (2008). *The Subprime Solution: How Today's Global Financial Crisis Happened and What to Do About It*. Princeton: Princeton University Press.

Singleton, R (1997). Competition policy for developing countries: A long-run, entry-based approach. *Contemporary Economic Policy*, 15(2), 1–11.

Siu, A (2001). *Earning Mobility of Hong Kong*. Hong Kong Institute of Economics and Business Strategy, University of Hong Kong.

Siu, W-S (2005). An institutional analysis of marketing practices of small and medium-sized enterprises in China, Hong Kong and Taiwan. *Entrepreneurship and Regional Development*, 17(1), 65–88.

Siu, W-S and DA Kirby (1999). A small firm marketing: A comparison of Eastern and Western marketing practices. *Asia Pacific Journal of Management*, 16, 259–274.

Sivalingam, G (2006). Competition policy and law in ASEAN. *The Singapore Economic Review*, 51(2), 241–265.

Smith, A (1759). *The Theory of Moral Sentiments*. In Raphael DD and AL Macfie (eds.), Indianapolis: Liberty Press.

Smith, A (1776). *An Inquiry into the Nature and Causes of the Wealth of Nations*. Reprinted in March (2003), New York: Bantam Dell.

Social Welfare Department, various years. *Statistics on the Comprehensive Social Security Assistance Scheme*. Hong Kong.

Social Welfare Department (1980–2003). *Number of CSSA Cases by Nature of Case*. Hong Kong.

Social Welfare Department (2004). *CSSA Monthly Key Statistics*. Hong Kong, August.

Solé, J (2007). Introducing Islamic banks into conventional banking systems. Working Paper, WP/07/175, Monetary and Capital Markets Department. Washington DC: International Monetary Fund, July.

Solow, RM (1957). Technical change and the aggregate production function. *Review of Economics and Statistics*, 39, 312–320.

Stiglitz, JE (1985). Credit markets and the control of capital. *Journal of Money, Credit and Banking*, 17(2), 133–152.

Stocker, ML (2005). Equity returns and economic freedom. *Cato Journal*, 25(3), 583–594.

Storey, DJ (1994). *Understanding the Small Business Sector*. London: Routledge.

Stroup, MD (2007). Economic freedom, democracy, and the quality of life. *World Development*, 35(1), 52–66.

Sun, T and X Zhang (2009). Spillovers of the US subprime financial turmoil to Mainland China and Hong Kong SAR: Evidence from stock markets. Working Paper, WP/09/166, Money and Capital Markets Department, International Monetary Fund, Washington DC, August.

Sung, Y-W (1991). *The China–Hong Kong Connection: The Key to China's Open Door Policy*. Cambridge, UK: Cambridge University Press.

Sung, Y-W (2004). *Hong Kong's Economic Integration With the Pearl River Delta: Quantifying the Benefits and Costs*. Department of Economics, Chinese University of Hong Kong.

Sutton, GD (2002). Explaining changes in house prices. *Bank of International Settlement Quarterly Review*, 46–55.

Swann, D, DP O'Brien, WP Maunder and WS Howe (1974). *Competition in British Industry*. London: George Allen and Unwin.

Szczepanik, EF (1958). *The Economic Growth of Hong Kong*. New York: Greenwood Press.

Tam, F-Y, K-L Moon, S-F Ng and C-L Hui (2005). The critical success factors of sourcing production for small and medium-sized clothing firms in Hong Kong. *Journal of Textile and Apparel Technology and Management*, 4(3) 1–11.

Tamura, R (2006). Human capital and economic development. *Journal of Development Economics*, 79, 26–72.

Tang, TKY (2003). Hong Kong productivity council — The i-Hub of productivity in Hong Kong. *Journal of Materials Processing Technology*, 139(1–3), 596–603.

Tarshis, L (1939). Changes in real and money wages. *Economic Journal*, 49, 150–154.

Taylor, JB (1992). *New Directions in Monetary Policy Research: Comments on the Federal Reserve System's Special Meeting on Operating Procedures.* Federal Reserve System Committee on Financial Analysis, Federal Reserve Bank of St. Louis, 18–19.

Taylor, JB (1993a). Discretion versus policy rules in practice. *Carnegie-Rochester Conference Series on Public Policy*, 39, 195–214.

Taylor, JB (1993b). *Macroeconomic Policy in a World Economy: From Econometric Design to Practical Operation.* New York: WW Norton.

Taylor, JB (2008). *The Financial Crisis and the Policy Responses: An Empirical Analysis of What Went Wrong.* Manuscript, November.

Taylor, JB (2009a). Surprising comparative properties of monetary models: Results from a new data base. National Bureau of Economic Research, Working Paper, No. 14849, MA: Cambridge, April.

Taylor, JB (2009b). *Getting Off Track: How Government Actions and Interventions Caused, Prolonged, and Worsened the Financial Crisis.* Stanford: Hoover Institution Press.

Taylor, JB and JC Williams (2009). A black swan in the money market. National Bureau of Economic Research, Working Paper, No. 13943, MA: Cambridge, April.

Tobin, J (1998). *Money, Credit and Capital.* Boston, MA: McGraw-Hill.

Toh, S and YS Lee (1995). *Trends in Mean Years of Schooling.* Paper and Analysis, Department of Statistics, Singapore, July.

Transparency House (2005). *Corruption Index.* Washington DC: Transparency House.

Tschoegl, AE (2000). International Banking Centers, Geography, and Foreign Banks. *Financial Markets, Institutions & Instruments*, 9(1), 1–32.

Tse, Y and A Tsui (2002). A multivariate GARCH model with time-varying correlations. *Journal of Business and Economic Statistics*, 20, 351–362.

Tse, YC (1998). Housing price, land supply and revenue from land sales. *Urban Studies*, 25(8), 1377–1392.

Tures, JA (2003). Economic freedom and conflict reduction: Evidence from 1970s, 1980s and 1990s. *Cato Journal*, 22(3), 533–542.

Ure, J (1991). Making ends meet–the other side of international telecommunications. *Hong Kong Center for Economic Research Letters.* University of Hong Kong, 7.

Utton, M (2000). Fifty years of UL competition policy. *Review of Industrial Organization*, 16, 267–285.

Vandenbussche, J, P Aghion and C Meghir (2006). Growth, distance to frontier and composition of human capital. *Journal of Economic Growth*, 11(2), 97–127.

Veblen, T (1932). *The Theory of Business Enterprise.* New York: Charles Scribner's Sons.

Veblen, T (1919). *The Place of Science in Modern Civilization and Other Essays.* New York: BW Huebsch.

Veblen, T (1933). *The Engineers and the Price System.* New York: The Viking Press.

Vega-Gordillo, M and JL Alvarez-Arce (2002). *The Chicken and the Egg: Economic Growth and Freedom.* Circulo de Empresarios, Madrid.

Vere, JP (2006). *Study on Earnings Mobility.* Commission on Poverty, CoP Paper 23/2006, Hong Kong, November.

Vickrey, W (1961). Counterspeculations, auctions and competitive sealed tenders. *Journal of Finance*, 16, 15–27.

Vietnam Country Commercial Guide (2003). Foreign commercial service, US department of state.

Vogel, E (1989). *One Step Ahead in China: Guangdong Under Reform*. Cambridge, MA: Harvard University Press.

Wade, R (1990). *Governing the Market: Economic Theory and the Role of Government in East Asian Industrialization*. Princeton, NJ: Princeton University Press.

Weinstein, JR (2001). *On Adam Smith*. Belmont, CA: Wadsworth/Thompson Learning.

Wicksell, K (1907). The influence of the rate of interest on prices. *Economic Journal*, 17(66), 213–220.

Williams, M (2007). The supermarket sector in China and Hong Kong: A tale of two systems. *Competition Law Review*, 3(2), 251–268.

Williamson, J (1995). *What Role for Currency Boards?* Washington DC: Institute for International Economics.

Wong, DTK and K-W Li (2010). Comparing the performance of relative stock return differential and real exchange rate in two financial crises. *Applied Financial Economics*, 20(1/2), 137–150.

Wong, H and KM Lee (2002). *Hong Kong Poverty Line Study*. Division of Social Studies, City University of Hong Kong (in Chinese).

Wong, MCS, WSC Leung and K-F Wong (1997). Risk, return and price linkage in China stocks. In Li, K-W (ed), *Financing China Trade and Investment*. Westport: Praeger, 239–274.

Wonnacott, P and R Wonnacott (1990). *Economics*. 4th Ed. New York: John Wiley & Sons.

Woodford, M (2001). The taylor rule and optimal monetary policy. *American Economic Review*, 91(2), 232–237.

World Bank (2005). *Aggregating Governance Indicators*. Washington DC: World Bank.

World Bank (2006). *World Bank Development Indicators*. Washington, DC: World Bank.

World Bank (2011a). *Global Monitoring Report*. Washington DC: World Bank.

World Bank (2011b) *Poverty at a Glance*, Washington DC: World Bank, March.

World Federation of Exchanges (2006). *Annual Report and Statistics*. London.

Wu, CL (1986). Government land sales in Hong Kong: Auctions and a proposed alternative. *Hong Kong Economic Papers*, 17, 51–63.

Wu, L (2005). *Understanding and Interpreting Chinese Economic Reform*. Ohio: Thomson Higher Education.

Yellen, J (2004). Innovations and issues in monetary policy. *American Economic Review Paper and Proceedings*, 94, 45–47.

Yeung, Y-M (1997). Planning for pearl city: Hong Kong's future, 1997 and beyond. *Cities*, 14(5), 249–256.

Yeung, Y-M and DKY Chu (eds.) (1998). *Guangdong: Survey of a Province Undergoing Rapid Change* 2nd Ed. The Chinese University Press.

Yeung, Y-M and DKY Chu (eds.) (2000). *Fujian, A Coastal Province in Transition and Transformation*. The Chinese University Press.

Yeung, Y-M and Y-W Sung (eds.) (1996). *Shanghai: Transformation and Modernization Under China's Open Policy*. The Chinese University Press.

Yeung, Y-M and J Shen (eds.) (2004). *Developing China's West: A Critical Path to Balanced National Development*. Hong Kong: The Chinese University Press.

Yeung, Y-M and J Shen (eds.) (2008). *The Pan-Pearl River Delta*. The Chinese University Press.

Yip, Y-Y and C Loh (2008). New generation, greening politics and growing civil society. In Ming, KC (ed.), *China's Hong Kong Transformed: Retrospect and Prospects Beyond the First Decade*. Hong Kong: City University of Hong Kong Press, 213–232.

Zakoian, JM (1994). Threshold heteroskedastic model. *Journal of Economic Dynamics and Control*, 18, 931–955.

Zee, HH, J King, B Russell and A Schenk (2001). *Hong Kong SAR: Policy and Administrative Issues in Introducing a Goods and Services Tax*. Fiscal Affairs Department, Washington DC: International Monetary Fund, January.
Zhang, W-B (1999). *Confucianism and Modernization*. New York: St. Martin's Press.
Zhang, W-B (2000). *On Adam Smith and Confucius: The Theory of Moral Sentiments and the Analects*. Commack, NY: Nova Science Publishers.
Zhou, X and K-W Li (2011). The impact of openness and domestic performance on growth using nonparametric estimation. *Applied Economics Letters*, 1–6.

Author Index

Subject Index